THE
HISTORY
OF
AMERICAN
METHODISM

EDITORIAL BOARD

THE

HISTORY

OF

AMERICAN

METHODISM

In Three Volumes

VOLUME II

ABINGDON PRESS
NEW YORK   NASHVILLE

Library of Congress Catalog Card Number: 64-10013

SET UP, PRINTED, AND BOUND BY THE
PARTHENON PRESS, AT NASHVILLE, TEN-
NESSEE, UNITED STATES OF AMERICA

THE WRITERS

THEODORE L. AGNEW, Professor of History, Oklahoma State University

WALTER W. BENJAMIN, Head, Department of Religion, Morningside College

EDWIN P. BOOTH, Professor of Historical Theology, Boston University School of Theology

RICHARD M. CAMERON, Professor of Church History, Boston University School of Theology

WILLIAM R. CANNON, Dean and Professor of Church History and Historical Theology, Candler School of Theology, Emory University

DOUGLAS R. CHANDLER, Professor of Church History, Wesley Theological Seminary

PAUL DOUGLASS, Professor of Government, Rollins College

BISHOP F. GERALD ENSLEY, Resident in the Iowa Area of The Methodist Church

WEBB GARRISON, Minister, Roberts Park Methodist Church, Indianapolis

JOHN O. GROSS, General Secretary, Division of Higher Education, Board of Education of The Methodist Church

BISHOP NOLAN B. HARMON, Resident in the Charlotte Area of The Methodist Church

LEONARD L. HAYNES, JR., Minister, Wesley Methodist Church, Baton Rouge, and Professor of Philosophy, Southern University

STUART C. HENRY, Professor of American Christianity, The Divinity School, Duke University

W. RICHEY HOGG, Professor of World Christianity, Perkins School of Theology

ARTHUR E. JONES, JR., Director of the Library and Professor of English, Drew University

BISHOP GERALD KENNEDY, Resident in the Los Angeles Area of The Methodist Church

BISHOP WILLIS J. KING, Retired, of The Methodist Church

DOW KIRKPATRICK, Minister, First Methodist Church, Evanston

MURRAY H. LEIFFER, Professor of Sociology and Social Ethics and Director of the Bureau of Social and Religious Research, Garrett Theological Seminary

GERALD O. McCULLOH, Director, Department of Ministerial Education, Board of Education of The Methodist Church

WILLIAM J. McCUTCHEON, Assistant Professor, Department of Religion, Beloit College

v

FREDERICK E. MASER, Minister, St. George's Methodist Church, Philadelphia

JAMES W. MAY, Associate Professor of Church History, Candler School of Theology, Emory University

ROBERT MOATS MILLER, Associate Professor of History, University of North Carolina

RALPH E. MORROW, Professor of History, Washington University

ARTHUR BRUCE MOSS, Minister Emeritus, John Street Methodist Church, New York City

BISHOP T. OTTO NALL, Resident in the Minnesota Area of The Methodist Church

J. ROBERT NELSON, Fairchild Professor of Systematic Theology, The Graduate School of Theology, Oberlin College

FREDERICK A. NORWOOD, Professor of History of Christianity, Garrett Theological Seminary

JAROSLAV J. PELIKAN, Titus Street Professor of Ecclesiastical History, Yale Divinity School

COEN G. PIERSON, John Clark Ridpath Professor of History and Chairman of the History Department, DePauw University

JAMES P. PILKINGTON, Personnel Manager, The Methodist Publishing House

J. MANNING POTTS, Editor, *The Upper Room*

MARTIN RIST, Professor of New Testament and Christian History, The Iliff School of Theology

LELAND SCOTT, Director, the Wesley Foundation, University of Arizona

LAWRENCE SHERWOOD, Minister, St. Paul's Methodist Church, Oakland, Maryland

DAVID C. SHIPLEY, Professor of Theology, Methodist Theological School in Ohio

GRANT S. SHOCKLEY, Professor of Religious Education, Garrett Theological Seminary

GEORGE A. SINGLETON, Editor, *The A.M.E. Review*

TIMOTHY L. SMITH, Associate Professor of History and Education, University of Minnesota

NORMAN W. SPELLMANN, Professor of Philosophy and Religion, Southwestern University, Georgetown, Texas

RALPH STOODY, General Secretary and Director, Commission on Public Relations and Methodist Information

CHARLES T. THRIFT, JR., President, Florida Southern College

FRANCIS C. WILSON, Executive Secretary, Communications Section, Board of Education of The Methodist Church

vi

THE CONTENTS

Part III. A Divided Church in a Divided Nation: 1844-76

Introduction 3
 FRANCIS C. WILSON

14. The Church Divides, 1844 11
 Sections 1-4, RICHARD M. CAMERON
 Sections 5-7, NORMAN W. SPELLMAN

15. The Organization of the Methodist Episcopal Church, South .. 86
 NOLAN B. HARMON

16. The Years of Disagreement, 1844-61 144
 ARTHUR E. JONES, JR.

17. The War Years 206
 JAMES W. MAY

18. Rebuilding the Southern Church 257
 CHARLES T. THRIFT, JR.

19. The Methodist Episcopal Church in the Postwar Era 315
 Sections 1-3, WALTER W. BENJAMIN
 Section 4, LELAND SCOTT

20. The Methodist Protestant Church, 1865-1900 391
 DOUGLAS R. CHANDLER

21. Methodism Goes West 420
 MARTIN RIST

22. Bilingual Work and the Language Conferences 469
 PAUL DOUGLASS

23. The A.M.E. and the A.M.E. Zion Churches 526
 GRANT S. SHOCKLEY; LEONARD L. HAYNES, Research Consultant

Part IV: A Flourishing Church in a Prospering Nation: 1876-1919

Introduction 585
    RALPH E. MORROW

24. The Theology and Practices of Methodism, 1876-1919 592
    Sections 1-2, 4-7, GERALD O. MCCULLOH
    Section 3, TIMOTHY L. SMITH

25. Early Efforts at Reunion 660
    DOW KIRKPATRICK

Bibliography 707

Index 726

Illustrations

(Following page 374)

1. Bishops of the Methodist Episcopal Church, 1848
2. Joshua Soule
3. James O. Andrew
4. William Capers
5. Robert Paine
6. Holland N. McTyeire
7. Secretary of War Stanton's letter to Bishop Ames
8. "Freedom" and "Slavery" from the *Ladies' Repository*
9. Summons to a member of the Methodist Episcopal Church to appear for trial
10. Early Sunday school certificate
11. Rules for scholars in the Sabbath school at John Street Church
12. The second Bethel Ship
13. William Nast
14. "Singing up a Crowd at the Old Adobe on the Plaza"
15. Mr. Butler and the alligator
16. Cottages at Ocean Grove

III

A
Divided Church
in a
Divided Nation

1844-76

A Divided Church in a Divided Nation

M ETHODISTS IN MID-CENTURY AMERICA WERE INEXTRICABLY CAUGHT UP IN the gathering storm that was to engulf the nation in the Civil War. The ferment over the slavery question, increasingly dominant in political discussions and overshadowing most of the domestic affairs of the country, was equally evident in church conferences. Sectional bickerings, often bitter and caustic, rumbled as freely from pulpits as from campaign platforms. There was no escaping the issues that were dividing the country.

Aged John C. Calhoun, debating with Whig giants Daniel Webster and Henry Clay over the Compromise of 1850, saw the snapping of "ecclesiastical cords" between Northern and Southern Methodists, Baptists, and Presbyterians as evidence of the inevitable dissolution of the Union. The church was part and parcel of the turbulent divisiveness that was everywhere in the air during the 1840's and again at the end of the '50's just prior to the outbreak of war. It is not unlikely that the division of the Methodist Episcopal Church into two sectional churches in 1844 was one of the contributing factors to the political disunity which led finally to the breach in the Union in 1861.

The bitter controversy over the slavery issue was a widening wedge of tension separating the nation, the church, and even many families. However, it was but one of the yeasting strains that permeated the land. Tremendous changes were taking place, affecting the social, cultural, and economic life of the nation as well as the political scene. The nation was growing up and expanding. The growing pains of national adolescence were forging a new national character to the United States. Colonial America had been individualistic, rural, provincial, agrarian. Now new influences were transforming the young country and its outlook. Immigration was importing new ethnic and cultural patterns. Agriculture was giving way to industry in the national economy. Embryonic efforts in international politics and export trade were shaping the beginnings of a new world view. The twin forces of urbanization and industrialization were moving the country forward with gigantic strides. Industrial development was lifting economic and living standards. Significant advances were being made in the natural sciences, and inventive genius was producing far-

3

reaching technological improvements for the home as well as the factory. New social and humanitarian forces were attacking the problems of poverty and public morals, giving attention to the welfare needs of the underprivileged and the afflicted. Free public education was becoming increasingly important and widespread. Colleges and universities were beginning to be seen not as the limited privilege of the wealthy few but the open opportunity for all young people who would aspire to wider knowledge and greater skills. Newspapers were to be found in every city and town. Books were widely read. Interest in music, art, and the theater provided a new dimension to life for many, except on the frontier and in the remote rural areas.

The great influx of immigrants from western Europe crowded the eastern seaboard cities, for a time producing critical problems of unemployment and inadequate housing but in the long run providing labor for the immense industrial development. Thousands seeking larger opportunities for their families headed west in search of land and fortune. Expansion westward went on unabated in the 1840's and '50's, even up to the attack upon Fort Sumter. During President Polk's administration the United States had extended her continental area practically to its present limits, although vast areas in the West were yet to be inhabited. Successful diplomatic negotiations with England had settled the Oregon boundary dispute, establishing the present line between the United States and British Columbia along the forty-ninth parallel to Puget Sound. After her hopeless defeat in the Mexican War, Mexico in 1848 relinquished all claims to Texas and ceded New Mexico (including present Arizona) and upper California to the United States. Texas was admitted into the Union in 1845 as a slave state. The admission of California as a free state in 1850 upset the balance between free and slave states. In 1854 Congress repealed the Missouri Compromise Act of 1820 by enacting the Kansas-Nebraska Act, in effect opening all territories to slavery and dispelling any hope that slavery could be contained in the states where it had previously existed. This incited extreme bitterness, especially among militant abolitionists throughout the North, and resulted in serious tensions within Methodist and other churches in Missouri and the rest of the border states. Irate protests appeared in church papers all over the North.

But these events together opened up the West and Southwest for settlement and greatly influenced the expansion of the church as well as the nation. Methodist circuit riders were uniquely effective in moving with the frontier. The political, economic, and sociological changes shaping the country's history in this explosive period had their effect also upon the growing life of Methodism throughout the land. The discovery of gold in California in 1848 triggered a mad rush westward. Oregon had already

been opened, largely through the pioneering efforts of Methodist missionaries, and the Far West became the target for unnumbered wagon trains
of settlers trekking across the prairies in search of new homes and fortunes. Meanwhile, the Middle West was being developed rapidly with
growing cities and tremendous agricultural expansion, made possible by
better means of transportation, plenty of cheap land, and the invention
of improved farm machinery.

A relatively high level of prosperity ensued in the whole country, both
North and South, during the early 1850's. Public agitation over the burning slavery controversy subsided somewhat after Congress accepted the
1850 Compromise. Higher prices for cotton boosted the economy of the
South, and great industrial development was going on throughout the
North. President Pierce exuded confidence in his 1853 inaugural, speaking of "unparalleled progression" marking the nation's growth in economic advances and population increase. In the North industry flourished.
Agriculture abounded especially in the South and Middle West. Gold
from California provided a steady flow of capital for eastern industry and
commerce, so that investments in manufacturing, mining, and fisheries
reached the high total of more than a billion dollars in the '50's. Mills in
New England and the Middle Atlantic states were in full production, increasing the output of textiles, shoes, lumber, foodstuffs, and other commodities. Individual purchasing power was high and the standard of
living advanced sharply over that of colonial America. Per capita wealth
had increased from $191 in 1790 to about $590 in 1860. The increase in
wages, coupled with mass production and abundant natural resources,
made it possible for people to spend increasingly more of their income for
consumer goods formerly regarded as luxuries.

The increasing need for jobs among the growing population together
with poor working conditions influenced the beginnings of the labor
movement, which had gained momentum following the panic of 1837.
The overproduction of consumer goods in the '40's and the immense immigration flooding the labor market accentuated the need for trade
unions to protect the rights of wage earners. The improved economic
situation in the '50's stimulated efforts to organize labor, and by 1860
there were at least ten national labor groups.

In the South the production of cotton had increased to nearly four
billion bales by 1860. Cotton exports amounted to over $330 million, the
largest single export of the nation, totaling 57 per cent of all commodities
exported. In contrast to the rapid rise of industry in the North, manufacturing in the South was meager. In the main, Southerners depended
upon the North and Europe for consumer goods. However, cotton mills
were being started in South Carolina and Georgia. In 1852 a cotton mill

in Columbia, South Carolina, was operating 120 looms with 5,000 spindles and was producing cloth more cheaply than New England could. By 1860 textile mills in the South were using 200,000 bales of cotton. But the feudal nature of the cotton culture held in check any attempt to start industrial development on a large scale, and war destroyed all hopes in that direction.

Cotton had settled slavery as an economic necessity upon the South and, as well, had solidified a powerful social and political stratification in the area. Keeping slaves was too costly and unprofitable for most lines of work and for most crops. In Virginia, where tobacco and rice were major crops, the use of slaves became less profitable to planters, who trafficked them southward to the Carolinas and Georgia. The raising of cotton was ideally suited to slave labor, and in the cotton-growing states the Negro slave became an important factor, symbolizing both wealth and status for his owner. The cotton culture, dependent in large measure upon the use of slave labor, developed a planter aristocracy which dominated the economic, social, and political life of the South. The exploitation of the soil in the wasteful agricultural methods of slave labor required more and more land to maintain cotton production. To obtain the land, planters moved their plantations from South Carolina and Georgia to Alabama and Mississippi and then on to Texas. The westward movement of the cotton culture carried with it the expansion of slavery as well as the grip of economic and political power.

The real wealth of the cotton culture was in the hands of a comparatively few. More than two thirds of the white population of 8,099,760 in the slave states in 1860 had no direct interest in slavery. The total population of 3,953,580 slaves were owned by only about 384,000 whites, but of that number it is estimated that only 1,733 slaveowners owned as many as 100 slaves. Only the wealthy plantation families held vast acreages and numerous slaves, thus sharing preponderantly in the rich proceeds of the cotton economy. The concentration of wealth, and with it social prestige and political power, may be seen in the fact that in 1850 a thousand families in the South received $50 million a year in income while the remaining 666,000 families received only about $60 million. Nine tenths of the Southern whites were small farmers, some small planters with several slaves, others tenant farmers who owned no slaves, and some with small land holdings. In the cities those who worked at various trades were always dependent upon the cotton planters for a livelihood.

Improved transportation was an important factor in mid-century developments in the country. Previously, poor roads and small incomes had limited people to a rather provincial outlook on life, with little knowledge of towns and states other than their own. Now railroads provided cheap, convenient, and fast transportation, making it possible for people to move about easily and more widely, opening new areas to travel. In 1860 one could travel in relative comfort from Boston to New Orleans, from Mobile to Baltimore, from New York to Nashville. During the '50's railway mileage more than tripled, with 30,000 miles of tracks in 1860 as compared to only 9,000 in 1850.

Although rail travel was swiftly supplanting the steamboat, the latter was still of major importance. The invention of the screw propeller and other improvements, as well as the construction of larger boats, stimulated river and coastal transportation. Stagecoaches linked outlying communities to railroad lines and steamboat docks. Means of travel were accessible to almost everyone in every town and village.

Technological progress and increased national wealth had little effect upon streets and sanitary conditions in the cities and towns. Streets were poorly paved and seldom lighted. Dogs, goats, hogs, and chickens roamed about at will. Cobblestones paved some of the streets in Boston and New York, while unpaved streets were common everywhere. In Washington, except for Pennsylvania Avenue, all streets were unpaved— wallowing holes for pigs in winter and dustbowls in summer. Roads in general were poor. Roadbuilding for the most part was done by farmers in lieu of paying the road tax, with little supervision and scant outlay of cash. Except for late spring and early fall, when the roads were fairly passable, travel was slow and tedious.

Public education at mid-century was moving ahead in the North, lagging in the South. Free schools were provided quite widely in the North, thanks to the persistent work of Horace Mann and other leaders, and to a lesser degree in the Middle West. Lack of public funds and the widely scattered population in the South retarded educational progress. In the North and East industrial growth made possible a rising standard of living and brought increasing demands upon cities and states to provide free schools. Competent teachers were often hard to find, and salaries were low.

Higher education was largely initiated and sponsored by church denominations. Of all colleges established by the time of the Civil War only seven were state schools. The 1840's and '50's saw a vigorous upsurge of activity in establishing colleges, with nearly a hundred founded in the '50's. Many of these were started in the South, where there was a growing distrust of the North and a dislike for Northern schools. Many were established also in the Middle West, which in spite of its sparse population came to have more colleges than the East. Practically all the colleges were small in student enrollment, financial support, and faculty. Only the older and better established schools such as Harvard, Yale, and Princeton were endowed at all, and those not too heavily. Methodists, with a long tradition of keen interest in education, could not but be deeply involved in the higher education of the period, as can be seen in the establishing of some of the outstanding Methodist colleges before and immediately after the Civil War.

Inevitably the slavery question would smash its political fury against the expanding economic and social progress of the country. Since the Missouri Compromise of 1820, the issue between adherents of slavery and proponents of its abolition had been joined. The debate erupted in every session of Congress and became vocal in every political campaign. Party conventions could not escape the heated controversy. Radical abolitionists in the North and rabid states' righters in the South kept the political pot boiling with ceaseless agitation over the issue. Every effort to keep the slavery question in the background failed.

Political and religious leaders in the North attacked slavery on moral grounds and maintained in the press, in church conferences, in political campaign debates that slavery should be outlawed by federal law. An aggressive antislavery movement in the North was led by William Lloyd Garrison, Wendell Phillips, and John Greenleaf Whittier. These and other militant abolitionist crusaders contributed voluminous writings and speeches against the inhumanity of slavery and in favor of immediate emancipation of all slaves. Antislavery newspapers and societies were numerous in New England, central New York, northern Ohio, and Michigan.

In the South, political and religious leaders alike espoused the conviction that slavery was not morally wrong and that neither hotheaded Northern abolitionists nor the federal government had the right to infringe upon the right to hold slaves. The slave was seen as legal property over which an owner had full legal right of ownership. Often the defense of slavery was argued in terms of biblical sanctions and the contention that the Negro was better off as a slave than free. In many states it was legally impossible to free slaves. Church people were as convinced as the nonreligious of the moral rightness of slavery. It is estimated that some 25,000 Methodists, including many preachers, together owned as many as 200,000 slaves.

Congress in passing the Kansas-Nebraska Act in 1854 provided that new territories could come into the Union in the future with or without slavery as their own citizens might decide. Franklin Pierce, the Democratic candidate, had been elected president in 1852 on the strength of wide support of the 1850 Compromise. Kansas and Nebraska now had the green light to allow slavery if they wanted it. Settlers or "squatters" moved into both territories in an effort to influence the constitutional vote on the status of slavery when it came up. "Bleeding Kansas" was torn by the ensuing bitter civil strife between proslavery settlers and "Free Soilers." Federal troops had to be sent in to quell the fighting, and, after several unsuccessful attempts to pass a referendum permitting slavery, Kansas in 1861 finally was admitted as a free state.

Meanwhile the Democratic Party, largely proslavery in sentiment, remained in power with the election of James Buchanan in 1856 to succeed Pierce. Buchanan defeated John C. Frémont, the Republican candidate, who ran on a campaign of "free soil, free speech, free men, and Frémont." The Supreme Court in the 1857 Dred Scott decision ruled in effect that Congress had never had power to exclude slavery from any of the territories. Heated political controversy caused in part by the court's decision seriously split the Democratic Party and foredoomed defeat in succeeding elections. The new Republican Party showed promising strength throughout the North in its first test in the 1856 voting for the presidency. In the 1858 campaign for United States senator in Illinois, Abraham Lincoln debated Stephen A. Douglas on the slavery issue. While losing the election, Lincoln gained national attention for his implacable stand against slavery and his stanch support of maintaining the Union at all costs. In the campaign of 1860 he was nominated by the Republicans and elected over the hopelessly divided Democratic forces, which fielded two factional candidates, Senator Douglas of Illinois and John C. Breckinridge of Kentucky.

Lincoln's election was greeted immediately by hostile Southern reaction against a president who openly and emphatically denounced slavery and denied the right of states to secede from the Union. South Carolina led a turbulent movement for secession, followed in time by other slaveholding states to form the Confederate States of America. There was no stopping the headlong surge toward civil war over the slavery question now joined with the issue of states' rights. The country, irreconcilably torn asunder, faced the devastation of four heartbreaking years of bloody conflict of intense fury and bitterness. When hostilities ended at Appomattox on April 9, 1865, an estimated 617,528 men had lost their lives, and the total cost in money of preserving the Union and abolishing slavery would probably total $10 million. It was costly to the entire nation.

After the war North and South faced the task of picking up the broken pieces of normal living, but each with differing problems. Difficult days lay ahead; but the Union was indissolubly one, and a new, stronger nation was to emerge out of the crucible of war. A divided country and a divided church faced similar situations, each affecting the other, with similar hopes for a brighter future.

The South was broken and demoralized, her lands devastated, her once proud plantations in utter ruins, her financial system shattered, her factories destroyed, the accumulated wealth of her people obliterated. The untimely death of President Lincoln by an assassin's gun less than a week after Appomattox removed all hope for a compassionate reconstruction. Carpetbag governments soon set up in the states were often corrupt and gave rise to added bitterness. They spawned retaliation from Southerners seeking to protect their homes and families through undercover groups such as the Ku Klux Klan.

In the North quick economic recovery, spurred by enormous war profits poured into capital investments, brought widespread prosperity. The postwar years became the era of the "robber barons," who dominated the business world with unprecedented concentration of ownership in manufacturing, finance, and transportation. Questionable business ethics of the day were matched by widespread political corruption. President Grant, skilled in war but naïve in politics, was able to do little to strengthen the national morality. But in spite of it all, the country forged forward in continuing expansion—except in the South, where progress was yet a long way off.

The Methodist church, divided and smarting from opposing sectional views as was the nation, also picked up the broken pieces and took faltering, timid first steps in both North and South in the direction of eventual reconciliation and reunion.

chapter 14

THE
CHURCH
DIVIDES

1844

**Methodist Slavery
  Legislation**

**The Abolitionist
  Struggle**

**The Wesleyan Methodist
  Church**

**The General Conference
  of 1844**

THE DIVISION OF THE METHODIST Episcopal Church into Northern and Southern sections was of fateful importance for the subsequent history of Methodism in this country. It may be of help, therefore, in understanding that event to give a connected account of the actions of the General Conferences up to that time on the question of slavery; for although the grounds of the separation were stated in terms of jurisdiction, the extent of the church's mission, and so on, it is obvious that slavery was at the bottom of it all. Such a recapitulation must of necessity consist chiefly of an account of positions taken or abandoned by the highest legislative body of the church, as recorded in the dry, dispassionate language of the conference *Journal*. But the decisions thus recorded grew out of the hopes and the ideals, the aspirations and the determination of forceful men and parties engaged in tense and dramatic struggle. In part the divergences grew out of the life of the Methodist Episcopal Church itself; in part they reflected the larger life of the nation in which the church lived and wrought. This larger context, charged with human emotion and conflict, can be read in more detail in other parts of this history. It can only be hinted at here. But the present account will be clothed with its full meaning only if this larger matrix of vigorous human and institutional life is constantly kept in mind.

1

The General Conferences Through 1832

The church's wrestlings with the problem of slavery in the late eighteenth and the early nineteenth centuries have already been recorded. Here it will suffice to recall that the high ground taken at the Christmas Conference, according to which even the *holding* of slaves by Methodists in those states which permitted their emancipation entailed expulsion, was quickly abandoned in the face of opposition which reached at times to threats of violence. Driven from this position the antislavery men struggled on, but with diminishing hopes of success, to effect the "extirpation" of slaveholding, of the trade, even domestic, in "the bodies or souls of men, women or children," and to keep those "in official station" free from entanglement of any sort with slavery. Agitation on the subject, while it never wholly died out in these early days, did not attain the importance it did in later times because the church was still engaged in hammering out questions of its organization and the allocation of authority. It was during these years that the constitution was formulated. The dissident movements of James O'Kelly and of the Methodist Protestants claimed a large share of the church's attention. These and other preoccupations kept antislavery agitation in a minor position among the church's concerns.

The General Conference of 1796 declared, "We are more than ever convinced of the great evil of African slavery." No slaveholder was to be admitted to membership until the preacher had spoken to him "freely and faithfully" on the subject. Every member who sold a slave was to be excluded from the society; those who purchased one were to submit to the decision of the quarterly meeting as to the time at which, having worked out his purchase price, the slave should be emancipated. This General Conference made a momentous concession of authority to the several Annual Conferences in that each was allowed to determine for itself under what conditions persons should be admitted to official stations.[1]

An enactment of the General Conference of 1800 had greater potential than actual importance. It provided that each of the Annual Conferences should appoint a committee to address the state legislatures from year to year, in favor of a gradual abolition of slavery.[2] This is one rather

[1] *Journals of the General Conference,* 1796-1836 (New York: Carlton and Phillips, 1855) , pp. 22-23.
[2] *Ibid.* (1800) , p. 41.

feeble indication that, though the Methodists might feel it incumbent upon them to obey the civil law with regard to emancipation, they were not wholly content to accept the laws as they were. It does not appear, however, that this "direction" of the General Conference was complied with to any extent. We have one instance of an effect being produced on a state legislature—but it was the reverse of gratifying. Asbury was informed that because of the Methodist petitions, the South Carolina General Assembly enacted "a law which prohibited a minister's attempting to instruct any number of blacks with the doors shut; and authorizing a peace officer to break open the door in such cases, and disperse or whip the offenders." [3] The apparent tendency of the Methodist antislavery position to make access to the Negroes more difficult gave its opponents another weapon for their attack, one which proved to be quite persuasive in the subsequent debate.

At this same General Conference of 1800 an enactment was passed requiring a traveling preacher who "by any means" became the owner of slaves either to forfeit his ministerial standing or to emancipate them "if it be practicable . . . agreeably to the laws of the state wherein they live." [4]

Succeeding General Conferences bear witness to still further concessions to the party which was becoming proslavery. That of 1804 reiterated the previous stand, but required the preachers to "exhort all slaves to render due . . . obedience to . . . their . . . masters," and went so far as to order two thousand copies of the "spiritual part" of the *Discipline* (that is, the part without the section on slavery) to be printed "for the use of the South." [5]

In 1808 a motion to strike out the section on slavery altogether failed; but a second concession was made to localism in the permission granted to each Annual Conference to make its own regulations concerning the buying and selling of slaves.[6] This gave rise to a wide and confusing diversity of practice which the General Conference of 1816 tried, without notable success, to reduce by gathering the reins into its own hands again. Later observers, both Northern and Southern, agreed that the buying and selling of slaves was carried on by Methodist laymen in the South pretty much as though no rule on the subject existed.[7]

Little was said and nothing at all done in the General Conference

---

[3] *Journal,* December 21, 1800.
[4] *Journals of the General Conference,* 1796-1836, p. 44.
[5] *Ibid.* (1804) , pp. 62-63, 65.
[6] *Ibid.* (1808) , p. 93.
[7] Lucius C. Matlack, *History of American Slavery and Methodism from 1780 to 1849; and History of the Wesleyan Methodist Connection of America* (New York, 1849) , p. 34.

of 1812 on the problem of slavery. Into that of 1816 a note of deep discouragement crept. A committee consisting of a member from each Annual Conference, entrusted with the task of examining the question, reported: "Little can be done to abolish a practice so contrary to the principles of moral justice. . . . The evil appears to be past remedy." They deplored the diversity of standards for admitting persons to official station which had grown up since 1800 and tried, not very successfully, to reduce it by this provision: "No slaveholder shall be eligible to any official station in our Church hereafter where the laws of the state in which he lives will admit of emancipation, and permit the liberated slave to enjoy freedom." [8]

In 1820, though much was said, nothing was done. There was a long and warm debate on the question of slavery, but possibly because the conference was much exercised over the "Canada question," the proposal to elect presiding elders, and Joshua Soule's election as bishop and subsequent refusal to accept the office, the matters in debate were not voted on. The questions debated are not even recorded in the *Journal* for that year. Four years later the section of the *Discipline* on slavery was amended for the last time. The amendment had to do with allowing certain improvement of status to the colored preachers, in those conferences which wished to adopt them and where "the usages of the country in different sections will justify." [9]

One more proposal was made in the General Conference of 1828 before the revival of the slavery question in the 1830's. S. G. Roszel of the Baltimore Conference and Peter Cartwright of the Illinois Conference proposed that inhumanity to slaves (by which they meant giving them insufficient food and clothing and separating families by trading) be treated as cases of immorality. This motion was laid on the table and never came up for discussion or a vote. Nothing of importance was done in the General Conference of 1832.

Thus the regulation of slavery in the Methodist Episcopal Church occupied less and less attention of the General Conferences during the first third of the nineteenth century. The fervor of the antislavery principles of the first generation cooled to a discouraged indifference; the standards were reduced to a minimum, so that it is safe to say that being a Methodist made comparatively little difference so far as slaveholding and even trading in slaves was concerned. The traveling ministry still, it would seem, kept comparatively clear of implication in the traffic.

[8] *Journals of the General Conference,* 1796-1836, pp. 169-70.
[9] *Ibid.* (1824), p. 294.

2

The General Conferences of 1836 and 1840

The troublesome question which many thought dead and safely buried in a shroud of qualifications and concessions was only sleeping. A breath from abroad revived it. The success of the parliamentary emancipation movement in England helped to rouse the abolition movement to life in this country under the aggressive leadership of William Lloyd Garrison and his disciples. This had little to do with the churches in its beginnings, and still less as time went on, but many churchmen caught the flame and began vigorous work in ecclesiastical circles. The spread of abolitionism in the North roused a countermovement for the defense of slavery in the South. Churchmen were among the leaders in the movement, and the biblical bulwarks of slavery were heavily relied on in the defensive strategy. The impetus to both the attack on and the defense of slavery came too late to make any impression on the General Conference of 1832, as we have seen. The antislavery forces were roused to new life in 1836 but made no progress whatever. In 1840 their increased strength was obvious; in 1844 the irresistible force met the immovable object, and disruption was the result.

The only out-and-out abolitionist delegations in the General Conference of 1836 were from the New England and the New Hampshire Conferences; only one other member, J. S. Barris of the Pittsburgh Conference, was found with them. A number of memorials presented to the General Conference, however, asked for a restoration of earlier and stricter rules on slavery. The committee appointed to consider them reported that it would be highly improper for the General Conference to change the rules, and that it was improper further to agitate the subject.[10]

The antislavery forces received an unexpected reinforcement from the fraternal address of the English Wesleyan delegate. From the eminence of the victory of the abolition cause achieved in 1833 in the British Empire, he spoke "with mildness, yet with plainness of speech," taking the position that "slavery is contrary to the principles of the Gospel." [11] He urged on his American brethren the duty of maintaining the *principle* of opposition to slavery.

The address aroused considerable excitement in the conference. Dr. Bangs indirectly complained of the transatlantic brethren's "interference." "The brethren from the South," said a Southern paper, "ex-

[10] *Ibid.* (1836) , p. 475.
[11] *Zion's Herald,* May 18, 1836.

pressed their opposition to abolition, but very delicately." [12] So strong
was the resistance to the sentiments of the address that the conference
refused to have it printed. The answer to it complained, "Had you been
able to view the subject from all sides . . . your tone of sympathy for us
would have been more pathetic." [13] The debate over the printing ranged
over the whole subject of the relation of the church to slavery. Dr. Bangs
was stronger in his condemnation of abolitionism than of slavery. It was
in this debate that Orange Scott of the New England Conference emerged
as the standard-bearer for the abolitionists in the church.

An instance of the knotty difficulties arising from the double mind of
the church on slavery is furnished by the report of the Judiciary Committee of this conference on an appeal from the Westmoreland and Lancaster Circuits of the Baltimore Annual Conference. The questions arising in that border conference were particularly acute because it had
always insisted that no slaveholder could enter its membership or be enrolled among its itinerants. The Westmoreland and Lancaster Circuits
were in Virginia. Some applicants for the ministry from those circuits
had been rejected. They petitioned this General Conference, alleging
that the exception in the paragraph of 1816 applied in their case, because
the laws of Virginia did not permit emancipation or the emancipated
slave to reside in freedom in the state. The committee had to walk cir-
cumspectly. It agreed with the petitioners in their claim that Virginia
laws entitled them to exception under the rule. But they refused to
change the Baltimore Conference's decision on the ground that it was
impossible to determine the motive for rejecting the petitioners, and that
the power of an Annual Conference to elect or reject with complete
freedom must be maintained.[14]

Perhaps the greatest excitement of the session was roused by the action
of two delegates from the New England Conference, who absented themselves from the General Conference sessions to make speeches at an
abolition meeting. The debate swirled about the disrespect shown by
the two delegates and the disrepute they had brought on the conference
by their inflammatory remarks in a city (Cincinnati) already excited over
the progress of abolition. There was debate over whether the number of
speakers should be mentioned in the censure, in order to show how few
there really were, and whether their names should be mentioned. The
last proposal was rejected as subjecting those so named to the possibility
of violent handling. Ultimately the conference dissociated itself sharply

[12] *The Virginia Conference Sentinel*, I (1836) , 46.
[13] *Ibid.*, p. 69.
[14] *Journals of the General Conference*, 1796-1836, pp. 465 ff.

from the culprits without naming or numbering them, and made a strong disclaimer of any intention "to interfere in the civil and political relation between master and slave as it exists in the slaveholding states of this Union." [15] Just to make sure their stand reached the ears of the whole church, the conference directed the framers of the Pastoral Address to "let our preachers, members, and friends know that the General Conference are opposed to the agitation of that subject, and will use all prudent means to put it down." [16]

The General Conference of 1840, in its dealings with the question of slavery, opened on the note with which the preceding conference had closed. "It was the solemn conviction of the Conference [1836]," said the bishops in their address, "that the interests of religion would not be advanced by any additional enactments in regard to [slavery]." [17] The address continued, as though in answer to the reproach implicit in the address of the Wesleyan Conference, by insisting that the General Rule on slavery had never been changed, and that, at the beginning as when the address was delivered, the simple owning of slaves had never rendered the master liable to excommunication. Subsequent regulation had constantly taken the laws of the states into consideration; they had changed from time to time and were a source of trouble to the church.[18] Not content with repudiating agitation in general, the bishops reproved the conferences of New England in particular for carrying on agitation in "such . . . a spirit as to disturb the peace of the Church." Such agitation, they said, was not making any contribution to freeing the church from slavery.

The fraternal delegate from the British Wesleyan Conference, in the address of this quadrennium, also struck the same note as four years earlier. He referred to that earlier address as containing sentiments to which his church still adhered. They were confirmed yet more in their views of the great moral evil of slavery. "Far be it from us to advocate violent and ill-considered measures. We are, however, strongly and unequivocally of opinion that it is . . . the paramount Christian duty of the ministers . . . in your country to maintain the *principle* of opposition to slavery." [19]

The General Conference's reply to this address was aimed at showing that the church's attitude toward slavery had not, in fact, changed. Buying or selling, it said, is forbidden in the General Rules as it has been since

[15] *Ibid.*, p. 447.
[16] *Ibid.*, p. 443.
[17] *Journal of the General Conference*, 1840, p. 134.
[18] *Ibid.*, p. 136.
[19] *Ibid.*, pp. 152-53.

1792; and the paragraph on slavery in the second part of the *Discipline* is still in force. The address implied that antislavery agitation was really inimical to carrying out the purpose of the section of the General Rules which required Methodists to be merciful to all, to their souls as well as their bodies. Such agitation prevented carrying out the work of evangelization among the slaves. The reply went on to explain the diversity of laws in the various states and said, "Each one of all these states is independent of the rest and sovereign, with respect to its internal government." For this reason it would be impossible to make one rule on slavery for all the states, and it would be wrong and unscriptural to contravene the laws of the states. "The question of the evil of slavery, abstractly considered . . . is a very different matter from a . . . rule of Church discipline to be executed . . . in defiance of the law of the land." The reply then cited the instructions Richard Watson, the great English Wesleyan missions secretary, had given to his workers in the West Indies before emancipation. He had admonished them to carry on their work of evangelization without "interfering with their [the slaves'] civil condition." [20]

How deeply the controversy over slavery permeated the discussions of this General Conference is illustrated by the debate over the report of the Committee on Itinerancy. The New England Conference was severely censured in the course of this report. This censure was finally stricken out, but only after a motion condemning a resolution of the Georgia Conference that "slavery, as it exists in these United States, is not a moral evil" had been laid on the table.[21]

One of the actions of this General Conference which roused the greatest excitement had nothing directly to do with the institution of slavery as such, and appeared before the conference under the noncommittal heading, "The Appeal of Silas Comfort." Silas Comfort was a New Yorker who had become a presiding elder in the Missouri Conference. In conducting a trial in this conference he had admitted the testimony of a colored person, and had been convicted of maladministration for so doing. On May 16 the General Conference heard his appeal and refused to sustain the conviction of his Annual Conference.[22] But two days later I. A. Few of Georgia introduced a resolution which was passed by a large majority: "It is inexpedient and unjustifiable for any preacher . . . to permit coloured persons to give testimony against white persons, in any state where they are denied that privilege in trials at law." [23] The con-

[20] *Ibid.,* pp. 154-56.
[21] *Ibid.,* pp. 106-7.
[22] *Ibid.,* p. 57.
[23] *Ibid.,* p. 60.

ference as a whole, however, had difficulty in reconciling itself with this resolution, and it came up for reconsideration several times. Bishop Soule had to explain that the resolution did not mean to prohibit the reception of testimony where the laws permitted it in civil trials; nor did it mean to cast any reflection on the integrity and piety of colored Methodists. But many Methodists obviously still felt that the Methodist Episcopal Church, in refusing to contravene the laws of the slave states, was adopting their sub-Christian standards as its own.

Talk of division in the church appeared in the formal debates in 1840. It was in connection with the question of receiving colored testimony that William Winans "talked loudly of a division of the church if the resolution [proposed by Mr. Few] were rescinded!" [24]

During the quadrennium just ended, the bishops and many of the presiding elders had acted in concert to repress the abolition movement which had reared its disturbing head in the General Conference of 1836. When presiding at Quarterly or Annual Conferences they had refused to entertain resolutions or receive memorials of an abolitionist tone. Often they adjourned a session to avoid having to countenance such proceedings. Daniel Dorchester, presiding elder of the Springfield District of the New England Conference, had adjourned a Quarterly Conference when it had introduced an antislavery resolution. A special convention petitioned Bishop Waugh for Dorchester's removal, and went so far as to propose several candidates to succeed him. Needless to say, the bishop did not see fit to comply with their request. Nevertheless, the New England Conference sustained charges against him of exceeding the powers of his office. Dr. Dorchester appealed to the General Conference, which reversed the New England Conference's decision.

This was but one of several cases involving the same principle. The procedure of the presiding officers was vindicated, not only in several specific cases but also by a blanket endorsement. The bishops themselves, in their address, asserted the constitutional right of presiding officers to refuse to admit questions; the Committee on Episcopacy approved their procedure and conduct during the quadrennium just ended; and finally the conference adopted a paragraph in the report of the Committee on Itinerancy which asserted the presiding officer's right to decline putting a question if, in his judgment, it did not pertain to the proper business of the conference. The paragraph, however, did require recording the president's refusal in the *Journal,* together with the conference's reasons for objecting thereto.[25]

[24] *Zion's Herald,* June 10, 1840.
[25] *Journal of the General Conference,* 1840, pp. 138, 99, 121.

Early in its session this General Conference was in receipt of a "communication" from the general secretary of the American Colonization Society. The Society was then over a quarter of a century old, and was the most "respectable" among the organizations devoted to the welfare of the Negroes. Its respectability, however, was greater than its effectiveness. Its objective was the establishment of a colony of free Negroes in Liberia; but during the first sixteen years of its existence it had transported thither only a few more than two thousand. When one considers that in spite of the outlawing of the slave trade, more than fifteen thousand Negroes were smuggled into the country every year, it becomes evident that the Colonization Society was not making much headway with the problem it existed to solve.

Nevertheless, it had enviable backing, not only from private philanthropists of high social standing but from state legislatures and religious bodies as well. The General Conference of 1840 responded favorably to the appeal of the Society and resolved that its efforts were deserving of approval and help. It was suggested that in Methodist churches a collection be taken annually for the Society's work on the Sunday nearest the Fourth of July.[26] For the abolitionists, however, this support was a ground of reproach. They were convinced that the Society was not only ineffective but a positive liability to the cause of emancipation. Many years before, William Lloyd Garrison had shown by an impressive accumulation of evidence from the Society's own representatives that they sang one song in the North and quite a different one in the South. Speaking to Northerners they presented their plans as an aid to the abolition of slavery; but in the South they stressed the beneficial effects of draining off the freedmen who might be centers of disaffection and revolt among the Negroes still in bonds. If the Society would ever bring about abolition of slavery, it would be only by the slow process of the centuries. The abolitionists were convinced that the Society was actually a channel by which the energies of emancipationists could be diverted into a safe dead end, and the General Conference's support of the Colonization Society was regarded as a defeat rather than a victory.

The Westmoreland Petition of this General Conference came from the same district and presented the same problem as the petition from the Westmoreland and Lancaster Circuits in 1836. It was considered and reported on in much the same way by the committee appointed for the purpose. The committee anxiously inquired concerning the general principles of right and wrong which underlay the questions presented by the petitioners. It asked: "May not the principles and causes giving birth and

[26] *Ibid.,* pp. 59-60.

perpetuity to great moral and political systems or institutions be regarded as evil, even essentially evil, in every primary aspect of the subject, without the implication of moral obliquity on the part of those involuntarily connected with such systems and institutions?" The report ended with a resolution which, adopted by the conference, read as follows:

The simple holding of slaves, or mere ownership of slave property, in states or territories where the laws do not admit of emancipation, and permit the liberated slave to enjoy freedom, constitutes no legal barrier to the election or ordination of ministers to the various grades of office known in the ministry of the Methodist Episcopal Church, and cannot, therefore, be considered as operating any forfeiture of right in view of such election and ordination.[27]

It is true that this paragraph contained nothing that had not been in the section of the *Discipline* on slavery since at least 1816. But this reiteration in a somewhat more positive form knocked one more bar off the barrier which many of the conferences, and not only Northern ones, had sought to erect against the involvement of the ministry of the church in slavery.

The General Conference of 1840 was indeed the low-water mark for antislavery sentiment in the church. It reiterated the reproof administered in 1836 to abolitionism. It tried (though unsuccessfully) to avoid further agitation of the subject. All the actions it took on the matter contravened the wishes of the antislavery party. It approved the authoritarian actions of officers presiding over conferences when they refused to put antislavery motions or to receive antislavery petitions. It refused to condemn a resolution to the effect that slavery was not a moral evil—though this was balanced by the deletion of censure for the conferences of New England. It repudiated (with some rather disingenuous arguments) the imputation of slackness in the cause of freedom brought by the English Wesleyan Conference. It approved the rejection of the testimony of colored persons in sections where it was not admitted in civil procedure. It approved the Colonization Society's ineffective and equivocal program. And finally it reiterated the legal right of access on the part of slaveholders to all grades of the ministry of the church.

The abolitionists, still very much in the minority in the church, were in despair. But after the conference the tide began to run the other way and bore in the spectacular events of 1844.

[27] *Ibid.,* p. 170-71.

3

The Abolitionists and Their Opponents in the 1830's

The Broader Conflict

Antislavery sentiments and antislavery organizations were not new in the 1830's. But in that decade, as the result of a number of forces, they assumed a new aggressiveness and were gradually transformed into an abolition movement. Most of these forces have already been mentioned but at this juncture need to be reconsidered in their connections with each other, and in their effect on church life in general and Methodist church life in particular.

Several of the most potent forces took their rise in the economic and political life of the nation. Abolitionism grew at an equal pace with the institution of slavery, and a defense of slavery kept pace with the attacks on it. We will have said much about the root cause of this newly intensified struggle when we remark that in the 1830's the climb of cotton to kingship accelerated in pace. Cotton was already on the verge of dominating not only the agrarian economy of the South but also a section of the manufacturing activities of both Old and New England. The spinning and weaving factories in both places were demanding more and more raw materials. In the effort to supply this demand the South did not altogether cease doing other things, of course, but her economy became more and more concentrated around producing cotton. Given the past history of the cotton industry it is not strange that many in the North as well as in the South were more and more firmly convinced that it could not be carried on without slave labor. And given the constantly expanding market, it is understandable that many believed that prosperity depended on the possibility of expanding the area in which slavery was as possible politically as it was profitable economically.

Under these circumstances the political representatives of the slave states not only insisted on freedom to expand their system to the westward but also battered away at the northern limit imposed by the Missouri Compromise of 1820. The Compromise Acts of the 1850's were, in effect, the abrogation of the arrangement of 1820. With the need to expand slavery came the need to intensify control of the slave population. A series of insurrections took place, the most formidable of which was led by Nat Turner in 1831—the very beginning of our decade. Many slave owners began to feel that they had a lion by the tail and that the only possible course was to tighten, not loosen, their hold over the entire Negro population.

Indeed, one of the facts of which we must constantly remind ourselves as we study this question is that slavery and antislavery sentiments and even actions did not, for a long time at any rate, correspond to geographical sections in the United States. But it is easy to overlook the early antislavery sentiment in the South precisely for the reason that during this crucial decade it began to disappear. It became either converted to or silent before a vigorous proslavery apologetic which grew up and gave the sanction of sectional unanimity to a proslavery outlook which could thereafter be increasingly considered as "Southern."

Here we will look briefly at the most obvious features of this apologetic as it emanated from the South as a whole, reserving for another time our consideration of the relation of Methodists to the movement.

Though they took second place behind the religious and biblical arguments, economic and secular arguments were not wanting. Slavery was often justified as a positive good for the Negro. See how much better off, this argument ran, the Negroes are here and now than they were in their native Africa. They have been rescued from intertribal warfare; their maintenance now is provided for, whereas they formerly had to eke out a precarious existence by wresting it from the jungle in a pestilential climate. Above all, they are now thrown into contact with our superior civilization and brought under the influence of the gospel in an enlightened and Christian land. Thus, even though they are slaves here, they have been much bettered economically and culturally by transportation from their original savagery and superstition.

Another argument compared the condition of the Negro slave favorably with that of the worker in the factories of the North and of Europe. The Southern Negro, though he is called a slave, is freer than the formally free worker in the North from the constant struggle merely to keep alive. The latter is at the mercy of the market and of an employer to whom his personal welfare means nothing if it conflicts with the profits of business. It is the wage earner of the North who is the real slave, though he is not called such. He lives in another man's house; if he cannot work, he and his family cannot eat, or find enough to wear, or have warmth and shelter from the rigors of winter.

The thought of the time was so completely cast in a biblical mode, and its expression so dominated by biblical images, that we are not surprised to find that the chief bulwark of the defense was drawn from the Bible. The highest sanctions of the Christian religion were therefore summoned to buttress slavery. One of the most thorough students of the legal and political aspects of the defense of slavery has come to the conclusion that the religious defense was the first to appear, and that it permeated all other kinds of apologetic. John Bachman, a prominent Lutheran clergyman of Charleston, wrote: "Our representatives in Congress used the argument contained in the Scriptures, and their opponents dared not tell them that the historical parts (and all that refers to slavery is historical) were uninspired and untrue." [28]

Given the literalistic approach to the Bible and the view of its authority then prevalent, it is not surprising that what the apologists for slavery sought there, they found. The patriarchs held slaves, and were the recipients of the marks of divine favor. The chosen people were given express permission to make slaves under certain circumstances. The classic verse on which this argument rested was Lev. 25:45: "You may also buy from among the strangers who sojourn with you and their families that are with you, who have been born in your land; and they may be your property." In the New Testament slavery is not only nowhere reproved, it is, by easy inference at least, approved. The favorite citation here is Paul's sending the slave Onesimus back to his owner Philemon without enjoining the latter to free him, but with an exhortation to treat him "no longer as a slave, but more than a slave, as a beloved brother." From there it was but a step to the conclusion of another clerical apologist who said, "The omniscient Saviour and his . . . Apostles . . . instituted regulations for the perpetual continuance of slavery." [29]

More intricate arguments were constructed from the sin of Noah's son Ham and the servitude which was to be the punishment for it. In keeping the Negroes (the sons of Ham) in servitude, slaveholders were vindicating the righteous law of God (Gen. 9:22, 25-27).

The clerical defenders of the system built up a secondary wall of defense in their conception of the church's task on earth. According to this view, the world was a place where the providence of a sovereign God determined conditions in order to make it the theater for working out his purposes. The church was to accept it as such rather than change it in the light of a social ideal of "human" origin. This was not limited to Calvinists, for, as we shall see later, Methodists relied heavily on it. The Calvinistic view of the world, however, was peculiarly adapted to support it. A Presbyterian minister, Dr. Thornwell, accordingly insisted that the church's business was not to remove all evil from the world or to change civil institutions. It had no more right to abolish slavery than to change a form of government from a republic to a monarchy. The

[28] Quoted in William Sumner Jenkins, Pro-slavery Thought in the Old South (Chapel Hill: University of North Carolina Press, 1935), pp. 206-7.
[29] [Iveson L. Brookes] A Defense of Southern Slavery Against the Attacks of Henry Clay and Alexander Campbell (Hamburg, S. C.: Robinson and Carlisle, 1851), p. 6.

church's duty *did* lie in teaching the mutual duties of master and slave—kindness to the former, submission to the latter.[30]

The religious defense of slavery was reinforced by a political theory, popularly called the "states' rights" theory. It maintained that the powers of the original colonies which had been delegated to the federal government under the terms of the constitution were strictly limited, and that each state retained sovereign powers of self-government in its internal affairs. As time went on, more and more stress was laid on the inherent right to withdraw from the confederation voluntarily entered into. But what interests us most at present is the contention that, so far as slavery within its own borders was concerned, each state had the right to regulate as it saw fit. The states' rights theory, in conjunction with the biblical defense of slavery, tended to become a hypersensitive localism, and went far to produce by direct and devious means of public pressure a unanimity of opinion in the South which was soon recognizable as sectional solidarity.

As counterpoise we have the rise of the antislavery movement which in its extreme manifestations (which were almost wholly confined to the North) became the abolition party. Neither antislavery ideas nor antislavery organizations were new in the 1830's. But an excess of zeal, determined aggressiveness, and above all an articulate organ of expression—William Lloyd Garrison's *Liberator*—were new. The first number of the *Liberator* appeared in the opening month of the decade we are considering—in January, 1831. The keynote Garrison struck is famous: "I will be as harsh as truth, and as uncompromising as justice. On this subject, I do not wish to think, to speak, or write, with moderation. . . . I am in earnest—I will not equivocate—I will not excuse—I will not retreat a single inch—*and I will be heard!*"

It was Garrison who wrote the statement of purpose of the American Antislavery Society, which was founded in 1833. Before long he was its president, and able more and more to impress his own ideas on its policy. His vigorous personality kept the loyalty of the Society behind his policies throughout the decade; but in 1840 it split, and the dissenters formed the National Antislavery Society. Three policies which he advocated with unyielding persistence alienated many: a place of equality for women in the movement; an attack on the churches for their inertia in the cause; and the restriction of the movement to nonviolent methods. His integrity, his courage, and his devotion were unquestionable. He was able to enlist the devotion of many able orators and men of action in his

[30] Thornwell, *Report on the Subject of Slavery Presented to the Synod of South Carolina, at Their Sessions in Winnsborough, November 6, 1851* (Columbia, 1852).

crusade. These, and the strident quality of his agitation, were his chief assets. That he was able to call attention to the wrongs inherent in the enslavement of the Negro and disturb the complacent lethargy of thousands, awakening them to the dangers of inaction, is undoubtedly true. It is also true that his denunciatory tactics were the most effective part of his activity. He coined a formula for the activities of the abolitionists: "Immediate abolition, gradually arrived at," which was more confusing than stirring. His capacity for alienating those who did not agree with him in all his principles, even those only remotely connected with abolition, proved an embarrassment to many of the workers in the cause. Finally, he was not nearly so effective in proposing practicable measures for remedying the evil of slavery as he was in denouncing the evil itself.

Just as in the South no defense of slavery was complete without the religious sanction, so in abolition circles no attack on it which omitted the religious factor and the services of religious people could have been successful. The church people whom Garrison alienated served under less spectacular leaders, but their quieter work was, in the end, more effective than his.

The mid-nineteenth century might be called the "age of philanthropy" in American life, just as the mid-eighteenth century has a good claim on the title in England. A host of "good causes" flourished—Bible societies, tract societies, missionary societies, societies for the promotion of this and for the prevention of that. Many of them had headquarters in New York City, so that their interlocking directorates have aptly been called "the benevolent empire." The source and the matrix of all this benevolent effort was the revivalism of the time. The prime figure in the revivals was the New School Presbyterian Charles Grandison Finney. Finney rather shocked his fellow Presbyterians with his "new measures" in evangelism, and still more by his espousal of a perfectionist theology. But he was a power in spreading the gospel and in imbuing his converts with zeal for labor in the evils that cried out for reform.

One of Finney's converts, Theodore Weld by name, claims our attention here because of his indefatigable work in the antislavery cause. Though he avoided publicity as studiously as Garrison sought it, his contribution to the cause of the slave was ultimately greater. He toiled long in the ranks of the American Antislavery Society, employing evangelistic techniques in the conversion of small towns in Ohio and other places to the cause, and fashioning local centers of antislavery action. It was Weld who converted James G. Birney, later to be the presidential candidate of the abolitionists, to his views. It was Weld who compiled the enormous collection of data from which Harriet Beecher Stowe verified the picture of slavery given in *Uncle Tom's Cabin*. Thus, less in the public eye but closer to the earnest Protestant folk of the North, and with more enduring results, did Weld and other evangelically minded men throw themselves into the greatest reform movement of the time. It is against this background that we should see the development of the abolition and antiabolition parties in the Methodist Episcopal Church of the 1830's.

The Abolitionist Struggle in the Methodist Episcopal Church

What attitude did Methodist writers take toward the defense of slavery? So far as the present writer has been able to discover, they took no part at all in the public defense of slavery as a positive good. Southern periodicals carried articles which *assumed* that it was such, but of the prominent publications which appeared in the course of the effort to convince men it was a positive good, none, it would appear, was by a Methodist. In the period after the separation the Methodist Episcopal Church, South, maintained that it was *not* a proslavery church. Northern Methodists were far from admitting the claim, but it could not even have been made if any prominent Methodist writings in behalf of slavery had been in existence to rise up and testify against them. Other less positive degrees of the polemic, however, were supported by Methodist writers.

Two approaches, perhaps the ones most frequently resorted to, are combined in the resolution which the Georgia Conference passed in 1838:

Resolved, That it is the sense of the Georgia Annual Conference that slavery as it exists in the United States is not a moral evil.

Resolved, That we view slavery as a civil and domestic institution, and one with which, as ministers of Christ, we have nothing to do, further than to ameliorate the condition of the slave, by endeavoring to impart to him and his master the benign influences of the religion of Christ, and aiding both on their way to heaven.[31]

For the Georgia Conference, slavery, if it was not a positive good, was not a moral evil. Another form of this argument, less sweeping and more defensible, was often used: Slaveholding is not a sin under all circumstances. Both paragraphs of the Georgia resolution were intended to justify the deference which the church had shown historically to state legislation on the subject and to excuse the church from current interference in the business. "It belongs to Caesar," said William Capers at

[31] Quoted from Orange Scott, "Appeal to the Methodist Episcopal Church," *The Wesleyan Antislavery Review,* 1838, p. 17.

another time, "not to the Church." [32] A resolution of the South Carolina Conference said, "We hold that the subject of slavery in these United States is not one proper for the action of the Church, but is exclusively appropriate to the civil authorities." Dr. Capers explained this, if Lucius Matlack's report is correct, by saying, "If slavery were a moral evil, that is, sinful, the Church would be bound to take cognizance of it; but our affirmation is, that it is not a matter for her jurisdiction, and, of course, not sinful." [33]

Even though Methodist writers took no prominent part in the wide dissemination of the idea that slavery was a good thing, there is no doubt that many of them actually believed it. Their opinions appeared in Methodist papers and were spoken on conference floors. Bishop Hedding wrote in the *Christian Advocate and Journal,* "The right to hold a slave is founded on this rule, 'Therefore, all things whatsoever ye would that men should do to you, do ye even so to them; for this is the law and the prophets.'" [34] Orange Scott noted a tendency toward a positive justification of slavery among some Methodist ministers in the late 1830's. "No Methodist minister," he said, "attempted to write a Bible argument thirty, nor even ten years ago, to justify slaveholding under any circumstances; but now our college and church officers, and even one of our bishops has done this!" Then he quotes from the professor of languages at Randolph-Macon College: "These extracts from Holy Writ unequivocally assert the right of property in slaves, together with the usual incidents of that right [such as the right to buy, sell, bequeath, etc.]." [35] Bishop Hedding, in addressing the Oneida Conference, reasoned thus:

If no case can be found where a man can own a slave, and in that act obey this [the golden] rule, then there is no case in which slaveowning can be justified. But if one case can be found where a man may hold a slave, and by the civil law own him, and in that act obey this rule, then there may be ten such cases, or ten thousand. And that there are many such cases among our brethren in the southern states, I firmly believe. . . . And I am not authorized to be the instrument of passing conference resolutions which even imply that they are all sinners.[36]

William Winans, arguing on the floor of the General Conference, asserted, "I am a slaveholder *on principle.*" He thought ministers *ought*

[32] *Ibid.,* p. 20.
[33] Matlack, *The Antislavery Struggle and Triumph in the Methodist Episcopal Church* (New York: Phillips and Hunt, 1881) , p. 104.
[34] October 20, 1837.
[35] "Appeal to the Methodist Episcopal Church," pp. 5, 13.
[36] *Christian Advocate and Journal,* October 20, 1837.

to be slaveholders, in order to be in a position to set a good example of kindness in treatment of them.

The expressions just quoted came from what Peter Cartwright used to call the "ultras" and went beyond those opinions which most Methodists held, or at least were willing to put into words. Until the 1840's most Methodists were, if not proslavery, at least antiabolitionist, and vigorously so. They held these sentiments either from a genuine conviction that the question was a civil rather than a moral one, and hence beyond the purview of the church, or else (what amounts to much the same thing) out of concern for the peace and unity of the church. The church's main reason for existence, these people thought, was to save souls; and the only consistent thing was to leave aside all questions which interfered with this pursuit. This was the main concern of the great majority of Methodists up through the '30's, and especially of the officiary, who felt themselves called upon to seek first the good of the Methodist Episcopal Church—its stability, its growth, the harmonious cooperation of all its parts. Again it must be noted that the antiabolition party was not sectional in its extent but numbered among its adherents members of Northern and border, as well as Southern, conferences. "Modern abolitionism," as it came to be called, was denounced as roundly in New York and Ohio as it was in Maryland and Georgia.

But denunciation could not prevent the movement, which had taken its rise outside the church, from making recruits within it. It made its way in spite of opposition and took firm hold first in the New England Conference. Thence it spread westward through the northernmost tier of states. Its adherents, however, were in the minority until well after the division of the church in 1844; and there never were many in the South.

One of the first concerns of the abolitionists was to counter the apologetic for slavery which we have already sketched. The sum and substance of what they had to say was: Slavery is unjust, it is sinful, and it should be stopped. This theme was capable of, and received, infinite elaboration. Since the most vigorous and resourceful of the advocates of abolition was Orange Scott, we can give an epitome of the party's arguments as he expressed them. His career as the architect of the first noteworthy schism over slavery will be described later. Here we have to do only with the ideas he brought to the attack on the institution of slavery. His was not a mind of great profundity; he was not even a steady master of literary expression. But his thoroughness, his depth of conviction, and his tirelessness in polemic made him the first among Methodist exponents of abolition ideology, and bore him at times to heights of convincing eloquence.

Scott drew up an address to the General Conference of 1836, a time when abolitionism was still odious. It was printed several times—sometimes alone and sometimes in connection with other pieces.[37] In this address, Scott emphasized that the great question was the justice or injustice of the claims of more than two million American citizens to the inalienable rights of free men. It would be wrong and improper for the General Conference to interfere with the *political* relations of master and slave, but as ministers they should have something to do with the *moral* principles involved. Slavery withheld the Bible from a sixth of the population. It separated husbands and wives and exposed a million females to insult without protection. Were not these moral questions?

Slavery could no more be justified from Scripture than the divine right of kings. The New Testament does condemn slaveholding as practiced among us in the most explicit terms. We should not delay to do justice to the slaves because at some period a white woman might happen to marry a black man. Slavery might be constitutional, but so was the attempt to abolish it. "Are there no interests to be consulted besides the peace of the Church? . . . She ought not . . . to give herself any peace till she cleanses the skirts of her garment from 'blood guiltiness!' " The expediency so much insisted on by the enemies of abolition ought not to weigh too heavily: "If public opinion is wrong, it ought to be braved!" Abolition is inevitable:

Blind though we be, aye, sir, blind as Samson in the Temple of Dagon, like him if we can do no more, we will grope our way along, feeling for the pillars of that temple which has been consecrated to the bloody rites of the Moloch, slavery—grasping their base we will bend forward, nerved by the omnipotence of truth, and upheave the entire fabric, whose undistinguishable ruins shall mark the spot where our grandest moral victory was proudly won!

The way to begin this reform, Scott felt, was to persuade Congress to abolish slavery in the District of Columbia and in the territories. The Colonization Society could not advance the cause; its program was based on wrong assumptions, the first of these being that the Negro had no rights in this country.

Many slaveholders in this country treated their slaves kindly. But cruel treatment—and there was plenty of that—was not the worst thing about

---

[37] The exposition which follows was taken from the copy in the Boston Athenaeum, of which the title page reads: *Address to the General Conference of the Methodist Episcopal Church by the Rev. O. Scott, a member of that body; presented during its session in . . . 1836. To which is added the Speech of the Rev. Mr. Scott, delivered on the floor of the General Conference.*

the institution. The worst feature of slavery was slavery itself. The attack on "modern abolitionism" was a repudiation of the historic teaching of Methodism in regard to the evil; for abolitionism is not "modern" but primitive in our church. It is but a revival of the vigorous sentiments of Wesley and the first American Methodist preachers on the matter. In this *Address* Scott gave a very able review of the history of the question in the church to support this contention.

In the Barbados, Scott continued, the danger of the amalgamation of the races decreased since emancipation. The cloud of fear of a black insurrection was dissipated, not increased, since that blessed event.

In his other polemic writings as well as in the *Address,* Scott tried from various starting points to dissipate the force of the biblical argument on which the defenders of slavery relied so heavily. In the process he and the other abolitionists managed partly to emerge from the rigorously literalistic interpretation of the Scriptures—without, however, arriving at a complete idea of a developing moral ideal.

Another way of vitiating the proslavery party's claim that the example of the patriarchs and apostles was authoritative was to show that the slavery of the Holy Land in Bible times was a very different and much less virulent form of it than that which prevailed in the United States of the nineteenth century. In addition to arguments on the meaning of the scriptural words for "slave," more ingenious than convincing, Scott was fond of quoting Wesley's superlatives in condemnation, as when he spoke of American slavery as "the vilest that ever saw the sun." Still, the abolitionists put their finger on the real weak spot of the proslavery apologetic when they said that justification from biblical example proves too much; one might, by the same argument, justify polygamy and the divine right of kings as well as slavery.

The story of the efforts of the abolition party to stay alive and propagate itself in the church, and the counter efforts to root it out, is not a happy one; but it must be told, for it was the most vital and absorbing facet of the life of the church at the time. As the struggle increased in intensity and bitterness, unchristian things were said and done on both sides. The consummation of the struggle is told in another section; here we recount its earlier stages—that is, those which transpired before the General Conference of 1844.

The methods of the abolitionists were the methods of all voluntary associations serving a cause: the formation of societies, the holding of conventions, agitation in bodies where a majority needed converting, the use of the written word, and so on. These methods, though now common property, were, it is interesting to note, first devised by Wilberforce and his lieutenants in their fight for abolition in the British Empire.[38] The antiabolitionist majority, at first irritated then alarmed by the persistence of these "fanatics," were not always careful to preserve the minority's right to expression. Various forms of gag rule were resorted to in the conferences, even as they were in the national Congress. The leading abolitionist agitators were charged and brought to trial for insubordination and slander, sometimes justifiably, sometimes under an unreasonably wide definition of those terms, as when attending an abolitionist meeting was regarded as transgressing the limits of due submissiveness to authority. The appointive power, the abolitionists said, was used in a punitive way. The abolitionists were driven to despair by these tactics, but the ebb of their fortunes was but the prelude to their ultimate victory.

The earliest Methodist Antislavery Society was formed in 1834 in New York City by La Roy Sunderland, an active abolitionist of the New England Conference. The Wesleyan Antislavery Society was formed at Lynn, Massachusetts, the next year, and in 1836 a similar society was formed in the New Hampshire Conference. After the split in the American Antislavery Society in 1840, the New Hampshire Conference Society felt it wise to proclaim its adherence to the aims set forth in the original constitution of that society.[39] By that time too it was felt expedient to make a declaration of loyalty to the Methodist Episcopal Church, repudiating the desire, which had been alleged by some, to reform the church by abolishing the episcopacy and introducing lay representation. The issue of church reform was driving a wedge into the Methodist antislavery movement just at the time when Garrison's insistence on women's rights and nonresistance was splitting the American Antislavery Society.

There were no antiabolition societies, for there was no need of them. The great weight of the official machinery of the church—most of the conferences, administrative officials, the church press—was arrayed against abolitionism. Moreover, the legislatures of some of the Southern states issued protests against the activities of the movement. The legislature of Virginia addressed a resolution to the nonslaveholding states requesting suppression of abolition societies. An address to the House of Delegates of that state complained of the "unhallowed attempt to array the sanctions of the pure and gentle religion" of Christianity against the institution of slavery, and deplored "unprovoked interference with our exclusive concerns." The "closest and most fraternal, . . . the most sacred [Union]

[38] G. M. Trevelyan, *English Social History* (London: Longmans, Green & Co., 1942), pp. 496-97.

[39] *Zion's Herald*, July 29, 1840.

that ever united Sovereign Powers" was being violated by some states.[40] Massachusetts, for instance, declared that a slave taken into that state was thereby freed. Maine, Ohio, and New York declined to co-operate in the suppression of abolition societies. The legislatures of South Carolina, North Carolina, Georgia, and Alabama also requested the nonslavehold-ing states to suppress abolition societies.

During the quadrennium between 1840 and 1844 a number of resolu-tions, vigorously antislavery in tone, were passed by the conferences, both Quarterly and Annual, in New England. Revulsion against the action of the 1840 General Conference in respect to the testimony of colored persons at church trials was especially evident. The New Hampshire Conference voted that it should be reconsidered or rescinded. It must be regarded, they said, "as a most fearful concession to slavery." [41] The Worcester Quarterly Conference was exercised over the same mat-ter.[42] The Quarterly Conference of St. Paul's Church in Lowell, Massa-chusetts, where Orange Scott was the admired pastor, not content with protesting the General Conference's action on colored testimony, drew up a whole list of its antiabolitionist acts which were vigorously disap-proved. The presiding elder, under the provision of the General Confer-ence, registered his dissent from the action of the Quarterly Conference as inconsistent with the spirit of abolitionism and of Methodism, though as an "old, decided and unyielding abolitionist," he consented to have the motion put.[43]

Just before the General Conference of 1844 many of the preachers of the Springfield (Massachusetts) District circulated a memorial through the columns of Zion's Herald for all who wished to sign. This resolution too deplored the action of 1840 on the testimony of colored people. It ex-pressed the hope, "in view of the fact that the constitution of the Method-ist Episcopal Church is decidedly anti-slavery in its character," that no slaveholder be elected to the higher offices of the church, such as bishop, missionary secretary, book agent, or editor; and concluded with an earnest petition "to take such constitutional measures as shall effectually separate the Methodist Episcopal Church from all connection with the practice of slaveholding." [44]

Many of the Annual Conferences before 1844 took a middle-of-the-road position—that is, they deplored slavery on the one hand and abolitionism on the other. Such was the Ohio Conference, for example. In its session

[40] The Virginia Conference Sentinel, I (1836), 165 ff.
[41] Zion's Herald, August 5, 1840.
[42] Ibid., August 19, 1840.
[43] Ibid., September 16, 1840.
[44] Ibid., January 10, 1844.

of 1835 it spoke of membership in the Methodist Episcopal Church as involving opposition to slavery, and it was in favor of "gradual peaceable emancipation." This meant approval and support for the Colonization Society. The resolution against abolition was sharper: "We deeply regret the proceedings of the abolitionists and anti-slavery societies in the free states; . . . and . . . we hereby recommend to . . . members within our bounds to abstain from any connection with them." [45]

The Baltimore Conference, on the borderline between slave and free states, reflected the same division in its statements. It too deplored abolition activity, and yet declared itself in 1836 to be "as much as ever convinced of the great evil of slavery." [46] The distinctive feature of the Baltimore Conference's stand on slavery was its continued determination to keep its membership and traveling ministry free of slaveholding. The early years of its Minutes have frequent references to applicants for ordination who were rejected until they had made satisfactory arrangements to clear themselves of entanglement in slave owning. The restriction persisted, but it was not so frankly recorded in later times. Its Journals are full of earnest wrestlings with cases of this kind; in 1843 it was still steadfast in its principle and ordered several members who had become owners of slaves "to take measures within the current conference year, to free themselves of the relation." [47]

A number of bodies, small and great, took action against the abolitionists. Zion's Watchman (published in New York by La Roy Sunderland to further the abolition cause) reported that the trustees of the West Circuit in New York City requested their pastor not to invite any preacher known to be an abolitionist into the pulpits of the circuit. Many were sure this measure was taken to shut out the delegates from the New England Conference, then in the city, from an opportunity to preach.[48] Sunderland himself was cited before the New England Conference, of which he was a member, for trial for misrepresentation and slander in his paper. The conference let him off with a light penalty, saying, in effect, "Not guilty—don't do it again." The Virginia Conference Sentinel published a letter disapproving of the New England Conference's leniency.[49]

For the whole decade after 1837 the Philadelphia Conference put the question to candidates for admission: "Are you an abolitionist?" and

   [45] Western Christian Advocate, September 11, 1835.
   [46] Zion's Herald, April 20, 1836.
   [47] Journals of the Baltimore Conference, III, 220. Quoted in this instance from mimeographed abstract by Edwin Schell, pp. 16-17.
   [48] Zion's Herald, May 4, 1836.
   [49] Vol. I (1836), 94-95.

accepted them only when the answer was in the negative. Lucius Matlack, who gives us this information, was himself twice refused admittance, in 1837 and 1838, on this very account.[50] This conference "heard with . . . regret" that Orange Scott and George Storrs had come within their boundaries and were lecturing on abolitionism. They protested strongly in a formal resolution and recommended that their brethren discourage all such activities as tending "to disturb the peace and prosperity within our bounds." [51] Similar resolutions were passed against abolitionists (without mentioning names, however) by the Ohio, the Baltimore, and the New York Conferences.

In the latter half of the decade simply engaging in abolition activities was enough to render the participants liable to prosecution, especially in cases where abolitionist publications criticized procedures or persons in the conservative bodies of the church. Bishop Waugh refused to put an antislavery motion in the New England Conference, refused to allow an appeal from his decision, refused to say whether memorials had been received to transmit to the committee, and finally refused to transmit such as he had received. In the New York Conference three members, Charles K. True, James Floy, and Paul R. Brown, were tried for aiding in the publication of an antislavery tract. True and Floy were suspended, but submitted and were restored. Brown refused to submit. He was subject to public rebuke by the bishop. His defense was: "As for pledging not to discuss the subject, I never can do it. If you think you must censure or suspend or expel me, why, you must take your course, and I must bear it. But I feel it to be my duty to plead for the slave, and I must have the liberty." [52] Matlack says he was the object of retaliatory use of the ap-pointive power. "The appointment of this noble-hearted brother . . . was in a distant field of labor, where he suffered much inconvenience and many privations." [53]

Henry Degen, employee of the Book Concern and a class leader, lost his classbook and was dismissed from his position for dividing his centennial offering between the cause proposed and the antislavery cause. The Erie Conference suspended Benjamin Preston for delivering an abolition lecture and denouncing the suspensions in the New York Conference. Bishop Hedding made a four-hour address in the New England Conference of 1838, which was made the basis of charges against Orange Scott; he pursued the matter the following year and even in the General Conference of 1840.

[50] *Antislavery Struggle*, p. 117.
[51] *Ibid.*, p. 83.
[52] *Ibid.*, p. 114.
[53] *History of American Slavery*, p. 261.

La Roy Sunderland was charged with slanderous insertions in the *Watchman* at three successive sessions of his conference (1836-38), but was acquitted each time. In 1840 he was tried on charges presented by the New York Conference and again acquitted. Finally he was tried by a committee in New York, himself not being present; but the proceedings were set aside by the New England Conference in the following year. He was tried once again for having slandered Bishop Soule, with Bishop Soule himself presiding at the trial, which gave rise to a good deal of adverse comment. The charge was sustained by a slight majority, but the penalty was light. Sunderland was ordered to print the facts of the decision in his paper without comment. He did this without *verbal* comment, but set the decision in large type and surrounded it with a deep mourning border. The height to which feelings were roused by these clashes is indicated by the fact that lay people took to writing jingles in the abolitionist journals, lampooning the "persecutors." Here is a verse from the one Sunderland printed on Bishop Soule, with the comment that every letter of it was justified—which brought on his trial for slander:

> Receive this truth—deep, dark, thy stain;
> Thy very soul is tinged with blood;
> Go, do thy first works o'er again—
> Go, cleanse thee in the Saviour's blood.[54]

Lucius Matlack later admitted that the abolitionists had gone beyond the bounds of charity in their spoken and their written comments on the church and its bishops:

Abolition writers assailed individual Bishops, by name, with severe and ill-advised criticism. These, in self-defense, preferred charges against their assailants, who were usually acquitted by their Annual Conferences. Thus a strife was engendered which produced alienation and disaffection with some leading Abolitionists, who, therefore, became objects of suspicion, and were charged with designing to divide the Church, or purposing to withdraw from its communion.[55]

Other signs of mounting party spirit appeared at the General Conference of 1836, though they did not get written into the records. A prominent Southern minister, a slaveholder, was proposed for the episcopacy. The antislavery forces, while admitting the qualifications of the man in question in all other respects, confidently asserted that as a slaveholder he could not be elected. Their confidence was justified, for

---

[54] Matlack, *Antislavery Struggle,* p. 131.
[55] *Ibid.,* p. 138.

of the three bishops elected none owned slaves. One, Wilbur Fisk (who declined the office), was a New Englander. The other two were both Virginians by birth: Beverly Waugh became a member of the Baltimore Conference, and Thomas A. Morris had been editor of the *Western Christian Advocate*. But the Southerners took it ill that the question of slaveholding had played a part in the election. A Georgian wrote:

We utterly deny, sir, that the provisions of the Discipline prevent a slave-holder from exercising the functions of a bishop, or any other office in the church, if the laws of the State in which he lives will not allow emancipation, or a manumitted slave to enjoy freedom. . . . The first blast of the abolition trump, announcing war against slavery, will . . . array the *entire South* in solid and indissoluble phalanx under one banner . . . with the motto "our domestic institutions." [56]

The *Virginia Conference Sentinel* disagreed with the opinion of its Georgia correspondent that the next General Conference should divide the church. It still had hope that the Northern brethren would withdraw from the controversy which could only issue in the ruin of both parties. Nevertheless, when the *Pittsburgh Christian Advocate* had earlier asked whether any Southern men were eligible for the highest church offices, the *Sentinel* termed the question "prophetic of the coming dismember-ment of Methodism." [57]

In the General Conference of 1836 direct threats of secession were heard—though to be sure they were uttered in caucuses rather than on the floor. But in 1840 they were heard in formal debate. It was by fore-stalling the election of additional bishops in 1840, Peter Cartwright said, that he and others probably prevented a complete break at that time.[58]

In the General Conference of 1840 a good deal of excitement was caused by the presentation of a memorial from New York City, purport-ing to be signed by over eleven hundred Methodist abolitionists. It fell into the hands of an unfriendly committee, who arranged for a quick investigation on the spot. It reported in horrified tones that many of the signatures were forged, many were written by nonmembers of the church, and many by *females*. Orange Scott, who had presented the petition, could only say that he had received it from people whom he thought to be trustworthy, and he had intended no deceit in the matter. The abolition-ists' reputation, low as it was, suffered still further from this episode. It is difficult to tell from this distance where the right of the matter lay.

[56] *Virginia Conference Sentinel*, I (1836), 127.
[57] *Ibid.*, pp. 118-19.
[58] *Autobiography of Peter Cartwright*, Centennial Edition (Nashville: Abingdon Press, 1956), pp. 238, 246.

Certainly the investigation was carried on by Scott's enemies; they refused him custody of the petition so that he could make his own investigation at the time. Matlack later asserted that those signers said to be non-members had been proved genuine.[59] Scott accounted for some of the discrepancies by saying that some of the signatures had been transferred from a petition on temperance by mistake. So far as that General Conference was concerned, however, the damage was done; in such cases later explanations make little impression.

By the second half of the decade, the abolitionists of the Northeast had attained enough strength to hold several antislavery conventions. The first was at Cazenovia, New York, in 1837; the second at Utica, New York, and the third at Lowell, Massachusetts, in the course of the next year. The fourth, the most ambitious of all, was called for New York City in the autumn of 1840.

The first three conventions had given rise to suspicion of disloyal tendencies. The *Christian Advocate and Journal* had spoken disparagingly of "radico abolitionists," and indeed criticisms and suggestions for reforming the church had been voiced. These reports did deter some from attending the fourth convention, but there were enough there to organize the American Wesleyan Antislavery Society. The convention affirmed its loyalty to the church and reiterated the belief that it could be "redeemed from the pollution and guilt of slavery." It listed and deplored the "proslavery" actions and failures to take action at the General Conference the preceding spring. It urged all abolitionists to continue to memorialize the conferences on the subject and to protest especially in the matter of receiving the testimony of Negroes. It drew up a constitution for the new society and proclaimed its objective to be the "entire extinction of slavery in the Methodist Episcopal Church in America." [60]

There was an exchange of messages between the convention and the editors of the *Christian Advocate and Journal,* the politeness of which did not conceal their irreconcilable hostility. The convention asked the editors whether they would receive communications on the progress of the abolition cause. The reply asserted personal friendliness for the representatives of the convention, but declared that it was impossible to recognize the activities of a body which had not been called under the authority of the *Discipline* and had no right to use the name "Methodist." This reply had two important consequences. Though the convention had first proposed to call the new society the American "Methodist" Antislavery Society, they abandoned that designation for "Wesleyan." The *Christian Advocate and Journal* in New York was manifestly closed

[59] *History of American Slavery,* p. 210.
[60] The reports of the convention appear in *Zion's Herald,* November 4 and 11, 1840.

to them, and they feared that with the imminent advent of Abel Stevens to the editorship *Zion's Herald,* which had up to that time been open to both sides of the question, would likewise be closed. So they instructed the abolitionists at the convention to choose their own religious weekly. This was of course regarded as flagrant disloyalty; but the abolitionists compounded it in the next few years by founding several papers of their own. In addition to *Zion's Watchman,* which had been edited by La Roy Sunderland in New York for the past four years, Luther Lee began the *New England Christian Advocate* in Lowell, Massachusetts, and Scott began the *True Wesleyan* in the same place but later moved it to New York City. There was also a *Wesleyan Journal* published for a time in Hallowell, Maine.

The American Wesleyan Antislavery Society died soon after its first anniversary convention. The leaders were greatly discouraged, for abolitionism had to all appearances been extinguished in the Methodist Episcopal Church, or at best driven to maintain a feeble existence underground. Its resurgence is closely bound up with the formation of the Wesleyan Methodist Connection, to which we now turn.

4

Orange Scott and the Organization of the Wesleyan Methodists

The leading figure in the abolitionists' struggle for recognition in the Methodist Episcopal Church was Orange Scott. Scott was born in Brookfield, Vermont, in 1800. His formal schooling amounted in all to only thirteen months. In spite of this handicap, he achieved genuine facility and purity in his use of both spoken and written English. Scott became a member of the New England Conference in 1822. In 1830 he was appointed presiding elder of the Springfield District. The turning point of his life came in 1833, when he first made contact with the antislavery movement. After his "conversion" to abolitionism, he continued to be a zealous preacher of the gospel. He pointed with pride to the revivals which attended his pastorates, citing them as proofs that abolitionism did not hinder but facilitated the spread of the gospel. He did not lose his love for the Methodist Episcopal Church, but he coveted for her above all else freedom from sinful complicity in slavery.

His first notable contribution to the cause was a series of stirring letters to *Zion's Herald* in 1835, the first material which that influential paper printed on the subject. His advocacy of abolitionism soon cost him his standing with his bishop. In 1836 he was not reappointed as presiding elder of the Providence District but was stationed, according to some accounts, in spite of, rather than with the authority of, the appointing powers in Lowell, Massachusetts. To Lowell came Lucius Matlack after he was refused membership in the Philadelphia Conference. Thereafter Matlack was Scott's trusted comrade-in-arms. Matlack left the Methodist Episcopal Church soon after his friend but returned to it after the end of slavery. He survived Scott by many years, and became in a sense his official biographer and the historian of the antislavery movement in Methodism.

Scott emerged into the notice of the whole church through his able *Address* to the General Conference of 1836. Thereafter, as the acknowledged leader of the abolition party in the church, he took part in most of the conflict we have already related. In 1837 he declined taking an appointment and served as agent of the American Antislavery Society. For them he made many addresses to all sorts of audiences, including Methodist conferences, as long as he was allowed. In 1838 he wrote the long "Appeal to the Methodist Episcopal Church," which comprised the first, and as it turned out, the only, issue of *The Wesleyan Antislavery Review*. He clung to the church till 1842, when he gave up hope that it would rid itself of entanglement in slavery. He then set forth on consolidating the fragmentary schisms which had already taken place and leading others like himself into a new church: the Wesleyan Methodist Connection of America.

Having presided over the preliminary convention which, in 1843, organized the connection, he declined the presidency which was offered him at the church's first General Conference. In 1846 he published a defense of his course called *The Grounds for Secession from the Methodist Episcopal Church*. Here he went over the history of the church's connection with slavery and also considered the justification of secession in general, concluding that it is a duty to separate oneself from a church which had proved obdurate in condoning a sin so grave as slavery. He lived but a year longer. On August 4, 1847, his friend Matlack preached his funeral sermon in Springfield.

Abel Stevens was perhaps his chief public opponent, especially during the time when Stevens was editor of *Zion's Herald*. Nevertheless, he paid tribute to Scott as second in influence only to Wilbur Fisk in the New England Methodism of his time. Stevens willingly acknowledged that though he loved polemics, he was a generous as well as courageous antagonist and acted "under the impulses of a sincere and courageous love of truth. . . . The people loved him." [61]

As leader of the "loyal opposition" in the General Conference of 1840, Scott had contended vigorously for the principles of the abolition party. After being repulsed all along the line, and after the refusal of the church papers to accept his partisan writings, he gave up hope of making an impression on the church. In February of 1841 he said in the *Watchman*, "I have little hope that the church will ever be reformed in relation to slavery." The following year in *Zion's Herald* he concluded, "There is, therefore, no alternative but to submit to things pretty much as they are, or secede." In the first issue of the *True Wesleyan*, November of 1842, appeared a public announcement of withdrawal from the Methodist Episcopal Church, signed by Scott, Jotham Horton, and La Roy Sunderland.

The chief reason they gave for taking this step was, of course, slavery; the Methodist Episcopal Church was both a slaveholding and a slavery-defending church. But to this they added another: The government of the church contained principles not laid down in the Scriptures or in the primitive church—principles which were subversive of the rights of both ministers and laymen. The separation between ministers and laymen in episcopal Methodism was traced to "the assumptions of Rome"! Here is an echo of the old cry of the Reformers of two decades earlier, who had erected the Methodist Protestant Church—and a foreshadowing of the features which were to appear in the polity of the new connection. The statement deplored the unqualified power of the bishops and presiding elders to curtail expression and to appoint the preachers where they liked, and concluded, in effect, that the appointive power is the power to destroy.

Scott elaborated the defense of his separation still further in a little periodical he issued in Boston called *The Wesleyan Companion*. Its purpose seems to have been to provide the members of the new connection with material for self-justification when objections were raised against their "come-outer" position. When a majority of any religious community, so the argument ran, become guilty of any wrongdoing, then the minority are under obligation to secede. To do otherwise makes them promoters of the sin. When the church spreads her folds so wide as to enclose sinners, she loses her identity, and her distinctive character is merged in the common character of the world.[62]

---

[61] William B. Sprague, ed., *Annals of the American Pulpit* (New York: Robert Carter and Brothers, 1861), VII, 670-71.
[62] Vol. I (1844), 76-78.

Even before the statement of withdrawal had been issued in 1842 by Scott, Horton, and Sunderland, small secessions had been taking place in various parts of the North. Matlack speaks of the "large amount of disaffected material" which had accumulated in the course of the attempt to suppress abolitionism in the Methodist Episcopal Church. There were young men on trial in the conferences who had been denied admission and local preachers who had lost their licenses. In Cleveland, Ohio, a whole station had been alienated because it had been attached to a circuit "for the purpose of dissolving the Quarterly Conference." [63]

Several secessions took place at the end of the 1830's. In the summer of 1839 some thirty persons in Munroe, Ohio, and a number in Williamsfield in the same state broke off from the Methodist Episcopal Church. A little later a group in Utica, New York, and in February of 1841 one in Wayne County, Michigan, likewise seceded. In New England Luther Lee had organized two separate churches in Providence, Rhode Island; Horton had led a secession in Boston, and some of Scott's sympathizers had withdrawn in Lowell. There were others, including one in Pittsburgh and one as far west as Iowa. Still others, in scattered places, seemed poised on the verge of departure and waiting chiefly for a more general exodus of abolitionists before acting. The public declaration of Scott, Horton, and Sunderland made them a kind of clearing house for such groups, and their correspondence indicates that they received news of many. In the circumstances they felt justified in taking steps toward combining these fragments into a whole, so that by common action they might perpetuate their witness.

A preliminary conference was held at Andover, Massachusetts, in February, 1843. To it were invited all who were in favor of organizing a Wesleyan Methodist Church, free from slavery and episcopacy. Both laymen and ministers were invited. Nine ministers and forty-three laymen responded. This convention appointed a Committee of Correspondence to assist the churches organized so far. It also appointed a committee to draft a *Discipline*. It resolved to hold a second convention after an interval of several months to act on the disciplinary proposals.[64]

The second convention assembled at Utica, New York, on May 31, 1843. It was attended by people from at least nine different denominations; in addition to Methodist Episcopalians, there were also Methodist Protestants, Protestant Episcopalians, Congregationalists, and Baptists. Orange Scott was elected president of this convention. In its sessions, and

[63] Matlack, *History of American Slavery*, pp. 301 ff.
[64] For a full discussion of the organization of the Wesleyan Methodists, see Ira Ford McLeister and Roy Stephen Nicholson, *History of the Wesleyan Methodist Church of America* (Marion, Ind.: Wesleyan Methodist Publishing Association, 1959), pp. 15-59.

in those of the first General Conference which was held the following year, the ground lines of the new connection's doctrine, practice, and government were laid down.

Since most of the participants in this new venture had been members of the Methodist Episcopal Church, it is not surprising that they followed the doctrinal position of the old church. This was a schism over discipline, not doctrine. The Methodist Episcopal Articles of Religion were the starting point for the new statement; most of them were adopted, and those which were left out were not rejected but regarded as superfluous. An Article on sanctification was adopted by the first General Conference and sent to the Annual Conferences for approval. It appeared in the *Discipline* printed after the General Conference of 1848. But for a number of years there continued to be objections against both the wording and the way it was adopted. Matlack speaks of a change made at the first General Conference of the new church in the matter of the Lord's Supper: "The semi-papal consecration of the elements of the Lord's Supper was abolished entirely." [65]

In matters of conduct, it is not surprising to find the General Rule on slavery returning to the early form which forbade the buying or selling of men, women, or children or holding them as slaves. It was further forbidden to claim that it was right so to do. The grand purpose of the founding of this new church was to exclude slaveholders from fellowship. The rule on intoxicating liquor forbade not only its manufacture, buying, and selling, but also its use, "unless for mechanical, chemical, or medical purposes." Some members of the organizing convention, but by no means all, had scruples against any connection with "oath-bound secret societies." These were described as "immoral in their tendency"; associating with them was declared inconsistent with Christian duty. One of the brethren shuddered when he heard Sunderland, Scott, Lee, and Horton avow themselves Masons. "If there is anything that will destroy us," he said, "it is Masonry." So there was a good deal of debate over whether there should be a mandatory rule against joining such societies or simply an advisory statement. It was left not only advisory but subject to the ruling of the respective Annual Conferences. But the first General Conference, meeting in 1844, adopted the following rule: "We will on no account tolerate our ministers and members in joining Secret, oath-bound Societies . . . as . . . it is inconsistent with our duties to God and Christianity."

Though the Wesleyan Methodists had left their doctrinal heritage unchanged save for minor matters, their unfortunate experience with cen-

[65] *History of American Slavery*, p. 350.

tralized authority in the church they had left made them determined
to modify radically the governmental plan. They took several leaves from
the Methodist Protestant *Discipline*. Laymen had equal representation in
both General and Annual Conferences. Though Scott would have been
content to let the episcopacy continue, under certain modifying limitations,[66] the majority insisted on substituting a president of the General
Conference, elective quadrennially. Chairmen of districts likewise were
elective. The appointments were made by a stationing committee of six
ministers and laymen. Both preachers and lay members had the privilege
of an appeal to the conference in case of dissatisfaction. In their reaction
to control from above the Wesleyans espoused something very like a congregational theory of the church. Because the local congregation itself
was a church, according to the New Testament, they refused to call the
entire group a church, and confined themselves to the name "Connection"
for the whole body. This did not last. Nearly half a century later they
changed the official title to "the Wesleyan Methodist Connection or
Church of America."

The first growth of the Wesleyan Connection was swift. When Orange
Scott seceded from the Methodist Episcopal Church, he had several
ministers but no laymen with him. They hoped to have perhaps two
thousand members in a year. But in six months there were more than
six thousand; a year later there were fifteen thousand. The first General
Conference in 1844 established six Annual Conferences. After the destruction of slavery had removed the chief reason for dissidence from
the Methodist Episcopal Church, a number, rather indefinitely given by
the *Cyclopaedia of Methodism* as "nearly a hundred ministers, and thousands of communicants," [67] returned to it. Among them was Lucius C.
Matlack, who, just thirty years after he had been rejected by the Philadelphia Conference, was made by unanimous action a member of that
body.[68]

It often happens that when a minority group takes a determined
stand on a matter of principle or secedes from a larger body, the results of
its action are felt quite as much in the inert body it has left as in its own
new entity, separate and free though it be. The Methodist Episcopal
Church began to move in an antislavery direction so swiftly and so soon
after the Wesleyan Methodists made it clear they meant business that it
can hardly have been mere coincidence.

The Methodist antislavery societies which had languished in the late

[66] Matlack, *Antislavery Struggle*, p. 143.

[67] Matthew Simpson, ed., *Cyclopaedia of Methodism* (Philadelphia: Louis H. Everts,
1880) , p. 924.

[68] *Antislavery Struggle*, p. 371.

1830's and early '40's took on new life and found a much more lively response in the Methodist Episcopal Church, at least in New England, than before. In Boston the ministers met after the withdrawal of Horton, Scott, and Sunderland to consult on preventing the spread of disaffection. They determined to set a backfire by holding antislavery conventions. Several of these were held; from them emanated statements which went beyond anything uttered by official Methodist bodies before.

The Massachusetts convention, meeting at Bromfield Street Church in Boston, said, "Slaveholding is a sin." For some the tension had become so high that the only choice was between reformation and division. The convention held in New Market, New Hampshire, said, "The only way to prevent an entire dissolution among us . . . is an entire separation from the South." It developed a plan to memorialize the next General Conference to divide the church, North and South, or to set off the New England conferences by themselves. In a similar convention held in Vermont early in 1844, words which had been spoken by the extreme abolitionists now began to be heard among the rank and file. Stoutly asserting their loyalty to the Methodist Episcopal Church, they nevertheless resolved that as Christians they could have "no fellowship with any man, whether he be a Methodist or otherwise, who can hold and treat any fellow being as a slave." [69] The officers presiding over conferences discontinued, at least to some extent, the policy which had dominated the preceding quadrennium and which had been approved by the General Conference of 1840, and began to entertain antislavery resolutions and to put motions of the same tenor. Not even Bishop Hedding tried any longer to obstruct them. The New York and Genesee Conferences proposed new forms of the rule on slavery. The former asked for the early form of the rule; the latter's proposal was that no slaveholder could be a member of the church if it were possible for him to free his slaves. The Baltimore Conference, though it continued to insist that its ministerial members keep clear of entanglements in slavery, would not hear of any change in the rule.

Thomas E. Bond, who had so firmly refused to entertain any communications from the Wesleyan Antislavery Society of 1840, now opened the columns of the *Christian Advocate and Journal* to discussion of the question. The Sparta Quarterly Conference in Georgia and the Russell Circuit of the Alabama Conference passed resolutions against this move, repeating that slavery was not a moral evil and even demanding Bond's removal as editor. Bond took an antislavery position himself, saying he would resign rather than defend the opinions contained in the resolutions

[69] *Zion's Herald,* February 21, 1844.

from Georgia and Alabama. He attacked a bill introduced into the legislature of Maryland, which would either drive free Negroes out of the state or to reduce them once more to servitude. However, so far as the church was concerned, he reiterated his position that the sinfulness of slavery depended on the circumstances.[70] He was severely taken to task by the Southern papers.

All this accelerated antislavery activity, which culminated in the actions of the General Conference of 1844, was thought by observers both at the time and since to have been a response in the Methodist Episcopal Church to the secession of the Wesleyans. Methodist officials had, up to that time, been vigorous antiabolitionists because they thought thus to preserve the unity and prosperity of the church. It is not unreasonable to suppose that once it became apparent to them that this attitude was not going to achieve the end desired, they might quickly change their policy. It was the threat of the Wesleyans which opened their eyes to the fact that their policy was more likely to produce schism than unity.

Several contemporary observers thought that the Wesleyan schism had a great deal to do with nerving the North to take its stand in the General Conference of 1844. Matlack himself, safely back in the mother church after the Civil War, was one of them. He was able also to cite the testimony of others in support of his own judgment. Bishop Thomson said to him in 1866 (the phraseology is Matlack's) that he had no doubt that "withdrawing as the Wesleyans did, when they did, for the reasons they assigned, and organizing just outside the lines of the Methodist Episcopal Church on an antislavery platform, they constrained a development of antislavery activity within the 'old Church,' which they could not have accomplished by remaining members of it." [71] Moses Hill, a prominent member first of the Erie then of the East Ohio Conference, a presiding elder, and a delegate to the General Conference, said, "It is evident that if the General Conference of 1844 had not dealt as they did with Bishop Andrew, the Wesleyans would have become a power in the land." [72]

All this does not mean that the indefatigable zeal of the abolition party in the church had suddenly converted a great many members of the church in the North. Neither does it mean that the antislavery stand the Northern Church finally took was a mere balancing of ecclesiastical expediencies. But it does mean that the pertinacious advocacy of abolitionism by a few Methodists, who were ready to leave the church rather than surrender their convictions, did finally bring a number of people in the church to a realization that keeping neutral on the subject was not

[70] *Christian Advocate and Journal*, August 30, 1843.
[71] *Antislavery Struggle*, p. 144.
[72] *Ibid.*, p. 145.

the safe way, ecclesiastically speaking, that they had thought. Thus released, they were able to express themselves effectively on a matter of conscience before and during the General Conference of 1844.

5

The General Conference of 1844

The Men Who Led

The ninth delegated General Conference of the Methodist Episcopal Church met in the Greene Street Methodist Church of New York City on Wednesday, May 1, 1844. One hundred and eighty preachers, elected as delegates from thirty-three Annual Conferences and representing 1,171,356 members of Methodist churches, came from all parts of the nation and from the Republic of Texas. For nearly six weeks they were to be housed in New York homes. On that opening morning, in addition to the elected delegates, who occupied the front pews of the church, there were present a large number of preachers and laymen not members of the conference. The small building was to continue crowded throughout the thirty-six days of business sessions—as issues momentous for both church and nation were debated—until the final adjournment of the conference just after midnight on Tuesday morning, June 11.

This General Conference was to be unique in American Methodism: It was the longest ever held; it had the greatest number of recorded roll call votes; and it debated and decided issues as poignant and divisive as any ever faced by an ecclesiastical body in American history.

The maturity and ability of the conference members is shown in this contemporary appraisal:

Among its members are many men hoary with age, whose venerable appearance, and serious though cheerful and benignant aspect, were calculated to inspire not only respect but veneration. There are also many in middle life, and in the full maturity of gifted intellect and eloquence. The number of young and inexperienced men is very small. Few public bodies in our country, perhaps none, whether civil or ecclesiastical, embrace a greater amount of effective talent than is comprised among the members of this Conference.[73]

[73] New York *Tribune*, May 2, 1844.

All five bishops were present: Joshua Soule, Elijah Hedding, James O. Andrew, Thomas A. Morris, and Beverly Waugh.

Soule (1781-1867), the senior bishop, was a native of Maine. Admitted on trial to the New England Conference in 1799, he was ordained deacon in 1802 and elder the following year, both ordinations by Bishop What-coat. An itinerant preacher and presiding elder in New England until he became book agent of the church in 1816, Soule was the first editor of *The Methodist Magazine* (1818). From 1820 to 1824 he was minister of churches in the New York and Baltimore Conferences. Soule was first elected to the episcopacy in 1820, but he refused to be consecrated when the General Conference persisted in making the office of presiding elder elective. In 1824 he was again elected bishop; and, the protested action having been rescinded, he accepted consecration. Assigned to the Western and Southern conferences, he moved his family to Lebanon, Ohio. Joshua Soule was the principal author of the constitution adopted by the General Conference in 1808.[74]

Elijah Hedding (1780-1852), born in New York and reared in Vermont, joined the New York Conference in 1801, was ordained deacon in 1803 by Bishop Whatcoat and elder in 1805 by Bishop Asbury. In that same year he became a member of the New England Conference where, as a pioneer circuit rider, stationed preacher, and presiding elder, he was one of the foremost agents of the extension of Methodism. Though his views later changed, he was a leader in the long-continued but unsuccessful movement to make presiding elders elective by the Annual Conferences. Elected to the episcopacy in 1824, he became known as a strict discipli-narian. In the 1830's and '40's he strongly opposed abolitionist agitation in the Northern conferences, bringing upon himself much abuse and criticism.[75]

James O. Andrew (1794-1871), son of the first native Georgian to enter the itinerant ministry of the Methodist Episcopal Church, joined the South Carolina Conference in 1812, was ordained deacon by Bishop Asbury in 1814 and elder by Bishop McKendree in 1816. After twenty years of ministry in the Carolinas and Georgia, Andrew went to the General Conference in 1832 seriously considering becoming a missionary to Africa. Instead, and with some reluctance on his part, he was elected to the episcopacy on the first ballot. In the following twelve years his work as a bishop was primarily in the Southern conferences. In 1842 his wife of twenty-six years died, leaving him a young Negro slave. Shortly before

[74] The standard biography of Soule is Horace M. Du Bose, *Life of Joshua Soule* (Nashville: Smith and Lamar, 1911).

[75] See D. W. Clark, *Life and Times of Rev. Elijah Hedding* (New York: Carlton and Phillips, 1856).

the General Conference in 1844 Andrew married again, and his second wife owned several slaves. It was the problem of how to deal with Bishop Andrew as a slave owner that placed the General Conference between Scylla and Charybdis.[76]

A native of West Virginia, Thomas A. Morris (1794-1874) entered the Methodist ministry in Ohio. Ordained deacon in 1818 by Bishop George and elder in 1820 by Bishop Roberts, he served as a preacher and presiding elder in Ohio and Kentucky until he was appointed editor of the *Western Christian Advocate* in 1834. He was a delegate to the General Conferences of 1824, 1828, 1832, and 1836, when he was elected to the episcopacy. Before 1844 he presided over conferences in the South and West, making the long journey to the Republic of Texas late in 1841.[77]

Another Virginian, Beverly Waugh (1789-1858), son of a veteran of the American Revolution, abandoned a business career to enter the Methodist ministry. Admitted to the Baltimore Conference in 1809, he was ordained deacon in 1811 and elder in 1813. Until 1828 he served in that conference, with eleven years in the cities of Washington and Baltimore. Although he had been a delegate to the General Conferences of 1816 and 1820, Waugh was not re-elected a delegate in 1824 because of his support of the election of presiding elders by the Annual Conferences. Subsequently he lost interest in the movement for reform, actively opposing the "Mutual Rights" men; he was again a delegate in 1828, when he was elected assistant book agent of the church. In 1832 he succeeded John Emory as the principal book agent. Due in part to his successful administration of the Book Concern, Waugh was elected to the episcopacy in 1836 on the first ballot. As a general superintendent he traveled as widely as any of his colleagues, presiding over conferences in all parts of the nation. In 1840 he presided over the organization of the Texas Conference. As slavery increasingly became an issue in the church, Waugh sought to avoid controversy. In 1837 he refused to allow abolitionists in the New England Conference to present antislavery petitions, declaring that consideration of the slavery issue was not a part of the business of an Annual Conference. In 1838, on the other hand, he would not ordain two slaveholding preachers in the Kentucky Conference until they executed bills of emancipation.[78]

[76] See George G. Smith, *The Life and Letters of James Osgood Andrew* (Nashville: Southern Methodist Publishing House, 1883).

[77] See John F. Marlay, *The Life of Rev. Thomas A. Morris* (Cincinnati: Hitchcock and Walden, 1875).

[78] A lengthy account of Waugh's life, based on his own manuscript journal, is found in Theodore L. Flood and John W. Hamilton, eds., *Lives of Methodist Bishops* (New York: Phillips and Hunt, 1882), pp. 225-62.

Two new bishops were elected at this General Conference: Leonidas L. Hamline and Edmund S. Janes.

Born in Connecticut of New England ancestry reaching back perhaps as early as 1639, Hamline (1797-1865) migrated to Ohio in the 1820's, where he was admitted to the bar. As the result of a conversion experience in 1828, he sought a license to preach, finally joining the Ohio Conference in 1832. Ordained deacon in 1834 and elder in 1836, he gained a wide reputation as a great preacher. In 1836 he was appointed assistant editor of the *Western Christian Advocate*. From 1841 until he was elected to the episcopacy in 1844, he was the first editor of the *Ladies' Repository*. He was a delegate to the General Conferences of 1840 and 1844.

Janes (1807-1876) and Hamline had much in common, for Janes was also a native of New England (Massachusetts) and had a brief career as a lawyer before turning to the ministry. Admitted to the Philadelphia Conference in 1830, Janes served churches in New Jersey until he was appointed agent for Dickinson College in 1834. From 1836 to 1840 he served churches in Philadelphia and New York City. In the latter year he was elected financial secretary of the American Bible Society, a position he held until his election to the episcopacy in 1844. Janes, only thirty-seven years old, was the youngest man ever elected bishop in the Methodist Episcopal Church. He never had been a delegate to a General Conference.[79]

The Growing Crisis in the Conference

The following day-by-day account is offered to assist the reader in appreciating the ever increasing sense of tension and impending crisis that hung over the conference from its early sessions, and to guide him in the later detailed attempt to interpret the significance of the conference.

Joshua Soule, senior bishop of the church, opened the proceedings of the conference at 9 o'clock, Wednesday morning, May 1, with a brief period of devotion. The succeeding two days were then spent in routine matters of organization—roll call, election of secretaries, appointment of committees, and establishing rules of procedure. On Thursday Bishop Soule presented the Address of the Bishops, which was basically a restatement of the constitutional foundation of Methodist polity.

You are now assembled in the ninth session of your body since its organization under a Constitution which, while it defines and restricts your powers, affords

[79] For biographical information on Hamline and Janes, see *Lives of Methodist Bishops*, pp. 289-324.

a permanent security of the rights and privileges of the great and growing body of ministers and people which you represent. . . .

According to our ecclesiastical organization, you are, under God, the constitutional body in which the conservative elements of the peace and unity of the Church repose. . . . If these principles are duly appreciated, no local or party views or interests will divide your counsels, consume your time, or give rise to useless or impassioned debate. . . .

The voice of wisdom admonishes us that any attempt to change or modify these constitutional principles, under such circumstances, is doubtful in policy, and dangerous in experiment.[80]

Reminding the delegates that the strength of Methodism lay in the itinerant nature of its ministry and general superintendency, Bishop Soule made specific suggestions for safeguarding this basic principle. Other recommendations were made concerning the missionary work of the church among the German, Indian, and Negro people. With reference to the "people of colour in these United States," Soule declared:

We may preach the Gospel of Christ to them, unite them in the communion of his Church, and introduce them to a participation of the blessings of her fellowship, and thus be instruments of their preparation for the riches of the inheritance of the saints in glory. This, as ministers of Christ, is our *work*, and should be our glory and joy. . . . But to raise them to equal civil rights and privileges is not within our power. Let us not labour in vain, and spend our strength for naught.[81]

In the light of a "mighty movement of Papal Rome to recover that domination and influence which she so reluctantly yielded to the champions of Scriptural truth and righteousness in the sixteenth century," Bishop Soule spoke of "the necessity and importance of a thorough course of Biblical literature and theological science, for the improvement of our ministry." Furthermore, the system of "Sunday-school instruction" needed to be revised and improved. "Much more might be done with a system better adapted to the capacities of the subjects of instruction, and with books suitable to different classes in the several stages of improvement." [82]

HARDING'S APPEAL

If the bishops had anticipated controversy, it was not long in appearing. Friday, May 3, as the conference began receiving memorials and pe-

---

[80] *Journal of the General Conference,* 1844, pp. 151-52.
[81] *Ibid.,* p. 165.
[82] *Ibid.,* pp. 167-70.

titions from Annual Conferences, the Providence Conference presented a petition concerning slavery. Despite objections from delegates from the South Carolina and Baltimore Conferences that slavery was not a suitable subject for General Conference legislation, the conference accepted the petition and ordered the appointment of a Committee on Slavery to receive this and similar memorials.

Memorials from the New Jersey and Oneida Conferences interjected another divisive issue on Saturday and Monday, calling for a limitation of the presiding elders' term of office. Then on Tuesday, Francis Harding of the Baltimore Conference appealed to the conference to reverse a decision of his Annual Conference. Harding had been suspended from his ministerial standing for refusing to free certain slaves who came into his possession by marriage. William A. Smith of Virginia represented the appellant, and John A. Collins presented the case for the Baltimore Conference.

The defense built its case on three factors: (1) Harding was not in his own person the owner of the slaves; (2) if he were the owner, the laws of Maryland did not permit manumission; and (3) the action of the preceding General Conference had declared that the ownership of slaves in states not permitting their emancipation was not in itself a barrier to any office in the church, including that of traveling elder.

The prosecution pointed out that the defendant might have freed the slaves by sending them to a free state or to Africa and that higher standards had always been maintained in the church for traveling preachers than for local preachers and lay members. Regardless of the merits or demerits of Harding's appeal on the basis of church law, the vote, when taken after four days of intensive debate, indicated that the antislavery group was now the majority of the General Conference. The vote was 117 to 56 to reject the appeal. Dr. Smith immediately declared: "A fair decision of this conference has not been given. And I wish my protest to go forth to the American Church, and American people, to serve as a beacon-light to warn the Church against the movements of a majority who can obliterate justice, and trample on the rights of a minority." [83]

The conference itself recognized the threat of division revealed in the rejection of Harding's appeal and in the more difficult case of Bishop Andrew, whose connection with slavery was a paramount subject of

[83] *Report of Debates in the General Conference of the Methodist Episcopal Church, Held in the City of New-York, 1844* (New York: Lane and Tippett, 1844), p. 52.

sub rosa conversation. On Tuesday, May 14, the conference unanimously accepted the following resolution:

In view of the distracting agitation which has so long prevailed on the subject of slavery and abolition, and especially the difficulties under which we labour in the present General Conference, on account of the relative position of our brethren North and South on this perplexing question; therefore,

Resolved, That a committee of six be appointed to confer with the Bishops, and report within two days, as to the possibility of adopting some plan, and what, for the permanent pacification of the church.[84]

The next day was set as a day of fasting and prayer to ask God's blessings upon the work of the committee.

The resolution had been drawn by Stephen Olin of the New York Conference, the highly respected president of Wesleyan University, and William Capers of the South Carolina Conference, one of the foremost leaders of the South. Olin discussed the predicament of the delegates with foreboding:

It appears to me that we stand committed on this question by our principles and views of policy, and neither of us dare move a step from our position. . . . I do not see how northern men can yield their ground, or southern men give up theirs. I do indeed believe, that if . . . this General Conference do not speak out clearly and distinctly on the subject, however unpalatable it may be, we cannot go home under this distracting question without a certainty of breaking up our conferences. . . . The men who stand here as abolitionists are as ardently attached to Methodist episcopacy as you all. . . . Your northern brethren . . . [have] come up here distressed beyond measure, and disposed, if they believed they could, without destruction and ruin to the Church, to make concession. . . . With regard to our southern brethren . . . if they concede what the northern brethren wish—if they concede that holding slaves is incompatible with holding their ministry—they may as well go to the Rocky Mountains as to their own sunny plains. The people would not bear it. They feel shut up to their principles on this point. . . . But if our difficulties are unmanageable, let our spirit be right. If we must part, let us meet and pour out our tears together; and let us not give up until we have tried. . . . I cannot speak on this subject without deep emotion. If we push our principles so far as to break up the connection, this may be the last time we meet. I fear it! I fear it! I see no way of escape.[85]

Others voiced the same apprehension. And the foreboding was justified. After four days of fruitless search, requests for more time, and separate caucuses of the Southern and Northern delegations, the in-

---

[84] *Journal of the General Conference*, 1844, pp. 42-43.
[85] *Debates*, p. 55.

evitable report of the committee was that they were "unable to agree upon any plan of compromise to reconcile the views of the northern and southern Conferences."

THE CASE OF BISHOP ANDREW

Against such a dark background the conference finally came to grips with the problem which had constantly been in the mind of all as other matters were discussed and which was to prove the precipitating cause of division. The fact that a beloved and respected bishop, James O. Andrew of Georgia, had become a slaveholder could no longer be evaded or ignored. "This fact," wrote Peter Cartwright, the famous Illinois presiding elder, "came upon us with the darkness and terror of a fearful storm, and covered the whole General Conference with sorrow and mourning." [86] The General Conference was compelled to face the issue openly and to render a final decision.

On Monday, May 20, the seventeenth day the conference had been in business session, John A. Collins of the Baltimore Conference brought into the open the issue which had been the subject of much private conversation and behind-the-scene maneuvering. On his motion the conference adopted the following resolution:

Whereas it is currently reported, and generally understood, that one of the Bishops of the M. E. Church has become connected with slavery; and whereas it is due to this General Conference to have a proper understanding of the matter; therefore,

Resolved, That the Committee on the Episcopacy be instructed to ascertain the facts in the case, and report the results of their investigation to this body tomorrow morning.[87]

But the conference was to have no respite from controversial issues, even for twenty-four hours. The discussion of the proposal to "limit the Episcopacy to continuing any preacher in the office of Presiding Elder more than four years at one time" was renewed in the meantime.

The Committee on Episcopacy had no difficulty in making the requested report the next day, since the case of Bishop Andrew had already been thoroughly explored by the committee. The report included a statement from Bishop Andrew setting forth the facts in the case. He confirmed the fact that he was the owner of a mulatto girl, bequeathed to him in trust, and a Negro boy, left to him from the estate of his first wife. Georgia law prohibited emancipation. The girl refused to go to

[86] *Autobiography of Peter Cartwright,* p. 271.
[87] *Journal of the General Conference,* 1844, p. 58.

either Liberia or to a free state, and the boy was not yet old enough to provide for himself. Bishop Andrew also readily acknowledged that his second wife was the owner of slaves inherited from her first husband. These the bishop had secured to his wife by a deed of trust in which he divested himself of any claim to the slave property of his wife. The bishop concluded his statement by declaring: "I have neither bought nor sold a slave; . . . in the only two instances in which I am legally a slaveholder, emancipation is impracticable. As to the servants owned by my wife, I have no legal responsibility in the premises, nor could my wife emancipate them if she desired to do so." [88]

These facts were never contested in the long debates that followed, nor was proof ever submitted that Bishop Andrew had violated the existing statutes of the Methodist Episcopal Church in regard to slaveholding. This immediately determined that the final decision would rest upon the issues of expediency and polity and not upon the questions of morality and religion involved in the holding of men, women, and children in bondage.

As soon as Bishop Andrew had publicly and officially admitted his connection with slavery, two delegates from the Baltimore Conference, Alfred Griffith and John Davis, offered this resolution: "Resolved, That the Rev. James O. Andrew be, and he is hereby affectionately requested to resign his office as one of the Bishops of the Methodist Episcopal Church."

Resignation was the solution which Bishop Andrew himself had proposed. When he arrived in Baltimore on his way to the General Conference, Andrew learned of the intense excitement caused by the news that he was a slaveholder, and that the matter would probably be investigated by the General Conference. At that time he resolved to resign. Upon reaching New York he made his intentions known to the Southern delegation in writing. On May 10 they replied:

Whereas, Bishop Andrew has signified to the delegates of the Conferences in the slave-holding States a purpose to yield to the present distressing urgency of the brethren from the Northern States, and resign his office of Bishop, and whereas in a meeting of said delegates to consider this matter, after solemn prayer and much deliberation, it appears to us that his resignation would inflict an incurable wound on the whole South and inevitably lead to division in the Church, therefore we do unanimously concur in requesting the Bishop, by all his love for the unity of the Church, which his resignation will certainly jeopardize, not to allow himself for any consideration to resign.[89]

[88] *Ibid.*, p. 64.
[89] Quoted in Smith, *Life of Andrew*, pp. 342-43.

Four days later Bishop Andrew wrote to his daughter in the South:

As to the General Conference, thus far it has done little else but quarrel. The old subject of slavery has come up in every shape and form. They are, some of them, in great trouble about having a slave-holding Bishop, and I should greatly relieve them if I would resign; but the delegations of the different slave-holding States have held a meeting and have unanimously protested against my resignation, under *any circumstances,* as ruinous to the whole Southern portion of our Church. In fact, I believe they are solemnly pledged, if I resign, that they will to a man secede from the Conference. I would most joyfully resign, if I did not dread the influence on the Southern Church.[90]

There was little else the bishop could do except await the final outcome of the conference's debates.

The Baltimore Conference delegates played a prominent part in the action against slavery in general and Bishop Andrew in particular. It was the Baltimore Conference that suspended Francis Harding when he refused to free his slaves. John A. Collins, who represented that conference in the Harding case, was also the delegate who offered the resolutions calling for a Committee on Slavery and for the Committee on Episcopacy to report on Bishop Andrew's status as a slaveholder. And the resolution requesting Bishop Andrew to resign was presented by two delegates from this same conference, Alfred Griffith and John Davis.

Some years later James Porter, a stanch abolitionist member of the New England Conference, wrote a detailed description of a private agreement made by leading representatives from the abolitionist and conservative parties before the General Conference in 1844. On reaching New York the day before the conference opened, Porter had been invited to a "private interview with a prominent actor in the scenes, whose influence was hardly equaled by that of any other man in the conservative party." [91] It is likely that this was John A. Collins.[92] Asked what New England wanted to keep her in the Methodist Episcopal Church, Porter demanded:

1. That Bishop Andrew should be required to purge himself of slavery or vacate the episcopal office. 2. That Baltimore [Conference] should be sustained in the case of Mr. Harding. 3. That the infamous Few resolution against allow-

[90] *Ibid.,* p. 355.

[91]Porter, "The General Conference of 1844," *Methodist Quarterly Review,* April, 1871, p. 242.

[92] John N. Norwood, *The Schism in the Methodist Episcopal Church, 1844: A Study of Slavery and Ecclesiastical Politics* (Alfred, N. Y.: Alfred University Press, 1923), p. 77 n.

ing colored members to testify against white persons in Church trials should be rescinded. 4. That no further abuse of abolitionists shall be perpetrated. 5. We added that we wanted several other things more decidedly antislavery in their character, but could hardly expect them under existing circumstances.

The conservative leader assured Porter that these demands were reasonable and that the Baltimore delegation would support them. This interview was then followed by a larger conference between "several Northern delegates with other leaders of the [conservative] party, who fully committed themselves and their associates as far as they could to these measures."

We then suggested that such was the *prejudice* in the Conference against abolitionists, that if we should make ourselves prominent in pushing the measures agreed upon they might be defeated, and proposed to them to take the laboring oar into their own hands, and leave us to vote, and otherwise aid the desired result as we might be able. By a private understanding this method was informally accepted and carried out to a successful issue in every particular.[93]

Norwood cites an incident which, while "none too well authenticated," supports the actuality of such an agreement. During the General Conference a Southern member reportedly asked an abolitionist why he and his brethren had so little to say. "Oh!" he replied, *"we* have nothing to do now. The Baltimore Conference is doing *our* work for us. And they will get all the odium; and we all the benefit." [94]

Intense debate on the Griffith resolution (requesting Bishop Andrew's resignation) continued through Wednesday, May 22, and into Thursday, May 23. Then, recognizing the untenability of the original resolution, two delegates from the Ohio Conference, James B. Finley and Joseph M. Trimble, proposed a substitute resolution that called for Bishop Andrew to "desist from the exercise of this office so long as this impediment remains." For the remainder of that day (May 23) and during six days of business sessions following, debate on this resolution dominated the conference. Finally, on Thursday, May 30, an attempt was made to call the previous question. Although a majority voted for the motion, 98 to 80, this was not the two-thirds majority necessary to end debate and to vote on the major motion.

At that critical moment the bishops made an attempt to save the church from division. On the request of Bishop Hedding the conference

[93] "The General Conference of 1844," p. 242.
[94] *Schism in the M.E. Church,* p. 77.

agreed to hold no session that afternoon in order that the bishops might consult in search of a solution. The next day Bishop Waugh presented unanimous recommendations from the bishops. They proposed that further action in the case of Bishop Andrew be postponed until the next session of the General Conference in 1848.

Until the cessation of the embarrassment, or the expiration of the interval between the present and the ensuing General Conference, the undersigned believe that such a division of the work of the general superintendency might be made, without any infraction of a constitutional principle, as would fully employ Bishop Andrew in those sections of the church in which his presence and services would be welcome and cordial.[95]

Immediately, John A. Collins (the Baltimore Conference again!) moved that consideration of the bishops' communication be postponed until the following day and that the statement be printed for distribution. This delay permitted a crucial caucus. James Porter later gave the following account of these behind-the-scene activities and their tragic result for the unity of the church:

Accordingly the delegates of the New England Conferences were immediately called together, and after due deliberation unanimously adopted a paper, declaring in substance that it was their solemn conviction that if Bishop Andrew should be left by the Conference in the exercise of Episcopal functions it would break up the most of our Churches in New England; and that the only way they could be holden together would be to secede in a body, and invite Bishop Hedding to preside over them. The proposition was also concurred in by some of our most distinguished laymen who were present, and a committee of two was appointed to communicate this action to Bishop Hedding before he should meet with his colleagues. But so much time was consumed by the meeting, and in copying the document, that we were too late, and did not see him, deeming it dangerous to our interests to call him out, believing it would be construed and used in a way to defeat our object. . . . On the morning of June 1 Bishop Hedding . . . was fully informed of the aforesaid action. He thought our fears well founded, and deeply regretted that he had not known of our action before he signed that report, and said that he would go right into the Conference and withdraw his name. He did so, stating that he had signed the document presented yesterday as a peace measure, but that facts had come to his knowledge since which led him to believe that it would not make peace, and that it might be productive of a lengthened debate, and instead of removing would only increase the difficulty. This so impaired the influence of the Bishops' recommendation that the Conference laid it on the table by a vote of ninety-five to eighty-four, showing very

[95] *Journal of the General Conference,* 1844, p. 76.

clearly that it would have carried had not Bishop Hedding withdrawn his name.[96]

John N. Norwood, author of the "standard history" of the division of Methodism in 1844, supported Porter's stress on the significance of this event:

The episcopal suggestion of postponement embodied the last faint hope of unity, and the abolitionists in self-defence had effectively blocked it. Postponement was generally satisfactory. . . . Had the bishops remained unanimous, it undoubtedly would have been adopted, and they would have remained unanimous but for New England. Secession and fear were rife in that section, its delegates reflected that fear, and a different direction was given to the course of events. This proved to be the turning point of the Conference.[97]

After the announcement of the vote rejecting the bishops' recommendations, the conference resumed debate on the Finley substitute on a motion by John A. Collins. The previous question was called and sustained by the necessary majority, and the vote was taken by roll call, "amid the most profound stillness." On Saturday morning, June 1, by a majority of 110 to 68, the conference adopted the substitute Finley resolution, calling for Bishop Andrew to cease his functions as a bishop as long as he remained a slave owner.

Immediately, Lovick Pierce of the Georgia Conference announced that a "manly, ministerial, and proper protest against this action of the conference, as an extra-judicial act" would be presented "at the earliest possible moment." [98]

The Plan of Separation

At the next session of the conference, Monday, June 3, William Capers presented a series of resolutions proposing the division of the Methodist Episcopal Church into two administrative areas, each having its own General Conference and bishops, but both abiding by the present constitution and *Discipline*. These resolutions were referred to a special committee; but two days later the committee reported that it could not agree on a report which would be acceptable to the conference. That afternoon, Wednesday, June 5, A. B. Longstreet of the Georgia Confer-

[96] "The General Conference of 1844," pp. 246-47.
[97] *Schism in the M.E. Church*, p. 80.
[98] *Debates*, p. 191.

ence, on behalf of the delegations from the Southern and Southwestern conferences, presented the following declaration:

> The delegates of the Conferences in the slaveholding states take leave to *declare* to the General Conference . . . that the continued agitation on the subject of slavery and abolition in a portion of the church; the frequent action on that subject in the General Conference; and especially the extra-judicial proceedings against Bishop Andrew, which resulted, on Saturday last, in the virtual suspension of him from his office as Superintendent, must produce a state of things in the South which renders a continuance of the jurisdiction of this General Conference over these Conferences inconsistent with the success of the ministry in the slaveholding states.[99]

On a motion by Charles Elliott (Ohio Conference), the conference referred this declaration to a Committee of Nine, with later instructions that "provided they cannot in their judgment devise a plan for an amicable adjustment of the difficulties now existing in the church, on the subject of slavery, to devise, if possible, a constitutional plan for a mutual and friendly division of the church." [100] Thomas Crowder (Virginia) attempted unsuccessfully to strike out the word "constitutional," ironically anticipating the later charge made by many Northern delegates. Bishop Hedding then appointed for this committee: Robert Paine (Tennessee), Glezen Filmore (Genesee), Peter Akers (Illinois), Nathan Bangs (New York), Thomas Crowder (Virginia), Thomas B. Sargent (Baltimore), William Winans (Mississippi), Leonidas L. Hamline (Ohio), and James Porter (New England).

While this committee was still at work, the "Protest of the Minority of the General Conference against the Action of that Body in the Case of Bishop Andrew"—usually called the "Protest"—was presented on Thursday morning, June 6. It was signed by sixty delegates, all but eight from Southern conferences. The tone of this protest was ominous for the continued unity of the Methodist Episcopal Church. It declared, in part:

> By pressing the issue in question, therefore, the majority virtually dissolve the government of the Methodist Episcopal Church, because in every constitutional aspect it is sundered by so crippling a co-ordinate branch of it as to destroy the itinerant general superintendency altogether. . . . The law of union, the principle of gravitation, binding us together, is dissolved, and the general superintendency of the Methodist Episcopal Church is no more!

The action of the majority, the "Protest" concluded, had placed the

[99] *Journal of the General Conference,* 1844, p. 109.
[100] *Ibid.,* p. 111.

minority in such "exigent circumstances" as would "render it finally necessary that the southern Conferences should have a *separate, independent* existence." [101]

On a motion by Matthew Simpson (Indiana Conference) the conference appointed Stephen Olin (New York), John P. Durbin (Philadelphia), and Leonidas L. Hamline (Ohio) "to prepare a statement of the facts connected with the proceedings in the case of Bishop Andrew." Obviously, this was to be a reply to the "Protest."

The next item of business was the other time-consuming problem before the conference: how far to limit the bishops' power to appoint the presiding elders. Despite motions to table, to amend, or to avoid the issue by adjourning, the conference finally adopted the following revision of the *Discipline:*

Question. How long may a Bishop allow a Presiding Elder to remain in office?

Answer. From any term not exceeding four years successively: after which he shall not be appointed to the same district for six years.[102]

Only the latter part of the proposal was new, for the four-year limit had been in the *Discipline* since 1792.

During the afternoon session Bishop Soule presented a communication from the bishops seeking "*official* instruction" from the General Conference concerning the status of Bishop Andrew. Just before the final vote had been taken on the Finley resolution the preceding Saturday, Soule had observed that the resolution was not clear and that "definite action must necessarily be hereafter taken to decide whether the resolution was mandatory or advisory." [103] Now the bishops were asking for that decision.

In reply to the three specific questions from the bishops, after considerable debate, the conference adopted the following resolutions offered by J. T. Mitchell of the Rock River Conference:

1. Resolved, As the sense of this Conference, that Bishop Andrew's name stand in the Minutes, Hymn-book, and Discipline, as formerly.

2. Resolved, That the rule in relation to the support of a Bishop, and his family, applies to Bishop Andrew.

3. Resolved, That whether in any, and if any, in what work, Bishop Andrew be employed, is to be determined by his own decision and action, in relation to the previous action of this Conference in his case.[104]

[101] *Ibid.,* pp. 197-98.
[102] *Ibid.,* p. 116.
[103] *Debates,* p. 190.
[104] *Journal of the General Conference,* 1844, p. 118.

These resolutions were considered separately, the vote being taken by roll call. The first was adopted by a vote of 155 to 17; the second by 152 to 14; and the third by 103 to 67. The opposition to the first two resolutions was entirely Northern, whereas 53 Southern votes were cast against the third.

Two days later (Saturday, June 8) the Committee of Nine, appointed to consider and report on the declaration of the Southern delegates, submitted a contingent plan of separation for guidance "should the Annual Conferences in the slaveholding states find it necessary to unite in a distinct ecclesiastical connection." This report came to be known as the "Plan of Separation."

Whereas, a declaration has been presented to this General Conference, . . . from thirteen Annual Conferences in the slaveholding states, representing that, for various reasons enumerated, the objects and purposes of the Christian ministry and church organization cannot be successfully accomplished by them under the jurisdiction of this General Conference as now constituted; and

Whereas, in the event of a separation, a contingency to which the declaration asks attention as not improbable, we esteem it the duty of this General Conference to meet the emergency with Christian kindness and the strictest equity; therefore, . . .

1. . . . The following rule shall be observed with regard to the northern boundary of such connection:—All the societies, stations, and Conferences adhering to the church in the South, by a vote of a majority of the members of said societies, stations, and Conferences, shall remain under the unmolested pastoral care of the Southern Church; and the ministers of the Methodist Episcopal Church shall in no wise attempt to organize churches or societies within the limits of the Church South, nor shall they attempt to exercise any pastoral oversight therein; it being understood that the ministry of the South reciprocally observe the same rule. . . . Provided also, that this rule shall apply only to societies, stations, and Conferences bordering on the line of division, and not to interior charges. . . .

2. That ministers, local and travelling, of every grade and office in the Methodist Episcopal Church, may, as they prefer, remain in that church, or, without blame, attach themselves to the Church South.

3. . . . That we recommend to all the Annual Conferences, at their first approaching sessions, to authorize a change of the sixth restrictive article, so that the first clause shall read thus: "They shall not appropriate the produce of the Book Concern, nor of the Chartered Fund, to any other purpose other than for the benefit of the travelling, supernumerary, superannuated, and worn-out preachers, their wives, widows, and children, and to such other purposes as may be determined upon by the votes of two-thirds of the members of the General Conference."

4. That whenever the Annual Conferences, by a vote of three-fourths of all their members voting on the third resolution, shall have concurred in the recommendation to alter the sixth restrictive article, the Agents at New York and Cincinnati shall . . . deliver over to any authorized agent or appointee of the Church South . . . all notes and book accounts against the ministers, church members, or citizens within its boundaries, with authority to collect the same . . . and . . . also convey to the aforesaid agent . . . all the real estate, and assign him all the property, including presses, stock, and all right and interest connected with the printing establishments at Charleston, Richmond, and Nashville. . . .

5. That . . . there shall be transferred to the above agent of the Southern Church so much of the capital and produce of the Methodist Book Concern as will, with the notes, book accounts, presses, & c., mentioned in the last resolution, bear the same proportion to the whole property of said Concern that the travelling preachers in the Southern Church shall bear to all the travelling ministers of the Methodist Episcopal Church. . . .

6. That the above transfer shall be in the form of annual payments of $25,000 per annum. . . .

7. That Nathan Bangs, George Peck, and James B. Finley be, and they are hereby appointed commissioners to act in concert with the same number of commissioners appointed by the Southern organization . . . to estimate the amount which will fall due to the South by the preceding rule, and to have full powers to carry into effect the whole arrangements proposed. . . .

8. That . . . the Agents at New-York are hereby authorized and directed to act in concert with said Southern agents, so as to give the provisions of these resolutions a legally binding force.

9. That all the property of the Methodist Episcopal Church in meeting-houses, parsonages, colleges, schools, Conference funds, cemeteries, and of every kind within the limits of the Southern organization, shall be for ever free from any claim set up on the part of the Methodist Episcopal Church. . . .

10. That the church so formed in the South shall have a common right to use all the copy-rights in possession of the Book Concerns at New-York and Cincinnati, at the time of the settlement. . . .

11. That the Book Agents at New-York be directed to make such compensation to the Conferences South, for their dividend from the Chartered Fund, as the commissioners above provided for shall agree upon.

12. That the Bishops be respectfully requested to lay that part of this report requiring the action of the Annual Conferences before them as soon as possible, beginning with the New-York Conference.[105]

The twelve resolutions were considered separately, with roll call votes being taken on the first (135 to 18), second (139 to 17), third (147 to 12),

[105] *Ibid.*, pp. 135-37.

and fifth (153 to 13). Final adoption came Saturday afternoon, June 8. Only eight members, representing an irreconcilable minority from the North, unwilling to let the South go without secession, were recorded in the negative on each of the four recorded votes.

On Monday, June 10, the closing day of the conference, the report of the committee appointed to prepare a statement of facts connected with the proceedings in the case of Bishop Andrew was presented by John P. Durbin (Philadelphia), the chairman. This was the formal reply of the majority to the minority's protest, and it is thus generally known as the "Reply to the Protest." By a vote of 116 to 26 this report was ordered to be entered on the *Journal* and printed.

Miscellaneous Conference Actions

Other acts of this General Conference included the election of two new bishops, Leonidas L. Hamline and Edmund S. Janes. The conference rescinded the resolutions adopted in 1840 which prohibited colored persons from giving testimony against white persons in church trials, in any state where they were denied that privilege in legal trials. Five new Annual Conferences were formed—Vermont, North Indiana, Iowa, Western Texas, and Florida. The bishops were requested to prepare a four-year uniform Course of Study for candidates for deacons' and elders' orders in the traveling ministry. The conference decided that a superintendent of the "missions to the coloured people" in the South Carolina, Georgia, and Alabama Conferences should be appointed by the presiding bishop. The conference also adopted, in place of the former rule on spirituous liquors, Wesley's original rule, which prohibited *"Drunkenness,* buying or selling spirituous liquors, or drinking them, unless in cases of extreme necessity." It authorized the book agents at Cincinnati "to publish a cheap Sabbath School Advocate, at 25 cents a year, for the benefit of the West." A new constitution for the church's Missionary Society and a "cent-a-week plan" for raising money were adopted "to enable the society to carry on more vigorously its missionary operations." The conference received a warning from the bishops on financing church construction:

It appears that the rules of Discipline requiring our members to build plain, cheap houses of worship, and to guard against contracting debts on the premises, have been too little regarded. In numerous instances costly houses have been erected on credit, or on a loan subject to lien or mortgage, which cannot be lifted by those immediately interested; and, as the last resort, agents have been sent out to solicit aid in distant parts.[106]

There was even a collection taken for two conference members who had been robbed of their pocketbooks and money.

Finally, "at a quarter after twelve o'clock, on the morning of the eleventh of June, and after prayer by brother Dunwody, Conference adjourned. . . . Thus ended the ninth delegated General Conference of the Methodist Episcopal Church." [107]

6

Interpreting the Conference

Focusing Agents in the 1844 Debate

Several historians of the division of the Methodist Episcopal Church have sought to interpret the crisis and separation in 1844 *solely* in terms of the slavery controversy. William Warren Sweet, a prominent example, wrote: "In the course of the debate the real issue, slavery, fell into the background, while its legal and constitutional phases became prominent." [108] The typical approach of this school of thought begins with a survey of General Conference and Annual Conference acts and statements concerning slavery, quotes social and economic historians on the development of slavery, and then, by way of the appeal of Francis Harding, centers on the attack upon Bishop Andrew—giving *exclusive* attention to the slavery controversy. There can be little doubt that slavery was a basic cause of the Methodist schism, but it was not the *only* cause.

Actually, only two delegates debated the issue of slavery: Samuel Dunwody of the South Carolina Conference and William Cass of the New Hampshire Conference.[109] The majority of the Southern delegates

---

[106] *Ibid.,* p. 88.

[107] *Ibid.,* p. 149.

[108] *Methodism in American History* (Nashville: Abingdon Press, 1953), pp. 246-47. Cf. Sweet's *Virginia Methodism,* pp. 188-226, and Norwood, *Schism in the M.E. Church,* p. 73. Other examples are J. M. Buckley's *A History of Methodism in the United States,* pp. 385-441; Charles Elliott, *History of the Great Secession;* and Luccock, Hutchinson, and Goodloe, *The Story of Methodism,* pp. 327-31.

[109] *Debates,* pp. 164-65, 108-9.

acknowledged the evil and curse of slavery.[110] As a historian of the Methodist Episcopal Church, South, has written: "Thus, then, it was not for slavery that they [the Southern delegates] contended, but for security from molestation in preaching the gospel to slave-owners and to slaves without running the risk of being denied access to both classes by interfering with existing institutions and civil relations." [111] Refusing to debate slavery, the Southerners took issue with their Northern brethren at their weakest point—on polity. Here the North seemed most vulnerable, for they had deviated considerably from the Asburian tradition. Although polity was not the *main* issue, it was nevertheless a real and vitally involved issue, with a long history of disagreement between the North and South going back at least as far as the General Conference of 1812. The "great debate" and the following separation, therefore, cannot be understood adequately unless more attention is given to the controversy over the nature of the general superintendency.[112]

In the course of the debates the slavery issue—the South's indefensible position—was pushed into the background; while an issue that was the North's most assailable point became prominent—a unilateral understanding of the locus of authority in American Methodism. Accordingly, a more illuminating approach to an interpretation of the debates and separation of 1844 begins with the presiding elder controversy, not the appeal of Francis Harding. The debate concerning the proposed limited tenure for presiding elders, the Griffith resolution, and the Finley substitute were the focusing agents pinpointing the issue of authority.

Originating perhaps with the memorials from the New Jersey and Oneida Conferences, a proposal was made by the Committee on the Revisal of the *Discipline* to limit a presiding elder's appointment to any one district to four consecutive years, "after which he shall not be appointed to the same district for six years." In the debate on this measure the party lines were clearly drawn: the four delegates favoring the proposal were from Northern and Eastern conferences; the seven opposed, from the South and West.

Opposing the report, William Capers (South Carolina) declared that it cast doubt on the bishops:

. . . venerable, tried, faithful, holy, and just men, and imbued with the spirit of knowledge, and wisdom, and grace, as that conference knew them to be; and

[110] Cf. *ibid.,* pp. 26-27, 44.

[111] Gross Alexander, *A History of the Methodist Church, South, in the United States* (New York: The Christian Literature Company, 1894) , p. 34.

[112] Cf. John J. Tigert, *A Constitutional History of American Episcopal Methodism* (Nashville: Smith and Lamar, 1916) , pp. 369-80.

although they travelled over parts of the country where other members of that conference never dreamed of going, yet the doubt must now be raised whether they were able to judge in a matter that was so directly in their providence. He (Dr. C.) begged to be allowed to confide in the episcopacy.[113]

William Winans of Mississippi said that there was no need for the restriction. Supported by delegates from Virginia and Tennessee, he held that the reappointment of a presiding elder to a particular district should be left to the discretion of the bishops.

The only justification, sir, that they can plead for the passage of this resolution is, that you desire to be relieved from the responsibility. But we do not wish to relieve you. For this purpose you were elected, to shoulder this responsibility. . . . And to relieve you from a responsibility, shall we cripple your power, and curtail those operations that may work for the glory of God and the salvation of deathless souls? . . . You are restricted within sufficiently narrow and local limits already. The rest should be left to your discretion, remembering the fearful responsibility under which you rest, and God forbid that you should ever be deprived of it.[114]

Other delegates pointed out the similarity of this proposal to the suspended resolutions of the 1820's. Peter Cartwright (Illinois) declared:

I think this resolution contemplates trammelling, curtailing, and eventually destroying the official power of the bishops. . . . This resolution is of the same family of little brats that have squeaked against presiding elders for thirty years. I think it will destroy effectually the official and healthy action of the presiding elders themselves. . . . I should not be surprised if they go next for "routine" in bishops, and want them to be changed every four years, or eight years at most.[115]

In supporting the proposed limit of tenure, on the other hand, Isaac Winner of New Jersey denied any novelty in the measure. He continued to say:

It has been further objected that it would trench upon the authority of the episcopacy. Why this, to some extent had been done already . . . . Brethren's fears that they should come in contact with the bishops, and thus mar and maculate the great enterprise in which they are engaged, were fallacious. Why, sir, the *General Conference* is *the* supreme power of the Church, not the

[113] *Debates*, p. 72.
[114] *Ibid.*, p. 79.
[115] *Ibid.*, p. 80.

episcopacy! Talk of power, and of bishops! . . . This body has the right to decide what power shall be intrusted in their hands.[116]

Thus the debate over limited tenure for presiding elders focused upon this issue: a unilateral (General Conference) versus a co-ordinate (General Conference and episcopacy) understanding of the locus of authority in the Methodist Episcopal Church.

The central figure in the divisive drama was Bishop James O. Andrew. As soon as his ownership of slaves was officially announced, Alfred Griffith offered the following preamble and resolution to the conference—quoted here because of their effect in further focusing upon the issue of polity:

> Whereas the Rev. James O. Andrew, one of the Bishops of the M. E. Church, has become connected with slavery, as communicated in his statement in his reply to the inquiry of the Committee on the Episcopacy . . . ; and whereas it has been, from the origin of said Church, a settled policy and invariable usage to elect no person to the office of Bishop who was embarrassed with this "great evil," as under such circumstances it would be impossible for a bishop to exercise the functions and perform the duties assigned to a general Superintendent with acceptance, in that large portion of his charge in which slavery does not exist; and whereas Bishop Andrew was himself nominated by our brethren of the slave-holding states, and elected by the General Conference of 1832, as a candidate who, though living in the midst of a slaveholding population, was nevertheless free from all personal connection with slavery; and whereas, this is, of all periods in our history as a Church, the one least favourable to such an innovation upon the practice and usage of Methodism as to confide a part of the itinerant general superintendency to a slaveholder; therefore,
>
> Resolved, That the Rev. James O. Andrew be, and he is hereby affectionately requested to resign his office as one of the Bishops of the Methodist Episcopal Church.[117]

The significance of slavery in this resolution is not denied, but also important is what is implied in the request—indeed, in the eyes of some of the delegates, the *demand* [118]—that Bishop Andrew resign his episcopal office. If the conference adopted the resolution, Andrew would have no choice except to resign. As Thomas Stringfield of the Holston Conference protested: "What we *intend* to do, let us *appear* to do. . . . If one of our most beloved and useful bishops is to be disrobed and degraded, let us not require him to do the deed himself; but let us have courage to do it in *form*, as we shall in *reality*." [119] Furthermore, there was no doubt in

[116] *Ibid.*, p. 78.
[117] *Journal of the General Conference*, 1844, p. 64.
[118] *Debates*, pp. 93-94, 96, 98, 100.
[119] *Ibid.*, pp. 93-94.

the mind of the author of the resolution that the General Conference was fully able to do what he intended it to do. Instead of arguing the slavery issue, Griffith came directly to the point in explaining his resolution: a bishop, "in the sense in which the word has been incorporated into our institutions," is "only an officer of the General Conference, created for specific purposes, and for no other than the purposes specified." Moreover, the General Conference has "full authority to regulate their own officers, to provide for any exigency which may operate as a barrier in the way of the accomplishment of the objects and purposes for which the officers were chosen." [120] Thus the Griffith resolution further focused the debates upon this issue: a unilateral versus a co-ordinate understanding of the locus of authority in Methodist polity.

The supporters of this resolution soon realized that their measure was too strongly worded. "This resolution was directly to the point, and should have been adopted," James Porter wrote. "But it was a little too explicit for the Conference and the times." [121] Accordingly, they presented the following substitute resolution:

Whereas, the Discipline of our church forbids the doing anything calculated to destroy our itinerant general superintendency, and whereas Bishop Andrew has become connected with slavery by marriage and otherwise, and this act having drawn after it circumstances which in the estimation of the General Conference will greatly embarrass the exercise of his office as an itinerant general Superintendent, if not in some places entirely prevent it; therefore,

Resolved, That it is the sense of this General Conference that he desist from the exercise of this office so long as this impediment remains.[122]

This resolution, submitted by J. B. Finley and J. M. Trimble of the Ohio Conference, placed the unilateralist or "conference" party on easier ground to defend. Whereas the Griffith resolution had left them open to the protest that *they* were destroying the general superintendency by forcing Bishop Andrew to resign, the Finley resolution charged the *bishop* with threatening to destroy the itinerant general superintendency by refusing to free his slaves. Instead of requesting Andrew to resign, the substitute stated the conference's desire that he "desist from the exercise" of his office until the slaves were freed. In a sense, the General Conference would thus be giving Bishop Andrew the necessary consent

---

[120] *Ibid.*, pp. 82-83.
[121] "The General Conference of 1844," p. 245. Cf. Jesse Peck, "The General Conference of 1844," *Methodist Quarterly Review*, April, 1870, pp. 178-79.
[122] *Journal of the General Conference*, 1844, pp. 65-66.

temporarily to "cease from traveling at large among the people." Nevertheless, the question was immediately raised whether this new resolution
was mandatory or advisory, indicating that in the minds of the opponents
of the substitute the issue was still the relationship between the General
Conference and the general superintendency.[123] As Tigert wrote a half
century later:

That sectional differences, particularly the contrast between the civil institutions
of the northern and southern portions of the Union, afterwards largely entered, directly and indirectly, into the estrangement of the two wings of
Episcopal Methodism, must be allowed, as a matter of course, by any one enjoy-
ing a tolerable acquaintance with the principles of human nature and the events
recorded on the broad page of history. But this fact must not blind us to an
antecedent difference, which radically divided the northern and southern sections of the Church on the nature of our ecclesiastical government, and particularly on the powers which the Delegated General Conference was entitled
to exercise under the constitution which had been given to it. In our Church,
as in our nation, the division was along the line of strict construction of the
powers delegated by the constitution, on the one hand, and a loose and broad
interpretation of those powers, on the other. These differences in the Church,
instead of fading away with the lapse of time, have been accentuated at critical
junctures, before, at, and since the division of Episcopal Methodism, until distinct
and opposed conceptions of our Church government, particularly of the powers
and relations of the General Conference, the Annual Conferences, and the
Episcopacy, have been crystallized in the Methodist Episcopal Church and the
Methodist Episcopal Church, South.[124]

When the Finley resolution was adopted, the vote was clearly along
sectional lines: the Northern and Eastern conferences unanimously in
favor, the Southern and Western unanimously in opposition, and the
border and Middle Western divided.

The "Conference" Party

An examination of the debates of the General Conference of 1844
reveals a clear division between two principal points of view, each held
and vigorously supported by a considerable number of delegates. The
majority party—hereafter referred to as the "Conference Party"—was
characterized by a unilateral understanding of the locus of authority in

[123] *Debates*, pp. 101-2, 106, 123-24, 128-34, 168-71, 190, 204, 207.
[124] *Constitutional History*, pp. 371-72.

Methodist polity. The major disagreement between the two parties was in their interpretation of the relationship of the general superintendency to the General Conference. The dominant and distinctive characteristic of the Conference Party's position was its unqualified insistence upon the supremacy of the General Conference, upon the General Conference as the unilateral locus of power in the Methodist Episcopal Church.

In the debate concerning limited tenure for presiding elders, it will be remembered, Isaac Winner declared: "Why, sir, the *General Conference* is *the* supreme power of the Church, not the episcopacy!" This theme was repeated and developed at length by Leonidas L. Hamline during the debate on the Finley substitute resolution. "Let it never be lost sight of," he admonished the delegates, "the General Conference is *'the sun of our system.'*" Not only is it "supreme," but "its supremacy is universal"; because it has "legislative, judicial, and executive supremacy."

Hamline explained the intent of these assertions by stating his purpose: "I shall argue our authority to depose a bishop summarily for improprieties morally innocent, which embarrass the exercise of his functions, *from the relations of the General Conference to the Church, and to the episcopacy.*" Speaking of the relationship of the General Conference to the general superintendent in terms of legislative supremacy, Hamline declared: "In clerical orders every man on this floor is his equal, but in legislative functions, his superior. Can you contribute the uplifting of a hand for or against a conference act? You may not do it. The Discipline, which we shape at pleasure, defies your touch. You may not, in this regard, breathe upon it." With reference to judicial supremacy, Hamline described the General Conference as "a court of appeals beyond which no parties can travel for the cure of errors."

It is the dernier resort, not only of appellants, but of original complainants. You, sir, must stand or fall by its sole decision. . . . Nor has a bishop part or lot in its court action. . . . His lips are sealed in this august body, except when himself is concerned. . . . So naked, sir, of judicial prerogatives is the bishop in this conference. . . . And in the mean time you are liable, as I suppose, to be stripped by us of those other high prerogatives of which, by our countenance, you now hold investiture. . . . Your station in the General Conference is a peculiar eminence. Your high seat is not at all terrific in concealed, or outbeaming power. It is like a gallery of disabilities, where, as a spectator of tragedy, you can do little more than admire or reprobate the piece, and smile or frown upon the actors.

The General Conference, according to Hamline, was not only the "ecclesiastical legislature and the high court—*curia maxima*—of the

Methodist Episcopal Church," it was also "clothed with supreme executive functions." Moreover, the conference could exercise its executive authority with or without the bishops. Because it was the *"fountain* of all official executive authority," the conference was the source of the bishops' powers.[125]

Closely associated with this stress upon the supremacy of the General Conference was the Conference Party's conviction that the bishops were the creation of the General Conference, that the bishops received their very existence as bishops from the General Conference. Nathan Bangs of the New York Conference argued, for example, that "inasmuch as the General Conference had created him [any bishop], they have power to depose or suspend him for just cause." [126] John P. Durbin (Philadelphia) also asserted that the episcopacy derived its power from the General Conference: "Solely, sir, from the suffrages of the General Conference. There, and there only, is the source of episcopal power in our Church. And the same power that conferred the authority can remove it, if they see it necessary." [127] The "Reply to the Protest" stated emphatically that "the bishops derive their power from the election of the General Conference, and not from their ordination." [128] Ordination simply confirmed that which had actually been conferred by the election.

Another theme of the Conference Party's argument which was closely related to its stress upon the supremacy of the General Conference was the contention that the bishops were the officers of the General Conference. They were created by the General Conference to serve as its executive, presiding officers. As Stephen Olin said, "It seems to me that we have large powers—plenary powers for carrying out through the episcopacy the general purposes of the conference and the Church." [129] Similarly, the "Reply to the Protest" quoted Bishop Hedding as saying: "The superintendents now have no power in the Church above that of elders, except what is connected with presiding in the conference, fixing the appointments of the preachers, and ordaining. . . . They are the servants of the elders, and go out and execute their commands." [130] (Note Hedding's failure to distinguish between the elders, collectively, and the delegated General Conference.) The clearest statement of this theme, however, was in Griffith's definition of the term "bishop": "We use it only and exclusively to denote and designate the chief officer of

[125] *Debates,* pp. 128-31.
[126] *Ibid.,* p. 127.
[127] *Ibid.,* p. 174.
[128] *Ibid.,* p. 236.
[129] *Ibid.,* p. 102.
[130] *Ibid.,* p. 236.

the General Conference. . . . A bishop among us is, therefore, only an officer of the General Conference, created for specific purposes, and for no other than the purposes specified." [131]

A third corollary of the Conference Party's stress upon the supremacy of the General Conference was their understanding of the amenability of the bishops to the General Conference. Hamline acknowledged that very many had privately urged that the General Conference had no authority to displace a bishop, except for crime and by a formal trial. He agreed that bishops should not be expelled from the *ministry* for "improper conduct" nor without due notice and trial, but they "may be deposed from *office* summarily, and for improprieties which, even if they be innocent hinder their usefulness, or render their ministrations a calamity." The rule in the *Discipline,* he continued, was "simply declaratory, recognizing a power already existing." "If there were no express rule for deposing a bishop, we should still be competent to depose." [132]

The power of the General Conference to remove a bishop from office without a trial was more emphatically stated in the "Reply to the Protest."

The "Protest" maintains, that "the General Conference has no right, power, or authority, ministerial, judicial, or administrative," in any way to subject a bishop "to any official disability whatever, without the formal presentation of a charge or charges, alleging that the bishop to be dealt with has been guilty of the violation of some law, or at least some disciplinary obligation of the Church, and also upon conviction of such charge, after due form of trial." . . . [This] is, in reality, an attempt to except, from the action of a general system, those who, least of all, ought to be excepted.[133]

At every General Conference, the "Reply" continued, the character of every bishop was examined, not just to determine whether there were grounds for formal presentation of charges leading to a regular trial; "but whether there is any 'objection'—anything that might interfere with the acceptance of the officer in question among his charge."

And it is doctrine novel and dangerous in the Methodist Church, that such difficulties cannot be corrected unless the person objected to be formally arraigned under some specific law, to be found in the concise code of the Discipline —doctrine not the less dangerous, because it is applied where "objections," unimportant in others, might be productive of the most disastrous consequences.[134]

[131] *Ibid.,* p. 82.
[132] *Ibid.,* pp. 132-33.
[133] *Ibid.,* p. 235.
[134] *Ibid.*

To support these contentions the "Reply" quoted passages from the
Discipline of 1785, Coke and Asbury's "Notes" to the *Discipline,* a
pamphlet by John Dickins—the "intimate friend" of Bishop Asbury—
Bishop Emory's *Defence of Our Fathers,* and concluded with the following quotations from Bishop Hedding, "who only concurs in the moderate,
truly Methodistic views of Bishops Asbury, Coke, and Emory."

The General Conference may expel a bishop not only for immoral, but for
"improper conduct," which means a small offense below a crime; for which not
even a child or a slave can be expelled but after repeated admonitions. . . .
The travelling preachers gave the bishop his power, they continue it in his hands,
and they can reduce, limit, or transfer it to other hands, whenever they see
cause.[135]

From a careful study of the thought of Asbury and the establishment
of constitutional government in American Methodism, it is apparent
that Durbin and his colleagues quoted these authorities out of their
original context. The passages from the 1785 *Discipline,* the Coke and
Asbury "Notes" (1798), and Dickins' pamphlet (1792) are pertinent
only to the period *prior* to the adoption of the delegated General Conference in 1808. For that period—1784 to 1808—they are eminently
relevant. The entire structure of Methodist polity was constantly subject
to radical change or revision by a simple majority vote in the yearly
conferences prior to 1792 and in the General Conferences thereafter. In
1808, however, the general superintendency and the delegated General
Conference were established as co-ordinate institutions, empowered,
limited, and protected by a constitution. The delegated General Conference was specifically forbidden by the Third Restrictive Rule to
"change or alter any part or rule of our government, so as to do away
episcopacy, or to destroy the plan of our itinerant general superintendency." Accordingly, the episcopacy was no longer "perfectly subject"
to the delegated General Conference, nor were the bishops—"their power,
their usefulness, themselves"—"entirely at the mercy" of that body. The
bishops were amenable to the General Conference for their conduct, but
that amenability was within constitutional limitations. The quotations
from an unidentified work of Bishop Hedding doubtless came from the
post-1808 period, but their context in the "Reply to the Protest" makes
an adequate interpretation difficult. If the several quotations all came
from the same work and referred to the episcopacy established by the
constitution, the bishop failed to make the necessary distinction between
the traveling preachers and the delegated General Conference. Other-

[135] *Ibid.,* pp. 174-75, 236-37.

wise, Durbin has placed them in irreconcilable juxtaposition. The delegated General Conference certainly did not have the authority to "reduce, limit, or transfer" the powers of the bishops "whenever they [saw] cause."

The widest divergence within the Conference Party was in their interpretation of the effect of the Finley resolution. Finley himself said that the resolution did not impeach the character of Bishop Andrew in any way. "We don't depose him as a bishop; we only say it is the sense of the General Conference that he ought to cease to exercise the office till this embarrassment ceases." [136] Hamline, on the other hand, interpreted the resolution as "a *mandamus* measure." "Its passage," he said, "will absolutely suspend the exercise of the superintendent's *functions,* until he complies with the prescribed condition." [137] The "Reply to the Protest," however, denied that the proceedings of the General Conference concerning Bishop Andrew were judicial: "The action of the General Conference was neither judicial nor punitive. It neither achieves nor intends a deposition, nor so much as a legal suspension. Bishop Andrew is still a bishop; and should he, against the expressed sense of the General Conference, proceed in the discharge of his functions, his official acts would be valid." [138] The "Reply" went on to say that Bishop Andrew's name would continue to appear in the official publications of the church as one of its bishops and that he would receive his salary in the customary way.

What, then, was the effect of the resolution? As chairman of the committee that drew up the "Reply," Durbin was probably most representative of the Conference Party's viewpoint. His answer was: "The substitute proposes only to express the sense of this conference in regard to a matter which it cannot, in duty and conscience, pass by without suitable expression; and having made the solemn expression, it leaves Bishop Andrew to act as *his* sense of duty shall dictate." [139] This statement received the endorsement of the conference when the resolutions proposed by J. T. Mitchell—concerning Andrew's status as a bishop of the church—were adopted.

That Mitchell's resolutions did not indicate the full scope of the viewpoint of the Conference Party, however, is implied in the previous rejection of two other measures. Before the adoption of the Finley resolution, the bishops presented a communication to the General Conference recommending the postponement of further action in the case of Bishop

[136] *Ibid.*, p. 100.
[137] *Ibid.*, p. 128.
[138] *Ibid.*, p. 232.
[139] *Ibid.*, p. 175.

Andrew until the next session of the General Conference, in 1848. A warm debate developed over whether or not to accept the bishops' recommendation, it will be remembered, and Bishop Hedding withdrew his signature from the communication. Then, after two days of discussion, Nathan Bangs moved that the communication be tabled. The vote was close and clearly along sectional lines: ninety-five for, eighty-four against; the Northeastern conferences unanimously in favor, the border and Middle West divided, and the South and West unanimously opposed.

Another significant act of the conference that further indicated the viewpoint of the Conference Party was the rejection of a resolution presented by two delegates from the Baltimore Conference, Henry Slicer and Thomas B. Sargent. The Finley resolution was adopted late Saturday afternoon, June 1, shortly after the communication from the bishops had been tabled. The following Monday morning, Slicer and Sargent presented this resolution:

> 1. Resolved, That it is the sense of this General Conference that the vote of Saturday last, in the case of Bishop Andrew, be understood as advisory only, and not in the light of a judicial mandate.
> 2. Resolved, That the final disposition of Bishop Andrew's case be postponed until the General Conference in 1848, in conformity with the suggestion of the Bishops, in their Address to the Conference on Friday, 31st May.[140]

After Slicer's introductory remarks, however, the measure was promptly tabled. Again the vote was along sectional lines; but on this occasion there was a majority of only seven votes—seventy-five to sixty-eight. Nevertheless, the Conference Party had rejected an advisory interpretation of the Finley resolution, at least by implication.

In summary, the Conference Party, as reflected in the debates as well as in the voting of the delegates to the General Conference of 1844, was characterized by a unilateral understanding of the locus of authority in the Methodist Episcopal Church—the General Conference being supreme. Although there was some recognition of the constitution as representing the ultimate authority of the traveling preachers, it was generally held that the constitution bestowed practically unlimited powers upon the General Conference. Indeed, there was an evident failure to distinguish between the sovereign General Conferences of the preconstitutional period and the delegated General Conference established in 1808. The bishops were strictly the executive officers of the conference, virtually without any constitutional protection or prerogatives.

[140] *Journal of the General Conference*, 1844, p. 85.

The "Constitution" Party

Standing in strong opposition to the Conference Party in the "great debate" in the General Conference of 1844 was a minority party which will here be termed the "Constitution Party." The principal characteristic of this party's viewpoint was its conviction that the locus of authority in the Methodist Episcopal Church was co-ordinately established in the General Conference and in the general superintendency. The ultimate authority was held by the traveling preachers collectively. Before the adoption of the constitution in 1808, this authority had been exercised by the yearly conference and, later, in the quadrennial General Conferences. In 1808, however, the traveling preachers established the delegated quadrennial General Conference and the general superintendency as co-ordinate institutions, empowered and limited by the constitution—which thereafter represented the continuing authority of the traveling preachers. Such convictions placed this party clearly within the tradition of general superintendency pioneered by Francis Asbury and written into the constitution by Joshua Soule.

Although the Constitution Party agreed that there were only two orders in the Methodist ministry, they were not willing to say that a bishop was only an officer of the General Conference. They used the word "officer" to describe a bishop, but he was a unique kind of officer.

In the first place, a bishop was an ordained officer. As A. L. P. Green of the Tennessee Conference asked:

When we make a book agent or editor, do we make him say that he believes that he is moved by the Holy Ghost to take on him the office of book agent or editor? No, sir. But we do a bishop when he is ordained, and we set him apart to the work by the imposition of hands. Will any brother say that this consecration is nothing more than a solemn mockery? [141]

"Episcopacy even in the Methodist Church is not a mere appointment to labour," the "Protest" declared. "It is an official consecrated station." [142]

In the second place, a bishop was elected for life, "or during good behavior"; whereas an officer of the conference was elected for a certain period of time. Again, as Green asked, "When a book agent or editor becomes old, or feeble in health, do we make him a superannuated book agent or editor? Not so, sir. But *once a bishop,* whether able to do the work of a superintendent or not, *always a bishop.*" [143]

[141] *Debates,* p. 124. Stephen Olin (New York) had made the comparison of the office of a book agent or editor to that of a bishop (*ibid.,* pp. 103-4).
[142] *Ibid.,* p. 209.
[143] *Ibid.,* p. 124. Italics mine.

In the third place, a bishop was an itinerant general superintendent. As such, he was not an officer of the General Conference but of the Methodist Episcopal Church in the United States of America. Bishop Soule declared, "I desire to understand my landmarks as a bishop of the Methodist Episcopal Church—not the bishop of the General Conference, not the bishop of any annual conference." [144] Or, as the "Protest" explained the position of the Constitution Party:

> As *executive officers* as well as *pastoral overseers,* the bishops belong to the Church as such, and not to the General Conference as one of its counsels or organs of action merely. . . . The bishops of the Methodist Episcopal Church, . . . instead of being the officers and creatures of the General Conference, are *de facto* the officers and servants of the Church.[145]

As has been seen, the Conference Party accused Bishop Andrew of having destroyed the general itinerant nature of the superintendency by becoming a slaveholder. William A. Smith of the Virginia Conference responded:

> It is in vain to plead that this course is called for by reasons arising out of the character of our episcopacy as a general superintendency. . . . The first ground on which the abolition argument rests the charge of "improper conduct" is, *that by his* [Bishop Andrew's] *marriage he has rendered himself "unacceptable" to a large portion of the north, and should therefore be deprived of his office.* "Unacceptable!" To whom? Abolitionists. . . . If he be "unacceptable" to the abolitionists and to those who associate with them, by reason of his having such connection with slavery as is provided for in the compromise rule, it is the fault of those to whom he is thus "unacceptable." . . . *They* then, and *not* Bishop Andrew or his friends, must suffer the consequences of his "unacceptability." [146]

The "Protest" also attacked the Finley resolution at this point.

> By pressing the issue in question, therefore, the majority virtually dissolve the government of the Methodist Episcopal Church, because in every constitutional aspect it is sundered by so crippling a co-ordinate branch of it as to destroy the itinerant general superintendency altogether. Whenever it is clearly ascertained that the compromise law of the Church, regulating slavery and abolition, is abandoned, every bishop, each of the venerable and excellent men who now adorn the Church and its councils, *ceases* to be a general superintendent. The law of union, the principle of gravitation, binding us together, is dissolved, and the general superintendency of the Methodist Episcopal Church is no more! [147]

[144] *Ibid.,* p. 169.
[145] *Ibid.,* p. 209.
[146] *Ibid.,* pp. 137-40.
[147] *Ibid.,* p. 211.

Another argument presented in defense of Bishop Andrew was based on the contention that there actually was no longer an itinerant general superintendency. "The plan of annually presiding in every conference, or once within the recess of the sessions of General Conference," one delegate declared, "expired with Bishop Asbury." He went on to show that Bishop Hedding had not visited the Southern conferences more than once in the past twenty years, and concluded: "A general superintendency, as interpreted by the practice of late years, implies eligibility to preside in any conference, but an actual presidency only when prudence demands it." [148] When another delegate proposed official sanction of this state of affairs, however, Henry Slicer of the Baltimore Conference asserted:

Every general superintendent must be as the life-blood of the human system, flowing out with constant vigorous action from the centre to circumference, and returning to the centre again with the same vitality, and one might as well talk of bandaging a man's arm, and have him remain in a state of health as to retain an itinerant general superintendent, and yet have him to remain within a district of the connection.[149]

The Constitution Party's understanding of the general itinerant character of the superintendency was in complete accord with Bishop Soule's concern that the bishops travel through the whole connection "in consecutive order." [150]

According to the Constitution Party, the general superintendency and the General Conference were co-ordinate branches of the government of the Methodist Episcopal Church. This relation was clearly stated in the "Protest." As the Methodist Episcopal Church was organized—that is, under the constitution—the episcopacy was "a co-ordinate branch, the executive department proper of the government." The bishops were the "executive officers as well as pastoral overseers" of the entire church. The other co-ordinate branch of the government, the General Conference, was "merely the representative organ of the Church, with limited powers to do its business, in the discharge of a delegated trust." Although the General Conference elected the bishops, it did so only as the church's "organ of action," exercising derivative rather than inherent power. Any assumption of power by the General Conference beyond its delegated authority would be a direct violation of one of the Restrictive Rules.

Despite the implications of the charges made by the Conference Party,

[148] *Ibid.*, p. 142.
[149] *Ibid.*, p. 107.
[150] *Journal of the General Conference,* 1844, p. 157.

the Constitution Party *did* acknowledge the amenability of the general superintendents to the General Conference. Bishop Soule spoke the convictions of the Constitution Party as well as his own convictions when he declared to the assembled delegates: "I hold that the General Conference of the Methodist Episcopal Church has an indisputable right— constitutional, sacred—to arraign at her tribunal every bishop; to try us there; to find us guilty of any offence with which we are charged on evidence, and to excommunicate—expel us. . . . I recognize fully their right." [151]

The bishops' amenability to the General Conference, however, did not mean that they were utterly at the mercy of the majority will of that body. The bishops were amenable *only* "in conformity with legal right and the provisions of law, in the premises. In this sense, and so viewed, they are subject to the General Conference, and this is sufficient limitation of their power, unless the government itself is to be considered irregular and unbalanced in the co-ordinate relations of its parts." [152] A formal trial was necessary. As Bishop Soule declared:

I had understood, from the beginning, that special provision was provided for the trial of a bishop. The constitution has provided that no preacher, no person was to be deprived of the right of trial, according to the forms of Discipline, and of the right of appeal; but, sir, if I understand the doctrine advanced and vindicated, it is that you may depose a bishop without the form of trial; you may depose him without any obligation to show cause, and therefore he is the only minister in your Church who has no appeal. It seems to me that the Church has made special provision for the trial of the bishop, for the special reason that the bishop has no appeal. [153]

The "Protest" emphatically declared:

We recognize in this General Conference no right, power, or authority, ministerial, judicial, or administrative, to suspend or depose a bishop of the Methodist Episcopal Church, or otherwise subject him to any official disability whatever, without the formal presentation of a charge or charges, alleging that the bishop to be dealt with has been guilty of the violation of some law, or at least some disciplinary obligation of the Church, and also upon conviction of such charge after due form of trial. [154]

The Constitution Party contended that they would have "submitted without remonstrance" had Bishop Andrew been "suspended according to

[151] *Debates,* p. 170.
[152] *Ibid.,* p. 209.
[153] *Ibid.,* p. 169.
[154] *Ibid.,* p. 204.

law, after due form of trial." Yet their "principal ground of complaint and remonstrance" was "the official refusal of the majority to abide the arbitrament of law." [155]

What was the effect of the Finley resolution, according to the viewpoint of the Constitution Party? During the debates on this resolution Bishop Soule declared his "deliberate opinion" of its effect: "The adoption of that resolution deposes Bishop Andrew without form of trial." Expressing a deeper concern, the principal author of the constitution continued:

You must know—you cannot but know, that . . . it will not be Bishop Andrew alone that your word will affect! No, sir. . . . I wish it to be distinctly understood, *it cannot affect him alone.* I mean specially in this point—I say that the resolution on which we are just about to act goes to sustain the doctrine that the General Conference have power and right to depose one of the bishops of the Methodist Episcopal Church without the form of trial—that you are under no obligation from the constitution or laws of the Church to *show cause* even. Now every man must see, and every man must know, that Bishop Andrew cannot be involved alone in the vote. It is the principle which is involved. It goes to say that when this conference shall vote on the subject—a simple majority of this conference, without form of trial, can depose a bishop of the Methodist Episcopal Church. . . . It involves the office; it involves the charge; it involves the relation itself. . . . I pray you hold to principles—to principles.[156]

In other words, passage of the Finley resolution would involve a fundamental change in the structure of Methodist polity. The essential nature of the general superintendency and the basic character of the relationship between the general superintendency and the General Conference—as established by the constitution—would be radically transformed, if not actually destroyed. Soule, therefore, begged the delegates to reject the proposal as contrary to constitutional principles.

The "Protest" gave a broader interpretation of the action of the General Conference. It declared that the "recent act of a majority" had degraded, punished, and suspended Bishop Andrew, "without the exhibition of any alleged offence against the laws or discipline of the Church, without any form of trial, or legal conviction of any kind, and in the absence of any charge of want of qualification or faithfulness in the performance of the duties pertaining to his office." [157] In reply to the contention that the resolution was a "mere matter of advice or recommendation," the "Protest" asserted that the resolution was "imperative and mandatory." The "entire proceedings of the majority in the case" sup-

[155] *Ibid.,* pp. 206, 211.
[156] *Ibid.,* pp. 171-72.
[157] *Ibid.,* p. 204.

ported such an interpretation. The Griffith resolution, which had "respectfully and affectionately requested" the bishop to resign, had been rejected in favor of the Finley substitute, which conveyed "no idea of request, advice, or recommendation." Also, a motion to declare the Finley resolution advisory had been promptly rejected by the majority. Therefore, the "Protest" concluded, the resolution was a "mandatory judgment." Even if the intention of the conference had been only to advise and request Bishop Andrew to "desist from his office," the action still would have had all the force of a mandate, "inasmuch as the officer [was] by such request compelled either to resign or remain in office contrary to the known will of the majority." When a body, "claiming the right to compel, asks the resignation of an officer, the request is, to all official and moral purposes, *compulsory,* as it loads the officer with disability, and gives notice of assumed unworthiness, if not criminality." [158]

The majority had not only acted without the support of any law, the Constitution Party further protested, but they had also acted "in defiance of the restraints and provisions of law." As a result, they had endangered the union and stability of the Methodist Episcopal Church and especially had jeopardized the general superintendency, "by subjecting any bishop of the Church at any time to the will and caprice of a majority of the General Conference." In fact, the majority had "virtually dissolve[d] the government of the Methodist Episcopal Church, because in every constitutional aspect it [was] sundered by so crippling a co-ordinate branch of it as to destroy the itinerant general superintendency altogether." [159]

The minority charged that the proceedings of the majority had created an irreparable breach in the church, necessitating "a *separate, independent* existence" for the Annual Conferences represented by the Constitution Party. The protesting minority, therefore, sought to "devise and adopt such measures and arrangement, present and prospective, as [would] secure an amicable division of the Church upon the broad principles of right and equity." [160]

[158] *Ibid.,* pp. 207, 210.
[159] *Ibid.,* pp. 204, 211.
[160] *Ibid.,* p. 211.

7

In Conclusion

The period from 1820 to 1844 was a time of increasing controversy and tension within the Methodist Episcopal Church. In each dispute, there was some disagreement over the nature of the general superintendency—the presiding elder controversy in 1820, the resulting appeal of Bishop McKendree to the Annual Conferences, and the two movements leading to the formation of the Methodist Protestant Church in 1830 and the Wesleyan Connection in 1843. Of particular importance for the present study is the fact that this church began to be divided along geographical lines in a debate over the relationship between the episcopacy and the General Conference in 1820. While the slavery question had been a troublesome issue in the Methodist Episcopal Church since its organization in 1784, the alignment on the polity dispute first came to light in 1820 at a time when the slavery problem—though never forgotten—was not prominently debated in the church. This, of course, does not rule out a possible correlation of the two issues. It is possible to theorize that the Southern ministers, perhaps realizing that they were already a minority in the General Conference,[161] sided with a strong episcopacy because they believed bishops could be expected to maintain the *status quo* and quell uprisings. Looking forward to a time when the Northern preachers might become militant abolitionists, the Southerners were possibly fighting for a powerful general superintendency as a line of defense. Such a view, however, would credit the Southerners in 1820 with unusual prescience.

Yet the sectional disagreement on polity did occur fifteen years before any bishop, acting in his official capacity, took definite steps to prevent discussion of antislavery or abolitionist views in a church conference.[162] At least, the polity issue must be recognized as a potentially divisive force within the Methodist Episcopal Church in the period following 1820. "Thus, nearly a quarter of a century before the division of the Church,

[161] For the first time in the history of the Methodist Episcopal Church, there was a minority of members in the South (the slave states) in 1818. Of the 229,627 total membership reported in the *Minutes* of that year, 114,569 were from the South and 115,058 from the remainder of the United States and its North American territories. These figures include white and colored members; a white Southern minority occurred for the first time in 1813.

[162] See Norwood, *Schism in the M.E. Church*, p. 34.

the Northeast and Southwest were solidly and determinedly arrayed against each other on a question purely constitutional, affecting the principles of ecclesiastical government alone." [163]

Whether Methodism ever would have actually divided over one or the other of these issues alone is strictly a matter of speculation. As a historical fact, the two issues were joined in the person and circumstances of Bishop James O. Andrew. By that time (1844) the withdrawal of the Wesleyan Connection in 1843 had shattered the hopes of the moderates or conservatives that the church could be held together by suppressing abolitionism and had caused a realignment of power blocks within the church. We have seen how the Baltimore Conference took the lead in seeking to purge the church's ministry and leadership of any connection with slavery. We have also seen how the Southern leaders refused to debate the issue of slavery. Charles S. Sydnor, historian of the South, has pointed out a characteristic of the South during this period which perhaps will shed some light on the situation in Methodism. In the 1830's and 1840's the Southerners

believed, and with good reason, that grave injuries had been done to the substantial interests of the South during the 1820's within the framework and through the procedures of democratic government. . . . Much thought was therefore given to devices for limiting and controlling self-government so as to protect smaller parts against the tyranny of the majority. . . . Inasmuch as the government to be held in check operated under a written constitution, the discussion turned into constitutional rather than philosophical channels.[164]

By 1844 the Methodist Southerner had good reason to fear that the same danger threatened the Southern minority in the Methodist Episcopal Church. It is quite possible that by that time Methodists in the South sought to hold the traditional Asburian co-ordinate relationship between the general superintendency and the General Conference and resisted all attempts to make the General Conference supreme as just such a "device." After all, had not the bishops faithfully prevented the Northern abolitionists from attacking slavery through the official agencies of the church since 1835? On the other hand, that defense would be sufficient grounds for a Northern attack on the episcopacy.

David M. Potter and Thomas G. Manning present an interpretation concerning the outbreak of the Civil War that possibly offers further illumination for an understanding of the situation in 1844:

[163] Tigert, Constitutional History, p. 371.
[164] The Development of Southern Sectionalism: 1819-1848 (Baton Rouge: Louisiana State University Press, 1948), p. 334.

Although secession would not have occurred without the slavery contest, it still remains true that the war would not have occurred without secession. The North was not at that time ready to go to war to abolish slavery, and the South was not ready to go to war to extend it into new places. But the South was prepared to fight for the right of secession. . . . The North was prepared to fight to prevent it. It was only when the irritation generated by the slavery question was translated into a constitutional form that a fighting issue appeared. Secession, then, was the explicit though not the basic cause of the war.[165]

Although the division of Methodism would not likely have occurred without the slavery contest, it still remains true that the division did not occur solely due to the slavery issue. The Northern Methodists were not ready to divide the church over slavery. Neither were the Southern Methodists determined to gain the right of slaveholding for the ministry and episcopacy where emancipation was permitted by state laws. But the Northerners were prepared to fight against slaveholding by any bishop, and they used the General Conference—as the supreme power in the church—to force a slave-owning bishop out of office. And the Southerners were willing to divide the church to defend the co-ordinate relationship between the General Conference and the general superintendency. It was only when the irritation generated by the slavery question was translated into—or combined with—a constitutional issue that a sufficient cause for division appeared. Slavery had been the foremost issue in the minds of all the Methodists, but the issue of polity was the only handle with which either side could grasp it. Therefore, the disagreement over the nature of the general superintendency, while not the basic cause, became the occasion of the division of the Methodist Episcopal Church in 1844.

[165] *Nationalism and Sectionalism in America, 1775-1877* (New York: Henry Holt and Company, 1949) , p. 252.

THE ORGANIZATION OF THE METHODIST EPISCOPAL CHURCH, SOUTH

Preliminary Measures, 1844

Methodist Response to Separation

The Louisville Convention, 1845

The First General Conference, 1846

The Southern Delegations Organize

THE GENERAL CONFERENCE OF 1844 adjourned as it had sat, in an atmosphere of frustration and bitter disappointment. The cleavage which had been felt as an all-pervasive spirit before the conference opened, and during its early sessions, was now an overt fact indelibly certified by the strict partisan vote of section against section. Until the final conclusive ballot had been recorded, unwearied efforts were made by many on both sides, in the vain endeavor to heal the breach and find some method to bridge that which was by its very nature an unbridgeable gulf. Subsequent moves on both sides were destined to widen that gulf continually.

The General Conference, by its adoption of the Plan of Separation, had provided under definitely stated conditions for the organizing of the conferences in the slaveholding states into a separate ecclesiastical connection. This was to be under the jurisdiction of a Southern General Conference, provided that those conferences involved should find such jurisdictional separation from the general connection necessary. It was, therefore, at once clear to the Southern delegation that some formal and effective means must be found to obtain the consensus of the Annual Conferences which presumably might wish to act under the plan. To clarify their own intent and act in full accord together, the Southern delegates agreed to meet and did meet (June 10-11, 1844), presumably in part on the afternoon of the day the General Conference adjourned, but certainly in full strength on June 11, the day after. The actions and recommendations of this post-General Conference meeting proved to be of the highest import.

It is noteworthy that at this preliminary meeting, and indeed throughout the whole of the subsequent moves in General Conferences, the General Convention, and in the separate Annual Conferences, the men involved were anxious to see that full, complete, and open records were unfailingly kept through each successive step.[1] The men of 1844 knew that what they were doing was important; they knew that each one of their moves would doubtless be scrutinized for its import, validity, and meaning by thousands then living, and by a posterity yet to come. So it was that the records even of small committees, and of many subsidiary groups which met here and there, were carefully kept and preserved, and in many cases published. The church and the world were certainly not to be left without a due record of plans, purposes, and events as these unrolled through this whole period.

Furthermore, the many resolutions, explanations, addresses, letters, etc., were always at great pains to set forth the meaning and intent of their respective authors. These separate documents and events may be interpreted differently, but the impartial historian must agree that everyone, every committee or conference which issued one of these documents, was at pains above all else to make the meaning clear. Ambiguity was not a fault of the Methodist leaders on either side of the great separation.

Reliance upon documents and publicity of action was made clear at this first meeting of the Southern delegation on June 11, 1844. The plan of action which they then agreed upon was carefully prepared and, as it turned out, adopted. Specifically the Southerners agreed that the following plan be recommended to the conferences represented by them:

With a view to promote uniformity of action in the premises, we beg leave to submit to your consideration the expediency of concurring in the following plan of procuring the judgment of the Church within the slaveholding States, as to the propriety of organizing a Southern division of the Methodist Episcopal

[1] The records and official documents relating to the organization of the Southern Church are found in *History of the Organization of the Methodist Episcopal Church, South: Comprehending all the Official Proceedings of the General Conference; the Southern Annual Conferences, and the General Convention; with such other matters as are necessary to a right understanding of the case.* (Nashville: Compiled and Published by the Editors and Publishers of the South-Western Christian Advocate, for the Methodist Episcopal Church, South, by Order of the Louisville Convention. William Cameron, Printer, 1845.) Most of the information in this chapter was gathered from this official record. The volume was reprinted by the Publishing House of the Methodist Episcopal Church, South, in 1925, with the Journal of the first General Conference of the Southern Church added to the original volume.

Church in the United States, and of effecting such an organization should it be deemed necessary:—

1. There shall be a Convention held in Louisville, Kentucky, to commence the 1st May, 1845,—composed of delegates from the several Annual Conferences within the slaveholding States, appointed in the ratio of one for every eleven members.

2. These delegates shall be appointed at the ensuing session of the several Annual Conferences enumerated, each Conference providing for the expenses of its own delegates.

3. These several Annual Conferences shall instruct their delegates to the proposed Convention on the points on which action is contemplated—conforming their instructions, as far as possible, to the opinions and wishes of the membership within their several Conference bounds.[2]

A lengthy "Address to the Ministers and Members of the Methodist Episcopal Church, in the Slaveholding States and Territories," prepared at this meeting, was designed to accompany and explain the specific recommendations for action. The address, which runs to something like fourteen hundred words, was an apologia for the benefit of the home constituency, and gave the whole of the events which had just transpired in New York. Naturally, it interpreted forcefully the Southern attitude and mind toward these events. The final paragraphs of the address deal definitely with the impending separation:

Some time before the adjournment, however, upon a *declaration* made by the Southern delegations, setting forth the impossibility of enduring such a state of things much longer, the General Conference, by a very large and decided majority, agreed to a *plan of formal and pacific separation,* by which the Southern Conferences are to have a distinct and independent organization of their own, in no way subject to Northern jurisdiction. It affords us pleasure to state that there were those found among the majority who met this proposition with every manifestation of justice and liberality. And should a similar spirit be exhibited by the Annual Conferences in the North, when submitted to them, as provided for in the plan itself, there will remain no legal impediment to its peaceful consummation.

This plan is approved by the undersigned as the best, and, indeed, all that can be done at present, in remedy of the great evil under which we labor. Provision is made for a peaceable and constitutional division of Church property of every kind. The plan does not decide that division shall take place; but simply, and it is thought securely, provides that it may, if it be found necessary. Of this necessity, you are to be the judges, after a careful survey and comparison of all the reasons for and against it.

[2] *History of the Organization,* p. 104.

As the undersigned have had opportunity and advantages which those at a distance could not possess, to form a correct judgment in the premises, and it may be expected of them that they express their views fully on the subject, they do not hesitate to say, that they regard a separation at no distant day as inevitable; and farther, that the plan of separation agreed upon is as eligible as the Southern Conferences have any right to expect at any time. We most respectfully, therefore, and with no common solicitude, beseech our brethren of the ministry and membership in the slaveholding States, to examine this matter carefully, and, weighing it well in all its bearings, try to reach the conclusion most proper under the circumstances. Shall that which, in all moral likelihood must take place soon, be attempted now, or are there reasons why it should be postponed?

We deprecate all excitement; we ask you to be calm and collected, and to approach and dispose of the subject with all the candor and forbearance the occasion demands. The separation proposed is *not* schism, it is *not* secession. It is a State or family, separating into two different States or families, by mutual consent. As the "Methodist Episcopal Church" will be found North of the dividing line, so the "Methodist Episcopal Church" will be found South of the same line. . . .

Disposed, however, to defer to the judgment of the Church, we leave this subject with you. Our first and most direct object has been to bring it fully before you, and giving you an opportunity to judge and determine for yourselves, await your decision. The minority from the South in the late General Conference, were most anxious to adjourn the decision in the case of Bishop Andrew, with all its attendant results, to the Annual Conferences and to the Church at large, to consider and decide upon during the next four years—as no charge was presented against the Bishop, and especially as this measure was urgently recommended by the whole bench of Bishops, although Bishop Hedding subsequently withdrew his name. The proposition, however, to refer the whole subject to the Church, was promptly rejected by the majority, and immediate action demanded and had. But as all the facts connected with the equivocal suspension of Bishop Andrew, will come before you in other forms, it is unnecessary to detail them in this brief address, the main object of which is to place before you, in a summary way, the principal facts and reasons connected with the proposed separation of the Southern Conferences into a distinct organization. . . .

Signed on behalf of the Kentucky, Missouri, Holston, Tennessee, North Carolina, Memphis, Arkansas, Virginia, Mississippi, Texas, Alabama, Georgia, and South Carolina Annual Conferences.

Kentucky.—H. B. Bascom, William Gunn, H. H. Kavanaugh, E. Stevenson, B. T. Crouch, G. W. Brush.

Missouri.—W. W. Redman, W. Patton, J. C. Berryman, J. M. Jameson.

Holston.—E. F. Sevier, S. Patton, T. Springfield.

Tennessee.—R. Paine, J. B. McFerrin, A. L. P. Green, T. Maddin.

North Carolina.—B. T. Blake, J. Jamieson, P. Doub.

Memphis.—G. W. D. Harris, S. S. Moody, W. McMahon, Thomas Joyner.

Arkansas.—J. C. Parker, W. P. Ratcliffe, A. Hunter.

Virginia.—J. Early, T. Crowder, W. A. Smith, L. M. Lee.

Mississippi.—W. Winans, B. M. Drake, J. Lane, G. M. Rogers.

Texas.—Littleton Fowler.

Alabama.—J. Boring, J. Hamilton, W. Murrah, G. Garrett.

Georgia.—G. F. Pierce, W. J. Parks, L. Pierce, J. W. Glenn, J. E. Evans, A. B. Longstreet.

South Carolina.—W. Capers, W. M. Wightman, C. Betts, S. Dunwody, H. A. C. Walker.[3]

We are at some pains to list the names of the conferences and the signers of this address, as all were participants in the post–General Conference consultation. These names will be recognized by many, even after the lapse of a century and more, as leaders of Methodist people in that crucial era. Their names and their subsequent actions have been handed down among Southern Methodists, as the names of the signers of 1776 are enshrined in the nation's annals. Many of these personages will be met with again in this history as further steps in the organization of the Methodist Episcopal Church, South, are enumerated.

These were men of strong minds, chosen leaders of great conferences, and seven of them—H. B. Bascom and H. H. Kavanaugh of Kentucky, Robert Paine of Tennessee, John Early of Virginia, George F. Pierce of Georgia, and William Capers and W. M. Wightman of South Carolina —were destined to be bishops in the Methodist Episcopal Church, South, an as yet uncreated entity, whose organization they were now driving forward to call into being.

The Roles of Bishops Soule and Andrew

The General Conference had declared it their "sense" that Bishop Andrew should cease to exercise episcopal functions, while encumbered with slavery. They did not, however, take away his office or title, or endeavor to implement their action in any further way. They left Andrew a bishop of the Methodist Episcopal Church, and ordered that his name should be so published in the *Discipline* and other official documents. They also saw to it that he should be supported out of the

[3] *Ibid.,* pp. 106-8.

fund then supporting all the bishops. It seems that the General Conference wished to leave it so that Andrew's taking or not taking "episcopal labor" should depend upon his own decision.

A decision of some sort, it was evident, would have to be made by Andrew or his brother bishops following the action of the General Conference. What the Board of Bishops might do about their comrade was itself an indeterminate matter—the General Conference resolution had simply said that it was their judgment that Andrew should "desist from the exercise of his office so long as this impediment remains."

The bishops knew, and Andrew himself later reminded them, that the conference had indeed tabled a resolution intended to explain the meaning of the Finley Resolution as being purely advisory. Andrew's letter to Soule of November 4, 1844, stated that it was his opinion—and the other bishops would probably have agreed—that this action in tabling a softer interpretation of the Finley Resolution made that resolution mandatory, not advisory.

This put the bishops in a quandary. If they should assign work to Andrew, they would seem to defy the deeply felt and overwhelming mind of the majority of the General Conference. Should they not assign Andrew work, they would themselves become the executioners of what could be regarded simply as a resolution calling on Andrew to do something himself. In this dilemma the bishops adopted a course which it was thought would keep them neutral and put the determination of the whole issue on Andrew.

They decided to make out two plans of episcopal visitation. One would be published without carrying the name of Bishop Andrew. A second plan of visitation, which did include Andrew's name and assignment—a so-called "reserve plan"—was made out privately. This was given to Bishop Joshua Soule, and he was instructed to let Andrew know that it would be the one put into effect if Bishop Andrew should apply *in writing* for episcopal work.

But Andrew himself had already gone. He had left New York on the adjournment of the conference and spent the next day in Newark, fulfilling a preaching engagement. From there he went south to his family in Georgia. He was not, therefore, available for any private counsel, had the bishops been minded to seek such, regarding his intent to take work or "desist" from doing so. Andrew later declared that he had no early notice at all of this plan, "except in vague rumor."

The storm which had been created by Andrew's status at the General Conference continued to rage around and about him following the adjournment of that body. Both friends and followers, as well as his active opponents, differed among themselves as to what course he should pursue. There were Southerners who felt that since the General Conference had no right to depose Andrew, he should go forthrightly ahead with his episcopal labors just as he had done hitherto. The greatest consensus in the South, however, seemed to be on the side of those who held that no matter how righteous his cause, he should not perform any episcopal labor, for it was argued that "if he did so, he would be impeached for a violation of the expressed will or 'sense' of the General Conference."

On the other side, his Northern opponents also proved to be divided, for when it appeared that Andrew was not going to take work, there were some who favored his suspension for that very reason. The very men who had voted for the suspension of Andrew—together with some of the Northern church papers—declared that since a bishop was supported by the church, he had no right to withhold his labors, and that if he did so, he could be impeached.

At this crucial time Bishop Soule made a move which served to alleviate much of the tension, certainly in the Southern mind, and put Soule himself far over on the side of the South. Joshua Soule had always been a powerful champion of the strongest sort of Methodist episcopacy. He had, as a young General Conference delegate in 1808, written the Restrictive Rule which had firmly put the episcopacy, as Asbury had embodied it, beyond the reach of General Conference action. He had refused to be consecrated a bishop in 1820 because he felt that the General Conference which elected him had, at the same time, changed the whole character of episcopacy by calling for an elective presiding eldership. Soule's refusal to be consecrated a bishop into the type of episcopacy which the General Conference of 1820 was calling for had caused that body to reconsider its stand and suspend its action for four years. Then in 1824 the General Conference, impressed by his stand, repealed its 1820 action and again elected Soule a bishop, and this time he was consecrated. The elements contending against him and his powerful view of the episcopacy withdrew and formed the Methodist Protestant Church.

Now, in the New York debates of 1844, Joshua Soule found himself heart and soul with the Southerners, not because of proslavery leanings but because of the view of episcopacy which the majority deposing Andrew had advanced. He and Andrew were personally very close, as well as of one mind regarding the powers of the great office they held. So in September of 1844, Soule helped settle the question of Andrew's taking work by inviting Andrew to join him in a joint superintendency of the Virginia Conference, soon to meet at Lynchburg. Soule's letter to Andrew makes clear many matters:

To the Rev. James O. Andrew, D.D., Bishop of the Methodist Episcopal Church:
Lebanon, Ohio, Sept. 26, 1844.

My Dear Bishop,—Since the close of the recent eventful session of the General Conference I have been watching, with deep solicitude, the "signs of the times," and tracing causes, as far as I was able, to their ultimate issues. Some *general* results, growing out of the action of the Conference, it required no prophetic vision to foresee. To prevent the measures which, in my judgment, would lead to these results with demonstrative certainty, I labored day and night with prayers and tears, till the deed was done,—the eventful resolution passed. From that perilous hour my hands hung down, discouragement filled my heart, and the last hope of the *unity* of our beloved Zion well nigh fled from *earth* to *heaven*. My last effort to avert the threatening storm appears in the joint recommendation of all the Bishops to suspend all action in the case until the ensuing General Conference. At the presentation of this document some brethren perceived that instead of *light* the darkness around them was increased tenfold. *Others will judge,* have judged already. And those who come after us will examine the history of our acts. The document was *respectfully* laid upon the table, probably under the influence of deep regret that "our Bishops should enter the arena of controversy in the General Conference." *But it cannot,—does not sleep there.* I have heard many excellent ministers, and distinguished laymen in our own communion, not in the slave States, refer to it as a measure of sound Christian policy, and with deep regret that the Conference had not adopted it. Many of our Northern brethren seem now deeply to deplore the division of the Church. Oh! that there had been *forethought* as well as *afterthought.* I have seen various plans of compromise for the adjustment of our difficulties and preservation of the unity of the Church. The most prominent plan provides that a fundamental article in the treaty shall be, That no abolitionist or slaveholder shall be eligible to the office of a Bishop in the Methodist Episcopal Church. Alas for us;—Where are our men of wisdom, of experience? Where are our fathers and brethren who have anaylzed the elements of civil or ecclesiastical compacts? who have studied man in his social relations? Who are the "high contracting parties," and will they create a *caste* in the constitutional eldership in the Church of Christ? Will this tend to harmonize and consolidate the body? Brethren North and South *will know* that the *cause* must be removed that the *effect* may cease. That the *fountain* must be dried up before the *stream* will cease to flow. But I must pause on this subject. The time has not fully arrived for me to define my position in regard to the causes and remedies of the evils which now agitate and distract our once united and peaceful body. Still I trust I have given such proofs, at different times, and under different circumstances, as not to render my position *doubtful* in the judgment of sober discriminating men, either North or South.—The General Conference spake in the language of wisdom and sound Christian policy when, in the pastoral address of 1836, it solemnly and affectionately *advised* the ministers and members of the Church to abstain from all agitation of the exciting subject of slavery and its abolition. Nor was the adoption of the Report of the committee on the memorial of our brethren from a portion of Virginia, within the bounds of the Baltimore Conference, less distinguished by the same characteristics of our holy Christianity, and the sound policy of our Discipline in providing for the case.

It has often been asked through the public Journals, and otherwise, "why Bishop Andrew was not assigned his regular portion of the Episcopal work for the four ensuing years, on the plan of visitation formed by the Bishops and published in the official papers?" It devolves on the majority of my colleagues in the Episcopacy, (if indeed we have an Episcopacy) rather than on me, to answer this question. Our difference of opinion in the premises, I have no doubt, was in Christian honesty and sincerity. Dismissing all further reference to the *painful* past till I see you in the South, let me now most cordially invite you to meet me at the Virginia Conference at Lynchburg, November 13th, 1844, should it please a gracious Providence to enable me to be there. And I earnestly desire that you would, if practicable, make your arrangements to be with me at all the Southern Conferences in my division of the work for the present year, where I am sure your services will not be "unacceptable." I am the more solicitous that you should be at Lynchburg from the fact that my present state of health creates a doubt whether I shall be able to reach it. I am now laboring, and have been for nearly three weeks, under the most severe attack of asthma which I have had for six or seven years—some nights unable to lie down for a moment. Great prostration of the vital function, and indeed of the whole physical system, is the consequence. But no effort of mine shall be wanting to meet my work; and the inducements to effort are greatly increased by the present position of the Church, and the hope of relief from my present affliction by the influence of a milder and more congenial climate. I cannot conclude without an expression of my sincere sympathy for you, and the second of your joys and sorrows, in the deep afflictions through which you have been called to pass. May the grace of our Lord Jesus Christ sustain you both.

Yours with sentiments of affection and esteem,

Joshua Soule.[4]

To this Bishop Andrew replied, accepting the invitation of Soule in part, and subsequently explaining his whole attitude in a published letter which he wrote from Charleston on November 4, 1844:

My Dear Brother,—I perceive from the resolutions passed at the various Church meetings in the South, that there is a very general expression of opinion in favor of my taking my appropriate share of Episcopal labor; and as I have received, both from public meetings and individual correspondents, from ministers and laymen, the most earnest and affectionate invitations to attend the sessions of most of the Southern and South-western Conferences, I deem it

[4] *Ibid.,* pp. 161-63.

due to all concerned to state definitely the course I have pursued, and had resolved to pursue, till the meeting of the convention at Louisville, Kentucky. Immediately after the passing of the memorable resolution in my case in the late General Conference, I left the city of New York and spent the next day, which was the Sabbath, at Newark, New Jersey, to fulfill an engagement previously made; after which I returned to the bosom of my family in Georgia. From Newark I addressed a letter to Bishop Soule, assigning the reasons for my departure, and stating in substance to the following effect, viz.: That I did not know whether the Bishops would feel authorized, in view of the recent action of the General Conference, to assign me a place among them for the next four years, unless that body should condescend to explain its action more definitely; but that if the Bishops should see proper to assign me my share in the Episcopal visitations, I should be glad that they would let my work commence as late in the season as convenient, inasmuch as I had been absent from my family most of the time for the last twelve months; but that if they did not feel authorized, in view of the action of the General Conference, to give me work, I should not feel hurt with them. It will be remembered that there was subsequently introduced into the Conference a resolution intended to explain the meaning of the former one as being simply *advisory;* this was promptly laid on the table, which left no doubt of the correctness of the opinion I had previously formed, that the General Conference designed the action as *mandatory.* I understand that the Southern delegates afterwards notified the Bishops in due form, that if they should give me my portion of the Episcopal work, I would attend to it. The plan of Episcopal visitation, however was drawn up and subsequently published without my name, as is well known. I have heard it rumored, indeed, that this plan was so arranged that I could be taken into it at *any time* when I should signify a wish to be so introduced; and some anonymous correspondents of the Western and South-western Christian Advocates have expressed themselves in a manner which indicated some surprise that I had not availed myself of this kind provision of the Episcopal Board. Now, in reply to all this I have only to say, that I presume those gentlemen are mistaken entirely as to the practicability of any such arrangement; for if the Bishops had contemplated the possibility of any such change in their plan, it is but fair to infer that either they would have appended to their published arrangement some note to that effect, or else that they would have informed me of it by letter; and forasmuch as they have done neither, I presume that the aforementioned rumor is altogether without foundation. However, I may be mistaken in this judgment, as I know nothing of the plans of the Bishops, other than what is published, not having received a line from one of them since the General Conference, save the accompanying letter from Bishop Soule. In view of all these facts, I came deliberately to the conclusion that the Bishops thought it most prudent, under the circumstances, not to invite me to perform any official action; and as I wished to be the cause of no unpleasant feeling to the Bishops or preachers, I determined not to visit any of the Annual Conferences at their respective sessions. At the urgent solicitation, however, of many of the preachers of the Kentucky Conference, I so far changed my determination as to make an effort to reach that Conference about the last day or two of the session; but a very unexpected detention on the road prevented the accomplishment of my purpose. Further reflection brought me back to my original purpose; and I abstained from visiting Holston and Missouri. On the important questions which now agitate us, I wished the Conferences to act in view of the great facts and principles involved, apart from any influence which my personal presence among them might produce. I had laid out my plan of work for the winter: I designed to visit different portions of the Church in the slaveholding States, and publish among them, as I was able, the unsearchable riches of Christ. The following communication from Bishop Soule furnishes me a sufficient reason to change my arrangements, and to attend in connection with him, the Conferences allotted to him during the winter, in the distribution of Episcopal labor.

And now permit me, in conclusion, to tender to my brethren both of the South and South-west, my most cordial and grateful acknowledgments for their kind expressions of sympathy for me in the storm through which I have been passing, and to invoke their most fervent and continued prayers for me and mine, and especially for the Church of God. I thank them for the many affectionate invitations to attend their Conferences, and most joyfully would I have been with them but for the reasons indicated above. May God abundantly bless us and guide us all into the way of truth and peace.

James O. Andrew.[5]

Some import of the vast questions then agitating the press, both South and North, can be seen in the Soule and Andrew letters, as well as the attitude of both men. The Soule invitation had the effect of getting Andrew officially at work again and taking an active part in the still undivided general superintendency. Both bishops, it developed, were present at the Lynchburg Conference when the Virginia Conference passed the resolutions dealing with the organization of the Methodist Episcopal Church, South.

2

The Methodist Response to Separation

The delegates of the South made their way from New York back to their home conferences, many by boat, especially those from inland

[5] *Ibid.,* pp. 159-61.

regions where the era of the steamboat had come to full flower on the Mississippi and its giant tributaries. Many went home by stage, and a few made part of the distance by the short railroads which even then had been built in the fast-developing nation. News of what had been done preceded them, and everywhere men were avid to hear what had transpired in the bitterly divided General Conference. Unrest and concern were seen written upon the faces of all those in responsible positions; nor were men of prominence in national life unaffected by the news. Henry Clay, then a leader in the Congress, wrote to W. A. Booth, "Scarcely any public occurrence has happened for a long time that gave me so much real concern and pain as this menaced separation. I will not say that it would necessarily produce a dissolution of the political union of these States, but the example would be fraught with imminent danger." [6] That there was a sense of national concern everywhere was greatly evident.

As the Southern delegates arrived at home, and as news of what had been done at New York continued to be talked of everywhere, throughout the South there began to stir unrest and anger, deep and profound. What in secular circles might be called a "newspaper war" at once began, and was destined to be carried on through many years with great vigor and effectiveness on both sides. It was an era of strong editors, and of powerful conference and sectional periodicals.

The central organ of the church at New York, the *Christian Advocate and Journal,* edited by Thomas E. Bond, M.D., "easily the first controversalist in the Church," opened what one Southern historian termed a "spirited attack on the South, which has been perseveringly sustained with consistent uncharitableness to the present time." [7] Southern editors, rejoining from their side, suggested that the bitter opposition of the New York *Advocate* was in part caused by the fact that the Southern delegations had supported another man than Dr. Bond for the editorship of that journal. Church papers in the South replied, of course, to all attacks, and gave free expression to their own opinion. These papers, organs of the several Annual Conferences, then and throughout the rest of the years of the Methodist Episcopal Church, South, powerful voices for the influence of Church opinion, began to overflow with messages of frustration, denunciation, and anger.

The Rev. John G. Jones, in his history of Mississippi Methodism, states:

[6] John F. Hurst, *History of Methodism* (New York: Eaton and Mains, 1902), V, 945-46.

[7] *History of the Organization,* p. 108.

From then [May and June] until the end of the year our Church papers were filled with . . . this unbrotherly and ruinous convulsion. Our ministers and members talked of little else, our churches and Quarterly Conferences debated the subject, and the entire portion of the year usually devoted to protracted meetings and efforts to save souls was taken up with this humiliating and much-to-be-deplored disaster to our glorious Church.[8]

As the Methodist Church has been an integral part of the development of the United States since its establishment as a nation, and as its membership to this day is more widely and perhaps more equitably distributed than that of any other church group, it is not surprising that this rift in a great ecclesiastical brotherhood caused repercussions in the public life of the nation itself. Already the fight over slavery, which had grown to an intense heat in the Congress, had made clear two opposing camps under the great dome of the Capitol itself. The whole nation was concerned. All thinking men viewed the division of the Methodist Episcopal Church ominously. "Neither side quite realized the might of the ideas and forces which separated them. Neither realized how fatefully this division in a national Christian church foreshadowed the soon-to-be-divided nation. In the debates over Methodist episcopacy in 1844 the historian can hear the drums of Gettysburg." [9]

Methodist people, meanwhile, in many places over the South met in various types of church assembly in order to take action supporting their delegates. This they did with fervor, expressing their disapprobation of the action of the 1844 Conference in strong language. "It is but a concession of candor," one editor of the South put it, "to admit that in many cases quite too much uncharitableness and even severity were indulged in." [10] The same authority truly stated, however, that the "official action of the Southern Annual Conferences" and not the "excited expressions of individuals or unofficial assemblies" showed the true temper of the South. This editor also points out that by the time the Southern conferences had met to take action—most of them during the fall of the year—some of the excitement created by the immediate news from New York had abated. But no one can read through the record of the meetings of the separate Annual Conferences and the formal resolutions which they adopted without seeing that the entire church throughout the whole South was stirred to its depths. Certainly it was

[8] *A Complete History of Methodism as Connected with the Mississippi Conference of the Methodist Episcopal Church, South* (Nashville: Printed for the Author by the Publishing House of the Methodist Episcopal Church, South, 1908), II, 501.

[9] Nolan B. Harmon, *The Organization of The Methodist Church* (2nd rev. ed.; Nashville: The Methodist Publishing House, 1962), p. 39.

[10] *History of the Organization,* p. 108.

of one mind with its delegates who had so bravely spoken for it in the great debates at New York.

The Action of the Southern Conferences

The Kentucky Conference was the first Annual Conference in what was termed the "Southern division of the Church" to meet after the adjournment of the General Conference. It convened on the eleventh of September, 1844. Naturally, the overwhelming topic was the contemplated division of the church. The conference set up a committee which it frankly called "The Committee on Division," and the report of that committee followed out and implemented the proposals and feelings of the Southerners who had talked together in New York.

The action of the Kentucky Conference set a pattern which was followed more or less closely by all the other Southern conferences. Each created a "Committee on Division" or a "Committee on Separation." Each of these committees, in making its report, first set forth the principles which guided its thinking (and action) and then gave its own judgment upon the actions of the late General Conference. Each expressed the deepest regret at the prospect of division. Each approved the "holding of a convention of delegates from the Conferences in the slave-holding States in the city of Louisville, on the first day of May next."

Since to the Kentucky Methodists it became apparent that they would in a sense act as hosts to the convention to be held in Louisville, they prepared for that event by some subsidiary resolutions "in reference to the contemplated Convention." The first of these subsidiary resolutions had to do with establishing the coming convention as a regular General Conference; the second proposed a "ratio of representation as now found in the 2d restrictive rule"; the third invited the "Bishops of the Methodist Episcopal Church, who may feel themselves disposed to do so" to be in attendance at the contemplated convention; and the fourth appointed the "Friday immediately preceding the day fixed for the meeting of the proposed General Convention" to be set aside "as a day of fasting and prayer for the blessing of Almighty God on the said Convention."

The Kentucky Conference, which pioneered in the course the other conferences were to follow, also appointed a committee to prepare an address for the members of the Methodist Episcopal Church within the bounds of the Kentucky Conference. That address was duly prepared and published. It is a lengthy one, running close to six thousand words.

The Kentucky address reviewed the entire matter of slavery in the church and *Discipline,* the storm about Bishop Andrew, and restated the Southern position with strength and vigor. It echoed the controversy over episcopacy by saying: "But while the episcopacy is thus degraded, the General Conference is exalted into an enormous irresponsible aristocracy, at whose feet the episcopacy must bow in submissive, not to say abject, dependence." The Kentuckians concluded, as did all kindred action in the other several conferences, by asserting that there was "no just and honorable alternative left, but a peaceable organization of two General Conferences."

This lengthy address came to a conclusion by inviting the "Northern brethren" to "join us, at least, in humbly asking the blessing of God on the South and North, and his direction and gracious guidance in the present trials, that all may result in the promotion of his glory, and the great good of the Church." [11]

Next met the Missouri Conference, likewise composed of Methodists in a divided state, who were as greatly concerned as were the Kentuckians. They too set up a Committee on Division, and at its behest the conference adopted a series of resolutions deploring the agitation over slavery and deeply regretting the prospect of separation, but approving the plan for a convention in Louisville. The Missourians were careful to state that in the event there was a separation, "the Southern and South-western Conferences shall not be regarded as a secession from the Methodist Episcopal Church, but that they shall be recognised in law, and to all intents and purposes, as a co-ordinate branch of the Methodist Episcopal Church in the United States of America, simply acting under a separate jurisdiction."

The practical-minded men of this conference, thinking also of the expense of the convention, included among their resolutions a proposal that "the preachers shall take up public collections in all their circuits and stations, some time before the first day of March next, for the purpose of defraying the expenses of the delegates to the above named convention." [12]

The Holston Conference followed along the same line, except that the Holston men inserted one novel resolution—and one much discussed later—in their particular series:

Resolved, That the Conferences in the non-slaveholding States and Territories, be, and they are hereby respectfully requested to elect one delegate from each Annual Conference, (either in Conference capacity or by the presiding elders,) to meet with one delegate from each of the slaveholding Conferences,

[11] *Ibid.,* pp. 111-24.
[12] *Ibid.,* pp. 124-27.

in the city of Louisville, Ky., on the first day of May, 1845, to devise some plan of compromise. And, in the event that the non-slaveholding Conferences, or any number of them, which, with the slaveholding Conferences, shall make a respectable majority of all the Annual Conferences, shall so elect delegates,—then, and in that case, the delegates which we will elect from this Conference to the Louisville convention, shall appoint one of their number on said committee of compromise. And the Southern and South-western Conferences are respectfully requested to agree to and act upon this plan.

Resolved, That if nothing can be effected on the foregoing plan, then the delegates from this Conference are instructed to propose to the Louisville convention the following or some similar plan, as the basis of connection between the two General Conferences—proposed in case of separate organization:—The said General Conferences shall appoint an equal number of delegates, (say ten,) who shall meet together in the interim of the General Conferences, to whom shall be referred for adjustment all matters of difference between the two General Conferences, or those Churches over which they exercise jurisdiction, their decisions or propositions for adjustment to be referred for ultimate action to the General Conferences before mentioned; and when both General Conferences have confirmed their decision, it shall be final and binding on both parties.

Resolved, That if both the foregoing propositions should fail, then the delegates from this Conference are instructed to support the plan of separation proposed by the late General Conference. And in so doing, we positively disavow secession, but declare ourselves, by the act of the General Conference, a co-ordinate branch of the Methodist Episcopal Church.[18]

As with Kentucky and Missouri, the Holston men invited all the bishops to attend the convention to be held in Louisville.

The Tennessee Conference, in approving the proposed convention, declared, "We honestly confess we see at present no prospect to avoid a separation." The Tennesseans also took cognizance of the threat that they might be called secessionists if the Plan of Separation were followed through, and acted, as did the others, to establish "the constitutional character and action of the Convention, as a General Conference proper." The bishops of the Methodist Episcopal Church were invited to attend the convention at Louisville, and the preachers of the Tennessee Conference were instructed to "lift a collection before the first day of April next, to defray the expenses of our delegates to the convention at Louisville, Kentucky."

In concluding its actions on this matter the Tennessee Conference, while joining the brethren of the Holston Conference in their regret for the necessity of a separation, refused to go along with them in their

[18] *Ibid.,* pp. 127-29.

plan to compromise the "existing difficulties." They affirmed that any plan which might be proposed with any degree of success "should come in an authoritative manner from the Northern section of the Church and believing the plan proposed by the Holston Conference, would, if generally adopted by the South, utterly fail to meet the object contemplated, therefore we cannot agree to the proposition." [14]

The Memphis Conference, through its Committee on Separation, acted as had the others. It approved the holding of the convention, and instructed its delegates that they "shall not be regarded as having by such division *seceded* from the Methodist Episcopal Church." Also, "being well satisfied with the Discipline of the Church as it now is, this Conference instructs its delegates not to support or favor any change in said Discipline, by said convention, only so far as is necessary to perfect a Southern organization."

Memphis "witnessed with sorrow and disapprobation, alike the violence manifested by some at the South, and the ultraism displayed by others at the North." It too invited "such of our Bishops, as may deem it proper, to be present at the contemplated convention in Louisville." The preachers were ordered to take up a public collection to defray the expenses of the delegates. [15]

The Mississippi Conference, as befitted its position in the deep South and the able men who had led it in the General Conference, defended with heat the position of these men in their attitude toward slavery, and particularly toward the deposition of Bishop Andrew. The Mississippians affirmed that "as no authorized plan of compromise has been suggested by the North, and as all the propositions made by the Southern delegates were rejected, we regard a separation as inevitable." They gave certain instructions to their delegates; set apart "the first Friday in May next . . . as a day of special fasting and prayer for the superintendence and direction of Divine Providence"; and also invited the general superintendents of the whole church to attend the proposed convention.

Taking notice of the Holston Conference resolution, the Mississippians stated: "Although we hold ourselves in readiness to accept any plan of pacification which obliterates the distinction between Northern and Southern Methodists, we do not regard the resolutions of the Holston Conference as sanctioned by the North, or practicable in itself. Therefore, *Resolved,* That this Conference do not concur." [16]

The Arkansas Conference took similar action to the others. That hope

---

[14] *Ibid.,* pp. 129-32.
[15] *Ibid.,* pp. 132-34.
[16] *Ibid.,* pp. 135-37.

had not quite been given up, however, is shown by an Arkansas resolution: "Should honorable and satisfactory propositions for pacification be made by the North, we shall expect our delegates to favor the perpetuation of the union." The usual actions to approve the convention, outline the rights, privileges, and duties of delegates, and to establish the convention itself as a General Conference should this be necessary, were taken by the Arkansas men. Their invitation to the bishops to attend the convention was slightly less enthusiastic than that of the other Southern Conferences: *"Resolved,* That the Bishops generally be, and they hereby are requested, if it be congenial with their feelings, to attend the convention at Louisville." A collection for the expenses of the delegates was ordered, and May 1 was set aside as "a day of humiliation and prayer." [17]

The Virginia Conference, large and influential in the connection, took substantially the same action as had the others. One new view of the situation was expressed by the Virginians when in the fourth resolution of their committee's report they held: "That while we do not propose to dissolve our connection with the Methodist Episcopal Church, but only *with the General Conference* of the Methodist Episcopal Church, we are, therefore, entitled to our full portion of all the rights and privileges appertaining to the property of the church." The idea that it was the *General Conference* which was to be separated from, and not the Methodist Episcopal Church, was one which was often set forth by Southern protagonists during these and the following years.

The Virginia Conference, of course, supported its committee in defending Bishop Andrew, and applauded his refusal to yield to an "unwarranted assumption of authority on the part of the General Conference." The Virginians declared that Bishop Andrew "has taken a noble stand upon the platform of constitutional law, in defence of the Episcopal Office and the rights of the South." It can be seen thus early that the support of Andrew and of a strong episcopacy was more and more becoming firmly established in the Southern mind.[18]

The North Carolina Conference stood exactly with the others, though a degree of forensic strength as well as of deep feeling was expressed by the North Carolinians apart from the usual resolutions.

The course of the late General Conference demanded a submission on the part of the ministers in the slaveholding Conferences, which the Discipline did not require and the institutions of the South absolutely forbade. . . . To have yielded would have been ruin. This, therefore, they *refused to do;* absolutely refused! With the Discipline in their hands, sustained and upheld by it, they

[17] *Ibid.,* pp. 137-39.
[18] *Ibid.,* pp. 139-41.

protested against the proceedings of the majority, with an unfaltering and manly voice, declaring them to be not only unauthorized but unconstitutional. . . . This, we sorrow when we say it, has opened a great gulf—we fear an impassable gulf—between the North and the South.

This strong pronouncement was backed up by its authors' citing the "numerous voluntary meetings within the bounds of the North Carolina Conference, both of ministers and people" in which these same sentiments were enthusiastically expressed. In brief words, North Carolina concurred with the others: "The time has come . . . to refuse to act in union with the North." [19]

The South Carolina Conference likewise went wholeheartedly along with the report of its Committee on Separation. The preamble to its final resolutions was much more lengthy than that of the other conferences. The South Carolina committee stated that it had made "diligent inquiry both out of Conference and by calling openly in Conference for information from the preachers, as to the number, if any, of local preachers, or other official members, or members of some standing among us, who should have expressed, in the meetings or in private, a different opinion from that which the meetings have proclaimed." The report went on to state that "in the whole field" of the conference, only one individual had been "heard to express himself doubtfully, as to the expediency of a separate jurisdiction for the Southern and South-western Conferences."

In keeping with their leadership in the national field, the South Carolinians went farther than the other conferences in their resolutions: "1. *Resolved,* That it is necessary for the Annual Conferences in the slaveholding States and Territories, and in Texas, to unite in a distinct ecclesiastical connection." But the South Carolinians, more optimistic of episcopal unity than the others, earnestly requested "the Bishops, one and all, to attend the said convention." Characteristically, they did not "consider the proposed convention competent to make any change or changes in the rules of discipline." They went ahead, however, to say that the convention might "nevertheless indicate what changes, if any, are deemed necessary under a separate jurisdiction of the Southern and and South-western Conferences." The resolutions closed with commending Bishop Andrew; thanking the delegates to the General Conference; and concurring in the change of the Sixth Restrictive Rule "so as to allow an equitable pro-rata division of the Book Concern." [20]

The Indian Mission Conference deplored the necessity for division

[19] *Ibid.,* pp. 142-43.
[20] *Ibid.,* pp. 143-47.

of any kind, but concurred in the same actions the other conferences had taken with respect to the Louisville Convention and kindred moves. There was more division, however, in the Indian Mission Conference than in the other conferences. The resolution approving the course pursued by the minority of the late General Conference was not unanimously adopted. There were eleven ayes, but three nays and four who declined to vote. On the matter of electing delegates to represent the Indian Mission Conference in the contemplated convention, unanimity came about again. This conference then proceeded to elect its delegates. It took an action the following day which will indicate the deep feeling of these sincere men:

Resolved, That in view of the condition of the Church at the present trying crisis, the members of this Conference will, when practicable, as near as may be, at the hour of twilight, in the evening of each day, until the close of the approaching convention at Louisville, meet each other at a throne of grace, and devoutly implore the blessing of God upon our assembled delegates in the discharge of their important duties.

This conference also called for Friday before the opening of the convention as "a day of fasting and supplication to Almighty God." [21]

The Georgia Conference, the territory in which Bishop Andrew lived, took a more decided action toward the pending separation. Their Committee on Division declared flatly that the action of the last General Conference "has rendered it *indispensable* that the Conferences, within whose limits slavery exists, should cease to be under the jurisdiction of that body." A lengthy preamble then defended with great strength and vigor the Southern position, especially as it revolved around Bishop Andrew. "We cannot admit that the framers of our Discipline ever intended to subject a Bishop to the monstrous injustice of being liable to be *expelled* by the General Conference . . . for an *impropriety* short of immorality, or official delinquency." They concluded their preamble by stating positively, "The foregoing views we consider the embodiment of public opinion throughout our Conference. The sentiments of our people in primary meetings, in quarterly conferences, as expressed in the most solemn forms, sustain the course of our delegation in the General Conference, and approve and even demand an organization which shall transfer the slaveholding Conferences from the jurisdiction of the North."

The Georgia Conference asked that the delegates chosen to go to the Louisville convention should "make a report to this body at its next session, of all their acts and doings in the aforesaid Convention, and

[21] *Ibid.,* pp. 147-48.

this body shall not be bound by any arrangements therein made, until after it shall have accepted and approved them in Conference assembled." The Georgians, apparently frightened by the action of the General Conference just concluded in New York, did not propose to approve in advance what any future Louisville Conference might do. They further instructed their delegates not to agree to any alterations in the *Discipline*. Characteristically, since the actions of Bishop Andrew had been involved in the General Conference and he himself was a Georgian, they resolved "that our beloved Bishop Andrew has endeared himself to the preachers and people of the Southern Church, by resisting the constitutional dictation of the majority of the late General Conference, and that we cordially approve his whole action in the case and welcome him to the unrestricted exercise of his episcopal functions among us."

It is significant also that this same conference took occasion to express high appreciation of "the devotion of our venerable senior Bishop to the constitution and discipline of the Church." This referred to Soule, who already had, by his speech and public actions, let it be known that he was well over on the Southern side. The Georgians struck down the Holston Conference resolution, regarding it as "tending only to embarrass the action of the convention, without the slightest promise of good to either division of the Church." It was further resolved that "the Bishops of the Methodist Episcopal Church be requested to attend the convention of Southern delegates to be held at Louisville in May next." [22]

The Florida Conference unanimously adopted the report of its Committee on Separation. It too approved the course pursued by "our venerable senior superintendent, Bishop Soule, in defending the Discipline of our Church." The Floridians declared that this "has served but to endear him to us more and more, and we heartily approve his course in inviting Bishop Andrew to assist him in his Episcopal visitations." The whole church now knew that whatever the General Conference had done with Andrew, Soule had invited him to be his co-worker and co-administrator in presiding over the Virginia Conference. The Holston Conference plan was noticed simply by saying that it was not concurred in.[23]

Texas was then a comparatively new conference, but growing rapidly, and with the Arkansas Conference was usually thought of as a "Southwestern Conference." Its Committee on Separation noted the effect of the great discussion which this whole matter had elicited in the church papers: "In view of the numerous expositions and arguments, *pro* and *con*, with which the Christian Advocates have teemed for some months,

[22] *Ibid.*, pp. 148-52.
[23] *Ibid.*, p. 153.

on the merits of the highly important subject upon which your committee have been called to act, they presume that the Conference is too well enlightened to need an elaborate and argumentative investigation of them, in their multifarious relations and bearings." The committee, therefore, went ahead to bring in six specific resolutions, each of which followed the action of the other Southern conferences.

In their fifth resolution the Texans repudiated the action of one of their own delegates to the late General Conference: "It is the sense of this Conference, that the Rev. John Clarke, one of our delegates to the late General Conference, entirely misrepresented our views and sentiments in his votes, in the cases of Rev. F. A. Harding and Bishop Andrew." [24]

Alabama, another state of the deep South, stood in line with Georgia and Mississippi with reference to the fateful moves of the General Conference. It paid its respects to the power the General Conference had exercised and strongly defended the episcopacy against the General Conference: "It can no more depose a Bishop for slaveholding than it can create a new Church." The Alabama committee, which was anything but calm, offered "to the calm consideration and mature action of the Alabama Annual Conference, the following series of resolutions."

The resolutions, of course, followed those of the sister conferences. They deplored the action in the case of Andrew; thought the late General Conference did one wise thing "in suggesting a duality of jurisdiction to meet the present emergency"; invited "all the Bishops to attend the proposed convention at Louisville" (which it heartily commended); and being "decided in its attachment to Methodism as it exists in the Book of Discipline" hoped that the Louisville Convention "will not make the slightest alteration, except so far as may be absolutely necessary for the formation of a separate jurisdiction." The conference further ordered every preacher to take up a collection as soon as practicable for the expenses of the convention; set aside "Friday immediately preceding the session of the convention . . . as a day of fasting and prayer"; expressed appreciation for "the commendable motives which induced the Holston Conference to suggest another expedient to compromise the differences existing between the Northern and Southern divisions of the Church" but stated flatly that it could not concur in the proposition. Its closing resolution was:

10. That this Conference fully recognizes the right of our excellent superintendent, Bishop Soule, to invite Bishop Andrew to share with him the responsibilities of the episcopal office, and while the Conference regrets the absence of

[24] *Ibid.*, pp. 154-55.

the *former,* it rejoices in being favored with the efficient services of the *latter*—
it respectfully tenders these "true yokefellows" in the superintendency the fullest
approbation, the most fervent prayers, and the most cordial sympathies.

About the entire resolution are the marks of Dr. Thomas O. Summers,
who later became a towering figure in the Methodist Episcopal Church,
South.[25]

This brief résumé of conference actions indicates the temper of the
Southern mind during the last half of the fateful year of 1844. "It is
from these official proceedings," states a Southern historian, "that
the real opinions and temper of the South are to be gathered, and not
from some unguarded expression, or ebullition of transient feeling, on
the part of individuals." This is true, and while the same history from
which we take this quotation goes on to reprove the Northern Church
for the "utmost uncharitableness" which was "manifested in the language
of those appointed to speak the sentiments of that portion of the Church,"
the Southern historian felt that "in the official action of the Southern Conferences a commendable moderation generally prevails." [26]

The Recoil of the Northern Conferences

As 1844 drew to a close, the attitude of the Northern conferences, as
expressed in their several meetings and through the various *Advocates,*
became more and more antagonistic to the whole idea of separation.
More and more were these conferences agitated by the actions put into
effect by the Southern conferences, moving forward under the Plan of
Separation. The invitation extended by Bishop Soule to Bishop Andrew
was severely censured. Charles Elliott of the *Western Christian Advocate,* Thomas Bond of the New York *Christian Advocate and Journal,*
and even the aging Nathan Bangs, editors and spokesmen of note in the
church, denounced Soule's invitation to Andrew as not only unauthorized
but in contravention of the decision of the General Conference and of
the Board of Bishops. Southern editors vigorously responded by saying:

That it contravened no action of the General Conference is very clear, from
the fact, that whether the Bishop should labor or not was to depend on his own
decisions. . . . As regards the Board of Bishops, the *spirit* of their decision was,
that if Bishop Andrew should signify a willingness to take work on the Episcopal

[25] *Ibid.,* pp. 155-57.
[26] *Ibid.,* pp. 157-58.

plan, it should be given him; and the *letter* of that decision was, that he should have work assigned him when he should make *written* application for it.[27]

Bishop Soule himself defended and explained his own course in a letter dated Augusta, Georgia, January 4, 1845. This letter is a response to the Northern editors, especially to Dr. Bond. Soule said:

It is very possible that in writing my letter of invitation to Bishop Andrew to meet me at the Virginia Conference, and accompany me to the others in my Southern tour, with a view to his affording me aid in the superintendency, I may have traveled out of the record of the *official* instructions of the General Conference for the government of the *"action"* of the superintendents in the Bishop's case, *according to Dr. Bond's "sense" of those instructions.* But *according to my best judgment* of those instructions, given to the Bishops, *not to Dr. Bond,* I have done nothing but what is fully provided for, and covered by the record. And I trust I may presume, without ostentation, that I have as good a "right" to judge of the meaning and import of such instructions as my good friend of the Christian Advocate and Journal; especially as I am amenable, not to him, but to the General Conference.[28]

Thus Soule versus Bond. However, continued complaints and questionings from the Northern conferences came in to the Board of Bishops, forcing Bishops Hedding, Waugh, Morris, and Hamline to feel it needful to give an explanation of their understanding of Andrew's position. For the first time the bishops made clear to the entire connection their own action with regard to Andrew and the episcopal visitation plan:

Dear Brethren,—The time has arrived, when, in the judgment of the undersigned, it is proper they should respond to calls which have been made, both privately and publicly, for authentic information in regard to the action of a majority of the Superintendents, by which the name of Bishop Andrew was omitted from the Plan of Episcopal Visitation, which was arranged at the close of the late General Conference, and published in the Christian Advocate and other official Journals of the Church. The statements which follow, will, it is believed, place that action and the grounds thereof in a view intelligible to all; and beyond this, they have neither desire nor intention to go in this communication.

On the first day of June last, the following preamble and resolution were adopted by the General Conference of the Methodist Episcopal Church:—

WHEREAS, the Discipline of our Church forbids the doing any thing calculated to destroy our itinerant general Superintendency, and whereas Bishop Andrew

[27] *Ibid.,* p. 163.
[28] First published in *The Southern Christian Advocate,* January 4, 1845; reprinted in *History of the Organization,* pp. 163-65.

has become connected with slavery by marriage and otherwise, and this act having drawn after it circumstances which, in the estimation of the General Conference, greatly embarrass the exercise of his office as an itinerant general Superintendent, if not in some places entirely prevent it; therefore,—

Resolved, That it is the sense of the General Conference, that he desist from the exercise of his office so long as this impediment remains.

On the 6th of June the following note was presented to the General Conference:—

Reverend and Dear Brethren,—As the case of Bishop Andrew unavoidably involves the future *action* of the Superintendents, which in their judgment, in the present position of the Bishop, they have no discretion to decide upon; they respectfully request from this General Conference *official* instruction in answer to the following questions:—

1. Shall Bishop Andrew's name remain as it now stands in the Minutes, Hymn Book, and Discipline, or shall it be struck off of these official records?

2. How shall the Bishop obtain his support? As provided for in the form of Discipline, or in some other way?

3. What work, if any, may the Bishop perform; and how shall he be appointed to his work?

> Joshua Soule,
> Elijah Hedding,
> Beverly Waugh,
> Thomas A. Morris.

To which the General Conference responded:—

1. *Resolved,* as the sense of this Conference, That Bishop Andrew's name stand in the Minutes, Hymn-Book, and Discipline, as formerly.

2. That the rule in relation to the support of a Bishop and his family, applies to Bishop Andrew.

3. That whether in any, and if in any, in what work, Bishop Andrew be employed, is to be determined by his own decision and action, in relation to the previous action of the Conference in his case.

In view of the aforesaid proceedings of the General Conference, the undersigned, on the 11th of June, appended their names to a paper written in the words which follow:—

It is our opinion in regard to the action of the late General Conference in the case of Bishop Andrew, that it was designed by that body to devolve the responsibility of the exercise of the functions of his office exclusively on himself. In the absence of Bishop Andrew at the time of arranging the Plan of Episcopal Visitation for the ensuing four years, and he not having notified us of his desire, or purpose, with respect to it, we should regard ourselves as acting in contravention of the expressed will of the General Conference, if we apportioned to Bishop Andrew any definite portion thereof. But if he shall hereafter make a written application for a portion of the general oversight, we should feel ourselves justified in assigning it to him.

After this paper was signed, and before the parting of the Superintendents, it was agreed to make out a reserved Plan of Episcopal Visitation, including Bishop Andrew in the apportionment of the work thereof, which was done, and intrusted to the safe keeping of Bishop Soule, with an explicit understanding, that if he should receive from Bishop Andrew a written application for his portion of the general Superintendence, he was then, and in that event, to publish the second or reserved plan in immediate connection with the said application, that the reason for the substitution of the second plan might accompany its publication. Such was the action of the undersigned in the case presented, and such the ground on which it was based. At present, this is all that they feel themselves called to make public.

Elijah Hedding,
B. Waugh,
Thomas A. Morris,
L.L. Hamline.[29]

This letter, appearing at a later date than the events which it delineates, makes clear the mind of the Board of Bishops toward their brother Andrew. It also indicates clearly the divided actions, if not divided mind, of the General Conference as the bishops saw it. The bishops continued to hold to the position that the General Conference wanted Andrew to make the decision himself as to whether or not he would "desist" from exercising episcopal functions, but did not refer to the fact that, as Andrew had pointed out in his letter, a motion to explain the Andrew resolution as merely *advisory* was tabled by the General Conference itself.

3

The Louisville Convention

As it became clear that the "Annual Conferences in the slaveholding States," as they then frankly called themselves, were of one mind as to the holding of a convention at Louisville in May, 1845, it became more and more certain that that meeting would be one of great import. Beside the regularly elected delegates, hundreds of ministers and members from far and near attended the convention to see what its deliberations might be. Among these were many stalwart Methodists of the North, men who

---

[29] *History of the Organization,* pp. 165-67.

had opposed before and were destined to oppose again everything done at Louisville. Matthew Simpson, soon to become a bishop in the Methodist Episcopal Church and always considered by Southerners their implacable foe, sat in the balcony during certain of the proceedings. The daily papers on both sides of the Ohio followed with interest everything that transpired. The entire church, North and South, awaited the final issue.

Intimations in the various resolutions adopted by the Southern conferences that this gathering might properly declare itself a General Conference were in the back of the minds of many delegates when they arrived at Louisville. In certain histories of the Southern Church it has been called a *conference* rather than a *convention,* but officially the gathering has been denominated by the majority of the Southern historians, and by its own records, "the Louisville Convention."

In practically all respects, however, the convention did not differ from what had become the fixed pattern of each quadrennial General Conference. Certainly the same organizational procedure was followed. The Annual Conferences represented in the convention were called in the order in which they then stood in the General Minutes, and the delegates of these conferences presented their certificates of election just as in a regular General Conference. Members who were not furnished with certificates of election were nevertheless granted seats, provided that the presiding officer of their respective conferences, or some member present, might attest their election.[30]

The conferences of the Methodist Episcopal Church (as they then were) sending delegates to the Convention were: Kentucky, Missouri, Holston, Tennessee, North Carolina, Memphis, Arkansas, Virginia, Mississippi, Texas,[31] Alabama, Georgia, South Carolina, Florida, and Indian Mission. Their delegates, as duly elected, met in the old Fourth Street Methodist Church in the city of Louisville, on the first day of May, 1845.

While all the bishops had been invited, there was considerable doubt

[30] The proceedings of the Louisville Convention are given in *History of the Organization,* beginning on p. 169. The account given here closely follows the official proceedings.

[31] The Texas Conference was divided in two by the 1844 General Conference, but the conference agreed to Littleton Fowler's proposal that all preachers in the state of Texas meet in conference at their next session to more effectively form their plans for future action. The reason for this was undoubtedly the pending separation of the church. The Texas preachers met for the last time together in January of 1845 and elected their delegates to Louisville. Thus there is some confusion as to whether there were fifteen or sixteen Annual Conferences present at the formation of the Methodist Episcopal Church, South. Technically, there were sixteen—but for all practical purposes, fifteen.

as to what members of the Board of Bishops, other than James O. Andrew and Joshua Soule, might be present. Andrew, it was known, was surely coming, and Soule had certified that he also expected to be there. The convention was called to order by Dr. William Capers of South Carolina. Dr. Lovick Pierce of the Georgia Conference, a venerable and distinguished leader, was elected president *pro tem.* He read the second chapter of the Epistle to the Philippians and had the convention sing "the 129th Hymn, containing an appropriate invocation of the Holy Spirit." Then Dr. Pierce offered what the Minutes call "a suitable and impressive prayer to the Throne of Grace."

Upon the call for the election of a secretary *pro tem* Thomas N. Ralston of the Kentucky Conference was chosen. The roll was then called, and the delegates were required to furnish their certificates of election. As the men who sat in this notable convention have always been considered not only the founding fathers but great stalwart leaders and preachers of the Southern Church, it will not be inappropriate to list their names by conferences:

Kentucky Conference—Henry B. Bascom, Edward Stevenson, Hubbard H. Kavanaugh, Benjamin T. Crouch, William Gunn, George W. Taylor, George W. Brush, John C. Harrison, Burr H. McCown, James King, John James, Thomas N. Ralston.

Missouri Conference—Andrew Monroe, Jesse Green, John Glanville, Wesley Browning, William Patton, John H. Lynn, Joseph Boyle, Thomas Johnson.

Holston Conference—Thomas K. Catlett, Thomas Stringfield, Rufus M. Stevens, Timothy Sullins, Creed Fulton.

Tennessee Conference—Robert Paine, John B. McFerrin, Alexander L. P. Green, Fountain E. Pitts, Ambrose F. Driskill, John W. Hanner, Joshua Boucher, Thomas Maddin, Frederick G. Ferguson, Robert L. Andrews.

North Carolina Conference—Samuel S. Bryant, Hezekiah G. Leigh, Bennet T. Blake, Robert J. Carson, Peter Doub, John T. Brame.

Memphis Conference—Moses Brock, George W. D. Harris, William McMahon, Thomas Joyner, Asbury Davidson, Wilson L. McAlister, Thomas Smith.

Arkansas Conference—John Harrell, John F. Truslow, Jacob Custer.

Virginia Conference—John Early, Thomas Crowder, William A. Smith, Leroy M. Lee, Abraham Penn, Davis S. Doggett, Henry B. Cowles, Anthony Dibrell.

Mississippi Conference—Lowell Campbell, John G. Jones, Green M. Rogers, Benjamin M. Drake, Samuel W. Speer, William H. Watkins, William Winans.

Texas Conference—Littleton Fowler, Francis Wilson, Robert Alexander.

Alabama Conference—Jefferson Hamilton, Jesse Boring, Thomas H. Capers, Eugene V. Levert, Elisha Calloway, Thomas O. Summers, Greenbury Garrett.

Georgia Conference—Lovick Pierce, James E. Evans, John W. Glenn, Samuel Anthony, Augustus B. Longstreet, Isaac Boring, James B. Payne, Thomas Sandford, George F. Pierce.

South Carolina Conference—William Capers, William M. Wightman, Hugh A. C. Walker, Samuel Dunwody, Bonn English, Samuel W. Capers, Whiteford Smith, Robert J. Boyd.

Florida Conference—Peyton P. Smith, Thomas C. Benning.

Indian Mission Conference—Edward T. Peery, David B. Cumming.

Such was the personnel of this remarkable body. Many of these men had already been in the stormy General Conference the year before; and many of them were to be in the first General Conference of the Methodist Episcopal Church, South, the succeeding year. All knew themselves to be at a decisive moment in the life of their church.

Augustus B. Longstreet, president of Emory College in Georgia, seconded by William Capers of South Carolina, moved that the bishops of the Methodist Episcopal Church who were then in attendance "be requested to preside over the meeting, under such arrangements as they may make from day to day among themselves." This resolution was adopted unanimously.

Bishop Soule informed the convention that he would express his views on the subject of this resolution, both on behalf of himself and his colleague Bishop Andrew, the next day. John Early of Virginia moved that all elections should be by ballot, "when more than one is nominated"; otherwise, if there were only one nomination, that name should be put forward at once for election.

Thomas O. Summers was nominated for permanent secretary and was duly elected on the first ballot. Thomas N. Ralston was elected assistant secretary. Various minor motions were made having to do with the drafting of rules for the convention and other kindred matters.

On Friday morning, May 2, the convention met at its own direction at eight-thirty instead of nine o'clock. Minutes of the day before were of course approved, and well knowing that all the proceedings of the body would be weighed carefully and examined minutely during subsequent years, a committee was created "to prepare a full and correct synopsis of the proceedings of the Convention, and furnish the Editors of the Louisville Journal with a copy each day, at 9 o'clock, P.M., for publication the next morning."

The committee (William M. Wightman, Leroy M. Lee, and John B. McFerrin) having been set up to report the actions of the convention, the matter of rules for the government of the body was next taken up. These followed the traditional parliamentary procedures. Rule 14, however, was somewhat novel: "Every member who shall be within the bar at the time the question is put, shall give his vote; unless the Convention, for special reason, excuse him." Apparently abstention from voting was a process not looked upon with favor by the fathers of 1845. They knew—and expected everyone else to know—their own minds.

A bit later during this second morning Bishop Soule arose and addressed the convention. His speech and the opinions and attitudes which he expressed therein, together with his own interpretation of many fundamentals of Methodist structure and law, has been considered of great import by subsequent Methodists, and we give it here in full as it is reported in the official *History of the Organization of the Methodist Episcopal Church, South:*

I rise on the present occasion to offer a few remarks to this Convention of ministers, under the influence of feelings more solemn and impressive than I recollect ever to have experienced before. The occasion is certainly one of no ordinary interest and solemnity. I am deeply impressed with a conviction of the important results of your deliberations and decisions in relation to that numerous body of Christians, and Christian ministers you here represent, and to the country at large. And knowing, as I do, the relative condition of the vast community where your acts must be extensively felt, I cannot but feel a deep interest in the business of the Convention, both as it respects yourselves, and the millions who must be affected by your decisions. With such views and feelings, you will indulge me in an expression of confident hope that all your business will be conducted with the greatest deliberation, and with that purity of heart, and moderation of temper suitable to yourselves, as a body of Christian ministers, and to the important concerns which have called you together in this city.

The opinion which I formed at the close of the late General Conference, that the proceedings of that body would result in a division of the Church, was not induced by the impulse of excitement; but was predicated of principles and facts, after the most deliberate and mature consideration. That opinion I have freely expressed. And however deeply I have regretted such a result, believing it to be inevitable, my efforts have been made, not to prevent it, but rather that it might be attended with the least injury, and the greatest amount of good which the case would admit, I was not alone in this opinion. A number of aged and influential ministers entertained the same views. And, indeed, it is not easy to conceive how any one, intimately acquainted with the facts in the case, and the relative position of the North and South, could arrive at any other conclusion. Nothing has transpired since the close of the General Conference to

change the opinion I then formed; but subsequent events have rather confirmed it. In view of the certainty of the issue, and at the same time ardently
desirous that the two great divisions of the Church might be in peace and
harmony within their own respective bounds, and cultivate the spirit of
Christian fellowship, brotherly kindness, and charity for each other, I cannot
but consider it an auspicious event that the sixteen Annual Conferences, represented in this Convention, have acted with such extraordinary unanimity in the
measures they have taken in the premises. In the Southern Conferences which
I have attended, I do not recollect that there has been a dissenting voice with
respect to the *necessity* of a separate organization; and although their official
acts in deciding the important question, have been marked with that clearness
and decision which should afford satisfactory evidence that they have acted
under a solemn conviction of duty to Christ, and to the people of their charge,
they have been equally distinguished by moderation and candor. And as far as
I have been informed, all the other Conferences have pursued a similar course.

It is ardently to be desired that the same unanimity may prevail in the
counsels of this Convention as distinguished, in such a remarkable manner,
the views, and deliberations, and decisions of your constituents. When it is
recollected that it is not only for yourselves, and the present ministry and
membership of the Conferences you represent, that you are assembled on this
occasion; but that millions of the present race, and generations yet unborn,
may be affected in their most essential interests, by the results of your
deliberations, it will occur to you how important it is that you should "do all
things as in the immediate presence of God." Let all your acts, dear brethren, be
accompanied with much prayer for that *wisdom which is from above.*

While you are thus impressed with the importance and solemnity of the
subject which has occasioned the Convention, and of the high responsibility
under which you act, I am confident you will cultivate the spirit of Christian
moderation and forbearance; and that in all your acts you will keep strictly
within the limits and provisions of the "plan of separation" adopted by the
General Conference with great unanimity and apparent Christian kindness.
I can have no doubt of the firm adherence of the ministers and members of the
Church in the Conferences you represent, to the doctrines, rules, order of
government, and forms of worship contained in our excellent book of discipline.
For myself, I stand upon the basis of Methodism as contained in this book, and
from it I intend never to be removed. I cannot be insensible to the expression
of your confidence in the resolution you have unanimously adopted, requesting
me to preside over the Convention in conjunction with my colleagues. And after
having weighed the subject with careful deliberation, I have resolved to accept
your invitation, and discharge the duties of the important trust to the best of
my ability. My excellent colleague, Bishop Andrew, is of the same mind, and
will cordially participate in the duties of the Chair.

I am requested to state to the Convention, that our worthy and excellent
colleague, Bishop Morris, believes it to be his duty to decline a participation

in the presidential duties. He assigns such reasons for so doing as are, in the judgment of his colleagues, perfectly satisfactory; and it is presumed they would be considered in the same light by the Convention. In conclusion, I trust that all things will be done in that spirit which will be approved of God. And devoutly pray that your acts may result in the advancement of the Redeemer's kingdom, and the salvation of the souls of men.

Having delivered this address, Bishop Soule walked over and took the chair, from which Dr. Pierce courteously arose, thus relinquishing the chairmanship.

The first major action was then taken. On motion of John Early and W. A. Smith of Virginia, it was resolved,

That a committee of *two* members, from each Annual Conference represented in this Convention, be appointed, whose duty it shall be to take into consideration the propriety and necessity of a Southern organization, according to the plan of separation adopted by the late General Conference; together with the acts of the several Annual Conferences on this subject, and report the best method of securing the objects contemplated in the appointment of this Convention.

The committee was set up by the respective delegations, thus creating a group of thirty. All memorials on church organization were to be referred "without vote" to this committee. The Friday adjournment was marked by the participation of Bishop Morris in what the Minutes call "religious exercises." He had declined to preside over the convention itself.

On Monday, May 5, the really important matter which had brought the convention together was put before the body in a resolution presented by William A. Smith of Virginia and Lovick Pierce of Georgia.

Resolved, By the delegates of the several Annual Conferences in the Southern and South-western States, in General Convention assembled, That we cannot sanction the action of the late General Conference of the Methodist Episcopal Church, on the subject of slavery, by remaining under the ecclesiastical jurisdiction of that body, without deep and lasting injury to the interests of the Church and the country; we, therefore, hereby instruct the committee on organization, that if upon a careful examination of the whole subject, they find that there is no reasonable ground to hope that the Northern majority will recede from their position and give some safe guaranty for the future security of our civil and ecclesiastical rights, that they report in favor of a separation from the ecclesiastical jurisdiction of the said General Conference.

On Tuesday morning Bishop Andrew presided. On that same day

there were strong speeches in favor of the resolution on separation. Indeed this resolution was debated again and again throughout the week. As the debating continued and it became clear that separation was inevitable, other important matters depending upon it began to assert themselves. Petitions began to come in asking that a Southern Book Concern be located in certain cities. The Louisville Methodist congregations got George W. Brush to ask for the location of the Book Concern and a newspaper in their city. A committee had early been created to look into the matter of a separate Book Concern.

A committee to look after missions and mission work on behalf of the Southern conferences had also been set up. Indeed, organizational structure quickly began to take shape even while the decisive resolution was impending. Time would fail to tell of the speeches and resolutions which were meanwhile offered, but in due time the Committee on Organization made its report through Dr. Henry Bascom, its chairman. The Publishing Committee was instructed to print one hundred copies of this report.

The formal action came on Saturday morning, May 17, with Bishop Andrew in the chair. The report of the Committee on Organization was taken up. The convention resolved to act upon it by *yeas* and *nays*. Surprisingly, it was allowed that sick and absent members should be permitted to enter their votes "at some subsequent period during the session." This action was at variance with the Methodist common law, which has always held that one must be present and voting to cast a valid Methodist ballot.

The crucially important first resolution, upon motion of John Early, was adopted:

Be it resolved, by the Delegates of the several Annual Conferences of the Methodist Episcopal Church in the Slaveholding States, in General Convention assembled, That it is right, expedient, and necessary to erect the Annual Conferences represented in this Convention, into a distinct ecclesiastical connexion, separate from the jurisdiction of the General Conference of the Methodist Episcopal Church, as at present constituted; and accordingly, we, the delegates of said Annual Conferences, acting under the provisional plan of separation adopted by the General Conference of 1844, do solemnly *declare* the jurisdiction hitherto exercised over said Annual Conferences, by the General Conference of the Methodist Episcopal Church, *entirely dissolved;* and that said Annual Conferences shall be, and they hereby *are constituted,* a separate ecclesiastical connexion, under the provisional plan of separation aforesaid, and based upon the Discipline of the Methodist Episcopal Church, comprehending the doctrines and entire moral, ecclesiastical, and economical rules and regulations of said Discipline, except only, in so far as verbal alterations may be necessary to a distinct organization, and to be known by the style and title of the METHODIST EPISCOPAL CHURCH, SOUTH.

All delegates voted for this, except William Gunn, George W. Taylor, and John C. Harrison of the Kentucky Conference.

The second resolution, on motion of Thomas Crowder of Virginia, was adopted as follows:

Resolved, That we cannot abandon or compromise the principles of action, upon which we proceed to a separate organization in the South; nevertheless, cherishing a sincere desire to maintain Christian union and fraternal intercourse with the Church North, we shall always be ready, kindly and respectfully, to entertain, and duly and carefully consider, any proposition or plan, having for its object the union of the two great bodies, in the North and South, whether such proposed union be *jurisdictional* or *connectional.*

Everyone present voted for this resolution.

An important additional report was then put forward by the Committee on Organization:

Resolved, That this Convention request the Bishops, presiding at the ensuing session of the border Conferences of the Methodist Episcopal Church, *South,* to incorporate into the aforesaid Conferences any societies or stations adjoining the line of division, provided such societies or stations, by a majority of the members, according to the provisions of the plan of separation adopted by the late General Conference, request such an arrangement.

The meaning of this paragraph was much disputed later, as under its provisions there was an invasion of some of the border conferences by other groups. The full text makes it clear why and how future difficulties could and did occur.

A further resolution proposed to amend the *Discipline* so that "the General Conference shall meet on the first day of May, in the year of our Lord, 1846, in the town of Petersburg, Virginia, and thenceforward in the month of April or May, once in four years successively; and in such place and on such day as shall be fixed on by the preceding General Conference." This change in the date of holding the General Conference was destined to become fixed in the procedure of Southern Methodism, and lasted throughout the entire lifetime of that organization—or until the year 1938, when the last General Conference of the Methodist Episcopal Church, South, was held in Birmingham, Alabama. It also seemed necessary to change the ratio of representation of elected delegates to the Southern General Conference. Therefore twenty-one was changed to fourteen in the legislation governing the ratio of Annual Conference members to delegates elected. This made for a more representative body than would have been the case had one to twenty-one remained the ratio.

Provision for Missions and Publishing

But there were other matters of general connectional work to be looked at. Noting that there might be something of a problem with respect to getting missions supported on a better basis by the Southern division of the church, the Committee on Missions recommended that "until a General Conference of the Annual Conferences represented in this Convention, shall have ordered otherwise, the Missionary Society of the Methodist Episcopal Church, in the city of Louisville, Ky., shall be regarded as the central or parent society for said Conferences,—said society having previously changed its title, and adopted a constitution agreeably to the purport of these resolutions."

Other resolutions in support of missionary work put forward by the Committee on Missions were adopted. Significantly enough, the whole report of this committee wound up by saying: "The missions connected with the Southern division of the Church *must* be sustained, and, with the blessing of God, *shall* be; and that this may be done with greater facility, it is enjoined on all missionaries to make quarterly reports of the work in their missions through one of our Church papers."

The Committee on Missions also felt it necessary to send out a lengthy letter dealing with the whole aspect of missions in the conferences represented in the convention. It is a strong and powerful appeal which, entirely apart from the structural work of the convention, shows that the men of the convention were alert to Methodism's duty:

And how numerous are the poor who must be destitute of the gospel without our ministry. Consider the many hundreds of thousands of the African race, who, though dwelling in our midst, cannot be served by the circuit appointments —German immigrants—the thousands of families scattered over the least favored parts of Florida and Arkansas, (where it is computed that the ministry cannot be sustained in the ratio of one to every fifty miles square) —East and West Texas—the tribes of Indians included in our Mission Conference—and the vast range of the farther tribes, from the borders of Mexico to the Rocky Mountains. How wide is the field! And what a call is this, of so many kindreds, colors, and conditions of men, in our national territory, crying to us for the gospel of Christ? This gospel they must have. The negro in his bonds—our citizen people in their far-off homes—the strangers among us from a foreign land—the Indian in the wilderness, whither he has retreated that we might possess his lands and become great in the earth—they *must* have the gospel. They all must have it, and we must give it to them. We have meant this, all this, and nothing but this, in all that we have done. We feel that our action in this Convention pledges us anew for the maintenance of that great motive principle of Methodism, that the gospel must be preached, with all our might, to as many as we can, and at all hazards.

This impassioned letter concluded by calling for a central society to be organized on the plan adopted at Louisville; a general treasurer should reside at Louisville, with assistant treasurers at Charleston, South Carolina, and New Orleans. It was requested that the letter be read over the church and acted upon at once.

There must be no delay, no holding back, no waiting for one another, no postponing the matter to a convenient season. We desire that every one should receive this letter as summoning him to begin, not by and by, not to-morrow, not the next hour, but with the paper in his hand. Read it to those about you— in the societies—in the congregations; and add what shall strike you to promote the cause. And may God, whom we serve in the gospel of his Son, send now prosperity.

The fathers of 1845 did not intend that there should be any laggards in this cause.

The convention created a committee to handle the matter of the Book Concern and church periodicals. It must be remembered that at that period—indeed during the whole formative period of the Methodist Church in America—the publishing interests of the church, embodied in the Book Concern and official organs and papers, loomed far larger than these do today. The Book Concern was the chief connectional instrument of early Methodism and a source of general revenue in a day that knew no World Service budget and very few conference collections. At a later date great causes such as world-wide missions, educational institutions, and endowments, and a plethora of gigantic enterprises usurped in the mind and program of the church something of the pristine priority long held by the Book Concern. But in 1845 this was not questioned.

The committee appointed at Louisville had to determine whether or not it should take its share of the money coming to it from the Book Concern—which it was understood was to be turned over to the separating conferences—and with these funds set up a separate Book Concern, or consider other possible measures.

The citizens of Louisville, Nashville, St. Louis, and Memphis were asking for the location of a Book Concern in their cities. The committee,

however, stated that while a Book Concern was considered indispensable
to the prosperity of the Methodist Episcopal Church, South, "yet we
deem the establishment of one at this time *premature.*" The committee
did recommend that two book agents be appointed, who should receive
propositions for the location of the Book Concern, and also "receive
moneys and contributions for building up the same." These were ordered
to report to the General Conference to be held at Petersburg the following
year.

In the meanwhile, the committee recommended that the Southern
ministers and members continue to patronize the Book Concerns at New
York and Cincinnati; also that they "patronize our Periodicals, viz.:
South-Western Christian Advocate, Southern Christian Advocate, and
Richmond Christian Advocate, as every way worthy of our support."

The report of the committee was adopted, and John Early of Virginia
and John B. McFerrin of Tennessee were unanimously elected book
agents.

That the members of the convention were still laboring under the
fear that their history might not be accurately told is made clear by
another motion of this committee—that there should be created a Publishing Committee, "whose duty it shall be to compile and publish a
work or book, which shall be called *The History of the Organization of
the Methodist Episcopal Church, South.*" Further resolutions directed
that this work should contain a full account of the acts of the 1844
General Conference in the cases of Bishop Andrew and the Rev. F. A.
Harding, the Protest of the Minority, the Declaration of the delegates
from the conferences in the slaveholding states, the General Conference
Address of Bishops Soule and Andrew, the Plan of Separation, the
address of the Southern delegates to the church in the South, and the
action of all the Southern Annual Conferences. To these were to be added
the addresses of Bishops Soule and Andrew before the convention and the
acts of the convention itself. Certain members of the convention were
requested to furnish the Publishing Committee a manuscript copy of
their speeches before the convention. Drs. Winans, Capers, Smith, Early,
Pierce, and several others were specifically named as "expected to contribute." Steps were taken to see that this publication be underwritten and
properly issued.

Toward Formal Organization

By the formal action of the Committee on Organization, Bishops
Soule and Andrew were "respectfully and cordially requested" by the

convention "to unite with and became regular and constitutional Bishops of the Methodist Episcopal Church South, upon the basis of the plan of separation adopted by the late General Conference." A resolution was also adopted

that should any portion of an Annual Conference on the line of separation, not represented in this Convention, adhere to the Methodist Episcopal Church, South, according to the plan of separation adopted at the late General Conference, and elect delegates to the General Conference of the Church in 1846, upon the basis of representation adopted by this Convention, they shall be accredited as members of the General Conference.

A committee of three was then appointed to prepare and report to the General Conference of 1846 "a revised copy of the present Discipline, with such changes as are necessary to conform it to the Organization of the Methodist Episcopal Church, South."

On Monday, May 19, Bishop Soule, in a formal response to the convention's invitation, stated that he felt himself "bound in good faith, to carry out the official plan of Episcopal Visitations as settled by the Bishops in New York, . . . until the session of the first General Conference of the Methodist Episcopal Church, South." At the time of this General Conference he would feel himself fully authorized by the Plan of Separation to unite with the Methodist Episcopal Church, South, "and if received by the General Conference of said Church, to exercise the functions of the Episcopal Office within the jurisdiction of said General Conference."

Bishop Andrew was under no necessity of being bound by a plan of visitation "as settled by the Bishops in New York." He therefore wrote:

I decidedly approve the course which the Convention has taken in establishing the Methodist Episcopal Church, South, believing as I do most sincerely, that it will tend, under God's blessing, to the wider spread and more efficient propagation of the gospel of the grace of God. I accept the invitation of the Convention to act as one of the superintendents of the Methodist Episcopal Church, South, and pledge myself, in humble dependence upon Divine grace, to use my best efforts to promote the cause of God in the interesting and extensive field of labor assigned me.

May the blessing of God be upon us mutually, in our laborious field of action, and finally, may we all, with our several charges, be gathered to the home of God and the good in heaven.

That education was also a matter to the fore in this convention is shown by the action of its Committee on Education, having to do with

Transylvania University in Lexington, Kentucky. Transylvania University was not then strictly under the control of the Methodist Episcopal Church, South, but, as the committee declared, did have "special claims" on its attention. The convention recommended that the Annual Conferences instruct their delegates to the General Conference of 1846 to take "such action as will consummate the proposed connexion between the Trustees of Transylvania University and the General Conference, and adopt it as the University of the Methodist Episcopal Church, South."

Knowing that the whole South was tremendously interested in the convention, and that this interest extended past the Methodist connection, a committee was appointed to prepare a Pastoral Address. This was ordered to be printed and read before those border charges or societies which might feel called upon to decide between the Northern and Southern branches of the church.

That the line of division between the conferences of the North and South was an indeterminate one was always in the minds of those in the convention. One of the final resolutions, therefore, offered by Thomas N. Ralston of Kentucky, held:

> That in the judgment of this Convention, those societies and stations on the border, within the limits of Conferences represented in this Convention, be constructively understood as adhering to the South, unless they see proper to take action on the subject; and in all such cases, we consider the Pastor of the society or station as the proper person to preside in the meeting.

After appropriate resolutions thanking the churches and pastors of Louisville for their hospitality, Bishops Soule and Andrew for their presidency, and the secretaries for fidelity, the journal and papers of the convention were entrusted to the newly elected book agents, Early and McFerrin. The convention adjourned on May 19. "The separation is made—formally, legally made—and let peace ensue."

Methodism's Reaction to Louisville

THE PART THE BISHOPS PLAYED

The connectional nature of Methodism, especially the way the polity of the church rests heavily upon its episcopacy, was never more clearly shown than immediately after the Louisville Convention adjourned. All the bishops had been invited to Louisville, but only Soule, Andrew, and Morris attended. Morris frankly declined to preside at any session; and while Soule and Andrew were formally requested to unite with the

Methodist Episcopal Church, South, and become regular bishops of it, Soule did not feel it wise to do so at Louisville.

On July 2, 1845, the Northern bishops met in New York to consider the status of the plan of episcopal visitation in the light of the organization of the Methodist Episcopal Church, South. Bishops Morris and Janes had been slated to preside over certain Southern conferences, and Bishop Soule, while theoretically in good standing, had given great offense to certain men in the North. It was declared that Soule, by attending the Louisville Convention and signifying that he would identify himself with the Southern Church, had seceded from the Methodist Episcopal Church and was no longer capable of exercising episcopal functions in it. Even before the bishops met to consider these matters, the conferences in the non-slaveholding states over which Soule was to preside were being besought "not to receive him as their presiding Bishop, as no act done under his administration would be legal—no ordination of his valid." [32]

In attendance at the meeting in New York were Elijah Hedding, Beverly Waugh, Thomas A. Morris, and Edmund S. Janes. Bishop Leonidas L. Hamline sent his opinion in writing, giving his judgment on the points to be acted upon. Bishop Soule did not attend, and of course Bishop Andrew was not invited.

Bishops Morris and Janes expressed a desire to visit and hold their assigned conferences in the South. Janes especially was liked by the Southerners. He had been elected a bishop by Southern votes and presented for ordination as bishop by William Capers of South Carolina and Lovick Pierce of Georgia. John J. Tigert called Janes a "last precious gift of the Southern to the Northern wing of Episcopal Methodism." [33] But after considerable discussion it was eventually decided that Janes and Morris should not go into Southern territory and that a new plan of visitation be worked up in which the Southern conferences would not be included. When it came to Bishop Soule's appointments, however, the bishops decided that they would not change or interfere in any way with his scheduled visitation of conferences north of the Ohio River. They agreed that if Soule did wish to be relieved of what might turn out to be hostile conferences, Bishop Morris should be ready to look after them.

Two formal resolutions were put forth by the bishops. The first affirmed that the much-discussed Plan of Separation was regarded by the bishops as of "binding obligation in the premises" insofar as their own administration was concerned. A second resolution affirmed that "in order to ascertain fairly the desire and purpose of those societies bordering on the line of division, in regard to their adherence to the Church, North or South, due notice should be given of the time, place, and object of the meeting for the above purpose." The latter resolution closed with instructions to see that "the sense of all the members present be ascertained, and the same be forwarded to the Bishop who may preside at the ensuing Annual Conferences; or forward to said presiding Bishop a written request to be recognized and have a preacher sent them, with the names of the majority appended thereto." This action was much applauded by the Southern connection and "was mightily influential in calming the troubled waters and settling the public mind." [34]

Bishop Soule was not unaware that there was great dissatisfaction with him in the Northern conferences. He had been assigned the Illinois, the Iowa, and the Rock River Conferences to preside over, but, after thinking matters over, he asked Bishop Morris to preside in these conferences for him. Soule happened to be in Cincinnati, however, when the Ohio Conference was in session September 3, 1845, and was invited by presiding Bishop Hamline to take part in some of its official proceedings. Great turmoil resulted. Many ministers stayed outside rather than sit under Soule's presidency. Hamline tried to allay the situation, but on a motion regarding Soule's presidency, the conference voted 145 to 7 against sitting in conference under him.

THE PRESS REACTS

Offsetting the official action of the bishops, the two leading connectional papers opposing the Plan of Separation—the *Christian Advocate and Journal* and the *Western Christian Advocate*—came out at once and with great heat and vigor, renewing their attack upon the Plan of Separation and heaping discredit upon the Louisville Convention and all its ways and works. Editors Bond and Elliott began to fan more and more the flames of angry partisanship. "They set themselves diligently to work to prove to the world, that the Southern organization was an actual *secession* from the Church, 'If not indeed a *schism* of the worst sort.' " [35] The Southern connection was called a "pro-slavery Church," and it was affirmed that the convention was not held in accordance with the Plan of Separation. Even if it were, they affirmed that the plan itself was unconstitutional and void. They further declared that those throughout the slaveholding states who would adhere to the Northern Church could claim Methodist church property in the South, and Southern

[34] *History of the Organization*, p. 237.
[35] *Ibid.*, p. 235.

ministers who disagreed with the Plan of Separation were urged to form themselves into separate conferences. They were assured that "however few in number, they would be recognized as the true Annual Conference —of Kentucky, Missouri, or Holston, as the case might be." [36]

Against this viewpoint Nathan Bangs and Stephen Olin, men of weight over the whole connection, contended strongly that the faith and honor of the church were deeply concerned in carrying out the Plan of Separation. Other church papers, contrary to the New York and Cincinnati *Advocates,* took the same "honorable ground"—as the Southern accounts expressed it.

THE PROBLEM OF BOUNDARIES

Meanwhile, the delegates from the Louisville Convention were making their way homeward. Everywhere they were received with acclaim, and what they had done in Louisville was wildly applauded. The South was more and more solidifying.

The Plan of Separation had ignored state lines. There had been an effort to see to it that local congregations, especially those in border conferences, should have the right to determine where their allegiance should be. But when congregations were divided and charges within the Annual Conferences began to divide from each other, there was laid the foundation for the great local antagonisms and neighborhood unrest which were to persist between the two branches of episcopal Methodism for the next fifty years.

Maysville, Kentucky, was one place where there was a division in the local congregation, with both Southern and Northern Methodists claiming to be the rightful holder of the church property. The church at Maysville was destined to be the focal point of a fierce legal battle— unhappily, one among many.

Bishop Thomas B. Neely, in commenting on the division of the church, wrote: "It is an error to think that all ministers and members of the Methodist Episcopal Church, south of Mason and Dixon's line withdrew . . . to the Church South, or to suppose that all in slave territory withdrew from the old Church." [37]

The publishing agents of the Methodist Episcopal Church had continued to travel through the South, for Leroy Swormstedt, Cincinnati agent, visited the Mississippi Conference in 1844 while some of these matters were pending. John G. Jones, the historian of Mississippi Methodism, who was present, said tartly of Swormstedt that he was "the man

[36] *Ibid.,* p. 236.
[37] *American Methodism: Its Divisions and Unification* (New York: Fleming H. Revell, 1915), p. 69.

whom he would not like to owe anything but love, unless we could have the money ready as soon as called for." [38] At the same time John B. McFerrin made plans to investigate locations for the Southern Book Concern. The Georgia Conference recommended to its preachers and members that they continue their patronage of the Book Concern just as they had hitherto done, "as long as the agents continue to pay on the Southern and Southwestern Conferences their annual dividends, and to pay the family expenses of the Southern Bishops as by law provided for the support of the episcopacy." [39] It should be noted that the publishing agents, who were the treasurers of the fund supporting the bishops, had continued to pay the salaries of the Southern bishops and did so continue until they obtained a ruling following the Petersburg Conference which stated that they should not.

It was an era of great unrest over all of Methodism, North and South. The convention in Louisville had definitely created a new church; but a structure as tightly integrated as episcopal Methodism was, and is, cannot possibly be torn apart without the difficult and painful severance of all manner of structural ties inhering in the Methodist organization.

THE PART THE RESTRICTIVE RULE PLAYED

The Plan of Separation adopted by the General Conference provided for the property of the Book Concern to be divided proportionately between the Northern and Southern branches. Its specific regulation was as follows:

3. *Resolved,* . . . that we recommend to all the Annual Conferences, at their first approaching sessions, to authorize a change of the sixth restrictive article, so that the first clause shall read thus: "They shall not appropriate the produce of the Book Concern, nor of the Chartered Fund, to any other purpose other than for the benefit of the traveling, supernumerary, superannuated, and worn-out preachers, their wives, widows, and children, and to such other purposes as may be determined upon by the vote of two-thirds of the members of the General Conference."

4. That whenever the Annual Conferences, by a vote of three-fourths of all their members voting on the third resolution, shall have concurred in the recommendation to alter the sixth restrictive article, the Agents at New York and Cincinnati shall, and they are hereby authorized and directed to deliver over to any authorized agent or appointee of the Church South, should one be organized, all notes and book accounts against the ministers, church members, or citizens, within its boundaries, with authority to collect the same for the sole use of the Southern Church, and that said Agents also convey to aforesaid

[38] Jones, *History of Methodism . . . the Mississippi Conference,* II, 504.
[39] *South-Western Christian Advocate,* February 20, 1846.

agent or appointee of the South, all the real estate, and assign to him all the property, including presses, stock, and all right and interest connected with the printing establishments at Charleston, Richmond, and Nashville, which now belong to the Methodist Episcopal Church.[40]

This, the technical matter of voting upon the change in the Restrictive Rule, promised to give the elements opposed to the action of the Southern conferences the power to block such action. Whatever might be thought of the Plan of Separation, or the attitude or actions of the 1844 General Conference, its record was now closed and it had adjourned. But in its recommendation that there be a change in the Sixth Restrictive Rule *if* the Southern conferences should decide to organize as a Church, the votes of the Northern conferences as well as of the Southern were required. And it was soon found—to the surprise of many—that the Northern conferences were not going along with the proposed change.

There were many reasons for this. The general feeling of disappointment and dismay that the church had to be divided was felt as keenly in the Northern conferences as in the Southern. Secession, a word freely used in the North, was as disliked in the churches there as it came to be in the nation at large. It was soon made clear by press, pulpit, and conference speeches that the whole move for a separate ecclesiastical organization in the South would be blocked if possible by many in the Northern conferences. The comparatively mild hope of the *Christian Advocate and Journal* on June 26, 1844, that "the South would cool down" was not helped by the storm now raging. Some felt that Bishop Andrew ought to resign completely, and that this would solve the problem. Some suggested that the Canadian and British Wesleyan Conferences ought to come in and arbitrate the division before it was too late. Holland McTyeire, who was later to become one of the strongest bishops of the Southern Church and one of its ablest historians, explained that a good many of the Northern people sincerely felt that if they did not agree to the Plan of Separation, they would be able thus to keep the church together.[41]

As it turned out, there was a debate upon changing the Restrictive Rule in practically all the conferences. The Northern conferences soon began to object, and those "calling themselves conservative" rejected the proposition by a strong vote. Southern historians noted that even some of those who had voted in favor of altering the Restrictive Rule when this was before the General Conference opposed it in their own

[40] *Journal of the General Conference,* 1844, pp. 135-36.
[41] *A History of Methodism* (Nashville: Southern Methodist Publishing House, 1884), p. 646.

Annual Conferences. Some sincerely felt that a refusal to allow the separating South to have its share of the Book Concern would block actual separation.

Meanwhile, Bishop Andrew, at Bishop Soule's invitation, was not "desisting" from his episcopal labors and travels, and this increased Northern hostility toward any Southern action. At any rate, before the Louisville Convention met it became clear that the Northern conferences were not going to vote to change the rule regarding the Book Concern. This, of course, would keep the South from having "an equitable and just division" of the property of the Book Concern—that is, if the South should separate, as it fully intended to do. It took the Supreme Court of the United States, a dozen years later, to determine the equities here and to issue a mandate which gave the Southern Church its share of the old Book Concern. The tale is not a happy one.

4

The First General Conference, Petersburg, 1846

Practically the same men who had composed the Louisville Convention were delegates to the first General Conference of the Methodist Episcopal Church, South. There were eighty-seven of these and, as it turned out, what they did in Petersburg was to continue and enlarge upon what was begun at Louisville, and to establish firmly, formally, and finally a new ecclesiasticism.

At a considerable time before the actual calling to order of the Petersburg Conference, the delegates necessarily had to leave their homes and begin, what was for many, a long journey to that historic city.

William Winans, that eccentric and colorful Mississippi leader, kept a journal of his trip to Virginia. He first went by rail to Bayou Sara, and then took the steamer "Rainbow" to New Orleans; thence back by steamer to Louisville, and from Louisville to Shelbyville, where "Annie Winans was in school"; then to Baltimore, Washington, and Petersburg, after a month and a day on the road—or the rivers. One might wonder why the Mississippi delegate had to first go down the river to New Orleans, then back up the river by another steamer, retracing hundreds of miles—but so the record is given.

The delegation from Georgia was delayed on the boat from Charleston to Wilmington, with Bishop Andrew on board. The colorful John W.

Hanner of Tennessee described in a letter to the *South-Western Christian Advocate* [42] some of the adventures he and his group had in getting to Petersburg up the Ohio River on the steam packet "Clipper," "running with one wheel only, crowded with passengers, most of whom mightily rush to eat at the first table." On board was Bishop Soule—"one of the leaders of the host." Also present were Robert Paine, soon to be a bishop; Drs. Green and Sehon; and editor John B. McFerrin. Fountain Pitts preached one night, and on another night, Dr. Green. The Southern delegates had to spend a Sunday in Cincinnati, and the fact that only one or two of them were asked to preach caused Hanner to write that "the Northern preachers in that city, disgraced themselves outright" by not inviting their brethren to preach. It was, said the Southerner, "unbrotherly hate." Finally they went overland by train to Baltimore, where the local ministers were much more friendly, and from that point they proceeded on to Petersburg.

All eyes in the South were upon that city as the General Conference began to convene. "On this date," observed the *South-Western Christian Advocate* (May 1, 1846), "our first Southern General Conference commences . . . at Petersburg, Virginia. The eyes of friends and foes will be upon its movements. . . . Let all the churches pray that wisdom from above may direct its deliberations." This same editorial went on to note with great interest—characteristic of all Methodists—that there would be bishops elected and that the selection of superintendents would not be the conference's least important task. Bishops ought to be, affirmed the editor, "men of deep piety; deeply read in evangelical theology; possessed of much general knowledge; prepared to expound and defend the doctrines and polity of our church; uniting as far as possible the different portions of the South—border, interior, and extremes—and [have a] standing which would command the esteem of the church." So the editor of 1846 would have a Methodist bishop be.

Arrived at Petersburg, the delegates assembled at the Union Street Church, which had just recently been sold to a Negro congregation. The Washington Street Church, which continues to stand in stately grandeur in Petersburg, had almost been completed but was not then ready for general occupancy.

In accordance with the action of the Convention of Delegates of the several Annual Conferences of the Methodist Episcopal Church, in the slaveholding States, which met in Louisville, Kentucky, in May, 1845, the First General Conference of the Methodist Episcopal Church, South, assembled in Petersburg, Virginia, in the Union street Church, on the first day of May, 1846.

[42] May 8, 1846.

Bishop Andrew not having arrived, and Bishop Soule not having, as yet, formally adhered to the Methodist Episcopal Church, South, the Delegates were called to order, at nine o'clock, A.M., by Dr. William Winans, of Mississippi Conference; and Rev. John Early, of Virginia Conference, was elected President *pro tem.;* whereupon he took the chair, and General Conference was opened— religious service conducted by Doctor Winans.[43]

In these terse, clear paragraphs the opening of Southern Methodism's momentous first General Conference is described. The usual processes of organizing the conference were put in motion, with delegates presenting their certificates or accredited vouchers of election and being properly seated. Thomas N. Ralston was elected secretary and Thomas O. Summers assistant secretary. The editors of the *Richmond, Southern,* and *South-Western Christian Advocates* were appointed a Committee of Publication, "whose business it shall be to supervise all publications of Reports of proceedings, with authority to employ a Reporter."

Crowds of visitors and interested persons crowded in and about the conference, observing its historic deliberations. One historian noted Lovick Pierce, "who ranked second to no man in the love and veneration of American Methodists," and his son, George F. Pierce, later bishop, "who was in the blossoming time of his genius and fame." [44] This distinguished father and son sat together, and an interested visitor from the balcony noted both their deep affection and their alertness toward unfolding events.

The next day was Saturday, and as Bishop Andrew had then arrived, he took the chair. The bylaws of the Louisville Convention were read and adopted as the bylaws of the conference, but on motion by John Early reconsideration was had, and it was finally decided to adopt the bylaws of the General Conference of 1844 for guidance in Petersburg.

A dramatic moment then occurred on this second day. "The venerable Bishop Soule, being present, proceeded to address the Conference in reference to the organization of the Methodist Episcopal Church, South —noticing the history of the controversy by which the Church has been so greatly agitated. . . . He now formally declared his adherence to the Methodist Episcopal Church, South." Benjamin M. Drake, of Mississippi, moved that Bishop Soule by a rising vote be received as one of the bishops of the Methodist Episcopal Church, South, and this was enthusiastically done. A moment later Henry B. Bascom moved that Bishop Soule "be requested to embody in writing the terms in which he

[43] *Journal of the General Conference of the Methodist Episcopal Church, South,* 1846, p. 5.

[44] O. P. Fitzgerald, *John B. McFerrin* (Nashville: Publishing House of the M. E. Church, South, 1889) , p. 179.

has formally announced his adherence to the Methodist Episcopal Church, South, and that a committee be appointed to respond to the same by resolution." [45]

Bishop Soule's communication, dated May 2, 1846, addressed to the "Rev. and dear Brethren," is a formal one, stating that he considered the body "as now organized, as the consummation of the organization of the Methodist Episcopal Church, South, in conformity to the 'Plan of Separation,' adopted by the General Conference of the M.E. Church, in 1844." He went on to say that it was in strict agreement with the provisions of that body "that you are vested with full power to transact all business appropriate to a Methodist General Conference."

Soule's dramatic personal declaration came toward the end of his statement:

And now, acting with strict regard to the Plan of Separation, and under a solemn conviction of duty, I formally declare my adherence to the Methodist Episcopal Church, South. And if the Conference receive me in my present relation to the Church, I am ready to serve them according to the best of my ability. In conclusion, I indulge the joyful assurance, that although separated from our Northern brethren by a distinct Conference jurisdiction, we shall never cease to treat them as "brethren beloved," and cultivate those principles and affections which constitute the essential unity of the Church of Christ. [46]

An appropriate response was made to this communication with Dr. Bascom and Dr. Winans acting as a committee.

The adherence of Soule to the Southern Church had a tremendous influence upon all Methodism. Southern historians have felt that his idea of the episcopacy was the motivating force which placed him upon the side of the South. He had with absolute inflexibility and at personal loss to himself stood during a long lifetime as a tower of strength for the Asburian episcopacy; and as the status of the episcopacy with relation to the General Conference had been challenged and marked down by the majority vote of the General Conference of 1844, Soule went with the Southern minority and remained with the South until he died.

Major Conference Actions

The usual General Conference committees, with some variations, were immediately set up. These consisted of a Committee on Episcopacy, "to

[45] *Journal of the General Conference,* 1846, p. 8.
[46] *Ibid.,* p. 9.

whom shall be referred the moral and official conduct of the Episcopacy for the two years last past: and the said committee shall inquire what additional number of bishops will be necessary in the M.E. Church, South, for the next four years, and report to the Conference." Then committees on itinerancy, boundaries, and finance were created. This latter was to have charge of all things that "relate to the interests of the M.E. Church, South, in the Book Concern at New York and Cincinnati; and the Charter Fund at Philadelphia, and who shall inquire into the best means to secure that interest according to the Plan of Separation, and also to inquire into the propriety of establishing a Book Concern in the M.E. Church, South, and the best method of establishing the same." As it turned out, this committee had much work to do. A Committee on Missions was of course created, and also one which was termed "on Literary Institutions"—which today we would equate with the Board of Education. Further committees on revisals, on Sabbath schools, on temperance, and on the American Bible Society were likewise created. Last, but not least, a committee was set up to ascertain "the expenses of the Bishops and Delegates, and the best method of defraying them." [47]

To counter the editorial attacks by the *Christian Advocate and Journal* and the *Western Christian Advocate*, the Committee on Episcopacy was ordered to look into whether Bishops Andrew and Soule had violated the spirit and letter of the Plan of Separation "in appointing ministers to border charges, stations, or societies, where the people, or members of the Church, had not adhered South, by a vote of the majority, as directed by the General Conference." Later in the conference, in a lengthy report that went into the whole controversial matter of boundaries, the committee reported: "Documentary evidence, in abundance, and perfectly satisfactory in its nature, has been furnished . . . that the administration of the Southern Bishops has been strictly conformed to the rule laid down in the Plan. . . . The Episcopal administration has united a praiseworthy caution with a firm maintenance of principle." [48]

THE BOOK CONCERN CONTROVERSY

Early in the conference a letter was publicly read from the book agents of the Methodist Episcopal Church, George Lane and C. B. Tippett, dated May 2. This letter was a formal inquiry "To the Bishops and Members of the General Conference of the M.E. Church, South,"

[47] *Ibid.,* pp. 10-11.
[48] *Ibid.,* pp. 48, 51.

regarding "the payment of the annual dividends to the Conferences within the bounds of the M.E. Church, South." The agents reported that they had laid the proposition of what to do before the Book Committee on March 26, and had specifically asked:

1. Whether the Book Committee would advise them to pay the annual dividends to the Conferences within the bounds of the M. E. Church, South, up to the next session of the General Conference of the M. E. Church in 1848?

2. If the dividends are not paid, whether they would advise the Agents to retain in their hands a sum equal to the portion of those Conferences, subject to the disposal of said General Conference?

3. Whether they would advise the Agents to pay the table expenses of the Bishops of the M. E. Church, South, up to the time of the said General Conference in 1848?

On the first and third of these questions, the agents reported, the committee said "No" unanimously; but on the second, they were unanimous in the affirmative. The formal communication of the agents to the Southern General Conference, therefore, let it be known that they would follow the advice of their Book Committee "and invest, in available funds, the whole amount that would fall to the share of the Southern Conferences; subject to the disposal of the General Conference of the M. E. Church in 1848." [49]

This letter, with all its implications, was referred by the General Conference to the Finance Committee. In turn, this brought back to the conference an extended reply, defending the whole idea of the Plan of Separation and the authority of the Southern delegates to create a new church. It is not without emotion.

Whence was the far larger portion of the money collected, by which your splendid edifices were erected? Whence have you realized the far larger portion of those profits by which you have divided from eight hundred to one thousand dollars per annum to the Conferences, and swelled your capital to the gross sum of *seven hundred thousand dollars?* But one answer, you well know, with your books before you, can be given to these questions. Southern and South Western men chiefly contributed to rebuild that Concern; and Southern and South Western trade mainly contributed to raise it to its present position of pecuniary profit and moral influence. All these facts . . . render it a dangerous experiment in the science of morals to deny us a single shilling of what is our due. . . . We do not relinquish our rights in the Book Concern under your management, but claim our full share of both the capital and its annual proceeds until there shall be a final settlement; nor do we relinquish the hope that a sense of

[49] *Ibid.,* p. 14.

justice will prevail with our Northern brethren, which shall in due time secure to us an equitable division of the property in question.[50]

This reply was adopted by the conference.

HIGHER EDUCATION

Of importance to the General Conference and to the South was a communication which came from the Board of Trustees of Transylvania University in Lexington, Kentucky. Transylvania University, this message said, should be in close relationship to the Methodist Episcopal Church, South.

That to remove any doubts that may exist on the subject, arising from the fact of the University having been actually conducted on the basis of the before-mentioned proposition, this Board will consider the University as open to be officered by the General Conference, about to be assembled at Petersburg, Virginia, according to the provisions of said proposition, when it shall have been accepted, and the contract consummated by such acceptance.[51]

Henry B. Bascom was then the president of Transylvania, and was anxious for the university to come wholly under the supervision of the Southern Church. Subsequently, "the offer of the control and management of the Academic Division of Transylvania University" was accepted upon the terms and conditions proposed. President Bascom and H. H. Kavanaugh were appointed to be the commissioners in behalf of the Methodist Episcopal Church, South. A Board of Curators was provided for, which was authorized to nominate the faculty; the curators and the trustees of the university were approved by the General Conference under certain expressed stipulations.

It is no part of this history to narrate the further record of Transylvania University, an institution which has had a noble career from that day to this. It passed from under the control of the Methodist Episcopal Church, South, after some years, but has continued its high work of education to the present in the heart of the bluegrass region of Kentucky. An older generation of Southern Methodists felt rather deeply the loss of Transylvania when this occurred.

Something of a modern touch came into the area of education with a resolution against appointing too many preachers to institutions of learning, thus taking them out of the pastorate. However, the Committee on Itinerancy reported that they did not consider it expedient to pass any

---

[50] *Ibid.*, pp. 33-34.
[51] *Ibid.*, p. 16.

new legislation on this matter at that particular time, as the remedy, they felt, lay with the bishops and the several Annual Conferences. They did recommend that "no man should hereafter be appointed to the Presidency, or to any Professorship in our institutions who has not travelled two full years, and been received, in the regular way, into full connection." [52]

THE ELECTION OF BISHOPS

As has been the case in every General or Jurisdictional Conference of Methodism when bishops are to be elected, such elections become the all-engrossing topic of conversation until the last ballot is declared. Petersburg proved no exception. On May 7 the Committee on Episcopacy, through its chairman William Winans, recommended the election of two additional bishops. Augustus Longstreet of Georgia moved to amend by "striking out the number *two* and inserting the number *one.*" His motion lost, and it was decided on motion of Benjamin Drake to ballot immediately upon the two persons to be elected bishop.

As upon all occasions of this sort, a moment of great solemnity then came. The bishops were requested by the conference to lead in prayer. The conference sang the first two stanzas of the old hymn:

> Father, if justly still we claim
> To us and ours the promise made,
> To us be graciously the same,
> And crown with living fire our head:
> Our claim admit, and from above,
> Of holiness the Spirit shower,
> Of wise discernment, humble love,
> And zeal, and unity, and power.

Bishop Andrew, suffering from an "affliction," asked to be excused from making the prayer, and Bishop Soule called on Lovick Pierce, "who also addressed the throne of grace."

Whether or not Bishop Andrew's stepping aside, and Bishop Soule's putting Lovick Pierce, another Georgian, before the conference just before the ballot, was an episcopal method of getting a prominent conference leader even more prominently in the minds of the men as they went to ballot, who can say? At any rate, the first ballot was cast and there was no election. On the second ballot William Capers of South Carolina and Robert Paine of Tennessee, both having received a majority of the total number of votes, were elected bishops of the Methodist Epis-

[52] *Ibid.,* p. 65.

copal Church, South. Ordination of these two brethren was set for a week from that particular day, in the new Washington Street Church, just being finished.

The two men thus elected were to prove worthy. William Capers was a native South Carolinian, born upon his well-to-do father's plantation near Charleston. In his ministerial career he had especially pioneered in insisting that Methodism must evangelize the Indians and the slaves. His "missions to the blacks," as his biographer terms it,[53] had served to awaken the Southern conferences to what should be done for the Negroes on the plantations and in the fields of the deep South. Capers had been elected by the General Conference of 1828 to serve as the first representative of the American Methodist Church to that of Great Britain—as he did very ably.

Robert Paine was a much younger man than Capers, and had no idea when he went to Petersburg that he would be elected a bishop. He did not wish it. "He had a young and growing family. He loved his home. . . . He almost rebelled. . . . He was not elated. The office had sought him. The honor came unbidden. Duty to God and man, made clear by the word of God and by the Holy Spirit, was the one great and all-sufficient reason for assuming such grave responsibilities." [54] Paine was "a Church statesman, Christian educator, McKendree's biographer, a Bishop who *filled* the office," said O. P. Fitzgerald.[55]

The conference paused at noon on Thursday, May 14, to go into solemn session for the consecration and ordination of the newly elected bishops. The Ordinal was read by Bishops Andrew and Soule, and the candidates presented by Lovick Pierce and John Early. Both these elders assisted in the imposition of hands, and "thus were William Capers, D.D., of the South Carolina Conference, and Robert Paine, D.D., of the Tennessee Conference, solemnly set apart to the office and work of Superintendents in the Methodist Episcopal Church, South." [56]

On the next day Bishop Capers took the chair from Bishop Andrew, and Bishop Paine took his turn in presiding on Saturday.

MISSIONS

The General Conference had created a strong Committee on Missions, with William Capers serving as chairman. This committee subsequently presented several reports which, in the main, were adopted. These looked

[53] William M. Wightman, *Life of William Capers, D.D.* (Nashville: Southern Methodist Publishing House, 1859), p. 288.
[54] R. H. Rivers, *The Life of Robert Paine, D.D.* (Nashville: Southern Methodist Publishing House, 1884), p. 82.
[55] *John B. McFerrin,* p. 178.
[56] *Journal of the General Conference,* 1846, p. 61.

forward to a continuation and expansion of the missionary activity which had been carried on in the various conferences now joined together in the new church, and toward the formation of an organization which would supervise the whole field of missions in its wider aspects. Methodism, South and North, intended to be missionary.

"Let each Annual Conference form itself into a Missionary Society, auxiliary to the Missionary Society of the Methodist Episcopal Church, South, under such regulations as the Conferences severally shall prescribe." [57] This was the opening statement of the first report brought in by the Committee on Missions, which gave all manner of details as to how mission work should be carried on. Later in the conference, on May 13, a regular constitution for the Missionary Society of the Methodist Episcopal Church, South, was presented and adopted with some modifications.

It was at first recommended that a secretary for the Missionary Society and also a general missionary agent, both to be elected by the General Conference, be in charge of mission work. Later, after some debate, this second office was decided against and a general secretary alone elected.

Edmund W. Sehon of Tennessee was elected on May 12 to be missionary secretary. Ten days later he resigned and Edward Stevenson of Kentucky was elected to this position.

Noteworthy among the reports of the Committee on Missions was that calling for the publication of a catechism "adapted to the purpose of communicating a knowledge of the doctrines, principles, and duties of our holy religion to the children and others requiring catechetical instruction in our missions." [58] Such a move today would be taken by the Board of Education, but in that formative period this was conceded to be the duty of the missionary enterprise.

That a world-wide view of missions was taken is shown by Report No. 6 of the Committee on Missions, looking toward Africa. It was known that the Methodist Episcopal Church already had a close tie with Liberia, and the Southern committee took occasion to disclaim any idea of "any unfriendly collision or interference with our brethren of the Northern Church, in any quarter, and most of all in the field of Missions, and could never entertain a thought of interfering with them in their work in Liberia." The report, however, went on to say that there were other points on the western coast of Africa which might be open and from which missionary operations might be commenced to advantage. It was therefore recommended that the bishop and the Board of Managers of

[57] *Ibid.*, p. 17.
[58] *Ibid.*, p. 23.

the Missionary Society "as soon as any providential opening shall appear" should send a missionary or missionaries thither.[59]

The Committee on Missions reported on what they called "the expediency and importance of instituting a Mission to China," noting that "half of the Pagan world belongs to the Celestial Empire, and the Emperor has recently, in the providence of God, opened a great and effectual door to Missionary operations." This report ended by soliciting the bishops to take measures for the appointment of two missionaries to China at their earliest convenience.[60] The possibility of missionizing the Jews was also discussed, and it was decided that where there was a conference "within whose bounds the Jews are numerous," the Annual Conference would solicit the bishop to appoint a special missionary.

Considerable time was given to establishing the headquarters of the missionary agent and to other matters having to do with organizational activities. It is quite evident that even though matters of supreme moment were facing the church in this organizational period, the whole drive of the Methodist Episcopal Church, South, in its missionary outreach was carefully nurtured, encouraged, and provided for.

PUBLISHING INTERESTS

Early in the conference the Finance Committee was authorized to investigate the "propriety" and the best methods of establishing a Book Concern for the Southern Church and to make a study of the periodicals, reporting on "what jurisdiction this Conference has over those papers established by the Methodist Episcopal Church within our bounds." Their first report recommended that a Book Concern be established, consisting of an Eastern and a Western division.

Action on this proposal occupied a good deal of time during the last ten days of the conference session. On May 13 the conference approved the establishment of the Eastern division of the Book Concern at Richmond and the Western division at Louisville—each division to have an agent, a book committee, and a periodical. A quarterly review was to be published at Louisville. All of this was reconsidered two days later, and there seem to have been lengthy debates over the cities to be chosen for the establishment of the Book Concern. Apparently, it was beginning to be strongly felt that it was "inexpedient" to establish a Book Concern, as one resolution put it, until the General Conference of 1850. The final action, coming on May 22 on a motion from William Winans, provided for one book agent to provide books for the Southern Church, "contract-

[59] *Ibid.*, p. 42.
[60] *Ibid.*, p. 37.

ing for such books where they can be obtained by him on the best terms," with book depositories at Louisville, Charleston, and Richmond. The agent was to receive all money collected either from Southern contributions or from the settlement with the Northern Church, but no money was to be invested in anything but books until the next General Conference. John Early was elected book agent.

Although the formal establishment of a Book Concern was postponed, the conference did approve the publication of weekly papers in Nashville, Charleston, and Richmond, and provided for a quarterly review. Editors were elected: For the *Nashville Christian Advocate,* John B. McFerrin editor, Moses M. Henkle assistant editor; for the *Southern Christian Advocate,* at Charleston, W. M. Wightman editor, Thomas O. Summers assistant editor; for the *Richmond Christian Advocate,* Leroy Lee editor. Henry B. Bascom was unanimously elected editor of the quarterly review.

The conference directed the book agent to publish the new edition of the *Discipline* then in preparation, and approved the publication of *The History of the Organization of the Methodist Episcopal Church, South,* as ordered by the Louisville Convention, recommending the same to "our preachers and people." An unusual resolution was passed asking the Southern editors to "allude as seldom as possible" to the controversy with the North. As if they—or anyone—could help it!

THE HYMNAL AND DISCIPLINE

When the matter of a new hymnbook came up, it was first laid upon the table. The conference finally decided that a committee be appointed to compile and publish such a book without reporting back to the conference. It was recommended that they increase "the number of the Common, Long, and Short Metres, by selecting from the authorized Wesleyan Hymn Book, and other approved sources," and exclude "some of the Particular Metres, which are unsuitable for the ordinary congregational singing." [61] Hymnody then, as now, was dear to the hearts of Methodist people.

The *Discipline* of the new church, published by John Early in 1846, was essentially that of the Methodist Episcopal Church. "All the doctrines, duties, and usages," stated the Pastoral Address, "the entire creed and ritual of the church before the separation, remain without change of any kind." [62] The major change was the addition of a section on the origin of the Methodist Episcopal Church, South, explaining briefly the reasons for so organizing. Other changes were in regard to the Book Con-

[61] *Ibid.,* p. 15.
[62] *Ibid.,* p. 109.

cern, editors, and such details of administration necessary to the separate church.

Interestingly enough, there was no change at all in the section on slavery—the tenth section of Part II in the 1844 *Discipline*. Earlier resolutions, not adopted by the conference, recommended that the statements on slavery adopted at the 1836 and 1840 General Conferences be appended to the present Section 10. A resolution that the committee on the Pastoral Address be required to "embody in their report a suitable exposition of the Tenth section of the *Discipline*" was also lost. Nevertheless, the Pastoral Address stated:

We re-avow, as our own, the declaration of the General Conference of 1836— "We wholly disclaim any right, wish, or intention to interfere in the civil or political relation of master and slave, as it exists in the slaveholding States of the Union." We agree with that body . . . in further declaring, that the subject of slavery in this country, is "put beyond the power of legislation by the General Government, as well as the control of ecclesiastical bodies." . . . We are well content merely to repeat the full and explicit declaration of the General Conference of 1840, "That the simple holding of slaves, or mere ownership of slave property, in States or Territories where the laws do not admit of emancipation, and permit the liberated slave to enjoy freedom, constitutes no legal barrier to the election or ordination of ministers, to the various grades of office known in the ministry of the Methodist Episcopal Church, and cannot, therefore, be considered as operating any forfeiture of right, in view of such election and ordination." . . .

We glance at these facts, not so much to satisfy you, as to show to others . . . that instead of any, the least departure from the law of the church respecting slavery, we have strictly adhered to it, throughout the whole struggle, and have been abused and denounced only because we would not submit to its violation by the Northern division of the church.[63]

OTHER CONFERENCE ACTIONS

The touchy problem of conference boundaries occupied a good bit of the conference's time and attention—particularly the matter of border conferences. The issues and disputes involved here are considered in the following chapter. An important move was the election of Henry B. Bascom, S. A. Latta, and A. L. P. Green as commissioners to deal with the commissioners of the Northern Church on the problem of the Book Concern. These men were given the authority to "take such measures as may best secure the just and equitable claims of the M.E. Church, South." Other matters coming before the conference were the election of

[63] *Ibid.*, pp. 111-12.

George F. Pierce as vice-president of Transylvania; the appointment of Lovick Pierce as fraternal delegate to the 1848 General Conference of the Methodist Episcopal Church; the selection of St. Louis as the meeting place of the next General Conference, to be held on May 1, 1850; and a request that Bishop Soule write a biography of William McKendree.

A lengthy Pastoral Address was prepared and subsequently distributed to the Southern conferences. It closes with these impressive words: "After all, personal piety is the one great interest that should engross us. Always important, beyond all power of thought, let it be with us the 'one thing needful,' that, elevated, by its aims and purposes, above all interests, we may exemplify in our own conduct and exhibit to others 'the doctrine of God our Saviour,' in all its truth and beauty." [64]

Thus, on May 23, ended the first General Conference of the Methodist Episcopal Church, South—and an organization that was to carry forward a banner of high churchliness and of tremendous vigor, in the best traditions of Methodism, had been launched on its career.

---

[64] *Ibid.,* p. 118.

chapter 16

THE YEARS
OF
DISAGREEMENT

1844-61

The "Paper Warfare"

Failure of the
  Plan of Separation

Border Troubles

The Book Concern Fight

Education

Missions

Growth of the
  Southern Church

E VEN BEFORE THE LONG GENERAL
  Conference of 1844 reached adjournment, the flames of disagreement, controversy, and bitterness were being fanned in other parts of the nation. Although the conference itself ended on a note of Christian forbearance and good will, if not actual harmony, the smoldering coals outside the city of New York were ready to burst into flame. The South had seethed over the treatment of Mr. Harding and Bishop Andrew for days before the almost unanimous acceptance of the resolutions reported by the Committee of Nine had apparently banked the fires in the conference itself. And when the Southern delegates met on the day following the adjournment of the conference in a caucus which proposed the convention to meet at Louisville, Kentucky, in May of 1845, it seemed to some in the North that the truce which had precariously promised a chance for the preservation of the Methodist Episcopal Church had been violated.[1]

As a matter of fact, the "irrepressible conflict" which produced the Civil War was even more inevitable in the Methodist Episcopal Church than in the nation. The series of compromises over the question of slavery, which were characterized by the strongly antislavery Hiram Mattison in 1859 as the "Downward Progress of the Church," [2] had increasingly run counter to the trend of opinion in the North. In the northern states the conviction of the evil of human slavery, always a part of Methodist thinking

[1] George Peck, *The Life and Times of Rev. George Peck* (New York: Nelson and Phillips, 1874), pp. 319-20.
[2] *The Impending Crisis of 1860* (New York: Mason Brothers, 1859), pp. 23 ff.

144

and its *Discipline,* became increasingly a matter of conscience that occupied men's minds and feelings and impelled them to speak out. The withdrawal of the Wesleyan Methodists in 1843 was simply a symptom of this increase. The slavery question was not merely a political issue separating citizens into political parties. It was a moral or ethical issue, and the church, by its very nature, was more sensitive to moral issues than was the nation at large. It is not surprising, therefore, that the separation in the church should have come fifteen years before the political separation or that the parallels between the course of events in the history of the largest and most widely national religious denomination and the course of events in the history of the nation itself should have been many and close, even to termination in warfare. For the Methodist Episcopal Church, the years between 1844 and 1860 have been called those of the "paper war." [3] The term is apt and accurate.

1

Reactions to the 1844 General Conference

For a decade and a half the actions of the General Conference of 1844 were debated, interpreted, and denounced in all sections of the country. The arguments of that great array of able churchmen were repeated, examined, extolled, ridiculed, and echoed interminably. The issues raised there were clarified, argued, and fought over, again and again. Was Bishop Andrew deposed or suspended? Was the action of the South secession or legal separation? Was the Methodist Episcopal Church divided into separate parts or simply subtracted from? Was the power of the General Conference over the episcopacy absolute? On which side was constitutionality, and what of expediency? In Minutes of conferences and meetings; in speeches, sermons, and addresses; in articles, pamphlets, and books; but above all, in the pages of the official *Advocates* and *Journals,* the charges and countercharges, and the protests and replies, poured from the presses. These were indeed the years of a paper warfare.

So all-enveloping was the argument over slavery and its place in the church that it obscures other developments. There were other issues, other disagreements, and the work of the church went on. Sometimes it went on

[3] The term was used at least as early as the resolutions adopted by the Holston Annual Conference of 1845.

the better for the separation with which historians have been preoccupied to the point of blindness. Pastoral labors, revivals of religious feeling, and the defense of Methodism as doctrine and organization continued. Debates over the need for theological education, lay representation, the preservation of the itinerancy, and the extension of missions engaged the attention of many. And yet, over all, these years were dominated by the contentions of the proslavery South and the antislavery North and their impact upon those caught between—geographically in the "border conferences" and emotionally or intellectually in "conservatism." [4]

Long before the last great speech of the 1844 General Conference the South was strongly agitated. News of the action of the Northern majority, in supporting the Baltimore Conference in the Harding case and in requesting Bishop Andrew to desist from his episcopal duties while connected with slavery, reached a people disturbed by the agitations connected with the failure of the Texas annexation treaty in the United States Senate. Throughout the slaveholding section there were meetings and resolutions were passed.

On June 8, 1844, a meeting on the Chesterfield Circuit in the Virginia Conference condemned the course of the General Conference and resolved that "we solemnly contemn the principles, and hold in sovereign contempt *the men who can, reckless of consequences, urge such principles* against the spirit and letter of our excellent Book of Discipline, in the attempt to degrade from his office the man who, in spite of men and devils, has filled to the full the high prerogatives of the Episcopal Chair." [5] Another meeting in Russell County, Alabama, on the same day, provides evidence that the events at the General Conference were watched throughout the South with concern and apprehension, even by non-Methodists. It "beheld, with unutterable indignation, the humiliating fact of a Bishop of the State of Georgia . . . put, in effect, upon his trial as a culprit, for the alleged sin of marrying a lady possessed of slaves," and strongly urged "the clergy of the Methodist Episcopal Church, at the South, to take immediate measures for their secession," assuring them of the "unalterable support of . . . every sect and denomination [in the South]." [6]

Only two days later in Wilmington, North Carolina, a meeting of both clergy and laymen insisted that the question of slavery was civil and po-

---

[4] Used often as a term of reproach by the abolitionist element in the Northern Church, "conservative" has usually the special force of seeking to preserve the unity of the church or the nation, hence, sometimes, "pro-Southern."

[5] A. H. Redford, *History of the Organization of the Methodist Episcopal Church, South* (Nashville: Redford, 1871), p. 386.

[6] *Ibid.*, p. 387.

litical, not ecclesiastical, that the "dignified, manly, and Christian firmness exhibited by the delegates from the Southern and Southwestern Conferences" deserved approval, that Bishop Andrew had been subjected to the "reckless and tyrannical conduct of a majority of the General Conference," and finally that "the present union of the Methodist Episcopal Church ought to be *immediately dissolved*." [7] Between July 4, 1844, and March 1, 1845, according to John N. Norwood's count, at least sixty-seven such resolutions were printed in the *Richmond Christian Advocate* alone.[8]

So unanimous and widespread were the Southern resolutions that Northern hints at a conspiracy of the Southern delegates and leaders can hardly be taken seriously. Even with the whole of the General Conference actions before them, the resolutions expressed strong support of Bishops Andrew and Soule, demanded the separation provided for by the work of the Committee of Nine, denounced abolition in the most vitriolic terms, labeled the attitude of the majority unconstitutional, and insisted that slavery was a civil matter, not something for ecclesiastical debate. At Milledgeville, Georgia, in resolutions cited for their moderate tone, the language was still strong enough to term the action of the conference "tyrannical, . . . governed by false views and unjustifiable prejudices—unconstitutional, impolitic, and oppressive," designed to retain "in Church-communion discontented fanatics and disorganizing radicals." [9]

Gradually the force of the Southern opposition, compounded variously of wounded pride and the sense of affront, genuine concern for what would happen to the work of the church, and elaborate rationalization of real convictions, penetrated the North. The policy of the various *Christian Advocates* to quote extensively from one another aided the spread. The moderate Northerners who had left the conference of 1844 grasping at the hope that compromise and the show of concession might yet hold the church together were soon of a different mind. The Rev. John McClintock summed up the situation. "The South will accept no such compromise," he wrote to his friend and president, Robert Emory, of Dickinson College, "and it is only treasuring up for ourselves, as you say, trouble for the future to agitate such projects. . . . We do not believe here that any compromise will be effected. The South will go off." [10]

[7] *Ibid.*, pp. 389-90.

[8] John N. Norwood, *The Schism in the Methodist Episcopal Church, 1844: A Study of Slavery and Ecclesiastical Politics* (Alfred, N. Y.: Alfred University Press, 1923), p. 88. This is by far the best-documented and most judicious study of the whole controversy.

[9] Edward H. Myers, *The Disruption of the Methodist Episcopal Church, 1844-1846* (Nashville: Redford, 1875), pp. 138-40.

[10] From Carlisle, October 31, 1844; quoted in George R. Crooks, *Life and Letters of the Rev. John M'Clintock* (New York: Nelson and Phillips, 1876), p. 135.

While Bishop Hedding was embarked on his episcopal tour after the General Conference, "he was greatly rejoiced to witness the gradual healing of party feeling, and the restoration of brotherly affection among many who had become alienated in the ultra-abolition excitement." [11] He was pleased to find the preachers in Boston and vicinity uniting in a formal request that he make his home in New England. Apparently the section had forgiven his seeming proslavery leanings in his attempt to save the church from distraction and dismemberment. His spectacular gesture in withdrawing his name from the bishops' signatures to the request for delay in acting upon the Andrew case may well have had something to do with the change. And the new feeling of unity may also have owed something to the remembrance of the bitter passages in the speech of the Rev. George F. Pierce on behalf of Bishop Andrew in which he called New England "a thorn in the flesh, a messenger of Satan," and exclaimed: "Let her go." [12] On the other hand, in Pennsylvania, John McClintock said:

It would be far better to let Maryland and Virginia go, and to keep the whole North united on an antislavery basis. . . . I am more and more disposed to believe, that if the curse of slavery is ever removed from us it must be by other people than slaveholders, and I do not intend to be backward hereafter in enlightening the people of these parts on the subject.[18]

The Course of Southern Opinion

It was in this atmosphere that the first of the Annual Conferences after the 1844 General Conference met in Kentucky in September, 1844. Its approval of the proposed Louisville Convention was set in the middle of assertions of the unconstitutionality of the action in the Harding and Andrew cases and the pious hope that separation might prove unnecessary. Its delegates to the Louisville Convention were instructed, in the event of "indispensable separation," to insist that the new organization was not to be considered a secession from the old, only a new and co-ordinate branch, and to make no change in the Discipline.

Most of the succeeding Southern conferences followed the Kentucky pattern closely. Some regretted the violence of partisanship, South as well as North. Some looked for last-ditch attempts at compromise, but such

---

[11] Davis W. Clark, *Life and Times of Rev. Elijah Hedding* (New York: Carlton and Phillips, 1856), p. 595.
[12] Peck, *Life and Times*, p. 266.
[18] Crooks, *Life of M'Clintock*, p. 135.

conciliatory gestures tended to come from the conferences on the border or from regions where slavery had not proved economically profitable. Essentially the South was united in its support of Bishop Andrew, the necessity for the Louisville Convention, and the need for separation. None of the dissenting voices seemed very significant, nor any of the proposals for compromise to hold out much hope.

The Course of Northern Opinion

While the course of the South had the smoothness of nearly universal assent, in the North things were different, notwithstanding the response to Bishop Hedding. When the Northern delegates returned to their homes from the General Conference, their reception was decidedly mixed. The small minority of the conference which had followed the lead of the outspoken Peter Cartwright in opposing the proposals of the Committee of Nine had expressed opinions that were now echoed widely. To some it seemed that the conference had sold out to slavery, and these resolved with McClintock: "That two hundred and fifty thousand slave-holders should rule this great empire is a thing not to be endured—and it can't be endured much longer." [14] To others their beloved church had been torn apart, injured by slaveholders and schismatics, with the connivance of their own delegates. Except in New England, which seemed happy at the prospect of eliminating slavery at any cost, the North was in a mood to count the cost and find fault with both the bargain and, ultimately, because so many of the 1844 delegates were not chosen for the 1848 conference, the bargainers.

In the spread of this feeling, the newspapers undoubtedly played a large part. A heated newspaper controversy concerning the constitutionality and expediency of the Plan of Separation was begun almost immediately after the conference adjourned. William Wightman blamed the policy of the New York *Christian Advocate* and Dr. Bond:

There is no doubt that, under the provisions of this plan of separation, the Southern organization would have been amicably carried through, and the Book Concern fund divided without an appeal to legal tribunals, had the official journal of the Northern Church adopted a pacific and conciliatory policy. Unfortunately, [it was] in the hands of a person wholly unsuited to the emergency.[15]

[14] *Ibid.*
[15] *Life of William Capers* (Nashville: Southern Methodist Publishing House, 1859), p. 410.

Actually there was no single Northern position in the controversies which arose. The so-called Plan of Separation had included three major provisions: a method of determining whether separation from the church was necessary, the responsibility to rest with the Annual Conferences in the slaveholding states; a very poorly defined scheme for determining the allegiance of the societies and circuits in the "border conferences" whose territory embraced both slaveholding and nonslaveholding territory; and a proposal, in the event that separation proved necessary, to make a division of church funds and property, most of which was represented by the capital and income involved in the operation of the Book Concerns, by a process of suspending the Sixth Restrictive Rule after a three-fourths vote of the members of the Annual Conferences. Each of these three major components of the Plan had its weaknesses which made it liable to attack. If the Southern conferences voted that separation was necessary, had the General Conference the right, under the provisions of the constitution adopted in 1808, to have established such a condition for separation in the first place? Even more basic, perhaps, was the church's government a limited one, like the federal government, with powers distinctly specified, or was it one of general powers with a few stated limitations? Again, was the Fifth Restrictive Rule, which prohibited the General Conference from abridging the rights of trial and appeal by ministers and members, violated in a separation which divided the body to which such an appeal would have to be made? Also, at least technically, would not a separation involve a constitutional violation by abridging the freedom of the general superintendency to travel over the whole of the connection as provided under the Third Restrictive Rule? Since the *Discipline* failed to provide for any body corresponding to the federal Supreme Court with final judicial power to decide on the constitutionality of legislative actions, there was room for all sorts of diverse opinions; and the newspapers, particularly in the North, permitted the editors and any correspondent to try their hands at being Chief Justice.

A letter from Dr. Robert Emory, published in the *Christian Advocate and Journal*,[16] and copied in the *Zion's Herald* of December 4, 1844, and the *Western Christian Advocate* of December 6, 1844, made a bitter attack on the General Conference for an "unconstitutional invasion of the rights both of the ministry and membership" in dividing the church without authority to do so. He proposed that all extremists—those who thought slaveholders necessarily sinners and those who thought that extirpation of slavery ought not to be sought by all scriptural means—should withdraw

[16] November 27, 1844, p. 61.

from the church. Dr. Nathan Bangs, on the other hand, in a long series of letters to the New York *Christian Advocate* during 1844 and 1845, maintained the constitutionality of the Plan, holding that the government of the church was vested in the General Conference with general powers to act in any instance except where specifically restrained by a few stated limitations.[17] In this view Bangs was supported generally by the respected Dr. Stephen Olin, president of Wesleyan, and later by William L. Harris.[18] But very few other readers of Dr. Bangs were able to agree with him. In fact, his views were at variance with those of the editor of the publication in which they first appeared. Dr. Thomas E. Bond had little enthusiasm for the whole plan from the beginning. As George Peck says, Bond "took ground against the constitutionality of the measures which were being pursued, and labored hard to persuade the people not to follow the preachers into the secession movement." [19] Bond particularly aroused the ire of the Southern leaders by addressing himself to their constituents. However, he was more consistent in his opposition than was Dr. Charles Elliott, the editor of the *Western Christian Advocate,* published in Cincinnati. Elliott had actually moved the report of the Committee of Nine with a strong speech in favor of the Plan on the floor of the General Conference. Between the conference and the Louisville Convention of 1845, he made a complete about-face, ending by opposing the Plan as strongly as he had previously supported it.

That this extended debate and the response it evoked from the South had an effect upon the voting of the Northern Annual Conferences in regard to the suspension of the Sixth Restrictive Rule seems fully attested by the pattern of that voting. The first conferences to vote strongly favored the proposal. The vote in the New York Annual Conference, which began the day after the General Conference ended, was reported in the *Christian Advocate and Journal* of June 26, 1844, as 143 for, 38 against; and, less than a month later, the vote in the Providence Conference was unanimously in favor. By the time the Philadelphia and New Jersey Conferences voted in April of 1845, with eight or nine months of constant debate intervening, the tables had turned completely. Philadelphia voted 12 for and 104 against; New Jersey, 2 for and 110 against.[20]

[17] Most clearly stated, perhaps, in a letter to the Rev. Albert Griffith, in the *Christian Advocate and Journal*, December 3, 1845, p. 65.

[18] *Christian Advocate and Journal*, September 10, 1845, p. 17; and William L. Harris, *The Constitutional Powers of the General Conference, with a Special Application to the Subject of Slaveholding* (Cincinnati: Methodist Book Concern, 1860), pp. 21-23.

[19] Peck, *Life and Times*, p. 266.

[20] *Christian Advocate and Journal*, April 16, 1845, p. 142; and *Minutes of the New Jersey Conference*, 1845, p. 11.

The Southern Bishops

The Northern newspapers were, however, but one factor in the developing opinion concerning the Plan of Separation. To see others, it is necessary to observe the actions of the bishops. The conference action on Bishop Andrew's case was ambiguous. Bishop Andrew had been requested to desist from his episcopal labors so long as he remained connected with slavery. At the same time, the conference had asserted that he was still a bishop whether or not he chose to comply with its wishes. Meeting on June 11, 1844, to arrange their itineraries, the bishops found themselves in disagreement concerning what to do about Bishop Andrew, who was absent. Since the latter had not indicated his decision on the question the conference had left up to him, the majority felt that he should not be included. Bishop Soule disagreed, and an alternative itinerary to include Bishop Andrew was entrusted to Bishop Soule, with the understanding that, if Bishop Andrew applied for assignment, Bishop Soule would publish the second plan with suitable explanation.

Bishop Andrew did not apply to the bishops for assignment, and it is highly unlikely that he personally requested it of the senior bishop, Soule. Bishop Soule, however, did issue an invitation in a letter dated September 26, 1844, in which he explained his own view that ministers and members of the church ought to abstain from discussion of the subject of slavery and its abolition, suggested that the rest of the bishops were responsible for Bishop Andrew's not having been assigned work, and invited him to "meet me at the Virginia Conference at Lynchburg, November 12, 1844," and to "make your arrangements to be with me at all the Southern Conferences in my division of the work for the present year." When Bishop Andrew accepted this invitation and Bishop Soule's letter was published in the *Christian Advocate and Journal* of December 4, 1844, Dr. Bangs immediately took exception, and Dr. Bond, Dr. Elliott, and others denounced Bishop Soule's action as unauthorized and opposed to the wishes of both the General Conference and the rest of the bishops. That Bishop Soule had taken the law into his own hands is clear enough. He had also indicated, if there were any who had doubts about it, where his attachment was to be. Although he had been reared in the North, Bishop Soule's reverence for the constitutional structure of the whole church in the formation of which he had played so large a part, his patriarchal sense of personal responsibility, and his sentimental attachment to the South and the Southern Methodist heroes of the past carried him into the Southern camp. While the North could question his methods and object to his position, no one could doubt his sincerity, and in the long run Soule's adherence to the South may have been a deciding factor in the judicial decision that the separation was a legal division of the church into parallel ecclesiastical organizations.

Under the attack of the editors, Bishop Soule was sufficiently annoyed to defend his action in a letter published in the *Southern Christian Advocate* and dated January 4, 1845. Here he takes issue with Bond's charge that he was claiming for one of the bishops the "right to decide on the legality of any act of the General Conference," refuses to accept the role of "scapegoat" for instituting new issues in the controversy, and somewhat testily suggests that the bishops, not the editors, constitute the superintendency and that Bond's conduct of the editorial office has hardly been calculated to support the ends of "unity and peace" which he purports to desire.

Ultimately Soule agreed to preside at the Louisville Convention and indicated that he would accept the invitation to serve as bishop for the newly organized church. Meantime the opposition to his course, his own failure to recognize the strength of this feeling, and his refusal, on principle, to accept the decision of the other bishops to confine their episcopal labors to the sections to which they intended to adhere, precipitated one of the most painful episodes of the whole controversy.

Despite many indications that the Northern conferences would not receive him as a bishop, Bishop Soule visited the Ohio Conference for its annual meeting in September, 1845. On the second day, Bishop Hedding, who was presiding, extended the courtesy due the senior bishop of the church by inviting him to take the chair. Bishop Soule began with the customary religious services, but when he was about to call for the regular business, the Rev. Jacob Young, a preacher of long standing, stood up to offer a resolution. When Bishop Soule showed an unwillingness to give Young's motion precedence, the Rev. James B. Finley spoke strongly for it. Young then offered his resolution, stating substantially that Bishop Soule's declared willingness to become a bishop of the Southern Church had, in effect, severed his connection with the Methodist Episcopal Church and that, therefore, it was "inexpedient and highly improper" for him to preside over any conference in that church.[21] Bishop Soule remarked to the conference that he would not leave the chair except at the instigation of the bishop who had invited him to assume it. However, Bishop Hedding, after attempting to make some other arrangement, finally took the chair himself in order to secure order. Young's motion carried by an overwhelming vote of 145 to 7.

[21] *Western Christian Advocate*, September 12, 1845, p. 86. For an account of the incident by a Southern interpreter see William A. Bowen, *Why Two Episcopal Methodist Churches in the United States?* (Nashville: Publishing House of the M. E. Church, South, 1901), p. 120.

Bishop Soule's stubborn insistence on complying with the instructions of the constituted authority in this instance seems hardly consistent with his actions in the Bishop Andrew situation. On the other hand, the action of Bishops Hedding, Waugh, Morris, and Hamline in assuming that the Plan of Separation would be implemented seems a no more realistic evaluation of the tenor of the Northern conferences.

Bascom's Book

In March of 1845, months before the Ohio Conference, while the Annual Conferences were voting on the Sixth Restrictive Rule, there appeared the grand compendium of the Southern arguments, what William Wightman called a "thorough armory" for the debate and then added: "This important publication has been delayed, of set purpose, in order . . . that the full impression which it is destined to produce throughout the whole border section, from Maryland to Missouri, might be felt just previously to the convention of the southern delegates at Louisville." [22] The "important publication" was Dr. Henry Bascom's *Methodism and Slavery*, which he had promised at the time of the General Conference and which, in its full title, he termed *A Review of the Manifesto of the Majority in Reply to the Protest of the Minority of the Late General Conference.*

Bascom's 165-page treatise covered all the ground of the Southern arguments from the time of the conference debate on Bishop Andrew. It surveyed the history of the Methodist compromises with slavery in order to determine the historic "intention" of the church, discoursed of the relationship between civil and ecclesiastical concerns, protested against the unconstitutional action against Bishop Andrew, with its false interpretation of the position of the episcopacy in the Methodist Church, and noted the crippling effect of the conference majority attitude upon the work of the church in the South. All this was done in the full panoply of elaborate argument and quotation, although it was so undocumented that the equally partisan Elliott termed it "a gemara, or a collection of the sayings of men, calculated to baffle the endeavors of reviewers." [23] George Peck, who later in the year at the urging of Drs. Elliott and Durbin produced a reply to Bascom's *Review*, said that it was "characterized by the same kind of logic which marked his 'Protest,' but far exceeding that document in virulence." [24] He also said

[22] *Southern Christian Advocate*, March 28, 1845.
[23] Charles Elliott, *History of the Great Secession* (Cincinnati: Swormstedt and Poe, 1855) , col. 466.
[24] Peck, *Life and Times*, p. 266.

of it that it was "saturated with wormwood and gall," marked "by remarkable strength of language and equally remarkable inattention to
facts." [25] To Elliott's mind, Bascom's production elevated the civil
powers over the ecclesiastical and adduced a doctrine of the episcopacy
"which leads to Puseyism and ends in Popery." [26] That it was an influence just at the time the convention was about to be assembled
seems incontestable.

2

Effects of the Louisville Convention

Since the work of the Louisville Convention in 1845 has already been
treated in the preceding chapter, it is unnecessary to speak of it here.
The sense of the importance of the decision demanded of the delegates
a ritualistic rehearsal of the reasons for separation, and the nearly
unanimous acceptance of the long report of the Committee on Organization and its seven resolutions established clearly the ultimate adoption of the name and polity of the Methodist Episcopal Church, South.

Bishops Soule and Andrew were invited to become its "regular and
constitutional" bishops under an organization which differed only by
"verbal alterations" from that provided by the *Discipline* of the Methodist Episcopal Church, although it was clear that the interpretation
of the role of a bishop differed from that of the majority in the
North. Bishop Andrew accepted the invitation immediately; Bishop
Soule chose to accept with the proviso that he should first "carry out
the official plan of Episcopal Visitations as settled by the Bishops in
New York." The consequences of Soule's decision have already been
noted in the Ohio Annual Conference of 1845.

Thus was the organization of the new church provided for. Similar
in almost every respect save in general attitude toward one social and
economic institution and toward one aspect of episcopal governance, the
church in the South was the "logical and inevitable consequence" [27]
of forces at work in shaping the destiny of the whole country. In the
parallels between events in the church and those in the nation, the
Southern insistence on retention of the *Discipline* with only such verbal

[25] *Ibid.*, p. 253.
[26] Elliott, *History of the Great Secession*, cols. 466-67.
[27] Norwood, *The Schism in the M. E. Church*, p. 100.

alterations as were indicated by the change in title has its counterpart in the later action of the Confederate States to adopt the United States constitution almost without change.

The interval between the Louisville Convention and the 1846 General Conference of the newly formed Methodist Episcopal Church, South, which it established, was filled with the actions of the individual Southern Annual Conferences, voting, one after another, following the lead of Kentucky: to declare their adherence to the Methodist Episcopal Church, South; to insist on no change in the *Discipline;* and to commend the conduct of Soule and Andrew.[28]

In the Northern conferences there was less agreement; but even there, one discerns some drawing together in opposition to the South. New England was relatively calm, except for some debate over the question of its present temper, whether it was abolitionist or merely antislavery. Editor Abel Stevens of *Zion's Herald* seemed to feel that the New England church had relaxed into the latter position; others disagreed. Everywhere the question of the constitutionality of the Plan of Separation was debated with even more vigor now that the South had assumed its validity and acted upon that assumption. And, of course, the problem of how or whether the Book Concern property should be divided followed upon the larger question. Both Bangs, who felt the action of the General Conference was constitutional, and Bond, who felt that it was not, agreed that the property should be divided as provided in the Plan. Others, like Peter Cartwright, James B. Finley, and Dr. Elliott, were not convinced.

In August, 1845, appeared George Peck's answer to Bascom's *Review.*[29] Temperate and objective in tone, for the most part, it nevertheless demonstrates the impossibility, given their separate orientations and prejudices, of the two churches at that date finding any area of agreement in the interpretation of the same facts and actions. Peck's arguments gained the full indorsement of the Northern Methodist papers; Bascom had nothing but praise from the Southern press, and even the non-Methodist political leaders joined the chorus. John C. Calhoun felt that the conduct of Southern leaders "was such as became patriots and Christians." [30] Henry Clay denied lack of sympathy with the sepa-

---

[28] For a full account of the conferences' actions, see *History of the Organization of the Methodist Episcopal Church, South* (Nashville: Compiled and Published by the Editors and Publishers of the South-Western Christian Advocate, for the M. E. Church, South, by order of the Louisville Convention. William Cameron, Printer, 1845), pp. 246-54.

[29] *Slavery and the Episcopacy: Being an Examination of Dr. Bascom's Review* (New York: Lane and Tippett, 1845).

[30] Letter from Calhoun to T. B. Stevenson, dated July 7, 1845; quoted by Elliott, *History of the Great Secession,* col. 520.

ration but asserted profound regret "for the cause which brought it about." [31] Peck defended the action of the General Conference in the case of Bishop Andrew. He was not inclined to defend its action on the Plan of Separation. Few in the North were.

3

The First General Conference of the Southern Church (1846)

The actions of the first General Conference of the Methodist Episcopal Church, South, meeting in Petersburg, Virginia, in May, 1846, have been treated in detail in the preceding chapter. Here it is necessary only to recall that none of the motions and resolutions suggesting change in the *Discipline* gained majority approval. If many of the delegates agreed with Dr. Boring "that slavery, as it exists in the United States, being a civil institution, *as set forth in the plan of organization of the M. E. Church, South,* is not a proper subject of ecclesiastical legislation," [32] they were not inclined to put it into the *Discipline*. Instead, the majority sentiment held with William Winans that, while the slavery legislation was wrong, it appeared inexpedient to make changes. What he and most of the others feared was the sensitivity of the border conferences to any action on the slavery issue and the way the proposed action might bear upon the question of whether the South had seceded or had been legally separated. From New York, Dr. Bond's comment was that "the lullaby of 'the same Church because the same Discipline,' must still be sung." [33]

The letter to the General Conference from Lane and Tippett, the agents of the Book Concern, saying that they could pay no more dividends to the bishops and conferences which united with the Methodist Episcopal Church, South, until directions were received from the 1848 General Conference of the Northern Church, drew much fire. At first, some members of the conference had been for sending an immediate and rather warm reply to the book agents, but cooler heads prevailed, the matter was referred to the finance committee, and, finally, the long

[31] Letter from Clay to T. B. Stevenson, dated August 12, 1845; quoted by Elliott, *History of the Great Secession*, cols. 520-521.
[32] *Christian Advocate and Journal*, June 10, 1846, p. 174.
[33] *Ibid.*, May 20, 1846, p. 162.

answer was approved by the conference in which the propriety of withholding money from the Southern Annual Conferences was seriously
questioned in view of the provisions of the Plan of Separation and the
evident justice of the Southern claim.

The emphasis upon missions in the Petersburg General Conference
had its connection with the relationship between the two churches.
It seems hardly fair to view this emphasis, as some in the Northern
conferences were inclined to, as owing primarily to a felt need to justify
the church by its expansion or to assuage feelings of guilt over the stand
on slavery. Much of the strength of the mission movement in the
Methodist Episcopal Church had always been in the South. It is not
so strange that the report of the Committee on Missions should have
paid special attention to the interests of the slave population and
stressed that "the duty [of giving the gospel to the slave population] is
binding on all, according to their ability, and it is binding on all as
they are severally able, with the same force of indispensable obligation." [34] The further adoption by the conference of the recommendation that missionaries be sent to China, that a mission to the Jews be
undertaken, and that a mission be sent to some place in Africa might
be seen as stemming from the same impulse. The New York *Christian
Advocate* suggested, however, that perhaps Dr. Longstreet and Dr.
Bascom might be sent "to convince the people of Africa that slavery
is 'a divine institution.' " [35]

Memorials were received by the General Conference in connection
with disputes in the border conferences. Difficulties in Maysville, Kentucky, led to a resolution that each Annual Conference was to supply
one hundred dollars to pay expenses incurred in a suit over the ownership of the church there. A petition from the Westmoreland Circuit of
the Baltimore Conference was received, expressing the desire of that circuit to be annexed to the Methodist Episcopal Church, South. The
Committee on Boundaries struggled with the problem of defining the
Kentucky and Virginia Conferences in such a way as to include Soule
Chapel of Cincinnati and the Kanawha District in the former and the
Westmoreland Circuit in the latter. Its full report with these inclusions
was adopted on the last day.

Also on the last day of the conference, May 23, at the motion of
Fountain Pitts of the Tennessee Conference, the conference "by a rising and unanimous vote" resolved: "That Dr. Lovick Pierce be, and
is hereby, delegated to visit the General Conference of the M. E. Church,

[34] *Journal of the General Conference of the Methodist Episcopal Church, South,* 1846,
p. 66.
[35] *Christian Advocate and Journal,* May 20, 1846, p. 162.

to be held in Pittsburgh, May 1, 1848, to tender to that body the Christian regards and fraternal salutations of the General Conference of the Methodist Episcopal Church, South." [36] The action was taken with what appeared to be a spontaneous feeling of good will born partly out of the sense of solid achievement which the General Conference of 1846 was certainly justified in feeling. It was an action, however, which was to bring increased bitterness and to enlarge the gap between the Methodist Episcopal Church and the Methodist Episcopal Church, South.

Where the Louisville Convention had glanced only indirectly at the problems of the area most violently affected by the slavery controversy throughout the years of disagreement, the General Conference of 1846 had had to face some of them head on. Difficulties in the border conferences had been directly involved in the study of the charges made by the Northern editors against the Southern bishops, and we have noted several conference actions in connection with memorials from embattled districts. To some extent the border conferences seem the battlefield where the infantry clashed, while the heavy propaganda guns, securely entrenched in the antislavery North and the proslavery South, fired salvos which fell short of their targets but which devastated the territory in between. If some of the troubles had been dimly foreseen at the 1844 conference, certainly the Plan of Separation was too vague and ambiguous in its specific terms to do more than encourage their growth.

4

The Fight for the Border Conferences

The Plan, it will be remembered, established what would seem to have been four fundamental principles concerning the territory along the tentative dividing line between the Methodist Episcopal Church and the area which was to become part of the Methodist Episcopal Church, South. First, the dividing line between the current slaveholding and nonslaveholding conferences should be the basic division between the churches. It could be modified or adjusted in compliance with

[36] *Journal of the General Conference*, 1846, pp. 100-101. Redford, *History of the Organization of the M. E. Church, South*, p. 511, includes the provision for the bishops to appoint a substitute in case of the inability of Dr. Pierce to attend.

other provisions of the Plan, but it constituted the starting place.[37] Second, "societies, stations, and conferences" on this line could, by majority vote, decide to adhere to the Southern Church. Third, when such a vote had registered the allegiance of the society, station, or conference to either the Methodist Episcopal Church or the Southern Church, the ministers of the one church were not to attempt to organize churches or societies within the territory so designated as under the jurisdiction of the other church. And fourth, only those stations, societies, and conferences directly on the border, not interior within any established jurisdiction, were to be allowed to make this choice. These provisions left many questions unanswered, and herein lay the seeds of much of the future trouble. Also, in the disparity of the interpretations of the Plan's provisions, we have a measure of the distance across the gulf between North and South.

Precisely what constituted a border society as opposed to an interior society? The line had been marked and provision made for stations, societies, and conferences adjacent to that line to declare allegiance one way or the other. But suppose a society adjacent to the line voted to adhere South—did this then change the location of the line so that another society was now adjacent to the line with the privilege of choosing its allegiance? And if this second society changed, what then? The North tended to feel that only the station, society, or conference whose territory was originally contiguous to the line had been intended to have the choice.[38] The South thought that an endless chain of proselyting was possible and that one society after another might vote to adhere either South or North until blocked by a society voting oppositely.

Must each of the stations, societies, and conferences on the Northern side of the border actually vote one way or the other in order to satisfy the provisions of the Plan? The North felt that the Plan was devised for the Southerners wishing to separate. Adherence to the original Methodist Episcopal Church could be assumed unless one of the specified bodies actually wished to test the wishes of its membership. Absence of vote was a vote for the *status quo*. The South, on the other hand, felt that the prohibition against extending the pastoral reach of its ministry only held where territories had actually voted to adhere North, otherwise they were free to establish such beachheads as, for instance, Soule Chapel in Cincinnati.

How long could the voting continue under the Plan of Separation?

[37] See Thomas B. Neely, *American Methodism: Its Divisions and Unification* (New York: Fleming H. Revell, 1915), pp. 110-16, for an extended discussion of this aspect of the Plan of Separation.

[38] "Where Is the Dividing Line?" *Christian Advocate and Journal,* February 4, 1846, p. 102.

On the whole, the North felt that the time for making the choice was a limited one; that is, a time limit was intended in the voting on the Sixth Restrictive Rule by the Annual Conferences, and some such limit was also intended in connection with the determination of the border. The position most common in the South took the view that a time limit for this choice was not intended.

Why were circuits not mentioned specifically in the Plan as it was presented? The South said, in effect, that they were intended, even though not specifically mentioned, because Methodist usage made stations, societies, and circuits synonymous and that, therefore, as units of the organization of the Methodist conferences, circuits could properly exercise the same option of adherence granted the other organizing units. The North maintained that circuits were deliberately excepted from the units which were to vote, and that the framers of the Plan, in this instance, had meant precisely what they said, nothing more.

Actually the conflict over the meaning of the Plan of Separation in regard to the border conferences reached its height early in 1847. The bishops of the Methodist Episcopal Church, meeting in Philadelphia on March 3-4, issued a series of resolutions which followed the line taken by the chief Northern editors. The bishops held that the Plan of Separation provided for "taking the votes by conferences, stations, and societies and not by circuits in fixing their church relations"; that the bishops would consider that the time for taking such votes in any of these divisions ran out at the time of the next regular Annual Conference after the organization of the Methodist Episcopal Church, South; that, when a border society or station north of the line of separation had received an assigned preacher from the Methodist Episcopal Church without remonstrance after the formation of the Methodist Episcopal Church, South, it could be assumed that this action finally fixed the church relation of that station; and that, because of the Chesapeake Bay boundary on the south, the Eastern Shore region of Maryland and Virginia would not be considered border territory within the meaning of the Plan adopted by the General Conference of 1844.[39]

These pronouncements of the Northern bishops brought renewed Southern concern. Editor Lee, in the *Richmond Christian Advocate* for April 1, 1847, called attention to the errors of the bishops. Editor Wightman, in the *Southern Christian Advocate* for April 9, expressed the belief that the bishops were nullifying the Plan of Separation by their interpretation and action—although the North might have complained equally that the bishops were assuming the validity of the Plan of Separation when it was fast becoming apparent that the Plan was to

[39] Elliott, *History of the Great Secession,* cols. 578-79.

be rejected, if indeed it had ever had legal status. Both Bishop Soule and Bishop Capers of the Southern Church entered the lists to record different interpretations. Capers' position seems to have been that the original line of separation was the Mason and Dixon Line. Wightman later remembered that in 1847, since "excitement was running high in the 'border' circuits, . . . it was thought desirable that [Bishop Capers] should travel through them." [40] And the bishop's exclamation on this trip reveals something of the attitude in that quarter: "No wonder that the Baltimore preachers feel sore. To lose such a country, and such a people! and with the aggravation of knowing that the loss is to be continually increasing, till all this fine portion of the Old Dominion has adhered South." [41] Bishop Soule, recognizing the difficulty of a literal interpretation of the Plan, attempted an interpretation "in the sense of the General Conference" which was not concerned with geographical boundaries but with a rule or regulation for societies which might be divided.[42] The North concluded that Bishop Capers claimed all the slaveholding states for the South, that Bishop Soule would add all those portions of the Northern conferences which might be induced to unite with the new church, and that the division of opinion between the Northern and Southern bishops was so sharp that "it is hard to say whether the plan means any thing at all." [43]

The arguments over the theoretical aspects of the border division were, of course, only reflections of practical difficulties and constant alarms which kept both churches agitated. On Sunday, July 12, 1846, the Rev. Valentine Gray of the Philadelphia Conference, while attempting to preach at Salem in the Northampton Circuit on the eastern shore of Virginia, had been interrupted in his conduct of the service by a mob which attempted to get him to leave a pulpit which he refused to leave voluntarily.

One of them came into the pulpit and took hold of my arm, while some cried, "Pull him over the top of the pulpit." Several of them reached over the pulpit, but could not get hold of me. While the one in the pulpit had me by the arm, another got upon a bench, and reaching over, caught me by the coat collar and cravat, and choked me considerably, also pulled my hair. Two or three others came into the pulpit and forced me out of it.[44]

When Gray still refused to leave, "they then seized hold of me again, and forced me out of the church. During this struggle they tore my coat."

[40] Wightman, *Life of Capers*, p. 420.
[41] *Ibid.*, p. 422.
[42] Elliott, *History of the Great Secession*, col. 581.
[43] *Ibid.*, col. 582.
[44] *Christian Advocate and Journal*, October 21, 1846, p. 42.

When Gray attempted to secure some kind of redress from the county court at Eastville the next day, he again encountered the hostile mob, and he concludes his story: "So I have been driven away without redress or protection." [45]

In commenting upon Gray's subjection to this kind of mob action, Dr. Bond blames two principal causes. He points first of all to remarks made before the quarterly meeting of the Northampton Circuit by John Early in which Dr. Early warned the people of the danger of suffering Northern preachers to have access to their slaves and pictured the Northern Church as composed wholly of abolitionists. The second, and perhaps more important, cause was not directly connected with Methodism. At a public meeting of the citizens of Accomac County, an address was delivered by Judge George P. Scarborough in which he harangued the people, "firmly remonstrating with the Methodists . . . , impressing upon them the dangers which [might] result to the safety of the people, and calling upon them . . . to sever their connection with the [Philadelphia] Conference . . . , and attach themselves to the Virginia Conference." [46] Later Bond secured the text of Scarborough's address and made this the occasion for a whole series of long editorials addressed to the Honorable Judge Scarborough of Accomac County, Virginia, in which Bond once again traveled the disputed course taken by the General Conference in its actions on the Rev. Mr. Harding and Bishop Andrew and the Plan of Separation and made this the occasion for complaints concerning the action of Judge Scarborough and the Southern attitude.[47]

Judge Scarborough's influence may have been felt in another affair which happened about four months after Gray was ejected from the pulpit in Salem. The incident took place at Guilford in Accomac County. The Rev. James Hargis had started his sermon, when a mob of rioters appeared. The mob commenced "shooting around the church, throwing missiles against it, and hallooing to such a degree" that some of the congregation left the church. Hargis, unable to proceed, invited his tormentors to come in and take seats so that he might talk to them. They refused, but they prevented the service from continuing and told Hargis that "if he came there any more they would put him in the mill-pond, which is near by." [48]

An editorial in the *Christian Advocate and Journal* for January 13,

[45] *Ibid.*

[46] *Christian Advocate and Journal,* November 11, 1846, p. 54.

[47] *Christian Advocate and Journal,* issues of January and February, 1847, pp. 10, 14, 18, 22, and 26.

[48] *Christian Advocate and Journal,* January 6, 1847, p. 2. See also Elliott, *History of the Great Secession,* col. 588.

1847, is entitled "Evils of the Division—Mournful Scenes Preparing on the Border." Here the editor recapitulates the Northern grievances against the "Superintendents of the new Church" who sent preachers "to the Eastern Shore of Virginia, Northampton circuit, in the Philadelphia Conference, and to a station in Cincinnati, and to Parkersburg, both within the bounds of the Ohio Annual Conference."

Parkersburg, Virginia (now West Virginia), in the Ohio Conference, was an early focal point of disturbance, as was, in fact, the whole of the Kanawha Valley region. After the Louisville Convention the question of affiliation North or South came to a vote and was decided in favor of the South by a rather narrow margin. This was reported to the Ohio Conference in 1845 by the Rev. Arza Brown, whose bias was Northern, as about an equal division of opinion, with the Methodist Episcopal Church faction strongly desirous of receiving a preacher as usual. The conference sent the Rev. John Dillon, whereupon the indignant opposing factions aligned themselves against the new preacher. A board of trustees had been called together in some haste before his arrival. They decided to refuse to receive any preacher sent by the Ohio Conference and closed the church against Dillon. The Northern adherents forced an entrance, and on Sunday, "notwithstanding the great disturbance made by a crowd around the church, and by some persons in the basement, he preached." [49] The next day a "committee of sixty" was appointed at an indignation meeting to wait on Mr. Dillon and give him five days to leave town before he was forcibly removed. The same report of the incident mentions that the Rev. Mr. Brown, returning to Parkersburg to remove his family, was threatened with a coat of tar and feathers.

In Cincinnati the conflict took on a slightly different form, although it is difficult at this distance to discern very clearly what happened. After the Ohio Conference of 1845, at which Bishop Soule was refused the right to preside, the presiding elder Michael Marley gave the missionary G. W. Maley permission to preach in the old Vine Street Church in the heart of the city. About ninety of the Cincinnati Methodists obtained transfer certificates to join the Vine Street membership and then voted unanimously to adhere to the South. Papers were presented to Bishop Andrew, who thereupon recognized the Vine Street group as a society of the Southern Church, a border society. The group then bought a new meeting house, which they named Soule Chapel. Between it and the tentative borderline interposed the Bethel charge of the Methodist Episcopal Church.[50]

[49] *Western Christian Advocate*, October 3, 1845, p. 98.
[50] See Norwood, *The Schism in the M. E. Church*, pp. 138-40, for the clearest account of the Cincinnati situation. It is the basis for the present version.

As John Norwood has pointed out, whatever the misunderstandings which permitted the situation to develop, Soule Chapel represents the "aggressive southern interpretation of the Plan of Separation which allowed the South to enter any unit north of the tentative line which had neglected to declare its continued allegiance to the old church." [51] Because the Ohio Conference had not voted (it had only rejected Soule), it did not matter whether Soule Chapel was a border society or not, in the Southern view. In any event, it was another brand for the fire of controversy.

In the fall of 1847, Bishop Soule established a Methodist Episcopal Church, South, district in the Guyandotte area of West Virginia, principally within the bounds of the Ohio Conference and its Kanawha and Guyandotte districts. In this move the situation concerning majorities and minorities may have been misrepresented to him, but it seemed to the Northern editors and others that the rights of the Northern Methodists had been infringed here, as in many other places, by unauthorized actions of the Southern bishops.

In St. Louis, in Mark Twain's Hannibal—in fact, in much of Missouri, where Southern adherents were particularly strong in their representation of the Methodist Episcopal Church as an abolitionist church—there were many incidents calculated to increase bitterness and tension. Two letters to the *Western Christian Advocate,* published on March 6, 1846, tell of injustices, congregations split, and voting manipulated to misrepresent the general will of the people involved. In Covington, Kentucky; in Washington, Arkansas; in Westmoreland and Warrenton, Virginia, the patterns of conflict repeat themselves. Legal actions in Alexandria, Virginia, were results of the border warfare, as it has been termed. Much of the spirit of the whole controversy as we have seen it was involved in the events at Maysville; furthermore, those events terminated in a legal suit which prophetically looked forward to the United States Supreme Court decision in connection with the Book Concern property.

The troubles at Maysville, located in Mason County, Kentucky, on the Ohio River, commenced after the Louisville Convention. Previous to its meeting, few Methodists had voted for separation. After it, two factions developed. The presiding elder, the preacher, and apparently the largest number of officials were Southern sympathizers. The other party was led by the layman John Armstrong and by Dr. Tomlinson,

[51] *Ibid.,* p. 139.

president of Augusta College. A heated campaign was waged. On August 31, 1845, was held the meeting at which the vote concerning affiliation was taken. Of those present, 109 voted to go with the South and 97 to remain with the old church. However, there had been some confusion over preliminary petitions circulated before the meeting for signature, and it was said that some of the Northern sympathizers remained away from the meeting under the misapprehension that they had already registered their vote. Indeed, 139 had signed the preliminary petition indicating their desire to remain with the Methodist Episcopal Church.[52] Before the secretary's report was sent to the Ohio Conference, someone added the names of some thirty-three absent members who were for adherence to the North. Thus the South claimed a majority of the formal meeting; the North, a majority of the whole charge.

Bishop Hamline, when the report was received by the Ohio Conference, found the proceedings too irregular to justify his sending a preacher to Maysville until there should be a formal meeting and evidence of a clear majority. Meanwhile, however, Dr. Tomlinson agreed to preach for them, and not long after, the presiding elder Michael Marley sent the Rev. Mr. Lawder to serve the charge and attached it to the Augusta Circuit. The Kentucky Conference, on the other hand, received the information about the vote in the formal meeting and sent the Rev. Mr. Grubbs to serve the church.

From announcements which appeared in the papers it became apparent that Dr. Tomlinson and Mr. Grubbs would be preaching in the same church at the same time. John Armstrong suggested a division of the time to permit both groups to use the meeting house at different hours. The offer was rejected, and the Northern group, acting upon advice of counsel, closed the meeting house. But Mr. Grubbs and his congregation reopened the building and held services. The Northern group countered by appealing to the court in Mason County, securing an injunction, and ultimately gaining a decree from Judge Reed ordering both groups to use the property jointly. The Southern group, with the financial support granted at the 1846 General Conference, took its appeal to the highest state court. This court set aside the lower court's decision and gave exclusive use of the meeting house to the South. This decision, handed down on July 27, 1847, was hailed everywhere in the South as an indication of the legal justification for the Southern position

[52] John Armstrong, "A Voice from Kentucky," *Christian Advocate and Journal*, February 25, 1846, p. 113. See also the excellent summary in Norwood, *The Schism in the M. E. Church*, pp. 142-44.

generally. And, of course, the Maysville opinion was just as widely denounced in the Methodist Episcopal Church.

Such instances of conflicts within and about the border conferences are legion. In judging their importance in the history of Methodism, one must remember, however, that individual Methodists were sometimes involved in conflicts over slavery which did not have anything to do directly with the church. Dr. John McClintock, for instance, rather innocently became involved in the Carlisle riots in June of 1847, when he offered to interpret the new Pennsylvania law concerning the rights of slaveowners and fugitive slaves. And, while he had acted as an individual under the direction of a social conscience, the storm of controversy and misunderstanding over the part that he played in defending the Negroes from unfair treatment brought the Methodists at Dickinson College and Dr. McClintock's friends all over the country into the situation. Since he was subsequently invited to take the presidencies of Genesee Seminary and of Allegheny College, a professorship at Wesleyan University, and the editorship of *The Methodist Quarterly Review,* it could be assumed that his actions were widely discussed, even if they had not been a matter of newspaper debate.[53] There was ample opportunity for feelings to be aroused even apart from the church strife. There was a widespread agitation over fugitive slaves and other manifestations of the "peculiar institution," and this agitation supplies a further source for the troubles which beset Methodism within the border areas.

Nevertheless, the border conflicts form a most important part of the climate under which the General Conference of 1848 met. They were a constant conditioning factor in church debates and newspaper controversies, because whatever was said anywhere was likely to be said with a weather eye on its effect upon the border territory. The border territory, then, was more than a source of igniting sparks. It was also, and in something like direct proportion to the distance the speaker was from the borderline itself, a conservative force acting to moderate positions. The North ridiculed the Southern Church's retention of the antislavery provisions of the *Discipline,* it is true. It is equally evident, however, that the rivalry to retain the border territory caused the antislavery sentiments of many Northern spokesmen to be couched in moderate terms, and it was 1860 before a stronger antislaveholding statement was adopted by the General Conference of the Methodist Episcopal Church.

[53] Crooks, *Life of M'Clintock,* pp. 145-85.

5

The 1848 General Conference of the Northern Church

As the 1848 General Conference of the Northern Church prepared to meet, the border troubles were particularly acute, although, if Dr. McClintock was right, there was a lull before the storm. In January, 1848, he wrote: "The Church controversy makes less stir than it did; but that is because men's minds are made up to break the plan of separation to pieces next May, and begin our missionary work South as well as North." [54] The actions of the Annual Conferences had swung strongly, as we have already seen, against the Plan of Separation and in favor of reversing the 1844 General Conference. The North Ohio Conference in August, 1845, had announced that it viewed the Southern separation as secession and resolved to request the General Conference of 1848 to ask provision for those brethren who wished to adhere to the Methodist Episcopal Church even though they were located inside the Southern borderline. The next month the Ohio Conference went on record as holding the Plan of Separation unconstitutional and a nullity and protested against the use of the word "North" in any designation of the Methodist Episcopal Church. The Illinois Conference had added that only Annual Conferences had the power to pass on the constitutionality of General Conference actions and praised Drs. Bond and Elliott, commenting that "the unmerited abuse which the Southern editors, and others," have heaped upon them "deserves the stern rebuke of all the friends of the Church." [55]

The sentiment to reverse the action of the 1844 General Conference ran strongly when it was time to select the delegates for the 1848 Conference, to be held in Pittsburgh. George Peck, in reporting his election by the New York Conference, commented:

The four years had been without precedent for stormy discussion and a spirit of revolution. During the whole period the Methodist papers, North and South, had been engaged in fierce controversies whose tendency was only to inflame and alienate. On the border . . . the war of passion raged till charity wept, and what had been a united, prosperous Church, now presented the appearance of two hostile armies. This conflict was at its height when the General Conference met.[56]

---

[54] *Ibid.*, p. 186.
[55] *Western Christian Advocate*, October 10, 1845, p. 103.
[56] Peck, *Life and Times*, p. 319.

While Dr. Peck was re-elected for the General Conference, the number of those who had voted for the Plan of Separation and who survived the change in sentiment was not large. Nathan Bangs, who missed only this one General Conference of all those from 1808 to 1852, attributed this failure to a "current of prejudice" which ran against him because of his defense of the constitutionality of the 1844 action on the Plan of Separation.[57] Edward Myers pointed out that only 41 of the 142 voting delegates who had attended the 1844 General Conference were returned to the General Conference of 1848. Further, of these 41, 11 had originally voted against the Plan of Separation. In other words, only 30 delegates who had voted *for* the adoption of the Report of the Committee of Nine were re-elected.[58]

Bishop Hedding called the General Conference to order on the first day of May in 1848, in the Liberty Street Methodist Episcopal Church, Pittsburgh. After the opening prayers and hymns, the presentation of credentials, and the election of Joseph Trimble of the Ohio Conference as secretary, the bishop announced that the superintendents had decided not to make a formal Episcopal Address to this conference. Instead, now in his eleventh General Conference, he spoke briefly concerning the gravity of the problems to be faced and the importance of prayer in the facing of them. Then the regular business of the conference was undertaken as committees were appointed and the conference organized. Matthew Simpson offered the resolution calling for a Committee on the State of the Church, to be composed of two members from each delegation. Although some thought the number too many, the motion carried, and the conference's most important committee was established.

On the second day some of the large number of memorials of grievances from the border churches and societies as a result of the division of the church were presented. These continued to pour in and to be referred to the Committee on the State of the Church. The credentials of the Canadian delegates were received, and as Dr. Green was present, he was invited within the bar of the conference. So, too, on the third day, were received the credentials of the Rev. James Dixon, appointed by the Wesleyan Connection of England, who thereupon addressed the conference and included a regret for the "sad division which has occurred between the North and the South" and the assurance that "our sympathies are entirely on the side of the emancipation of slaves." [59]

[57] Abel Stevens, *Life and Times of Nathan Bangs* (New York: Carlton and Porter, 1863), p. 375.

[58] Myers, *Disruption of the M. E. Church*, p. 144.

[59] *Daily Christian Advocate*, May 4, 1848.

The Problem of Fraternal Relations

In contrast to the Rev. Mr. Dixon's reception, and immediately after several more memorials concerning difficulties stemming from the division, came an event which was to have many repercussions and which, even now, poses many problems in interpretation. The *Daily Christian Advocate* reported simply that a communication was presented from "Dr. L. Pierce, a representative of the M. E. Church, South," and that the communication was referred to the Committee on the State of the Church. In an editorial comment about it, William Hunter characterized the letter as one of inquiry and speculated that it was referred to the committee with the tacit understanding that it would sleep in that committee. He thought that Pierce would have done better to have presented his credentials at once, although in correcting his view the next day, he had been given to understand that the credentials were in Bishop Soule's possession and the latter had not yet arrived.

It will be remembered that the first General Conference of the Methodist Episcopal Church, South, had appointed Dr. Pierce a delegate to the Pittsburgh Conference "to tender to that body the Christian regards and fraternal salutations of the General Conference of the Methodist Episcopal Church, South." [60]

In view of the arguments which arose over the treatment of Dr. Pierce, it is worth examining his letter, which he addressed "to the Bishops and Members of the Methodist Episcopal Church, in General Conference assembled":

Reverend and Dear Brethren:—The General Conference of the Methodist Episcopal Church, South, appointed me as their delegate to bear to you the Christian salutations of the Church, South, and to assure you that they sincerely desire that the two great bodies of Wesleyan Methodists, North and South, should maintain at all times a warm, confiding, and brotherly, fraternal relation to each other; and that through me they make this offer to you, and very ardently desire that you, on your part, will accept the offer in the same spirit of brotherly love and kindness.

The acceptance or rejection of this proposition, made by your Southern brethren, is entirely at your disposal; and as my situation is one of painful solicitude until this question is decided, you will allow me to beg your earliest attention to it.

And I would farther say, that your reply to this communication will most gratify me if it is made officially in the form of resolutions.

[60] *Journal of the General Conference,* 1846, p. 101.

I have the honor to be, very respectfully, yours in the unity of Wesleyan Methodism,

L. Pierce, Delegate from the M.E. Church, South.

Pittsburgh, May 3, 1848.[61]

As Bishop Neely has pointed out, Pierce's letter could hardly have been better designed to evoke a negative response from the conference.[62] In the first place, it reached the conference before Pierce's credentials were presented. In the second place, it goes well beyond the commission given Pierce by the General Conference of the Southern Church. By inserting the paragraph concerning the acceptance or rejection of the proposal of the Southern brethren, he effectively introduced the notion that there might be a question as to whether the conference would be willing to accept him as a fraternal delegate. In addition, the request for a reply to be made in the "form of resolutions" would seem to be suggesting to the conference what would be proper procedure and, even more likely to arouse opposition, that important official consequences waited upon the reply of the conference, as though, perhaps, the legal status of the Southern Church were involved. Thus to express himself as painfully solicitous or anxious about the action of the conference and, at the same time, to seem to be desiring to put the conference on record in a hasty action could hardly have had any outcome except to put the delegates on guard, even to arouse suspicion.

On Friday, the fifth day of the conference, George Peck reported for the Committee on the State of the Church. This committee recommended the adoption of the following resolution accompanied by a brief preamble:

Whereas, a letter from Rev. L. Pierce, D.D., delegate of the Methodist E. Church South, proposing fraternal relations between the Methodist Episcopal Church and the M. E. Church South, has been presented to this Conference, and whereas, there are serious questions and difficulties existing between the two bodies; therefore,

Resolved, That while we tender to the Rev. Dr. Pierce all personal courtesies, and invite him to attend our sessions, this General Conference does not consider it proper, at present, to enter into fraternal relations with the Methodist E. Church, South.[63]

After considerable debate, much of it concerned with the effect of

---

[61] Quoted here from Redford, *History of the Organization of the M. E. Church, South,* pp. 533-34.

[62] Neely, *American Methodism,* pp. 72-86.

[63] *Daily Christian Advocate,* May 6, 1848.

such an action in the border states and with the precise intention of
the motion, it was amended at the motion of Dr. Tomlinson to include
the following:

Provided, however, that nothing in this resolution shall be so construed as to
operate as a bar to any propositions from Dr. Pierce, or any other representative
of the Methodist E. Church South, towards the settlement of existing difficulties
between that body and this.[64]

With the amendment, the committee's recommendation was adopted
unanimously, although a motion the next day, designed to make it clear
that Dr. Pierce was invited within the bar of the conference, was readily
adopted. To the whole matter, the General Conference had devoted
more than a full day's attention. Its action is a commentary upon the
relations between the two churches, although the motives of the prin-
cipals are not easy to discern clearly. On May 9, the same day on which
his official credentials were presented to the conference, Dr. Pierce sent
the following letter to the "bishops and members" of the General Conference:

Reverend and Dear Brethren:—I have received two extracts from your Journal of the 4th and 5th instant. From these extracts I learn you decline receiving
me in my proper character, as the accredited delegate of the M. E. Church, South,
and only invite me to a seat within the bar as due to me on account of my
private and personal merits. These considerations I shall appreciate, and will
reciprocate them in all the private and social walks of life. But within the bar
of the General Conference I can only be known in my official character.

You will therefore regard this communication as final on the part of the M. E.
Church, South. She can never renew the offer of fraternal relations between the
two great bodies of Wesleyan Methodists in the United States. But the proposition can be renewed at any time, either now or hereafter, by the M. E. Church.
And if ever made upon the basis of the Plan of Separation, as adopted by the
General Conference of 1844, the Church, South, will cordially entertain the
proposition.

With sentiments of deep regret, and with feelings of disappointed hopes, I
am yours, in Christian fellowship.[65]

The authoritativeness with which Dr. Pierce undertakes to speak for
the Southern Church in declaring that his letter is its final communication, that there can be no further renewal of the offer of fraternal
relations, and that henceforth any such offer must come from the Northern Church, is puzzling. It lends support to the view that Dr. Pierce

[64] *Ibid.*

[65] *Journal of the General Conference of the Methodist Episcopal Church, South,* 1850,
p. 190. Redford, *History of the Organization,* pp. 537-38, terms the letter "replete with
manly and Christian sentiments."

"came with the desire, if not a plan, to score a diplomatic and controversial point, rather than to win the Conference and to remove the difficulties." [66] He seems to have come to Pittsburgh to get himself formally recognized and to get the General Conference committed to a position. If he failed in this, he succeeded in becoming something of a *cause célèbre* and in making his rejection a key issue in the conflict between the two churches.

The Repudiation of the Plan of Separation

The second major issue dealt with by the General Conference was the question of the validity of the Plan of Separation. Through days occupied with appeal cases and with what under ordinary circumstances were matters of moment, the Committee on the State of the Church struggled. Before its report was made, the bishops had asked consideration of the possible advisability of the delegated Annual Conference with representatives from each of the Annual Conferences, this conference to assume a judicial function to try appeals and to decide on the constitutionality of conference actions. While the bishops' request did not produce action, the fact that it was made indicates the recognition of the need that had accompanied the debate on the Plan of Separation. On the tenth day the motion to establish a California and Oregon Mission Conference was given back to committee and was to be later approved. On the eleventh a question about the vote of the Annual Conferences on the Sixth Restrictive Rule, in connection with the division of church property, met the response that no report had been received from the Southern conferences which had been connected with the Methodist Episcopal Church when the vote was taken. The General Conference of 1844 had established no method or responsibility for collecting the vote it authorized. On this same matter, communication was received from the commissioners appointed by the Methodist Episcopal Church, South. The Rev. Messrs. Green, Parsons, and Pierce, with John Early, formally announced their presence and preferred the claims of the Southern Church to its share of the Book Concern property. The communication was turned over to the Committee on the State of the Church. A letter from Bishop Soule was read. He requested investigation by the General Conference of charges which he had heard indirectly had been made against him. On the latter matter the conference acted promptly the next day, although there was considerable debate, during which James Finley announced that he was quite prepared to make the charges referred to if necessary. What the conference did was to declare

[66] Neely, *American Methodism,* p. 83.

that, since Bishop Soule had withdrawn from the Methodist Episcopal Church, the General Conference could exercise no ecclesiastical authority over him. The conference could not, therefore, properly act upon the bishop's request.[67]

Finally, on May 24, the Committee on the State of the Church made its report. And there was extended debate before, two days later, a section-by-section vote secured the passage of the recommendation as amended by Matthew Simpson and Daniel Curry. As finally passed, the original wording, to the effect that the General Conference did not possess authority to make a division of the church or to violate the right of an individual to church membership guaranteed by the Fifth Restrictive Rule, was discarded. The conference simply declared that the report of the select Committee of Nine in the 1844 conference was adopted as a peace offering to secure harmony in the Southern borders and was dependent upon the concurrence of three fourths of the members of the Annual Conferences and observance of "certain provisions respecting a boundary by the distinct eccclesiastical connection separating from us, should such a connection be formed." The plan had not been ratified by the Annual Conferences, and the provisions concerning the boundary had been "violated by the highest authorities of said connection"; therefore, the Plan was declared null and void.[68]

The Plan of Separation was thus officially pronounced dead. The tide of opposition which had been building since June of 1844 had attained overwhelming force, and, for better or for worse, the conference of 1848 had undone the work of the 1844 conference, which had been hailed then as Christian, charitable, and equitable. The verdict of history would seem to hold that this new step was mistaken but understandable. Legal questions aside, it is hard to disagree with Professor Norwood when he says that "the Plan was a wonderful exhibition of christian charity, manifested in a situation as baffling as any that ever confronted a great religious assembly," and for one half of the "supposedly dissolved partnership" to "act as judge in its own case" seems hardly fair or sound.[69] Some might argue that the repudiation worked good by simplifying the situation for both the separated churches, but this would be a difficult thesis to maintain in view of the increased bitterness it engendered, the financial limitations it placed on the development of the Southern Church, and the barriers it helped to erect against eventual unification.

The decision against the validity of the Plan of Separation affected directly the decision of the General Conference upon the "property

[67] *Journal of the General Conference of the Methodist Episcopal Church*, 1848, p. 47.
[68] *Ibid.*, pp. 80-85.
[69] Norwood, *The Schism in the M. E. Church*, p. 125.

question," although the South had tried to keep them separate issues. The Annual Conferences had voted upon the suspension of the Sixth Restrictive Rule, as we have already noted, and, while the General Conference had difficulty receiving an official report of the voting, the results were capable of tabulation. The total vote in 1844 and 1845 of all the Annual Conferences showed a clear majority in favor of suspending the rule and, thereby, approving the action of the 1844 General Conference and the division of the Book Concern property. However, the constitutional requirement called for a three-fourth majority, and, even with the almost unanimous Southern vote, it was evident that the majority was not nearly this large.

With an insufficient vote in favor of suspension of the Sixth Restrictive Rule, the conference felt that there was nothing it could do, even if it wished, toward dividing the property. The commissioners from the Methodist Episcopal Church, South, were told that the General Conference had no authority to negotiate with them. It could take no action beyond advising the Northern commissioners to seek legal counsel or to submit the matter to arbitration. And inevitably the situation seemed designed to increase the tension between the churches. To the South it seemed that fair dealing required the division of the Book Concern property, particularly since the majority in the church favored such a division. Furthermore, some of the conferences had given reasons for voting against the division which indicated that they might change their positions. Both the Illinois and Baltimore Conferences had expressed themselves as favoring division of the property but unwilling to approve such a division until a separate church was established, since to do so sooner would encourage separation. The tide had so changed by 1848, however, that the proposal to resubmit the question of suspending the Sixth Restrictive Rule hardly offered a chance of changing the verdict. The South felt it had a clear grievance, that it was being treated unjustly. On the other hand, the North could counter by pointing out that the Southern Church had just assumed the right to the property of the Southern *Advocates;* that a division with the seceding South might encourage such earlier secessionists as the Wesleyans to put in claims; and that the South had not complied with the provisions of the Plan in other respects.

Other Actions

Of course, the General Conference dealt with matters other than those pertaining to the relations between the churches. It considered and acted upon what seemed unending appeal and boundary questions; it pro-

vided for a revision of the hymnbook. It heard and queried Dr. Dixon
of the British Wesleyan Methodist Church. It requested Bishop Hedding to prepare his biography. It appointed Dr. Charles Elliott to write
a history of the past quadrennium, and it elected capable editors to serve
its interests in the periodical presses. Abel Stevens was elected editor
of the *Christian Advocate and Journal* despite a rather stormy earlier
session in which objections to his editorial report of the General Conference for the *Zion's Herald* were recorded; but when he declined, the
appointment went to George Peck. John McClintock was chosen editor
of the *Quarterly Review;* Matthew Simpson, of the *Western Christian
Advocate;* and William Hosmer, of the *Northern Advocate.* But it was
the conference actions on the Plan of Separation and the book funds
which captured most attention and brought the most immediate response.

Shortly after the adjournment Dr. Bascom issued another of his sizable
pamphlets, this one entitled *A Brief Appeal to Public Opinion, in a Series
of Exceptions to the Course and Action of the Methodist Episcopal
Church, from 1844-1848, Affecting the Rights and Interests of the Methodist Episcopal Church, South.* If the title is misleading in its allusion to
brevity, it accurately describes the contents as an "appeal to public
opinion." It repeats all the old arguments, brings them up to date, and
clothes them heavily in invective. It asserts of the Northern Church
that "it is so mixed up with the whole machinery of abolition and
anti-slavery agitation . . . that its own chosen colors will not allow
us any longer to distinguish it from the common enemy. It has become
a pander to political agitation. It is an Abolition church. . . . They
have no fixed principles or settled views. They are the victims of a mania,
constantly involving them in contradiction and inconsistency." [70] George
Peck says of the pamphlet that "the author infused all the asperity and
gall of which he was master. He charged the Methodist Episcopal
Church with 'perjury and subornation of perjury, . . . want of reverence
for the word of God, . . . bad faith, [and] deception utterly irreconcilable
with any virtue belonging to the Christian character.' " [71] Although he
was urged to make formal answer, Peck said that he refrained because he
saw no prospect of any good result. The pamphlet had been written
"to fire the Southern heart" and "to inspire hatred of the North." He
also said that his one brief editorial on the spirit of the "Appeal" and
the "inconclusiveness of its reasoning" brought upon his head the "storm
of southern wrath." [72]

[70] *Brief Appeal* (Louisville: Morton & Griswold, 1848) , p. 61.
[71] *Life and Times,* p. 323.
[72] *Ibid.*

6

The Struggle for the Book Concern Property

In part, Bascom's pamphlet, which was issued by the Southern "Commissioners for the Settlement of the Property Question between the Two Churches," was intended as an explanation and justification for their final action, taken at a meeting on September 9, 1848. There the commissioners, Bishops Soule, Andrew, Capers, and Paine, and the book agent, John Early, agreed that, not having received any proposal from the Northern Church since the adjournment of the General Conference, it was necessary to seek other recourse. They could not avoid "regarding the action of the late General Conference in their attempt at the destruction of the Plan of Separation" as an action which would place in jeopardy "rights and claims previously admitted and provided for." The conference action was "a gross, unlawful trespass, and therefore null and void in all its aspects and bearings." Hence, they resolved "that it is expedient and necessary, in view of the rights and interests in controversy, that the necessary suits be instituted as soon as practicable, for the recovery of the funds and property falling due to the Methodist Episcopal Church, South, under the contract of the Plan of Separation, adopted by the General Conference of 1844." [73] Thus began the phase of the controversy which was termed by Bishop McTyeire the "appeal to Caesar."

Although the commissioners' resolution to institute suits was dated September 9, 1848, no immediate move was made. Meantime, the New York agents had sought legal counsel which advised them "that neither they, nor the General Conference, nor the Annual Conferences, could legally perform any act" toward the division of the Book Concern property and they could not submit the Southern claim to a legal arbitration. In fact, there was nothing they could do, except await legal decision.[74] On December 22, 1848, they so indicated to the Southern commissioners in a letter whose publication renewed Southern charges of a plan to defraud the Southern Church.[75]

Since no suit had in fact been started and the recommendation of the General Conference to seek voluntary arbitration had come to nothing, the Northern bishops went ahead with the proposal to resubmit the sus-

[73] Bascom, *Brief Appeal*, pp. 200-202.
[74] Peck, *Life and Times*, p. 324.
[75] See the *Christian Advocate and Journal* for January 25, 1849, and the *Richmond Christian Advocate* of the same date.

pension of the Sixth Restrictive Rule to the Annual Conferences. The voting commenced in the spring of 1849. The Baltimore, Pittsburgh, and Philadelphia Conferences voted for the suspension almost unanimously. The New England, Troy, Black River, and Providence Conferences, on the other hand, voted by substantial majorities against the proposal. The voting stopped when it was learned that the South had brought suit.

Three suits were filed. The one in Philadelphia involved the Chartered Fund and was never brought to trial; settlement was made without it. The second was filed on June 15, 1849, in the United States Circuit Court for the southern district of New York against George Lane and others. The third was entered about a month later on July 12, 1849, in the United States Circuit Court for the district of Ohio.

The New York case came up for hearing first. Nevertheless, almost two years had elapsed between the filing and the appearance before Judges Nelson and Betts of Daniel Lord, Reverdy Johnson, and his son for the plaintiffs and Rufus Choate, George Wood, and E. L. Fancher for the defendants. Until May 29 the arguments stretched out, and, as they are printed in Sutton's book *The Methodist Church Property Case*,[76] they represent a full and able review of the opinion and evidence on both sides.

At the conclusion of the hearing, Judge Nelson pointed out that it would be some time before a decision would be rendered, and he recommended strongly the advantages of amicable settlement out of court. To this suggestion both parties apparently were willing to listen. In fact, there had been from the beginning a great reluctance on the part of many Methodist Episcopal Church leaders to be settling differences in the civil courts and to appear to be arguing over money. A certain similar feeling would explain the delays by the Southern commissioners in seeking a court decision. A correspondence was begun in 1851 in the hope of establishing some kind of arbitration. The fact that it closed almost immediately is evidence of the depth of divergence between the two viewpoints. To the Methodist Episcopal Church arbitration meant a consideration by arbiters of the whole basis for the claim and, if some measure of it could be allowed, a consideration of plans for a fair division. To the Southern Church the only matter to arbitrate was the size of the South's share and the method of payment. There could be no questioning of the validity of the claim or of the binding nature of the Plan of Separation as a contract. Obviously no meeting of the minds could be achieved, negotiations stopped, and the court had to decide.

[76] (New York: Lane and Scott, 1851). The arguments are ably summarized by Norwood, *Schism*, pp. 164-68.

On November 11, 1851, Judge Nelson delivered the decision of the court in favor of the South. He accepted and repeated most of the Southern attorney's arguments. He gave the opinion that the General Conference of 1844 had proceeded on the assumption that it had the power to erect the church into two separate ecclesiastical establishments, and the Southern conferences, in accepting and acting upon this assumption, had not forfeited their rights to a fund previously held in common. The judge's decision was jubilantly hailed in the South and attacked in the North in all of the church papers except the *Pittsburgh Christian Advocate*, although the attacks by Peck, Bond, and Simpson aimed chiefly at the logic of the decision and the erroneous conception of the nature of the church's government and indicated, at the same time, a willingness to pay the claims.

Meantime, the Ohio suit, filed in July of 1849, was not argued before Judge Leavitt until June of 1852, six months after the New York decision had been rendered, yet its result was exactly opposite. Judge Leavitt found for the defendants on every count. It was his opinion that the General Conference, as a delegated body with limited powers, had no authority to divide the church and that, indeed, the Plan of Separation made no claim to the possession or exercise of such power. As he saw it, the profit of the Book Concern was specifically designated for a particular purpose to be used in a particular way, and the Annual Conferences had refused to sanction any alteration in this use. Any members of the Methodist Episcopal Church could withdraw from that church at any time, but when they did so, they took with them no rights of property. The Southern conferences' withdrawals were voluntary, not induced by positive necessity, and they involved no retention of property rights.

It need hardly be said that feelings were reversed from those which prevailed after the New York hearing. Northerners were highly elated over Judge Leavitt's support of their views. The Southern papers claimed that pressures had overcome clear convictions of "moral equity and legal right," or they expressed great concern over what the decision might mean to widows or orphans who might, by it, "lose their chief means of support." [77]

Some writers in the church papers had urged the Methodist Episcopal Church to appeal the decision in the New York court case, but although there was an announcement in the *Christian Advocate and Journal* for January 1, 1852, no appeal was carried up to the Supreme Court. Instead, Judge McLean, voluntarily taking the initiative, managed to get the agreement of agents on both sides to undertake negotiations toward

[77] *St. Louis Christian Advocate,* October 28, 1852.

a final settlement. [78] Because he chaired the meetings of the agents himself and because the difficulty of appraisal of the Book Concern or of an appeal promised longer delays, difficulties, and costs, the Southern commissioners and the eastern agents worked out the details of a settlement. Under its terms, the Southern Church was awarded a total of $275,000, made up of $191,000 cash, to be paid over a ten-year period, assumed debts, and the valuation of printing presses and equipment at Richmond, Charleston, and Nashville. This agreement was reached in December of 1853.

The suit in Ohio was, on the other hand, appealed by the Southern commissioners to the Supreme Court of the United States. Appealed in time for the December term, 1853, it was not tried until April, 1854. Then the Court, headed by Chief Justice Taney and including Judge McLean, who disqualified himself as an interested Methodist from sitting on the case, and Judge Nelson, who had given the New York decision, heard arguments of the lawyers. For the plaintiffs, it was Henry Stanberry, prompted by William Smith and A. L. P. Green; for the defendants, it was T. Ewing and George Badger, coached by George Peck and Nathan Bangs. The case was decided in favor of the Methodist Episcopal Church, South, without dissent, and Judge Nelson was chosen to deliver the opinion of the court, which, quite naturally, followed his reasoning in the lower court. That Judge Nelson was selected to write the opinion was a source of some dissatisfaction in the North,[79] but in the South the authority of the Supreme Court was felt to have established once and forever the legality of the action of the Southern conferences and, in a sense, to have justified it. The practical result of the decision was to give to the Southern Church $60,000 in cash, payable within five years, and $20,000 in book stock. The intangible results were of greater importance. As Myers put it, the separation was legalized; the two branches of Methodism appeared co-ordinate in the eyes of the law; [80] neither one could claim to be the "original church," the "old mother church," or the "old Methodist church."

The litigation over the property cases was but one aspect of the rivaling development of the two churches. It does, however, keep in focus the conflicts which influenced both churches through these years. The paper war continued, more sporadically perhaps. George Peck reported that the Southern Methodist papers kept up a constant war with the North. As editor of the *Christian Advocate and Journal*, he felt it his duty

---

[78] For the most detailed treatment of these negotiations, see Elliott, *History of the Great Secession*, cols. 726-36.

[79] *Ibid.*, col. 800.

[80] Myers, *Disruption of the M. E. Church*, p. 183.

"to correct some of their more glaring misrepresentations." Although he sought, he said, to avoid acrimony, "the asperity of the Southern press, both religious and secular, was aggravated by a revival of the antislavery controversy [resulting from] the abrogation of the Missouri Compromise and the passage of the Fugitive Slave Law." [81] National events aroused both extreme factions, and Peck, trying to keep discussion of the Fugitive Slave Law out of the *Advocate,* found himself attacked on both fronts —by the South, and by the "radical prints" which he said raised a clamor about his "cowardice" and "non-committalism" or charged him with favoring slavery and the Fugitive Slave Law.

7

The Second General Conference of the Southern Church

The Methodist Episcopal Church, South, held its second General Conference in St. Louis in 1850. It was a brief one, cut short by the epidemic of cholera which took the life of one delegate, Isaac Boring of Georgia. No business was transacted the first day, May 1, because the difficulties of travel in that year prevented the attainment of a quorum until the second day. And adjournment finally came on Tuesday, May 14, although a committee had actually conferred with the bishops on May 6 to decide whether the session should be continued in St. Louis.

The Episcopal Address set the general tone of the conference. It was read by Bishop Andrew and signed by Bishops Andrew, Capers, and Paine only. The address itself called attention to Bishop Soule's "increasing infirmities" and made it the occasion to ask for additional strengthening of the episcopacy.[82] The venerable bishop reached St. Louis by the seventh, although he was too ill to attend the conference immediately and did not attempt to take the chair for any sessions.

The Episcopal Address laid particular emphasis upon the subject of missions, clearly calling for a major effort by the Southern Church in this area. It announced the carrying out of the instructions of the 1846 General Conference by the sending of two missionaries—Charles Taylor

[81] Peck, *Life and Times,* pp. 326-28.
[82] *Journal of the General Conference,* 1850, p. 134.

and Benjamin Jenkins—to Shanghai, China. Here the language of the
bishops in speaking of their appeal for help is indicative of the militant
element in the missionary thrust: "Certainly, if we are in earnest," they
said, "in our attempts to aid in subjugating China's teeming millions to
the Cross of our Lord Jesus Christ, *two men* can hardly be regarded as
our full quota of troops for the grand army of invasion and occupation." [83] Missions among the Indians and the sending of three missionaries to California received their share of attention, but particular emphasis was placed upon the missions to the slaves. The bishops noted
that "interest among the planters is extending," and stressed: "To this
work we are especially called of God, and woe be to the Church if we
neglect it." [84] Such evidence as is available indicates that this work was
not being neglected, and reports like that of J. F. W. Toland that
"many who belonged to no Church themselves were foremost in their
efforts to help the missionary in his work," [85] point to the encouragement given by slaveowners, however motivated, to the Methodists engaged in plantation preaching.

The bishops commented bitterly on the actions of the Northern
Church at the 1848 Pittsburgh General Conference. In their view, the
manifestation of kindly feeling in 1844 turned out to be "only the show
of kindness, a mere transient impulse," and at Pittsburgh they "pursued
such a course of action as destroyed all hope on the part of the Southern
Church, that she should either be able to obtain justice, or that fraternal
relations would be established." [86] The bishops told the conference:
"Your Messenger was rejected, and your offers of peace were met with
contempt. Your Commissioners . . . were treated with like discourtesy"
and "your claims were disposed of in summary manner." They charged
that "the very men who, from sheer hatred of slavery, drove the South
into separation, proved their sincerity and consistency by not only retaining all slave-holding members already under their charge, but in
making arrangements to gather as many more into the fold as practicable.
The Plan of Separation was repudiated for the avowed purpose of in-
vading Southern territory"; and, as evidence, the bishops referred to
the formation of the West Virginia Conference—"entirely within the
limits of the Southern Church." Because of the position assumed by
the Northern Church, the bishops said that they "felt ourselves at liberty
to accept invitations to occupy stations and circuits heretofore within its

[83] *Ibid.*, p. 136.
[84] *Ibid.*, p. 137.
[85] Reported in W. P. Harrison, ed. *The Gospel Among the Slaves* (Nashville: Publishing House of the M. E. Church, South, 1893) , p. 288.
[86] *Journal of the General Conference,* 1850, p. 141.

limits." And finally the bishops blamed the North for "their attempt to alienate the Indian tribes." All in all, it was an inflammatory declamation, hardly designed to encourage peace or understanding, and some of the General Conference actions seemed to have had their source in it.

On May 6 a recommendation of the Committee on Boundaries was adopted and a new Annual Conference established. This was the Western Virginia Conference, designed to include all the state of Virginia "which is, or *may be,* under our jurisdiction, not included in the present Virginia, North Carolina, or Holston Conference," [87] and designed also as an answer to the West Virginia Conference established by the Northern Church.

The Report of the Commissioners Appointed to Manage the Property Question was presented by Henry Bascom on May 9. It announced the institution of those suits in the circuit courts for New York, Pennsylvania, and Ohio which have already been discussed. It seemed to anticipate the eventual appeal of both cases to the United States Supreme Court, and it announced that the commissioners had drawn upon the book agent for $2,650 to defray the heavy expenses incurred or to be incurred. It asked the General Conference for some action to permit the commissioners, or one of them, to be made available to the South's lawyers for "free and frequent conversation," listing the counselors with Daniel Webster's name at the head, although eventually he was withdrawn from the case. To this report the General Conference responded by appointing a committee to confer with the bishops and, at the committee's recommendation, by resolving unanimously to give full approval to the action of the commissioners in bringing suit and to request and instruct the commissioners and to supply them with the necessary funds "to prosecute the claim with vigour, until the final decision of the Supreme Court of the United States be had in the suits now pending." [88]

The relationship between the two Methodist churches may even have entered somewhat into the election of the new bishop requested in the Episcopal Address. On the first ballot Henry Bascom, Joseph Boyle, and George F. Pierce were the leading candidates. On the second, Bascom, certainly the leading spokesman for the Southern Church in the paper war, had more than the necessary margin. The ordination of Bishop Bascom, with the aged Bishop Soule leading the laying on of hands, was one of the two most impressive ceremonies of the conference, the other being the funeral of Isaac Boring.

On May 13, Lovick Pierce made his report to the conference concerning his attendance at the Pittsburgh Conference as fraternal emissary.

[87] *Ibid.,* p. 153.
[88] *Ibid.,* p. 186.

Substantially his report agrees with the account which has already been given, except that the *Journal of the General Conference* does not include Pierce's complete initial letter to the conference with its request for recognition by formal action. Pierce explained that he had addressed his letter to the conference because he had not been furnished with any official testimonial by the Petersburg Conference or by the bishops. He summed up his rejection in dramatic phrases, concluding: "We did affectionately endeavor to make and preserve peace, but our offer was rejected as of no deserving," and he complained of his not being invited to preach from Methodist pulpits in Pittsburgh, asking: "And if one of their chief ministers, or even clever ministers, was at a General, or even Annual Conference with us, could we have the heart to treat him as an unworthy brother?" After a long digression concerning his meeting with Dr. Dixon and Brother Ryerson, he concluded his report by recommending a resolution which would make official policy the position taken in Pierce's last letter to the Northern conference, in which he announced his communication as the final attempt to restore friendly relations between the two churches, and insisted that any future step in this direction must come from the Northern Church.[89] But the conference acted simply to receive Pierce's report without special notice of the recommended resolution.

The conference gave considerable attention to its official publications and to their strengthening. It re-elected Editors Lee, Wightman, and McFerrin, thus endorsing the policies they had been pursuing. The only other major action of the conference was in respect to the rule on slavery. The Committee on Revisals reported the recommendation that Part II, Section 9, of the *Discipline*, which contained all that was said about slavery, be expunged, but a 43-to-39 majority voted against the recommendation, chiefly because of its probable effect in the border states. Another motion, that the part be omitted in *Disciplines* prepared for those conferences which wished it left out, was laid on the table. Finally the conference compromised with appearance by adding the following paragraph of explanation: "This section was inserted by a majority of votes when the M. E. Church embraced the whole country; and as the M. E. Church, South, still embraces a wide extent of country, with various views and conflicting interests, it is not removed, though it has long since become inoperative, and ceased, by common consent, to set forth a practical rule or principle."

And so the General Conference of 1850 adjourned. Over it had hung the shadow of the cholera epidemic. Over it also had hung the shadow of the conflict with the Northern Church. And if the shadows had some-

[89] *Ibid.*, pp. 190-91.

what affected its actions, nevertheless, the conference had transacted its business and charted its course for another four years.

8

The Churches in the 1850's

In fact, the two years between the adjournment of the 1850 conference of the Southern Church and the 1852 General Conference of the Northern Church saw some slackening in the frequency of the newspaper conflicts, if not in their virulence. Of course, the actions of the Southern General Conference and its Episcopal Address brought some rejoinders in the Northern papers, and Editor Wightman's denunciations of the Northern response brought an article entitled "Indignation Let Loose" in the *Christian Advocate and Journal,*[90] but Peck restrained both himself and the New York *Advocate* much of the time. Judge Nelson's decision in the New York Circuit Court on the property question stirred controversy and much advice to appeal the decision, but there were other controversies within the churches which absorbed some of the attention. A convention in favor of lay delegation and lay representation at General and Annual Conferences met in Philadelphia and drew up resolutions to be presented to the General Conference. Thomas Bond published several long articles against the proposal in the *Christian Advocate and Journal.* And the establishment of colleges and conference seminaries continued apace. Willamette in Salem, Oregon; Baldwin Institute in Berea, Ohio; and Mount Union Seminary in Mount Union, Ohio, were followed by Mount Pleasant College, Mount Pleasant, Iowa, in 1849; California Wesleyan, later to be University of the Pacific, in 1851; and Northwestern University, in the same year. Both churches lost able leaders. Bishop Bascom died in 1850 after holding but one Annual Conference. Stephen Olin, one of the most respected of the Northern leaders, died in August of 1851. And in April, 1852, less than a month before the opening of General Conference, Bishop Hedding died.

The 1852 General Conference of the Northern Church

The 1852 General Conference of the Methodist Episcopal Church gathered in the city of Boston at the Bromfield Street Chapel. In de-

[90] August 15, 1850, p. 130.

scribing the assemblage of 188 delegates, Abel Stevens wrote in *Zion's Herald:* "The number of aged men in it is larger than has been the case for three or four sessions." [91] While he did not say so, one reason for the "good proportion of hoary heads" was the return to the General Conference of men like Nathan Bangs, Gardner Baker, Homer Clarke, Charles Adams, and Elihu Scott, who, because of the reaction against those who had indorsed the Plan of Separation, had missed the Pittsburgh conference.

Unlike the 1850 Episcopal Address of the Southern Church, the message addressed to the General Conference by Bishops Waugh, Morris, and Janes made no reference to the other Methodist Episcopal Church. It spoke of the death of Bishop Hedding. It urged the avoidance of modifying the general superintendency to result in diocesan episcopacy: the itinerancy must be preserved both in the general ministry and the superintendency. The address reported the expansion of the mission movement and the numerical increase in collegiate institutions, although for a moment the bishops reflected that perhaps fewer institutions better endowed with stronger faculties might serve the cause of education better. Finally, the bishops called for an expansion of the episcopacy to include at least six effective superintendents.

With this keynote, the General Conference worked with as much thoroughness and dispatch as was possible under the load of a tremendous number of petitions and appeals and memorials of one sort or another. Particularly burdensome were the appeals by individuals against actions taken by Annual Conferences. The cases of Sprague, Inskip, McAbee, and Taylor consumed a great deal of the time of the conference and intensified the sentiment for some sort of judicial-review procedure. Although no satisfactory answer was found by this General Conference, the need for a solution was more urgently apparent than ever before.

Of particular importance among the actions of the 1852 General Conference were those connected with Bishop Hamline's resignation, the election of new bishops, lay delegation, and seating in the churches, although the adoption of the *California Christian Advocate,* the establishment of the *Northwestern Christian Advocate* in Chicago, the formation of a Kentucky Conference, and the debate over the idea of missionary bishops were highly important developments.

On May 11 the Committee on the Episcopacy reported that it had prepared three resolutions in response to Bishop Hamline's request that he be permitted, for reason of health, to resign his office and return his ordination papers. The committee proposed: (*a*) an expression of sym-

[91] May 5, 1852, p. 70.

pathy with their beloved superintendent in his afflictions, (b) a state-ment approving his administration and character, and (c) an acceptance of the proffered resignation. There was no question about the first two resolutions, but the third brought an extended discussion and a counter-motion to return the Bishop's parchments, declining his resignation and granting him unrestricted permission to pursue any course for the restora-tion of his health. At issue in the debate was the conception of a bishop's position. While J. A. Collins and the opponents of the third resolution would not maintain the doctrine of "once a bishop, always a bishop," certainly the huge majority which voted to accede to Bishop Hamline's request, a request wholly consistent with his speech at the 1844 General Conference, were voting approval of a doctrine which held that the episcopacy in the Methodist Church was an office merely, not a third ec-clesiastical order. Behind their action lay the majority view in Bishop Andrew's case and a distinction never really resolved between the positions of the churches, North and South.

Numerous petitions and memorials asking the General Conference to introduce lay representation in the Annual and General Conferences of the church were referred to the Committee on Lay Delegation. On May 27 it reported that it had considered the petitions and arguments and concluded unanimously that such a change would not be advantageous to the interests of the church. Its recommendation was overwhelmingly accepted by a vote of 171 to 3, which left no doubt where the preachers themselves stood in 1852.

On May 21 the Committee on the Episcopacy recommended the elec-tion of three new bishops, and an amendment from the floor changed the number to four. The election on May 25 surely has had few parallels. On the very first ballot all four new bishops were chosen. They were Levi Scott, Matthew Simpson, Osmon C. Baker, and Edward R. Ames. A native of Delaware, Bishop Scott had been assistant book agent in New York. Matthew Simpson had been a professor at Allegheny College, president of Indiana Asbury, and editor of the *Western Christian Advocate*. Bishop Baker was a member of the New Hampshire Conference, had taught in Newbury Seminary, and later became a professor at the Concord Biblical Institute. Bishop Ames's career had included preaching in Indiana and Illinois, service as missionary to the Indians, and appointment as mission-ary secretary for the frontier. Like Matthew Simpson, he was a member of the Indiana Conference when elected.

The conference had received a number of memorials, petitions, and appeals connected with seating in the Methodist churches and meetings. On May 31, the next to the last day of the conference, the Committee on Revisals brought in its report recommending that the matter be optional with each Annual Conference. A substitute motion was made to remove the prohibition against mixed seating and to prevent, wherever possible, the selling of pews. A move by Charles Elliott to postpone action was lost. Eventually, with Nathan Bangs, Peter Cartwright, Jacob Young, and J. A. Collins speaking to the issue, the conference voted the substitute motion, ninety-eight yeas to fifty-five nays, thereby striking out of the *Discipline* the statement that there should be no exception to the rule requiring men and women to sit apart and shortening the statement urging free seating by substituting: "Let all our churches be built plain and decent, and with free seats wherever practicable." [92] Liberal and democratic sentiments prevailed.

The General Conference took no action to establish an office of missionary bishop; however, the resolution which was introduced by Peter Sanford and Abiathar Osbon to amend the Third Restrictive Rule in order to remove any bar to such an appointment put the whole matter before the church, and the very able speeches of John McClintock and Jacob Young, on opposite sides of the question of whether the appointment of a missionary bishop for Africa alone would fall under the Third Restrictive Rule, certainly did much to pave the way for actions by later conferences.

The vote to establish a Kentucky Conference of the Methodist Episcopal Church was accompanied by a debate on the floor which was to echo long after the conference adjourned. Actually, this was the only occasion in which slavery and slaveholding became an issue or even an important element in the deliberations of the 1852 conference. Petitions and memorials concerning slavery were referred to the Committee on Revisals and then turned over to an appointed Committee on Slavery, of which George Peck was chairman. A report was made, but no action taken. The debate over the advisability of a Kentucky Conference did bring in the question of whether slaveowners ought even to be permitted to be members of the Methodist Episcopal Church, a question that the majority apparently preferred not to have asked. Opposition to the establishment of a Kentucky Annual Conference was unsuccessful in rallying the most strongly antislavery conferences in New England and upper New York to oppose the new conference. But discussion on the larger issue did not end there.

Some of the conference appointments were of considerable interest. John McClintock's policy of increasing the practicality of *The Methodist Quarterly Review* by seeking constantly to improve the scholarship and

[92] *Journal of the General Conference of the Methodist Episcopal Church,* 1852, pp. 107-8.

importance of the contributions earned the indorsement of a second tour of duty as editor. Thomas Bond was returned to the editorship of the *Christian Advocate and Journal* and Charles Elliott to the *Western Christian Advocate*. Homer J. Clarke became editor of the *Pittsburgh Christian Advocate* and J. V. Watson of the new *Northwestern Christian Advocate*. William Hosmer was again to edit the *Northern Christian Advocate,* and Abel Stevens was elected editor of the newly provided-for monthly, the *National Magazine.*

After the adjournment of the General Conference a warm discussion developed in the Northern papers concerning the proper attitude of the Methodist Episcopal Church toward slavery and the moral position of slaveowners. Bond, Elliott, and Clarke, in their respective papers, maintained that the church could properly include those who happened to own slaves. On the other side, Daniel Wise of *Zion's Herald,* Hosmer, and Watson condemned all slaveholding and favored excluding from the church all those who would persist in owning slaves. For those who held the latter view, Bond coined the term "Hosmerites." As contributors joined in the controversy, the discussion of slavery was conducted with, perhaps, as J. M. Buckley suggested, "greater zeal and force" than ever before.[93]

The 1854 General Conference of the Southern Church

Meantime, the third General Conference of the Methodist Episcopal Church, South, met in May, 1854, at Columbus, Georgia. Rather ironically, the only bishop present at the opening session was Bishop Soule, whom many had not expected to live to see another conference. The bishop announced that Bishop Paine was in the city but confined to his room with illness and that he had heard nothing of Bishops Andrew and Capers. The senior bishop, feeble himself, presided at all sessions until the arrival of Bishop Capers on May 8 permitted him relief.

Many of the problems raised in the Columbus conference were also those with which the Northern Church had been dealing. The continuance of the itinerancy, whether there should be lay delegation, and the need for additions to the episcopacy were considered here too. And the statistics of the growth of the Southern Church showed a gratifying increase in membership and in traveling preachers.[94]

[93] *A History of Methodism in the United States* (New York: Christian Literature Company, 1897), II, 159.
[94] See Gross Alexander, *A History of the Methodist Church South* (New York: Christian Literature Company, 1894), p. 62.

The conference heard with approval the report of the commissioners charged with the settlement of the property question. They were told officially of the settlement with the New York book agents and of the decision of the Supreme Court of the United States in the Ohio suit. The results were gratifying, and there was a certain magnanimity in the report itself. "We should not do justice to our feelings if we forbore to express our great satisfaction with the Christian courtesy and kindness which marked the intercourse of the Northern Commissioners and Agents," the report said. "They met us on the platform of candor, liberality and strict justice, and we are happy to say that our long contested difficulties were readily adjusted." [95]

The General Conference voted on May 30 to adopt the report and to express its gratitude to the Southern commissioners for the "vigilance and ability with which our interests have been guarded," and "in view of the labor performed and losses sustained by the Commissioners," to permit each of them and the widow of Bishop Bascom to draw upon the book agents for the sum of one thousand dollars.[96]

With the financial affairs of the Southern Church all but finally settled on a secure basis, the conference was in a position to establish a publishing house of its own, or, as the resolution put it, a "book concern proper." The major problem was its location. After hearing the rival claims of a number of sites, the conference voted on the place. On the first ballot Memphis, Louisville, Prattville, Atlanta, Nashville, St. Louis, and Columbus all received votes. By the fourth ballot the choice had clearly narrowed to Nashville, Louisville, and Memphis. The withdrawal of Memphis after the fifth ballot permitted the selection of Nashville on the sixth, sixty to fifty-seven. Edward Stevenson and F. A. Owen were elected the first agents and authorized to invest as much as $75,000 in the new establishment, more than that if the bishops and the Book Committee concurred. The revision of the *Discipline* to incorporate these changes provided for a Book Committee of five; editors for the *Quarterly Review,* the *Ladies' Companion, Sunday School Visitor,* and the Sunday school books and tracts; depositories at Richmond, Charleston, New Orleans, St. Louis, Galveston, Louisville, Memphis, and San Francisco; and official recognition of ten papers with the General Conference responsible only for those at Nashville, Richmond, Charleston, and St. Louis.[97]

On May 19, Report No. 3 of the Committee on the Episcopacy was adopted. It consisted of a long preamble to justify a short resolution

[95] *Journal of the General Conference of the Methodist Episcopal Church, South,* 1854, pp. 336-37.

[96] *Ibid.,* pp. 331-33.

[97] *Ibid.,* pp. 323-25.

which must have seemed obvious to most of the delegates: the episcopacy needed three new bishops. On the first ballot, although thirty-two names received votes, George F. Pierce of Georgia received a majority and was declared elected. On the fifth ballot John Early of Virginia was elected. And finally, on the seventh, Hubbard H. Kavanaugh of Kentucky was chosen, and the delegates from the border states had achieved a preconference objective.[98]

The specially appointed committee on the slavery section of the *Discipline,* with A. L. P. Green as chairman, presented three reports on May 25-26. The first report contained the resolution that the whole Ninth Section of the Second Part of the *Discipline* be stricken. It was adopted by a rising vote with only one nay, although its preamble was referred to the bishops to revise and publish as seemed best to them. The second report recommended the striking out of the proviso that no slaveholder should be eligible for the office of deacon or elder. It was likewise adopted. The third report provided for the expunction of the General Rule on slavery, and it encountered the same strong opposition that such a move had met before. Laid on the table for one day, it was moved again on the next. This time it had the support of a majority, sixty-six to forty-three, but this was not a constitutional majority sufficient to effect a change in the *Discipline.* Primarily it was the delegates from the border conferences who blocked the move. Finally, a supplemental explanation of the rule was adopted: "Resolved, that the General Rule on the subject of 'the buying and selling of men, women, and children, with an intention to enslave them,' is understood as referring exclusively to the slave trade, as prohibited by the Constitution and laws of the United States." [99] The next step could be clearly foreseen.

The General Conference of 1854 closed with the affairs of the Methodist Episcopal Church, South, in good order. Once again it had a full complement of vigorous episcopal leaders. It had provided for a new conference in the state of Arkansas, to be organized by Bishop Kavanaugh in November after the adjournment. It had established the Kansas Mission Conference to include Kansas Territory and part of the territory of New Mexico. It had reorganized committees, and it had established a publishing house at Nashville, which was to play its part in helping that city earn its title of "Athens of the South" and heart of Southern Methodism. Although there had been little spectacular about the General Conference, its achievements were solid ones.

[98] A. H. Redford, *Life and Times of H. H. Kavanaugh* (Nashville, 1884), p 382.
[99] *Journal of the General Conference,* 1854, pp. 300-301.

Problems on the West Coast

Because even the problems of Methodist missions in the far West entered into the controversy between the churches, there is reason to stop
at this point in 1854 to look at developments in an area where the problems were chiefly of another sort. Here, naturally, the Northern Church
had inherited the lead.

The first Methodist sermon in San Francisco had been preached on
April 24, 1847, by William Roberts of the New Jersey Conference, who
simply stopped there en route to Oregon, where Jason Lee and Marcus
Whitman had pioneered mission establishment. Apparently it was
Roberts' recommendations which led to a grant of $2,000 from the Mis-
sion Board and the decision to send missionaries to California as well as
to the Oregon Territory. Bishop Waugh appointed Isaac Owen of Indiana and the indomitable William Taylor of the Baltimore Conference.
And the General Conference of 1848 had responded to a memorial from
the Oregon Mission requesting the formation of an Annual Conference
by acting to establish a single Mission Conference comprising Oregon,
California, and New Mexico. The geographical impracticality of this step
was only one difficulty. The same year saw the temporary eclipse of the
work in Oregon when the New Jersey mechanic James Marshall, erecting
a sawmill for J. A. Sutter, discovered gold in the American River and the
resultant gold rush depopulated the Oregon Territory. But the setback
was only temporary. The land-donation law of 1850 brought settlers, not
just fortune hunters, back to Oregon in such numbers that in ten years
the population more than tripled. Under the leadership of Roberts the
work there prospered.

Meantime William Taylor, traveling by sea, arrived at San Francisco on
September 21, 1849; and a month later, Owen, who had come by the
laborious overland route, also reached the town. When they arrived, they
found the local preacher Asa White in his famous blue tent preaching
evangelistic sermons. Owen went to Sacramento, where the Methodist layman Dr. William Grove Deal had already organized a group to whom he
preached. Taylor, concentrating for a time on San Francisco, organized
the Powell Street Church, which held its first Quarterly Conference on
November 30 and, by January 1, 1850, numbered sixty-nine members.
Taylor also began regular street preaching next to a saloon on the plaza.
Under his leadership Methodism made strong gains, and it is not surprising that, when the missionaries of the Southern Church, sent as a
result of the action of the 1850 General Conference, reached the coast,

they found the Northern Church well entrenched in both California and Oregon.

Reinforcements sent to Roberts in 1851 included two college graduates, and then, in 1853, Gustavus Hines and his two younger brothers were transferred to Oregon from the Genesee Conference. Active recruiting by John Durbin and Bishop Janes had assured some supply of missionaries and preachers. And the task became easier when the 1852 General Conference accepted a recommendation of its Boundary Committee which made two regular Annual Conferences of what had been a single Mission Conference covering an extent of territory which was impossibly large.

Theological Education

One controversy of considerable significance which occupied attention during these years developed over the question of theological education and the formal educational requirements for the ministry. While the public arguments upon the question were rehearsed chiefly in the Northern papers, discussion was by no means confined to the North. In a series of articles on literary attainments for the ministry which ran in the *Christian Advocate and Journal* during late 1846 and early 1847, James Sewall had taken the conservative position, arguing from traditional American Methodist practices that what made the Methodist ministry effective was inspirational preaching, the common appeal, the close touch with the average person, the openness to experience rather than to books. In his view too much education or formal training would detract from these, and the system of informal courses of reading which prevailed was best designed to produce the desirable results which gave Methodism its numerical superiority over other denominations.

Despite Sewall's views, a biblical institute under the control of the church was opened in Concord, New Hampshire, in 1847. Named the Methodist General Biblical Institute, it was designed to train young men for the ministry and had the special interest of Bishop Hedding and later Bishop Baker. Eventually it was moved to Boston in 1868, was reorganized as the Boston Theological Seminary, and then became part of Boston University. In its early years, however, it was variously regarded as an object of suspicion or a sign of progress, depending upon the views of the controversialist.

In 1853, James Strong penned a letter for the December 22 issue of the *Christian Advocate and Journal* which brought on an extended discussion and warm debate. Strong proposed a central theological seminary for the Methodist Episcopal Church, to be located in the vicinity of New

York, and suggested a meeting at the Book Concern of both preachers and laymen to discuss the subject and take measures for its realization. He maintained that such an institution was necessary to provide a superior theological training to satisfy congregations increasing in number, wealth, learning, and refinement. Unless there is good preaching to adapt itself to the "upward tendency of Methodism," the church will be unable to hold its congregations or its ministry.

An answer was immediately forthcoming from James Sewall,[100] who seized upon the rather unfortunate phrase about the "upward tendency of Methodism" to attack Strong's position. Sewall held that success in the study of theology "depends more upon the *state* of the *heart* than on the *culture* of the *head*," and he resented the implied strictures upon the present ministry as unfair and untrue. Dr. Bond, as editor, defended the inclusion of Strong's letter in the *Advocate,* but, at the same time, stated his opposition to the "scholastic training of our preachers." In the *Christian Advocate and Journal* for January 19, 1854, appeared George Hughes's satiric expansion of Strong's proposal, sketching plans for a "Central Salvation Seminary," which would have a professor of prayer meetings and another of class meetings and would inculcate a "higher style of sermonizing" for the "higher stratum" of society. Hughes's extravagance was taken to task by R. S. Moran, who asked what Methodism might not be able to do if its preachers had the advantages of its founder.

For several months the letters appeared regularly on the subject. F. A. Morrell on February 9 dissented wholly from Strong's views, indorsing the competence of the ministers who had built "the Church, the beautiful edifice raised by the toil and sacrifice of our fathers, exceeding in numbers and influence any other Church in this land," and calling upon those who loved Methodism "to quench this firebrand." D. D. T. Leech, on the other hand, felt that the age of progress demanded such an institution. Who could contend reasonably that a minister could be too thoroughly educated? E. E. Griswold very ably asked the crucial question of whether seminary training and ministerial service were really antagonistic to each other. Strong, in a second letter on March 2, 1854, held that a theological seminary could be so organized as to comport "with the essential economy and genius of Methodism." Isaac Winner called attention to the view of the bishops in 1840, which was somewhat unfavorable to the idea of seminaries but insistent that, if established, they be kept under the control of the General Conference. For that reason he opposed Strong's committee of interested people and urged that the matter be presented to the General Conference.

[100] *Christian Advocate and Journal,* January 5, 1854, p. 1.

No end of the argument was in sight when Garrett Biblical Institute was incorporated by the Illinois Legislature in 1855. Probably at the suggestion of P. M. Borein, under whose ministry she had been converted, Mrs. Eliza Garrett, widow of the mayor of Chicago, resolved to devote a portion of her property to ministerial education. Her resolve, the fortunate presence and labors of John Dempster, who had founded the Concord Institute, and the advice of Judge Grant Goodrich and John Clark led to the establishment of Garrett Institute, to which Mrs. Garrett presented gifts and bequests totaling more than $300,000.

Also in 1855, Randolph S. Foster published, "at the request of the New-York East Conference," *A Treatise on the Need of the M. E. Church with Respect to her Ministry*.[101] The essence of Foster's argument for formal theological training is that the change which had taken place in the first half of the nineteenth century in the Methodist body, in other denominations, and in general society "requires that we should have a more thoroughly educated and liberally informed ministry." Scholars are necessary to maintain the relationship between Methodism and theological truth. The church has both an intellectual and a spiritual life. It needs a more spiritual and consecrated ministry; it also needs a more intellectual apprehension of truths; and the two are interdependent. Foster's pamphlet was followed quickly by J. H. Perry's *Defense of the Present Mode of Training Candidates for the Ministry in the Methodist Episcopal Church*.[102] The latter took the position that the conference request for publication of Foster's sermon was a courteous formality that Dr. Foster should better have neglected to comply with, since Perry's opposing arguments would probably have had the indorsement of five sixths of the members of the conference. Basically, both Perry and Alfred Brunson, who published a tract in the following year,[103] attempted to defend the prevailing system of ministerial training and to "deprecate all foolhardy attempts at revolution."

In the controversy over the mode of ministerial training may be recognized some of the same issues as were involved in the ill-fated founding of Cokesbury College and which were to appear later in the fundamentalist controversy and, later yet, in the discussions of the relation of the theological schools to the Methodist Church and the preaching ministry. The arguments during the "years of disagreement" resulted finally in the establishment of Drew Theological Seminary in 1867 in the very center of the field of controversy. And it is worth noting that both James Strong

[101] (New York: Carlton and Phillips, 1855).
[102] (New York: Carlton and Phillips, 1855).
[103] *The Gospel Ministry: Its Characteristics and Qualifications* (New York, 1856).

and Randolph Foster (later Bishop Foster) were among the first to be called to professorships at that institution.

Meantime, however, the controversy received some attention at the 1856 General Conference of the Methodist Episcopal Church, which convened in Indianapolis. There, in their Episcopal Address, the bishops repeated substantially what had been said in 1840, although with the recognition that "Biblical schools" were already established. They said: "If it be the judgment of the Church that Biblical schools are desirable, then we would suggest . . . that they should be of a connectional character, and in some way responsible to the General Conference, so that their management and teaching shall be in harmony with the doctrines and Discipline of the Church." [104] The conference itself approved a series of resolutions which, in effect, approved of biblical institutes, provided sufficient safeguards were established, emphasizing that mere educational qualifications were not sufficient for acceptance into the ministry, that trustees of such institutions all be members of the Methodist Episcopal Church, that there be no attempt to multiply these institutions greatly, that no candidate for the ministry be admitted to a biblical institute without certificate from the Quarterly or Annual Conference, and that the bishops act as an advisory committee to counsel the trustees of Garrett Biblical Institute and "such other Biblical Institutes as may exist in accordance with the provisions of the above resolutions." [105]

When the Methodist Episcopal Church, South, met in General Conference two years later, it merely approved a report which saw no need for the establishment of such theological institutions, although it indorsed the striving for a better-educated ministry. Instead of a fundamental cleavage between North and South on the issue of theological education, it is clear that there was great divergence in the North and that the Southern position was related to the financial straits of so many of its educational institutions.

The 1856 General Conference and Slavery

After occupying a subordinate position in 1852, slavery was again the major matter of debate at the Indianapolis General Conference of the Northern Church. Should slaveholders be permitted to remain members in good standing within the Methodist Episcopal Church? What action, if any, ought the General Conference to take, and what were its consti-

---

[104] *Journal of the General Conference of the Methodist Episcopal Church,* 1856, p. 196.
[105] *Ibid.,* pp. 150-51.

tutional powers? These were the issues as the slavery debate resumed.

Charles Elliott's massive, exhaustive, and highly partisan examination of the documents and opinions involved in the "Great Secession" had been published the year before. Antislavery feeling was continuing to spread in the Northern states and abolitionism beginning to be regarded as more than merely fanatical radicalism. Conflicting pressures in the border states were reaching new heights. Against this tide, the bishops urged moderation. The Episcopal Address reported that resolutions originating in the Troy, Erie, North Ohio, and Wisconsin Conferences asking for a change in the General Rule on slavery had been laid before the Annual Conferences without receiving any constitutional majority. Under the circumstances, the bishops doubted that "in view of the restricted powers of a delegated General Conference, any measure equivalent to a change in the General Rules can be constitutionally adopted without the concurrence of the annual conferences." Further, they thought that the existence of Methodist Episcopal Church conferences and churches within slaveholding territory "does not tend to extend or perpetuate slavery" because of the general attitude of the church and the statements in the *Discipline*.[106]

Despite the minimization of the issue and its difficulties by the bishops, the General Conference was deluged with petitions and memorials on the slavery question—on both sides! Some asked for action to eliminate slaveholding; others requested that there be no change in the rules.

To some extent, the alignment of opinion on the slavery issue dominated the General Conference. At one point a member objected to any attempt to elect officers and editors for the coming quadrennium until the vote on the report on slavery could be taken. He wanted to see where each man stood. The slavery question also contributed to an alignment which strengthened the power of those whom Hiram Mattison called the "brakemen." These were the men who, on every issue, whether it was African episcopacy, slavery, presiding elderships, or the length of time a preacher could be assigned to a charge, invoked constitutionality, anticongregationalism, and old-time Methodism to resist any change.

On the slavery issue the brakemen won for the moment, and the General Conference took no action. But the subject was debated ably and at great length. As George Peck said, "The discussion this time was long and spirited." [107] Miner Raymond of the New England Conference, chairman of the Committee on Slavery, and John A. Collins, chairman of the minority members who presented a counterreport, were key

---

[106] *Ibid.*, pp. 199-200.
[107] Peck, *Life and Times*, p. 353.

figures. Hiram Mattison, Abel Stevens, George R. Crooks, John Dempster, Samuel Y. Monroe, Edward Thomson, Israel Chamberlayne, and John McClintock were principal speakers.

The report of the Committee on Slavery was read on May 21. It pointed out the inconsistencies involved in attempting to distinguish between mercenary slaveholding and benevolent, concluded that the time had come when it was the duty of the church to revise its statutes so as to express its real sentiments, and offered a series of resolutions. It recommended that the Annual Conferences amend the General Rule on Slavery so as to read: "the buying, selling, or holding a human being as property"; that the *Discipline* be further amended to state that, because no man has a moral right to hold a fellow being as property, no slaveholder should be eligible to membership in the church hereafter, where emancipation could be effected without injury to the slave; and that the preacher in charge should assume the responsibility for prudently enforcing the rules and for calling together committees to investigate cases of slaveholding and to determine when slaves should be freed.[108]

The following day the minority report held that the proposed change was unconstitutional; that the change was unnecessary because the *Discipline* and the church are clearly understood to be opposed to slavery; and, perhaps most important, that "any increased stringency of the *Discipline* on the subject of Slavery, will greatly weaken, if not destroy our church in the slaveholding States, and along the border." [109]

Once again constitutionality and expediency were opposed to any change. George Peck and others supported the minority position because "our Church on the border was suffering fearfully in the collisions of the North and the South. . . . Extreme measures on the part of the Conference would be fatal to them." [110]

Representatives from Baltimore, Western Virginia, and Missouri deplored a move which would make ownership of a slave a bar to membership in the church.

In the end, as Matlack's study emphasized, action was averted by a vote in which the majority refused to suspend the order of the day in order to take further action on the subject of slavery. Previously, however, a large majority had expressed themselves as favoring the prohibition of all slaveholding, provided there was a concurring vote of the Annual Conferences, the prohibition to be effected by a change in the General

---

[108] *Proceedings and Debates of the M. E. General Conference, 1856* (Syracuse: Matlack, 1856), pp. 121-22.

[109] *Ibid.*, pp. 125-28.

[110] Peck, *Life and Times*, p. 354.

Rule. The failure of the conference to act was the result of a coalition of the conservatives (ninety-six votes) and the constitutional abolitionists (thirty-one votes) against the radical abolitionists (ninety-one votes), a coalition which threw the balance in favor of postponing further action.[111]

In other matters the General Conference was able to accomplish more. After much debate it was voted to propose to the Annual Conferences that the constitution be altered to permit the Liberian Conference to elect to the new office of missionary bishop an elder in good standing who should act as superintendent, his jurisdiction being limited to Africa. The missionaries of the Methodist Episcopal Church in Germany were united in a Mission Conference to be effected in that country. The conference heard and approved the final settlement between the Western Book Concern and the commissioners of the Southern Church. It also adopted two new papers: the *Pacific Christian Advocate* at Portland, Oregon, and the *Central Christian Advocate* at St. Louis, which had been taking a leading part in the paper war with the Southern Church. It increased the number of Annual Conferences to forty-seven.

No official action was taken over a redefinition of the function of presiding elders. Likewise, the conference resisted attempts to extend the length of time that preachers could be assigned to a particular charge. In this instance the change had the support of the Canadian Conference representatives, Ryerson and Jones, who actually participated in an unprecedented fashion in the debate on the issue. Abel Stevens was elected editor of the *Christian Advocate and Journal,* replacing Dr. Thomas Bond, who had died in March. D. D. Whedon was chosen to edit *The Methodist Quarterly Review*. Other editors elected were: Daniel Wise, the *Sunday-School Advocate;* James Floy, the *National Magazine;* D. W. Clark, the *Ladies' Repository;* Calvin Kingsley, the *Western Christian Advocate;* F. G. Hibbard, the *Northern Christian Advocate;* I. N. Baird, the Pittsburgh *Advocate*; Thomas H. Pearne, the Pacific; Eleazar Thomas, the California; and Joseph Brooks, the Central. J. V. Watson was elected editor of the *Northwestern Christian Advocate,* but he died a few months after the conference adjourned, and Dr. Thomas M. Eddy was chosen to take his place.

Intensified Assault on Slavery

After the 1856 General Conference the discussion about the means of extirpating slavery was intensified. Abel Stevens' speech, which had been

---

[111] Lucius C. Matlack, *The Antislavery Struggle and Triumph in the Methodist Episcopal Church* (New York: Phillips and Hunt, 1881), pp. 293-94.

read by Dr. McClintock, had affirmed boldly that the membership of slaveholders was protected by the constitution of the Methodist Episcopal Church. His upholding of the bishops' position in this respect may have been instrumental in securing his election to the editorship of the New York *Advocate,* but to many this insistence on the necessity for a change in the constitution and the General Rule on slavery seemed contrary to the position Stevens had taken earlier in *Zion's Herald* and quite contrary to the logic of the situation. Dr. E. O. Haven, the new editor of *Zion's Herald,* took issue with Stevens, and the two papers joined in warm debate. Dr. Haven published an attack upon Stevens' arguments in a series of articles written by Professor W. L. Harris which he later gathered into the book *Constitutional Powers of the General Conference.*

Harris argued that the General Conference possessed full power to make or revise any rule which did not conflict with a General Rule. A mere statutory rule excluding slaveholders would not revoke or materially change any General Rule, and, therefore, the General Conference had the power to refuse to tolerate slavery any longer. Stevens dissented and was, in turn, replied to by D. D. Whedon. Daniel Wise of the *Sunday-School Advocate,* who was condemned by some for introducing antislavery views into that paper, and F. G. Hibbard, who had replaced William Hosmer as editor of the *Northern Christian Advocate,* strongly indorsed the idea of immediate statutory action. William Hosmer's new *Northern Independent* argued for antislaveholding action with even more vehemence.

While both positions represented in the debate over constitutionality were against slaveholding, it should be recognized that a few Annual Conferences were opposed to any further antislavery action. Some opposed it because they feared further disruption in the work of the churches on the border. Some conservatives felt that no worth-while purpose could be served by further change and that no change could be effected either by constitutional amendment or by General Conference action.

In December, 1857, an antislavery convention of 205 members from the five conferences in western New York met to consider the questions of whether the slaveholders in the church were protected by constitutional right; whether to undertake directing efforts to change the General Rule; what change, if any, should be proposed; and whether anything further could be done to secure the extirpation of slavery. This Rochester Convention concluded that "even if it were expedient and desirable to change the General Rule on Slavery, it was . . . impossible. . . . We could not come within a thousand votes." [112] Thus, in its resolutions, the convention objected to any attempt to change the General Rule as an "unnecessary and dangerous experiment," insisting that direct legislation by the General Conference was not only right but essential.

Meantime, such pamphlet publications as Hiram Mattison's *Impending Crisis of 1860* [113] and J. Mayland McCarter's *Border Methodism and Border Slavery* [114] were concerned with demonstrating in detail the extent of slaveholding in the Northern Church and substantiating the charge of Dr. McFerrin that the principal difference on the slavery issue was only that "the South, occupying a much larger slave territory than the North, has a greater number of ministers and members connected with slavery than are found in the North!" [115] And Mattison concludes bitterly: "We are an 'anti-slavery' slaveholding Church!" [116]

One center of controversy during this period of extreme agitation was the matter of the various specific proposals of rules to be substituted for the General Rule on slavery. One had been presented at the 1856 General Conference and had failed to secure there the necessary two-thirds vote to send it to the Annual Conferences. It had forbidden "the buying, selling, or holding a human being as property." Three other proposals were voted upon in various Annual Conferences. The Cincinnati Rule prohibited "the buying or selling of men, women, or children, or holding them, with an intention to use them as slaves." The Erie Rule prohibited "the buying, selling, holding, or transferring of any human being, to be used in slavery." And the Providence Rule prohibited "slaveholding, the buying or selling of men, women, or children, with an intention to enslave them."

Not all conferences voted upon any single proposed rule. In tabulating reported votes, Mattison represents the Cincinnati Rule as actually defeated by the voting conferences 97 to 545. The Providence Rule had a majority of 968 to 569. The Erie Rule, the most popular, obtained a majority of 1,255 to 485, well within the two-thirds figure. But none of these counts includes the votes of the border conferences, which would have been sufficient to preclude absolutely the possibility of a favorable

[112] Hiram Mattison, *What of the Night?* (New York: Anti-Slavery Union of the Black River Conference, 1860), p. 9.

[113] In full: *The Impending Crisis of 1860; or, the Present Connection of the Methodist Episcopal Church with Slavery, and Our Duty in Regard to It.*

[114] *Border Methodism and Border Slavery, Being a Statement and Review of the Action of the Philadelphia Annual Conference Concerning Slavery, at Its Late Session at Easton, Pa.* (Philadelphia: Collins, 1858).

[115] Nashville *Christian Advocate,* December 4, 1856.

[116] *The Impending Crisis,* p. 70.

result and the introduction of an extirpatory rule by constitutional change.[117]

Abel Stevens' views were gathered together in *An Appeal to the Methodist Episcopal Church Concerning What Its Next General Conference Should Do on the Question of Slavery*.[118] In effect, because of the danger to the border work, the threat of a new division of the church, and the reluctance to introduce an "unscriptural term of membership," [119] he favored merely a declaration of the "sense of the Church on the whole subject" in a pastoral address and in a marginal notation in the *Discipline* opposite the General Rule on slavery. Whedon's position, published originally in the New York *Tribune,* was reprinted as *Letter to Rev. Dr. Stevens on the Subject of His Late Appeal to the Methodist Episcopal Church*.[120] He believed that constitutional change was possible, safe, and secure. Even more directly for action was J. K. Peck's pamphlet which objected strongly to so much deference to the border and indorsed the attempt to secure passage of the Providence Rule.[121]

Also indicative of the turbulence of the agitation pro and con, a Ministers' and Laymen's Union, with Nathan Bangs as its president, was formed in 1859 at the New York Conference to protest against proposed changes in the rule on slavery and to preserve the unity of the church. In answer, the Anti-slavery Society of the New York East Conference, with Dr. Curry as principal spokesman, vigorously opposed the views and general position of the Ministers' and Laymen's Union. Out of the slavery controversies and the joining together of ministers and laity came much of the impetus for the lay-delegation or lay-representation movement within the Methodist Episcopal Church.

The 1858 General Conference of the Southern Church

In the midst of the Northern Church's internal struggle over what to do about slaveholding, the Methodist Episcopal Church, South, opened its General Conference of 1858 in the hall of the Tennessee House of Representatives at the state capitol in Nashville. Nashville was the home of the new publishing house, and it was appropriate that the city which was becoming the ecclesiastical center of Southern Methodism should have

---

[117] Mattison, *What of the Night?* pp. 16-17.
[118] (New York: Trow, 1859).
[119] *Ibid.,* p. 33.
[120] (New York: Alvord, 1859).
[121] *Stevens Answered in His Appeal to the Methodist Episcopal Church* (Montrose, Pa.: "Republican" Steam Power Press, 1859), p. 44.

received this conference, welcoming the delegates who converged on the city by steamboat, stagecoach, and railroad.

Once again old Bishop Soule opened the conference. In fact, this conference was attended by all the bishops who had signed the *Journal* of 1854 except William Capers, who had died. Again the recommendations in the address of the bishops were particularly important. As is often the case, these recommendations are more revealing than the statistics of growth and the signs of prosperity which the bishops reported. Much of the emphasis in the Episcopal Address of 1858 was placed upon the need for the missionary function. The death of Bishop Capers provided additional reason for dwelling on the missions to the slaves as the "crowning glory of our church," but foreign missions came in for their share of attention too. To some extent the emphasis reveals the rankling over English nonrecognition of the Southern Church and an awareness of a special concern well expressed in such a statement as this: "The position we, of the Methodist Church, South, have taken for the African, has to a great extent cut us off from the sympathy of the Christian Church throughout the world; and it behooves us to make good this position in the sight of God, of angels, of men, of churches, and to our own consciences." [122] The bishops called for a "careful revision of our whole missionary plan of operations." [123] They suggested that the church was perhaps not aggressive enough—although its rate of growth was far greater than that of the Northern Church in the same period.

The bishops called attention to the importance of missions even in the older states. In general, signs of the rivalry with the Northern Church appear in the bishops' comments about the difficulties of the California missionaries' facing a "strong tide of opposition in California," where the Northern Church men were first on the scene and had the advantage of the publications of the New York Book Concern. Again, in connection with the German people in Missouri, the bishops noted that the Southern consent to leaving the German Methodist churches under Northern control after 1844 had now left them out of sympathy with their neighbors, and the bishops were led to urge that it would be better "to take more decided measures for occupying that ground." [124] There may even be signs of the rivalry in the bishops' criticism of many of the church papers: there were too many of them to support creditably, and some

[122] Charles F. Deems, ed., *Annals of Southern Methodism for 1856* (Nashville: Stevenson & Owen, 1857), p. 198; extracted from the Eleventh Annual Report of the Missionary Society of the Methodist Episcopal Church, South.

[123] *Journal of the General Conference of the Methodist Episcopal Church, South,* 1858, p. 396.

[124] *Ibid.,* p. 393.

editors seemed insufficiently zealous to defend the institutions of Methodism and too ready "to discuss and promote innovations upon our established doctrines or usages." [125]

The bishops decried proposed changes in the itinerancy and agitation over lay delegation as unfortunate. They spoke against the sectionalizing influences in favor of a general church with an itinerant ministry and traveling superintendents. In these matters the differences in polity of the churches, South and North, appear to the historian very small indeed.

One action of the General Conference of 1858 was a direct reply to the action of the Northern Church in 1856 which had authorized the raising of funds to erect a Methodist Episcopal Church in the nation's capital. On May 7 a resolution to co-operate in the building of a Southern church in Washington was adopted when the reported petition urged support for a "little band of Southern Methodists . . . manfully stemming the tide of opposition from the thousands who hold connection with an avowedly abolition Church." [126]

The General Conference also dealt with complaints made against the administration of Bishop Early. The bishop had been reported as arbitrary and discourteous, and the Committee on the Episcopacy had accepted the allegations to the extent of recommending that the conference approve his character but release him from regular episcopal work. Ultimately the General Conference turned down this suggestion, at the same time that it excluded mention of Bishop Early from the formal announcement of approval of the course of episcopal work during the quadrennium.

The report of the Committee on Books and Periodicals presented a clear summary of the difficulties besetting the publishing enterprise. Heavy liabilities demanded extended support and patronage by both clergy and laity if the publications were to survive in a period of financial difficulty. Ultimately the able John B. McFerrin was elected agent to head the affairs of the publishing house. He succeeded admirably until the Federal Army entered Nashville in 1862.

The major action of the Nashville General Conference of 1858, however, was taken after the introduction of the motion to approve the Alabama Resolution. The Alabama Conference had passed a resolution to expunge the General Rule on slavery, and the bishops had placed the resolution before all the Annual Conferences except the Kansas, Pacific, and Indian Mission. The reported results indicated a vote of 1,160–311. The conference debated for several days as some delegates from the

[125] *Ibid.*, p. 397.
[126] *Ibid.*, p. 416.

border conferences sought to block action. Finally, however, on May 19, the conference approved a series of resolutions by an overwhelming margin which effected the removal of the rule on slavery from the General Rules of the Methodist Episcopal Church, South, subject to the concurrent action of the Annual Conferences. Thus, in 1858, the Southern Church took the action which many had insisted was demanded by the position taken in 1844.

As Bishop Pierce explained it, the Southern Church had held from the beginning that it was not the province of the church to deal with civil institutions. The action of the conference had merely squared the *Discipline* with this profession and removed legislation that was "contradictory and absurd." Now, having "surrendered to Caesar the things which are his, . . . we can . . . preach Christ alike to the master and the servant, secure in the confidence and affection of the one and the other." [127]

By its action the Southern Church had completed the definition of its position. The struggle in the Northern Church continued until long after Civil War fighting commenced. In fact, the 1860 General Conference of the Northern Church was debating its course and preparing majority and minority reports in Buffalo when news of the nomination of Abraham Lincoln as Republican candidate for the presidency of the United States reached the conference. And there is some evidence that it took the actual outbreak of hostilities eleven months later to avert yet another secession or at least a further splitting of the Methodist Episcopal Church.

[127] *Ibid.*, p. 586.

chapter 17

THE
WAR YEARS

Participation in the War

Influence of Church
Spokesmen

The New Status of
Methodism

The Mission to the South

The Emancipated Negro

A LTHOUGH NATHAN BANGS HAD PREACHED and written against slavery for over a quarter of a century, he came to the end of his life in 1862 believing that God, having thrust aside the "original party leaders," had "taken the problem into his own almighty hand." The divine resolution of the bitter strife, Bangs believed, would visit "such retributions, on Church and State, North and South, as should astonish all the civilized world." [1] Although the younger men who succeeded Bangs and his contemporaries in the leadership of American Methodism did not question the fact of divine governance in the affairs of the nation, they were not prepared to resign their own initiative in matters so crucial. The wartime leaders of Methodism, both North and South, were not only confident in their reading of God's purpose; they also assumed, on behalf of their respective churches, the burden of a generous contribution toward what they envisioned as its fulfillment. The contradiction which Bangs resolved by leaving the issue in the hands of God, each of the two largest Methodist churches obscured by embracing the cause of one of the parties in the armed conflict. Methodists of neither side could comprehend the extent to which they identified their own sectional and institutional interests with the will of God. "Hence there arose the passions of conflict which accompany the strife of those who cannot understand the apparent moral obtuseness of their enemy." [2]

[1] Abel Stevens, *Life and Times of Nathan Bangs* (New York: Carlton and Porter, 1863), p. 322.

[2] H. Richard Niebuhr, *The Social Sources of Denominationalism* (New York: Meridian Books, 1957), p. 195.

By 1861 each of the two Methodist bodies that had separated in 1844 had become the largest and wealthiest Protestant church in its geographical area, and the members of each church were widely dispersed in the general population of its region. Moreover, the connectional character of Methodism, in both North and South, tended to give to each of the churches a large measure of uniformity of attitude and habits of thought and to increase the hostility of each toward the church from which it was separated. It was no matter of surprise, therefore, that upon the outbreak of war each church should rally at once to the cause with which it, in fact, already was identified.

The differences distinguishing Northern from Southern Methodists were not merely sectional. The two churches were also separated by divergent understandings of the church's function in society and the scope of its responsibilities. Many Methodists in the North believed that the church must influence political action on the slavery question. This view, although bolstered by strong abolitionist sentiment in some quarters, actually reflected a growing sense of responsibility on the part of the church for the moral quality of the whole of public life. Matthew Simpson's biographer has noted that Simpson, while editor of the *Western Christian Advocate* from 1848 to 1852, broadened "his concept of Christian responsibility . . . from evangelism and the doctrine of Christian influence . . . to the belief that the Christian must do battle for what was right, and that *right* was inextricably bound up with public affairs." [3] Simpson stood among those who, while eschewing the radical tenets of abolitionism, nevertheless held the church to be responsible for the reform of national life. This interest in reform, as Timothy L. Smith has pointed out, sprang partly from the joining of the perfectionist fervor of the mid-century revivals with the millennial ferment of the times.[4] When debate gave place to military contest, the sense of responsibility for public righteousness merged with patriotic support of the nation at war. The pulpit and the press once dedicated to the reform of national life now saw their immediate task as augmenting the support of the military enterprise. The 1862 resolutions of the East Baltimore Conference stated the case simply: "In our patriotic efforts . . . to sustain the government . . . we are not justly liable to the charge of political teaching, and in the inculcation of loyal principles and sentiments we recognize the pulpit and the press as legitimate instrumentalities." [5]

In the eyes of the leaders of the Southern Church the statement by the

[3] Robert D. Clark, *The Life of Matthew Simpson* (New York: The Macmillan Company, 1956), p. 160.

[4] *Revivalism and Social Reform in Mid-Nineteenth-Century America* (Nashville: Abingdon Press, 1957), p. 206.

[5] *Christian Advocate and Journal*, March 13, 1862, p. 85.

East Baltimore Conference was only further evidence that the Northern Church was, indeed, a "political" church. The Southern Church held to what it regarded as the "strictly Scriptural mission for the church." [6] As tensions became heightened, Southern editors urged the church to "preach repentance and faith and holiness" and "allow the people who are competent to attend to the affairs of the Nation and the State." [7] With the coming of the war Methodists of the South saw no alternative to defending their altars and firesides against an invasion incited in part, as they believed, by a "political" church and pulpit. Two weeks after the firing on Fort Sumter the editor of the Nashville *Christian Advocate* wrote under the heading "Civil War—Our Duty":

We exhort our countrymen, as they begin in the right, so to keep in the right. This itself is strength: it is more than armies. Preserve local order. Avoid swearing and drunkenness. Remember the Sabbath day. Patriotism is a duty which the Christian religion enjoins and has illustrated by glorious examples. Let prayer be made at the head of regiments.[8]

To the very end the Southern Church held to its view that the church must avoid political involvement. The pastoral letter of the Southern bishops in 1866 noted with satisfaction that the church had in no way "become complicated with political affairs," but had "been satisfied to perform her legitimate duties." [9]

These two views of the function of the church will be further illustrated as we trace the full story of American Methodism in the great conflict of the 1860's. Other differences, as well as similarities, will appear. The story deals with the rationalizations employed by the churches to justify their participation in the war; the various ministries provided for military personnel; the new institutional forms called forth in the war years; and the new leadership emerging. The account also touches upon the response of the churches to the changing fortunes of war; the advance of the Northern missionaries into the South; the disorganization wrought in the Southern Church; and the effects of the war upon Negro Methodists. Especially complex is the picture of the conflict in the border states. Here were the early arenas of military engagement; and here also were many communities in which the contest between Northern and Southern

---

[6] Hunter Dickinson Farish, *The Circuit Rider Dismounts: A Social History of Southern Methodism 1865-1900* (Richmond: The Dietz Press, 1938), p. 14.

[7] William Warren Sweet, *The Methodist Episcopal Church and the Civil War* (Cincinnati: Methodist Book Concern, 1912), p. 45.

[8] April 25, 1861.

[9] *Journal of the General Conference*, 1866, p. 17.

Methodism had flamed in bitterness since 1844. Because the controversy on the border affected in a number of ways the course of other events, it is with this portion of the story that we begin.

1

The "New Chapter" and the Struggle on the Border

Although the Methodist Episcopal Church had taken a strong anti-slavery position in the decade preceding 1860, the vigor and consistency of its stand had been qualified by a concern to retain the support of its border conferences, which were either wholly or in part within slave territory. Roughly 15 per cent of the total membership of the Northern Church in 1861 was in six border conferences: Baltimore, Baltimore East, Philadelphia, Western Virginia, Kentucky, and Missouri.[10] Prior to 1860 the church forbade slaveholding by its ministers, the buying or selling of slaves by its lay members, and the owning of slaves by lay members where state laws permitted emancipation. Not until 1860 did the more radical antislavery forces in the General Conference succeed in modifying the existing rule. The new statement—the "New Chapter"—adopted at Buffalo declared:

> We believe that the buying, selling, or holding of human beings, to be used as chattels, is . . . inconsistent with . . . that Rule in our Discipline which requires all who desire to continue among us "to do no harm," and "to avoid evil of every kind." We therefore affectionately admonish all our preachers and people to keep themselves pure from this great evil, and to seek its extirpation by all lawful and Christian means.[11]

Acceptance by the General Conference of the modification describing the new legislation as advisory and admonitory did not allay the fears of more conservative elements in the border conferences that the church was moving to an absolute position. Indeed, if there were any doubt that the church was moving toward an even firmer stand, it should have been dispelled by the election of Edward Thomson and Charles Elliott, respectively, to edit the *Christian Advocate and Journal* of New York and the *Central Christian Advocate* of St. Louis. Both men, known for their

[10] Figures from Sweet, *The Church and the Civil War*, pp. 46-47.
[11] *Journal of the General Conference*, 1860, p. 260.

pronounced antislavery opinions, replaced more conservative editors. As Sweet points out, the contest over the slavery question in the Methodist Episcopal Church was practically settled before the war began. To be sure, it would remain for the General Conference of 1864 to make the holding of slaves an unqualified impediment to Methodist membership. But by 1860 the church, with the exception of the border conferences, where a few slaveholders remained in the church, was practically unanimous in its repudiation of slavery. "The great majority of the membership . . . was in the Free States, and a very large majority of them were ready to identify themselves with any political movement which might rid the Nation of the institution of slavery, which they regarded as a sin, and which they had almost completely driven from the Church." [12]

As was feared, the "New Chapter" of 1860 stirred immediate protest in the border conferences. Some ministers and members withdrew from the Northern Church, and many of these entered the Methodist Episcopal Church, South. The most pronounced opposition came from the Baltimore and East Baltimore Conferences; but only in the former, a considerable part of which lay in the state of Virginia, were there extensive defections. In its 1861 session the Baltimore Conference discussed resolutions calling for immediate withdrawal from the jurisdiction of the Northern General Conference. Conditions proposed for return to the Northern body included the revocation of the "New Chapter" and the transfer to the Annual Conferences of the right to determine their respective positions on slavery. Further, the resolutions called for giving the slaveholding conferences a representative voice in the editorial policies of the church papers. Although Bishop Levi Scott declared the proposed resolutions out of order and refused to put the question, the split in the Baltimore Conference had been brought into the open. From 1862 through 1865, the Virginia section of the conference, having affirmed its independence of the Northern Church, convened separately. At its first meeting after the war, the General Conference of the Southern Church received into its membership the Baltimore Annual Conference, consisting of some twelve thousand lay members and over a hundred ministers.[13]

Of the other five border conferences in the Northern Church only East Baltimore and Philadelphia called for repeal of the "New Chapter." The Philadelphia Conference concurred in the action of the East Baltimore Conference, which had demanded repeal and defended the

[12] Sweet, *The Church and the Civil War*, pp. 45-46.
[13] William Warren Sweet, *Virginia Methodism: A History* (Richmond: Whittet & Shepperson, 1955), pp. 264-69, 294.

proposition that each Annual Conference should be given power to determine its own policies on the slavery issue. The Western Virginia and Kentucky Conferences expressed their opposition to the "New Chapter" but declined to reopen the question. The Missouri Conference recorded its sympathy with the other border conferences, but held that, since the new rule was advisory only, it would not renew the controversy. All the border conferences met in March, 1861, shortly after the inauguration of President Lincoln; and each of them, with the exception of Baltimore, adopted resolutions affirming support of the national government. A year later, after its proslavery preachers had withdrawn, the Baltimore Conference repudiated the rebellion and gave its endorsement to the Union.[14]

Some of the sharpest and most uncharitable exchanges among Methodists took place in those border communities where a sizable minority group of Methodists confronted a larger group belonging to the other branch of the Wesleyan family. The existence of both groups in the same community made for bitter conflict between them and intensified suspicion within each. Bitterness was compounded in western Virginia, Kentucky, and Missouri. In 1861 the Methodist Episcopal Church, South, had 10,898 white members in western Virginia, 41,043 in Kentucky, and 40,593 in Missouri. Methodist Episcopal membership in these three states in 1861 was: western Virginia, 21,792; Kentucky, 3,405; and Missouri, 6,245.[15] Southern Methodists constituted a clear majority in Missouri and Kentucky, but Northern Methodist membership in western Virginia was almost twice that of Southern Methodists. The acrimony in these three states during the war reflected a continuation of the controversy that had torn the border conferences since 1844.

When the attempt of Kentucky to maintain a neutral position gave way to open support of the Union cause, the stage was set for intensified strife among the Methodists. The sympathies of Northern Methodists, who stood in the minority, were clearly with the Union. An example of the extremes to which the excitement of these days could lead is seen in these words from a patriotic sermon by a minister of the Methodist Episcopal Church:

I trust our troops will rally and wipe out the disgrace of Manassas, though it cost the life of every rebel under arms. Let Davis and Beauregard be captured, to meet the fate of Haman. Hang them up on Mason's and Dixon's line, that traitors of both sections may be warned. Let them hang until vultures shall eat their rotten flesh from their bones; let them hang until the crows shall

---

[14] Sweet, *The Church and the Civil War*, pp. 48-50.
[15] Figures from *ibid.*, p. 53.

build their filthy nests in their skeletons: let them hang until the rope rots, and let their dismembered bones fall so deep into the earth that God Almighty can't find them in the day of resurrection.[16]

Southern Methodists in Kentucky found their house divided. Strong Union loyalties found expression in both the Louisville and the Kentucky Conferences of the Southern Church. A majority of the preachers of the Kentucky Conference were Union men, and in 1862 some of these preachers refused to go to appointments within the Confederate lines. Two years later, in resolutions making them in effect practically independent of the Methodist Episcopal Church, South, the Kentucky Conference preachers affirmed their devotion to the Union and stated that the conference had always been loyal to the North. In the spring of 1865 eighteen members of the conference withdrew and entered the Methodist Episcopal Church.[17]

The people of the western counties of Virginia owned few slaves and were predominantly supporters of the Union. Quite aside from the issues of slavery and secession, however, the western part of the state had little in common with the eastern section; and prior to the war this difference was registered in the adherence of the majority of the Methodists of western Virginia to the Northern Church. The movement to form a separate government was set on foot in 1861, and a year later Congress passed the bill admitting the state of West Virginia into the Union. Members of the Methodist Episcopal Church in West Virginia preached boldly in support of the Union. In the words of one of them, the Methodist Episcopal Church was a "heaven-appointed instrumentality" for the preservation of the integrity of the Union.[18]

None of the border states saw more rancor, or suffered more cruelty practiced in the name of Christianity, than did Missouri. In terms of reported membership, the Methodist Episcopal Church, South, outnumbered the Methodist Episcopal Church over six to one in Missouri in 1861. Missouri Methodists were for the most part descendants of old Southern families who had been associated with the institution of slavery in the states from which they had migrated. If the majority of the Southern Methodists in Missouri did not favor secession, the greater part of their leadership was vocal in its support. During the early stage of the secession controversy the Southern Methodist majority made life so difficult for the Northern Methodists that numbers of the latter fled from the state. Persecution of the Northern Methodist minority became

---

[16] Quoted, *ibid.*, p. 57.
[17] *Ibid.*, p. 57.
[18] *Ibid.*, pp. 54-55.

so severe that one presiding elder traveled with two revolvers on his person, and Charles Elliott, editor of the *Central Christian Advocate,* advised his fellow Northern Methodists to suspend all public church services outside the city of St. Louis.[19]

With the retreat of Governor Price into Arkansas, and with the occupation of Missouri by Union forces, persecution now came to be directed against the Methodist Episcopal Church, South. When it had become clear that Missouri would remain in the Union, the Southern Church adopted a stand of neutrality and asserted its loyalty to the government. Its Northern opponents, however, were reluctant to recognize its claims to be a nonpolitical, nonsectional body, and under the aggressive encouragement of the *Central Christian Advocate* lost no opportunity to capitalize on public suspicions of the Southern Church and its leaders.

The Missouri Conference of the Methodist Episcopal Church loudly proclaimed its loyalty. Loyal editors printed with enthusiasm accounts of members and preachers changing from the Southern to the Northern Church on the issue of loyalty to the government. In 1863 the Missionary Society of the church appropriated $7,000 to aid the conference in extending its work in Missouri and Arkansas. The 1864 session of the Missouri Annual Conference heard reports of the affiliation of four ministers and over a thousand laymen who formerly had belonged to the Methodist Episcopal Church, South.[20]

Even after the war Missouri Methodists continued to inflict cruelties upon one another. Each side stated its case in volumes which are important today chiefly for depicting the harvest of the bitter fruit of suspicion and recrimination. Charles Elliott's *South-Western Methodism*[21] devoted several chapters to the "persecutions of the M. E. Church." Merely to be a member of the Methodist Episcopal Church in those days, Elliott explained in his Preface, "was the greatest crime known by the pro-slavery men." It was "synonymous with *negro thief,* incendiary, insurrectionist and the like." [22] The other side of the controversy produced a two-volume work, the extended title of which suggests the material from which it drew: *Martyrdom in Missouri, A History of Religious Proscription, the Seizure of Churches, and the Persecution of Ministers of the Gospel, in the State of Missouri During the Late Civil War.*[23] Said the author, who already had gathered material for a third volume: "If an accurate record were preserved of all the

[19] *Central Christian Advocate,* May 15, 1861.

[20] Sweet, *The Church and the Civil War,* pp. 60-62.

[21] *South-Western Methodism. A History of the M.E. Church in the South-West from 1844 to 1864* (Cincinnati: Poe and Hitchcock, 1868) .

[22] *Ibid.,* p. 3.

[23] W. M. Leftwich (St. Louis: Southwestern Book and Publishing Company, 1870) .

sufferings endured in Missouri by the children of God at the hands of military and ecclesiastical persecutors, it would require volume after volume." [24]

The struggle on the border comes into intelligible perspective only as it falls into place in the larger conflict between two churches of common heritage now further alienated by the warfare that tore the nation asunder. We turn, therefore, to consider the kind of support that each church offered to the civil authority and its military operations.

2

Patriotism and Religion in the North

For the first three years the extensive war activities of the Methodist Episcopal Church were conceived and directed without official action by the highest governing body of the denomination. To be sure, the General Conference of 1860 had confirmed and strengthened the anti-slavery stand of the church, but that conference adjourned almost a year before Lincoln issued his first call for troops. Hence, from the beginning of hostilities until the convening of the next General Conference the posture of the church was determined by the aggressive leadership of the bishops, the church press, and the Annual Conferences, all supported by the wide popular endorsement of clergy and laity. When the General Conference assembled on May 2, 1864, the war was already closer to its end than national or ecclesiastical leaders dared to believe.

A week after it convened in Old Union Church in Philadelphia, the 1864 conference determined "to present to the President of these United States, in a suitable address, the assurances of our Church that we are with him heart and soul in the present struggle for human rights and free institutions." [25] The address, prepared by the Committee on the State of the Nation, was calculated to elicit the President's support of Methodist interests; and Lincoln's reply betrayed the concern of the chief executive to retain the backing of the largest Protestant church at a time when Methodist assistance was of critical political importance. Notwithstanding the political considerations, however, the Methodist address and the President's reply are of special interest at this point

[24] *Ibid.*, p. 14.
[25] *Journal of the General Conference,* 1864, p. 98.

for what they reflect, in dramatic and prestigious setting, of the broad and effective support already given to the war effort by the church.

The conference designated five of its members to bear the address to Washington: Bishop Edward R. Ames, Joseph Cummings, George Peck, Charles Elliott, and Granville Moody. In the presence of his cabinet the President listened to the statement prepared by the Methodists:

> *To His Excellency Abraham Lincoln, President of the*
> *United States*
>
> The General Conference of the Methodist Episcopal Church, now in session in the city of Philadelphia, representing nearly seven thousand ministers and nearly a million of members, mindful of their duty as Christian citizens, takes the earliest opportunity to express to you the assurance of the loyalty of the Church, her earnest devotion to the interests of the country, and her sympathy with you in the great responsibilities of your high position in this trying hour.

Continuing, the address pointed proudly to a Methodist record "never . . . tarnished by disloyalty," and to the "many thousands" of Methodist members and the "large number" of their ministers who had "rushed to arms to maintain the cause of God and humanity." It condemned the "unnatural, utterly unjustifiable rebellion, involving the crime of treason against the best of human governments and sin against God." It congratulated the president on the recent victories of the Federal arms and commended his "proclamations of liberty . . . and all the acts of government designed to secure freedom to the enslaved."

The statement also placed the church on record in support of the reconstruction of the South. "We trust," said the General Conference to the president, "that when military usages and necessities shall justify interference with established institutions, and the removal of wrongs sanctioned by law, the occasion will be improved, not merely to injure our foes . . . , but also as an opportunity to recognize our obligations to God and to honor his law." Methodists prayed for the early coming of the day when America should be "truly a republican and free country," with slavery unknown in any of its states or territories.[26]

President Lincoln, having seen the address in advance, took from his desk a prepared reply and read it to the assembled dignitaries:

> Gentlemen,—In response to your address allow me to attest the accuracy of its historical statements, indorse the sentiments it expresses, and thank you in the nation's name for the sure promise it gives.

[26] *Ibid.,* pp. 378-79.

Nobly sustained as the government has been by all the Churches, I would utter nothing which might in the least appear invidious against any. Yet without this it may fairly be said that the Methodist Episcopal Church, not less devoted than the best, is, by its greater numbers, the most important of all. It is no fault in others that the Methodist Church sends more soldiers to the field, more nurses to the hospitals, and more prayers to heaven than any. God bless the Methodist Church! bless all the Churches! and blessed be God! who in this our great trial giveth us the Churches.[27]

The sheer numbers of the Methodists made them a decisive factor in any enterprise drawing freely upon their resources of men, wealth, and moral force. Yet, there were other characteristics of the denomination which enhanced and facilitated its support of the nation at war. The nature of its organization, the distribution of its membership, the vigor of its press, and the aggressive personal leadership of its bishops served the nation as well as the church. Beyond these more tangible resources, however, lay an ideology, not wholly peculiar to the denomination, to the service of which the Methodists provided moral and spiritual sanctions, and dedicated their seemingly boundless energies. To the Methodists the nation was indebted not only for their generous contributions of men and materials, but also for their service in mobilizing public opinion, and in discerning and interpreting a transcendent meaning in the great fratricidal conflict.[28]

Zealously the church marshaled public opinion. "The spirit of Methodism," Bishop Morris told the General Conference, "is the spirit of patriotism." [29] In their address to the conference the bishops proudly announced: "In this great crisis of our national affairs . . . the Methodist Episcopal Church has proved herself to be eminently loyal." Her loyalty, continued the bishops, extended beyond resolutions of approval and sympathy and contributions of money. "Her members in large numbers, and many of her ministers, have flocked to the national standard, and have fought side by side with brother patriots on every battle-field of this dreadful war." [30] To all Methodists everywhere the conference directed a pastoral exhortation begging them to remember "how heartily we are identified with the nation in her struggles," and calling for continued sacrifices until "the nation's new life shall be placed beyond the reach of the bloody hands which seek to destroy it." Solemnly the conference

---

[27] *Ibid.*, p. 380.
[28] Ralph E. Morrow, *Northern Methodism and Reconstruction* (East Lansing: Michigan State University Press, 1956) , pp. 15-25, discusses these specific contributions.
[29] *Journal of the General Conference*, 1864, p. 290.
[30] *Ibid.*, p. 274.

charged its constituency: "All true patriots ought to regard their lives and treasures, without reservation, as subject to the exigencies of this conflict, until it is honorably and triumphantly ended." [31]

If in its work near the border the Northern Church met peculiar difficulties in establishing a posture of loyalty, its other conferences presented on the whole a solid phalanx of patriotism. Such controversies as troubled Kentucky and Missouri were exceptional in those conferences where the preponderance of Methodist membership resided. Flags were a common sight in churches, especially at the sessions of the Annual Conferences. On some occasions the raising of the flag and the reading of resolutions was accompanied by addresses and the singing of patriotic songs. Charles Elliott displayed in all the conferences he visited a large silk flag made by "five excellent Union, Christian, Methodist ladies in St. Louis." The fiery editor's account before the Illinois Conference of his defense of Northern Methodism in St. Louis had led the Illinois preachers to take up a collection of fifty dollars to purchase him a flag. Among other mottoes embroidered on Elliott's flag and its pendants were the words, "The Central Christian Advocate of the Methodist Episcopal Church of 1784." [32] (This date emphasized the unvarying antislavery witness of the church since its founding.)

Patriotic demonstrations in Methodist gatherings sometimes took on the character of revival meetings. Descriptions of audience response to the addresses of Bishop Matthew Simpson picture the explosive excitement greeting many a Methodist orator less distinguished than the bishop. When Simpson spoke, "men clenched their hands, shouted, stamped, stood on their feet, and were left at the end in a tumult of patriotic excitement." At Chillicothe, Ohio, "ladies threw away their fans and handkerchiefs; men threw their hats in the air, stood erect, and mounted the seats." At Philadelphia, where Simpson substituted for President Lincoln at the opening of the Sanitary Fair, the bishop's peroration brought from the audience shouts of "Amen! Amen!" When Simpson paid dramatic tribute to the "war-torn, shot-riddled flag" of the 55th Regiment, five thousand listeners in the New York Academy of Music rose to their feet and gave three cheers for the flag.[33] Simpson's biographer says of him: "The cause of the Union possessed and overwhelmed him. The mingled emotions—his hatred of slavery, his frustration from the long years of struggle with the southern church,

[31] *Ibid.*, pp. 434-35.
[32] Elliott, *South-Western Methodism*, pp. 311-13.
[33] Clark, *Life of Simpson*, pp. 237, 240, 242.

his intense love of country and church, . . . the fluctuating griefs and joys of war—all boiled within him and overflowed in a torrent of words." [34] In Simpson, Methodist patriotism reached out to touch audiences far larger than any offered by the church. His celebrated "War Address," delivered repeatedly on patriotic occasions, would itself have made him a national figure. One editor thought that Simpson should travel at large "to address the public mind upon those great questions which concern so vitally the Church and the nation." [35]

Patriotism as spelled out by the Methodists called for more than passive adherence to the Union side in the conflict. "We continue to discountenance faint-hearted endorsement as well as avowed opposition to the Government, whether by ministers or laymen." So resolved the Rock River Conference in 1861.[36] The Wisconsin Conference stated the issue more sharply: "At such a time as this, neutrality is treason, silence crime, and inaction unpardonable." [37] The Genesee Conference in 1863 declared they would not receive into conference membership "any one whose patriotism could justly be called into question." [38] It was not unusual for an entire conference to have the oath of allegiance administered by a federal officer. The Minutes of the New York East Conference referred to such an occasion as exhibiting a "happy union of religion and patriotism," and carried a list of all who had signed the oath. At the same session the conference voted approval of one of its members who, because he would not bind himself to avoid political sermons, had not been accepted by the charge to which he had been appointed. Bishop Baker presented to this preacher a collection of $238.50 raised in his behalf by his fellow ministers.[39]

Northern Methodism was no less outspoken in some of the western conferences, where political opposition to the administration and to the continuation of the war manifested considerable strength. Sweet holds, "with a considerable degree of certainty," that the "copperhead" element was very small among Methodists, even in those areas where it was most prevalent.[40] In the southern parts of Ohio, Indiana, and Illinois, where strong sympathies for the South were not uncommon, one rarely found a Methodist preacher who was a Democrat. Indeed, such a preacher would have found it hard to gain a hearing or to collect his

[34] *Ibid.*, p. 236.
[35] *Ibid.*, p. 238, quoting clipping from the Rochester *Democrat*, n.d.
[36] Sweet, *The Church and the Civil War*, p. 84.
[37] *Ibid.*, p. 85.
[38] *Ibid.*, p. 75.
[39] *Ibid.*, p. 71.
[40] *Ibid.*, p. 83.

salary. An Ohio presiding elder reported that he countered the "Butter-nut" sentiment in his district with a war sermon every Sunday.[41]

"God Cannot Do Without America"

In the ready mingling of the sentiments of patriotism and religion Methodist orators helped partisans of the Union cause find transcendent meaning in the tragic struggle between the Blue and the Gray. The divine purpose which they discerned in the conflict not only undergirded their appeals for loyalty, unity, and unremitting effort, but also, as victory became certain, shaped the attitudes of the victors toward the vanquished South. It would not be just, to be sure, to read uniformity into all the patriotic expressions in Methodist sermons, editorials, and resolutions, or to impugn indiscriminately the sincerity of statements of simple benevolence toward the South. But the uses of religion in the service of patriotism were many and varied.

Bishop Simpson's lecture on the eve of the 1864 presidential election was chauvinistic. He believed it to be the "design of Providence" that the nation, "having passed through this fiery ordeal, [should] come out of it purer, stronger, and more glorious than ever before." America's democracy and religious freedom, her education of the masses, and her hospitality to the oppressed were indications of her election to fulfill a great national destiny. "This nation has the sympathy of the masses all over the earth, and if the world is to be raised to its proper place, I would say it with all reverence, God cannot do without America." [42]

The Pastoral Address of the General Conference ended in a more humble tenor. "We are yet a haughty and rebellious people," the Meth-odists were told. "There can be no good reason to expect the restoration of order and unity until we properly deplore our sins and turn to God with deep self-abasement and fervent prayer." [43] But the boundary between humility and self-righteousness was not easily identified. The fires that cleansed the victor could also burn the vanquished, and the same rationale that explained the suffering of the North justified the punishment of the South. The scourge that purified the North could be read as divine judgment executed by the hands of the North upon the sins of the South. Moreover, the divine visitation that smote the Confederacy made of the South a challenging field of missionary

[41] *Ibid.*, pp. 79, 86.

[42] George Richard Crooks, *The Life of Bishop Matthew Simpson* (New York: Harper & Brothers, 1890), p. 380.

[43] *Journal of the General Conference*, 1864, pp. 435-36.

activity for Northern evangelists. With the establishment of peace, Bishop Morris reminded the General Conference, "we shall have such a revival of the work of God as the world has never seen. We have the dawning of this glorious day already, and we believe the sun will soon arise in full splendor, and from every hill and valley will go up the shout, 'Hallelujah! the Lord God omnipotent reigneth.' " [44] In fairness to the senior bishop it must be granted that his vision encompassed horizons beyond the South; but Simpson had already spoken before the Missionary Society about the "vast field opening" in the South. The Northern Church must enter it, Simpson urged, "or be derelict in Christian Duty." [45]

As Northern victories pointed conclusively toward the return of peace, Methodist visions of a united church extending to the Gulf became enticing. Missionary enthusiasm did not always allow for nice distinctions between the prospect of a united nation and that of a united church, or between conversion to Christ and the restoration of law and order. Ralph E. Morrow's study of the roots of Northern Methodist interest in the South after the war underscores the strain of cultural imperialism running through Methodist pronouncements and editorials. The victory of Northern arms would vindicate Northern principles and validate the North's assumption of cultural superiority. Since Methodism was believed to carry with it the highest civilization of all times, its mission to the South was now clearly revealed, and only the defects of Southern character stood in the way of the rejuvenation of the vanquished territory.[46] The story of Northern Methodist expansion into the South, however, can be more easily understood after we have first viewed the work of the Northern chaplains and the wartime activities of the Southern Church.

Ministries to the Union Troops

A total of 510 Methodist chaplains served in the Union armies.[47] Within a month after President Lincoln's first call for troops the War Department issued a general order allowing one chaplain to each regiment, to be appointed by the regimental commander on the vote of his officers. Before the end of the year the president also recommended provisions for the appointment of regular hospital chaplains. Certain abuses in the appointment of chaplains soon became apparent, and the

[44] *Ibid.,* p. 291.
[45] *Christian Advocate and Journal,* February 18, 1864, p. 53.
[46] *Northern Methodism and Reconstruction,* pp. 20-25.
[47] This paragraph and the one following are summarized from Sweet's chapter on the chaplaincy in *The Church and the Civil War,* pp. 133-41.

Methodists, no less than other denominations, found that some unqualified men were representing them in the chaplaincy. To give a single example, certain local preachers in Pennsylvania received ordination from an independent Congregational Church in order to qualify for appointment. Congressional legislation passed in July, 1862, provided more rigid standards in an effort to ensure that only ordained men with proper ecclesiastical certification should serve. Further legislation in 1864 determined the rank of the chaplain and prescribed his duties. He was to submit monthly reports to the adjutant general regarding moral conditions among the soldiers, conduct appropriate burial services, and provide public religious services on Sundays wherever practicable.

Chaplains also distributed tracts, Bibles, and various items provided for the comfort of the troops. Many chaplains wrote communications to the church papers, some as regular correspondents, describing their work in the regiments and presenting the needs of the soldiers to the home churches and the various agencies contributing supplies for their work. Because in most cases the regimental commander had chosen him directly, the chaplain tended to be a man already popular with officers and men. In instances where a considerable number of volunteers came from a single church it was not uncommon for the pastor to be selected as the chaplain. Some preachers who enlisted as privates later received chaplain appointments. On the whole, Methodist chaplains served faithfully. The chaplain in many instances organized a regimental church, which held regular services and afforded other channels for sustained pastoral relationships. When his troops remained in camp, he held revival meetings, in which he was often assisted by delegates of the Christian Commission.

No man symbolized the Union chaplaincy in the public mind more completely than Charles C. McCabe, the popular "singing chaplain" from Ohio who later was to become a bishop in the Methodist Episcopal Church. McCabe's eloquence contributed to the raising of the 122nd Regiment of Ohio; and in the fall of 1862, a few days before his twenty-sixth birthday, the young minister accepted appointment as chaplain of the 122nd. He had hardly completed eight months of service, however, when he was captured while tending the wounded of his retreating regiment and was sent to the celebrated Libby Prison in Richmond. During the five months of his confinement McCabe assisted in educational and morale work with the prisoners. Brought near death by an attack of typhoid fever, he weighed less than a hundred pounds when exchanged. In later years his prison experiences became familiar to thousands who heard his popular lecture on "The Bright Side of Life in Libby Prison." [48] McCabe himself estimated that over a period of forty years audiences attending his lecture contributed $150,000 for the erection of churches and parsonages and the support of poor preachers.

Six months after his release McCabe had recovered sufficiently to return to the camps. In the meantime he had resigned his chaplaincy and accepted appointment as delegate of the United States Christian Commission. He now began a period of intensive evangelistic work in the camps in Virginia. Soon brought to exhaustion, he returned home once more for recuperation and next took an assignment as home agent of the Christian Commission with responsibility for raising funds in Iowa, Illinois, and Wisconsin. He set his own goal at $250,000 and toward its achievement secured the largest single gift to the commission, a $10,000 contribution by a wealthy Illinois farmer.[49]

McCabe's promotional work in behalf of the Christian Commission had further significance in that it foreshadowed the new kind of promotion and fund-raising for church-wide benevolent causes which the Methodists were to employ extensively in the period after the war. The chaplain appeared, as he put it, "doomed to raise money." [50] For the remainder of his life he was to be associated with the causes of church extension, missions, education of the freedman, and other forms of Christian philanthropy to the support of which the church came to apply the zeal which earlier it had directed toward evangelistic activity.

Methodists and the Christian Commission

Much of the Methodist support of the Union cause was channeled through the service activities of the United States Christian Commission, which was launched at a convention in New York City in November, 1861.[51] The commission combined the efforts of the Young Men's Christian Associations and various relief organizations already serving the troops, and drew to its banners a host of workers from the evangelical churches. Twelve members comprised the original commission, but the membership was later expanded to forty-seven. An efficient executive committee of five members directed the multiform activities from commission headquarters in Philadelphia. The plan of organization ultimately adopted provided for a general field agent, with one or more

[48] Frank Milton Bristol, *The Life of Chaplain McCabe* (New York: Fleming H. Revell Company, 1908), pp. 118-45.

[49] *Ibid.*, pp. 174-80.

[50] *Ibid.*, p. 164.

[51] See C. Howard Hopkins, *History of the Y.M.C.A. in North America* (New York: Association Press, 1951), pp. 89-94.

assistants in each army. The general agent established stations as needed and assigned delegates to the stations. A permanent station agent in each corps directed the work of the delegates.[52] Auxiliaries in the larger cities augmented the promotional work of the central commission, and the auxiliaries were strengthened in turn by a network of tributary organizations in the towns and villages.

Over 4,000 delegates, two thirds of them laymen, served under the commission in hospitals and camps and on the battlefield. Among these workers were 458 ministers of the Methodist Episcopal Church.[53] Delegates served for terms of six weeks without pay. Addressed as "Chaplain" by the troops, they performed most of the duties of chaplains, visiting the sick and wounded, conducting religious services, burying the dead, distributing religious literature and various "stores," and discouraging the vices usually associated with camp life. Not the least of the delegates' contributions was their support of civilian morale through the firsthand accounts of military life they were able to bring back to their communities. Delegates were also effective in raising funds for the commission. When a Methodist minister in Clearfield County, Pennsylvania, left his charge for service as a delegate, a public meeting raised an offering of $875.25.[54]

The Christian Commission derived much of its support from various denominational agencies and through denominational channels. With no general organ of its own, it depended largely upon the religious and secular press to publicize its activities. Methodist *Advocates* carried reports from delegates and urged financial support of the commission. Annual Conferences supported the commission in a variety of ways. The Newark Conference, for instance, resolved that each of its districts should keep one of its preachers in service as a delegate "all the time that the exigencies of the army require" and that the presiding elder, assisted by two other preachers, should supply the appointments of the delegate during his absence. Methodist churches received collections for the commission on the various thanksgiving and fast days observed during the war.[55] The 1864 General Conference endorsed both the Sanitary Commission and the Christian Commission as "sublime manifestations of benevolence." It commended these organizations to the "enlarged liberality" of all Methodists, and urged the church to take action necessary

[52] Lemuel Moss, *Annals of the United States Christian Commission* (Philadelphia: J. B. Lippincott & Co., 1868) , p. 145.
[53] Sweet, *The Church and the Civil War*, p. 164.
[54] Moss, *Annals of the Christian Commission*, pp. 522-23, 541-47.
[55] Sweet, *The Church and the Civil War*, pp. 163, 165-66.

to furnish its "due proportion of Christian men, and especially Christian ministers, for this holy work." [56]

The Tract Society of the Methodist Episcopal Church co-operated with the Christian Commission in supplying religious publications. To the 1864 General Conference the Tract Society reported that it had donated to the commission hundreds of thousands of copies of its publication, "Good News," and over two million pages of tracts.[57] The church made further, though indirect, contributions to the commission through its increased support of the American Bible Society, which contributed Scriptures for the commission's use.[58]

Edmund S. Janes, bishop of the Northern Church, was one of the four Methodists listed among the original twelve members of the Christian Commission. Bishop Janes was also one of the two Methodists on the five-man executive committee in the first year.[59] On two occasions the bishop visited the War Department in the interest of expediting access of the commission's workers to the troops. Secretary Stanton assured Janes "that every facility consistent with the exigencies of the service" would be opened to the commission "for the performance of their religious and benevolent purposes in the armies of the United States, and in the forts, garrisons, and camps, and military posts." [60] Bishop Janes also represented the commission in an unsuccessful attempt to visit Union men in Confederate prisons. Amid increased reports of the poor treatment of Northern captives in military prisons the commission secured War Department approval for its representatives to seek passage through enemy lines for the purpose of carrying supplies to Federal prisoners in the South. Bishop Janes and Bishop Alfred Lee of the Protestant Episcopal Church proceeded as far as the flag-of-truce boat on the James River; but General Grant's agent was unable to obtain permission from Confederate authorities for completion of the mission.[61]

Bishop Simpson also became a member of the Christian Commission and at the end of the war was one of the five trustees appointed to liquidate the commission's work. Simpson spoke at the first public anniversary of the commission in the Philadelphia Academy of Music in 1863, and delivered the concluding address at the fourth and last anniversary in the Hall of the House of Representatives in February, 1866. The Methodist bishop's summary of the achievements of the com-

[56] *Journal of the General Conference*, 1864, pp. 264-65, 435.
[57] *Ibid.*, pp. 432-33.
[58] Sweet, *The Church and the Civil War*, pp. 166-68.
[59] Moss, *Annals of the Christian Commission*, pp. 106, 108.
[60] Memorandum quoted in *ibid.*, p. 131.
[61] *Ibid.*, pp. 189-98.

mission not only reflects the support given by his own church to the organization's wartime activities, but also indicates the extent to which piety and patriotism had become identified during the war years. The Christian Commission, Simpson reminded his distinguished audience, had contributed immeasurably to the triumph of the Northern armies. The labors of the delegates had "sanctified the War in the hearts of the soldiers." [62] The reports which the returning delegates brought back to the homes and the churches of the nation made the war "sacred in the eyes of the people." The work of the commission had helped to identify the government "with every feeling of religion and every act of mercy." [63] Moreover, the influence of the commission had reached beyond America to strengthen the "cause of Christianity throughout the world." For the first time in history the "whole Christian Church" had been united on a strictly voluntary basis in a benevolent ministry on the field of battle. "Here men of all denominations mingled freely. Men of all creeds stood side by side, engaged in works of mercy, emulous only in performing humble services and deeds of love. And thus the churches, bound together in one great effort for the cause of Christ, have exemplified true Christianity. As citizens they rallied under one flag, as Christians under one cross." [64] To be added to the achievements of the commission, the bishop continued, was its demonstration of the ability of woman to "stand side by side with man" in the ministry on the battlefield and in the hospitals. "What part she is to have in the future of humanity I know not, but I fancy that her aid in some active form will be essential in correcting those forms of vice which now especially degrade humanity." [65]

Bishop Simpson envisioned the spirit of the Christian Commission living on in other fields. Its workers would find new places of service in the evangelization of the cities, the education of the freedmen, and the reconstruction of the nation. "When the law and the sword have accomplished their utmost work, they cannot change unwilling minds. The moral work remains to be done." [66]

Another indication of Methodist support of the war effort was the enthusiastic encouragement by its clergy in the promotion of enlistment. In some communities the Methodist preacher was the chief assistant of the recruiting officer. He might stand with the officer within the chancel and urge his people to come forward for enlistment. Or he might first enlist himself and then urge others to follow his example. Some preachers

[62] *Ibid.*, p. 272.
[63] *Ibid.*, p. 273.
[64] *Ibid.*, p. 274.
[65] *Ibid.*, p. 276.
[66] *Ibid.*, p. 277.

raised more than one company in this fashion. Many large churches raised companies composed almost exclusively of their own members, and conferences as well as local churches valued the prestige derived from large enlistments. Church papers mentioned regiments made up largely of Methodists. During the Gettysburg campaign in the summer of 1863, when emergency companies were being recruited for defense in southeastern Pennsylvania, one company was made up of Methodist preachers from Philadelphia and vicinity. Many of these preachers wielded shovels and picks in erecting fortifications for the defense of Philadelphia.[67]

The number of Methodists serving in the Northern armies can only be estimated. Bishop Morris reported in 1864 that at least one hundred thousand Methodists had been mustered into service.[68] General Clinton B. Fisk, himself an ardent Methodist, claimed in 1862 that 15 per cent of the Union armies were Methodist. Sweet considers this percentage too high, and suggests that a total of something over 125,000 Methodist men served during the war. Membership of the Methodist Episcopal Church declined from 990,447 in 1861 to 929,259 in 1865. This loss of 61,188 Sweet attributes largely to enlistments of Methodist men in the army.[69]

Methodist women were organized for a variety of activities in support of the war. Many churches sponsored sewing societies for knitting socks, making underwear, and pulling lint. Women from a particular church in some cases were responsible for the service work in a hospital.[70]

Granville Moody: "Gallant Fighting Preacher"

Besides the Methodists serving as chaplains and as Christian Commission delegates, a large number of preachers became commissioned officers, and others enlisted as privates. Among the delegates to the General Conference of 1864 were three ministers who had fought as colonels for Northern regiments.[71] One of these was the colorful Granville Moody, onetime commander of the 74th Ohio Regiment. Pastor of Morris Chapel in Cincinnati, Moody in 1861 recruited volunteers for what he termed the "holiest [war] the world ever knew." When Governor Dennison offered him the command of the 74th, the Methodist Episcopal Preachers Association of Cincinnati termed the call "providential" and

[67] Sweet, *The Church and the Civil War*, pp. 77-78.
[68] *Journal of the General Conference*, 1864, p. 290.
[69] Sweet, *The Church and the Civil War*, pp. 93-95.
[70] *Ibid.*, pp. 77-78.
[71] *Journal of the General Conference*, 1864, p. 290.

"cordially" approved his acceptance. Moody took the appointment on condition that Major Alexander von Schrader, who had served in the Prussian army, would become lieutenant colonel of the regiment. Moody's friends considered that his sound judgment and his burning zeal for the Union compensated for his lack of military experience. Temporarily detached from his regiment, Moody, to quote a newspaper account, "greatly improved himself in military knowledge" while assigned as post commander of Camp Chase, and rejoined his regiment in the summer of 1862.[72]

Moody assisted the chaplain of his regiment and often preached in the regimental church, which was known as the "Church of the Living God." On one evening the colonel baptized nine soldiers.[73] Of one of his Sundays Moody wrote to a church editor:

After attending to all my duties of a military character, I said to the officers and men at the stations, as they stood drawn up in line, that I had some orders from the head-quarters of the King Immortal, Eternal, and Invisible, and proceeded to declare to them the gospel of the grace of God, "teaching them to observe all things whatsoever were commanded" by the Captain of our salvation. In this way I had the opportunity of preaching to hundreds of my fellow-sinners, citizens, and soldiers, and I assure you I found great delight in this work of faith and labor of love, which I pursue with the patience of hope. It seemed like the old circuit preaching that we were accustomed to in the olden time.[74]

An Illinois officer who heard Moody preach before a soldier congregation in Nashville wrote to his sister: "It was one of the most eloquent sermons I ever heard, one which I shall always remember. I could have listened to him for hours without experiencing the least weariness." [75]

After seventeen months in the Army of the Cumberland, Moody was so weakened by exposure and wounds that he resigned his commission. In accepting his resignation General Rosecrans recommended the fighting parson for the position of post chaplain, should an opening occur. The United States Senate, in March, 1865, conferred upon him the rank of brigadier general, by brevet.[76] Even while in command of his regiment Colonel Moody had found opportunity to address patriotic rallies in his

[72] Granville Moody, *A Life's Retrospect: Autobiography of Rev. Granville Moody*, ed. Sylvester Weeks (Cincinnati: Cranston and Stowe, 1890), pp. 337-38, 364.

[73] Sweet, *The Church and the Civil War*, p. 140.

[74] *A Life's Retrospect*, pp. 349-50.

[75] Quoted by Bell Irvin Wiley, *The Life of Billy Yank, the Common Soldier of the Union* (New York: Bobbs-Merrill, 1952), p. 268.

[76] Moody, *A Life's Retrospect*, pp. 366-68.

native state. The Springfield, Ohio, *News* reported in 1863 a stirring Washington's Birthday address by the "gallant fighting preacher" in which he paid his respects to "traitors to our holy cause." These Moody described as "these craven gray-backs, butternuts, Knights of the Golden Circle, . . . and other jayhawking sympathizers with rebels." [77]

The New Status of Methodism

If the picture presented by Northern Methodists in the Civil War period is one of wholehearted patriotism and loyal support of the government, one ought to bear in mind that their motives were not always unmixed. Just as the Northern Church had developed a maturer sense of social responsibility, so had it become more concerned as to its relative position among the other denominations; and Methodist assistance in the prosecution of the war was not unrelated to the Methodist search for status. A generation earlier the old established denominations had scorned the Methodists for their heretical doctrines and emotional worship and had ridiculed them for their uneducated leadership. Now, Methodist bishops enjoyed the confidence of the White House and were consulted by members of the cabinet. Methodists were especially proud of the political leadership of Matthew Simpson, who more than any of the wartime bishops symbolized the Methodist struggle for status. Simpson believed not only in the ultimate triumph of Christianity and the peculiar destiny of the American nation. He also believed in the greatness of the Methodist Episcopal Church, and he was jealous of its claim to distinction. Intellectually superior to his contemporaries in the church, experienced in the frontier politics of Indiana, and an able tactician in political maneuver within his own denomination, Simpson proved a formidable representative of the Methodists in dealing with the new political leaders in Washington.

The first substantial appointment given by the Republicans to a Methodist was that of John Evans as governor of Colorado Territory. Evans, the Chicago real-estate operator for whom Evanston was named, was a founder of Northwestern University. He and Simpson both recognized the advantage of having a Methodist in the governorship and made their plans accordingly. Methodist office-seekers plagued Simpson with their pleas for his assistance; but the bishop was sensitive to the criticism of "political" bishops, and, further, he was anxious to exert his influence in the most strategic fashion. He was particularly desirous of

[77] *Ibid.*, p. 375.

securing a cabinet post for James Harlan, a graduate of Indiana Asbury and United States Senator from Iowa. Simpson declined for himself an appointment offered him by Stanton as head of a commission to investigate conditions among Negroes in certain occupied areas in the South.

It would not be fair to imply that Simpson bargained Methodist support of the Union for political favors; but it is no disparagement of Methodist patriotism to say that he lost no opportunity to make the Republican administration aware of the strength of the Methodist vote and respectful of the political claims of Methodist leaders. Lincoln instituted a more thoroughgoing housecleaning of officeholders than any of his predecessors; but Methodists were disappointed in the recognition accorded them. Simpson complained to the president himself, and, seconded by Ames and such lesser lights as John Lanahan, he began to cultivate members of the cabinet. If the proportion of Methodist privates was commensurate with the total Methodist population, the dispensers of patronage must be apprised of the validity of Methodist claims upon the larger rewards to the faithful.

In fairness to the Methodist leaders one must judge their political activities in terms of the standards of their own day. Their patriotism should not be called into question merely on the grounds of its association with the political self-assertion that accompanied the struggle for status. The nation was being pressed to recognize that if the Methodists were loyal citizens, they also had come of age. As the Northern Church entered its centennial observance in 1866, *Harper's Weekly* commented: "For good or for ill, this form of Protestantism has become the predominant ecclesiastical fact of the nation. The official census places it, numerically far in advance of any other American religious body, and the general religious statistics of the country show that it comprises nearly one-half of all our Protestant communicants." [78] Men would question Bishop Simpson's suggestion that God could not do without America; but the years of the Civil War made it clear that no great movement, political or otherwise, could disregard the interests of the Methodist Episcopal Church.[79]

Methodists of the Confederacy were no less loyal to their government. But the problems they faced left small room for concern with status and political preferment. They were not unaware, however, of the political interests of Methodists in the North.

[78] October 6, 1866.

[79] Clark, *Life of Simpson*, pp. vii-x, 224-29, provides an excellent discussion of Bishop Simpson's concern for Methodist status and of his political influence with the Lincoln administration.

3

The Southern Church and the Confederacy

On July 3, 1861, Chancellor William M. Wightman addressed the graduating class of Southern University at Greensboro, Alabama. North and South still were engaged in slow and quiet preparation, and neither side had seriously tested its arms. Before his election to the chancellorship Wightman was president—the first—of Wofford College in his native South Carolina. For fourteen years he had edited the *Southern Christian Advocate*. In 1866 he would be elected bishop. He spoke, therefore, as an acknowledged leader of the Southern Church. Before the end of the year his address was circulated in the *Quarterly Review*.[80]

With the establishment of the Confederate government, said Wightman, the world beheld "a new nationality . . . —a union of eleven homogeneous states." His words reflected the confidence of the South in the justice of its cause, the superiority of its culture, and the purity of its moral claims.

The life of the new Government is one; the people, in blood, institutions, interests, manners, and customs, one. . . . It is the type of the highest civilization. It is strong enough to stand against the world. Its domain is the most productive on earth; its people as brave as the bravest; . . . its resources, . . . its intelligence, its religion—all point to an illustrious destiny in the future. . . . The position of commercial inferiority to which we have hitherto submitted, and by which millions of Southern money have built up Northern cities, and moved the countless wheels of Northern industry—repaid now by the base attempt to subjugate us—is changed. Henceforward, we build up our own commerce, manufactures, literature. The sceptre has already fallen from the hands of New York. Grass will ere long grow in her streets, and solitude reign in her palaces and avenues. The grand, historic hour has struck . . . , and a new order of things begins.[81]

What had destroyed the free institutions of the North, the chancellor reminded the graduates, was "something more terrible than the shot and shell that rained upon Fort Sumter."

It was *corrupt ambition!* It was lust of power for the sake of public plunder. It was the 50,000 offices that constituted the stupendous bribe for which public liberty, free institutions, security and prosperity, were sold!—universal suffrage

---

[80] "Baccalaureate Address of W. M. Wightman, D.D., L.L.D.," *Quarterly Review of the Methodist Episcopal Church, South,* October, 1861, pp. 525-31.
[81] *Ibid.,* pp. 527-28.

in the hands of an unintelligent population, demoralized by corrupt intrigues!—a moral pestilence in the very heart of the nation, contaminating their religion at its fountain-heads, infecting their literature, and rendering the masses of the people servile tools in the hands of corrupt party leaders! [82]

Wightman's baccalaureate anticipated themes often to be repeated in the Southern Methodist press and pulpit. These themes were common to the pronouncements of most of the Protestant churches in the South. The general position of Southern religious leadership was comprehensively stated in the "Address to Christians Throughout the World, by the Clergy of the Confederate States of America," issued from Richmond in 1863.[83] The address reflected Confederate optimism following General Lee's victory at Chancellorsville and gave expression to Southern resentment over the Emancipation Proclamation. It originated within a conference of ministers in the Confederate capital, and the signatures affixed to it were confined to prominent representatives of the various Protestant churches in the Confederacy. The names of three bishops, James O. Andrew, George Foster Pierce, and John Early, headed the list of seventeen signatures from the Methodist Episcopal Church, South. Three Methodist Protestant ministers also signed the document.

Disavowing "any inclination to meddle with political questions," and disclaiming any desire to resume old controversies or to discuss the causes of the war, the Southern ministers proposed to offer a simple and dignified statement of their position. They entertained no fear as to the "final issue" of the conflict. They appealed only to an "enlightened Christian sentiment . . . against war, against persecution for conscience' sake, against the ravaging of the Church of God by fanatical invasion." Their first major point was that the war proposed to achieve that which in the very nature of the case could not be achieved by violence, namely, the restoration of the Union. It was inconceivable that violent means could "reunite independent States, . . . or coerce a people to brotherly kindness, unity, and devotion to each other." The war, these ministers insisted, had been forced upon them. "After a conflict of opinions between the North and South in Church and State, of more than thirty years, growing more painful and bitter daily," the South had withdrawn "to secure peace." Invasion had now destroyed its peace, polluted its sanctuaries, violated the sacredness of its homes, and robbed its people of their property. Such violence had contradicted the professions of the North and revealed its real aim—the subjugation of the South.

[82] *Ibid.*, p. 530.
[83] The address is printed in full in Edward McPherson, *The Political History of the United States of America During the Great Rebellion* (2nd ed., Washington: Philp and Solomons, 1865), pp. 517-21.

The second general point of the address was that the separation of
the Confederate States was regarded as final. The political and
ecclesiastical line drawn between North and South was distinct, deliberate, and fixed. "Our institutions, habits, tastes, pursuits, and religion,
suggest no wish for reconstruction of the Union." After an invasion
lasting for two years the Union armies had achieved nothing but cruelty.
Their only gain within Confederate territory was the ground on which
they pitched their tents. The conflict had achieved no good result, and
offered no promise of good.

Particularly objectionable to the Southern church leaders was President Lincoln's Emancipation Proclamation. The inevitable result of the
Proclamation—assuming that its provisions were enforceable—would be
insurrection. Should the slaves revolt, the Southerners held, the interests
of public safety would require the "slaughter of tens of thousands of
poor deluded insurrectionists." The Christian sensibilities of the Confederate churchmen recoiled from such a vision. On the other hand,
the protesters believed that the Proclamation was actually a "mere
political document, devised to win favor among the most fanatical of
the Northern people." It represented an attempt, "under the disguise
of philanthropy," to win the approval of mankind for a wicked, reckless,
and useless war. Yet, far from being an act of philanthropy in behalf of
the slaves, it was really an act of malice against their masters. Indeed, so
the address pointed out, the restriction of enforced emancipation to
the slaves of those who were fighting against the United States was proof
enough that the Proclamation was more political than philanthropic.

The protests concluded with an appeal to the civilized world to appreciate the "moral and spiritual interests of the South."

> The relation of master and slave among us, however we may deplore abuses
> in this, as in other relations of mankind, is not incompatible with our holy
> Christianity, and . . . the presence of the Africans of our land is an occasion of
> gratitude on their behalf before God; seeing that thereby Divine Providence
> has brought them where missionaries of the Cross may freely proclaim to them
> the word of salvation, and the work is not interrupted by agitating fanaticism.
> The South has done more than any people on earth for the Christianization of
> the African race.

In all its dealings with the slaves the South had followed the scriptural
plan.[84] Fanatical abolitionism interfered with the ways of Providence
and resulted only in hatred, bitterness, infidelity, and moral degeneracy.

As Northern troops advanced deeper into the South, Methodist leaders
joined in the condemnation of reported cruelties of enemy soldiers.

[84] I Tim. 6:1-6.

Bishop Pierce denounced the "proud, rapacious, malignant foe, who, without right or reason, against law and right and humanity," came down upon the South "full of hate and rage to enslave or exterminate us." [85] The Georgia Conference censured the "unprincipled modes of warfare" of the invaders and resolved: "It is the duty of the Christian nations of the earth to pronounce them enemies of the human race, and to brand their principles and measures as infamous." Moreover, the Georgia preachers were confident that, even if the war should consume all the resources of the South, the Confederacy would not violate the "principles of humanity" in its own military operations.[86]

Bishop Pierce Addresses the Legislature

Southerners took pride in the religious professions of their political and military leaders and expressed admiration for their "prudence, moderation and magnanimity" in the conduct of the war.[87] They noted with approbation the willingness of their leaders to recognize their dependence upon God "in the formal and humble celebration of His goodness." [88] Methodists met in their own churches and joined congregations of other denominations to observe the various days of fasting and thanksgiving proclaimed by President Jefferson Davis.

March 27, 1863, was such a day of "fasting, humiliation and prayer." On that day Bishop Pierce, who had come to Milledgeville, the state capital, from his plantation near Sparta, preached before the General Assembly of Georgia. Pierce's address before the legislature went beyond the conventional endorsement of the Southern cause to an examination of the relation between government and religion and to a defense of the theocratic position. The Confederacy was not inconsistent in seeking divine support, the bishop reminded the Assembly. "Our religion has never resolved itself into conventional fallacies—into a geographical conscience, and erected the fancied rights of any people into a 'higher law' than divine revelation." The North had erected "their reason into a counsellor of the Almighty," and had made "a majority vote higher authority in morals as well as politics than the Constitution of the land and the Book of heaven." If the South would gain divine approval, it must "plant the government on the Bible, talk less of the rights of the people and more about the rights of God, extirpate the political heresies

[85] George G. Smith, *The Life and Times of George Foster Pierce* (Nashville: Hunter & Welburn, 1888), p. 466.

[86] *Minutes of the Georgia Annual Conference*, 1862, p. 39.

[87] *Ibid.*

[88] McPherson, *Political History of the Great Rebellion*, p. 520.

which have demoralized society, abolish party tactics, and let all the ends we aim at be God and country and truth." [89]

The bishop was not content, however, merely to point out the fallacies of the religion of his "Northern enemies." Now that the public mind was "loosened from old ideas and broken up by the ploughshare of war," the South was in position to "amend what was faulty and . . . incorporate . . . principles conservative of law, order, and morals." It was well, to be sure, that the constitution of the Confederacy had appealed to Almighty God. But the language employed was that of natural religion rather than that of Christianity. Therefore, he urged:

> Let us avow our faith in [God's] revelation, identify our government with his honor, and commit our interests to the power that is pledged to perpetuate the Church and to insure her dominion. Then, amid the rise and fall of kingdoms and all the mutations of time, our Republic shall embody one element—pure, true, eternal—an element which shall ally us in friendship with heaven and stamp upon all our prosperity the seal of the divine blessing.

Indispensably related to the government of God, for example, is the observance of the Christian Sabbath. "Every legislative enactment which requires or sanctions its violation ought to be repealed." [90]

Pierce claimed that he was pleading, not for the formal establishment of religion, but for the "solemn acknowledgment" of God's Word "as well as his providence." This would be "specially harmonious" with the South's "high and holy" mission to Christianize the African race. He considered a reform of the abuses of slavery one of the moral objectives of the war. Those statutes regarding slavery which were "adverse . . . to the will of God" should be repealed. In particular, he criticized the law forbidding the teaching of slaves to read. It is the Negro's right "to read for himself the epistles of his Redeemer's love." Further, "all laws and parts of laws which authorize or allow arbitrary interference with the connubial relations of slaves ought to be rescinded." [91]

Bishop Pierce's sermon turned in conclusion to a theme prominent in his preaching throughout the war—the evil of speculation and extortion. In addition to his ecclesiastical responsibilities he gave himself zealously during the war years to the supervision of his plantation, and he deemed this contribution to the Confederate war effort a matter of conscience. He spared no blows against that patriotism which "puts off its nobility and works for hire." [92] Now he warned the legislature of that selfishness

[89] Smith, *Life of Pierce*, pp. 468-70.

[90] *Ibid.*, pp. 470-73.

[91] *Ibid.*, pp. 471-75.

[92] William W. Bennett, *A Narrative of the Great Revival Which Prevailed in the Southern Armies* (Philadelphia: Claxton, Remsen & Haffelfinger, 1877), p. 44.

from within which is fully as dangerous as violence from without. "Pitiless extortion is making havoc in the land. . . . Avarice, with full barns, puts the bounties of Providence under bolts and bars, waiting with eager longings for higher prices." He deplored the speculation in salt, bread, and meat, which ran riot "in defiance of the thunders of pulpit, executive interference, and the horrors of threatened famine." [93] Finally, the bishop appealed to the Assembly to "cultivate personal piety," and to "promote religion" by work, example, and prayer. "With a Christian constitution, a faithful administration, a moral and religious people, we may look for peace ere long, an honorable nationality," and an enduring and abundant prosperity.[94]

Hardly three months had followed Pierce's Milledgeville sermon before the face of the war was changed for the Confederates. On July 3, two years to the day after Chancellor Wightman had spoken to the Greensboro graduates about grass in the streets of New York, Lee's forces fell back at Gettysburg. On the very next day Pemberton surrendered at Vicksburg. By the end of November, Chattanooga was in Union hands. "Our temporal condition looks none the brightest," E. H. Myers wrote in the *Southern Christian Advocate* in July. "The high hopes . . . which we entertained a few weeks since, have been in a measure disappointed, and we may be doomed to yet greater disappointment." But Myers found in the "fruits of the cultivation of personal religion" a refuge of comfort in the midst of calamity. "He who, in the dark hour, feels that he grows in grace and maintains soul-communion with God, stands upon a rock. He shall never be moved." [95] After the fall of Atlanta, over a year later, Bishop Pierce wrote to his son: "I cannot see through the gloom of the times, and dread the discipline of heaven in this matter. God pity us and help us. I shall try to do right and trust God." [96]

Even as the hopes of the Confederacy receded, however, missionaries and chaplains in the Southern armies began to reap their own harvest of the "fruits of the cultivation of personal religion."

Southern Chaplains and the Army Mission

Despite the readiness of Southern church leaders to invoke religious sanctions in defense of the Confederacy, religion did not thrive in the

[93] Smith, *Life of Pierce,* p. 476.

[94] *Ibid.,* p. 477.

[95] Quoted in J. William Jones, *Christ in the Camp* (Atlanta: The Martin & Hoyt Co., 1904) , p. 607.

[96] Smith, *Life of Pierce,* p. 486.

camps during the early months of the war. The festive spirit accompanying the departure of volunteers from their homes, and the excitement among thousands of troops, most of them from rural areas, thrown together in a life freed of customary moral restraints, was not conducive to the cultivation of piety. The supply of chaplains was inadequate, and their work was poorly organized. Some chaplains were unqualified, morally and otherwise, for their work. Some became discouraged and returned home.[97] There were, to be sure, exceptions to the general desuetude of religious life in the camps, but it was not until 1863 that the Southern churches marshaled their resources sufficiently to begin meeting the needs for religious leadership and supplies.

Because of the loss of conference Minutes and the failure of some conferences to meet during the war, reliable figures on the number of Methodist chaplains in the Confederate armies are not available. Sweet lists 209 Confederate chaplains from the Methodist Episcopal Church, South, but adds that the list is "far from complete." [98] A number of ministers from Southern conferences on the border served as chaplains with the Union armies. As in the North, the ministry to the troops was augmented by a considerable number of missionaries, whose work was similar to that of the chaplains. Their work resembled that of the delegates of the Christian Commission, although it lacked the interdenominational support and supervision which the commission provided in the North. Sweet lists 32 such missionaries.[99] In addition to the general missionaries sponsored by the church at large there were other missionaries appointed and supported by the Annual Conferences.

Early in 1863 the Chaplains' Association in Jackson's Corps addressed an urgent appeal to the churches of the Confederacy to supply chaplains for the armies. Despite General Jackson's well-known personal interest in the religious welfare of his troops, the association reminded the churches, some entire brigades in his corps were without chaplains. Less than half the regiments had chaplains. "The Church," continued the statement, "should clearly understand and fully estimate the relation which it sustains to the war, and the duty which it owes to the army. In an important sense, the cause of the country is the cause of the Church." [100]

Within a few weeks of the publication of this appeal the bishops and the Board of Missions of the Methodist Episcopal Church, South, meeting in Macon, Georgia, initiated plans for the Army Mission, which

[97] Bell Irvin Wiley, *The Life of Johnny Reb* (Indianapolis: Bobbs-Merrill, 1943), pp. 174-75. See also Wiley's article " 'Holy Joes' of the Sixties: A Study of Civil War Chaplains," *Huntington Library Quarterly,* XVI (1952-53), 287-304.

[98] Sweet, *The Church and the Civil War,* pp. 219-22.

[99] *Ibid.,* p. 223.

[100] Jones, *Christ in the Camp,* p. 233.

would become a branch of the operations of the Missionary Society of the Southern Church. The bishops were requested to appoint one general missionary to each army corps as soon as funds became available and needs were established. Each general missionary should "travel through the department assigned to him, preach to the soldiers, visit [the] sick and wounded, and report to the bishop having charge of his department the condition and wants of the army, and suggest proper persons to be engaged as laborers in the field." He was to co-operate with the Confederate States Bible Society, Annual Conference agencies, and the religious journals in circulating the Scriptures and religious literature.[101]

E. W. Sehon, missionary secretary of the Southern Church, traveled at large soliciting funds for the Army Mission and appealing for workers. The bishops called upon Methodists to "fill the treasury of the Lord," that the church might "send the gospel of peace to every army of the Confederacy." [102] Bishop Andrew, himself nearing seventy, suggested that the "refugee preachers" volunteer for this service. "Were I not so old," the bishop wrote, "I should have been there long before now." [103]

Methodists in the South joined early with other denominations in support of various state and local Bible and tract societies at work among the soldiers. The Soldiers' Tract Association of the Methodist Episcopal Church, South, began operations in March, 1862, and by mid-summer had ten colporteurs in the field. Before the end of the war the association employed twenty-five ministers and laymen in its three depositories, from which it distributed publications to its own agents and colporteurs and to chaplains. Superintendent of the Tract Association was William W. Bennett, who in later years was to become president of Randolph-Macon College. In addition to tracts, Scriptures, and hymnals, the Tract Association, on the request of the bishops, distributed the "Southern Methodist Primer," the "Infant Manual," and catechisms. Many of its publications were used in army Bible classes and Sunday schools. Bennett reported to the bishops that in one of the armies Tract Association workers had conducted classes for teaching soldiers to read and write. The association also issued two semimonthly papers, *The Soldier's Paper*, published in Richmond, and *The Army and Navy Herald*, published in Macon, Georgia.[104] An editorial in the first issue of *The Army and Navy Herald* promised "to furnish the reader with such original productions and eclectic Christian literature as will in some humble measure compensate for the absence of books . . . and elevate his conceptions to the

---

[101] Bennett, *Narrative of the Great Revival*, pp. 267-68.
[102] *Ibid.*
[103] Jones, *Christ in the Camp*, p. 607.
[104] Bennett, *Narrative of the Great Revival*, p. 76; Jones, *Christ in the Camp*, p. 612.

comprehension of a purer and more peaceful area . . . than the strife of
the times." The same issue carried articles entitled "Come to Jesus," "A
Model Boy," "The Whiskey Erysipelas," and "The Soldier's Death." [105]

Revivals in the Southern Armies

By the early months of 1863 evidences of a heightened religious interest
appeared in the Southern armies. To be sure, revivals had been reported
from some quarters as early as 1861; but these were sporadic and not so
general as the waves of evangelistic fervor sweeping over the Southern
encampments from 1863 to 1865. Bennett estimated that 150,000 Confederate soldiers were converted during the war, and that "fully one-
third of all the soldiers in the field were praying men and members of
some branch of the Christian Church." [106]

One memorable episode of revival activity centered in the neighborhood of Dalton, Georgia, where the Army of Tennessee, retreating southward after the Battle of Missionary Ridge, entered winter quarters late
in 1863. Two members of the Tennessee Annual Conference were
among the chaplains and missionaries working with troops in Dalton and
in other encampments in northwest Georgia. Their reports afford a
vivid picture of the religious activities of these winter months. S. M.
Cherry was central distributing agent of the Soldiers' Tract Association,
and John B. McFerrin, still officially book agent of the Methodist Episcopal Church, South, was in charge of all Methodist missionary work in the
Army of Tennessee. Cherry stored his supplies in a room near the town
square and the depot in Dalton. "I . . . soon had a counter arranged,"
he wrote, "for my army papers, tracts, Bibles, Testaments, hymn books,
and other religious literature. This became at once the head-quarters
of chaplains, missionaries, evangelists, preachers, and all who sought
religious reading. . . . I had pens, ink, and stationery for those who wished
to write. . . . The citizens who remained in Dalton tendered us the
different church edifices for the use of the soldiers, and we had a protracted meeting lasting for five months in them." [107]

While chaplains and missionaries of all denominations preached in
the Dalton revival, other protracted meetings got under way in the
camps around the town. The concentration of troops in their winter
encampments enabled chaplains and missionaries to reach great numbers

[105] Quoted by Wiley, *The Life of Johnny Reb*, p. 177, from issue of October, 1863,
among the Van David Papers, University of Texas.
[106] Bennett, *Narrative of the Great Revival*, p. 412.
[107] Jones, *Christ in the Camp*, p. 580.

of men and to preach in units which did not have chaplains of their own. Cherry found revivals in a Texas brigade and a Louisiana brigade, neither of which had a chaplain.[108] McFerrin preached often in Dalton and also "traveled up and down the lines, working wherever there was a call." He wrote:

The soldiers erected stands, improvised seats, and even built log churches, where they worshiped God in spirit and in truth. The result was glorious; thousands were happily converted and were prepared for the future that awaited them. Officers and men alike were brought under religious influence. Our custom was to admit persons into any Church they might choose, while in an army association we were all one.[109]

Cherry reported that "about 300" were baptized on the first of May, and "not less than five hundred professed to find peace in believing the first week of the month." As the Union army resumed its pressures in the direction of Atlanta, many Confederate soldiers "literally went from the altar to their entrenchments . . . still singing the songs of Zion." [110]

Wiley suggests several causes of the mounting revivalism in the Southern ranks. Increases in the numbers of chaplains and missionaries and in the circulation of religious literature were contributing factors. The character of the Southern soldier was another factor. "Most wearers of the gray," says Wiley, "came from communities where the church was fervid, aggressive, and influential, and where revivals were common." Furthermore, a new seriousness in the wake of Southern reverses created an atmosphere more conducive to revivals. When, toward the end of the war, casualties thinned many regiments, the ever-present imminence of death made the soldier more responsive to the calls for repentance and "decision." [111] From Bennett's earlier perspective, the cultural homogeneity of the Southern troops appeared an important factor in the revival. The Confederate forces were "strictly native Americans, of the Southern type," manifesting the "respect and reverence of their race for all the ordinances and institutions of religion." Another factor, Bennett believed, was the orthodoxy of the Confederate soldier's background. He was not disturbed by "false theories" and the "strange jumble of opinions" that prevented the "simple truths of the gospel" from having their full effect.[112]

[108] *Ibid.*, p. 582.
[109] O. P. Fitzgerald, *John B. McFerrin* (Nashville: Publishing House of the M. E. Church, South, 1889), p. 276.
[110] Jones, *Christ in the Camp*, p. 583.
[111] *The Life of Johnny Reb*, pp. 183-84.
[112] *Narrative of the Great Revival*, pp. 23-24.

In view of recent studies of the mid-century revivals in the North, one may question the implication that revivalism was more prevalent in the Southern armies.[113] The extensive evangelistic activity that had stirred the cities, towns, and villages of the North for over a decade preceding the war had mounted to a climax in the "prayer-meeting revivals" of 1857 and 1858. Nonsectarian in scope and strongly emphasizing lay participation, the movement created "attitudes of concern and expectancy" which were intensified under conditions of war. McCabe wrote of the "everlasting protracted meeting" going on in his regiment.[114] Alfred Cookman's reports on his preaching in the Army of the Potomac in February and March, 1864, reflect a religious interest not unlike that described in McFerrin's reports from the Army of Tennessee.[115] By 1865 the revivals under way in the Union armies had become a "major interest of the times." [116] Apparently, churchmen on neither side were aware of the awakenings in the opposite camp.

The significant contrast between North and South is to be found, not in the prevalence of revivalism, but in the content of the evangelist's message. The preaching of the Northern chaplains and missionaries, even while employing the traditional terminology of the revival exhortation, bore the perfectionist and millennialist overtones of the revivals of the 1850's. It fostered faith in a God immediately involved in the momentous issues of the day. The outpouring of the Holy Spirit for which the revivalists prayed was a Pentecostal visitation which would cleanse the nation of its evils and make Christ "king of the nation's affairs, economic and political, as well as religious." [117] Charles McCabe taught the Libby prisoners and thousands in the Army of the Potomac to sing:

> I have seen him in the watchfires of a hundred circling camps;
> They have builded him an altar in the evening dews and damps;
> I have read his righteous sentence by the dim and flaring lamps;
> His day is marching on.

As Christ "died to make men holy," so the Union soldier would "die to make men free." [118]

On the other hand, the religious aspirations of the Southern soldier

---

[113] See Smith, *Revivalism and Social Reform*, pp. 76-79, and Hopkins, *History of the Y.M.C.A.*, pp. 81-84. Contrast Wiley, *The Life of Johnny Reb*, p. 183.

[114] Bristol, *Life of McCabe*, p. 123.

[115] Henry B. Ridgaway, *The Life of the Rev. Alfred Cookman* (New York: Harper & Brothers, 1873), pp. 259-76.

[116] Smith, *Revivalism and Social Reform*, p. 77.

[117] *Ibid.*, pp. 222-23.

[118] Bristol, *Life of McCabe*, pp. 192-203.

were expressed in terms of the otherworldliness of traditional piety. The Confederate chaplain disdained "political" questions. He had little, if anything, to say of the causes of the war and of the issues of the day. J. C. Granberry, superintendent of Methodist missionaries in Lee's army, thus described the preaching in the Southern armies:

The sermons in the camp would have suited any congregation in city or country, and with even less change might have been preached to the Union armies. . . . The hearers were besought to immediate and uncompromising action, for the time was short. The songs, prayers, lay testimonies and exhortations, in a word, all the exercises, were in the same line. There was no stirring up of bad blood; no inflaming of malice and revenge. The man of God lifted up, not the Bars and Stars, but the cross, and pressed the inquiry, "Who among you are on the Lord's side?" [119]

No less than their counterparts in the North, representatives of the Southern churches entered freely into interdenominational arrangements for meeting the moral and religious needs of the troops. Early in the war General "Stonewall" Jackson, himself a Presbyterian, insisted that chaplains not touch upon denominational distinctions. A chaplain who preached denominational sermons, said Jackson, ought not to be in the army.[120] If the South lacked such formal interdenominational structures as the Christian Commission, the informal co-operation of chaplains and missionaries in voluntary associations provided an interdenominational milieu for religious work. Christian Associations appeared, often spontaneously, in many regiments and brigades. The association afforded an opportunity for public confession and Christian fellowship. It facilitated and conserved the work of the chaplains and missionaries and became a base for lay-directed religious work in the absence of a chaplain. Southern Methodist chaplains and missionaries noted with approval the harmonious relations among denominations. "We know no distinctions here," W. H. Browning wrote from Chattanooga. "Baptists, Cumberlands, Old [School] Presbyterians, Episcopalians, and Methodists, work together, and rejoice together at the success of our cause." [121] Atticus G. Haygood, missionary to Bryan's Brigade in East Tennessee, wrote: "Anything looking like controversy would be considered an intolerable impertinence in the army. I think the unity and brotherly love among the Christians of our noble armies will, when those armies return home, effectually rebuke the intolerant bigotry that has so often reared its foul crest by the altars of God." [122]

[119] Jones, *Christ in the Camp*, pp. 14-15.
[120] Bennett, *Narrative of the Great Revival*, p. 52.
[121] *Ibid.*, p. 315.
[122] Jones, *Christ in the Camp*, p. 618.

A Refugee Preacher and the "Army Church"

The story of Enoch M. Marvin affords a view of a peculiar kind of religious leadership in the Confederate forces, that of a refugee preacher living as guest at an army headquarters.[123] As the popular pastor of Centenary Church in St. Louis, Marvin enjoyed the friendship of many prominent Missourians, a number of whom were serving in the Confederate army. He had been elected delegate to the General Conference scheduled to meet in New Orleans, May 1, 1862. Anticipating that the Federal authorities then occupying St. Louis might prevent his crossing the Confederate lines, and apprehensive, too, lest he might be asked to take the oath of allegiance to the United States, Marvin determined in February to leave for the South at once. Having laid away supplies for his wife and five children and the two household slaves, he slipped out of St. Louis after a Sunday evening service, and, with the help of friendly guides, made his way into Arkansas and thence to Memphis. When he learned at Memphis of the postponement of the General Conference, he moved on to Vicksburg, and from there to Woodville, a vacant charge which he supplied until the meeting of the Mississippi Annual Conference in November.

In December, Marvin went to the army of General Sterling Price, a former Governor of Missouri, who had brought five thousand men of the State Guard into the Confederate forces. He remained a guest at Price's headquarters for most of the time until surrender. Bishop Paine offered him an appointment as missionary chaplain of one of the army corps of the Trans-Mississippi Department, and army friends from Missouri sought an appointment for him as military chaplain with appropriate rank and pay. Marvin chose, however, to remain "acting chaplain" of Price's division, supported only by voluntary contributions of his friends.

In March of 1863 General Price moved his command to Little Rock, and here Marvin preached for several months in a Presbyterian church. It was in Little Rock that he presided over the meeting of six Methodist and three Presbyterian ministers that drew up plans for an "Army Church," which soon was organized in the various regiments and contributed to a period of revivals in the winter of 1863-64 similar to those in the Army of Tennessee. The articles of faith and constitution of the Church of the Army were as follows:

The Christian men of the army, believing that the habitation of God by his Spirit constitutes the Church, agree for their edification and for the conversion

[123] See Thomas M. Finney, *Life and Labors of Enoch Mather Marvin* (St. Louis: James H. Chambers, 1880), pp. 357-421.

of their fellow-men, to organize the Church of the Army, with the following Articles of Faith and Constitution:

Article I. We believe the Scriptures of the Old and New Testaments to be the word of God; the only rule of faith and obedience.

Art. II. We believe in one God, the Father, the Son and the Holy Ghost, the same in substance, equal in power and glory.

Art. III. We believe in the fall in Adam, the redemption by Christ, and the renewing of the Holy Ghost.

Art. IV. We believe in justification by faith alone, and therefore receive and rest upon Christ alone as our only hope.

Art. V. We believe in the communion of saints and the doctrine of eternal rewards and punishments.

Constitution

The Christian men who have been baptized, adopting these "Articles of Faith," in the regiment, shall constitute one church, who shall choose ten officers to take the spiritual oversight of the same. Of the officers so selected, the chaplains or one selected by themselves shall act as moderator. The officers will meet once a month, or oftener if necessary, and in the exercise of discipline will be governed by the teachings of Christ. They will keep a record of the names and the manner in which their ecclesiastical connection with the Church is dissolved.[124]

Marvin's only combat experience came on July 4 in the disastrous attack upon Helena, in which Price suffered high casualties and lost a large part of his command into the hands of the enemy. A severe eye infection in the fall almost cost Marvin his eyesight, but he soon resumed his preaching in various encampments and nearby communities, wearing a leather patch over one eye and reciting his scripture from memory. He made preaching tours into East Texas and Louisiana and visited sessions of the Wachita, Texas, East Texas, and Louisiana Annual Conferences. During the last months of the war he lived in the home of a Methodist preacher in Greenwood, Louisiana, whence he continued to journey to preach in the encampments in Arkansas. In March, 1865, Mrs. Marvin and the children, traveling on a special permit from President Lincoln, left St. Louis to join her husband, whom she found, after a month of travel, in Homer, Louisiana.

After the surrender Marvin and his family moved to Texas. On his earlier visits in East Texas he had preached at Marshall, which for a time was headquarters of the military governor of Missouri. Now he was appointed supply for the Marshall station, where he remained until his election to the episcopacy in the General Conference of 1866. He was not a delegate to the conference, nor was he present at the time of his

[124] *Ibid.*, p. 378.

election. He was the church's first bishop from the trans-Mississippi West.

Charles Elliott's comment on Marvin's election echoed all the unhappy quarrels of Missouri Methodists. "Mr. Marvin's rebel notoriety," observed the wartime editor of the *Central Christian Advocate,* "promoted him to the Episcopacy in preference to men of far greater intellectual and moral worth. Surviving his 'lost cause,' because traitors are not hung, Bishop Marvin is evidently determined that the embers of rebel prejudice, passion, and hate shall burn as long as possible." [125]

Disorganization in the Southern Church

The churches shared in all the disorganization, demoralization, and impoverishment which the war years brought to the South. The Annual Conferences, with some exceptions, met regularly; but attendance was often poor, and in some instances the bishops were unable to reach their conferences. The Texas conferences did not see a bishop for five years. The occupation of New Orleans by Federal forces in the spring of 1862 prevented the holding of the 1862 General Conference, which had been appointed to meet in that city. A pastor in Atlanta in 1862 later described a "sort of missing link in the series of General Conferences," which met in the parlor of an Atlanta home on April 10, 1862. Bishops Andrew, Pierce, and Early attended this two-day informal meeting, and Bishop Andrew presided. "This . . . was shortly after the downfall of Forts Henry and Donelson and the dear bought victory at Shiloh. The political and ecclesiastical outlook was unpromising, if not discouraging." The small group which came together represented the Mission Board and other connectional interests. J. B. McFerrin, book agent and missionary secretary, and Holland N. McTyeire, editor of the Nashville *Christian Advocate,* only a few weeks earlier had been forced out of Nashville by the arrival of Union forces. The Atlanta meeting apportioned the episcopal salaries, decided to consolidate the Nashville *Christian Advocate* with the *Southern Christian Advocate,* and appealed to the church for funds to support the China Mission.[126]

Except for its work with the armies the operations of the Missionary Society of the Southern Church came to a virtual halt. Of the eight missionaries appointed to China before 1860 only Young J. Allen and J. W. Lambuth were still on the field when the war began. Drafts in the hands of the China missionaries at the beginning of the conflict were

[125] *South-Western Methodism,* p. 448.

[126] W. J. Scott, "Bishop J. O. Andrew," *Quarterly Review of the Methodist Episcopal Church, South,* April, 1883, pp. 329-30.

honored by the treasurer of the Missionary Society of the Northern Church; but thereafter the two men remained without support from, or communication with, their home base. Allen found employment in translation and editorial work for the Chinese government. In 1866 the Missionary Society reported an indebtedness of $60,200.

Work in the Indian missions suffered radical losses and disorganization. From a reported total of 4,160 in 1860 the Indian membership declined to 701 in 1866.[127] With the Indian territory overrun by marauding troops, and with tribes and families dispersed, it appeared doubtful for a time that the Indian work could be reorganized.

The institutions of the church suffered equal disorganization and attrition. Most of the schools and colleges were closed, their endowments partially or totally dissipated, and their property deteriorated. By the end of the war all the weekly *Advocates* had suspended publication. The *Richmond Christian Advocate* suffered disastrous losses from fire at the time of the evacuation of the Confederate capital in 1865. The *Southern Christian Advocate* fled Charleston in front of the Federal troops, published for a time in Augusta, Georgia, and then moved to Macon, where it soon suspended publication. The most serious property loss of the Southern Church was its Publishing House. Seized by Federal authorities in 1862, it was used, among other things, for a government printing office. Its stock was confiscated, its machinery badly damaged, and its business prostrated. The decline in the Publishing House assets between 1862 and 1866 was reported as nearly a quarter of a million dollars.

Losses at the level of the local church were extensive and embraced intangibles beyond enumeration. In some areas the itinerant system was disrupted, and ministers were forced to turn to other pursuits to earn or supplement their support. Some churches saw their pastors enter the army. Some pastors became refugees in front of advancing enemy troops; others were removed by occupation authorities. Over all the churches hung the pall of poverty bred by destruction and economic dislocation. Patrons who had contributed liberally, especially those in the planter class, were now in ruin. Hundreds of churches were destroyed, many were severely damaged, and some were dismantled. Some remained in the hands of the military or of ministers of the Northern Church, and others were simply abandoned by their congregations.

Although statistics reflect only partially the nature and extent of losses suffered by the Southern Church, a comparison of figures reported in 1860 and 1866 reveals critical losses in membership and leadership. The

[127] P. A. Peterson, *Hand-Book of Southern Methodism* (Richmond: J. W. Fergusson & Son, 1883), p. 115.

total membership declined from 754,421 to 508,676. Over half of this loss was in Negro membership, which was reduced from 207,766 to 78,742. The number of traveling preachers declined from 2,784 to 2,485, and the number of local preachers, from 5,353 to 3,829. The number of preachers admitted on trial fell from 266 in 1860 to 114 in 1866.[128]

A review of the episcopal leadership of the Southern Church during the war years suggests more subtle dimensions of the predicament in which the church stood. Whatever may be said in appreciation of the personal qualities of the Southern bishops, their effectiveness was seriously limited by their age, the restrictions on their travel, and the many contingencies of day-to-day living. Bishop Soule was seventy-nine when the war began. Bishop Early was seventy-five, and Bishop Andrew, sixty-six. All three were to be superannuated in 1866. Bishop Kavanaugh was fifty-eight, and Bishop Paine, sixty-one. Bishop Pierce, the youngest, was forty-nine. Soule remained at his home near Nashville throughout the war and had little or no contact with his episcopal colleagues. Paine and Pierce remained on their farms, leaving only for the minimal travel required by their episcopal duties. Andrew, living near Selma, Alabama, turned briefly to farming. Pierce's plantation, "Sunshine," near Sparta, Georgia, became widely known for its hospitality to transient preachers and soldiers. Paine, who had accumulated considerable property, including a number of slaves, continued to supervise his farming interests at Aberdeen, Mississippi, although rumors that he was being sought by Federal authorities caused him to leave home for brief periods. His home served for a time as a hospital for wounded soldiers.

All the Southern bishops, moreover, were essentially conservative. Pierce took little part in politics before 1861. Andrew, says his biographer, "was an old-time Whig of the Webster school, and probably voted for John Bell and Edward Everett in the election of 1860." [129] Paine, who before his elevation to the episcopacy had served sixteen years as president of LaGrange College in Alabama, told President Buchanan in 1860 that he had not voted in a presidential election for thirty years. This, he said, was "in order to give an example to younger ministers, and thus to reserve my influence for moral and religious ends." [130] When resolutions in sympathy with the secession movement were introduced in the South Carolina Conference, Bishop Paine ruled them out of order.[131] Soule and Andrew were both at the Alabama Conference in

[128] Ibid.
[129] George G. Smith, The Life and Letters of James Osgood Andrew (Nashville: Southern Methodist Publishing House, 1883), p. 436.
[130] R. H. Rivers, The Life of Robert Paine (Nashville: Southern Methodist Publishing House, 1884), p. 142.
[131] Ibid., p. 145.

December, 1860, and the two were agreed that "political" resolutions, should they be introduced, would be declared out of order.[132]

Hubbard H. Kavanaugh, who maintained his residence at Versailles, Kentucky, through all the war, was the only one of the Southern bishops to spend any considerable time outside the Confederate lines. The sharp differences that divided Kentucky politically extended into the Louisville and Kentucky Conferences and required skill and impartiality on the part of the presiding and appointing officer. Kavanaugh, a native of Kentucky, presided at most of the sessions of the two conferences. "I have deemed it my duty as a minister of the Gospel," he wrote, "not only to abstain from participating in political affairs, but, on the contrary, to mitigate as far as practicable the asperity of feeling which prevails so widely." [133]

Responding to appeals from California to ordain some young men, Kavanaugh presided at the Pacific Annual Conference in 1864. While he was on the west coast, Federal officers, prompted by charges that Kavanaugh was on a political mission, arrested him and searched his baggage. The bishop was treated courteously and freed on the following day. Of the charges against him he wrote:

Since the commencement of the war, I have never crossed the military lines, nor entered any State in rebellion, except on a visit to Nashville, Tenn., then in possession of the Federal troops and under their control, together with the whole line of road from my residence to that city. I have never been a politician, nor in any manner participated actively in political affairs, and have never preached politics, either before or since the war. On the contrary, I have invariably discouraged it in the ministry of the Church over which I had in some sense the supervision.[134]

4

The Mission to the South Gets Under Way

No action of the Northern Church was more productive of lasting bitterness than was its organized expansion into territory which the Methodist Episcopal Church, South, considered its own. A recent study

[132] Smith, *Life of Andrew*, p. 473.
[133] A. H. Redford, *Life and Times of H. H. Kavanaugh* (Nashville, 1884) , p. 418.
[134] *Ibid.*, pp. 417-18. See also J. C. Simmons, *The History of Southern Methodism on the Pacific Coast* (Nashville: Southern Methodist Publishing House, 1886) , pp. 299-313.

of this period describes the missionary activities of the Northern Methodists in the South as a "tale of ecclesiastical conquest, aided and abetted
by the federal government itself." [135] The policy of Northern Methodism
in regard to its expansion in the South began to take shape early in
1863, but it remained for the General Conference of 1864 to adopt the
disciplinary changes, provide the funds, and set up administrative
structures for implementation of policy.

In their address to the General Conference the bishops directed attention to the "large and inviting fields of Christian enterprise and labor"
that lay in the territories of the Southern Church already behind the
Federal lines. The Methodist Episcopal Church once occupied these areas,
the bishops noted, and she ought never to have consented to exclusion
from them on any grounds. "Now that the providence of God has opened
her way, she should not be disobedient to her heavenly calling, but should
return at the earliest practicable period." The Northern Church must
re-enter these fields, the address continued, "preaching Christ and him
crucified to all classes of people." Moreover, she must welcome back
into her communion all ministers and members involuntarily cut off,
although she must be careful to exclude the slaveholder and the traitor.
The bishops added that, already, they had explored thoroughly the
territory within the Federal lines, and had "temporarily appointed a few
preachers." [136]

The mission to the South claimed much of the delegates' time in the
1864 General Conference. They revised the constitution of the Missionary
Society to provide for a third class of missions (i.e., neither foreign nor
domestic) to consist of work in the United States and its territories not
included in the bounds of an Annual Conference. They delegated liberal
executive authority to the bishops for administration of the new missions
and provided for allocation of supporting funds.[137] They founded the
Church Extension Society, which, though charged with duties extending
beyond a single region, proved a valuable adjunct to the work in the
South. Finally, to strengthen leadership for its enlarged missions program,
the conference elected three additional bishops. All three of the new
bishops were war editors of Methodist journals—Edward Thomson, of
the *Christian Advocate and Journal;* Calvin Kingsley, of the *Western
Christian Advocate;* and D. W. Clark, of the *Ladies' Repository.*

The legislation of the General Conference, therefore, gave sanction to,
and provided implementation for, a policy already adopted by the
bishops. The "exploration" of the bishops had involved more than a

[135] Morrow, *Northern Methodism and Reconstruction*, pp. 32-33.
[136] *Journal of the General Conference*, 1864, pp. 278-79.
[137] *Ibid.*, pp. 387-88.

preliminary investigation. As early as 1861 Northern Methodist clergy had urged the church to carry its banners into the territories of the Methodist Episcopal Church, South. In the ensuing months, as soldiers, chaplains, and civilian officials wrote from the South, or returned home to tell of needs there, the cry increased for the Methodists to send preachers and missionaries to take over abandoned churches and replace disloyal ministers. Loyalist Methodists remaining in the wake of retreating Confederate forces added their appeals to the cry for help.

At their regular fall meeting in 1863 the bishops discussed temporary arrangements for the occupied territories and agreed upon the "exploration" of their "providential" openings. The Missionary Society appropriated $35,000 for the emergency work. Bishop Ames, having notified Simpson of his intentions, consulted his good friend Secretary Stanton in Washington. The War Department Secretary, on November 30, ordered the generals commanding the Departments of Missouri, the Tennessee, and the Gulf to place at Ames's disposal "all houses of worship belonging to the Methodist Episcopal Church, South, in which a loyal minister, who has been appointed by a loyal Bishop of said Church does not officiate." The efforts of the government "to restore tranquility to the community and peace to the Nation" required "that Christian Ministers . . . support and foster the loyal sentiment of the people." The War Department order affirmed "entire confidence" in Bishop Ames and directed the generals to support the "execution of his important mission" and, specifically, to furnish him with transportation and subsistence. Before the end of the year similar orders went to the Department of the South in behalf of Bishop Janes, and to authorities in Kentucky and Tennessee in behalf of Bishop Simpson.[138]

The protest aroused by Stanton's order was not confined to the Southern Church. Union commanders, with an eye on their need of the church property for use as hospitals, barracks, and stables, were not co-operative. The most vigorous protest came from the slavery territory within Union lines. Senators and representatives from the border states sought Congressional legislation in relief of the threatened property. In April a convention of ministers of the Southern Church, largely from Kentucky, Tennessee, and Missouri, met in Louisville, protested against the execution of Stanton's order, and requested the president "to restrain and prevent its enforcement." Actually, Lincoln had already pressed Stanton to modify his order. After a vigorous protest to the president by loyal Methodists of Missouri, Stanton, in February, 1864, restricted the application of his previous order "to such States as are by the President's

---

[138] McPherson, *Political History of the Great Rebellion*, p. 521.

Proclamation designated as being in rebellion." [139] Sweet says that the president "was certainly never in favor of this plan of military interference with the Churches." [140] At least, he was not openly sympathetic with Stanton's policy. Fortunately for the Southern Church, the directives were never enforced to the full letter. In the meantime, however, Ames and his colleagues were out to make the most effective use of their right of occupancy.

Early in 1864 Ames made his way down the Mississippi, taking over Methodist churches in Memphis, Little Rock, Pine Bluff, Vicksburg, Jackson, Natchez, Baton Rouge, and New Orleans. The bishop placed John P. Newman of New York in charge of Methodist churches in New Orleans. Before a large audience assembled in Carondolet Street Church to welcome him to his new appointment, Newman offered his justification of the ecclesiastical invasion. The Methodist Episcopal Church, he claimed, was not a sectional church. Because it took the world for its parish, it had as much right to send ministers to the South as to Bulgaria and Scandinavia. Moreover, the church would not entrust its men then in the South "to the exclusive influence of Southern teaching." Finally, Newman held that the entry of the church into the South was justified because the Southern ministers had "either fled or been silenced, or imprisoned, or banished." It had therefore become the "solemn duty of the Mother Church to send shepherds to these deserted and scattered flocks." [141]

By mid-January Bishop Simpson arrived in Tennessee, where his coming had been heralded by "Parson" William G. Brownlow, vitriolic editor of the Knoxville *Whig and Rebel Ventilator*. Simpson established Michael J. Cramer, brother-in-law of Ulysses S. Grant, as his agent in Nashville and designated Chaplain Calvin Holman as his representative in Chattanooga. He gave to the Union chaplains the assignment of investigating the loyalty of members and ministers.

The remaining bishops entered their designated territories as soon as military operations opened the way. Each bishop appointed one or more preachers as resident agents. These representatives were to supervise the appropriated churches, correlate the work of Methodist chaplains and missionaries, and, wherever possible, form Methodist congregations. Twenty-one ordained ministers from Northern conferences were appointed to missionary work in the South in the last two years of the war.[142] In several places the Northern Church established monopoly

[139] *Ibid.*, p. 522.
[140] *The Church and the Civil War*, p. 107.
[141] McPherson, *Political History of the Great Rebellion*, p. 523, quoting the *True Delta*, March 28, 1864.
[142] Sweet, *The Church and the Civil War*, p. 100.

control of Methodist work. In New Orleans, for most of 1864 and 1865, every Southern church was under the control of Northern Methodists. Simpson's agents controlled both the Nashville churches that were not appropriated for use by the military. For a year and a half before the close of hostilities Northern Methodist preachers, operating under Federal protection, proselyted freely in central Tennessee, along the Atlantic Coast from Charleston to Florida, and in the area around the mouth of the Mississippi. Methodist chaplains proved effective agents of the Northern Church in the vicinity of Federal army posts. By the middle of 1864 laymen and preachers in eastern Tennessee, encouraged by "Parson" Brownlow's paper, were prepared to organize the first Annual Conference of the Methodist Episcopal Church in territory claimed by the Southern Church. In June of 1865 Bishop Davis W. Clark presided at the first session of the Holston Annual Conference of the Northern Church.

5

Methodism and the Negro in the War

More urgent, however, than the need for establishing churches in the South was the situation presented by conditions among the recently emancipated slaves. The advance of the Union lines into the South multiplied demands for relief measures to aid the freed Negroes. Military commanders adopted a variety of expedients in dealing with the colored population, and only gradually did the Federal government and the churches establish policy for working with the displaced bondsmen. The policy of the government at the beginning of the war was to avoid interference with slavery. Escaping slaves were at first denied sanctuary in Union camps and with the troops, and were returned to their owners. The rapid turn of events, however, soon required abandonment of this policy. As early as the summer of 1861, Union commanders were employing "contrabands," as the fleeing slaves were called, on numerous labor details. As the number of fugitives increased, military officials organized departments of Negro affairs to provide sustenance, employment, and, in some cases, education.

By the beginning of 1862 a number of societies were already active in the North in raising funds and collecting clothing for the freedmen. Early in the same year the board of managers of the Missionary Society of the Northern Church took action to establish a mission for colored people in and near Port Royal. Increasingly, Methodists heard appeals for teachers, missionaries, and gifts of money and clothing. Three relief organizations with which Methodists co-operated extensively were the National Freedmen's Relief Association, the Western Freedmen's Aid Commission, and the Northwestern Freedmen's Aid Commission. In the last two years of the war most of the Annual Conferences appointed a special committee on freedmen's aid, and reports of the committee usually contained an endorsement of one of the relief organizations.

The church in general gave support to the movement for emancipation and registered impatience with the government's reluctance to effect immediate emancipation. Many Methodists expressed approval of General Frémont's order freeing the slaves in Missouri early in the war. Calls for immediate emancipation came more frequently and urgently from pulpit and press. Methodist leaders gave enthusiastic endorsement to President Lincoln's Emancipation Proclamation, which became effective at the beginning of 1863. The General Conference of 1864 described the proclamation as a providential instrument, fully implementing the national policy on slavery and producing results of interest to Christians and all philanthropists everywhere.[143]

The General Conference also urged the Congress to establish a Bureau of Freedmen's Affairs. The conference declared that it was the duty of the national government not only to assist the freedmen but also to protect those who were working for their "relief and elevation." Methodists were urged to give liberally to the United States Commission for the Relief of the National Freedmen, an organization representing the claims of a number of freedmen's aid societies.[144] It was not until 1866, however, that the Northern Church, following a pattern already established by other denominations, organized its own Freedmen's Aid Society.

The 1864 General Conference sent down to the Annual Conferences a resolution changing the General Rule on slavery so as to prohibit slaveholding as well as the buying and selling of slaves.[145] Affirmative action by the Annual Conferences removed the last vestige of the church's sanction of the institution of slavery. Northern Methodists, however, were not yet clear as to the place of the Negro in the life of the church. If Gilbert Haven, the "best-known Methodist abolitionist," spoke boldly in favor of social equality, his position was not representative of the view of Methodist leadership, not to mention the rank

[143] *Journal of the General Conference,* 1864, p. 440.
[144] *Ibid.,* pp. 440-42.
[145] *Ibid.,* pp. 167, 376.

and file of the laity. Even Bishop Simpson, uncompromising as was his opposition to slavery, suggested as late as 1864 that the Negroes should be given a "state of their own, perhaps on the border between Mexico and Texas." [146]

The 1864 General Conference addressed itself to the question of colored membership in the church. Its committee studying the matter estimated that, before the start of the war, the border conferences had about 27,000 colored members and that over 100,000 Negroes attended Methodist worship. Moreover, the committee report assumed that after the war the colored members of the Southern Church would, "in the nature of the case, seek a home with some other branch of the Methodist family." Although the Northern Church had been deprived of its "appropriate jurisdiction" over the slave in the extreme South, it had remained sympathetic and would welcome him back to its protection.[147]

The committee did not explore the implications of the "protective" relationship to Negro Methodists. It was more concerned with the organization and supervision of Negro local preachers. If these could be "properly marshaled," the committee pointed out, the Northern Church would be enabled to "possess the land." In dealing with the Negro preachers the church faced several alternatives: (a) They could be advised to join one of the independent African Methodist Churches, with some kind of subsidy extended from the Methodist Episcopal Church; (b) they could remain as local preachers, serving under white presiding elders as needed; (c) they could be received into the existing Annual Conferences; (d) they could be organized into mission conferences. The General Conference endorsed the latter alternative. It was the duty of the church, the conference voted, "to encourage *colored pastorates* for *colored people* wherever practicable, and to contribute to their efficiency" by every possible means. Inasmuch as a distinctive conference organization of their own was deemed most conducive to the efficiency of Negro Methodists, the General Conference authorized the bishops

to organize among our colored ministers, for the benefit of our colored members and population, Mission Conferences—one or more—where in their godly judgment the exigencies of the work may demand it; and should more than one be organized, to determine their boundaries until the meeting of the next General Conference. . . . *Provided,* that nothing in this resolution be so construed as to impair the existing constitutional rights of our colored members on the one hand, or to forbid, on the other, the transfer of white ministers to said conference or conferences where it may be practicable and deemed necessary.[148]

---

[146] Clark, *Life of Simpson,* p. 242.
[147] *Journal of the General Conference,* 1864, pp. 485-86.
[148] *Ibid.,* pp. 486-87.

As the war drew to its close, Northern Methodism, whatever may be said in appreciation of its official attitude toward the Negro, had only begun to deal with the question of the place of the Negro Methodist in the life of the church.

The Southern Church, on the other hand, was not yet ready to examine critically the inferior status conferred upon its Negro members by a feudalistic culture. Mission work among the slaves persisted in some areas of the Southern Church throughout most of the war. The South Carolina Annual Conference received a report from its Mission Board in December, 1863, commending the "heroic fidelity of the missionary pastors" and noting the "salutary effects of the Gospel they preach, upon the minds of the African race." Methodist missionaries, the report continued, sought not only to improve moral conditions among the slaves; they also helped the servant to understand "his civil relation to that master, to whose government and protection Providence had committed him." South Carolina Methodists found in these missionary activities one explanation for the loyalty of those slaves who had remained with their owners and refused "to purchase their homes and comforts at the fictitious value of a nominal freedom under Northern misrule." It was a "matter of no ordinary gratification to know that . . . neither Abolition Proclamations tending them liberty, nor the alluring promises of a level-ling democracy," had been able to sever "those domestic ties that bind the slaves to their masters." [149]

Reluctantly, and pained by the failure of others to appreciate its position, the Southern Church came at length to see that, for all its concern with their welfare, it had not won the loyalty of its Negro constituency. The words of the General Conference of 1866 in effect mark the end of the old relationship:

We have expended our means and strength liberally and patiently for many years for their salvation and improvement, and if in anywise our conduct has not been appreciated by some on earth, nevertheless, our witness is with God, and our record on high. It is grateful to our own feelings to know that if the colored people do not remain under our pastoral care, their departure reflects no discredit upon our labors in their behalf, and is necessitated by no in-difference on our part to their welfare. Many of them will probably unite with the African M. E. Church, some of them with the Northern Methodist Church, while others, notwithstanding extraneous influences and unkind misrepresenta-tions of our Church, will remain with us.[150]

---

[149] *Minutes of the Seventy-Sixth Session of the South Carolina Conference,* pp. 17-18.
[150] *Journal of the General Conference,* 1866, p. 18.

Missionaries from the Negro Methodist churches entered the South well before the end of the war. Representatives of the A.M.E. Church came to South Carolina from New York in May, 1863, and began work at Port Royal, Edisto, and Beaufort. Two years later the church organized the South Carolina Annual Conference, its first in the South. One of the bishops of the A.M.E. Church was Daniel A. Payne, who as a youth in 1835 had been forced to close his school for colored children in Charleston and flee the state. In December, 1863, Bishop Payne came to Nashville and welcomed two congregations of Negro Methodists into his connection. Members, stewards, and trustees of Capers Chapel and Andrew Chapel transferred their membership from the Southern Church and changed the names of their churches to St. John's and St. Paul's.[151]

Missionaries of another Negro church, A.M.E. Zion, began work in New Bern and other communities of eastern North Carolina early in 1864 and, before the end of the year, organized the Old North Carolina Annual Conference. In the same year the A.M.E. Zion Church also opened missions in Florida and Louisiana, and in 1865 it organized its Louisiana Annual Conference.[152]

Thus were the foundations laid for the phenomenal growth of African Methodism in the South after the war. By 1865 both churches were prepared to bid for the allegiance of Negro Methodists in the former Confederate states.

This chapter has by design centered attention on the life and thought of the two largest branches of American Methodism as they confronted the issues and events of the war. But the study gains adequate perspective only as one keeps in view the great transformations which the war accelerated in every area of American life. Not until the return of peace would either of the churches begin to comprehend the extent of these changes and their implications for the life of the nation and its churches. The Southern Church of 1865 found itself absorbed in a struggle for its very existence, and it would not easily or quickly be liberated from its identification with an antebellum culture. The Northern Church, whatever its losses, emerged from the war with its institutions largely intact, and its leadership steering it into the mainstream of American political life. Bishop Simpson could boast of his church's wealth, its influence, its refinement, and its "great enterprise."[153] If Southern

---

[151] Daniel A. Payne, *A History of the African Methodist Episcopal Church,* ed. C. S. Smith (Nashville: Publishing House of the A.M.E. Sunday-School Union, 1891), pp. 471-72.

[152] David Henry Bradley, Sr., *A History of the A.M.E. Zion Church, 1796-1872* (Nashville: The Parthenon Press, 1956), pp. 160-62.

[153] Crooks, *Life of Simpson,* p. 507.

Methodism remained bound by its ties to a prewar culture, the Northern Church showed disturbing signs of a comfortable adjustment to the culture of America's Gilded Age. This contrast in cultural orientation had been sharpened by the war, and, no less than the bitterness engendered by military conflict, it widened and deepened the division between the two churches.

chapter 18

REBUILDING THE SOUTHERN CHURCH

Conditions After the War

The 1866 General Conference

The Colored Methodist
  Episcopal Church

Missions and Publishing

Constitutional Reform

Education and Sunday Schools

Social and Spiritual Outlook

WHEN THE ARMIES OF THE UNION AND of the Confederacy were disbanded in 1865 two matters had been settled beyond further dispute: the Negro was to be free and the Union was to be perpetuated. Though slavery and state sovereignty were no longer at issue, the Civil War, like most wars, had created new problems in the solving of old ones. For almost an entire generation following armed hostilities the political, economic, and social reconstruction of the South occupied the chief attention of the entire nation.

The bewildering set of problems which arose in 1865 was almost as difficult and ominous as slavery and disunion had been in 1861. The greatest dilemma was the political status of the Negroes, now set free. If they were not permitted to vote, they would probably become virtual peons of the white people of the South. If they were given the right to vote, they would at once become objects of the most corrupting sectional competition. In any case, with Negroes counted as full citizens, the defeated South would have many more votes in Congress and in the electoral college than it had had prior to the war. The way out of this dilemma was found in what is called Reconstruction—a policy quite different from what President Abraham Lincoln had envisaged and one that was applied with drastic and cruel intent to the defeated section for ten years and then abandoned as a hopeless and almost immoral experiment.

Since the war was fought largely in the South, here its destruction was heaviest. Towns, cities, homes, railways, bridges, livestock, foodstuffs, and personal belongings—the things all invasions feed

257

upon—were destroyed. General William Sherman, who was most proficient in carrying the rigors of war to the people, made these comments two years after the war to veterans who had accompanied him:

Look to the South, and you who went with me through that land can best say if they too have not been fearfully punished. Mourning in every household, desolation written in broad characters across the whole face of their country, cities in ashes and fields laid waste, their commerce gone, their system of labor annihilated and destroyed. Ruin, poverty, and distress everywhere, and now pestilence adding to the very cap sheaf to their stack of misery; her proud men begging for pardon and appealing for permission to raise food for their children; her five million of slaves free, and their value lost to their former masters forever.[1]

So acute was the distress throughout the South that there was the threat of starvation for hundreds of whites and blacks alike.[2] The crops of 1865 turned out badly, in large part due to the fact that most of the former soldiers reached their homes too late for a successful planting and the Negro labor supply was not dependable. The critical distress continued until 1867. Even then, privation and destruction were everywhere. While many became discouraged and left the South for the West or the North, the great mass of the people accepted the situation and made the best of it. In addition to the cost of war, the South had to bear the price of peace. To a South already impoverished came additional burdens in the form of high federal taxes. All Confederate currency became worthless, and all war debts were forcibly repudiated as a part of the condition of re-entering the Union. The greatest single possession a Southerner lost was his property in Negroes, with a money value which has been estimated all the way from one billion to four billion dollars. This was total and just as real as if the same amount of money had been invested in a Confederate bond. However, the South's most pathetic disaster was that it was forced to skip almost a generation of young men, dead of disease or killed on the field of battle—or wounded into economic incompetency. The losses among the whites are usually estimated at about half the military population, but since accurate records are lacking the exact numbers cannot be ascertained.

---

[1] *Weekly Constitutionalist*, Augusta, Georgia, November 27, 1867, quoted in E. Merton Coulter, *The South During Reconstruction 1865-1877* (Baton Rouge: Louisiana State University Press, 1947), p. 2.

[2] See Richard Irby, *History of Randolph-Macon College, Virginia* (Richmond: Whittet and Shepperson, n.d.), p. 165.

1

The Church at the Close of the War

The churches and church people were more involved in the Civil War than in any war of modern times. Since the church was an extremely important institution in the South, possibly more so than in the North, and probably in both sections more so than at the present time, it was inevitable that ecclesiastical Reconstruction should give rise to bitter feelings. The influence exerted by the churches on political conditions was never so potent as during the slavery controversy, the war, and the Reconstruction period. All the churches, North and South, took a conspicuous part in the slavery controversy. From 1845 to the outbreak of the Civil War, slavery was the chief theme of the church press and the all-absorbing topic of church controversy. When the war came, it was looked upon by the church people of the North as though largely a moral and religious struggle, and it appealed quite strongly to their religious zeal. Despite the religious enthusiasm over the issues, the churches in the North and in the South experienced wartime losses in membership. As one Methodist historian says, the war and the political agitation preceding it "had a demoralizing effect upon all church work." [3] The popular notion that in time of crisis people turn to the church did not prove true in the South, and a recent study points out that the churches "at home experienced no revival or religious excitement comparable in any manner to that experienced by the men in camps." [4] Though numerous revivals were attempted, there appears to have been a complete lack of religious enthusiasm. There was, however, a remarkable degree of interdenominational co-operation among southern Protestant churches during and immediately following the war.

When the war closed, Northern churches and church leaders considered the problem of the freedmen not only as a national problem but as one peculiarly for the churches and church people to solve. Even before the war ended, practically all the Northern churches had entered the South with a determination to solve that knotty question in their own way, most of them thinking that there was but one way to solve it and that was through the church's efforts. By 1865 all the Southern churches were in a greatly disorganized and impoverished condition. Their

---

[3] Macum Phelan, *A History of Early Methodism in Texas, 1817-1866* (Nashville: Cokesbury Press, 1924), p. 467.

[4] W. Harrison Daniel, "The Protestant Church in the Confederate States" (Unpublished dissertation, Duke University, 1957), p. 219.

properties destroyed, their buildings burned or badly in need of repair, and the church treasuries empty, it was doubtful whether some of them could survive. Many Northern churches acted upon the principle that the question of separate churches had been settled by the war along with that of state sovereignty.

The end of the war found the Methodist Episcopal Church, South, with six bishops: Joshua Soule, James O. Andrew, Robert Paine, George F. Pierce, John Early, and Hubbard H. Kavanaugh. Bishops Soule and Andrew were enfeebled by advanced age, while Bishop Early was handicapped by illness. This in effect left only three bishops to serve all the Annual Conferences of 1865. The ranks of the episcopacy were depleted, an extensive preparatory and college educational program was disrupted, well-developed publishing interests were destroyed, the vast missionary program was wrecked and heavily in debt, and many church buildings either completely demolished or in the hands of the Methodist Episcopal Church. There is little wonder that many despaired of survival, some even believing that affiliation with another denomination was desirable. Of this one historian wrote as follows: "Then some of the Church, losing faith in her future, were coquetting with an Episcopal Bishop for a union of churches—the M.E. Church South and the Protestant Episcopal South; and some were proposing to give up and go back to the M.E. Church." [5] The great majority, however, were strongly opposed to any such action. Talk of merger and the loss of members to other denominations were still matters of concern to Bishop Pierce two years later when he wrote:

Much of our labor is bestowed upon fields unfenced, left open, and the devil and the world, to say nothing of better folks, forage upon our plantation, and we are left to glean where we ought to have reaped. . . . We need [more spiritual life] to save the Church from the schismatic plans of Northern Methodists and the subtle proselytism of the Episcopalians. These last, despairing of building up their own sect by conversions from the world, are beguiling some of our people by shallow talk about succession, confirmation, mother church, our beautiful liturgy. Our young people they are bribing with an assurance of larger liberty in worldly amusements, fasting in Lent purchasing the privilege of dancing the rest of the year.[6]

In its meeting in 1864, the Kentucky Conference practically declared its independence of the Southern Church, definitely asserting that it was not responsible for the actions of the other Annual Conferences. A resolution of loyalty to the Union was unanimously adopted at the same session.

[5] George G. Smith, *The Life and Times of George Foster Pierce* (Nashville: Hunter and Welburn, 1888) , p. 492.
[6] *Ibid.,* pp. 504-5.

However, this did not satisfy some of the more pronouncedly loyal ministers, some of whom left for the Kentucky Annual Conference of the Northern Church the next year. The situation in Kentucky was described by Bishop Kavanaugh in a letter dated May 24, 1865, addressed to Bishop Soule. In the letter Bishop Kavanaugh says:

I have had some uneasiness lately lest the radical Union sentiment of some of our brethren both of the laiety and the ministry might turn them to the M.E. Church. To satisfy myself of the truth of things on the subject, I have traveled pretty extensively lately, and find that we have but a very little to fear. There are slight disaffections in the cities of Covington, Newport and Louisville, the balance of the state with the exception of some disaffection in the mountains, are firm in their adherence to the M.E. Church, *South*. They are for no ecclesiastical change whatever but there is a general desire on the *border everywhere* that the word "South" should be removed from our church designation by our next General Conference.[7]

Removal of "South" from the title was all that many felt was necessary to establish reunion with the Northern Church.

Leaders of the Southern Church began to talk of fraternal relations and eventual reunion with the Northern Church almost immediately after the cessation of hostilities. It was assumed that church properties would be returned to their Southern owners and that an acceptable plan for restoring the unity of the church similar to Lincoln's magnanimous plan for restoring unity in the nation might be evolved. The Southern bishops issued individual pleas to Methodist ministers and laymen in behalf of national loyalty, unity, and peace, and called upon the churches to pray for those in authority. D. D. Whedon, in an editorial including many excerpts from Southern Methodist church papers under the caption "Spirit of the Southern Press," says:

Indeed, we understand the unanimous and settled ground of the Church South to be this: *We, the Church South, made the last formal proposition for recognition or union, and that was formally rejected; we now stand permanently ready, not to make further official offers, but to hear and consider in a Christian spirit whatever propositions the Methodist Episcopal Church sees fit to make.*[8]

This was written before political Reconstruction, with Federal army units stationed throughout the South, was undertaken. The same editor, writing in 1873, said:

The Southern papers unanimously applauded our publication [of January, 1866], and accepted for the time our terms. But in our own Church a most

[7] MS letter in Emory University Library.
[8] *Methodist Quarterly Review* (Northern), January, 1866, pp. 129-30.

irrational opposition arose. . . . Meanwhile, by the delay of this opposition, and the long friction of the debate, the temper of the South began to turn, and the golden hour was lost. The Southern rebel politicians . . . breathed their Copperhead inspiration into a Church that was always proud to be a political appanage.[9]

This last statement was a direct jibe at the often expressed Southern opinion that one of the most serious impediments to reunion was that the Northern Church was too seriously involved in politics.

Following the war, there were many Southern people who wanted to see the militant sectionalism of the Old South replaced by a sincere national loyalty. In 1865 there were occasional influential leaders who were unafraid to express such a view in advocating some act that would reunite separate groups of similar organizations in the North and in the South. The wartime president of Trinity College, Braxton Craven, was such a man. He is described as "educator, author, minister, and former slaveholder and supporter of secession in North Carolina." [10] Serving as pastor of Edenton Street Church in Raleigh during the last two years of the war while not needed for his college responsibilities, Craven addressed a letter in July, 1865, to Northern Methodist Bishop Edward R. Ames, director of Southern work for his church and the one to whom most Southern Methodist church property had been released. Craven felt that a mutually voluntary effort toward reunion of the two branches of Methodism in 1865 would have constituted at least a gesture toward national solidarity. The letter maintained, quite accurately it developed, that if such a union could not be agreed upon immediately, it would be many years before effective action could be taken. Craven had just learned of the action of the Northern bishops, who on June 15 had issued a statement affirming, first, that they had no authority to originate any proposals or pleas for union, and, second, that they recommended for postwar evangelism a continuation of the policy approved by the wartime General Conference of 1864 of establishing as much work as possible among both Negroes and whites in the South. In his letter to Bishop Ames, Craven says:

Our relations to each other will, I hope, excuse me for saying, that I regret the action of the Bishops of the Methodist Episcopal Church, at their late meeting, in reference to Methodism in the Southern States. . . . Immediate regular official action is the more important, because time will inevitably increase

[9] *Ibid.,* April, 1873, p. 332.
[10] Nora C. Chaffin, "A Southern Advocate of Methodist Unification in 1865," *The North Carolina Historical Review,* January, 1941, p. 38.

the difficulties in the way of successful operation or adjustment. Already not a few very harsh and very unnecessary things have been published in the papers. . . . The difficulties between the Church North and South, could now be easily adjusted; but if passion, prejudice, ambition, and intemperate zeal shall belabor the question till 1868, I fear "it will be past mending." . . . The great Methodist heart in the South beats with warm, true life; it is neither dead in sin, nor corrupt in the practices of the traitor. . . . I will not suppose that Northern Methodists are so self-righteous, so self-confident, or so intolerant as to reject fellowship with a people whom they have striven so hard to retain in the Union.[11]

When it became apparent that the wartime policy toward the Southern churches, frequently described as one of "disintegration and absorption," was to be continued in peacetime, fierce resistance was met from those whose churches and associations were to be subjected to the process. Southern Methodist leaders who had advocated fraternity and reunion soon began to urge continuance of the Southern Church rather than submit to the conditions under which Southerners might be readmitted to the Northern Church. Southern ministers applying for membership were required to give satisfactory assurance of loyalty to the government and approval of the antislavery doctrines of the Northern Church.[12] Those who had been in rebellion were to be admitted only after they had confessed their sin, for it was felt that certain tests must be applied to the Confederate sinners asking for admission in order that the enormity of their crimes should be made plain to them. This policy was generally unsuccessful because the Confederates objected to being treated as "rebels and traitors" and to "sitting upon stools of repentance" before they could be received into the church.[13]

The Episcopal Church in the Confederate States of America, meeting in November, 1865, voted to reunite with its counterpart in the United States, and the two groups of the Methodist Protestant Church united a few years later. The other principal denominations of the South, with a longer history and experience of separate existence, soon determined to continue their separate ways. These sought to recover for their own use the church property turned over by the military to the representatives of the corresponding Northern denominations or missionary societies which had followed the army to the South. These representatives, in most instances, seem to have looked upon military conquest as a sufficient grant of ecclesiastical authority.

---

[11] *Ibid.,* pp. 42-43, 45.

[12] *Journal of the General Conference,* 1864, p. 241.

[13] Walter Lynwood Fleming, *The Sequel of Appomattox* (New Haven: Yale University Press, 1919), p. 198.

The Northern Church connections, insofar as the whites of the South were concerned, remained largely on a missionary footing, though some permanent readjustments occurred in the border states. The establishment of the Freedmen's Bureau in 1865, headed by General Oliver Otis Howard, a man greatly interested in the church, was considered a direct invitation to the Northern churches to send missionaries and teachers into the South. Throughout the entire Reconstruction period, the great field for Northern missionary effort was among the freed people.

The Presbyterians, Baptists, and Methodists were the major denominations of the South, and as the period of Reconstruction progressed the likelihood of reunion within these groups deteriorated. One prominent historian, writing in recent years, said of the Methodists:

The most uncompromising clerical gladiators throughout the nation were the Northern Methodists, whose church polity and practice became so steeped in the new isms of the age as to make it difficult to distinguish them from a wing of the Republican Party. . . . As radical and uncompromising as Thaddeus Stevens himself, they believed in Negro suffrage, the confiscation of Southern property, and death to traitors. The most extreme advocated miscegenation.[14]

More serious for the future of the church than the losses in membership and property was the extreme poverty which hung like a pall over the entire church. In 1866 an editor of the church declared that

in our Church, there was probably, before the war, more wealth than was ever held by the same number of professing Christians. . . . Let us pray God to lead us into temptation no more. And it does seem sure enough, that in that direction we shall be gratified; that the field which we now cultivate will be noted henceforth for its poverty, as it was once remarkable for its wealth.[15]

Many Methodist ministers were forced by necessity to sell their horses in order to provide for their families. Further indication of the general poverty throughout the church was indicated in the fact that while the amount raised for retired ministers and orphans and widows of ministers

[14] Coulter, *The South During Reconstruction,* p. 332.

[15] Quoted in Hunter Dickinson Farish, *The Circuit Rider Dismounts: A Social History of Southern Methodism 1865-1900* (Richmond: The Dietz Press, 1938) , p. 30. This is the most important study of the Southern Methodist Church in this period ever made, originally being prepared as a dissertation at Harvard University. Another important work on the Southern Church in Reconstruction is Comer Hastings, "The Methodist Episcopal Church, South, During the Reconstruction Period" (Unpublished dissertation, Duke University, 1932) . Briefer, but likewise valuable, is William Larkin Duren, *The Trail of the Circuit Rider* (New Orleans: Privately printed, 1936) .

in all the conferences in 1860 was $67,030, only $35,444 could be raised in 1866, even though needs were greater.

There is little wonder that the zeal with which the Northern Methodists attempted to hold church property in the South should have caused such a violent reaction in the Southern Church. With the perspective of a very few years, some of the missionaries themselves were a little surprised at their earlier attitudes and actions. Of the position taken by many of the Northern missionaries one of their number later wrote:

No other denomination did just as we did in that matter. Temporary occupancy of pulpits, in some instances, occurred with others; but our ministers stood in the attitude of conquerors. They differed little in appearance from . . . invaders. It did not so appear to them. It did so appear to the Church, South. It is so esteemed by them now. They may stigmatize it with unwonted severity, we may think; but their ox is gored by our bull, and we do not feel the pain. We should remember that.

If our occupancy of the pulpits of the Church, South, had been only for the purpose of suffering the preaching of the word to deserted congregations, and, on the return of their pastors and the restoration of peace, had been yielded up gracefully, it would have been better for the peace of the Methodist family. But such was not the case. Claims were set up to the property on questionable grounds. Possession was retained until compelled to relinquish by civil authority.

If this statement be correct, then our ecclesiastical relations with the Southern Methodist are, in this aspect, most unfortunate.[16]

Along with many other questions, two major ones faced the Southern Church leaders. One related to the calling of a session of the General Conference of the church and the other related to an expression of the official attitude of the Southern Church toward the Northern Church. While there were many diverse opinions being expressed about relationships between the two churches, there was no way to make an official statement of the attitude of the church except at a General Conference. The regular quadrennial General Conference had been omitted in 1862 because of the difficulties of travel and the fact that the city of New Orleans, where the sessions of the conference were to be held, had fallen into Federal hands prior to the date of the meeting.

The need for new legislation and an opportunity to make official statements in behalf of the church was so urgent that many church leaders considered the possibility of calling a special session of the General Conference shortly after the end of hostilities. Bishop Kavanaugh wrote to Bishop Soule on May 24, 1865, saying:

[16] L. C. Matlock, "An Interesting Statement of the Case," Nashville *Christian Advocate*, April 2, 1870.

I have very many things about which to talk to you. . . . about the propriety of a called Genl. Conference; or, of waiting until the regular time in 1866. It occurs to me, Bishop, that it will take a large part of a year to get our annual conferences properly arranged. . . . I crave your opinion in regard to our delegates. It appears to me, that should there be a called General Conference, that the delegates now elected, are properly the members of the body; but should there be no Genl. Conference until the Spring of 1866 then there should be an election of delegates to that Genl. Conference, the two conferences in point of *time* being different? [17]

No special session was held and new delegates were elected for a session called to meet in New Orleans in the spring of 1866. It was highly significant for the future of the church that a regular session with newly elected delegates was held, rather than a special session with the delegates elected in 1861. The conference of 1866 proved to be one of the most significant General Conferences ever held in Methodism, and the composition of the body was highly important for the problems to be faced.

Meanwhile, the need for an official expression of attitude of the Southern Church on a number of problems, particularly relationships with the Northern Church and the disposition of Negro members of the Southern Church, became urgent. The cause of unity might have been helped considerably if some type of official statement could have been made in behalf of each side immediately after the war. The General Conference of the Northern Church had met in 1864, while the war was still in progress, and statements adopted during the heat of war might have been tempered considerably had there been an opportunity soon after the cessation of hostilities. It is impossible to generalize on exactly what Methodists in the North thought of Methodists in the South, or those in the South of those in the North, or what either thought about the Negro; there are abundant publications from which isolated quotations may be taken to confirm almost any position. It is possible to present many statements indicating that persons in the North felt that the responsibility for educating the Negroes was with the South. On the other hand, the prevailing opinion in the North seemed to be that, if not the responsibility of the North, it must be assumed by the North if it were ever to be accomplished. The prevailing opinion in the South seemed to be that if given time, sufficient education for the Negroes would be supplied. Many people in the South, however, felt that since the North was responsible for the current situation it should bear the brunt of providing educational facilities for the Negro.

[17] MS letter, Emory University Library.

The view is generally expressed that "the deathblow to any attempt at union of the Churches, North and South, at this time was struck by the bishops of the Methodist Church South in a pastoral letter which they sent out over the South at the close of the war." [18] In spite of all that had transpired, this letter was not sent out until August whereas hostilities had ceased in April. There is considerable evidence to show, as Hunter Dickinson Farish said,

If, during the first days after the War, the Northern Church had manifested a conciliatory and charitable spirit toward the Southern Methodists, a reconciliation might have been effected and a union consummated between the two bodies. . . . But the leading officials and the press of the Northern body rapidly assumed an attitude of hostility towards the Southern organization and its members that gave the final blow to any prospect for a reunion of the two Churches at that time. They did not for a moment leave in doubt their enmity to the Southern Church or their determination to impose stringent conditions upon the return of Southern Methodists to the Methodist Episcopal fold.[19]

Amidst the perplexities of the time, the leaders of the Southern Church soon made plans to make more or less authoritative public statements about the future of the church pending the meeting of the General Conference. Personal words of courage and faith in the mission of the church came from all over the South, but the first expression from any sizable assembly of church leaders came in June, 1865, in the form of the "Palmyra Manifesto." This document was the report from a group of twenty-four ministers and about a dozen laymen called together by Andrew Monroe, one of the elder statesmen of the denomination in Missouri. Border areas like Missouri were in the most urgent need for clarification on the future status of the denomination, for in such areas the church "scarcely knew, under existing circumstances, whether she, as an ecclesiastical organization, was alive or dead." [20] All the preachers and official members within the bounds of the Missouri Conference were invited to meet at Palmyra, Marion County, Missouri, on June 22, 1865. Bishop Kavanaugh met with the group during most of their sessions. The report was a very long one, specifically setting forth reasons for the continued existence of the Southern Church, and it served as a manifesto against those who wished to absorb Southern Methodism into other groups. The report outlined the chief differences between the Northern and Southern Churches since the time of their separation and affirmed

---

[18] William Warren Sweet, *The Methodist Episcopal Church and the Civil War* (Cincinnati: Methodist Book Concern, 1912), pp. 103-4.

[19] *Circuit Rider Dismounts*, pp. 40-41. Used by permission of Mrs. A. B. Howard.

[20] W. H. Lewis, *The History of Methodism in Missouri for a Decade of Years, from 1860 to 1870* (Nashville: Privately printed, 1890), p. 171.

that these differences had in no way been totally abolished by the abolition of slavery. It went on to assert that were the Southern Methodists
to go into any other church it would be tantamount to admitting the
charge that they stood or fell on slavery.

The report closed in these words: "It is due [to] every principle of
self-respect and ecclesiastical propriety that we maintain, with firm
reliance upon the help of the Great Head of the Church, our organization without embarrassment or compromise. . . . [while desiring] most
ardently to cultivate fraternal relations with all the evangelical
Churches. . . ." [21]

The message from Palmyra was carried rather quickly throughout the
Southern Church press. It was felt that if the Missouri preachers, who
had suffered so much, could maintain their loyalty to the church, surely
so could all others. It was reported that in some areas, particularly in
Virginia and the Carolinas, the message came "like life from the dead." [22]
It gave courage and confidence to Methodists in all parts of the South
and had a large influence in shaping a statement issued by the bishops.
The bishops assembled in Columbus, Georgia, in August, 1865, and
summoned Holland N. McTyeire, who had edited the Nashville *Christian
Advocate* from 1858 until February, 1862, when the Federal army
captured Nashville and commandeered the printing presses for its own
needs. McTyeire was to become the outstanding leader of Southern
Methodism throughout the entire period of Reconstruction. He was the
architect of most of the progressive actions taken by the Southern
Methodist Church from the time of his first election as a member of the
General Conference in 1854, when he was under thirty years of age,
until the time of his death in 1889.

The bishops, after conferring with McTyeire, decided to issue a
Pastoral Address to the entire church which would be also a notice to
the world of the "will to live" of the church, with a clarion call for a
General Conference in New Orleans the following year. McTyeire was
assigned the task of preparing this address to the church. One leader of
the church described McTyeire's contribution as follows:

Under their direction, he wrote an address to the Church which was like the
blast of a trumpet: the Methodist Episcopal Church, South, yet lived, and in
all of its polity and principles was unchanged; neither disintegration nor
absorption was to be thought of, all rumors to the contrary notwithstanding;
whatever banner had fallen, that of Southern Methodism was still unfurled;
whatever cause had been lost, that of our Church still survived; and the General

[21] *Ibid.*, p. 178.
[22] *Ibid.*, p. 179.

Conference was summoned to meet in New Orleans in April, 1866, though its adjournment had occurred eight years before.[23]

The address stated emphatically that the questions raised in the division of 1844 were not settled by the war. The incorporation of social dogmas and political tests into their church creeds brought forth the assertion that "a large proportion, if not a majority of the Northern Methodists have become incurably radical." Tolerance toward former foes was advised, especially for those in sections in which brethren held opposing views. Bearing testimony to the poverty of the times, pastors were exhorted, whenever it was impossible for the charges to support them, to follow the example of the Apostle Paul and work with their hands. All suggestions of reunion were rejected. The continued invasion of Southern territory and the usurpation of Southern pulpits were severely denounced, while the Annual Conferences were urged to present a united front against the invasion. The platform of the church was restated in these words:

Preach Christ and him crucified. Do not preach politics. You have no commission to preach politics. . . . Keep in view that rule of our faith which declares that "the Holy Scriptures contain all things necessary to salvation; so that whatever is not read therein nor may be proved thereby, is not to be required of any man."

This last sentence was a reiteration of one found earlier in the statement which stated that the Northern Methodists "have gone on to impose conditions upon discipleship that Christ did not impose." [24] The bishops' Pastoral Address clearly marked the turning point in the "health" of the Southern Church. Once it was determined that the church intended to continue its separate existence, many who had earlier advocated reunion expressed approbation. Journals of the Southern Church expressed full approval of the stand taken by the bishops. As was to be expected, many of the Northern Church publications expressed surprise that the statement took such a look to a past that was long dead and apparently had no vision of a "dawning new day."

The fortunes of the Southern Church improved slowly. By the end of 1865 most of the churches (except some held by Negro congregations) occupied by the Northern Church under the authority of the Secretary of War were restored to their former owners by President Andrew Johnson. The Publishing House in Nashville was restored in 1865, and the

[23] John J. Tigert, Fraternal Address, *Journal of the General Conference*, 1892, p. 575.

[24] *Minutes of the Mississippi Annual Conference*, 1865, pp. 25-29.

publication of the Nashville *Christian Advocate* was resumed soon after-wards. The various conference publications were gradually revived. A number of schools and colleges throughout the church resumed opera-tions by the end of 1865. Most schools for men were forced to close for from one to four years, with a few being closed even longer than this.

Instead of showing an increase of 150,000 members in the six years before 1866, a figure which would have been easily attained with its annual pre-war increase, the Southern Church showed a loss of ap-proximately 250,000. Including probationers, the total number of mem-bers reported in 1860 was 748,968, served by 2,615 traveling preachers and 5,353 local preachers. The full members included 454,203 whites, 171,857 Negroes, and 3,295 Indians. Losses during the war period reduced these figures so that in 1866 the report showed 498,847 members, served by 2,314 traveling preachers and 3,769 local preachers. This included 419,404 white members, 78,742 Negro members, and 701 Indian members, with no probationary members reported.[25]

2

The General Conference of 1866

A quality of daring and determination characterized the sessions of the General Conference from the outset, when it convened in New Orleans on Wednesday, April 4, 1866. The bishops in their Pastoral Address had urged the Annual Conferences to send their ablest men as delegates to the conference. Able and forward-looking men comprised the group of 153 ministers who were chosen as delegates. There were no lay members of the General Conference, since neither the Northern nor Southern Church had yet yielded to the requests to authorize lay mem-bership in either General or Annual Conferences.

The conference of 1866 proved to be one of the most significant ever held in Methodism, for in its actions are found the beginnings of many practices which have come largely to characterize American Methodism. The significance was recognized almost immediately and it has been acknowledged in various ways during the intervening years. Of it one writer says:

[25] *Minutes of the Annual Conferences of the Methodist Episcopal Church, South.* 1860, p. 293, and 1866, p. 94.

Only the Christmas Conference which assembled in Lovely Lane Chapel in 1784 could compare in significance with the postwar Conference of 1866; in the former, American Methodism was born, and in the latter, a great segment was to arise Phoenix-like from ashes and continue the unprecedented growth which had hitherto characterized it. This required constructive statesmanship of a high order and fundamental reorganization.[26]

William Warren Sweet, one of the most prominent historians of American Methodism, spoke of the session in these words: "The Conference was forward looking to an extraordinary degree, for even conservative men having become accustomed to great changes now gave their support to what they would have considered a few years before as radical legislation." [27] Another historian characterized it as "one of the most important in the history of Church councils in America." [28]

Not all the leaders of the church called the conference "progressive." A conservative group headed by Bishop George F. Pierce felt that it was "radical." Bishop Pierce was quite outspoken and opposed one of the actions of the conference so vigorously that he indicated he would resign at once if the action were made operative. The action related to the removal of the time limit on pastoral appointments, and in the light of the bishop's attitude the conference agreed on a four-year limit to replace the older one of two years. Bishop Pierce's biographer says:

There was a party of progressives in the Church who found him always in their way. They were bright, gifted, pious, conscientious young men. They had hinted before the war at changes which were to be great improvements. . . . It was evident that in the . . . General Conference radicalism was to have sway. The elections to the body indicated the fact.[29]

In the course of the conference, Holland N. McTyeire emerged as the most influential person in its deliberations, and he probably exerted greater leadership than anyone else in the determination of its acts and policies. It was McTyeire who introduced the resolution leading to the most far-reaching change ever made in American Episcopal Methodism when he offered the following: "*Resolved*, That it is the sense of this General Conference that Lay Representation be introduced into the Annual and General Conferences." [30] The resolution was adopted by a huge majority, though by something less than the two-thirds majority

[26] John J. Tigert IV, *Bishop Holland Nimmon McTyeire, Ecclesiastical and Educational Architect* (Nashville: Vanderbilt University Press, 1955) , p. 135.

[27] *Methodism in American History* (Nashville: Abingdon Press, 1953) , p. 309.

[28] Farish, *Circuit Rider Dismounts*, p. 63.

[29] Smith, *Life of Pierce*, pp. 492-93.

[30] *Journal of the General Conference*, 1866, p. 62.

that would be required for submitting the proposal to the Annual
Conferences. Writing later of this strategy, McTyeire said:

The principle once admitted, even by a numerical majority, every thing was
gained. Men who were doubtful, or so indifferent to the new measure as to
vote on the old side, saw that the Church could not well stand in that attitude
on such a subject—excluding laymen on a minority expression of the ministry;
and enough of them consented to waive their preferences on the final record to
make a two-thirds majority.[31]

Though by all odds the most important single piece of legislation, the
action on lay representation was only one of many important actions.
The bishops' address to the conference had anticipated that there would
be numerous and far-reaching proposals for changes when they said:

If we are to judge from the tone of the religious press, and the action of many
of our Conferences, great concern is felt in respect to certain changes in our
economy. . . . Well for us if we can happily avoid extremes and do neither too
little nor too much. Let us remember that while innovations are not necessarily
improvements, wisdom may demand in the department of ecclesiastical expediency new applications and developments of fundamental principles. The
efficiency of Methodism finds its first condition in the prevalence of deep spiritual life; and alterations on our economy are valuable as they coincide with this
condition, calamitous when they ignore it.[32]

Fearing that divisions of opinion on proposed changes would lead to
great bitterness and even to withdrawal by the defeated minority, Bishop
James O. Andrew urged the delegates to maintain a spirit of brotherly
love. His remarks included the hope that they would conduct all their
discussions with a "calm, Christian temper," refraining from condemning
beforehand all those who proposed changes as being enemies of Methodism, realizing that they were perhaps "as good friends of the Church
as others who oppose them." [33]

Constitutional Changes Considered

So many memorials and petitions for changes in polity were submitted
to the General Conference by the various Annual Conferences, churches,
and delegates that the regular committees of the conference could not

[31] *A History of Methodism* (Nashville: Southern Methodist Publishing House, 1884),
p. 668.
[32] *Journal of the General Conference,* 1866, p. 20.
[33] *Ibid.,* p. 27.

handle them properly. This led to the creation of a special committee on "Changes of Economy" to which all proposals for constitutional changes were referred. The committee was composed of one delegate from each Annual Conference. E. H. Myers of the Georgia Conference, one of the acknowledged leaders of the progressives, was named chairman of this committee. The committee made seven different reports to the conference on the following subjects: (1) lay representation; (2) a change in the name of the church; (3) the reception of members into the church; (4) district conferences; (5) extension of the pastoral term; (6) formation of episcopal districts; and (7) the adoption of a new constitution for the church.

LAY REPRESENTATION

Lay representation was the commanding question in these reports and in all the actions of the conference. The acute interest manifested in the conference foretold the importance of this innovation in the life of the church. Agitation for lay representation in the Annual and General Conferences of American Methodism was not new. As early as 1816, a special committee had advised against lay representation, saying it would "be inconsistent with the present constitution." [34] The early struggle for lay representation was not a separate issue of its own, but was connected with the desire on the part of local preachers to have a part in formulating the legislation of the church. In an effort to appease the local preachers without granting lay representation in General and Annual Conferences, the General Conference of 1820 had created a "District Conference" of which all the local preachers in the district were members.[35] To these conferences had been assigned the responsibilities of licensing preachers, renewing licenses for local preachers, and recommending traveling preachers. Trying, suspending, expelling, and acquitting local preachers, as well as examining them on "doctrines and discipline" were also prescribed as responsibilities. The failure of these conferences to satisfy the advocates of lay representation, coupled with an assertion by the General Conference of 1828 that a divinely instituted ministry could not permit its functions to be controlled by "others," was largely responsible for the first major division in American Methodism which had led to the formation of the Methodist Protestant Church in 1830. In the face of the rising tide of democracy throughout the United States it is surprising that the subject of lay representation was so nearly dormant within episcopal Methodism for a score of years following the

[34] *Journals of the General Conference, 1796-1836* (New York: Carlton and Phillips, 1855), p. 166.
[35] *Ibid.*, p. 219.

organization of the Methodist Protestant Church. While the subject had been the chief center of action of the General Conference of 1828, the succeeding conference in 1832 devoted no attention whatever to the matter. The conference of 1840 dismissed proposals for lay representation as "not expedient." Various proposals for lay representation were put forward in the General Conferences of the Southern Church from 1850 until one was finally passed in 1866 and made fully operative in 1870. A financial plan had been adopted in 1850 providing for the optional use of a form of lay co-operation which provided for one lay steward from each district who would "have the right to vote and speak in the Annual Conference on all questions relating to the financial and secular interests of the Church." [36] This optional plan was continued at ensuing conferences, thereby enabling the laymen through this limited participation to reveal the value of their counsel in the administration of church affairs.

Agitation for enlarged lay participation in church affairs was not confined to the Southern Church. In March, 1852, prior to the General Conference of the Northern Church, a convention was held to consider the propriety of petitioning the General Conference to provide for lay representation in the conferences of the church. In the course of the discussion attention was called to the progress being made by the Southern Church under the optional plan of 1850, and the convention "broke into cheers when the statement was made that the division of the church would not have occurred, had there been lay representation in 1844." [37] In spite of the optimistic opinion of the group on how lay representation might have preserved union, such representation in the Methodist Protestant Church did not prevent disruption there. The petition was not granted by the General Conference of 1852. The General Conferences of 1860 and 1864 of the Northern Church expressed a willingness to admit laymen to the General Conference but not the Annual Conferences "whenever the people should desire." Not until two years after the Southern Church granted lay representation was any action taken, and then only two lay delegates in the General Conference from each Annual Conference and no lay representatives in the Annual Conferences were provided.[38]

Since the General Conference was primarily a legislative body, the Southern Church decided to give laymen equal representation with ministers in this body. Provision was made that whenever as many as one fifth of all the members of the General Conference requested it,

[36] *Journal of the General Conference,* 1850, p. 215.
[37] Duren, *Trail of the Circuit Rider,* pp. 282-83.
[38] *Journal of the General Conference,* 1868, p. 275.

the lay and clerical delegates might deliberate and vote as separate groups, but where the vote was so taken no legislation could become effective until it was approved by a majority of the members of each group. Two other provisions to safeguard the rights of each group were adopted: lay delegates would have no vote on any question concerning ministerial character and relations; and lay delegates would be elected by laymen only and clerical delegates by ministers only.[39]

As Annual Conferences were considered primarily as administrative groups, it was deemed unnecessary to establish a balance of power with equal representation of lay and clerical members of these conferences. The plan provided for four lay delegates from each presiding elder's district to be chosen in such manner as might be determined by each Annual Conference. After the plan was ratified, laymen began to take their places in the Annual Conferences immediately, and lay delegates were elected to the General Conference in 1870 for the first time in the history of American Episcopal Methodism.

The success with which the new program of lay representation functioned reconciled most of its opponents. Even Bishop Pierce, who had not approved the new program, soon acknowledged its merit. Bishop Robert Paine summed up the general attitude in remarks to the conference of 1870 on its closing day when he said, "The inauguration of the system of lay representation has worked admirably, confirming our conviction that the laity can greatly aid in managing the great interests of the Church." [40] This new provision, which brought new energy and new talents into the counsels of the church, has been characterized as a voluntary relinquishment of power on the part of the clergy "unprecedented in any major ecclesiastical body." [41]

CHANGE OF NAME

Numerous proposals came before the conference relating to changing the name of the church, the word "South" being considered a handicap to most of the border conferences as well as a target for ridicule from many Union sympathizers. The conference voted overwhelmingly to change the name and by a vote of 111 to 21 selected from the nine proposed, "The Methodist Church." This name, however, did not prove as appealing as it did nearly seventy-five years later when it was adopted as the official name of united American Methodism, for, upon reconsideration by the conference the following day, another of the proposed names was recommended to the Annual Conferences for approval. The

[39] *Journal of the General Conference,* 1866, pp. 108-9.
[40] *Journal of the General Conference,* 1870, p. 347.
[41] Farish, *Circuit Rider Dismounts,* p. 65.

name finally agreed upon was "The Episcopal Methodist Church"; but when submitted to the conferences it was not sanctioned, and the old name was retained.

So confident were the bishops that the change would be made, Bishop Doggett advised a group seeking union to adopt the new name. Consequently, when in 1867 the members of the Council of the Christian Union Church in Southern Illinois resolved to unite with the Southern Church, they voted to enter "The Episcopal Methodist Church." [42] The Council was accepted under the name and organized into the Illinois Conference with its first session in October, 1867. Although the proposed name was ultimately rejected by the Annual Conferences, the Illinois Conference continued as a part of the "Episcopal Methodist Church" until the General Conference of 1878 granted permission to change it to the Methodist Episcopal Church, South. Aside from the confusion on names, the establishment of the Illinois Conference is of interest even more so because for the first time the work of the Southern Church penetrated north of the agreed dividing line and into the territory of the Northern Church.

LOCAL CHURCH MEMBERSHIP

Another report proposed far-reaching changes relating to membership and the holding of certain meetings in the local church. The plan proposed abolition of the six-month probationary period to which a candidate for membership had to submit before being admitted into full church membership, and the abolition of compulsory attendance upon class meetings. A new group was established called the "church meeting" in which all business affairs of the congregation would be transacted. These proposals were all approved by the conference and ultimately found their way into the program of the church.

DISTRICT CONFERENCES

Anticipating the adoption of the proposal for lay representation by districts in the Annual Conferences, the committee felt that a district group of some type was the logical body to elect these representatives. Establishment of a new conference was recommended and the name "District Conference" was revived. The proposed conference was not to be the same as the one that had been created by the General Conference of 1820 and abolished in 1836; the original District Conference had been limited to certain duties relating to the regulation of local preachers.

[42] William Thomas Mathis, *The Organization of the Illinois Conference of the Methodist Episcopal Church, South* (Murphysboro, Ill.: Privately printed, 1927), p. 96.

The General Conference, however, tabled the report of the committee and provided that for the immediate future lay representatives to Annual Conferences would be elected in such manner as each conference might determine.

EXTENSION OF THE PASTORAL TERM

From its beginning, Methodism has been characterized by the itinerant system. While all appointments were on an annual basis, the Southern Church by 1866 had extended the maximum time in which a minister might serve in one pastoral charge to two consecutive years (except in New Orleans, where a man might serve longer because it was felt it took at least two years to build up any immunity to yellow fever). Many of the leaders of the church felt that the church could be improved by a much more settled pastorate than it had previously had. Consequently, the committee recommended the removal of all time limits and that the bishops be authorized to appoint men annually with no limit whatsoever on the total length of service in any one pastorate. The proposal was adopted overwhelmingly by the conference but on the following day was modified to place a maximum limit of four consecutive years on the pastoral term. Conservative members of the conference led by Bishop Pierce, who threatened to resign if the unlimited tenure proposal was actually placed in effect, were responsible for securing the reconsideration and change. Of Bishop Pierce it was said: "He accepted these changes, but never indorsed them all, and he held to it that four years was too long for any man to stay in one charge, and whenever he could he invariably changed him at the end of two years." [43]

EPISCOPAL DISTRICTS AND A NEW CONSTITUTION

Two other reports were made by the Committee on Changes of Economy. One proposed that the Annual Conferences be grouped into districts or areas under the direction of a resident bishop. This proposal was rejected by the conference as being opposed to the Methodist theory of the episcopacy which maintained that the bishops were "general superintendents" and not diocesan or area leaders. The other report related to the proposed adoption of a new constitution for the church. This was not recommended by the committee because it felt that "only a few changes in the present Constitution are all that is needed." [44]

All proposed constitutional changes required a two-thirds majority in the General Conference and the approval of three fourths of all the votes cast in the Annual Conferences. The only proposal of the General

[43] Smith, *Life of Pierce*, p. 494.
[44] *Journal of the General Conference*, 1866, p. 68.

Conference which failed to receive the required support of the Annual Conferences was that relating to the change of the name of the denomination.

Other Actions of the Conference

The General Conference of 1866 took many other far-reaching actions which were not dependent upon the Annual Conferences for approval. The strengthening of the missionary program of the church, both foreign and domestic, was one of the more important. Prior to 1866 all of the missionary work of the church had been conducted through the church Missionary Society; the foreign work was confined largely to a mission in China, while domestic work centered largely around certain Indian and Negro undertakings. By the end of the war the Missionary Society was almost entirely inactive and was burdened with a rather substantial indebtedness. The conference took steps to revitalize the defunct missionary program by organizing two separate boards, one called the Board of Foreign Missions and the other the Board of Domestic Missions. Much attention was devoted to re-establishing the publishing interests of the church. Education likewise came before the General Conference, though more attention was given to securing a more efficient and better-educated ministry than to the projection of new schools or even the rebuilding of the war-wrecked educational institutions. Action was also taken looking to the establishment of chairs for instruction in Bible in the existing institutions of learning.

Heated discussion took place over the extension of the bishops' right to pass upon actions of the General Conference. The General Conference of 1854 had empowered the bishops to suspend conference actions which they deemed to be unconstitutional. Though this extension of power to the bishops itself related to the structure of the church and thereby became a constitutional matter rather than a statutory one, it had been adopted as simple legislation and was never submitted to the Annual Conferences for ratification. In spite of this defect in its adoption, it was inserted in the *Discipline* as a limiting factor on the power of General Conferences. When its legality was questioned in the General Conference of 1866 the debate became so heated that action was postponed indefinitely. The General Conference of 1870 deleted the earlier action from the *Discipline,* then enacted virtually the same provisions in the form of a constitutional amendment. This was sent to the Annual Conferences, where it received overwhelming ratification and thus became a part of the constitution of the church.

The Negro membership of the Southern Church was steadily declining and the conference took timely action to deal with this problem. The Negro members were to be organized into separate missions, churches, circuits, districts, and Annual Conferences. When there were sufficient Annual Conferences they were to be assisted in forming a separate jurisdiction for themselves.

The bishops recommended enlarging the group of bishops so that closer supervision might be given to the rebuilding of the church in the war-torn states. Recommended also was a bishop who might devote the greater portion of his time to the Pacific coast, where the Southern Church had organized an Annual Conference in 1852. Bishops Soule, Early, and Andrew were relieved of the responsibilities of active administration by the conference, and the Committee on Episcopacy recommended the election of six additional bishops. The conference reduced the number to four, though thirteen members voted to elect ten, twelve voting for seven. The General Conference thus increased the number of active bishops by only one, while at the same time it urged the bishops to assign one to the Pacific coastal conferences.

Among the men chosen for bishop was Holland N. McTyeire, who had already established himself as one of the leaders in the efforts to revitalize and expand the Southern Church. In the ensuing decades he became the acknowledged leader of most of the progressive movements in the church, especially distinguishing himself in the Reconstruction era in the field of higher education while entrusted with the responsibility for launching Vanderbilt University. Others elected as bishops were William M. Wightman, Enoch M. Marvin, and David S. Doggett. These men, along with others who were elected before the end of the century, one writer says, "constituted what was probably the ablest body of ecclesiastical leaders in the South during that period." [45]

3

Work With Negro Members

One of the inevitable consequences of emancipation was the withdrawal of the Negroes from the churches of their former masters. All

[45] Farish, *Circuit Rider Dismounts*, p. 64.

the efforts of the Southern churches for the Negro, consequently, were more or less in vain. In many cases the Negroes were suspicious of the Southern churches, with the result that the Negro membership of these churches decreased very rapidly. During the war, the Methodist Episcopal Church, South, lost over 60 per cent of its Negro membership to independent Negro churches. Of the Negro membership of the Southern Presbyterians, it is estimated that 70 per cent went to the same type of churches.[46] In 1860 the number of Negro members in the Methodist Episcopal Church, South, was 207,776; by 1866 their membership had been reduced to 78,742; and in 1869 it was only 19,686. Two northern Negro churches, the African Methodist Episcopal and the African Methodist Episcopal Zion, reaped the largest benefits from the Negro withdrawals from the Southern Church. Almost half of the Negro church members in the South in 1859 had been Methodist, but the two northern Negro churches had no southern membership previous to the Civil War. Even before the war ended, representatives of both churches had entered the South with the intention of winning the southern Negro. Their success is indicated by the fact that the 70,000 membership of the A.M.E. Church at the opening of the war had grown to 391,044 ten years later, while the A.M.E. Zion Church had increased from 42,000 in 1860 to 164,000 in 1868. These two Negro groups along with the Methodist Episcopal Church competed keenly for the Negro members of the Southern Church. In many instances the Negro members of Southern Methodist churches separated with the approval and assistance of the white members. One minister thus describes the formation of a Negro congregation:

> My Negro membership was large and a somewhat puzzling factor in our work . . . now they were free and began to assert their independence. I told them of the organization of their people . . . the Zion Methodist, and believing they would be better in that church than ours, I called their leaders together and explained it to them to go into that organization.[47]

Many such transfers were made, though not very amicably when the Northern Church was the one to which the group was going. Some Negro congregations became bewildered and moved from church to church. One Negro pastor led his congregation first into the Northern Church and then later into the A.M.E. Church.

[46] William Warren Sweet, "Negro Churches in the South: A Phase of Reconstruction," *The Methodist Review* (Northern), May, 1921, p. 412.
[47] *Ibid.*, pp. 412-13.

Missionary Endeavors

Northern Methodist missionaries working in the South seemed to feel that the success and perpetuity of the work there depended largely upon the triumph in Congress of the radicals and their Reconstruction policy. It should not be inferred from this, however, that the pre-eminent motive of the Methodist Episcopal Church in working in the South was a political one or was primarily selfish. Most of the Methodist leaders in the North were absolutely sincere and unselfish in their feelings that their church was needed in the South to perform a work which could not be performed by the Southern Church on account of its poverty and disorganized condition. Many of them also felt that their church was needed in the South as a center about which whites who were unsympathetic with the Southern attitude might congregate.

Immediately after the war the Southern churchmen, in their poverty-stricken condition, set out to do all that they could for the Negro and rather generally welcomed Northern aid. One Methodist editor urged in 1865 that Northern missionaries who came into the South to do good be met "in the spirit of Christ," and he went on to say that Southerners did not intend to be outdone in deeds of kindness toward the Negro race.[48] Another editor declared that the people of the South would rejoice if the Northern Christians did half as much as they declared they intended to do for the Negro.[49] That a number of missionaries sent into the South took an interest in politics and in many instances became office holders during the period of Negro supremacy is not surprising. The political activity displayed by the Negro ministers and their white leaders from the North soon changed the kindly feeling that had been exhibited toward both. However, the Southern Church continued work among the Negroes for several years after the war. Engrossed in its own poverty-stricken fight for survival, it was unable to do much for Negroes until its own continuance was assured and the Southern states had experienced a measure of economic recovery. Beginning in 1882, the Southern Church started an active financial and educational program in behalf of the Colored Methodist Episcopal Church.

The Southern Church since its organization in 1845 had concentrated nearly all of its missionary energy upon the Negroes, and it was perfectly natural for this effort to be continued during the war and in the years following, insofar as the resources of the church would permit. Southern

[48] *Southern Christian Advocate*, October 5, 1865.
[49] *Richmond Christian Advocate*, October 26, 1865.

whites, both within and outside the churches, had taken a keen interest in the welfare of the Negroes. Immediately following the war most people of the South believed that learning must be substituted for slavery, and it was their belief that some form of intellectual training had to be established if friendly relations between the two races were to remain. Annual Conferences throughout the South expressed the hope that the education of the Negroes would progress rapidly. The Montgomery Conference resolved that it would recommend "to our people to countenance and encourage day schools for the education of colored children, under proper regulations and trustworthy teachers." [50] In Russell County, Alabama, the Southern Methodist minister was enlisted to hold classes for Negroes in his own back yard, outbuildings, and porches, and this he did for more than two years, assisted by members of his family.[51] It is significant that as late as 1869, one half of the 405 native white teachers in the public schools of South Carolina were conducting schools for Negroes.[52]

That there was soon a change of attitude on the part of the Southern whites there is little doubt. Most lost interest in the education of the Negro while many openly opposed it as the Reconstruction program progressed. The forces that caused this general shift in attitude were also at work in the Southern Church, where the attitude shifted from one of keen interest to one of utter indifference. Bishop Andrew stated that the Northern missionaries were causing the Negro to take "such a course of conduct as to induce in the mind of the white man a state of feeling which caused prejudice against the Negroes." [53] When Southerners began to ostracize the Northern teachers, the teachers in return taught the Negroes songs calculated to irritate the Southerners.[54]

The most successful aspect of the Northern Methodist attempt to reconstruct the South was their work in the education of the freedmen. Their efforts to evangelize the Southern whites were almost a complete failure, for they gained no real support outside of such border areas as eastern Tennessee and the contiguous hill country. The freed Negro, on the other hand, convinced that there was magic in learning, flocked to schools supported by various denominations, of which the Northern Methodist was most prominent. The schools were used as agencies for

[50] *New Orleans Christian Advocate*, January 27, 1866.

[51] Walter Lynwood Fleming, *Civil War and Reconstruction in Alabama* (New York: Columbia University Press, 1905), p. 460.

[52] Francis Butler Simkins and Robert Hilliard Woody, *South Carolina During Reconstruction* (Chapel Hill: University of North Carolina Press, 1932), p. 423.

[53] *New Orleans Christian Advocate*, March 2, 1867.

[54] Simkins and Woody, *South Carolina During Reconstruction*, p. 433.

spiritual guidance and recruitment for church membership. Of the Northern Methodist work one recent author points out that no other church tried "more earnestly to release the Negro from the shackles of ignorance." [55] The same author maintains, however, that the church might well have spent its funds and energies to greater advantage, e.g., in a fast-growing and rapidly industrializing East where social problems among the immigrants in the urban areas were mounting.[56] Some of the church leaders in the program for freedmen's betterment called all social legislation wrong and inexpedient and opposed a shorter working day and higher wages for labor, and concluded that "only slavery itself is . . . more inimical to the common good" and "the rights of the individual" than labor unions.[57] The effectiveness of the church's program in other areas of the country was undoubtedly reduced because of concentration of its work in the South, where a better means of bestowing help might have been found.

Following the organization of their former Negro members into a church of their own in 1870, the conferences of the Southern Church during the following decade devoted very little attention or effort to the matter of Negro education. It was not until shortly before 1880 that any determined effort was again made to provide educational facilities for Negroes. A real change in attitude came in 1881 when a prominent Methodist minister, Atticus G. Haygood, later to become a bishop, published a volume on Negro education entitled *Our Brother in Black*. It was later said that this book did more "to bring to both sections sanity of thinking concerning the negro problem" than had anything else.[58] Haygood advocated that the ensuing General Conference of the Southern Church should take vigorous action to establish an educational institution for the church to which it had transferred most of its remaining Negro members in 1870.

Organization of the Colored Methodist Episcopal Church

With the Negro membership rapidly deserting, the General Conference of 1866 took action designed to keep the remaining members united in one church, even though it obviously would not be the Southern

---

[55] Ralph E. Morrow, *Northern Methodism and Reconstruction* (East Lansing: Michigan State University Press, 1956) , p. 248.

[56] *Ibid.*, p. 247.

[57] An editorial, New York *Christian Advocate*, September 5, 1867, p. 264.

[58] Horace M. Du Bose, *A History of Methodism* (Nashville: Lamar and Smith, 1916) , p. 128.

Church. Legislation was taken to provide for the organizing of Negro members into separate missions, churches, charges, districts, and Annual Conferences of their own. It was also provided that when two or more Annual Conferences were formed they might be organized into a separate General Conference. However, even after making these provisions the conference, seeking to act for the very best possible interest of Negro members, passed a resolution stating:

That in order to promote union and harmony among the colored people, our bishops . . . are . . . authorized to confer with the Bishops of the African M.E. Church as to the propriety of a union of that Church with the M.E. Church, South, upon the basis of the plan adopted by this General Conference, for a separate organization for the colored people; and that they report the result to the next General Conference for their action.[59]

Another action provided that whenever an entire congregation that had sole use of a building voluntarily left the Southern Church to join the A.M.E. Church, trustees should allow the members to keep the building. Difficulties between the two churches from 1866 to 1870 were such that the bishops recommended to the General Conference that the new Negro church be established immediately and did not even make a report on the proposal for merger with the A.M.E. Church. Conflict over church property between the new church and the A.M.E. Church continued for a number of years. Meanwhile, the organization of the separate Negro church proceeded, and early in 1870 the first Negro Annual Conference was organized at Carthage, Texas, called the Texas Colored Conference. Similar conferences in Tennessee, Mississippi, Georgia, and Alabama were organized about the same time with three more being created during the summer of 1870. Nevertheless, the Negro membership of the Southern Church continued to decrease.

All of the plans except the organization of a Negro General Conference had been carried out prior to the meeting of the General Conference of the Southern Church in the spring of 1870. This conference made final plans for the organization of the Negro churches into an autonomous ecclesiastical organization with its own General Conference.

The Colored Methodist Episcopal Church in America was chosen as the name for the new denomination when the delegates met for organization in Jackson, Tennessee, on December 15, 1870. A proposed name for the new group had been discussed at the General Conference of 1870, and the Committee on Religious Interests of the Colored People stated in its report that the committee was of the opinion that they would

[59] *Journal of the General Conference,* 1866, p. 73.

"naturally take the name of 'Colored Methodist Episcopal Church, South,' being the colored members of the M.E. Church, South, simply set up to themselves." [60] The conference took no final action on a name and it is interesting to note that when the group organized it did not include the word "South" in its title. The conference did sponsor a church publication, named the *Christian Index,* for the new Negro denomination and elected Samuel Watson as editor. The new church elected William H. Miles of Kentucky and Richard H. Vanderhorst as bishops. They were consecrated to this office by Bishop Robert Paine and Bishop Holland N. McTyeire, delegated by the Southern Church to assist in the organization. Watson was confirmed as editor of the *Christian Index* and in describing the new bishops wrote: "Bishop Miles is *bright,* but Bishop Vanderhorst, as a Kentucky brother said in the General Conference, is *black* enough for any of us." [61]

The church organization was perfected and, after "taking out and putting in such things as would be for the highest interest of the Church," the *Doctrines and Discipline of the Methodist Episcopal Church, South,* was adopted by the new church as its own.[62] One of the provisions added was that no white person could become a member of that church, and when a white man later applied for admission into one of the conferences he was refused. The Southern Church had intended that all of its Negro members would be transferred to the new church but while this was generally done, as late as 1895 there were still 389 Negro members reported.

The new church realized the serious trouble that was being caused by the use of Negro churches and schools for political activity and influence. With this in mind, and undoubtedly with strong suggestions from leaders of the church from which they were leaving, the Colored Methodist Episcopal Church provided in its *Discipline* that church buildings were not to be used for political speeches and assemblies.[63]

Though entirely separated, the new church had to fight for its very existence. Internal weakness and external pressure made its early life difficult. Whenever possible, the A.M.E. Church, the A.M.E. Zion Church, and the Northern Church continued their policy of absorbing entire congregations which had belonged to the Southern Church. Occasionally a congregation of one of the other churches would unite with the C.M.E.

[60] *Journal of the General Conference,* 1870, p. 217.

[61] Quoted in C. H. Phillips, *A History of the Colored Methodist Episcopal Church in America* (Jackson, Tenn.: Publishing House of the Colored Methodist Episcopal Church, 1900), p. 51.

[62] *Ibid.,* p. 46.

[63] Reported in the *Journal of the General Conference,* 1874, p. 459.

Church and this would serve to intensify the already bitter feeling. Other Negro denominations reproached them for their connection with the Methodist Episcopal Church, South, and proceeded at various times to call them the "Rebel," the "Democratic," and the "Old Slavery" Church. Of these names, one member wrote:

> These were powerful weapons used against us, for the reason that our people were naturally credulous. . . . Some were odiously inclined to the Church, South; others refused social relations with those who in any way affiliated with that Church. Thus the credulity of the ignorant was played upon with ease, and they joined in the rabble cry: "Demolish the new Church!"—the "Democratic Church." [64]

Buildings of the new church were frequently burned, and such a fire caused the first sessions of the Missouri and Kansas Annual Conference in 1872, scheduled for Sante Fe, Missouri, to be held in the open. Writing of this experience, Bishop W. H. Miles said: "The Church having been burned just before the Conference, we held the sessions in the woods, and had a very pleasant time." Of a fire in Thomasville, Georgia, in 1873, Bishop L. H. Holsey wrote: "The church . . . has been burned by our enemies, but a new one has been erected on the smoky ruins." [65]

The death of one of its two bishops in 1872 and the resignation of the book agent left the C.M.E. Church so depleted in its leadership that a special session of its General Conference was held in March, 1873. L. J. Scurlock, the book agent, left his post "for a more lucrative field" and became a member of the Mississippi legislature. To this conference the A.M.E. Church sent fraternal greetings and in its message referred to the touchy subject of church property. In its reply the conference said: "Touching the question of property, we are willing to act strictly according to the principle of equity and right, and earnestly hope that all disputes regarding the same may be amicably adjusted." [66]

The bishops of the C.M.E. Church wrote in 1874 that their church was "suffering more from the want of a better-informed ministry than from any other cause." [67] In an effort to alleviate this condition, the C.M.E. Church General Conference of 1874 authorized the establishment of a "Central University" in Louisville, but the project was abandoned several years later for lack of funds. It also expressed approval of the steps taken by the Southern Church for its Negro members, for "setting up" and not "off" the new ecclesiastical organization. A committee was

[64] Phillips, *History of the C. M. E. Church*, pp. 71-72.
[65] *Ibid.*, pp. 72-73.
[66] *Ibid.*, pp. 54, 66-67.
[67] Reported in the *Journal of the General Conference*, 1874, p. 460.

established for negotiations with any other branch of Negro Methodism, and the conference placed itself on record as favoring organic union, the only proviso being "as the Bible authorizes." [68] Little progress, however, was made toward union with any other Negro groups.

In spite of reproach, the new church continued fairly close association with the Southern Church and received some assistance from the parent body. Substantial support, however, did not come until after 1880, following Reconstruction, when the latter was in a greatly improved economic condition. All the property which had been used by Negro members was transferred at the outset.[69]

The C.M.E. Church not only held its own but was able to show modest expansion during the Reconstruction period. In 1874 it had 15 Annual Conferences, 4 bishops, 607 traveling preachers, 518 local preachers, 74,799 members, 535 Sunday schools, 1,102 Sunday-school teachers, and 49,955 Sunday-school members.[70] By 1875 the church had approximately eighty thousand members, a substantial increase over its membership when organized but barely larger than what the Negro membership of the Southern Church had been in 1866. With this membership it was a low fourth among the Negro Methodist groups, being scarcely one third as large as two of them and substantially less than half as large as the Negro membership in the South reported by the Northern Church.

The cultural and social importance of the independent Negro churches is not always understood. The creation of these churches was one of the most important consequences of emancipation and Reconstruction. A contemporary historian says: "It meant religious freedom for the blacks for the first time in their history and opened up to Negro leadership at least one field of social endeavor. To this day not even the most reactionary Southern white challenges the right of the Negro to determine his own religious concepts." [71]

---

[68] Phillips, *History of the C. M. E. Church*, p. 96.

[69] *Journal of the General Conference*, 1874, p. 458.

[70] *Ibid.*, p. 543.

[71] Francis Butler Simkins, *A History of the South* (New York: Alfred A. Knopf, 1959), p. 307.

4

Rebuilding Missionary and Publishing Programs

The war left the missionary and publishing programs of the Southern Church in shambles. Of the situation one historian writes: "The Missionary Society of the church was found to be $60,200 in debt, and the Publishing House was practically in ruins. The General Conference of 1866 'patched up these two wrecks and sent them forth to sink or swim.' " [72]

The mission work of the church was administered by its Missionary Society and had consisted before the war in foreign work in China, Indian mission work in the Indian Territory, work among German settlers in Louisiana and Texas, and work among the Negroes. An Indian Mission Annual Conference had been organized in 1844, but the German work was not organized into an Annual Conference until 1874.[73] During the war the entire missionary program was disrupted because of the interruption in communications and the lack of resources. Practically all of the wartime energies of the Society were directed toward the maintenance of missionaries with the Confederate armies. Following the war, the Society's currency and securities were worthless, and it was also faced with a debt which had been incurred for its China program at the outset of the war, forcing the missionaries there to support themselves.

Treaty ports had been opened in China in 1842, and missionary societies the world over rushed to move in. Undivided Methodism had at its last General Conference in 1844 made plans for the opening of work in China, and the Missionary Society of the Southern Church took steps immediately to establish a mission there. The first missionaries from the Southern Church arrived in Shanghai in September, 1848. The mission work in China grew rapidly and in 1859 was extended to Soochow when that city was opened up to foreigners. During the Civil War the missionary strength of the China mission was reduced so that by the time the General Conference met in 1866 it consisted of only two men, Young J. Allen and J. W. Lambuth, their families, and one native preacher. These missionaries had received little or no support from America during the previous six years. Allen had found employment with the Chinese government, and the Lambuth family was being supported

[72] Gross Alexander, *A History of the Methodist Church, South, in the United States* (New York: Christian Literature Company, 1894), p. 85.

[73] A. W. Wilson, *Missions of the Methodist Episcopal Church, South* (Nashville: Southern Methodist Publishing House, 1882), pp. 31, 47.

partially by work for the Chinese government and partially by the teaching efforts of Mrs. Lambuth. These families labored in China for many years following the war and rendered distinguished service.

Edmund W. Sehon had been elected Secretary of the Missionary Society in 1850, and he continued to direct its activities until 1866. In April, 1863, J. B. McFerrin was placed in charge of all the Methodist missionary work in the army of Tennessee. He was the book agent of the church but because of the destruction of the Publishing House was available for this assignment. Of his work he wrote: "I entered immediately on my work in the army, and as rapidly as I could engaged as many preachers as I thought the Missionary Society could sustain. There was, however, no lack of men or means. Many faithful preachers were ready for the work and the people were willing to contribute to sustain them." [74]

The General Conference of 1866 made provision for the payment of the missionary debt by dividing the amount needed among the twenty-four Annual Conferences in such a manner that it was expected that the debt would be discharged soon. Substantial progress was made on reducing the indebtedness during the ensuing four years, and though sufficient funds seemed to have been raised by 1872 the debt was not completely settled until after 1878. Of the amount raised for application on the debt approximately $10,000 appears to have been invested in stocks which proved worthless, necessitating the raising of additional funds later.[75]

In an effort to strengthen the entire missionary program of the church, the General Conference of 1866 divided the work into two separate parts and organized a Board of Foreign Missions with offices located in Baltimore, Maryland, with Sehon as its secretary. A Board of Domestic Missions was organized and located at Nashville, Tennessee, and placed under the direction of McFerrin. The work of the foreign mission group was to be financed by special collections taken for the purpose, while the work of the domestic mission group was to be financed from a levy of 10 per cent of all monies raised in Annual Conferences for domestic missions. In this manner, 90 per cent of the money raised for domestic missions would be retained for use within the conference, while the remainder would be sent to the board located in Nashville.[76] This method of organization and financing proved very unsatisfactory because little money was raised for the Board of Foreign Missions, which in addi-

[74] O. P. Fitzgerald, *John B. McFerrin* (Nashville: Publishing House of the Methodist Episcopal Church, South, 1889) , p. 272.

[75] James Cannon, III, *History of Southern Methodist Missions* (Nashville: Cokesbury Press, 1926) , p. 53.

[76] *Journal of the General Conference,* 1866, pp. 52-56.

tion to work in China was also responsible for work among the American Indians.[77]

The General Conference of 1870 abolished the system of dual boards as being too extravagant for a poverty stricken denomination and placed all of its missionary work under the direction of the Board of Missions located in Nashville, with McFerrin as secretary. The plan of financing was changed entirely with 40 per cent of all missionary funds raised being forwarded to the central board in Nashville, while the remaining 60 per cent was retained in the Annual Conference for domestic missionary work within the conference.[78] The new organization did not provide the results expected, because under the newly consolidated missionary program the bulk of expenditures still went for domestic missions while the foreign missionary program was neglected.[79] The General Conference of 1874 left the organizational pattern the same and re-elected J. B. McFerrin as secretary but took action to place practically all domestic missionary work under the direct supervision of the Annual Conferences, thereby freeing the general church agency to devote its energies largely to the foreign missionary program. It was not until after the General Conference of 1874 that the China mission received its first addition after the war, when A. P. Parker went out to join the staff in 1875.[80]

The following year Bishop Enoch M. Marvin visited the China mission and ordained several native preachers. This first visit of a Southern Methodist bishop to China not only gave great encouragement to the missionaries but served as a stimulus for missionary enthusiasm and support in the church at home. Bishop Marvin's visit has been called "a dividing point between the time of beginnings and development of policy and that of intensive development and expansion." [81]

Meanwhile, the foreign missionary work of the church was expanding very slowly. Mexico, both along the Texas border and in Mexico City, became in 1871 the scene of limited missionary activity. Brazil became, in 1876, the third foreign country into which missionaries of the Southern Church were sent. J. J. Ransom did pioneer work there before a permanent mission was established in 1881. The limited work before 1878 was scarcely an intimation of the vast missionary program that was to be developed by the church during the last quarter of the century. Japan, Korea, Siberia-Manchuria, and Cuba, along with the earlier work in China, Mexico, and Brazil, became scenes of extensive missionary activity

[77] Ibid., p. 52.
[78] Journal of the General Conference, 1870, p. 330.
[79] Journal of the General Conference, 1874, p. 383.
[80] Alexander, History of the Methodist Church, South, p. 122.
[81] Cannon, History of Southern Methodist Missions, p. 106.

before the end of the century. Africa and Europe were not added until the early years of the twentieth century.[82]

From 1861 to 1878 McFerrin directed most of the missionary activity of the church, serving as treasurer of the Missionary Society from 1861 to 1866, as secretary of the Board of Domestic Missions from 1866 to 1870, and secretary of the united Board of Missions from 1870 to 1878. In the latter year he summarized his work as follows:

> We had a degree of success—kept the Board out of debt and established new Missions. During my term of service we greatly enlarged our field in China, established our Missions in the City of Mexico, on the border between Texas and Mexico, in Brazil, and kept up the work among the Indians, the Germans, and among the whites on our borders.
>
> When the General Conference met at Atlanta, May 1, 1878, I had all my reports ready and recommended the organization of a Woman's Missionary Society. Here ended my work as Missionary Secretary. . . . We began in debt to the amount of some $80,000, wrecked and ruined by the war, with a membership of about 400,000 whites. . . . No one, perhaps, as well as myself knew the difficulties I had to overcome. Our people were just out of a disastrous war, their property gone, their spirits in a great measure broken; their minds and hearts full, and intensely moved against the world at large because they considered the world was against them on account of their connection with slavery—a connection which they themselves did not make. Never before did I feel so forcibly the powers of these words, "Charity begins at home;" "The Greeks are at your doors." But we fought it through, and lived to witness a brighter day for ourselves and the heathen world abroad.[83]

Organized missionary work by women received official recognition for the first time in the General Conference of 1878, although isolated and sporadic work had taken place before the division of the church in 1844 and had continued in the Southern Church. The earliest authentic record of the organization of women for foreign missionary work is that of a group formed in 1858 on the Lebanon Circuit of the Tennessee Conference. Organized primarily to raise funds to be sent to the wife of a missionary in China for her work with women and children, this organization was a casualty of the war; but Mrs. Margaret Lavinia Kelley, the prime mover, organized another such society in Nashville in 1874. Mrs. Juliana Hayes, of Trinity Church, Baltimore, Maryland, had organized a similar society there in 1869. The leaders of the societies in Baltimore and in Nashville established correspondence and were largely

[82] The full story of the Southern Church's missionary work is given in chapter 27 and in Cannon, *History of Southern Methodist Missions.*

[83] Fitzgerald, *John B. McFerrin,* pp. 301-2.

responsible for a request being made by the Board of Missions to the General Conference of 1874 to authorize a connectional missionary agency for women. The General Conference did not grant permission, but the missionary activity among the women of the church continued to increase. The work had grown so much by 1878 that the General Conference meeting that year adopted overwhelmingly a constitution providing for the Woman's Missionary Society of the Methodist Episcopal Church, South. On the day following this action, May 23, an organizational convention of women was held in the First Methodist Church of Atlanta, signaling the beginning of a group that gave great strength to the missionary program for many decades.[84]

One of the most involved questions following the division of 1844 revolved around an equitable distribution of property between the two churches. The original Plan of Separation had provided that property consisting largely of the assets of the Book Concern should be distributed to each section in proportion to the number of traveling preachers each had of the total. Law suits growing out of this plan had finally been settled by 1854 in favor of the Southern Church. Consequently, at the General Conference of 1854 steps were taken to establish a denominationally owned and controlled printing and publishing house in Nashville. The new buildings and equipment of the recently finished Publishing House had been the center of attention when the General Conference of 1858 met in Nashville. With the printed word taking a place second in importance only to preaching, it is understandable that it was with considerable esteem that the church held its publishing interests.

J. B. McFerrin, who until that time had edited the Nashville *Christian Advocate,* was elected book agent in 1858. Under his leadership the Publishing House developed a large and prosperous business and continued to function until February, 1862, when the Federal army occupied Nashville. The army used the printing facilities for military purposes. In the process the stock of paper and ink was consumed and the machinery greatly damaged.

The publishing fortunes of the church were at a very low ebb in 1866, when A. H. Redford was elected book agent "with no books to sell, no facilities for making books, and no suitable place for keeping them when made." [85] The prospects for ever re-establishing a satisfactory publishing arrangement were so unfavorable that many of the delegates to the conference had favored the abandonment of the enterprise. Debt-ridden, the fortunes of the Publishing House, already bad in 1866, became much

    [84] Lewis Edward Mattingly, "A History of the Board of Missions of the Methodist Episcopal Church, South" (Unpublished dissertation, Emory University, 1939), p. 34.
    [85] Alexander, *History of the Methodist Church, South,* p. 85.

worse by 1878. A disastrous fire in 1872 which destroyed most of the building and equipment only served to compound the problem. By 1878 the liabilities exceeded the assets by approximately $125,000, while the actual indebtedness amounted to more than $350,000. The publishing program was adjudged insolvent and the General Conference of 1878 was faced with solving this problem.[86] In the face of this crisis the church turned to McFerrin, then in his seventy-first year, and again elected him book agent, in which capacity he served until his death nine years later. Despite the depressed condition of the publishing interests, the poverty of the South, the disheartened state of the church, and the many opportunities for more profitable investments in safer enterprises, McFerrin succeeded in disposing of enough bonds carrying 4 per cent interest to retire the entire indebtedness. Of this phenomenal achievement, Mc-Ferrin's biographer says:

To the whole Church belongs the honor of this achievement, to its entire ministry and his immediate official co-laborers, much credit is due; but to McFerrin's wonderful hold upon the confidence and affection of the Church, and his masterful leadership, more than to what was done, or could have been done by any other man, must this deliverance be ascribed.[87]

The denominational press was one of the most effective agencies of the Southern Church during the Reconstruction period. In spite of the financial difficulties of the Publishing House, the Nashville *Christian Advocate* was published weekly under the editorship of Thomas O. Summers and circulated throughout the entire church. The General Conference of 1870 assumed sponsorship of a quarterly publication devoted to literary and theological essays, an earlier one having been suspended because of the war. The conference also instituted a biweekly German paper for circulation among the German missions of the church in Louisiana and Texas. In addition there were thirteen weekly periodicals being published by 1874 in the various Annual Conferences.[88]

[86] *Ibid.*, p. 101.
[87] Fitzgerald, *John B. McFerrin*, p. 367.
[88] Hastings, *The M. E. Church, South, During Reconstruction*, pp. 62-63.

5

Constitutional Reform at the 1870 and 1874 Conferences

By comparison with the bold ventures undertaken by the General Conference of 1866, the conference of 1870 was unusually conservative. The mounting problems over relations with the Northern Church, the disposition of the Negro members of the Southern Church, the rehabilitation of church edifices, and the remaining debts of both the missionary and publishing enterprises tended to subdue the delegates. The very extent of the sweeping changes four years earlier probably contributed to holding down additional innovations in church organization. The General Conference of 1870 marked the introduction of lay representation into the highest legislative body of either the Northern Church or the Southern Church. Consequently, the actions of the conference were watched with extreme interest because many had felt that the introduction of laymen might lead to even more far-reaching changes. Lest there be attempts at radical changes, the bishops in their address to the conference warned against unnecessary or hasty legislation and urged the delegates to judiciously consider the actions of the previous session.[89] Whereas the previous conference had proposed sweeping constitutional changes, all of which were ratified by the Annual Conferences except the change in name, the conference of 1870 proposed only two constitutional revisions, both of which were approved by the conferences, actually having been taken to legalize actions of earlier General Conferences. The one relating to providing a test for the constitutionality of legislation of the General Conference stemmed from an action taken by the conference of 1854, and the proposal to create District Conferences came from an action of the conference of 1866.

Plan for Constitutional Review—1870

Prior to 1854 there had been no check on the legislative power of a General Conference. In an effort to correct this situation the conference of 1854 granted the bishops the right to veto any legislation which they regarded as unconstitutional. This action, passed as simple legislation by

[89] *Journal of the General Conference*, 1870, p. 163.

a majority vote of the conference and never submitted to the Annual Conferences for approval, had nevertheless been inserted in the *Discipline* of the church. Many questions had been raised about the legality of the provision, so the General Conference of 1870 took action to remove it from the *Discipline* and made a substitute proposal which was adopted overwhelmingly in both the conference and in the ensuing Annual Conferences. The new action provided that

when any rule or regulation is adopted by the General Conference, which, in the opinion of the Bishops, is unconstitutional, the Bishops may present to the Conference which passed said rule or regulation, their objections thereto, with their reasons, in writing; and if then the General Conference shall, by a two-thirds vote, adhere to its action on said rule or regulation, it shall then take the course provided for altering a restrictive rule [confirmation by a General Conference majority of two thirds and by three fourths of the members voting in all the Annual Conferences], and if thus passed upon affirmatively, the Bishops shall announce that such rule or regulation takes effect from that time.[90]

The action of 1854 and the constitutional change of 1870, which received almost unanimous support, were important in themselves, but their greatest significance lies in the fact that they constituted the beginning of a movement which led ultimately to the creation of a Judicial Council with appellate jurisdiction to pass judgment on the acts of the bishops and the General Conference.

Provision for District Conferences—1870

The second important change which was effected by the conference of 1870 was practically necessitated by ratification of the action of 1866 which provided for lay representation in the Annual Conferences. The new legislation provided for four delegates from each presiding elder's district, but left to each Annual Conference the privilege of determining the manner in which its lay members would be selected. The Committee on Changes of Economy had submitted a report to the General Conference of 1866 recommending the establishment of District Conferences and, among other things, assigning to these conferences the responsibility for selecting delegates to the Annual Conference. This report was tabled and the Annual Conferences left to work out their separate methods. Most conferences deemed some representative meeting within each presiding elder's district as the most logical group to name the lay

[90] *Ibid.,* p. 331.

delegates. There was little disagreement about the desirability of the district meetings, even among leaders who differed sharply on other matters. Bishop Pierce, the acknowledged leader of the conservatives, encouraged District Conferences and attended all that he could, as did Bishop McTyeire, who was the undoubted champion of the progressive wing of the church.

While many districts had assemblies of one type or another largely for evangelistic purposes, such groups became almost universal throughout the church after 1866, though their composition varied widely from conference to conference. The action taken in 1870 provided for a District Conference annually, to be composed of all traveling and local preachers in the district and of laymen, the exact number of whom was to be determined by each Annual Conference. Supervision of all religious, educational, and mission work within the district as well as the election of the lay delegates to the Annual Conference were among the duties assigned to this body. Religious services such as preaching, love feasts, and the administration of the sacrament of the Lord's Supper were also to be given prominent places.[91]

The district meetings were always well attended and became the scenes of unusual religious activity. Revivals frequently began here and spread to churches throughout an entire district. There is little doubt that the District Conferences were a very important factor in the revitalizing of the Southern Church during the period of Reconstruction. Of them Bishop McTyeire wrote that they

had shown admirable fitness for serving the Church to edification. This was not that District Conference which obtained from 1820 to 1836—confined to local preachers, and never popular or useful. It was rather a return to the earlier practice, when a Yearly Conference was held by Bishop Asbury in every District. Simple in organization, and bringing together various elements of power within a range wide enough for variety and narrow enough for coöperation; promoting Christian fellowship; taking cognizance of a class of subjects which neither Annual nor Quarterly Conferences can well handle; and bringing to bear upon given points, for days, the best preaching, where Christian hospitality and love-feasts and sacraments may be enjoyed—the District Conference fell at once into place.[92]

Of the new conferences, especially of their value for religious edification, Bishop Pierce wrote:

My experience of these district meetings confirm me in my original convictions of their use and value to the Church. . . . I came. . . . to attend the Rome

[91] *Ibid.*, pp. 192-93.
[92] McTyeire, *History of Methodism*, p. 668.

District Meeting at Dalton. . . . The meeting was one of the best in all respects. Over one hundred delegates were present, and all alive and awake. I preached every day, as usual. Some bright conversions—some at the altar and one in the closet at home. This looked like old times. The religious element was strong and active in our business meetings. On Saturday afternoon for an hour or two we were "quite on the verge of heaven." The Spirit did not come as a rushing mighty wind, but he did distil as a gentle dew—soft and refreshing. Our hearts warmed and mellowed and melted. . . . It was a divine baptism, rich in present enjoyment and promising yet better things to come. It was a blessing which will tell on whole households, and, I trust, on generations to come.[93]

The District Conference remained an important part of the Methodist organizational pattern for the more than seventy-five years before each pastoral charge was granted a lay delegate to the Annual Conference. District Conferences have continued in united Methodism, although many of the original responsibilities have been assigned to other groups.

Temperance—1874

Due to absorption in other matters, particularly relations with the Methodist Episcopal Church, the General Conference of 1874 devoted very little attention to constitutional matters and as a result proposed only one change, this later failing to receive the concurrence of the Annual Conferences. The proposed constitutional amendment dealt with beverage alcohol and proposed a substitute in the reasons for exclusion from church membership the words "Making, buying, selling, or using, as a beverage, intoxicating liquors" for the regulation reading "Drunkenness or drinking spirituous liquors, unless in cases of necessity." [94] Considerable distinction was made by many between the phrases "spirituous liquors" and "intoxicating liquors," the latter generally being used to include wine and beer whereas the first was understood to mean distilled spirits only.

The phraseology that the conference sought to replace was the same that the church had used for many years prior to the division of 1844. The Northern Church had strengthened its rule in 1848, and, though the Southern Church frequently took action against members on the grounds of immorality for dealing in spirituous liquors, there was no specific rule making "buying and selling" a reason in itself for exclusion from membership. Never once was this failure of the effort to strengthen

[93] Smith, *Life of Pierce*, pp. 502, 514-15.
[94] *Journal of the General Conference*, 1874, pp. 440, 535-36.

the regulation on beverage alcohol charged to the fact that laymen had recently been introduced into the legislative processes of the church. On the contrary, the new proposal received the required approbation in the General Conference, where laymen had equal representation, but failed in the Annual Conferences where laymen had only limited representation. The strongest opposition to the proposed new regulation came from clergymen, one of whom was the venerated Lovick Pierce, father of Bishop Pierce, of Georgia. He wrote:

No one would ever have thought of conforming our General Rules to this idea on the subject of liquor, but for this temperance enthusiasm—we mean to say total abstinence enthusiasm. For no one of safe mind will say that total abstinence from anything that may be temperately used, ever was, or ever can be, a moral obligation *per se.*[95]

Despite these and other arguments, the Southern Church became increasingly energetic in attacking the problem.

6

Activity and Growth to 1874

An apparently amiable separation agreement on the division of assets and the establishment of territorial "rights," agreed upon when the Southern delegates withdrew from the General Conference of the Methodist Episcopal Church in 1844, was soon followed by misunderstandings, recriminations, and lengthy and bitter litigation eventually taken to the Supreme Court of the United States. Conflicts in the border states of Maryland, Virginia, Kentucky, and Missouri, where each group claimed exclusive rights and accused the other of trespassing, served to intensify the hard feelings between the churches. Bitter controversy was caused in Maryland when a portion of the Baltimore Conference adhered to the Southern Church, thereby setting the stage for prolonged dispute over the division of property. The withdrawal of eighteen members of the Southern Church in Kentucky who later affiliated with the Northern Church gave rise to considerable bitterness. Eastern Tennessee and

[95] "Shall the General Rules Be Changed?" Nashville *Christian Advocate*, August 29, 1874, p. 14.

Missouri were also scenes of persecution and even violence on the part of partisans of each church.

The Civil War enabled the Northern Church to push south of the border states when Bishop Edward R. Ames obtained an order from Secretary of War Edwin M. Stanton on November 30, 1863, granting him possession of certain church buildings in the South which were not occupied by a loyal minister appointed by a loyal bishop.[96] Similar orders were issued as the federal troops spread, and soon much property of the Southern Church was under the control of representatives of the Northern Church, thus increasing the bitter feeling. The expansion was sanctioned by the General Conference meeting in Philadelphia in 1864, as the bishops announced that the advance of the federal armies had opened the South to the Northern Church. They further stated that it was their conviction that the South was a legitimate mission field and that it was the solemn duty of the church to care for the people there who were neither slaveholders nor "tainted with treason."[97] To cope with the situation the conference provided for missions in the South and authorized the bishops to organize Annual Conferences there whenever in their judgment the interests of their work should require it. The entire region was mapped out for occupation.

The Beginnings of Fraternal Relations

Following the cessation of hostilities the bishops of the Northern Church issued a statement in which they noted that since slavery was no longer a point of issue they hoped the day was not far distant when "there shall be but one organization, which shall embrace the whole Methodist family of the United States."[98] It was this statement calling for union, the tenacious hold on captured church property, and the very offensive conditions outlined for individual Southern whites who might seek to join the Northern Church that called forth the Palmyra Manifesto from Missouri and a statement from the bishops of the Southern Church asserting that the abolition of slavery was not in itself a sufficient reason for termination of the church. The bishops stated that they felt that talk of reunion was calculated to disturb and confuse their members to such an extent that they might be absorbed individually into the

[96] Edward McPherson, *The Political History of the United States of America During the Great Rebellion* (2nd ed., Washington: Philp and Solomons, 1865), p. 521.

[97] *Journal of the General Conference,* 1864, pp. 278-79.

[98] George R. Crooks, *The Life of Bishop Matthew Simpson* (New York: Harper & Brothers, 1890), p. 432.

Northern Church. The General Conference of 1866 overwhelmingly endorsed the opinion that the church should continue its separate existence.
The conference received no fraternal greetings from the bishops of the
Northern Church but did receive a telegram from the New York East
Conference suggesting a joint day of prayer for the "full restoration of
Christian sympathy and love between the Churches, especially between
the different branches of Methodists within this nation." [99] Another
message was received from the New York Conference "proposing arrangements for reunion of the Methodist Churches." This was referred to the
bishops, who suggested in their reply that fraternity must be restored
before the question of unity could be discussed.[100]

The General Conference of the Methodist Episcopal Church at its
meeting in 1868 created a "Commission on Reunion" to treat with any
other Methodist Church desiring union. The following year the bishops
sent two of their number to bear fraternal greetings to a meeting of the
bishops of the Southern Church being held in St. Louis. In their formal
message, they stated that they were quite aware that there were historic
as well as contemporary difficulties in the way of reunion but that they
would like to discuss "the propriety, practicability, and methods of
reunion." [101] The Southern bishops responded with a letter in which
they stated:

> Permit us, then, to say, in regard to "reunion," that in our opinion there is
> another subject to be considered before that can be entertained, and necessarily
> in order to it—we mean the establishment of fraternal feelings and relations
> between the two Churches. They must be one in spirit before they can be one
> in organization. . . . Heart divisions must be cured before corporate divisions
> can be healed.[102]

They then went on to refer to the manner in which their fraternal
delegates had been rejected by the Northern Church in 1848 and the
farewell remarks to that conference by the delegates who said that
fraternal relations would always be welcomed but that the next overtures would have to come from the Northern Church. They were still
convinced that fraternal relations should precede organic union.

To the General Conference of the Southern Church in 1870 came representatives of the Commission on Reunion who were cordially received

---

[99] *Journal of the General Conference,* 1866, p. 26.

[100] *Ibid.,* p. 42. See also Aubrey G. Walton, "Attempts Toward Unification of the
Methodist Episcopal Church and the Methodist Episcopal Church, South, 1865-1926"
(Unpublished dissertation, Duke University, 1931), p. 54.

[101] *Formal Fraternity* (New York: Nelson and Phillips, 1876), p. 8.

[102] *Ibid.,* p. 10.

and permitted to speak to the delegates. However, John C. Keener of the Louisiana Conference, who was elected bishop later in the session, called attention to the fact that the commission whose communication was then being considered had been created to confer with a group from the A.M.E. Zion Church and in addition had been empowered "to treat with a similar Commission from any other Methodist Church that may desire a like union." He stated that he understood this to mean that the commission was to converse "with any Churches that may be knocking for admission at the door of the M.E. Church, and not to knock for admission at the door of any other Church." [103] The conference concurred in Keener's objection and refused to consider any proposal of reunion but did authorize a committee of nine to study the whole matter. The conference passed resolutions expressing high regard for the visitors but stating that it did not regard the commission which they represented "as having been constituted by that General Conference a Commission to make proposals of union to the General Conference of the Methodist Episcopal Church, South"; and even if such commission were fully clothed with the necessary authority, it was their judgment that the "true interests of the Church of Christ require and demand the maintenance of our separate and distinct organization." [104] The fact that the commission had been originally created to confer with a Negro church may have had some effect, but the concluding words of the reply seemed to indicate that no matter what the original power of the commission had been, it would still have met with failure in its effort to place reunion ahead of the re-establishment of fraternal relations. Every indication was given that fraternal relations would be welcomed but that the first move for such would have to come from the Northern Church.

The next Northern General Conference, meeting in 1872, adopted a report of the Committee on the State of the Church which referred to conditions existing which seemed to make it necessary for that church to continue its work in the territory occupied by the Methodist Episcopal Church, South. The committee also stated in its report that it believed there was abundant room for both churches and that God would use both in the promotion of its cause. The report pointed out, however, that truly fraternal relations should be established since this course was being demanded by the sentiments of the people. It was then suggested that the conference appoint a fraternal delegation consisting of two ministers and one layman to convey fraternal greetings to the next General Conference of the Southern Church.[105] The report was adopted

---

[103] *Journal of the General Conference,* 1870, pp. 198-99.
[104] *Ibid.,* p. 231.
[105] *Journal of the General Conference,* 1872, pp. 402-3.

and the bishops authorized to name such a delegation. The appointment of these fraternal delegates and their subsequent visit to the General Conference in Louisville in 1874 was the first real step toward restoring friendly relations between the two bodies of episcopal Methodism in the United States and ushered in what has been accurately defined as a "period of fraternity." [106]

The fraternal delegates were received with warm cordiality and one of them said in his formal remarks: "Differences there are between us, but can they not be adjusted by the great law of love? Is there not intelligence and piety sufficient in these two great Methodist bodies to work out an enduring peace on the basis of justice and honor to all parties?" [107] The conference responded with a series of resolutions that expressed pleasure over the fact that the fraternal delegates had been sent but made clear that organic union was not involved in fraternity. The resolutions indicated, however, that fraternal relations between the two bodies were most important and desirable, and the two concluding resolutions actually provided for formal relations between the two churches. These resolutions were as follows:

Resolved, 1. That this General Conference has received with pleasure the fraternal greetings of the Methodist Episcopal Church, conveyed to us by their delegates, and that our College of Bishops be, and are hereby, authorized to appoint a delegation, consisting of two ministers and one layman, to bear our Christian salutations to their next ensuing General Conference.

Resolved, 2. That, in order to remove all obstacles to formal fraternity between the two Churches, our College of Bishops is authorized to appoint a Commission, consisting of three ministers and two laymen, to meet a similar Commission authorized by the General Conference of the Methodist Episcopal Church, and to adjust all existing difficulties.[108]

The bishops appointed the three fraternal delegates, naming among them Lovick Pierce, who was spurned by the General Conference of the Northern Church in 1848. Unfortunately Pierce was too ill to make the trip, but his colleagues bore his address to the conference. The delegates were cordially received and the conference responded with the following resolution:

That we gladly welcome among us the distinguished representatives of the Methodist Episcopal Church, South . . . greatly regretting, . . . the inability to be present with us of their associate, the venerable Rev. Dr. Lovick Pierce,

[106] Walton, "Attempts Toward Unification," p. 64.
[107] *Formal Fraternity*, p. 34.
[108] *Journal of the General Conference*, 1874, pp. 547-48.

whom, for his eminent character and services, it would have especially delighted us to receive; and we heartily recognize their coming as the harbinger of better relations henceforth between the two chief branches of our American Methodism.[109]

The conference later instructed its bishops to appoint a commission to confer with the commission already appointed by the Southern Church. The joint commission met in Congress Hall at Cape May, New Jersey, on Thursday, August 17, 1876, and became generally known as the "Cape May Commission." Its work signaled the final establishment of fraternal relations between the two branches of episcopal Methodism.

Several other churches exchanged fraternal greetings with the Southern Church during the years following the war, but it was not until 1874 that greetings from a foreign church were received. To the General Conference of that year came greetings from the Wesleyan Methodist Conference of Great Britain, which stated: "We cannot overlook the fact that so many years have elapsed since the commencement of your separate existence as a Church without our having sought intercommunion with you. The causes existing at the time, from which this arose, have now passed away." [110] The General Conference responded by saying that because of heated and misunderstood sectional views the church had not sought recognition by other Christian bodies but that such recognition was welcomed. The reply continued: "We have not been able to see why your venerable body has failed to recognize us hitherto. But we rejoice to know that an era of clear views has dawned." [111]

Colleges and Theological Education

More than one hundred high schools, academies, and colleges, some of them among the finest in the region, were under the patronage and control of the Southern Church in 1858.[112] However, military demands for manpower and the depleted financial condition of the South caused the closing of almost all the colleges, even those for women, and efforts to establish a central university, for which a charter was issued in 1858, were thwarted.[113] Perhaps the most serious handicap resulted from the loss of endowment funds. A number of Methodist colleges had had sizable endowments, but almost all of the funds had been invested in Con-

[109] *Journal of the General Conference*, 1876, p. 211.
[110] *Journal of the General Conference*, 1874, p. 375.
[111] *Ibid.*, p. 539.
[112] *Journal of the General Conference*, 1858, pp. 523-32.
[113] *Ibid.*, p. 569.

federate bonds or stocks of southern corporations, both of which were now worthless.

After the war, many colleges resumed activity with inadequate resources and even less adequate physical facilities. New educational institutions were also founded at a rapid rate. This re-awakened interest received considerable impetus from the General Conference of 1866, which declared its alarm over the fact that the preceding four years had been blank as far as education was concerned and said that if an entire generation was to be saved from ignorance it must be done immediately.[114] The conference counseled the church that its first obligation was to the maintenance of existing institutions.[115]

Some colleges were aided in their reopening by indirect governmental help—such as in Georgia, where the state had agreed to pay the tuition of all disabled Confederate veterans who would agree to teach school for a few years. Emory College reopened in January, 1866, with only about twenty students, but when the regular academic year started in the autumn the state appropriation helped swell this number to 120, of whom 93 were veterans. During the first year $9,866 was paid to the college and by the end of 1869 it was estimated that appropriations had exceeded $100,000, this being more than two thirds of the total income during the period. One result of this dependence on veterans' funds was the college's first departure from its rigid classical curriculum; in 1867 the board of trustees felt the need for "practical" education to meet the conditions of the Reconstruction period and voted to award the degree of bachelor of science and English literature and to omit Latin and Greek from the requirements therefor.[116]

For almost a decade after the war Methodist colleges furnished the most ample facilities for higher education that could be obtained in a number of the Southern states and frequently attained stability and a creditable level of instruction more quickly than many of the secular schools. Throughout the Reconstruction period they prepared a great number of educated leaders for the South.[117] The educational facilities of church and state combined were so grossly inadequate in meeting the needs of a progressive age that it is not surprising that the whites of the South made little educational progress during the first fifteen or twenty years after the war. In the state of South Carolina alone the number of

[114] *Journal of the General Conference,* 1866, pp. 131-37.
[115] *Ibid.,* p. 136.
[116] Henry M. Bullock, *A History of Emory University* (Nashville: Parthenon Press, 1936), pp. 151-57.
[117] Farish, *Circuit Rider Dismounts,* p. 260.

white illiterates over twenty years of age rose from 14,792 in 1860 to 34,335 twenty years later.[118]

The struggle for a better-trained ministry developed at the same time the church was endeavoring to rebuild its shattered school and college program. Some leaders of the church had been seeking this for years and felt that such a ministry could only be provided through the establishment of strong biblical departments in the colleges and perhaps even a central university for the entire church. For years though, the larger portion of the Southern Church had consistently opposed theological education as being inconsistent with Methodist emphasis on "heart religion." The bishops in their address to the General Conference of 1866, however, urged the establishment of an institute "for the proper training of . . . young preachers," and called upon the conference to seriously consider this matter, thereby securing for the church the "invaluable advantages" they felt their provision alone could supply.[119] The conference endorsed the suggestion but felt that the condition of the country made the establishment of a theological school or institute impractical at the time. It urged that for the present the improvement of ministerial education be sought in strong "biblical schools" in existing colleges. It was recommended that these departments should include instruction in original languages of the Scriptures, ecclesiastical history, biblical criticism and hermeneutics, dogmatic and practical theology, and homiletics and pastoral duties.[120] Lest there might be objection to this recommendation, the conference tempered its action by asserting its belief of the divine call to the ministry and a spiritual preparation for it, and its intent to subordinate every conceivable plan of ministerial education to this principle.

The request for the establishment of biblical schools or departments met with favorable response. Wofford College, Southern University, Emory College, and Trinity College responded by creating such departments within a year, although there was considerable opposition. The fact, however, that they had been recommended by the General Conference and that they were being established in these colleges with the consent of the various controlling Annual Conferences was indicative of the development of a more liberal attitude toward theological education than had existed before the war. That these departments were not considered permanent solutions to the problem was recognized, but no other method was deemed expedient because of economic conditions. The bishops called to the attention of the General Conference of 1870

---

[118] Simkins and Woody, *South Carolina During Reconstruction*, p. 422.
[119] *Journal of the General Conference*, 1866, pp. 19-20.
[120] *Ibid.*, p. 136.

the need for continued attention to the problem and the conference instructed its Committee on Education to make a special report on the subject.[121] The committee, however, could not agree and a majority report recommending a central theological institute and a minority report recommending expansion and improvement of college biblical departments were presented. The conference adopted the minority report and as a consequence a number of colleges expanded or established biblical departments.

Some of the leaders, notably Bishop George F. Pierce, opposed the expansion, even in the colleges, of educational facilities for ministers. While holding the Holston Conference in 1871 he encountered a number of preachers who wished to terminate their pastoral duties so that they might attend college. Concerning this he said:

Education is very desirable; but there is a time for, and a fitness in, things. The sentiment in Holston, I think, is unsound, unwholesome, and will work detriment to the men and the work. . . . I do not sympathize, as much as might be judged, with the rage for an educated ministry. I want the Conference mixed —some of all grades, save the lowest stratum; for we have every grade of work to do, and our system is one of adaptation.[122]

The proponents of a new central educational institution, of whom Bishop McTyeire was the leader, were not idle. When the General Conference of 1858 had been asked to receive the charter of the proposed central university, the conference had declined on the grounds that it existed only briefly each four years and was therefore not the proper group to supervise an educational institution. The suggestion was made, however, that the Tennessee Annual Conference, with such other conferences as might desire to participate, might "take said institution under its care and management." [123] Consequently, in 1871 the Tennessee Conference appointed a committee to meet with similar committees from any interested Annual Conferences to discuss plans for a new university. This action met with an immediate response, and committees were established by the Memphis, Alabama, North Alabama, Louisiana, Mississippi, North Mississippi, Arkansas, and White River Conferences. These committees met on January 24, 1872, at Memphis with Bishops Paine and McTyeire in attendance.

Out of this session came a resolution setting forth the need for establishing a new institution of learning and proposing plans for one. The institution was to afford the youth of the church and the country a place

[121] Journal of the General Conference, 1870, pp. 166, 169.
[122] Smith, Life of Pierce, p. 553.
[123] Journal of the General Conference, 1858, p. 570.

where theological, literary, scientific, and professional studies of the highest order might be pursued. The school was to be called the "Central University of the Methodist Episcopal Church, South." It was to be controlled by as many Annual Conferences as desired to co-operate. Theological, literary, normal, law, and medical schools were proposed, with one million dollars set as the minimum amount necessary for the projected institution and no department to be started until half that amount was secured. A board of trust was created to carry out the plans, and the bishops of the Methodist Episcopal Church, South, were requested to act as a board of supervisors and share in the government of the new university, and also to select the location of the proposed new university. The bishops acceded to the requests after being careful to point out that in so doing they were not in any way discriminating between any other institutions of the church and the proposed new institution.

This action had been unanimous, but, following his return home from the meeting of the bishops, Bishop Pierce engaged in a lengthy correspondence with Bishop McTyeire over the value of the proposed university, especially its theological department. In one of his letters, he said:

It is my opinion that every dollar invested in a theological school will be a damage to Methodism. Had I a million, I would not give a dime for such an object. . . . I cannot "conscientiously help forward the work" of providing a theological school, and *therefore* I "feel obliged to hinder it," if I can fairly. I am against it—head and heart, tongue and pen—"now and forever, one and indivisible." . . . I pray most sincerely that the theological scheme may go down to the shades of oblivion.[124]

The controversy was not limited to the two bishops, however, for the pages of most of the church papers were filled with communications relating both to the proposed university and to the matter of ministerial education. An editorial by Thomas O. Summers had this to say:

It has been suggested that the projected University can be nothing more than another of the same grade as those now in existence; that money enough cannot be collected to endow a University of the grade proposed; that its establishment would interfere with those institutions now struggling for life; that it would not do to locate it in the country—that it would not do to locate it in a city; and that, if we have it at all, it should be originated by the General Conference. . . . As to the theological feature of the undertaking, various objections have been raised. Some are opposed to any education for the ministry. Pray the Lord, when he is sending laborers into his harvest, to send

[124] Smith, *Life of Pierce,* pp. 558-59.

some fully prepared to do all that demands the highest culture. It is a great deal better to have the corn put into our cribs (or, for that matter, the bread put upon our table) than to get merely rain from heaven and fruitful seasons, and the divine blessing upon the labor of our hands. We had some "denominations" that eschew all training for the ministry—but ours is not one of them. The friends of special training for the ministry are twitted with the charge of setting up "preacher-manufactories," providing "man-made ministers," "aping other denominations." [125]

The editorial goes on to say that the people making these charges know they are false because only those with a recognized "call" will be permitted to take the theological courses. Summers continues:

The Methodists have always favored a training of some sort for this important work. The only question has been one concerning the best means of securing it. . . . [Some say] there would be castes in the ministry, and circuits and stations would snub those preachers who may not [be trained]. On the other hand, it has been suggested that if a special training for the ministry were to become the order of the day, there would not be uneducated men enough to supply those regions in which they are in demand. [126]

Though some feared that the proposed new university with its theological school would adversely affect existing institutions, the friends of several colleges began to sound the merits of their respective institutions as a nucleus of the proposed new university. [127] The conferences co-operating in the establishment of the central university expressed great pleasure over the proposed plans, and in 1872 several appointed agents to begin raising money for the project. Such, however, was the exhausted condition of the South, and so slow its recuperation under the disorganized state of its labor trade and government, that the first efforts to raise funds showed the almost utter impossibility of raising the half million dollars required before any department could be established. The plan had already been adjudged a failure by some of its warmest friends when Cornelius Vanderbilt came to the rescue of the proposed central university. On March 17, 1873, Vanderbilt made through Bishop McTyeire an offer to the Board of Trust of Central University in which he agreed to give not less than $500,000 for the university. Vanderbilt had never had any direct connection with the Southern Church, but his wife was a

[125] "The New University Project," Nashville *Christian Advocate*, January 13, 1872, p. 8.

[126] *Ibid.*

[127] Clarence Moore Dannelly, "The Development of Collegiate Education in the Methodist Episcopal Church, South, 1846-1902 (Unpublished dissertation, Yale University, 1933), p. 213.

cousin of Bishop McTyeire's wife and had belonged to the church in Mobile, and the Vanderbilts attended a nondenominational church in New York City of which a former pastor in the Southern Church was minister.

Vanderbilt's gift was made subject to the condition that Bishop McTyeire become president of the board of trust and that the university be located in or near Nashville. The gift was accepted in March, 1873, and in appreciation the board authorized that the name of the institution be changed to Vanderbilt University. Before his death Vanderbilt increased his contribution to one million dollars. In speaking of the significance of Vanderbilt's action, Bishop McTyeire said:

A citizen of the North, Mr. VANDERBILT . . . to the South . . . looked, and extended to her people what they needed as much as pecuniary aid—*a token of goodwill.* The act, timely and delicately as munificently done, touched men's hearts. It had no conditions that wounded the self-respect, or questioned the patriotism of the recipients. The effect was widely healing and reconciling, as against any sectional animosities which the late unhappy years had tended to create. A distinguished statesman remarked: "Commodore VANDERBILT has done more for reconstruction than the Forty-second Congress." [128]

The General Conference of 1874 was evidently satisfied with the biblical departments in the colleges and the way in which plans for the biblical department in the new university in Nashville were progressing, for it took no action on these matters. Not only was there no objection to the establishment of Vanderbilt University, with its biblical department, but a resolution was adopted endorsing the establishment and endowment of institutions of learning and expressing deep appreciation to Vanderbilt for his generosity. Vanderbilt University was formally opened in 1875, with biblical, philosophy, science, and literature departments. Instruction in medicine and law had started the previous year when the university assumed responsibility for existing programs in these areas. Vanderbilt ushered in a new era for higher education in the South, with high scholastic standards inspiring better work in other colleges and in preparatory schools. As educational levels rose there was an increasing demand for a better-educated ministry.[129]

[128] Quoted in Tigert, *Life of McTyeire,* pp. 184-85.
[129] See Charles T. Thrift, Jr., "The History of Theological Education in the Methodist Episcopal Church, South, 1845-1915" (Unpublished dissertation, Duke University, 1932).

Sunday Schools

The Methodist movement had from its beginning recognized the efficacy of religious instruction for youth, and Sunday schools for such instruction had received substantial support from all Methodist groups. The American Sunday school movement became interdenominational in character and sponsored numerous union schools in areas too sparsely settled for denominational groups to operate separately. The Southern Church had always been an ardent supporter of Sunday schools and for this sponsorship had founded its Sunday School Association. With the entire educational system in chaos in the postwar years, it soon became apparent that many children would receive no other formal education than what could be acquired in Sunday schools. The church undertook to make these schools effective agencies of religious instruction, the General Conference of 1866 removing them from the jurisdiction of the Sunday School Association and making them an integral part of the church itself. Supervision of the program was assigned to the book agent who was instructed to make provision for greatly improved instructional materials. Further effectiveness was given to the program in 1870 when the General Conference created the office of Sunday school secretary and elected Atticus G. Haygood to the position.[130] Under his able leadership the quality of materials increased, the number of publications was enlarged, the number of schools grew remarkably, and a church-wide Sunday school convention was held in Nashville in May, 1871. The loose affiliation of Sunday schools with the regular church organization prior to 1866 frequently had given rise to friction between Sunday school superintendent and pastor. An effort to make the superintendent responsible to the Quarterly Conference failed in 1870, but in 1874 the General Conference assigned the election of the Sunday school superintendent to this body and required approval by the pastor before election.[131] All these changes resulted in making this portion of the church's educational program quite effective in imparting religious instruction.

Revivalism and Holiness

In addition to its emphasis on education, Southern Methodism had always laid stress upon a deep emotional experience. In the postwar years, such an experience tended to turn attention from the blasted

[130] *Journal of the General Conference*, 1870, pp. 193-96.
[131] *Journal of the General Conference*, 1874, p. 419.

hopes, impoverishment, and humiliation that were everywhere apparent. Revivalism with its emphasis on emotionalism played an important part in the life and phenomenal expansion of the church during the Reconstruction days. Revivals were held in every conference, resulting in the conversion of thousands who were added to the membership. Though the time of the professional evangelist was to come later, certain preachers became widely known for their ability as revival preachers. Stemming from the revivalism of these years was the emphasis upon Christian perfectionism which gave rise to what came to be known as the holiness movement. The Southern bishops called attention in their address to the General Conference of 1870 to the fact that the doctrine of perfect love, "which casts out fear and purifies the heart, . . . is too much overlooked and neglected." [132] By 1875 the interest in holiness had spread throughout the entire church. Relief from concern for the social problems of the day was found by many in the doctrine of entire sanctification, which placed almost its entire emphasis on individual religious experience. The movement gained a large following within the Southern Church and in time became such a source of contention and division that the bishops were forced to warn the church of its dangers. In their address to the conference of 1878 the bishops, though calling on the church to reassert the doctrine of entire sanctification, warned of distortions being taught by "factious leaders." [133] The emphasis on other-worldliness and its "anticipation of the pre-millennium days" were found to be unfavorable to practical religion.[134] Organizations made up of only those professing entire sanctification were formed within the regular churches, disparaging those who had not received the "second blessing" and those who were judged not to possess "heart religion." The situation was to become so acute before the end of the century that the bishops were forced to issue a very strong statement on the subject in 1894.

Temperance and Other Moral Questions

While a "desire to flee from the wrath to come, and to be saved from their sins" was the only condition imposed on those seeking membership, Southern Methodists were required to live morally superior lives by abstaining from "taking such diversions as cannot be used in the name of the Lord Jesus." [135] Moral suasion was constantly employed to

[132] *Journal of the General Conference,* 1870, p. 164.
[133] *Journal of the General Conference,* 1878, p. 33.
[134] Farish, *Circuit Rider Dismounts,* p. 74.
[135] *Discipline,* 1870, p. 28.

induce men to keep themselves free from immoralities and worldliness. The moral laxity which was manifested throughout the entire nation in the postwar years was gradually followed by an awareness that religious welfare was dependent upon social conditions and that men could not be disassociated from their social surroundings. As the important relation of humanitarian to moral reform was better understood, the Southern Church not only endorsed various reform movements from which it had earlier remained aloof but also began to encourage the enactment of legislation for moral and humanitarian elevation. The most vigorous efforts for enforcing personal and social morality were those directed against alcohol and its attendant problems. The failure of adoption in 1874 of a proposed constitutional amendment to strengthen the regulations relating to liquor was not indicative of any willingness to compromise or temper the opposition, but was rather a disagreement on methods. Indeed, one of the leading opponents of the proposed change wrote approvingly of John Wesley's attitude toward the "useless use of liquor." [136] The increased use of alcoholic beverages in the postwar decade seemed to intensify the church's opposition to the use of liquor and to serve as the stimulus for encouraging the Southern Church to take a leading part in temperance and prohibition movements during the last quarter of the century. Other moral and humanitarian matters to which the Southern Church gave increasing attention were: gambling, Sabbath observance, divorce, rights of labor, rights of women, and "worldly amusements," meaning usually theater going, card playing, horse racing, and dancing. Of these, dancing and gambling came in for the largest concern in the postwar period, the attack on gambling being intensified because of the chartering of a lottery in Alabama in 1866 and in Louisiana in 1867. Attention to all of these matters became more pronounced during the two closing decades of the century.

7

Leadership and Survival

The decade following the war found the Methodist Episcopal Church, South, fighting for its very existence. Its shattered fortune and uncertain future certainly did not portend the profound influence that the church

[136] Nashville *Christian Advocate,* August 29, 1874.

was to have "upon social relations of every kind in the South during the remainder of the nineteenth century." [137] With its ministry depleted, many buildings destroyed or in hostile hands, and many white and most of its Negro members gone, the prospect for survival in 1865 was a rather forlorn one. A missionary endeavor disrupted, an excellent college program wrecked, a publishing plant destroyed, and relentless opposition from the Northern Church all added to the woes of the struggling church. However, rehabilitation and readjustment characterized the work of the postwar decade.

The determination of the future in this situation depended largely on the leadership it might generate. That leadership was clearly in the hands of the bishops, though the bold actions of the General Conference of 1866 were of great importance. The tendency before the war had been to increase the power and influence of the bishops, and the General Conference of 1854 gave them a place no Methodist bishops had ever previously held. Fortunate it was for the postwar church that the episcopal leadership was so able. Six bishops were living in 1865, though three, who died during the ensuing decade, were virtually incapacitated at the time. Four new bishops were elected in 1866 and a fifth was added in 1870, the last raising the total number of active bishops to eight: Paine, Pierce, Kavanaugh, Wightman, Marvin, Doggett, McTyeire, and John C. Keener, who was elected in 1870. These eight constituted the episcopal leadership during the difficult days of Reconstruction, for no additional ones were elected until 1882.

The bishops traveled widely and not only presided at the Annual Conferences but visited most of the District Conferences. They preached frequently and were generally known for their eloquence as speakers. There was a remarkable unity in action, though the two acknowledged leaders of the group, George F. Pierce and Holland N. McTyeire, sometimes engaged in heated controversy. To able leadership much credit is due for the remarkable recovery made by the church.

There were many others, too, who made vital contributions to the fight for survival. Most notable were several who were elected to positions of general responsibility by various sessions of the General Conference, some of these later being elected to the episcopacy. The contributions of J. B. McFerrin have already been sketched. Though never elected a bishop, he ranks with the bishops as being one of the outstanding leaders of the period. Few ever served the Methodist Church so long, so well, and in so many different capacities as did McFerrin. Two others who rendered distinguished service in helping restore the church were T. O. Summers and Atticus G. Haygood. Summers, earlier book editor

[137] Farish, *Circuit Rider Dismounts*, p. 362.

and editor of the *Quarterly Review,* was elected editor of the Nashville *Christian Advocate* in 1870; Haygood, later elected bishop, was elected Sunday school secretary in 1870. James A. Duncan, president of Randolph-Macon College, and Landon C. Garland, a layman, one-time president of Randolph-Macon and first chancellor of Vanderbilt University, gave able leadership in helping to restore the educational program of the church. These two, along with another able leader, Lovick Pierce, were the fraternal delegates received by the Northern Church for the first time in 1876.

The year of 1874 marked the turning point in the struggle for survival. The church had finally made it clear that reunion at that time with the Northern Church would not be considered and that fraternity of equals was all that was desired. Fraternal relations between the two groups were established at the General Conference of 1874. Substantial economic recovery and political reconstruction a few years later made the return to a place of leadership much easier. A white membership that reached a record low in 1866 of 419,404 equalled its 1860 figure for the first time in 1869, and in 1874 this membership had risen to 715,951. Meanwhile, the Negro membership of 207,766 in 1860 dropped to a low of 19,686 in 1869. Following the organization of the Colored Methodist Episcopal Church in 1870 the Negro membership was virtually eliminated, amounting in 1875 to only 2,083, who had elected not to join the C.M.E. Church. The Indian membership of 701 reported in 1866 increased to 4,335 in 1875. The total gain in membership from 1866 to 1875 was reported as 226,260. Financially, the Southern Church by 1875 equalled its 1860 attainments in most areas and, for the first time, was beginning to exceed in a few. The decade had witnessed the turning of disaster and defeat into a great triumph. Though great tribute is due many individuals, particularly the bishops, for their part in the remarkable recovery, the General Conference of 1866 stands as the great force that charted the way.

When one regards the wonderful career which has been made possible for the Southern church because of the boldness of the New Orleans decisions, one wishes that other churches might more frequently be backed against a wall and made to feel that they were fighting for their lives, as the Southern church then felt. In a crisis such as those delegates faced the only possible course was to take a great venture of faith into untried, untrodden ways. But that leap of faith proved to be the way of salvation.[138]

[138] Luccock, Hutchinson, and Goodloe, *The Story of Methodism* (Nashville: Abingdon Press, 1949), p. 344.

chapter 19

THE
METHODIST
EPISCOPAL
CHURCH
IN THE
POSTWAR ERA

The Age of Methodist
    Affluence

Social Concerns

The Free Methodists

Freedmen's Aid
    Society

Concern for Theology

THE CIVIL WAR MARKED THE GREAT watershed in American social and economic history. With the rifles stacked and the cannon muffled at Appomattox, America rapidly evolved from primarily an agrarian economy to become the industrial colossus of the world. Where we were once a land of the hoe, spade, and ax, the jackhammer, lathe, and drill press now became the tools of our trade. We became less known for our "plains of waving grain" than for our belching Bessemers of steel. Rapid urbanization and industrialization, however, with their birth pangs and growing pains, severely wrenched and tore the American social fabric. Mushrooming cities created slums, fostered corruption, developed large pockets of unassimilated foreign-born, and opened the door to "bossism." Not only did ruddy farm boys in unprecedented numbers seek their fortune in the cities of the land, but during the "immigrant invasion" eastern ports opened their doors to destitute millions from central and southeastern European countries. They were destined to be the human raw material for the ever-rapacious maw of the industrial machine.

With the rapid rise of the "robber baron," a social stratification structured primarily on wealth tended to alter traditional social patterns. Before 1870 America was a nation with a rather broad diffusion of wealth, status, and power, in which the man of moderate means, as the resident of a small community, could command much deference and exert considerable influence. As the industrial revolution progressed, however, the position and power of the old gentry—the small manufacturer, merchant, professional man, lawyer, physician, clergyman, and professor—was gradually usurped by the *nouveau riche*. In the short space of one generation a new race of men had come up from slum and log cabin to take possession of the seats of the mighty. With a cut-throat, dog-eat-dog, "root-hog or die" philosophy the rape of both human and natural resources by the "barons" proceeded apace. In the scramble for a share of what Parrington called "the Great Barbecue," [1] the names of Baker, Carnegie, Drew, Duke, Gould, Hill, Harriman, Morgan, Rockefeller, Stanford, Stillman, and Vanderbilt came to the fore. Unhindered by restrictive social and economic legislation, these masters of capital dominated not only their own particular industrial bastion but virtually controlled the economic and political affairs of the nation as well.

1

The Age of Methodist Affluence

Throughout the postwar era the Methodist Episcopal Church, like Protestantism in general, suffered from a socio-economic myopia. It seemed oblivious to America's emergence from its agrarian cocoon. Its Puritan ethic, strengthened by frontier individualism, increasingly revealed little understanding of or impact upon the collective and complex problems of a burgeoning urban culture. Profiting immensely numerically and financially during the "Barbecue," the church revealed a reluctance to bring to judgment a movement which statistically bore ecclesiastical fruit. Neither Methodist journalism nor ecclesiastical pronouncement during the 1860's or 70's reveals any serious and sustained indictment of uninhibited capitalism. To be sure, as scandal after scandal was brought to light during the Grant administration, each in turn was suitably castigated. Such exposés, nevertheless, were regarded as "unhappy departures from the norm," and pastors continued to regard their capitalistic "pillars" as men to be emulated and their millions as morally pure.[2] During the heyday of graft and corruption Daniel Curry opined that "the earnest and acquisitive devotees of Mammon comprise but a comparative-

[1] See Vernon L. Parrington, *Main Currents in American Thought* (New York: Harcourt, Brace, & Co., 1927, 1930), III, 23-25.

[2] Henry F. May, *Protestant Churches and Industrial America* (New York: Harper & Brothers, 1949), pp. 54-55.

ly small part of society." [3] Thus, it seemed that with the vindication of the abolitionist cause much of the dynamic went out of the idealism and reform movements of previous decades, not to return until the social gospel era. The period between 1861 and 1876 has been characterized as the "summit of complacency" in American Protestantism.[4]

The ideological basis for Methodism's social and economic complacency during the Gilded Age found its locus in the Social Darwinism of Herbert Spencer as it filtered into American thought through his disciple, William Graham Sumner. The Yale professor's antireform rationalization for the law of the jungle in human affairs was tersely put: "The truth is, that the social order is fixed by laws of nature precisely analogous to those of the physical order. The most that man can do . . . by his ignorance and conceit [is] to mar the operation of the social laws." [5] Such unmitigated naturalism asserted that men were powerless of their own will either to prevent or hasten human improvement and that socio-economic ameliorists who refused to let "ill enough alone" were interfering with natural and therefore moral laws. Overwhelmingly the Protestant ethos acceded to the dictum, noting how "right" and characteristically "American" it sounded. "The 'Protestant ethic' of thrift, hard work and success, once preached as a means of testifying to God's glory," now found added support in the latest findings of social science.[6] However hostile Methodist ministers might have been to predestination, Calvinism's ethic of frugality and industry, which held individuals morally responsible for their destitution, was widely accepted by them. Although many would have disagreed with the liberal theology of Henry Ward Beecher, few would have dissented with respect to his economic philosophy:

God has intended the great to be great and the little to be little. . . . The trade union, originated under the European tradition, destroys liberty. . . . I do not say that a dollar a day is enough to support a working man. . . . But it is enough to support a man! Not enough to support a man and five children if a man insists on smoking and drinking beer . . . but the man who cannot live on bread and water is not fit to live.[7]

Methodism had a share in developing the cult of the self-made man, which served not only to buoy up the discouraged and downhearted but to confirm the faith of those high on the economic ladder of the right-

[3] New York *Christian Advocate*, February 15, 1872, p. 52.

[4] May, *Protestant Churches and Industrial America*, pp. 39-40.

[5] Cited by Eric F. Goldman, *Rendezvous with Destiny* (New York: Alfred A. Knopf, 1952), p. 91.

[6] May, *Protestant Churches and Industrial America*, pp. 143-44.

[7] George E. McNeil, *The Labor Movement* (New York, 1887), p. 210.

eousness of the established order. Secular proverbs sprouted by the dozens —"Genius thrives on adversity," "Sweat and be saved," "There's always room at the top," "You can't keep a good man down"—and were endowed with all the sanctity of Holy Writ. Not until the end of the century did Methodist apologists of *laissez faire* realize that they had substituted Adam Smith and Herbert Spencer for Amos and Isaiah, and that political economy was not a science but an "ingenious and plausible theory of business details." [8]

In spite of its deficient social ethic the church was a young, aggressive, and growing giant during the postwar era. Twenty years after the great schism of 1844 it seemed as if those who had foretold the event would mean new life rather than death had been right, for there were more than a few reasons for self-congratulation. In the almost one hundred years since the Christmas Conference, the growth of the church had paralleled that of the Republic, so that in numbers, wealth, influence, and vigor it was in the van of American Protestantism. During the Centennial of 1866 it paused to catch a second wind and then rushed on to set new records. Although the war resulted in a loss of 61,000 members, from 1864 to 1876 the membership rose from 923,000 to over 1,642,000— or a net increase of almost 60,000 communicants a year. Such statistics in part reflect the growing interest in religion by the postwar citizenry, for although a mere 22 per cent were church affiliated in 1850, by 1890, 34 per cent were listed on some ecclesiastical roll.[9] With the rapid rise of cities and towns church construction proceeded apace with 2,319 new churches built during 1868-72 and with church property valuation jumping from 36 to over 56 million dollars.[10]

Methodists were not alone in noticing their rags-to-riches ecclesiastical success story. Noting the typical quarter-million membership gain during the preceding quadrennium, one brother testily affirmed, "The time is now past when sneers and derision are . . . a legitimate part of the Christian courtesy to be accorded to the followers of Wesley. Instead of this we see a tendency . . . almost universal, to copy the Methodist style of doing the work of God." [11] Not a few Methodists were nonplused over their rapid rise to eminence and suggested a combination of factors as the cause. Some stressed Methodism's mediating theology, which saved the gospel from being wrecked between the Scylla of "old theological predestinarianism" and the Charybdis of Unitarian rationalism and Uni-

[8] Edward H. Rogers, *The Relations of Christianity to Labor and Capital* (Boston, 1870), p. 5.

[9] Wade Crawford Barclay, *The History of Methodist Missions* (New York: Board of Missions of The Methodist Church, 1957), III, 1.

[10] *Journal of the General Conference*, 1872, p. 454.

[11] *Zion's Herald*, June 3, 1869, p. 258.

versalist sentimentality. The church revealed how to be "evangelistical-ly liberal without being Pelagianly liberalistic, . . . kept away from the pitfalls of a limited atonement, . . . a cast-iron necessity upon free-will, . . . infant damnation, . . . [but] flung open the glorious gates of the gospel day by the free offer of a full salvation to *all.*" [12] Its catholicity of spirit spelled out through the doctrines of free grace, free will, and sanctification harmonized easily with the American ethos and the political liberalism of the time. Correctly relating a sect and church type ecclesiology it emphasized both Christian individualism and Christian community so that neither was destructive of the other.[13]

Its itinerancy, moreover, spoke the idiom of the farm and frontier un-burdened by the robes, jargon, and theological intricacies of other denominations. Through a "marvelous pragmatism" Methodist polity had reached a high degree of organizational efficiency and was "at once flexible enough to keep pace with an ever dynamic geographic frontier yet sufficiently rigid to restrain an often turbulent membership." Seeds of schism seldom germinated in its bed of theological speculation because the intellect and the heart were reconciled by "the frank subordination of the first," and Methodists found their bond of unity lay "not in the fine print of prayer books" but in a "strange warming of the heart" which was common to all although variously expressed. It had succeeded in "institutionalizing the gospel of revivalism" and by some was considered the "high church of evangelism." [14] Permeating the entire membership was a fierce and unashamed loyalty to the Wesleyan heritage. Long before the tide of ecumenical endeavor made a rugged denominational spirit seem suspect, if not sinful, Bishop Simpson, at a Centennial gathering in New York, enunciated the ethos of the church: "Do anything for a Methodist because he is a Methodist . . . . For myself, I am free to say I have no faith in bringing up my sons or my daughters to be hewers of wood or drawers of water for any other denomination in the land (great applause) ." [15]

Nevertheless, under the impact of urbanization, industrialization, and an increasingly sophisticated American culture, the constituency of the church was rapidly changing. That which its founder had long feared, Methodist affluence, had become a reality in the Gilded Age. In less than one hundred years a "peculiar people" had bootstrapped their way up

[12] *Ibid.,* December 3, 1868, p. 579.
[13] S. D. Hillman, "The United States and Methodism," *The Methodist Quarterly Review,* January, 1867, pp. 40-41.
[14] Ralph E. Morrow, *Northern Methodism and Reconstruction* (East Lansing: Michigan State University Press, 1956) , pp. 6-7.
[15] *Zion's Herald,* June 20, 1866, p. 179.

the socio-economic ladder by practicing the Puritan ethic of thrift, sobriety, and hard work until they were close to the seats of the mighty. An
ever decreasing number of Methodists wore overalls, carried a lunch
pail, smelled of sweat, and came home with dirty and calloused hands.
Instead, they had migrated into the occupations and professions of the
middle class and were practicing law and medicine, operating small business establishments, teaching, clerking, and accounting. It had been an
arduous, if short, journey to "respectability," and there were some who
were not unhappy about it:

By virtue of the habits which religion inculcates and cherishes, our Church
members have as a body risen in the social scale, and thus become socially removed from the great body out of which most of them were originally gathered.
This tendency of things is natural and universal, and its results unavoidable;
perhaps we might add, also, not undesirable.[16]

With a burgeoning membership discipline declined, and the line between the church and the world was blurred. Church trials and expulsions became infrequent, probationary membership was a dead letter,
class meetings ceased to exist, revivalism was increasingly left to the
"professionals," and Methodists were no longer looked upon as a "peculiar people." In manners and customs Methodists picked up practices
of other religious groups. Distinctiveness in dress was gone, and the Puritan Sabbath was increasingly profaned by the reading of Sunday newspapers and playing sports and games. Whereas it had once been difficult
to get into the Methodist Church and very easy to be expelled, now it
was the reverse: indeed, death did not always remove one's name from
the membership rolls! Although the General Conference of 1864 attempted to reinforce discipline through revising a statement on "Neglect
of the Means of Grace," [17] organization and efficient church administration were stressed. Bank account levels and community status, rather
than the possession of spiritual graces, determined the selection of some
trustees. Official board meetings increased in importance and prayer
meetings decreased in attendance. Discipline among the clergy declined,
with ministers overly concerned with place, rank, and office. On furlough
from India and attending the General Conference of 1864, James M.
Thoburn was shocked by ecclesiastical politicking for preferential offices. "This kind of thing may be all right among the politicians of

---

[16] New York *Christian Advocate*, February 8, 1866, p. 44.
[17] *Journal of the General Conference*, 1864, p. 416.

this world, but . . . it seemed wholly out of place, to put it very mildly, in an assembly of Christian ministers." [18]

While the church still retained the poor in the West and rural areas, class lines were beginning to structure membership in the East. As J. M. Buckley observed, the membership, viewed as a pyramid, had its base in the eighteenth century among the poor. Now the figure was inverted, with only the point touching the poor. Moreover, another pyramid, with its base rising from the middle class, had its apex in the upper strata of society.[19] However nice in theory, the multiclass church had a difficult time in maintaining fellowship. The tension between the Methodists of Jerusalem's Upper Room and those of Athens' Academy was deep and real. Buckley lamented that "the rich will not worship in plain churches, and the poor will not come to grand edifices where the plainness of their attire is made more obvious by the magnificence of the surroundings." [20] With the poor, "Only the ordinary evil tendencies of human nature disturb the Church; when all are rich and successful . . . semi-aristocratic feelings . . . [and] persistency of personal opinion . . . cause friction; but when the different classes are united in a democratic organization . . . the want of homogeneity continually produces discord." [21]

The prosperity of the time, together with Methodism's pride of "arrival," reflected itself in church architecture and construction. Heretofore satisfied with a nondescript log cabin or frame building for worship, Methodists competed with much vigor with the Presbyterians, Congregationalists, and Episcopalians in the construction of elaborate Gothic, Romanesque, and Classic structures; as early as 1852 the Episcopal Address affirmed that "very costly edifices lay heavy taxes on our pecuniary resources" and do not "tend to edification or godliness, but rather gender pride." [22] The defenders of the "gilded church," however, affirmed that the magnificent cathedrals were merely representative of the new social and economic stature of the membership and an "inspiration to lavish gifts and noble achievements." [23] Nevertheless, with the tendency toward carpeted isles and cushioned pews, pipe organs and paid choirs, stained glass windows and ushers with "tails," it was clear to many that metropolitan Methodism was catering to the possessors of wealth, style, and fashion. Periodically the despisers of culture fought the onrushing trend and served notice that not all members of Free Methodist sympathies had

---

[18] Thoburn, *My Missionary Apprenticeship* (New York: Phillips and Hunt, 1886), p. 112.

[19] *Zion's Herald,* February 18, 1875, p. 49.

[20] *Ibid.,* February 25, 1875, p. 58.

[21] *Ibid.,* p. 57.

[22] *Journal of the General Conference,* 1852, p. 159.

[23] New York *Christian Advocate,* January 18, 1872, p. 17.

left the mother church. During 1870-76 in the North Indiana Conference an "organ war" continued unabated, with conservative "anti-organites" nocturnally crawling into churches to cut the organ bellows, whereupon the next Sabbath "both choir and minister were greatly chagrined." At the Annual Conference in Kokomo in 1870 the anti-organites filled the pipes with pepper, "which set the choir and congregation to sneezing and coughing." [24]

Toward an Educated Ministry

Others traced the church's class friction and consequent loss of the poor to a change in the training and character of the ministry. The seminary-trained pastor, they maintained, replete with classical and theological education, no longer wanted to be considered the apostolic "offscouring of all things" but desired a "station neat and complete" where scholarly articles could be written and the affairs of the mind pursued. They would have revised Tertullian's dictum to read: "What has the Holy Club to do with seminary; the Methodist pulpit to do with Greek, systematic theology, and homiletics?" The new ministerial image with its "professionalism" of culture and refinement separated sheep and shepherd. Knowledge and high culture made a minister "abstract in . . . discourse, [promoted] a horror of coarse manners and coarse speech, of dirty houses, and . . . filthy clothing. While it broadens his theory of human rights, . . . it works in him a social transformation, an aesthetic taste, which shrinks from and repels the coarseness and ignorance of the lower classes." [25] Fledgling intellectual "Samsons" were leaving the straight and narrow road of perfectionism and free grace to stalk the demons of rationalism, deism, and Darwinism. "Only misshapen bodies," affirmed one member of the old guard, "need the *adornment* of dress. . . . Learned phrases do not make a learned man. Great-swelling words not only indicate 'vanity' of heart, but . . . emptiness of head." [26] Seminary graduates were accused of having low sermonic voltage, and thus were ill fitted to wage "aggressive war on the masses." The church was spread-eagled between the poor, who were leaving because of too much polish and refinement, and the *nouveau riche*, who were migrating

[24] H. N. Herrick and William Warren Sweet, *A History of the North Indiana Conference of the Methodist Episcopal Church* (Indianapolis: W. K. Stewart Company, 1917), p. 111.

[25] B. H. Nadal, "Educational Qualifications for the Ministry," *The Methodist Quarterly Review*, April, 1867, pp. 230, 224.

[26] Samuel Dunn, "Our Ministry," *The Methodist Quarterly Review*, October, 1867, p. 600.

to the Presbyterians and Episcopalians because of Methodism's cultural paucity. The church was losing at both ends of the line.[27]

Nevertheless, an increasing majority of clergy and laymen wanted Sunday worship to be something more than an enclosed camp meeting. With the rapid upward social and educational evolution of the constituency, the "old time religion" with its chorus of congregational "amens" gradually was replaced by liturgical formality and reasoned sermonic discourse. The founding of Boston (1847), Garrett (1855), and Drew (1867) theological seminaries reflected the need for an academically proficient and professional ministry which would not only relate the gospel to an age of ever-increasing complexity, but would hold the large white-collar, college-trained membership. That the old guard, nurtured on the fiery eloquence and exhortation of the circuit rider era, were unaware of the change in the times, and thought they were the recipients of an adulterated gospel is understandable; hence their complaints against "a cold delivery," "manuscript readers," "lack of spirit," and "current-event preaching." The church periodicals, however, strongly defended the necessity for theological education and poured forth a deluge of articles on the curriculum, professors, financial support, and importance of the seminaries. "We have never heard a minister regret the length and fullness of his preparation," stated *Zion's Herald*. Granted that the Holy Spirit once spoke through Balaam's ass, "when He anoints the lips of 'an eloquent man,' . . . one 'instructed in the way of the Lord,'" the effect is overwhelming on "doubters and gainsayers." [28] Daniel Curry defended the diminishing emotionalism by stating that Jesus was probably the "most solitary human being" and that "honest and ingenious minds have an instinctive dislike of cant" and prefer to remain silent rather than fall into the "detested practice." [29] A pastor from Illinois in 1866 lamented the fact that Garrett was hung with the epithet "Biblical Institute" in order to keep the anti-intellectuals happy and remonstrated, that when the seminary at Concord, New Hampshire, is relocated in Boston, "I pray that it may be properly christened." [30] That the Wesleyan movement had begun within a university was constantly pointed out by the defenders of an educated ministry.

Urbanization also meant a modification of Methodism's traditional itinerancy. While the pro's and con's of the circuit rider versus the settled pastorate were endlessly debated during the era, the most populous areas in the North and East had already accepted the resident pastor-

[27] Nadal, "Educational Qualifications," p. 229.
[28] August 13, 1874, p. 260.
[29] New York *Christian Advocate*, August 29, 1872, p. 276.
[30] *Zion's Herald*, September 26, 1866, p. 321.

ship. Its partisans affirmed that the pattern would attract a more educated minister, allowed time for indoctrination from "Genesis to Revelation," inculcated warm relations between pastor and flock, and prompted the "sweetest notes of song" to waft through the church aisles. Surprisingly, some of the strongest defenders of the itinerancy came from the East. The New York *Christian Advocate and Journal* maintained that it made for a more "fervid pulpit," strengthened ministerial recruitment and financial support, extended the gospel through better utilization of ministerial personnel, and developed and preserved a prophetic ministry. "A minister settled desires to remain so"—and was apt to deal gently with the distiller, stock gambler, and swindler. The rural itinerancy made it almost impossible to rely on a manuscript, and thus an orator was not allowed to ruin his effectiveness by retreating to his study and his pen. Since I Corinthians indicated that little human wisdom was needed to preach, the itinerant exhorter seldom took sermonic byways into natural theology, philosophy, and book reviews.[31] Nevertheless, urbanization increased the pressure for longer ministerial tenure, and the General Conference of 1864 extended the possible pastoral term from two to three years, and in 1888 to five years. In 1887 the *Western Christian Advocate* lamented that the number of Methodist ministers who had published volumes of sermons could be numbered on one hand. "The itinerancy is the death of literary effort," the editor continued. "It is time we . . . do our share." [32]

The Decline of the Camp Meeting

The decline and fall of the summer camp meeting was another feature of the Gilded Age. Although Methodist periodicals spoke with one voice in defense of the frontier-inspired institution and faithfully reported every July and August their great achievements, increasing urbanization, larger churches, better transportation, and other areas for social expression prompted their demise. Before the Civil War the camp meeting had been an annual seven-day spiritual tonic that broke the drudgery of chopping trees, breaking ground, doing chores, and opened up social contacts unknown in the depressing monotony of the isolated settler's cabin. After the war it increasingly received bad publicity, with opponents charging that the meetings were rampant with drunkenness, immorality, and fanaticism. Ministers with college and seminary degrees

[31] April 28, 1864, p. 132.
[32] May 11, 1887, p. 296.

depreciated revivalism's "ranting and raving," emphasized educational means for spiritual growth, and charged that the meetings conflicted with church attendance.

Forced on the defensive, camp meeting zealots warned that the institution would cease only "when the old heroic fire of Methodism dies out." Extravagances should be overlooked, for "no powerful movements, religious, social or civil, can be made without eccentricities. The ocean foams and surges because it heaves sublime depths." [33] The camp meeting attacked the problem of class by placing "the poorest clerk or sewing girl on a level with the richest lord or lady." [34] It alone dispensed what church members needed: not relaxation, social enjoyment, educational development, but a "baptism of fire." A participant at the 25,000-member National Camp Meeting at Manheim, Pennsylvania, in 1868 beheld a "spontaneous burst of agony and of glory" after a holiness sermon. "It was the most sublime spectacle ever witnessed. Waves of glory rolled from the stand to the outer circle. . . . No one who witnessed that scene need regret not being present at Pentecost. It was Pentecost repeated." [35]

Camp meeting devotees discovered that "the world" crept into their leafy Bethel in subtle ways. Railroad companies refused to heed the pleas of camp trustees not to run Sunday excursion specials through the camps. Troops of picnickers inundated the camps during the week ends, and gangs of howling ruffians vied with one another to break up evangelistic services. Gates had to be locked and guards stationed in order to maintain decorum. At the same time camp participants were also responsible for the changing character of the religious retreat. One observer was obliged to present a lengthy defense against the fact that many came "half in search of health and half in quest of religion" and tended to "mix Christianity and sea-bathing a little too confusedly." [36] Socializing rather than "spiritual intensification" seemed to be the motive of many, for officials complained of meeting friends and trains, family reunions, and the "running from tent to tent to pass a bit of gossip." [37] Others saw little virtue in scanty board, cotton roofs, and musty straw ticks, and desired their annual dose of hell fire and holiness to be dispensed in more pleasant surroundings. A few felt that the rustic pulpit of the camp meeting had become an oratorical gladiatorial arena, a "platform for trial sermons with reference to future appointments." [38] Neverthe-

[33] *Zion's Herald*, July 30, 1868, p. 372.
[34] *Ibid.*, October 27, 1870, p. 510.
[35] *Ibid.*, August 6, 1868, p. 381.
[36] New York *Christian Advocate*, August 29, 1872, p. 276.
[37] *Zion's Herald*, August 13, 1868, p. 390.
[38] *Ibid.*, September 17, 1874, p. 300.

less, Methodism attempted to keep alive the purpose of the camp meeting, albeit a gradual metamorphosis took place. In time the permanent church camp with its substantial, well-screened cottages, its tabernacle seating hundreds on comfortable benches, and lighted by electric lights took the place of exhorting under the spreading oaks.

Under the impact of urbanization, industrialization, and immigration, Methodism's agrarian-structured and pietistic ethic not only suffered defeat after defeat but no longer related the constituency meaningfully to the basic problems of American society. With discipline declining, incongruous though it seemed, sectarian standards of conduct respecting amusements, the Sabbath, diversions, meat and drink, were pitched higher and more zealously insisted upon. Prosperity played havoc with Puritan manners and morals for, as the prophet Micah had found out, imperial cities and the simple life seldom go together.

The Temperance Crusade

With the demise of slavery, the liquor problem became the primary ethical interest among postwar Methodists. Seeking additional sources of revenue, Congress in 1862 passed an Internal Revenue Act that licensed liquor interests, thus giving them governmental sanction. Further stimulated by the tide of immigrants with whom drink was a matter of custom, by industrialism where the saloon was a haven from the grinding routine of work, the traffic jumped from $29 million in 1860 to $190 million in 1880.[39] The foreign-born felt legal restriction upon drinking was an infringement upon personal liberty, while brewers and distillers, as state after state dropped prohibitory enactments, were jubilant about the future: "The enormous influx of immigration will in a few years overreach the Puritanical element in every state in the Union." [40]

The church fought "the demon Rum" valiantly if not too sagaciously by supporting the formation of the National Prohibition Party in 1869, the Woman's Temperance Crusade and the Woman's Christian Temperance Union in 1873. Frances E. Willard, for many years the dynamic and brilliant head of the W.C.T.U., possessed insight far beyond her time in seeing the connection between alcohol and social disorganization. Her pioneering work for universal suffrage, regulation of monopolies, direct voting for president, confiscation of land not in use, government

[39] William Warren Sweet, The Story of Religion in America (New York: Harper & Brothers, 1930) , p. 478.
[40] Cited by Barclay, History of Missions, III, 55.

issue of all money, free and unlimited coinage of silver, and support of social and economic amelioration caused many to stigmatize her as a radical. Bishop Gilbert Haven, while editor of *Zion's Herald,* saw the importance of woman's suffrage in fighting municipal sin in general and John Barleycorn in particular. As early as 1869 he asked that the fairer sex be given the ballot to cool the "seething caldron of corruption," for a woman's "nature is higher than the man's in tone. It more readily heeds the laws of morals. The wives of drunkards will not vote as they do." [41]

The General Conference of 1868 permitted the appointment of a full-time temperance agitator. Successive conferences took more advanced positions in recommending support of legal restriction of liquor, the organization of Sunday school temperance societies, the use of "unfermented wine" in the sacrament, a Committee on Temperance at each charge, and the promotion of temperance literature.[42] While the official position of the church was "complete legal prohibition," differences existed as to whether political action through the Prohibition Party was sound strategy. Many felt that the party would be "the retreat of cranks and visionaries . . . the rejected material of the other parties," [43] and the General Conference of 1892 cautioned that its antiliquor statement should not be construed as endorsement of any party. As time progressed, revivalistic methods in treating the problem, while never given up, slowly gave way to more scientific methods and the indoctrination of the young.

Granted the gravity of the problem, the fixation on John Barleycorn revealed an unfortunate myopia with respect to the larger social, economic, and political issues of the era. "The cries of the hour," stated Gilbert Haven in 1869, "are 'The Negro, Drunkard, Woman'!" [44] The phrase that Wesley had used of slavery, "the sum of all villainies," was transferred after the Civil War to liquor, with the expectation that a reign of social and political righteousness would be inaugurated when demon rum was exorcised. The tremendous amount of journalistic ink spilled on the subject—many weeklies ran an article a week—revealed a one-sided attack on the kingdom of evil. Such zealotism against a habit that was part of the immigrant's culture caused him to be repelled by the church. Since most of the foreign-born drank, many churchmen used liquor pro-

[41] *Zion's Herald,* June 17, 1869, p. 280.

[42] *Journal of the General Conference,* 1872, pp. 383-84; 1876, pp. 336-38; 1880, pp. 397, 399.

[43] "The Prohibition Movement," *The Methodist Review,* March, 1885, p. 280.

[44] *Zion's Herald,* June 17, 1869, p. 280.

nouncements as a foil against the immigrant's claims for social and economic justice.

Discipline in the Gilded Age

True to their English Puritan tradition, Methodists also decried the increasing desecration of the Sabbath. They were astounded by the "continental Sunday" habits of the immigrant and his desire to change the fourth commandment from "Remember the Sabbath, to keep it holy" to "Remember the Sabbath day, to keep it hilarious." An observer in Chicago in 1872 lamented the compulsion the Irish and German settlers felt to give the city the "honor and felicity of an European Sabbath" and noted that Sunday there was like "Berlin in the morning and a Paris in the afternoon." [45] Neither pulpit nor pen understood the Old World conception of Sunday as a day of recreation as well as worship, or the workers' desire for Sunday excitement and amusement after six days of routine and grinding toil.

In fighting the trend the lists of "baneful employments" were expanded far beyond the protest against Sabbath cooking, as in earlier days. Criticisms of steamboat excusions, picnics, baseball, printing and reading secular papers, parades, open livery stables, beer gardens, and ice cream "saloons" were unceasing. The railroads were especially excoriated for running Sunday trains. "The Pacific trains are starting on the Sabbath," cried *Zion's Herald* in 1860; "Let no minister encourage them in this desecration." [46] In reporting the systematic looting of freight from the Panhandle Railroad by its employees, the *Western Christian Advocate* in 1887 pontificated that since the railroad broke one of the Ten Commandments by running Sunday trains, it should not be surprised that its employees broke another and stole from them.[47]

The church fought the post–Civil War trend toward amusements and professionalism in sports and games with stepped-up pietistic admonition and prohibitory legislation. Whereas Wesley had held that "the sanctified person will not indulge in . . . trifles," too many of his followers made a significant inversion: "Those who avoid such things are the sanctified, and the only sanctified persons." [48] Unable to see that worldliness and increasing laxity were but symptomatic of a deeper evolution

[45] Cited by Sweet, *Story of Religion in America,* p. 334.
[46] May 27, 1869, p. 248.
[47] April 20, 1887, p. 252.
[48] Richard M. Cameron, *Methodism and Society in Historical Perspective* (Nashville: Abingdon Press, 1961), p. 218.

in American culture, and overlooking the wholesale moral corruption in all phases of political, commercial, and social life, many ministers fixated upon the trivial. "Having lost the center of the matter precious to their forefathers, the Methodists mistakenly clung to a portion of the periphery." [49] Thus, the General Conference of 1872, reflecting the pressure from many memorials against "sinful amusements," amended the *Discipline* chapter on "Imprudent Conduct" to include "dancing, playing at games of chance, attending theaters, horse races, circuses, dancing parties, or patronizing . . . other amusements as are obviously of misleading or questionable moral tendency." [50] Even the martyred Lincoln was taken to task for his theatergoing by the New York *Christian Advocate* less than a month after his assassination: "Millions of hearts . . . feel that a theater is not a very good place to die in; that the transition from the playhouse to the bar of God is fearfully abrupt." [51] Novel reading perverted history, "kept thousands from coming to Christ," and took time away from reading the Bible and Methodist literature." [52] Although such admonitions were incapable of enforcement and not shared by all the clergy, they were reflective of Methodism's agrarian bias and its distrust of the wealth, novelty, and increasingly complex fascinations of urban life. Granted the fact that some amusements and sports were coarse, if not vulgar, such pietistic legalism shackled the church with the image of being against fun and fostering a "long-faced religion."

Expansion and Denominational Rivalry

The denominational rivalry and competition during the 1870's and '80's was indicative that the Civil War brought political but not social and religious unity to the nation. The sensitive twentieth-century ear is shocked not only by the heckling between various Methodist journals but also by their ceaseless carping against everything from Unitarianism and Mormonism to Rum and Romanism. It was an era of "rugged denominationalism" without ecumenical hopes or programs, and Methodist editors did not have to pull their journalistic punches for fear of hurting religious sensitivities. The New Testament church never "was a mass of independent atoms," stated *Zion's Herald* in criticizing the Congregationalists while lampooning the Baptists for immersing children so young their feet could not touch the baptistery floor.[53] One probable

[49] *Ibid.*
[50] *Journal of the General Conference*, 1872, pp. 379-80.
[51] May 4, 1865, p. 140.
[52] Cameron, *Methodism and Society*, pp. 221-22.
[53] August 31, 1871, p. 414.

aim of such journalistic fisticuffs was to increase subscription levels. Gilbert Haven of *Zion's Herald* had few satirical peers. Having welcomed an ex-Baptist parson into the Methodist clergy, he was chagrined to see him go back to his first ecclesiastical love within the week. Nonetheless, he sped his parting guest on with the observation "that, after all, he was an aquatic animal, and had only come to the surface long enough to blow." [54]

In the Midwest "church racing," as Haven called it, was the favorite sport among the Methodists, Baptists, Congregationalists, and Presbyterians.[55] "Denominations, weak as well as strong, felt called of God to put forth herculean efforts to gain a foothold in or to capture the civilization of the West—the weak in order to lift themselves, . . . the strong to retain their inherited prestige." [56] Although the hardships of the frontier produced impulses for co-operation, rivalry, engendered by doctrinal seriousness and a lack of the sense of sin over sectarianism, was far stronger. Methodists were aggressive because they were convinced that free grace and perfection in love were authentically Christian, whereas the Baptist demand for immersion and the Presbyterian "divine despot" God were false. Denominational journals in the East alternately rejoiced and wept over news from the "front." When the *Macedonian,* the missionary organ of the Baptist Church, exulted over wiping out a Methodist church and baptizing its "preacher, steward and class leader," *Zion's Herald* regretted the fact that Methodist's foremost rivals were operating under a spurious Macedonian cry, "Come over and be baptized." [57] When city fathers granted financial inducements to the first denomination to erect a chapel in a given locality, sectarian competition became fierce. Once when a Methodist itinerant neglected to clinch an offer for $600, a Congregational "chapel stealer" came along the next day and wangled a better deal with the town council, and raised a chapel to Congregationalism.[58]

With the formation of the Church Extension Society in 1864, two years after the Homestead Act of 1862, Methodism made rapid strides in providing suitable church buildings for sod-housed settlers on the trans-Missouri plains. By making direct gifts and loans to societies it stimulated the building of thousands of churches. By a donation of $250, hundreds of Methodists were directly responsible for the construction of churches

---

[54] George Prentice, *The Life of Gilbert Haven* (New York: Phillips and Hunt, 1883), p. 353.

[55] *Zion's Herald,* November 19, 1874, p. 369.

[56] Peter G. Mode, *The Frontier Spirit in American Christianity* (New York: The Macmillan Company, 1923), p. 120.

[57] January 23, 1868, p. 41.

[58] *Ibid.,* November 19, 1874, p. 369.

that cost less than $1,250 each on the frontier.[59] During its first six years the society had collected from churches and individuals $489,303.64, with which it had aided 733 churches.[60]

"Chaplain" C. C. McCabe, for many years secretary of the Church Extension Society, had no peer in extracting money from well-heeled eastern Methodists. A banker who regularly contributed twitted him by beginning his letters, "The Great American Champion Beggar, Chaplain C. C. McCabe," but invariably signed off, "Take the enclosed check." A friendly Presbyterian contributor besought him to "please get out of this region while I have something left," and ended with the admonition, "When you get the country well 'underbrushed' we will send out some Presbyterians and put on the finishing touches." [61] His success as a preacher was due to the fact that his announced topic was seldom church extension but rather "The Bright Side of Life in Libby Prison," and when people turned out in droves, he let "them in free and charged them for going out." [62] When the freethinker Robert G. Ingersoll pronounced a funeral over the Christian church in advance, McCabe wired him that the Methodists were building a church a day and soon hoped to raise it to two. The retort inspired the Rev. Mr. Alfred J. Hough to pen the famous hymn that McCabe sang from coast to coast:

> The infidels, a motley band,
>   In council met and said:
> "The Churches die all through the land,
>   The last will soon be dead."
> When suddenly a message came,
>   It filled them with dismay:
> "All hail the power of Jesus' name!
>   We're building *two* a day." [63]

Macedonian calls from the western-plain states appeared with greater frequency in the correpondence columns of the weeklies in the East. Conferences with burgeoning memberships tried to entice ministerial talent west by exclaiming over the unique opportunities, climate, soil, industrious people, and inexpensive land in their areas. A plea from Nebraska City, Nebraska, in 1871 asked whether there were "no wide-awake, energetic young men in the New England Conferences or colleges who would like to ride a border circuit," and, while admitting the hard-

[59] Frank Milton Bristol, *The Life of Chaplain McCabe* (New York: Fleming H. Revell, 1908), p. 246.
[60] Barclay, *History of Missions,* III, 137.
[61] Bristol, *Life of McCabe,* pp. 243-45.
[62] *Ibid.,* p. 120.
[63] *Ibid.,* p. 259.

ships of a society "less refined" and small salaries, compensation was promised through more hearty human relationships and a lower cost of living.[64] Living conditions were Spartan. A Minnesota pastor reported the homestead log cabins of his parishioners were fifteen or twenty feet square, suitably "chunked and daubed," and contained but one room with a loft overhead and loose boards on the floor. In one of the homes where he preached, he could stand upright only between the ceiling joists.[65] Thus, Asa Turner's advice, as a member of the "Iowa Band," was starkly realistic to prospective ministers:

Don't come here expecting a paradise. Our climate will permit men to live long enough, if they do their duty. If they do not, no matter how soon they die. Office and station are but little regarded here. People will not speak of you or to you, as the Rev. Mr. So-and-so, but will call you simply by your name, and your wife Peggy or Polly, or whatever her name may be.

Come prepared to expect savage things, rough things. Lay aside all your dandy whims boys learn in college, and take a few lessons of your grandma there before you come. Get clothes, firm, durable, something that will go through the hazel brush without tearing. Don't be afraid of a good, hard hand, or a tanned face. If you keep free from a hard heart, you will do well. Get wives of the old Puritan stamp, such as honored the distaff and the loom, those who can pail a cow, and churn the butter, and be proud of a jean dress or a checked apron.[66]

Methodism and Roman Catholicism

Methodism had an extremely difficult time accepting the policy of unrestricted immigration during the era that brought a flood tide of Roman Catholics to American shores.[67] Although the Civil War had shunted much anti-Catholic feeling onto the battlefield, Methodists, like Protestants in general, were infected by a residual but strong religious nativism which regarded Catholics as outsiders and aliens by nationality, religion, custom, and class to the American dream. American nationalism and

[64] *Zion's Herald*, April 13, 1871, p. 175.

[65] New York *Christian Advocate*, September 28, 1871, p. 306.

[66] Quoted by George M. Stephenson, *The Puritan Heritage* (New York: The Macmillan Company, 1952) , p. 269.

[67] Roman Catholic population jumped from 1,606,000 in 1850 to 7,362,000 in 1890. A spot check of the religious affiliation of the immigrants during 1899 revealed: Roman Catholic, 52.1 per cent; Protestants, 18.5 per cent; Jewish, 10.4 per cent; miscellaneous, 15.2 per cent. In 1890 Roman Catholics numbered 386,200 in New York City; 201,063 in Brooklyn; 163,658 in Philadelphia; and 262,047 in Chicago (Barclay, *History of Missions*, III, pp. 2, 12) .

democracy had automatically been identified with Protestantism; and with the immigrant's Sabbath pleasures, liquor habits, and amusement tastes contrary to the Puritan ethos, the Methodist consensus that the Roman Catholic "didn't belong" was enforced. A visiting British Methodist undoubtedly expressed the views of his American counterpart in 1856 when, after "looking in" at a Catholic service in New York and seeing the "show and glare of popery," he was of a mind to shout, "Idolatry! Idolatry! as loudly as Latimer himself." [68] The fact that many foreign-born priests did not throw themselves into the channels of American life, and that their church exerted pressure in New York and New England to obtain public funds for its budding parochial school system, strengthened the sentiment that there was a "Catholic plan" afoot which was antithetical to public education, democracy, and liberty. The Episcopal Address of 1872 warned that the "Romish Church" was intent on destroying public education and asked Methodists to unite with "all intelligent Christians and all true patriots" to protect the "free institutions" granted by "our Protestant forefathers." [69]

While hagridden by Catholicism's rapid expansion in the New World, Methodism rejoiced that signs in Italy, Spain, France, and Austria indicated that the tide of events was running against "popery." "So in the Old World the Catholic Church is waning, while in our Protestant America, by means of immigration, she is putting forth an exuberant growth." [70]

Dollinger, the German Roman Catholic church historian, later excommunicated, was praised for not acceding to the dogma of papal infallibility; Austria commended for breaking a concordat; Garibaldi and Victor Emmanuel II acclaimed for uniting Italy and forcing the pope to sulk in the Vatican, albeit there was some fear that the Papal See might be transferred to this country. In spite of statistics to the contrary, such events produced a "wonderful satisfaction" that the "Roman Church has not the shadow of a promise . . . that her dogmas and ceremonies will be the dominant Christianity of this continent." [71] The *Zeitgeist* in America—with its liberal training in education, free circulation of the Scriptures, and freedom of individual judgment—would speedily cause all people to see the spiritual bankruptcy of Rome. "The great forces of the age—the energy, the enterprise, the intelligence, the virtue—are Protestant. Protestant peoples lead the van, are the formative, the colonizing,

[68] Stephenson, *Puritan Heritage*, p. 226.
[69] *Journal of the General Conference*, 1872, p. 456.
[70] *Zion's Herald*, June 10, 1869, p. 270.
[71] *Ibid.*, November 7, 1872, p. 529.

the trading agencies of the world." [72] Thus the Bishops' Address of 1892, while expressing no desire to limit immigration, called for the "speedy Americanization" of "Old World peoples" with "Old World ideas, habits, and excesses . . . incompatible with our most cherished principles and institutions. . . . The policy of encouraging communities of foreign-born citizens and their children to continue foreign in their language, schools, churches, tastes, and social habits, we regard as both unwise and unsafe." [73]

As time wore on, the query would not down as to why the immigrant horde had remained loyal to its ancestral faith, and not a few wondered where Methodism had erred. Editor Buckley admitted that the Catholic Church was "free to all comers" but warned, with a characteristic pietistic reaction, that Methodism should not "broaden the base morally" to attract converts. He opined that Catholics came from mass "with the books all balanced" but spent the rest of the Sabbath in frolic and the remainder of the week without a thought of growing morally or spiritually.[74] Although there were periodic suggestions for team ministries in the inner city, institutional churches with weekday programs, the construction of inexpensive chapels in workingmen's districts, and the establishment of foreign language missions, it was a question of being too late with too little.

Occasionally Protestant anxiety took the form of complaining to city authorities about Catholic Sabbath parades and bands, affirming that they interfered with parishioners getting to church and interrupted services. After one such complaint in New York in 1868, the Catholic *Tablet* taunted the Protestants for their "airs of superiority," and added that Catholicism "is joy, and worship is a perpetual feast. . . . You can never make them accept the Puritanic gloom, put on the Puritanic long face, and whip the beer-barrel if it works on Sunday." [75] Sometimes the journal dispensed sound advice:

The real enemies to us . . . are the Methodists, admirably organized for aggression, and who, in their appeals to the animal nature and sensible devotion, acquire no little power over the sensitive, the ignorant, and the superstitious. They, however, are laying the foundation of their own ruin. They are becoming wealthy, are building fine churches, founding colleges and theological

---

[72] *Ibid.*, June 10, 1869, p. 270.
[73] *Journal of the General Conference*, 1892, p. 54.
[74] *Zion's Herald*, March 27, 1873, p. 100.
[75] Cited by H. Mattison, "Romanism in the United States," *The Methodist Quarterly Review*, October, 1868, pp. 508-9.

seminaries, and they are taking their place among the *respectable* sects of the country. . . . They are ruined the moment they lose sight of the poor.[76]

Methodism and the Working Classes

Unquestionably the developing bourgeois orientation of the church did cause Methodism, both in thought and action, to neglect the proletariat. Zealous of making membership capital at the expense of the prostrate Southern Church and of being the pioneering church in the West, the Methodist Episcopal Church overlooked crucial economic and social problems on its own urban doorstep. Once the religion of the poor, it now displayed an almost frantic solicitude for the souls of those on Park Avenue. With immigrants and workers crowding into the old city, churches followed the migration of their rich constituents along the broad avenues uptown. By 1865 fifty Protestant congregations had deserted lower New York, and Bostonians were evacuating historic meeting houses for "sumptuous edifices in the Back Bay." Rationalizations followed: "If there are heathen in the lanes," stated one Protestant assembly in 1869, "there are heathen in the stately avenues also." [77]

The church was hindered in developing a *rapprochement* with labor by its entrenched Puritanism, which viewed the close affiliation between godliness and wealth as altogether natural since the virtues of thrift, honesty, and industry were authentically Christian. The strong individualistic element in the Wesleyan heritage caused many to see *laissez faire* as divinely ordained and to affirm that religious conversion of the capitalist lion and laboring lamb would cause them to feed together on the straw of economic harmony. The danger of wealth lay not in its accumulation or power but in the temptation to become ostentatious. Riches were "the legitimate growth of Christian life," stated one correspondent of the New York *Christian Advocate,* and only to be condemned when the possessors "walk the street with haughty airs or sweep out church aisles with surplus silks." [78] The rule of thumb seemed to be that a well-heeled Methodist should neither by manner nor dress reveal the state of his bank account.

Wesley's old formula, "Gain all you can, save all you can, give all you can," was used by church-patronizing industrialists as the Gilded Age's conscience money. Religious journalists seldom wandered into the byways of novel social and economic philosophy. Methodist "barons" such as

[76] Cited by the New York *Christian Advocate,* March 11, 1869, p. 76.
[77] Aaron Ignatius Abell, *The Urban Impact on American Protestantism, 1865-1900* (Cambridge: Harvard University Press, 1943), pp. 4-6.
[78] January 4, 1872, p. 1.

Daniel Drew, Isaac Rich, Lee Claflin, and Jacob Sleeper were assiduously cultivated for donations to pet ecclesiastical projects, and their demise was sure to bring a black-columned three-thousand word obituary of the most laudable variety. Uncritical admiration of such self-made industrialists led many churchmen to give labor the stone of Horatio Alger philosophy in place of the loaf of economic justice. While granting "the present order of business affairs" in 1872 made "the rich richer, and the poor poorer," the New York *Christian Advocate* editorialized:

> The whole secret of the difference between pecuniary increase and hopelessly continuous poverty lies in the adjustment of incomes to expenses of living. In almost any case a healthy man . . . may live on something less than his current wages; and whoever does that must soon become a capitalist. Let young men remember this, and abstain from their senseless whinings about the antagonism of capital against labor . . . . Correct the manners, and the finances will soon come round all right.[79]

During the time that Cardinal Gibbon was giving yeoman leadership in the Knights of Labor, influential Methodists saw little but evil in the struggling trade union movement. In 1888 J. W. Mendenhall, editor of *The Methodist Review,* berated union leaders for thinking and acting as "members of the laboring class" instead of "citizens of the republic." "It is undemocratic, anti-American, anti-Christian, and shows how deeply the movement is rooted, not in intelligent desire to promote the general good, but in the selfism of human nature." [80] Three years later, somewhat chastened but forgetting the eighth-century Hebrew prophets, he stated: "The criticism of the Church for its alleged inattention to social and industrial questions is not wholly justified, for such questions are new, and it is a problem to know what more to do than discuss them." [81] William Nast of the German Methodist *Christliche Apologete* denounced the crusade for an eight-hour day as a stratagem to exploit labor by "drones and demagogues" and feared workers would use their leisure time hanging around bars and engaging in frivolous pleasures. The zealous advocate of freedman uplift, Daniel Curry, opposed higher wages, since they would discourage thrift and industry; believed that public regulation of wages and hours would "trammel the free working of our labor system"; opined that all special labor legislation was "wrong and inexpedient"; and concluded that "only slavery itself is . . . more inimical to the com-

---

[79] March 7, 1872, p. 76.
[80] "Sentimental Sociology," *The Methodist Review,* January, 1888, p. 139.
[81] *The Methodist Review,* November, 1891, p. 923.

mon good" and the rights of the individual than labor unions.[82] Evidently trying to temper the antilabor bias of the church, the Episcopal Address of 1876 stated that it was not only "Christ-like" but "expedient" to cultivate the poor. "The Church which preaches to most of the poor of this generation . . . will preach to most of the rich in the next generation." [83]

Theologically rather than sociologically oriented clergymen strained at the gnat of "Romanism, Mormonism, and Alcoholism" while swallowing a camel of economic injustice. Not a few were mystified why a seamstress who made $7.50 a week and lived in a cold water walk-up would not sit in the same pew as her employer, whose salary ran into five figures. Many felt that liberal doses of charity would salve the exacerbations of labor and that moral suasion was the solvent for the collective egotism of the capitalists. Nevertheless, when five hundred Protestant ministers in New York were petitioned by the bakers' union to preach sermons against compulsory Sunday labor, even their entrenched Sabbatarianism was not strong enough to cause more than a half dozen to do so. As blood flowed freely from strike violence in the 1870's, ministerial aversion to violence not only increased their sympathy for capital but prevented recognition that coercion was a necessary ingredient in securing economic justice. Many, the disciples of Herbert Spencer, considered the price of labor, like that of corn and cabbage, a commodity to be sold. "Labor is a commodity, having its prices varying from time to time, and in various places, according to the relative demand and supply, and it is great folly to attempt to regulate prices by law." [84]

During the '80's, however, there were signs that the church was finally awakening to its responsibility to labor. The abstention from churchgoing by workers and the increasing anticlericalism of their leaders, who classed the church as the pawn of bourgeois interests, could no longer be ignored. The pleas of Frances E. Willard, who was initiated into the Knights of Labor in 1887, and the institutional church programs of J. W. Magruder of Cincinnati, Henry Morgan of Boston, and others, began to fall on sympathetic ears. In 1872 E. H. Rogers, a prominent Methodist layman of Chelsea, Massachusetts, was one of the founders of the Christian Labor Union of Boston, whose platform declared that Jesus taught spiritual principles "which pertained to the temporal life of man" and that the poverty of the poor, not their natural depravity,

[82] New York *Christian Advocate*, September 5, 1867, p. 284.
[83] *Journal of the General Conference*, 1876, p. 404.
[84] New York *Christian Advocate*, January 21, 1869, p. 20.

was the cause of their absence from church.[85] In 1888 for the first time the Episcopal Address included a long section dealing with labor. Affirming that the Golden Rule was the "antidote to all the evils" between rich and poor, but holding "millions of laborers compactly organized" as a "danger . . . too palpable to be concealed or overlooked," the bishops, in their soul searching, were speaking the mind of the church:

Are they drifting away from us? . . . Have we forgotten our mission as we have increased in wealth? . . . Is this alienation [of church and worker] a fact? If so, what is its cause? If we have given too much attention to the rich, or cherished too much regard for social position, or have in any wise neglected the poor, we have departed from the spirit of our calling. . . . If fine churches are in the way they do not honor us, and it were better never to have them than that they should stand as monuments of unchurchly pride or as barriers. . . . This fact reveals a portentous evil, and demands a remedy at whatever cost.[86]

Four years later, in Amos-like tones, they denounced the "grinding and soulless arrogance of monopolies," which excited hate, riot, and revolution, and asked the church not to be a "mere idle spectator" but side with the "toiling multitudes." [87]

Thus did Methodism, after much stumbling, respond creditably if slowly to the challenge of modern, urbanized industrial America. The focus began to change from the concentration upon individual morals to the discovery of a social ethic capable of understanding social sins. Those outside the American dream—tenement residents, sweated children, blackened miners, twelve-hour-day and seven-day-week steel workers, exploited women, sharecroppers, and migratory laborers—were found, and the premises of the system that put them there, laissez faire, were called into question. The urban masses were to be won not by pontificating about a better world in the by-and-by but through endorsing unions, supporting strikes, writing reform legislation, and working for social amelioration, by lifting them out of a this-worldly hell. That the social gospel was desperately needed, few question; that Methodism was guilty of contributing to the religious ethos of the Gilded Age which made its coming imperative, only the most zealous Wesleyan would doubt.

[85] The Union complained that wealthy churches were actually indifferent if not antagonistic to human brotherhood and that the clergy should teach capitalist "pillars" how to morally acquire property instead of how to dispense it. A founder of the Union declared: "So the church says that, to build a theological seminary is serving God; and she accepts half a million of money from a man, Daniel Drew, who got it by the most iniquitous service of Mammon, and names the seminary after the man." (E. H. Rogers, Like unto Me. Boston: 1876, p. 15.)

[86] Journal of the General Conference, 1888, pp. 57-58.

[87] Journal of the General Conference, 1892, p. 56.

Buttressed by the nearly unanimous opinion of academic authorities, sustained by the growing wealth and power of the churchgoing middle class, American Protestantism maintained its support of the combined social and religious orthodoxy developed in the prewar period. Christian America was still being guided by the Unseen Hand; church and nation were sound. Greed at the top could be ignored or accepted as a tool of progress. Misery at the bottom could be waved aside as inevitable or, at most, treated by a program of guarded and labeled philanthropy. The only vigorous dissent came from isolated and ineffective radicals. Until they were shocked by a series of violent social conflicts, most Protestant spokesmen continued to insist that all was well.[88]

2

The Free Methodists

The creation of a separate Free Methodist Church immediately prior to the Civil War lay in the polarization of two groups in the Genesee Conference with respect to theological, cultural, and ecclesiastical ideology. Though the theological cause involved the place and importance of holiness in Methodist doctrine and practice, the cultural and ecclesiastical reasons for the rupture are important albeit exceedingly difficult to unravel. Both before, during, and after the schism, partisans of both the church and the new sect wrote with such passion as to sometimes obscure the issue in question. After the break both parties tended to justify the righteousness of their particular action by fabrication or discovery of additional grounds for the separation.

During the fifth and sixth decades of the 1800's a conference minority, known by the epithet "the Nazarites," became increasingly convinced that Methodism's American success story had caused a repudiation of the Wesleyan birthright of entire sanctification. They viewed with a jaundiced eye the growing spirit of self-congratulation that permeated ecclesiastical councils, as reports of immense wealth, burgeoning membership, and increased prestige multiplied. Wesley's premonition that Methodists would lose their spirituality when they had bootstrapped their way to material and cultural respectability had proved unfortunately true. Hitherto a "peculiar people," Methodists had waxed and grown fat, and like the chosen people during the reign of Solomon desired to be as "other nations."

[88] May, *Protestant Churches and Industrial America*, pp. 62-63; used by permission.

Self-gratulations soon made its evil effect visible. Why should a people who had become so numerous, strong, wealthy and influential continue to be so singular? Why erect such plain houses of worship as they had done in the former times? Why insist upon modesty and plainness of attire? Why continue to be so unlike the nations round about them? Why incur the displeasure of those in lofty stations, of those who abounded in wealth, of those who were the *elite* of society, who otherwise might patronize their services and be drawn into their communion? Had they not hitherto been too narrow and exclusive? Would it not be wise to broaden Methodism so as better to adapt it to the higher social classes? [89]

Holiness, the doctrinal touchstone of Methodism, fell into disrepute in some circles. Considered by some a "counsel of perfection" for a few elect souls, it was openly ridiculed by others. One holiness preacher was told not to overdo a good thing, "lest he should drive away men of influence *needed to the church*." [90] By accepting the old "Moravian heresy" of the identification of justification and sanctification, or by flirting with "gradualistic" notions of regeneration, many ministers lowered the tone of "all that is vital to Christian experience, discipline, character and fruitfulness." [91] Nathan Bangs in 1851 lamented that Methodists had become lukewarm concerning entire sanctification, and even the saintly Peter Cartwright, although he protested strongly against the acculturation of the church during the era, was "strangely silent" concerning holiness.[92]

The Nazarites were convinced that the drift from holiness had opened the door to worldliness and lax discipline. Primitive Methodism expected its clergy and laymen, whether rich or poor, to dress in plain garb without jewelry, ornamentation, and frills. The decline of the revival, the diminishing camp meeting, the forgotten love feast were symptomatic of a church enmeshed in a culture that was turning rancid. Overdressed ladies in selected pews during the Sabbath fashion parade drove the poor away. The stringent rules prohibiting specific items of dress adopted at the Christmas Conference in 1784 were reduced to a simple apostolic directive by the General Conference of 1856. Holiness ascetics and proponents of a "Christ against culture" ethic were shocked at Bishop Simpson's proclivity for Gothic cathedrals and criticized his spouse for breaking the stereotype of the Methodist parson's wife.

[89] Wilson T. Hogue, *History of the Free Methodist Church* (Chicago: Free Methodist Publishing House, 1915) , I, 17. Used by permission of the Light and Life Press.
[90] Benjamin Titus Roberts, *Why Another Sect?* (Rochester: The Earnest Christian Publishing House, 1879) , pp. 72-73.
[91] Hogue, *History*, I, 14-15.
[92] Leslie R. Marston, *A Living Witness* (Winona Lake, Ind.: Light and Life Press, 1960) , pp. 141-42.

On one occasion she brought consternation to a Presbyterian banker's wife who was entertaining them during the conference session. Thinking of the Methodists as plain, illiterate people, the hostess, wishing not to overawe her guests at their first dinner, twisted her hair in a tight knot, took off her rings, wore a "big-flowered tycoon-rep wrapper" and a white apron. She had not yet seen her guest, who had been shown to her room by a servant. At dinnertime Mrs. Simpson swept down the stairs, a tall, stately woman in black silk ruffled to the waist, with expensive laces and jewelry, and her hair done in the latest style. The banker's wife, embarrassed and chagrined, sat silent through the meal while Mrs. Simpson, a splendid talker, "charmed everybody." [93]

Declining spirituality revealed itself in the loss of simplicity in worship. Some conservatives decried the "abominable practice" of sitting down during prayer, and implored heaven to save Methodism from the worldly allure of pews, choirs, organs, instrumental music, and a congregational ministry that had ensnared "heathen churches" in its midst. Although the *Discipline* had never forbidden instrumental music, a committee on the state of discipline of the Genesee Conference in 1846 took a mediating position between the extremists. Stating its preference for vocal singing it recommended that a "company of singers"—the term "choir" was carefully avoided—be trained to guide the congregation and that instrumental music be employed only for "regulating the key, or assisting those parts which are weak or unreliable." [94] Nevertheless, the Nazarites saw that choirs, organs, "tune books," and other paraphernalia of "scientific music" tended to make worship less emotionally demonstrative and catered to the aesthetic sensitivities of the more cultured Methodist. They viewed with alarm the lessening participation in the service by the laity. "It does appear strange," twitted one brother, that when a pastor announces a hymn, " 'we will *join* in singing,' to hear, after deliberation, a very select choir, at a very select distance from the audience, discourse a new-fangled tune that nobody knows—to the edification of nobody." [95] Henry Ward Beecher noted the lowered volume of Methodist singing in 1857: "How I long for the good old Methodist thunder! One good burst of old fashioned music would have blown this modern singing out the window like a wadding from a gun." [96] A Genesee visitor from the Philadelphia Conference expressed a distaste for the congregation "turning their rear part to the pulpit" to hear the choir in the back or

[93] Robert D. Clark, *The Life of Matthew Simpson* (New York: The Macmillan Company, 1956), p. 276. Used by permission.
[94] F. W. Conable, *History of the Genesee Annual Conference* (2nd ed.; New York: Phillips and Hunt, 1885), p. 532.
[95] *The Northern Independent,* March 29, 1860.
[96] *Ibid.,* September 10, 1857.

side of the church.[97] Others wanted choirs abolished because "professional singers" had the reputation for partying into the early Sabbath hours, playing cards, and dancing. Thus, when a Nazarite preacher, Joseph McCreery, discovered a paid choir on his Lyndonville Circuit in 1854-55, he "drove out the doves who were billing and cooing in the gallery" and reinstated congregational singing.[98]

Another pattern of worship that rankled the Nazarite sensitivity was that of the "pewed" church. In spite of the fact that a few of Wesley's churches had been supported through pew rental, they viewed the refusal of the General Conference in 1852 to sustain the Ohio Conference's censure of a minister who erected a pewed church as an example that official Methodism had tacitly allowed a caste system to develop within its membership. In spite of the fact that pew rental helped retire the debt on magnificent urban cathedrals, the practice was a contradiction to the doctrine of free grace, discriminated against the poor, and kept the masses from the church.

The toleration of slavery was still another factor contributing to the schism. The Nazarites felt that all true sons of Wesley would be united in fulfilling their founder's last command to extirpate the "vilest [institution] that ever saw the sun." They perceived little wisdom in the go-slow, protect-the-unity-of-the-church, hold-the-border-conferences strategy that emanated from those high on the ecclesiastical ladder. The Christian social ethic was being compromised when powerful forces within the church feared the abolitionist as much as it did the slaveholder. They detested the temporizing on so grave an issue as represented by Bishop Waugh before the New England Conference in 1837: "I would that it [slavery] were obliterated from the earth; but in view of the terrific consequences that are likely to follow the agitation . . . I cannot consent . . . in those measures which are advocated by modern abolitionists." [99] Although there was no proslavery sentiment in the strongly abolitionist Genesee Conference, the Nazarites felt that the church, in allowing laymen to own slaves until 1864, had sold its prophetic birthright for the pottage of denominational unity. "Up to the day that slavery was abolished by the sword," affirmed Benjamin T. Roberts, the founder of the Free Methodist Church, "there were thousands of slaveholders in good standing in the Methodist Episcopal Church. . . . [It] tolerated slavery to the last." [100]

The final and most immediate cause that alienated the Nazarites and

[97] *Ibid.*, February 15, 1859.
[98] Roberts, *Why Another Sect?* p. 140.
[99] *Zion's Herald*, June 28, 1837.
[100] *Why Another Sect?* p. 46.

the "Regency"—as the Genesee Conference majority party was called— was that of lodge membership. The rural-oriented, pietistic-permeated holiness party felt not only that the urban-dominated "Regency" modernists were leading Genesee Methodism away from the straight and narrow path of Wesleyanism, but that its members were the "bishop's men" and controlled conference patronage. Although the Genesee Conference had on at least three separate occasions taken action against Masonic Lodge membership, the General Conference of 1852 ruled that an Annual Conference could not discipline a pastor unless his lodge membership conflicted with the rules of the church.[101] Holiness advocates believed that the devotees of Masonry were struggling to rise above Methodism's humble origin and frontier culture to a sense of belonging and status through the "cabalistic, ritual, closed-group chumminess, and pompous pageantry" of the lodge.[102]

The Genesee Conflict

The first indication of trouble occurred during the 1848 Conference when a Nazarite sympathizer, Eleazer Thomas, distributed C. D. Burlingham's anti-Masonic tract to all members. Although "the wildest excitement followed," a compromise exhorted each party to do nothing to disturb conference tranquility. Nevertheless, Roberts affirmed a "breach thus begun was never healed" and the Regency "took the Church into the lodge and the lodge into the Church." [103] During the 1850's it became increasingly apparent to the Nazarites that they were "unequally yoked" with "secret-society preachers" whose bond of lodge togetherness was stronger than the comradeship of Christian fellowship.

The leader of the Nazarites and founder of the Free Methodist Church, Benjamin Titus Roberts, was a graduate of Wesleyan University, Middletown, Connecticut, who chose the ministry in place of the legal profession shortly before being admitted to the bar. Strongly influenced by a campus revival under the stimulus of John Wesley Redfield, Roberts revealed an early interest in temperance and slavery re-

[101] In spite of the fact that Freemasonry united the colonies during the Revolutionary War and laid the foundation for the doctrine of the separation of church and state, a widespread anti-Masonic movement swept America after the mysterious killing in 1826 of William Morgan, a bricklayer of Batavia, New York, who reportedly was about to publish a revelation of Masonic secrets. Many conferences subsequently passed resolutions against Masonry, feeling it was dangerous to democracy and encroached upon the proper domain of the church. The Nazarite campaign, however, was late, for resentment to lodge membership had died down before mid-century.

[102] Marston, *A Living Witness*, p. 168.

[103] *Why Another Sect?* p. 52.

form and taught a class of young women in an African church. Although financial necessity enforced periodic discontinuance of his school work, he graduated with honors and gave junior and senior class orations. When invited to the presidency of Wyoming Seminary at Kingston, Pennsylvania, a secondary school of the church, he declined by accepting the advice of Wesleyan President Olin: "There are more who are ready to teach than to preach." [104]

Upon graduation in 1848, at twenty-six years of age, he joined the Genesee Conference on trial and held successive pastorates at Caryville, Pike, and Rushford. In 1852 he was appointed to the Niagara Street Church of Buffalo, the choice parish of the district, and rumor had it that the presiding eldership was not far off. Although revivals were frequently initiated in his rural pastorates, Roberts couldn't "strike fire" in pagan Buffalo. Like Micah he believed the stronghold of evil to be in the city—in American Methodism, in the city parish. On one occasion a promising revival had its spirit dissipated by competition with a Missionary Society convocation whose aim was the raising of money. Key members of the church were opposed to revivalism, Roberts' measures, and instantaneous holiness. As an observer at the General Conference of 1852 he became disheartened that a strong stand was not taken against pew rental but offered to stay and see the Niagara Street Church free if it became a "free church." Frustrated in reforming his own parish, and with plans for building a "free" church for the poor never materializing, he was appointed to Brockport in 1853 and then to Albion in 1855, in a conference increasingly torn by intrafraternal skirmishing.

During the summer of 1855 a pamphlet purporting to be "Documents of the Nazarite Union" fell into the hands of editor John Robie of the Regency-sympathetic *Buffalo Advocate*. Stating that the Nazarite "order" should be labeled "Preachers'-Come-back-to-the-Discipline Society," the document made for provocative discussion. "Practical Propositions" called for the establishment of "old line" Methodism, including required class attendance, family prayer, quarterly fasts, and congregational singing. The Regency ministry was portrayed as

clerical professors in Odd-Fellow regalia, "shawled to the nose and bearded to the eyes," reading foolscap sermons one day, and praying to open secret Lodges the next;—pipelaying and managing in the Conference to oust out some, and hoist in others—and its lay professors rigged out in brass and feathers, and imitation posies, together with all its artifices to entice the world to love and support the Church; such as its sham donations, post-offices, lotteries, grab-bags,

[104] Benson Howard Roberts, *Benjamin Titus Roberts* (North Chili, N. Y.: The Earnest Christian Office, 1900), p. 29.

and oyster suppers for God. . . . They have other Masonic duties than building the walls of Jerusalem; other tents to pitch than the goodly tents of Jacob.

Regency-nurtured laymen were "adorned in artificial, if not costly, array, and 'sit in beauty side by side,' in our galleries, and in the rear of our congregations. But their voice is never heard in our love-feasts, our class-meetings, or our prayer-meetings." Those engaged in reformation were "cloven down from behind by unseen hands," thus proving the current proverb: "He who attempts the enforcement of the *Discipline* . . . is starved in his circuit, and damned in the Conference." [105]

Chagrined, the Nazarites struck back, affirming that the "Union" or "Band" existed only on paper and was nothing more than "a mere proposal" in the fertile, if unstable, mind of Joseph McCreery. McCreery was an early, if periodically an embarrassing, lieutenant of Roberts whose brand of perfectionism in time became repellent even among the Free Methodists. Although McCreery three years later confessed: *"I alone was responsible for the whole concern,"* the Genesee Conference in 1855 accepted the existence of the Nazarite "Band" as fact and passed its "disapprobation upon such associations." Party lines became more clearly drawn in 1856, and pressure on the Nazarite faction increased. Two presiding elders, Loren Stiles, Jr., and I. C. Kingsley, assigned to "stamp out fanaticism" in their districts became themselves seekers after holiness. Whether Regency pressure was responsible for their transfer to the Cincinnati Conference in 1856 is unclear,[106] but such was their standing in the conference that a petition signed by 1,500 members brought them back the subsequent year.

Meanwhile, the ecclesiastical jousting via the printed word increased in tempo. An article in the Medina *Tribune*, September 11, 1856, by "Junius" incensed the Nazarites because the Regency satirist concealed his identity in castigating their cause. "Spurious reformers are as plenty as blackberries. They go forth before the world, putting on strange and uncouth airs, . . . repeating nonsensical and claptrap phrases. . . . The ridiculous figure they cut excites the laughter and jeers of all—save those who are addled and silly as themselves." "Junius" continued:

They probably felt the motion of something within them—it may have been wind in the stomach—and mistook it for the intimations of a heaven-derived commission. . . . To them, religion . . . [is] outward forms and symbols . . . corporal manifestations, of animal influence and nervous sensations. With them,

[105] Quoted in Hogue, *History,* II, 376-408.
[106] Conable stated Stiles's dismissal of charges against McCreery developed "strong opposition" to his reappointment and he "indignantly asked Bishop Morris to transfer him to the Cincinnati Conference" (*History of the Genesee Conference,* p. 643).

a long face and sanctimonious airs answer for inward purity and goodness of heart. . . . A high-sounding profession takes precedence of a holy life, and getting happy in a religious meeting is laid down as an indubitable proof of the divine favor. With them, a broad-brimmed, bell-crowned hat is equivalent to "the helmet of salvation," and a shad-bellied coat to the robe of righteousness.[107]

The Nazarite-holiness party suffered still another defeat in 1856 when the General Conference replaced William Hosmer, editor of the *Northern Christian Advocate* and radical abolitionist, with the moderate F. G. Hibbard. Hosmer's friends united and formed *The Northern Independent* and placed him in charge, with publication beginning January, 1857. Although devoted primarily to slavery reform, Hosmer opened his columns to Nazarite protestations of ecclesiastical tyranny and injustice. Benjamin Roberts first submitted his conference-shaking "New School Methodism" to the *Northern Christian Advocate,* but Hibbard demurred at publishing it since it would not be "prudent" and would involve "hopeless controversy." *The Northern Independent* published it without hesitation and won the immediate plaudits of Roberts: "In intellect and courage, Hosmer was the John Knox of his day." [108] The article destroyed the uneasy truce pledged in 1848 and precipitated the crisis that led to the formation of the Free Methodist Church.

Roberts' polemic accused a coterie of thirty ministers of departing from historic Methodist doctrine. Labeling the Regency as "New School Methodists," he cited extracts from the *Buffalo Christian Advocate* to show their theological affinity for Theodore Parker, Newman, Thomas Paine, and Voltaire. Devotion to God was subordinated to the "benevolence" of the Transcendentalist, while justification and entire sanctification were not distinguished as two separate manifestations of grace. Since the two groups were alienated theologically, they differed fundamentally in church extension and cultivation. While "Old School Methodists" favored "simplicity and fervency in worship" and sponsored revivals, "deep and thorough," the liberals treated "with distrust all professions of deep Christian experience." The Regency furnished their Gothic churches with such trappings as "organs, melodeons, violins, and professional singers" in an attempt to secure the "patronage of the worldly, the favor of the proud and aspiring; and the various artifices of worldly policy." The Nazarites as "preachers of the old stamp" met budgetary obligations through inculcating self-denial and appealing to the love of Christ, while "New School Methodists" auctioned pews to the highest bidder and conducted "parties of pleasure, oyster suppers,

---

[107] Quoted in Hogue, *History,* I, 120-21.
[108] *Why Another Sect?* p. 47.

fairs, grab-bags, festivals and lotteries." The latter held clandestine meetings and had "free access at all times to the ears of the Episcopacy," and through control of patronage and appointments drove the adherents of "primitive Methodism" from the conference. Roberts closed his article by holding the "New School Methodists" responsible for the slow growth of the conference.[109]

With this indictment coming but a few days before the conference convened in LeRoy, New York, the storm broke. Regency sympathizers may have met in secret to move in concert against the Nazarites, although the reputed Minutes of such a meeting are rather innocuous.[110] In spite of the fact that Roberts promised a "humble confession" and retraction printed in church papers from "Maine to California" if it were found that he had misrepresented anyone, a conclave of fifty Regency ministers combined the talents of "Jesuits," "Jacobins," and the "Jewish Sanhedrin" and "worked under the cover of darkness" to rid the conference of the Nazarite incubus.[111] Sure of its majority the Regency was not interested in discussing the article, but, as one member stated: *"Nazaritism must be crushed out, and we have the tools to do it with!"* [112] Having lost a petition for trial by committee, by the narrow margin of fifty-two to forty-three, Roberts was sentenced to be reproved by the chair. Admonished for "immoral and unchristian conduct" he was assigned to a miserable rural charge at Pekin.

Other key Nazarite leaders slipped down a few rungs on the ecclesiastical ladder. William C. Kendall, a man who made "holiness his hobby," was sent to the "starvation circuit" of West Falls and advised by the presiding elder that "if he pleased the people pretty well, they might board him and his wife around, from house to house, but they would not be able to support him if he kept house." [113] The Nazarites were shocked that a man of such piety, whom they believed capable of filling the very best pulpits of the land, should be treated with such injustice. Kendall brushed away the tears, nevertheless, as the appointment was read and vowed *"to make them repent that they ever sent me to West Falls to cure or punish me."* [114] The embattled holiness minority attributed his unexpected demise several months later to the hardships and indignities heaped upon him while holding the fort of primitive Methodism. Nor

---

[109] Roberts' article is quoted in Hogue, *History,* I, 97 ff.

[110] See Marston, *A Living Witness,* p. 193; Hogue, *History,* I, 69.

[111] Richard R. Blews, *Master Workmen* (Winona Lake, Ind.: Light and Life Press, 1939), p. 34; Hogue, *History,* I, 68-70.

[112] Roberts, *Why Another Sect?* p. 149.

[113] *Ibid.,* p. 76.

[114] Hogue, *History,* I, 86.

were they placated when "those who had been his violent persecutors" vied with each other to sing his praises at the funeral.[115]

Meanwhile, Roberts' reputation for "immorality" had preceded him to Pekin, and he wondered whether "any itinerant ever had a colder reception." [116] Warm revivals were soon ignited, however, which overcame the chilly atmosphere. "Father Chesbrough," later a prominent layman in the Free Methodist Church, remarked after Roberts' inaugural sermon that he had once again heard the Methodism of the "old Baltimore Conference," not now "preached in western New York." In spite of opposition from some official board members, an indifferent presiding elder, and a steward who ran competitive prayer meetings, the "tide of salvation began to rise"—with young people putting off their "jewelry and finery" and with Roberts having one of the largest tents at the district camp meeting that summer.[117] Just as it appeared that the controversy might be waning, George W. Estes, a local preacher of the Clarkson charge, in a misguided attempt to defend Roberts, republished his "New School Methodism" and added a libelous account of the trial. Stating that the Regency had a custom of an "annual sacrifice of a human victim," albeit the "religious rites and ceremonies . . . assume a legal complexion," he named the ministers who voted to sustain the charge against Roberts:

> No man is safe who dares even whisper a word against this secret Inquisition in our midst. Common crime can command its indulgences—bankruptcies and adulteries are venal offenses—but opposition to its schemes and policies is a "mortal sin"—a crime "without benefit of clergy." The same fifty men who voted Brother Roberts guilty of "unchristian and immoral conduct" . . . voted to readmit a brother from the regions round about Buffalo, for the service performed of kissing a young lady in the vestibule of the Conference room. . . . Nero fiddled while the martyrs burned.[118]

"Sham trials" and "starvation appointments," Estes went on, were the means by which the best men in the conference were being "cloven down, one after another." He issued a call for all sympathetic laymen to withhold financial support of Regency clerics as the means of exterminating "this incubus, which is crushing us into the earth." Promising he would "neither run a step, nor pay a cent" to anyone who condemned Roberts, he signed off: "I agreed to support the M. E. Church as a Church of the living God; not as the mere adjunct of a secular or political clique.[119] Roberts was suspected of collusion with Estes concerning

---

[115] Roberts, *Why Another Sect?* p. 79.
[116] *Ibid.*, p. 155.
[117] Hogue, *History*, I, 152-53.
[118] Quoted in *Ibid.*, p. 159.
[119] *Ibid.*, pp. 161-62.

the printing and distribution of the article and ordered to stand trial at Perry in 1858. The Nazarites were nonplused, however, when a later Quarterly Conference renewed Estes' local preacher's license after he had admitted authorship of the article.

With partisanship now at a fever pitch, Roberts was convinced he would not receive a fair trial. Denied a change of venue to either the Oneida Conference or a civil court and prohibited from counsel outside the conference and trial by committee, he was expelled by a fifty-four to thirty-four vote. Since conference membership totaled 116, holiness advocates felt the abstentions were due to the fear of the "New School Methodists." Roberts was mystified, moreover, how Regency justice was tempered with mercy. During a recess of the trial he was the unanimous selection to give the funeral oration of William C. Kendall and chaired the public meeting of the American Bible Society. "Was this in imitation of the old idolators," he mused, "who first crowned with garlands the victims they were about to sacrifice?" [120]

Although Estes testified that Roberts had nothing to do with the document in question, the Rev. Mr. John Bowman affirmed the accused had delivered a bundle of them to him on a train and was responsible for its publication. Roberts was thoroughly disgruntled with the proceedings. Some men were "gathering chestnuts" during testimony and came back only to vote. The prosecution declined to have the printer of the document testify, although it brought him "seventy miles across the country," because it would have served to acquit the defendant. After Roberts had been expelled from the conference and the church, Bishop Janes shook his hand and said: "Do not be discouraged, Brother Roberts —there is a bright future before you yet." [121] Along with the also ejected McCreery, Roberts appealed to the General Conference, scheduled to meet at Buffalo in May, 1860.

A Nazarite sympathizer characterized the intervening two years as a "Reign of Terror" in which the "madness of Saul of Tarsus . . . scarcely exceeded the rage" with which the "worldly-minded, apostate majority" hunted down the true sons of Wesley.[122] Roberts and McCreery, however, welcomed the pleasant support of a sizable group of laymen who, with the covert encouragement of some pastors in the Genesee Conference, were organizing for the defense of the "sacred

[120] *Why Another Sect?* p. 178.
[121] *Ibid.*, pp. 173-86.
[122] Quoted by Hogue, *History*, I, 181. Hogue unquestionably has overdrawn the conflict in stating that the Nazarites were driven from worship in churches, schools, barns, and courthouses, with some of them being carried off to prison in irons and their personal property destroyed. He admits that the "grosser forms of . . . persecution emanated from the rowdy elements" in the communities affected (pp. 181-92).

doctrines of Methodism." Almost two hundred laymen, as yet excluded from ecclesiastical channels of protest, responded to the call of Isaac M. Chesbrough and met on December 1, 1858, at Albion, New York, in what was to be called the First Laymen's Convention. *"We know what Methodism is,"* the laymen protested. "Some of us were converted, and joined the Church under the labors of her honored pioneers." The charge against Roberts and McCreery of inciting "fanaticism" they judged as *"utterly false and groundless."* Stating that they had "not the slightest intention of leaving the Church of our choice," they quoted several volumes of Methodist Church polity to support their plan of throttling the Regency by not paying "one farthing to preacher or Presiding Elder" who voted against Roberts and McCreery. They took the "contumacious" twosome to their bosom and promised them $1,000 and $600 respectively if they would "travel at large, and labor as opportunity" presented itself in the Regency vineyard.[123]

Although he had received a call from a "superior charge in Brooklyn," Roberts moved his family to Buffalo, the lair of Regency strength, and itinerated at will through the conference. While waiting his appeal to the General Conference he joined the church at Pekin, his last charge, as a probationer and was granted an exhorter's license. Upon the termination of this irregular relationship a few months later, Roberts disclaimed any need of ecclesiastical authority for preaching and protested but a desire to fulfill the apostolic ideal, "to flee from the wrath to come." "The Lord has opened a wide door, into which I have entered. I disclaim all authority from man . . . and [the Lord] blesses me it in." [124] In March of 1859 he journeyed to St. Louis to contact John Wesley Redfield, a "western" Nazarite, and his flock of 150 pilgrim perfectionists who had left the church.

Tensions were near the explosive stage when Bishop Simpson convened the Genesee Conference at Brockport in October, 1859. The Nazarite sympathizer Fay Purdy, a lawyer-evangelist, had "pitched a large tabernacle" seating three thousand people within sight and almost within sound of the conference church. Roberts spoke on one occasion, and night after night holiness sympathizers, both clergy and laymen, streamed into the tent from the hinterlands. Notwithstanding Hosmer's opinion that the revival was intended as an olive branch and Purdy's affirmation that his exhortation would relax tensions, it was quite apparent that the holiness party wanted to embarrass the bishop and run competition with the conference. Bishop Simpson revealed his discomfiture in a letter to his wife: "Women have come by troops—one crowd by a canalboat, others

[123] Quoted in *Ibid.,* pp. 198-202.
[124] *Why Another Sect?* p. 202.

from Utica, and some . . . from St. Louis. They are in attendance in the galleries, and some have their knitting busily employed. They are all Nazarites, and use . . . many epithets denunciatory of the Conference." [125] "These Nazarites are like Canada thistles," was the acrid remark of one Genesee pastor; "you cut one down and ten will spring up in its place." [126]

The episcopal power, nevertheless, was sufficiently strong to defeat the challengers. Conference resolutions rebuked misguided brethren who fraternized with and opened their pulpits to "expelled ministers," stating that such behavior was "subversive of the integrity and government of the Church" and productive of "discord and division and every evil work." Simpson reminded his shepherds of their pledge upon being admitted to the conference, that they would not be governed by their own will but "act in all things like a son of the Gospel." [127] The bishop, "as much a believer in discipline as in holiness," was successful in drying up the participation of clergy from other conferences in Purdy's extravaganza, and the session ended with four dismissals—Loren Stiles, Jr., John A. Wells, William Cooley, Charles D. Burlingham—and several "voluntary" locations. Simpson, nevertheless, had a parting shot for the victorious Regency. "Hearty prayers and responses," he affirmed, and "praising God aloud" were "the privilege of his children" and fully in keeping with the spirit of Methodism. [128]

John Robie of the *Buffalo Advocate* was gratified that since the holiness "crazy men [would] not be orderly" and "having coveted martyrdom" they were given their desires. [129] William Hosmer of *The Northern Independent* deplored the expulsions as great "ecclesiastical blunders" and protested that the charge of "contumacy is often a virtue." He was particularly incensed that a conference resolution, in an attempt to suppress Nazarite propaganda, disapproved of any member acting as agent for, writing for, or giving encouragement and support to the *Independent*.

The Conflict Becomes Church Wide

The Second Laymen's Convention, which met in Albion on November 1-2, 1859, also struck back at the "contumacy" charge, stating that there was not "an honest man in the Conference but may be expelled [if]

---

[125] Quoted in Marston, *A Living Witness,* p. 218.

[126] Roberts, *Why Another Sect?* p. 263.

[127] Conable, *History of the Genesee Conference,* p. 652.

[128] Timothy L. Smith, *Revivalism and Social Reform in Mid-Nineteenth-Century America* (Nashville: Abingdon Press, 1957) , p. 130.

[129] Quoted in Marston, *A Living Witness,* p. 217.

. . . a majority can be obtained. . . . Let some mandate be issued that cannot in conscience be obeyed, and the guilt of contumacy is incurred." It found evidence neither in Bible nor *Discipline* that "contumacy" was a crime, but suspected it to be an excuse *"to prevent the work of holiness from spreading among us—to put down the life and power of godliness in our churches, and to inaugurate in its stead the peaceable reign of a cold and heartless formalism."* [130] It strengthened the administrative spadework of the First Convention and provided for the organization of "Bands" and the financial support of deposed clergymen. By early 1860 "Salvation Bands" began springing up in Syracuse, Rochester, and Albion, with Roberts establishing two "Free" Methodist churches in Buffalo. A Third Laymen's Convention at Olean on February 1-2 attempted to exert pressure for reform upon the coming General Conference by presenting a 1,500-member petition for a review of the judicial actions of the Genesee Conference in expelling the six Nazarite ministers. It asked that slaveholders be denied membership, commended Roberts for inaugurating the publication of the holiness journal *The Earnest Christian,* and established executive councils for the seven districts to supervise camp meetings and general quarterly meetings and exercise oversight of the new movement. Surprisingly enough, although reiterating "unfaltering attachment to the M. E. Church" and exhorting "brethren everywhere not to secede," the convention looked with favor on the "prosperity" of Loren Stiles's "Free" Methodist Church at Albion.

Meanwhile, John Wesley Redfield, medical doctor and holiness local preacher, by itinerating on the St. Louis-Chicago "axis" during the late 1850's, had provoked considerable opposition from "superficial, false, and fashionable professors of religion." Roberts had first met Redfield when the latter ignited a revival during his student days at Wesleyan. In 1852 he had hoped that the phenomenon could be duplicated at his Niagara Street Church in Buffalo to pull it out of the spiritual doldrums, but Redfield's only effect was increased factionalism, and he had to leave without having his expenses paid. As early as 1856 the free-wheeling itinerant was sowing the tares of enthusiasm in the field of Illinois and Missouri Wesleyanism and had blessed Elgin, Marengo, Woodstock, and St. Charles with his ministrations. Redfield was convinced that holiness reform meant schism. "As God lives," he stated, "there is no rational hope but separation, . . . for you cannot then keep out the spirit of carnal warfare, and that will be the death to spirituality." [131]

Opposition to his "spiritual quickening" arose within the Rock River

---

[130] Quoted in Hogue, *History,* I, 249-50.
[131] Quoted in Marston, *A Living Witness,* p. 227.

Conference in 1858 and 1859, with some laymen ostensibly being "read out of the church" for attending his revivals. In early 1859 he was pastoring a flock of 150 souls that had separated with his blessing from the Ebenezer Methodist Church in St. Louis. In March of that year, Benjamin T. Roberts was called in and an independent "Free Methodist Church" was organized. It was Redfield's plan to structure the "fruits of revivals" into "organized but independent and self-directing societies," so as to exert pressure on the General Conference toward "reform and reconciliation." [132] Thus, whether *de jure* or *de facto*, a new sect had come into being in the West. In spite of the fact that Redfield lacked organizational ability in comparison to Roberts, that he was a local instead of a conference preacher, and that there had been less "persecution" in the West than in the East, only ecclesiastical formalities and connectional ties were needed after the General Conference was over.

By the eve of the General Conference the Redfieldites were committed both in action and sentiment to separation. "You think there is hope of restoration to the church," wrote Mrs. Kendall, who was privy to Redfield, to Mrs. Roberts on May 19, 1860. "I wish I could say I believe it would be so . . . [but] it is God's will to raise up another people whose God is the Lord." [133]

By the time of the General Conference in May, 1860, the controversy had left too much hurt in its wake for the Regency lion and the Nazarite lamb to continue to bed down in the same Wesleyan stall. Moreover, with the nation on the brink of the Civil War other issues were of crucial importance. A primary concern was to keep the border conferences in Kentucky, Maryland, West Virginia, and Missouri within the church, thus helping to forestall the secession of those states from the Union. "Sustaining an appeal from abolitionists, even sanctified ones, would hardly serve this purpose." [134] Nevertheless, a committee of forty-seven members, one from each conference delegation, was appointed to investigate the judicial procedures that lay behind the nature of the Genesee trouble. Several days later, when the committee petitioned for additional conference records, the Regency was adamant in its resistance. James M. Fuller protested his conference "would not submit . . . to any Star-chamber investigations," and that such an action would transcend the constitutional powers of the General Conference. With the petition tabled by the narrow margin of ninety-seven to eighty-four, one of the Buffalo group asked that the special committee be discharged and its papers transferred to appropriate standing committees, stating that in "politics

[132] *Ibid.*, pp. 231-32.
[133] *Ibid.*, p. 240.
[134] Smith, *Revivalism and Social Reform*, p. 131.

he was a State's Rights man, and in religious matters a Conference Rights man!" Immediately a Baltimore delegate, "in a violent speech, of the plantation style," led off a wave of supporting speeches.[135] The vote was ordered without further debate, and the committee was dismissed by a vote of 104 to 81. "Herod and Pilate became friends," wrote Roberts, to whom the procedure was but a brazen example of ecclesiastical logrolling. "Baltimore helped Genesee to dispose of the 'Nazarites'; and Genesee helped Baltimore to substitute for the *rule* against slaveholding." [136]

Roberts' appeal from the sentence of reproof in 1857 resulted in a nineteen to nineteen tie, thus allowing the verdict of the Genesee Conference to stand. The General Conference Committee on Appeals also declined to review his petition against expulsion in 1858 since he "tacitly confessed the justice" of the verdict by becoming a probationer, continued to preach after being relieved of ministerial authorization, and had "connected himself with another organization, contemplating Church ends independent of and hostile to the Church to whose General Conference he now appeals." [137] The cardinal sin of Methodism was disobedience to discipline, and when it supported schism, it was especially despicable. If innocent of such offenses in 1858, by the time of the General Conference Roberts and the other expelled Nazarites were most assuredly guilty. Nevertheless, Roberts maintained the decision of the Committee on Appeals was "one of the unsolved mysteries," although even the sympathetic *Northern Independent* admitted, as do Free Methodists today, that he had prejudiced his case by his free-lance itinerating.[138]

The Bishops' Address foreshadowing this action was surprisingly restrained. Affirming that a "remarkably harmonious . . . doctrinal unity still prevails among us," they nevertheless noted that a few brethren presented Christian perfection "in the terms and forms of expression used" somewhat contrary to "our standard authors." They continued:

These individuals claim to be strictly Wesleyan in their views of the doctrine, and probably are so substantially. Nor do we impugn their motives. But in our judgment, in denouncing those in the ministry and laity who do not sympathize with them and adopt their measures, . . . by employing and encouraging erratic and irresponsible persons to conduct religious services, they have erred, and unhappily agitated some of our societies, and in a few instances caused secessions.

[135] Hogue, *History,* I, 296.
[136] *Why Another Sect?* p. 300.
[137] *Journal of the General Conference,* 1860, p. 253.
[138] See Marston, *A Living Witness,* pp. 205-6, 243.

It is our opinion there was no occasion for these specialties. Our ministers are *generally Wesleyan in their faith and preaching touching this subject.*[139]

Organization of the Free Methodist Church

In less than three weeks after Roberts lost his appeal, a group of Genesee Nazarites met to cement the final bricks in the Free Methodist edifice. They invited Regency-persecuted Wesleyans to form "Free Methodist Societies," recognized as valid the ordination of expelled clergy, and appointed a committee to prepare a code of General Rules and Regulations so that "primitive Methodism be restored and secured." [140] On August 23, 1860, at Pekin, New York, a delegated convention of fifteen ministers and forty-five laymen reluctantly consented under heavy pressure from the Redfieldites to formal organization. In actuality, goaded on by Redfield, a Western Laymen's Convention of twenty-one members, meeting at St. Charles, Illinois, on July 1, 1860, had already created a new denomination. The convention transacted business as if it were an Annual Conference and appointed Redfield as superintendent over the Western work. Many noteworthy Easterners, however, among them S. K. J. Chesbrough, felt the new Zion to be premature; that Bands were sufficient until a "great swarm from the M. E. Church" could be persuaded to join. McCreery felt that "many of the sheep of the Methodist fold had been so starved by the Regency preachers that they were unable to jump the fence, and he wished to remain in a position where he could salt them through the rails." [141]

The impatient Redfield, however, would brook no delay: "Brethren, when fruit is ripe, it had better be picked, lest on falling it bruise. In the West we are ready for an organization. . . . If you are not ready, wait until you are." [142] Anticipating an East-West split among the perfectionists if he hesitated, Roberts grudgingly consented to organization, and was named a "general superintendent." A minority of five ministers and two laymen abstained, and in forming their own Nazarite Bands promptly "went to seed" in an orgy of fanaticism that shocked even the Free Methodist perfectionists.

The Pekin sect chose the name, "The Free Methodist Church," to testify that the new church was delivered from secret societies, slavery,

---

[139] *Journal of the General Conference,* 1860, p. 317. Italics mine.
[140] Quoted in Marston, *A Living Witness,* p. 249.
[141] Quoted in Hogue, *History,* I, 321-22.
[142] *Ibid.*

rented pews, outward ornaments of pride, and was at liberty to have "the freedom of the Spirit" in its worship. The twenty-five Articles of Religion were reduced to twenty-three through four deletions and two additions: "Of Purgatory," "Of Both Kinds," "Of the Marriage of Ministers," "Of the Rulers of the United States of America," and all but the first paragraph on "Of the Sacraments" were omitted, for although acceptable theologically, they were no longer thought necessary. Added were statements on "Entire Sanctification" and "Future Rewards and Punishments," constructed from the writings of Wesley.

The article on sanctification read:

Justified persons, while they do not outwardly commit sin, are nevertheless conscious of sin still remaining in the heart. They feel a natural tendency to evil, a proneness to depart from God and cleave to the things of earth. Those who are sanctified wholly are saved from all inward sin—from evil thoughts and evil tempers. No wrong temper, none contrary to love, remains in the soul. All their thoughts, words, and actions are governed by pure love. Entire sanctification takes place subsequently to justification, and is the work of God wrought instantaneously upon the consecrated, believing soul. After a soul is cleansed from all sin, it is then fully prepared to grow in grace.

That this was the crucial doctrine is evident, for when Stiles held the article allowed a "gradualistic interpretation," he was silenced by Redfield's rebuttal: "Brethren, I would not make a threat, but unless we go straight on the question of holiness . . . we had better halt where we are. The gradualistic theory is what has made so much mischief." [143]

Unquestionably the one-sided interpretation of sanctification in terms of the instantaneous rather than the gradual had its origin in frontier attitudes, revivalistic promotion, and sectarian rivalry. Instantaneous perfection, albeit but one facet of Wesley's theology, was overemphasized and separated from the long-term nurture, guidance, and "growth in grace" which both preceded and followed "perfection in love." The sacramental setting that Wesley presupposed was replaced by the frenzy of the camp meeting. And although Wesley was fairly tolerant of method, the Free Methodists, as part of the holiness movement,

maintained a strict and unvarying methodology. And opponents of the method were apt to be considered opponents of the doctrine. Wesley had encouraged testimony only when the time, place, and motive were propitious. In the later emphasis testimony was pronounced a duty, to be given however adverse the reaction. . . . It was now being presented as almost wholly comprehended in

[143] Quoted in Marston, *A Living Witness*, pp. 258-59.

the specific experience, any prior or subsequent nurture being merely incidental—sometimes irrelevant.[144]

Because of their experience with "ecclesiastical tyranny" the Free Methodists developed a modified episcopacy without adopting local autonomy. Laymen were given equal representation with clergy on all boards and conferences. Evidently thinking a change in nomenclature would somehow restrict the power of the office, the more proletarian and less fearsome designation, "general superintendent," replaced the magisterial appellation "bishop." Elected for a term of four years with unlimited re-election possible, holders of the office won back their episcopal birthright and were officially called "bishops" as a result of General Conference action in 1907. District superintendents, who might also pastor a charge, were elected by the Annual Conference, and class leaders by the congregation.

Rules for church membership were tightened up. Six months of probationary status was granted only upon testifying to a "desire to flee from the wrath to come," having an "assurance of sins forgiven," and consenting to the "general rules." Evidence from the witness of the Spirit that one was a child of God and possession of a "perfect love which casteth out fear" were part of a seven-point covenant necessary for full membership.[145] Worship services were simple, with an emphasis upon prayer, testimony, hymn singing, scripture reading, and exhortation. Choirs and musical instruments were forbidden. This proscription troubled Free Methodism for decades, and finally in 1955 the church broke the long-guarded tradition and allowed musical exercises if the participants sought no "display of talent, however excellent."

The new church grew progressively, if slowly, and by 1878 had 313 ministers and 10,682 members. On the other hand, the Genesee Conference, with 10,999 members in 1859, was hurt by the separation, and although some loss can be attributed to the effect of the Civil War, it was not until 1878 that the conference membership rose above the 1859 figure.

The "official" historians of each side—Conable and Hogue and, to a lesser extent, Roberts—reveal an understandable partisanship and prejudice. The passage of time, however, drew mother and child some-

---

[144] John L. Peters, *Christian Perfection and American Methodism* (Nashville: Abingdon Press, 1956), p. 190.

[145] The *Discipline* first adopted contained this provision: "Question 4: Will you forever lay aside all superfluous ornaments, and adorn yourself in modest apparel, with shamefacedness and sobriety, not with broidered hair, or gold, or pearls, or costly array, but, which becometh those professing godliness, with good works?" (Quoted in Hogue, *History*, I, 330. This is not in the present *Discipline* of the Free Methodist Church.)

what closer together. During the celebration of its centennial in 1910, in a remarkable confession of institutional sin, the Genesee Conference returned the parchments of Benjamin T. Roberts to his son, the Rev. Benson H. Roberts. In a fraternal address the latter justified the position his father had taken, and asked "in the name of Christian courtesy" that "expelled" be replaced with "for violation of ecclesiastical censure" after the names of the banished Nazarites in the conference obituary column.

Roberts' later writings on holiness were neither fanatical nor un-Wesleyan, and his administration moderated the spirit of antinominanism and insubordination that was characteristic of some early Free Methodists. He maintained the distinction between justification, wherein power is received to live without committing sin, and entire sanctification, where the inner impulses to sin are purged away. The latter state was more than a change in relationship with God; it came not through self-discipline, but was a work of grace through the Holy Spirit changing the core of man's being. The eradication of a "carnal mind," however, did not make a man less human, destroy free will or the possibility of backsliding. "If one is sanctified wholly his mind, his will, is so changed that earthly things lose their attraction. . . . But their minds are not destroyed . . . as to do away with the freedom of the will." [146]

Both Methodist Episcopal and Free Methodist partisans shared the guilt for the rupture. If the majority of the Genesee Conference had been more sympathetic to perfectionism and had attempted to guide and structure the holiness movement, purging it from coarse and fanatic elements, the conference may have remained at peace. If the urban pastors had been less interested in developing a Gilded Age constituency and had provided a sacramental setting for the many sincere souls seeking the holiness experience, the rural ministers may not have been so one-sided in its advocacy. Until schism threatened, some of Methodism's most prominent bishops, ministers, educators, and professional people were numbered among the advocates of holiness. All saw in the revival of this aspect of Wesleyan doctrine the antidote to a threatening "modernism" and a worldly-minded church. Benjamin T. Roberts, moreover, was not an irresponsible schismatic. A man of high intelligence, great literary ability, and a warm heart, he remained calm and unvituperative amid provocation. He declined establishing a denominational paper after the break by affirming it would but add to controversy through a rehearsal of old wrongs.

For their part, the Nazarites did not recognize the economic, personal,

[146] *Holiness Teachings Compiled from the Editorial Writings of the Late Rev. Benjamin T. Roberts* (North Chili: N. Y.: The Earnest Christian Publishing House, 1893) , p. 242.

and sociological factors in the rupture. The conflict over holiness would not have divided the conference without the "struggle for place and power in which platforms of moral reform in church and state played a major part." The plea for the restoration of "primitive Methodism" and a place for "second blessing" were emotional symbols as well as vital issues in the contest. Moreover, the sharp urban-rural cleavage may have developed in part from the fact that the doctrine of second blessing was most frequently held by those whose material blessings were meager. That the Oneida and East Genesee Conferences underwent holiness revivals during the Regency-Nazarite fracas without unfortunate results seems to underscore the importance of the nontheological factors in the schism.[147]

If the fault of the Regency was acquiescence to spiritual mediocrity, the failing of too many Nazarites was pharisaism. Their "Christ against culture" position, structured from an ultraindividualistic Puritanism, prevented a sympathetic understanding of the evolution in thought, custom, and circumstance within the church and society during the nineteenth century. They emphasized the "accidental as well as essential peculiarities" with which Methodism was born.[148] In their eyes the church was not a hospital for worldly sinners but a pietistic-oriented rest home for holy men whose proof of sainthood was an adherence to a set of stringent and sacrosanct regulations. Ribbons and bows, brooches and "broidered hair," hat feathers and rings, were clear evidences of personal worldliness. Concerned with the "outside of the cup," many failed to see that a concern for plainness of dress could be a cloak for pride, just as perfunctory shouting and weeping could cover a paucity of piety.

Some of the Nazarite advocates of holiness were its poorest recommendation. Among the many earnest seekers after perfect love, a few zealots "mistook censoriousness for sanctity, denunciation for devotion, and high profession for holy practice." [149] For example, McCreery never found an ecclesiastical home to his liking, while Stiles, after being expelled in 1859, encamped for thirty days in his former charge and evacuated the premises only after the trustees threatened legal action. Driven by their detractors, many Nazarites ultimately became guilty of the charges made against them.

While one sector of the church was intent upon a revival of the traditional emphasis, another sector was restive under that tradition. It welcomed instead

[147] Smith, *Revivalism and Social Reform*, pp. 132-33.
[148] Conable, *History of the Genesee Conference*, p. 629.
[149] Peters, *Christian Perfection*, p. 191.

the sweep of nineteenth-century theological optimism. Between a confident humanitarian morality and a traditional piety which appeared unconcerned with the society of which it was a part, the sympathies of . . . the church were with the former. Thus two groups with antithetical points of view were mutually repelled by the extremes each saw in the other. The result in some instances was the rise of "come-outism" and "crush-outism." Reaction provoked reaction, and extreme begot extreme.[150]

3

The Era of Reconstruction: the Freedmen's Aid Society

Awake, awake, put on thy strength,
Thy beautiful array;
The day of freedom dawns at length,
The Lord's appointed day.

Rebuild thy walls, thy bounds enlarge,
And send thy heralds forth;
Say to the South, "Give up thy charge!"
And, "Keep not back, O North!"[151]

In the Grant-Sherman juggernaut that slowly crushed the life out of the Confederacy in the early days of 1865, Northern Methodism saw Providence opening up a field of missionary endeavor unparalleled in human history. The most populous, prosperous, and energetic Protestant church in America saw in Appomattox, the Second Inaugural, and the parallel of the Good Samaritan sufficient sign and justification that it must move south and possess the land. Portrayed as a realm where "mulattos swarmed like locusts, pride, luxury and idleness were general, all the commands of the Decalogue trampled" and where "tyranny and lust reigned," the "God-smitten" South desperately needed the ministrations of Methodist mercy.[152] Clearly the Northern Church had to do what Grant, Lincoln, and the Grand Army of the Republic could not do —make a more perfect Union by lifting the South spiritually, educationally, and morally.

Nevertheless, the Southern invasion by Northern Methodism revealed a strange amalgam of altruistic and sectarian motivation. While the hu-

[150] Ibid., p. 192.
[151] Hymnal of the Methodist Episcopal Church, 1878 edition, No. 909.
[152] Quoted in Morrow, Northern Methodism and Reconstruction, p. 19.

manitarian viewed the South as a fertile field upon which to make amends to a race sorely persecuted, clerics possessing the "wisdom of the serpent" saw the ex-Confederacy with her four million freedmen as "black unto harvest" for Methodism. The voice of the former pleaded: "There are two Africas. One is beyond the seas, the other is at our doors. One is thousands of miles away. The other lies bruised and bleeding under our feet." [153] Thousands rose to the challenge as did one lady who, in teaching in Maryland in 1865, responded: "I am glad that I have a part, however humble in the noble work now before our nation, of recompensing for the oppression and injustice of the past." [154]

For those still embittered by the schism of 1844, however, the defeat of the Confederacy was sufficient proof that the Southern Church had proved a poor steward to the sons of Ham and had forfeited all rights to a continued spiritual monopoly below the Mason-Dixon line. With the war still in progress during the General Conference of 1864, the Episcopal Address announced that the nineteen years of "wrongful exclusion" were over and the "days of exclusive occupancy" at an end. "The wall of partition is broken down by that very power whose dreadful ministry was invoked to strengthen it. . . . [The Northern Church] ought never to have been excluded from any portion of the territory of the United States; she ought never to have consented, on any ground, to such exclusion." [155] The national interest and that of Northern Methodism neatly coincided: "The flag of the republic and the flag of Methodism must go forward over the revolted territory side by side." [156]

Yet, during the war years the church was not of a single mind as to what its ideology and practice concerning the Southern Negro should be. John Reid, editor of the *Western Christian Advocate,* surmised that Northern Methodism without Negroes would be "free from . . . perplexing questions," [157] while others advocated their cultivation by African Methodist Churches. A few felt that a modification of the Pauline dictum—to the white first, and then to the black—should guide basic strategy. Hence, John Newman, in charge of Methodist work around New Orleans in early 1864, finished his inaugural sermon with the charge "that if the Caucasian should reject the gospel and refuse to fill the churches . . . we turn to the sons of Africa." [158] Almost universally Northern educators and evangelists were shocked by the "unrepentant spirit" of Southern Methodists and hurt because "old Mother Church" was not

[153] *Ninth Annual Report of the Freedmen's Aid Society,* p. 30.
[154] *Zion's Herald,* January 17, 1865.
[155] *Journal of the General Conference,* 1864, pp. 278-79.
[156] New York *Christian Advocate,* March 16, 1865, p. 84.
[157] *Western Christian Advocate,* July 12, 1865, p. 220.
[158] Morrow, *Northern Methodism and Reconstruction,* p. 125.

welcomed after her long exile. Their negrophile sentiment increased thereby and gradually flooded into more effective channels. As one Methodist woman put it, "It is not only the African who needs uplifting but it is the African alone that can be reached." [159] Four fifths of all Methodist expenditures in the South during Reconstruction went to evangelize and educate the freedman.

The church began aiding the emancipated Negro more than two years before Appomattox. Not only did most of its editors ceaselessly petition the government to establish a Freedmen's Bureau, but a resolution of the General Conference of 1864 stated that "the best interests of the freedmen and of the country demand legislation that shall . . . protect this people." [160] This concern found its outlet in the federal Freedmen's Bureau and in the dozens of nonsectarian freedmen's commissions and relief associations spawned during the war years. General Clinton B. Fisk, a prominent layman, oversaw the Bureau's affairs in Tennessee and Kentucky, while Northern Methodist clergymen at different times held state superintendencies of education in Alabama, Florida, Tennessee, and Virginia. Although such ecumenical endeavor was supported by Methodist time and treasure, and although Bishop Simpson was president of the American Freedmen's Union Commission in 1866, a "complex of motives" created the Methodist Freedmen's Aid Society in the late summer of that year.

Unquestionably the primary factor in causing denominational atomization of freedmen endeavor was an ideological rift over the educational philosphy of the Freedmen's Union Commission. Most evangelical denominations, Methodists included, desired religious beliefs and values taught in conjunction with the three R's. The Unitarians, on the contrary, were horrified that both educational and religious needs were served by the same organization and wanted to draw the line between "teacher and missionary, civilizer and evangelizer." In July, 1866, O. B. Frothingham, the spokesman of New England Unitarianism, likened the "sectarians" to "Romanists," and demanded that teachers sent to the South have nothing to do with "churches, creeds or sacraments" because "ceremonial religion" caused mental instruction to be "warped." [161] Within a month after the assault, Bishop Simpson began to retire from participation in the Freedmen's Union Commission and the Northern Church had given birth to its own Freedmen's Aid Society.

The organizing convention, composed of eleven clergy and laymen, met at Trinity Methodist Church in Cincinnati on August 7-8, 1866.

[159] *Ibid.*, p. 127.
[160] *Journal of the General Conference*, 1864, p. 442.
[161] Cited by Morrow, *Northern Methodism and Reconstruction*, pp. 156-57.

Members of the Convention were: Bishop D. W. Clark; the Revs. Adam Poe, J. M. Reid, R. S. Rust, J. M. Walden, J. R. Stillwell, Luke Hitchcock, B. F. Crary, Robert Allyn; Mr. J. F. Larkin, and the Hon. Grant Goodrich. Seven of these had in the past espoused abolitionist sentiment and were still suspicious of the conservatives in the Missionary Society, especially its secretary, John P. Durbin, who was reputed to be indifferent if not hostile to the evangelization of the Negro. Significantly, no invitations were extended to executives of the Missionary Society, ostensibly because of a lack of time "to call in . . . our brethren from the East"; but the excuse seemed weak to the *Central Advocate,* inasmuch as rumors about the formation of the new society had been abroad for a year.[162]

The founders made a strong case for a distinctively Methodist freedmen's society. The ecumenical tent had by then, they pointed out, all but collapsed with the Friends, Baptists, United Brethren, Congregationalists, United Presbyterians, and Episcopalians supporting their own educational programs in the South and increasingly turning a deaf ear to the financial pleas of the Freedmen's Union Commission agents. They estimated that the Northern Church was contributing half of all the funds expended by the commission—a small fraction of which, if diverted to "languishing" Methodist mission schools, would pump new life into them. A letter from General Fisk strengthened their case, while an epistle of Walter S. Carter protested, "It was a mistake that the Methodists ever united at all with any outside agency. From the start . . . Methodist hands should have handled Methodist funds . . . to pay Methodist teachers, to found Methodist schools." [163] The constitution stated that the purpose of the society "shall be to labor for the relief and education of the Freedmen." Bishop Davis W. Clark was elected president; Clinton B. Fisk, Grant Goodrich, and I. W. Wiley, vice-presidents; Adam Poe, treasurer; and R. S. Rust, general field superintendent.

The new benevolent venture evoked strong editorial support. In place of teachers selected "indiscriminately from various sects, or with no religion whatsoever," [164] Methodism could now actualize the educational dictum of her founder and thus unify "sound learning with vital piety." Literary education and spiritual redemption would be the double fare for the downtrodden race. And while a few lamented the pell-mell exodus southward for the souls and minds of four million Negroes, Methodists in general were satisfied that they had gone the second mile in freedmen ecumenical endeavor and that the Southern field was wide

---

[162] *Central Advocate,* August 15, 1866.
[163] *First Annual Report of the Freedmen's Aid Society,* p. 11.
[164] *Zion's Herald,* September 5, 1866.

enough so that there "need be no unhealthy rivalry." [165] The society moved swiftly; at the end of the first year it had hired fifty-two teachers, established fifty-nine schools enrolling five thousand students, and spent $60,000.[166]

Experiments in Education

How the Freedmen's Aid Society could best utilize its talent and treasure came as a result of the experience of its earliest years. Initially it focused almost entirely upon primary education, and the schools, with their wide teacher-student ratio, were more noteworthy for quantity than quality. Primary schools declined from a high of sixty in 1868 as a shift towards qualitative improvement and quantitative retrenchment gradually evolved. Richard Rust, who did yeoman service as secretary for the society for over three decades, recalled in 1878 that, "Our work commenced with primary study and . . . gradually advanced with the progress of the pupils, until we . . . reached the higher branches." [167]

The reasons for the gradual move toward higher education were compelling. With limited financial and personnel resources, the society realized that the normal school or teacher-training institution was the most effective means of combatting Negro ignorance. The freedman was reminded that in the advancement of any race "help must come from its own ranks." [168] The strategy evolved was known as "seed-sowing," with the hope that Methodist-trained Negro educators would be broadcast throughout the South to lift up their own race.[169] The shift away from primary education was also hastened by the promises and practices of Republican-dominated state legislatures with regard to Negro public instruction. Finally, the decision in 1870 by the Freedmen's Bureau to discontinue subsidies to charitable institutions sharply curtailed the work.

In 1866 Congress directed the bureau's commissioner, General O. O. Howard, to pay the travel vouchers of teachers to the field and to work with private benevolent associations, and appropriated half a million dollars for construction, rental, and repairs of school buildings. The society was not lacking in gratitude, for their Annual Report of 1869

[165] New York *Christian Advocate*, December 27, 1866, p. 412.
[166] *Second Annual Report*, pp. 10, 12.
[167] *Eleventh Annual Report*, p. 22.
[168] *Fourth Annual Report*, p. 7.
[169] See S. G. Arnold, "Education Among the Freedmen," *The Methodist Quarterly Review*, January, 1878, p. 55.

thanked Howard for "liberal appropriations" without which "emancipation would have been but a doubtful boon." [170] Two years later it expressed "deep regret that no additional appropriations can be expected from the Government" and moved to "retrench its operations." [171] However, the elimination of subsidies and the final demise of the national bureau in 1872 was due more to sectarian bickering over federal handouts than to any theoretical query about violation of the separation of church and state. Discontented Methodists, seldom forgetting that Commissioner Howard and John W. Alford, chief of the bureau's educational division, were Congregationalists, sulked over their thin slice of the federal financial pie. Bishop Ames told Howard that Methodism was "not treated fairly" and that its "agents were repulsed with . . . coolness" by the bureau.[172]

Bookkeeping intricacies frustrate any attempt to know how much Methodist schools lost with the cessation of federal funds, although the entire operation was severely restricted for some time after 1870. During that year the society maintained 58 schools of various levels and employed 110 teachers, whereas one year later the totals were 35 and 75 respectively. The church did not easily accept the suspension of federal grants. As late as 1875 the society affirmed that "the Government should have continued its aid," [173] and its report to the General Conference of 1876 petitioned for "liberal support from the Church and Government." [174]

With hope of federal support evaporating and primary instruction both unprofitable and increasingly taken over by the states, Methodism moved vigorously into higher education. By 1882 the society had founded twenty-five institutions variously labeled as universities, colleges, institutions, seminaries, normal schools, and academies. With the exception of Virginia, every state in the old Confederacy was represented. Chartered institutions were: Central Tennessee College, Nashville; Clark University, Atlanta; Claflin University, Orangeburg, South Carolina; New Orleans University; Rust University, Holly Springs, Mississippi; Wiley

[170] Federal money was granted for remodeling and construction of church educational structures only if the benevolent association guaranteed the building would always be used for educational purposes and that no student would ever be excluded because of race. The Freedmen's Bureau allowed the churches to retain title because it had legal authority to pay rent but not teachers' salaries. In some instances the Bureau erected a building on church-owned land and then asked the church to bill it ten dollars a month for each teacher employed. See George R. Bentley, *A History of the Freedmen's Bureau* (Philadelphia: University of Pennsylvania Press, 1955), pp. 172-73.

[171] *Fourth Annual Report*, p. 14.

[172] Cited by Morrow, *Northern Methodism and Reconstruction*, p. 164.

[173] *Eighth Annual Report*, p. 5.

[174] *Journal of the General Conference*, 1876, p. 624.

University, Marshall, Texas; Centenary Biblical Institute, Baltimore; Gammon Theological Seminary, Atlanta; Baker Institute, Orangeburg; Thomson Biblical Institute, New Orleans; Meharry Medical College, Nashville. Institutions not chartered were: Bennett Seminary, Greensboro, North Carolina; Cookman Institute, Jacksonville; Dadeville Seminary, Dadeville, Alabama; Haven Normal School, Waynesboro, Georgia; Huntsville Normal School, Huntsville, Alabama; Houston Seminary; La Grange Seminary, La Grange, Georgia; La Teche Seminary, La Teche, Louisiana; Meridian Academy, Meridian, Mississippi; Morristown Seminary, Morristown, Tennessee; Rome Normal School, Rome, Georgia; Walden Seminary, Little Rock; West Texas Conference Seminary, Austin; West Tennessee Seminary, Mason. Since a scant total of ninety-five pedagogues served the schools, it was evident that the label an institution wore revealed little concerning its academic fare. "The Methodists had the mischievous habit of magnifying the character of institutions by the magnificence of their titles." [175] An observer from New England, after surveying Central Tennessee College in 1874, remarked that it was a "school which . . . is no more like a university than an egg is like a full-sized rooster." [176] Even the best "colleges" and "universities" for many years were on a par with Northern academies or high schools. The titles were chosen, undoubtedly, with the fond hope of what the schools expected to be in the future.

Most freedmen institutions attempted to encompass the entire academic gamut. With adequate finances and persistent motivation, a student could progress from primary school through intermediate and college preparatory work to liberal arts and professional training at the same institution. The curriculum was patterned after Northern institutions. Clark University of Atlanta, one of the few schools able to sustain the cost of printing a catalog, offered the typical educational fare. In 1879 instruction in the "lower English branches" included reading, elocution, spelling, penmanship, composition, English grammar, arithmetic, and United States history. Students planning on college added Latin, Greek, and mathematics "from Algebra to Quadratics." The four-year liberal arts program included additional work in language together with "Natural, Moral and Political Science . . . and Metaphysics." Schools accomplished this academic wizardry with as few as three to five or—if they were fortunate—six to eight teachers, including the president.

Since the society accepted the theory that the Negro had to "lift himself," professional training emphasized teaching and the ministry. In

[175] Morrow, *Northern Methodism and Reconstruction*, p. 165.
[176] *Zion's Herald*, September 24, 1874.

order to keep church funds flowing south, each institution annually boasted how many teachers and preachers it had sent into the field. An analysis of the 2,490 students enrolled at 20 schools in 1880 reveals that 1,100 planned on teaching and almost 400 on preaching. The number would undoubtedly be higher except that 1,359 indicated no vocational designation. The fact that only slightly more than 100 were planning on law or medicine reveals the limited facilities in these areas.[177]

By the early 1870's, educators began to realize that the academic repast fit for the cultured New Englander was not necessarily digestible for their Negro charges. There was a loss of idealism over the intellectual capability of the Negro, with some teachers seeing them as "mere children" who needed to be taught how to keep house and work with their hands as much as to read and write. Moreover, many Negro teachers had difficulty finding employment in the slowly developing public school system, and even if they did, salaries were so parsimonious as to keep them almost destitute. Hence, with Booker T. Washington, it was felt that "the training of the mind shall not unfit them for the 'stern realities' of life." Not every Negro could be a minister, teacher, or doctor but he could achieve greater liberty and have time for intellectual affairs if he could "cut out a coat, shoe a horse, build a wagon, or erect a house." [178] In 1879 President Braden of Central Tennessee College asked that Negro women be taught how to sew, care for the sick, prepare food, and make their homes attractive.[179] "At length I clearly saw," said another educator after six years of experience, "that industrial education lay at the bottom . . . of the future prosperity of the blacks." [180] The antidote to Negro idleness, the raiding of watermelon patches, "invasion of smoke houses," "dram drinking," card playing, dancing, and running with "loose women" lay in channeling interest into "useful arts and agriculture."

Financial difficulties hindered the society in emphasizing that treasure was in the hand as well as in the head. It was far easier to buy an abandoned warehouse or church and put in a blackboard and a few chairs than it was to buy a farm or equip a carpentry or printing shop.[181] However, in 1872 the South Carolina Legislature located the State Agricultural College for Negroes at Claflin University and until 1896 made annual appropriations to the school. In 1884 the agricultural department made four hundred dollars above expenses and, together with the school

[177] Thirteenth Annual Report, p. 9.
[178] Sixteenth Annual Report, pp. 19, 16.
[179] Twelfth Annual Report, p. 14.
[180] Zion's Herald, September 24, 1874, p. 306.
[181] Morrow, Northern Methodism and Reconstruction, p. 167.

of carpentry and printing department, helped students work their way through school. Through the herculean efforts of Bishop Warren, Clark University in 1881 had erected four frame buildings for its schools of carpentry, agriculture, and domestic economy.

The freedmen possessed an overpowering passion for schooling. In education lay the key to status, success, and, more important, the elevation to full manhood. An army chaplain overheard his Negro servant, upon spelling out his lesson, address himself in rapture: "John Green, you have it. You can read. *John Green, you are a man!*" [182] There was a greater desire for instruction, however, among the young and in the urban centers than among the elderly and in the rural areas. "What's de use ob niggers pretendin' to larnin'?" mused one venerable fieldhand. "Wat'll dey be but niggers wen dey gits through?" [183] Some of the strongest opponents to enlightenment were unlettered Negro preachers. They were shrewd enough to realize that as their people became educated, their occupation was restricted, and it was hard to find a rebuttal to an elderly clergyman who would ask, "Did Christ ever go to college?" [184]

Hardships and Resentments

The freedmen went to school amid superhuman difficulties. Poverty was their constant companion and made school attendance highly irregular. Pretheological students at Central Tennessee College in 1875 could stay only "as long as their conscience, the voice of the Church, and their money would permit." [185] Many found it necessary to teach, preach, or do manual labor six to nine months a year. Even so, now and then a white employer would withhold wages because "none of his money should go to send a nigger to school." [186] Discouragement came easy to some who found that a trained intellect did not "grow osmotically," and they left with the parting shot, "I ain't learnin' nuffin' 'tall." [187] Of the total number of 240 theological students that Central Tennessee College had enrolled from its founding until 1879, only a few had been able to finish their academic program.

The society employed heroic means in an attempt to keep the freedman in pursuit of his sheepskin. Tuition ranged from ten cents to a dollar a month, with many of the destitute carried gratis. The names and

[182] Bentley, *History of the Freedmen's Bureau*, p. 170.
[183] Cited by Morrow, *Northern Methodism and Reconstruction*, p. 153.
[184] *Ibid.*, pp. 173-74.
[185] *Eighth Annual Report*, p. 16.
[186] *Seventh Annual Report*, p. 11.
[187] Morrow, *Northern Methodism and Reconstruction*, p. 174.

addresses of needy students were provided for patrons who could contribute as little as twenty-five to fifty dollars a year toward their education. In most cases ministerial students did not have to pay for tuition, room, or textbooks, while some boarding students were given permission to raise vegetables on small college-owned plots. Students arriving for the fall term "with their mulecart of provisions, meal, bacon, and cowpeas" [188] were no cause for surprise, since such items stocked their own larders.

For over a decade after the war Methodist weeklies were bombarded with Macedonian calls from the South for men and money to help school and student. One optimistic brother estimated that "fifty thousand dollars put into this place will affect the whole South for good for generations. . . . Where are the men who want to bless themselves?" [189] Another educator set his sights lower: "Hundreds of colored . . . with the aid of twenty-five dollars could attend school. . . . For Christ's sake, help!" [190] Every appeal and motive—Roman Catholicism's rapid advance, Negro superstition, white brutality, the poverty and ostracism of teachers, the Ku Klux Klan, the pride of endowing a chair or scholarship or building a school—were employed in an attempt to channel the residual passions of wartime into more humanitarian goals. The liberal *Zion's Herald* was so overwhelmed by appeals from "all quarters of the South" which if heeded "would drain our eyes and purses" that even sympathetic Gilbert Haven protested, "We cannot turn our columns completely into a begging lecture." [191]

Measured against any standard, Northern pedagogues faced almost insuperable odds during their Southern sojourn. They crossed the Mason-Dixon line with no little naïveté and great idealism, and it is amazing that many continued year after year at their posts. Frontier-like conditions faced the staff, two thirds of whom were women, and many found themselves teaching in warehouses, barns, under trees, and in "old shanties." One schoolmarm in Maryland during the late '60's related that she and her students were on "the most friendly relations with pigs that . . . are visible through the floor and . . . come up and dip their long noses in the school waterpail." Another instructor in Augusta, Georgia, found she was "obliged to give up sick" after the first day of school because the January "wind blew in all around and from beneath . . . the school." [192] As late as 1874 Clark University had only one dilapidated building with

[188] New York *Christian Advocate*, April 9, 1868, p. 114.
[189] *Zion's Herald*, April 9, 1874, p. 114.
[190] *Ibid.*, July 23, 1874, p. 234.
[191] December 19, 1867.
[192] *Ibid.*, March 14, 1866.

"no plaster, paper, nor ceiling," and "the light shines through its crevices." The president lamented that he could not keep it warm during the coldest weather and begged a Northern church to forego the luxury of a spire and send the money South. During the same year the principal of Haven Normal School deplored the fact that his school was housed in "one of the extremely uncomfortable churches which are so common in this country." [193]

With the expenditure of around $100,000 a year by the society, material improvements gradually came. Central Tennessee College is a good example of the physical evolution of freedmen institutions. Begun in a basement of a Negro church in Nashville in 1866, it later moved to an abandoned Confederate gun factory and by 1875 had four buildings "composed of brick" valued in excess of $70,000. Its administration boasted that one was *three* stories *high* and that together they housed music and recitation rooms, library, cabinet, dormitories, chapel, "society rooms," and a dining hall.[194]

The society staffed its schools through summer recruitment and relied upon the reservoir of learning in the North. Advertisements of vacancies and persuasive pleas for help constantly flowed northward. A hard-pressed brother of La Grange, Georgia, cried: "Whoever will now come forth . . . in spite of hard speeches, sour looks, repulsive acts, and social proscription" will do more for "truth and righteousness" than all the Southern churches put together.[195] As late as 1875 Bishop Haven found the supplication of self-denial a powerful motive in recruitment: "Here is a chance to serve Christ and your generation. . . . 'Count yourself the last and least.' Reckon yourself a 'nigger.' Accept the approbrium, that you may share the glory that shall follow." [196] On rare occasions when Northern idealism faltered, the secretary with reluctance filled out the complement of teachers with Southern converts. The number of teachers employed began with 52 the first year, rose to above 100 in 1868, reached a peak of 110 in 1870, and then dropped and stabilized near 75. Half of the teachers in Northern Methodist institutions, however, drew salaries from other sources, and many other Methodist educators were supported in other institutions through state aid and private subscription.

Salary contracts had a "pleasantly informal character" about them. Although the society took care of travel expenses, many teachers were warned that they could not expect more than fifteen dollars a month,

[193] *Eighth Annual Report*, pp. 31, 34.
[194] *Ibid.*, p. 15.
[195] John H. Caldwell, "Relations of the Colored People to the Methodist Episcopal Church, South," *The Methodist Quarterly Review*, July, 1866, p. 435.
[196] *Zion's Herald*, August 19, 1875, p. 257.

including board. Since salaries depended largely upon church solicitation, which frequently incurred deficits, periodic rumblings of discontent and of financial neglect were heard from the Southern hinterland. One teacher was compelled one winter to sell her prized organ to avoid starvation, yet modestly wrote the society to "afford me some aid this year, for I greatly need it." [197] On the other hand, an exasperated evangelist-teacher stationed in Georgia, after months of vain promises, mourned: "If I don't get help soon I shall consider that I am in the employ of nobody as nobody pays me anything." [198] A Louisiana instructor was paid in corn, potatoes, and peanuts, while others had to sell articles of clothing and furniture to keep from cold and hunger. The poverty of the teachers not only revealed the destitution of the South, but their pleas helped untie purse strings in the North.

Great as its accomplishments were, the Freedmen's Aid Society would have made a far greater contribution to Negro enlightenment had its schools not aroused Southern resentment and prejudice. Although a segment of the citizenry favored Negro education through the Reconstruction era, the vast majority detested the educational invasion and viewed it as simply a different form of hostility against their culture. Billy Yank with rifle and cannon had physically crushed the South; now foreign pedagogues, through lectern and radical ideology, would destroy her soul. Their interest, the Southerner was convinced, lay in stamping a made-in-the-North image of custom and character upon the Negroes. The animus of the ex-rebel focused not so much upon the schoolmarm as it did on the *Yankee* schoolmarm. He was convinced that the teachers' interest focused upon politics and sociology and that the three R's were prostituted to "Reading, Riting, and Republicanism." In Republicanism the Southerner saw everything he loathed—abolition, emancipation, Negro troops, military reconstruction, civil rights, social equality, Negro suffrage—and because the Methodist Episcopal Church was protected and furthered by the Republican carpetbag government, it shared the hatred of an embittered and defeated people. Whereas in the North it was the church of wealth, status, and influence, in the South both its clergy and laymen were treated as the "offscouring of all things."

The South believed, in spite of the wreckage of war, that it could solve its own educational problems. The platitudes of pure selflessness that heralded the advance of the legion of Northern educators fell on cynical ears. The Negro was but the innocent and unwitting pawn in the religious-political machinations of schemers who continued the post-Appomattox rape of the South. The general feeling was that "schooling

[197] *Seventh Annual Report*, pp. 11-12.
[198] *Zion's Herald*, February 22, 1872.

ruins a nigger." A white member of the Louisiana legislature, upon passing a Negro school shortly after the end of the war and seeing children playing, asked, "Is this a school?" "Yes," was the reply. "What, for niggers?" "Evidently." He threw up his hands. "Well, well," he said, "I have seen many an absurdity in my lifetime, but *this is the climax!*" 199 "Nigger teacher" thus became one of the most scurrilous epithets of the Southern vocabulary during Reconstruction.

The cross of social ostracism, then, was added to the Northern teacher's burden of misery wages, hard work, limited equipment, and constant privation. On the streets, in shops, and in church the Southerner allowed his animosity to shine forth. "We are shut out from all white society," sighed one teacher, "until it is really a treat to have a white child speak to us." 200 "My wife has not enjoyed the privilege of speaking with a white woman in over two years," grieved a pedagogue in Georgia. A transplanted New England schoolmarm reported a hostile reception from townsfolk in eastern Maryland: "Men bandied rude insulting jests at my expense, and coupled my name with curses, . . . and even from the children I heard . . . 'she's nothing but a damned nigger teacher.' " 201 "No man in Mississippi," pleaded a lonely one, "was ever more hated by the Rebels—and ninety-nine hundredths are Rebels—than myself." 202 Some found themselves treated as counterfeiters and horse thieves, and reported that unrepentant rebels would scurry into shops or cross the streets to avoid meeting them. Bishop Haven, in his travels through Texas in 1869, discovered that the recipient of Southern hospitality had to denounce the government and Negro and Freedmen agencies, but that the "greatest sin of all" was to join the Methodist Episcopal Church.203

Many educators, therefore, found it difficult to engage lodgings. "The Jews were to have no intercourse, no dealings with the Samaritans. . . . Southern ladies refused to take boarders into their houses from the North, no matter how worthy, intelligent, or refined they might be." 204 A certain Miss Barnes, who opened a school in an unfinished, dilapidated church in Gainesville, Florida, obtained board "with the greatest difficulty" at the exorbitant price of thirty dollars a month "from a hotelkeeper who feared her presence might drive his other customers away." 205 Some teachers were forced to stay with sympathetic Northerners and in

---

199 W. E. Burghardt Du Bois, *Black Reconstruction* (New York: Harcourt, Brace, & Co., 1935) , p. 637.
200 *Seventh Annual Report,* p. 13.
201 Cited by Morrow, *Northern Methodism and Reconstruction,* p. 237.
202 *Zion's Herald,* April 22, 1869, p. 188.
203 *Ibid.,* March 18, 1869.
204 N. E. Cobleigh, "Southern Reconstruction," *The Methodist Quarterly Review,* July, 1870, p. 385.
205 Cited by Bentley, *History of the Freedmen's Bureau,* p. 179.

the homes of their Negro pupils. Unquestionably, some took delight in tormenting prejudiced Southern sensitivity. Bishop Haven, the bête noire of the segregationists, employed twentieth-century freedom-rider and sit-in tactics during his travels. In 1873 in Mississippi he rode in a train car "reserved" for colored passengers and ate in a Negro hotel in Vicksburg. While dining with Negro guests in a white hotel in Jackson, his party was relegated to a corner and "screened off." When he moved his table to the middle of the dining hall, he was not served, and left for another establishment.[206]

Southern hostility was high against the persons and property of Northern Methodism. A flood of atrocity reports came out of the South in the late '60's. The "assassin's bullet and the incendiary's torch," as well as "clubs, stones, green apples, and rotten eggs," were the vehicles of hatred.[207] Because of war propaganda the church was psychologically prepared to accept such tales as the report that the forests from Charleston to Augusta "are fetid with the decaying bodies of colored men." [208] That the defeated white Southerner resorted to acts of violence cannot be doubted; that clerical propagandists were prone to exaggerate rumors without validating them, and sent doubtful tales northward to ready ears and editors in the interest of larger appropriations, is also not open to question.

Violence was greatest in the rural areas away from federal military posts. A school principal in 1874 wrote that he had stayed up many nights "guarding our buildings against fire" from bands of armed and masked men. "To be for weeks in constant expectation of being murdered or burned out, and without losing faith in God, is something of a strain on the nerves." [209] When his assassination misfired, one brother in Mississippi bewailed the fact that "ministers, lawyers, doctors and merchants united in an attempt to whitewash the matter." [210] Harassment and coercion were proportional to the effect desired. Anonymous dispatches informed some zealous educators that their services were no longer desired, and they were "invited" to leave the community within twenty-four hours.[211] A Georgia evangelist who ignored two prior ultimatums was curtly informed not to "prech her . . . enny more" because "the nixt warnen el be the led or the steal." [212] At Walhalla, South Carolina, some whites "hired a perennially drunken Negro to go to

[206] *Zion's Herald*, October 16, 1873, p. 330.
[207] Cited by Morrow, *Northern Methodism and Reconstruction*, p. 239.
[208] Washington *Chronicle*, July 11, 1865.
[209] *Seventh Annual Report*, p. 11.
[210] *Zion's Herald*, April 22, 1869, p. 188.
[211] *Seventh Annual Report*, p. 11.
[212] Morrow, *Northern Methodism and Reconstruction*, p. 238.

school" and constantly harass the teacher as she walked down the streets. One resourceful lady of Oxford, North Carolina, retaliated effectively, however, by purchasing a revolver, and "let herself be seen at target practice during her noon recesses." [213]

Exiled in an inhospitable land full of embittered people, Northerners reacted diversely to such treatment. Some accepted it as necessary cross-bearing in bringing enlightenment to a region of darkness and bigotry. Many learned from bitter experience not to engage in politics and thus lessened the cause for offense. For those who saw Providence in Appomattox, it was an enigma that the angelic had not replaced the beast in the Southern heart. As late as 1870 Cobleigh was astonished at Southern resistance to social, religious, and moral reconstruction. "They had not sinned, they had not done wrong, they had simply been unsuccessful. They had no pardon to ask, no confession to make; they were not ashamed of either their cause or their course." [214] Many felt that progress would be speeded up only by "Butler-like administration," President Johnson's impeachment, "drum-head court martials," hangings, and more federal troops. Others vented their frustration by sending back vignettes of the domestic helplessness of aristocratic but slaveless white ladies and their ludicrous attempts at cooking, sewing, and washing.

Particular Problems in the South

NEGRO MINISTERIAL TRAINING

One of the great challenges which the society faced was to upgrade the intellectual and moral requirements of the Negro Methodist minister. Only four of the first thirty colored clergymen enrolled by the church in South Carolina, Mississippi, and Texas could read "simple large print," and none could write. "In lieu of scholarly attainments the colored pastor relied on his natural repertoire of a strong diaphragm, graphic volubility, and uncomplicated faith." [215] One of the crosses consistently borne by the educators was the lack of appreciation of scholarship by the freedman parson. Many had known good work done by illiterate exhorters and felt that with "ignorance and strong lungs, success will crown their future efforts." Others were but "panderers to superstitious notions," whose preaching aimed at producing an emotionl excitement "often unhealthy to soul and body." The liturgical sensitivities of North-

---

[213] Bentley, *History of the Freedmen's Bureau*, p. 182.
[214] "Southern Reconstruction," p. 380.
[215] Morrow, *Northern Methodism and Reconstruction*, p. 146.

The North

1. The bishops of the Methodist Episcopal Church, 1848: seated, Morris, Hedding, Waugh; standing, Janes, Hamline. A daguerreotype taken at the 1848 General Conference (here reproduced from the *Ladies' Repository*, June, 1849). "The likenesses are said to be . . . about perfect, there being only a slight tinge of high-headedness about Bishop Morris, and a degree of despondency in the expression of Bishop Waugh."

The South

2. Joshua Soule
(from Flood and Hamilton,
Lives of Methodist Bishops)

3. James O. Andrew
(from Flood and Hamilton,
Lives of Methodist Bishops)

4. William Capers
(from Flood and Hamilton,
Lives of Methodist Bishops)

5. Robert Paine
(from Rivers, *Life of Paine*)

6. Holland N. McTyeire
(from Tigert, *Bishop McTyeire*)

Secretary of War Stanton to Bishop Ames

War Department
January 30: 1862

To the
Reverend Bishop Ames, &
The Honorable Hamilton Fish.
Gentlemen,

Persons who have been in the
military service of the United States as Officers
and soldiers are now held as Prisoners in the City
of Richmond, Virginia and in other places in the
South; some of them are sick, some wounded, many
in a state of destitution, and all are objects of
public sympathy and deep solicitude to this
Government.

You have been appointed to the humane
and Christian duty of visiting these prisoners in the
places where they are confined and to relieve their
necessities, supply their wants, and provide for their
comfort, according to your discretion.

You are also requested to make or procure
a list of all the prisoners so held in captivity, designating their names, the time and place when captured,
the service to which they belonged, their present state
and condition, their wants and necessities, and
all other particulars that may be interesting and
proper for their families to know, or useful to be

known by this Government, for the purpose of effecting their exchange or release. Your message being purely an errand of mercy, this Government expects and desires that you should not seek, obtain, or report information, or have communication on any subject, not immediately relating to its humane and Christian object.

To enable you to supply immediate relief to these prisoners, the sum of twenty five thousand dollars is placed in your hands with authority to draw at sight on the Assistant Treasurer of the United States at New York for the further sum of twenty five thousand dollars. And a depôt of clothing, medicines and other necessaries, to be supplied upon your requisition, for the use of the prisoners, is established at Fortress Monroe.

You will proceed, directly, to Fortress Monroe and communicate with General John E. Wool, commanding there, who is instructed to take such measures as may be right and proper, to procure you a safe-guard and passage to Richmond or other places, to enable you to perform the duties of your appointment.

You will conform to such police regulations as may be prescribed for your visitation and relief of the prisoners. And may give assurance that, on like condition, prisoners held by the United States may receive visitation and relief. You will be accompanied by the prisoners, now at Fortress Monroe, that have been heretofore taken and held by the military force of the United States, and they will be unconditionally released and delivered up.

In case General Wool shall not be able to procure for you a satisfactory safe-guard for your benevolent visitation, you will return to Washington and report to this Department; and, if successful, full and speedy report is requested.

Very respectfully
Your Obt. Servt,
Edwin M. Stanton
Secretary of War

7. The original of this previously unpublished document is in the Library of the Methodist Publishing House, Nashville.

8. While the bishops and the church as a whole were facing such grim documents as Stanton's authorization, the *Ladies' Repository* on the eve of the Civil War (August, 1860) used this to illustrate "Freedom" and "Slavery."

Frankford Pa., March 19th 1851

To Mr. Daniel Wilcox,

Dear Brother You are hereby notified to appear before a committee of your brethren, tomorrow evening, the 20th inst. at ½ past 7 oclock, in the Lecture-room of the Methodist E. Church, Frankford, to answer to the following charge

Viz Wilful neglect of class

Yours very truly

James H. McFarland

9. The importance of the class meeting is shown by this document from St. George's, Philadelphia:

> "Frankford Pa. March 19th, 1851
> To Mr. Daniel Wilcox
>   Dear Brother
> You are hereby notified to appear before a committee of your brethren, tomorrow evening, the 20th . . . at ½ past 7 oclock, in the Lecture-room of the Methodist E. Church, Frankford, to answer to the following charge
>   viz Wilful neglect of class
>   Yours very truly
>   James H. McFarland"

SUNDAY-SCHOOL CERTIFICATE OF ADMISSION.

The Children walking in Wisdom's way.

having complied with the rules of admission to   Sunday-school,   attached to the   Church, in   is this day enrolled as a member thereof, and is henceforth entitled to all its privileges.

May God guide and keep   , and bless the instruction   may here receive, to the everlasting good of   soul.

Superintendent,

10. Reproduced from Warriner, *Old Sands Street Church of Brooklyn*

RULES

IN RELATION TO THE GOVERNMENT OF SCHOLARS

CONNECTED WITH THE

JOHN STREET

METHODIST EPISCOPAL SABBATH SCHOOL

RULE 1.—It is expected of Scholars connected with this School, that they will remain in the Class assigned them by the Superintendents, until they shall consent to a change.

RULE 2.—When the Scholars enter the School-room, they must conduct themselves as becometh the Sabbath and the House of God, by abstaining from loud talking, or laughing, or otherwise acting improperly.

RULE 3.—During the opening or closing of the School, or when the School is being addressed from the desk, Scholars will not be permitted to leave their Class.

RULE 4.—No Scholar will leave their Class without permission from their Teacher, and no Teacher must allow more than one Scholar to leave the Class at a time.

RULE 5.—During the time of Prayer, every Scholar must kneel down and observe strict silence.

RULE 6.—Every Scholar in the School must commit to memory the Ten Commandments and the Lord's Prayer.

RULE 7.—The Librarian will attend on each Class in the morning and collect the Libraries, and in the afternoon will distribute the books. No Scholar will be permitted to go to the Library. Each Scholar must provide themselves with a strip of paper with the number of the books they would like to read thereon.

RULE 8.—When the School is dismissed, the Scholars will proceed in procession up into Church, headed by their Teachers. No Scholar will be permitted to stop around the door of the Church.

RULE 9.—Scholars who do not sit with their Parents in the Church, must sit with their Teachers in the gallery.

10.—Any Scholar who will persist in disobeying the Rules of this School *shall be expelled*.

NEW-YORK, NOVEMBER 5TH, 1858.

11. Reproduced from the copy at John Street Church

12. The second Bethel Ship of the Swedish Harbor Mission, 1857-79

13. William Nast, father of German Methodism, with daughter Josephine and son Albert. Albert Nast's handwritten note on the back says that this photograph was taken about 1850.

14. "Singing up a Crowd at the Old Adobe on the Plaza"
(from William Taylor, *Seven Years' Street Preaching in San Francisco*)

15. The perils of missionary life are dramatized in this drawing from William Taylor's *Christian Adventures in South Africa*. The account of Mr. Butler's narrow escape from this improbable-looking alligator is told on pp. 484-85 of that book.

16. Successors to the frontier camp-meeting tents: cottages at Ocean Grove Campmeeting Association, New Jersey—built in the 1870's, still in use.

ern churchmen were shocked at the "extravagant utterances, moanings, and gesticulations of ignorant, misguided, and often egotistical preachers." [216]

Educators, however, remembered that Methodism had begun with a "heart strangely warmed" and were cognizant of the dangers in imposing a religion of cold formality upon the spontaneous freedmen. Care was taken not to shape the Negro theological student into the image of his Northern white counterpart, lest he be unfitted to deal with his flock. Since they came not from "homes of refinement, but from plantations and hovels and poverty," and would work among the "poor and ignorant," it would be folly to lift them too high. Colored congregations neither desired nor appreciated "ministers of scholarly attainments" but asked for men of "eminent piety, good sense, and respectable acquirements." Thus, while many "indulge in a mode of life and worship displeasing to intelligent Christians . . . great allowances should be made." [217] A rudimentary knowledge of Christian doctrine and the *Discipline* usually sufficed for conference membership. At Thomson Biblical Institute, in New Orleans, in 1872 a series of lectures on the Bible was provided for pastors and "licentiates," with a manuscript prepared and delivered "with great care as to pronunciation." By 1885 the theological department of Central Tennessee College was subjecting students to such heavyweights as *Pope's Theology, Ecclesiastical Law, Harman's Introduction to the Study of the Holy Scriptures, Christian Evidences, Binney's Theological Compend,* and *History of Doctrine.* A five-year pastor's correspondence course attempted to clothe educationally naked novices who had slipped into the clerical estate at an earlier time.

FINANCES

Throughout the history of the society, its officials, in characteristic Methodist fashion, affirmed that their institution's yeoman service was not sufficiently rewarded. Through the late '60's and '70's they pleaded that additional funds were imperative if facilities were to be repaired and enlarged, the pitiful salaries increased, and endowments and scholarships created. Nevertheless, Richard Rust lamented in 1874 that the budget of $55,000 amounted to a meager response of but four cents per member, and that only two thirds of the assessment had been raised. With the belief that "no other organization . . . has yielded so much fruit upon the amount expended" the board of managers asked $100,000 for the next year, and begged the clergy to "take this holy cause to their

[216] *Fourteenth Annual Report,* p. 8; *Sixth Annual Report,* p. 16; *Twelfth Annual Report,* p. 15.

[217] *Fifth Annual Report,* p. 8; *Eighth Annual Report,* p. 12.

hearts, to their closets, and to their pulpits." [218] Although receipts increased almost $12,000 the following year, Rust was still chagrined that "only a little more than one-half of the pastoral charges" had taken a collection for the society as directed by the General Conference.[219]

During the first twelve years the annual budget averaged about $65,000, and it was not until 1884, with increased tuition costs, annuities, donations, and bequests, that expenditures went beyond $150,000. Significantly, in 1886, the collections from the Annual Conferences totaled but $69,836 of a budget of $168,747. The society invariably had a rough time in the financial infighting with four other agencies—Missionary Society, Church Extension, Sunday School Union, and Tract Society—for the benevolent dollar. In 1873 it came in third, with 60 per cent of what the Church Extension Society was granted but with only 8 per cent of what the Missionary Society received. The Negroes, however, gave all out of proportion to their ability to keep the schools solvent. The principal of Bennett Seminary in Greensboro, North Carolina, reported that a collection in one church "amounted to *one hundred and five dollars,*" with much of it coming from "Sabbath-school children bringing their pennies." [220] Nevertheless, because of "their heritage of poverty" the 270 students of Central Tennessee College in 1873 contributed less than $1,400 in room rent and tuition.

EDUCATION FOR WHITE MEMBERS

By the middle 1870's the work of the society had earned the respect if not the financial support of Southern Methodism. Educators reported "a growing sentiment in favor of our work," and while admitting that social barriers still existed, maintained that "a brighter era is awaiting us." [221] Amicability was unquestionably hastened by the General Conference request in 1880 for the society to enlarge its work to include the poor whites, "but not to the embarrassment of the work among our people of color." [222] The motives, however, for opening this new field were varied. With no hope for union with Southern Methodism in the foreseeable future, the church found itself too deeply committed in the South not to take care of the educational needs of its white members. Fifteen years of sacrificial labor within the ex-Confederacy had resulted in over 200,000 white members and property valued at $6,700,000. Cognizant that strong church colleges meant strong conferences, it felt

[218] *Seventh Annual Report,* pp. 16-19.
[219] *Eighth Annual Report,* p. 54.
[220] *Ibid.,* p. 37.
[221] *Twelfth Annual Report,* p. 34.
[222] *Journal of the General Conference,* 1880, p. 345.

its Southern fledging had to be strengthened or abandoned to the Southern Church. Not only did the poor whites deserve help in education because of their reputed "loyalty to the Government and the old Church" during the war, but the sentiment was universal that Northern Methodists would regard the colleges with greater financial affection if their "own kind" were being helped. The General Conference, consequently, reminded pastors to inform their people that "a portion of the appropriations" went to "the white population connected with our Church." [223] In 1881 one observer felt the timely aid to white schools had "saved to [Northern] Methodism thousands of whites" who otherwise would have been lost to other denominations or "to the world." [224]

Whereas hostility and suspicion marked the opening of Negro schools, financial inducements and flattery from the seats of the mighty attended the founding of white institutions. When in 1881 Bishop Warren and Secretary Rust called a public meeting to test the sentiment concerning the founding of Little Rock University, the governor, city mayor, superintendent of public instruction, principal of union schools, and other eminent citizens were present to give their support to the venture. Subsequently, Little Rock and Chattanooga were to raise $8,000 and $15,000 respectively for their universities. By 1887 the society had established or was aiding fifteen institutions in the amount of $17,138, or one sixth of its annual budget. The lion's share of such aid was channeled into Little Rock University and Chattanooga University in the hope that two high-caliber and strategically placed institutions could be created around which smaller "seminaries might cluster and act as feeders." [225]

Chartered institutions were Andrews Collegiate Institute, Andrews Institute, Alabama; Chattanooga University; Grant Memorial University, Athens, Tennessee; Little Rock University; and Texas Wesleyan College, Fort Worth. Institutions not chartered were Baldwin Seminary, Baldwin, Louisiana; Bloomington College, Bloomington, Tennessee; Ellijay Seminary, Ellijay, Georgia; Kingsley Seminary, Bloomingday, Tennessee; Mt. Union Seminary, Mt. Union, Alabama; Mt. Zion Seminary, Mt. Zion, Georgia; Powell Valley Seminary, Well Spring, Tennessee; Roanoke Seminary, Roanoke, Virginia; Tullahoma College, Tullahoma, Tennessee; Warren College, Fullen's, Tennessee.

The society's aid and supervision of white institutions, appreciated though it was by the South, raised the vexing problem of segregation. Although a nondiscriminatory policy in 1878 was sustained by the General Conference of 1884 ruling that "no student shall be excluded from in-

[223] Ibid.
[224] Fourteenth Annual Report, p. 37.
[225] Eighteenth Annual Report, p. 5.

struction in any and every school under the supervision of the Church because of race, color, or previous condition of servitude," the administration of Chattanooga University denied admission to several colored students in 1886. School trustees protested that "in the present state of society" Negro students would "be fatal to the prosperity of the institution" and would "excite prejudice and passion." Moreover, they based their case on another resolution of the General Conference, which allowed under certain conditions of "expediency" that administration of the problem should be left in the hands of those "immediately concerned." This rather seemed to be a case of the society withholding with its right hand what had been confirmed with the left, and the executive committee was asked to "use all proper means . . . to induce the trustees . . . to rescind the order." It also called for the resignation of a certain Professor Wilford Caulkins, who was reputed to have refused to shake the hand of a Negro Methodist minister of a nearby church.[226] That the university was ultimately "persuaded" to follow society policy was undoubtedly due more to economic coercion and a loss of an appeal to the General Conference than from an institutional change of heart. Thus, a religious Plessy vs. Ferguson pattern evolved, with racial matters left in the hands of local boards and the society's institutions continuing to be described as "for whites" or "for Negroes."

Ultimate Results

No other church in America gave so unstintingly of her sons and her substance to free the Negro from ignorance, poverty, and environmental debasement as did the Methodist Episcopal Church. After twenty years in the Southern vineyard the society had spent nearly two million dollars, had an annual budget approaching $200,000, and employed 204 teachers (some of whom were Negroes), with 6,500 pupils at work. Nonetheless, statistics made little impression upon a vocal minority of malcontents who were influenced by the perennial poverty of the Southern stepchild. To the boast that Methodism had achieved results "without a parallel in the history of all missionary movement," they cynically responded, "The Southern field is a dry and withered land that has swallowed up . . . thousands [while] giving little back." [227] Many continued to feel the schools were a permanent financial millstone around the neck

[226] *Nineteenth Annual Report*, pp. 23-29.
[227] Cited by Morrow, *Northern Methodism and Reconstruction*, p. 246.

of the church, that they had stimulated denominational animosity and wasted men and money.

Given the advantage of historical hindsight, it might have been in the best interest of the church to have channeled some funds for Negro education through the Southern Church. One factor which contributed to the swift reunion of the Northern and Southern dioceses of the Protestant Episcopal Church was the financial generosity which the former gave their destitute brethren. Funds for Negro education were spent in accordance with the wishes of Southern whites. A few voices in the wilderness prophesied that had such institutional selflessness been followed by the Northern Church, it would have won the Southern sister by an invincible love.

There is little doubt that the society strengthened the Southern fixation of the church and hindered the recognition that the mushrooming city was the most important missionary field during the crucial decades after the war. If the church had pursued the spiritual, educational, and economic welfare of the Celtic, Latin, and Slavic immigrant with the same fervor as it did the freedman, Methodism's progressive retreat from the metropolitan areas might have been arrested. Unfortunately, while the immigrant was judged an undesirable and an alien to the American Protestant dream, the nobility and progress of the African was shouted from the rooftops. While reports with monotonous regularity streamed up from the Southern field asking for increased aid to keep Romanism's tentacles from throttling a virgin territory, the immigrant deluge settled on Methodism's eastern flank without any concerted effort made toward evangelization.

There were too many signs of progress in the '70's and '80's, however, for the society to seriously question its labor. Epistles by the hundreds bore the eloquent testimony of teachers who were ecstatic about the progress of their charges. "A pupil to whom he gave instruction during the evenings of less than one month advanced during that time from the primer to become a tolerable reader, a good penman, and went through the fundamental rules of arithmetic. At the close of the month he was missing, and we hear from him as a teacher in North Carolina!" [228] A society-trained Negro minister could but testify: "The old Church . . . put clothes on our backs, and shoes on our feet, and hats on our heads, and . . . they's put brains in our hats, bless the Lord!" [229] Even the opposition, a Southern clergyman of long experience, grudgingly admitted that "the colored Methodists in the South who have had the

---

[228] New York *Christian Advocate*, April 9, 1868, p. 114.
[229] *Tenth Annual Report*, p. 67.

advantage of your . . . training are far in advance of any [other] colored people in that section." [230]

Methodist bread cast upon the Southern waters, then, was not lost. Statistics emanating from Southern statehouses and from Washington told of an ever-increasing number of Negroes becoming landowners, professional people, businessmen, skilled laborers, and taxpayers. In helping to make this possible, the church was truly *alma mater* to infant institutions which in time would win renown. The concentration of Methodist membership and educational institutions in the South is a permanent testimony of the work done in a bygone era in a then-alien land, to guide the freedman in his stride toward freedom.

4

The Concern for Systematic Theology, 1840-70

It is to be remembered . . . that the Arminian scheme has yet to be reduced to a systematic and logical form. . . . It has furnished us, indeed, with some detached negations and philosophical theories. . . . It is clear that an exposition of this theology which shall satisfy the logical consciousness is indispensable to its perpetuity, otherwise it cannot take possession of . . . minds, educated by the Word and Spirit of God, and disciplined to exact analysis and argument.[231]

Early Attempts at a More Systematic Theology

American Methodism in the early nineteenth century—greatly swelled in numbers after two generations of intense evangelical effort—*did* gradually face the problem of introducing its people into the broader, more "systematic" phases of historic Christian understanding and experience. Many agreed with President Stephen Olin of Wesleyan University, who observed (according to B. F. Tefft) that the great lack in the theology of Methodism was "the reduction of its tenets to a scientific system." [232] Actually, many Methodists hoped it would be Olin himself who would commit the Wesleyan motifs to such treatment, but the

[230] Cited by Morrow, *Northern Methodism and Reconstruction*, p. 176.

[231] E. P. Humphrey, *Our Theology and Its Development* (Philadelphia: Presbyterian Board, 1857).

[232] Tefft, *Methodism Successful* (New York: Derby and Jackson, 1860), p. 168.

demands of administration and, more particularly, the desperate instability of his health restricted the ultimate extent of his own writings. Olin died in 1851. There were others, such as William F. Warren, who began anticipating that Methodism's seminaries would gradually provide the opportunity for such a genuinely "scientific exposition" of Methodism's total doctrinal heritage.

This desire to pass beyond mere controversial theology did not, in itself, constitute any deviation from the basic theological attitude of Wesleyan Methodism. Methodist interest had always been simply to emphasize "first principles" of evangelical truth, except where the very possibilities of experimentally appropriating such truth were obscured by what was considered erroneous doctrine. Nevertheless, during this mid-century period there was a noticeable contribution, to the theological literature of American Methodism, of works dealing systematically with the various elements of Christian doctrine.

A common theme runs through the prefaces of such works: There is a need for a summary statement of the fundamental doctrines of the Bible in terms which the laity as well as the younger ministry of the church can understand. For some, this meant an exposition of Methodism's twenty-five Articles of Religion; [233] for others, it meant an independent attempt at dealing summarily with the great evangelical truths;[234] and for still others, it meant an American rewriting of Richard Watson's early-nineteenth-century, British Wesleyan *Theological Institutes.*[235]

It was Watson's systematic treatment of the theological motifs of Wesley and Fletcher (in the style and with some of the content of his own contemporary English "systems") which proved to be the standard theological source in American Methodism for at least three decades following the early 1840's. Watson's treatment of (I) the Evidences, (II) the Doctrines, (III) the Morals, and (IV) the Institutions of Christianity not only provided a norm for subsequent doctrinal studies, but gave direction to the whole theological enterprise within American Methodism—integrating Methodist theology into the polemic categories of contemporary anti-deistic, anti-Calvinistic theology.

[233] See Silas Comfort, *An Exposition of the Articles of Religion of the Methodist Episcopal Church* (New York: Published for the Author at the Conference Office, 1847) ; and A. A. Jimeson, *Notes on the Twenty-five Articles* (Cincinnati: Applegate and Co., 1853) . Jimeson, incidentally, indicates no awareness of Comfort's work.

[234] Asbury Lowrey, *Positive Theology* (Cincinnati, 1853) ; Moses M. Henkle, *Primary Platform of Methodism; or, Exposition of the General Rules* (Louisville: Published by the Author and Company, 1851) .

[235] Thomas N. Ralston, *Elements of Divinity* (1847) ; Luther Lee, *Elements of Theology* (1853) ; Samuel Wakefield, *A Complete System of Christian Theology* (1858) . These dates on the first editions of Lee and Wakefield are given in F. A. Archibald, ed., *Methodism and Literature* (New York: Phillips and Hunt, 1883) , p. 172.

The intention of adapting Watson's *Institutes* is quite explicit in Wakefield's *Complete System of Christian Theology*. Besides his abridgment of Watson, Wakefield included certain original matter at various points in the discussion. He also prefixed "a brief Introduction to the Study of Theology, principally derived from the theological writings of Knapp, Dick, and Horne" (Knapp was an early-nineteenth-century pietist theologian at Halle, in Germany; the other two were contemporary British theologians). In 1863 Wakefield's volume received an extended review by Daniel Whedon, then editor, in the January issue of *The Methodist Quarterly Review*. Whedon's remarks are indicative of the concern of many in the church for a genuinely indigenous and wholly independent Methodist systematic theology. The review concludes:

There are points in which the author bases himself upon Watson, in which we concur with neither. There are points of philosophy in which Mr. Watson followed the prevalent theories of the Locke philosophy which Dr. Wakefield has preserved, and which we should have expunged and replaced with the reverse view. There are some minor points of theology in which we differ from him [Wakefield]. . . . Yet, as a whole, as to the main outlines of our Arminian Wesleyan theology . . . the volume before us [is representative].

Whedon himself was to become a major factor in diverting the mind of nineteenth-century American Methodism away from any unqualified appeal to the doctrinal positions of Richard Watson. Through his articles and reviews as editor of *The Methodist Quarterly Review* (1856-84), through his *Freedom of the Will*, and through his definitive article in the *Bibliotheca Sacra* (1862) on the "Doctrines of Methodism," Daniel Whedon proved a formative influence in the emergence of an indigenous theological tradition within American Methodism. His *Freedom of the Will as a Basis of Human Responsibility* [236] proved to be a major instance within American Methodism of the influence of Edwardean Calvinism in substantially revising and delimiting traditional issues between Calvinistic and Arminian theological orientations.

The writings of William Fairfield Warren are further indicative of the new theological independence characteristic of American Methodism in this mid-century period. Warren, who became the first dean of Boston University's School of Theology (as well as first president of the university itself), published an introduction to systematic theology [237] in 1865, while serving as theological professor at the Methodist seminary

---

[236] (New York: Carlton and Porter, 1864).

[237] *Systematische Theologie einheitlich behandelt: Einleitung* (Bremen, Verlag des Tractathauses, 1865; Cincinnati: Poe and Hitchcock, 1865). Warren's work was not published in English; some passages are translated in McClintock's review.

in Bremen, Germany. In a review of Warren's work John McClintock writes:

> To state and vindicate the Methodist system of doctrines, with reference to the theological and philosophical relations of the time, is a task that must have fallen to some one; and we are thankful it has fallen to one so well qualified to accomplish it. . . . American Methodism, whose birth was some forty years later than that of English Methodism, has waited as many years after the publication of Watson's great work for the appearance of its first work of systematic theology. Not that she has produced nothing in the field of theological literature; on the contrary, the practical and controversial demands of this period of her development have been most ably met in the writings of Bangs, Emory, Fisk, Olin and others, now among the dead; and of Elliott, Whedon, Peck, Porter, Foster, and many others of the living. But an original . . . work on systematic theology has not yet been brought out in American Methodism. The work . . . by Dr. Warren forms the introduction to such a work; but, as yet, it is only a noble beginning.[238]

Unfortunately, the main body of Warren's proposed systematic theology was never completed; but his supplementary writings in methodology and in soteriology proved to be quite significant.

There were several systematic writings in preparation during this period. Thomas Summers, dean and first professor in systematic theology at Vanderbilt University's Biblical Department, prepared his extended lectures on the Articles of Religion during the late 1870's, although they were not published until 1888. L. T. Townsend's *Outline of Theology* and *Elements of General and Christian Theology* were published in the 1870's, while Townsend was professor of practical theology in Boston University's School of Theology. John Miley's *Atonement in Christ,* first published in 1879, was completely incorporated into his later *Systematic Theology.* Actually, the first original and complete system of theology to be published within American Methodism was that of Miner Raymond of Garrett Biblical Institute. Raymond succeeded John Dempster in the chair of systematic theology at Garrett in 1864; his *Systematic Theology* was published in 1877-79.

Methodism and Advanced Intellectual Developments

"A little before and after the year 1840 we witness the first considerable effects of German philosophy and criticism on American religious thought. This oceanic current reached us by two channels, one direct,

---

[238] *The Methodist Quarterly Review,* January, 1866, pp. 106, 104.

the other by way of Great Britain." [239] What were the points of contact between American Methodist thought in this middle period and the dynamic intellectual developments which so characterized nineteenth-century Europe? The first two continental figures to receive significant attention in *The Methodist Quarterly Review* were A. Tholuck (the "conciliatory" theologian at Halle, following 1826), and Victor Cousin (the French romanticist philosopher). In quite broad terms it may be said that the elements of pietism and theological ability in Tholuck, and the emphases on intuitional realism and the voluntary self in Cousin, were factors making these men attractive to their Methodist reviewers. Herder, Schlegel, and Kant also were reviewed—Kant's reviewer being careful to distinguish his transcendental philosophy from "modern transcendentalism."

It was under the editorship of John McClintock (1848-56) that the readers of *The Methodist Quarterly Review* were made most keenly aware of that world of thought which proved so definitive of nineteenth-century intellectual history. Even before McClintock's election as editor, he personally had contributed some of the most significant of the earlier review articles on continental thought. As editor he insisted—even in the face of severe criticism—that Methodism's intellectual horizons be expanded still more. During the eight years of McClintock's editorial supervision he himself contributed or directly solicited articles and reviews on Bushnell, Channing, Morell, Hamilton, Comte, and Coleridge.

One of McClintock's most important contributions to the theological literature and thought of American Methodism was the introduction of regular sections of "Literary Intelligence—Theological." In these pages appeared critical notices of the publications, journals, and major intellectual developments in England, France, and Germany. The October, 1850, issue, for example, included the announcement that Professor J. L. Jacobi of the University of Berlin had been secured as a regular correspondent for the *Review*. Jacobi's initial contribution was a favorable notice of the theological work of Schenkel, Roth, Müller, Neander, Nitzsch, Sack, and Hagenbach, with strong critical remarks directed against David Strauss and Bruno Bauer. William F. Warren served as foreign theological correspondent for the *Review* during the early 1860's. Following 1867, these review notices—especially those re-

[239] William F. Warren, "American Infidelity: Its Factors and Phases," in *History, Essays, Orations and Other Documents of the Sixth General Conference of the Evangelical Alliance*, ed. by Philip Schaff and S. I. Prime (New York: Harper & Brothers, 1874), p. 252. The German philosophies, in various forms, had been penetrating American thought since early nineteenth century—Coleridge and Emerson being among the chief mediators in this earlier period. Cf. *The Life and Letters of Stephen Olin* (New York: Harper, 1853), II, 346 ff.

garding German theological publications—were furnished by John Fletcher Hurst.

Daniel Whedon was elected editor of *The Methodist Quarterly Review* in 1856, and continued the tradition of attending editorially to the broad stream of contemporary intellectual and theological developments. For instance, during Whedon's first decade and a half as editor he either contributed or directly solicited reviews on Cousin, Mansel and Hamilton, Maurice, Darwin, Spencer, DeWette, and Schleiermacher, as well as the more conservative such as Knapp, Tholuck, Hagenbach, Hengstenberg, Harms, Lange, Ullmann, and Schenkel. There also were notices of such American theological contemporaries as Theodore Parker, Horace Bushnell, Charles Hodge, George P. Fisher, Laurens P. Hickok, Edwards A. Park, and Henry B. Smith. Whedon encouraged articles by fellow Methodists—Warren, B. F. Cocker, Alexander Winchell, Borden Parker Bowne, *et al.*—dealing with some of the most advanced phases of philosophical, scientific, and theological thought in the nineteenth century. With respect to doctrinal articles more directly involving Methodist standards, Whedon's policy was to exclude only that which was quite clearly contrary to such standards. On articles involving variances he added his own editorial notes and qualifications.

In such an intellectually revolutionary time American Methodism, together with American Protestantism, found itself involved in the concomitant—and sometimes antagonistic—pull of two methodological concerns: (1) a stubborn determination to sustain the essentials of biblical theism and Christian evangelicalism; and (2) a desire to encourage contemporary intellectual relevancy, even if it meant the revision of traditional doctrinal formulations. Actually, the critical period of intellectual-theological adjustment did not come until the 1870's, a period especially marked by the publication of Darwin's *Descent of Man*. In this instance, it may be said that American Methodism's more advanced thinkers defended the reasonableness of biblical theism (in the face of the new evolutionary science and thought) in one or both of the following manners: (1) divorce the evolutionary naturalist of any scientific ground for his atheism; (2) explicate the inevitability of the theistic solution to the question of ultimate causation.

The Methodist Quarterly Review was not the only major theological journal in American Methodism during this period. Beginning in 1847 there was a *Quarterly Review* for the newly formed Methodist Episcopal Church, South. Interestingly enough, the great division of 1844 did not determine, in any significant way, the transitions into this important theological middle period. Those characteristics which defined this newer theological period—the concern for a more systematic statement of evangelical belief and the growing awareness of the larger currents of nineteenth-century thought—were quite evident in the Southern Church.

In 1858 Thomas O. Summers was named to succeed D. S. Doggett as editor of the Southern *Quarterly Review*. He continued to edit this journal until late in 1861, when the War Between the States forced its discontinuance.[240] Summers' editorial policy, as he himself expressed it, was to conserve, express, and encourage the truest evangelical orthodoxy of Arminian Methodism. He conceived the province of the *Quarterly Review* to be quite properly a conservative one—"to reflect rather than to direct the thought and opinion of the Southern Methodist Episcopal Church." [241] And yet, Summers was not wholly averse to admitting articles which reflected differences of opinion on biblical, theological, and philosophical matters. He even acknowledged that he could "tolerate a little scientific heresy, however pertinacious he may be in regard to theological orthodoxy." [242] His most succinct statement of his editorial method came in 1880, upon resuming the editorship of the *Quarterly Review:* "Scientific and theological speculations of a vagarious character are not desired—nothing contrary to our recognized standards should appear in its pages, except to be refuted—it is a *Methodist* Review; yet, in keeping with the genius of Methodism, no pragmatic shibboleths will be enforced upon any writer." [243]

During Summers' first editorial term (1858-61), he admitted articles on Comte, Hamilton, German theology, German philosophy, and Kant.[244] He himself contributed reviews of Mansel's Bampton Lectures on the *Limits of Religious Thought,* and of Darwin's *Origin of Species* (which, to his mind, simply did not settle "the vexed question of the origin and variation of species and fertility of hybrids").

Methodism's Theologians and Emergent Religious Philosophies

What, more specifically, were the Methodist reactions to those revisionist religious philosophies which were emerging from Germany and

---

[240] Between 1861 and 1879 a certain nominal support was given by the Methodist Episcopal Church, South, to A. T. Bledsoe's *Southern Review*. Bledsoe's periodical dealt with matters of general literature and history; it included sporadic articles and reviews on religious topics. The *Quarterly Review* of the Methodist Episcopal Church, South, was revived in 1879, and Summers assumed the editorship in 1880.

[241] *Quarterly Review*, January, 1859, p. 143.

[242] *Ibid.*, October, 1859, p. 624.

[243] *Ibid.*, January, 1880, p. 179.

[244] See, e.g., W. J. Sasnett, "German Philosophy," July, 1858, pp. 321-47. In his editorial section of the same issue (p. 619) Summers quotes a notice on this article from the Texas *Christian Advocate:* "We are proud to know that the Church has a mind so capable of appreciating the German Philosophy."

England? Although generally sympathetic with the transcendental revolt against empiricism (or sensationalism), and although themselves
broadly influenced by the principles and methods of that intuitional
realism which characterized the writings of Reid and Cousin, the American Methodists tended to be quite critical of those efforts at a Christian
rationale which characterized the writings of Coleridge, Schleiermacher,
the American transcendentalists, Bushnell, and Maurice. The tendency
toward philosophical romanticism which characterized the theological
writings of this latter group seemed, to the Methodists, to constitute a
fundamental capitulation to an ever-encroaching rationalistic age—employing "the formulas of ordinary theology in a sense diverse from their
apparent original intention." This was a serious charge, for in the Methodist view the realities of evangelical experience could only be sustained
in a context which upheld the essential affirmations of historically or-
thodox evangelicalism.[245] To interpret Christianity in terms of "the
modernly so called *transcendental philosophy*," wrote Miner Raymond
in 1854, meant either reducing the central truths of Christianity to nonen-
tities or rendering them wholly inoperative "for any purpose of experimental or practical godliness." [246]

Were the American Methodists opposed to all efforts at dealing intellectually with the fundamentals of evangelical experience? There were
many who defended the assertion that Methodism, essentially, was "religion without philosophy"; doctrinal formulation, according to some
Methodist interpreters, was an obscuration of the stress on evangelical
experience—a stress which belonged uniquely to Methodism. But it is
important to note that leaders in American Methodist thought—Bangs,
Olin, McClintock, Stevens, Whedon—strongly repudiated any such radical disjunction between experience and theology.[247]

[245] Whedon, review of *Tracts for Priests and People, The Methodist Quarterly
Review*, January, 1863, pp. 163-65. Cf. Whedon's criticism of Bushnell's *Christian
Nurture* for its diminution of Christian experience—an appraisal based on the practical
imperceptibility therein of any doctrine of radical conversion (MQR, October, 1861,
pp. 698-700); also Whedon's summary estimate of Schleiermacher (MQR, January,
1860, p. 155). See also Summers' comment on Schleiermacher, "whose pantheism
utterly precludes all objective Christianity," in Summers' *Systematic Theology* (Nashville: Publishing House of the Methodist Episcopal Church, South, 1888), I, 456.

[246] *A Sermon . . . before . . . the legislature of Massachusetts at the annual election*
(Boston: White, 1854).

[247] See Nathan Bangs, *The Present State, Prospects, and Responsibilities of the
Methodist Episcopal Church* (New York: Lane and Scott, 1850) for a specific treatment of this charge. Cf. John Dempster's review of Volume III of Stevens' *History of
Methodism*, in *The Methodist Quarterly Review*, April, 1863, pp. 204-26; and Whedon's
remark in the October, 1872, MQR: "The vague depreciation of 'creeds' and 'theologies' is rather new in our Methodism" (p. 667).

It was at this very point that Methodism's theologians entered a methodological protest against emergent nineteenth-century religious philosophies. Both Whedon and McClintock criticized the tendency in Coleridge, Maurice, and Bushnell to denounce systematic ("scientific") doctrinal statements or historically oriented apologetics. The Methodists
generally insisted that the evident character of religious experience had
reference value for Christianity only in a context of objective historical
testimony, systematically related. "What we most disapprove . . . is . . .
setting the conscious experimental evidence of religion in *opposition* to
the historical and logical, instead of presenting them as co-ordinate and
harmonious reciprocal conditions to each other. Historical Christianity
is largely the basis and body of that religion which evidences itself to the
soul." [248] It was this conviction which led Whedon to reject an assertion
by Frederic H. Hedge, a Unitarian transcendentalist, that Methodism had
proved a practical "corrective" to the evils of the "Paleyan age." The
reference here was to William Paley, whose *View of the Evidences of
Christianity* (1794) contained the apologetics of Christian faith so characteristic of eighteenth-century English theology—the arguments from
prophecy, miracle, and historical-literary vindication to the unique and
authoritative fact of the Christian revelation. Whedon, and the greater
portion of American Methodism, remained stanch advocates of the
Paleyan method of cumulative historical "Christian evidences."

We are not . . . to be fascinated out of that firm maintenance of Christian
FACTS, for the masterly statement of which William Paley's name is illustriously
trite. With all our Methodism [and its appeal to experience], we would not
give one ounce of Paley's solid evidential sense for the entire volume of
transcendental gas that exhilerates the brains of . . . glowing intuitionalists. [249]

But was there not a certain affinity between Methodism's stress on
Christian experience and that religious empiricism which was emerging in the nineteenth century? Although the overly subjective nature of
the religious epistemology of Schleiermacher and Coleridge quite generally was stressed, still there were those within American Methodism (e.g.,
Olin, McClintock, Curry) who saw in such writings a vindication of
Methodism's own traditionally unique emphasis on experimental religion. "To Methodism Christianity is primarily a new life in God, medi-
ated to the believer by the Church through the preaching of the word

---

[248] Whedon, *Statements: Theological and Critical* (New York: Phillips and Hunt,
1887) , p. 183.
[249] *Ibid.,* pp. 257 ff.

and prayer; so to Schleiermacher." [250] That there was "conscious experimental evidence of religion" was seen to be the testimony "of Augustine, Bernard, Coleridge, Schleiermacher, and others"; but "more effective expositions" of the intrinsically self-evidencing power of Christianity could be found in the writings of Wesley, Fletcher, and Watson.[251]

Perhaps even more significant than the notice of such affinity was the recognition on the part of a few sensitive observers that American Methodism—in its own theological presentations—had failed to integrate that emphasis on experimental evidence which had been such a promising aspect of its earlier heritage. Its academic apologetics were limited almost completely to the methodology of natural theology (the traditional, rational arguments for the existence of God, etc.). J. A. Reubelt, of Indiana Asbury University, concluded his article on Schleiermacher with these penetrating remarks:

Both Methodism and Schleiermacher's theology deny that the natural man, the unchanged and unsanctified intellect, has any insight into the mysteries of religion; but this identity is only partial. When we go to a revival meeting, to a class meeting, or love-feast, we cannot be mistaken as to the completeness of the identity; but when we go to the recitation-room in our higher institutions of learning, and our theological seminaries, if we examine the course of study prescribed for our young preachers, then this identity is greatly marred; not only the identity of Methodism and Schleiermacher's theology, but also the identity of *Methodist life* and *Methodist theology*. This is the case with nearly all our apologetical literature. Here we meet as highest authority Paley, Butler [Analogy], and other writers from the deistical period. None of these men viewed Christianity *as a new life from and in God, none referred to the testimony of the Spirit,* none makes a change of heart the *conditio sine qua non* of understanding the Bible; but all endeavor, as Supernaturalism did, to construe from miracles and prophecies an argument amounting, if it could have been completed, to a demonstration.[252]

The self-apparent inconsistency (as Reubelt termed it) here was, at best, only partially comprehended by American Methodism. The method of traditional apologetics (set forth, for instance, in Watson's *Theological Institutes*) was followed with care and attention, although some sporadic efforts were made at supplementation in accord with the dimensions of internal evidence and the appeal to experience. There were to be some few attempts at the type of integration urged by Reubelt, but American Methodism generally did not grasp the unique relevance of its methodo-

[250] J. A. Reubelt, "Schleiermacher: His Theology and Influence," *Methodist Quarterly Review,* April, 1869, p. 227.
[251] Whedon, *Statements,* p. 183.
[252] "Schleiermacher: His Theology and Influence," p. 227.

logical heritage to the contemporary discussions in theology.[253] Actually, Methodism's primary attention was drawn to the necessity of sustaining a theological context adequate to the demands of truly Christian experience. Methodism conceived itself to be one of the leading forces in the evangelical "front" against materialistic and rationalistic elements in the contemporary intellectual scene.

[253] A somewhat later exception to this generalization is R. S. Foster's *Philosophy of Christian Experience* (New York: Hunt and Eaton, 1891), which is an apologetic based on the rational significance and theological implications of the concrete facts of Christian experience. The fact remains, however, that American Methodism did not respond creatively to the emergent emphasis on empirical methodologies.

chapter 20

THE
METHODIST
PROTESTANT
CHURCH

1865-1900

The Methodist Church

Reunion and
  Union Proposals

Publishing

Missions

Schools

B EGINNING IN 1858, AS A RESULT OF THE slavery controversy, the conferences in the East and South and the conferences in the North and West met in separate General Conferences or Conventions. Each branch claimed to be the true and original Methodist Protestant Church. It was not until 1877 that the split was healed and there was once again one Methodist Protestant Church in the United States. The history of their separation is often complex—involving changes in name and organization—and there were, for example, two different General Conferences of the Methodist Protestant Church meeting in 1866.

1

The War Years, East and South

The Eastern and Southern conferences of the Methodist Protestant Church experienced at close range most of the disasters that accompany war. Their Baltimore paper, *The Methodist Protestant*, suspended publication for two weeks in 1861 and was reduced in size and limited in circulation. Its beloved editor, Eli Y. Reese, took his own life in frustration and despair as military regulations were clamped down on the city, and Baltimore pastors assumed editorial responsibility for a time. When the "strictly religious" character of the paper was demonstrated, in that it consistently avoided mention of slavery and other political issues, Secretary of War Stanton authorized its circulation among

391

the subscribers in the South, but mail irregularities soon put a stop to this effort.[1]

Yadkin College in North Carolina, which had been opened in 1856, closed its doors almost immediately at the beginning of the war when sixty out of eighty boarding students volunteered for service in the Confederate Army. The school remained closed for six years.[2]

The General Conference, when it convened in Georgetown, D.C., in May, 1862, had only Maryland delegates present, and adjourned after going through the motions of organization. Francis Waters was elected president and Daniel E. Reese secretary, and they were authorized to call an adjourned session as soon as practicable. This was attempted three years later, again in Georgetown, but only ten delegates from Maryland and one from Illinois attended. Although no journal was kept, a Baltimore delegate, Dr. Lawrence W. Bates, reported the proceedings. The most important actions were plans to revise the ritual, an official visit to President Andrew Johnson at the White House, and passage of a resolution "not only to submit to the powers that be, but most earnestly pray for those in authority." [3]

The disorder and poverty caused by the war in the Southern conferences were still reflected in the limited representation at the General Conference in Georgetown in 1866. Only four of the fifteen Southern conferences sent delegates—Alabama, Maryland, North Carolina, and Virginia. Some minor changes were made in the ritual and in membership requirements, and editors were elected. The plight of the churches throughout the South was the most pressing problem. A ruling on military service by ministers was urged by the Marylanders, referred to the Judiciary Committee, and adopted for insertion in the *Discipline:* "The voluntary bearing of arms, in military service, by Ministers of the Methodist Protestant Church, is inconsistent with their professional calling and the nature and intent of their ordination vows." [4]

On the sixth day a committee was appointed "to wait on the President of the United States to ascertain his pleasure in regard to receiving the Conference in a body." That afternoon Dr. John J. Murray reported for the committee that "his excellency had expressed his pleasure in regard to

---

[1] Edward J. Drinkhouse, *History of Methodist Reform* (Baltimore: Board of Publication of the Methodist Protestant Church, 1899), II, 449.

[2] Olin Bain Michael, *Yadkin College, a Historic Sketch* (Salisbury, N.C.: Rowan Printing Company, 1939), p. 31.

[3] Ancel H. Bassett, *A Concise History of the Methodist Protestant Church* (Pittsburgh: Press of Charles A. Scott, 1877), pp. 167-69. See also: *The Methodist Protestant,* May 20, 1865, p. 3.

[4] *Discipline of the Methodist Protestant Church,* 1866, p. 63. This paragraph was dropped in 1877 when the Northern and Southern sections reunited.

the reception of the body," and would expect them the following day sometime between ten and two o'clock "at the pleasure of the Conference." William H. Wills of North Carolina, president of the Conference and spokesman for the visitors, apologized for the "meagerness" of their number and for their appearance. Their clothing, he said—particularly his own, which had been made by his wife and daughter—was evidence of the "fiery ordeal through which the southern portions of the country and the churches had so recently passed." [5] The customary official compliments were exchanged.

The most disturbing question to the Methodist Protestants in 1866 was the relationship between the General Conference and the nineteen Annual Conferences of the North and West which, after the 1858 separation, had revised the constitution and *Discipline* on the issue of slavery. A committee was appointed to study the matter, and a paper by John J. Murray was adopted. The conclusion stated: "It is evident that the conferences which have adopted said Constitution and Discipline [of the antislavery Cincinnati Convention], having voluntarily separated themselves from this Conference have no right to representation therein." There was, however, no "unkind feeling for those who have gone from us" but a willingness to receive any conference that showed a desire to return by repudiating the Cincinnati Articles and reaffirming the original constitution and *Discipline* of the church.[6]

Late in the conference great excitement followed the reading of a letter from Bishop McTyeire of the Methodist Episcopal Church, South, a letter authorized by the General Conference of that church at its recent session in New Orleans. The bishop stated that his church had adopted lay representation; and since this, the chief cause of division, was now removed, discussion looking to union of the denominations was invited. The Methodist Protestant delegates were almost swept off their feet by this overture. A special session of their General Conference, with convention powers, was called to meet in Montgomery, Alabama, in May of the following year (1867) to discuss the proposed merger. For the next decade union was the most popular subject, and hopes of union with other branches of Methodism led to several futile discussions. The reunion in 1877 of their own divided house was to be their one success.

---

[5] *The Methodist Protestant,* May 19, 1866, p. 3.
[6] *Journal of the General Conference,* 1866, pp. 24-25.

2

The Union Decade, 1867-77

Actions in the Southern Conferences

Only forty-one of the seventy-one elected delegates were able to attend the Montgomery Convention in May, 1867, but the church's chief historian wrote that "considering the disruption of the railroads and the poverty of the men the attendance was remarkable." [7] Although union with the Methodist Episcopal Church, South, was the primary interest of the convention, actions on several other matters were pressed.

The troublesome word "white" in Article XII of the constitution was made still more offensive to the Northern and Western conferences by a rewording of the paragraph so as to exclude Negro ministers and preachers, as well as members, from voting and from eligibility to the General Conference. At the same time resolutions were adopted "for the improvement of the colored race" and for retaining "our colored membership in our own connection." On the strength of this at least nine Negro Methodist Protestant Annual Conferences were eventually organized, with a total membership of 5,786 members reported in 1900. [8] Delegates from Maryland brought with them $800 for distribution among their more needy brethren in the South. A Board of Missions was organized, with headquarters in Baltimore. The strength of the Maryland Conference was demonstrated in that eight of the twelve members of this board were Maryland delegates, including the chairman, the Rev. S. B. Southerland.

These items of business seem to have been interspersed in fragments of time through the more demanding considerations of church union. Bishops George F. Pierce and Holland McTyeire, Dr. L. M. Lee, and the Rev. J. E. Evans, all of the Methodist Episcopal Church, South, were introduced and their pressing invitations to unite were warmly applauded. A few days of discussion, however, revealed that the proposal was premature. The lay representation plan adopted by the Southern Church [9] was an insignificant inducement to union when placed beside

[7] Drinkhouse, *History*, II, 487.
[8] *Journal of the General Conference of the Methodist Protestant Church*, 1900, pp. 127-28.
[9] The plan provided for equal representation of laymen in the General Conference and for four lay delegates for each district in the Annual Conferences.

the fifteen demands made by the Methodist Protestants. Their "terms of union" included several difficult items: the addition of the word "Protestant" to the name of the united church, if the word "Episcopal" were retained; abolition of the presiding eldership; the creation of as many bishops as Annual Conferences; the selection of the first newly elected bishops from the Methodist Protestants; the right of appeal of ministers; no transfer of ministers (from conference to conference) without their consent; the parity of local and itinerant ministers; equal delegation (lay and ministerial) in all Annual Conferences; no veto power of the bishops; and the autonomy of the Maryland Conference with respect to name, membership, and boundaries.[10]

Nine days of reports, addresses, and parliamentary maneuvering ended in a resolution, adopted by a vote of twenty-six to fifteen, "that the Convention take no decisive action at this time" but that the "disagreeing propositions" be referred to commissioners representing the two churches with authority to call another convention at Lynchburg, Virginia, in May of 1868 "if it deems it proper, to conclude any proposed union." [11] But no other convention on union with the Southern Church was called. The official exchanges soon ceased.

Several Methodist Protestant churches, however, and much of what survived after the Civil War of their Virginia Conference accepted invitations to join the Methodist Episcopal Church, South. The Virginia Conference was almost dismembered, and "within a year six ministers of the Alabama Conference withdrew and united with the Methodist Episcopal Church, South, in some cases carrying societies with them. The same occurred in the Mississippi Conference." [12] The *Methodist Recorder* gave the Western and Northern opinion of the Virginia defection: "We can not see how the members of the Virginia Conference can exchange our real lay delegation for the mere shadow of it which is found in the Methodist Episcopal Church, South. . . . We regret their action." [13]

The Northern and Western Conferences

From 1858 to 1864 the Northern and Western Annual Conferences of the Methodist Protestant Church met in General Conventions—in Springfield, Ohio, in 1858; in Pittsburgh in 1860; and in Cincinnati in 1862.

[10] *Journal of Proceedings of the Convention of the Methodist Protestant Church held in Montgomery, Alabama*, May, 1867, Appendix A, pp. 37-38.
[11] *Ibid.*, p. 22.
[12] Drinkhouse, *History*, II, 509.
[13] *Methodist Recorder*, December 15, 1869, p. 4.

On the last day of the Cincinnati Convention a declaration restoring the General Conference and implying that the Northern and Western branch was the true Methodist Protestant Church was presented by Dr. George Brown, the convention president. It was unanimously passed. It stated that the Methodist Protestant Church, by her original organization and by her Twenty-third Article of Religion ("Of the Rulers of the United States of America"), stood firmly bound in her allegiance to the nation; and that the Southern states, including the Methodist Protestant Church in those states, had renounced their allegiance to the United States and were now in "the double sin of slavery and rebellion." "The position assumed by the Methodist Protestant Church in the rebel states . . . must be considered in the light of a revolt from the Methodist Protestant Church in the free states." Therefore: "Be it resolved . . . that the General Conference of the Methodist Protestant Church . . . is hereby restored to its full original authority under the Constitution of the Methodist Protestant Church." [14]

This spirit of division deepened as the war years passed, and the Michigan Annual Conference fairly represented the Northern sentiments in an 1864 pledge of renewed devotion to the Federal government:

We do indignantly frown upon any measures or propositions of peace . . . which might secure less than an undivided nation. . . . We have no sympathy with those whose sympathies are with the rebellion. . . . Therefore we will sustain Caesar, and call upon him to bear not the sword in vain, and sheathe it not, until every rebel shall have laid down his arms and submitted to his rightful authorities.[15]

Reunion of the divided church was to wait for more than a decade. Meanwhile a plan of union among nonepiscopal Methodists in the North and West seemed for a brief interval to be a dramatic ecumenical adventure. Its rise and failure can be briefly summarized.

CONVERSATIONS WITH THE WESLEYANS

At the Springfield Convention in 1858 The Rev. Cyrus C. Prindle of the Wesleyan Methodist Church was introduced, and the paper he read was referred to the Committee on Communications. Prindle was speaking for a committee appointed by the General Conference of his church to "fraternize and correspond with other reformatory, religious bodies with a view to attaining a more intimate union." His speech was warmly received, and the convention at once appointed a committee of

[14] *Proceedings of the General Convention of the Methodist Protestant Church, held at Cincinnati, Ohio,* 1862, p. 30.
[15] *Western Methodist Protestant,* November 2, 1864, p. 2.

five to carry on negotiations "for the ultimate purpose if possible of becoming one body." [16]

These two committees met together in the First Methodist Protestant Church in Pittsburgh on February 18, 1859. George Brown was chosen chairman and W. H. Brewster secretary. Ancel Bassett of the Methodist Protestants and Cyrus Prindle of the Wesleyan Methodists were named to prepare a "plan of co-operation"; each submitted a plan the following morning separately and without consultation but with surprising similarity "in spirit and sentiment." [17] It was recommended that both churches unite in religious efforts, in revivals, in protracted, quarterly, and other meetings; that isolated members or families be urged to join the nearest church of either branch; that vacancies be filled by ministers of either church; that the publications of each be freely exchanged and read; and that harmony and fellowship be encouraged in all things.

As a first step, a joint hymnbook was authorized, and Dr. George Brown was selected to compile it. But the Methodist Protestant action in the enterprise was too fast for the Wesleyans. When the hymnbook was published in Cincinnati in 1860, its popularity and sale were strictly limited to the Methodist Protestants, and the general effect of the hymnbook was divisive.

The advocates of union among nonepiscopal Methodists were active if not effective. Two fraternal delegates were sent by the Methodist Protestants to the Wesleyan General Conference in 1864 "with a proposal of church union and a joint ownership of Adrian College." Without doubt the college, begun by the Wesleyans, needed more support than either denomination could provide, alone, at that time. But now the Wesleyans became cautious. Their historian says, in explanation, that about twenty "self-appointed" men, in their eagerness, moved ahead independently of their General Conference to persuade the Annual Conferences to support union.[18] Reluctance on both sides increased to opposition.

ORGANIZATION OF THE METHODIST CHURCH

At a called convention in Cleveland in 1865 fifty-six Methodist Protestants and sixty-three Wesleyan Methodists and a half-dozen independent delegates adopted, without dissent, L. C. Matlack's proposals for union; and another convention of nonepiscopal Methodists was called to meet

[16] *Proceedings of the General Convention of Delegates from the Northern and Western Conferences of the Methodist Protestant Church, Springfield, Ohio,* 1858, pp. 15-16.

[17] Bassett, *Concise History,* pp. 188-89.

[18] Ira Ford McLeister, *History of the Wesleyan Methodist Church of America,* rev. by Roy S. Nicholson (Marion, Ind.: Wesleyan Methodist Publishing Association, 1959), p. 81.

in Cincinnati the following year to work out the details. In this interval, however, so many protest meetings were held by the Wesleyans that their delegation to the Cincinnati Convention was reduced to 38 while the Methodist Protestants numbered 138. The Free Methodists were not represented. In an honest attempt to ignore objections of a more local character the convention agreed to form a united body, "the Methodist Church." A constitution was adopted which varied but slightly from the constitution of the Methodist Protestant Church as revised by the Northern and Western Conferences in 1858.[19] It was ordered that the first General Conference of the Methodist Church meet in Cleveland in May of 1867, and a committee was appointed to prepare a *Discipline* and to report at the Cleveland Conference. In keeping with the spirit of union and the name of the new church, the name of the official weekly was ordered changed from the *Western Methodist Protestant* to the *Methodist Recorder*.

All of this was frowned upon by the Southern and Eastern sections of the Methodist Protestant Church. In 1866 the Maryland Annual Conference declared its intention "to hold fast and maintain the *doctrines,* the *government* and the *name* of the Methodist Protestant Church"; [20] and at the General Conference in Georgetown that year Dr. Waters' proposal of fraternization with nonepiscopal Methodists was discreetly withdrawn after brief debate.

The "cooling off" on the part of those Wesleyans who had initiated union was described for the Methodist Protestants in their *Methodist Recorder* in 1868. A series of articles lamented the failure of the Methodist Church to become a successful union, and attached most of the blame to the Wesleyans.[21] One of the disputed questions was their strong anti-secret society stand which the Methodist Protestants could not accept.[22] Another grievance was the feeling among the Wesleyans that they were losing their Adrian College, that it was being taken over by a new organization.[23] The aloofness of the Primitive Methodists was also puzzling. The *Methodist Recorder* marveled that they did not seek "to blend with the new Methodist body now forming," for it is "thoroughly anti-episcopal, anti-priest domination, anti-alcoholic beverages, anti-diabolism of all sorts." Furthermore, the Primitive Methodists should have been attracted because the new church was republican in polity, and was stressing lay authority and the itinerancy.[24]

[19] Bassett, *Concise History*, pp. 207-8.
[20] *Minutes of the Thirty-eighth Session of the Maryland Annual Conference*, Baltimore, 1866, p. 7.
[21] *Methodist Recorder*, February 5, 1868, p. 6 (and successive issues).
[22] *Western Methodist Protestant*, December 13, 1865, p. 3.
[23] McLeister and Nicholson, *History of the Wesleyan Church*, p. 89.
[24] *Methodist Recorder*, June 23, 1869, p. 2.

As the result of all this, "the Methodist Church" was little more than a name standing for the Methodist Protestants of the North and West, and as such the title was easily discarded at the time of union in 1877.

There was little in the 1860's to encourage friendship between the Northern and Southern sections of the church. However, there were occasional exchanges of friendliness, and some correspondence developed. Several of the Annual Conferences on both sides sent and received fraternal delegates after 1866. At the Methodist Protestant General Conference in Baltimore in 1870 papers from fraternal messengers of the Methodist Church, the Methodist Episcopal Church, and the Methodist Episcopal Church, South, were read and answered in a friendly manner; but the reply to the Methodist Church clearly stated that the only hope of reconciliation with this body lay in the return of the Northern and Western conferences to the fold.[25]

In 1871 the Methodist Church held its second General Conference in Pittsburgh. Fraternal messengers from the Maryland Conference were heard, and five fraternal messengers were appointed to the next General Conference of the Methodist Protestant Church. These delegates were asked to act as a commission "to receive any propositions looking toward union" of the two sections.[26] There seems to have been an understanding that the commission would not *make* any propositions for union.

The Reunion of the Methodist Protestant Church

The first clear proposal of a step toward union was adopted at the General Conference of the Methodist Protestant Church at Lynchburg, Virginia, in 1874. This was a resolution, presented by John Paris, which called for a General Convention on constitutional changes and for a committee of nine persons "to confer with any like commission from any Methodist body in America . . . on the subject of union . . . and especially with a committee of 9 . . . of the Methodist Church, which has made overtures to us for a reunion." [27] The words and actions on both sides were cautious, each branch being determined to show that initial overtures and suggestions for union came from the other.[28]

Proposals and plans now multiplied, and the ground swell toward reunion was strong at the General Conference of the Methodist Church

[25] *Journal of the General Conference of the Methodist Protestant Church,* 1870, p. 15.

[26] *Minutes of the Second General Conference of the Methodist Church,* 1871, p. 78.

[27] *Journal of the General Conference of the Methodist Protestant Church,* 1874, p. 19.

[28] John Scott, *Recollections of Fifty Years in the Ministry* (Pittsburgh and Baltimore: Methodist Protestant Board of Publication, 1898) , pp. 155-56.

at Princeton, Illinois, in 1875. The first paragraph of the report of the Committee on Union stated that "inasmuch as the cause for suspension of official relations by the Conferences of the North . . . is now entirely removed by the providence of God," and since the "General Conference of the South [Lynchburg, 1874] . . . did elect nine commissioners . . . to deliberate together and devise plans for reunion alike honorable and desirable to each; therefore this committee unanimously recommend the election of nine persons as commissioners for said purpose." [29]

The commissioners of both branches met together in Pittsburgh before the year was out, and in three days of amicable discussion achieved a "Basis of Union" acceptable to both sides. The word "white" as a membership and suffrage limitation was removed from the constitution, and it was agreed that the name of the reunited church should be the Methodist Protestant Church. The constitutions and *Disciplines* of the two divisions were easily harmonized with few changes. A convention of the Methodist Protestant and Methodist Churches was called to meet in Baltimore in May, 1877. All the Annual Conferences in the Methodist Church approved the call of the convention, as did all but four of the Methodist Protestant Annual Conferences. The four dissenting conferences were Colorado (Texas), Mississippi, North Mississippi, and North Carolina (in the latter the vote was twenty-nine to twenty-six) .[30]

Extensive arrangements were made in Baltimore for a dramatic ceremony of merger. The Methodist Church Convention assembled in the West Baltimore Church, at Greene and Lombard Streets; the Methodist Protestant Convention in the East Baltimore Church, at Fayette and Asquith Streets. Both conventions opened on the same date, May 11, 1877, and deliberated separately for a week on the Basis of Union. The Convention of the Methodist Church on the second day honored the venerable Thomas McCormick of Baltimore, the "only surviving one of the eleven ministers expelled as Reformers" in 1827. McCormick had been one of the twelve pallbearers who carried the body of Asbury in 1816 to the Eutaw Street Church, followed by the whole General Conference and many residents of the city. Now the whole convention rose to greet him, and the feeble patriarch spoke simply but effectively in support of the proposed reunion. Ancel Bassett's description of these events is brief but reliable, and can be followed with confidence.[31]

A strong uneasiness for some days developed in the Methodist Church Convention over suffrage rights, and this would not be quieted until a resolution was adopted which interpreted those rights to mean "that no

[29] *Journal of the General Conference of the Methodist Church,* 1875, p. 96.
[30] *The Methodist Protestant,* December 30, 1876, p. 2.
[31] *Concise History,* pp. 245-46.

person who enjoys the right of suffrage and eligibility to office in the State, shall be deprived of these rights in the church," and that "Annual Conferences respectively may confer these rights, if they shall see fit, upon members of the church within their bounds who do not enjoy them in the state." [32] This would, in some measure, it was hoped, protect the Negro membership in the South; the constitution, however, when finally adopted made such special injunction unnecessary.

When the Basis of Union had been adopted by both conventions, the Committee of Arrangements "for assembling and merging the two Conventions" took charge and submitted its "programme of formal exercises to be observed." Bassett describes the procedure for Wednesday afternoon, May 16:

The two Conventions, headed by their respective Presidents and Secretaries, marched along Lombard Street, one from the East, the other from the West, to the intersection of Fremont Street, where they met, single file. Here, the members of the Methodist body joined arm in arm, two by two, with the Methodist Protestants, and marched to the Starr Methodist Protestant Church, on Poppleton Street. Presidents Bates and Smith, arm in arm, took the lead, followed by the Secretaries, and then the entire body of the representatives paired in the same manner. The entire line of procession extended the distance of about a block and a half, the process of mingling and consolidation attracting much attention. In the process, one of the North Carolina brethren, who had voted against the union and the Basis, first and last, took the arm of the writer. And how could we two walk together, unless we were agreed? [33]

Starr Church was filled. There were hand clasps, embraces, smiles, tears, hymns, prayers, and speeches. An hour was given to "voluntary five-minutes' addresses" by the members. An hour was given to the presidents' greetings and informal greetings. The union was formally announced by President Bates and the Doxology was sung. It was late that night when the weary delegates found their way to their lodgings.

The following days, May 17-23, were busy with organizational matters. The constitutions and *Disciplines* of the two churches were "collated" and portions voted on daily. The first General Conference of the reunited church was ordered to meet in Pittsburgh the third Friday in May of 1880. The quadrennial General Conference was adopted, and the ratio of representation was to be one minister and one layman for every 1,500 members. The Committee on Colleges reported favorably on Adrian, Western Maryland, and the college in North Carolina. The official hymn-

[32] *Ibid.*, p. 248.
[33] *Ibid.*, p. 251.

books of the two churches, published in Baltimore and Pittsburgh, were recognized and approved to be used for the present.

A committee of seven visited the president of the United States on Monday, May 21, and "each made brief addresses." President Hayes congratulated them on the successful reunion and expressed the hope that the Presbyterian and Methodist Episcopal Churches would soon heal their schisms.

The General Rules were dropped, and in their place the Rules of Christian Duties in the *Discipline* of the Methodist Church were adopted; the clause against slavery was, of course, omitted, and a prohibition of the use of tobacco was inserted. The conference adjourned near midnight of the seventh day (May 23). The Doxology was sung, and the Benediction was pronounced by Professor G. B. McElroy of Adrian.[34]

3

Activities of the United Church

Lawrence W. Bates, president of the General Conference of the Methodist Church, closed his address at the merger service in Starr Church with the confident hope that the Methodist Protestant Church "should now be a stronger, holier and more successful church." [35] Accurate statistics are wanting to show fulfillment of these hopes, for either size or holiness, because early records are meager.

The forty-four Annual Conferences of the united church gave a total of 113,405 members; 1,314 itinerant ministers and preachers; 925 unstationed ministers and preachers; 1,351 churches; and church property valued at $2,662,736. The Northern section could report equal or slightly larger figures for all items except membership; in this respect they were 1,400 fewer than the Southern section. Over half of the entire membership was in six of the conferences: Maryland (12,383), North Carolina (10,806), Ohio (5,604), Muskingum (9,506), West Virginia (9,480), and Pittsburgh (7,088). Indiana reported 4,835 members; North Illinois and Wisconsin, Iowa, and Virginia were in the 3,000 bracket; and Min-

[34] For details of this General Convention see Bassett, *Concise History*, pp. 254-58, and Drinkhouse, *History*, II, 555-72. The published *Minutes*, also available, are, however, brief.
[35] Bassett, *Concise History*, p. 252.

nesota, Oregon, Nebraska, Tennessee, and South East Missouri had fewer than 500 each.[36]

In the first two years following reunion forty new churches were dedicated and fifteen were under construction. Yet, with several Annual Conferences failing to submit reports, it is evident that growth was slow in the first quadrennium. Their historian deduces some comfort in discovering that in these years over against these small increases the Methodist Episcopal Church showed an even smaller percentage of gain.[37]

Comparison of a few figures for 1877 and 1900 may be helpful:

	Members	Ministers and Preachers	Unstationed Ministers and Preachers	Churches	Property Value
1877	113,405	1,314	925	1,351	$2,662,736
1900	184,097	1,647	1,135	2,400	4,754,721

More important evidences of new life and health in the church are seen in some ventures in publishing and in educational and missionary concerns.

Publishing

The two Book Concerns (Baltimore and Pittsburgh) continued their separate and distinctive activities after 1877 until union with other Methodists in 1939. However, they were put directly under the authority of the General Conference through a Board of Publication composed of five men from each Book Concern—or Directory, as they were called. The two official papers, *The Methodist Protestant* and the *Methodist Recorder,* were continued, with frequently improved style and appearance. The complete plan of unification of the publishing offices occupied more time and filled more pages than any other constitutional matter. The relationships between the Baltimore and Pittsburgh interests presented grave problems.

Immediately after reunion, in order to promote unity throughout the church and to dramatize the good will determined upon by the official periodicals, the editors of both papers, E. J. Drinkhouse and Alexander

---

[36] Edward J. Drinkhouse and Ancel H. Bassett, historians, constituted a committee on statistics authorized to compile a report for the Minutes. See Drinkhouse, *History,* II, 571-72. The number of conferences at the time of union is given in the *Proceedings of the Joint Convention,* pp. 55-56.

[37] Drinkhouse, *History,* II, 593.

Clark, traveled together, chiefly throughout the West and South. Wherever possible they spoke in Annual Conferences for the support of both journals. A line of able editors continued the work. Drinkhouse served the Baltimore paper until 1892; he was followed by F. T. Tagg, who was editor until 1916, when F. T. Benson assumed the duties—three *Methodist Protestant* editors in fifty-four years. The *Recorder* was directed by Alexander Clark until his death in 1879. Then John Scott began his second term as editor, serving until 1888. He was followed by D. S. Stephens of Adrian, Martin Luther Jennings, and Lyman E. Davis.

A popular and useful church periodical, begun in 1878 by E. J. Drinkhouse and published by the Baltimore Directory, was the *Bible School,* a monthly journal of four pages, featuring commentary on the International Sunday School Lessons. Before its discontinuance in 1885 it had a circulation of twenty thousand, for the most part in the East and South. The *Bible School Quarterly,* begun by Drinkhouse in 1880, was added to the Sunday school "helps" by the Baltimore Directory. At the same time the Pittsburgh Directory was publishing *Our Morning Guide* and *The Child's Recorder* under the direction of John Scott. In 1884 the General Conference ordered the consolidation of the Sunday school papers under a separate editor, and the Board of Publication chose John F. Cowan as Sunday school editor. Cowan served until 1898, becoming then the associate editor of the *Christian Endeavor World. Our Young People* became the official organ of the Christian Endeavor. In 1892 the average yearly circulation of the six Sunday school papers was 129,300.[38]

In the last two decades of the nineteenth century several other Methodist Protestant publications appeared, but they soon failed. The trans-Mississippi conferences began a local *Western Protestant* which was published first at Haynesville, Louisiana, then in Dallas, Texas, for a few years. It was followed by a few issues of a *Protestant Recorder,* published in Magnolia, Arkansas, and at Indianapolis the *Western Record* made a brief appearance. Other papers, of even shorter life, were *The National Methodist* (Indiana), *The Southern Christian Advance* (Texas), *The Protestant Advocate* (Georgia), *The Central Protestant* (North Carolina), and *The Pennsylvania Methodist Protestant.*

Church Polity

After the Civil War many of the leaders among the Methodist Protestants began to feel that the fathers of the denomination had created, in

[38] See Crates Johnson, "The History of our Sunday School Literature," *The Methodist Protestant* (Centennial Edition), May 16, 1928, p. 36.

their passion for democracy, a connection too loose and free for effective church life. This need for "a more decisive executive branch" than that provided by the constitution was back of the Annual Council. The Methodist Church, in its General Conference of 1875, had authorized this annual meeting of the president of the General Conference with the president of the college (Adrian), the editor and publisher, and the corresponding secretaries of the different boards. This plan was carried over into the reunited church in 1877 and became a part of the *Discipline*. The council met yearly until 1892, when it was abolished. Its powers were more hoped for than real, as it was regarded by all except its members as purely advisory. Requests for more authority were promptly rejected by the majority of Methodist Protestants, who feared centralization. The Annual Council's enemies said that "it was a gosling which after a while would become a bishop gander." [39]

This dread of episcopacy, coupled to the fear of any clerical power, was a favorite theme until well into the twentieth century. For example, *The Methodist Protestant* issued a seventieth anniversary issue, November 9, 1898. Thirty-two large pages were well filled with reform history, biographical sketches of nearly forty reform leaders, and articles on church freedom and liberty. Particularly conspicuous was the embellished cover with its bold reassertion of the historic three-line motto:

Mutual Rights—Liberal Methodism

A Church without a Bishop in a country without a King

Free Grace—Free Speech

The bottom of the cover was decorated with a scroll containing the words, "One is your Master, even Christ and all ye are brethren"; and the whole concluded with the significant *"Fides, Libertas, Amicitia, Praecipua Animi Humani Bona Sunt."* Probably no other printed pages from Methodist Protestant presses declared their principles more graphically than did this 1898 poster-cover of their Baltimore weekly.

Some of the conferences were disturbed by necessary changes in line with the freedom stressed by growing ideas of reform. One problem was thrust upon the New York Conference in 1880, when Miss Anna M. Shaw was elected to elder's orders and received ordination. The ordination of women generally and this act specifically, when referred to the Judiciary Committee, were declared to be "unauthorized by the law of the church," and therefore Miss Shaw was not entitled to recognition as an elder in the Methodist Protestant Church. Long debates buried the real question underneath parliamentary maneuvers, but the New York

<hr>

[39] Drinkhouse, *History,* II, 574.

Conference continued to recognize her orders and work. In 1892 the General Conference recognized Mrs. Eugenia F. St. John as an elder from the Kansas Conference, and three other women were recognized by the Committee on Certificates and seated as lay delegates. Conference debate and voting by "orders" (laymen and ministers voting separately) resulted in the adoption of a minority report which admitted the women to their seats but referred the principle of the election and ordination of women to the Annual Conferences. No constitutional change was won by this procedure, the matter being essentially left to the Annual Conferences to interpret.

The Ecumenical Methodist Conferences

Methodist Protestants were well represented and active at the first and second Ecumenical Methodist Conferences. At the first, which met in City Road Chapel, London, September 7-20, 1881, the five Methodist Protestant delegates were Dr. G. B. McElroy, president of Adrian College, the Rev. J. H. Robinson, Dr. S. B. Southerland, J. J. Gillespie, and Charles W. Button. Dr. Southerland presided over the sessions one day, read one of the scheduled papers, and spoke on nonepiscopal Methodism in America. He was introduced by General Clinton B. Fisk of the Methodist Episcopal Church, as from "the Protestant Methodist Church," an error which Dr. Southerland promptly corrected. (Frequent, and unintentional, slights of this kind were exchanged. The *Christian Advocate* was called to task by *The Methodist Protestant* for such carelessness, and the *Advocate* became piqued when *The Methodist Protestant* spoke of the "Episcopal Methodist Church.")

The Second Ecumenical Methodist Conference met in the Metropolitan Methodist Episcopal Church, Washington, D. C., October 7-20, 1891. Here the Methodist Protestants had nine delegates. Dr. J. T. Murray of Maryland presided on the seventh day, and the Rev. T. J. Ogden of North Carolina and the Rev. T. B. Appleget of New Jersey read papers. The English New Connexion Methodists seemed to be on common ground with the Methodist Protestants. Dr. J. T. Ward, president of Westminster Theological Seminary, entertained the New Connexion delegate, J. C. Watts, and Western Maryland College conferred on him the Doctor of Divinity degree.[40]

[40] *Ibid.*, p. 651.

4

Missions

At the General Conference of the Northern and Western conferences of the Methodist Protestant Church in Allegheny City, Pennsylvania, in 1866, the Committee on Missions confessed that it "felt at a loss what to say." The failure of all its plans and programs was a source of great "pain and mortification." The receipts for the past four years, although higher than for any previous quadrennium, were "but a trifle over two thousand dollars per annum, from a membership of forty to fifty thousand ministers and members." [41] All the committee could do, their report concluded, was to lament these facts and urge the Annual Conferences to "require their ministers and preachers to make greater efforts" in this cause. The missionary reports for several succeeding General Conferences are but variations of this 1866 admission of inaction. In the 1870's some Annual Conferences quickened with missionary interest. The Maryland Conference authorized the woman's missionary society in Baltimore to co-operate with the Woman's Foreign Missionary Society of the Methodist Episcopal Church. This they did for one year. A similar co-operation was achieved in Pittsburgh, when Methodist Protestant women began to contribute to the support of Miss Elizabeth Guthrie, who had been in Japan for six years under the interdenominational Woman's Union Missionary Society. It was as a result of one of Miss Guthrie's speeches that the Woman's Foreign Missionary Society of the Methodist Protestant Church was founded in 1879. The Methodist Protestants then took over the support of Miss Guthrie. Home on furlough in 1880, she died suddenly in San Francisco on her way back to her work and Miss Harriett Brittain was selected by the Society to replace her. With the work in Japan as inspiration, a new missionary response was felt throughout the church.

In 1879 the *Methodist Protestant Missionary* first appeared, edited by C. H. Wilson, and at the General Conference in Pittsburgh in May, 1880, a Board of Home and Foreign Missions was created. At the same time the Woman's Foreign Missionary Society was recognized as one of the permanent agencies of the church. Eight years later, at the General Conference in Adrian, Michigan (1888), a Board of Home Missions and a Board of Foreign Missions were created. F. T. Tagg was the first corresponding secretary of the Board of Foreign Missions, and Benjamin Stout of the Board of Home Missions.

[41] *Proceedings of the Ninth General Conference of the Methodist Protestant Church,* 1866, p. 17.

Japan was the only foreign mission field of the Methodist Protestants before 1900. There in October, 1880, Miss Brittain opened a school in Yokohama. The agreement was that the Board would pay her expenses and that the Woman's Foreign Missionary Society would pay her salary, but Miss Brittain purchased property with $9,000 of her own funds and was later reimbursed by the Board.[42] In 1882 the Rev. Fred C. Klein was appointed as the first ordained missionary of the Methodist Protestant Church, and he and Mrs. Klein arrived in Japan in 1883. The work then consisted of one school of forty-seven pupils. Soon a Sunday school, preaching services, and a night school for young men were started. The first church was organized in Yokohama with twelve members, on July 11, 1886. Another church at Nagoya was started by Dr. Klein the next year. He also was the founder of Nagoya College (1887) and for many years, with his talented wife, brought wise and energetic leadership to the Japan work. Dr. T. H. Colhouer accompanied Dr. Klein and shared heavy responsibilities. He guided the building of the first Methodist Protestant Church in Japan. The Japan Conference, consisting of three Americans and one Japanese minister, was organized in 1892.

5

Later Union Proposals

In 1880, at the Methodist Protestant General Conference in Pittsburgh, three fraternal messengers were introduced at an evening session set aside for hearing them. They were the Rev. W. P. Harrison and the Hon. Patrick Hamil of the Methodist Episcopal Church, South, and the Rev. William H. Black of the Cumberland Presbyterian Church. Following their speeches, "Blest Be the Tie That Binds, etc. was sung," and the conference president responded, "fully reciprocating the kind words and cordial greetings of the esteemed brethren." [43] The president was then authorized "to send one ministerial and one lay Fraternal Messenger to each of the bodies represented by these distinguished brethren." [44]

At the next General Conference, in Baltimore, 1884, the report of the

[42] Proceedings of the Annual Council, 1880, p. 32.
[43] Journal of the General Conference, 1880, pp. 23-24.
[44] Ibid., p. 31.

Committee on Fraternal Relations was devoted entirely to the Cumberland Presbyterians, for by then exchanges with the Methodist Episcopal Churches had subsided to the level of perfunctory pleasantries with the Southern and into complete silence with the Northern branch. Five commissioners were appointed to "confer with a like Commission of the Cumberland Presbyterian Church on the subject of organic union and report to the next General Conference." [45] A telegram was dispatched with this news to the General Assembly of the Cumberland Presbyterians, then in session in McKeesport, Pennsylvania. The telegram arrived too late for action that year, but it was courteously acknowledged, and the next year the General Assembly appointed their own union commissioners. The two commissions met together at the Maxwell House Hotel in Nashville, Tennessee, May 13, 1886. G. B. McElroy was elected chairman and W. H. Black secretary. It was the "unanimous opinion" of the Methodist Protestant commission that in the creeds of the two churches there was "no difference whatever except that which grows out of the doctrines of the 'Preservation of Believers' and 'Apostacy,' which we agree are not essential to the Christian System"; and in polity there was "no serious impediment to an organic union." They added that they could "see no sufficient reason why two bodies of Christians so alike in doctrine, government and practice should long remain as separate organizations." [46]

The 1888 General Conference Committee on Communications, however, did not agree with the Committee on Fraternal Relations. They urged "a calm and judicious consideration" of this and all proposals of union which might encourage "a departure in the least degree" from "certain fundamental principles" of the Methodist Protestant Church. Any sign of a want of confidence in these principles, now that the Methodist Episcopal Church was beginning to adopt them, would be a "grievous blunder." As long as the Methodist Protestant General Conference talked of "organic union," the church "will be in a continual confusion and a state of unrest. . . . Further overtures in this direction should now cease." [47]

The enthusiasm for union with the Cumberland Presbyterians immediately died. One member of the committee, J. J. Smith, probably did as much as all others to quiet the issue when he pointed out the really serious differences involving the authority of conferences, sessions, elders, and the stationing system. Only one further mention of this effort oc-

[45] *Journal of the General Conference*, 1884, pp. 25-26.
[46] *Journal of the General Conference*, 1888, pp. 69-73.
[47] *Ibid.*

curred, when the General Conference of 1892 resolved to send one minister and one layman "to bear fraternal greetings . . . to the next official conference of that [the Cumberland Presbyterian] Church." [48]

In the last two decades of the nineteenth century several other unions were discussed. These were brief but unsuccessful considerations of mergers with the Reformed Episcopal Church, the Congregational Methodists, the United Brethren, and the Primitive Methodists. No more than the casual exchange of fraternal greetings came out of these talks, and no real feeling for union was noticeable throughout the church until that historic outburst of enthusiasm which followed the famous "little Benjamin" address of Thomas Hamilton Lewis at the General Conference of the Methodist Episcopal Church in 1908. (The Methodist Protestants seemed to have thought of themselves for many years as "a little Benjamin among the tribes of Israel.") Here Dr. Lewis, president of the General Conference of the Methodist Protestant Church, made the first significant appeal for a full union of the three largest and most influential Methodist denominations. His address, because of the excitement it created, has often been regarded as of historic importance in the story of Methodist union.[49]

6

Schools and Colleges

On the fourth day of the Joint Convention of the Methodist Protestant and Methodist Churches in 1877, the report of the Committee on Colleges, as read, amended, and adopted, briefly presented three colleges: one, in North Carolina, was "an opening as yet undeveloped," three thousand dollars being needed before purchasing "a building in process of construction, beautifully adapted to educational purposes." Two colleges, Adrian in Michigan and Western Maryland, were at that time well established and ready to serve the reunited church as officially recognized Methodist Protestant schools.[50]

[48] *Journal of the General Conference,* 1892, p. 102.
[49] See the *Christian Advocate,* June 18, 1908, p. 1035; *The Methodist Protestant,* June 3, 1908, pp. 5-7.
[50] *Proceedings of the Joint Convention,* 1877, pp. 37-39.

Adrian and Other Western Schools

In 1877 Adrian had been for nearly a decade under the full control of the Methodist Protestants. Begun in 1852 as a Wesleyan Methodist college at Leoni, near Jackson, Michigan, it had been moved to Adrian in 1859. As early as 1862 the board of trustees voted to invite the Methodist Protestants to co-operate at Adrian, "with equal rights and responsibilities." [51] This seems to have been a proper move, as both the Wesleyans and the Methodist Protestants of the North and West expected a union of nonepiscopal Methodists to be completed at once, and the Methodist Protestants were attempting at that time, through their "collegiate association" in Ohio, to start a church college somewhere in the West. In 1866 the General Conference of the Methodist Protestants of the North and West recorded that "the inauguratory steps taken toward a union of non-episcopal bodies of this country, have culminated in a joint proprietorship of Adrian College." [52] The union plans failed and the Wesleyans withdrew; but the trustees of the college, caught in a financial crisis, felt the necessity of putting the control of the institution in the hands of a church that would be responsible for the entire debt and for securing a proper endowment fund.[53] In 1868 the Methodist Protestants, agreeing to these terms, were given full control.

Many columns of the *Methodist Recorder* were devoted to Adrian, and there were many appeals in the 1860's and '70's for the church to support their "College of the West." Revival news was particularly welcomed by the *Recorder's* readers. The issue of January 29, 1868, reported the conversion of thirty students and the good news that "with the exception of some four or five cases we believe every member of the four regular college classes is now a professor of religion." In the same issue Cornelius Springer, the venerable editor and leader in the Ohio Conference, described his "sojourn" with his wife as guests at the college. The institution, said Springer, was "very prosperous," with 155 students, "although many had gone out to teach school during the winter." Religion was prominent: daily chapel for faculty and students, two sermons every Sabbath, several weekly prayer meetings, daily private prayer meetings in dormitory rooms, and "few representatives of sin." The four large edifices were "splendid," but a "floating debt of some twenty thousand

[51] Fannie Hay, Ruth Cargo, and Harlan Feeman, *The Story of a Noble Devotion: A Short History of Adrian College* (Adrian College Press, 1945), p. 30.
[52] *Journal of the General Conference,* 1866, p. 9.
[53] Hay, Cargo, and Feeman, *Story of a Noble Devotion,* p. 32.

dollars was most embarrassing and should be payed off by the church at once." [54]

Cornelius Springer was a little too optimistic in 1868 about Adrian's prosperity. The debt was not "payed off by the church at once," as he hoped. Instead, such adverses as fire loses in 1869 and 1880, the financial panics of 1873 and 1893, and the repeated failure of supporting Annual Conferences to raise their quotas of both money and students, caused President D. C. Thomas to say in his message to the 1894 General Conference:

> But the marvel is how could our College maintain such standing during all these years with insufficient endowment and with inadequate equipment? It has been because of the self-sacrificing devotion of men who have given themselves wholly to the cause of our beloved faith. Adrian College is a monument more to the spirit of unselfish devotion and honorable service than to the munificence of our church. [55]

President Thomas could have illustrated his General Conference address by recalling voluntary 10 per cent reductions in faculty salaries in at least one crisis. [56]

The reputation of Adrian's presidents was high in the church both East and West. Asa Mahan, the first (1859-64; 1867-71), had been a well-known leader in antislavery reforms at Oberlin. While pastor of the Plymouth Congregational Church in Adrian, he took the initiative in getting Michigan Union College moved from Leoni to Adrian and reincorporated as Adrian College in 1859. Mahan advocated coeducation in his inaugural address that year. George B. McElroy (1873-80) directed the college in a particularly trying decade; and Thomas Hamilton Lewis (1902-4), president of Western Maryland College, divided his time between the two colleges for two years, "going back and forth every two weeks between Westminster, Maryland, and Adrian and without expense to Adrian save his travelling expenses and necessary assistance in the president's office at Western Maryland." [57] The encouraging reports both by the trustees and President Lewis to the General Conference of 1904 showed how well deserved was the church's confidence in the energy and administrative skills of the "drafted" Lewis. [58]

[54] *Methodist Recorder*, January 29, 1868, p. 7.
[55] *Journal of the General Conference of the Methodist Protestant Church*, 1896, p. 122.
[56] Hay, Cargo, and Feeman, *Story of a Noble Devotion*, p. 39.
[57] *Ibid.*, pp. 65-66.
[58] *Journal of the General Conference of the Methodist Protestant Church*, 1904, pp. 132-42.

In Illinois, Methodist Protestants complained that appeals for Adrian cut into their support of their own college at Henry City, begun about 1855 and chartered by the state legislature "with university privileges and powers." This was North Illinois Institute. George B. McElroy was president until 1867, when John Kost took charge. Methodist Protestants were reminded that "Adrian was not the only college recognized by the highest authority of the church," and that "the North Illinois Conference was not to be solicited for Adrian" [59] but for their own school. In spite of these protections and warnings, North Illinois Institute was forced by debts to close in 1870, and a concentration of church support and able leadership gave to Adrian a temporary educational monopoly among Methodist Protestants in the West.

The feeling was strong that Adrian's location was somewhat peripheral, and Ohio and Illinois were always eager to establish their own conference schools. The General Conference of 1880 recommended Gittings Seminary at La Harpe, Illinois, "now under the control and supervision of the North Illinois Conference; and . . . intended to be everything that is desirable as a Methodist Protestant Seminary where our people may educate their children under our own denominational influence. . . . It is designed as a preparatory school for our colleges." [60] In 1892 Gittings Seminary was being supported by the conferences in Illinois, Iowa, and Missouri; it was free from debt and had four faculty members, three of whom were Adrian graduates.[61] The school was not reported in later conferences.

Three other Western educational ventures, of more continuing success, should be recognized. Kansas City University was projected by a commission or board of twenty trustees appointed by the General Conference of 1888 to take steps toward "the establishment of an institution of learning in the West." The plans of this board were adopted in 1892. A gift of "120 acres or more" of land and the support of "the Kansas City people" seemed encouraging, and during the General Conference of 1896, meeting in that city, the cornerstone for the "experiment" was laid. In 1900 the report to the General Conference described Mather Hall (named after the principal benefactor, Dr. S. F. Mather) "erected and equipped for University Work," property valued at over $214,428, and "a practical course of university instruction" arranged with "the Allopathic College of Physicians and Surgeons, the Homeopathic College of Medicine and Surgery and the School of Elocution and

[59] *Methodist Recorder*, June 2, 1869, p. 1.
[60] *Journal of the General Conference*, 1880, p. 70.
[61] *Journal of the General Conference*, 1892, p. 101.

Oratory, all of Kansas City." [62] David S. Stephens, formerly president of
Adrian (1882-88) and editor of the *Methodist Recorder*, was chancellor of
Kansas City University from 1894 to 1914. He was followed by John H.
Lucas and, in 1919, by Albert Norman Ward, who had been vice-president
of Western Maryland College from 1913 to 1916.

In 1895, Westminster College was founded at Westminster, Texas. Dr.
James Lisbon Lawlis was the first president and continued in charge of
the School of Theology after 1896, when he was succeeded by Professor
Charles O. Stubbs. In 1902 the school was moved to Tehuacana, Texas,
but retained the name Westminster in spite of the recommendation to
change made by the General Conference of 1904. The college enrollment in 1903 was 72; in 1904 it was 63, but the preparatory school and
the department of music and elocution brought the total of students to
more than 200.[63]

West Lafayette College was begun when the Muskingum (Ohio) Annual Conference accepted land valued at $20,000 donated by the Hon.
Vincent Ferguson. The General Conference of 1900, upon the report of
the Committee on Education, gave the enterprise "friendly recognition."
The school opened in the fall of that year. Four years later the Committee on Education, basing its findings on the annual catalogue, reported
the college to be "in a prosperous condition" with an "average attendance
of between 100 and 125 students." [64] It was recommended that "West
Lafayette College be recognized as one of the official colleges of the Methodist Protestant Church." By 1920 the college had merged with
Adrian.[65]

Colleges in the East

The North Carolina school briefly mentioned in the 1877 report of
the Committee on Colleges was Yadkin College in Davidson County. Begun as Yadkin Institute in 1856, largely through the initiative and
generosity of Henry Walser of the state legislature and Thomas C. Crump,
it had been chartered as a college in 1861. It was closed during the Civil
War years, reopened as an academy in 1867, and transferred to the North
Carolina Conference in 1871.[66] In 1873 it achieved college standing again
and reported eighty students.

[62] *Journal of the General Conference,* 1900, p. 78.
[63] *Journal of the General Conference,* 1904, p. 162.
[64] *Ibid.,* p. 99.
[65] *Journal of the General Conference,* 1920, p. 62.
[66] J. Elwood Carroll, *History of the North Carolina Conference of the Methodist
Protestant Church* (Greensboro, N. C.: McCulloch and Swain, 1939), p. 52.

The catalogue of 1879 listed fifty-three male and twenty-five female students in the college and twenty-six undergraduates. Some other students, not listed, were "irregular" or "in the Preparatory Department." A faculty of five was named: the Rev. Shadrach Simpson, A.M., president and professor of ancient languages, metaphysics, rhetoric, and logic; A. Baker, A.B., professor of mathematics and English literature; G. M. Smithdeal, professor of penmanship; Miss Swannanoa Harris, teacher of music; and R. T. Pickens, A.B., professor in the Female Department.[67] A short course was advertised by which students with "energy, pluck, determination and fair capacity . . . will be graduated in three years, otherwise they remain four years."

A description of some general advantages in Yadkin's location stated that

a village presents fewer causes of diversion from study, fewer temptations to extravagance and, a thing which is of the greatest importance, fewer temptations to dissipation. . . . there is here no local cause of disease; the sale of ardent liquors within two miles of the College is forbidden by law . . . so that parents may rest assured that their sons are as favorably situated at Yadkin College as it is possible for them to be any where.[68]

Particular business advantages also were cited in the 1879 college catalogue:

Yadkin College is an incorporated town of about one hundred and fifty inhabitants. There are four stores and one Tobacco Factory. Messrs. Dale and Jordan manufacture Plug, Twist and Smoking Tobacco. These gentlemen are business men, and are prompt in filling orders. Mr. Dale furnishes Kerosene Oil regularly at fifteen cents per gallon. This low price of fuel, together with the cheapness of many other articles and general simplicity in style of life, makes Yadkin a very desirable point for education.[69]

Yadkin's church connections were not advertised in promoting the school. Religious services were briefly mentioned under "Morals," and although students were "required to attend Sabbath School . . . the doctrinal points of denominations receive no attention." The school illustrates the grim struggles and honest achievements of many small church-related colleges of the South in the post–Civil War era. Continually burdened with debt because of inadequate support, it wavered between collapse and temporary security with a persistent devotion to character improvement, good manners, classical learning, hard work, and moral in-

[67] Michael, *Yadkin College*, pp. 52-76.
[68] *Ibid.*, p. 68.
[69] *Ibid.*, p. 70.

tegrity. George S. Wills, professor at Western Maryland College; Charles E. Forlines, professor and president at Westminster Theological Seminary; W. T. Totten, professor and president at Yadkin, and many others continued the school's idealism and spirit well into the twentieth century.

Yadkin trustees were directed by the North Carolina Annual Conference in 1895 to ask the state legislature to annul the college charter, and the school was known thereafter as Yadkin High School. In 1924 the institution was closed, its work and traditions being perpetuated in High Point College, which was opened that year.[70]

The third of the colleges reported to the Joint Convention in Baltimore in 1877 was Western Maryland. The college by then was just ten years old. Begun as an academy by Professor Fayette R. Buell in the town of Westminster, Maryland, it asked for the support of the Maryland Conference. This was granted in 1866 when the conference "commended [the institution] to the patronage of the Church." [71] The cornerstone of the first building ("Old Main") was laid in September, 1866. The next year the Maryland Conference took "supervisory control" and chose a board of directors. In 1869 the purchase of the property by the board was ratified by the conference, and the college became an institution of the church. The first president (1867-86) was James Thomas Ward, "a man of strong personality and great influence [who] laid firm foundations for the institution." [72] The second president, Thomas Hamilton Lewis, gave brilliant leadership to Western Maryland from 1886 to 1920. Lewis was one of the greatest preachers of the Methodist Protestant Church. He was the real founder of Westminster Theological Seminary in 1881, the president of Western Maryland for thirty-four years, president of the General Conference from 1920 to 1928, and in the last two years of his life contributing editor of the church periodicals. For nearly fifty years he was the outstanding leader of the Maryland Conference. His devotion to church union, particularly Methodist union, marked all his many activities.[73]

The Committee on Colleges reported to the General Conference of 1880 that Western Maryland seemed to be "in a highly prosperous condition." Student enrollment had averaged 110 for each year since the institution came into existence, and a total of 70 graduates in that year in-

[70] Carroll, *History of the North Carolina Conference*, p. 53.

[71] J. T. Murray and T. H. Lewis, *History of the Maryland Annual Conference of the Methodist Protestant Church* (Baltimore, 1882) , p. 54.

[72] John D. Makosky, *Western Maryland College in the Nineteenth Century* (Westminster, Md., 1940) , p. 5.

[73] See the *Minutes of the Maryland Annual Conference*, 1930, pp. 133-36.

cluded 18 ministers of the Maryland Conference. The property was described as consisting of "a spacious edifice five stories high, with ample accommodations for a large number of students, and grounds embracing eight acres, allowing sufficient range for the exercise of students during the time not allotted to study. The finances of the college are in good condition. . . . The debt upon the property will, it is believed, be entirely paid off in the course of another year. . . . The estimated value of the entire property is $35,000." [74]

In 1904 President Lewis' report to the General Conference demonstrated his wise leadership. Although the debt had increased to $17,000, property worth $248,475 had been secured. Twenty buildings showed material growth and expansion, and the average annual attendance was 242 for the quadrennium, with 118 graduates for the same period—an average of 29 in each class.

In keeping with the times, a coeducational system was advertised, but Lewis explained that "it was co-equal rather than co-incident education. The sexes were assigned the same work, but not mingled in the same classes." [75]

Ministerial Education

Methodist Protestants, like other churches after the Civil War, felt the increased pressures for a better-educated ministry; they also shared in the ancient conflict between "spiritual" and "intellectual" gifts in ministerial acceptability. When the *Western Methodist Protestant* as early as 1855 appealed for educated ministers, it was bold enough to say that although a college education should not necessarily be required, nevertheless, "To set an individual to preach the gospel who is a loggerhead . . . is abominable. . . . We have every means to educate our ministers and if they will not be educated they should stay at home, on their farms or in their shops." Then, admitting the dangers to the ministry in both education and excesses of emotionalism, the writer ventured what he no doubt hoped would be a rhetorical question: "Why can not a minister of letters be as spiritual as one who is ignorant?" [76]

Concern moved into action when the Western and Northern General Conference of 1866 organized a Board of Ministerial Education. This move grew out of an association formed at Springfield, Ohio, the year be-

[74] *Journal of the General Conference,* 1880, p. 69.
[75] *Journal of the General Conference,* 1904, p. 147.
[76] *Western Methodist Protestant,* July 26, 1855. A series of articles in this and later issues by J. H. Richards of North Wilna, New York.

fore "to raise means to assist young men in obtaining an education for the ministry." [77] James B. Walker, who had been active in this cause for many years, was elected corresponding secretary, and in this office he became in a real sense the "father" of ministerial education in the Methodist Protestant Church. Walker gave himself to this task with consecrated enthusiasm until his retirement in 1890. Then James C. Berrien directed the board's work until 1908, when George R. Brown became the secretary. These three gave admirable leadership during the fifty years of the board's life, until 1916. The joint tasks of examining and financing (through loans) the education of ministerial candidates were then assumed by the newly created Board of Education.

Long, detailed, and carefully prepared reports to General Conferences exhibit the remarkable work and interest of the Board of Ministerial Training.[78] Its records were accurate and its requirements specific. Every ministerial candidate was expected to answer before the conference several plain questions about his religious experience, his motives, his morals, his conduct, and his debts. He promised to withdraw from the denomination "in an orderly manner" if his theology changed, and "to refrain from the use of tobacco, wine and all intoxicating liquors." Frequent inquiries and reports determined the candidate's eligibility to borrow from the board's funds.

It became increasingly clear that theological education, or ministerial training, could not become a major responsibility of the church colleges. Hopes that Adrian and Western Maryland, particularly, might staff and finance departments of theology soon faded. In 1881 the Maryland Conference named a committee "to mature and report plans to the next Conference" for a school of theology. In 1882 the Westminster Theological Seminary was established at Westminster, Maryland, and its first board of governors was incorporated in 1884. That year the school was advertised in The Methodist Protestant as offering "a collegiate course and two years in theology for complete course" and "accommodational course with elective studies to those not graduates of a college." Total expenses, board and tuition, for one year were $100. Thomas H. Lewis, the first president, taught Hebrew language and literature. Four other men completed the faculty: J. T. Ward (systematic theology), J. D. Kinzer (pastoral theology), A. T. Cralle (historical theology), and A. M. Merrill (instructor in elocution).

[77] Bassett, Concise History, p. 212.
[78] See the General Conference Journals, particularly 1880, 1884, and following years. The report by J. C. Berrien in 1892 is unusually important (p. 76).

After four years, in 1886, Dr. Lewis went to the presidency of Western Maryland College, and Dr. Ward served as the seminary president until his death in 1897, when Dr. Hugh Latimer Elderdice began his thirty-five year term of careful leadership in administration and scholarship.

In 1900 five professors constituted the faculty: President Elderdice taught Hebrew and historical theology; Benjamin Franklin Benson, systematic and practical theology; James William Reese, New Testament Greek and exegesis; and Thomas H. Lewis, Christian evidences. There were "special lectures" by visiting ministers, for the most part in practical subjects.

Two classes of students were provided for, according to the catalogue of 1900: college graduates, who "after two years of successful study and the presentation of an approved thesis on some theological subject" received the Bachelor of Divinity degree; and nongraduates who, after three years of successful study and the completion of a thesis, would "secure a certificate of graduation and be enrolled among the Alumni." The total enrollment in 1901 was twenty-five. The list of graduates since 1884 totaled fifty-eight. Charles Edward Forlines and James Henry Straughn were two of the 1901 graduates. Dr. Forlines, of encyclopedic mind and with unique skills in teaching and inspiring ministerial students, was professor of theology and church history in the seminary and president from 1936 to 1943. Dr. Straughn, after years of leadership, as president of the Maryland Annual Conference and the General Conference and in other church positions, dramatized Methodist Union in 1939, when he was elected by the Methodist Protestants, along with John Calvin Broomfield, to the episcopacy of The Methodist Church.

chapter 21

METHODISM GOES WEST

Expansion from the Mississippi to the Pacific Coast

METHODISM BEGAN TO MOVE WEST OF the Mississippi River several decades before Horace Greeley urged: "Go West, young man." Those states nearest the Mississippi began to be settled soon after the turn of the century. Before long, missions and schools began to be established for the Indians in Kansas and in Indian Territory to the southwest, as well as in faraway Oregon. Methodism began to penetrate Texas while it was still a foreign country. The push of the white man to the West was inexorable. It was accelerated by a number of factors in addition to the urge to migrate, among them the popular-sovereignty law as it affected Kansas and Nebraska; the discovery of gold, first in California and later on in other areas; the unique Mormon settlement of Utah; the Civil War, which many people North and South sought to escape; the Homestead Act; the development of trails and roads; the building of the railroads; and the use of steamships on navigable rivers.

Where does the West begin? Where does it end? Obviously, it ends with the Pacific Ocean. In this study it begins west of those states which have the Mississippi as their eastern border or through which the great river flows—Minnesota, Iowa, Missouri, Arkansas, and Louisiana. Those are more Middle West and South, it would seem, than West and are not included. The whole comprises sixteen of our present states with a total area of more than 1,600,000 square miles. Parts of this great region were, at one time or another, under the control of at least six foreign nations—Spain, France, Russia, England, Mexico, and the Republic of Texas. One of the states, Oklahoma, was opened up to settlement by the

420

white men at so late a date, 1889, that for the most part it lies outside this purview.

Almost every geographical feature is to be found in the West—plains, plateaus, hills, mountains, streams and rivers, deserts, forests, and coastal regions. Its climate ranges from extremes of cold to extremes of heat, from high humidity to low, from excessive rainfall to almost none at all. It contains vast resources, mineral deposits, forests, and agricultural lands. In the earliest period, fur was a magnet for traders and trappers. For a time much of the West was reserved for the Indians, with white settlers excluded. However, save for Indian Territory and the Indian reservations, the white man settled where he wished to settle, and the Indians were pushed out or died as a result of disease and war.

The immigrants were mostly Americans of western European stock. However, long before they arrived, the Spaniards had begun to settle in the southwestern section and in California. They frequently married native women, and their offspring came to be known as Mexicans. Many of the Indians retained their native dialects. The Mexicans spoke Spanish. However, in most of the West, English was the prevailing language. The Indians also had their native religions, but a number had been more or less converted to Christianity by Protestant and Catholic missionaries. The areas once controlled by Spain and Mexico were Roman Catholic; Utah, of course, was predominantly Mormon.

In the early period much of the American population was migratory, constantly shifting. Very few of the trappers and miners thought of making the West their permanent home. This was true as well of those who came West in a later period. The Great American Desert was a vast expanse to cross in order to get to the mountains or to the coast, not a place to live in. The mountains would be valueless, it was believed, once the gold and silver were extracted. There was also a countermigration; many became discouraged or restless and returned to their homes. However, an increasing number of families began to move in and to make more or less permanent homes, engaging in farming, ranching, lumbering, trade, and other occupations in addition to mining. The settlements were mostly small villages, if even this large, and the distances between settlements were usually great. Save in a few localities the population was, and remained, quite sparse.

Much of the migration was the growing edge of the push to the West, as was the case with Texas, Kansas, and Nebraska. In other instances the immigrants leapfrogged across the plains and mountains to California and Oregon, across the plains to Colorado. As a result many of the new settlements were isolated from the East, the Middle West, and the South.

This was true of the churches as well. For example, the first Protestant Episcopal church in Denver was named St. John's in the Wilderness, for the nearest church of this denomination at the time was in eastern Kansas some six hundred miles away.

There were constant changes in the political divisions which are not generally known. A territory, such as Kansas, Nebraska, or Oregon, might contain much more land than is now comprised in the states by these names. Again, a given area which is now a state, such as Wyoming or Montana, might have been divided among two or three territories at a given time. The Methodist ecclesiastical divisions, the conferences, usually followed the political divisions, but this was not always the case. At times an Annual Conference might extend beyond its natural boundaries for missionary purposes.

For very practical reasons, a conference would be organized with but several hundred church members and a few preachers; a district, when there were but a few score of church members; and a class or society—actually a church—with less than a dozen, including the preacher's wife, on numerous occasions. For example, a Methodist preacher was sent to organize a class in Loveland, Colorado. He found no Methodists in the community, but formed a class out of three people—a Baptist couple and a member of the United Brethren Church. Unlike many of these first classes, the Loveland church has had a continuous history to the present. Some of the conferences were designated as missionary—even "foreign" missionary—conferences, with the preachers retaining their membership in their home conferences, making it easier for them to return, as far too many of them did.

On occasion, but far too infrequently, the missionary societies initiated missionary work in a new region. At times Annual Conferences assumed responsibility, as did some of the bishops. Frequently a presiding elder would establish new circuits, or a preacher would enlarge his circuit. Let us not forget the local preachers, who on numerous occasions were the first clergymen in a new settlement or region, even going there primarily to mine, to farm, or to engage in some other lay occupation. Frequently they would preach on Sundays and would start Sunday schools and classes, thereby preparing the way for the preachers sent there under official appointment. Moreover, even after this occurred, they rendered valuable service as class leaders, as Sunday school superintendents, and as preachers when the preacher was elsewhere on his circuit. Frequently they were the only persons available to be appointed to circuits. Without them Methodism would have made a far poorer showing on the frontier than it did.

In the main, the immediate supervision of the field was under the direction of the presiding elders. Without them many sections would have been left without attention. For the most part the bishops visited the frontier only to preside over conference sessions and to make appointments, and at times they failed to do this. There were some notable exceptions, such as Bishop Kavanaugh's visit to California in 1856 and Bishop Marvin's to Montana in 1871. The latter made such a favorable impression that a number of Montana babies were named Marvin. Few of the missionary officials visited the field. Again, in 1840, when E. R. Ames—later a bishop—was put in charge of the Indian missions, he made an extensive visit among the Indians of the upper Mississippi Valley and the plains in the West and Southwest. More direct personal acquaintance with the frontier on the part of bishops and officials would have been most valuable.

The order of treatment in this chapter will follow both regional and state lines. Where both the Northern and Southern Churches are involved in a given state, they will be treated separately, rather than together, for they actually were separate. Both for reasons of their location —one in the southeast corner of the West, the other in the northeast— as well as for the time when Methodism became established in these areas, Texas will be considered first and the Dakotas, last. Following a brief study of the Indian missions on the plains, there will be a survey of Methodism in Kansas and Nebraska, in Colorado, in Montana, in Wyoming, in Utah, and in New Mexico. Geography, not the time of beginnings, takes us out to the coast, first to Oregon and its two satellites, Washington and Idaho, and then to northern and southern California, and its neighbors, Nevada and Arizona.

1

Texas

The beginnings of Methodist missions in Texas, though among Americans, were carried on in a foreign land. During the Spanish and Mexican periods a number of Americans settled in Texas, mainly in three regions: the Red River district—which many thought was United States territory —the "redlands" of the east, and the colonial grants in the south-central section. As many as four thousand had settled by 1820, and twenty thousand a decade later. Prior to the time of the Republic, Protestant worship services were forbidden by law. Even so, Methodist and other Protestant preachers began to preach and hold services as they could.[1]

William Stevenson of the Missouri Conference was one of the first; about 1817 he crossed over from Arkansas and apparently founded a society at Pecan Point. Others soon followed him, among them Henry Stephenson, who was in Texas briefly in 1824 and again in 1834, when he entered from Louisiana, preaching and holding a camp meeting. He is said to have organized two societies, one of these twelve miles east of San Augustine, which later occupied the McMahan Chapel and had a continuing existence. In November, 1834, the Mississippi Conference appointed him to the Texas Mission, the first formal recognition of Texas in Methodist records. He moved to Texas in 1835, settling on a branch of the Sabine River west of Louisiana.

In April, 1837, the year after Texas obtained its independence from Mexico, Dr. Martin Ruter, the president of Allegheny College, was appointed superintendent of the Texas Mission, with Robert Alexander and Littleton Fowler as his assistants. His assistants preceded him to the field, Alexander arriving in August, Fowler, in October; they preached, held camp meetings, and looked for building lots for churches. Ruter, fifty-two years old at the time, came in November. Within the next six months this remarkable man, the real founder of Texas Methodism, rode two thousand difficult miles, preached almost daily, shrank from no danger or hardship, founded societies as he went, made provision for the building of churches, mapped out circuits for preachers to travel, and made plans for a college. In April of 1838 he left to attend the annual meeting of the Missionary Society, to recruit preachers for the mission, and to bring his family to Texas. However, he became fatally ill, and died May 16 in Washington, Texas. According to a report he wrote on April 26, there were 20 societies in Texas with 325 members. A number of Sunday schools had been started, church buildings at San Augustine and Nacogdoches were nearing completion, and others were to follow. In 1840, Rutersville College, named in his memory, was opened.

Fowler, his successor, became the presiding elder of the Texas Mission District of the Mississippi Conference in December, 1838. It had five circuits and seven preachers. In the 1839 General Minutes, six circuits—San Augustine, Jasper, Montgomery, Washington, Rutersville, and

---

[1] The main sources on Texas Methodism are: Macum Phelan, *A History of Early Methodism in Texas, 1817-1866* (Nashville: Cokesbury Press, 1924); Olin Nail, *The First Hundred Years of the Southwest Texas Conference of the Methodist Church* (San Antonio: Southwest Texas Conference, The Methodist Church, 1958); Wade Crawford Barclay, *History of Methodist Missions* (New York: Board of Missions of The Methodist Church, 1949, Vol. I).

Brazora—reported 754 members for the year, with a much higher average membership per circuit than was normal for a frontier. The prospects were so good that on December 25, 1840, the Texas Conference was organized. Eighteen ministers and probationers were available; there were 3 districts, 16 circuits, and 1,878 members (230 colored). Fowler, needing additional preachers, recruited some from Northern conferences.[2]

In 1844, with a membership of 4,970, the conference was divided into the Eastern Texas Conference and the Western Texas Conference. These two conferences, as was to be expected, lined themselves up with the Southern Church. Delegates from both attended the Louisville Convention in 1845 as simply the Texas Conference. Annexation and statehood served but to increase the number of settlers, among them a number of Germans. To meet the needs of the Germans Henry P. Young (Jung) had been appointed in 1845 to work among his fellow countrymen. In 1846 Littleton Fowler died as a result of his great exposures "in discharging his official duties." Further expansion occasioned the formation of the Rio Grande Mission Conference in November, 1859, with 1,418 members. The growth continued at an unprecedented rate, for by 1861 Texas Methodism had 25,061 white members and 4,968 colored. During the war and Reconstruction years the Texas conferences, along with other Southern conferences, suffered severe disruptions with marked losses in membership. However, within a few years a remarkable recovery occurred insofar as the white membership was concerned, for by 1870 it totaled 34,772, nearly 10,000 more than in 1861. However, the colored membership had declined to 1,987.

The Northern Methodists experienced scarcely any success in Texas following the separation in 1844. In 1853 the Arkansas Conference established a Texas Mission, appointing three preachers to the field. Only 113 members were reported in 1854. In the following year the Texas Mission District was authorized, with five circuits in the Northeast— Bonham, Grayson, Millwood, Clear Fork, and Denton. Anthony Bewley, an experienced preacher, was the presiding elder. The presence of the Northern preachers, who were considered to be abolitionists, was deeply resented. In March, 1859, despite growing hostility, the Arkansas Conference quite ill-advisedly met at Timber Creek near Bonham. During the Sunday preaching service a crowd of citizens surrounded the place of worship, and one of the party read Bishop Edmund Janes a set of declarations which in substance ordered the Northern preachers to suspend operations. The Texas District was discontinued soon after-

[2] Membership records used throughout come from the annual *Minutes* of the Methodist Episcopal Church and of the Methodist Episcopal Church, South, for the years indicated.

wards, but Bewley was appointed to be superintendent and missionary to Texas. Accused of belonging to a secret abolitionist organization, he fled to Missouri, where he was apprehended and brought back to Texas, and reportedly hanged without a trial. This marked the end of the pre-war efforts of the Northern Church in Texas. Following the war the Texas Mission Conference was formed in 1867, with 19 circuits and 1,093 members. In 1870 the Texas Conference, organized the year before, reported a marked increase to 5,846 members.

2

Indian Missions

An overlooked aspect of the move westward is the missions to the Indians, many of whom were displaced from the Middle West, the East, and the South.[3] Early in the nineteenth century quite a number had migrated more or less voluntarily in order to escape the constant encroachments of the white men upon their lands, resulting in mutual hostility. After the Indian Removal Act of 1830, which provided for the exchange of lands east of the Mississippi for lands to the west side, others migrated West, frequently most unwillingly. Some had been Christianized prior to their migrations; in a number of instances their white missionaries as well as their native preachers moved out West with them.

During the decade ahead, Indians in increasing numbers settled, or were settled, in the Great Plains region, in Arkansas, and in Indian Territory. Five Indian nations—the Cherokees, Creeks, Seminoles, Choctaws, and Chickasaws—were settled in Indian Territory. Most of those who migrated under government orders suffered hardships and, in too many instances, tragedy as well. None suffered more than those Cherokees who followed the so-called "trail of tears" in 1838. Due to a variety of causes, including government mismanagement and heartlessness, nearly 4,000 of the 11,500 who started West died along the way; a Choctaw group lost nearly 2,000. Embittered before their departure, with sad experiences during their enforced migrations, many of the Indians gave up the white man's religion, Christianity, and others became quite antagonistic to-

---

[3] Information on the Indian missions is from: S. H. Babcock and J. Y. Bryce, *History of Methodism in Oklahoma* (1935, Vol. I); Barclay, *History of Methodist Missions*, Vol. II.

ward it. In some instances Christian Indians were subjected to ostracism and persecution.

In 1831 the new and relatively weak Missouri Conference began to assume responsibility for Indian work, forming the Shawnee, "Kanzas" (Caw), Cherokee, and Creek missions. Thomas and William Johnson, assigned to the Shawnee and "Kanzas" missions respectively, were to end their lives in Indian work. Bishop Robert R. Roberts personally appealed to the Tennessee Conference for volunteers for an expansion of Methodism into Arkansas; eight responded. As a result, in 1832 the Arkansas District of the Missouri Conference was formed with A. D. Smith as the presiding elder and superintendent of the Indian missions. Also, Joseph Edmundson was the presiding elder of the Missouri District and the superintendent of the Kanzas missions. In the following year the Indian Missionary District of the Missouri Conference was created, with Thomas Johnson, quite deservedly, the superintendent. Four missions were listed—Shawnee, Delaware, Iowa and Sac, and Peoria—with schools in each place. Similarly, six schools were given for the Creek Mission and four for the Cherokee. In 1831 Alexander Talley had been appointed by the Mississippi Conference to the Choctaw Mission west of Mississippi.

In 1836 the work among the Cherokees, Creeks, and Choctaws—which by now included 1,225 Indian members, plus a few white and colored—up to now shared by the Missouri and Mississippi Conferences, was assigned to the newly organized Arkansas Conference. The Shawnee, Delaware, Peoria, Kickapoo, and Kansas missions remained under the jurisdiction of the Missouri Conference, and reported but 427 members.

In 1840 Edward R. Ames became one of the corresponding secretaries of the Missionary Society, with the Indian missions as his special responsibility. Accordingly, he made an extensive trip among the Indian missions, becoming acquainted with the field at first hand. This responsibility no doubt accounts in part for his interest in the frontier when he became a bishop. A new phase opened with the organization of the Indian Mission Conference, which took place on October 23, 1844, at Riley's Chapel, two miles east of Tahlequah. It assumed charge of the Indian missions previously attached to the Missouri and Arkansas Conferences. It was divided into three districts—the Kanzas River, the Cherokee, and the Choctaw—with a total of 14 appointments and 3,237 members, 112 of whom were white, 133, colored. Jerome Berryman was appointed to be the superintendent.

With the division of the church in 1844, the Indian Mission Conference became attached to the Southern Church. In 1850 the conference restricted itself to the Cherokees, Creeks, and Choctaws in Indian Territory, with the St. Louis Conference assuming responsibility for the Indians of Kansas. In 1871 the Indian Mission reported 4,952 members, 188 of whom were white, 434, colored. It was not, of course, until 1889 that Indian Territory, which included most of Oklahoma, was thrown open to white settlement on any large scale. Meanwhile, the Northern Methodists were continuing with missions among the Indians of Kansas, assigning them to the Missouri Conference, with but 172 Indians reported for the Wyandott Mission in 1849. The number of missions and members increased in succeeding years, but the inexorable pressure of the white settlers coupled with the Civil War pushed the Indians further and further west.

The missions and schools conducted by the Methodists among the Indians west of the Mississippi during this period of settlement were invaluable Christianizing and civilizing agencies. A byproduct was the training they provided for preachers who later on were to labor effectively among the white settlers, such as William H. Goode, who formally introduced Northern Methodism into Kansas, Nebraska, and Colorado; and L. B. Stateler, who was to be the pioneer of Southern Methodism in Montana.

3

Kansas and Nebraska

Until 1861, when two conferences were organized, beginnings and development of Northern Methodism in Kansas and Nebraska were interrelated.[4] As early as 1831, when the region was largely inhabited by Indians, Methodism had been introduced with the establishment of the Shawnee Mission in the Missouri Conference. Beginning with 1853 a number of free-lance preachers, including W. D. Gage, had preached on occasion to the few white settlers in the territory. In 1852 the General Conference, aware of future developments, attached the Indian Mission portion of the territory of Nebraska—including Kansas—to the Missouri Conference. With the passage of the Kansas-Nebraska Bill in 1854, which

---

[4] The major sources for this section are: David Marquette, *A History of Nebraska Methodism,* 1854-1904 (Cincinnati: The Western Methodist Book Concern Press, 1904); Everett Jackman, *The Nebraska Methodist Story* (Nebraska Conference Methodist Historical Society, 1954); William Goode, *Outposts of Zion, with Limnings of Mission Life* (Cincinnati: Poe and Hitchcock, 1864); E. J. Stanley, *Life of Rev. L. B. Stateler* (Nashville: Publishing House of the Methodist Episcopal Church, South, 1907).

created the territories of Kansas and Nebraska, opening them up to white settlers and providing popular sovereignty to determine whether they should be free soil or slave, settlers began to stream in, especially into Kansas.

The story of "bloody" Kansas as a prelude to the Civil War is pertinent to the history of religion in the territory. Immigrants representing both sides came in large numbers, many from Missouri and the Southern states, and many more eventually from the Middle West and New England. New England in particular organized companies of free-soil colonists to go to Kansas in order to make it a free state. Towns, such as Lawrence and Topeka, were organized as free-soil towns; others, including Atchison, Lecompton, and Leavenworth, as proslavery. With radical elements on both sides, a great deal of hostility, which at times resulted in bloodshed, developed. As a consequence, not only were both Southern and Northern Methodists well represented in Kansas, but, quite understandably, they were not on the most friendly terms. On the other hand, Nebraska did not become too greatly involved in the popular-sovereignty conflict.

In June, 1854, Bishop Ames appointed William H. Goode, the experienced missionary to the Indians, to survey Kansas and Nebraska and to make a full report. Goode immediately left his home in Indiana, reaching his field early in July. Three dangers confronted him—hostile Indians, the threat of border warfare, and an outbreak of Asiatic cholera. Undaunted, he visited the Wakarusa Mission, and appointed the missionary, Abraham Still, to be in charge of the work in that immediate region. On July 8 he preached what he believed to be the first sermon in the area to white settlers by a regularly appointed preacher.

Although he was all but prostrated by some mysterious disease, he continued his survey, reaching the house of Thomas B. Markham near Kickapoo and engaging him to be preacher in charge in the section around Fort Leavenworth. Next, he went to Nebraska, to the deserted site of old Fort Kearney—soon to be the site of Nebraska City—and then to the site of Omaha where as yet there were no buildings, only a single pile of lumber. He spent a Sunday with the Presbyterian preacher at the Bellevue Indian mission, and here he preached his first sermon in Nebraska. As he had done in Kansas, he assigned two preachers to be in charge of the circuits until conference time.

Returning to his home in Indiana on August 18, 1854, he reported that although there were probably not more than five hundred families in Kansas and Nebraska, provision should be made for the large increase in population that was expected. He recommended that Kansas and Nebraska should be formed into a single district, with a presiding elder who should travel at large, with power to open up new fields of labor and to employ and assign preachers to their circuits. As a result, the Missouri Conference meeting during October 12-16, 1854, created the Kansas and Nebraska Mission District, with seven missions—not including the Indian missions—and appointed Goode as the presiding elder to carry out the plans he had envisioned. This he proceeded to do with his characteristic energy and wisdom. The results appear in the report to the 1855 conference: 631 white members distributed, quite unevenly, among the Wakarusa, Fort Leavenworth, Omaha, Old Fort Kearney, Marie de Cygnes, Fort Scott, Fort Riley, Nemahaw, Wolf River, and Wyandott and Delaware missions. In addition there were 127 Indian members.

We seldom learn what the wives of the frontier preachers thought about their husbands' occupation. Consequently the observations of Mrs. C. H. Lovejoy, whose husband was appointed to the Fort Riley Mission, are of interest:

His field of labor extends from Pottawatomie Mission, thirty miles on the south[east], to seventy or eighty miles west from here beyond the Fort, and [he] finds twelve places where they need constant Sabbath preaching. Drones that cannot work hard or live on coarse fare, or sleep in cabins with or without a bed, or in the open prairie need not come here.[5]

She was quite correct in her views.

The church at Manhattan, Kansas, had an unusual origin. In part it was composed of free-soil colonists who organized it on their arrival. However, another group, under the leadership of John Pipher, was formed into a Methodist class of twenty-three members on April 30, 1855, while on a steamboat on the Ohio River on the first stage of their journey to Kansas. On arriving in Manhattan the class joined the church that had been previously established there.

In 1855 Nebraska became a district of the Iowa Conference with eight circuits. Goode was appointed to be the presiding elder of the new district. Kansas, the more populous territory, remained with the Missouri Conference, and was divided into two districts. Two able presiding elders were appointed—L. B. Dennis to the North Kansas District, and Abraham Still to the South Kansas.

A further change, in anticipation of increased migration, was effected in 1856 when the three districts were organized as the Kansas-Nebraska Conference. The organization took place on October 23 in the Lawrence church, a combination frame building and tent. The political situation at the time was exceedingly tense, so tense that some of the preachers

---

[5] *First Methodist Church, Manhattan, Kansas, 1855-1955; One Hundred Years of Christian Service and a Consecrated Future* (1955), p. 13.

attending the session were armed. This new conference extended to the Rocky Mountains in the west, and was divided into three districts—the Leavenworth, the Topeka, and the Nebraska. By 1860 the population of Kansas was 107,206, of Nebraska, 28,841. During this same year the membership of the conference was 3,881, with Kansas furnishing 2,997, Nebraska, 884. As was customarily true of the western frontiers, the church membership fell far short of keeping pace with the population.

With future expansion in mind, the new conference was divided into two in 1861. On March 21-26, about two months after Kansas was admitted as a free state, the Kansas Conference was organized, with eight districts, including one in Colorado and the St. Joseph German mission, which overlapped into Nebraska and Missouri. By now there were 78 effective preachers, 71 charges, and 4,038 members.

The Nebraska Conference was organized during April 4-8, with 2 districts, 22 effective preachers, 20 charges, and 948 members. Nebraska, with a much smaller population, did not become a state until 1867.

The Civil War, grasshopper plagues, drouths, and a constantly shifting population created great difficulties for the churches. Despite these impediments to progress, both conferences had a steady growth, so that by 1870 the Kansas Conference reported 103 effective preachers, 95 charges, 233 local preachers, and 10,290 members, and the Nebraska Conference reported 36 effective preachers, 33 charges, 2,670 members, and 46 local preachers. By this time, both conferences had extended their fields of activity to the plains further west.

As for the Southern Methodists, who were more in evidence in Kansas than in Nebraska, in 1850 their Indian missions in Kansas were attached to the St. Louis Conference. Southern preachers as well as Northern crossed the borders to preach in Kansas and Nebraska on occasion. In September, 1854, following the enactment of the Kansas-Nebraska Bill, the St. Louis Conference created the Kansas Mission District, with Andrew Monroe as the superintendent. In addition to the Indian missions it consisted of eight circuits. In 1855 the district reported 619 white members, 248 Indian, and 1 colored. The white membership almost equaled that of the Northern Church in Kansas, which reported 631.

A change was made the following year (1855), for on October 24 the Kansas Mission Conference was organized with two districts, Lecompton and Kickapoo. William Bradford was the presiding elder of the first and Nathan Scarritt of the second, both of them able men. It included ten circuits—one of them Santa Fe, New Mexico—three Indian missions, and an Indian school. The last available statistical report of this conference is for 1860. By then it comprised three districts and the Pike's Peak Mission, with 25 charges, 1,039 white members, 130 Indian, and 5 colored. In the light of the increasing hostility of Kansans toward the Southern preachers this was a remarkable achievement.

The next and last session of this conference was held in the fall of 1861, after the war had broken out. In order to avoid any possible pretext for a disturbance, instead of the conference being held at Atchison as planned, it was convened at a farm on Grasshopper Creek several miles west of the town, almost in secret. No records of this final session are in existence. The preachers were assigned to their posts, which some attempted to fill, despite the dangers involved in doing so. L. B. Stateler was threatened with hanging if he remained. Accordingly, he went to Denver, planning to have his wife and daughter join him there. During his absence his house was burned down, and his wife and daughter barely escaped being burned to death. For the most part the Southern Church suspended its operations in Kansas during the war years. That it revived at all following the war is remarkable. The details of the revival are lost, but the outline may be recovered in part.

As was previously stated, the Kansas Mission Conference came to an end with the session of 1861. Some of its circuits became attached to the St. Louis Conference; others, to the Missouri; still others disappeared. In 1866 the Missouri Conference formed the Leavenworth District, but it apparently did not last out the year. Instead, we find some of the Kansas points listed in the St. Joseph District, and, in 1867, others, along with the Nebraska circuit, in the Savannah District. In 1867 the St. Louis Conference established the Kansas Mission District, comprising seven circuits and the Shawnee Indian Mission.

Enough progress was made in the next few years to justify the inclusion of Kansas and Nebraska in the Western Conference, organized in Leavenworth September 8-10, 1870, along with Colorado and Montana. This was one of a number of conferences, both North and South, whose boundaries seem to be quite unrealistic. Fifteen points are listed for Kansas and Nebraska alone, with a total conference membership of 1,549 whites, 133 colored people, and but 37 Indians. The greater number, of course, were in Kansas rather than in Nebraska. Indeed, in the following year 1,802 white members are given for Kansas, 258 for Nebraska.

In studying the history of the two Methodisms in Kansas it is of interest to see how closely they paralleled each other in their methods of operation. It is also significant to note how, in both situations, conferences rather than missionary societies assumed responsibility for missionary work in territories other than their own. This same assumption of responsibility by Annual Conferences for missionary work came into evidence in other frontier situations in the West as new areas were settled.

To be sure, the missionary societies were not inactive and at times provided necessary funds; but, even so, they seemingly should have been more deeply involved than they were.

4

Colorado

In a very real sense, Colorado Methodism was an extension of Methodism in Kansas and Nebraska. Furthermore, both branches of Methodism were present; and, as in Kansas, the Civil War had an adverse reaction upon the Southern Church. But there were some major differences; for, unlike the territories to the east, the settlement of Colorado was not the growing edge of settlements moving across the border. Instead, the settlers leaped over the vast plains of western Nebraska, Kansas, and eastern Colorado, the "Great American Desert," in their search for gold. Furthermore, few of the early settlers planned to stay permanently, but hoped to return home when they had made their stake or when the gold mines played out. Thousands came, but as many thousands left, for the population in 1870 was little more than that of 1860. It is obvious that the establishment of permanent religious work in such a situation was most difficult.[6]

Colorado was sparsely settled by wandering Indians, some Mexicans along the New Mexico border, and trappers and traders prior to 1858, when the first of a series of gold discoveries was made. In 1846 Mormons had wintered at Pueblo, and a decade later the Roman Catholics founded a church at Conejos, near the New Mexico border, which is still in existence. But with the beginning of the gold rush, occasional preachers began to arrive with the gold miners.

The first of these, it appears, was George W. Fisher, a Northern Methodist local preacher, carpenter, wagonmaker, and housebuilder, who arrived with the party of General William Larimer. At the request of

[6] Sources on Colorado Methodism are: Lowell Swan, "A History of Methodism in Colorado, 1863-76" (Unpublished Th.D. dissertation, Iliff School of Theology, 1951); Kenneth Metcalf, "The Beginnings of Methodism in Colorado" (Unpublished Th.D. dissertation, Iliff School of Theology, 1948); William Goode, *Outposts of Zion;* E. J. Stanley, *Life of Stateler;* Isaac Beardsley, *Echoes from Peak and Plain, or Tales of Life, War, Travels and Colorado Methodism* (Cincinnati: Curts and Jennings, 1898).

Larimer, a devout Presbyterian, on November 1, 1858, he conducted the first religious service on record in Denver and the gold-mining region. It was held in one end of a double log cabin owned by two gamblers. His congregation consisted of members of the Larimer party, the two Indian "wives" of the gamblers, and their children. Gambling continued uninterrupted during the singing of hymns, the saying of prayers, and the preaching. It is reported that he began his sermon by saying, "Boys, when there is any good to be done, consider me in," an attitude that typified most of the preachers who came out to the West. Among the other preachers in the area there was a Rev. Mr. Porter of the Southern Church from Georgia, who is otherwise unidentified. He probably came with a mining party from Georgia.

The Northern Church was the first Protestant denomination to begin officially in Colorado. In 1859 Bishop Levi Scott, who had observed the migration to the Pike's Peak and Cherry Creek region when he presided over the Kansas and Nebraska Conference, enlisted Dr. William Goode, who had introduced Methodism into Kansas and Nebraska, and Jacob Adriance to go to Colorado as missionaries. They arrived in Denver on June 28, and on July 3 held morning and afternoon preaching services in an unfinished hotel. Young Adriance, who had a good voice, attracted the congregations "by singing them up." Going to the gold mines on July 10, Goode preached at Central City out of doors to a large group of miners, using "treasures in earthen vessels" as his theme. On the day following he organized a church consisting of forty-five members, many of them Welsh hard-rock miners—"Cousin Jacks"—which is in existence today, with its stone building dating back to 1864. Leaving G. W. Fisher in charge, they went on to Golden City, where Goode preached on July 17 in a large, round gambling tent, but by arrangement gambling was suspended for an hour. A second church was organized here. Then they returned to Denver and on August 2 founded a church now known as Trinity Methodist Church. Goode soon departed for his home, leaving Adriance in charge of the Golden and Denver circuits.

In 1860 Colorado became a district of the Kansas and Nebraska Conference, with the redoubtable John M. Chivington as the presiding elder. Under his aggressive leadership the membership grew from 27 in 1860 to 348 a year later, with seven circuits at gateways to the mountains— Denver, Golden, Colorado Springs, and Canon City—and in the mountain mining camps. Chivington gained fame as "Major Chivington"—the officer chiefly responsible for the defeat of a hitherto victorious Confederate Army at Glorieta Pass in New Mexico, which ended Confederate dreams of the conquest of Colorado, New Mexico, and the Southwest to California. However, in 1864 he was bitterly criticized for the destruction of an Indian village and the death of many of its inhabitants at Sand Creek, Colorado. "Father" John L. Dyer, one of the early preachers, was known as the "Snow-Shoe Itinerant," since he made his preaching rounds in the mountains in winter on homemade skis. His autobiography, *The Snow-Shoe Itinerant,* provides a fascinating account of experiences in the mining camps.

During the summer—June or July—of 1860 William Bradford came to Denver from the Kansas Mission Conference of the Southern Church. He soon had a congregation of twenty-six members as well as an attractive chapel, the first church building in Denver. The conference met in the fall and created the Pike's Peak Mission, with Bradford as superintendent and preacher at Denver. Six additional circuits were authorized, but were left to be supplied. It is doubtful that any of them were supplied; for with the outbreak of the Civil War, the congregation disbanded— for Union sentiment was high in Colorado—Bradford departed; and the Episcopalians acquired the chapel. Unaware of the situation, in 1862 Learner B. Stateler came from inhospitable Kansas to inhospitable Colorado to take charge of the Denver circuit, only to find that he had no congregation, no chapel. For a time he preached from place to place, and his wife ran a boarding house, but in 1864 they departed for Montana.

On July 10, 1863, Bishop Ames presided over the organization of the Rocky Mountain Conference—next year named the Colorado Conference—of the Northern Church, with 15 local preachers and 241 white members and 14 colored. It comprised two districts and thirteen circuits. Oliver A. Willard, Frances Willard's brother, was the presiding elder of the Denver District, and B. T. Vincent, brother of John H. Vincent, went to Central City, where in 1864 he began the publication of a Sunday school journal, the *Rocky Mountain Sunday School Casket,* Colorado's first magazine. The conference authorized Colorado's first school of higher learning, Colorado Seminary—now the University of Denver—which was founded in 1864.

Colorado's future seemed to be assured with the coming of the railroad in 1870 and with statehood in 1876. In 1872 the German Methodists had made a start in Denver with a church with a membership of twelve. In 1866 the Missouri Conference of the Southern Church appointed Stateler a superintendent of missions in Colorado and Montana, but he never resumed any activity in Colorado. In 1870 the Western Conference appointed W. H. Lewis as presiding elder of the Colorado District and pastor at Denver. However, it was not until the arrival of A. A. Morrison in 1871 that the Denver church was reorganized, with twenty-five members. In 1872 the Southern Church appointed seven preachers to Colorado, with 258 members reported the next year, a very good beginning. For the most part the churches extended from Denver to the west and southwest. One, however, was founded at Sterling in the northeast by former Confederate prisoners of war and their families. In this same year—1872—the Northern Church reported 31 churches in the Colorado Conference with 1,070 members, located either in the mountains or on the eastern edge of the mountains. It was not until later that settlers and the churches moved into the arid eastern plains.

5

Montana

Prior to 1862 there were very few settlers within Montana with its vast area of nearly 150,000 square miles. But with the finding of gold in the southwestern section ("Old Montana"), at Grasshopper Creek (Bannack) in 1862, at Alder Gulch (Virginia City) in 1863, and at Last Chance (Helena) in 1864, a typical gold rush developed, with gold seekers by the thousands streaming in from East, South, and West. Towns sprang up in a few weeks, many of them to dwindle away or die as the gold gave out or when richer strikes were reported elsewhere. In these early days very few settlers went to the other parts of Montana.

As was to be expected, preachers of various denominations who mined or did other work during the week and preached when and as they could on Sundays were among the newcomers. A Northern Methodist class was formed at Virginia City during the winter of 1863-64 with William Florkey as the leader.[7] Hugh Duncan, a miner and local preacher, preached at Junction and Virginia City at about the same time, as did W. W. Alderson in the Gallatin Valley. A Southern Church preacher, a Brother Hardgrove, preached at Norwegian Gulch. All of this was preparatory, but not of lasting quality.

In July of 1864 Stateler, of the former Kansas Mission Conference of the Southern Church, came to Montana with his wife from Denver, in part to escape the inhospitality if not hostility of Coloradoans toward Southern preachers. Finding the group of Southerners at Norwegian

---

[7] For further information on Montana, see: Edward Mills, *Plains, Peaks, and Pioneers* (Portland, Ore.: Binfords and Mort, 1947); Barclay, *History of Methodist Missions,* Vol. III; Stanley, *Life of Stateler.*

Gulch, he made plans for preaching services. He erected a rude preaching place, a kind of arbor made of forked limbs stuck upright in the ground, with poles, placed horizontally in the forks, which were covered with brush for the roof. Here he shared preaching with Brother Hardgrove. He preached, in addition, at Virginia City, and also at Willow Creek, where he organized a class of six members. He supported himself by farming. Finding the situation somewhat unsettled, in 1866 he moved to Oregon, where he was appointed to the Albany Circuit of the Columbia Conference.

The Northern Church was the first to enter the field officially. In 1864 Bishop Edmund Janes urged A. M. Hough, of the New York Conference, to go to Montana as superintendent of the proposed mission there to recover his health. When his wife was told that she should not go with him since there was not a respectable woman in the territory, she replied spiritedly, "If there is not a respectable woman in the territory of 15,000 or 20,000 inhabitants, then it is time there was one." After a long and arduous seventeen-hundred-mile stagecoach ride they arrived with his assistant, E. T. McLaughlin, in Virginia City on October 23. With his health apparently restored despite the difficult trip, he entered upon his new duties with great vigor, both preaching and seeing to the completion of a $1,500 log chapel. The chapel was dedicated on November 6; the collection to wipe out the building debt amounted to $704.50. His wife had been misinformed concerning all of the Montana women, for Hough reported that there were a number of ladies in the town of much refinement who regularly attended his services. By January the membership had reached ninety persons; accordingly, an addition was made to the chapel.

Soon afterward, however, thousands of miners began to leave Bannack and Virginia City for the new fields in Last Chance Gulch (Helena). After surveying the situation in Helena, Hough sent McLaughlin to be in charge, and he preached his first sermon there standing on a pile of logs which soon were to be used in building the church. In August of 1866 James King went to Virginia City, and with "true Methodist enthusiasm and energy," to quote the Episcopalian Bishop Daniel Tuttle, he proceeded to raise $3,000 for a new frame church. However, because of some mismanagement, the church was sold under a mechanic's lien and came into the possession of the Episcopalians, who had money if not enthusiasm and energy. In September of 1867 Hough organized a class in Bozeman, where a church had recently been dedicated. It was most unusual for a building to be erected before a society had been formally founded.

In 1868 Hough went to Southern California, this time for his wife's health, and McLaughlin left for Ohio. George Comfort, who had come to Virginia City in April, was the only traveling preacher remaining. He moved to Helena, and preached at Bozeman. By this time the membership had fallen to about fifty. Among the replacements was T. C. Iliff, who later on was to be the superintendent in Utah. He came to Helena in the spring of 1871, but in the fall he moved to Missoula, where he performed much of the manual labor in building a church. It was not until June of 1872 that the renowned William W. Van Orsdel (Brother Van) came to preach, sing, and pray.

It was on August 8 of this same year that the Rocky Mountain Conference, comprising Utah, Montana, Idaho, and part of Wyoming, was organized. Despite the untiring labors of consecrated preachers the Montana Mission reported a total of but ninety-five members, one church building, and *one half* of a parsonage. J. A. Van Anda became the presiding elder of the Helena District, which had seven circuits.

In the meantime in 1866 Stateler, out in Oregon, read that the Southern Church's Missouri Conference—which had absorbed some of the territory of the Kansas Mission Conference—had appointed him to be superintendent of missions in Colorado and Montana. Accordingly, in 1867 he returned to Montana to take up his duties. He had no congregations, no churches, no preachers, no money appropriated for the task ahead. However, confining all his attention to Montana, he began to farm and to reorganize former classes and form new ones. He appointed B. R. Baxter, a local preacher, to be in charge of the newly organized church in Helena. In 1870 the newly formed Western Conference appointed him as the presiding elder of the Montana District, which included seven circuits. Three circuits materialized, with a total membership in 1871 of ninety-three, just two less than that reported by the Northern Church in the following year. Stateler attended the 1871 conference session and recruited preachers, with the result that the membership increased to 131 in 1872. During this time, and for many years to come, he supported himself by farming—his wife taking care of the farm during his absences—and in addition he gave a good deal of money to further the work of the church. He truly was the father of Southern Methodism in Montana. The Southern Church restricted most of its activities to Old Montana. The Northern Church, on the other hand, followed settlers as they moved into other sections of the territory.

6

Wyoming

Wyoming, with its more than 97,000 square miles, has always been sparsely settled. There was little to attract settlers in the early days of westward migration; instead, it provided a passageway along the Oregon Trail and, beginning in 1867, by means of the Union Pacific Railroad. Mormons for a time had settled in the Southwest region; but, with the coming of General A. S. Johnston's army in 1857, they departed for Utah. The discovery of gold, in limited quantities, to be sure, in 1867 in the south-central region provided a stimulus to settlements. From time to time portions of Wyoming were claimed by other territories. Its present boundaries were not determined until it gained territorial status in 1868. The population in 1870 had grown to but 9,118, and to only 20,789 by 1880. Among the discouraging factors in settlement was the hostility of Indians, the Sioux and the Cheyennes in particular. Most of the early settlements were along the Union Pacific right of way, as was but natural.

Not only was Wyoming politically divided, but insofar as Methodism was concerned, it was ecclesiastically parceled out as well.[8] The southwest corner was contained in the Utah Mission, the northeast was included in the Black Hills Mission when it was formed in 1880, and the southern and eastern regions, for the most part along the Union Pacific Railroad, at first were in the Colorado Conference. It was not until 1888 that the Wyoming Mission Conference was formed, with seven circuits, all but Sundance in the northeast corner being situated in the southern section of the territory. There were about half-a-dozen preachers, with the able D. L. Rader as the superintendent, and only 329 members. The Southern Church did not become established in Wyoming.

The first two Methodist churches in Wyoming, one at Cheyenne, the other at Laramie—both important towns along the Union Pacific Railroad—were organized in a strikingly similar manner. In both instances Methodist preachers, one a supernumerary, the other a local preacher, and both of them practicing physicians who had come to Wyoming for their health, played important roles in establishing these two churches.

Cheyenne, for a time the end point of the railroad construction, was

[8] See: Barclay, *History of Methodist Missions,* Vol. III; Malcolm L. Cook, "The Methodist Episcopal Church in Wyoming, 1867-88" (Unpublished A.M. thesis, University of Denver, 1955).

laid out in 1867. It is estimated that about 6,000 persons, most of them described as riffraff, were in the settlement at this time. On September 20, 1867, W. W. Baldwin of the Colorado Conference preached in the City Hall to seventy persons. Soon afterward a Methodist society was formed with nine members under the direction of Dr. D. W. Scott, practicing physician and local preacher. Later a Sunday school, with Scott as superintendent, was begun. Nearly a year later, in July, 1868, a Sunday school was started in Laramie, with five children in attendance. Within a few months, in December, a society, also with five members, was formed by Dr. G. F. Hilton, a supernumerary of the Wisconsin Conference and also a physician.

In 1868 both Cheyenne and Laramie were in the "Dacotah" District of the Colorado Conference. Andrew W. Cather was appointed both as the presiding elder and pastor of the two churches. The name was changed to the Wyoming District in 1869, and in August of that year Cather was succeeded by Lewis Hartsough, who had taken a supernumerary relationship with the Central New York Conference in April to become the agent of the American Bible Society from North Platte westward along the railroad. However, he left in December to become the superintendent of the newly formed Utah Mission.

This constant change of presiding elders and preachers was all too common a feature of Methodism in the West; Wyoming was especially stricken by this migrant ministry. Even though a church was built at Cheyenne in 1870 and another at Laramie in 1871, the increase in membership was lamentably small.

Further west, in Evanston, also on the railroad, on October 19, 1870, G. M. Pierce, superintendent of the Utah Mission, preached in a railroad section house to a small group. Later on in the year a church was organized under his direction; and, despite a very small membership, a church building was erected in 1871. The church, however, experienced difficult times in the days ahead, partly because of the strength of the Mormons in that region.

Although efforts were made to establish churches at the mining camps of South Pass and Atlantic, and in the railroad towns of Rock Springs and Rawlins, these met with very little success at first. However, by 1876 a church was begun in Rawlins, and in 1877 in Rock Springs. It was not until later on that churches were organized at other settlements. As was previously noted, when the Wyoming Mission, including all of Wyoming, was formed in 1888 there were but a half-dozen or so churches and not many more than three hundred members.

7

Utah

Utah, which was essentially a Mormon theocracy under Brigham Young, was unlike any other western frontier. Its population, largely Mormon, grew rapidly: 11,380 in 1850; 40,273 in 1860; and 86,786 in 1870. In the late 1860's there may have been no more than a thousand Gentiles (non-Mormons) in Utah. This, coupled with the opposition, if not at times open hostility, toward both Protestant and Catholic missions made their establishment most difficult. The Methodists, usually among the first to work in newly settled areas, were somewhat laggard in Utah. The Southern Church made little if any effort to enter the field, and the Northern was slow to do so.[9]

In 1855 the Committee on Domestic Missions recommended that it would be desirable to establish a mission in Utah, but no definite action was taken. In this same year the California Conference optimistically listed Salt Lake City among its appointments, but sent no preacher to the Utah capital. Bishop Matthew Simpson went through Utah in the fall of 1862 while en route from the West Coast, but this chance visit produced no immediate results. In 1867 the Nevada Conference included Salt Lake City among its appointments. J. L. Trefren, the presiding elder, visited Salt Lake City during the winter, and reported that it would not be feasible to establish a mission there; accordingly no preacher was sent to this post.

During the following year A. N. Fisher, also a presiding elder of the Nevada Conference, was in Salt Lake City. He accepted Brigham Young's invitation to preach in the Mormon Tabernacle, and was subjected to ridicule by the Mormon audience. Bishop Calvin Kingsley, while on his way to preside over the Nevada Conference, accepted a similar invitation, but fared no better. For in his sermon he spoke movingly of the glorious prospect of going to Abraham's bosom after death. Whereupon Brigham Young said that, if the bishop did so, he would be going to the bosom of an old polygamist!

In 1869 Lewis Hartsough, then an agent for the American Bible Society—and for a brief time, beginning in August, the pastor of the

---

[9] The major sources of information on Utah are: Henry Merkel, *History of Methodism in Utah* (Colorado Springs: Dentan Printing Co., 1938) ; Barclay, *History of Methodist Missions*, Vol. III; J. M. Reid and J. T. Gracey, *Missions and Missionary Society of the Methodist Episcopal Church* (New York: Eaton and Mains, 1895, Vol. I) . *Minutes of the Twenty-fifth Anniversary of the Utah Mission* (J. D. Gillilan and E. C. Hunt, 1895) .

Laramie, Wyoming, church—made a number of trips to Utah. As a result of his observations, he called the attention of both Bishop Kingsley and Bishop Simpson to the need and opportunity in Utah. The Utah Mission was authorized in November; Hartsough was appointed superintendent; and he was in Salt Lake City to assume his duties in December. This was about fourteen years after the first recommendation to initiate a mission in Utah had been made.

On his arrival he called on Bishop Daniel Tuttle, of the Protestant Episcopal Church, who offered him the use of his church's place of worship, Independence Hall, on the following Sunday evening. He also made an additional offer: "Our choir will do the singing, wife will play the organ—won't you, dear, and I will sing bass." Hartsough gratefully accepted both of these gracious offers. In addition to preaching in Salt Lake City, every fortnight he visited such places as he could during the winter, occasionally preaching in Corinne—the chief Gentile town— and in Ogden. It should be said that he served without pay, accepting but $300 for expenses.

In the spring he attended his own conference, the Central New York, and enlisted Gustavus M. Pierce to become the pastor at Salt Lake City. Pierce arrived with his family early in May, 1870, and preached his first Salt Lake City sermon in Independence Hall on the fifteenth. He organized a Methodist class on May 20, and on May 22 about forty persons attended his services in Faust's Hall, the misleading name of an unfinished loft over a livery stable, which was to be the church home for a year. Soon afterward Hartsough departed with his family for a lower altitude, and Pierce became the superintendent.

Three preachers were there to assist him. By 1871 classes had been started at Corinne, Ogden, Tooele, and Evanston, Wyoming, with a total membership in the mission of 120. A church building at Corinne, which is still standing, was dedicated in 1870 by Chaplain C. C. McCabe, agent of the Church Extension Society. In addition to Sunday schools, the Methodists, like the other denominations, had a system of mission day schools, partly because the existing schools were inadequate and thoroughly under Mormon control, and partly as a means of doing missionary work among the Mormon pupils.

In 1872 Utah became a part of the Rocky Mountain Conference, with 2 districts, 15 appointments—9 of which were left to be supplied—and but 106 members. In 1877 Utah became a separate conference, with but 7 traveling preachers and 143 members. In 1880, by its own request, the conference once more became a mission. Not a great deal had been accomplished during this period of time, despite the devoted work of the preachers and teachers and the expenditure of considerable sums of money. As has been well stated, Methodist work in Utah was and continued to be "peculiar and difficult."

8

New Mexico

When New Mexico became a territory in 1850, it was essentially a conquered province with an alien population of more than 60,000, composed of Mexicans, Indians, and Anglo-Americans, with Spanish as the predominant language. Indian religions persisted, at times under the cloak of Christianity, but Roman Catholicism was the prevailing faith. Protestantism was practically nonexistent until Baptist, Presbyterian, and Methodist missionaries began to arrive. When they did come, their missions differed but little from foreign missions in Latin America.

It was in 1850 that Enoch G. Nicholson was sent out by the Northern Church to Santa Fe to minister to persons who spoke English.[10] He was under appointment, strange to say, of the Oregon and California Conference. The result of this endeavor was to determine whether or not the mission should be extended to the Spanish-speaking population, a rather strange test, it seems. By November he had organized a small society, composed of residents and army personnel. With the removal of the army headquarters, his congregation declined sharply. This, coupled with his wife's illness, induced him to depart for the East.

He returned in 1853, with two assistants; one, the Rev. Walter Hansen, a New Mexico native who spoke Spanish, the other, Father Benigno Cardenas, a disaffected priest, whom Nicholson had met during his first stay. Despite the active opposition of the Roman Catholic bishop, Cardenas preached his first sermon in the public square. Then he dramatically turned over his credentials as a priest to Nicholson and requested that he authorize him to be a Methodist preacher working with

[10] Information on New Mexico can be found in: Thomas Harwood, *History of New Mexico Spanish and English Missions of the Methodist Episcopal Church from 1850-1910* (Albuquerque: El Abogado Press, 1908, 1910, Vols. I, II); Barclay, *History of Methodist Missions*, Vol. III; James Cannon, *History of Southern Methodist Missions* (Nashville: Cokesbury Press, 1926); Harriet S. Kellogg, *Life of Mrs. Emily J. Harwood* (Albuquerque: El Abogado Press, 1908).

the mission. It was by this irregular method that the Methodists acquired the first of a series of Spanish-American workers in New Mexico.

Since the illiteracy rate was high and schools were few, Hansen started a school with some thirty to thirty-five pupils. The opposition of the Catholic bishop helped to bring about its dissolution, and Hansen left the mission soon afterward. With the energetic help of Cardenas, Nicholson was able to form societies at Peralta and Socorro and to make a number of converts in other places. A start had scarcely been made among the Spanish-speaking people when Nicholson, pleading ill health, left the mission in June of 1854, leaving the converted priest in charge.

Dallas D. Lore arrived as superintendent on July 24, 1855. He made a round of inspection, and reorganized the societies at Peralta and Socorro. He planned a monthly circuit of four appointments. He also began to spend some time with the Indians, whom he believed would be receptive to evangelization. Even so, the Board discontinued the mission in 1856, partly because of questions concerning Cardenas. However, Thomas Harwood, who arrived in 1869, stated that the entire success of the mission up to the time of Lore's arrival was due to the preaching of the ex-priest.

In 1864, the General Conference requested that a mission and mission school be established in New Mexico, but nothing was done at this time. The Colorado Conference of 1868 appointed John L. Dyer, the "snow-shoe itinerant," who had urged that a mission be formed in New Mexico, as the presiding elder of the Rio Grande District, which was to include New Mexico. He made Elizabethtown, a mining camp, his headquarters, and formed a class of seven persons there. During the year he preached in many places, including Santa Fe, where he assisted the Presbyterian preacher in a two-week revival. During the following year he made Santa Fe his headquarters; and, without "a solitary assistant, not even a wife," he was not only presiding elder but pastor for all New Mexico and the San Luis Valley in Colorado.

Without minimizing what Dyer did, no doubt his greatest contribution to the mission was to persuade his capable and dauntless friends of Wisconsin days, Thomas Harwood and his wife Emily, who was a college-trained teacher, to come to New Mexico to take his place. Their arrival in the fall of 1869 marked the beginning of a long and fruitful career in New Mexico which was an epic in missionary history. They made their headquarters at La Junta (Tiptonville), in the northeast corner of the territory, and wisely began to learn Spanish. Harwood lost no time in making his rounds, visiting established points and organizing both English- and Spanish-speaking churches and Sunday schools. Emily

Harwood began to establish much-needed mission schools. The first one, at Cherry Valley near La Junta, using a renovated henhouse for a schoolhouse, was the beginning of a series of self-supporting schools. Harwood found the class at Peralta functioning, with Ambrosio Gonzales as the leader.

The New Mexico Mission of the Colorado Conference was formed in 1872, with Harwood as superintendent, a position which he held until 1884 with great distinction. By 1884 there were 24 charges in the mission, 14 church buildings, 488 members, and 22 Sunday schools. In addition, there were six elementary schools and two academies by 1886. The Harwoods trained and made use of a number of natives in their work. Much of what they did was self-supporting. Insofar as the history of Methodist missions in the West is concerned, their work among the native people is outstanding.

Apparently the Southern Church paid but little attention to New Mexico in the early period. To be sure, Santa Fe was listed as an appointment of the Kansas Mission Conference from its beginnings in 1855 through 1859, but it was always left to be supplied, and no reports from Santa Fe appear in the records. Evidently the conference sent no preachers there. Later it was for a time a part of the West Texas Conference, then of the Mexican Border Conference. In 1890 a New Mexico Annual Conference was formed.

9

Oregon

By a treaty of 1818 England and the United States had joint occupation of Oregon, which was later a region of some 443,000 square miles, extending from the forty-second parallel—the northern boundary of California—to parallel 54-40, and from the Pacific Ocean to the Rocky Mountains. The Hudson's Bay Company exercised a monopoly over the only industry, the fur trade; and under its factor, Dr. John McLoughlin, it virtually ruled the region and provided whatever law and order were needed. Although he realized that settlements would destroy the fur trade in time, McLoughlin was hospitable to newcomers, including American missionaries. However, he was averse to any American settlements north of the Columbia River. In 1846 the two nations agreed upon the forty-ninth parallel as the dividing line. The Territory of

Oregon, organized in 1848, comprised Oregon, Washington, Idaho, and parts of Wyoming and Montana. In 1859 "southern Oregon" became a state; the remainder was included in Washington Territory. It has been estimated that before settlement the region had a population of 100,000 Indians. The number, however, was drastically reduced by their susceptibility to diseases introduced by the white men. By 1845 over five thousand settlers had arrived over the Oregon Trail; a much smaller number came by the long sea voyage.

The often-told account of the Flathead and Nez Percé Indians, who came from the Oregon country to St. Louis in 1831 to learn about the white man's God and his wonderful Book, is probably apocryphal. However, it was a factor in initiating the missions to the Oregon Indians under Jason Lee, Marcus Whitman, and H. H. Spalding.[11] In 1833 the Methodist Missionary Society appointed young Jason Lee as missionary to the Indians of Oregon. He selected his nephew, Daniel Lee, and Cyrus Shepard, a teacher, as his assistants. Going overland, they arrived at McLoughlin's headquarters at Fort Vancouver on September 15, 1834. Their genial host advised them to establish their mission in the Willamette Valley. Following this advice, which was not entirely disinterested, they chose a location near French Prairie, where some French Canadians, former employees of the Hudson's Bay Company, were farming. They immediately began to construct a mission house, which was to be the headquarters for a number of years.

Lee's main purpose, of course, was to Christianize the Indians. He also desired to civilize them, giving them at least an elementary education, and teaching them useful arts, such as farming, various manual crafts, and homemaking. Furthermore, he wanted the mission to be as self-supporting as possible. Accordingly, the missionaries began to farm as well as to preach, and Shepard started both a Sunday school and a day school. Reinforcements arrived in 1837, among them some women and a much-needed physician, for disease had taken a heavy toll of the Indians at the mission. In 1838 a branch was opened at The Dalles, on the Columbia River some eighty miles east of Fort Vancouver. A number of well-attended camp meetings were held here in later years.

In 1838, leaving David Leslie in charge, Lee returned to the States to make a report and to obtain more missionaries, more financial

[11] On Oregon Methodism see: H. K. Hines, *Missionary History of the Pacific Northwest* (Portland: H. K. Hines, 1899); Cornelius Brosnan, *Jason Lee: Prophet of the New Oregon* (New York: The Macmillan Co., 1932); James Bashford, *The Oregon Missions* (New York: The Abingdon Press, 1918); Barclay, *History of Methodist Missions*, Vols. II, III.

aid, and more supplies and equipment. A ship, the "Lausanne," was chartered in 1839 for the trip to Oregon. The missionary party consisted of fifty-one men, women, and children. The freight included household goods, tools, farm implements, machinery for both a sawmill and a grist-mill, and many "missionary barrels" of clothing for the Indians. The arrival of the "Lausanne" at Fort Vancouver on June 1, 1840, marked the real beginning of the settlement of Oregon by American families.

On his return, Lee, who had been away twenty-six months, embarked on an ambitious program of expansion. In addition to the home mission near French Prairie and The Dalles, missionaries were assigned to Willamette Falls (Oregon City); Clatsop (near modern Astoria), at the mouth of the Columbia River; Nisqually (Tacoma); and Umpqua, in the south. The mission center near French Prairie was soon transferred to Cheme-keta (Salem), where the sawmill and gristmill were being set up. Also, an Indian Manual Labor Training School, costing about $10,000, was erected there. Likewise, Oregon Institute, a school for white children— and the forerunner of Willamette University—was being planned in 1842 for Salem.

Time, however, was running out for Jason Lee. Disease and other factors had brought about a great decrease in the Indian population. Moreover, an increasing number of white settlers were arriving. Willamette Falls was becoming a white church rather than an Indian mission. Umpqua proved to be a poor location. The Roman Catholic mission already established at Nisqually made the Methodist prospects there rather poor. Some of the missionary staff were unsuited for their exacting positions, and a certain amount of dissension had developed. Furthermore, some of the missionaries began to engage in private business affairs. The actual results had fallen far below the original sanguine expectations of Lee and of the Missionary Society. For example, in March, 1840, Leslie reported that in addition to the white membership of twenty-six at the central station, there were but three half-breeds, four Indians, and one Hawaiian, a most disappointing showing after nearly six years of endeavor.

Consequently, damaging reports, some of them true, others not, had reached the Mission Board. On December 25, 1843, Lee embarked for New York, hoping to explain matters satisfactorily. In Hawaii he received the disconcerting news that his successor, George Gary, had already been appointed and was on his way to Oregon! Lee pleaded his case when he reached New York, but to little avail. He never returned to Oregon; instead, before many months had passed he was taken ill and died on March 12, 1845, nearly a dozen years after his appointment to

Oregon. This marked the tragic end of a most nobly conceived, but in some respects poorly executed, missionary endeavor.

George Gary arrived in the Willamette Valley, June 1, 1844, and in accord with his instructions he began to liquidate much of the missionary establishment. He abandoned and sold the land and equipment of all the mission stations save two, The Dalles and the central mission at Chemeketa (Salem). The Indian Manual Labor Training School building was sold to the Oregon Institute for $4,000. About $25,000 in all was realized from the liquidation. All but one of the lay workers were dismissed. Thus, in about a decade the Oregon Mission to the Indians was born, flourished, and all but died. The total cost in money, to say nothing of the human costs which cannot be evaluated, may have been as much as $250,000.

William Roberts, the "apostle" of Pacific Coast Methodism, was appointed superintendent during this process of closing the missions. With his assistant, James Wilbur, he stopped over at San Francisco on his way to Oregon in April, 1847, and in May founded a society, the first Protestant church in California. He did not reach Oregon until June, 1847. He completed the liquidation, and then began to center attention upon the white settlers rather than on the Indians. About a year after his arrival he had eight missionaries to assist him. These were appointed to four circuits in the Willamette Valley—Oregon City, Salem, Yamhill, and Calapooia. The number of circuits grew to seven in 1848—the year when southern Oregon became a territory—with 443 members. The rush to the California gold fields brought about a temporary decline in population. However, immigration was induced by the prospects of free land, so that in 1850 the population was 12,093, and in 1860, 52,465.

On September 5, 1849, Roberts—who would have been an excellent bishop had the General Conference seen fit to elect him—organized the Oregon and California Mission Conference, containing a vast area in its boundaries, with himself as superintendent. Including himself there were but six of the preachers who were active members of any Annual Conference. All six, two of them representing California, four, Oregon, were outstanding Christian leaders. Two of them, Isaac Owen and William Taylor, who was later to gain world-wide note as a missionary bishop and evangelist, were not in attendance, but en route to their posts in California. Vast though its boundaries—for it supposedly included all the United States west of the Rocky Mountains—the new conference actually comprised but a few circuits in the Willamette Valley and northern California. When this conference held its last session in 1852, prior to its division into the Oregon Conference and the California Conference, the Oregon District reported 7 circuits and 475 members. The Oregon Conference was organized March 17, 1853, Bishop Ames presiding, with 11 circuits and 706 church members. By now, missions to the Indians, begun with such high hopes nineteen years previously, had practically been given up.

The Southern Church made a rather late start in Oregon; however, it may be surprising that it entered this far-northern field at all. In 1858 Oregon was assigned to the San Francisco District of the Pacific Conference, and in the following year the Independence Circuit reported forty-six members. At this time the Oregon District was formed, with the very capable Orceneth Fisher as the presiding elder. He was able to provide four preachers for the ten circuits on his district. The report to the conference in 1860 gave a total of 268 members in the following circuits: Portland, Salem, Independence, Corvallis, and Eugene. This was far fewer than the membership of the Oregon Conference of the Northern Church for the same year, which was given as 2,231. Even so, considering the late start and the opposition encountered by the Southern preachers, the showing is quite commendable. No records for the war years seem to be available. However, despite the obvious handicaps the work continued, for in 1866 there were enough members to warrant the formation of the Columbia Conference with two districts and seven circuits in Oregon. Fourteen traveling preachers were listed, and the membership was given in round numbers as 500. The next year the membership was 732.

10

Washington

What is now the state of Washington was included in the Oregon Conference of the Northern Church, formed in 1853. By now a few hundred settlers had gone north of the Columbia River to the Puget Sound region. For the most part the area was largely dense forests and water. Frequently the only mode of travel was by canoe. Benjamin Close had been assigned to Olympia in 1852. He preached his first sermon there on December 26 in a new schoolhouse. The congregation had scarcely left the building following the close of the service when the roof, heavily weighted with snow, came crashing down. A possible tragedy was barely avoided.

The conference made provision for a Northern Oregon (i.e., Washington) District. In 1853 Close was appointed to the Puget Sound Mission as superintendent. He reported thirty-one members by conference time in 1854. The circuits had grown to six, with preachers assigned to four of them. J. F. Devore, appointed to Steilacoom on Puget Sound, needed lumber for a church. Accordingly, dressed in his good suit and wearing kid gloves, he went to a mill owner in Olympia and asked for a donation of lumber. The latter, supposing from his dress that Devore was above doing any physical labor, told him that he could have all the lumber that he could carry from the mill to the Sound in one day. The preacher arrived at dawn the next day dressed in working clothes, and by sunset had moved enough lumber to the Sound not only for a church but for a parsonage as well.

David E. Blaine was appointed to Seattle in 1854. A graduate of Auburn Seminary, he and his wife Catherine came from New York on their honeymoon. Seattle at this time was a hamlet of some thirty rude cabins surrounded by dense forests. On Sunday, December 4, he preached in a boarding house and organized a society of four persons, including his wife. They rented a shack with cracks so wide that they needed no windows. His wife, who also was well educated, started a school, the first one in Seattle. Within two months fourteen children were studying in the "parsonage" five days a week. Largely by his own physical labor Blaine soon had both a church and a parsonage built, and painted them both white. Painted buildings were such a rarity that the church came to be known as the "white church." Blaine, in addition to his pastoral duties, taught an evening school and also became deputy county clerk. He, like many preachers on the frontier, needed to supplement his income, for his collections for the year totaled only about $150.

The Northern Methodists were the first Protestant group to establish churches east of the Cascades. In 1859 the conference assigned George M. Berry to Walla Walla. Before long he was able to have a church building constructed, and he reported a membership of thirty by the end of the year.

The growth of Methodism in Washington was very slow. The conference of 1855 listed but 66 members for Puget Sound, and somewhat less than double this amount, 123, in 1860, or, with Walla Walla added, 153. As a result of the slow development most of the Methodist work in Washington continued to be attached to the Oregon Conference. It was not until 1884 that the Puget Sound Conference, with 20 charges, 22 local preachers, and 1,204 members, was organized.

There is little evidence of activity in Washington by the Southern Church. In 1870 Walla Walla was attached to the Umatilla District of the Columbia Conference; B. F. King was appointed to this new charge.

Fifty-three members were reported at conference time, 1871. After this, the circuit was left to be supplied until 1873, but with the same number of members reported each year. In 1874, however, but seven members were given. There is even less evidence of work by the Southern Church in the Puget Sound region.

11

Idaho

Idaho, at first a part of Oregon Territory, next, of Washington, and later, in 1863, organized as Idaho Territory, was a very sparsely settled region. There were a few trading posts in the early period. On July 27, 1834, Jason Lee stopped at one of these in eastern Idaho, Fort Hall, and preached to a motley congregation of immigrants, trappers, and Indians; it was thirty years, however, before a Methodist preacher was assigned to Idaho. A few Indian missions were established by Protestants and Catholics. In 1860 some Mormons founded a permanent settlement at Franklin, in the southeastern corner, thinking that they were in Utah. In the main, Idaho was largely a passageway to and from the West until this same year, 1860, when gold was discovered in the western part. Gold seekers arrived like quicksilver from various parts of the country, including the mining camps of California, Nevada, and Colorado—few of them, as Bancroft has noted, with any "Puritan prejudices to overcome." By 1864 Idaho City had become the leading town, with about six thousand inhabitants, followed by Placerville, Centerville, and Pioneer City. In 1862 gold was also discovered in the extreme southwest region, and Owyhee, Boonville, and Silver City sprang up.

In 1864 the Oregon Conference of the Northern Church appointed C. S. Kingsley, a supernumerary, to Idaho City. He preached, and soon built a church, the first house of worship in Idaho, save for a Roman Catholic church erected the previous year. However, it was destroyed by the disastrous fire of 1865 set by miners who raided the food stores for food. No report of his work is given in the conference records. In this same year Idaho became a third-class mission of the Interior Department, under Bishop Calvin Kingsley's direction. On September 20, 1865, he appointed the experienced missionary, William Roberts, as "missionary to Idaho." He expressed the opinion that missionary work in Idaho was more difficult than on the coast, in part because of the constant shifting of the population, and in part because of the large proportion of Roman Catholics—Pioneer City, for instance, was at the time called "New Dublin." He could also have added the Mormon influence as a third factor. No church organization was reported at conference time; however, there is a record of two Sunday schools with a round-number enrollment of a hundred. Roberts was reappointed in 1866, 1867, and 1868, as superintendent of the Idaho Mission, but there is no report of the results of his endeavor. He may have organized a church in Idaho City, but even this is not certain. If so, it was one of only three Protestant churches which, according to Bancroft, were in Idaho prior to 1871. The Idaho Mission was discontinued in 1869, a sure indication of its failure, and Roberts was appointed to Portland.

However, when the Rocky Mountain Conference was formed in 1872, three Idaho circuits, Boise City, Silver City, and Salmon River, along with some Utah circuits, comprised the Corinne District. The presiding elder, J. M. Jamison, preached in Idaho City and at Boise City. He stated that there had never been a regularly organized Methodist church in Boise City, probably not in all of Idaho. Accordingly, on November 17, he organized a church in Boise City and held what probably was the first Quarterly Conference in Idaho. As a result of his visit, Boise City reported seventeen members, Rocky Bar, twelve, at conference time in 1873, when the Idaho District was formed. Jamison was made presiding elder, and there were five circuits—Boise City, Idaho City, Payette, Rocky Bar, and Silver City. The next year the district reported 139 members, 1 parsonage, and no church building.

However, the way ahead was difficult, and became more so, perhaps, when Idaho was parceled out among three conferences—the Columbia River, the Montana, and the Utah. It was not until years later, 1884, that the Idaho Conference came into being.

12

California

In relating the beginnings of Methodism in California it should be recalled that there were two Californias, north and south, which differed not only geographically but culturally and economically as well. Furthermore, there were two Methodisms, far removed from their home bases, both the Northern and Southern churches, which became established in both northern and southern California, and almost on equal terms. As is quite well known, in 1848, soon after California was acquired from Mexico, gold was discovered at Sutter's Mill in the northern section, and the forty-niners and their successors began to pour into the gold fields by the thousands.

Northern California

But even before this influx had begun, Methodism had made a start in this region.[12] For, as was mentioned earlier, on April 24, 1847, while en route to Oregon to take over as superintendent of the Oregon Mission, William Roberts of the Northern Church, together with his assistant, James H. Wilbur, stopped over at a small, adobe village, called Yerba Buena (San Francisco). On the following day they held religious services on shipboard and, while drinking and billiards were temporarily suspended, in a hotel in the settlement. Before long they organized a Methodist class of six persons, the first Protestant organization on the coast south of Oregon, and started a Sunday school. Since the ship was to be in port for forty-five days, they visited a number of nearby communities. As a result of his survey, Roberts sent back a report, to be delivered by Colonel J. C. Fremont, calling attention to the need for missionaries in California.

However, before these were appointed, Elihu Anthony, an industrious local preacher, founded Methodist classes at San Jose, Santa Cruz, and Pajara. He kept in touch with Roberts, now in Oregon, who approved his activities. However, with the discovery of gold most of the new members left for the mining camps. Early in the summer of 1849, Roberts, as superintendent of the Oregon and California Mission, returned to California. He visited Sacramento, Stockton, San Jose, and other places, preaching as he went and securing lots for churches. In San Francisco he met Asa White, a local preacher, and his family consisting of "his

---

[12] Sources on California are: Edward Jervey, *History of Methodism in Southern California and Arizona* (Nashville: Parthenon Press, 1960); Leon Loofbourow, *In Search of God's Gold* (San Francisco: Historical Society of the California-Nevada Annual Conference of The Methodist Church, in co-operation with the College of the Pacific, 1950); William Taylor, *California Life Illustrated* (New York: Carlton and Porter, 1859); Elmer Clark, *Healing Ourselves* (Nashville: Cokesbury Press, 1924); C. V. Anthony, *Fifty Years of Methodism. A History of the Methodist Episcopal Church Within the Bounds of the California Annual Conference from 1847 to 1897* (San Francisco: Methodist Book Concern, 1901); James Cannon, *History of Southern Methodist Missions;* J. C. Simmons, *The History of Southern Methodism on the Pacific Coast* (Nashville: Southern Methodist Publishing House, 1886).

wife, two sons, eight daughters, six sons-in-law, and thirty grandchildren."
He held Sunday services and weekly prayer meetings in a blue tent, which
became almost legendary after it was used in other settlements as well.
His family alone would have made a good-sized frontier congregation. A
lot was obtained for erecting a church, lumber for which had been
shipped from Oregon. Roberts apparently left White in temporary
charge of the Methodists in the town.

On September 5, 1849, as previously noted, shortly after his return to
Oregon, Roberts organized the Oregon and California Mission Conference, with two of its members, William Taylor and Isaac Owen, absent
because they were en route to California at the time. Taylor, traveling
by sea, arrived on September 21. He was well received by the San
Francisco Methodists, whose society grew from twenty to sixty-nine by
the first of the year. Owen, going by land, arrived a month later, and
was assigned to Stockton and Sacramento. Lumber and a tin roof for a
chapel which Taylor had shipped from Baltimore were piled up on the
church lot where Owen preached his first Sacramento sermon. Pointing
to this pile he predicted, "We will occupy our new church next Sunday,"
and they did. Owen had shipped books to the value of $2,000 to San
Francisco, for a book room, which he and Taylor helped to build next
to the church.

They pressed local preachers into useful service; before long other
missionaries came out to help them. When Roberts presided over the
meeting of the district conference in August, 1851, nine preachers were
present. They reported 507 members, 12 churches, and 5 parsonages, a
remarkable achievement. Owen, described as a plain, earnest, indefatigable minister, became the presiding elder of this California District.
In this same year the *California Christian Advocate* began publication,
and a charter was obtained for California Wesleyan College, reincorporated in 1852 as the University of the Pacific. About ten additional
missionaries arrived in 1852, but this was not a net gain, for some had
departed.

As a result of the growth that had been attained, coupled with good
prospects for the future, the California Conference of the Methodist
Episcopal Church was organized during February 3-8, 1853, with 1,436
members. Thirty-five preachers, including supplies and candidates for
admission to the conference, were present. By 1860 the conference had 8
districts (including 1 German), 111 stations and circuits, 81 local
preachers, 73 church buildings, and 3,441 members. Far distant Honolulu
was one of the appointments.

Since many Southerners had come to California, in May of 1849 the bishops of the Southern Church established California as a "foreign" mission under the direction of Bishop Robert Paine. He appointed Jesse Boring as the superintendent, with D. W. Pollock and A. M. Wynn as associates. Arriving on April 15, 1850, Boring chose San Francisco as his headquarters and assigned Pollock to Sacramento, Wynn to Stockton. However, before leaving for Stockton, during Boring's temporary absence in May, Wynn organized a society in San Francisco, marking the formal beginning of the Southern Church in California. Arriving in Stockton in July, Wynn soon founded a church there; and at about the same time Pollock started one in Sacramento, and in addition built a church, Asbury Chapel, and a parsonage. By fall a class had been started at Sonora; and Southern Methodism soon spread to Sonoma, Napa, Benicia, and San Jose. Before long chapels were built at San Francisco and San Jose. The Southern preachers encountered opposition, even hostility, from Northern antislavery sympathizers, which at times provided difficulties for them; but they tried to maintain the policy that their church was a religious, not a political, organization, and that their own function was to preach the gospel and to look after the religious needs of their people.

In order to obtain additional missionaries both to aid him and to constitute enough preachers for a conference, Boring inaugurated the novel plan called the "Thousand-Dollar Proposition." He proposed that each conference of the Southern Church provide $1,000 and one missionary for the California Mission. Despite strenuous opposition, eight conferences responded, sending out thirteen preachers and presumably raising $1,000 for each one sent out. With these reinforcements, on April 15, 1852, Boring organized the Pacific Conference with eighteen preachers present. It was divided into two districts, the San Francisco and the Sacramento, with twenty circuits. There were 294 members all told, and 10 church buildings. The organization of this conference antedated that of the Northern Church's conference by ten months. Boring had already established a paper, the *Christian Observer*—with several columns in Spanish—which was replaced by the *Pacific Methodist* later. The conference authorized four schools—two were already in operation—and a college. They were keeping pace with their Northern brethren; and in one area, camp meetings, they definitely excelled. These were held frequently, were well attended, and reported numerous conversions.

The church grew steadily; the Minutes of 1860 report 6 districts, including Oregon; 53 circuits and stations; and 2,500 members, 268 in Oregon. This compared favorably with the Northern Church report for the same year, cited above. In one respect it was better, for the Southern circuits, though fewer in number, had a larger average membership.

It is obvious that the two churches were rivals; not infrequently they both had societies in the same town. But there were also indications of good fellowship and brotherhood. Bishop H. H. Kavanaugh of the Southern Church and Bishop Levi Scott of the Northern were both in California in the summer of 1856. Surprisingly enough, Bishop Kavanaugh dedicated the second Northern church to be built in Sacramento; and in San Jose he sat alongside Bishop Scott as he was presiding over the California Conference, and preached to the conference on Sunday evening. However, when Kavanaugh came back in 1864 to preside over the Pacific Conference, he was arrested by the military as a Confederate agent while he was at a camp meeting.

Returning to 1856, as a result of the good feeling that had been engendered, in November two committees of three each from the two conferences conferred concerning the possibility of union, or at least, of more fraternal fellowship. Indeed, in their isolation there was a suggestion that the two conferences might unite as an independent Western Methodist Church. Nothing, however, resulted from this meeting; the Southerners, rightly or wrongly, felt that the Northern conference wanted to swallow them up.

Southern California

Turning to the southern part of California, gold was one of the factors that divided the state into two sections. Southern California, derisively called the "cow country," had no gold to support its economy. By comparison it was sparsely settled; the towns were few in number and quite small; the population consisted to a considerable degree of Spanish-speaking Roman Catholics. Much of the land was semi-arid; drouths, occasional floods, grasshopper plagues, and epidemics discouraged American settlers. The prospects for establishing Protestant missions were not very good.

James W. Brier, of the Northern Church, was apparently the first Methodist preacher in Los Angeles. He had left the Middle West with his wife and three children in April, 1849. Taking a wrong trail which led them by Death Valley, reportedly so-named by Mrs. Brier, the heroine of the expedition, their party all but died of hunger and thirst. However, the Briers finally reached Los Angeles in the spring of 1850. Few Americans were living here, and probably seven eighths of the population could not speak English. Nevertheless he began to preach and conduct religious services. But in time he became discouraged and went north, being assigned to Sonoma in 1853.

The real founder of Northern Methodism in southern California was Adam Bland. In 1853 the California Conference appointed him to be the missionary to Los Angeles, which reportedly had few Protestants and no Methodists among its inhabitants. He leased the El Dorado Saloon, a two-room building, one room for a chapel and a schoolroom, the other for the parsonage, on February 16, one day after his arrival. By April he had a congregation of fifty, a Sunday school of over twenty-five scholars. He also raised $1,000 toward a church building. His wife's school for girls proved to be successful. By the end of the year he had fifteen church members to report. A lawyer's wife wrote that this Methodist preacher and his wife were "trying to civilize the place." He also preached in places near Los Angeles as well. He predicted that southern California would become the "big-end" of the state, but reported that its people were the worst he had ever seen.

In 1854 he was made the presiding elder of the Southern California District, with its five charges—Los Angeles, Lexington, Santa Barbara, Tulare, and, hopefully, San Diego. The next year only twenty-two members were reported at conference time, one alone, surprisingly, at Los Angeles, fifteen at Lexington, and six at Santa Barbara. Accordingly, the district was discontinued, and the work was almost at a standstill; indeed, it seems to have been practically discontinued during the war. The circuits were left to be supplied, and no reports were received from them at conference time. However, in 1866, Bland, now the presiding elder of the Santa Clara District, paid a visit in an attempt to revive the churches. As a result, Los Angeles reported a membership of fourteen to the conference session of 1867; and preachers were assigned, under his direction, to Los Angeles, San Luis Obispo, Santa Barbara, and San Bernardino. These four charges reported 128 members to the conference of 1868.

The expectation that the railroad which had reached San Francisco in 1869 would soon be extended to Los Angeles brought about a land boom, and many settlers went to southern California. In keeping with the brightening prospect, the Los Angeles District of the California Conference was authorized in 1870 with ten charges. From here on the growth was steady, so that during September 6-10, 1876, the Southern California Conference was organized with 2 districts, 27 charges, 23 preachers, 22 local preachers, 1,257 members, 13 churches, and 9 parsonages, twenty-three years after Bland first went to Los Angeles.

The Southern Church entered southern California following an unusual set of circumstances. In 1854 J. F. Blythe, presiding elder of the Stockton District of the Southern Church, read in the *California Christian Advocate,* of the Northern Church, that certain members of the Northern Church at Los Nietos—near Los Angeles—had become dissatisfied with an abolitionist sentiment, which, they claimed, had developed in the church, and desired a preacher of their own kind. Accordingly, he visited the settlement and found that they had withdrawn, and that a layman, Alexander Groves, had formed a class. Blythe formally organized them into a class of sixteen members of the Southern Church, and in 1855 sent them a colorful preacher, J. T. Cox, well known for his evangelistic and camp-meeting fervor. He also assigned E. B. Lockley to Los Angeles. Lockley wrote that he almost starved, for his collection in six months amounted to about $10. The two circuits were reduced to one, the Los Angeles, and later two preachers in succession did die shortly after reaching their post, but of disease, not of starvation. The Los Angeles District, despite a reported membership of forty, was created in 1858, but was soon discontinued. During the war the Southern Church was apparently more active than the Northern. In 1862 societies were formed at Carpinteria and San Bernardino, and in 1864 Los Angeles had fifty-six members. Even so, but one preacher at a time was appointed to southern California until 1868, when the Los Angeles District was reconstituted, with W. A. Spurlock as the presiding elder.

Four of the charges under his supervision—Los Angeles Station, San Bernardino, Santa Barbara, and San Diego—reported 389 members in 1869. From here on, the growth was steady, justifying the organization of the Los Angeles Conference during October 26-30, 1870, which included southern California and east to the Rocky Mountains. This occurred six years before the Southern California Conference of the Northern Church came into existence.

The situation in California was unique, in that the two churches practically paralleled each other and were somewhat equal in strength. Save for Boring's unusual "Thousand-Dollar Proposition," their methods were quite similar. Both had unusually strong leaders, Boring and Roberts, during the initial stages. Both were more or less at a standstill in southern California during the war years, but both had about the same membership in northern California in 1866 as they had in 1860. In 1876, when the Southern California Conference was organized, there was not a great deal of disparity in membership in the southern part of the state—996 for the Southern Church, 1,257 for the Northern. But the Northern Church began to pull away by this time in northern California, for in this same year the Southern Church reported 3,836 members in the Pacific Conference; the Northern, 7,640 in the California Conference.

13

Nevada

Nevada, known as the Washoe Country, was a part of California until 1850, when most of the present state was incorporated into the newly formed Utah Territory. The discovery of gold in California resulted not only in a steady stream of immigrants passing through the Washoe Country but also in small settlements of traders, Mormons for the most part, along the trails. The first settlement was in the valley of the Carson River in 1849. When a Federal army was sent to Utah to deal with the Mormon "problem," Brigham Young recalled the Mormons in Nevada to Utah; 985 men, women, and children heeded his summons. Carson City itself was not laid out until 1858. In 1859 the exceedingly rich Comstock Lode, containing silver as well as gold, was discovered. This, of course, led to a typical influx of miners seeking the precious metals. The principal camp was Virginia City. In 1860 the population of Nevada was 6,857—with only 710 women—but before long it was about 20,000. In 1861 Nevada Territory (comprising little more than half of the present state) was formed. Very shortly, in 1864, Nevada became a state, in order to give Lincoln the votes of an additional free state. The history of mining fluctuated with the finding of ore bodies. Twelve were located between 1859 and 1872. But in 1873 the Big Bonanza, the largest of them all, was discovered, with a consequent revival of the state's economy and population, which rose from 42,491 in 1870 to 62,266 in 1880, after which it declined. There were but three permanent towns of any consequence, Carson City, Virginia City, and Reno, in 1890.[13]

It is obvious that the Nevada of those days was largely dependent upon mining. This resulted in a floating population which made it a difficult field for the establishment of churches. Furthermore, the residents were especially disinterested in religion and in religious living. The Rev.

---

[13] For further information on Methodism in Nevada, see "Methodist Episcopal Church," in Myron Angel, ed., *History of Nevada* (Oakland, Calif.: Thompson and West, 1881).

H. Richardson, an agent of the American Bible Society who traveled widely, queried:

Is there a state in our whole Union where there is so little religious restraint, such ignorance of the Bible, such flaunting of its teachings, such Sabbath breaking, such heaven daring profanity, such drunkenness, such unblushing licentiousness, and such glorying in shame, in short is there another state where the people so generally feel as though they were almost or quite out of God's moral jurisdiction?

This severe indictment, in all fairness to Nevada, might also have been directed with equal validity against other frontier mining camps.

Aside from the Mormons, the Methodists were the first to establish an outpost in Nevada, although quite hesitatingly. Carson Valley was listed as an appointment of the California Conference of the Northern Church as early as 1855. It was to be supplied, and there is no evidence that a preacher was sent there. It was left to be supplied for the next three years as well. There is a statement to the effect that Ira P. Hale was assigned in 1857, but again there is no record that he went to Nevada until several years later.

In 1859 a local preacher, Jesse L. Bennett, called the Father of Nevada Methodism, began preaching in Carson Valley at Genoa, Eagle Branch, and Virginia City—where he reputedly received a collection amounting to several hundred dollars. He organized a class at Carson City, but this apparently dissolved when he departed in 1860. More officially, A. L. S. Bateman was appointed by the conference in 1859 to Carson Valley, where he, too, organized a society. Ten members are reported for Virginia City in the Minutes of 1860, twelve for Carson Valley, and five for Walker River. Furthermore, Carson Valley had a building lot valued at $300, the first tangible evidence of any permanence to Methodist activity in Nevada. This somewhat detailed account indicates the difficulties that were encountered in establishing the church on any firm basis in the mining camps.

In September, 1861, coincident with the formation of Nevada Territory, the Nevada Territory District of the California Conference was authorized, with N. R. Peck as the presiding elder. The district was assigned ten circuits. At conference time all but one, Carson City, were left to be supplied. Even so, preachers were found, and in 1862 the first district report gave a total of eighty-one members. The prosperity of Virginia City is reflected in the building of a $20,000 church and a $2,000 parsonage in 1862 during the pastorate of C. V. Anthony.

Despite the fact that the membership in the district had risen to but

166 in 1863, the Nevada Conference was organized in 1864, at the session of the California Conference. The chief reason for this was the great difficulty of reaching Nevada across the Sierra Nevada Mountains. The conference met in Virginia City in the following year. The two districts included 13 circuits which reported 267 members. Not long afterward the $20,000 church building was badly damaged by what was termed a "Washoe zephyr," and soon after this mishap the damaged structure was completely destroyed by fire.

It was stated earlier that Reno was one of the three permanent towns of any size. There had been preaching at its site as early as 1863, but no regular services were conducted there until after the townsite was laid out in 1867. It first appears as an appointment in the following year.

That the frontier preachers and their families suffered many hardships is well known. However, very few suffered starvation. The tragic story of Valentine Rightmyer, who died on April 11, 1873, marks an exception. He had a large family and a small income. In order to keep his family properly fed he denied himself food to such an extent that he died of "inanition" (starvation). This would not have occurred had he informed his people of his dire need. Ironically, the circuit he served was Gold Hill and Silver City.

Despite its limited number of charges—twenty-eight as the maximum— and small membership, the Nevada Conference continued until 1884, when it was made into a mission. This was a prudent change, for in the decade of 1880-90 the population of the state declined from 62,266 to 47,355.

14

Arizona

Arizona, which was largely a thoroughfare to and from California in the early days, was for a long period of time sparsely settled by Americans. Even as late as 1870 there were only 9,658 whites and "civilized" Indians occupying its 113,956 square miles; it is estimated that there were also some 20,000 "uncivilized" hostile Indians living there as well. It was at first largely pro-Southern in its sentiments. It was occupied by a Texas expedition in 1861 and declared for the Confederacy; but the Texans retired before a Union force in 1862; and in 1863, despite its very small population, Arizona became a territory of the United States.

For these and other reasons it did not appeal to the Protestant churches as a fruitful field for missions, either among the Indians or among the few white settlers. To be sure, in February of 1859 Horace S. Bishop and David Tuthill of the Northern Church were transferred from their conferences in the East to the California Conference to be missionaries in Arizona. By April, Bishop had preached in several small settlements to audiences, one third of whom were Mexicans with little or no knowledge of English. Tuthill made Tubac, some fifty miles south of Tucson, his headquarters, from which he planned to travel to preach at a half a dozen places. Apparently their mission was a failure; for by September, Bishop withdrew from the Methodist connection, and Tuthill was appointed to a charge in California.

In 1860 and in 1864 the General Conference made some proposals for missions in Arizona, which was to be considered a "foreign mission," but these were not carried out at the time. The individual effort by Charles P. Cooke illustrates the official reluctance to enter Arizona. He had been stationed as a soldier in the territory, where he observed the plight of the Indians at first hand. Following his conversion, for a time he was a local preacher and city missionary in Chicago. Learning about an appeal for missionaries to the Indians, he applied to the Missionary Society, which was not ready to act at this time. Accordingly, in 1869 he went to the Pima Reservation on the Gila River, where he obtained a position as a government teacher. In addition to his teaching, he preached and did some "solid" missionary work. According to one report he eventually joined the Presbyterian Church, which supported him in his missionary endeavors. Early in the spring of 1870 John L. Dyer, presiding elder of the Santa Fe District, preached three times at Fort Defiance in the northeastern corner of Arizona, but this visit was without lasting results. In the fall of this same year Alexander Gilmore, an army chaplain, preached in Prescott, about a mile from his army post, and in the following February started a Sunday school. He may well have prepared the way for Methodism in this settlement.

With official interest revived, in 1872 Bishop Matthew Simpson sent G. A. Reeder of North Ohio to be the superintendent of the reactivated Arizona Mission. Soon after his arrival he reported that there was no Protestant church building in the territory, and that he had not met a single Methodist. He was struck with the utter disregard of the majority of the people for the claims of religion. Other difficulties included the open hostility of the Apache Indians, the influence of the saloons, the prevalence of vice, and the opposition of the Roman Catholic Church. However, he was not unsuccessful, for when he resigned in 1874, he left the names of forty-six members and probationers. During his stay he had been quite industrious, for he had held 5 protracted meetings and 1 camp meeting, had preached 422 times, and had traveled 14,000 miles, sleeping on his blankets, on boards, and on "the bosom of the earth." His departure did not leave the field entirely unattended, for D. B. Wright, a supernumerary, was at Prescott; and, later on, in 1877, J. M. Winnega came to Florence. However, little was accomplished during this interim except to hold the ground.

Even so, a new day was at hand. First of all, on September 5, 1879, G. H. Adams, an experienced frontier preacher from Colorado, arrived as the superintendent of the Arizona Mission and pastor at Prescott. An additional factor was the completion of the Southern Pacific Railroad in 1880, which made the southern part of Arizona more accessible and led to further settlements. Adams improved the church building at Prescott, started the erection of a parsonage, and transformed a "union" Sunday school into a Methodist one. He was quite industrious, with the result that two years later, in 1881, there were church buildings in Globe City, Tombstone, Phoenix, Pinal, and Tucson, with the total church property valued at $35,000. The Arizona Mission Conference was organized in July, 1881, with Adams, quite fittingly, as the superintendent, a post which he retained until his retirement in 1890. His first report, in 1883, gave the membership of the mission as 143, a slow growth, but still a growth.

Despite the Southern sentiment in Arizona in the first days of settlement, the Southern Church did not enter the territory officially, it seems, until 1870, when the Los Angeles Conference appointed Alexander Groves—who had organized a class at Los Nietos, California—to Arizona. He evidently organized two circuits, Prescott and Salt River, each of which reported twelve members at the next conference. Franklin Mc-Kean was assigned to help him at Salt River, but in 1872 he was alone again. In 1873 Groves was made the presiding elder of the new Arizona District. He had the same two circuits, Prescott and Salt River, with but seventeen members, and a preacher to assist him. In 1876, when Lewis J. Hedgpeth became presiding elder, Groves was sent to the Verde River territory to the north. As with the Northern Church, progress was very slow, if, indeed, not at a standstill. For the sake of comparison, in 1883 the combined membership of the two stations, Prescott and Phoenix, was only 51, and the Northern Church had but 143 in the Arizona Mission. The observation of Wright, who earlier had served the Northern Church in Prescott, is understandable: "When you think of poor, neglected Arizona, let your heart raise a prayer to God that He may pass this way."

15

The Dakotas

Finally, we retrace geographically to the northeast, to Dakota Territory.[14] The settlement of South and North Dakota—which constituted Dakota Territory in 1861—was delayed. It was not until the treaty with the Yankton Indians in 1858 that even the southeastern corner of South Dakota was opened up to settlement. Two years later, in 1860, the Upper Iowa Conference of the Northern Church sent a young preacher, S. W. Ingham, Jr., to be in charge of the "Dacotah" Mission, which included only that "portion of the country lying between the Big Sioux and the Missouri Rivers," a triangle that was just being settled. On October 14 he preached at Vermillion, and then visited Yankton, Fort Randall, Canton, Richland, and Sioux Falls. On January 13, 1861, a society of nine members was formed at Vermillion, probably the first religious organization in Dakota. The first church building, of logs with a sod roof, was erected there in 1862. This project was aided by a gift of $130 from the preachers of the conference, and, surprisingly, by a gift of $325 from the Presbyterian missionary society for the purchase of the necessary "hardware." A second society was organized at Richland. Even so, the work was discouraging, for when Ingham left after two years of conscientious service the total membership was but twenty-eight.

In 1864 "Dacotah" was attached to the newly organized Des Moines Conference. Circuits were added and some abandoned, all in the original triangle. In 1872 Dakota was assigned to the Northwest Iowa Conference, becoming a district in the following year. This district reported 15 circuits and 529 members to the conference session of 1876, rather meager results after fifteen years of missionary activity.

Conditions in North Dakota were far less favorable. It was not until 1871, when James Gurley was assigned to the North Pacific Railroad Mission of the Minnesota Conference, that we have any official Methodist concern for North Dakota. He preached at Fargo, preparing the way for the organization of a society there in 1872. A second church was founded, at Grand Forks, in the following year. For some undisclosed reason, in 1873 the North Pacific Mission was transferred to the Northwest Iowa Conference, with John Webb in charge, becoming a district in

[14] Information on the Dakotas can be found in: C. A. Armstrong, ed., *History of the Methodist Church in North Dakota and Dakota Territory* (Nashville: Parthenon Press, 1960); Barclay, *History of Methodist Missions*, Vol. III.

the following year with four circuits—Fargo and Jamestown, Bismarck, Grand Forks and Pembino, and Goose River. The results of the missionary efforts were not very encouraging; two circuits alone reported to the conference in 1876, and their total membership was but fifteen.

In 1874 and again in 1876 the region was devastated by severe grasshopper plagues which all but brought starvation to some areas, so that Congress appropriated $150,000 for food for the hungry. For this and other reasons the outlook for the Dakotas was gloomy. As a result, the two districts were discontinued. In 1877 the circuits in South Dakota were assigned to the Sioux City District of the Northwest Iowa Conference, as was true of Fargo of the North Pacific. However, within a few years conditions in the Dakotas began to change for the better, and with this improvement the church began to make substantial gains. Accordingly, in 1880 the Dakota Mission was organized, taking in "all that part of Dakota south of the Minnesota Conference and east of the Black Hills Mission," with 28 charges and 1,299 members. On October 8, 1885, the Dakota Conference was organized, with 4,497 members. Meanwhile, the greater number of the North Dakota circuits were being assigned to the Red River District of the Minnesota Conference along with numerous Minnesota circuits. The growth was satisfactory enough to warrant the detachment of the North Dakota charges, which were now formed into the North Dakota Mission in 1884, composed of two districts and thirty-one circuits. On October 15, 1886, the North Dakota Conference came into being, with 2,341 members.

A very different situation developed in the southwestern corner of Dakota Territory when gold was discovered in the Black Hills in 1874. A typical gold rush developed; thousands of gold seekers arrived; the Indians were dislodged; mining camps came and went, a few of which survived; and, of course, there were a number of preachers.

The most striking of these was the Methodist Henry Weston Smith, a black-bearded veteran of the Civil War, who on May 7, 1876, conducted the first religious service of record in Custer, if not, indeed, in the Black Hills. Later on he went to Deadwood, working at hard manual labor during the day, and preaching on street corners at nights and on Sundays. While traveling to Crook City to preach, he was killed by hostile Indians. They apparently killed him by mistake, for they usually respected the preachers, whom they called "Black Robes" and "Godmen." In any event, they respected his body, which was found unscalped and otherwise unmutilated, with his Bible in his outstretched hand.

The General Conference of 1876 failed to act upon the request to send preachers to the Black Hills. However, in 1878 the Northwest

Iowa Conference appointed James Williams to this region. In the following year he became the presiding elder of the newly formed Black Hills District, and in 1880 he was appointed superintendent of the Black Hills Mission. By this time churches had been organized at Central City (1878), Crook City (1879), Lead City (1880), and Custer (1880). The seed sown by Smith was beginning to grow. The mission when formed had 5 missionaries, 97 members, 1 church building, and 3 Sunday schools with 160 scholars. In the year following, a church was organized at Rapid City, the eastern gateway to the hills. Later on, the wide open spaces between the Black Hills and the eastern part of South Dakota began to be settled.

16

Some Concluding Observations

A few observations may be noted from this study. First of all, in the main neither the Northern nor the Southern Church had the foresight to make provision for effective work on the Western frontier. The church officials, in general, were seemingly indifferent to the needs of the West, and in the main made no plans, provided no money, and assigned no preachers to be on hand as the new places were being opened up and settled. The popular story to the effect that the Methodist circuit rider was at the site of a new settlement to greet the settlers as they arrived is myth, not fact. A notable exception—and there were others—was the sending out of William Goode, an intelligent and capable preacher, to Kansas and Nebraska soon after they were opened to white settlers to survey the field, and to make a report. In addition, he made recommendations which were followed. As a result, the Methodists were ready, in some measure at least, for the settlers when they began to arrive in considerable numbers in these territories.

Another observation is that, despite the contributions of the local preachers and the circuit riders, the presiding elder was frequently the key clergyman in the frontier situations. It was he who mapped out the circuits, helped to organize churches, obtained preachers for them when and how he could, supervised the preachers and churches of his district, and visited the churches frequently, once a quarter when feasible. Unfortunately, his supply of missionary money to pay preachers and to help build churches was very limited. Moreover, his tenure, as a general rule, was much too brief. There were instances of presiding elders being assigned to a district for a number of years, but all too frequently the tenure was one or two years. It is also true that the preachers stayed on their circuits for much too short a time—one, two, or three years at most. This was due in large measure to the Methodist polity, which in this case might well be questioned. However, it was also due to the fact that all too many of the preachers, like many settlers—often a misnomer—were restless, footloose, migratory. This, of course, is why many of them were in the West in the first place.

It is also observable that there was an apparent lack of any real effort, any creative attempt, in general, to find a new, a different, a more effective approach to meet the conditions of the frontier in the West. The methods used on the eastern side of the Mississippi were followed with little change on the western side. An outstanding exception was Jesse Boring's "Thousand-Dollar Proposition" by which he obtained badly needed preachers and money from Annual Conferences of the Southern Church for the work he was supervising in northern California. Save for the possibility, as was averred, that in some instances the conferences used this as an opportunity to rid themselves of certain preachers, the proposal was successful in its results. Even so, it apparently was not repeated by the Southern Church, nor was it copied by the Northern.

It has frequently been stated, and with some measure of truth, that the Methodist ecclesiastical system of Annual Conferences, bishops, presiding elders, circuit riders, and local preachers, coupled with its Arminian theology, helped to make the Methodists more effective and more successful on the frontier than other denominations were. On the other hand, when compared with the total population of a given frontier territory or state, not with the membership of some other denomination, the number of Methodist members in proportion to the population was extremely—it is fair to say appallingly—low, and remained low for a good many years.

On the more positive side, the interest of the frontier church in education was commendable. Conferences with but a few hundred members and with very little financial backing established schools, elementary and secondary, and in some instances, of a higher rank. In addition, wives of preachers not infrequently taught schools in their homes or elsewhere, not merely to augment the always meager income of the frontier preacher, but also because of an earnest desire to meet the glaring need of providing the frontier children with an education. Many of the churches had libraries. One of these is extant, with a number of its books, in the St. James Methodist Church of Central City, Colorado, whose building was begun in 1864. At times the conference reports listed the number of volumes in each of the church libraries. Preachers and preachers' wives taught singing. In fact, to cite again the statement of an early resident of Los Angeles, a lawyer's wife, the Methodist preacher and his wife were attempting "to civilize the place," along with Christianizing it. Poorly, yes, frequently miserably, paid, sacrificing with glad hearts, and sharing the discomforts, hardships, and dangers of the frontier, far away from home and friends, the preachers and their wives, unsung and unhonored all too frequently, were the vanguards of Christianity and of civilization as Methodism went West.

chapter 22

BILINGUAL
WORK
AND THE
LANGUAGE
CONFERENCES

The Mission to the French

German Methodism

Swedish Methodism

Norwegian-Danish Methodism

Bilingual Missions

T HE MINISTRY TO LANGUAGE GROUPS DE-
veloped as a response to the challenge of immigration into the United
States. For a hundred years between the
defeat of Napoleon at Waterloo in 1815
and the outbreak of World War I in
midsummer, 1914, an ocean of human
beings poured into America and surged
across the continent, creating communities of particular peoples in particular
geographic areas. Circuit riders, ministering to them, received their appointments on one frontier; by the next
Annual Conference time they found
themselves in the rear of pioneers who
had advanced beyond their stations. In
growing industrial cities and mining
towns, as well as in spacious agricultural
areas, newcomers joined those who spoke
their language and shared their culture.
In the twelve decades following 1820
more than 38,000,000 human beings arrived from abroad to make their home
in the land of political freedom, religious liberty, and economic opportunity.
When Oscar Handlin wrote *The Uprooted: The Epic Story of the Great
Migrations that Made the American
People,* he said: "Once I thought to
write a history of the immigrants in
America. Then I discovered the immigrants *were* American history." [1]

The development of the language
work by Methodists bore a relationship
to the number and nationality of immigrants (Table 1). The various immigration waves reached their peak at
a procession of different dates extending
from the middle of the nineteenth into
the first quarter of the twentieth century.
Two historical dates block out a time

[1] (Boston: Little, Brown & Co., 1951), p. 3.

469

span of some 102 years during which the principal developments in the
ministry to the foreign-language groups took place. The period extends
from the organization of the Missionary Society of the Methodist Episcopal
Church in 1819 to the enactment of the Quota Law of 1921, which
drastically limited new admissions by the application of a national-
origins formula. During these years the United States experienced intercontinental population movements on a scale new in history. The
church in America had little experience to guide it in a situation of
such magnitude. Soon after its founding, however, the Missionary Society
recognized the need for new approaches to the extension of the gospel.
"Experiment is the truest test of all thrones," the society pointed out.[2]

Table 1: Principal Sources of Immigration into the United States (1820-1950) [3]

COUNTRY	CUMULATIVE TOTAL RANK ORDER	PEAK YEAR
Germany	6,248,529	1882
Italy	4,776,884	1907
Ireland	4,617,485	1851
Great Britain	4,386,692	1888
Austria-Hungary	4,172,104	1907
Russia	3,343,895	1913
Canada and Newfoundland	3,177,446	1924
Sweden	1,228,113	1882
Mexico	838,844	1924
Norway	814,955	1882
France	633,807	1851
West Indies	496,686	1824
Greece	439,581	1907
Poland	422,326	1921
China	398,882	1882
Turkey	362,034	1913
Denmark	340,418	1882
Switzerland	306,227	1883
Japan	297,146	1907
Netherlands	268,619	1882
Portugal	263,467	1921
Spain	173,021	1921
Belgium	170,374	1913
Romania	158,021	1921
South America	143,133	1924
Czechoslovakia	128,360	1921

[2] *Second Annual Report of the Missionary Society,* 1820-21.

[3] From data in Francis J. Brown and Joseph S. Roucek, eds., *One America* (3rd
ed.; © 1952 by Prentice-Hall, Inc., Englewood Cliffs, N.J.), p. 16. Reprinted by
permission.

1

The Language Ministry of John Wesley

Methodist precedent existed for religious work carried on in native tongues. To John Wesley languages provided a channel for the communication of the gospel as natural to the religious vocation as prayer and scripture reading. Even before his ship set sail for Georgia in 1735, John Wesley commenced to study German in the privacy of his cabin in the forecastle of the ship. "I began to learn German," he noted in his *Journal*, "in order to converse [a little] with the Moravians." [4]

He studied German grammar in systematically scheduled periods of unbroken application ranging from three to four hours in length, practiced spoken German in conversations on deck and at public services, sang with the Moravian brethren aboard. He read and translated hymns from the *Gesangbuch*. During his Georgia mission between February 6, 1736, and December 2, 1737, John Wesley translated from German into English some thirty-three hymns. He is credited with introducing the German style of singing into English church life. Bishop Nuelsen in his definitive study asserts that the influence of the German hymn was one of the most powerful factors at work in conditioning Wesley for his Aldersgate experience on May 24, 1738.[5] Knowledge of German, however, proved to be insufficient to meet the linguistic needs of the Georgia mission.

On June 28, 1736, Wesley began the study of Spanish, for three good reasons: to read Spanish devotional literature so that he could better minister to the Spanish-speaking Indians and some colonists in Georgia; to converse with Jewish parishioners who spoke the language; to be helpful to officers who sometimes came to him for assistance with Spanish correspondence.[6] Toward the end of his Georgia mission Wesley was preaching to groups in five languages: English, German, French, Spanish, and Italian.

Thus to John Wesley the ability to speak languages contributed indispensable working equipment for an adequate ministry in the New World. His example, however, left little mark upon the administrative imagination or policy planning of the church. Almost a century passed before the language movement began to take form with an identifiable

---

[4] October 17, 1735.

[5] John L. Nuelsen, *John Wesley und das deutsche Kirchenlied* (Bremen: Anker-Verlag, 1938), p. 8.

[6] *Journal*, ed. by Curnock; editor's note for diary entry of July 2, 1736.

history and administrative structure—and even then without clear strategy or considered tactics. In its report to the 1924 General Conference of the Methodist Episcopal Church, the Foreign Language Commission candidly stated:

The Methodist Episcopal Church has never developed a policy in regard to its responsibility for work among foreign-language peoples in America. All of this work has sprung up in sporadic manner, with little or no regard for guiding principles. . . . Over against this opportunism is an accomplishment among certain nationality groups of the older immigration that has all the earmarks of a providential movement.[7]

The main streams of the ministry to the immigrants, which had been initiated by the Missionary Society of the Methodist Episcopal Church with a concern for the French, remained for the most part the work of the Northern Church during the 109 years of separation of the Methodist Protestant Church and the 94 years of division following the organization of the Methodist Episcopal Church, South, in 1845. When unification came in 1939, the specialized language work had largely been assimilated into the English-speaking parishes of The Methodist Church.

2

Efforts to Reach the French

Following the purchase of Louisiana from France in 1803, popular interest developed in the vast territory which extended from the Gulf of Mexico to Canada and from the Mississippi to the Rocky Mountains. The French-speaking peoples brought within the jurisdiction of the nation included persons born in France, families descended from French citizens, French-Canadian fur trappers and dealers trading at the mouth of the Mississippi River in the early 1800's, Acadian exiles, and a mixture of races resulting from the intermarriage of the French with the Spanish, Indian, Negro, and English.

The mission to the French was the first foreign-language work to concern the church in the nineteenth century; it remained one of the most unresponsive. A knowledgeable missionary to the French gave it as his opinion that "among all the foreigners who come to this new

[7] *Journal of the General Conference,* 1924, p. 1681.

world to find homes, the French seem to be the least accessible to Protestant missions." [8]

Two years after the purchase of Louisiana, Lorenzo Dow, a circuit rider from Massachusetts, itinerated through the Lower Mississippi region. He made reports which led to the appointment of Elisha Bowman as a circuit rider to southern Louisiana. When his efforts failed to give Methodism root in New Orleans, Bowman shifted his efforts to the countryside.

While from its beginning the Missionary Society took a major interest in "aboriginal missions" directed toward the evangelization of the American Indian, the annual meeting held in John Street Church in the spring of 1820 devoted attention to the foreign-language ministry. Bishop William McKendree, who had been a powerful religious leader on the westward-moving frontier, directed a letter to the Society, describing conditions of religious need in Canada, Florida, the state of Louisiana, and the Missouri territory,[9] and urged the Society to send itinerant missionaries to the "western frontiers, to preach to these inhabitants in French."

The New York Conference took the initiative in appropriating support for a language missionary during the conference year 1820-21. Ebenezer Brown proceeded south with instructions to preach, if possible, to the French inhabitants of Louisiana. Experiencing disappointment in his efforts, he redefined his mission, remaining in New Orleans to assist in the work of an English-speaking congregation. Then he returned to his conference. In 1846 the Methodist Episcopal Church, South, attempted work among the French in New Orleans. Although the missionary reported twenty-three members as a result of his first year of work, he quit and withdrew from the church.

Beginning in the 1830's, French immigrants entered the United States in numbers more constant than newcomers from any other country, reaching a high tide in 1851. From the end of the Civil War until the turn of the century, moreover, French Canadians in substantial numbers migrated to the United States. They settled principally in New England, Michigan, and Illinois.

Sizable French-speaking colonies developed in New York, Detroit, Chicago, and San Francisco, but Louisiana and New England continued to be the principal areas of concentration. In 1838 the New York Conference authorized the appointment of a missionary to the French population in the city of New York. Again the work failed to take root. In 1841 the Missionary Society noted in its Proceedings that the

[8] J. B. Cocagne to the Missionary Society, *Thirty-fifth Annual Report*, 1854, p. 72.
[9] *First Annual Report of the Missionary Society*, under date of April 17, 1820.

French mission in New York had been temporarily suspended and the missionary transferred for the season to the border of Lake Champlain.[10] The Society, however, made a hopeful policy statement about the language work.

In the spring of 1851, Thomas Carter, responding to a request expressed by a few French persons to hear the gospel preached in their own language, went from New York to Detroit. He began his mission by holding services on Sunday afternoons in the Second Methodist Episcopal Church. In the summer of the same year John B. Cocagne was transferred from the Black River Conference to New York to develop work among the French initiated a dozen years before by Charles H. Williamson.

The work in Detroit seemed promising. In the spring of 1853 a thriving congregation occupied Sunday-school rooms in a basement auditorium. The edifice was dedicated as the first French Methodist church in the United States. The society, however, failed to develop durable strength. When Carter left for Buenos Aires in 1856, Cocagne moved from New York to Detroit to succeed him. On a voyage to France, Cocagne lost his life. The Detroit society, failing to find suitable leadership, disintegrated.

During his mission in New York, Cocagne took the trouble to write a letter to the Missionary Society in which he specified difficulties encountered in his work among the French.[11] He said that many of the families were poor. Frequently he saw them begging from house to house. "Many arrive here without any means to commence business, or even to live upon for a week," he reported. The French immigrants were ignorant of the English language. The majority were influenced by "ignorant and bigoted Jesuits and priests." Some few who ventured to think for themselves became skeptics. The indifference to religious subjects was "almost unbounded." Among the more educated French a deeply rooted rationalism made the evangelical approach to the immigrants difficult. He emphasized the necessity of showing the French the "palpable and irreconcilable differences which exist between Popery and the Protestantism of America." "They know *nothing* about the new birth," he added. He observed that some referred to him as a "false prophet." Cocagne guessed that not one out of thirty French-speaking persons in New York City was attached to any church. Commenting on his own work, he said that he was preaching to an average congregation of about twenty-five. He specified his needs: (*a*) a suitable place of worship; (*b*) a day school connected with the mission; (*c*) a program to

---

[10] *Twenty-second Annual Report*, 1841, p. 17.
[11] *Thirty-fifth Annual Report*, 1854, pp. 73-76.

teach English to the French; (d) two assistants; and (e) more money for the work. Statistics showed three French missionaries at work and sixty-two members.[12]

The Methodist Episcopal Church, South, on its part felt its obligations to work among the French in Louisiana. In 1879 it attempted to establish a mission with a day school and a Sunday school in rural parishes. The work proved to be as disappointing as efforts in New Orleans had been more than thirty years before. In 1885 the Central Illinois Conference of the Northern Church appropriated $500 to re-establish work begun in New Orleans more than six decades before. By 1890 French services were being held in two chapels, and Sunday schools were well attended.

The migration of French-speaking families from Canada into the states along the northern boundary provided a missionary field for cultivation that was first given attention, with disappointing results, by the Troy Conference as early as 1856. Mission programs developed by the conferences in New England in scattered efforts gave promise, but failed to develop strong and durable societies.

A review of the obstacles faced by the workers among the French showed the chief difficulty to be the lack of able bilingual missionaries.[13] Moreover, pressures brought to bear on Methodist converts from Roman Catholicism by their priests were strong. Because of their migratory industrial habits, French-Canadian families had no firm roots in the community. Their culture was generally alien to the warm evangelical message of Methodism.

It was not until 1908 that the Methodist Episcopal Church, South, established a mission which had durability. In Martin Hebert, a Creole, the church found a preacher who himself was a part of the culture and had a genius for recruiting and training Creole leadership.

The work among the French carried on by the Southern Church developed its center at Houma, Louisiana, a Mississippi River town at the junction of six navigable bayous. In 1912 Hebert asked the Woman's Missionary Council to assign deaconesses to a community house. Their service added a new dimension to the program. A school for French children provided another functional service. By 1920 Hebert, as superintendent of the French Mission District of the Louisiana Conference, had under his administrative care seven charges, twenty-three churches, and eight hundred members.[14]

[12] Ibid., p. 36.
[13] Thirty-eighth Annual Report of the Missionary Society, 1857, p. 82.
[14] Minutes of the Annual Conferences, Methodist Episcopal Church, South, 1920, p. 245.

The fruitful effort of the Methodist Episcopal Church, South, showed the importance of developing from among the French-speaking people themselves preachers who had been educated in a Protestant environment, who were equipped with an evangelical message, and who had a concern for education and social service.

3

German Methodism

The early concern which the Missionary Society had shown for the French in the South was directed on the western frontier to the immigrants from Germany, who were settling in large numbers in the Ohio River Valley and particularly around Cincinnati, the industrial and merchandizing center of the expanding western territory. The mission to the Germans developed as Methodism's most effective language work.[15] And the character of the German mission was most profoundly influenced by William Nast (1807-99).

The Pioneering Work of William Nast

In a sense Nast became a prototype of the Methodist leader engaged in language work and an inspiring legend among the peoples of other immigrant groups. He combined in his person qualities of linguistic competence, intellectual power, demonstrated scholarship, evangelical passion, sense of mission, emotional durability, and pioneering zest. Nast had come to a clear direction for his life as a result of an agonizing self-appraisal extending over nearly a decade of restless intellectual activity and spiritual searching. After unsettling theological studies in the Protestant Evangelical Theological Seminary of Blaubeuren in southern Germany and further work at the University of Tübingen, he migrated in 1828 to America, where, he had heard, there was a dearth of men capable of teaching languages and literature.

As a librarian and instructor at West Point, Nast was deeply in-

[15] This movement within Methodism is comprehensively discussed by Paul F. Douglass, *The Story of German Methodism* (New York: The Methodist Book Concern, 1939).

fluenced by a sermon preached by President Wilbur Fisk of Wesleyan University. Fisk corresponded with Nast. In a historic letter to the still-questing young German scholar, he suggested: "You only need to go to Christ that you may have light and strength." [16]

In the spring of 1834 Nast became an instructor in ancient languages at Kenyon College, in Gambier, Ohio, and assistant to the principal of the senior department, Kenyon Preparatory Schools. While thus professionally employed, he attended a revival meeting in Danville, Ohio. During the service he obtained the "long-sought witness of the Spirit, clearer than the light of the sun." [17] The vivid date was January 17, 1835; it became a historic point in the story of German Methodism. Nast's intellectual and spiritual preparation now seemed sufficient to him to justify his offering himself as a missionary to the Germans in America.

For half a decade the need for such a missionary had been discussed in Ohio Conference circles and particularly in the columns of the *Western Christian Advocate*. Now that a qualified man was ready to undertake the task, influential leaders within the conference raised objections to the establishment of a German mission. Adam Miller, who was a participant in the development of the project, observed that "there had been no deep-laid plans, no great preparations or calculations on the part of the Church for carrying on this work." [18] Because of the adventitious nature of the development, German Methodists took satisfaction in the feeling, as Miller phrased it, that "God opened the way and carried on this work." [19]

On August 19, 1835, Bishop Joshua Soule, presiding over the Ohio Conference, appointed Nast a missionary to the Germans. Upon the adjournment of the annual session, Nast proceeded to Cincinnati with his entire equipment: a general directive, the promise of $100 voted by the conference as the annual stipend of the German missionary, and his religious experience. At the end of his first year of work, he reported to the Ohio Conference three converts—a woman and two men. One was Edward Hoch, who volunteered to serve as Nast's bodyguard in areas known in Cincinnati as "Over the Rhine," where German saloon keepers resented his missionary intrusion and his constant admonitions to abstinence. Hoch was to be the father of Edward W. Hoch, two-term governor of Kansas and temperance leader. The other man was John

[16] Dated March 12, 1833; preserved in the archives of the Museum of German Methodism, Nippert Memorial Library, Bethesda Hospital, Cincinnati.

[17] Adam Miller, *Experience of German Methodist Preachers* (Cincinnati: Methodist Book Concern, 1859), p. 87.

[18] *Ibid.*, p. 88.

[19] *Ibid.*

Zwahlen, a Swiss-born Cincinnati clerk, who became one of the stalwart leaders of the German work.

The 1836 Ohio Conference received Nast's report with disappointment. After superficial discussion, the conference decided to substitute the extensive for the intensive type of mission carried on during the previous year in Cincinnati. Nast's second appointment committed to his care the Germans throughout the whole state of Ohio. He traveled a three-hundred-mile circuit each month, preaching in twenty-two places. During the conference year he covered some four thousand miles on horseback. When the conference received Nast's second annual report, it reversed its policy, now substituting intensive for extensive missions. Nast returned to Cincinnati. In the summer of 1838 he organized the first German Methodist society of nineteen members in Burke's Chapel on busy Vine Street.

When the Ohio Conference met in 1838, a strong faction favored abandonment of the German work. L. L. Hamline, an influential conference member and editor of the *Western Christian Advocate,* led a movement to support the continuation of the language mission and won authorization for the publication of a religious journal in the German language. The *Pittsburgh Christian Advocate* volunteered to serve as a clearing house for $10 contributions toward a $3,000 fund necessary to underwrite the venture. The Board of Bishops unanimously approved the publication, provided it could be issued without loss to the Methodist Book Concern. The bishops appointed Nast editor of the yet-to-be-named magazine. *Der Christliche Apologete* began publication on January 4, 1839. It provided spiritual, intellectual, and organizational leadership for the German movement at a time when there were only fifty German Methodists. Rarely has the influence of a publication been so powerful in the development of a mission. It began with a list of forty subscribers. Within two years its circulation increased to twelve hundred.[20]

During the first missionary year in Cincinnati, Nast won the friendship of James Gamble, an Irish soapmaker and active Methodist layman. Gamble opened his home for German Methodist class meetings. Out of the association between Gamble and Nast, a family romance developed: Nast's daughter Fanny married Gamble's son William. Thus two great immigrant families were united in Christian service to the benefit of the German mission.

[20] *Twenty-second Annual Report of the Missionary Society,* 1841.

The Development of German Work in America

From the very beginning the mission to the Germans recruited its preachers from converts. First they were licensed as exhorters. Quarterly Conferences accepted the most promising ones as local preachers. Annual Conferences received them on trial and, when they were qualified, into full relationship. Annual Conferences made appropriations for their subsistence support, and bishops appointed them to mission territories.

The following example will suggest the pattern by which the German work grew. In the course of his preaching in Cincinnati, Nast had been instrumental in bringing about the conversion of a young German named Francis Nuelsen. By family tradition the Nuelsens were Roman Catholics. When by letter Francis informed his mother of his religious experience, she persuaded her husband to sell the family home and business in Germany and move to America, there to recover their son from his apostasy. The Nuelsen migration failed splendidly in its purpose: two daughters and two of four sons experienced conversion and joined the Methodist Episcopal Church.

Amelia Nuelsen, sister of Francis, was a devout but questioning Catholic who roomed with the Nasts in Cincinnati. She rebelled at Protestant ways as she observed them in the Methodist family, but she was torn by inner conflict between two allegiances as she compared the faith of her landlords with her Roman Catholic practices. The doubts in her mind were resolved while she was listening to a sermon preached by Peter Schmucker, a former Lutheran preacher who had succeeded Nast in Cincinnati.

Within Methodist circles Miss Nuelsen made the acquaintance of Ludwig S. Jacoby,[21] a young Jew of twenty-six who was rooming on the upper floor of the Western Methodist Book Concern. Jacoby was teaching German in the city and industriously developing a German grammar for successful publication. Moved by the preaching of Nast one Sunday evening and his remark that "there may be a Saul among us, whom God will convert into a Paul," [22] Jacoby joined the church on the Sunday before Christmas, 1839. He married Amelia Nuelsen. Granted an exhorter's license, he began to preach among the laborers along the canal in Cincinnati.

Early in 1841 a member of the Missouri Conference traveled to Cin-

[21] For a biography of Jacoby, see Heinrich Mann, *Ludwig S. Jacoby: Sein Leben und Werken* (Bremen: Verlag des Traktathauses, 1892) , p. 274.
[22] Miller, *Experience of German Methodist Preachers,* p. 126.

cinnati to talk with Nast and Bishop T. A. Morris about the desire of English-speaking pastors to have a German-speaking missionary assigned to St. Louis. Bishop Morris asked Jacoby to accept the call. With his wife and baby daughter, Jacoby arrived in St. Louis on August 1, 1841.

The work in St. Louis thrived under Jacoby's imaginative leadership. He extended his ministry by holding services in the home of a German family some eight miles outside the city, preaching there once a week. In the southern section of the city he began to preach Sunday afternoons from a butcher's block in the market house. On his second Sunday in the location, ruffians pushed him from the block, assaulted him, and protested his mission. Police took the situation in hand. Jacoby applied to the mayor for "watchmen." During the course of the year one of these—a German—was converted. Undeterred by opposition from secular Germans and some German newspapers, Jacoby continued to distribute tracts, Testaments, and Bibles, braving "opprobrious epithets" and sometimes bombs of mud hurled at him.[23]

At the first Quarterly Conference, held on March 18, 1842, forty members of the society authorized construction of a church. The edifice was dedicated on August 7, 1842. Further to meet the needs of the German community, Jacoby organized a day school and installed his brother-in-law, Henry Nuelsen, as first teacher. Nuelsen's son John became the first German to be elected to the episcopacy by Methodists.

From the center in Cincinnati, missionaries pushed out in all directions. Nast, touring the East both as circulation manager of the *Apologete* and missionary at large in 1841, visited a class meeting in New York to see what might be done for the Germans settling in such large numbers in the great cities along the Atlantic coast. Addressing the New York Conference, he was instrumental in encouraging a decision to authorize a German mission in New York. Work was initiated also in other cities in the Middle Atlantic states. In the spring of 1842, Peter Schmucker went south to New Orleans, organized a class, and in 1843 entrusted the work to Karl Bremer, a young man converted in Germany and licensed as a local preacher in America.

In 1841 the Missionary Society recorded eleven German missions operating under the jurisdiction of four conferences: the Ohio, Pittsburgh, Indiana, and Kentucky.[24]

In less than a decade after Nast's appointment as missionary to the Germans in Cincinnati, the work had grown to such proportions that

[23] *Ibid.*, p. 135.
[24] *Twenty-second Annual Report*, 1841, pp. 15-18.

questions about the proper administrative supervision were being raised. How was the German mission to be integrated into the work of the English-speaking conferences? Although among themselves the Germans were seriously discussing the necessity of language conferences, Peter Schmucker in a compromise proposed consolidation in two German districts, one attached to the Ohio and the other to the Missouri Conference. The 1844 General Conference adopted a resolution enabling the creation of German-speaking districts. Pursuant to this authorization three German-speaking districts were established: the Pittsburgh, the Cincinnati, and the St. Louis, with Charles H. Doering, Peter Schmucker, and Ludwig Jacoby respectively as presiding elders.

A decision of even greater importance was made in September, 1845, in Cincinnati. The action was the outcome of a resolution of twenty-seven German preachers attending the Ohio Conference to set aside a prayer-meeting hour for an instructive discourse on the duty, necessity, and blessedness of spreading the gospel. They asked the Sunday School Union of the Methodist Episcopal Church to make an appropriation to provide for the publication of Sunday-school literature in the German language at the plant of the Western Methodist Book Concern. The Germans pledged themselves to support their own request by endeavoring to pay a quarterly assessment of one cent for every pupil and teacher enrolled toward the support of the Union, in addition to such annual collections as the Ohio and Illinois Conferences might order. Thus in 1845 the Germans took the first step in developing a teaching literature.

The Establishment of Methodism in Germany

While German Methodism was spreading over the American continent, seeds were being sown which presently led to the extension of the mission back to the fatherland. As Germans were converted in America and became active in the Methodist fellowship, they wrote letters home to their relatives. In these communications they often vividly described their religious experiences. Such correspondence led to requests for Methodist preachers. In the spring of 1849 the Board of Managers of the Missionary Society, impressed with the magnitude of the German migration to America, took action to establish the long-discussed mission at Bremen, the principal port of embarkation. Recommending the appointment of two missionaries, the society noted that in 1849 sixty thousand emigrants embarked on seventy vessels from the port of Bremen for New York. It estimated further that emigrants departed from Hamburg for the United States on thirty-two ships.[25]

The bishops placed the administration of the new work in Germany under the direction of Bishop T. A. Morris, a leader well qualified by heartfelt interest and experience with the language work. Morris discussed the selection of the first missionary to be sent by American Methodists to Germany with Nast. Then he invited Jacoby, presiding elder of the Quincy District, Illinois Conference, to initiate the program. Jacoby sailed from New York on October 20, 1849, equipped with $5 worth of tracts and a few New Testaments provided by the American Bible Society with a promise of more.

Jacoby disembarked at Bremen on November 9 and proceeded to establish his work much as he had done in St. Louis. From the first the work prospered. Jacoby, overburdened as a solitary missionary and in poor health, begged for reinforcements. The next year the Missionary Society authorized assistance for the ailing pastor. Charles H. Doering and Louis Nippert, the two preachers who arrived from America to help him on June 7, 1850, were strong leaders.

The assistance now available enabled Jacoby to itinerate about Germany in response to demands for Methodist preaching. In the spring of 1851 two other missionaries, Englehardt Riemenschneider and Jacoby's brother-in-law Henry Nuelsen, arrived from America to strengthen the work.

The Methodist work was introduced into Switzerland in 1856 by two separate missions. With Jacoby's approval, Ernest Mann, converted in Bremen, preached his first sermon in Lausanne. Jacoby, recognizing Zurich as a city of historic charm, industry, and strategic power, assigned Herman zur Jakobsmüllen to build the work there.[26]

From the moment of his arrival on the Continent in 1849, Jacoby experienced difficulties from established ecclesiastical authorities. As the Methodist work strengthened, resistance encountered from the state churches stiffened. The pressure became so serious that in 1855 Jacoby and his associates in Germany felt compelled to submit a petition through the Missionary Society to United States President Franklin Pierce, asking the good offices of the government through diplomatic channels to intercede with the German governments to obtain more lenient treatment of Methodist missionaries by political authorities.[27] The solution, as

[25] *Thirty-first Annual Report,* 1849-50, p. 28.
[26] The record of the development of the work in Switzerland is summarized in L. Peter, *Geschichte der bischöflichen Methodistenkirchen in der Schweiz* (Zurich: Christliche Verlagsbuchhandlung, 1893) , p. 229.
[27] *Thirty-sixth Annual Report of the Missionary Society,* 1855, p. 18.

William F. Warren pointed out, came providentially as a result of the Prussian victory over Austria in 1866.[28]

The dedication of a headquarters known as the Tract House, in Bremen, on April 1, 1855, became a milestone in the development of the mission in Germany. The three-story structure included a chapel seating four hundred, a bookstore, the office of the superintendent of the mission, and living quarters for the preacher in charge. By the end of the year Methodist statistics showed 18 missionaries and assistants in 9 stations; 596 full members; 44 probationers; and 26 Sunday schools with an enrollment of 1,512 scholars. During the first nine years of the mission only 7 missionaries had been sent from America to Germany; the movement had produced its own preachers.

The 1856 General Conference of the Methodist Episcopal Church faced serious problems related to the German mission. Nast nevertheless succeeded in obtaining authorization for the publication of the *Sonntagschule Glocke* for church-school circulation and consented to wait another quadrennium for legislation which would make possible the organization of German-language conferences. Jacoby, who urged an act enabling the establishment of a Mission Conference, was elated at a resolution authorizing the conference in Germany, and in parts of France and Switzerland where German was spoken as a language.[29] The Mission Conference was organized in Bremen in September, 1856.

The Organization of German Methodism

In America the desirability of continuing German-language districts within English-speaking conferences lessened. The fundamental policy question was this: Would a language conference encourage growth which could never be obtained within the English-speaking framework? Or would such an organizational pattern widen the gulf between the German- and English-speaking pastors and societies? Would the Germans be isolated behind a language barrier? By 1860 the German work was being carried on as parts of 9 conferences and 18 districts in the United States, 4 districts in Germany, 210 appointments in America, and 17 appointments in Germany.

While the proper policy was under discussion, Bishop Edward R. Ames decided in 1862 to administer a strong medicine to the Germans, who seemed unable to agree among themselves about the pattern of organization. He dissolved the Cincinnati District and divided its charges

---

[28] *True Theory of Missionary Work* (pamphlet; 1869), pp. 21-25.
[29] *Journal of the General Conference*, 1856, p. 143.

among three English-speaking districts. Likewise in the Southeast Indiana Conference he divided the German appointments among four English-speaking districts. The situation which resulted was so unsatisfactory that Germans came to agreement on policy. Seven German-speaking churchmen went to Philadelphia as delegates to the 1864 General Conference. The Committee on German Work of the Cincinnati Conference[30] recommended that the interests and proper development of German Methodism would be most successfully promoted by organizing, as far as practicable, the German missions and pastoral charges into separate Annual Conferences. German Methodism came of age in Philadelphia when the 1864 General Conference and the subsequent quadrennial session enacted legislation enabling the organization of German-speaking Annual Conferences.

By 1915 the ten German-language conferences in the United States were reporting 60,271 full members in 761 churches and 67,297 scholars in 723 Sunday schools.

The work on the Continent was strengthened in 1897 by the merger of the programs of the Methodist Episcopal Church and the Synod of the Wesleyan Methodist Church. Wesleyan Methodism had been brought to Winnenden, citadel of German pietism, in 1831 by Christopher Mueller. In 1844 Nast had visited Winnenden to establish fraternal relations. Steps toward unification had been begun in 1894.

The Troubles of Two World Wars

During the 108 years between the appointment of Nast as German missionary to Cincinnati in 1835 and the disbanding of the East German Conference in 1943, Methodism in its German relationship experienced the strain of political events on both continents. In America the early developments of the mission took place in a period of controversy over the issue of slavery.

The outbreak of World War I initiated a period of prolonged stress. During most of these years administrative leadership was given to Methodism on the Continent by John L. Nuelsen, elected bishop in 1908 and assigned to Europe in 1912.

Austria declared war on Serbia on July 28, 1914. Bishop Nuelsen declared that his duty compelled him to remain in Germany with the Methodist people. In 1916 the German Conference petitioned the General Conference to have Nuelsen returned as their bishop. When, how-

[30] *Journal of the Cincinnati Conference*, 1863, pp. 22-25.

ever, the United States declared war on Germany on April 16, 1917, Nuelsen withdrew to Switzerland, placing his administrative duties in the hands of his district superintendents.

After America declared war and joined the Allied Powers, English-speaking Methodists were inclined to look with suspicion upon the patriotism of Germans in the United States. Within church circles relationships became strained. Secret Service agents visited German Methodist administrative officers and attended German Methodist services to hear what was being said.

From the day the war broke out in 1914, Bishop Nuelsen was determined that the conflict should not divide Methodists. He discussed ideas with the preachers under his episcopal supervision in Germany. He pointed out that Methodism in Germany was still financially dependent upon support from the United States; that neither the Methodist work in Germany nor that in Scandinavia commanded undivided sympathy in America; and that after the war Methodists on the Continent would be in serious need of brotherly assistance. He recalled the influence which Methodism in Germany had exercised upon the church in America. Pointing out the threat of nationalism to Christianity, Nuelsen declared in a polemic tract issued to German Methodists early in 1917: "Christianity is supranational. In the kingdom of Christ there are no trenches and no customs barriers. . . . Our battle is against sin, the flesh, the devil, and his works." [31]

German Methodism survived World War I without separation of the work in America from that on the Continent.

Immediately after the peace German Methodists in the United States mobilized a program of relief and reconstruction. Contributions to the assistance fund exceeded half a million dollars. Bishop Nuelsen toured the nation to raise money. Southern planters contributed cotton to provide textiles for clothing; people in the North paid ocean freight. German Methodist families in the United States bought "vacation certificates" to provide rest for ailing German children. Swiss and Scandinavian Methodists joined in the relief programs.

Political difficulties in Germany were not at an end. The Weimar Republic (1919-33) reeled through the National Socialist revolution into the Third Reich in early 1933. As the agents of Adolf Hitler moved forcefully to co-ordinate religious with political life in a Nordic racial state, Methodist conferences in Germany took steps to maintain their connectionalism. At the same time they found it necessary to devise an organizational pattern acceptable to the National Socialist government.

[31] *Der Methodismus in Deutschland nach dem Krieg* (Bremen: Buchhandlung und Verlag des Traktathauses), pp. 29-31.

The 1936 General Conference enacted legislation enabling the Annual Conferences in Germany to form a Central Conference and elect a bishop.[32] On September 17, 1936, Bishop Nuelsen called the five conferences together in Frankfurt am Main to organize the Central Conference of Germany. On the first ballot the delegates elected F. H. Otto Melle, head of the Methodist Theological Seminary in Frankfurt, to the office of bishop.

On March 13, 1938, Germany absorbed Austria. The union of two German-speaking nations in Central Europe was generally welcomed by Methodists in both states. The merger of the political states, however, necessitated changes in the Methodist organization. Bishop Nuelsen promptly transferred the five pastors of the Austrian Mission Conference to the Central Conference of Germany under the jurisdiction of Bishop Melle and left the pulpits to be filled by Melle. On April 21, 1938, the Board of Foreign Missions announced the official dissolution of the Austrian Mission Conference.

The Dissolution of German-Speaking Conferences

The strains, suspicions, and aftermath of World War I accelerated sociological forces long at work among the German population in the United States to bring about a thoroughgoing discussion of the organizational pattern of German-speaking Methodists in language conferences. Immigration was declining. Membership seemed to have reached a plateau. Increasingly preachers sought transfer from German- to English-speaking conferences. Difficulties in parish administration increased; more than three out of five German-speaking parishes overlapped English-speaking appointments. Duplication of effort and intradenominational competition generated administrative friction. Finally, by force of environment and economic pressure Germans had become bilingual. In 1924 the English language predominated in 57 per cent of some 530 German congregations.

The assimilation of the German-language into the English-language conferences followed a general pattern. In an effort to bridge the gap between the cultures, the German churches began by introducing English partially into Sunday-school teaching and young people's meetings. Next came an occasional English-language Sunday-evening service. As the process accelerated, the German-language service was maintained on Sunday mornings; all other services with the exception of prayer meet-

---

[32] The conferences in Germany in 1936 were: Central Germany; Northeast Germany; Northwest Germany; South Germany; and Southwest Germany.

ings, adult Bible classes, and the ministry to the aged were carried on in English. However much some leaders of German Methodism sought to ward off the certain outcome of the trend, it became apparent that the time was approaching for the liquidation of the movement which had written such a glorious chapter in the history of Methodism.

First by special legislation of General Conferences and then pursuant to a general enabling act, the adjustment proceeded. The North German Conference was first to dissolve (1924); the East German Conference the last, completing its seventy-eighth and final session on April 11, 1942.

According to the general pattern of pastoral assignment as the conferences dissolved, geographic location of the German congregations within the boundaries of English-speaking conferences determined official connectional relationships, while joint commissions on mergers worked out particular plans for the assimilation of specific connectional institutions and programs.

The Achievements of German Methodism

While the story of German Methodism stands in the history of the Christian church as an epic of evangelical action, the institutions established by it on both continents expressed personal faith in collective action through camp meetings, the deaconess hospital movement, academies and colleges, theological schools, homes for children and the aged, and a memorable literature.

Because the gregarious German Methodists "felt" their religion, the camp meeting developed as a cardinal event in the annual calendars of the congregations. In the summer of 1839, German Methodists held their first camp meeting in Mill Creek Valley seven miles outside Cincinnati. From this gathering the German Methodists, chiefly from the end of the Civil War to World War I, developed three dozen camp grounds across the continent. From their scanty incomes the Germans systematically set aside savings to cover their expenses to "the meetings." German preachers, who rarely took vacations, scheduled the camp meetings as the annual event on their family calendars. Small congregations often pooled their funds to help selected persons attend. They prayed for specific souls to be saved.

EDUCATIONAL INSTITUTIONS

If the camp meeting provided a primitive locale for spiritual fellowship of the spread-out German congregations, the educational institutions

established by the German Methodists on both continents shared a common respect for the mind. In founding their schools, colleges, and
seminaries German Methodists held to a primary purpose: adequately to
prepare their leadership. Hence they gave first attention to the education of ministers and teachers. Probably the seminary for the professional
training of ministers in Germany was most far-reaching in its influence
and most durable in its educational service. Established in 1858 in
Bremen, it was the first educational institution of the German Methodists.
It was later moved to Frankfurt am Main.

While the seminary was the first and most durable of the German
Methodist educational institutions, it was only one of a number of
efforts undertaken to unite theological literacy with evangelical passion.
In 1858 William Nast and Jacob Rothweiler, with the authorization
and support of the Cincinnati and North Ohio Conferences, negotiated
an arrangement with Baldwin University in Berea, Ohio, under which
twelve German students began study on the campus. The language
work developed so successfully that in 1864 a group of German preachers and laymen obtained a charter for German Wallace College. Perhaps
no institution founded by German Methodists in America maintained a
closer relationship with the seminary in Frankfurt am Main.

The steady growth of German Wallace College in buildings, endowment, faculty, prestige, student body, and alumni loyalty side by side
with Baldwin University presented the situation of two friendly educational establishments performing almost identical functions. A logical
step was merger. In 1913 the two institutions united to form Baldwin-
Wallace College.

In 1864 a group of preachers in Quincy, Illinois, began to explore
their Christian duty of ministering to orphans left fatherless by Civil
War casualties. Their concern led to the founding of the Western
Orphan Asylum and Educational Institute in Warrenton, Missouri. As
the years went by, it became clear that a separation of the educational
program from the charitable work would be desirable. In 1869 the name
of the institution was changed to Central Wesleyan College and Orphan
Asylum. Thus the relative position of the two operations was reversed.
In 1884 the educational institution was fully separated from the asylum.
The divorce proved advantageous to both divisions.

In 1919, Central Wesleyan absorbed Mount Pleasant German College
of Mount Pleasant, Iowa. Central Wesleyan continued as a four-year
liberal-arts college, offering also a four-year preparatory academy course
until 1933. With the development of public high schools in Warrenton
and other towns in the county, the need for the academy decreased. The
financial crash in 1929 so reduced the endowment fund that Central

Wesleyan faced a choice of alternatives: either to close or to operate on a reduced budget as a junior college. The board of trustees chose the junior-college plan. The last four-year class was graduated in 1930. In the fall of the same year Central Wesleyan opened as a junior college.

Shortly after the Civil War a group of preachers of the Northwest German Conference purchased a marine hospital in Galena, Illinois. They reconditioned it for educational purposes. In 1868 the institution opened for academic work with a primary school for children. As its program grew and its usefulness was demonstrated, the Northwest German Conference recognized the project as the Normal School of Galena, Illinois, accepted conference responsibility for it, and had title to the property transferred to its trustees. The name was changed to the German-English College of Galena. In 1891 the college was transferred to Charles City, Iowa, and changed its name to Charles City College. In 1914 it merged with Morningside College, Sioux City, Iowa.

In the South, German Methodists were active in educational ventures. Emmanuel Institute was opened in Brenham, Texas, in 1876. Closed for lack of financial support, the institution was reopened in 1883. Another college had been started by the Germans in Rutersville. Unable to support two institutions which competed with each other, the South German Conference closed the institution at Rutersville and concentrated the educational programs at Brenham. Christian Blinn, New York businessman traveling through Texas, became interested in the educational project. He donated a building which served for both academic and residence purposes. In gratitude, the trustees changed the name of the institution to Blinn Memorial College in 1889.

When the conference discontinued support in 1933, citizens of Brenham reorganized the institution as a private and then public nonsectarian junior college. It continued from 1937 under the name of Blinn College as the first county district tax-supported junior college in Texas.

Two other educational programs of the German Methodists met with only temporary success. In 1889 the North German Conference opened St. Paul's College in Minnesota. In 1917 the Minnesota Conference took over the college buildings as a home for the aged. The students were transferred to Parker College, Winnebago, Minnesota. In the fall of 1896 the West German Conference opened the Enterprise (Kansas) Normal Academy and Commercial School. This institution closed in 1917.

The German conferences of the Methodist Episcopal Church took as their special foreign-missions project the support of an institution in Kiukiang, China. In 1902 an institution, founded in 1881, was renamed William Nast College. As the strength of German Methodism ebbed after World War I, William Nast College, no longer sponsored by the Germans, was turned over to the Board of Foreign Missions of the Methodist Episcopal Church.

LITERATURE

The Germans believed in Christian literature quite as much as in education. From the early beginning of the movement, German Methodists issued publications of persuasive influence and high quality. For a hundred years *Der Christliche Apologete* gave German Methodism its voice under three editors: William Nast (1838-92), Albert Nast (1892-1918), and August J. Bucher (1918-37). John A. Diekmann served as volunteer editor (1937-41).

Following World War I the *Apologete* continued publication under increasingly difficult conditions. The conflict had shaken the unity which once characterized the German Americans. Teaching of German in schools and colleges had been suspended; only slowly did it regain status in curriculums. Immigration, both as a result of the war and quota restrictions, fell sharply. The talk of merger with English-speaking conferences increased. The aging readers were dying at the rate of three or four hundred a year. Despite heroic budgeting and sacrificial service on the part of editors, deficits mounted. Loyal readers insisted that the publication was "indispensable." The last issue was published under date of December 3, 1941, completing 103 years.

The publication of the *Apologete* was only the first of the journalistic efforts of German Methodism. In 1856 *Die Sonntagschule Glocke,* a church-school paper, appeared. By 1871 the growth of Sunday-school enrollment made a weekly lesson guide necessary. This was called *Die Bebelforscher.* In 1873 *Haus und Herd* took its place among the periodicals as a monthly edited for the whole family. By 1893 the German publications were reaching their golden age.

Beyond the publication of periodicals German Methodism produced books in the German language. In religious publishing history there was never any program quite like the one the Germans developed. Books fell into three classifications: first, publications dealing with the mechanics of faith, doctrine, ritual, and worship; second, inspirational volumes of religious experiences; and third, books which constituted a library of self-education. Probably the third category was most unusual. The "ABC" books for children were introduced in 1848. Between 1849 and 1865 fifty volumes of a "Youth Library" were published. During this same period the "Library A for Small Children" grew to sixty volumes. The graded popularization program received a new impetus in 1865, when Henry Liebardt joined Nast as an assistant editor.

His genius for simplification without the sacrifice of scholarly respectability expanded the "Youth Library" to a hundred volumes. Perhaps the most influential of all volumes was *Life Compass for Old and Young*, written by George H. Simons. Almost every German Methodist family aspired to own the book.

The printing press played a fundamental role in the development of the mission to the Germans. There was persistent emphasis on reading. As a primary force German Methodist literature was educative; it oriented the immigrant mind to American society through the genius of evangelical Protestantism.

DEACONESS WORK

Through the deaconesses-and-hospital movement German Methodists provided a channel of Christian service for women. Beginning with the organization of the Bethany Society in 1874, the deaconess movement on the Continent came to be the strongest institutional branch of German Methodism. The mother house of the Bethany Society was developed at Frankfurt am Main. When the Wesleyans united with the Methodist Episcopal Church in 1897, distinguished institutions of the Bethany Society and the Martha and Mary Society, with mother house in Nuremberg, were associated. By 1936, when the Central Conference of Germany was organized, German Methodist deaconesses were at work in well-equipped and -administered hospitals and stations in thirty-six German, Swiss, and Austrian cities.

In 1888 the Elizabeth Gamble Deaconess Home and Christ Hospital had been opened in Cincinnati, with Isabella Thoburn, first head-mother of the Chicago Deaconess Training School, as head deaconess. The institution took its name from Elizabeth Gamble, the wife of James Gamble, the Irish soapmaker who had assisted Nast in his early mission. Christ Hospital had become the special project of James N. Gamble, ingenious chemist who developed Ivory soap. In 1895, Louise Golder, at the age of forty-two, entered the Elizabeth Gamble Deaconess Home to become the first German Methodist deaconess in America. In 1896, Christian Golder, with his sister Louise, rented a little house in Cincinnati to found a German hospital. Six German nurses were released from Christ Hospital to assist the Golders. To help support the work, a Bethesda Society was organized in 1897. Out of this beginning of hospital and society grew the Bethesda Institutions, a complex of hospitals, homes, and training schools in Cincinnati. By 1926 Bethesda included twenty-five separate buildings spread out over eighty-five Cincinnati acres and representing a debt-free value of $3,000,000. The mother house maintained branch homes and stations in Chicago, Milwaukee, Kansas City, Detroit, Terre Haute, Los Angeles, and Akron.

Within the framework of Bethesda Institutions, Dorcas Institute opened in 1910. Originally planned to educate parish deaconesses, in 1917 its program was extended to provide studies designed to prepare young women for entrance into the Bethesda School of Nursing. Dorcas Institute was absorbed by the Cincinnati Training School affiliated with Bethesda Institutions.

The East German Conference in 1901 broadened a deaconess work which it had begun in Brooklyn in 1893 by the organization of the Bethany Society. As the need for hospital service increased, the Bethany Society borrowed money for the Harbor Mission Society, acquired a new site, and on September 16, 1902, dedicated the Bethany Deaconess Home and Hospital. In 1907 the modern hospital facility was enlarged to include a new deaconess home. For fifty years, from 1894, Martha Binder, born in Würtenburg, served as the head deaconess nurse.

In 1895 Jacob Rothweiler, who had been very instrumental in the development of German Methodist educational institutions, took the initiative to convene a meeting in Louisville to explore means of providing a deaconess hospital service in that city. In the fall of 1896 a group of German preachers and laymen accepted a gift of the Southwestern Homeopathic College to serve as an initial base for a hospital. The public response to the facility was such that during the next year the hospital was moved to larger quarters. Plans for still further enlargement were developed, and on February 24, 1898, well-equipped facilities were dedicated. A still larger and more adequate hospital building was placed in service in the summer of 1904.

German Methodism was strong in its emphasis on religious experience, uncompromising in its Protestant affirmation, effective in its training of its young preachers, outspoken in its moral positions, and effective in the expression of faith in social service and institutional ministry.

4

Swedish Methodism

Methodism developed its second strongest language ministry among the immigrants from Sweden. They provided the eighth largest blood stream of the nation. In the century between 1830 and 1930 some

1,300,000 Swedes arrived in the United States; the movement reached its peak in 1882. For the most part, they settled in the north-central and northeastern states. The Swedes came to America for economic, political, and social reasons; a primary factor motivating emigration in the middle of the nineteenth century, however, was religious. The state church of Sweden looked upon dissenters as apostates and upon a free-church movement as subversive of established relationships. Protests against compulsory military training caused some young men to leave the country. The social status of the industrial and agricultural workers was dreary; economic distress aggravated the discontent. During the 1840's the immigration from Sweden began to swell to large proportions. From 1820 to 1868, United States immigration statistics lumped the arrivals from Norway and Sweden together. The Methodist Episcopal Church in its mission followed the same pattern under the general classification of "Scandinavian work."

The people who came from Sweden were predominantly Protestant. They were literate, skilled in craftsmanship, imaginative in the arts, adaptable to industry and agriculture, and readily assimilable into American culture. Some had been influenced by an evangelical movement set in motion by the Scandinavian work of the Wesleyan Missionary Society.

The Bethel Ship

The mission to the Swedes built its own pattern and developed differently from German Methodism. As an identifiable movement it took root in New York in 1845 through the leadership of Olof Gustav Hedström (1803-77), who had been a circuit rider for ten years.

The influx of Scandinavians in the 1840's and a concern for the welfare of the sailors who manned the ships that brought the immigrants to New York had motivated a New York Swedish layman, Peter Bergner, to initiate shipboard services. Through the good offices of the Missionary Society a handful of generous laymen provided funds by which Asbury Church bought a condemned two-masted brig lying at Pier 11, North River. The ship, known as the "Henry Leeds," was fitted out as a meeting place and renamed the "John Wesley." At the end of the 1845 session of the New York Conference, the presiding bishop sent O. G. Hedström, with whom Bergner had corresponded, to this appointment, called the North River Mission.[33]

---

[33] The story of Swedish Methodism is told in Nils M. Liljegren, N. O. Westergreen, and C. G. Wallenius, *Svenske Metodismen i Amerika* (Chicago: Svenska M. E. Bokhandes-Föreningens Förlag, 1895), especially pp. 129-92.

The mission opened in May, 1845. Assisted by what he called some "families of sound Protestant principles, and ardent piety," [34] Hedström succeeded in bringing about the organization of the first Swedish Methodist Sunday school in America.

From the moment of his first sermon on the brig, Hedström became the symbol of the Swedish Methodist movement as, a decade before, Nast had come to represent German Methodism. As a pastoral routine he met incoming ships from Scandinavian countries, distributed tracts, gave out Bibles provided by the American Bible Society, and invited immigrants to the "John Wesley," or "Bethel Ship," a name which in Scandinavian circles meant, from Gen. 28:19, a "hallowed place" and in the vocabulary of seamen a chapel afloat in a harbor.

Pastor Hedström organized his program to meet the needs of the situation. He visited the sick in hospitals and boarding houses. Being the only Protestant Swedish-language missionary in New York at the time, he served in many instances, as he said, as "physician, nurse, and amanuensis for those who are sick and dying." [35]

The Spread of the Work in America

Commencing with the Bethel Ship, the mission to the Swedes in a decade developed from one vessel and one missionary to seven churches and seventeen missionaries in the United States, one missionary in Sweden, and one in Norway.

Pastor Hedström received fruitful support in the extension of the work from his brother Jonas. Four years after his marriage Olof Hedström had returned to Sweden to visit his family. In his native land he was instrumental in bringing about the conversion of his father and two brothers. Jonas, the younger of the two brothers and a blacksmith by calling, emigrated to America. He practiced his trade in New York and Pennsylvania. Toward the end of the 1830's he moved west to Knox County, Illinois. Between 1846 and 1857 he effectively collaborated with Olof, who counseled the immigrants arriving in New York, advising them to frugality and often directing them to areas favorable for settlement. One of the colonies recommended by Jonas Hedström developed in Illinois at Victoria. Jonas, who had advanced from exhorter to local preacher and member on trial in the Rock River Conference, organized a society in Victoria in December, 1846. From this base he made it his responsibility to visit Swedish

---

[34] *Twenty-seventh Annual Report of the Missionary Society*, 1846, p. 95.
[35] *Twenty-ninth Annual Report of the Missionary Society*, 1848, p. 101.

communities, to preach, and to urge the formation of Methodist societies. Through his concern churches developed in Andover, Galesburg, Knoxville, LaFayette, Rock Island, and Moline in Illinois, and New Sweden in Iowa. He encouraged converted Swedes to itinerate among the settlers with schedules of visitation and preaching. In 1848 he was appointed to the Swede Mission of the Rock River Conference.

In 1850 Olof and Jonas Hedström joined together to conduct revival services in Chicago, where Swedes were beginning to concentrate. From this effort a Chicago mission developed. In 1853 it was placed in charge of Sven B. Newman, an extremely effective worker who in 1851 had transferred north from the Alabama Conference of the Methodist Episcopal Church, South, to help Pastor Hedström on the Bethel Ship in New York.

Like Jonas Hedström, Newman extended the reach of his ministry and was instrumental in establishing societies in a number of Illinois and Indiana communities. The vitality of the work in Chicago was demonstrated after the great Chicago fire in 1871. This catastrophe brought heavy losses to Swedish Methodists in the northside area of the city. After the conflagration new churches developed at Market Street, May Street, Shurtleff Avenue, and South Chicago.

In the late 1870's and 1880's small Swedish Methodist societies developed in Massachusetts. By 1895 the New England Conference was reporting ten Swedish churches with 1,541 members.[36]

In the early 1880's the West Texas Conference of the Methodist Episcopal Church was carrying on work among Scandinavians on the Austin District in Austin, Round Rock, Fort Worth, and Dallas.

In New York, Pastor Hedström recognized that a harbor ship was only a temporary, even though a symbolic, location for a durable ministry. Convinced of the need for a permanent church center, he took the leadership to raise funds to build Swedish Immanuel Church in Brooklyn. The edifice was dedicated in May, 1872. It was said at the time that Swedish Methodism had "gone ashore."

As small, scattered societies developed westward, finally reaching the Pacific coast, the Swedes, like the Germans, came to feel the need for lingual and cultural unity in the administration of their affairs. The evolution of the administrative pattern followed the same general line as that of the German-language conferences. Thus the Peoria Conference, at its first session in 1856, included all Scandinavian societies under a general category of Swede Mission. In 1857 it provided a Swedish Mission District to include eight mission circuits, placing

[36] *Minutes of the Annual Conferences,* Spring, 1895, p. 169.

the district under the administrative supervision of a presiding elder. By 1866 this district included circuits in the three states of Illinois, Iowa, and Indiana. The range of the Andover Circuit in Illinois gives an idea of the extended nature of the work: it included nine preaching places, some of which were as much as forty miles apart. In 1859 the Minnesota Conference formed a Scandinavian Mission District to include Swedish missions in Minnesota, Norwegian and Danish work in Upper Iowa, and certain circuits in Wisconsin. In 1872 separate Swedish and Norwegian districts were established.

In 1868 the General Conference denied a request of Scandinavian preachers to enable them to organize an Annual Conference to include all Scandinavian work, but in 1876 legislation authorized the step "within such bounds as may at the same time be agreed upon." [37] Pursuant to this enabling act, the first Swedish Annual Conference, the Northwest Swedish Conference, was organized in Galesburg, Illinois, in September, 1877. It embraced the Swedish work in the Central Illinois and Minnesota Conferences. From the creation of this first Swedish Annual Conference, subdivisions were made in following years to provide for administration and supervision of the growing work. Pursuant to enabling legislation of the 1892 General Conference, the Northwest Swedish Conference was divided in 1894 into the Central Swedish Conference, the Western Swedish Conference, and the Northwest Mission. Changes from time to time were made in conference structure, territory, and names. At the outbreak of World War I, Swedish Methodism was organized in four Annual Conferences and two Mission Conferences. The work was being carried on by 167 effective ministers, among 19,815 full members and 21,365 Sunday-school scholars.

Methodism in Sweden

Swedish Methodism spread to the Continent in much the same fashion as had German Methodism. Like the Germans, Swedish converts in America wrote the good news about their spiritual experience home to relatives in their native land. Sailors, returning to their home ports, testified to the meaning of the grace of God in their lives.

John P. Larson, shipwrecked in 1852 en route to America from Sweden, was picked up by a British ship and returned safely to his native land. His powerful testimony and fruitful, if solitary, effort encouraged Pastor Hedström to make a recommendation to the Mis-

---

[37] *Journal of the General Conference,* 1876, p. 380.

sionary Society to appropriate $200 a year to support Larson in his work.[38] Itinerating from Kalmar, he distributed Bibles, visited homes, and held meetings. In 1855 he was appointed to Scandinavia as "Missionary, Sweden." [39]

The work in Sweden was given strength by a visit which Pastor Hedström made to the country in 1863. Beginning in Karlskrona, the kingdom's chief naval base and important industrial community on the Baltic Sea, he preached in adjacent towns.

A Chicago businessman by coincidence invited Victor Witting, editor of the *Sändebudet,* to visit Sweden with him. Witting at the time was serving as an unpaid editor of the Methodist Swedish periodical established in 1862. He preached fruitfully during the visit.

The presence of men of the caliber of Hedström, Larson, and Witting in Sweden appealed to people outside the circle of sailors and their families. A broader base of interest in the Methodist message developed. Up to the middle 1860's, however, no systematic effort had been made to provide an administrative structure for the ministry in Sweden.

In 1868 the growing work in Sweden was separated administratively from the mission work in Norway and Denmark. Witting was given responsibility for the development and management of the work in Sweden. His designation inaugurated a new era in the work in Sweden. In Karlskrona, Witting began to build on the durable result of the work of Hedström, who had preached there in 1863. He found Methodism alive among some naval seamen. During long voyages converts were often made on board ship; these men returned to strengthen the mission. In 1870 Emmanuel Methodist Chapel was dedicated in Karlskrona. This was the first Methodist chapel to be built in Sweden.

The work of Methodism spread contagiously during the early 1870's. But achievement often met dramatic opposition. From their first presence in Sweden, Methodists found their efforts circumscribed by restrictions of the Church of Sweden, just as Jacoby and his associates in Germany had experienced resistance to their work from the state church. Three examples will suffice to indicate the nature of the difficulties encountered. One evening a group of farm hands, incensed by the preaching of their parish pastor against the Methodists who were meeting in the community, dragged a ship's cannon from the waterfront, loaded it with stones, and fired a broadside into a house where Methodists were meeting. In another town a mob, faces blackened with charcoal and led by a strong man disguised by an animal mask,

[38] *Thirty-sixth Annual Report,* 1855, p. 67.
[39] *Thirty-seventh Annual Report of the Missionary Society,* 1856, p. 41.

invaded a service and seized the preacher. Unfrightened, the preacher tore off the leader's mask and identified him with the words: "So it's you, Carlson." He sat him down on the front pew to listen to his sermon! In still another community an exhorter was stoned into unconsciousness. He died praying for those who had committed the assault and battery.

Methodists found themselves confronted with a dilemma: they must either obey the laws of the kingdom relating to the Church of Sweden or obey their consciences. The need to choose between such alternatives was finally resolved by actions taken in 1875 and 1876. In 1873 Sweden promulgated a law for the benefit of dissenters. Pursuant to the legislation a committee of Methodist preachers and laymen in 1875 prepared a petition and asked for an audience with the king. They requested permission to withdraw from the Church of Sweden so that they could establish an independent denomination. The committee supported the request with signatures of fourteen hundred Methodists in Sweden and presented the king with copies of the *Discipline*, the *Hymnal*, and a volume of John Wesley's *Sermons*. The sovereign granted the petition. Thus in 1876 the Methodist Episcopal Church became the first denomination officially to be recognized by the state as a haven for persons withdrawing from the state church.

The 1876 General Conference enacted enabling legislation[40] which led to the organization of the Sweden Conference. Under the Sweden Conference, Methodist work in Finland was organized in 1884 into a Finland District. Through Finland word came from St. Petersburg that conditions were ripe for the formation of a Methodist society in Russia if a preacher could be sent. Bishop Charles H. Fowler appointed Carl P. Carlsson, a presiding elder in the Sweden Conference, to undertake the mission. The first Methodist class was formed and the Lord's Supper first administered by Methodists in Russia in November, 1889.

Education for pastoral leadership in Sweden was given attention, as it had been in Germany, by the establishment in 1874 of a seminary in Örebro. The institution was later moved to Stockholm, and finally in 1883 permanently located in Uppsala.

Swedish Methodist Work

When the General Conference authorized the appointment of the Foreign Language Commission in 1920, the Swedish work in the United

---

[40] *Journal of the General Conference*, 1876, p. 300.

States was composed of 150 effective ministers in four Annual Conferences and two Mission Conferences in the United States, 19,451 full members, and 19,365 scholars enrolled in Sunday schools. In Sweden the conferences reported 111 effective preachers, 16,021 full members, and 21,492 Sunday-school scholars.

The Swedes in America were not so ambitious in the founding of educational institutions as the Germans. Except for a small college started in Austin, Texas, Swedish Methodists confined their educational responsibilities to ministerial training. A Swedish Theological Seminary, opened in 1870 at Galesburg, Illinois, was moved to Evanston in 1875, with the encouragement of Northwestern University. Here it entered into a working agreement with Garrett Biblical Institute. In 1934 the seminary merged with an educational institution founded by the Norwegians and Danes to become Evanston Collegiate Institute.

In their ministry of Christian service the Swedes, like the Germans, developed important institutions: for the aged, Bethel Swedish Home, Ossining, New York; Bethany Home, Chicago; Emmanuel Home, Clay Center, Kansas; Adone Seaman Bethel Home, Galveston, Texas; for working girls, Swedish Epworth Home for Employed Young Women, New York; Susanna Wesley Home for Employed Young Women, Chicago; for the unfortunate, Scandinavian Home of Shelter for Fallen Women, Minneapolis; for the cities, Immigrant and Port Mission, Brooklyn; City and Immigrant Mission, Chicago; and for the tubercular, the Swedish National Sanatorium for Consumptives, Denver.

5

Norwegian-Danish Methodism

For English-speaking Methodists it was convenient to classify Swedes, Norwegians, and Danes together as Scandinavians. The administrative convenience did not reckon with linguistic differences or nationalistic sentiments. Further, the publication of the *Sändebudet* as the chief periodical of the movement in the Swedish language irritated the Norwegians and the Danes.[41]

Added together, immigrants from Norway and Denmark were almost

[41] The story of Norwegian Methodism is told by Andrew Haagensen, *Den Norsk-Dansk Methodismes Historie paa begge Sider Havet* (Chicago: Den Norsk-Danske Boghandels Officin, 1894).

as numerous as the Swedes, and the period of their coming to the United States corresponded. While religious pressures exercised a considerable first impetus in the Swedish migration, economic and social factors predominated in the decision of Norwegians and Danes to settle in America. An acute social crisis in the 1840's and 1850's expressed itself in Norway and Denmark by spreading poverty, increasing prison population, a rising illegitimate birth rate, and a sensitive reaction to world economic conditions. The early immigrants from Norway came mostly from the rural areas and the small proprietor classes, but after 1875 emigration originated more among the urban and industrial section of the population. For the most part the churchgoing Norwegians in America continued as Lutheran in their denominational allegiance, but many went unchurched or joined non-Lutheran English-speaking congregations.

Especially during the thirty years between 1880 and 1910 a condition of unrest produced major and sustained emigration from Denmark. Arriving chiefly through the port of New York, some Danes settled in the East around Perth Amboy, New Jersey. Encouraged by the Homestead Act and railroad expansion, others moved to the Midwest, developed a settlement in Chicago, reached into Wisconsin, pushed westward into Iowa, Minnesota, and Nebraska, and reached to the Pacific coast.

The leader among the Norwegians, like Nast among the Germans and Hedström among the Swedes, was Ole Peter Petersen. In 1843 Petersen, a young Norwegian sailor, became associated with Methodists in Boston. Three years later he responded to an altar call while attending a service on Bethel Ship in New York. Thus awakened under the preaching of Pastor Hedström, he thought seriously about his religious life while on a voyage to his native city of Fredrikstadt. In Norway he found opportunity as a layman to give testimony and encourage Lutherans to seek freedom in Christ. Returning to the United States in 1850, he was licensed as a local preacher. Bishop Edmund S. Janes appointed him a missionary to the Norwegians in Upper Iowa.

Back in 1839 Norwegians had established a colony at Muskego, near Milwaukee. This area now became a magnet which drew Methodists. They overflowed to the northern tier of Iowa counties. They moved into the southeastern counties of Minnesota; up to the Dakotas; and on to Montana, Washington, and Oregon.

Petersen's appointment was to a dynamic area. The mission was given power by strong convictions held by some Norwegians which asserted the authority of lay preaching.

In 1856 the Wisconsin Conference formed a Norwegian Mission District with nine missionaries appointed to eight circuits located in the three states of Wisconsin, Minnesota, and Iowa.[42] Sixteen years later, in 1872, the conference separated the Scandinavian work into Swedish and Norwegian Districts. The growth of the program led in 1876 to the division of the Norwegian District to form the Minnesota and Iowa Districts. Four years later the 1880 General Conference enacted enabling legislation authorizing a Norwegian Annual Conference.[43] Pursuant to this action, the Northwest Norwegian Conference was organized in 1880. Four years later, in 1884, the name was changed to the Norwegian and Danish Conference. The General Conference further authorized the organization of the Northwest Norwegian and Danish Mission.[44] The 1892 General Conference changed the name to the Western Norwegian-Danish Mission Conference.[45]

Some of the administrative difficulty experienced in the language work may be appreciated from the fact that in 1932 Norwegian and Danish work was being carried on in the states of Massachusetts, New York, New Hampshire, Rhode Island, Pennsylvania, Maryland, Michigan, Illinois, Wisconsin, Minnesota, North Dakota, South Dakota and Nebraska.[46] The loneliness and isolation of the preachers and their families is indicated by the fact that thirty-five counties had no more than one charge each; five counties had only two.

Just as the German and Swedish missions had reached back into the old countries, so the Norwegian mission was extended to Norway. Influenced by converts made aboard Bethel Ship as they returned to the old country and by reports about Methodist experiences elsewhere, people in Norway began to request Methodist preachers. In the summer of 1853 Bishop Beverly Waugh ordained Petersen deacon and elder and assigned him from Upper Iowa to Norway with headquarters in Fredrikstadt.

Lonely in his mission, harassed by leaders of the Evangelical Lutheran Church, physically exhausted by the strenuous demands of his task, and intellectually determined to make conversion something more than a mere transfer from a Lutheran establishment to a free church, he asked for reinforcements, as Jacoby had done a half decade before from Germany.

Bishop T. A. Morris responded by appointing Christian Willerup

[42] Minutes of the Annual Conferences, 1856, p. 179.
[43] Journal of the General Conference, 1880, p. 389.
[44] Journal of the General Conference, 1884, p. 410.
[45] Journal of the General Conference, 1892, p. 415.
[46] The Methodist Year Book, 1932 (New York: Methodist Book Concern, 1932), p. 246.

superintendent of the Scandinavian Mission. He arrived in Norway in 1856. The withdrawals from the state church to Methodist societies— after careful deliberation, as Petersen insisted—continued. Andrew Haagensen was one of the young men choosing the Methodist Episcopal Church as his haven. He joined with others in a petition requesting permission from the government, under a law effective in 1845, to organize a free-church congregation with Petersen as pastor. The request was granted, and the Methodist Episcopal Church became the first dissenting body to benefit from the law. In 1857 the congregation in Sarpsborg erected the first Methodist church building in Norway without financial assistance of the Missionary Society.[47]

In 1857 Bishop Matthew Simpson, on the first episcopal visit made to Norway, appointed Willerup to Copenhagen. In the Danish capital city Willerup found a substantial group of Danes preparing to separate from the Lutheran Church and join Methodist societies.

The first Methodist Episcopal society in Denmark was organized in 1859. A Byzantine-type brick chapel in Copenhagen was dedicated in 1866 as Saint Paul's Methodist Church.

In 1868 missionary leaders, disappointed at the slow growth of the work in Norway, provided what they believed to be a more effective administrative structure. The Scandinavian work was divided into three missions, each with a superintendent, for Norway, Sweden, and Denmark. Petersen returned to have charge of the Norway Mission and continued effectively in charge until 1871. By 1875 work was being carried on at eighty-two preaching points with 1,870 members. The General Conference in 1876 recognized the growth of the work by enacting enabling legislation which led to the organization of the Norway Conference that year.[48] In 1920 the Norway Conference had 42 effective preachers, 59 churches, and 14,010 Sunday-school scholars.[49]

Among Norwegians and Danes, Methodist missionaries experienced the influence of the Mormons. Under encouragement from the Mormon missionaries, Danes by the hundreds were emigrating to Utah. In 1883 Martinus Nelson, pastor of the Second Norwegian Methodist Church of Chicago, was appointed under funds appropriated by the General Missionary Committee to superintend the work of the Utah missions. He organized the First Norwegian Methodist Church of Salt Lake City, established day schools, and opened a camp meeting. Nelson was outspoken in his attacks on Mormon tyranny, which he alleged made a

[47] *Thirty-ninth Annual Report of the Missionary Society*, 1858, p. 66.
[48] *Journal of the General Conference*, 1876, p. 351.
[49] *Minutes of the Annual Conferences*, 1920, pp. 1056-61.

farce of what the Mormons themselves claimed to be religious freedom, and he preached against polygamy.

The Norwegian-Danish work, organized first in the Utah District under the authority of the 1888 General Conference, became the Western Norwegian-Danish Mission in 1892 and a full-fledged Annual Conference in 1895. Mormon territory, however, was difficult soil for the Methodists to cultivate among the Scandinavians.

In 1869 the publication of a Norwegian monthly periodical known as the *Missionaren* was initiated. In 1887 *Den Kristelig Talsmand* succeeded it as the journal of Norwegian Methodists.

Like the Swedes, the Norwegians and Danes developed institutions: Elim Old People's Home, Minneapolis; Bethany Old People's Home, Stockton, California; Deaconess and Women's Home, Chicago; Lyng Home for Girls, Seattle; and the Norwegian-Danish Girls' Home, Los Angeles.

The only educational institution developed by the Norwegians and Danes in America grew out of a proposal, in 1866, to establish a "Scandinavian School" for training ministers for both Swedish and Norwegian-Danish churches. Teachers were appointed and money raised, but plans fell through at this time and the two groups went their separate ways. The Norwegian-Danish seminary was first opened at Evanston in 1870, but it was January of 1886 before classes were held regularly. A building was begun in 1887. For more than a third of a century this seminary was headed by Nels E. Simonsen. In 1934 it merged with the Swedish institution to form the Evanston Collegiate Institute, which in 1950 became Kendall College.

Like the German, the Swedish, Norwegian, and Danish missions experienced the inevitable socializing effects of American life. In 1921 *Den Kristelig Talsmand* ceased publication after fifty-two years of continuous service to the Norwegians. On September 24, 1936, the *Sändebudet* capitulated after having served the Swedes as their journal for seventy-four years. The Eastern Swedish Conference dissolved on April 20, 1941. Slightly more than two years later the Norwegian-Danish Conference disbanded on May 30, 1943, as the last of the language conferences formed to meet spiritual needs of the historic period of immigration.

6

Bilingual Missions

The language ministry to the Germans, Swedes, Norwegians, and Danes as organized into conferences constituted one pattern of operation. The other took the form of a series of dispersed approaches, often by fits and starts, to miscellaneous groups of immigrants. For the most part these efforts responded to obvious need, but lacked clearly thought-through policy and adequate and sustained implementation. In many cases the activities suffered for want of linguistically competent and emotionally durable personnel. Even taking this administrative inadequacy into consideration, a historian is compelled to point out the difficulty of the task involved in developing a productive ministry within the context of cultural heritages, strangeness to the ways of evangelical Protestantism, and the modest economic circumstances of the newcomers. An examination of the approaches made to the Welsh, Chinese, Japanese, Italians, Mexicans, and Cubans will reveal the hope, disappointments, and achievements of the church.

Among the Welsh

The language ministry to the immigrants from Wales seemed promising because the Welsh had ties to the Methodist tradition. Probably the work of John Wesley and George Whitefield in Wales was the most significant event in Welsh history since the struggle of Owen Glendower as the champion of Welsh independence at the end of the fourteenth and the beginning of the fifteenth century. The Welsh took pride in their language. Moreover, they expressed one of the most intense non-political nationalisms of any successful minority group. Protestants to the core, they were versed in theology and conversant with the meaning of a free church. They were emotionally warm, loved to sing, and were gregarious. Although they were inclined, as a result of the Whitefield controversy, toward the presbyterian and congregational forms of church government rather than the episcopal, they had a closer natural affinity to the Methodist way than to any other denomination.[50] Despite this orientation the Welsh Calvinistic Methodists in 1920 united with the Presbyterian Church U.S.A.

[50] Daniel J. Williams, *One Hundred Years of Welsh Calvinistic Methodism in America* (Philadelphia: Westminster Press, 1937), pp. 258-75.

The trickle of Welsh immigrants arriving at the end of the eighteenth century increased toward the middle of the nineteenth with small settlements centered in central New York. Colonies of Welsh developed in New York City, spread into Pennsylvania, and later west to Ohio, Illinois, Iowa, Wisconsin, Minnesota, Nebraska, and a few to Colorado and California. In the late nineteenth century Welsh slatemakers began to move in numbers to eastern New York, southwestern Vermont, and Pennsylvania.

As early as 1828 the Methodist Episcopal Church began missions to the Welsh in and around Utica, New York. This area became the center for the principal work among the Welsh by Methodists. In the early 1840's Welsh missions were formed in the Black River and Pittsburgh Conferences. Although the Welsh immigration remained small, compared with the arrivals from major countries, the General Conference in 1848 scouted the need for a more extensive mission and set up machinery to explore the feasibility of increasing the number of missionaries. A society was formed in Trenton, New Jersey, in 1848. By 1851 small Welsh missions were operating in four Annual Conferences. By the summer of 1854 the work looked promising. Missions were active in the Oneida, Black River, Pittsburgh, Cincinnati, New York, Wyoming, Baltimore, Ohio, and Wisconsin Conferences. At the end of June, 1854, twelve Welsh missionaries from these nine conferences met in Utica to share their experiences and review their approach.

Along the Ohio River efforts found encouraging response. In Ironton and in Lawrence and Gallia counties societies throve. Indeed, the Ironton Welsh Mission Circuit published a hymnal in the Welsh language and was making requests for books and a *Discipline* in the native tongue. Probably the high point in the mission to the Welsh was reached in Utica in 1886 with the erection of Coke Memorial Church. The cost was $15,000, contributed by the congregation and neighboring English-speaking churches. In 1888 a small church was dedicated in Wilkes-Barre, Pennsylvania. In 1893 the five missions in Utica, Bangor (Pennsylvania), Chicago, Fond du Lac, and Wilkes-Barre were receiving assistance from the Missionary Society in total amount of $2,000.[51]

Before the beginning of the twentieth century the language work among the Welsh had all but disappeared. Among the reasons for the disappointing effort were: The Welsh immigrants were never numerous; the average number arriving through the port of New York from 1867 to 1874 was only 1,057 a year. The people were poor; the Welsh churches failed as a rule to become self-supporting. The church experienced dif-

[51] *Seventy-fifth Annual Report of the Missionary Society*, 1893, p. 312.

ficulty in recruiting competent missionaries. Further, the Welsh held uncompromising convictions which leaned toward congregational government and Calvinistic theology. And finally, they were easily assimilated into the English-speaking congregations.

Among the Chinese

Despite an authentic need rooted in sociological, economic, and political circumstances creating conditions which cried out for an effective ministry, work among the Chinese immigrants developed slowly. Constituting one of the small minority groups,[52] the Chinese were nevertheless the first immigrant people to experience legislated discrimination. This political attitude hurt the spiritual mission.

From the time of the passage of the Chinese Exclusion Act by Congress in 1882 up to its repeal in 1943, Chinese arrivals were reduced to a trickle. For the most part the Chinese concentrated in western-seaboard cities. The 1870 census showed that four out of five Chinese in the United States resided in California. San Francisco, New York, Los Angeles, Seattle, Portland, and Chicago as major cities had their Chinatown sections, but a few Chinese found their way into almost every city of substantial size. Fewer than one out of ten lived in rural areas.

Belatedly the Methodist response to the Chinese need took form. In 1868 Otis Gibson, a Dickinson College graduate who had gone to Foochow in 1855, initiated work among the Chinese in California. A committee of the California Conference had studied the situation, and the General Missionary Committee appropriated $4,000 to finance the initial effort. Gibson began his mission by organizing two Sunday schools in San Francisco and one in San Jose. On Christmas Day, 1870, a headquarters building in San Francisco was dedicated and called the Chinese Mission Institute.[53] In 1872 a second center was opened in San Francisco as Foke Yam Tong Chapel, remodeled from a storehouse. At both facilities the response of the Chinese was encouraging.

The mission to the Chinese, however, sorely needed native leadership. Hopes were dimmed by disappointment as two China-born workers returned home after two years of work. From the beginning the lack of competently trained bilingual preachers was a persistent difficulty. Added to the personnel shortage was the human factor expressed in a political climate of growing racial tension. The Chinese had first been

[52] In the years between 1820 and 1950, Chinese immigration totaled 389,882, reaching its peak year in 1882.

[53] *Fifty-second Annual Report of the Missionary Society*, 1870, p. 126.

encouraged to migrate to America by employers seeking unskilled labor. The Chinese played a useful part in railroad building and in the early development of California. Indeed, under the Burlingame Treaty (1868), the United States extended to the Chinese the same rights in America as those enjoyed by the citizens of other favored nations. The treaty also recognized the inherent and inalienable right of human beings to change their political allegiances.

Objections to the Chinese were based chiefly on economic grounds: they deprived white persons of employment. The campaign against the Chinese, indeed, marked the first occasion in which racism was used as an argument for immigration restriction. It was claimed that the Chinese worshiped idols; that they were unable to distinguish between right and wrong; that they were impregnable to the influences of Anglo-Saxon culture; that their labor was servile; that they remitted money out of the country; that they shipped their dead to China for burial; that they were vicious; that among themselves they operated their own private racial government; that they would not assimilate with Caucasians; and that they were addicted to prostitution, gambling, and disease. It was pointed out that Chinese males in the United States outnumbered females and that, to rectify this imbalance, opportunists engaged in the practice of the recruitment, transportation, and exploitation of women. The situation was ripe for a warmly evangelical and action-oriented Christian mission.

In 1878 A. J. Hanson, a member of the California Conference, was appointed to assist Gibson. From San Francisco the ministry to the Chinese spread. Day schools, Sunday schools, and Methodist societies developed in Chicago; in San Diego, Los Angeles, Stockton, Pasadena, Monterey, Alameda, Napa City, and San Jose in California; and in Washington and Oregon.

While the work was being extended on the Pacific coast, a mission to the Chinese was begun in 1878 in New York by a theological student assisted by a preacher of the Five Points Mission. Handicapped by inadequate facilities, the New York mission nevertheless gained strength, especially under the leadership of Mary A. Lathbury from 1883 to 1894.

In California, Gibson was compelled by ill health to give up his appointment as superintendent of the Chinese mission in 1884. As he reviewed his experience, he said that his greatest embarrassment had stemmed from the failure of the mission to "develop native Chinese preachers who feel called of God to devote their lives to the ministry of the Gospel among their countrymen in America." [54] Hanson, who had gone from San Francisco to superintend the Chinese work in

---

[54] *Sixty-sixth Annual Report of the Missionary Society,* 1884, p. 213.

Oregon and Washington, echoed this judgment when he said that there was crying need for an experienced native to preach on the streets, to assist in the school, to instruct probationers, and to aid in other places of the work.[55]

In an earlier report Gibson had pointed out some of the difficulties encountered in the work. He mentioned the "unsettled state" of the Chinese, their many dialects, their origin in provinces in China where Methodists had neither laborers nor converts, and the absence of family roots.[56] In 1885, F. J. Masters succeeded Gibson as superintendent of the Chinese mission of the California Conference. Experienced as a missionary in Canton under the auspices of the British Wesleyan Society, he seriously reviewed the strategy and tactics of the mission, which had developed around a program of teaching English and preaching in the Chinese vernacular. Too often, he felt, the Chinese came to the Methodist schools more to learn English than to study the Bible. He doubted that it was necessary to offer English as a "bait to draw people to our preaching services" and held the opinion that the Christian religion would never become a power among the Chinese until the churches gave less attention "to A B C schools" and undertook more thorough evangelistic work. He proposed a shift in emphasis from primary English instruction to aggressive direct evangelism among the masses.[57]

The political situation had its effect upon the mission work as anti-Chinese agitation generated an anti-American reaction. As one student of the movement said: "What reply could the missionary give to those who asked why the government had broken a solemn treaty made with China, or why missionaries exhorted Chinese to prepare to go to Heaven with Americans forever when so many church members were unwilling to live in association with them a few years upon earth?" [58] Masters reported the hazards of the San Francisco work in this paragraph:

Every week Chinese were beaten, kicked, and stoned when found alone on the streets. . . . Some were cowardly attacked and wounded while on their way to our school. Women on their way to our services had their ear-rings torn out in broad daylight. Our school windows were broken, and filthy refuse was cast through the open windows upon the heads of the Chinese while

[55] Seventy-fourth Annual Report of the Missionary Society, 1892, p. 359.
[56] Forty-ninth Annual Report of the Missionary Society, 1867, pp. 124-25.
[57] Seventy-sixth Annual Report of the Missionary Society, 1894, p. 345; Seventy-seventh Annual Report, 1895, p. 311.
[58] Wade Crawford Barclay, The History of Methodist Missions (New York: Board of Missions of The Methodist Church, 1957), III, 291-92.

sitting at their desks. One of the senior scholars in our school, a clerk in a pawnshop, had his eye cut out one night while quietly walking to school.[59]

At Unification the Pacific Chinese mission work of the Methodist Episcopal Church was reporting 11 effective preachers, 428 full members, and 773 Sunday-school scholars.[60]

Among the Japanese

The response of the mission to the Japanese was emotionally warmer and organizationally more substantial than that of the work among the Chinese. A third smaller in numbers than the Chinese, Japanese immigration reached its peak a quarter of a century later, in 1907.[61] Politically, the Japanese sector of the population experienced sustained discrimination.

The initial political opposition to the Japanese came from trade unions and developed as a result of competition in the labor market. In 1900 a San Francisco mass meeting urged Congress to exclude Japanese immigrants, to restrict Japanese entry to protect American workers. Four years later the California and Nevada legislatures urged Washington to take immediate action. Sentiment developed to segregate Japanese children in schools. Following the San Francisco fire in the spring of 1906, popular agitation led the Board of Education in the fall to order the transfer of most Japanese pupils to an oriental school in the center of the city. The Japanese government by diplomatic representations in Washington protested the policy. Public agitation increased. President Theodore Roosevelt summoned Mayor Eugene Schmitz and the San Francisco School Board members to Washington. As a result the board rescinded its order, and the federal government dropped certain litigation pending to test the California school law. In 1907 Japan entered into a gentlemen's agreement to limit emigration. The general climate of hostility to the Japanese, however, continued. Political parties included exclusion planks in their platforms. Legislatures in California, Oregon, Nevada, and Montana considered legislative action. In 1913 the California legislature enacted a land law which limited the right of Japanese to lease agricultural lands to three years and prohibited the bequeathing of such lands to heirs under penalty of a citizenship disability.

[59] *Sixty-eighth Annual Report of the Missionary Society,* 1886, pp. 297-98.
[60] *Minutes of the Annual Conferences,* 1939, pp. 514-21.
[61] Between 1820 and 1950, Japanese immigrants totaled 279,146.

Anti-Japanese sentiment flared up again following World War I. Alarmed by gains made by Japanese farmers during the war years, the public resumed agitation. The attitude was strengthened by resentment against the award of Shantung to Japan; by Japanese imperialism in Siberia, Manchuria, and Korea; and by pseudo-scientific assertions made concerning the Japanese biology and culture. Popular movements claimed that the Japanese were nonassimilable; that the worship of the Mikado was incompatible with American citizenship; and that Japan extended its sovereignty to claim the allegiance of Japanese born in the United States. California, Oregon, Washington, Idaho, Nebraska, Texas, Delaware, Colorado, and New Mexico strengthened discriminatory land legislation.[62]

Following the war the Asiatic Exclusion League, formed in the early years of the century, reorganized with the support of patriotic, military, labor, and agricultural organizations such as the American Legion of California, the State Federation of Labor, the Native Sons of the Golden West, and the California State Grange.

Indeed, the Immigration Act of 1924 included an exclusion clause. In signing the law President Calvin Coolidge expressed regret that the section was included in the legislation.

When in 1940 news spread that Japan had joined the Nazi axis, a new wave of suspicion developed. Pursuant to an executive order of President Franklin D. Roosevelt on February 19, 1942, United States military authorities evacuated 110,000 persons, 70,000 of whom were American citizens, from their places of permanent settlement on the Pacific coast and relocated them, for the announced reason of military necessity. For a half decade the Japanese community in America was uprooted.

This review of the political climate in which the mission to the Japanese was carried on indicates the character of the difficulties which confronted Methodist missionaries among the Japanese. In their work they were compelled to defend the Japanese against charges which ranged from clannishness to espionage and disloyalty. The achievement of the Methodist mission to the Japanese is therefore to be recognized as a performance of a high order.

When World War II broke out, more than four out of five Japanese were living in California, and most of them in Los Angeles County. Unlike the Chinese, at least half the Japanese in California were

[62] For a summary discussion of anti-Japanese agitation, see the report of the Select Committee Investigating National Defense Migration, *Findings and Recommendations on Evacuation of Enemy Aliens and Others from Prohibited Military Zones* (Washington Printing Office, 1942), pp. 72-90.

engaged in agriculture. By preference many of them sent their children to Japanese-language schools, and some registered their children with the Japanese consul in California. Most of the older Japanese were Buddhists.

Sociologically, the Japanese divided into two groups. The niseis represented the American-born generation; in 1939 their average age was nineteen. The older, immigrant stock was known as isseis; in 1939 the average age was fifty-eight. There was no middle generation, because of the effect of the restrictive immigration policy. The younger Japanese, educated in American schools for occupations and professions, were generally members of active Christian denominations. They tended to be alienated from the culture of their parents. In 1929 niseis organized the Japanese-American Citizens League for the purpose of "building toward responsible citizenship." This society became an active force in religious, cultural, social, recreational, and civic life.

Methodist work among the Japanese in California began in 1877, when the Japanese in San Francisco numbered probably not more than half a hundred. The history began with Japanese who attended the Chinese mission, took instruction from Otis Gibson, and joined the Methodist Episcopal Church. In the next two years a half dozen Japanese were baptized. The impetus to the Japanese mission, however, came with the formation of an interdenominational "Gospel Society" of some thirty-three members. The group met regularly each week in a rented room in the Chinese Mission Institute. In 1881, Kanichi Mieyama, one of the two Japanese who had taken instruction from Gibson in 1877, began to study for the ministry. In 1884 he was admitted on trial to the California Conference.[63]

In 1886 about one out of eight of the estimated eight hundred Japanese in San Francisco had become members of the Gospel Society. Seventy had joined the Methodist Episcopal Church. Fifty-seven were attending schools and colleges.

The growth of the mission to the Japanese in numbers was accompanied by a sense of responsibility. They pledged over $2,000 toward a mission of their own. After temporarily renting a chapel and parsonage from Central Methodist Church, they opened a Japanese Mission House of fourteen rooms. The first Japanese Methodist Church in America was dedicated on the site on December 4, 1894.

From San Francisco the Japanese mission extended north, south, and east. A unit of the Japanese Gospel Society, organized in Oakland a half dozen years after Otis Gibson had begun the instruction of

[63] *Minutes of the Annual Conferences,* Fall, 1884, p. 240.

two young Japanese, was organized as a church society in 1889 and became self-supporting. This church established branches at Berkeley and Alameda and maintained an evening school. Likewise in the spring of 1889 two Japanese students, with the assistance of the Fort Street Church, opened a mission house in Los Angeles. After six months of financial assistance extended to the Japanese by the Chinese Mission in San Francisco, the Fort Street Church assumed financial responsibility for the maintenance of the work. In 1892 a mission circuit was established in Sacramento with a plan for visiting work camps and ranches as well as preaching places. In the fall of 1892 a Japanese from San Francisco traveled through Oregon, Washington, and Idaho. In the winter of 1893 a mission was opened in Portland. Converts began to preach to laborers engaged in the construction of the Union Pacific Railroad in Idaho and Wyoming. A Japanese local preacher in Seattle pushed up to Port Simpson in British Columbia. The Japanese preachers in the 1880's and 1890's had imagination, morals, and conviction.

As might have been expected, when they received reports that Japanese immigrants had arrived in Hawaii in 1885, Japanese Methodists in San Francisco raised a fund to send Mieyama, converted through the ministry of Otis Gibson eight years before, to study and report on conditions in the Islands. Mieyama preached, organized a Japanese Mutual Aid Society, and within eight months organized a society with twenty-eight members in Honolulu. A temperance society was established. Following Mieyama's return to San Francisco in the late summer of 1889, the church in Honolulu suffered for want of leadership. As a temporary expedient, A. N. Fisher, a member of the Genesee Conference, in California for health reasons, assumed supervision of the work. He reported 5 Japanese ministers, 15 preaching places, 41 full members, 7 evening schools, 8 Sunday schools, and 184 scholars. He pointed out the need to double the number of preachers. During his eighteen months in Hawaii, Fisher organized five more congregations, erected two chapels, and baptized seventy-four adults.

The personnel involved in the Hawaiian Japanese mission was fluid. For a period of three years sixteen different persons served on the staff. Organizational confusion was resolved in 1893, and the California Conference sent two Japanese preachers to the Islands to develop and extend the work.

As in other language missions, the Japanese felt the need for a Japanese District. This was formed in the California Conference in 1893.

The Methodist Episcopal Church, South, like the Methodist Episcopal Church, was concerned with oriental missionary work on the Pacific coast, but its pattern was different and its activity more modest. A mission was initiated in 1897 as a result of visits of two women to the area. After the earthquake in 1906, the Methodist Episcopal Church and the Methodist Episcopal Church, South, divided responsibility for the oriental missions, the Korean work being assigned to the Southern Church. Churches for Japanese and Koreans, with native preachers, developed in San Francisco, Oakland, Stockton, Manteca, Sacramento, Maxwell, Willows, Reedley, Dinuba, Alameda, and Walnut Grove in California and at Terry, Texas. C. F. Reid, the first superintendent of the Pacific missions of the Southern Church, was assisted by T. S. Ryang, a native Korean preacher. Educated at the Union Methodist Theological Seminary in Seoul, Ryang became superintendent of the Siberian Korean Mission in 1923 and president of the Korean Annual Conference, South, in 1930. In 1950 he disappeared into North Korea.

Among the Italians

Immigrants from Italy comprised the second largest non–Anglo-Saxon stream in the American population, standing second only to the German.[64] The Italians came to the United States primarily for economic reasons, to find their "pot of gold" in the New World and to win relief from the growing pressure of rising population against the meager resources of their peninsula. Two thirds of those who arrived in the high tide of Italian migration, which reached its peak in 1907, had lived on the soil. In America, however, nearly nine out of ten of them settled in cities. For the most part the Italians became unskilled wage earners. About half of them made their homes in New York near the port of arrival. They overflowed in large numbers into Pennsylvania, New Jersey, Massachusetts, Illinois, California, and Louisiana; the south Atlantic and south central states received a comparatively small proportion of the newcomers. Almost every manufacturing and industrial city, however, found an Italian colony within it. Often these settlements were referred to as "Little Italy."

By language, dialect, customs, close-knit family organization, culture, and Roman Catholic religion, the Italian immigrants confronted American churches with a formidable missionary task. Except for a few who had been influenced in Italy by Protestant ideas, their outlook was alien to the Methodist way. Many Italians returned to Italy; the counter-migration created a high degree of mobility, which added to the difficulty of the work. The Methodists found the task of developing a

[64] In the 130 years beginning in 1820, German immigration totaled 6,248,529; Italian, 4,776,884.

responsible ministry among the Italians in America exceptionally perplexing.

Methodist work among the Italians began in New York informally
under financial support provided by a layman under the pastoral leadership of Vito L. Calabrese, who had been a member of the Italy Conference of the Methodist Episcopal Church. Calabrese initiated Sunday-
afternoon services in the chapel of Five Points Mission of the New
York Conference. During the conference year of 1890 the Missionary
Society assumed responsibility for the project and provided funds to
rent rooms for the work. By 1894 the society was reporting a hundred
members.[65]

In 1889, which found Calabrese opening work in New York, a mission
was initiated in New Orleans. Three mission stations, a deaconess work
related to the home and children, an industrial school with scheduled
classes two afternoons a week, and a Sunday school provided vehicles
of institutional service.[66] In 1890 a broad institutional program was
started in Philadelphia under the leadership of T. D. Malan. Malan
developed an association for young men, a night school, a sewing class,
and open-air meetings.[67]

In 1894 Italian missions were opened in Boston and Chicago. The
Missionary Society appropriated $5,271 during the year to support
the Italian work in the Philadelphia, New York, New England, Rock
River, and Louisiana Conferences.[68]

When World War I broke out, the Italian-language mission of the
Methodist Episcopal Church had 3,259 full members and 3,323 scholars
enrolled in Sunday schools.[69]

By 1924, when the Foreign Language Commission reported to the
General Conference, statistics showed that the Methodist Episcopal
Church was carrying on work among Italians at fifty-four appointments
with 3,408 full members.[70]

The establishment of the Italy Conference as a result of enabling
legislation of the General Conference in 1880 had no similarity in
its pattern of development to the conferences in Germany, Norway,
and Sweden. It was not the response to language-mission work initiated
in the United States, but rather the result of long-considered and
deliberated projects to bring the warm evangelical message of Methodism to the Italian peninsula, where the Waldensians had performed

[65] *Seventy-sixth Annual Report of the Missionary Society,* 1894, p. 357.
[66] *Seventy-first Annual Report of the Missionary Society,* 1889, p. 353.
[67] *Seventy-third Annual Report of the Missionary Society,* 1892, p. 361.
[68] *Seventy-sixth Annual Report of the Missionary Society,* 1894, p. 358.
[69] *Minutes of the Annual Conferences,* 1915, p. 455.
[70] *Minutes of the Annual Conferences,* 1924, pp. 538, 1116-17.

a significant work and the Wesleyan Methodist Missionary Society had made initial effort as early as 1861.

Like the Methodist Episcopal Church, the Methodist Episcopal Church, South, was seriously concerned with the Italians, half a million of whom by 1920 were probably living within the territory served by the Southern Church. Italian work developed chiefly in Florida, Alabama, Louisiana, Missouri, and Texas. In Ybor City, a foreign-speaking quarter of Tampa, Florida, a flourishing Italian work grew up at San Paulo Church and at Russell Mission. Probably the largest Italian work of the Southern Church was developed at St. Mark's Hall, New Orleans, in very adequate facilities.[71]

The Italian activities of the Southern Church often included teamwork arrangements carried on by collaboration of the Board of Missions, the Woman's Missionary Council, the Board of Church Extension, and city mission boards.

The Italian-language mission, like the mission to the Germans, was confronted with political problems at the time of its most important growth. Over a period of nearly a quarter century from the time that Benito Mussolini executed his planned march on Rome on October 28, 1922, the Italian work in America felt the detrimental effects of events that plagued the old country. Among some Italians there was a feeling that *Il Duce* might be a good leader for Italy. Within the context of the American mood of the early 1920's, some Americans came to look with suspicion upon the loyalty of the Italians. The feeling intensified in the next decade when in October, 1935, Italy, defying the League of Nations, invaded Ethiopia. In 1936, Mussolini with Hitler openly intervened in the Spanish Civil War on the side of General Francisco Franco. On October 1, 1936, Rome and Berlin secretly formed an axis, and they openly proclaimed an alliance in the spring of 1939. From December 11, 1941, Italy and the United States were declared enemies in war. From 1922 until the war ended in 1945, the Italians in America shared an opprobrium reflected from the mother country.

Despite significant developments in scattered cities, Methodism's language mission among the Italians proved disappointing. The culture and religious orientation of the Italians themselves; the failure of the Methodists to develop an adequately trained ministry; the meagerness of the facilities and institutional programs provided—all these factors combined to make difficult a language mission which promised an opportunity of large proportions.

[71] James Cannon, III, *History of Southern Methodist Missions* (Nashville: Cokesbury Press, 1926), p. 314.

Among the Cubans

On October 10, 1868, a group of Cubans, rebelling against the tyranny of Spanish administration under the Bourbon restoration, declared Cuba's independence at the plantation of Yara in Oriente Province. The frightful decade which followed, known as the Ten Years' War, ended in the Treaty of Zanjón, the reassertion of Spanish sovereignty, and continuing political unrest. Many Cuban patriots, fleeing the island, found haven from persecution in Key West, Florida. Here the Florida Conference of the Methodist Episcopal Church, South, established a mission through the leadership of C. A. Fulwood (1846-1905), pastor of Stone Church. Joseph E. Vanduser became the first full-time missionary to the Cuban refugees. He died at the age of twenty-two. Six characteristic words were carved on his gravestone as expressive of his last wish: "Don't give up the Cuban mission." Standing by this memorial one day, H. B. Someillan as a young Methodist made a covenant with God to devote his entire life to a ministry to Cubans. From Key West, Cuban cigar makers moved to Ybor City, a Latin quarter of Tampa. In 1894 Someillan followed them. Beginning with classes in the home of Rosa Valdez and assistance from the Woman's Missionary Council, he laid the foundations for a Florida Latin District. This grew to include the churches of San Mateo in West Tampa, San Marcus in Ybor City, San Lucas in Palmetto Beach, San Juan and San Giovanni in Roberts City, San Lucia in East Tampa, La Trinidad and El Selvado in Key West, a mission to Cuba proper, and Italian work carried on at San Paulo Church in Ybor City. In 1917 some 481 full members and 1,212 Sunday-school scholars were being reported by the Florida Latin District. By 1930, however, the Florida Latin District ceased to be reported in the list of Florida Conference appointments. The work survived modestly as a "Latin Mission."

Among the Mexicans

Mexican immigrants, moving north from the neighboring nation to the south, concentrated chiefly in a narrow chain of southwestern counties stretching from Los Angeles, California, to Brownsville and Corpus Christi, Texas. Distinct in physical appearance, culturally oriented to their Indian-Spanish inheritance, and earning their living mostly as laborers, unskilled workers, and agricultural hands, the Mexicans settled primarily in territory for which the Methodist Episcopal Church, South, was responsible. In 1914 the Council of Protestant Missionary Societies working in Mexico developed an agreement under which the Southern Church in 1918 assumed the programs of the other church societies in the northern states of Mexico and administered them as a part of the ministry already being carried on among Mexicans in the Southwest. The work among the Mexicans in the United States became the most extensive enterprise of the Home Department of the Board of Missions of the Methodist Episcopal Church, South.

The mission to the Mexicans in the United States had begun with a sermon preached in El Paso in 1878. Spreading from this center, the work developed in New Mexico, Arizona, California, and West Texas. For more than forty years John F. Corbin served as a leader of the Mexican work in the Southern Church, erecting more churches on the border than any other Methodist. In 1924 the Home Department, General Work, of the Methodist Episcopal Church, South, was assisting twenty preachers in the Western Mexican Mission and twenty-nine in the Texas Mexican Mission, as well as the Valley Institute, the Wesleyan Mexican Institute, the Mexican Community Center, some day schools, and a language periodical called *Evangelista Mexicana*.

The language missions conducted by both the Northern and the Southern Churches were extended to various other national groups in varied locations—by the Southern Church to Bohemians in Texas, Greeks in southern cities, and Syrians and Greeks in Mississippi; and by the Northern Church to Bohemians in Chicago, Cleveland, the Pittsburgh Conference, and the East Baltimore Conference. Efforts were made by the Northern Church to reach the Portuguese in Massachusetts, and through the Church of All Nations, conducted under the New York East Conference, Spaniards, Poles, and Rumanians.

7

Liquidation and Assimilation of the Language Mission

The tense years of World War I and the aftermath of the hostilities following the armistice in 1918 created a climate which brought to a focus, for fundamental policy consideration by the church, an accumulating series of problems relating to the foreign-language ministry. The war experience had intensified the spirit of nationalism. A suspicion about the patriotism of "foreigners" encouraged emphasis on programs to accelerate Americanization. A quest for cultural security believed to be inherent in ethnic and linguistic homogeneity became apparent. National policy restricted immigration on the basis of national quotas. Philosophies tinged with racial ideologies appeared. An attitude of political isolationism was strengthened.

In addition to these war-stimulated factors, the language ministry faced problems which were inherent in its own achievement during the days of the high tide of immigration. The foreign-born and the first, second, and third generations of their children were being Americanized. The older national groups were speaking English as their mother tongue. In the great American melting pot the powers of social change and cultural assimilation were transcending historical and sentimental cultural loyalties. Administrative leaders, aware of competitive inefficiencies resulting from the overlapping of foreign-language with English-speaking parishes, saw the need to rethink the whole language work. In the depression years of the 1930's declining World Service receipts added an element of financial urgency to the desire for ameliorative action.

Even while World War I was being fought, the Methodist Episcopal Church gave serious forward thought to the needs of the language work as one phase of *The Centenary Survey*. The report of this imaginative study group proposed enlarged programs for the Chinese, Japanese, Italians, Latin-Americans, Eastern Europeans, Bohemians, Poles, Magyars, Jews, Finns, Syrians, French Canadians, Armenians, and Greeks.[72] During the three quadrenniums between 1920 and 1932, the Methodist Episcopal Church gave a factual consideration to the language work in terms of basic policy which exceeded the attention accorded to it at any time during the preceding century of unparalleled immigration. When the General Conference met in 1920, an Inter-Board Conference,[73] which began work on the preparation of data in 1919, had in readiness a study which suggested general guidelines for a fresh approach to the language ministry. Its reconsideration within the Methodist Episcopal Church was seriously undertaken by the 1920 General Conference with the establishment of a Committee of Six on Foreign Language Publications and a Commission of Seven on Foreign Language Work.[74]

[72] *The Centenary Survey of the Board of Home Missions and Church Extension of the Methodist Episcopal Church* (New York: Joint Centenary Committee, 1918). See especially "Missionary Work Among Recent Immigrant Peoples," pp. 31-45.

[73] Membership was composed of institutional and board personnel. *Journal of the General Conference*, 1920, p. 128.

[74] *Ibid.*, pp. 128, 292, 446, 606-7.

The Committee of Six, with two representatives each from the Board of Home Missions, the Methodist Book Concern, and the Board of Education, was discontinued by action of the General Conference of 1932.[75] Reasons given by the committee for the discharge were: (a) the decline of permanent foreign-language residents as a result of the federal restricted-immigration policy; (b) the rapidly increasing proportion of the English-speaking constituents among children from the homes of America's foreign-language groups; (c) the access to an adequate supply of "penny Gospels" in the language of all foreign-language groups; and (d) the necessity to curtail activity on account of the continued shortage in World Service receipts.

The Commission of Seven, appointed on December 2, 1921, by the Board of Home Missions and Church Extension, was directed to study the past development and needs of the "foreign-speaking people in our midst" and to recommend the most effective methods for organizing and promoting the work, together with suggestions for any desirable administrative change.[76]

The General Conference, which met in Springfield, Massachusetts, in 1924, received two important reports for its policy determination. The fruitfulness of the historic language mission was apparent from the presence there of delegates from some nineteen language conferences which had developed directly from the missions which the Methodist Episcopal Church had undertaken since Nast was first appointed as a missionary to the Germans. The conferences represented in this seating were: California German, Central Swedish, Chicago German, East German, Eastern Swedish, North Germany, Northern German, Northern Swedish, Northwest German, Norwegian-Danish, Pacific German, St. Louis German, South Germany, Southern German, Sweden, Switzerland, West German, Western Norwegian-Danish, and the Western Swedish.[77]

In the Episcopal Address the bishops anticipated the consideration of the reports on the language work. While recognizing the policy of restricted immigration as "wise," they urged placing "at the service of these prospective citizens every constructive agency that makes for an intelligent, patriotic, and Christian citizenship." The bishops said: "They [the immigrants] will become either an ominous peril or an invaluable national asset. We unhesitatingly affirm that their assimilation into American ideals is impossible until they are Christianized, for American idealism at its best has its sources in the idealism of

[75] *Journal of the General Conference,* 1932, pp. 1480-81.
[76] *Journal of the General Conference,* 1920, p. 508.
[77] *Journal of the General Conference,* 1924, pp. 1864-68.

Christ." The Episcopal Address concluded the discussion of the foreign-language work with these words:

Believing that the nation cannot live half American and half un-American, and believing also that the kingdom of God cannot come on earth until all tongues and tribes, all regions and races come under the complete sway of Christ our Redeemer-King, we call upon this Conference to face with fearless faith the problem of making adequate provision for the manifold interpretation of the Gospel of Christ to these peoples whom God has providentially sent to us. . . . No question before this Conference ought to have a more complete and a more courageous consideration than the report of that Commission [the Commission of Seven].[78]

The report of the Commission of Seven on Foreign Language Work came before the General Conference three days before the end of the session, when the body was confronted with the clearance of a crowded calendar before adjournment. The delegates faced a historic moment in the life of the Christian church in America. E. D. Kohlstedt, a product of German Methodist missions and presently (1926) to become the corresponding secretary of the Board of Home Missions and Church Extension, commented on the nature of the deliberations on the report:

Only a fractional portion of the delegates could possibly have realized, at the time and under such circumstances, the far-reaching significance of the several proposals embodied in the Commission's report.

In the past, the lack of any stated policy of procedure or eventual objective with reference to organizational relationships between our foreign and English language conferences and churches has proven to be a very weak link in the golden chain of our general Methodist brotherhood; like Topsy, we had no policy to mother our development in these particulars.[79]

The reports as presented brought together a formidable array of statistics on the language work to inform the delegates and propose policies. Upon assuming its responsibilities in 1920, the Committee of Six had proceeded to inventory the language literature of the church. In 1924 it submitted its findings: one journal published in German under authority of the General Conference;[80] hymnals, *Disciplines,* and other publications in German, Swedish, Norwegian-Danish, Filipino, and Spanish; periodicals subsidized by the Board of Home Missions in Portuguese and Slovak; and materials subsidized jointly by the Board of Home Missions and the Methodist Book Concern in Italian.

The Commission of Seven, for its part, described the scope of the

[78] *Ibid.,* pp. 168-69.
[79] *Zion's Herald,* September 10, 1924, p. 1180.
[80] *Der Christliche Apologete.*

foreign-language work in the United States: ten German, four Swedish, and two Norwegian-Danish Annual Conferences; two Swedish Mission Conferences; five missions known as the Hawaii, the Pacific Chinese, the Pacific Japanese, the Latin American, and the Southwest Spanish; and unorganized work in 303 churches in English-speaking conferences. Among these 303 churches, definitely planned language work was being carried on in 136. The statistical tabulation (Table 2) summarizes the scope of the work.

Table 2: Scope of Foreign Language Work, 1924 [81]

LANGUAGE WORK	NUMBER OF CHARGES	EFFECTIVE PASTORS
A. Organized Conferences		
10 German	467	375
6 Swedish	186	128
2 Norwegian-Danish	86	64
Total 18	739	567
B. Missions		
Pacific Chinese	7	7
Pacific Japanese	22	15
Latin American	28	21
Southwest Spanish	21	15
Hawaii	31	17
JAPANESE (11)		
KOREAN (9)		
FILIPINO (11)		
Puerto Rico	39	15
Total	148	90
C. Unorganized		
Eastern Norwegian-Danish	13	12
Newer immigration groups	123	71
Total	136	83
Grand Total	1,023	740

The Committee of Six concluded its report with this suggestion: "The Church should, therefore, look forward to a very large extension of the work of producing evangelistic and missionary literature for foreign-language groups." [82] The Commission of Seven described the ministry

---

[81] Special appointments excluded. Compiled from "The Foreign Language Commission Abstract of Findings," *Journal of the General Conference,* 1924, p. 1661.

[82] *Ibid.,* p. 1639.

through languages as "America's most important, though vexing problem
and the Church's richest opportunity." [83] In broad outline, the administrative policy for the language ministry as established by the 1924 General Conference included (a) enabling legislation to provide for the
self-determined dissolution of the language conferences; (b) the creation of a Bilingual Mission within the Board of Home Missions and
Church Extension; and (c) steps to merge the cultural streams into
the English-speaking congregations. The program, so far as the language
conferences were concerned, recognized the principle of self-determina-
tion implemented with procedures designed to simplify and expedite
their dissolution. To co-ordinate the language work not organized into
conferences, the General Conference set up a Bilingual Mission operating under the direction of the bishop of the Philadelphia Area and
attached this agency to the Board of Home Missions and Church Extension. According to this program, pastors of bilingual churches received
their appointments from a single bishop, while superintendents of
districts geographically including the language charges presided at
Quarterly Conferences. The plan further called for the appointment
of a superintendent of the Bilingual Mission. Finally, the new program
anticipated the convening of informal conferences of language pastors
for the purposes of fellowship and sharing of information. Bishop E. G.
Richardson, of the Philadelphia Area, to whom all foreign-language
work other than that of the language conferences had been assigned,
proceeded spiritedly with his task.

The administrative job which confronted the Bilingual Mission from
its inception was formidable. Responsibility for 136 churches serving
some twenty nationalities was as complicated as it was diverse. Geographically the missions were so widely separated that unified administration and equitable appointment were almost impossible. The two
chief problems of the period of assimilation, however, proved to be
finance and ministerial personnel.

As the language work moved forward into a new epoch of policy,
church leaders were generally distressed because the societies had
matured so slowly toward self-support. A memorandum for internal
administrative circulation explained the poor financial support of the
Italians, who "had been trained for generations to bargain with the
church somewhat as they bargain for clothing and vegetables in the
market. A church that dispenses the benefits of salvation sets its price
too high. In many cases people preferred or had to go without. When
Protestant missions were opened and the word went out that every-

[83] *Ibid.*, p. 1690.

thing was free, we were taken at our word and are being still held to it." [84]

The finance problem had a further deleterious effect on the work. The language pastor felt that he had to show results to justify, by membership statistics, continuing support by the Board of Home Missions and Church Extension. His dilemma was that if he pressed for self-support, he would lose numbers. Moreover, when the language groups came to contribute some fraction of the cost of their support, they wanted more of a voice in the selection of their pastors and more to say about their activities. Movement toward self-support thus made the work administratively more complicated.

As continuing decline in World Service collections during the depression years of the 1930's forced further retrenchment in the work of the Bilingual Mission, ways and means had to be forthcoming to bolster up the operations. Increasing self-support was one obvious answer. "I believe," W. I. Shattuck, superintendent of the Bilingual Mission since 1925, said, "that most of our bilingual pastors are convinced now that their self-support is the only way out." [85] Some English-speaking churches budgeted aid to their foreign-speaking neighbors. Some of the language churches demonstrated a surprising vitality, substantially increasing their own giving. Some district superintendents designated funds in their own budgets to assist the language pastors; others diverted funds appropriated for bilingual work to aid their own English-language district programs.[86] Some language churches slowed down their efforts toward self-support because the district superintendent seemed to be able to provide additional funds from some magic sources; other societies dwindled to extinction.

While financial consideration precipitated serious problems, the human issue concerning the welfare of the language pastors emerged as one of special difficulty. What was to be done with them? In desperation, Shattuck declared: "The Good Book says, 'There is a path no bird of prey knowest and neither hath the falcon eye seen it.' I believe that somewhere there are openings for these language pastors who have been left in a very critical situation by the change of immigration laws and the new deal." [87]

The personnel problem involved in the assimilation of the language pastors became a responsibility as administratively difficult for the

[84] "The Administration of Finance," staff memorandum of the Board of Home Missions and Church Extension (undated, but probably 1928).
[85] Staff memorandum, March 2, 1934, p. 7.
[86] Ibid.
[87] Ibid., p. 6.

church authorities as it was excruciatingly painful to the pastors themselves. The men were aging. Their ministry was specialized. They were
not particularly acceptable to English-speaking congregations. Efforts
were made to find congenial work for some of the men outside the
pastorate, in Goodwill Industries, business, manufacturing, education,
and even labor unions. To fit language pastors to appointments which
might be pried open, Shattuck developed a comprehensive personnel
album complete with photographs and life records. Problems of fairness
emerged when two or more language pastors possessed equal qualifications for appointments to only one available pastorate.

Interdenominational relationships intensified the difficulties. If, for
example, the Bohemian work in Baltimore should be given over to the
Presbyterians, what appointment would be forthcoming for the Methodist pastor? If Presbyterians turned over Italian work to Methodists,
what would the Presbyterians do with the Presbyterian pastor?

The district superintendents, moreover, were ill prepared and un-
trained to cope with the transition. They rarely spoke the language of
the Quarterly Conferences or comprehended the cultural patterns. The
language constituents, on the other hand, were not versed in the intricacies of the *Discipline* nor patient with the mechanical application
of its paragraphs to their problems. In many cases the superintendents
relied upon the "little black book," as the *Discipline* was often called
by the foreign-language Methodists, as a guide to the solution of extremely tense human situations which emerged from linguistic and
cultural differences and from administrative assumptions as far apart
as the poles. In the Troy Conference prolonged court litigation resulted.[88]

Some district superintendents, on the other hand, performed out-
standingly in obtaining placement for language pastors and encouraging
their acceptance by congregations. In the New Jersey Conference an
Italian pastor was appointed to an English-speaking congregation in a
section nine-tenths Italian. He performed with satisfaction. With this
demonstration, it was hoped that churches similarly situated in certain
other cities might follow suit. Shattuck tried to place the pastors. By
May 1, 1934, eighty-six bilingual projects served by eighty-eight pastors
distributed over thirteen episcopal areas, twenty-seven conferences, and
forty-three districts had been administratively assimilated. By 1936 the
Board of Home Missions and Church Extension could report to the

[88] See *Miller v. Musso* (38 N.Y. Supp. 2d., 51; 265. App. Div. 57, 1942; 269 App. Div.
5, 1945. 54 N.Y. Supp. 2d., 86). The appeal record of the case of Salvatore Musso, plain-
tiff, against Cassius J. Miller, defendant, illustrates the problems of the language
ministry in the 1930's, and is, at the same time, an important event in American ecclesiastical history. The issue involved the authority of the state to intervene in
church administrative matters.

General Conference that the Bilingual Mission had been incorporated into the Department of City Work.[89]

Step by step the unstructured and dispersed language movement outside the language conferences, appearing during a germinal epoch of ethnic interaction, pronounced spiritual need, and unique opportunity, was assimilated into the administrative structure of the English-speaking conferences, districts, and churches without general provision for special administrative organization. Bishop Nuelsen referred to the process as the merging of the "creeks and small rivers" with the "mighty stream of life of our great Methodist Church." To him the ministry through foreign languages had been a "means of molding the shape and structure of the Church of Jesus Christ within the nation." [90] It belonged part and parcel to the history, sociology, and cultural pluralism of the unique human interaction under democratic institutions which make America. Unification of the Methodist churches in 1939, on the threshold of the outbreak of World War II, found the church facing new problems posed by refugees from racial and authoritarian regimes. The cycle of the specialized language ministry as a movement within American Methodism, however, had run its course and performed its service.

In perspective, the ministry to the immigrant peoples enriched the life of the church, extended its brotherhood in warm intercontinental relationships, provided a cosmopolitan association which often was lacking within English-speaking congregations, and performed an important role in the assimilation of human beings of diverse cultures and blood streams into the life of American democracy. From its achievements as well as from its failures, American Methodism learned lessons helpful in other movements to extend the Christian message.

On a new continent of moving geographic, commercial, intellectual, and spiritual frontiers, uprooted men, reaching to establish a new life and to discover roles in the American community, found in the Methodist churches a haven which contributed stability to their outpouring energy. Methodism met the new peoples speaking foreign languages at the points of arrival and settlement, and contributed a balance and earnestness of soul to their lives.

[89] *Journal of the General Conference,* 1936, p. 967.
[90] Introduction to Douglass, *The Story of Methodism,* p. xviii.

THE A.M.E.
AND THE
A.M.E. ZION
CHURCHES

Growth and Spread

Polity

Education

Missions

Publishing

The A. M. E. Church

THE DEVELOPMENT OF THE AFRICAN Methodist Episcopal Church, the oldest organization of any kind established by Negroes in the United States, has passed through several phases. It originated in 1786 at Philadelphia as a small prayer band in St. George's Church under the leadership of Richard Allen (1760-1831). This group subsequently developed into the Free African Society in 1787. With Allen was Absalom Jones, the founder and organizer of St. Thomas' Protestant Episcopal Church in 1794, also an outgrowth of the Free African Society. He was the first Negro rector-priest of the Episcopal Church in America. From the Free African Society also emerged the semi-independent Bethel Church, which later became completely autonomous and the organizing nucleus for the new denomination in 1816. The details of this earliest phase of A. M. E. history are given elsewhere in this *History* and will not be dealt with here, since this chapter is particularly concerned with A. M. E. origins and growth since the 1816 Organizing Convention.

The singular fact that characterizes the several African Methodist societies that met at Philadelphia in 1816 to form a united body was their desire to be free from control and discrimination and to have wider participation and fuller expression in the total life of the church than had been available in the churches from which they had seceded. In the words of Benjamin T. Tanner, in his famous *An Apology for African*

Methodism, Negro Methodists then as now were anxious "to think for themselves, . . . to talk for themselves, . . . to act for themselves; [and to] support from their own substance, however scanty, the ministration of the Word which they receive." [1] This fact pervades the record of the earliest churches that united with the denomination and those throughout its history. It is true of the Negroes who remained in the Methodist churches as well as of those who left. It also accounted for the attempt on the part of the Methodist Episcopal Church finally to ameliorate the situation. The founding of Zoar Church in Philadelphia, the mother church of Negro Methodism, is the classic example. "In 1794 . . . the Methodists of St. George's, viewing with . . . chagrin the widespread withdrawal of Negroes, . . . established a mission at Camperdown . . . which eventually became the present Zoar Church." [2]

It was following discrimination, together with gross personal indignities, that the sizable group of Negroes withdrew in a body from St. George's Church in Philadelphia in 1787 and formed the Free African Society.

African Methodism in Maryland had a similar background. It began as early as 1787 when the white members of the Log Meeting House, Lovely Lane, and Strawberry Alley Societies in Baltimore refused to let Negroes occupy the same pews or receive the sacrament of Holy Communion with them in the same church buildings. This situation precipitated the withdrawal of the Negro membership of these societies and the formation of a Baltimore African Church. This body, while Methodistic in doctrine and polity, was for all practical purposes an independent organization until 1812, at which time Daniel Coker, the organizer of African Methodism in Maryland, formed the Negro membership of this and of other Methodist congregations in Baltimore and vicinity into the society that presented itself at the Organizing Convention.

The Spread of the A. M. E. Church

WORK IN THE EAST

The earliest record of an African Methodist organization in New Jersey is the Mount Pisgah Church at Salem, organized by Reuben Cuff in 1800. Here, after many years of joint worship, the white and Negro members mutually agreed to worship separately. From 1800 to 1815 Cuff apparently

---

[1] (Baltimore, 1867), p. 16.
[2] W. E. B. Du Bois, *The Philadelphia Negro* (Philadelphia: Publications of the University of Pennsylvania, No. 14, 1899), p. 22.

served as the leader of this small group. In 1816 he and his church responded to Richard Allen's invitation to meet in "general society" and form an African Methodist denomination. Following the convention Cuff was returned to Mount Pisgah as its first A. M. E. pastor. Richard Wright, reported that Clayton Durham, one of the local preachers from Bethel Church in Philadelphia, was appointed to this work in 1817.[3]

In 1805 Peter Spencer and forty-two Negro members of the Asbury Church at Wilmington, Delaware, withdrew to form a separate church meeting because they were denied equality in the church's administration of Holy Communion. In 1805 they erected their first church, Ezion. In 1813 a dispute arose between the Asbury trustees and the Ezion membership. They were told that they must accept any preacher sent by the Methodist Episcopal conference. A statement of clarification known as the "Articles of Association" was drafted to relieve the tense situation, but it failed to achieve its purpose. Consequently, in June, 1813, Spencer and his group severed their connection with the Methodist Episcopal Church and became an independent body taking the name, Union Church of Africans. Apparently some Negroes remained at Ezion and later became the nucleus for the first Negro Methodist church in Wilmington, probably the second oldest in the Delaware Conference. In September of that same year the Union Church of Africans was legally incorporated. Between 1813 and 1816 Peter Spencer, and a colleague, William Anderson, seem to have established another Union Church of Africans at Attleborough, Pennsylvania, and created a connectional relationship with Mount Pisgah at Salem. It was these three churches which comprised the Union Church of Africans at the Organizing Convention called by Allen. The mother church of this Union, Wilmington, for reasons that will be discussed later, never affiliated with the new denomination, although the Salem and Attleborough churches did. As a consequence of this first schism "Allen" African Methodism did not gain another foothold in Delaware until the establishment of Bethel Church in Wilmington in the 1840's.

Coming now to the Attleborough Church, Pennsylvania, the problem of unclear evidence for its date of establishment arises. Wright indicated that it was the first work in Pennsylvania outside Philadelphia and the oldest work in the Philadelphia Conference, excepting Bethel, but this claim is not substantiated by a date earlier than 1822.[4] It was represented at the Organizing Convention by William Anderson, Jacob Marsh, and

[3] *The Encyclopaedia of the A. M. E. Church* (2nd ed., Philadelphia: A. M. E. Book Concern, 1947), p. 449.
[4] *Ibid.*, p. 464.

Edward Jackson. It is probable that the Attleborough Church was organized later than 1812 but before 1816.

The second phase of the story of the growth and expansion of the newly organized African Methodist Episcopal Church was the division of the work of the new denomination into territories, circuits, and stations among the seven traveling preachers who were to give pastoral oversight to local congregations with a combined numerical membership of approximately five thousand persons, located in a dozen or so widely scattered eastern-seaboard communities. This responsibility was dealt with by the Organizing Convention when it authorized the establishment of two Annual Conferences, the Philadelphia and the Baltimore. The original boundaries of the Philadelphia Conference included the territory in eastern Pennsylvania and the states of New Jersey and Delaware. The oldest boundaries of the Baltimore Conference included the territory of western Pennsylvania and the state of Maryland. This particular territorial allocation seems to have been influenced by two major factors—the location of accessible travel routes and the scarcity of itinerant pastors.[5]

Following the Organizing Convention the development of the connection must be traced through the records of the Annual Conferences. The first one held was the Philadelphia, which convened following the adjournment of the Organizing Convention, April 14-20, 1816. There are no extant Minutes of this session, but the collateral evidence consisting of recorded recollections and later conference proceedings confirm, at least in part, some of its important activities.

Within the boundaries of this new conference the first circuit of the connection was formed, consisting of Bucks County in the southeastern portion of the state of Pennsylvania. The preacher-in-charge of this first circuit was William Paul Quinn, who in later years was to render yeoman service to the church as a missionary and bishop.

The first recorded meeting of this conference took place in Philadelphia on May 9, 1818.[6] Five ministers were admitted on trial and six gained full conference membership. Morris Brown, the organizer of the work at Charleston, South Carolina, and later the successor to Allen as general superintendent, was among these latter. At this same session the Snow Hill Society, on the eastern shore of Maryland, and the Colored

[5] Jabez P. Campbell, "Our Episcopacy," *A.M.E. Church Review*, VI (1889), 1-6.

[6] Information on these conferences comes from Daniel A. Payne, *History of the African Methodist Episcopal Church*, ed. C. S. Smith (Nashville: Publishing House of the A.M.E. Sunday School Union, 1891); and the continuation of this work: Charles S. Smith, *A History of the African Methodist Episcopal Church* (Philadelphia: Book Concern of the A.M.E. Church, 1922).

People's Church at Trenton, New Jersey, organized by Allen in 1817, were received. Other accessions by 1818 were: in New Jersey: Woodbury, Gouldtown, (New) Brunswick, and Princeton; in Pennsylvania: Bridgeport, Lancaster, Frankford, New Hope (now extinct), Plemeth (Plymouth), Westchester, Whitemarsh, and in Philadelphia, a second church (Union); in New York work in Brooklyn also existed by this time. By 1822 there were seven circuits of work—three in Pennsylvania, two in New Jersey, and one each in Delaware and Maryland.

In 1827 the conference was presented with a petition to form western New York and Canada into a mission and to send them a preacher. This request was the result of the labors of church extension in this area which had planted churches in Utica, Rochester, and Buffalo in New York, and at Erie, Niagara, Gambia, and Malden in Canada. After careful consideration this matter was referred to the New York Conference. In 1828 the African Methodist Society in Albany was received on petition, and in 1830 the Ohio work of the Pittsburgh Circuit became a part of the Ohio Conference organized in that year.

In 1832-33 Black Code restrictions, which strictly forbade nonresident Negroes to enter the state except as slaves or servants of whites, seriously threatened the work of the eastern-shore—Maryland and Delaware—churches. The conference was petitioned by these churches to ordain "native sons" for the work there that it might continue. The 1840-60 period in the Philadelphia Conference is characterized by expansion northward to the Canadian border and westward to Harrisburg and the Susquehanna River.

A significant event at the 1822 Baltimore Conference was the petition of the Israel Bethel Colored Methodist Church in Washington, D.C. Like many other Negro Methodist churches in this period, it had arisen as a protest movement against the humiliation of Negroes by whites in the churches of that city. In 1820 a group of Negroes had withdrawn from the Ebenezer Church and organized Israel Bethel. About the same time, however, other groups of Negroes from various Methodist churches in southeast Washington and Georgetown had been doing the same thing. It was this composite group of "secessionist" Negro Methodists that sought annexation. The petition presented was granted; and David Smith, who had organized this white-church-exodus movement as a missionary, was returned by the conference as the first pastor.[7]

Prior to the War Between the States, several other things occurred within the Baltimore Conference. Missionary preachers pushed north-

[7] John W. Cromwell, "First Negro Churches in the District of Columbia," *The Journal of Negro History,* January, 1922, pp. 65 ff.

ward into central Pennsylvania and westward toward West Virginia. In 1847 the First Colored Wesleyan Methodist Independent Society of Baltimore was received into the conference. Kent County, Maryland, was formed into a circuit. In 1848 the "new" mother church in Baltimore, Bethel, was dedicated. Finally, a mission church was established in Baltimore under Bethel's guidance. St. Paul's in Washington, D.C., and Ebenezer in Georgetown were dedicated in 1857, and in 1862 a church was organized at Annapolis, Maryland.

The New York Conference, authorized in 1822, was organized by Allen on June 8 of that same year at New York City. It represented the consummation of the missionary labors of William Lambert, who had established a mission there in 1817. The original territory of this conference included all the New England states as well as the state of New York. Its first list of appointments read as follows: New York City: Bethel, Harlem, and Wesleyan (Brooklyn) ; Long Island: Jamaica, (Glen) Cove, Flushing, and White Plains Circuit. The records for the period 1822-30 have been lost. In 1831 Albany was added, and in 1832 Jeremiah Miller was sent to Canada as a missionary. In 1838 work was reported at Buffalo, New York, and at Niagara and St. David, Canada. In 1841 the Binghamton Circuit was received; and in 1842 a Negro congregation in Providence, Rhode Island, seceded from the Zion Wesley Connection (A. M. E. Zion) and united with the conference. By 1843 the strong Haverstraw (New York) Circuit had been formed, and in 1852 the Negro membership of the First Congregational Church in Schenectady, New York, withdrew in a body and petitioned for affiliation with Bethel.

An A. M. E. society existed in New England before 1821. There was a Bethel Church at New Bedford, Massachusetts, in that year pastored by Charles Spicer, a deacon under the supervision of Bethel in New York City.

Work at New Haven was established in 1837; in Boston in 1839; and in 1842, at Providence. In 1843 Eli N. Hale organized other work at New Bedford, and Henry J. Johnson started the northernmost post of the connection at Portland, Maine. About 1845 Johnson also opened work at Newport, Rhode Island, and in 1847, at Lynn, Massachusetts.

In 1848 the New England itinerants petitioned the General Conference "to set off the New England district." The petition was approved, and the New England Conference was authorized for organization in 1852. Its official territory included the traditional New England States.[8]

---

[8] John T. Jenifer, *Centennial Retrospect History of the African Methodist Episcopal Church* (Nashville: A.M.E. Sunday School Union, 1916), pp. 44-50.

THE WEST

During the decade of the 1820's the young denomination moved west-ward. The story began in Ohio in 1815 at Cincinnati, where the white members of Wesley Chapel (Old Stone Church) objected to the emotional expressions of its Negro members during worship. Eventually they proceeded to "crowd" them into one section of the church. This humiliated and infuriated the Negroes, and in 1815 steps were taken to separate the two groups during worship. This division took the form of a separate church, Deer Creek, which the Negroes established rather than be segregated. They worshiped separately until 1823, but even then such undue influence and control was being exerted by the whites in the direction of the affairs of the Deer Creek Church that a sizable group of the membership seceded to unite with the African Methodist Episcopal Church. This was probably the origin of Allen Temple in Cincinnati, the acknowledged mother of all Negro churches in the city, claiming a founding date of February 4, 1824.

While the Deer Creek situation was fairly typical of many accessions in the expansion of African Methodism until about 1820, it cannot be regarded as a typical method of accession after 1820, particularly in the West. The opening of the Ohio Territory presented the young denomi-nation with a challenge of a different type, namely, "frontier evangelism." Here churches had to be established under extremely difficult circum-stances, not merely organized from an existing congregation or received "on petition." Du Bois, in his study of the Negro church, interpreted this fact sociologically when he said, "In the West it may be stated that colored churches were not the result of secessions or irregular, wholesale withdrawals from the white churches as in the East. They sprang up directly in the path of the westward migration of colored people from the South and East." [9] Some of the records of this westward thrust will now be reviewed. Under the leadership of such pioneer preachers as George Bowler, Moses Freeman, and William Quinn, work was estab-lished at Chillicothe as early as 1822, and by 1824 two circuits had been formed. By 1824 the Ohio work was ready for conference organization. This was formally done by Superintendent Morris Brown in August, 1830, at Hillsborough, Ohio. Its original boundaries included the terri-tories of western Pennsylvania, Ohio, and northwestern Virginia. There are no records of the Ohio Conference until 1833. It is known, however, that Quinn established the first Negro organization in Cleveland, St.

[9] *The Negro Church* (Atlanta University Publications, No. 8: Atlanta: Atlanta University Press, 1903), p. 33.

John's Church, in 1830. In 1836 the Ohio Conference created the Richmond Circuit, which included Indiana territory. A North Ohio Conference was formed out of the Ohio in 1882, and about 1920 the South Ohio Conference was created.

The General Conference of 1840 authorized the organization of the Indiana and Upper Canada Conferences.

Since 1836, when the Richmond Circuit first appeared in the list of Ohio appointments, there had been evidence of A. M. E. activity in the Hoosier State. From 1837 to 1840 annual appointments appear to have been made to this circuit. The Indiana Conference was formally organized at Blue River, near Carthage in Rush County, on October 2, 1840. It was created out of a portion of the former Ohio Territory, and its original boundaries included Indiana, Illinois, Michigan, Missouri, Alabama, and Louisiana. Wright estimates that one fourth of the conferences of the connection have come from this territory. In 1848 the Society of Methodists in New Orleans, composed of free Negroes requested assistance in the establishment of an A. M. E. church there; and in 1855 the conference founded a mission at St. Paul, Minnesota, and one in the state of Wisconsin to include Racine, Milwaukee, Madison, and Kenosha.

At least two factors militated against the advancement of A. M. E. work in the Southwest. First, the territory of the Indiana Conference was so vast that travel and administration were extremely difficult. Second, pastors who had received appointments from a conference in a free state to a church in a slave state were finding it increasingly difficult to gain community acceptance. The Missouri Conference was created to meet the situation posed by these two problems. This body was authorized by the 1852 General Conference "to embrace all the churches in the slave-holding states of the West and Southwest." Its boundaries, therefore, arbitrarily included the states of Missouri, southern Illinois, western Kentucky, Tennessee, Mississippi, Louisiana and Alabama. Formal organization took place on September 13, 1855, at Quinn Chapel in Louisville.

The closing of the fourth decade of work by the A. M. E. Church found wide gaps in the locations of its western mission churches. By 1856, except for a church in Sacramento, there were no churches west of St. Louis.

Jordan Winston Early, a zealous missionary of this period, did much to close this gap in Missouri. His first establishment seems to have been Carondelet, about 1851 and he later organized churches and missions throughout the state. By 1882 the North Missouri Conference was founded, and by 1916 the Southwest Missouri Conference was at work in the state.

In 1849 Bishop Quinn assigned T. M. D. Ward, later a bishop, as a missionary to California, but he did not arrive at his destination until 1852. In 1851 the first Colored Methodist Church in Sacramento had petitioned for, and received, membership. In 1852 Charles Stewart, a local preacher, had established the first mission church on the Pacific Coast at San Francisco. By 1862 the Placerville Circuit had been established; and by 1864 churches were found at Oakland, Petaluma, San Jose, Stockton, Marysville, and Coloma in California, and at Virginia City and Carson City in Nevada.[10] The General Conference of 1860 had set the boundaries of this work, but the California Conference was not formally organized until April 6, 1865, by Bishop J. P. Campbell.

The genesis of the Pittsburgh Conference was in the old Philadelphia Conference, where as early as 1824 it was mentioned as the "Western District, State of Pennsylvania" and included Pittsburgh, Washington, Uniontown, Brownsville, Geneva, and Monmouth. By 1830 this work was the Pittsburgh Circuit, and as such was placed under the jurisdiction of the Ohio Conference, organized in that year. At the time of its formal organization, April 3, 1868, at Pittsburgh by Bishop A. W. Wayman, its boundaries were set to include all the western portion of the state of Pennsylvania not included in the Philadelphia Conference. The West Virginia Conference, an outgrowth of the Pittsburgh Conference, was organized in 1902.

African Methodism was temporarily halted in her southwestern thrust by the events preceding the Civil War. Nevertheless, as early as 1859 a missionary was in the state of Kansas. John Wilkerson from the Missouri Conference organized the first work there at Leavenworth City later that same year. About this same time a church was founded at Kansas City, Kansas. The Annual Conference was organized at Fort Scott, Kansas, on October 4, 1876, by Bishop J. A. Shorter. In September, 1883, the South Kansas Conference was formed.

The history of the Illinois Conference reaches back to the beginning of the 1830's, when the Brooklyn Circuit in Illinois was established by Quinn, then an Ohio Conference missionary. It continued with the granting of a license to preach to Jordan W. Early by George W. Johnson, another missionary from the Ohio Conference, in 1836. The Brooklyn Circuit was assigned to Quinn as a western missionary district as one of the first appointments of the Indiana Conference in 1840. Quinn reported Illinois churches in his Report on Missions to the General Conference of 1844. Early began work at Galena about 1845. In 1847

[10] Benjamin Tanner, *An Outline of Our History and Government for African Methodist Churchmen* (Philadelphia: Grant, Faires & Rodgers, 1884), pp. 199-200.

Quinn Chapel, Chicago, was founded. In 1884 the Illinois work was separated from that of Indiana.

The histories of the Chicago and Iowa Conferences are so interrelated that it is necessary to discuss them as a unit. The Chicago Conference was organized in 1882 with boundaries including northern Illinois, Iowa, Wisconsin, Minnesota, the Dakotas, and Gary, Indiana. In 1883 the Iowa Conference was organized, diminishing the Chicago territory by including parts of Iowa, Minnesota, and Wisconsin. In 1912 the Iowa Conference was discontinued and its work placed in the Chicago Conference, where it remained until the creation of the Northwestern Conference in 1920, at which time a part of its work was placed in that new body.

A. M. E. history in Michigan began in 1839, when, as a result of the missionary labor of Quinn, the Colored Methodist Society there was organized. In 1841 this society was re-organized as an A. M. E. church, taking the name Bethel. By 1860 there were churches at Calvin Center (1849), Ypsilanti (1859), Battle Creek (1855), and Adrian (1855). Between 1861 and the formal organization of the Michigan Conference in 1887, ten more churches had been founded.

In that same year, 1887, the Colorado Conference was organized by Bishop J. M. Brown. Its territory embraced Colorado, Utah, Wyoming, Montana, Arizona, and New Mexico. The first Colorado Conference church was Shorter Chapel in Denver, organized in 1868. Its first two districts had appointments in Phoenix, Arizona; Salt Lake City, Utah; and Cheyenne, Wyoming. Between 1884 and 1906 the Puget Sound and the Oklahoma Conferences were organized. The Puget Sound Conference included Oregon, Washington, Montana, Idaho, the territories of Alaska and the provinces of British Columbia, while the Oklahoma Conference comprised the then Oklahoma and Indian Territories. By 1916 the Central Oklahoma and the Northeast Oklahoma Conferences had been organized.

THE SOUTH

The most productive years of growth in the history of African Methodism are those following the Civil War, 1865-85, in the South. In those two decades thirty-six or one third of the denomination's conferences were founded. New churches were formed in seventeen states, twelve of which were below the Mason-Dixon Line.

Prior to the manumission of the Negro slaves in the South, independent Negro churches were practically nonexistent. "Outside of the few ministers of the A. M. E. and the A. M. E. Zion churches in the border states, it is doubtful if there were a score of colored pastors in full control of colored churches in the South before the Civil War." [11] Among these few, however, were three African Methodist Episcopal societies in Charleston, South Carolina; Mobile, Alabama; and New Orleans, Louisiana.

While the A. M. E. Church was establishing itself in the North, Morris Brown and others were organizing free—and some slave—Negroes in Charleston into an African Methodist Church society. Prior to 1816 many of these had been members of the white Methodist churches in and around Charleston. By 1817 a sizable number had withdrawn from the white churches, purchased land for an edifice, acquired a burial ground, and requested one of their number, Morris Brown, to seek ordination from Allen. In 1818 this church had its own Quarterly Conference and a membership of approximately two thousand. The years 1818-22 found the young church and its leaders involved in the antislavery movement—which activity resulted in the usual imprisonment for such a charge. In 1822 Brown and other church leaders were allegedly guilty of involvement in the Vesey insurrection plot. The church and its activities were legally suppressed. At this point, Brown and others went to Philadelphia, and the church, which now had approximately three thousand members, apparently dissolved.

The "dissolution" of the African Society in Charleston was more apparent than actual. It is almost certain that secret meetings of the old church were held, in addition to the formal services which these evicted refugees then attended in the white churches, to which many of them returned. This was the only indigenous religious activity among Negroes in the South generally, and in South Carolina particularly, from 1822 until the Civil War period. In 1863 James Lynch and James D. S. Hall, the first commissioned A. M. E. Southern missionaries, were sent out. In 1864 the General Conference called for the building up of the church in the South. Bishop Payne went to Charleston to re-establish the work there and to organize the first Southern conference, the South Carolina, in May, 1865. The original boundaries of the conference included South Carolina, North Carolina, Georgia, and east Florida, and the first appointments sent missionary preachers to points in each of these four states.

The next conference to be organized was the Louisiana. Jordan Winston Early, the pioneer African Methodist missionary, stated that he was in New Orleans "about the year 1842," and at that time assisted in establishing a church there and securing a charter for the "free people of

[11] Du Bois, *The Negro Church*, p. 33.

color" to organize a Methodist society.[12] In 1858, when all Negro churches were closed in compliance with a city ordinance designating them as illegal, the New Orleans churches became "invisible" and were conducted secretly. Following North-South hostilities, religious freedom was restored to Negroes in Louisiana and other parts of the South where it had been abrogated. Shortly after this, the Negro churches resumed their normal activity. The formal organization of the Louisiana Conference occurred in November, 1865. Its initial boundaries were fixed to include Louisiana, Mississippi, Arkansas, Texas, Alabama, and western Florida.

During 1867 three conferences were formed out of the original mission territory of the South Carolina Conference. The North Carolina Conference was organized in March at Wilmington; the Georgia, in May at Macon; and the Florida, in June at Tallahassee. In this same year the Virginia Conference was formed at Richmond on May 10. African Methodist work existed in Virginia prior to this date. Cromwell claimed that the "A.M.E. Church . . . had already got a foothold in Norfolk and Portsmouth as early as 1863." [13] In 1867 the west Florida work was combined with the East Florida Conference to form the Florida Conference. July, 1868, witnessed the formation of the Alabama Conference at Selma. "African Methodism was known to exist in the city of Mobile as early as 1820, but . . . 'the walls of slavery were towering high, therefore the little band had to bow low again.' " Possibly these African Methodists were from Baltimore and Charleston and were resold via the slave-trade route. Since no trace of the Mobile church can be found after 1830, it can be concluded that it was not visibly active until the legal re-establishment of civil liberty for Negroes following the Civil War.[14] The Mississippi Conference was organized at Vicksburg on October 8, 1868, and on October 22 the Texas Conference was founded at Galveston. Three other conference organizations in this year complete the conference structure of the South: the Kentucky (September 8), at Louisville; the Tennessee (September 10), at Nashville; and the Arkansas (November 19), at Little Rock, all originally missionary outposts of the Missouri Conference and extensions of the earlier labors of Quinn, Early, and others.

With the organization of the Southern states, the structure of African

[12] Sarah J. W. Early, *Life and Labors of Rev. Jordan W. Early* (Nashville: A.M.E. Sunday School Union, 1894), p. 32.

[13] "First Negro Churches in the District of Columbia," p. 67.

[14] Wesley J. Gaines, *African Methodism in the South* (Atlanta: Franklin Publishing House, 1890), p. 225; George A. Singleton, *The Romance of African Methodism* (New York: Exposition Press, 1952), p. 27.

Episcopal Methodism became national. Every state except New Hampshire, Vermont, Montana, and Idaho claimed at least one church.

The next phase of A. M. E. history, 1884-1906, was one of consolidation. The state conferences, responding to population increases and membership gains, subdivided their work into intrastate conferences, as the Northern and Western conferences had done. Between 1884 and 1916, the ten southern-state Annual Conferences had increased by twenty-eight to make a total of thirty-eight conferences. Only the Virginia Conference found it unnecessary to subdivide its work.

A. M. E. Polity

In matters of doctrine and polity, African Methodism was from the beginning in close accord with the Methodist Episcopal Church. "We do acquiesce and accord with the Rules of the Methodist Episcopal Church for our Church government and discipline, and with her creeds and articles for our faith." "In some respects we are *more Methodistic* and in others *more episcopal* than many of our sister M. E.'s." Such an attitude indicated that Methodism was admirably suited both to the spiritual and temporal needs of Negroes. "To a people whose circumstances are what ours have been, and are, no other form of Church government is better adapted than the Episcopal as modified by *'Methodist'*; . . . than that modified by *'African.'*" [15]

A sketch of the development of African Methodist Episcopal polity can best be viewed in historical perspective. Almost the first official act of the new Negro denomination was the securing of a *Discipline*. To meet this situation the A. M. E.'s adopted the *Discipline* of the Methodist Episcopal Church, after deleting its alleged proslavery allusions and its references to the office of presiding elder. The term "African" was prefixed to the title, and the revised product has been known since 1817 as the *Doctrines and Discipline of the African Methodist Episcopal Church*. After laying off the work of the church into circuits, the matter of election of an episcopal head was discussed. It was decided to constitute their episcopacy precisely like that of the mother church, and, with this in mind, Richard Allen was consecrated the first bishop of the African Methodist Episcopal Church in 1816, the first Negro to hold so high an ecclesiastical office in America.

Theoretically the center of power and control was placed in the Gen-

[15] Tanner, *An Outline of our History and Government*, pp. 11, 20-21.

eral Conference by the new *Discipline*. Actually, however, it took almost two decades for the General Conference to claim its prerogatives.

Prior to the meeting of the first General Conference in 1820, the organization and government of the church was determined by the two original Annual Conferences—Philadelphia and Baltimore. The first recorded meeting of the Baltimore Conference in 1818 examined, tried, and convicted Daniel Coker and expelled him from the connection. It also elected Don Carlos Hall as the first book steward and ruled that itinerants should be appointed at the conference, with the laymen concurring in the appointments. Finally, it acted as a General Conference by deciding "that two deacons were sufficient to present [candidates] for ordination."

The General Conference of 1820 was presumably held at Philadelphia, but since there are no records of it there is some uncertainty about this. This fact is also further evidence of the General Conference's lack of power in this early period. In 1822 the Philadelphia Conference acted in a similar fashion as the Baltimore in assuming General Conference authority. It repealed its own previous ruling limiting a preacher to a two-year tenure, elected Morris Brown as an assistant superintendent (bishop), set the salary of the superintendent, created an Annual Conference (New York), and denied the right of the Quarterly Conference, given in the *Discipline*, to recommend the admission of licentiates. The election of delegates to the 1824 General Conference was another instance in which it was ignored by the Annual Conference. The manner of these elections, in 1823, was determined by the Baltimore Conference rather than by the *Discipline*. Payne recorded the motion "that the Annual Conference have the prerogative of legislating in behalf of the selection of delegates . . . to attend the General Conference." [16]

This second General Conference did meet, but there are only scant records from it. In any case it was not, at this time, a determinative body for the denomination. The 1828 General Conference was held, but apparently it was only an interlude between the sessions of the Philadelphia Conference for the purpose of electing a bishop, Morris Brown. It was not until 1836 that the General Conference came of age. This body revised the *Discipline*, elected a general book steward, George Hogarth, and another assistant to the bishop, Edward Waters.

Beginning with 1844, the General Conference gave significant leadership to the denomination. The phenomenal report of the missionary labors of William Paul Quinn were reported at this session, which inspired the creation of the Parent Home and Foreign Missionary Society. The *Discipline* was amended, deleting the titles "junior" and "senior"

[16] *History of the A.M.E. Church*, p. 39.

bishop and designating bishops as "joint" bishops. Token representation was granted to laymen in the General Conference, i.e., a local preacher could represent the laity; and Quinn was elected to the general superintendency. The 1848 General Conference defeated a motion to create presiding elders; elected Daniel A. Payne as historiographer; approved new liturgical material for public worship; expedited the procedure for the trial of a bishop; increased episcopal power and remuneration; defined and clarified the authority of local trustees; reset eligibility qualifications for local preachers.

In 1852 motions to license women to preach and to create presiding elders did not prevail, but remarriage following separation or divorce was made permissible under certain circumstances. Three episcopal districts were formed. Visitors from conferences other than that of the district in which the General Conference was being held were denied the right to speak or vote at the sessions. Willis Nazrey and Daniel A. Payne were elevated to the episcopacy.

The tenth General Conference, 1856, was spirited and constructive. The book committee, later the Book Concern, reported legal incorporation in the state of Pennsylvania. The Canadian church was peacefully separated from the parent body. Following a long and acrimonious discussion of the slavery issue, a firm antislavery, rather than a moderate abolitionist, resolution prevailed. The question of the remarriage of divorced persons was postponed, despite an action of the General Conference of 1852 that was strangely never printed in the *Discipline*. Uniformity in ministerial dress as recommended in the *Discipline* was reinforced by an amending action allowing conferences to suspend violators. The motion to create a cabinet of elders, a bishops' council, to "advise" the bishop in matters of policy and appointment, was defeated, and a measure requiring episcopal residence and quadrennial supervision was postponed indefinitely. Amendments to the *Discipline* included a reconstitution of the composition of the General Conference and the manner of the election and ordination of bishops. The tenure of itinerants at stations and in cities was limited to two and four years, respectively.

The 1864 meeting considered a proposal for organic union with the A. M. E. Zion Church and voted to submit the matter to the Quarterly and Annual Conferences. (The proposal was rejected after the vote.) A. W. Wayman and J. P. Campbell were elected bishops. The next quadrennial meeting, 1868, authorized the use of the presiding-elder system on an optional basis in the conferences. The General Conference became an elected body, and full lay representation was introduced. The board of stewardesses and the new general office of corresponding secretary of missions were created at this meeting. Bishops elected were J. A. Shorter, T. M. D. Ward, and J. M. Brown.

The 1872 General Conference, which met at Nashville, was the first delegated General Conference and the first one to meet in the South. At this meeting the Colored Methodist Episcopal Church requested the return of certain properties which some A. M. E. pastors had evidently possessed prior to the organization of the C. M. E. Church in 1870. A series of resolutions favoring civil rights for Negroes were adopted. A financial department was created; the name "book concern" became "publication department." In 1876 a petition to change the name of the denomination from "African" to "American" Methodist Episcopal was denied, and a petition of the former schismatic Independent Methodist Episcopal Church for organic reunion was granted with certain specific provisions. The sixteenth General Conference, of 1880, instituted an important polity change, namely, the assignment of bishops to their episcopal districts by the episcopal committee and not by themselves, as had previously been the case. This General Conference was also the first one to be held west of the Mississippi River, at St. Louis, Missouri. Bishops elected at this session were H. M. Turner, W. F. Dickerson, and R. H. Cain. This session was followed by the controversial 1884 meeting, at which Bishop John M. Brown in the quadrennial sermon advocated an emphasis on "apostolic succession," which he stoutly defended. The conference did not concur in this interpretation, and went on record deploring the fact that this kind of doctrine was being preached from some pulpits. The British Methodist Episcopal Church which had amiably separated from the denomination in 1856 reunited with the A. M. E. church at this time.

The 1888 session of the General Conference again considered a report on organic union with the A. M. E. Zion Church, but no positive action was taken. General officers were disqualified from being members of the General Conference unless elected by their respective Annual Conferences. Bishops were requested to "consult" on dissatisfactions over appointments. W. J. Gaines, B. W. Arnett, B. T. Tanner, and A. Grant were elected bishops.

The accomplishments of the General Conferences for the next quadrennia to 1916 can be considered together. In 1892 the Church Extension Society was created, and all foreign missions were related to the General Board of Missions.

In 1896 it was required that ministerial candidates be examined and recommended by a district conference; the basis of ministerial representation at the General Conference was changed from one delegate for every twenty-five members to one for every thirty members. The 1900 meeting of the General Conference adopted and legalized the Articles of Incorporation; instituted the Order of Deaconess; sanctioned the work of women evangelists; required general officers of new departments to raise their salaries from within their departmental budgets; and approved the incorporation of A. M. E. churches in other countries. The issue of lay rights and representation occupied the attention of the 1904 General Conference. It decided to have lay representation at the Annual Conference level as well as at the General Conference. Five bishops were elected in 1908, three were assigned to the United States and two to South Africa and West Africa. This same General Conference, 1908, recorded the first meeting of the Tri-Council of Colored Methodist Bishops, a meeting of the bishops of the A. M. E., A. M. E. Zion, and C. M. E. Churches. At this meeting it was jointly agreed by the bodies present to meet triennially and discuss such matters as federation, liturgy and uniformity of service, a common hymnal, and a catechism. The 1912 General Conference restored the words, "He descended into hell," to the Apostles' Creed, a standard act of worship in the A. M. E. liturgy. The centennial General Conference of 1916 ordered "the Episcopal Committee to report the boundaries of the districts before assigning the bishops" and to change "Bishops' Council" to "Council of Bishops."

Education

SUNDAY SCHOOLS

The first efforts toward education in the A. M. E. Church were in the area of Sunday schools. In 1795 Richard Allen organized the first Negro Sunday school in America at Philadelphia. During the following year, "a day and a night school was maintained by the members of Bethel Church." The two decades following these early developments, however, witnessed a decline in educational activity. In 1819 Payne commented: "At the end of this first decade we find no traces of any efforts . . . for the education of the rising generation through any agency of the Conferences." [17]

John Charleston, a native Virginian, was purportedly the first convert of America's first Sunday school, organized by Francis Asbury in Hanover County, Virginia. Charleston left Virginia as a boy and went to Ohio,

[17] *Ibid.*, p. 52.

where he became a local preacher in the Methodist church in Chillicothe. Later he united with the A.M.E. church there and became one of their most effective missionary preachers.[18] The first Negro Sunday school in the West was founded in the A. M. E. church at Chillicothe in 1829. In 1833 Lewis Woodson of the Ohio Conference offered its first resolution on the subject of education, pleading that "common schools, Sunday-schools, and temperance societies are of the highest importance to all people; . . . that it shall be the duty of every member of this Conference . . . to promote . . . these." [19] After its adoption, copies of this resolution were sent to the Baltimore, New York, and Philadelphia Conferences; and under the inspiration of the Ohio action, adoptions were obtained in each conference. At this point words became deeds. Education was discussed by ministers and laymen. Bethel Church in Baltimore opened a school, kept by John Fortie, about 1835. When the first report of Sunday schools was made by the Baltimore Conference in 1841, it reported two schools in Baltimore with 208 pupils and 19 teachers. Washington, D. C., reported 2 schools with 204 pupils. Columbia Circuit, Lancaster, Carlisle, Gettysburg, and Lewistown, Pennsylvania, each had a Sunday school. That following year, 1842, the conference had twelve Sabbath schools and two day schools. Quinn's Missions Report of 1844 indicated that he had organized 40 schools with 920 pupils and 40 teachers. He also reported that he had organized 50 Sunday schools with 2,000 pupils and 200 teachers as well as 40 temperance societies.

The climax of this early phase of the educational movement in African Episcopal Methodism came with the action of the 1848 General Conference which decreed a plan for common schools, encouraging every pastor "to establish a high school wherever practicable." This same body also made it the responsibility of all exhorters "to employ their talents and time in the Sabbath-schools as teachers." [20]

The Sunday school also went to the mission field. J. W. Early, who worked in the home field in the 1830's, 40's, and 50's, said, "The Sabbath-schools were made a necessary appendage of the church, and the question received much attention in the Conferences." [21]

In the years immediately following the Civil War Sunday school work spread throughout the South, beginning in Louisiana, where it had existed before the Civil War, and where 16 Sunday schools with 85 teachers and 1,029 pupils, as well as a library, were reported in 1866. During

[18] B. W. Arnett, Colored Sunday Schools (Nashville: A.M.E. Sunday School Union, 1896) , p. 5.
[19] Payne, History of the A.M.E. Church, p. 98.
[20] Ibid., p. 220.
[21] Sarah Early, Life and Labors of J. W. Early, p. 48.

the 1880's Sunday schools reached both Canada and the West Indies following the organization of African Methodism in those places.

Following this missionary phase of the Sunday school movement was its connectional organization period. In 1882 Charles S. Smith, later a bishop, had petitioned the Bishops' Council for authorization to organize the Sunday schools of the connection in a Sunday school union, "to systematise the Sunday-school work among the colored people, to provide them with a literature and text-books, to extend the work of the Sunday-schools, . . . to provide for Sunday-school institutes, and to aid improvident schools." [22]

Smith's petition had been granted but no funds provided. In the next few years a constitution was drawn, Children's Day was established, Sunday school literature and a Sunday school press were created. By 1884 most of the conferences had endorsed the agency, and at the General Conference of that year it received recognition as an official department. Smith became its first corresponding secretary. In 1888 a highpoint was reached when the union purchased a building for publishing in Nashville.

Somewhat parallel to the development of the Sunday school movement was the leadership training program. In 1874 W. H. Coleman organized and conducted the first leadership training enterprise, known as a Sunday school institute. This arose out of the need to prepare Sunday school teachers to use the then new Uniform Lesson system, which practically all of the churches of the denomination had adopted. The procedure followed in these institutes was known as the "Cincinnati Plan," an in-service teacher-training program combining teacher training in religious education and biblical studies. By 1876 the General Conference provided that there should be Sunday school "institutes" in Annual Conferences, and in 1886 this same kind of training was made obligatory in all presiding elder districts.

YOUTH WORK AND ADULT EDUCATION

The development of youth work in the A. M. E. Church began with the random formation of Christian Endeavor Societies in local churches in the 1880's. In 1896 the General Conference adopted a resolution designating these local Christian Endeavor Societies as the official youth groups for the denomination. In 1900 these local groups were formed into a connectional society and designated the Allen Christian Endeavor League; the bishops were authorized to draft a constitution; and B. W. Arnett was appointed the first secretary. The constitution was presented

[22] Payne, *History of the A.M.E. Church,* pp. 493-94.

establishing the Young Peoples' Department with the official name of Allen Christian Endeavor League. The major objectives of these groups were: "To promote intelligent and practical Christian living among the young members. . . . To train them in the proper methods of Christian work and helpfulness. . . . To strengthen and purify the social life of our young people." [23] Somewhat later the league founded a publication, the *Allen Christian Endeavorer,* which became their connectional organ.

About 1850 evidences of adult education appeared. One of the best examples could be found in the Israel Lyceum of the then Israel Bethel A. M. E. Church of Washington, D. C., which in its day successfully attracted "the most intellectual men to listen to lectures, participate in discussion, and read dissertations on timely topics." Another instance was the Bethel Literary society, established by Bishop Payne in 1881, "for the general mental and moral improvement of young people . . . and for . . . a forum." Another effort in the 1880's that was directed toward the education of adults took the form of a theological and literary association, "having for its object the promotion of the study of science, art, literature, and religion." These associations were modeled closely after the Methodist-inspired Chautauqua movement of the 1870's. Still another adult-education opportunity was the Normal School Training Course, often connected with the associations, thus affording day school or Sunday school teachers an opportunity to improve their knowledge and skills during the summer-vacation period. By 1884 a connectional Literary, Historical and Educational Association was formed by the General Conference for "the cultivation of literature, and the study of history, science, philosophy, and the promotion of Christian education." [24]

Summarily, by 1916 practically every conference had united with the Sunday School Union. Christian Endeavor Leagues were flourishing. Several outstanding adult-work programs could be cited. Leadership training institutes were being held, and liaison relationships were being developed with other church departments to care for the educational needs of the membership.

HIGHER EDUCATION

Some of the earliest efforts at theological and higher education among and by Negroes in America are traceable to A. M. E. endeavors. The resolution on education adopted by the Ohio Conference in 1833, and subsequently by the other conferences, initiated these ventures. The

[23] Smith, *History of the A.M.E. Church,* p. 236.

[24] Cromwell, "First Negro Churches in the District of Columbia," p. 70; Jenifer, *Centennial Retrospect History,* p. 24; H. M. Turner, *The Genius and Theory of Methodist Polity* (Philadelphia: Publication Department, A.M.E. Church, 1885), pp. 290-91.

Baltimore Conference in 1838 passed a resolution obligating its ministers to speak on education quarterly. Following a contentious struggle, the General Conference of 1844 adopted a Course of Study which was made a requirement for those seeking ordination. In 1845 a national educational convention was held in Philadelphia to devise a plan to educate the ministry and to establish a connectional school. Actions of the 1848 and 1880 General Conferences made major revisions of the Course of Study. Correspondence schools of theology were instituted in 1896. In 1900 it was recommended that the seminaries receive appropriations from general church funds, and in 1912 all deans of theological schools were included in the membership of the General Conference.

Prior to 1865 the A. M. E. Church was involved in two movements that were to eventuate in the establishment of the first Negro institution of higher education in the United States. The Ohio Conference in 1844 purchased land near Columbus for a "seminary of learning on the manual trade plan" for instruction in "various branches of literature, science, theology, agriculture, and the mechanic arts." Until 1854 its classes met in Bethel Church in Columbus, thus also providing for that city its first public school for Negroes. Meanwhile, between 1853 and 1855, the Cincinnati Conference of the Northern Church was initiating the Ohio African University. This institution was approved by the 1856 Northern General Conference and renamed Wilberforce University. From 1856 to 1862 the A. M. E.'s and the Northern Church conducted Wilberforce as a co-operative venture. The school was closed at the outset of the Civil War; and when it was decided to reopen it, the A. M. E. Church purchased the property and became sole owners. Its first Negro president was Daniel A. Payne, the first American Negro college president. In 1867 the liberal arts department was organized, and in 1887 the state of Ohio established a normal and industrial department. Finally, in 1891 the addition of a theological department was authorized by the church and trustees, later to be called Payne Theological Seminary of Wilberforce University.

From 1866 to 1886 eight schools were established by the A. M. E. Church. In 1866 at Live Oak, Florida, Edward Waters College was begun as Brown Theological Institute. In 1876 it was renamed Brown University. It moved to Jacksonville in 1891, and in 1892 it assumed its present name. Allen University at Columbia, South Carolina, was that state's first Negro college. It began as Payne Institute in 1870. Ten years later Bishop W. F. Dickerson moved it to its present location and renamed it. Paul Quinn College was established at Waco, Texas, in 1872. Its charter, which dates from 1881, makes it the oldest Negro liberal arts school in that state. In 1881 three colleges were founded—Turner College at Hernando, Mississippi, Western University at Quindaro, Kansas, and Morris Brown College at Atlanta. The latter institution began operation in May, 1885. St. James Academy and Industrial Institute was founded at New Orleans in 1882. In North Carolina, Kittrell College—discontinued in 1942—was established by that conference in 1885 as a normal and industrial school. The following year Shorter College, Little Rock, came into being as Bethel Institute. The name was changed to its present title when it received its charter in 1892.

In the next decade, 1886-96, six more schools were founded. In 1886 W. A. Rice founded Ironsides Normal Institute in New Jersey, later Bordentown Training and Industrial Institute. Payne University at Selma, Alabama, opened for instruction in 1889 as a parish school for the Brown A. M. E. Church there. Three schools were established in 1890: Campbell College (an incorporation of Stringer and Disney Academies, pioneer Negro schools in Mississippi), founded in Bethel Church, Vicksburg; Lampton College (merged with Campbell in 1932), located originally at Delphi and later at Alexandria, Louisiana; and Wayman Institute, a Kentucky Conference school established at Harrodsburg. In 1915 Wayman merged with Turner College in Tennessee; and in 1917 Flipper-Key-Paris College was established at Talihina, Oklahoma. Most of these schools had developed theological departments as well as liberal arts and normal departments by 1916.

The General Conference of 1876 authorized the formation of a General Board of Education, "to supervise the higher educational work of the Church." J. C. Embry was elected the first secretary of this unit. In 1884 the educational work was reorganized and the church was divided into "four educational districts with a General Secretary and assistant district secretaries." [25]

Publishing

The literary efforts of the A. M. E. Church include the publication of the *Discipline,* official General Conference Minutes, church periodicals,

[25] Payne, *History of the A.M.E. Church,* pp. 423-38; C. L. Jordan, "African Methodism's Stake in Higher Education, 1863-1963," *Journal of Religious Education of the A.M.E. Church,* Vol. 23, No. 3, 14-16; W. A. Daniel, *The Education of Negro Ministers* (New York: Doran, 1925), pp. 146-61; B. W. Arnett, *The Budget, Containing the Annual Reports of the General Affairs of the A.M.E. Church of the U.S.A.* (Xenia, Ohio, 1887), pp. 147, 154 ff.; *The Budget* (1884), p. 167; "Quadrennial Address of the Bishops of the A.M.E. Church to the General Conference, Washington, D.C., May 4, 1896," p. 40.

hymnals, Sunday school literature, histories, and miscellaneous writings by members of the connection.

The first *Discipline* was published in 1817. The first major revision of the *Discipline* was made in 1836, and since that time periodic revisions and changes have been made as needed. The first printing of the *General Minutes* of the denomination was in 1822. After this they were published intermittently until after the Civil War. In 1840 the first discussion of a connectional periodical occurred. This came to fruition in the founding of the *A. M. E. Church Magazine* in 1841. George Hogarth was the first editor. This paper, originally intended to be a weekly, became a quarterly in its first year and continued in existence for seven years. In 1848 it was made a weekly, renamed the *Christian Herald,* and published by Major Delaney's militant race newspaper, *Pittsburgh Mystery,* which was purchased by the denomination for that purpose.[26] Augustus R. Green was its first editor, and in 1852 the *Christian Herald* became the *Christian Recorder* by action of the General Conference. There have been two other regional *Recorders.* The *Southern Recorder,* authorized by the General Conferences of 1880 and 1884, was finally started in 1886 by Henry M. Turner. It was purchased by the denomination in 1888 and became the *Southern Christian Recorder.* The *Western Christian Recorder* was founded by Frank M. McDonald as a private venture in 1891. In 1900 it became one of the official organs of the church, and in 1912 its editor became a general officer.

Between 1858 and 1864 the need for a more sophisticated type of journal began to crystallize, and a new type of publication was instituted "to furnish the race with the thoughts of the leading men and women," and to give "opportunity to [those] who have talent as writers." The earlier of the two forms of this journal was the *Repository of Religion and Literature,* edited by John M. Brown and published at Indianapolis for the first time in April, 1858. This effort expired in 1864. In 1883 a revival of this type of publication was suggested by Benjamin T. Tanner, which eventuated in the action of the ensuing General Conference of 1884 authorizing the publication of the *A. M. E. Church Review.* Tanner became the first editor.

Two A. M. E. missionary periodicals have been developed. The *Voice of Missions,* the official organ of the Missionary Department of the General Conference, was begun in 1892 and continues until the present. The

[26] F. G. Detweiler, *The Negro Press in the United States* (Chicago: The University of Chicago Press, 1922), p. 43.

Woman's Missionary Recorder, established in 1912, served as the editorial organ of the women's auxiliary missionary societies.

The first hymnbook compiled and published by Negroes in America was the A. M. E. *Hymnal.* Its history reaches back to an 1807 copy of the *Pocket Hymn Book, Selected from Different Authors.* This early collection by Richard Allen was apparently published privately by him in 1807 and revised in 1818 with the assistance of Jacob Tapsico. The preface to this edition states:

> Having become a distinct and separate body of people, there is no collection of hymns we could with propriety adopt. However, we have for some time been collecting materials for the present work. . . . We have not passed over a selection of hymns because esteemed and used by a particular denomination, but have endeavoured to collect such as were applicable to the various states of Christian experience.

From 1818 to 1835 no reference to a hymnal can be found. Payne insisted that up to 1826 there is no proof of the existence of a hymnal and that "probably the Hymn Book of the M. E. Church was used." [27] This statement may indicate the fact that either the 1818 edition was not connectional but local; and if connectional, it was not used widely. There have been several editions of the hymnbook since these early days. Payne related that the subject of the publication of a hymnal was discussed by the Philadelphia Conference in 1835; and that Joseph M. Corr, then general book steward, reported that a thousand copies had been published. In 1854 the Philadelphia Conference learned that a revision of the hymnal was nearly complete, and that "it was the design of the book steward to publish two forms of the hymn-book, one for the pews, . . . the other for the pulpit." The General Conference of 1856 voted "to revise the present hymn book, [and] to publish it as soon as practicable." [28] A revision with minor changes was ordered by the General Conference of 1864. The 1868 body appointed Henry M. Turner to revise the old hymnbook completely, "which was equivalent to authorizing him to compile a new one." This revision, which appeared in 1873, served as the authorized revision until 1893. It was the first of the omnibus hymnals including "spiritual songs" and chants, liturgies, rituals, and other church ordinances. In 1888 the General Conference appointed another hymnal-revision committee and instructed it to compile what became known as the 1893 hymnbook. Under the editorship of J. C. Embry, a smaller edition, with the hymns grouped according to meter, was presented to the church. Chants were deleted from this edition,

[27] *History of the A.M.E. Church,* p. 52.
[28] *Ibid.,* pp. 110, 315, 358-59.

and the ritual for the administration of baptism and Holy Communion, which had been deleted from some former edition, were restored. The first musically scored hymnal was published in 1897, again under the editorship of Embry. This edition was not revised until 1941.[29]

In connection with the movement to organize the council of the bishops of the three major Negro Methodist bodies in 1908, an attempt was made to develop a common hymnal and liturgy. These failed to materialize, as did the continuance of the council.

A. M. E. Sunday school literature, "the first . . . ever published in this country for the exclusive use of Negro Sunday schools,[30] has been successfully published and widely used since the late 1880's through the facilities of their Sunday School Union Press, the publishing unit for religious education materials. By 1881 a Child's Recorder was being published and in popular demand by all the Sabbath schools. H. M. Turner's Catechism was also in general use as teaching material. The second Annual Report of the Publication Department in 1882 indicated a continued demand for the Child's Recorder, and the interesting fact that "We have also, by authority of the Publishing Board, arranged for, and secured with our imprint on it, a Teacher's Quarterly, Scholar's Quarterly, and Little Learner's Paper." [31]

In addition, the then traditional catechisms, "Milk for Babes" and "Children's Bread," were being printed. In the 1884 report of the Sunday School Department it was learned that in January, 1883, a new publication, Our Sunday School Review, had been introduced, and in March of that same year the Jubilee Gem had been presented. Curriculum materials such as the Teacher's Quarterly, Scholar's Quarterly, Juvenile Lesson Paper, Gem Lesson Paper, Primary Lessons for Beginners, and the Young Allenite, had been added. The ten graded publications were "fully adapted to every feature of . . . Sunday School work." In the youth field, by 1912 the Allen Christian Endeavor League was publishing "all kinds of literature," e.g., a Young Peoples Quarterly was being done by Augustus Young of Akron; and there was a connectional youth organ, the Allen Christian Endeavorer. By 1916 a teacher's guide and quarterlies for each age group in the Sunday school had been developed and improved; and the Allen C. E. League Star, a youth periodical, had appeared.

[29] The A.M.E. Hymnal (Nashville: The A.M.E. Sunday School Union, 1954), pp. 543-44.

[30] J. B. F. Shaw, The Negro in the History of Methodism (Nashville: Parthenon Press, 1954), pp. 50-51.

[31] Arnett, Budget (1882), p. 43.

Missionary Work

HOME MISSIONS

The missionary enterprise of the A. M. E. Church has been an integral part of its life and work in both the national and world fields since its independence as a denomination. The home missionary endeavors of the church grew out of the needs of an expanding ministry and membership in the early pioneer days of the country's history. At first—1816-24— missionary activity was in the form of sporadic and unorganized assistance to struggling mission churches and poor preachers. The earliest organizational expression of this impulse was the Dorcas Society, formed by Richard Allen about 1824, which had as its purpose, "to see to it that the ministers were well clad when they came to conference." The next effort in this direction was the formation of the women of the Annual Conferences into an organization known as the Daughters of the Conference. This movement was initiated by Sarah Allen, wife of Bishop Allen, about 1827, to increase the benevolent giving of the churches at the Annual Conferences. In 1840 William Paul Quinn was commissioned by the General Conference as its first home missionary. His assignment was to organize churches, temperance societies, and schools. Quinn's outstanding accomplishments in the ensuing quadrennium—1840-44—inspired the creation of the Parent Home and Foreign Missionary Society in 1844. Probably the first home-missions institution founded by an Annual Conference was the Home for Aged and Infirm Colored People at Philadelphia. This home, one of the first of its kind anywhere in America, was established about 1845 by Stephen Smith of Bethel Church, a local preacher and philanthropist. Smith gave the land for this home; and his legacy still supports it, although it has not been a church institution for many years. Beginning in 1846 with the Ohio Conference, home missionary societies were organized throughout the connection at the conference level and usually divided into "missionary" districts corresponding to the later presiding-elder districts.

During the California gold-rush years, 1846-56, the A. M. E. Church followed hundreds of its own people and many other Negroes who left the South, Midwest, and East to set out for the "New Eldorado." In the interest of efficiency and order the General Conference of 1848 required an annual report of each of its missionary points at home and abroad, and from all levels of the connection from the local church to the General Conference. It also instituted the practice of having a sermon preached on the subject of missions at every annual session of the conferences.

In 1855 the Philadelphia Conference Committee on Missions made three significant requests and recommendations: the establishment of a Home and Foreign Missionary Society; the supervision of the Strouds-burg Mission, Pennsylvania; and the funds to support a city missionary "over Philadelphia and its vicinity." [32] In 1864 the General Conference created an office of corresponding secretary of missions and an elected general board for supervision. Following the Civil War elementary and preparatory schools—anticipating the denomination's future colleges—were organized in most of the Annual Conferences throughout the South and were known as "district schools." These schools, inadequate as they sometimes were, met a critical need in a section where educational facilities for Negroes were still more inadequate or lacking altogether. Some of these schools were: Selma Institute (Alabama); the Abbeville School, the Flegler High School, and the Sumter District School (South Carolina); Payne High School and Cartersville Normal and Preparatory School (Georgia).

Home missionary work began among the American Indians about 1870 in the territory that was then called the Indian Reservation, an area of approximately 71,000 square miles, "lying between Kansas on the North, Arkansas on the East, and Texas on the South and inhabited by Cherokee, Chickasaw, Choctaw, Seminole, and Osage Indians." This work was first listed as the Schulyville Indian Territory Mission Circuit. In 1872 it was included in the work of the Pulaski District of the Arkansas Conference. In 1879 the Indian Mission Conference was organized.

In 1874 the first women's missionary group was organized and designated the Woman's Parent Mite Missionary Society, an auxiliary to the general missionary organization. The activities of this group were limited to the northern churches. In 1894 the southern church women were formed into the Woman's Home and Foreign Missionary Society. The General Conference of 1896 recognized both groups as connectional agencies.

The establishment of hospitals was also a concern of A. M. E. missions. African Methodist Episcopal clergy and laymen were largely responsible for the establishment of the Provident Hospital and Training School for Nurses in Chicago in 1891 and the Douglas Hospital at Kansas City, Kansas. By 1897 the connectional Preachers' Aid and Mutual Relief Association was established, through which "preachers with a little means might make provision for their families in case of death." The General Conference of 1900 authorized it as an official organization and elected

[32] Payne, *History of the A.M.E. Church,* p. 319.

J. T. Jenifer as its first secretary. That same year the denomination saw the need for a new approach to the religious life of the urban Negro and established the first of many institutional churches. Du Bois commented, "The institutional church, established in Chicago by the A. M. E. denomination, is the most advanced step in the direction of making the church exist for the people rather than the people for the church." [33] Another action of the General Conference that year was the authorization of the Church Extension Society, which had been created in 1892, "to prepare plans and specifications for church buildings and parsonages." [34] The General Conference of 1908 authorized the Woman's Parent Mite Society to incorporate. The conference of 1912 constituted the Home and Foreign Missionary Department, which was subsequently incorporated in the state of New York in 1914.

FOREIGN MISSIONS

The missionary outreach of the A. M. E. Church in the foreign field began in Africa in 1820, when Daniel Coker, as a representative of the American Colonization Society, organized the first A. M. E. churches in both Liberia and Sierra Leone.[35] The first official missionary, Charles Butler, was appointed by the church to Africa in 1822. The fact is, however, he never left the United States for his assignment. The first missionary to reach Africa—Liberia—and reside there was John Boggs, who went out in 1824, but established no permanent work. Again in 1856 the General Conference set apart Africa as a foreign mission field and appointed J. R. V. Morgan as the missionary-pastor. Little is known of him except the fact that he had to return because he could not be supported.

The first permanent work in Africa was finally established in Liberia in 1878. It grew out of a congregation organized by Bishop John M. Brown and A. T. Carr in the Morris Brown Church in Charleston, South Carolina. Appointed to lead this small group of approximately thirty members was S. F. Flegler. The group landed in Liberia at Monrovia later that same year and proceeded immediately to organize and build a church and a school at Brewersville. In 1891 Bishop Turner organized the Liberian Conference. Two schools grew out of this work before 1916, namely, the Eliza Turner School at Monrovia and the Monrovia College and Industrial Institute.

The work in Sierra Leone, then a British colony that had been established originally by the British as an asylum for Africans rescued from

[33] *The Negro Church,* p. 85.
[34] Smith, *History of the A.M.E. Church,* p. 219.
[35] *Ibid.,* pp. 174-75, 179.

slave traders, dated from the time of Coker's mission there in 1820. It was not heard of again until J. R. Frederick of the New England Conference was appointed there as a missionary in 1866. When he finally arrived in 1887, he was welcomed by a large British Methodist African congregation whose ancestors had come there from Nova Scotia in 1792. In 1891 Bishop Turner organized the work in this West African country into the Sierra Leone Conference. In 1902 the Bishop Cornelius T. Shaffer High School was founded, and in 1908 a seminary was established at Freetown, the country's capital city.

The years 1892-1900 witnessed the rise and growth of the A. M. E. Church in South Africa. In 1892 a schism occurred in the Wesleyan Methodist Church (British) in Pretoria, Transvaal, occasioned by the fact that "up to 1886 the white and colored ministers in the Wesleyan Church had met together," but "in that year the color line was drawn and each side was required to meet apart from the other; yet the colored brethren were compelled to have a white chairman and secretary." 36 The African membership withdrew and under the leadership of M. M. Mokone became the independent "Ethiopian" Church. In 1896, under the leadership of Mokone, this body petitioned the A. M. E. Church for membership. Their petition was granted; and James M. Dwane, who had been sent to America to unite with the A. M. E. Church on behalf of the South Africans, returned with the authority to superintend the work in South Africa. The following year the South African or Cape Colony Conference was organized. In 1898 Bishop Turner organized the Transvaal Conference. By 1904 Bishop Levi J. Coppin reported the organization of three more Annual Conferences: the Orange River Colony, the Natal, and the Zambesi. Bethel Institute, at Cape Town, the precursor of Wilberforce Institute, had also been established by this time.

A. M. E. activity in Haiti and the Dominican Republic began in 1824, when President Jean Boyer of Haiti invited the Negro church to establish work there. In response to this, several members of Bethel Church in Philadelphia, including Henry Allen, Richard Robinson, and Scipio Beanes, embarked for the island that same year. Before the end of the year they had built the first Protestant church there at Port-au-Prince and named it St. Peter's. In 1827 Scipio Beanes returned to the United States, received ordination at the Baltimore Conference, and was reappointed to Haiti as pastor-in-charge. In 1830 the Haitian church formally united with the connection. Following the death of Beanes in 1835, St. Peter's was neglected by the home church, and about 1840 Henry

---

36 *Ibid.*, p. 181.

Allen formed the independent "Haitian Union Methodist Society." The General Conference of 1880 voted to re-establish contact with the Haitian group; and by 1887 an Annual Conference had been formed, which reported 3 churches, 450 members, and 1 school.[37]

In addition to the work that was founded in Haiti and Santo Domingo, Dominican Republic, A. M. E. missions were initiated on Cuba and Jamaica. Work was established at Antigua and on the Virgin Islands, and missions were founded at Dominica, Tobago, Barbados, Trinidad, and St. Thomas. Outside the West Indies there were mission points in the Bahama and Bermuda Islands.[38]

In Central and South America African Methodism has had some continuous work since the 1850's at Paramaribo (Dutch Guiana) and Georgetown (Demerara, British Guiana), the location of the Missionary and Industrial Institute.

2

The A. M. E. Zion Church

The history of the African Methodist Episcopal Zion Church falls naturally into three periods: the formative phase (1796-1821), the developing phase (1821-63), and the "flourishing" phase (1863-96). For the purposes of this chapter, a fourth phase (1896-1916) will be discussed. The first period, describing the early founding of the denomination and the establishment of its itinerancy, is adequately detailed elsewhere in this *History* and will not claim major attention. The proposed task here is to chronicle the main events and circumstances that affected the growth and expansion of this segment of American Methodism from the first yearly conference, held in 1821.

Growth and Spread

The growth of the A. M. E. Zion Church after 1820 can be followed best through the proceedings and appointments of its yearly and Annual

---

[37] E. L. Newsome, "Early Figures in Haitian Methodism," *Phylon*, V (1944), 59; Jenifer, *Centennial Retrospect History*, pp. 123-24.

[38] Horace Talbert, *The Sons of Allen* (Xenia, Ohio: The Aldine Press, 1906), pp. 208-9.

Conferences.[39] In speaking of "conferences" before that time, Hood said, "The preachers of the African Methodist Episcopal Zion Connection had occasional Conferences as early as 1812; but the first regular meeting of the New York Conference of which we have a record was held in New York city June 21, 1821." [40] This first yearly conference was presided over by William Phoebus, a minister of the Methodist Episcopal Church, elected in the absence of a Methodist bishop. The appointments for this first year were: Zion, New York City, Abraham Thompson; Long Island Church, William Carman; Wesley Church, Philadelphia, Simon Murray; Easton, Pennsylvania, and New Haven, James Anderson. This conference concluded with the self-authorization of the group to designate themselves as the New York Conference.

The second yearly conference met in Philadelphia in 1822. James Varick, Abraham Thompson, and Leven J. Smith were ordained elders on June 17, 1822, becoming the first in the connection. Abraham Thompson was elected to preside at this session and at the subsequent adjourned session in July, thus becoming the first Negro to preside over the deliberations of the connection. Varick was elected as the first super-intendent of the connection at this conference.

The third yearly conference convened May 21, 1823, in New York City. Superintendent Varick presided. News reached the conference that there was internal strife in the Wesley Church at Philadelphia. Probably for this reason they were not represented at this session. Ordinarily the fourth yearly conference would have met in May, 1824. It was postponed, however, because it was hoped that the Methodist Episcopal General Conference, which was scheduled to meet at about that same time, would take some favorable action respecting Zion's request for establishment and the ordination of her preachers. When this did not happen, the yearly conference convened on July 15, 1824.

The fifth yearly conference which met on May 19, 1825, in New York City was not attended by any except the New York preachers. A new society was noted at Harlem, in upper Manhattan. The sixth yearly conference, 1826, witnessed James Varick's reappointment as superintendent and the appearance of the first circuits—one on Long Island, to

[39] See Christopher Rush, A Short Account of the Rise and Progress of the African Methodist Episcopal Church in America (New York, 1843), pp. 69-87, for proceedings to 1833; David H. Bradley, Sr., A History of the A.M.E. Zion Church, Part I, 1796-1872 (Nashville: Parthenon Press, 1956), pp. 94-170, for coverage up to 1872; John J. Moore, History of the A.M.E. Zion Church in America (York, Pa.: Teachers' Journal Office, 1884), pp. 87-106, for data to 1876; and J. W. Hood, One Hundred Years of the African Methodist Episcopal Zion Church (New York: A.M.E. Zion Book Concern, 1895), pp. 93-94, 213-520, for the record to 1892.

[40] One Hundred Years, p. 213.

which William Carman and George Tredwell were appointed, and two in New Jersey, to which Timothy Eatto and Charles Anderson were assigned. Christopher Rush went to Mother Zion that year, and Peter Vanhas to the young church at Harlem. The establishment of a church at Buffalo, New York, represented by Joseph P. Hopkins was indicated at the seventh yearly conference, 1827.

In 1828 Leven Smith was urged to accept the superintendency of the connection but declined. Following this Christopher Rush was elected to the position, becoming the second superintendent of the Zion movement. There is some confusion about the dates, election, and tenure of Varick and Rush.

The ninth yearly conference, which met in New York City beginning May 21, 1829, is of particular interest. The Wesleyan Church of Philadelphia officially affiliated with the connection. New work was reported in Pennsylvania. The climactic event of this session was the creation of the Philadelphia Conference, the second one in the denomination. The appointments at this conference were made for the New York Conference only, the Philadelphia Conference having been authorized to convene later.

EXPANSION IN THE EAST AND WEST

The decade and a half (1830-45) between the founding of the second and third Annual Conferences is a convenient period to discuss at this time. The newly organized Philadelphia Conference met in its first session at Philadelphia beginning June 14, 1829. Its original boundaries included all of the state of Pennsylvania and southern New Jersey. The following were its first appointments: Wesleyan, Philadelphia, Edward Johnson; Western District, Jacob Richardson, assisted by missionaries, David Smith and Richard Phillips. About the same time came the rise of Zion Methodism in the District of Columbia. There was an A. M. E. Zion Church in Washington in 1837 and probably as early as 1833.

By 1843 the Philadelphia Conference made the following creditable progress report: two churches each in Philadelphia, Pittsburgh, and Baltimore, and one organization established or being established in Harrisburg, York, Carlisle, Shippensburg, Lewistown, Bellefonte, Williamsport, and Johnstown, Pennsylvania. At the Philadelphia Conference held in 1844, one of the two Baltimore churches mentioned above, the First Colored Wesley Methodist Independent Society of Baltimore, was formally annexed to the connection. By 1848 the formation of the Baltimore Conference had decreased the area of the Philadelphia body. Again about 1849 the formation of the Allegheny Conference, whose boundaries included western Pennsylvania, further constricted its geographic jurisdiction.

The organization of the New England Conference in Hartford in 1845 was the second conference territory to be taken out of the original jurisdiction of the New York Conference. Its first boundaries included the New England states and parts of Canada. The founding churches in this northeastern-Canadian section of the denomination were seven: Nantucket, Massachussetts; Providence, Rhode Island; Middletown, New Haven, Hartford, Stonington, and Bridgeport, Connecticut. Between 1845 and 1849 charges were founded at Worcester and Springfield in Massachusetts and at Norwalk, Connecticut. The work at Springfield and Norwalk did not survive its early establishment. Springfield was later revived and became an effective work. Though none of the Zion histories mention the fact explicitly, an A. M. E. Zion church existed in New Bedford by 1838. Hood substantiated this when he reported that Frederick Douglass, Negro orator and leader, joined the Zion connection at New Bedford in that year.

Following the separation of the New England work from the New York Conference in 1845, the next important development was the creation of the Genesee or Western New York Conference in either 1849 or 1851. It was the last conference established by Rush and the fourth one that he had helped to create. Its early boundaries embraced western New York and northeastern Pennsylvania. A relatively small Negro population in this area at that time limited the growth of the work.

The westward extension of Zion Methodism is the least brilliant chapter in the entire history. From the beginning it was the story of failure and frustration. Several reasons can be advanced for this. First, the Zionites took to the field in the West—and elsewhere—later than the A. M. E.'s. Second, they were not sufficiently established in the Midwest early enough before the Civil War to be able to launch a strong and effective missionary thrust toward the far West and the Southwest. Third, they often lacked sufficient manpower to take advantage of the opportunities that did present themselves. Fourth, the emancipation of the slaves and the consequent opening of the South for expansion diverted their attention from their western mission. Finally, the schism of 1852, which divided the church into two factions on the issue of the office of assistant superintendent during the critical years 1852-60, so preoccupied the church that its responsibility in the West languished.

The work in Ohio never prospered. As late as 1891, when the Ohio Conference was finally organized, there were only four churches in the state. In 1906 there were only 9 churches and a scant 386 members reported. Since it was not reported as a conference in 1906, it must have been merged temporarily with a neighboring one. Between 1906 and 1916, however, it reappeared as a separate conference and reported 14 churches and 1,389 members. The story of the A. M. E. Zion Church in Indiana is only slightly better than in Ohio. The work here was not strong enough to require an Annual Conference until about 1906, when it reported 8 churches with a total of 1,281 members. In 1916 there were 19 churches with 2,465 members.

The situation was much the same in Michigan. The Canada-Michigan Conference was organized in 1879, largely in response to a request on the part of some Canadian Negro Methodists in 1860. Lack of ministers and funds for missionary advancement, however, prevented any real progress in this area until ministers had been recruited from the Southern churches and funds made available. Thus, the work of this conference lay dormant until the Southern field was cultivated during the Reconstruction era. By 1906 there were only two churches and sixty members in the state. No conference was in existence. In 1916, 6 churches reported 515 members. The Missouri Conference, organized in 1890, showed some vitality. In 1906 it reported 11 churches and 1,765 members, while in 1916 these figures increased to 16 churches and 4,046 members.

Bishop J. J. Moore had established three churches in California in 1852. In 1868 the California Conference was organized by Bishop J. J. Clinton. Here again, as in the case of the other western conferences, the lack of leadership and funds lost many opportunities for establishing new work. When Bishop Lomax visited the work there in 1881, the number of churches was still the same. By 1906, 11 churches were added to the original 3, and the membership reported was 902. By 1916 the number of churches more than doubled, to 30, and the membership rose to 1,577. The Oregon Conference was organized out of the original territory of the California Conference and also included the state of Washington, and in 1916 it reported 10 churches and 158 members.

Before the end of the flourishing period, the last eastern Annual Conference, the New Jersey, was formed. Bishop J. J. Clinton, presiding at the New York Conference of 1874, had suggested in his annual address that the body in its present size and extent was unmanageable and recommended the creation of a "New Jersey" state conference. This recommendation was accepted, the territory delimited, and authorization granted to organize in July, 1874. The first boundaries of the new conference included New Jersey and Staten Island, New York.

FORMATION OF THE SOUTHERN CONFERENCES

The work of the A. M. E. Zion Church in the South presaged the Civil War. Between 1856 and 1860 the Southern Conference was organized, with boundaries originally including Maryland, the District of Columbia, western Virginia, Kentucky, and Virginia, north of the James River, including Richmond. The Southern Conference was not productive. Until about 1868, when it seems to have been redesignated the Baltimore Conference, only two churches had been established by it south of the Potomac River. In 1872 the old Southern Conference was merged to form the Philadelphia-Baltimore Conference.

The earliest and the most successful effort at Southern work was in North Carolina. In 1862 the Zion Church at New Haven instigated a move on the part of the New England Conference to respond to the "Macedonian call" of the church at New Bern, North Carolina. This church, Andrew Chapel, had been a separate Negro Methodist congregation since about 1838, when it was set apart by the Methodist Episcopal Church. It was the home church of many of the New Haven Zionites, including Christopher Rush. The conference appointed John Williams a missionary to New Bern, to leave early in 1863. Williams had not gone by the end of 1863, and Bishop Clinton appointed J. W. Hood to leave immediately. Hood reached Washington, D. C., in December, 1863. The frozen Chesapeake Bay detained him until the middle of January, but he arrived at New Bern on January 20, 1864. Following a siege of intrigue and litigation Andrew Chapel, with its membership of about four hundred persons, was officially received into the A. M. E. Zion connection, thus becoming the first A. M. E. Zion church of the South.

Churches were founded later at Beaufort, Roanoke Island, and Washington. In December, 1864, the North Carolina Conference was organized by Bishop J. J. Clinton, embracing southern Virginia, North Carolina, and Tennessee. After its formation this conference created several other bodies including the Central North Carolina, the Western North Carolina (1891), and Blue Ridge (1892) Conferences. By 1916 the Albemarle and the Cape Fear Conferences were added.

A natural territorial outgrowth of the North Carolina Conference was the Tennessee, organized at Knoxville in October, 1868. By 1872 it had a lay membership of more than six thousand dispersed over an area that included eastern Tennessee and western North Carolina.

The second successful conference to be organized in the South was the Louisiana. After supervising the founding of the North Carolina work, Bishop Clinton went directly to New Orleans, which by 1864 was in the custody of the Union armies, and set up the work of that area as authorized by the 1864 General Conference. On March 13, 1865, the Louisiana Conference was organized, including the whole of the lower South, except the work already allocated to the North Carolina Conference. In 1867 Alabama and Georgia, Florida in 1869, and Texas in 1883, were formed into conferences out of its original territory. By 1891 a Northern Louisiana Conference had been formed.

On June 6, 1866, the Kentucky Conference was organized by Bishop Sampson Talbot in the Center Street Church, Louisville, with an initial membership of almost two thousand persons. This conference was responsible for the reclamation and salvaging of many of the earlier attempts at A. M. E. Zion church extension in Indiana, Illinois, and Missouri. It was also the parent body of both the Arkansas and Missouri Conferences, set apart in 1882 and 1890, respectively. Its own division into a Kentucky and West Kentucky Conference occurred between 1895 and 1906.

In October of 1866 the Virginia Conference was formed out of the North Carolina. It was laid off to include southern Virginia, except Tennessee Conference territory in that area, and fourteen counties in northeast North Carolina.

South Carolina, although technically a part of the old Louisiana Conference, was organized by the North Carolina Conference. In 1866 Horace Clinton and Titus Hogans of Lancaster County, South Carolina, walked to New Bern, North Carolina, to petition the North Carolina Conference, then in session, for aid in organizing one for South Carolina A. M. E. Zionites. The emissaries were promptly ordained deacons and instructed to return to South Carolina as missionaries. When in March, 1867, Bishop Clinton and other elders formally organized this new conference, its geographic limits were made to coincide with the state boundaries. In 1891 Bishop C. C. Petty organized the second and only other state organization in South Carolina, the Palmetto Conference.

The large and prominent Alabama Conference, second in influence and strength only to the North Carolina, was organized in April, 1867. It was the first body to be formed out of the large region assigned to the Louisiana Conference for cultivation. In 1881 the West Alabama Conference was created, and by 1895 an East Alabama Conference existed. Prior to 1906 Central, North, and West Alabama Conferences had been formed and East Alabama eliminated. By 1916 there were six conferences in the state: Alabama Central, North, South, Southeast, West, and Cahaba.

The Georgia Conference was organized in June, 1867, by Bishop Clinton. At first there was high promise for its work, until Augusta, a strategic center, was lost by the withdrawal of Trinity Church from the connection. After that time the progress of the work was difficult. In 1885 this conference divided, creating the North and South Georgia Conferences. By 1906, however, the "North" Georgia designation had been deleted but the "South" Georgia continued.

The organization of the Florida Conference in April, 1869, at Pensacola climaxed the work of Wilbur G. Strong, a missionary to Florida, Louisiana, and Alabama as early as 1864. In 1891 the South Florida Conference was organized out of the Florida, which was then renamed the West Florida Conference for a period before reclaiming its original designation.

The West Tennessee–Mississippi Conference was organized by Bishop Clinton, also in 1869. It was the result of the effort of the North Carolina Conference missionary thrust to the west and a similar impetus from the Louisiana and Alabama Conferences northward. In 1891 a South Mississippi Conference was formed.

Doctrine and Polity

The doctrine and polity of the African Methodist Episcopal Zion Church was practically identical with that of the Methodist Episcopal Church. "Our Church Polity . . . originally embraced and does now embrace all the doctrines of religious faith and Christian practice contained in the government of the mother Church, which [we] see in full, in the present form of Discipline." [41]

The earliest meetings of the Negro members of John Street Church dealt primarily with ways and means of providing a time and place for their separate common worship. Recollections and records reveal that their desire was to remain an integral part of the Methodist Episcopal Church. In reflecting upon the Founders' Address, Hood said,

The great respect that these men had for the mother Church is seen in the care they took not to use language which might be offensive. . . . This . . . characterizes every document emanating from them during the twenty years or more that they were in correspondence with the bishops and Conference of the Methodist Episcopal Church trying to get that body to assist them in their effort to establish in a regular way an ordained ministry.[42]

When they realized that the General Conference of the Methodist Episcopal Church was not going to establish them as a separate conference or ordain their preachers, they sought to perfect an organization on their own. Adapted from the Methodist Episcopal Discipline, a Discipline, au-

---

[41] Moore, History, pp. 76-78.
[42] One Hundred Years, p. 9.

thorized and published in 1820, became, as originally intended, the law of the church. Under this dispensation the first yearly conference was established and met in June 21, 1821, in Zion Church at New York City. According to their *Discipline,* they desired to elect a Methodist bishop as "superintendent." Since, however, none was present they selected an elder of the mother church, William Phoebus, to chair the conference and Joshua Soule as secretary. A "district chairman" to supervise the work of the "annual district" was established, since the newly created *Discipline* did not provide for presiding elders, and James Varick elected the first holder of that office. Still hoping that the Methodist Episcopal Church would respond to their petition to aid in establishing them and ordaining them, they did nothing about further organization or ordination at that sitting of the conference. On September 27, 1821, however, a special call meeting was held on the subject of ordination. Three distinct opinions were in evidence. Some favored returning to the government of the Methodist Episcopal Church as a means of securing ordination. Another faction favored petitioning the Stillwellites for this service, while still others counseled the maintainence of elected elders until ordination could be secured. The vexing question was finally resolved in 1822 with "the imposition of hands" from James Covel, Silvester Hutchinson, and William Stillwell, all of whom had been formerly elders in the Methodist Episcopal Church, but were then elders in the Stillwellite group. They ordained three elders; and, in July of that same year, in the adjourned session of the second yearly conference, six deacons were ordained, among them Christopher Rush.

During this same session James Varick was appointed superintendent of the connection, as provided in the *Discipline,* thus instituting its earliest form of the episcopacy and the first "bishop" in the denomination. The prerogatives of this office, formerly including only the supervision of preachers, Quarterly Conferences, and churches, were now extended to permit the supervision of Annual Conferences.

In 1824 the denomination's "limited episcopacy" was expanded further with action to elect superintendents for four-year terms instead of annually as had been the case. The 1828 yearly conference may also be referred to as the first General Conference of the connection. From this year the General Conference has met quadrennially.

The next consequential event in Zion's history relating to polity was its first major schism of 1852. Since, however, the events preceding and following this separation are inextricably interwoven with General Conference activity, it will be discussed together with the proceedings of the General Conferences which met from 1840 to 1860.

The genesis of the split in Zion Methodism is to be found in the creation of the office of "assistant superintendent." From the death of Varick, about 1828, until 1840, Rush was the only superintendent. In 1840 Rush was re-elected and William Miller elected with the understanding that he would "assist" Rush in this office. Others understood that Miller would also have the right of succession. In 1844 both Rush and Miller were re-elected. Miller died in 1846.[43] In 1848 Rush was first elected and George Galbreath elected second, the second superintendent serving as assistant by custom. Galbreath and others interpreted this election to include the right of succession as some had claimed Miller's did. In 1852 the aging Rush was defeated, and Galbreath elected superintendent to succeed him. At this same session the General Conference proceeded to elect William Bishop "assistant" superintendent. Many felt that the election of Galbreath as superintendent from the position of "assistant" or "second" superintendent and the election of an assistant superintendent with the implication of the right of succession to the superintendency had been an unconstitutional innovation in their polity, and as such it was patently illegal. Apparently this sentiment prevailed, and both elections were declared null and void. Rush was recalled to the chair, and voting for the office of superintendent was begun de novo. This time Galbreath and Bishop were nominated. Bishop was elected first. A second ballot elected Galbreath as superintendent, which position he declined on the grounds that this was the same position that he had served previously. A resolution was then presented recommending the abolition of the general superintendency.

This action was so effectively opposed by a strong minority that it was then decided to have three superintendents, including the two which had already been elected, and to have them serve on an equal basis. George A. Spywood was elected the third superintendent. This 1852 decision also initiated the episcopal district as a unit of administration in A. M. E. Zion polity. A schism resulted, during which Bishop was called to trial and refused to submit; Galbreath died; and Bishop withdrew to form the Wesleyan Methodist Church.

A verbal overture toward reunion was made first by the Bishop faction to the regular 1856 General Conference of the remainder, meeting in New York. Late in 1859 or early in 1860 representatives of both factions met in Newburgh, New York, and drew up the Newburgh Reunion Platform. This was subsequently presented to the Wesleyan General Conference but not acted upon by them. On June 1, 1860, S. T. Gray,

---

[43] See Bradley, History, pp. 127-28, for the question of the date of Miller's death and of the superintendency.

representing the mother church—Zion in New York City—invited the "Wesleyans" to hold their conference at Zion that week. The regular General Conference had already decided to meet there, so the strategy of the mother church was obvious. At this conference the Wesleyans did adopt the Newburgh Platform, and by the end of June were reunited with the regular connection.[44]

Summarily, several achievements can be credited to the General Conference of 1860. The church was united for the first time since 1852, and it was resolved "that all matters pertaining to former difficulties be laid aside forever." The principle of the supremacy of the General Conference and the equality of all superintendents elected by it was established. The new *Discipline,* which had been revised and adopted by the interim regular General Conference in a special session in 1858, was adopted, "with such revision as the wants of the connection demanded." The office of "assistant superintendent" was abolished and the term "general superintendent" discontinued. The corporate title of the denomination was changed to include "Zion," thus legalizing the designation of the denomination which the 1848 General Conference had approved, and which from its earliest history had been used to recognize the place of honor of the mother church, Zion, in New York City. Peter Ross, J. J. Clinton, and W. H. Bishop were elected to the superintendency and assigned to three districts according to a plan of two-year rotation. The *Discipline* was revised and the General Conference adjourned.

Several noteworthy things happened in the General Conference of 1864. The crucial principle of the supremacy of the General Conference and the equality of all superintendents elected by it was reaffirmed. Lay delegates were found taking their places in the General Conference that quadrennium, although equal lay representation did not come until 1928.[45] The superintendents urged organic union with the A. M. E. Church. The basis for this was the report of a committee stating that the leadership of both churches were favorably disposed to the idea. The recommendations of a subcommittee appointed later in the session were: a delegated convention should be called to consummate the union, and a committee should be appointed to prepare the constituency for the change. This report was adopted and the necessary delegates and committees appointed with the power to act. The conference voted the election of four superintendents: Joseph J. Clinton, John D. Brooks, Samson Talbot, and Jeremiah W. Loguen. Four episcopal districts were

[44] See Bradley, *History,* pp. 131-44, and Hood, *One Hundred Years,* pp. 71-79, for the story of the schism.

[45] J. W. Eichelberger, *Manual for Directors of Christian Education in the A.M.E. Zion Church* (Nashville: Parthenon Press, n.d.), p. 14.

determined and assigned. The two Southern conferences (North Carolina and Louisiana) and the one Western conference (California) were
placed in the new Fourth District.

At the 1868 General Conference, apart from receiving a negative
response from the Northern Methodist Church on the subject of reunion which Zion had offered, several important actions were taken.
The term "superintendent" was changed to "bishop" by a vote of this
body. A discussion of episcopal tenure was initiated but not concluded.
John J. Moore and Singleton T. Jones were elected bishops. Two new
episcopal districts were also added at this conference. A significant concluding action of the body was the deletion of the term "male" from
the requirement in the *Discipline* for ordination. Pursuant to this, Julia
A. Foote received ordination as a deacon in 1896, and Mary J. Small was
admitted to the order of elder in 1898.[46] This conference, also received
a report from the A. M. E. Committee on Union, stating that they were
not able at this time to consummate union but were desirous of another
effort to do so. The A. M. E. Zion body felt that they had extended themselves as far as possible on this issue already. The petition was not
granted, and the matter was tabled.

A second division almost enveloped the denomination in the interim
between the General Conferences of 1868 and 1872. This particular conflict, referred to as "the struggle of the giants," Bishops J. J. Clinton and
S. T. Jones, originated in a misunderstanding about the place of meeting
for the 1872 General Conference. Jones favored New York City as the
site of the conference, since this would also be the location of the Methodist Episcopal General Conference, with whom union conversation
could possibly be carried on as per the mutual agreements of the two
bodies in 1868. Clinton, voicing the growing doubt that union with
the Methodist Episcopal Church was any longer a live option, proposed
that the conference meet in Charlotte, North Carolina. The Annual
Conferences divided over the matter under the leadership of Jones and
Clinton, each of whom convened a General Conference in 1872 at New
York and Charlotte respectively. Jones capitulated, adjourned his body,
composed of the Genesee and Philadelphia-Baltimore Conferences, to
meet the group at Charlotte, and the matter was adjusted amicably by
the end of the conference.[47]

By 1875 the temporal economy of the church had been well established. Originally all church property was deeded to the trustees of

    [46] F. Claude Spurgeon, ed., *A.M.E. Zion Handbook* (Washington, D.C.: 1952-56),
p. 20.
    [47] Moore, *History*, pp. 265, 276-77; C. R. Harris, *Zion's Historical Catechism* (Char-
lotte: A.M.E. Zion Publishing House, 1916), pp. 33-35.

local churches to be held in trust by them for the churches. By 1880 the conveyance procedure was to deed all church property to the local trustees to be held in trust by them for the Annual Conference and the denomination. This arrangement gave to ministers, as members of the conference, and laymen, as members of local churches, proportionate equity in the property of the connection. A second feature of the temporal economy of the A. M. E. Zion Church was the office of steward. A steward was elected by the Quarterly Conference and held office for one year. In churches which were not legally incorporated, stewards acted as incorporated trustees and cared for the temporal life of the charge. This position altered some after the 1880's, and stewards gradually became responsible for the pastoral support of the church. In cases where there were no stewards, the trustees came into this responsibility.

The A. M. E. Zion ministry was in all respects governed by the same rules and practices as the Methodist Episcopal Church. It was both local and itinerant. In the matter of the episcopacy in 1868, bishops constituted an elevated office but not a separate order. The rituals for the ordination of deacons and elders—and the laying of the cornerstones of churches—were first adopted in 1872 and first inserted in the *Discipline* in 1888. In 1880 the General Conference voted to eliminate quadrennial elections of bishops, and to elect them for life or during good behavior. In 1896 an extended churchwide program was launched to increase the then very inadequate remuneration of their episcopal leaders.

In a manner similar to American Methodism generally, Zion has three "instituted conferences"—the Quarterly Conference, the Annual Conference, and the General Conference. It was probably first among American Methodist churches to grant to the laity representation in the Annual and General Conferences.

The General Conferences between 1900 and 1916 did several things that should be noted. The Conference of 1900 created a Connectional Council. This was an executive body composed of the bishops, general officers, and members of the general boards and agencies elected by the General Conference. It met annually at the place of the meeting of the Board of Bishops. Since its creation its membership composition has been revised to include the president, secretary, and treasurer of each administrative board appointed by the General Conference. The important duties of this body were to correlate the total program of the connection.

The General Conference of 1904 organized the denomination's general program and agencies into departments. Home missions, church extension, foreign missions, and Christian education were placed under the supervision of General Conference boards. Support for the agencies was apportioned to the churches as well as received from voluntary offerings.

Allocations to each agency were then to be proportionately shared among the needs and askings of the particular agency's work on the counsel of a denominationally selected board of management.

As of 1916 even further consolidation had taken place. Home missions and church extension were placed under one board, the Board of Church Extension and Home Missions. Foreign missions were assigned to the Foreign Missions Board; and educational interests, including schools and colleges, Sunday school work, and Varick Christian Endeavor Societies, remained under the Board of Education. A death benefit fund was also organized within the ministerial brotherhood in 1904.

In 1908 the General Conference authorized its bishops to participate in the first Tri-Council of Colored Methodist Bishops, held at Washington, D. C., in the Metropolitan A. M. E. Church. In 1912 an important advance was made in Christian education with the appointment of James W. Eichelberger as the first fulltime executive secretary of the A. M. E. Zion Sunday School Union.

A statistical summary of the organizational strength of Zion Methodism in 1916 revealed: bishops, 12; general officers, 24; Annual Conferences, 45; presiding elders, 126; churches, 2,716; value of churches, $7,591,393; ministers and local preachers, 3,962; members, 257,169; Sunday school teachers and pupils, 254,084; colleges and schools, 12.

Education

The earliest reference to education in the history of the A. M. E. Zion Church is in connection with the use of its New York church for public education. Bradley found this allusion in the *Minutes of the Common Council of the City of New York:* "Returns were received from the following churches of the monies given to them for the use of Schools agreeably to law wit, the German Lutheran Church, the Methodist Episcopal Church, the Scotch Presbyterian Church, and the African Church." [48] The next reference to education is found in the building plan of their first permanent edifice in 1818: "The number of the members . . . of the congregation, so rapidly increased that the Trustees . . . found their house of worship too small . . . and they were induced to consult about building a larger and more substantial house, with a school room underneath." [49] Plans for this schoolroom were abandoned after it was clear that they would not be granted the usual and necessary financial aid from the state of New York.

[48] *History*, p. 65.
[49] Rush, *A Short Account*, pp. 29-30.

RELIGIOUS EDUCATION

Subsequent efforts toward educational advancement came in the area of Sunday school work. By 1857 the New England Conference "reported 223 scholars with 36 teachers in seven schools." The connection as a whole reported to the General Conference of 1864 a total of 131 organizations, 988 teachers, 9,369 pupils, and 64,000 library books. A Sabbath School Union was also formed at this conference.

In 1888 the General Conference was memorialized to establish a denomination-wide board or organization to embrace the concerns of Sunday schools, Sunday school literature, and Annual Conference programs of religious education. This memorial was acted upon favorably, and the Board of Bishops authorized the creation of the Sunday School Union in 1889. It was placed under the supervision of the Publication Board pending the action of the ensuing General Conference of 1892. This body approved the action and elected an editor. The 1916 General Conference elected two administrative officers known as the general superintendent of Sunday schools and an editor of Sunday school literature. The Sunday School Union was redesignated the Sunday School Department and placed under the authority of a Sunday School Board elected by the General Conference.

A further development of the Sunday School Board was A. M. E. Zion youth work. Following the general pattern of the then current "Christian endeavor" movement of the 1880's, Zion religious educators organized the Varick Christian Endeavor Society. This plan for conducting youth work throughout the connection was subsequently authorized by the General Conference in the early 1900's. These societies provided a graded program of study and fellowship for intermediates (ages 12-14) and senior young people (ages 15-24).

A third educational development in Zion Methodism was the Literary Society. In the General Conference of 1860, the following resolution offered by W. F. Butler was adopted: "Resolved, that there be a Literary Society organized in this Conference, and that we recommend to the Annual Conferences to raise funds for its encouragement, and each elder establish auxiliaries to this institution in his charge." [50]

Pursuant to this resolution Literary Societies appeared in Annual Conferences and local churches. That same year the New England Conference organized a society. The Literary Society movement was basically an adult education program. Membership in it entailed the presentation of a paper on some literary, philosophical, or theological theme. These

[50] Quoted in Rufus E. Clement, "The Educational Work of the A.M.E. Zion Church, 1820-1920" (Unpublished master's thesis, Northwestern University, 1922), p. 45.

papers were read at the ensuing Annual Conference or local meeting, judged, and awarded prizes on the basis of grammar, writing, style, and logic. After having met a real need in the life of a culturally deprived and educationally neglected people, this institution expired as a general thing sometime prior to World War I.

HIGHER EDUCATION

In the field of theological and higher education the A. M. E. Zion story began with Rush Academy. Named for the venerable Christopher Rush, who in 1848 envisioned an institution for the education of ministers, this school would have been one of the first institutions for the higher education of Negroes in America. Rush Academy never claimed its destiny. Literally years of litigation to secure a clear title and deed to the property, intradenominational strife, and dereliction of responsibility on the part of those appointed by the church to attend its affairs eventuated in the abandonment of the effort by default about 1868.

Prior to 1865 an educational venture was begun in the area of ministerial training. As early as the 1850's some Annual Conferences were experimenting with courses of study. The New England Conference in 1856 required a "Course of Studies for Graduates to Holy Orders." Among other things the course included: grammar, arithmetic, geography, rules and *Discipline*, Bible, the sacraments, "Scripture doctrine," theology, and history. These subjects were to be studied with the aid of an approved list of books in these fields. The General Conference of 1860 authorized a Course of Study to be placed in the *Discipline* for local preachers and exhorters. Clement inferred from this that some academic and literary requirements were made long before this for deacons and elders.[51]

Following the Civil War, during the Reconstruction period, innumerable opportunities presented themselves to all churches and agencies in the staggering task of educating more than four million emancipated Negro slaves. Illiterate for the most part, these persons had to be provided first with the basic tools for living and working. The A. M. E. Zion Church made its contribution to the solution of this problem. Before the cessation of hostilities J. W. Hood was in North Carolina establishing churches and Sunday schools. Before 1865 an Annual Conference had been organized, 11 churches formed, and 5 Sunday schools were operating with 1,215 pupils. Under the auspices of the Negro churches, then, one of the first efforts of both secular and religious education was fostered. Other early efforts were from the various government agencies and white denominations of the North, especially the Northern Methodists. Preparation for this task and participation in it by the A. M. E.

[51] *Ibid.*, pp. 47-48.

Zion Church took the form of conference resolutions, conference organizations for religious education, specific mandates and plans to each local church for the administration of Sunday schools, and the contribution of relatively considerable sums of money for the work of the Freedmen's Bureau and similar agencies of national and state governments.

The major and unique contribution that is to be related here, however, is the establishment of a system of schools and colleges, some of which today are ready to enter their second century of service.

The first effort in this major development period was the 1868 General Conference action that, the Rush Academy plan being abandoned, an institution for manual training by the same name be started in one of the Southern states. Between 1868 and 1872 funds were collected for this proposed school, through conference "Rush University Fund" drives. It was finally decided to locate this school in North Carolina. This decision caused some disaffection on the part of the Northern conferences and accounted for the poor and nonenthusiastic response of some of the Northern conferences to the project. The end result of all of this was the founding in 1880 of the first A. M. E. Zion school, Zion Wesley Institute, at Concord, North Carolina. Previous to this, two other schools had been opened by A. M. E. Zion conferences or ministers: short-lived Zion Hill Collegiate Institute, near Pittsburgh, purchased by the Allegheny Conference and opened in 1876, and Petty High School in Lancaster, South Carolina, opened after the passage of a South Carolina law expelling Negroes from all state schools.

Other educational activity prior to 1880 was the institution of the Preacher's Institute, an in-service theological education plan conceived by the North Carolina Conference. Also during this period some of the conferences organized educational societies for the purpose of assisting "pious young men" who planned to enter the Christian ministry.

The years between 1880 and 1920 were the most active and fruitful of all in Zion Methodism's contribution to higher education. Not all of the ventures were successful. Jones University, founded about 1890 at Tuscaloosa, Alabama, by Bishop C. C. Petty, who also served as its first president, existed for about two years and is not heard of thereafter. It did have a student body of 175 and a teaching staff of 7 during the school year 1891-92. There were other similar futile attempts to establish schools at Lincolnton, North Carolina, in 1892 (Moore's Academy) and at Mobile, Alabama (Zion Institute). Parochial schools appeared in a sporadic fashion throughout the connection, lasting for unknown periods of time and leaving scant data upon which any evaluation can be made concerning their effectiveness. Clement recalled an illustrious example of one of these parochial schools related to the A. M. E. Zion Church at Tuskegee, Alabama. He stated that Booker T. Washington used the facilities of this A. M. E. Zion parochial school for two years while searching for a place to commence his work which was to eventuate in the world-famed Tuskegee Institute.[52]

Several successful school ventures were launched by the A. M. E. Zion Church between 1880 and 1920. In South Carolina, Lancaster Normal and Industrial Institute was founded by C. C. Petty in 1879. Zion Wesley Institute, previously mentioned, was founded by C. R. Harris, later a bishop, in his own home, in January, 1880. This institution, located in Salisbury, North Carolina, was renamed Livingstone College in 1882 to honor the memory of the famous missionary, David Livingstone. In 1881 Walter's Institute, the first A. M. E. Zion school west of the Mississippi River, was established in Ashley County—later moved to Warren —Arkansas, by Bishop C. R. Harris. In 1892 Zion opened Atkinson Literary and Industrial College at Madisonville, Kentucky. At this time it was the only school in western Kentucky offering a secondary education to Negroes. In 1893 Edenton Normal and Industrial Institute was founded by H. B. Pettigrew at Edenton, North Carolina. It aided greatly in supplementing the meager provisions made for Negro secondary education in the state. The second A. M. E. Zion school in South Carolina also appeared in 1893. It was the Clinton Normal and Industrial College at Rock Hill. About 1894 Greeneville College at Greeneville, Tennessee, was founded. The Lomax-Hannon High and Industrial School was established in Greenville, Alabama, in 1898. The first school founded in Georgia was the Macon High and Industrial School. Around 1899-1900 B. T. Bridges started this work near Macon. Again, in 1902 in North Carolina, William Sutton founded the Eastern North Carolina Industrial Academy at New Bern. In Virginia the A. M. E. Zion Church obtained control of the Dinwiddie Normal and Industrial School in 1907. This school had been established in 1898 and was for many years the strongest secondary school of the connection and state. In 1910, after many digressive attempts, a theological seminary—Hood—was established on the campus of Livingstone College. Sometime between 1918 and 1922 its program was reorganized and the B. D. degree was offered in addition to the diploma course.

In 1908 the General Conference at Philadelphia established the Board of Education, by which all connectional schools were to be owned and controlled. Prior to that time the various institutions were under the ownership and supervision of their respective founding conferences.

[52] *Ibid.*, pp. 82-84.

Publications

The first publication issued by the A. M. E. Zion Church was its *Discipline.* Apparently this first *Discipline* was used without revision until the 1840 General Conference. Following this, quadrennial revisions were made incorporating General Conference action. The schism of 1852-60 witnessed the rise of two *Disciplines,* but with the reunion of the warring factions, a single *Discipline* was used again and revised following each General Conference as necessity required.

Probably the earliest concrete action taken by the A. M. E. Zion Church in the publishing field was the attempt on the part of the New York Conference to initiate a connectional journal in 1841. This newspaper, which was to have been called *Zion Wesley,* never materialized. By 1860 there was another insistent demand brought before the General Conference for a monthly periodical. In this session a resolution was presented and adopted to publish a paper. The final action of this body was the adoption of the newspaper *Anglo-African* as the official organ of the connection. This arrangement seems to have continued until the meeting of the General Conference in 1868 but was never entirely satisfactory. In 1868 the Board of Bishops recommended the purchase of the *Zion Standard and Weekly Review* from Zion Church in New York. This was done, but the paper failed within a year. In 1872 or 1873 the *Zion Church Advocate* was begun in Washington, D. C., by J. P. Hamer and J. E. Price. The General Conference agreed to make this the connectional publication and manage it in 1876 but it too failed. At this point, Hood arranged for the publication of a paper at New Bern, North Carolina. This paper, the *Star of Zion,* was the first successful publication experience, and in 1880 the General Conference took charge and made it an official paper. A. S. Richardson was elected editor. In 1884 the *Star of Zion* became a weekly and has continued since as the official organ of the church. In addition to the official *Star of Zion,* there is also the *A. M. E. Zion Quarterly Review,* "a national literary and homiletic magazine," founded in 1899 by Bishop Joseph J. Clinton. The most recent publication is the *Missionary Seer,* official organ of Home and Foreign Missions for the denomination, founded in 1901.[53]

Though there are only scant records about the religious education literature for Sunday schools and Varick Christian Endeavor Societies, it was an important phase in the literary development. We have noted that

---

[53] J. Garland Penn, *The Afro-American Press and Its Editors* (Springfield, Mass.: Willey and Co., 1891), pp. 83-89; Clement, "Educational Work," pp. 42-44, 79; Hood, *One Hundred Years,* pp. 107-10; Spurgeon, *Handbook,* p. 22.

Sunday schools had existed in A. M. E. Zion churches from the very earliest period. The educational materials used in these schools from their inception to the establishment of the editorial department were probably the same as those used in the Methodist Episcopal Church. With the establishment of the publishing house the creation of some indigenous materials was possible, but many schools still relied on Methodist Episcopal materials or materials from other denominations.

The lack of necessary factual data about the evolution of the A. M. E. Zion hymnal in any of the histories or elsewhere makes the task of tracing its origin and development difficult. It can certainly be assumed that one of the several Methodist hymnals—and rituals—was used at least until the establishment of the A. M. E. Zion connection. Following their separation from the Methodist Episcopal Church, it is also reasonable to assume in view of the sentiment of the Founder's Address a Methodist Episcopal hymnal was used. On the strength of these assumptions, then, and without the evidence that there was an A. M. E. Zion hymnal up until this period, we must proceed to the first recorded words about the matter in Moore's *History*. He indicated that by 1841 there was an A. M. E. Zion hymnal. In speaking about the formation of the first publishing committee in that year he said, "They published our hymnbooks, disciplines, minutes, and other connectional matter." [54] The General Conference of 1860 "reported the Book Concern as having a stock in hymnbooks," and the same body in 1868 declared that hymnbooks were needed but not available—and the general book agent was authorized "to publish the old hymn book and the disciplines." In 1872 the General Conference heard from its publishers that it had been "unable to supply or print hymn books or disciplines . . . for want of means." At this same meeting it was suggested that "we adopt the hymn book of the M. E. Church." This recommendation was received and adopted. The Methodist Episcopal *Hymnals* were secured and imprinted with the A. M. E. Zion seal. Again in 1876 the Book Concern was in financial difficulty and hymnals were not available. This time the Book Concern sought financing from other A. M. E. Zion agencies to republish until it was completely reorganized and made solvent in 1877, at which time they immediately printed a thousand hymnals. Thus it can be seen from this survey of the Book Concern's financial dilemmas that the first A. M. E. Zion hymnal came into existence between about 1824 and 1841. This hymnal was apparently used until 1872, when the Methodist Episcopal hymnal was "adopted" and used as a substitute. In 1876, however, a new edition was probably brought out. It is not known how many revisions have been

[54] *History*, p. 318.

made since 1876. *The New Hymn and Tune Book: An Offering of Praise for the Use of the African M. E. Zion Church of America* appears to have been adopted in 1888. "The Bishops' Address" in the current hymnal, 1957, mentions, "For some time we have realized the need of a Hymn book containing more of the modern hymns than the one we have been using."

In 1908 the effort to develop a common hymnal by the A. M. E., A. M. E. Zion, and C. M. E. initiated a series of joint meetings which lasted for thirty years. The C. M. E.'s first withdrew from such conversations, but the A. M. E. and the A. M. E. Zion groups continued until 1940.

The A. M. E. Zion Publishing House has a full and interesting background. It began as the New York Conference Book Concern in the mother Zion Church, New York City, about 1841. Jacob D. Richardson was appointed as the first general book steward; and together with a small committee they published the hymn books, *Disciplines, Minutes,* and connectional pieces. In 1844, following the death of Richardson, the General Conference appointed a committee to manage the concern —J. P. Thompson, W. H. Bishop, and T. Eatto. In 1856 the General Conference appointed a General Book Committee to supervise the Book Concern. In 1860 trustees were elected and in 1864 a printer named. From 1860 to 1880 the Publishing House encountered recurring periods of financial difficulty. In 1880 it was moved to Petersburg, Virginia. As the A. M. E. Zion Church began to expand southward, the plant was moved to Salisbury, North Carolina; and by 1900 it was permanently located in the then new and commodius Varick Memorial Building in Charlotte, North Carolina.

Missions

The missionary work of the A. M. E. Zion Church functioned under two auspices, the Woman's Home and Foreign Missionary Society, founded in 1880, and the Department of Foreign Missions of the General Conference Board of Foreign Missions, established in 1892. Missionary activity in the church, however, antedates these organizations by more than two decades. Moore mentioned that the General Conference of 1856 called for a report of the Demerara (British Guiana, South America) Mission; and, "after several letters from the mission were read, in which Rev. R. C. Henderson informed the Conference that he could not be present, his term having expired, he was not re-elected Superintendent of the mission." From this interchange of correspondence Demerara seems to have been the earliest foreign mission of the church, and apparently it had been in existence for several years. The fate of the Demerara work is not known, since no further mention was made of it.

At the 1856 General Conference Moore also reported that "the Conference then by resolution set off an Annual Conference in the province of Nova Scotia and authorization was granted for the convening of this body in September, 1857." [55] The work in Canada grew slowly. In 1860 it was represented at the General Conference, but the intervening war years and preoccupation with the new Southern work, 1861-78, saw this mission neglected. In 1879 the Canadian work was merged with that of the Michigan Conference.

The earliest successful foreign missionary work of the A. M. E. Zion Church began in Liberia, to which Andrew Cartwright was sent in 1876. The next permanent work was established in the East Gold Coast (Ghana) Colony at Keta in 1898 by Thomas B. Freeman. Work on the West Gold Coast did not begin until 1903, when a national, Osam-Pinanko, organized a mission at Cape Coast. Both Freeman and Osam-Pinanko opened their respective missions under the supervision of Bishop John B. Small, A. M. E. Zion's first resident African bishop.[56] Missionary work in South America was resumed at Georgetown, British Guiana, by William A. Deane in 1911.

3

Relations with Other Groups

The rise and growth of the two major independent Negro Methodist churches has not been one of uninterrupted accord. Since their early beginnings in the 1780's until as late as the 1930's, each group has experienced divisions and schisms. In connection with the A. M. E. Zion Church, between 1800 and 1812 Abraham Thompson and June Scott of Zion Church in New York defected and organized an ill-fated and short-lived Union Society, and in 1813 Thomas Sipkins and William Miller formed the Asbury Church, which they had intended to be Methodist but separate and distinct from Zion. In the A. M. E. Church as early as 1816, at the seat of the Organizing Convention and just prior to the ratifica-

[55] *History*, p. 221.
[56] Cameron C. Alleyne, *Gold Coast at a Glance* (Pelham, N.Y.: published for the author, 1931), pp. 52, 113-14, 116-18.

tion of the Ecclesiastical Compact, the first schism of that body occurred when the African Union Church in Wilmington, Delaware, withdrew from the Convention and formed a separate church. Thus, they never became a part of the A. M. E. connection.[57]

The development of A. M. E. work in Canada produced two divisions. One was a voluntary, nonschismatic separation from the American body (British Methodist Episcopal) while the other (Independent Methodist Episcopal) was a schismatic division of the B. M. E. Church.

African Methodist societies had existed in Canada since 1826. In 1827 a preacher was requested, and in 1832 Jeremiah Miller of the New York Conference was sent there as a missionary. By 1839 churches existed at Niagara, St. David, St. Catherine's, Toronto, Malden, Hamilton, and Brandford. In 1840 the A. M. E. Upper Canada Conference was organized at Toronto under Bishop Morris Brown. This territory was especially promising for A. M. E. missions because large numbers of Negro fugitive slaves had taken refuge there as an asylum from the stringencies and atrocities of the various slave laws of the United States. Following the organization of the Canadian work, however, for various reasons it was neglected. The Canadians sought to remedy this by electing a superintendent of their own, for which they were severely rebuked and individually impeached. In 1856 Benjamin Stuart petitioned the A. M. E. General Conference to form an independent body of African Methodists in Canada. The resolution was adopted and the formation of the new church begun. The last session of the A. M. E. Canadian Conference was held in Chatham on September 29, 1856, at 10:00 A.M. At 12:00 noon that same day the organizing convention of the new denomination was convened, with Samuel H. Brown as chairman. The name adopted was British Methodist Episcopal Church. The Articles of Faith in the *Discipline* of the A. M. E. Church were adopted, except the twenty-third, for which a substitute was prepared acknowledging the sovereignty and protection of the Queen of England. The A. M. E. *Discipline* was adopted with such changes as might be necessary for its use and authority in Canada. The hymnal of the parent body was also put into use. After considerable discussion concerning the election of an episcopal leader, Bishop W. H. Nazrey was duly elected. The boundaries of the new denomination were set to be Canada and South America. Circuits and stations were set off, and the first General Conference was appointed to meet in Toronto in September, 1860. The history of the B. M. E. Church began with its first Annual Conference at Toronto in October, 1856. The Nova

[57] John M. Brown, "Richard Allen and His Co-adjutors," *Repository of Religion and Literature,* January, 1861, pp. 1-4.

Scotia Annual Conference was organized at Liverpool, July 31, 1868; the British Guiana Conference at Georgetown on April 8, 1873; and the Bermuda Conference at Hamilton on May 13, 1873.[58]

Some time between 1860 and 1870 a schism took place in the B. M. E. Church. Augustus R. Green and his son A. M. Green, together with others of like persuasion, withdrew and organized the Independent Methodist Episcopal Church. Green was elected a bishop of this group, and they remained together as a separate and independent body until 1876. In that year they petitioned the Indiana Conference, which in turn petitioned the A. M. E. General Conference of 1876 that they be reunited. The petition was granted with the proviso that Green resign his episcopal office. This was complied with, and the I. M. E. Church reunited with the A. M. E. Church at the close of that session of the General Conference. Efforts toward reunion by the B. M. E. Church were initiated in 1880. A joint committee was raised to reunite the Canadian church, and by 1884 the two bodies were one again.[59]

There were other smaller schismatic groups that split off from the A. M. E. and A. M. E. Zion bodies. In 1840 numbers of Negro members of various Negro Methodist churches in and around Baltimore met in Elkton, Maryland, and established the Colored Methodist Protestant Church. They were probably influenced by the Methodist Protestant movement of more than a decade before, but they were not related to it organically. Shaw pointed out that this group was not to be confused with the six small Annual Conferences of Negroes who were to be found in the Methodist Protestant Church at the time of unification in 1939. These were from South Carolina, Alabama, and Texas. Their forebearers had followed their masters when the Methodist Protestants separated from the Methodist Episcopal Church. In Alabama and Texas in 1852 a Colored Congregational Methodist denomination was formed. This body was an outgrowth of the white Congregational Methodists of that region, themselves a split from the Southern Church over matters pertaining to the episcopacy and itinerancy.[60]

A third small independent Negro Methodist denomination that appeared after the Civil War was the Reformed Zion Union Apostolic Church in southeastern Virginia. The origin of this body is interesting. The Negroes were no longer welcome to attend the white Methodist churches in their region, and they did not wish to affiliate with either the A. M. E. or A. M. E. Zion Churches. They had no ministerial leader-

[58] Payne, *History of the A.M.E. Church*, pp. 361-92.
[59] Jenifer, *Centennial Retrospect History*, pp. 371-75, 338-40.
[60] Shaw, *Negro in the History of Methodism*, pp. 89-90. Du Bois, *The Negro Church*, p. 44.

ship among them, yet they still desired to remain Methodist. Their situation was aided by James R. Howell, an A. M. E. Zion preacher from New York. Howell met with the leaders of this group at Boydton, Virginia, in 1869 and there organized them into the Zion Union Apostolic Church. Howell became their first president and later their first bishop. Following a period of disorganization, John M. Bishop reorganized the group in 1881 and reunited the warring factions. In 1882 their name became Reformed Zion Union Apostolic Church.

Another small schismatic group was the Free Christian Zion Church of Christ. This body was founded by E. D. Brown, a conference missionary of the A. M. E. Zion Church in Redemption, Arkansas, in 1905. Its membership had withdrawn from Methodist Episcopal, A. M. E., A. M. E. Zion, C. M. E., and Baptist Churches. The ostensible cause for the separation of the several ministers from their denominations was a protest movement against overhead connectional taxation. It was their belief that such matters were for local church determination. In 1916 this body, composed of about thirty-five local churches and claiming more than six thousand members, was essentially Methodistic in all matters of doctrine and polity excepting a few. A "chief pastor" was selected from among them to preside over the entire denomination. All appointments to pastorates and other offices were made by him. A "general assembly" replaced the Methodist General Conference, and laymen were prominent in its church affairs.

In 1873 at Baltimore an African American Methodist Episcopal Church was organized. This group represented a small number of Negro Methodist ministers who had come from various other Negro Methodist connections "to form a more modern and reformed Methodism and Christian religion." They did not differ significantly from their several parent bodies in doctrine or government. They made appointments to churches in Maryland, Virginia, Delaware, Pennsylvania, Ohio, Indiana, New York, Illinois, Massachusetts, New Jersey, and the District of Columbia. As of 1916, the first report year of this denomination, it claimed 28 churches, 1,310 members, 6 Sunday schools with 200 pupils, and 35 ministers.

The Reformed Methodist Union Episcopal Church was founded in 1884, when a sizable number of ministers and laymen withdrew from the A. M. E. Church because of the manner of electing ministerial delegates to the General Conference. The issue was their disapproval of the action of Bishop William F. Dickerson, who, in conducting the election of the delegates of the South Carolina Conference to the ensuing General Conference, insisted upon electing them by voice vote rather than by ballot. In 1885 a convention of delegates from South Carolina and Georgia concerned about this issue met under the leadership of William E. Johnson and organized the "Independent Methodist Church" with Johnson as president. In 1896 this name was reconsidered and changed to "Reformed Methodist Union Episcopal Church." In 1899 E. Russell Middleton was elected to the episcopacy of this body by their General Conference and consecrated by a white bishop of the Reformed Episcopal Church, Peter F. Stevens. Later bishops elected by the R. M. U. E. Church were consecrated by the imposition of hands by other elders.

An Independent A. M. E. Church was organized in 1897 at Jacksonville, Florida. Its establishment was the result of the dissatisfaction of some A. M. E. pastors with certain presiding elders regarding matters of church administration. This body adopted their own *Discipline,* but retained the Articles of Religion and General Rules of African Methodism. In 1900 there was a split within the Independent A. M. E. Church originating in the same cause that occasioned the break with the A. M. E.'s in 1897. This body, which likewise referred to itself as the Independent A. M. E. Church, organized at Coldwater, Mississippi, in July of that same year. Their polity excluded presiding elders altogether. From 1900 until 1919 the two branches of the I. A. M. E. Church remained apart. In 1919 "Articles of Confederation" were drawn up by a joint body of their bishops, which were later ratified, thus reuniting these factions in 1920.

Union Proposals

The contacts and relationships of the A. M. E. and A. M. E. Zion Churches with the Methodist Episcopal Church from 1816 to 1916 were many and varied. In the founding period of the A. M. E. Church, while the vicissitudes of separation were being experienced, and after this event, Negroes felt that the Northern Church was hostile. Payne said,

The animosity shown by the Methodist Episcopal Church does not reflect any lustre or glory, but rather stands as a strain upon her credit—not wanting the colored people, yet unwilling to let them go; and when of their own accord the despised members separated, resorting to subterfuge, and invoking the action of the law to compel them to return to their position of vassalage and ill-usage.[61]

[61] *History of the A.M.E. Church,* p. 52.

Hood's observation reinforced this feeling as he spoke for the A. M. E. Zion Church: "The ministers of the several denominations were opposed to the movement [independent Negro churches], especially the Methodist ministers, including a majority of the bishops; and the episcopal form of government was favorable to the purpose of the Methodist ministers to hinder the success of the colored brethren in their effort to be free." [62]

During the first organizational years of both African Methodist denominations, however, there were many needs that bound these fledgling churches to their parent. Both churches adopted the *Discipline,* doctrines, hymnody, and ritual of the Methodist Episcopal Church. Hood spoke to the matter of ritual specifically when he observed, "Our ministers have long used the ritual of the Methodist Episcopal Church in performing the ceremonies." [63] The problem of ordination for the A. M. E. Zionites, however, proved to be more than the mother church felt it could solve, and they were finally forced to seek satisfaction elsewhere. Despite this fact Zion used individual preachers of the Methodist Episcopal Church who were kindly disposed to their independent church. Rush stated in 1829, "The preachers of the old connexion of our white brethren manifested a very friendly disposition towards us, so that Jacob Matthews . . . easily effected arrangements with them to fill appointments [to preach]." [64] As Bradley indicated, "The deep feeling of resentment was not against the ministry of John Street but rather the New York Conference." [65]

The A. M. E.'s experienced the same relationship to the Methodist Episcopal Church in some of their contacts with them. In speaking of the A. M. E. General Conference of 1844, held in Pittsburgh, Payne had this to say: "Their churches were kindly opened for the preaching of our clergy, and many of them daily attended the deliberations of the Conference." [66]

It is perhaps in the field of religious education, however, that the greatest liberality of spirit and deed were manifested toward the young Negro Methodist bodies. In 1856 Wilberforce University opened under the joint sponsorship of the A. M. E. and the Northern Methodist Churches. This relationship continued until 1863, when the A. M. E.'s bought the institution from the Northern Church and operated it for themselves. A similar spirit of Christian aid was shown by "the unselfish

[62] *One Hundred Years,* p. 7.
[63] *Ibid.,* p. 97.
[64] Rush, *A Short Account,* p. 84.
[65] *History,* p. 104.
[66] *History of the A.M.E. Church,* p. 173.

and self-sacrificing . . . men and women who . . . established schools . . . under the auspices of the Freedmen's Aid Society of the Methodist Episcopal Church" during and after the Civil War.[67] In addition to this there is some indication that Negroes were rather generally admitted to most of the white Methodist colleges in the North and West.

The first provision for A. M. E. Sunday school literature was made possible through a plan of co-operative use involving the publishing press and facilities of the Southern Church at Nashville, from 1886 to 1888. Arnett reported: "In 1886, through the goodwill and great liberality of the Publishing House of the M. E. Church, South, we were able to complete arrangements that would enable the [Sunday School] Union to furnish quarterlies and lesson papers to our schools." [68]

The Civil War period produced some interesting contacts with the Methodist Episcopal Churches. In 1863 "a Rev. Mr. Lee of New York city, a minister of the Methodist Episcopal Church, visited the [Baltimore] Conference with the view of securing some colored ministers to go as missionaries to South Carolina." When it was explained to him that the A. M. E. Church had once operated in South Carolina and intended to do so again independently, he said, "The field is yours; go and occupy it." The Southern Church in 1863 gave their North Street Church in Portsmouth, Virginia, to the A. M. E.'s. In 1864 Northern Church fraternal delegates came to the A. M. E. General Conference for the first time, beginning a continual though intermittent practice.[69]

This period also produced strife and rivalry. Often the Northern Church in its zealous attempts to enlarge its denominational holdings would obstruct the work of the Negro denominations in recruiting the emancipated slaves. A case in point was the situation that developed around the New Bern, North Carolina, church, in which the claims of the A. M. E. Zionites, Northern Methodists, and white Congregationalists had to be adjudicated by the Union Army authorities.

Apart from the inter-Methodist relationships and co-operative ventures that have been mentioned, there were other areas and levels of contact between the Negro Methodist groups and the Northern and Southern Churches in the various interdenominational and ecumenical movements here and abroad. Since 1881 both A. M. E.'s and A. M. E. Zionites have been active in the Ecumenical Methodist Conferences. In 1884 they also united to celebrate the Centennial of American Methodism. Both hold membership in the National Council of Churches and the World Council.

[67] Smith, *History of the A.M.E. Church*, p. 73.
[68] *Centennial Budget*, pp. 150-51.
[69] Smith, *History of the A.M.E. Church*, pp. 51-57.

IV

A
Flourishing
Church
in a
Prospering
Nation

"Building two a day!"

1876-1919

A Flourishing Church in a Prospering Nation

THE HISTORIAN'S PREOCCUPATION WITH CHANGE IN HUMAN AFFAIRS MAY easily yield a distorted picture of the later nineteenth century. Without probing very deep a long list of similarities between the America of 1900 and that of 1860 can be compiled. The people still lived predominately on farms and in villages; the main interests of Americans continued to be largely confined within national boundaries; and individualism, self-help, unlimited opportunity, and progress persisted as the principal constituents of the popular creed. Even the group and sectional conflicts, population movements, industrial growth, and urbanization that gave an immensely dynamic quality to the period have histories that long antedate the Civil War. Yet if flux and newness were not the whole of the period, they were among its prominent realities. Strong-running social and economic currents were rapidly eroding the forms, habits, and attitudes of a society that by the standards of the twentieth century was simple and innocent. The odyssey which that scion of a great American family, Henry Adams, recorded in his autobiography was shared by many other sensitive Americans. The social order that they had understood and felt secure in at mid-century seemed to have slipped away by 1900.

An era that so readily boasted of creation and progress began in an orgy of destruction. In the human and material resources that were commandeered to fight it, and the depth of sacrifice it demanded of the entire people, the Civil War was "total." It is one of the ironies of our history that the results of the war varied so widely from the exalted purposes proclaimed by each side as reasons for doing battle. Contrary to the often confident predictions, the war did not bring to the South political or economic independence or heightened respect among the peoples of the world. Rather, its harvest was sectional humiliation, relegation to an inferior position in national affairs, and blight to the economy of the region. The North, though victorious, must be counted only partially successful in enforcing its trinity of aims—union, freedom, and equality—announced during the war or immediately thereafter. While the threat to national unity was turned back, the restored South became more solid in its politics than ever before and remained wedded to salient features of its traditional culture. Freedom, defined merely as

585

the abolition of slavery, was an irreversible consequence of the war, but the failure to link effectively equality with freedom often gave to the latter a restricted practical meaning. Negro and white Americans alike felt the effects of this failure. For the Negro they were registered in his economic degradation, his cultural poverty, and his social ostracism. For the whites was posed the acute moral dilemma of upholding freedom, justice, and equality as universal rights yet suffering a racial line to be drawn around the full enjoyment of them.

As older sections of the nation wrestled with the legacy of war, the lineaments of a new society emerged in the broad reaches of the trans-Mississippi West. On the eve of the Civil War, the region bounded roughly by the ninety-sixth meridian, the Pacific slope, Canada, and Mexico, comprising more than two fifths of the land surface of the country, was little known and lightly esteemed. Most Americans looked upon it chiefly as an inhospitable barrier to communications between the states of the Mississippi Valley and settlements along the Pacific. Save for isolated Spanish and Mormon settlements, it was the preserve of widely scattered Indian peoples. After 1860, however, the abundant mineral wealth of the region, a growing acquaintance with its potentialities for food production, and public land policies that often seemed to seek the most rapid disposition of the public domain instead of its wisest use helped to lure population over the plains and even into mountain and desert regions. By 1900 twelve states had been carved out of a geographical area that many, fifty years earlier, had declared unfit for human habitation. The settlement of the last continental frontier carried with it a resolution of the centuries-long struggle waged by Indian peoples in defense of their distinctive civilizations. Their strength of resistance finally sapped by military defeat and, more covertly, by aggressions against the economic foundations of their aboriginal cultures, the Indians everywhere had been restricted to reservations before the end of the century. There, under federal supervision, policies were applied that intended the eradication of their traditional folkways and their eventual integration into a larger society.

The courage, perseverance, and ingenuity that went into the settlement of the West have been memoralized in the folk literature of the nation. Too easily overlooked is the part played by the prosaic and impersonal forces of economics. Without the mechanization of agriculture and land transportation the natural environment of much of the trans-Mississippi region would have slowed or, for a long time, prevented the westward flow of population. The transformation of the West, however, was only one of the results of the technological innovations and industrial expansion that were moving over America at a rapid rate. The statistics of growth in basic industries forcibly indicate the economic momentum and direction of the later nineteenth century. The railroad mileage of the nation increased by 650 per cent between 1860 and 1900. In the same period the output of coal multiplied almost twenty-five times, crude iron and steel almost thirty times, and petroleum more than six hundred times. These sensational gains were echoed through the whole economy. While the nation's population increased only two and a half times in the forty years after the Civil War, the amount of capital invested in manufacturing establishments was multiplied by fifteen and the value of their products grew more than tenfold. The census of 1890 related the monumental change that had taken place in the economic base of American life. For the first time in the history of the United States, the total value of manufactured commodities exceeded that of agriculture.

The foundation the nineteenth century laid for an economic establishment that one day would be capable of fantastic abundance ranks perhaps as its greatest achievement. Even before the end of the century untold numbers of Americans had experienced the benefits of industrialization in enlarged conveniences and more luxuries. More immediately, however, the great material rewards of industrialization were conspicuously concentrated in the class which owned or controlled industrial property. The progress in equitably distributing wealth ran behind the progress in producing it. In 1900, a year in which the average annual wage of the American worker was little more than five hundred dollars, a steel tycoon enjoyed a personal income well in excess of twenty million—without having to share any of it with the income tax collector.

The immense fortunes that were accumulated, the prodigality with which they were spent, and the ostentatious display they sometimes induced led Mark Twain to dub the period the "Gilded Age." The hundred-room mansions that sprang up on New York's Fifth Avenue and the fifty-room "summer cottages" at Newport symbolized the arrival of a plutocracy striving to become an aristocracy. By his success the captain of industry reshaped not only the physical environment of his fellow citizens but often their values and aspirations. "Get rich! Get rich! I say it is your duty to get rich" was one of the popular texts of the post–Civil War generation. Americans in more rustic times had found their heroes in the statesman-farmer, the soldier-patriot, and the frontiersman. In the flush years of the nineteenth century they often looked for them in the financier and the industrial magnate.

Yet the celebration of the new order fell far short of unanimity. Industrial change involved the disruption of traditional forms of workmanship, the rupture of old economic relationships, and a redistribution of property and influence which welled up in social protest. A center of this protest was among the industrial wage earners, a class whose rate of increase between 1860 and 1900 was almost twice that of the total population. The unrest of labor was compounded from a myriad of factors. The obsolescence of ancient skills by mechanization, periodic downturns in the business cycle, the tendency of wages to increase more slowly than living costs, the high frequency of accidents, the insecurity of job tenure, and disappointed attempts to rise to the ranks of businessmen each contributed a portion. On several occasions this discontent flared into violence. In 1877, 1892, and 1894 strikes in major industries degenerated into open warfare. The massive bitterness exhibited by both sides in these encounters shocked a people who were accustomed to think of employment merely as a matter of personal negotiation between owner and worker. A more common and, in the long run, a more effective response to industrialization was the resort to unionization. By 1880 organized labor had begun to recover from the shattering blows delivered by the depression of 1873, and with the formation of the American Federation of Labor in 1886 the labor movement approached unprecedented heights of unity. Although the American Federation of Labor could claim the adherence of only a minor fraction of workers and was relatively ineffective in organizing the great mass-production industries, the modern labor movement may be dated from its founding. Taking a leaf from the book of business, it sought to enlarge labor's power and influence in the industrial state through organized bigness.

The waves of unrest set up by industrialization rose even higher among agricultural interests of the South and West. Stung by the growing disparity between commodity prices and the costs of agricultural production, many farmers imitated labor in seeking protection through organization. Agricultural alliances, associations, and granges sprang up in profusion after 1870. These organizations attacked the plight of the farmer on the economic and political fronts. In an effort to relieve the squeeze caused by declining farm income and increased capital expenditures they instituted co-operatives for the marketing of farm products, the purchase of supplies and equipment, and the financing of agricultural projects. Before 1860 co-operatives made little headway among farmers, but by 1900 nearly half of the farm families of the nation had subscribed to the movement.

Agricultural distress also found an outlet in several splinter political parties in which the antipathy to industrial and financial concentration ran strong. The failure of either the Democrats or Republicans to pay adequate heed to the rumblings from rural sections turned some farmers to the support of the Granger, Greenback, and Anti-Monopoly parties

of the 1870's and '80's. In the last decade of the century these were succeeded by the Populist party which, more than any other important
political movement in American history, spoke for a single economic
interest. Although it faded almost as rapidly as it blossomed, Populism
momentarily swelled to proportions that seemed to seriously threaten
the existing party structure. Despite a poorly conducted campaign the
Populist candidate for president in 1892 polled more than a million
votes, and the party became a potent element in the politics of a dozen
states. The inroads of Populism stirred the major political organizations to move off dead center. Under the threat of party destruction the
Democrats in the presidential election of 1896 tailored a platform to fit
rural unrest and nominated a son of the middle border, William Jennings
Bryan, as their standard-bearer.

But the meaning of Populism was not summed up in its protests
against "monopolistic bankers and industrialists." In the fullest sense
it was a reaction to the decline of rural influence in national affairs and of
agriculture as a way of life. The most dramatic demographic trend between 1860 and 1900 was not the westward drift of population but its
growing concentration in towns and cities. According to the census of
1860 less than 20 per cent of all Americans lived in communities of
2,500 or more. By 1900 the percentage had risen to 40. Towns and cities
sprang up in open fields, and older cities became the nucleuses of metropolitan areas that held vast hinterlands tributary to them. In each of
the last four decades of the nineteenth century the population of New
York City grew by a half million, and that of Chicago rhythmically
doubled. Only eleven American cities could count more than a hundred
thousand inhabitants in 1860. The total in 1900 stood at forty-five.

In these great urban centers the promise and the threat of a civilization undergoing metamorphosis swung into sharpest focus. The schools,
museums, theaters, libraries, concert halls, and public gardens that dotted
the urban landscapes heralded the bountiful opportunities that city life
afforded. Yet the leavening effects of urbanization were mixed with grim
symptoms of social and political disorganization. The hasty and un-
planned growth of cities almost guaranteed that facilities conducive to
health, comfort, and security would drag behind. Noise, congestion, and
filth reduced legions of city dwellers to brute levels of existence and, too
often, official venality held them there. An illustrious British observer of
life in the United States declared that the late-nineteenth-century city
represented the most conspicuous failure of American democracy. His
verdict was incomplete, but it pointed to soft spots in the American
social order worthy of the fullest energies of reformers.

To a degree not always appreciated urban growth fed off a large, if incalculable, exodus from the countryside. Between 1860 and 1900 the growth rate of the nonfarm population was at least eight times greater than that of the farm, and much of the difference must be attributed to the cityward movement of people who had been born to agricultural occupations. In the northeastern states, parts of the country deserved the poetic description that Goldsmith in "The Deserted Village" earlier gave to the rural areas of England. More than half the townships of New England lost population between 1880 and 1900. While opinion-makers continued to preach that contact with nature and the soil was necessary to the good life, many in their rural audiences acted out a contrary belief.

The cities, however, were safety valves for rural depression and failure in Europe as well as in the United States. From 1860 to 1900 fourteen million Europeans immigrated to the United States, more than twice the total of the preceding forty years. The swelling tide of immigration was accompanied by a shift in its sources from northern and western Europe to the southern and eastern parts of the continent. In the 1870's the British Isles, Germany, and Scandanavia contributed 90 per cent of the newcomers. By the end of the century more than half came from Italy, Russia, and the Austro-Hungarian Empire. But irrespective of place of birth, the vast majority of immigrants were of peasant stock, uprooted from familiar soil by overpopulation, innovations in the use and ownership of land, and political oppression. Even though thousands managed to resume agricultural pursuits in their adopted land, the city became the typical home of the immigrant in America. In 1900 one seventh of the American population was foreign born, and of these fully three fourths were classified as urban. That urban society withstood the shock of an immense immigration bespoke its strength and flexibility, but heavy strains were put upon it. The nagging social problems of the city, when sliced another way, often were the problems of the immigrant.

Any historical sketch true to the facts of nineteenth-century America will be largely an account of internal affairs. While some Americans—scientists, scholars, and men of letters, in particular—were members of an international community, the common run of their fellows were engrossed in domestic affairs. The century-long period of peace in Europe which followed the overthrow of Napoleon in 1815 reinforced the sense of national sufficiency latent in the geographical isolation of the United States. The acquisition of Alaska in 1867 and simultaneous overtures to annex Canada and islands in the Caribbean were not real exceptions to the introverted character of American interests. They were, instead, primarily outgrowths of personal adventures in diplomacy which lacked a solid base in public opinion. Into the 1890's arguments of the needless-ness of American commitments beyond the continent were effectively used to keep the military and diplomatic arms of government the smallest by far of those of any major country in the western world.

Towards the end of the century, however, unmistakable evidences appeared of an incipient breakdown of American insularity. For scores of years American missionaries and merchants had been at work in distant lands. To the interest they had generated were added, in the last quarter of the century, the need of an expanding economy for foreign markets and materials and the bumptious energies left unexpended from the settlement of the continent. The short and victorious Spanish-American War of 1898 is a convenient place from which to mark America's entry into internationalism. The acquisition of the Philippines from Spain forced the United States into an attentive concern with events in the Far East, while the addition of Puerto Rico and the establishment of a protectorate over Cuba swelled public interest in Latin America. Hawaii, in 1898, and Samoa, in 1899, were other territorial prizes grasped by a nation growing conscious of empire. Involvement in the technologically backward areas of the world also pulled the United States closer to the ken of Europe, for in Latin America, the Orient, and the South Pacific American ambitions mingled and clashed with those of various European powers. Tentative and inchoate as these overseas entanglements were, they nonetheless harbingered the era in which no knowledgeable citizen could say, if indeed he ever could, that the United States was a nation entire in itself.

A balance sheet for the late nineteenth century is not easily prepared. The best-informed students of the period differ sharply in their judgments. Generally, these judgments divide along the line that separates material accomplishment from equity in the dealings of man with man. The record of the era in regard to the first is fairly clear. The post–Civil War generation inherited a partially settled continent, vast reservoirs of untapped natural wealth, and an economy that in its productive capabilities was infantile. It bequeathed to the twentieth century a settled continental domain, together with the organized technological means of turning the natural endowments of the nation to human purposes. These were not contemptible gains. However, in the sphere of human relationships the returns are not as bright. The bigotry visited upon persons whose race, color, or creed seemed alien and the recurrent disregard of human dignity in the name of economic progress were stark reminders that all was not well in the land. Yet the generation often excused even its glaring failures as mere detours on the road to a better tomorrow. Fortunately, there were always Americans who insisted that tomorrow must come.

chapter 24

THE
THEOLOGY
AND
PRACTICES
OF
METHODISM

1876-1919

Theological Emphases

Holiness Crusade

Worship

Discipline

Training Youth

The Ministry

R APID AND FAR-REACHING CHANGE IN belief and practice was in store for the Methodist people as they entered the last quarter of the nineteenth century. Within forty years the reliance upon revelation as man's sole source of the knowledge of God was challenged by the appeal to reason in the quest for religious knowledge. Man's understanding of himself was expanded through the insights of psychology. The strongly pietistic legacy of the revival movement was confronted by a growing ethical interest in the nature of the good and man's moral obligation. Individualism encountered a sociological emphasis upon the implications of racial continuity and solidarity. The heavenly hope was qualified by the recognition of truth to be found through study of the science of the world. The liberating influence of German idealism was active in the mind of Methodism.

As may be expected, such extensive developments in belief and their influence upon practice met resistance and aroused antagonism. Groups of Methodists intent upon retaining a central emphasis upon individual and personal holiness were formed. Before the end of the century the holiness reaction was organized in opposition to the general trend in Methodist thought and behavior. Controversy was precipitated also over the fundamentalist-modernist issue. The rigors of personal discipline were relaxed in practices, dress, and diversion. Social activities introduced into the program of the church influenced the architecture of the church building. Class meetings were replaced by organized classes in the Sunday school. A better-educated Methodist constituency began to demand a more adequately trained ministry. To some it seemed that prosperity was sapping the spiritual vitality of the church. For the great majority these changes were recognized as the characteristics of the Methodist movement growing in breadth and maturity to minister to men in a period of accelerated change in the life of a growing nation.

1

The Changing Theological Emphases

In 1876 American Methodism, in spite of being divided in its organizational structure, was predominantly of one voice in its theology. The evangelical Arminianism which it had received from John Wesley guided the main stream of Methodist preaching. The pages of *Zion's Herald* and the *Christian Advocate* rang with the clash of armaments in encounter with Calvinism. The columns of *The Methodist Quarterly Review* continued to support the Arminianism of its founder and mentor, Nathan Bangs. Although the first American Methodist Journal, *The Arminian Magazine,* had survived only a few issues, its emphasis upon God's universal grace, freely given and freely received, had not been displaced nor weakened. A description of Methodist preaching during the first century of the movement can be applied with accuracy to the theology of Methodism at the beginning of the last quarter of the nineteenth century:

> With almost ceaseless iteration the preachers taught the doctrines of universal depravity, universal redemption, the witness of the Spirit or Christian assurance, the duty of testimony, and sanctification or Christian perfection . . . and they proclaimed the five universals: that all men needed salvation; that all men might be saved; that all men might know themselves saved; that all should declare their salvation; and that all might perfect holiness in the fear of the Lord.[1]

The sources of Methodist theology were the Bible, John Wesley's standard sermons, his *Notes upon the New Testament,* and Richard Watson's *Theological Institutes.* The insights gained through this reading were to be tested by experience and proclaimed with evangelizing concern. These works, together with W. B. Pope's *A Compendium of Christian Theology,* made up the core of the theological studies in the Conference Course of

[1] W. J. Townsend, H. B. Workman. George Eayrs, *A New History of Methodism* (London: Hodder and Stoughton, 1909), I, 305-6.

Study in both the Methodist Episcopal Church and the Methodist Episcopal Church, South. Watson's *Institutes* began by tracing the "Evidences of the Divine Authority of the Holy Scriptures," continued with an investigation of the traditional structure of doctrines derived from the Scriptures, and closed with sections dealing with "The Morals" and "The Institutions" of Christianity. "The doctrine of the redemption of all mankind" was elaborated in opposition to the Calvinist teaching, with its doctrines of election, predestination, and partial redemption.[2]

Methodism was justified to continue its existence, it was held, only as it could be shown to be "eminently personal and experimental." The Christian life was regarded as including both faith and personal discipline.[3] Methodist theology, as it was preached and popularly accepted, was regarded as a restatement of the postulates of apostolic Christianity, interpreted in the light of actual or possible personal experience.

Many of the teachers of theology in the theological seminaries added their voices in the cause of evangelical Arminianism. T. O. Summers at Vanderbilt published his *Systematic Theology* as a "Complete Body of Wesleyan Arminian Divinity." William Fairfield Warren and Henry C. Sheldon at Boston continued to trace the footprints of Arminius and to stress God's gracious purpose to extend salvation to all men. John J. Tigert and Wilbur Fisk Tillett carried forward in Southern Methodism the doctrinal discussion with Arminian emphases. Milton S. Terry and Miner Raymond at Garrett interpreted the atonement as the fulfillment of the universal divine saving will. At Drew the voices of John Miley, Olin A. Curtis, and Randolph S. Foster were raised in strong support of the rights of Arminian theology against the Calvinism which Methodism was encountering.

Yet there were also new influences at work shaping the mind of Methodism in the days of restored peace and prosperity, both North and South, in the decades following the Civil War. Popular skepticism regarding the adequacy of revelation as the source of knowledge led to greater attention to reason in religion. John Miley, who was professor of systematic theology at Drew Theological Seminary, was a strong champion of the rights of reason. Faith without a rational foundation, he held, could not long be maintained. The paths of advanced theological study led to the German universities. When men who had received their training on the European continent began to teach in the Methodist theological semi-

[2] Richard Watson, *Theological Institutes* (New York: Emory and Waugh, 1831), pp. 351 ff.

[3] Daniel Curry, "Possible Perils of Methodism from Modern Skepticism," *Proceedings of the Oecumenical Methodist Conference . . . 1881* (London: Wesleyan Conference Office, 1881), p. 263.

naries and universities, the influence of rationalism, philosophical idealism, and biblical criticism was soon apparent in Methodist ministerial and
higher education. The problem of skepticism was not limited to the
schools. It laid its hand upon the very life of the church. The Bishops'
Address to the General Conference of the Methodist Episcopal Church
in 1888 called attention to "the subtle and ever-varying forms of skepticism rife in our times." [4]

Historical criticism challenged the sovereignty of purely textual study
of the Scriptures. Although the acceptance of the historical approach to
biblical study was strongly resisted, there were leaders of Methodist
thought in the theological schools who not only recommended this type
of critical research but saw that it must inevitably supersede uncritical
literalism.

The appearance of scientific materialism and the theory of biological
evolution presented new problems for the previous views of man and the
world. Methodist theologians and philosophers such as Olin A. Curtis
and Borden Parker Bowne, through their teaching and writing, explored
the new philosophies of man and nature, and expressed their answers in
psychological and cosmological theories which established the case for a
spiritual understanding of personality and the natural order. Bowne began publishing his critical evaluation of the materialism of Herbert Spencer with the article "Herbert Spencer's Laws of the Unknowable," in the
New Englander in 1872, and his first book, The Philosophy of Herbert
Spencer, in 1874. He carried on his criticism through forty years, culmi-
nating with his volume Kant and Spencer in 1912. As a theist "Bowne held
that the decisive argument for theism is the intelligibility of the universe." [5] As a personalist Bowne contended that man's relation with the
intelligible universe lies in his thinking, his self-consciousness, and his
self-direction, in which he experiences immediately the nature of the
universe.

Another development in Methodist theology is seen in the emergence of
a broad ethical concern and the structuring of this concern in a new
emphasis upon the relation between the Kingdom of God and the struggle for a Christian society. This change from the extreme individualism
of the mid-nineteenth century should be regarded as essentially a development of early Methodism. At the outset the Wesleyan movement
expressed its social concern in a program of care for the orphans, the imprisoned, and the social outcasts. Attention to the social demands of the
Christian faith as a concomitant of a strong sense of personal morality

[4] *Journal of the General Conference*, 1888, p. 40.
[5] Francis J. McConnell, *Borden Parker Bowne* (Cincinnati: The Abingdon Press,
1929), p. 122.

was, for the Methodist movement, something of a recovery of its birth-right. Methodism had never surrendered its original emphasis upon man's freedom and moral responsibility. The theological basis for the social concern which was urged upon the Methodist people may be very simply stated: God, through his church, makes the Christian to be a fellow laborer with Christ for the salvation of the world. The Christian must therefore pray and work for the coming of the Kingdom of God upon earth among men.

In society this resulted in the emergence of church-related institutions dedicated to social service. In the schools and the Conference Course of Study attention was given to the study of ethics, both personal and social. In the church emphasis was placed upon meeting human need in a wide variety of circumstances.[6] The list of social problems which were dealt with in the deliberations of the Second Ecumenical Methodist Conference in Washington, D. C., in 1891 shows the awareness of the relation of theology to ethics and the development of the Christian conscience in social concern. The conference traced the implications of Christian social responsibility in the areas of temperance, labor and capital, poverty and wealth, agriculture, war and peace, international arbitration, vice, gambling and lotteries, marriage and divorce, amusements, and Sabbath observance. Methodist efforts were perhaps somewhat delayed in moving into the cities with the rapid urbanization of the late nineteenth century, but "in the 1890's an effort was made to place at least one institutional church in every city."[7] By 1900 many Methodists were working at the task of social amelioration in the cities of America. The Methodist Federation for Social Service was formed in 1907, the General Conference of the Methodist Episcopal Church adopted the Social Creed of Methodism in 1908, and the first chair in the sociology of religion in a Methodist seminary was established at Drew in 1909.

These sweeping changes in Methodist theology were not achieved without criticism and controversy. Contrary to wide popular opinion, Methodists have taken their theology seriously enough to struggle for its understanding and expression. While Methodism has not expended extensive energy in doctrinal formulation or in defense of a particular creed, yet the essentials of the Methodist understanding of the Christian faith and the Christian life have been remarkably consistent. This consistency has

[6] An extensive recent study of the involvement of Methodism in the emerging interest in social issues and the influence of the social gospel has been made by Richard M. Cameron in *Methodism and Society in Historical Perspective* (Nashville: Abingdon Press, 1961). See especially chapters 6 and 7.

[7] Walter G. Muelder, "Methodism's Contribution to Social Reform," in William K. Anderson, ed., *Methodism* (Nashville: The Methodist Publishing House, 1947), p. 201.

not been achieved without open challenge to variants nor without controversy among leaders of Methodist thought. In the holding of "opinions" Methodism has, since Wesley, granted wide latitude. In the retention of "essentials of right religion" Methodism has scarcely wavered from Wesley's threefold basis of authority in belief. Concerning doctrines, Methodists have asked: Are they biblical? Are they rational? Are they experimental, i.e., verified in experience?

Because of the determination to retain these bases for faith, there emerged in the period under review the two most famous accusations of doctrinal heresy in the history of American Methodism. One of these accusations was made in 1895 against Hinckley G. Mitchell, professor of Hebrew and Old Testament exegesis at Boston University School of Theology. Professor Mitchell had earned the Ph.D. degree at the University of Leipzig in 1879. He was a brilliant teacher who reflected the rising interest in biblical criticism, sometimes calling attention to the inconsistencies and inadequacies of Old Testament scriptures. Some of his students became aroused and made accusations of heresy. The accusation was renewed in 1900 and in 1905. Sentiments expressed among the students brought forth scathing charges and countercharges in the pages of *The Methodist Review* and the *Andover Review*. In 1905 the bishops of the church, whose confirmation of the appointment of all theological professors was required, refused to endorse Professor Mitchell. In self-defense Mitchell requested to be tried by the Central New York Conference, of which he was a member. He was defended by a rising young minister, Francis J. McConnell. The conference refused to institute a formal trial, but passed a resolution of censure for teachings which were contrary to the Holy Scriptures and to the doctrinal standards of Methodism. The General Conference of 1908 held that the Central New York Conference action was illegal and set it aside. The Judiciary Committee of this General Conference ruled that the bishops had no legal right to investigate and report charges of erroneous teaching in the seminaries. Although this step toward academic freedom was gained, and Professor Mitchell was officially vindicated, yet his teaching service was lost to the church. In the absence of episcopal approval he had transferred to the Theological School of Tufts College, a Universalist seminary.

The other heresy charge was made against Borden Parker Bowne, also a Boston University professor, in 1904. There was little likelihood that the charge would be sustained, but the trial was held with Bowne's full consent. Francis J. McConnell, in his biography of Borden Parker Bowne, reports that Bowne was requested to stand trial so that the charges would be thrown out and thus clear the accusatory mood from the theological air. McConnell comments: "Why the air could not have been even better cleared by the refusal of the Conference to entertain the charges is a mystery." [8] Bowne's skill in controversy was such that his vindication was expected, and was unanimously voted by the Select Number of Fifteen of the New York East Conference, before whom the trial was held. He was charged with teaching: (1) doctrines contrary to the Articles of Religion; (2) doctrines contrary to the established standards of doctrine of the Methodist Church, on the Trinity, miracles in the Old and New Testaments, the atonement, divine governance of future punishment of the wicked and reward of the righteous, sin, salvation, repentance, justification, regeneration, and assurance of salvation through the witness of the Spirit.[9] Concerning the outcome Bowne wrote in a letter, "The decisive and unanimous declaration of my doctrinal soundness is a great gain." [10]

A controversy which stirred American Christianity widely, and produced no small contention in Methodism, came over the fundamentalist-modernist issue. The fundamentalists represented the general interest in conservative theology. They championed the "old-time gospel" and the "verbal inspiration of the Bible" against the acceptance of the socio-ethical view of the progressive improvement of man and the critical approach to biblical study which seemed to breach the wall of the absolute authority of the Bible. Premillennialism, although not overly strong in Methodist fundamentalism, also challenged the emerging scientific views of man and the world.

Within the Methodist Episcopal Church, "The program of the conservatives was twofold: first, to compel the Commission on Courses of Study for young ministers to choose only those books which the conservatives considered in harmony with Methodist doctrinal standards; second, they urged upon the General Conference to declare 'the binding authority of our Articles of Religion and other established standards of doctrine.' " [11] The extensive changes in the Course of Study in the Methodist Episcopal Church in 1916 and in the Methodist Episcopal Church, South, in 1918 show that the liberal influence was not to be uprooted. Strong statements of the liberal point of view, such as Harris Franklin Rall's *Modern Premillennialism and the Christian Hope* and Francis J. McConnell's *The Essentials of Methodism,* gathered constructive support for the acceptance of liberalism. It was clear that Methodism embraced men of good faith in both the fundamentalist and modernist groups. It was inevitable that, in some instances, "the bibliolaters discovered iconoclasts standing

[8] McConnell, *Borden Parker Bowne,* p. 189.
[9] Cf. *The Methodist Review* (Northern), May, 1922, pp. 399-413.
[10] Quoted in McConnell, *Borden Parker Bowne,* p. 189.
[11] William Warren Sweet, *Methodism in American History* (Rev. ed., Nashville: Abingdon Press, 1953), p. 392.

behind their altars." [12] There was an unfortunate waste of pulpit oratory in partisan conflict. Yet Methodism discovered that brethren of different theological persuasions could live and work together. The real adversary was not in the household of faith, but abroad in the world.

By its inclusiveness of variety of opinion, its strong adherence to the essentials of doctrine received from historic Christianity and verified in experience, its evangelistic zeal which it had never surrendered, and its concern to see its faith manifested in personal and social righteousness, Methodism was theologically armed to meet the secularism, the humanism, and the materialism of the succeeding decades of opulence and depression.

2

The Continuing Message

A historic turn of a phrase has characterized Methodism as "Christianity in earnest." In some periods of its history the Methodist Church has been less attentive to its theological position than at other times. But there has been a constancy about its message that has survived many changes in method and manners. One of Methodism's elder theologians, born before the opening of the period here being considered, Harris Franklin Rall, has written: "The insistent Methodist emphasis has been on Christianity as a gospel and a way of life." [13] The commission of Methodism was and is "to spread scriptural holiness throughout the land." The message of Methodism likewise has been and is "the gospel of salvation in Jesus Christ for all men." The message is grounded in the biblical revelation. It must become, for the individual, authenticated in experience. The systematic structure of the message will depend upon the Christian's use of his rational powers. Salvation is at once both a gift and a demand. It is received through grace, obeyed in the disciplines of Christian living, and shared through the witness which its possession demands. The lists of the duties of Methodist preachers have from the first contained this admonition: "You have nothing to do but save souls." This task was seen to require the preacher "to bring as many sinners as you can to repentance,

[12] Edwin Holt Hughes, *I Was Made a Minister* (New York and Nashville: Abingdon-Cokesbury Press, 1943), p. 167.

[13] "The Methodist Church," in R. Newton Flew, ed., *The Nature of the Church* (New York: Harper & Brothers, 1952), p. 329.

and with all your power to build them up in that holiness without which they cannot see the Lord." [14]

Changes in the method of communication and in the manner of articulating the duties of the Christian life can be traced in the period from 1876 to 1919. But the message which Methodism has proclaimed from its beginnings has been the good news of the love of God made manifest in Jesus Christ, and operative unto righteousness and holiness in the experience of the individual and society through the Holy Spirit. The community of faith finds nurture and expression through the fellowship of the "society" and the communion of the church.

Universality of Sin

Methodism has recognized and emphasized in its preaching the sinfulness of man. In the Articles of Religion (VII) it is called "original or birth sin," which is taken to mean "the corruption of the nature of every man," whereby he is by nature inclined to evil.

The Methodist movement from time to time has focused attention upon and openly denounced particular sins. The list of activities prohibited to Methodists in 1872 added strength to the impression that Methodism was narrow and puritanical in its view of sin. Preoccupation with temperance, theater-going, dancing, and the wearing of bodily adornment seemed to be defining sin by the naming of specific sins. In the era of revivals many Methodist preachers harangued their hearers for their blatant and besetting sins. Such a procedure, although often effective as a preparation for evangelism, was negative pleading. The positive counterpart in the message expressed the more realistic purpose, which was to show that all men need salvation. Preaching in the 1870's vividly portrayed the damnation which was the destiny of every man, woman, and child who failed to respond to the gospel call.

A clear example of this doctrine of sin appears in the opening exhortation by the minister in the ritual for the Administration of Baptism to Infants. The statement, "All men are conceived and born in sin," was all inclusive. In the case of the baptism of "Such as Are of Riper Years," the following was added: "And that which is born of the flesh is flesh, and they that are in the flesh cannot please God, but live in sin, committing many actual transgressions." [15] If these words were used in the holy mo-

---

[14] *Discipline of the Methodist Episcopal Church*, 1884, ¶¶ 118-19.

[15] *Discipline of the Methodist Episcopal Church*, 1884, ¶¶ 401-2; *Discipline of the Methodist Episcopal Church, South*, 1886, ¶¶ 178-79.

ment of expectancy before the altar, when the decision to seek salvation was to be sealed by the sacrament, how much more strongly must the universal sinfulness of man have been expressed in the revival sermon, when the "hardened sinners" must be brought to see the errors of their ways and repent.

By 1919 the opening words of the baptismal office for infants read very differently. In the Methodist Episcopal Church the ritual observed that "God in his great mercy hath entered into covenant relation with man, wherein he hath included children as partakers of its gracious benefits." The minister in the Methodist Episcopal Church, South, read on like occasion, "All men, though fallen in Adam, are born into this world in Christ the Redeemer, heirs of life eternal and subjects of the saving grace of the Holy Spirit." Those of "Riper Years" were now admonished that "all men have sinned and come short of the glory of God," and that "all men do inherit a nature so fallen that no man, of his own strength, can so live as to please God." [16] The language and the mood had changed, but the message of man's sinfulness and need of God remained. All must receive salvation as a gift of divine grace.

Salvation for All

The gospel of salvation in the Methodist message matched the universality of man's sin and the total corruption of his nature with the affirmation of God's forgiving grace which was extended to all. John Wesley had discovered a new power in his preaching when he found himself led "to declare strongly and explicitly that God willeth 'all men to be saved' [and] that 'Christ gave himself a ransom for all.' " [17] "The grace or love of God, whence cometh our salvation, is FREE IN ALL, and FREE FOR ALL." [18] In the recognition that man is justified by faith and that he is saved only through the gift of grace, the Methodist message was clearly in the Reformation tradition. But in promising this gift to all who would receive it, the departure from the Calvinist doctrine of predestination and the inscrutable decrees of election was unmistakable. The preaching of a universal atonement and grace freely offered to all men drew immediate and open opposition from the Calvinist camp. Even under attack from his close friend and associate, George Whitefield, Wesley would not

[16] *Discipline of the Methodist Episcopal Church*, 1916, ¶¶ 511-12; *Discipline of the Methodist Episcopal Church, South*, 1918, ¶¶ 795, 797.
[17] *Journal*, April 26, 1739.
[18] Sermon, "Free Grace,"

retreat from the proclamation of free grace offered to free men that they might accept Christ and be converted.

This Arminian keynote which was sounded by the founder was not allowed to be silent in Methodist preaching. Through the revival services of the nineteenth century, in song and in sermon, "whosoever will" was an ever-recurring theme. The books in the Course of Study from which the preacher learned his theology traced the scriptural authority for extending the call to all men in Christ's name. Watson's *Theological Institutes* was the text in theology for Methodist ministers, both North and South, from the 1870's to the turn of the century. Its pages are filled with the Arminian opposition to predestination and special election. "Our Lord Jesus Christ did so die for all men, as to make salvation attainable by all men." Scripture passages were cited which showed that Christ died "for all men," and which spoke of his death as an atonement for the "sins of the whole world." The effects of Christ's death were seen to be equal in extent to the effects of the fall of our first parents. Christ died not only for those who are saved but also for those who by rejecting him shall perish. It is the duty of all men to believe and receive the gospel. Men's failure to obtain salvation is the fault of their own opposing wills. "He willeth all men to be saved." [19]

As the years moved onward, the Sunday schools and youth organizations provided new instruments for communicating the message. The primary purpose of these organizations was to bring all children and youth to conversion and to instruct them in the knowledge of the Scriptures. The Methodist leaders in the emerging emphasis upon social reform found in this new movement an opportunity for "social salvation." Frank Mason North saw "in haunts of wretchedness and need" the extent of sin and the need of salvation. In 1893 he wrote that the problem of poverty "lies very close to the problem of sin. Sin is a primary cause of poverty, poverty a constant occasion for sin." [20] Bishop Herbert Welch, in an article on "The Church and Social Service," in 1908 stressed the evangelistic purpose of social service. "Our need," he said, "is not evangelism or social service, but evangelism and social service, now and forever, one and inseparable! This is not revolution, but the old, the natural, the inherent meaning of the religion of Jesus Christ." [21]

One of Methodism's most intrepid campaigners for Christ in this period walked almost around the globe in the succession of his missionary journeys. William Taylor, elected missionary bishop of Africa in 1884, carried the message of the saving love of God, revealed in Christ, to India,

---

[19] Pp. 320 ff.

[20] "City Missions and Poverty," *Zion's Herald* (1893), p. 33.

[21] *The Methodist Review* (Northern), September, 1908, p. 714.

South America, and Africa during the period of rapid missionary expansion. He preached "a plain Gospel 'short-cut' into the way of salvation." He noted "the aptitude of the heathen mind to receive divine truth on the foundation of faith in God implanted in every human breast" as the basis of their response to his emphasis upon their personal responsibility.[22] From city slum to African bush, the message with which Methodism was entrusted was proclaimed: "Salvation is for all."

The Witness of the Spirit

Methodism's message has further affirmed the possibility of the assurance of one's own salvation as an inner experience, through the "witness of the Spirit." John Wesley held that the knowledge of the truth comes to man by way of scripture, reason, and experience. To the light of scripture and reason is added the testimony of God's Spirit when one has turned from sin and received salvation. "The testimony of the spirit," Wesley said, "is an inward impression of the soul, whereby the Spirit of God directly witnesses to my spirit, that I am a child of God; that Jesus Christ hath loved me, and given Himself for me; and that all my sins are blotted out, and I, even I, am reconciled to God." [23] Wesley sought to guard against confusing this witness with the vain and self-satisfied imaginings of the natural man that his state is one of righteousness and that his good feelings about himself are an effect of the Spirit of God. In self-satisfaction man resists God. On the other hand, Wesley warned against limiting the genuine witness of God's Spirit to the apostles in the New Testament age. He insisted that an authentic and assuring witness of the Spirit is possible for the genuine Christian. He further held that the possibility of this assurance was a significant part of the message which God had given to Methodists to bear to all mankind.

A corollary of Christian assurance is the responsibility to testify to others concerning the joy of salvation. This testimony is to be given by word, as one testifies to another concerning the new life in Christ which he has received. Testimony also involves another kind of conversation: "The meaning thereof is exceeding broad, taking in our whole deportment. . . . It includes every motion of our heart, of our tongue, of our hands and bodily members. It extends to all our actions and words; to the employment of all our powers and faculties; to the manner of using

[22] William Taylor, *The Flaming Torch in Darkest Africa* (New York: Eaton and Mains, 1898), pp. 539 ff., 543.
[23] Sermon, "The Witness of the Spirit."

every talent we have received." [24] The witness of the Divine Spirit within must be expressed in outward evidences in simplicity, sincerity, and love.

Methodism has continued to offer the inner assurance of salvation and to demand the external witness of "a vast and mighty change" in the outward life as the blessings of Christian experience. This part of the Methodist message, with the expectancy which it engendered, was a factor in the drawing power of the revival meetings. Men and women came, resisting but seeking, eager for regeneration and renewal. It was the reality of the experience of salvation which lifted religion out of dead ceremony and dead theology, into "a living, creative, glorious reality," as recognized beyond Methodist circles by such a preacher as George A. Gordon, minister of Old South Church in Boston, in his sermon "Religion as Experience."

The Methodists in their singing asked the soul's most searching question:

> How can a sinner know
> His sins on earth forgiven?
> How can my gracious Savior show
> My name inscribed in heaven?

They pleaded for the revealing and redeeming Spirit:

> Spirit of faith, come down,
> Reveal the things of God;
> And make to us the Godhead known,
> And witness with the blood:
> 'Tis thine the blood to apply,
> And give us eyes to see,
> That he who did for sinners die,
> Hath surely died for me.

In the assurance of reconciliation the answer was given:

> My God is reconciled;
> His pardoning voice I hear:
> He owns me for his child;
> I can no longer fear:
> With confidence I now draw nigh,
> And, "Father, Abba, Father," cry.

Then the testimony arose from the joyful heart:

> What we have felt and seen
> With confidence we tell;

[24] Wesley Sermon, "The Witness of Our Own Spirit."

> And publish to the sons of men
> The signs infallible.[25]

The "signs infallible" were the fruits of the Spirit manifest in a life of obedience and righteousness.

Bishop C. B. Galloway, in a sermon preached at the Ecumenical Methodist Conference in London in 1901, voiced the fruits which Methodism had reaped through its reliance on Christian experience. He saw the life of Methodism to be a conscious experience of personal regeneration. He spoke also of the irrepressibility of Christian testimony: "God has made us a great people because we have been a witnessing people. Our itinerants, from Wesley to the present day, have preached doctrines verified by their own experiences." [26] In experience Methodism found the authority of its message and the mandate to proclaim it. That Methodism had not lost its sense of responsibility for the promulgation of experiential religion in 1919 is to be seen in an article in *The Methodist Review* by Bishop E. D. Mouzon. He wrote: "We cannot be too often reminded that all religion begins in experience—an experience of need and an experience of satisfaction. . . . Methodism does come to the world with a definite type of Christian experience, and when we cease to enjoy and proclaim that experience, then do we cease to fulfill our God-appointed mission in the world.[27]

The Methodist view of the validation of knowledge and faith in experience was a factor in the development of liberal Protestant thought in the latter part of the nineteenth century and the early years of the twentieth. The primacy accorded to experience, as Maximin Piette, the Roman Catholic scholar, has noted, helped to pave the way for Schleiermacher's theological inquiries into *feeling* as a basis for religious knowledge and certainty and for William James's monumental studies, *The Principles of Psychology* and *The Varieties of Religious Experience.*[28] The immediate awareness of God, of which man was held to be capable by the personalist theological tradition, was grounded in the Methodist insistence that the Divine Spirit bears direct witness within man's consciousness.

[25] Hymn stanzas from the 1878 *Methodist Hymnal*, Nos. 437, 435, 438. These hymns of Charles Wesley also appear in the official hymnals of the Southern Church and the Methodist Protestant Church of this period.

[26] "Christian Experience: Its Supreme Value and Crowning Evidence," *Proceedings of the Third Ecumenical Methodist Conference* (New York: Eaton and Mains, 1901), p. 19.

[27] "Methodism Facing the New Era," *The Methodist Review* (Northern), October, 1919; pp. 670-71.

[28] Piette, *John Wesley in the Evolution of Protestantism*, tr. J. B. Howard (New York: Sheed & Ward, 1937), pp. 478-79, 568n.

The Call to Christian Perfection

Probably the most demanding word in the message of Methodism has been the call to Christian perfection. John Wesley, in his sermon "Christian Perfection" and in "A Plain Account of Christian Perfection," set this expectation solidly within the requirements of those who would undertake to be not only *almost* but *altogether* Christian.

He knew that anyone who preached perfection, either as a requirement or a possible attainment, would be accounted by some to be "worse than a heathen man or a publican." But since the call to perfection was scriptural, he felt it to be binding on all who would strive to live in obedience to "the oracles of God."

Christian perfection did not mean perfection in knowledge, total escape from ignorance, freedom from mistake, immunity to infirmity, nor deliverance from temptation. Perfection was, Wesley held, another name for holiness. Perfection meant "being grown up to the measure of the stature of the fulness of Christ." Such a person is made free from outward sin, delivered from evil thoughts and evil tempers, and so filled with Christ that his only motive is pure and holy love.[29]

The expectation of perfection in the Methodist message has been alternately stressed and neglected. It has never been entirely silenced, however, inasmuch as it has been held formally before the mind of every young preacher who has entered a Methodist conference since Wesley's day.

The call to perfection, seen as "entire sanctification" or "holiness," was the occasion for some of the divisions which came in the unity of Methodism. Where sanctification was regarded as a second act of grace after justification, there arose controversy between those who claimed to have been "sanctified" and those who were certain only that they were "justified." A fuller account of the holiness controversy is given below. The value of the emphasis upon Christian perfection in Methodism lies in its insistence upon the complete consecration of all of the Christian's talents and powers to the service of God. God's part in sanctification is the transformation of man into the likeness of Christ. When God's act and man's responsibility in holy love have been seen in relation to each other, Methodism has been strengthened and purified in its life and witness. When the negative implications of holiness have been stressed, pharisaism and self-righteousness have resulted.

Shortly after the Civil War the church entered a period of general re-

[29] Sermon, "Christian Perfection."

ligious awakening with a resurgence of spiritual activity and revitalized experience, particularly noticeable in the South:

A sound of revival was heard from one border to the other. The connectional journals teemed with news of a fruitful evangelism. The bishops sent out an address exhorting the church to a consideration of the doctrine of "perfect love." The membership was urged to "go on to this perfection of sanctifying grace." The old Wesleyan doctrines were being preached in their purity.[30]

The spirit of revival spread throughout the church, with a general return, in both North and South, to the historic Methodist doctrines and concern for personal discipline and the experience of holiness. Unfortunately ministers and congregations found themselves being divided over the holiness question. In the years that followed many groups separated themselves from Methodism and formed holiness associations.

The benefit which accrued to Methodism through this experience was the rediscovery of the original Wesleyan emphasis upon the ethical requirements of the life of salvation. As if by fire there was a cleansing of life in the recognition of the demands of righteousness, personal and social. Harris Franklin Rall observed in 1920 that what remained was "the emphasis upon the fact that religion means holiness of life, a holiness which is alike the gift of God and the task of man." [31] Perfection for man was seen as a goal toward which he must constantly strive.

Methodism has not been willing to surrender the call to perfection from its message. Francis J. McConnell, writing on "Entire Sanctification" in 1916, said: "It is essential to Methodism to keep alive the ideal at which it [sanctification] aims; that is, the bringing of all parts of the life under subjection to the law of the Kingdom." [32] If the ideal is retained, it will serve to motivate the expression of perfect love in ways unforeseen from one generation to the next.

In the era of the social gospel the "new sanctification" was seen to require the redemption of society, the purification of the social order from all sin.[33] In the tensions of war perfect love strove for peace. The call to Christian perfection remained a vital summons to holy love and righteousness, to purity of heart and life.

[30] Horace M. Du Bose, *A History of Methodism* (Nashville: Lamar and Smith, 1916), p. 17.

[31] "Methodism Today," *American Journal of Theology*, XXIV (1920), 488.

[32] McConnell, *The Essentials of Methodism* (New York: The Methodist Book Concern, 1916), p. 22.

[33] See C. W. Barnes, "The New Sanctification," *The Methodist Review* (Northern), January, 1912.

3

The Holiness Crusade

The religion of the Methodists was from the beginning centered in Christian experience. The doctrines which attracted their chief attention had to do with personal salvation and personal holiness. Their principal arguments were over the manner by which ethical and evangelical aspirations could be realized in the lives of individuals. Did deliverance from the bent to sin which remained in believers come by growth or by a miraculous "second blessing"? Was it achieved through solitary introspection and prayer or group testimony and confession? Was it attested more by Puritan discipline or perfect love? Should those who believed they had found this experience make public profession of it, so as to inspire faith in others, or let Christlikeness bear its own witness?

John Wesley had taught the early Methodist preachers that man's moral ability was a gift of God's grace. Divine love had preserved the sons of Adam from the total depravity which otherwise would have resulted from the fall, endowing them with the capacity to respond to the gospel. When the light came to a man, it was not his "natural ability" but his faith in the atonement of Christ which made regeneration possible. The Holy Spirit raised the penitent from the death of sinning to a new life of obedience to God's will.

Wesley taught, however, that the progress of this new life was hindered by another order of evil, which he called "sin in believers." Sometimes referred to as the carnal nature or the "seed" of sin, this inclination to evil was most clearly described as a diseased condition of the soul. The early Methodists considered original sin to be not so much guilt for Adam's transgression as a sinful condition stemming from it. But Wesley was much less concerned with theological diagnosis of the disease than with declaring God's grace to cure it—initially in the "new birth" of regeneration, and entirely in a second crisis of Christian experience called "perfect love." [34]

[34] European students have led the way in exploring this aspect of Wesley's teaching. The best study is Harald Lindström, *Wesley and Sanctification,* tr. H. S. Harvey (London: Epworth Press, 1946). Cf. R. Newton Flew, *The Idea of Perfection in Christian Theology* (London: Oxford University Press, 1934), pp. 313-42; W. E. Sangster, *The Path to Perfection* (New York and Nashville: Abingdon-Cokesbury Press, 1943); social implications of the doctrine in Wellman J. Warner, *The Wesleyan Movement in the Industrial Revolution* (London: Longmans, Green & Co., 1930), pp. 61-72; and George Allen Turner, *The More Excellent Way: The Scriptural Basis of the Wesleyan Message* (Winona Lake, Ind.: Light and Life Press, 1951).

Wesley chose this term because it called to mind both the grace of God and the believer's ethical responsibility to live by the Sermon on the Mount. Christ's work at Calvary was not a substitute but a foundation for our holiness. The purpose of the atonement is both to justify and sanctify men. The believer's experience of conversion, Wesley taught, brought such fellowship with Christ as to make him deeply discontent with the residue of sin within. If he walked in the light, he would give himself to a period of agonized soul-searching climaxed in an experience which combined entire consecration and complete trust. At this point "the love of God," as the New Testament promised, would be "shed abroad" in the seeker's heart, purifying him of inward sin and empowering him to live the new life victoriously. Imperfect judgment, the physical and mental passions common to men, temptation, and the freedom by which, through willful disobedience, he might again fall into sin, would remain real. But the bent of the sanctified soul would now be toward God's will, not away from it.

Interestingly, Wesley never left a completely clear testimony to his own enjoyment of perfect love, although he recorded, studied, and used as examples the experiences of hundreds of others. Moreover, he so carefully emphasized the processes of self-examination and consecration which preceded its attainment and the godly discipline which must follow it as to allow the question whether he really understood it to be achieved through spiritual growth rather than, as he often said, by a "second blessing, properly so-called." Recent studies, however, have demonstrated conclusively that Wesley did teach that sanctification was an instantaneous experience which believers might hope to receive "now, and by simple faith." But he never ruled out completely the possibility of its realization through growth, so long as entire consecration and faith in the atonement played their part at some point in the process.[35]

The Crusade Begins

During the twenty-five years preceding the outbreak of the Civil War, the doctrine of Christian perfection excited great interest among American Methodists, particularly in the Northern Church. Bishops and prominent pastors began calling for its revival in the early 1830's. In 1839 Timothy Merritt launched in Boston a monthly periodical entitled the *Guide to Christian Perfection*—later called the *Guide to Holiness*. By

---

[35] See Lindström, *Wesley and Sanctification;* Turner, *The More Excellent Way,* pp. 168-72; John L. Peters, *Christian Perfection and American Methodism* (Nashville: Abingdon Press, 1956) , pp. 27-66, 201-15.

that date Phoebe Palmer, a laywoman active in the Allen Street Methodist Church, New York City, had become a leader in the movement. The
"Tuesday Meeting for the Promotion of Holiness," held each week in the
parlors of her home, inspired hundreds of preachers to seek and to find
what they believed was "perfect love." The most honored leaders of Methodism—Nathan Bangs, George O. Peck, Bishops Edmund S. Janes and
Leonidas L. Hamline, educators Stephen Olin and John Dempster, to
mention a few—were friends and admirers of Mrs. Palmer, and endorsed
the crusade heartily.

Several factors help to account for the growth of this distinctive "holiness movement" in pre–Civil War days. One was the fact that revivalism,
with its characteristic stress upon free will and free grace, was at high
tide in nearly all denominations. Perfectionism, inevitably, was the crest
of the wave. Charles G. Finney and Asa Mahan led their friends and
associates at the new Congregationalist college at Oberlin, Ohio, into the
experience of sanctification in 1839. Thereafter, despite heated controversy, both of them championed the doctrine faithfully. In 1858 William
E. Boardman, a young Presbyterian minister active in the American Sunday School Union, published a volume entitled *The Higher Christian
Life*. His express aim was to present the idea of holiness in a terminology
which would be acceptable to persons outside the Methodist tradition.
The book became a best-seller at once, making Boardman's name well-
known on both sides of the Atlantic. The following year A. B. Earle, by
then the most prominent Baptist evangelist in the nation, sought and
found the experience described in his book *The Rest of Faith,* and began
preaching about it constantly in city-wide revivals all over the country.

Other factors were social and intellectual rather than simply religious.
American thought in the period is best described by the terms "romanticism" and "transcendentalism." Ralph Waldo Emerson's essays and addresses illustrate the perfectionist implications of both these themes. The
ethical ideals to which Emerson and Henry David Thoreau aspired on
a highly sophisticated level, plain men of the time sought at a Methodist
mourners' bench or class meeting. Entire sanctification was a kind of
evangelical transcendentalism which thrived amidst the optimism, the
idealism, and the moral earnestness which were so much a part of nineteenth-century American character. The growing complexity of urban
life and the emerging role of women in religious affairs seem to have
encouraged it. American Christians were practical, also; they would listen
to preachers who promised to make religion work. Thus the life of James
Caughey, a well-known Methodist evangelist of this period, is described
as *Earnest Christianity Illustrated*. Boardman wrote of "gospel efficiency,"

and one of Phoebe Palmer's famous tracts was entitled *Faith and Its Effects.* Their trust in God must get results. To a nation awe-stricken by the crisis over slavery, fearing at once the moral consequences of maintaining it and the social consequences of abolishing it, such a call to perfection seemed the need of the hour.

Among Methodists, it is true, two controversies demonstrated the divisive potentialities inherent in the promotion of the doctrine. In 1857 Nathan Bangs and other ministers raised the question whether Mrs. Palmer and her husband, Dr. Walter Palmer, were emphasizing in their writings and camp-meeting exhortations the role of faith in attaining sanctification so much as to undervalue the importance of the witness of the Holy Spirit to it. Two years later, in western New York, zeal for holiness combined with radical abolitionism and the rural Methodist's fear of the "worldliness" growing in fine city churches to spark the secession of the Free Methodists from the denomination.[36]

Despite these controversies, however, the main body of Wesley's followers in the United States and Canada were by the end of the Civil War unanimous in the conviction that personal sanctification was, in the words of the title of a famous book by Jesse T. Peck, *The Central Idea of Christianity.*[37] The centenary observance of 1866 dramatized this fact to all observers. John C. McClintock, chairman of the committee in charge of the celebration and soon to be the first president of Drew University, pleaded in a centennial oration delivered in his former pulpit, St. Paul's, New York, that the Methodist ministry must hold to this "great central idea of the whole Book of God," even though critics called it fanaticism. "If we keep to that," McClintock said, "the next century is ours. Our work is a moral work, that is to say, the work of making men holy." [38]

Walter and Phoebe Palmer, who had recently purchased the *Guide,* enjoyed one of their most successful tours that year. They conducted a revival of three weeks' duration at Evanston, Illinois, where Frances Willard joined many students at the infant Northwestern University in seeking sanctification, and then proceeded to McKendree College, in the southern part of the same state. They preached also at conference cen-

---

[36] For fuller discussion of the material in the preceding paragraphs, see Timothy L. Smith, *Revivalism and Social Reform in Mid-Nineteenth-Century America* (Nashville: Abingdon Press, 1957), pp. 114-47; and Peters, *Christian Perfection,* pp. 90-132.

[37] (Boston: H. V. Degen, 1856).

[38] Quoted in *Proceedings of Holiness Conferences Held at Cincinnati, November 26th, 1877, and at New York, December 17, 1877* (Philadelphia: National Publishing Association for the Promotion of Holiness, [1878]), pp. 139-40. Cf. *The Guide to Holiness,* L (1866), 123-25.

tennial camp meetings in Albion, Palmyra, and Ann Arbor, Michigan; Des Plaines, Illinois; Lima, Indiana; Greenbush, Ontario; and Watertown, New York. Wherever the Palmers went, great numbers professed the second blessing and pledged to "uphold the banner of holiness" in their home communities. Anthony Atwood, president of the Philadelphia preachers' meeting, reported at the end of the year that "the work of holiness never took hold of our ministers and people in this city as now." [39]

The mounting perfectionist fervor was due in part to the work of a remarkable group of urban pastors, of whom Alfred Cookman is perhaps the best example. Cookman professed the experience of sanctification in 1857, while serving the Green Street Church, Philadelphia. At successive pastorates in that city, and in New York, Wilmington, and Newark, he organized weekday meetings for the promotion of holiness, patterned on Mrs. Palmer's example, and carried on an intensely "spiritual" program. He spent every summer making the rounds of Methodist camp meetings in the East, preaching on perfect love with great success. At Cookman's death in 1871, Bishop Simpson delivered the funeral address, and Randolph S. Foster, McClintock's successor at Drew, declared that "the most sacred man I have known . . . is enshrined in that casket." [40]

Among the many presiding elders encouraging men like Cookman was William B. Osborn, of the South Jersey Conference. In the summer of 1867 Osborn and John Swannell Inskip, pastor of the Greene Street Church in New York and chairman of the city's Methodist preachers' meeting, persuaded a distinguished group of pastors to join them in sponsoring a general "national camp meeting" at Vineland, New Jersey. Extensive advertising in the religious press combined with convenient travel on the new railroads to bring to the little New Jersey town Methodists from all the states of the northern seaboard. Scores professed the coveted blessing. When the sponsoring committee met to consider plans for the future, they organized the "National Campmeeting Association for the Promotion of Holiness," elected John Inskip its president, and laid plans for a camp the next year at Manheim, Pennsylvania, completing all the business while on their knees in prayer.[41]

Within three years the National Association had become an important

[39] See *The Guide to Holiness,* L (1866), p. 188; cf. pp. 58-59, 88-92, 122-25, 152-54; and LI (1867), 155.

[40] Henry B. Ridgaway, *The Life of the Rev. Alfred Cookman* (New York: Harper & Brothers, 1873), p. 456; cf. pp. 193-307.

[41] A. McLean and Joel W. Eaton, eds., *Penuel; or, Face to Face with God* (New York: W. C. Palmer, Jr., 1869), contains the most nearly contemporary account, pp. 3-20, 148-57. Cf. George Hughes, *Days of Power in the Forest Temple. A Review of the*

Methodist institution. The Manheim encampment attracted hundreds of parishioners from urban congregations, and deeply influenced as well the spiritual life of the Evangelical Association, a German-speaking arm of Methodism which flourished in rural Pennsylvania.[42] At the 1869 gathering, held at the Troy Conference camp grounds on Round Lake, New York, 150 clergymen were present, and attendance reached 20,000 the first Sunday, despite an agreement barring trains to the grounds on the Sabbath. As at Manheim the year before, Bishop Matthew Simpson preached the opening sermon. His impassioned exhortation at the sacramental service which followed was long remembered. "Dear ministers of Jesus," Simpson cried, "if there is anything you have not given up, now is the time to consecrate fully your all to Christ. You need, and may have a fresh anointing just now." Then he added: "Brethren, there never was a day when we needed more power than now. We are called to meet, in this land, the tide of heathenism rolling in upon our shores. Infidelity is making its fiercest onset. We need and must have apostolic power." [43] Nearly four hundred persons testified at the love feast on the final Sunday morning to "receiving during this meeting the consciousness of sanctifying grace." [44] Among them were representatives of every state in the union except Texas, Louisiana, and Florida. A preacher from the Old Dominion declared the Methodists were "reconstructing Virginia upon the basis of holiness."

In 1870 the association sponsored three regional camp meetings, at sites near Baltimore, Boston, and Chicago. The next year they returned to Round Lake, then proceeded to Urbana, Ohio, where Asbury Lowrey, the presiding elder, had recently begun to emphasize sanctification. A correspondent to *The Methodist,* an independent New York City weekly, wrote that "doctors of divinity, professors in literary institutions, officers of the General Conference, [and] men of wealth, position, and power" appeared at the altar in quest of perfect love.[45] Meanwhile, Inskip and one party of workers invaded the Far West, equipped with a great circus tent. They conducted meetings of eight days each at Sacramento, Santa Clara, San Francisco, and Salt Lake City. An eyewitness reported that at Santa

Wonderful Work of God at Fourteen National Camp Meetings from 1867 to 1872 (Boston: John Bent and Co., 1873) , pp. 39-60; Phoebe Palmer, ed., *Pioneer Experiences, or the Gift of Power Received by Faith* (New York: W. C. Palmer, Jr., 1867) , pp. 52-60, 346-51.

[42] Cf. Ridgaway, *Life of Cookman,* pp. 349-50; Hughes, *Days of Power,* p. 65; and Raymond W. Albright, *A History of the Evangelical Church* (Harrisburg, Pa.: The Evangelical Press, 1942) , pp. 268-78.

[43] McLean and Eaton, *Penuel,* p. 468; cf. pp. 158-59, 254-68.

[44] Ridgaway, *Life of Cookman,* p. 360.

[45] Quoted in *ibid.,* p. 422.

Clara he saw "presiding elders, pastors, and other ministers . . . stricken to the ground by the power of God" and lying for hours "filled with glory." At the Mormon capital Brigham Young obliged by appearing nightly with his elders in an effort to overawe the congregation, and was roundly denounced by the fiery Inskip in a sermon on the last judgment—a fact duly reported in the religious press back East.[46]

During the next five years, twenty-eight national camp meetings— including three at Knoxville, Tennessee, three at Old Orchard, Maine, three in Iowa and Nebraska, and four in the cities of Baltimore and Washington—extended the influence of the movement far and wide. Inskip and a half-dozen of the other leaders gave up the pastorate to become full-time evangelists. William B. Osborn spent most of the decade developing Ocean Grove Camp Meeting on the Jersey coast, soon the largest such gathering in the nation and an annual forum for Dr. and Mrs. Palmer's ministry.[47]

The friendliness of the bishops, in both North and South, was an important factor in the early success of this organized crusade. Of those in office in the Northern Church before 1872, Edmund S. Janes and Edward Thomson earnestly supported the "second blessing" doctrine, though they stood officially aloof from the national camp meetings. Matthew Simpson, as we have seen, was an active participant. And Edward R. Ames helped Inskip launch his career as an evangelist in 1871 by inviting him to serve as evening speaker at the St. Louis, Kansas, Missouri, and Nebraska Annual Conferences. Of eight new bishops elected at the General Conference of 1872, four—Jesse T. Peck, Randolph S. Foster, Stephen M. Merrill, and Gilbert Haven—were decided friends of the holiness movement, and none of the others could be classed among its opponents. Peck led an unsuccessful attempt at this conference to define the doctrine of Christian perfection in such a way as to commit the denomination unreservedly to the "second blessing" view. Foster had published only three years earlier a revised edition of his most important book, Christian Purity, or The Heritage of Faith. In it he declared that a careful reconsideration of the question of the mode of sanctification had convinced him that although growth in holiness was one way, "we can and ought to be sanctified now, by faith." [48]

Two years earlier the Southern bishops had declared that their church

---

[46] Holiness Conferences . . . 1877, pp. 127-28, 132.

[47] See a complete list, through 1894, in The Double Cure, or Echoes from the National Camp-Meetings (Boston: The Christian Witness Co., 1894), pp. 7-8.

[48] Foster, Christian Purity (rev. ed., New York: Carlton and Lanahan, 1869), preface and pp. 180-221.

and section needed more than anything else "a general and powerful revival of Scriptural holiness." In 1878 they criticized their preachers sharply for the insufficient stress laid upon Christian perfection. "The infrequency of its proclamation from the pulpit and the irregularity of its experimental power in the Church," the bishops warned, "have proved a serious detriment to . . . our mission. . . . Let us more than ever reassert this grand doctrine." [49]

Wise leadership by the holiness advocates was, however, an important factor in the spread of their movement. Cookman, Inskip, and William McDonald, editor of *The Advocate of Holiness,* were capable men, widely respected. They were determined to organize and direct an intensely spiritual crusade which would steer clear of fanatical and divisive tendencies. The long periods of silent prayer at their camp meetings, the solemn communion services, and the firm control of the programs by a small group effectively curbed any outbreaks of religious rowdyism. They urged converts to avoid unnecessary controversy in their home churches, to maintain a tolerant spirit, and to shun extravagant claims to spiritual power or testimonies lacking in proper humility. No critic ever dared to charge them with disloyalty. They were, after all, appealing to Wesley, and to the memory of Asbury, Bangs, and Hamline. By these means they convinced many Methodists that the revival was "loyal to the entire history of the church" and to "the cardinal ideas of its founder." [50]

They also seized every opportunity to advertise the holiness crusade in the popular religious press. The New York *Christian Advocate,* published at the national headquarters of the Northern Church, and conference newspapers such as *Zion's Herald* and the *Northern Christian Advocate,* were open channels to the mind of the denomination. The Methodist Book Concern published the biography of Cookman and devotional books by several of the leaders. The office of Dr. and Mrs. Palmer's *Guide to Holiness,* which by 1870 served 30,000 subscribers, meanwhile issued a stream of books and pamphlets, notably those written by Phoebe Palmer herself. Forty-seven editions of her tract, *Faith and Its Effects,* had appeared by 1867, and fifty-two of *The Way of Holiness* by 1885. The National Association began as early as 1870 the publication of two new periodicals, *The Christian Standard and Home Journal,* printed at Philadelphia and edited by John Inskip, and *The Advocate of Holiness,* edited by William McDonald in Boston. The presses of both magazines issued numerous books as well.

When the depression of 1873 set in, these enterprises were placed un-

---

[49] *Journal of the General Conference,* 1870, p. 165; 1878, p. 33.
[50] Hughes, *Days of Power,* pp. 422, 425.

der an affiliate organization, the National Publishing Association for the Promotion of Holiness, directed by Washington C. DePauw, the Indiana glass manufacturer whose generosity to Indiana Asbury later gave that institution a new name.

Throughout the decade of the 1880's, in fact, official expressions of Methodism's loyalty to the doctrine and experience of entire sanctification seemed more frequent and positive than ever before. At the first world conference of Wesley's followers, held in London in 1881, John P. Newman, pastor of the Metropolitan Church, Washington, D. C. and soon to be a bishop of the Northern Church, delivered the principal address at the session devoted to "Scriptural Holiness, and the Special Fitness of Methodist Means of Grace to Promote It." In the discussion which followed, prominent leaders of English Methodism as well as key spokesmen for the several branches in America insisted that although differences of opinion did exist, Methodists generally supported the "second blessing" view. The session was then turned into an hour-long love feast of personal testimonies, despite the objections of James M. Buckley that such witnessing invariably aggravated the divisions which existed on the subject.

At a second American centennial celebration, held in 1884, many of the speeches reflected an awareness of growing tension over the issue. But the pastoral address, read by Bishop Stephen M. Merrill, climaxed with a ringing appeal to Methodist ministers to make holiness the answer to the heresies which were infiltrating the church "under the guise of liberality and loyalty to Christ." At their General Conference held four years later, the Northern bishops reiterated the warning that the denomination could not successfully resist the "loose thought of the times" unless her ministers emphasized more "the office and work of the Holy Spirit in renewing and sanctifying the soul." [51]

Meanwhile, in the young theological seminaries of the denomination champions of traditional Wesleyanism held sway. The books of John S. Miley at Drew, of Miner Raymond and Milton S. Terry at Garrett, of T. O. Summers at Vanderbilt, and of Daniel Steele and Olin Curtis at Boston University, all emphasized earnestly the doctrine of perfect love—though Miley, in his major work, was careful to insist that advocates of both gradual and instantaneous sanctification were heirs of a common tradition. Down until the 1890's historians of the church also seem to have agreed with Philip Schaff's remark that Methodists thought the doctrine of sanctification their "crowning glory." Henry K. Carroll, super-

[51] *Proceedings, Sermons, Essays, and Addresses of the Centennial Methodist Conference* (New York: Phillips and Hunt, 1885), p. 320; *Journal of the General Conference, 1888*, pp. 59-60.

visor of the federal census of 1890, wrote that the belief that Christian perfection was "obtainable instantaneously between justification and death" was a chief article of their faith.[52]

Neither bishops nor seminary professors, pastors nor evangelists, however, could have made the idea of personal holiness so compellingly attractive had it not seemed to contemporaries to meet the religious needs of the age. When George Hughes attributed the church's spiritual poverty to the decline of class meetings, the growing pomp and display of formal worship in fine church buildings, the urban laity's increasing indulgence of "worldly" amusements, and the ministry's conformity to "the spirit of the age," he was echoing a general opinion. "Apostolic power" seemed indeed the demand of the day. The first inroads of the new science and of liberal theology only intensified this conviction among conservative bishops and editors.[53]

Outside the Methodist fold, indeed, the same concern was evident. In 1869 a writer in *The American Presbyterian Review* warned that moral force could be recovered in Christendom only if the new hopes for the coming of Christ's kingdom on earth were accompanied by a "profounder practical understanding of the vitalizing energy of the Holy Spirit of God" in transforming individual lives.[54] During succeeding years William E. Boardman, Asa T. Mahan, former president of Oberlin College, and the Baptist evangelist A. B. Earle, author of *The Rest of Faith,* frequently found Presbyterians, Congregationalists, and Baptists inquiring after what Boardman's famous book had called *The Higher Christian Life.*[55] The western yearly meetings of the Society of Friends likewise fell under the influence of the holiness revival. David B. Updegraff, an Ohio evangelist, and Dougan Clark, professor of Bible at Earlham College, Richmond, Indiana, worked closely with the leaders of the National Association. An International Friends Assembly which met at Earlham in 1887 adopted a thoroughly Wesleyan statement on entire sanctification, treating that experience as simply a corollary of George Fox's doctrine of the

[52] U.S. Census of 1890, *Bulletin No. 195,* June 24, 1892 (Washington: Government Printing Office) , p. 4.

[53] Hughes, *Days of Power,* pp. 10-26.

[54] Ray Palmer, "The Want of Moral Force in Christendom," *The American Presbyterian Review,* I (1869) , 464-74. Cf. "Justification and Sanctification," *The Congregational Review,* VII (1867) , 321-31; W. W. Patton, "Revivals of Religion," *The New Englander,* XXIII (1874) , 38-50; and Amos S. Chesebrough, "A Critical Examination of the New Testament Teachings with Respect to the Office of the Holy Spirit," *The New Englander,* XXVII (1878) , 462-89.

[55] See A. B. Earle, *Bringing in the Sheaves* (Boston: J. H. Earle, 1869) , pp. 54 ff., 280-94; Asa T. Mahan, *Out of Darkness into Light* (Boston: Willard Tract Repository, 1876) , pp. 190-92.

inner light.[56] Little wonder, then, that at the centennial conference of
1884, a speaker who was chronicling "the influence of Methodism on
other denominations" should have declared that Christian perfection
had been so widely adopted "in fact, if not in form" by other churches
that Wesley's followers could hardly claim it as their peculiar heritage.[57]

What is often overlooked is that this optimistic belief in man's perfecti-
bility by grace was the contribution Methodists made to the romantic
idealism which underlay so much of the movement for social reform in
the late nineteenth and early twentieth centuries. It was fully as important as the "progressive orthodoxy" being taught at Andover Seminary during these years. It required, moreover, no break with the denomination's heritage. Wesley's followers could and in many cases did embrace the emerging social idealism without rejecting their founder's
message. Ethical earnestness, a belief in the immanence of God's sanctifying spirit, a readiness to accept the call to consecrate oneself and one's
resources to the Kingdom of God, and an unreserved acceptance of the
law of love—these were as much the hallmarks of the new social Christianity as they had been the foundations of old-time Methodist religion.
To this fact William and Catherine Booth, leaders of the Salvation Army,
gave unforgettable testimony. Zeal for personal holiness, to be sure,
pulled some men into isolation from social needs; but the larger number
found service and sacrifice for humanity the essence of the divine compulsion they called perfect love.

Controversy and Disruption, 1880-1900

As time passed, however, a growing cleavage separated the denomination's official leaders from those who made a specialty of the second blessing. The tension stemmed in part from the rise after 1875 in the Midwest and South of a rural and more radical phase of the holiness revival.
A company of evangelists appeared who were seemingly more intent upon
Puritan standards of dress and behavior than on perfect love, and certainly less attached to Wesleyan tradition and discipline. Several independent sects emerged with their blessing, long before the crisis of the
1890's drove many of the older and more urban "loyalist" party out of
the church.

[56] See Dougan Clark and Joseph H. Smith, *David B. Updegraff and His Work* (Cincinnati: The Methodist Book Concern, 1895) ; Dougan Clark, *The Offices of the Holy
Spirit* (Philadelphia: The Christian Standard, 1879).

[57] *Proceedings . . . of the Centennial Methodist Conference*, p. 281.

Typical of the radical leaders was John P. Brooks, editor of *The Banner of Holiness,* published in Bloomington, Illinois. Although at first a loyal Methodist, Brooks left the denomination about 1885. Two years later he published *The Divine Church,* an attack on organized denominations which became a textbook of "come-outism" from that day onward. Brooks was by that time editing *The Good Way,* a magazine published by the group in Missouri and Kansas which later adopted the name Church of God (Holiness). Another such figure was Daniel S. Warner, who founded the Church of God, with headquarters in Anderson, Indiana, in 1880, on an antidenominational platform. Hardin Wallace, an Illinois evangelist, initiated the holiness camp meeting and "band" movement in rural east Texas in 1877, then went on to southern California to lend inspiration to what later became the Holiness Church. S. B. Shaw, of Lansing, Michigan, after several unsuccessful attempts to unite the radical wing of the movement in that state on a nondenominational basis, formed a short-lived sect of his own known as the Primitive Holiness Mission.

These early secessions seriously embarrassed the more conservative leaders of the revival, whose strategy had been to convince everyone of their entire loyalty to Methodism. In the Lone Star state B. F. Gassaway, Hardin Wallace's first convert, led Methodist clergymen in setting up the Northwest Texas Holiness Association, intending thus to counteract the radicalism flourishing in the older, undenominational Texas Holiness Association. When Shaw and Brooks called a General Holiness Assembly to meet in Chicago in 1885, loyalist members of the conservative party appeared in force, elected George Hughes, then editor of *The Guide to Holiness,* as chairman, and firmly rejected any discussion of organizing independent churches. Of the family of older Wesleyan denominations, only the Free Methodists benefited from the radical agitation. They were too conservative, however, for the more independent leaders. The spiritual crisis of the 1890's seems to have divided the radicals into two parties, one rigidly Puritan and the other intensely emotional. From the former arose such groups as the Pillar of Fire Church, in Colorado, and the Metropolitan Church Association, in Chicago. The latter spawned by 1907 numerous "pentecostal" sects. These drew a sharp distinction between the experience of entire sanctification and the "baptism of the Holy Ghost," a "third blessing" which they believed was evidenced by speaking in an unknown tongue.[58]

But the Methodist bishops had other grounds as well on which to op-

[58] For a fuller treatment, with references to the primary sources, see Timothy L. Smith, *Called unto Holiness: The Story of the Nazarenes: The Formative Years* (Kansas City, Mo.: Nazarene Publishing House, 1962), chapter 2.

pose independent organizations devoted to cultivating sanctification. In 1881 a company of the most eminent sponsors of the perfectionist awakening, including the scholars John Miley, Daniel Steele, Asbury Lowrey, and Milton S. Terry, appealed to the leaders of the Northern Church to arrange under their own chairmanship a great national convention for the promotion of Christian holiness. The revival which had made such progress in the previous decade, the petitioners declared, could "never become universal in the church if left to independent organizations and unrecognized agencies." The bishops replied in a public letter which professed their "entire allegiance" to Wesley's doctrine but which bluntly rejected the proposal. "It is our solemn conviction," they wrote, "that the whole subject of personal experience . . . can be best maintained and enforced in connection with the established usages of the church." And it was all too true, they added, that holiness associations segregated a part of the church from the whole, producing an unhappy alienation. This declaration by the bishops gave opponents of the second blessing an officially acceptable line of attack. Moreover, it drove a wedge between the champions of that doctrine and the great body of moderate men in the denomination who believed in but did not make a specialty of Christian perfection.[59]

The National Association could scarcely be expected, however, to abandon overnight the agencies which had brought the interest in sanctification to such a high pitch. The organization of regional, state, and local associations had only recently begun. The "holiness" press was expanding rapidly, and weekday meetings for the promotion of the higher life, patterned on Mrs. Palmer's, were multiplying in cities large and small. Before the decade was over, more than two hundred holiness evangelists were giving all their time to the work. Yet to encourage these activities seemed a direct challenge to the advice of the bishops.

J. E. Searles framed the response of the leaders of the movement to this dilemma in 1887. Methodism still needed the National Association, he said, both to expand the work already begun and to shield the state and local associations, many of which were loosely organized interdenominational bodies, from unsound and fanatical tendencies. Even though the doctrine of holiness "is clearly and fully taught in our schools," Searles declared, "it seldom finds its way into the pulpits and prayer-meetings of the churches." Too many ministers knew of sanctification only from theory, not experience—and this when the growing worldliness of urban life was undermining personal consecration. "Our danger increases," he

[59] *The Central Christian Advocate*, January 18, 1882, printed both letters—as did many conference journals.

warned, "with our increase of numbers, and popularity, and wealth." [60]

The election of the free-lance missionary evangelist, William Taylor, as missionary bishop of the Northern Church in 1884 illustrates both the strength of the holiness advocates and the problems which their array of extra-constitutional activities posed to the organization. Taylor was one of Phoebe Palmer's converts. He spent the years following the Civil War establishing self-supporting missions in South America, Australia, and India. An incorrigible individualist, he ignored the Methodist Board of Foreign Missions, securing both money and volunteers at holiness camp meetings from Maine to Oregon. In 1882, however, the General Missionary Committee denied the right of Taylor or any person other than its regular appointees to organize Northern Methodist churches outside the United States. His South American congregations were declared "out of order" and their pastors commanded to return home. The committee could not, however, dissolve the South India Conference, erected from Taylor's labors in 1880. Taylor himself accepted the status of a local preacher and appeared at the General Conference of 1884 as a *lay delegate* from South India. Toward the end of that conference Daniel Curry, newly elected editor of *The Methodist Quarterly Review,* secured adoption of his proposal to elect a new missionary bishop for Liberia, hoping thus to place a Negro on the episcopal board. An obscure delegate, however, nominated William Taylor. The idea took the conference by storm, and Taylor was elected on the first ballot.

The new bishop immediately launched an aggressive program. He spurned the $3,000 annual salary which the Missionary Committee set aside for his use after the Book Committee, regularly responsible for episcopal support, refused to pay him, and raised the money both for his own needs and for his missionaries at camp meetings and holiness conventions all over the country. The General Conference of 1888 only partially sustained Taylor's position, amidst general embarrassment all around. The long address of the bishops to that assembly, which began with a ringing affirmation of their belief in the doctrine and experience of holiness, laid bare the problems which independent agencies presented to a denomination accustomed to tight discipline. They defended their recent policy of refusing to appoint regular ministers to the office of evangelist, and urged the conference to provide for "some official supervision or limitation" of the work of "voluntary alliances, leagues, unions and associations." [61]

A similar impasse developed in Southern Methodism as soon as holi-

[60] J. E. Searles, *History of the Present Holiness Revival* (Boston: McDonald and Gill, 1887), pp. 29-32.

[61] *Journal of the General Conference,* 1888, pp. 47-48, 59-60.

ness associations became numerous there. Spokesmen for the latter insisted that they were the most loyal of churchmen. Far from being responsible for the "fanatical extremes" of "come-outism" which had "brought the cause of holiness into such disrepute in California, Missouri, and in parts of Texas," their prime objective was to channel the yearning for perfection into paths of loyalty to the church. Leonidas Rosser, a Virginia editor and presiding elder who was later to be a bishop, pointedly noted that Methodism itself had begun as "a great holiness association" in the Church of England, and had suffered from a like misunderstanding.[62] The Bishops' Address for 1894, however, denounced the party which had sprung up proclaiming "holiness as a watchword" and maintaining "holiness associations, holiness meetings, holiness preachers, holiness evangelists, and holiness property." The bishops did not question the sincerity of these men and indeed hoped the entire church would profit by their godly example. But they deplored their claim to "a monopoly of the experience, practice, and advocacy of holiness" and their tendency to "separate themselves from the body of ministers and disciples." The delegates responded with legislation, strengthened at the General Conference held four years later, forbidding evangelists to conduct meetings in the bounds of a Methodist charge without the pastor's consent.[63]

From this point on, events within individual conferences of the Southern Church moved rapidly to the crisis stage. The Northwest Texas Conference adopted "peace" measures whose practical effect was to outlaw holiness associations and evangelists. Henry Clay Morrison, the founder of Asbury College at Wilmore, Kentucky, was tried and temporarily expelled from the Kentucky Conference for disregarding the rule against unauthorized evangelistic campaigns. E. C. DeJernett, founder of Texas Holiness University at Greenville, evangelist "Bud" Robinson, and many other Texans broke with Southern Methodism over this issue, migrating first to the Gulf Mission Conference of the Northern Church and thereafter to one of several parent bodies of the Church of the Nazarene.

In central Tennessee, at the headquarters of Southern Methodism, B. F. Haynes, a former presiding elder and editor of the conference journal, *The Tennessee Methodist*, committed that paper to the twin causes of prohibition and perfectionism in 1894, at the very point when the Nashville *Christian Advocate*, newspaper for the whole denomination,

[62] Rosser, "Sanctification," *The Methodist Review* (Southern), November, 1887, p. 237. See also John A. Porter, W. B. Godbey, *et. al.*, *Christian Perfection, an Address by the Southern Holiness Associations* (Nashville, [1890]).
[63] *Journal of the General Conference*, 1894, p. 25.

was taking the opposite stand. Within two years Haynes's fellow ministers had disowned their journal. The embattled editor eventually sold out to J. O. McClurkan, a Cumberland Presbyterian minister who founded in 1899 the Pentecostal Mission, an organization which later merged with the Church of the Nazarene. Haynes accepted the presidency first of a tiny Methodist school at Pulaski, Tennessee, and, thereafter, of Asbury College. In 1909 he moved on to Texas Holiness University, joined the Church of the Nazarene, and soon became the first editor of *The Herald of Holiness,* the national organ of that denomination.[64]

The outbreak of a doctrinal controversy in which the teachings of Wesley himself came under frank attack had meanwhile immeasurably complicated the argument over independent holiness agencies. J. M. Boland, a preacher in the Southern Church, published in 1888 a volume called *The Problem of Methodism,* in which he declared that Wesley got his notion of "sin in believers" from the Calvinists and that he erased it from the Articles of Religion in 1784. Boland maintained further that regardless of Wesley's conclusions, the Bible taught that sanctification was accomplished in the initial experience of conversion. A brief notice in the Southern *Quarterly Review* praised Boland's book highly and called for the elimination from Methodist doctrine of "all that recognized 'a second change.' " Forceful rejoinders appeared at once, both in the *Review* and elsewhere. George H. Hayes added fuel to the fire in 1891 with *The Problem Solved,* a volume which shared Boland's rejection of the second blessing, but for opposite reasons. The Calvinists were correct, Hayes argued, in teaching that depravity was inseparable from the mortal state. This prompted an even more formidable defense of Christian perfection spearheaded by John J. Tigert, O. E. Brown, and T. O. Summers, all professors at Vanderbilt. When Tigert became editor of the *Review* in 1894, he promptly closed its columns to all material which contradicted the traditional Wesleyan doctrine.

The next year a similar public debate broke out in the Northern Church, sparked by Bostonian James Mudge's volume *Growth in Holiness Toward Perfection, or Progressive Sanctification.* Mudge was much less radical than Boland had been. He did not deny the traditional doctrine that believers were to be sanctified after they were justified. He did, however, reject the idea of an instantaneous experience and acknowledged that in doing so he was departing from Wesley's view. Mudge also took the occasion to denounce the sectarian and divisive tendencies of the second blessing movement. Here was middle ground clearly accep-

[64] See B. F. Haynes, *Tempest-Tossed on Methodist Seas* (Kansas City, Mo.: Nazarene Publishing House, 1914).

table to many thoughtful Methodists. Segments of the official press issued favorable reviews at once. Within the year the Methodist Book Concern published book-length replies by Daniel Steele and Lewis R. Dunn, the chief literary lights of the holiness party, and denominational periodicals of all sorts pitched into the fray.[65]

The noise of this battle had not diminished when D. W. C. Huntington, chancellor of Nebraska Wesleyan University, provoked another with *Sin and Holiness,* an elaborate reworking of J. M. Boland's thesis. Meanwhile, Wilbur F. Tillett, dean of the theological faculty at Vanderbilt, adopted Mudge's line of attack, and Olin A. Curtis left the field at Boston University to Borden Parker Bowne, to whose thought the entire issue was irrelevant. The holiness leaders realized at once that some Methodist colleges and universities would no longer shelter their defenders. Several of the bishops in both sections were disturbed. Northern Bishop Willard F. Mallalieu wrote in 1904 an introduction to George W. Wilson's attack on the intellectuals, entitled *Methodist Theology vs Methodist Theologians.* Wilson declared that "New England Methodism, where much of this new theology is born, is slowly dying. . . . An increasing proportion of our members dance, play cards, attend theaters, [and] absent themselves from revivals." Spiritual compromise in urban congregations, he believed, had made the atmosphere favorable to theologies which explained away the call to Christian perfection.[66]

The doctrinal controversy brought deep gloom to those holiness advocates who had determined to remain loyal to the church. "Spiritual matters with us are not specially hopeful," William McDonald, Inskip's successor as head of the National Association, wrote from Boston in 1895. "Fairs, church theatricals, and higher criticisms seem to take the lead, and those who inquire the way to Zion are only here and there a traveler." [67] Beverly Carradine, of St. Louis, who was fast becoming the movement's most prominent evangelist, and Isaiah Reid, veteran leader of the Iowa Holiness Association, declared that the time had come to separate entirely holiness publishing ventures from denominational identification and to begin the establishment of separate colleges as well. Between 1895 and 1905 Asbury College, Texas Holiness University, Meridian College (Meridian, Mississippi), and Trevecca College (Nashville) emerged in the South and God's Bible School (Cincinnati), Tay-

---

[65] Mudge, *Growth in Holiness Toward Perfection* (New York: Hunt and Eaton, 1895); Steele, *A Defense of Christian Perfection* (New York: Hunt and Eaton, 1896); Dunn, *A Manual of Holiness and Review of Dr. James B. Mudge* (Cincinnati: Cranston and Curts, 1895).

[66] (Cincinnati: Jennings and Pye, 1904); see introduction and pp. 329 ff.

[67] Quoted in *Peniel Herald,* I (1895), 5.

lor University (Upland, Indiana), Chicago Evangelistic Institute, and Central Holiness University (Oskaloosa, Iowa) appeared in the Midwest. Reid urged his fellows, however, not to withdraw from Methodism unless compelled to do so. Those in Texas and Kentucky who were transferring from the Southern to the Northern Church were merely moving "out of one frying pan into another." The "war to extermination" which had begun in the South would, he predicted, spread throughout the country.[68]

Most of the older members of the conservative party followed Reid's advice, and lived and died in the church of their fathers. Such secessions as did occur among this group were intermittent and disorganized, and arose in response to grievous local ruptures. Indeed, the decisive factor which alienated many of them from Methodism was their determination to participate in undenominational mission and social work which their bishops refused to approve.

By the 1890's urban holiness ministers were active in hundreds of missions to the poor. Some of these offered a helping hand to the victims of drink and vice on skid row. Others, however, served uprooted families who had recently moved from the countryside to the city. In New York, for example, A. B. Simpson's Christian Alliance Bible School trained young people for the foreign field by sending them out in bands to the missions, hospitals, and jails of the metropolis. In St. Louis the First Methodist Church sponsored a mission to poor families; by 1895 this was called "the natural rallying center for the holiness movement in the city." In Spokane, Washington, D. N. McInturff, formerly a leading Methodist pastor, established the People's United Church, which was entirely Methodist in doctrine and polity, save for a strong stand favoring women's rights.

Such missions inevitably produced a class of converts who could not feel at home in stylish downtown congregations. Moreover, they nurtured a sense of freedom and fellowship among their sponsors which offered a welcome respite from bitter and fruitless controversy. The result was the organization by 1900 of scores of independent holiness congregations, in cities large and small. The earliest Church of the Nazarene congregations—in Providence, Lynn (Massachusetts), Nashville, Brooklyn, Little Rock, Spokane, Chicago, and Los Angeles—all originated in this way, without any of the leaders seemingly planning to found a new denomination.

The story of Phineas Bresee, the founder of the western arm of the Church of the Nazarene, illustrates this fact well. Bresee had already

[68] *The Christian Witness,* January 10 and September 12, 1895.

occupied most of the important Northern Methodist pulpits in southern California when, in 1894, Mr. and Mrs. T. P. Ferguson invited him to join them in the conduct of Peniel Mission. Bresee agreed to do so, apparently with no thought of breaking with the conference in which he had recently been a presiding elder, a delegate to the General Conference, and a leader in missionary and educational enterprises. At the conference of 1894, however, Bishop J. N. Fitzgerald refused to grant him permission to accept the assignment. After three days of thought and prayer, Bresee asked for location, an honorable release from his obligations as a traveling minister. His close friend, Joseph P. Widney, a wealthy physician who was then serving as president of the University of Southern California, joined him in the work at Peniel Hall, conducting a training institute for the study of the Bible and practical nursing. Twelve months later these two had decided that the poor must have a church and not simply a mission. Both withdrew from the Methodist connection and became joint superintendents of the Church of the Nazarene. Many years passed, however, before the vision of establishing a national holiness denomination became dominant in Bresee's thinking; Widney had long before that time returned to Wesley's fold.[69]

Thus throughout the twenty years following 1880, Methodist leaders in both the North and the South witnessed a growing disruption of fellowship in their communions which they seemed powerless to halt. The bishops were generally sane, conservative, and deeply religious men. They were anxious to keep Methodism evangelical and thoroughly Wesleyan. On the one hand, however, wealthy city congregations and their cultivated pastors had rebelled against the class meeting, the revival, and the old standards which an earlier generation had thought to be evidence of holiness. Recently this part of the church had seemed an easy prey to the young university men who were rapidly forsaking traditional Methodist theology. Some of the bishops believed the church needed the perfectionist awakening to stave off this attack from the liberal left. But the second-blessing preachers had become increasingly critical of episcopal authority. Some of them had maintained fellowship with the radicals who took part in the earliest secessions. Now, in the 1890's, all of them seemed bent on missionary and evangelistic activities which were independent of the bishops' control.

None should forget, however, that for many years after the crisis of the mid-1890's Methodist leaders in both the North and the South sponsored a serious campaign to bring the great body of their preachers back to the quest of perfect love. Samuel Ashton Kean, an Ohio pastor and

[69] See Smith, *Called unto Holiness*, pp. 47-53, 91-150.

presiding elder, held "pentecostal services" at scores of Annual Conferences in both churches, by appointment of the presiding officers. In Ohio, Indiana, Iowa, Nebraska, the Dakotas, and Washington state, as well as in border conferences of both the Southern and Northern Churches, this campaign was remarkably successful. One result, of course, was simply to produce a second crop of prospects for a distinctively holiness church and to keep alive the camp meetings where suspicion of the hierarchy flourished year by year. But a more important result was that Christian perfection retained a place for itself in the household of Methodist faith, enabling thousands of preachers and laymen who heartily believed in it to keep the charge of fidelity and devotion they had received from their fathers.

4

Changing Patterns of Worship

In the form and practice of public worship Methodism has been found in tension between two tendencies. Freedom of order, extempore prayer, and the extensive use of "popular" hymn singing have always had their place, and at times have moved into the ascendancy. Equally characteristic, however, has been the concern for an established and historic order of worship, the use of ritual and formal prayers, and a catholicity in hymnody which has retained the great hymns, canticles, and chants from all Christendom. Adherence to both of these emphases in worship is discernible during the last quarter of the nineteenth century and the first two decades of the twentieth. The general direction of movement, however, is from freedom to form, from revivalism to ritual.

Form and Freedom

It will be remembered that John Wesley had prepared for American Methodism, *The Sunday Service of the Methodists in North America,* containing orders of worship for Sunday, together with the ritual for the sacraments, ordinations, and "various occasions." Although this order was adapted in wording and doctrine to American Methodist use, its various services were closely parallel to the *Book of Common Prayer* of the Church of England. In Wesley's opinion the Anglican liturgy was the most exalted in Christendom. As long as the Methodists in America were dependent for the sacraments upon the Anglican priests, it had not been necessary for the Methodists to have a ritual of their own. In 1784 the results of the War of Independence and the emergence of the new nation had made it inevitable that a new and independent church should be established. A liturgy for the new church would be required. This Wesley supplied, and the Christmas Conference adopted it.

As the Methodist circuit riders followed the movement of population westward, there was little time and opportunity for the amenities of ceremony, either secular or sacred. Preaching was carried on often without any ecclesiastical setting. Services were held in a pioneer cabin, a plain meeting house, or in the open air. The itinerant Methodist preacher carried tracts and pamphlets in his saddlebags. The hymnbooks, privately owned and used in family singing and as resources for personal devotion, guided the song service in the congregation. Rough garments which would give protection from the elements were more suited to the life of the circuit rider than the linens and embroidery of priestly vesture. Lack of education and formal training for the ministry gave further occasion to the itinerant preachers to rely upon preaching drawn from the Scriptures and personal experience more than upon the other "means of grace" for the spiritual edification of their hearers. Under these circumstances the urgent need of the people was felt to be a call to repentance and conversion. On the Methodist circuits the visit of the preacher was an occasion for hearing the call to turn and receive salvation. In the classes which were formed for the nurture and discipline of the converts interim leadership was in the hands of class leaders who were not authorized or equipped to perform the priestly office.

Separation from the Church of England carried with it a reaction against the formal and the sacerdotal. Even *The Sunday Service*, the basis of American Methodist liturgy, showed significant deletions and changes from the Anglican liturgy from which it was drawn. Wesley's changes had made provision for free prayer, which had no place in the liturgy of the Church of England. He had substituted a prayer for pardon for the pronouncement of absolution. This changed an objective ecclesiastical act to a subjective plea addressed by the penitent to his God. The reaction thus begun was carried further. American Methodism became a movement in revolt against formalism. "Methodism became a pioneering church in more than one way. It was thoroughly infused with evangelistic fervor and with new spiritual force. The spiritual life that characterized it was too vital to be confined within the limits of a fixed order of worship." [70] The spirit of freedom and democracy which was abroad in the land was reflected in the worship practices of the Methodist people.

Article of Religion XXII, concerning rites and ceremonies, had stated the principle of freedom:

It is not necessary that rites and ceremonies should in all places be the same, or exactly alike; for they have been always different, and may be changed according to the diversity of countries, times, and men's manners, so that nothing be ordained against God's Word. . . . Every particular church may ordain, change, or abolish rites and ceremonies, so that all things may be done to edification.

This manifesto had been accepted and made the basis for action. The style of worship which developed in the first century of American Methodism was indigenous to the frontier circuits and plain city meeting houses. It lacked many of the elements of form and nicety, just as the pioneer cabins lacked the formal order of the English country cottage and garden. But there was rugged vitality and stirring enthusiasm in Methodist worship which was suited to the robust life of the new land.

At the same time, the Methodist movement never lost its consciousness that it was a church in full recognition of its continuity with the Christian heritage. By 1824, the *Discipline* required that in the administration of the sacraments of baptism and the Lord's Supper the ritual invariably be used. Orders for the solemnization of matrimony and the burial of the dead were also provided, and on these occasions the amenities of the ritual were scrupulously observed. The ordination of ministers to the offices of deacon and elder and the consecration of bishops were performed with formal prayer and ritual. When a cornerstone was laid or a church was dedicated, it was done with suitable ceremony.

The Order of Service

The Sunday morning service had been generally exempt from the greater freedom which characterized the revival services and other meetings. Requirements for order and uniformity in public worship were clearly stated in the 1886 *Discipline* and were binding alike on preacher and congregation in Methodism. These provided that the morning service should include the following:

[70] Ilion T. Jones, *A Historical Approach to Evangelical Worship* (Nashville: Abingdon Press, 1954), p. 152.

(1) Singing—the congregation standing.

(2) Prayer—the congregation kneeling.

(3) Reading a lesson out of the Old Testament, and another out of the New.

(4) Singing—the congregation sitting.

(5) Preaching.

(6) Singing—the congregation standing.

(7) Prayer—the congregation kneeling.

(8) Benediction.

This list is drawn from the 1886 *Discipline of The Methodist Episcopal Church, South* (paragraph 100). The parallel paragraph in the 1884 *Discipline of The Methodist Episcopal Church* makes essentially the same requirements, adding: "Let a Doxology be sung at the conclusion of each service and the Apostolic Benediction (2 Cor. 13:14) be invariably used in dismissing the congregation." The Lord's Prayer was to be repeated by all. This was not the liturgy which Wesley had prescribed, but it expressed a determination that there should be order, dignity, historicity, and uniformity in Methodist worship.

Undoubtedly "shouting Methodists" shouted Amens during the prayers and "Praise the Lords" to punctuate the preaching. In class meetings there were noisy testimonies, and in the revivals cries arose from the mourners' bench. Clamor and confusion sometimes reigned in the congregation. Worshipers were moved, and they were encouraged to make their responses known. The free worship form emerged as an expression of a stirring evangelistic movement, and often exhibited more spontaneity than structure. But it was praise, confession, petition for pardon, and thanksgiving. These were experiences, and they were being offered to God.

As the country became more settled, and the movement of population into the cities increased, there was a change of emphasis in worship. Greater opportunities for ministerial education through the seminaries brought knowledge of the historic rubrics of Christian worship. The training of a younger minister by apprenticeship to a senior preacher on a circuit had tended to limit the experience of the learner, and to perpetuate the current practices. Formal training in theological schools enabled the ministers to call upon wider resources in leading the worship experiences of the congregation. Longer pastorates afforded opportunity for the minister to give attention to the means of Christian nurture and growth in grace. Economic improvement made possible the building of better church edifices. In the planning of many of these attention was given to providing a suitable "house of worship." There was an increase in the use of choirs in the service of worship. Immigration provided contact with other Protestant groups which brought with them their liturgical worship practices.

Participation by the congregation in the service took place, as has been observed, both formally and informally. The shouts which were characteristic of Methodist meetings were examples of spontaneous sharing. Opportunity to participate verbally in the service was also given in the call for a season of extempore prayers, the unison praying of the Lord's Prayer, the singing of hymns, and of responses such as the Gloria Patri and the Doxology.

An innovation in congregational participation was the responsive reading of the Psalter, introduced in the 1905 *Hymnal*. The poetic parallelism of Hebrew poetry had always been observed, and now historical biblical study focused attention upon the antiphonal use of certain psalms in the temple worship in Jerusalem. The influences leading to the introduction of the responsive reading of the psalms are not clearly traced. The Psalter, said by all, was in Wesley's *Sunday Service*, but there is no indication of its responsive use.

Some responsive readings had been included in a book of popular religious songs, *The Epworth Hymnal*, in 1885, and had since been in use in Epworth League meetings and Methodist social gatherings.[71] *The Methodist Hymnal* issued in 1878 contained no Psalter other than those psalms included for singing among the "Occasional Pieces and Chants." *The Methodist Hymnal* of 1905, the first joint hymnal of the Northern and Southern Churches, included "The Psalter for Responsive Readings in the Sunday Services," with a selection for morning and evening for each Sunday of the year. Additional selections were included as "Readings for Special Days," with attention given to missions, education, temperance and moral reform, and the nation. By 1919 the Old Testament lesson in the Sunday service in many Methodist churches was read responsively by the congregation.

Freedom continued in Methodist worship in accordance with its charter in the Articles of Religion, but this freedom had come to express itself in a form which had recovered much of the structure of *The Sunday Service* adopted in 1784.

[71] "Responsive Services for the Sunday-School and Social Meetings," *The Epworth Hymnal* (Cincinnati: Cranston and Stowe, 1885), pp. 4-7.

Hymns

Both the spirit and the message of the Methodist movement were in no small part developed through singing. John Wesley was the preacher, organizer, and publisher. Charles Wesley was the hymn writer. The placing of the two together on a single memorial tablet in Westminster Abbey reflects vividly and accurately their co-operative leadership in the Methodist revival. In true Wesleyan fashion admonitions such as the following appeared: "In every society let due attention be given to the cultivation of sacred music." And lest the values of full congregational participation not be achieved, every member was to be exhorted to sing, "not one in ten only, as singing is a part of divine worship in which all ought to unite." [72]

Careful attention was given also to the doctrines which the hymns expressed. In John Wesley's Preface to *A Collection of Hymns for Use of the People Called Methodist,* first published in 1780, a concern for theological content is seen in these words:

It [the hymnal] is large enough to contain all the important truths of our most holy religion, whether speculative or practical; yea, to illustrate them all, and to prove them both by scripture and reason: and this is done in a regular order. The hymns are not carelessly jumbled together, but carefully ranged under proper heads, according to the experience of real Christians. So that this book is, in effect, a little body of experimental and practical divinity.

This book was used, to some extent at least as Wesley intended, in the early years of American Methodist worship. In 1808, Francis Asbury directed the compilation of another hymnbook which was approved and ordered published by the General Conference. In his Preface he also called attention to the importance of the theological content of the hymns. He wrote: "In examining the arrangement, you will find every particular head well furnished with suitable hymns, in which are contained a body of excellent divinity, explanatory of and enforcing the fundamental doctrines of the gospel." [73]

The publishing of an official Methodist hymnbook, after the approval of the 1820 General Conference, indicated that the Methodists were determined not to let the strength gained through singing subside.

A mood of subjectivism and strong sentimentality prevailed in the

---

[72] *Discipline of the Methodist Episcopal Church,* 1884, ¶ 56.
[73] *A Selection of Hymns from Various Authors* (New York: Wilson and Hitt, 1808), p. iv.

singing of the Methodist societies in the era of revivalism. During the middle decades of the nineteenth century many small books of religious songs with tunes and choruses to appeal to popular taste made their appearance. Theologically these songs spoke almost exclusively of the sinner's plight and the atoning sacrifice of Jesus. Their appeal was for the sinner to step forward and claim the prize of his salvation.

> Come to the Savior, make no delay,
> Here in His Word He's shown us the way;
> Here in our midst He's standing today,
> Tenderly saying, "Come." [74]

The titles of the books, such as *The Prize* (1870), *The Little Sower* (1870), *Songs of Love* (1874), *Songs of Redeeming Love* (1882), *Purest Gems* (1891), *The Gospel Pilot Hymnal* (1899), indicate their content and purpose.

A new edition of the *Methodist Hymnal* was authorized by the Northern General Conference of 1876. The committee which prepared it sought to keep it in the finest tradition of the hymnody of the church universal, and of the Wesleyan hymn books. Of the tunes the editors said: "The music is mainly of a solid, enduring kind." The importance of "a choir or a precentor, and an organ, if possible, to lead the people," was also recognized. The use of this book was recommended not only for Sunday morning worship but also for "praise meetings," the Sunday school, and social meetings. The chief purpose was that this new hymnal should "contribute somewhat to the spirituality of divine worship through the power of sacred song upon the heart." [75] The book contained a wide selection of excellent hymns arranged according to their topical and theological content, plus hymns and chants from the preceding centuries and traditions of Christian worship.

Between the types represented by this official hymnal and the revival songbooks, yet another hymnal appeared. *The Epworth Hymnal* was published in 1885 by the authority of the General Conference to be used primarily in the Sunday schools and social services. John H. Vincent was chairman of the editorial committee. This hymnal brought together some of the hymns of the ages with "songs full of strength and sweetness." The Preface voices a suggestion of defensiveness as it notes the inclusion of " 'popular songs' which hold much truth rhythmically told. The severest criticisms might point out slight defects in them which,

[74] George F. Root, "Come to the Savior," *The Prize* (Chicago: Root & Cady, 1870), No. 5.

[75] Preface to the *Hymnal of the Methodist Episcopal Church*, 1878, pp. vi-vii.

although sufficient to exclude them from the classic lists, do not justify
their omission in a book 'for the people.' " The editors kept faith with
their statement of purpose. Most of the hymns included were of excellent quality. But among them were some in which "the gospel bell is ringing," or the sinner is plunged in "the crimson wave," in the vivid im-
agery of the revival songs.

A *Young People's Hymnal* was issued in 1897 by the Methodist Episcopal Church, South, through its Sunday School Board, "Adapted to the
Use of Sunday Schools, Epworth Leagues, Prayer Meetings and Revivals." The problem which plagued the church in its hymnody was well
expressed in the Preface of *The Young People's Hymnal* No. 2 (1903),
which said:

> It often happens in the use of a Sunday school song book that two or three
> dozen of the showier and shallower pieces are learned and used till they are
> worn out, and the conclusion is reached that the book is exhausted, when, in
> truth, its resources have scarcely been touched. The more difficult pieces and
> those which do not at first so strongly strike the youthful taste are usually the
> ones which are truly the most beautiful when once mastered, and by far more
> enduring than the other class.[76]

The need for Methodism to recover her heritage of great hymns is more
evident in this book than in *The Epworth Hymnal*.

The loftiness of the poetry in the great hymns was generally recognized.
Hymnbooks of the livelier sort were defended on the grounds that the
more "popular" tunes were more conducive to full congregational participation in singing. One writer in *The Methodist Review* stated the
case vividly in these words: "If some competent tune-maker would revise our excellent body of theology as found in our *Hymnal*, we could
in a short time drive out swarms of *Gems* and *Charms* and *Shouts* and
ad omne genus from our Sunday Schools, social, and revival services." [77]
There was no desire to reduce the use of hymns in worship. Rather, the
hope was expressed that more popular tunes would cause the singing
to become more "spirited and spiritual."

The recovery of the awareness of a common heritage in hymnody was
one of the influences strengthening the will of the major branches of
Methodism toward reunion. A joint commission was authorized to explore steps by which Methodism, North and South, might move together.
The commission recommended a common catechism, a common hymn-

---

[76] *The Young People's Hymnal No. 2* (Nashville: Publishing House of the Methodist Episcopal Church, South, 1903), p. 2.
[77] W. R. Goodwin, "Church Music," *The Methodist Review* (Northern), July, 1898,
p. 633.

book, a common order of worship, and co-operation in missionary work overseas. One of the first fruits of this program was the publication in 1905 of *The Methodist Hymnal, Official Hymnal of the Methodist Episcopal Church and the Methodist Episcopal Church, South.* The music editors chosen were musicians of distinction, Karl P. Harrington of Wesleyan University and Peter C. Lutkin of Northwestern University. Although the 1905 *Hymnal* contained fewer of the hymns of the Wesleys than were included in 1878,[78] the total collection was enriched by wise selections from both ancient and modern sources. Concern was given to expressions of "sound doctrine and healthful Christian experience," and the desire that the new hymnal "will greatly enrich our worship."

Among the hymns included for the first time in 1905 were such examples of classical and Reformation hymnody as "Come Ye Faithful," by John of Damascus, and "Now Thank We All Our God," by Martin Rinkart. Some newly written hymns included have demonstrated their permanence. "Lead On, O King Eternal," by E. W. Shurtleff, and "He Leadeth Me," by J. H. Gilmore, were new to the 1905 *Methodist Hymnal.* Mary Ann Thompson's mission hymn, "O, Zion, Haste," and C. T. Winchester's hymn on education, "The Lord Our God Alone Is Strong," made their first appearance. The theme of social service, which was to gain greatly in emphasis in the social gospel era of the next two decades, was represented by "Where Cross the Crowded Ways of Life," by Frank Mason North, and "O Master, Let Me Walk with Thee," by Washington Gladden.

The growing interest in liturgy is immediately apparent in the 1905 *Hymnal.* The Order of Public Worship, facing the title page, includes the following:

    I. Voluntary, instrumental or vocal.

    II. Singing from the Common Hymnal, the people standing.

    III. The Apostles' Creed, recited by all, still standing.

    IV. Prayer, concluding with the Lord's Prayer, repeated audibly by all, both minister and people kneeling.

    V. Anthem or Voluntary.

    VI. Lesson from the Old Testament, which, if from the Psalms, may be read responsively.

    VII. The Gloria Patri.

    VIII. Lesson from the New Testament.

    IX. Notices, followed by collection.

[78] Cf. Benjamin Franklin Crawford, *Theological Trends in Methodist Hymnody* (Carnegie, Pa.: Carnegie Church Press, 1939), p. 45. Charles Wesley's hymns were reduced from 308 in 1876 to 121 in 1905. The number of John Wesley's hymns declined from 31 to 19.

    X. Singing from the Common Hymnal, the people standing.
    XI. The Sermon.
    XII. Prayer, the people kneeling.
    XIII. Singing from the Common Hymnal, the people standing.
    XIV. Doxology and the Apostolic Benediction.

The Psalter was arranged as responsive readings for each Sunday in the church year and for special days. The ritual for baptism, reception of members, the Lord's Supper or Holy Communion, matrimony, the burial of the dead, and for the dedication of a church followed the Psalter. The minister was admonished "to make faithful use of the forms and orders here provided, and without other deviation than that here indicated as permitted." Further, "We urge all pastors to encourage and train their congregations to participate audibly in those portions of the service provided for this purpose, particularly in the celebration of the Lord's Supper. The portions to be used by the congregation are specially indicated by black face type." [79]

By 1919 Methodism had passed through its period of greatest informality in worship. In 1881 "formality" had been classed with "worldliness" and "improper amusements" as a peril to Methodism.[80] The proper place for the "rags of ritualism" was then said to be "in the wastebasket." But now, in the first two decades of the twentieth century, liturgy and the established ritual were being restored to use in Methodist churches.

5

The Administration of Discipline

A distinctive feature of the Methodist movement from its beginning has been methodical attention to the personal and social discipline of its members in both spiritual and ethical matters.

John Wesley called on all who would be made perfect in love to give themselves to the daily discipline of obedience. "All who expect to be sanctified at all expect to be sanctified by faith. But meantime they know that faith will not be given but to them that obey." [81] Ministers and laymen alike were held responsible for a kind of scrutiny and surveillance of one another's lives whereby every appearance of evil might be avoided.

[79] *The Methodist Hymnal*, 1905, p. 88.
[80] Cf. J. W. McKay, "Possible Perils of Methodism from Formality, Worldliness, and Improper Amusements among our own Members," *Proceedings of the Oecumenical Methodist Conference . . . 1881*, pp. 278-83.
[81] *Letters*, to Dorothy Furly, August 19, 1759.

The organization of the class meetings and the appointment of class leaders were designed in part to ensure that every member of the church should be regularly subject to pastoral oversight. Within the classes the opportunity and obligation of group fellowship, religious worship, instruction, encouragement, and admonition for the members were provided. Leaders of the classes were to make regular reports to the minister. Since the class leaders were members of the congregation, this system provided a way for the itinerant minister to have intimate and up-to-date knowledge concerning the faith and life of each of his members.

Bishop Elijah Hedding published in 1842 *A Discourse on the Administration of Discipline,* which vividly portrays the place of discipline in the Methodist movement. He traced the responsibilities of the bishop, the presiding elder, the preacher in charge, the local preacher, the class leader, and the lay member in the maintenance of the laws and observances of the Methodist order:

The great work of discipline is to instruct, educate, and govern the people, and thus help them on towards heaven: to restrain and keep them from evil, or warn, reprove, and reclaim them when they may have erred, or fallen into sin. To accomplish this, the pastor is to labor "publicly, and from house to house; to be instant in season, out of season; reprove, rebuke, exhort, with all long-suffering and doctrine." The sick, the aged, the bereaved and sorrowful, are to be visited, admonished, encouraged, and comforted, as their conditions and wants may require. The youth and the children are to be objects of the care of the faithful shepherd. To perform these important and benevolent duties, he must avail himself of all the helps under his control. His colleague is his assistant in this work, and has his portion of care and labours, as well as the preacher in charge. The local preachers are to be associated with the itinerants in these services. . . . A minister is bound *to take heed to all the flock over which the Holy Ghost has made him an overseer.*[82]

Insofar as this concept of discipline was held within Methodism, the pattern was not that of officious nosiness into private affairs but an intimate concern for the personal welfare of each of the members. Provision was made for investigation, report, admonition, reproof, charges, trial, and expulsion from the means of grace and the fellowship. But it was recognized that the necessity of expelling a member was evidence that the preacher and fellow members had failed to use the power and influence to save which reside in the church. Nevertheless, resort to expulsion was felt to be necessary "to prevent the Church from being corrupted, by

[82] Hedding, *A Discourse on the Administration of Discipline* (New York: Lane and Sandford, 1842) , pp. 39-40, 53.

retaining in her bosom unrighteous and ungodly persons." [83] The purpose of this discipline was "to help them on towards heaven."

The Northern General Conference of 1872 adopted a rule on "imprudent and unchristian conduct" which added to the specifications of the
General Rules prohibitions on the buying, selling, and using of intoxicating liquors, dancing, games of chance, theater-going, horse races, circuses,
and the patronizing of dancing schools. These specific examples of conduct for which the church member would be brought to trial were not
added to the *Discipline* of the Methodist Episcopal Church, South. However, both branches of Methodism provided censure and the possibility
of expulsion for immorality, neglect of duty, the indulgence of sinful
tempers or words, sowing dissension among the members, attacks upon
the doctrines and discipline of the church, refusal to submit to arbitration
of a dispute with another member, and the nonpayment of debts. When
charges were preferred on any of these offenses, a trial was to be held
before a committee of the offender's fellow members. If he were judged
guilty by a majority of the committee, he was to be suspended or expelled
by the preacher. The General Rules, upon which Methodist discipline
was based, were identical in the Northern and Southern Churches, with
the single exception of the deletion of the item against "slave-holding;
buying or selling slaves" from the *Discipline* of the Methodist Episcopal
Church, South.[84]

The pattern of requirements for life and conduct, both general and
specific, continued essentially unchanged until Methodist unification in
1939. Any change in the General Rules, except by a very elaborate process of amendment, has been prohibited by a restrictive rule adopted in
1808.

In spite of the continuity which was maintained in the laws governing the trial of a church member for persistent violation or neglect of the
rules, in the period from 1876 to 1919 the administration of discipline
in Methodism was greatly relaxed. Departures from historic doctrines in
the Wesleyan heritage were noted in the section on theology. As Methodist members shared in the economic growth of the nation, less attention was paid to the provisions on indebtedness and the lending of money
at interest to fellow members. European immigration served to introduce into the tradition of Sabbath-observance many of the liberties and
employments characteristic of the Sunday practices of Europe. Methodists shared in this change in the keeping of the Sabbath.

The attitude toward amusements and recreation underwent perhaps

[83] *Ibid.*, p. 62.
[84] Cf. *Disciplin: of the Methodist Episcopal Church, South*, 1886, ¶¶ 28, 125-31; *Discipline of the Methodist Episcopal Church*, 1884, ¶¶ 32, 230-46.

the most thoroughgoing change of any of the areas of personal and social conduct. In the difficult days immediately after the Civil War there was little opportunity for the pursuits of leisure. But with economic recovery, both North and South, attention was again turned to diversion and amusement. The propriety of amusements suitable to the full enjoyment of life was recognized, as the distinction was drawn between innocent amusements and those which were still regarded as improper. J. M. Buckley, editor of the *Christian Advocate,* gave expression to the conservative but changing attitude regarding amusements at the first Ecumenical Methodist Conference in London in 1881. He indicated that he thought the list of amusements proscribed by the action of the 1872 General Conference was partial and unsatisfactory, and was being largely ignored. While he yielded nothing in his opposition to card-playing, dancing, and theater-going, yet he admonished the church to accept and make a place for those diversions which were not evil in their associations and tendencies.[85] These views represented a significant difference from those of some of his contemporaries, who held that all play and diversion should be prohibited, even charades in the family parlor and impromptu theatricals in the drawing room. The fear was expressed that these experiences would but "create a desire for stronger excitements."

A decade later, at the next Ecumenical Methodist Conference, a paper on "The Attitude of the Church Toward Amusements" was presented by Bishop C. D. Foss. He gave principles for the choice of amusements which would add joy to the Christian life and experience. He advocated the candid recognition of man's need for amusement and recommended cordial approval of constructive diversions as having a place in the recreation program for young people in the church. The pastor must not be "a lynx-eyed critic or a stern police justice." Bishop Foss had come to see in the Epworth League an organization through which tens of thousands of young people would find the experience of applied Christianity. Along with work and study there should be "hours of delightful recreation . . . merry conversation, reading, music, and games." [86] The standard of choice was to be the ethics of the New Testament, which allows personal liberty without harm to others, and the Methodist General Rule which excepts "the taking of such diversions as cannot be used in the name of the Lord Jesus."

The Episcopal Address to the Northern General Conference of 1900

---

[85] Buckley, "General Remarks," *Proceedings of the Oecumenical Methodist Conference . . . 1881,* pp. 287-88.

[86] *Proceedings of the Second Ecumenical Methodist Conference . . . 1891* (New York: Hunt and Eaton, 1892), p. 587.

noted the change in attitude in respect to the disciplined life in these
words:

The rigid and minute Church discipline of former years is relaxed: is this a sign
of pastoral unfaithfulness, or is it a sign of growing respect for individual
liberty and a better conception of the function of the Church? The plainness of
the early Methodist congregations has disappeared: is this simply vanity and
worldliness, or is it, in part, the natural and justifiable development of the
aesthetic faculty under more prosperous external conditions?[87]

No answer was given, but the reader senses a wistful feeling of loss in the
surrender of certain distinctive characteristics of the Methodist way of life.

Although the practices of Methodists were liberalized in the acceptance of diversions which were to be found in the culture surrounding
them, the specific rule on dancing, theater-going, and circuses was not officially altered until the General Conference of 1924. An "Address on
Worldliness," prepared by the bishops of the Methodist Episcopal
Church, South, and published in the *Discipline* for 1922, recognized
the importance of recreation, relaxation, sports, and play, while ad-
monishing against indecent theater shows, obscene literature, and
"those forms of needless self-indulgence that unfit the believer for communion with God or for faithful and effective service of man." [88]

The historic stand of Methodism had included the avoidance of
"drunkenness, buying or selling spiritous liquors, or drinking them,
unless in cases of extreme necessity" as one of the ways by which the
Methodist people "shall continue to evidence their desire of salvation." [89]
To this express prohibition a paragraph of general advice appears in the
1884 *Discipline:*

Both science and human experience agree with the Holy Scriptures in condemning all alcoholic beverages as being neither useful nor safe. The business
of manufacturing and of vending such liquors is also against the principles of
morality, political economy, and the public welfare. We, therefore, regard
voluntary total abstinence from all intoxicants as the true ground of personal
temperance, and complete legal prohibition of the traffic in alcoholic drinks
as the duty of civil government.[90]

[87] *Journal of the General Conference,* 1900, p. 60.
[88] ¶ 823.
[89] *Discipline of the Methodist Episcopal Church,* 1884, ¶ 32. This admonition is
among the General Rules and has been set forth with some variance in each *Discipline*
of the three main branches of Methodism in the United States. It is interesting to note
that in the *Discipline* of the Southern Church for 1886 the item reads: "Drunkenness,
or drinking spiritous liquors, unless in cases of necessity." The ban on "buying and
selling" was not included (¶ 28) .
[90] ¶ 36.

Methodism was thus committed to abstinence in its ideal and its proclamation.

The importance and difficulty of making its practice coincide with its preachment was noted by an American Methodist representative to the first Ecumenical Methodist Conference in 1881. He observed: "If any of us have not the grace to do this [practice abstinence], then we should cease preaching Christian perfection until we have learned to practice the first principle (s), self-denial." [91] The methods which Methodists were to employ in pursuit of this objective were education of the young, active participation in the work of the temperance societies, and the marshaling of popular support for general prohibition legislation. Church trials by which erring individuals were excluded from the fellowship for intemperance were few. The nurture of individual members in ideals and practice, as well as giving the weight of Methodist support to the call for legal reform, largely characterized Methodist discipline on the temperance issue.

The disciplining of church members extended also to divorce and the remarriage of divorced persons, lending of money at usury and contracting burdensome indebtedness, and idle or vile speaking. Fasting was enjoined as a means of keeping mentally and spiritually alert, and thus was defended on ground of being instrumental to good health as well as providing an exercise in obedience to the Scriptures.[92]

Criticism increased concerning the list of forbidden amusements and other action which had been introduced into the *Discipline* in 1872. While the importance of discipline within the church was fully acknowledged, yet it was recognized also that investigations, trials, and exclusion from the church could well represent a failure on the part of the church to elicit willing obedience to its rules. There was honest doubt as to the wisdom and practicality of rigid enforcement of violations of the *index expurgatorius* of 1872.[93]

In 1884 laxness in the administration of discipline was deplored: "The result is, offenders remain in the Church, elements of weakness to it, and stumbling blocks in the way of its progress." [94] By 1898 the mood had clearly changed to a concern for getting persons into the church for their cultivation in godliness, rather than putting them out for the sake of

[91] Alpha J. Kynett, in *Proceedings of the Oecumenical Methodist Conference . . . 1881*, p. 218.

[92] See John E. Godbey, "Is Fasting a Religious Exercise Enjoined by the Bible?" *The Methodist Review* (Southern), November-December, 1895, p. 222.

[93] See George P. Mains, "Our Special Legislation on Amusements: Honest Doubt as to Its Wisdom," *The Methodist Review* (Northern), May, 1892, pp. 375-89.

[94] William N. McElroy, "The Administration of the Discipline," *Methodist Quarterly Review* (Northern), January, 1884, p. 80.

cleansing the fellowship. An article in *The Methodist Review* emphasized the value of inclusiveness in these terms: "We do not believe anything is gained by holding up the extreme penalty of excommunication
for acts of doubtful character, or, at the worst, vanities or follies. . . . The
church is not a punitive institution. It succeeds, not by casting out men,
but by getting them in and developing all their capabilities for good.
Christ was not a maker of rules and regulations." [95]

Protestantism had surrendered the confessional and penance as means
of discipline within the church. Now Methodism was witnessing the decline of the class meeting as an instrument of group discipline, and was
moving out of the era of excommunication for violations of its ethical
legislation. In 1916 the rule on amusements came under extensive discussion, and within two quadrennia specific prohibitions on amusements
yielded to the more general admonition to Methodists "to make their
amusements the subject of careful thought and frequent prayer, to study
the subject of amusements in the light of their tendencies, and to be
scrupulously careful in this matter to set no injurious example." [96] Legalism in ethics and discipline had largely disappeared.

6

Training Methodist Youth

The Sunday School

In 1876 Methodism was helping to shape a structure of formal Christian education for American Protestant youth. The Sunday school movement had gained wide acceptance since Robert Raikes had gathered the
children from the streets into his home for Sunday instruction in 1780.
John Wesley had sensed the promise of the Sunday school plan immediately and had incorporated it into the Methodist program. The first Sunday schools in America were established in the 1780's by Methodist
preachers. The 1790 Conference in Charleston, South Carolina, had
voted "to establish Sunday Schools, in, or near the place of worship," and

---

[95] H. K. Carroll, "Is Methodism Catholic?" *The Methodist Review* (Northern),
March, 1898, p. 183.
[96] *Discipline of the Methodist Episcopal Church,* 1924, ¶ 69.

had decided to "compile a proper schoolbook to teach them learning and piety." [97]

From these simple parochial beginnings the Sunday school movement had gained international recognition and interdenominational organizational structure in less than a century. The interdenominational American Sunday School Union was established in 1824. In the Methodist General Conference of the same year a report of the Committee on Education advised greater attention to the Christian education of the youth. Martin Ruter, chairman of this committee and manager of the Western Book Concern in Cincinnati, immediately undertook the publication of instruction books for the Sunday schools. The Sunday School Union of the Methodist Episcopal Church was organized in 1827, and was approved the next year by the General Conference. The churches responded to the urgency of providing religious instruction so completely that by 1876 almost every Methodist church had its Sunday school. The number of students enrolled was reported to exceed the total number of church members. In the Methodist Episcopal Church in 1875 there were 19,106 Sunday schools with an enrollment of 1,398,731 scholars.

The improvement of religious instruction had been recognized as essential to the effectiveness of the Sunday school. Dr. John H. Vincent (later bishop) presented to the Rock River Conference in 1860 a report from the Sunday School Committee calling for the holding of teachers' institutes, to be conducted by the ablest religious educators, "to elevate our standards and improve our religious culture." [98] These words reflect a new concern in respect to the purpose of the Sunday schools, moving from the earlier concern to teach youth to read the Bible in order to bring them to conversion and prepare them for a glorious eternity.

In 1872, in response to an urgent proposal by B. F. Jacobs, a layman, and Dr. Vincent, both from Illinois, the International Sunday School Convention approved the establishment of an International Lesson Committee. An experimental system of uniform lessons was already in use. Dr. Vincent, who was to serve from 1868 to 1888 as secretary and editor of the Sunday School Union, was named chairman of the committee. The content of the curriculum was at first almost exclusively biblical, but in the years ahead church history, biblical archaeology and geography, doctrine, and Christian biography were added in the interest of broadening

[97] *Minutes of the Methodist Conferences Annually held in America, from 1773 to 1794, inclusive* (Philadelphia: Printed by Henry Tuckniss and sold by John Dickins, 1795).

[98] Quoted by Arlo Ayres Brown, *A History of Religious Education in Recent Times* (New York: The Abingdon Press, 1923), p. 69.

the cultural and religious growth of the students. The Sunday school, which had begun to outstrip the revival as an evangelizing agency of the church, came also to supply the means of Christian nurture for those who were being saved.

Significant advances in public education challenged and guided the Sunday schools in their development. Often charged with being "strong at the heart but weak at the head," Sunday schools were now led to a rethinking of objectives, content, method, and physical facilities. Under the influence of the educational theories of Herbart, Pestalozzi, and Froebel, mere memorizing of verses from the Bible was seen to be inadequate as religious instruction. The curriculum was graded to adjust to age differentiations of "kindergarten and beginners," "primary," "juniors," and "intermediates." The differentiation of age groups and the educational value of small classes, as well as the inspiration of the large assembly, were determinative of the architecture of buildings designed for church-school use. A Sunday school building erected in Akron, Ohio, in 1867 became the model for the hundreds of Akron-plan buildings which made their appearance in the fifty years that followed.

Changes in theology and in educational theory and the advent of the historical-critical approach to Bible study inevitably led to a rethinking of the adequacy of a lesson system devoted exclusively to study of biblical materials. The National Primary Union, formed in 1884, provided a rallying point for the opposition to the International Uniform Lesson plan. The selection of suitable biblical materials for a particular age and stage of development of the child, the grading of lessons for various age groups, and the introduction of extra-biblical materials were the major objectives of the Union and of the Graded Lessons Conference of 1907. These new considerations in curriculum-making were strongly resisted for more than two decades by the International Lesson Committee. The Religious Education Association, which was organized in 1903, carried forward the more liberal and experimental emphases which were emerging in the growing attention to the Christian education of youth. In 1908 the International Sunday School Association accepted the proposals of the Graded Lessons Conference to issue a series of graded lessons in addition to the uniform lessons.[99] The continued use of both types of lessons in the years that followed demonstrated that each was suited to meet the needs of churches of different backgrounds and teacher competence.

[99] For a summary of this development see Brown, *History of Religious Education*, pp. 81-112.

Youth Movements

Major attention in the Sunday school movement had been focused upon instruction in the Bible. The full development of the Christian person requires experiences of personal participation in programs of learning, social service, group leadership, and fellowship of a broader scope than the exclusively biblical study which had been provided. Attempts were made to meet this need by the organization of various young people's societies within the church. Early attempts in the Northern Church to secure General Conference approval for youth organizations in 1864 and 1872 were unsuccessful. In 1876 such approval was granted to the Church Lyceum, a program which had begun in the Fifty-first Street Church in Philadelphia. The purpose of the Lyceum was to provide encouragement in the reading of Christian literature. In 1884, under the leadership of John H. Vincent, an organization was formed called the Oxford League. Bible study, devotional exercise, reading of the Christian classics, and participation in Christian service programs were included in the statement of the League's purpose. Many of the Lyceum groups were superseded by chapters of the Oxford League as its popular program met with wide acceptance.

The Young People's Methodist Alliance was organized at the Des Plaines Camp Meeting Ground near Chicago in 1883. A Young People's Society of the Detroit Conference was formed in Michigan, and the Young People's Christian League in Boston, both in 1887. The youth of the North Ohio Conference formed the North Ohio Conference Methodist Episcopal Alliance in 1888. The popular response to these organizations of youth indicated the need to unify their efforts and thus to extend their influence. Representatives of the organizations met at the Central Methodist Church in Cleveland, Ohio, on May 14-15, 1889. A single Methodist youth organization was formed, to be called the Epworth League, "commemorating the birthplace of the founder of Methodism." Jesse L. Hurlbut, who had succeeded John H. Vincent as secretary of the Sunday School Union, became the corresponding secretary of the Board of Control. In 1890 the official periodical of the League was named *The Epworth Herald*. General Conference approval of the new youth organization was granted in 1892.

The Epworth League through its four departments—spiritual work, mercy and help, world evangelism, and literary and social work—provided opportunities for a variety of interests and the means of growth in spiritual leadership to Methodist youth. The pledge of the youth members "to take some active part" in the religious meetings of the church proved to be widely fulfilled as inexperienced young people took their first steps in Christian leadership in "leading League." The place which the Epworth League came to occupy was accurately foretold in the Episcopal Address at the General Conference in 1892: "There had long been a real chasm between the adult Church and the Sabbath-school which was not adequately provided for. The young manhood and womanhood of the Church lacked a place and opportunity for the best use and development of their powers. The Epworth League is a natural supply for this want." [100] The Epworth League was adopted as the official youth organization of the Methodist Episcopal Church, South, and the Methodist Church of Canada.

In 1881 the Christian Endeavor Society was founded in Portland, Maine, as an interdenominational youth organization. It became also international, with wide and effective influence in the nurture of Christian understanding and service, in response to the need within all churches for a fellowship of youth. In the Methodist Protestant Church the Christian Endeavor movement was "zealously espoused" by the young people of the church, and by 1899 had grown to nearly one thousand societies. *Our Young People* was the Methodist Protestant youth weekly magazine.

Methodist concern for the spiritual growth of its youth further led to the development of programs especially adapted to students in colleges and universities. The Y.M.C.A. and the Y.W.C.A., lay associations which had been founded at the middle of the nineteenth century, had extended their work to include youth on the campuses. The associations' purpose included evangelism and Christian nurture on a nondenominational basis. Missionary interest was expressed, and the calling of youth to vocations in Christian missions was centered in the Student Volunteer Movement. Many groups of the Y.M.C.A. and Y.W.C.A. and local chapters of the S.V.M. were active on the campuses of Methodist colleges. Where the desire was sufficiently strong for the retention of denominational ties in the student years, an extension of the Epworth League provided a basis for student religious organization.

In the church-related colleges religious instruction was included in the curriculum, in courses in Bible, church history, philosophy of religion, and religious education. The state colleges and universities, however, observing strictly the American principle of the separation of church and state, did not provide instruction in religion. Early in the twentieth century a new program came into being called the Wesley Foundation.

[100] *Journal of the General Conference of the Methodist Episcopal Church*, 1892, p. 52.

The Wesley Foundation sought to provide group fellowship, worship, and courses of instruction in religion for Methodist young people during their student years in public institutions of higher learning. James C. Baker (later bishop) established the first Wesley Foundation at Urbana, Illinois, to serve the Methodist students at the University of Illinois. This was incorporated in 1913. In 1914 the General Board of Education of the Southern Church authorized a study of the need for religious training for Methodist students in state schools. As a result of this study, a plan for financing special student ministries in co-operation with local churches and Annual Conferences and for the appointment of an educational secretary was approved by the board in 1916. Student work at state colleges and universities was extended to fifty centers by 1920, many with full-time directors and accredited courses in religion.

Teacher Training

One of the problems encountered in the development of Sunday schools and the religious education movement was that of providing training for an adequate staff of teachers. From the first days of the Sunday schools pastors had given instruction to their teachers in informal classes. The first formal step in teacher training was the organization of a normal course for teachers by John H. Vincent in 1867. This was expanded in the establishment of the Assembly at Lake Chautauqua, New York, in 1874. The Chautauqua Assembly provided an attractive setting where lectures and study were offered for Sunday-school teachers in a summer institute. Textbooks and lesson materials were published by the Methodist Sunday School Union, of which Vincent was the editor. These included Bible study, principles of education, and teaching methods. Jesse L. Hurlbut became editor when Dr. Vincent was elected to the episcopacy at the General Conference of 1888. Hurlbut continued in this office until 1900, writing as well as editing an impressive list of books for the normal courses. Teacher training was continued in classes in the local churches and communities, through summer institutes, by correspondence, and through courses in religious education in institutions of higher education. In 1909 the Board of Sunday Schools of the Methodist Episcopal Church published *The Worker and His Work Series* of texts for correspondence study; these covered the whole range of teaching from cradle roll through adult classes, and included a course for school superintendents.

Courses in religious education were being offered in fifteen Methodist colleges by 1920. Opportunity for graduate study was provided through the establishment of a chair of religious education at Boston University School of Theology in 1911. Interest in this work increased so that in 1919 the School of Religious Education of Boston University was organized. The first professor of religious education at Garrett Biblical Institute was appointed in 1912. Northwestern University in 1919 established a department of religious education. Antecedent to these formal courses were the interests and enthusiasms of the earlier seminary teachers for the Sunday school program. Daniel P. Kidder, who was from 1844 to 1856 editor of Sunday school books and tracts, served in the years that followed as professor of practical theology at Garrett Biblical Institute and later at Drew Theological Seminary. His passion for the Sunday school was undoubtedly communicated to the seminary students in his classroom, though the title of the course was "homiletics" or "practical theology."

Weekday Religious Instruction

Another development in the religious education of youth during this period provided for weekday instruction of children in addition to the programs scheduled on Sunday. Between 1900 and 1919 several experiments were in progress designed to give weekday time for religious studies and also to relate religious instruction to the educational program of the public schools.[101]

The daily Vacation Bible School had its beginnings almost simultaneously in New York City and in Traux Prairie, Wisconsin, at the opening of the century. Length of the schools varied widely, from two to six weeks. Study materials also showed the variety which differing leadership would dictate. Bible study, worship, music, missions, health and hygiene, patriotism, handicrafts, recreation, and field trips all found their place in the Vacation Bible School program. Since the schools were held on weekdays, the inclusion of matters other than biblical study did not incur wide criticism. While some of the schools were sponsored by a single church or denomination, many were conducted as community enterprises interdenominationally.

Other plans provided for a regular period of religious instruction outside school hours one or more days a week during the school year. In some states the laws permitted the offering of courses in religion for credit at the high school level. Experiments of this kind were undertaken in Colorado in 1910, North Dakota in 1911, and Indiana in 1913. The in-

[101] See Brown, *History of Religious Education,* pp. 195-227.

struction was given outside the regular school schedule in Colorado and North Dakota. In the latter, a syllabus was provided by the State Board of Education. In Indiana the plan provided for instruction during specified hours when the students were released from the public school schedule. The Methodist church in Gary, Indiana, was one of the first to pioneer in this "released-time" program. In Van Wert, Ohio, and in Batavia, Illinois, a plan was devised whereby for an entire day a staff of skilled teachers taught a succession of classes in religion as the pupils attended in rotation by grades. This provided graded instruction with the possibility of the fuller use of the time of competent teaching personnel. In 1920 there were more than three hundred weekday schools, of various types other than parochial schools, in operation.

Two particular values prompted the wide interest in experiments in weekday religious instruction. One was the opportunity to relate religious learning to the rest of the learning experience, and thus to facilitate wholeness in the pupil's personal development. The other was the challenge and opportunity to make religious instruction develop competence and effectiveness so that it would not suffer by comparison with general educational standards and practice. The achievement of either of these values was not clearly assured in 1919, but the experiments were to continue and expand with the increase in interdenominational and ecumenical programs in the years ahead. Over the years, legal difficulties developed in many states in connection with the attempts to relate religious instruction to the program of the public schools with the result that many of the experimental programs have been discontinued.

7

The Methodist Ministry

Underlying all other requirements for one who would serve in the ministry of Methodism has been, and is, the necessity that he be "called of God." Descriptive of this call was another phrase, rich in authentic Christian meaning, "moved by the Holy Ghost to preach." From the beginning of Methodism persons so moved have been required to meet four additional requirements. (1) Concerning their personal spiritual experience, the question was asked: "Do they know God as a pardoning

God? Have they the love of God abiding in them?" (2) Concerning their talents and promise of usefulness, the inquiry was, "Have they gifts, as well as grace, for the work . . . and has God given them any degree of utterance?" (3) In regard to their industry and diligence, they were required never to "be triflingly employed," "to mind *every* point, great and small, in the Methodist *Discipline*," "to spend and be spent" in the saving of souls. (4) In the matter of preparation for the task, the preacher was required to qualify by "walking closely with God," prayer, "searching the scriptures," fasting, partaking of the Lord's Supper "at every opportunity," and by "appropriate reading, study, and private devotion, from six in the morning until twelve." If any preacher failed to spend "at least five hours in four and twenty" in reading because he had no taste for reading, he was summarily advised to "contract a taste for it by use, or return to your trade." [102] Many specific requirements have been added and dropped in the course of the years. But the essentials—personal spiritual experience, talent, diligence, and preparation—have remained.

John Wesley gave constant attention to the qualifications of the Methodist preachers. At the first conference in 1744 a "seminary for labourers" was proposed by Wesley. In 1747 at the Orphan House in Newcastle, and in 1749 at Kingswood, he gathered some of his preachers for lectures, Bible study, and instruction in ministerial duties during Lent.

In early American Methodism the need for training was recognized, but formal theological education was neither required nor desired. The Methodist circuit riders who carried the gospel across the continent were trained in the "college on horseback." Bishop Asbury held that the books and tracts in the saddlebags were the best means of education for the traveling preachers.

The circuit system made it possible to appoint a "junior preacher" on a circuit with one who could teach him in the school of experience. When a proposal for a theological school was made about fifty years after the Christmas Conference, it was strongly opposed on the grounds that formal seminary education would actually make men unfit for the rigors of the itinerant ministry and would "educate them away from the people."

The Course of Study

The need for study and for books was, however, clearly recognized. In 1820 the *Discipline* stipulated:

[102] *Discipline*, 1785, pp. 11-12, 16-24.

It shall be the duty of the bishops or of a committee which they may appoint at each annual conference, to point out a course of reading and study proper to be pursued by candidates for the ministry. . . and before any such candidate is received into full connection, he shall give satisfactory evidence respecting his knowledge of these particular subjects, which have been recommended to his consideration.[103]

It was the responsibility of the presiding elder (district superintendent) to direct the candidates in their studies. Two years at first appears to have been the extent of the period of probation and the course of instruction, but the course was soon extended to include two additional years following admission into full membership in the conference. The list of books recommended appears first in the *Discipline* of 1848 in the Methodist Episcopal Church, and in 1878 in the Methodist Episcopal Church, South. Examinations were conducted by a committee of examiners either appointed by the bishop or elected by the conference.

In 1876 about one third of the preachers in Methodism were conference members who had completed the Course of Study, and the other two thirds were local preachers. Men were entering the traveling ministry at the rate of about seven hundred annually.[104] With the passing of the circuit system the need for local preachers decreased. Yet the number of local preachers still available, and the continuing opposition to seminary training, discouraged some very promising young men from the ministry. Concern was widely expressed over the lack of suitable candidates.

Some significant changes had already taken place in the concept of educational preparation for the ministry. There were four theological schools in full operation at this time, and others were soon to appear. Boston University School of Theology had developed from the first seminary to be founded in American Methodism, the Newbury Biblical Institute, at Newbury, Vermont, which began theological instruction in the 1840-41 academic year. It was renamed the Methodist General Biblical Institute and moved to Concord, New Hampshire in 1847. In 1868 it moved to Boston and became the first department of Boston University. The establishment of Garrett Biblical Institute was approved by the Rock River Conference in 1854, with the opening of classes on the new campus in Evanston, Illinois, in 1855. And Drew Theological Seminary, an outgrowth of the centennial of Methodism, had opened at Madison, New Jersey, in 1867. The Swedish Theological Seminary had also been

---

[103] Pp. 33-34.
[104] "Education for the Ministry," *The Methodist Review* (Northern), July, 1885, pp. 597 ff.

in operation in Evanston, Illinois, since 1870. Although the General Conference of the Southern Church rejected a proposal for a theological school in 1870, the Central University of the Methodist Episcopal Church, South, later Vanderbilt University, was chartered at Nashville in 1872. The first department listed in the proposal for Central University was "a theological school for the training of our young preachers." Theological departments were included in many of the colleges, their special purpose being to provide ministerial education. By 1885 about one hundred ministers with formal theological education were being received into conference membership annually.[105]

The Methodist Protestant Church had expressed its concern for ministerial training by the authorization of a Board of Ministerial Education at its General Conference (of the Western and Northern branch) in 1866. The first graduate seminary in Methodist Protestantism was the Westminster Theological Seminary, Westminster, Maryland, incorporated in 1884.

The opposition to seminary-trained ministers had not entirely subsided, however, even in the high echelons of the church. Daniel Curry, editor of *The Methodist Review,* observed in 1886 that the average minister was not expected to be a scholar, that theological professors were "bookish," and that neither the methods nor the graduates of the seminaries were satisfactory for the ministry of the church.[106] Yet there was a widespread call for a new program of ministerial education to be developed in the colleges. More than thirty colleges and universities were founded in the fifteen years from 1875 to 1890. Since all of them had departments of Bible, and biblical studies were regarded as the core of ministerial education, it was inevitable that the colleges should be regarded with hope for a new scheme of ministerial training to meet the needs of men who could not secure a seminary education. "Conference seminaries" which would provide courses for ministers without college preparation were called for. Wilbraham Academy, with its "comprehensive course of Bible study," and the Chicago Training School of the Women's Foreign Missionary Society were cited as examples to be emulated. "There is room for a less learned ministry, full of faith and the Holy Ghost." [107] There was no general response to this proposal. The immediate future was to favor rapid development of the Course of Study and the conference examinations.

Since Methodism was demanding more adequately trained men for her

[105] *Ibid,* p. 598.
[106] "Ministerial Education," *The Methodist Review* (Northern) , July, 1886, p. 588.
[107] D. Steele, "Non-Classical Methodist Theological Schools," *The Methodist Review* (Northern) , May, 1886, p. 455.

ministry, steps were taken to improve both the content and the administration of the Course of Study. *The Methodist Review* in the 1890's carried numerous articles and editorial comments supporting the improvement of ministerial education through "our largest school of theology," the Course of Study, in preparation for the conference examinations. The actual Course of Study for the next quadrennium was published in the *Review* in 1892. Practical suggestions on how to study particular books were featured for those who were enrolled in the course.

The focusing of attention upon the Course of Study resulted in its general strengthening as an educational program. Inadequacies were seen in the course itself, in the qualifications of the students for independent study, and in the procedure of conducting the examinations. The Wilmington Conference pioneered some improvements in the 1890's which resulted in changes in the handling of the examinations in many other conferences. The plan in the Wilmington Conference included the election of a permanent board of examiners, the organization of the course into departments, the requirement that all examinations be in writing, a provision for mid-year examinations which relieved the pressure at the session of the Annual Conference, and the submission of all examinations to the secretary of the board in order that a paper be identified for the grader by a code number rather than by the student's name. The last, clearly intended to reduce personal favoritism, provides an interesting commentary on one of the problems in the system of conference examinations. It is interesting to observe that after unification all of these changes became standard procedure in the administration of the Course of Study on a church-wide basis by the Department of Ministerial Education. Anonymity is not maintained in the grading of papers, but the graders are selected nationally and are thus "external examiners" from the point of view of a particular Annual Conference.

A Bureau of Correspondence to prepare the Course of Study was authorized by the General Conference of the Methodist Episcopal Church, South, in 1902. The work of the bureau demonstrated the effectiveness of a general church agency in supervising ministerial studies. In 1914 this agency was expanded into the Department of Ministerial Supply and Training, whose purpose was "to develop a more efficient ministry by keeping before the church its responsibility in raising up young men for this service, . . . thorough preparation, . . . financial assistance from the Ministerial Education Loan Fund, [and] correspondence courses for the benefit of preachers, teachers, and other Christian workers." [108] A permanent Commission on Course of Study appointed by the Board of Bishops was provided in the 1916 *Discipline* for the

[108] Du Bose, *History of Methodism*, p. 112.

Methodist Episcopal Church. These church-wide agencies were designed to unify and standardize the work of the Annual Conference board of examiners and to direct and aid students in their studies, as well as to prescribe the Course of Study.

As stated earlier, the first list of books in the Course of Study was published in the 1878 *Discipline* of the Southern Church, a procedure which had been followed in the North since 1848. The intent of the bishops to provide materials for serious study is evident in the courses which appeared.

The Course of Study for conference membership in the Methodist Episcopal Church in 1876 and 1880 included the following books: Angus, *Handbook of the Bible;* Blackburn, *History of the Christian Church;* Butler, *Analogy of Religion; Catechism of the Methodist Episcopal Church; Discipline of the Methodist Episcopal Church;* Garbett, *God's Written Word;* Harman, *Introduction to the Holy Scriptures;* Haven, *Rhetoric;* Hibbard, *Baptism;* Hill, *Rhetoric;* Kidder, *Homiletics;* Miley, *Atonement in Christ;* Nast, *Introduction to the New Testament;* Pope, *Compendium of Christian Theology;* Porter, *Compendium of Methodism;* Porter, *Elements of Intellectual Science;* Rawlinson, *Ancient History;* Ridpath, *History of the United States;* Smith, *Scripture History;* Stevens, *History of American Methodism;* Thalheimer, *Ancient History;* Thalheimer, *Medieval and Modern History; The Bible, Old and New Testaments;* True, *Logic;* Upham, *Mental Philosophy;* Waddington, *Church History;* Watson, *Theological Institutes;* Wayland, *Moral Science;* Wesley, *Plain Account of Christian Perfection;* Whatley, *Logic.*

In addition to these upon which examinations were given, an imposing list was appended for required reading in Wesley's sermons, Bible geography, manners and customs, ecclesiastical law, history of missions, history of rationalism, biblical hermeneutics, and preaching. There was also a separate four-year course for local preachers, and full courses in German, Norwegian, Danish, and Swedish for candidates in these language conferences.

The courses in the Methodist Episcopal Church, South, for 1878 and 1882 included some of the same books but with significant differences. The books required for examination were: Alford, *The New Testament;* Bickersteth, *The Spirit of Life;* Bingham, *Antiquities;* Blackburn, *History of the Christian Church;* Bloomfield, *The New Testament;* Bond, *Evidences of Christianity;* Broadus, *Preparation and Delivery of Sermons;* Butler, *Analogy of Religion;* Claude, *Essay on the Composition of a Sermon;* Conybeare and Howson, *Life and Epistles of St. Paul;* Coppee, *Rhetoric;* Coppee, *Logic; Discipline of the Methodist Episcopal Church, South;* Edgar, *Variations of Popery;* Farrar, *Life of Christ;* Henry, *Ex-*

position; Hickok, *Moral Science;* Hoppins, *Homiletics;* Jacobs, *Ecclesiastical Polity of the New Testament;* Jevon, *Lessons in Logic; Manual of the Discipline;* McTyeire, *Catechism on Church Government;* Mosheim, *Church History;* Neander, *Planting and Training of the Christian Church;* Olshausen, *The New Testament;* Paine, *Life of William McKendree;* Porter, *Elements of Intellectual Science;* Powell, *Apostolical Succession; Preacher's Manual;* Ralston, *Elements of Divinity;* Redford, *History of the Organization of the Methodist Episcopal Church, South;* Rivers, *Mental Philosophy;* Smith, *Elements of Divinity;* Summers, *Baptism; The Bible, Old and New Testaments;* Watson, *Exposition;* Watson, *Theological Institutes;* Watson, *Sermons;* Wesley, *Explanatory Notes on the New Testament;* Wesley, *Sermons;* Young, *Christ of History.*

A separate course was provided for the local preachers, and a special list was indicated in 1886 for the Mexican preachers.

It is not surprising that wide variations were noted in the administration of examinations in the several conferences. Yet every Methodist preacher was required to present a certificate of having passed these studies before he could be admitted to conference membership. Although the courses were revised each quadrennium, many books were retained throughout an entire generation. In the Southern Church the long-time favorites were McTyeire's *History of Methodism* and Paine's *Life of William McKendree.* Both were required for over fifty years. In the North Watson's *Theological Institutes* was the standard for forty-four years, Butler's *Analogy* for sixty years, and Wesley's *Christian Perfection* was retained for more than three quarters of a century.

Theological Schools

With the growth of the theological schools in acceptance and competence, the young preachers were officially "earnestly advised" to attend them. "But they shall not, on account of such attendance, be excused from examination on any part of the Conference Courses of Study." [109] By the end of the nineteenth century proposals were being made that a conference should accept a certificate of graduation from a theological seminary as a substitute for the Course of Study examinations.[110] The substitution of a seminary degree for the Course of Study was not accepted at this time. The *Discipline* of the Methodist Episcopal Church for 1916 (paragraph 596.3) stipulated that an Annual Conference could

[109] *Discipline of the Methodist Episcopal Church,* 1884, Appendix, p. 319.
[110] *The Methodist Review* (Northern), July, 1898, pp. 635-38.

not admit a man either on trial or into full membership unless he had passed the conference examinations. The "seminary rule," under which exemption from the Course of Study was permitted, was not adopted until 1928.

Intellectual and economic advancements led the Methodist people to demand increasingly better equipped ministers. The station appointment in a settled community called for a minister with a different type of educational qualification than that presented by the itinerant preacher under the circuit system. The need increased for ministers who were seminary trained and, under this demand, theological schools grew in acceptance and support. Their right of academic freedom was clearly established in 1908. When the bishops of the Methodist Episcopal Church, who had the power to veto the appointments of ministers to the seminary faculties, refused to approve Professor Hinckley G. Mitchell at Boston in 1905, the issue was carried to the following General Conference. The result was that the bishops were "relieved from the duty of investigating and reporting upon charges of misteaching in our theological schools," [111] although their formal approval of faculty appointments was required until 1928. Bishop Edwin Holt Hughes observes in his autobiography that this veto of seminary faculty appointments was a "power they [the bishops] had not sought and which later they were glad to surrender." [112] The outcome of the General Conference action at once assured and acknowledged the seminaries' place in the church at large.

Immediately upon the termination of the relationship between the Methodist Episcopal Church, South, and Vanderbilt University, with the loss of the Southern Church's only theological seminary, the General Conference of 1914 took steps to provide for the immediate establishment of a school for the training of ministers. A commission was appointed for this purpose, and before the year was past the Candler School of Theology was opened in the Wesley Memorial Building in Atlanta, Georgia. Asa Candler donated one million dollars to provide for its continuing support. The commission also recognized the newly founded school of theology at Southern Methodist University in Dallas, Texas, to be the church's seminary in the West.

In 1919 there were nine theological seminaries related to the Methodist Episcopal Church, two operated by the Methodist Episcopal Church, South, and one serving the Methodist Protestant Church. These were:

Methodist Episcopal Church: Boston University School of Theology, Boston, Massachusetts; Drew Theological Seminary, Madison, New Jer-

[111] *Discipline of the Methodist Episcopal Church,* 1908, ¶ 197.
[112] *I Was Made a Minister,* p. 36.

sey; Gammon Theological Seminary, Atlanta, Georgia; Garrett Biblical Institute, Evanston, Illinois; Iliff School of Theology, Denver, Colorado; Kimball School of Theology, Salem, Oregon; Maclay College of Theology, Los Angeles, California; Norwegian-Danish Theological Seminary, Evanston, Illinois; Swedish Theological Seminary, Evanston, Illinois.

Methodist Episcopal Church, South: Candler School of Theology, Atlanta, Georgia; Southern Methodist University School of Theology, Dallas, Texas.

Methodist Protestant Church: Westminster Theological Seminary, Westminster, Maryland.

Two other schools which were in fact theological departments of undergraduate colleges rather than graduate seminaries were the Central Wesleyan Theological Seminary, Warrenton, Missouri, and the Nast Theological Seminary, Berea, Ohio.

The minister was now expected to be a man of broad education and competence in many fields. Forty years earlier the articles in Methodist periodicals dealing with ministerial education had cited the needs for doctrinal and biblical studies. By 1919 the same journals featured articles with such titles as "The Preacher as a Reader of General Literature," "Shorthand and the Ministry," "Comparative Religion and the Preacher," and "Ministers as Reformers." [113]

With the establishment of the Commission on Course of Study in 1916 in the Methodist Episcopal Church, a new program of in-service training and continuing education for the ministry was developed. Pastors' schools of one or two weeks' duration were begun in many of the Annual Conferences. These served as coaching schools for the students in the Course of Study, and as institutes with lectures and refresher courses for the ministers who were already members of the conferences.

Preparation and Ordination

Methodism has required that the first step into its ministry be taken in the local church. When a member of the church felt that he[114] was "moved by the Holy Ghost to preach," he was expected to make his call known to his pastor. If the pastor felt that he should be encouraged to enter the ministry, his name was presented to the Quarterly Confer-

---

[113] *The Methodist Review* (Northern), September, 1916; March, 1918; May, 1918; November, 1918.

[114] The use of the masculine pronoun is significant. Women were first included in all provisions governing the ministry by action of the General Conference of 1956 (*Discipline*, 1956, ¶ 303).

ence of the circuit or station for recommendation to the bishop or the presiding elder for a license to preach. With this recommendation and the completion of "such course of Study as the Bishops shall prescribe," he could be licensed. Only then could he appropriately begin to preach. "No member of the church shall be at liberty to preach without such license." When he had passed the examination in the Course of Study for Admission on Trial, if he were duly licensed, he could be admitted to conference membership by vote of the ministerial members of the Annual Conference as a probationer or a preacher-on-trial. The minimum period of probation was two years. When he had served for two successive years in the regular service under appointment, and passed the examination in the prescribed studies, he could be received into "full connection," i.e., full membership. The requirements for his continuance were effectiveness in the work of the ministry and obedience to the discipline of the church.

The Methodist Episcopal Church and the Methodist Episcopal Church, South, provided two separate ordinations for the minister. A man was first ordained deacon, and after two years in the office of deacon he could be elected and ordained elder. A mission conference could elect a man to elder's orders sooner if it were deemed expedient. Ordination of a deacon was by election by the ministerial members of the Annual Conference and the laying on of the hands of a bishop. In the ordination of an elder some of the other elders joined the bishop in the laying on of their hands. In the Methodist Protestant Church there was a single ordination, that of the office of elder, which a man received by election of the Annual Conference and the laying on of hands of other elders.

The duty and authority of a traveling deacon was to administer baptism, to solemnize matrimony, to assist an elder in administering the Lord's Supper, and to perform all the regular duties of a traveling preacher. To these duties and authority was added the administration of the Lord's Supper when a man was ordained elder. A preacher could be ordained traveling deacon one year after admission on trial in the Northern Church, or after two years in the Southern Church. He could be ordained traveling elder only after serving two years as a deacon.

Methodism also provided for ordination of a local preacher as local deacon, upon the recommendation of the Quarterly Conference of the church of which he was a member, the completion of the qualifying studies, and after he had preached four years from the time he was licensed. Ordination as local elder could be granted upon fulfilling the qualifications of character and study, and having preached four years as a local deacon. The person receiving local ordination was authorized to preach, to baptize, and to receive members into the church, but he was not authorized to administer the sacrament of Holy Communion.

Technically the local preacher, though ordained, remained a layman. The ministers were those, ordained or unordained, who were probationary or full members of the Annual Conferences. This distinction between "preachers" and "ministers" is traceable in American Methodism from the time of Francis Asbury. Before the Christmas Conference the lay preachers preached and received members into the societies. The ministers were the Anglican clergymen who, on the occasion of their periodic visits throughout the connection, would administer the sacraments. Asbury, in a letter to Wesley in England, requested that "a minister, and such preachers as you can fully recommend" [115] be sent to carry on the work in America. Local preachers eventually came to receive ordination, both as deacons and as elders, but they continued to be regarded as ordained laymen. Only those ordained preachers who were received into membership in the conferences were ministers in the traveling connection.

[115] *Letters*, March 20, 1784

chapter 25

EARLY
EFFORTS
AT REUNION

The Cape May Conference

The Negro Churches

The Centennial of 1884

Ecumenical Conferences

S TANDING WHERE WE DO THIS HOUR, WITH
the old strifes sinking out of mind with
their obsolete causes, and in the presence of
so many converging Methodisms, and face
to face with the common foes of our common convictions and common history, we
cannot close this epistle of love and solicitude
without placing upon the heart of all Methodists every-where some sense of gratitude
for consummating fraternity between long-
estranged brothers, and an earnest prayer for
the hastening of that fullness of time in the
near future when there shall be one Methodism for mankind.[1]

The "hour" was May, 1876, and the
"where" was Baltimore—the General
Conference of the Methodist Episcopal
Church. Such high-flown language is expected in a general pronouncement of
the General Conference. In so many
generations faithful churchmen have
wondered about such pronouncements.
Do they completely ignore the true situation? Or do they deliberately speak above
the truth of the situation that the best
in men may be called forth?

"The old strifes sinking out of mind
with their obsolete causes" had been
painfully slow in sinking out of mind—
if, indeed, one could believe they had.

Though the clear intent of this pastoral address of the Northern General
Conference was forward, rather than
backward, it must be remembered out of
what kind of strain and misunderstanding it had come.

Occasionally the absence of a certain
man from a historic moment carries more
drama than the presence of a score of
other men. Dr. Lovick Pierce was not

[1] *Journal of the General Conference of the
Methodist Episcopal Church*, 1876, p. 411.

present at Baltimore in 1876. He had been designated the senior fraternal messenger from the General Conference of the Methodist Episcopal Church, South. A delegation of fraternal delegates to the Northern General Conference had been authorized at Louisville in May, 1874.[2] The College of Bishops of Southern Methodism, meeting in May, 1875, had appointed James A. Duncan, president of Randolph Macon College, Dr. Pierce and Dr. Landon C. Garland, chancellor of Vanderbilt University.[3]

Only the two arrived at the Baltimore Conference. Lovick Pierce began the journey but, being at the advanced age of ninety-two, found further travel impossible. He interrupted his trip but sent to the Conference a letter which was appropriately read instead of the address he would have delivered.[4]

The advanced age of this man would have restrained any body of wise men from laying on him the necessity for such strenuous travel, had it not been for the fact that his long life, in itself, represented an appropriate bridge with the early days of disruption.

In 1848—two years following the heated days of the separation—Dr. Pierce had gone from the Southern branch to the first General Conference of the Northern branch, meeting in Pittsburgh, as a fraternal delegate. He had been rejected, and there then set in what he calls in his letter of 1876 the "wintry night of 21 years." [5]

The twenty-one years of wintry night bring the calendar to 1869. In May of this year Bishops Janes and Simpson made a visit to the meeting of the bishops of the Southern Church in St. Louis. They had been appointed to bear a fraternal communication from the meeting of the bishops of the Methodist Episcopal Church, held in Meadville, Pennsylvania, in April of the same year. Bishop Morris had been appointed to accompany them but was unable to do so.[6]

This Northern deputation began its communication with the Southern bishops by saying: "It seems to us, that as the division of those Churches of our country which are of like faith and order has been productive of evil, so the reunion of them would be productive of good." They

[2] *Journal of the General Conference of the Methodist Episcopal Church, South,* 1874, pp. 540-49, 553-63.

[3] *Formal Fraternity, Proceedings of the General Conferences of the Methodist Episcopal Church and of the Methodist Episcopal Church, South, in 1872, 1874 and 1876, and of the Joint Commission of the Two Churches on Fraternal Relations, at Cape May, New Jersey, August 16-23, 1876,* p. 40.

[4] *Journal of the General Conference of the Methodist Episcopal Church,* 1876, pp. 211, 259, 416-20.

[5] *Ibid.,* p. 417.

[6] *Formal Fraternity,* p. 7.

continued: "As the main cause of the separation has been removed, so has the chief obstacle to the restoration." [7]

As early as the Erie, Pennsylvania, meeting of the Board of Bishops of the Northern Church in June, 1865, recognizing that the "great cause which led to the separation" [8] had passed, the hope was expressed that the day was not far distant when the whole Methodist family of the United States should be one organization.

Reference was then made to the action of the General Conference in Chicago, 1868, in appointing a commission "to confer with a like Commission from the African M. E. Zion Church" and be also "empowered to treat with a similar Commission from any other Methodist Church that may desire a like union." [9]

What Bishops Janes and Simpson did not specifically say to the Southern bishops was that this commission was appointed primarily to consider union with the Negro churches. Bishop Singleton T. Jones of the African Methodist Episcopal Zion Church, represented his General Conference meeting in Washington, D. C., at the same time. He had come to say to the Methodist Episcopal Church that the A. M. E. Zion Church was ready to enter into arrangements to affiliate on the basis of equality.[10]

The Chicago General Conference expressed deep interest and agreed to appoint a commission to meet with a similar one from the A.M.E. Zion Church and to report to the next General Conference. It was then ordered that this commission be empowered to treat with a similar commission from any other Methodist Church that might desire a like union.

They urged the Southern bishops to give attention to the commission referred to, and should a commission be appointed by the Southern General Conference, the two could meet and report to the next General Conferences.

The response of the Southern bishops at first seems on the verge of accepting the invitation to consider reunion, but then states that the subject of fraternal feelings and relations between the two churches must be considered first. The bishops moved, then, to recall the rejection of Lovick Pierce, to dispute the statement that slavery was the cause of separation, to deny that the Southern branch "separated" from the main body of the church, and to object to the conduct of missionaries and agents sent into the Southern states.

[7] *Ibid.*, p. 8.
[8] *Ibid.*, p. 9.
[9] *Journal of the General Conference of the Methodist Episcopal Church*, 1868, p. 264.
[10] John Jamieson Moore, *History of the A.M.E. Zion Church in America* (York, Pa.; Teacher's Journal Office, 1884) , p. 262.

Thus the thaw in that long wintry night had begun. It was followed by a fraternal visit of Bishop Janes and the Rev. Harris to the General Conference of the Methodist Episcopal Church, South, in Memphis in May, 1870. It was appropriate that Bishop Janes should have been a member of both delegations—the one from bishops to bishops and the one from General Conference to General Conference. He had been elected at the 1844 conference before the withdrawal of the Southern delegates, and his election was made possible by the support of Southern voters. These visitors came having been appointed by the commissioners appointed by the Methodist Episcopal General Conference of 1868. They were cordially received, but doubt was expressed as to their full authority to make proposals of union to the General Conference of the Methodist Episcopal Church, South.[11]

In 1872 the Northern General Conference ordered that fraternal delegates be sent to the next Southern General Conference—the first since the rejection of Lovick Pierce in 1848. The Board of Bishops later appointed Dr. A. S. Hunt, Dr. C. H. Fowler, and General Clinton B. Fisk. Bishop Janes, in a letter informing Dr. Fowler of the appointment, revealed the attitude of the Northern bishops toward this move:

I think it would be well for the commissioners to have some correspondence with each other before the time. I think also it would be well for the commissioners to meet in Cincinnati and spend one or two days together before you go to Louisville. You need to have your address or communication that you send in prepared. Of course it will be short and simple, but that is the very reason why it needs study and much care in its preparation. Every word needs to be weighed. It is not only necessary to look at what you mean by it, but also what enemies can by torture make it mean. There will be bitter enemies in the conference. You will want to be frank and open in all you say and yet observe the strictest rules of diplomacy. You will do well to look over carefully the history of the two churches since 44 that you may be prepared to meet any references that may be made to past events.

You will only propose fraternal relations not organic union. The latter will come in due time. They may possibly complain of our going into the South. You know the history of the whole movement and our reasons for it. I should be very careful not to anticipate in any statements any objections but stand entirely on the defensive.

I do not anticipate any unbrotherly conduct towards you. I believe you will be received most cordially and treated with the highest respect. Still there may be persons who will start troublesome questions which it will be well to be prepared to answer. The majority of ministers and laymen in the South are . . . in favor

[11] *Journal of the General Conference of the Methodist Episcopal Church, South,* 1870, pp. 191, 196-200.

of union, even organic union. Some of the leaders are bitterly opposed to even fraternal relations. Excuse these suggestions. I have the fullest confidence in the wisdom of yourself and colleagues. God and Duty

Yours Fraternally
E. S. JANES [12]

There was, therefore, some reason in 1876 to hope "for the hastening of that fullness of time in the near future when there shall be one Methodism for mankind." The "near" future was, however, no nearer than sixty-three years.

The Southern delegation had brought to Baltimore the Louisville resolution which stated "that in order to remove all obstacles to formal fraternity between the two churches, our College of Bishops is authorized to appoint a Commission, consisting of three ministers and two laymen, to meet a similar Commission authorized by the General Conference of the Methodist Episcopal Church, and to adjust all existing difficulties." [13] The Baltimore Conference heard the Pierce letter and addresses by Duncan and Garland. The conference, on the recommendation of a committee of the conference, adopted the wording of the Southern General Conference. A commission was appointed consisting of Morris DeCamp Crawford, Enoch L. Fancher, Erasmus Q. Fuller, Clinton B. Fisk, and John P. Newman.

This brings us to Cape May, New Jersey, August 16-23, 1876.

1

The Cape May Conference

The Board of Commissioners of the Methodist Episcopal Church, and of the Methodist Episcopal Church, South, appointed under the action of their General Conferences, met as a Joint Commission on Fraternal Relations in rooms of Congress Hall at ten o'clock A.M. on Thursday, August 17.[14]

[12] MS letter dated February 25, 1874, in the library of the Methodist Publishing House, Nashville.

[13] Journal of the General Conference of the Methodist Episcopal Church, South, 1874, p. 560.

[14] The Minutes of the Joint Commission and the Minutes of the separate meetings of the Southern commissioners in the handwriting of the secretaries are in the library of the Candler School of Theology, Atlanta. The Journal of the General Conference of the Methodist Episcopal Church, South, meeting in Atlanta in 1918, carries this

The Southern commissioners had been together for a few days in Philadelphia. At their morning session on August 14 they had recorded their common mind:

After full Conference the Commission were unanimously agreed that it is invested with plenary powers for the full and final adjustment of all existing difficulties and removal of all obstacles to formal fraternity between the M. E. Church and the M. E. Church South, subject only to the limitations that said adjustments of difficulties and establishment of formal fraternity shall not ignore The Plan of Separation adopted, by the General Conference of 1844, under which the M. E. Church, South claims to be a cognate and co-equal section of the original Methodist Episcopal Church of the United States of America organized in 1784, and, also, asserts certain inherent property rights:—the provisions of said Plan, however, touching territorial limits, being subject to such revision as may lead to a solution mutually satisfactory.[15]

In careful observance of the amenities so customary to that day, the two commissions arrived in Cape May the day prior to the opening of their consultations and exchanged correspondence. The commissioners of the Methodist Episcopal Church, South, sent a note to Dr. Morris DeCamp Crawford, chairman of the commissioners of the Methodist Episcopal Church, in which they said they had the "honor to report to you our presence, and our readiness to enter upon the work intrusted to us." [16]

Commissioners of the Methodist Episcopal Church, South, were E. H. Myers, R. K. Hargrove, Thomas M. Finney, Robert B. Vance, and David Clopton.

The niceties of the occasion did not prevent a frank statement in this opening letter of the issue at debate from the beginning:

In his address to your General Conference, that revered patriarch of Methodism —Dr. Lovick Pierce—postulated what seems to us may constitute a happy term of agreement between our respective Churches, namely, That there is but one Episcopal Methodism in the United States, and you and we together make up this Methodism, our two General Conference jurisdictions being each rightfully and historically integral parts of the original Methodist Episcopal Church constituted in 1784.[17]

reference: "J. E. Dickey, of the North Georgia Conference, presented to the Conference the original Minutes of the Cape May Commission, which had been found among the records of First Church, Atlanta, and ordered by that body to be turned over to the General Conference. Dr. Dickey moved that the document be presented to Emory University, in the custody of the Chancellor" (p. 19).

[15] *Journal of the Proceedings of the Board of Commissioners of the Methodist Episcopal Church, South, 1876*, pp. 101-2.
[16] *Formal Fraternity*, p. 60.
[17] *Ibid.*, pp. 60-61.

The letter presses its point again and again by asking for assurances that the Northern commissioners accept the postulates of Dr. Pierce. It further states that the advances made by recent General Conferences of Northern Methodism were interpreted by Southern Methodism "as the official recognition of the Methodist Episcopal Church, South, as a legitimate organization of the Methodist Episcopal Church into a second General Conference jurisdiction, as provided for in 1844 by the last Ecumenical General Conference of the Methodist Episcopal Church." [18]

Offering these suggestions and hoping and praying for a harmonious session, the communication called on the Northern commission to designate the hour and place for assembling in joint commission.

The same day the response was delivered to Dr. E. H. Myers, chairman of the Southern delegation. It reciprocated the expression of the hopeful spirit contained in the first letter. From the outset it was believed that no insuperable difficulty stood in the way. The letter quoted as acceptable the "language of that venerable patriarch of Methodism, Dr. Lovick Pierce, 'There is but one Episcopal Methodism in the United States.'" [19]

The Northern commissioners were not prepared, they went on to declare, to adopt some of the views referred to in the previous letter touching the action of the General Conferences referred to, but it was not believed material that such constructions of such actions should be adopted. At this point, the right to differ in sincerity was accorded to both sides. It was believed, however, that upon every important and essential matter both commissions could meet upon a common ground.

We venture to suggest one such basis, for example: Each of the aforesaid Churches is a legitimate Branch of Episcopal Methodism in the United States, and since the organization of the Methodist Episcopal Church, South, was consummated in 1845, by the voluntary exercise of the right of the Southern Annual Conferences, ministers and members, to adhere to that Communion, she has been an evangelical Church, reared on scriptural foundations, and her ministers and members, with those of the Methodist Episcopal Church, have constituted one Methodist family. "You and we together," as Dr. Pierce remarks, "make up this Methodism." We can, thus understood, accept the postulates of Dr. Pierce to which you refer.[20]

It is not easy to determine whether the two commissions were able to meet because they had reached an agreement on the basic issue of separation or whether they were able to meet because they carefully skirted the issue.

[18] *Ibid.*, p. 61.
[19] *Ibid.*, p. 63.
[20] *Ibid.*

The Minutes of the Southern commissioners, meeting alone on August 17 just prior to the 10:00 A.M. opening of the Joint Commission, show the mind of the group: "Reserving for consideration differences of opinion mentioned in said letter, there was expression of satisfaction as to its conciliatory spirit and tenor, and the time having arrived for the meeting of the Two Commissions in Joint Session this Commission adjourned for that purpose." [21]

Present-day Methodists must not overlook the presence in these communications of the word "jurisdiction." A word so early with us may be expected to remain with us late. History does not always teach us the solution to our problems, but more frequently it reminds us of the basic issues. Here, then, was and is the stubborn question: Was Southern Methodism a group of disloyal rebels who "went out" from the Methodist Episcopal Church, and now could only return by repentance? Or were Northern and Southern Methodisms two jurisdictions of the same original and continuing ecumenical episcopal Methodism?

To understand the true depth of this dilemma, one must understand that this is the same dilemma the nation found itself in. Were the Southern states disloyal rebels, or was the conflict between two parties equally loyal to the ideals of the whole nation?

It was possible on the evening of the opening day of joint deliberations for the commissioners to adopt unanimously the following:

DECLARATION AND BASIS OF FRATERNITY between said Churches, namely: STATUS OF THE METHODIST EPISCOPAL CHURCH, AND OF THE METHODIST EPISCOPAL CHURCH, SOUTH, AND THEIR CO-ORDINATE RELATION AS LEGITIMATE BRANCHES OF EPISCOPAL METHODISM:

Each of said Churches is a legitimate Branch of Episcopal Methodism in the United States, having a common origin in the Methodist Episcopal Church organized in 1784.

Since the organization of the Methodist Episcopal Church, South, was consummated in 1845, by the voluntary exercise of the right of the Southern Annual Conferences, ministers and members, to adhere to that Communion, it has been an evangelical Church, reared on scriptural foundations, and her ministers and members, with those of the Methodist Episcopal Church, have constituted one Methodist family, though in distinct ecclesiastical connections. [22]

The Southern commissioners had met at 6:00 P.M. that day to consider the paper which had been prepared by E. L. Fancher of the Northern Church and E. H. Myers of the Southern Church before its proposal at 8:00 P.M. to the Joint Commission:

[21] *Journal of the Proceedings of the Southern Commissioners*, p. 111.
[22] *Formal Fraternity*, p. 67.

It was noted that the form of statement in a certain connection would exclude several colored church organizations from the classification of Episcopal Methodisms of this country, but it was concluded that, as those organizations did not come into view in any wise in the appointment and functions of this Joint Commission, the omission of reference to them could not be properly construed as an oversight of those Episcopal Methodisms; It was also suggested and agreed that after the words of the final clause, to wit: "have constituted one Methodist Family" there be added the words, to wit: "though in distinct ecclesiastical connections." With this amendment it was declared by each of the Commissions, that the proposed paper was satisfactory.[23]

After its adoption, the chairman, E. H. Myers of Savannah, Georgia, called on Morris Crawford of New York to lead in a prayer of thanksgiving to God. The commissioners united in singing, led by General Clinton B. Fisk of St. Louis. The secretaries carefully noted in the Minutes the full text of the familiar verse:

> Blest be the tie that binds
> Our hearts in Christian love;
> The fellowship of kindred minds
> Is like to that above.

"The Chairmen of the Boards, in token of the meaning and effect of the action just consummated, joined hands, which was followed by the same token exchanged between the Commissioners of the two Boards." [24]

Now, however, the jubilation had to find an end so the hard work could be done on such matters as the practical details of property settlements. Though there were singing and hand-shaking at Cape May, in many a town and village in the South and especially in the border states there were bitterness and disputes over church property.

The Cape May commissioners were well aware of the years of storm behind these questions of property settlement. Many Northern writers and preachers had expressed their moral rage at a church which they believed to be the "illegitimate offspring of slavery." Slowly there developed in the Northern branch a missionary motivation to invade the territory of the Southern branch and take over. Bishops had used the power of the presidency of the United States and the force of the War Department to take over pulpits and property in the South. Out of this tangle of human emotion, however, the commissioners did arrive at "Rules for the Adjustment of Adverse Claims to Church Property."

[23] *Journal of the Proceedings of the Southern Commissioners*, p. 112.
[24] *Formal Fraternity*, p. 68.

Not only were rules devised, but certain specific cases of adverse property claims were investigated and adjudicated.

Rule I. In cases not adjudicated by the Joint Commission, any Society of either Church, constituted according to its Discipline, now occupying the Church Property, shall remain in possession thereof, *provided,* that where there is now in the same place a Society of more members attached to the other Church, and which has hitherto claimed the use of the property, the latter shall be entitled to such possession.

Rule II. Forasmuch as the Joint Commission have no power to annul decisions respecting Church Property made by the State Courts, the Joint Commission ordained in respect thereof:—

1. In cases in which such a decision has been made, or in which there exists an agreement, the same shall be carried out in good faith.

2. (Here a lengthy paragraph provides for arbitrators—one to be chosen by each claimant from their respective Societies, and the two thus chosen shall select a third person, not connected with either of said churches—where settlements cannot otherwise be speedily settled.)

3. In communities where there is but one Society, Rule I shall apply.

Rule III. Whenever necessary to carry the aforegoing Rules into effect, the legal title to the Church Property shall be accordingly transferred.

Rule IV. These Rules shall take effect immediately.[25]

On the afternoon of the final day, August 23, an address to the bishops, ministers, and members of the two branches of Methodism was delivered which included the statement of agreements, and further exhortations to fraternity.

We cannot restrain the expression of our united congratulations to both of the great Churches whose Commissions we have executed, in uniting between them the broken cords of affectionate and brotherly fraternization. Henceforth they may hail each other as from the auxiliary ranks of one great army. The only differences they will foster will be those friendly rivalries that spring from earnest endeavors to further to the utmost the triumphs of the gospel of peace. Whatever progress is made by the one Church or by the other will occasion general joy. They will rejoice in each other's success as a common good; and, amid the thousand glorious memories of Methodism, they will go forward devoted to their one work of spreading Scriptural holiness over these lands.[26]

Comparisons are then drawn between two such branches of the same church and the apostles who went out two by two to witness. An astronomical illustration was also used—that of dual-stars revolving together

[25] *Ibid.,* pp. 69-70.
[26] *Ibid.,* pp. 80-81.

so much the complement of each other as to produce a pure white light of exceeding brilliancy.

The strong sense of "fraternity" which developed at Cape May was not immediately conveyed to the whole of both churches. Many took vigorous exception to the spirit and decisions of those meetings. Bishop Thomas B. Neely, writing as late as 1915 in his *American Methodism: Its Divisions and Unification,* betrayed a strain of sarcasm:

> According to this the arrangement was not only final but also complete. Everything had been adjusted. No further unpleasantness could be possible. Never again would there be, or could there be, any occasion for difficulty or unfraternal difference, but, anywhere and everywhere in the South, the two Churches could, and would, without friction, work side by side. Paradise was restored.[27]

Bishop Neely was quite convinced that the Northern commissioners had been "conciliatory in the extreme, and so much so, that possibly without fully perceiving its bearing, on one point they conceded too much. So anxious were they to reach harmony and fraternity that they apparently were blinded to an historical inaccuracy which was issued in the declaration of the joint commission." He is taking objection to the statement which makes both churches branches of Episcopal Methodism. "As a matter of fact the Methodist Episcopal Church did not branch from anything in 1844 or 1845." "It is not a branch but the main stream. It is not a branch but the original tree with its roots reaching back to 1784." [28]

Morrow points out that within the Methodist Episcopal Church the reaction to the agreements was generally distributed with some reference to geography. "In the North, sentiment generally endorsed the settlement, except for New England and upper New York. *Zion's Herald,* the journal of the New England clergy, was noncommittal in its editorial comment, and waited three weeks to print even an abbreviated account of the proceedings at Cape May." [29]

New York Methodists violently objected to making legitimate the Southern branch. In a vote, 113 to one, they called on the next General Conference to disapprove the work of the commissioners.

Northern Methodists working in the South saw the whole affair as a surrender. "Nevertheless, the importance of the Joint Commission of 1876 should not be reduced to a cipher. For the first time in thirty years,

[27] Thomas B. Neely, *American Methodism: Its Divisions and Unification* (New York: Fleming H. Revell Co., 1915), p. 231. Used by permission.

[28] *Ibid.,* pp. 232-33.

[29] Ralph E. Morrow, *Northern Methodism and Reconstruction* (East Lansing: Michigan State University Press, 1956), p. 88.

accredited agents of the opposite denominations used ordered conversations rather than anathemas in an effort to resolve differences. Probably the Peace Commission was worth less in concrete achievement than as a symbol." [30]

2

The Question of Union in the Negro Churches

So much had resulted from a commission appointed initially to canvass the possibilities of union with Negro churches. Giving it authority to deal with Southern Methodism was clearly an afterthought.

The two major Negro churches had been making efforts to find a way to union between themselves. In 1864 both General Conferences, of the A.M.E. Church and of the A.M.E. Zion Church, were meeting in the city of Philadelphia. Early in the month of May of that year John Turner called the attention of the A.M.E. General Conference to a deputation appointed by the General Conference of the Methodist Episcopal Church. A resolution was offered by a Dr. Revels that a similar deputation be appointed to wait upon the Northern General Conference. At this same point in the conference, H. M. Turner offered a lengthy preamble and resolution recommending the union of the African Methodist Episcopal Church and the African Methodist Episcopal Zion Church. This was referred to a special committee of eight.[31]

The report of this committee of the A.M.E. Church to its General Conference was:

We, your committee, to whom was referred the subject of the union of the African Methodist Episcopal Church and the African Methodist Episcopal Zion Church, after giving the subject the most careful attention, beg leave to report as follows:

Your committee find in existence in the various parts of the United States two separate and distinct religious organizations, to wit: the African Methodist Episcopal Church and the African Methodist Episcopal Zion Church, both professing the same faith and preaching the same gospel, and being separated by only a few points upon which hang no important issues.

[30] *Ibid.,* pp. 90-91.
[31] Charles Spencer Smith, *A History of the African Methodist Episcopal Church* (Philadelphia: Book Concern of the A.M.E. Church, 1922) , pp. 466-67.

And your committee, firmly believing in the universally received maxim that weakness follows division, and strength follows union, and that this principle is exemplified by the continued separation of the two aforementioned bodies, we can but lament its further continuance. And in view of the momentous events daily transpiring, plainly indicating to every thoughtful mind the expediency and the vital importance of a union among all colored people, social and ecclesiastical; and while the light of the civilization and the claims of our holy religion, as well as the vast harvest to be gathered into the garden of our Lord and Master, call upon us to arise in the majesty of a noble purpose; releasing ourselves from all the embarrassments which a separate existence has unfortunately occasioned, we offer to our sister Church a friendly and Christian negotiation, having in view the combination of the two bodies.

Therefore, to consummate so desirable an object your committee would respectfully recommend the appointment of one elder from each Annual Conference District, in connection with two bishops, to confer with the same number of elders, and the two Superintendents of the African Methodist Episcopal Zion Church, who may have received an appointment, and are endorsed with power to act in the matter aforesaid, by their General Conference.

Said committee of their General Conference shall have power to call a convention consisting of such a number of delegates as may be agreed upon by them from each Connection. This convention, when once assembled, shall have power to agree upon articles of consolidation. Said articles of consolidation must be submitted to all the Annual Conferences of each Connection, and if ratified by a majority of the same, they shall be final.

Your committee further reports that in view of the fact that the Methodist Episcopal Church has, in the most Christian manner, interested itself in this important office by appointing its highest officers, even its bishops, to act as friendly mediators in this matter; therefore, be it

Resolved, that we accept this mediation and kindly invite them to a friendly participation in the above mentioned conference.[32]

A subcommittee of three was appointed to inform the A.M.E. Zion General Conference of this action.

The next day a committee of delegates from the A.M.E. Zion Church came to the A.M.E. General Conference and presented the following resolution:

Resolved, by General Conference of the A.M.E. Zion Church, that the body cordially receive the representation just made to it by the subcommittee on Church union created by the General Conference of the A.M.E. Church, and that we promise to give the subject that Christian and fraternal consideration which its importance so earnestly demands, at the earliest opportunity.[33]

[32] *Ibid.,* pp. 371-72. See also Appendix, p. 491.
[33] *Ibid.,* p. 493.

This resolution had come out of the Eleventh Session of the General Conference of the A.M.E. Zion Church, where the question of consolidation was committed to a joint convention "to consummate a union upon a basis which will be satisfactory to all concerned." [34]

The *Discipline* of the African Methodist Episcopal Zion Church fixed May 25 as the time of the assembling of its General Conference. The General Conference of the African Methodist Episcopal Church, which convened the first Monday in May, delayed final adjournment in order that it might be in session when the General Conference of the African Methodist Episcopal Zion Church should convene.[35]

On the last evening of the A.M.E. General Conference (there is some confusion as to whether this was May 26 or May 27 [36]) the whole matter was approved and delegates elected to the convention set to meet in the same city of Philadelphia in Wesley African Methodist Episcopal Zion Church on the second Tuesday in June, 1864.[37]

On May 27 the A.M.E. Zion committee, headed by the Rev. S. T. Jones, afterward a bishop, reported on the matter to its General Conference, as follows:

Whereas, by the working and control of an all-wise and gracious Providence, circumstances and events have so conspired during the present great struggle as clearly to indicate that the time to favor Zion has fully come; and

Whereas, we should prove ourselves false alike to the principles of our holy religion, our obligations as the representatives of Christ, and our duty and responsibilities as the leaders of a people weak because divided, if we should fail from any minor consideration to improve the present favorable opportunity, having in view the future peace and prosperity of the Church, and the moral, social, and political interests of the race with which we are immediately identified; therefore,

Resolved, That the great principle of Christian union and brotherhood we fully endorse, and that all proper means be employed in furtherance of that principle, and that our warm sympathies are with those who are heartily engaged in the effort to unite in one body the African Methodist Episcopal Zion Church and the African Methodist Episcopal Church.

Resolved, That as an evidence of our sincerity, and with a view of facilitating the consummation so ardently desired, this Conference appoint a committee of nine with the Bench of Superintendents forthwith, who shall be authorized and empowered to confer with a similar committee in connection with the Bench of Bishops of the African Methodist Episcopal Church on all matters touching a consolidation of the bodies represented.[38]

[34] Moore, *History of the A.M.E. Zion Church,* p. 235.
[35] Smith, *History of the A.M.E. Church,* p. 374.
[36] *Ibid.,* pp. 494-95.
[37] *Ibid.,* p. 373.
[38] *Ibid.,* pp. 374-75.

A committee of three—J. W. Hood, J. H. Smith, and J. P. Hamer—was appointed to inform the General Conference of the African Methodist Episcopal Church that in compliance with their wishes a committee had been named to confer with them on the consolidation of the connections. On returning they represented that six o'clock that evening had been fixed upon for the joint meeting. The committee of nine reported to the A.M.E. Zion Conference that it had been agreed to submit the subject to a convention composed of twenty-five on each side, and to have their action submitted to all the Annual Conferences for confirmation.

Whereas, the committee of the A.M.E. Zion and the A.M.E. General Conferences met in joint committee, and having interchanged sentiments on the great question of union between the bodies represented by them; therefore,

Resolved, that it is the opinion of this meeting that the great question of consolidation may be safely committed to a convention to consummate a union upon a basis which will be satisfactory to all concerned.

Resolved, that it is the sense of this joint committee that such a convention be held in the city of Philadelphia, commencing on the second Tuesday in June, 1864, in Wesley Church on Lombard Street, at 10 o'clock, A.M., and that twenty-five delegates from each connection shall compose said convention; and the result of said convention shall be submitted to the Annual Conferences of both Churches, and if agreed to by a majority of each, shall be final; all of which is respectfully submitted.[39]

It was approved and the delegates elected.

The Joint Convention of 1864

The convention met at the time and place agreed upon and continued in session for two days. The following platform was approved:

Whereas, the great principles of Christianity, as taught by Christ and his Apostles, call upon the Church militant to labor for the spread of God's kingdom among men throughout the whole world, by means of preaching, teaching, and a general diffusion of knowledge; and

Whereas, there has been a growing tendency among the members of the said Churches for a union of the two Connections, and action has been taken in the Annual Conferences of the African Methodist Episcopal Zion Church on this subject; and also many articles have appeared in the Christian Recorder and Anglo-African, discussing the propriety of a union which cannot be properly effected without the action of the General Conferences of both Churches; and, deeply convinced of the importance of Christian union and fellowship, and of

[39] Moore, History of the A.M.E. Zion Church, pp. 235-36.

the retarding and pernicious influences usually consequent upon division; therefore,

Resolved, That the undersigned members and representatives of the African Methodist Episcopal Zion, and the African Methodist Episcopal Churches in America, with a sense of their responsibility to God, as well as a sense of the grave and delicate responsibilities resting on them as the conservators of the dearest rights and interests of that portion of the great family of God for whom they act, respectfully present to the Convention the following articles as the basis of a permanent union of the respective bodies of the same represented by the delegates.[40]

Then follows the listing of the articles of agreement. First the "Points on Which We Already Agree"—doctrine, mode of worship, system of the itinerant ministry, the fact of being Methodists. Class meetings, love feasts, and prayer meetings are the same. The General Rules are the same. Each has Official Boards and Quarterly, Annual, and General Conferences. Both are episcopal Methodists.

It was agreed in the event of union to change both connectional names and adopt "The United African Methodist Episcopal Church in America." Matters of lay representation, trustees, the ministry, etc., were agreed to. Then the method of submitting this plan to the male members of each connection through Quarterly and Annual Conferences was outlined. Finally, ratification was to come at the 1868 General Conferences.[41]

The Twelfth Session of the A.M.E. Zion General Conference, meeting in Washington in 1868, on the first day appointed a committee to prepare an address to forward to the Methodist Episcopal General Conference, then in session in Chicago, Illinois.[42]

On the sixth day a motion passed changing the title of superintendent to bishop, "in order to complete the plan of consolidation of the African Methodist Episcopal Zion Church with the African Methodist Episcopal Church." [43]

A committee from the A.M.E. Church came to the conference on the next day. When their address was read and acted upon, a preamble and resolution were offered by David Stevens on the subject of the General Conference's communicating with the General Conference of the Methodist Episcopal Church, then in session at Chicago, Illinois, on the ques- of union with the Methodist Episcopal Church. The matter was discussed at some length, and afterward a telegram was sent to the Methodist Episcopal General Conference.[44]

[40] Smith, *History of the A.M.E. Church,* pp. 376-77.
[41] *Ibid.,* pp. 377-79.
[42] Moore, *History of the A.M.E. Zion Church,* p. 247.
[43] *Ibid.,* p. 256.
[44] *Ibid.,* p. 257.

The following day the conference met in executive session to consider further the matter of union with the A.M.E. Church. The following preamble and resolution offered by J. J. Moore was adopted:

WHEREAS, This General Conference has been officially informed by a committee from the African Methodist Episcopal Bethel Church that they are not prepared to unite with us on the plan agreed upon by the convention of the two connections held at Philadelphia in 1864, and submitted to the Annual Conferences of each connection for ratification, and

WHEREAS, They decline uniting on the basis agreed upon, but now ask us to meet with them to unite on some other basis or plan; and

WHEREAS, Our people in adopting the plan proposed by the said convention did it in good faith and did not authorize us to offer or accept any other plan; therefore

Resolved, That we deem it inexpedient to meet with them according to their proposal.[45]

Later in the conference the committee brought word from the A.M.E. Church that they were rejecting the plan of union because in the voting by the people of the connection there had not been "that fulness of the members of our church which is their right." [46] Union was still favored, but not on the basis of the 1864 convention. A new plan was called for. The matter was laid to rest with the adoption of the following report to be taken to the A.M.E. Church:

To the General Conference of the A.M.E. Bethel Church:—We have been appointed a committee to inform your honorable body that according to the action of your body on the subject of consolidation, taken on Saturday last, a copy of which is herewith presented, that our body must respectfully and peremptorily decline to take any further action on the subject at the present session. J. P. Hamer, Sec., Wm. F. Butler, Chairman.[47]

The Minutes of the 1868 General Conference of the A.M.E. Church were not printed. "The only known reason is that the General Book Steward, Joshua Woodlyn, did not see his way clear to print them. What parsimony! What shortsightedness!" [48] Smith reports that at this conference it was found that while the conferences of the African Methodist Episcopal Zion Church had voted in favor of the plan of union, the A.M.E. Church conferences had voted against it. It was proposed that

[45] Ibid., p. 258.
[46] Ibid., p. 259.
[47] Ibid., pp. 261-62.
[48] Smith, History of the A.M.E. Church, p. 78.

negotiations be continued but on a different basis. To this suggestion the A.M.E. Zion Church objected, as seen in the adoption of the above resolution.[49]

So historian Smith concludes that, "despite the amount of time, energy, and talent expended in an effort, which undoubtedly on the surface was honest and sincere, to effect organic union between the two churches in question, it proved a dismal failure."[50]

Proposals to the Northern Church

During this same session of the A.M.E. Zion General Conference, a committee was appointed to draft proposals to the Methodist Episcopal Church of union with that body; which committee reported to the conference the following:

To the Bishops and members of the M.E. General Conference:—We are ready to enter into arrangements by which to affiliate on the basis of equality, and to become one and inseparable now and forever. On the condition of full equality with the most favored of the church, we desire the further stipulation, that a sufficient number of those whom we may select to exercise the episcopal oversight of the colored element of the body may be set apart to that office, on the basis of the perfect equality with all other Bishops of the M.E. Church; as we have practically demonstrated that a lay representation, especially in the law making department of the church, is at once sound, safe and productive of harmony among the people. We hope if at all compatible with views of religious progress that you will adopt the same as the rule of the church.[51]

This resolution was carried in person by Bishop Singleton T. Jones from the A.M.E. Zion General Conference in Washington to the Methodist Episcopal General Conference meeting at the same time in Chicago. The Methodist Episcopal Conference adopted the following:

Resolved, 1. That we, having received the official communication of the African Methodist Episcopal Zion Church proposing union with the Methodist Episcopal Church in the United States, and also the representations of the Rev. S. T. Jones on the same subject, with great satisfaction, we hereby express to them our Christian regards and deep interests in their progress and prosperity as a Church of the Lord Jesus Christ.

[49] Ibid., p. 80.
[50] Ibid., p. 56.
[51] Moore, History of the A.M.E. Zion Church, pp. 262-63.

Resolved, 2. That this Conference entertains favorably the proposal of union between the two bodies aforesaid.

Resolved, 3. That whereas the time of the sessions of these two General Conferences is so far spent that it will be impracticable to have the necessary negotiations, and to discuss and determine the details of the terms of union before their adjournment, that eight members of this body be appointed, who, with the Bishops, shall constitute a commission to meet and confer with a similar commission of the African Methodist Episcopal Zion Church, and report to the next General Conference.

Resolved, 4. That a copy of the foregoing action of this body be given to the delegate, and by him be forwarded to the General Conference of the African Methodist Episcopal Zion Church.[52]

This was the action which became the basis of the Cape May meetings, somewhat to the understandable irritation of the Southern delegation.

Bishop Jones returned to the seat of his General Conference on its closing day, and the following resolution was adopted:

Resolved, That while we gratefully acknowledge our thanks to Almighty God for the safe return to us of our beloved bishop, Singleton T. Jones, from his mission to the M. E. General Conference, in session at Chicago, Ill., we return our thanks for the manner in which he expressed the sentiments of this conference to that body, and the prospective success attained by his mission.[53]

No mention further of this matter of union is to be found in the A.M.E. Zion General Conferences of 1872, 1876, 1880, with the exception of this strong statement in the Episcopal Address of 1872:

Dear Brethren, you can more fully appreciate our need of money to extend and support our connection, when we remind you of the two great monied religious bodies we have to grapple with—the M.E. Church north, and the M.E. Church south, who make their money a means of proselyting our preachers, in many cases, especially the former body, and the step taken by our body at our last General Conference toward consolidation with the M.E. Church has been used by unscrupulous agents of that church to proselyte our ministers and members, creating distraction among us and sometimes ruptures in our churches, which course no Christian body could sanction, in the light of the golden rule: "Do unto others as you would have them do unto you." In relation to the question of affiliation and consolidation with the M.E. Church, we could wish, as expressed in our General Conference in 1868, that all branches of Methodists on this continent were united; but from the unfortunate develop-

---

[52] *Journal of the General Conference of the Methodist Episcopal Church,* 1868, pp. 199, 227, 238, 471-76.

[53] Moore, *History of the A.M.E. Zion Church,* pp. 271-72.

ments connected with this movement, we are compelled to recommend the suspension of future action on the subject until the great obstacle to this happy result is farther removed; that is, the prejudice of caste that still exists in the mother [the M.E.] church; yet we shall still cultivate a friendly and Christian feeling toward our mother until she has reached the proper position on this question of caste.[54]

Bishop Singleton T. Jones sent a letter to the 1872 General Conference of the Methodist Episcopal Church in Brooklyn stating that on account of disaffection in the A.M.E. Zion Church on the subject of union with the Methodist Episcopal Church, he desired that further negotiations looking to that end might be stayed for the present.

To the Bishops and Delegates of the General Conference of the Methodist Episcopal Church assembled in Brooklyn, N. Y.

Christian Brethren: We have been delegated by the General Conference of the African Methodist Episcopal Zion Church, sitting in New York, to convey to you its Christian greetings, and to inform you of the present attitude of that Church on the subject of affiliation and union as proposed by us in 1868. We beg leave respectfully to thank your reverend body for the cordial manner and generous spirit in which our proposal was met and entertained, as also for the distinguished consideration with which our delegate was received by your body at its last session. We sensibly appreciate the respect shown our Church in the distinguished character of the commission appointed by you to conduct the negotiations for union with the commission appointed on our part; and we desire here to bear grateful testimony to the uniformly kind, patient, and Christian bearing and action of said commission pending these negotiations. The mutual spirit of accommodation and agreement which characterized the proceedings of the joint meeting of these commissions in 1869 inspired the hope that the work of unification, so far at least as these Churches were concerned, would be happily consummated during your present sitting. We regret to say, however, that a wide-spread disaffection, originating, as we fear, in a willful misrepresentation of the commendable objects mutually sought to be attained by friends of the proposed union in both Churches, now exists among the membership, and more particularly the ministry, of the Church we represent, precluding, for the present at least, the possibility of the consummation of the union in any manner which is likely to prove satisfactory to either body. We most respectfully ask, therefore, that further negotiations may be stayed until pending efforts with a view to harmony in our own ranks shall have been exhausted, or developments shall warrant further action. And we pray that, in any event, the mutual feelings of friendship and fraternal regard heretofore existing between us as parts of the great family of the Redeemer may be perpetuated.

[54] *Ibid.*, p. 286.

Signed in behalf of the African Methodist Episcopal Zion Church in General
Conference assembled, New York, May 3, 1872.

                          S. T. Jones)
                          George H. Washington)   Committee [55]
                          Samuel Sherman)

A fraternal letter to the General Conference of the African Methodist
Episcopal Church, in session in Nashville, Tennessee, was read and
adopted. This letter was in answer to a telegram received from that conference a few days previously.[56]

And now, dear brethren, we desire to express what we know is the prevailing
desire among all Christians, that there may be a closer union between all
branches of the Church of God; and to us a closer union between all branches
of the Methodistic family seems especially desirable. . . . It may be that we are
not ready to enter into organic union now, but this should receive that prayerful
consideration which its importance demands. . . .

From this point, 1872, the story of union between the Northern
Church and the Negro churches is almost entirely told in a series of
visits by fraternal delegates to one another's General Conferences. These
visits were characterized by expressions of close and sincere brotherhood
and the desire for union. In each General Conference they were accepted
with gratitude, and no further specific action was taken to work out the
problems preventing union.

Proposals of the Southern Church

The Southern branch of Methodism had an eight-year period without
a meeting of the General Conference (1858-66) because of the War Between the States. In the first meeting following the conflict (New Orleans,
1866) some interesting recognition of desires for reunion within Methodism is recorded.

The Committee on the Religious Interests of the Colored People presented the following report, which was adopted:

That in order to promote union and harmony among the colored people,
our Bishops be, and they are hereby, authorized to confer with the Bishops of
the African M.E. Church as to the propriety of a union of that Church with
the M.E. Church, South, upon the basis of the plan adopted by this General

[55] *Journal of the General Conference of the Methodist Episcopal Church*, 1872, p.
534.
[56] *Ibid.*, pp. 196, 394, 541-42.

Conference, for a separate organization for the colored people; and that they report the result to the next General Conference of their action.[57]

In an earlier report the same committee had obtained General Conference approval of the plan referred to. This plan made provision for organization of colored members separately as desired by them on all levels—pastoral charges, Quarterly Conferences, District and Annual Conferences. The proposal was that "when two or more Annual Conferences shall be formed, let our Bishops advise and assist them in organizing a separate General Conference jurisdiction for themselves." [58]

It was, therefore, in terms of a separate jurisdiction for colored members that the Southern branch offered union with the A.M.E. Church in 1866.

This same General Conference made its first efforts toward the Methodist Protestant Church. The last act of the last day records a resolution which called for a commission "to confer with a commission, if one be appointed, from the General Conference of the Methodist Protestant Church . . . on the subject of union between the Methodist Protestant Church and the Methodist Episcopal Church, South, with power to settle terms of union." [59]

This resolution had grown out of a report by the Committee on Correspondence with other Churches,[60] which had expressed the conviction that the Methodist Episcopal Church, South, "stands this day, as she has always stood, ready and willing to consider, with Christian candor, any unequivocal and scriptural overtures for sympathy and fellowship which may be tendered her by any body of Christians in their general representative capacity."

The 1870 General Conference carries no reference to the continuation of this effort of reconciliation with the A.M.E. Church. This was, however, the conference which set the colored members of the Methodist Episcopal Church, South, apart into a General Conference of their own.

Obstacles to Union of the Negro Churches

In 1872 the African Methodist Episcopal General Conference meeting in Nashville received a communication from the recently organized Colored Methodist Episcopal Church asking that steps be taken to settle some property disputes which had arisen between the two Negro Method-

[57] *Journal of the General Conference of the Methodist Episcopal Church, South,* 1866, p. 73.
[58] *Ibid.,* p. 58.
[59] *Ibid.,* p. 138.
[60] *Ibid.,* pp. 49-51.

ist denominations in the South.[61] No mention of union with anybody is found in the Episcopal Address, and a resolution calling on the General Conference to try to mature plans for consolidation of the A.M.E. Church with the A.M.E. Zion Church was referred to a special committee of one from each Annual Conference. The report of this committee set up no channels for achieving unity, but contented itself with such general expressions of good will as: "We would therefore extend the hand of friendship . . . avowing our purpose to co-operate." "We believe the good time is coming and ought to be now, when all the members of the great Methodistic family shall be one." [62] The conference objected to racial prejudice in the Methodist Episcopal Church and welcomed all colored Methodists to join the A.M.E. Church.

In 1876 the A.M.E. General Conference met in Atlanta, and the only mention of unity was in connection with the exchange of fraternal delegates. The 1880 General Conference of the same church, meeting in St. Louis, received a letter from the A.M.E. Zion General Conference which said: "While as unselfish christians (judging from past efforts which have failed) we see at present no probability of a closer, or an organic union, between the A.M.E. and the A.M.E. Zion Churches of this country." [63]

However, the two churches did carry on further conversations through their respective Commissions on Organic Union, in session at Washington, D. C., July 15-17, 1885. Articles of Agreement were adopted. One of these was that these articles should be first submitted to a joint meeting of the bishops. This was done in Philadelphia in 1886. The bishops agreed on all except Article VII, in relation to the name ("First United Methodist Episcopal Church"), and Article X, in relation to the episcopacy. Being unable to come to an agreement, the bishops adjourned, to meet again in Atlantic City in August, 1887. A majority of A.M.E. Church bishops appeared at Atlantic City, but only one of the A.M.E. Zion bishops—Singleton T. Jones. After waiting forty-eight hours, they resolved to take no action, but to call another joint meeting. December 15, 1887, was designated as the date for a meeting in Mobile, Alabama. The bishops of the A.M.E. Church later found that they would be holding Annual Conferences at that time. So the senior bishops of both churches agreed upon an indefinite postponement.[64]

In 1878 at the General Conference of the Southern Church meeting in Atlanta, fraternal messengers were received from the A.M.E. Church.

[61] *Journal of the General Conference of the A.M.E. Church*, 1872, p. 25.
[62] *Ibid.*, pp. 79-80.
[63] *Journal of the General Conference of the A.M.E. Church*, 1880, p. 245.
[64] Smith, *History of the A.M.E. Church*, pp. 380-83.

The *Journal* records that the speeches were frequently interrupted by hearty responses.

The Conference then arose spontaneously, and sung,
When that illustrious day shall rise, etc.

The Chair (Bishop McTyeire) then addressed the Fraternal Messengers in his happiest style, expressing the heartiest congratulations on the kindly relations subsisting between the two Connections. The Bishop made a pleasant allusion to the Colored M.E. Church in America, and expressed an earnest desire for the unification of all the colored Methodist organizations.[65]

The Second Ecumenical Conference, which met in Washington, D. C., in October, 1891, was the inspiration for the Southern Methodist General Conference to appoint in Memphis, in May, 1894, a Commission on Federation. A letter from them to the Northern General Conference in Cleveland in May, 1896, proposed that they appoint a like commission. This was done.

On January 7, 1898, the commissioners met in joint session in Washington. A report of agreements was made to the General Conferences following and the actions approved. The commission was continued.

This Commission on Federation then became the only instrument for talks on union between the Northern Church and the Negro churches. In the 1904 General Conference of the Northern Church the report of the commission was adopted which recommended "that the Commission on Federation take such steps as it may deem wise and necessary to bring about a closer unity and a greater fraternity and co-operation in Christian work between the colored Methodist Churches having an episcopal form of government." [66]

It is noteworthy that at this point a decided shift in the negotiations took place. Hereafter there seems to have been no effort on the part of the Northern or Southern Churches for union between themselves and the colored branches, but all efforts were directed toward helping the colored branches unite among themselves.

The Commission on Federation reported to the 1908 General Conference meeting in Baltimore,[67] and the following was approved as the third paragraph in the report: "We rejoice in the increasing evidences of closer fellowship and prospective union between the various branches of colored Episcopal Methodism in the United States as one of the most

[65] *Journal of the General Conference of the Methodist Episcopal Church, South,* 1878, p. 193.

[66] *Journal of the General Conference of the Methodist Episcopal Church,* 1904, p. 535.

[67] *Journal of the General Conference of the Methodist Episcopal Church,* 1908, pp. 623-24.

striking and hopeful indications of the growth of the spirit of Christian unity, and hereby instruct the Commission on Federation to further these results as far as may be practicable." Paragraph 4 in the same report set up a separate Commission for Federation of Colored Churches and invited the General Conference of the A.M.E. Zion Church, meeting in Philadelphia; the A.M.E. Church, meeting in Norfolk; and the C.M.E. Church, to meet in two years, to set up similar commissions for consultation.

Both Northern and Southern General Conferences (Baltimore, 1908, and Birmingham, 1906) adopted the resolution from the Joint Commission on Federation to set up a "Federal Council" for these two churches, which,

without interfering with the autonomy of the respective Churches, and having no legislative functions, shall yet be invested with advisory powers in regard to world-wide missions, Christian education, the evangelization of the unchurched masses, and the charitable and brotherly adjustment of all misunderstandings and conflicts that may arise between the different churches of Methodism.[68]

The Joint Commission, as has been seen, made certain overtures to the colored Methodist churches. These were reported to the Southern General Conference as a part of the Minutes of the Joint Commission, but no action seems to have followed.[69]

The *Journal* of the General Conference of the African Methodist Episcopal Church in 1904 lists "Commissioners to meet the AME Zion and the CME Churches on the Federation of Colored Churches." The Episcopal Address that year had a section on the Federation of Methodist Bodies:

It will be borne in mind that the spirit of the age invites to federation separate bodies pursuing similar lines of work, particularly when there is agreement in principle, doctrine, aims and methods; and that there was much said regarding the Federation of Methodism at the Third Ecumenical Methodist Conference, London, England, September 1901. Since then the Methodist Episcopal Church and the Methodist Episcopal Church, South, have provided for federation to the extent of a common hymn book, a catechism, a uniform service for public worship, and of certain interests connected with foreign missionary operations.

It seems to us that much good would ensue from a federation of like interests by the various colored branches of American Methodism; and we

[68] *Ibid.*, pp. 622-23; *Journal of the General Conference of the Methodist Episcopal Church, South*, 1906, pp. 356-57.
[69] *Journal of the General Conference of the Methodist Episcopal Church, South*, 1906, pp. 357-59.

recommend that a committee be appointed to confer with the General Conference of the African Methodist Episcopal Zion Church now assembled in
St. Louis, Mo., and the Colored Methodist Episcopal Church of America, so as
to obtain their views and opinions as to the desirability of forming a federation
for purposes similar to those underlying the federation between the Methodist
Episcopal Church and the Methodist Episcopal Church South, said committee
to consist of four Bishops, three ministers and two laymen.[70]

The fraternal delegate from the A.M.E. Zion Church, the Rev. J. Harvey Anderson, referred to past union attempts:

Three unsuccessful attempts have been made to effect organic union between
the A.M.E. and the A.M.E. Zion Churches: the first by the church authorities
in New York City, August 17, 1820, in the home of William Brown, an official
representative of the A.M.E. Zion Church in Lenard Street. The second attempt
was by a joint commission from the two denominations appointed by the
several General Conferences, and which Joint Commission met in Philadelphia,
Pa. in May [June], 1864. The third attempt was inaugurated and the
second Joint Commission appointed by the General Conference—the one,
A.M.E. in Philadelphia: the other, A.M.E. Zion in Pittsburg, Pa.—met in the
A.M.E. Zion Church, Harrisburg, Pa., May, 1892. Both the rather elaborate
attempts were miserable failures. The speaker is favorable to organic union, but
with the very few men of his church, fail to discover so desireable consummation
in the near future.[71]

The chief point in the way of an agreement at Harrisburg seems to
have been the name of the unified church. The name proposed was
African Zion Methodist Episcopal Church. The *Journal* of the A.M.E.
Church General Conference is confused, as the debate undoubtedly was.
At any rate, this confusion ended another attempt at union.[72]

The fraternal speaker to the 1904 conference further elaborated on
his feeling that previous attempts had been too hurried. "Hasty senti-
mentalism, unstudied zeal, and a desire to accomplish in a single quadrennium a work which requires fifty years for consummation from the
beginning, will always prove miserable, humiliating failure." [73]

The conference adopted the report of the Committee on Church Federation calling for implementation of the suggestions in the Bishops'
Address.[74]

Four years later in Norfolk the General Conference of the A.M.E.

---

[70] *Journal of the General Conference of the A.M.E. Church*, 1904, pp. 95-96.
[71] *Ibid.*, p. 220.
[72] Smith, *History of the A.M.E. Church*, pp. 383-87.
[73] *Journal of the General Conference of the A.M.E. Church*, 1904, p. 221.
[74] *Ibid.*, pp. 235-36.

Church heard Bishop W. J. Gaines in the welcome address to the conference say:

There is one recent event that looms up with great significance and I cannot pass it by without mention. The convocation of the three leading Negro Methodist bodies early this year was far reaching in its view to promote Christian unity and the welfare of the race, reaching as it did an agreement on so many points of vital interest to race and Church. God was glorified and unity was foreshadowed with a dignity befitting the moment. With this great council of churches a long step has been taken toward the day when there shall be no difference in creed or church relations but we shall stand as one before the God we all serve. I consider this occurrence of great portent and I look for great fruit from this brotherly Christian Council of the bishops of the A.M.E., of the A.M.E. Zion and of the C.M.E. Churches in this country.[75]

The Episcopal Address likewise spoke with favor regarding the Conference on Federation.[76] The fraternal delegate from the C.M.E. Church spoke at length of the Bishops' Council of all Negro Methodist churches and called for the union of all Negro Methodist churches.[77] A communication was received from the Methodist Episcopal General Conference, in session in Baltimore, calling for continuation of the Commission on Federation. It was approved.

The bishops brought a statement to the conference which approved the formation in Washington, D. C., in February, 1908, of "The United Boards of Bishops of the A.M.E., A.M.E.Z., and C.M.E. Churches." They further recommended to the respective connections the uniting in connectional confederation, and authorized a commission to co-operate.[78]

The Southern General Conference in Asheville in 1910 acted to elect members to the Federal Council according to the terms of the 1906 resolution. It also expressed "hearty accord with the hope expressed by the Fraternal Messenger from the African Methodist Episcopal Zion Church, that a united Methodist Church for the negroes of our country may, in the near future, bring together our colored brethren, and that we authorize our representatives in the Federal Council of Methodism to coöperate, so far as they can, with any plans looking toward this consummation." [79]

When the Commission on Federation of Colored Churches reported to the 1912 General Conference in Minneapolis, it was evident that the

[75] *Journal of the General Conference of the A.M.E. Church,* 1908, pp. 42-43.
[76] *Ibid.,* p. 53.
[77] *Ibid.,* pp. 181, 184.
[78] *Ibid.,* pp. 274-76.
[79] *Journal of the General Conference of the Methodist Episcopal Church, South,* 1910, p. 238.

concern of the commission was not at all the union of the Negro churches with the Northern branch of white Methodism. Rather, it conceived its role to be that of encouraging the three Negro branches to be more co-operative among themselves and perhaps move toward unity. The commissions had not been able to meet together. There had, however, been held a meeting of the "Federated Methodist Bishops" in Mobile in 1911. So the report to the Northern General Conference was:

We are glad to report the advance made in federation by the three great colored churches under the leadership of their Bishops and the evidences of readiness to receive and welcome any encouragement our Church can give them in their efforts to make their Methodism among Negroes one coöperative body. ... It is plainly our duty to assist in every practical way in allaying the competition among the colored Methodist Churches, and thus increase the efficiency of Methodism's combined service to the Negro race.[80]

The A.M.E. Church Episcopal Address of 1912 refers to the second meeting of the Tri-Council of Colored Methodist Bishops (this body seems to be spoken of under many and various titles) in Mobile. It also refers to the world-wide nature of Methodism and the Fourth Ecumenical Methodist Conference in Toronto in October, 1911. The bishops made a general expression of desire for unity and a recognition of one another's ministry.[81] The report of the Committee on Federation of Colored Methodist Churches was exceedingly general.[82]

The General Conference of the Southern Church met in Oklahoma City in 1914 and received a report which said in part:

We rejoice that after twenty years of faithful, sympathetic, and honorable service by able representatives of the Methodist Episcopal Church, South, and the Methodist Episcopal Church in a Commission on the Federation of Methodism, the Federal Council of Methodism has been fully established with well-defined powers, conferred by the General Conferences, to hear and finally determine, without appeal from its decision, all cases of conflict or misunderstanding between the two branches of Methodism. . . . We indorse the action of our Commissioners during the last quadrennium in entering upon the responsibility of conducting negotiations with the Commissions of the Methodist Episcopal Church and the Methodist Protestant Church looking toward the unification of the Methodist bodies in the United States, and especially since they were charged to further, as far as was consistent and practicable, closer relations between ourselves and these two and other Methodist bodies.[83]

[80] Journal of the General Conference of the Methodist Episcopal Church, 1912, p. 744.
[81] Journal of the General Conference of the A.M.E. Church, 1912, pp. 82-83.
[82] Ibid., pp. 374-75.
[83] Journal of the General Conference, 1914, pp. 259-60.

One careful reservation was added concerning the Negro members:

2. The Methodist Episcopal Church, South, regards the unification of the Methodist Episcopal Church, the Methodist Protestant Church, and the Methodist Episcopal Church, South, by the plan proposed by the Joint Commission on Federation, as feasible and desirable, and hereby declares itself in favor of the unification of the Methodist Episcopal Church and the Methodist Episcopal Church, South, in accordance with this general plan of reorganization, and in favor of the unification of all or any Methodist bodies who accept this proposed plan after it has been accepted by the Methodist Episcopal Church. However, we recommend that the colored membership of the various Methodist bodies be formed into an independent organization holding fraternal relations with the reorganized and united Church.[84]

By the time of the report of the Commission on Federation to the 1916 Northern General Conference a "Declaration of Agreement" had been worked out containing principles in three areas: "A Plan for Co-operation," "A Plan for Federation," and "The Plan for Organic Union."

The plan for co-operation included the same standards in each Negro branch and the Northern branch for the ministry, curriculum in schools and colleges, etc., co-operative evangelistic and financial campaigns.

The plan for federation called for an end to duplication and over-lapping in the establishment of churches and in Africa, the establishment of a common Negro Methodist theological seminary, and mutual recognition of ministerial standing.

The Plan for Organic Union welcomed the day of union, and asked that the commissions be continued. This report was approved by the Northern General Conference.[85]

The Journal of the 1920 General Conference shows no report of this commission.

Articles of Agreement were again drawn up by a committee appointed by the Tri-Council of Bishops at Louisville, Kentucky, February 16, 1918, touching the subject of organic union among the three denominations composing the said Tri-Council, namely, the African Methodist Episcopal Church, the African Methodist Episcopal Zion Church, and the Colored Methodist Episcopal Church. The agreement failed because of the nonconcurrence of a majority of the Annual Conferences of the Colored Methodist Episcopal Church. "This adverse action was chiefly stimulated and promoted by Bishop C. H. Phillips, who circulated a

[84] *Ibid.*, pp. 263-64.
[85] *Journal of the General Conference of the Methodist Episcopal Church*, 1916, pp. 1316-18, 307.

manifesto containing Fourteen Points against organic union on the basis of the 'Birmingham Plan.' " [86] A further attempt in 1922 also failed.

3

The Centennial of 1884

During these years when General Conferences were appointing commissions and hearing their reports, perhaps one of the most potent influences toward unity had been the centennial observance of 1884 and the Methodist Ecumenical Conferences.

The Episcopal Address at the Northern Church's General Conference of 1884 could not, of course, ignore the fact that it was the centennial year of American Methodism. This fact set the tone of the entire address. In a section specifically dealing with the plan of centennial, reference was made to the preparations made by the 1880 conference.[87]

In that earlier conference a series of recommendations provided for the preaching of centennial sermons and the holding of centennial celebrations on all levels from the local church to the General Conference. It also called for a special offering of a minimum sum of ten million dollars for education, church debts, superannuates, missions, and evangelism.[88]

In the 1884 conference the plans for a Christmas Conference, December 9-17, were laid and approved. These plans were reported as having been made jointly by six branches of American Methodism.[89]

Up to this point there had been considerable difference of opinion over the matter of an appropriate centennial date. The report of the Committee on the Centenary of American Methodism to the 1866 Southern General Conference rehearses the various dates suggested. Should Methodism observe centenaries for the Aldersgate experience in 1738, or for the arrival of Embury and Strawbridge in America in 1766, or for the Christmas Conference in 1784? The date of 1766 for the begin-

---

[86] Smith, *History of the A.M.E. Church*, p. 391.

[87] *Journal of the General Conference of the Methodist Episcopal Church*, 1884, pp. 32-39.

[88] *Journal of the General Conference of the Methodist Episcopal Church*, 1880, pp. 330-31.

[89] *Journal of the General Conference of the Methodist Episcopal Church*, 1884, pp. 380-84.

ning of Methodism in America was challenged by many. According to some authorities, there were societies of Methodists organized in the United States as early as 1760. Others marked the vital beginning of Methodism in America from 1769.

There is one date, however, which is undisputed, and it marks the great historic event, which gave organic form and permanency to Methodism in this country, to-wit, the combination of the Wesleyan Society elements into a regular ecclesiastical body, recognized as the Methodist Episcopal Church in America, of which the Methodist Episcopal Church, South, is a living representative.[90]

There was, of course, another very good reason why the Southern Church could not see itself joining in a centennial celebration in 1866. This is referred to by the committee's report:

As the circumstances of our Church and country do not favor any demonstrations of such nature as usually characterize centennial celebrations, and as no definite date can be assigned for the origin of Methodism in America in its inchoate character as a Wesleyan Society, like that of 1784, which marks its organization as a duly constituted Episcopal Church, the committee do not recommend that any formal centennial celebration take place until 1884.[91]

It was appropriate, therefore, that the first call for a centennial celebration in 1884 should originate in the South. Thomas O. Summers, who was one of the secretaries at Cape May, and A. G. Haygood, later bishop, initiated the matter with the 1878 General Conference in Atlanta. The Southern bishops were requested, on behalf of the conference, to open correspondence on the subject with the bishops of the Methodist Episcopal Church, the presidents of several Canadian conferences, and of all other Methodist bodies on this continent.[92]

The Episcopal Address of the Southern bishops in 1882 in Nashville referred to the tentative action taken four years earlier and expressed the belief that it now was time to take advanced steps for concerted action including designating the projects for the thank-offerings to be received. "The centenary of the organization of American Methodism is an event too rich in suggestion, and too important in its bearings on the religion

[90] *Journal of the General Conference of the Methodist Episcopal Church, South,* 1866, p. 67.

[91] *Ibid.*

[92] *Journal of the General Conference of the Methodist Episcopal Church, South,* 1878, pp. 137-38.

and civilization of our land, to pass without suitable celebration." [93]

The General Conference called for the raising of two million dollars, to be applied equally to the causes of education, church extension, and foreign missions.[94]

The General Conference of 1886, in Richmond, Virgina, received the report. The leading object of the centenary observance was declared to have been the spiritual improvement of the people. That in no small measure was believed to have been done. As for the two million dollars, considerable explanation was given to show that the goal had in fact been realized. The great bulk of this money, however, was raised and spent in local churches, and one gathers the impression that the connectional interests of missions, education, and church extension did not receive substantial strength from the offering. The report refers more than once to a period of "monetary stringency that paralyzed our industries." [95]

No concrete proposal for a further study of the possibilities of union within the diverse branches of American Methodism was made at the centenary conference. On the contrary, several speakers were careful to state that organic union was not a subject for discussion at the centennial celebration. On the evening before the formal opening of the conference, the delegates gathered in the First Methodist Episcopal Church of Baltimore, the lineal successor of Lovely Lane Chapel, in which the Christmas Conference of 1784 had assembled. Bishop E. G. Andrews, of the Methodist Episcopal Church, delivered the address of welcome, during which he said:

To-morrow, if it please God, we shall enter on grave deliberations. They will concern, not questions of speculative philosophy, or even of dogmatic theology, but of the organic life and work of Methodism.

We shall naturally, in the first place, turn to the organization of the Church, and to the particular form of organization which, upon the advice of Mr. Wesley, our fathers with perfect unanimity adopted. . . .

But whether or not new light shall come to us from this Conference, for one thing we confidently hope. It will declare, it will increase, fraternal affection. I speak not of the reknitting of sundered ecclesiastic ties—with that question we have here and now no concern. But to love one another, to value one another's character, work, and success, to have mutual forbearance, co-operation, and helpfulness, this surely will come from a week spent as it were around the

[93] *Journal of the General Conference of the Methodist Episcopal Church, South,* 1882, p. 24.
[94] *Ibid.,* pp. 163-65.
[95] *Journal of the General Conference of the Methodist Episcopal Church, South,* 1886, pp. 45-49.

family hearthstone, in tender remembrance of our common parentage, in mutual prayer, in deliberation concerning the kingdom of our common Lord and Savior.[96]

The opening sermon of the conference was delivered by Bishop R. S. Foster, of the Methodist Episcopal Church. "For more than two hours the bishop held the unwearied attention of the Conference, and the power of the Lord was manifest in the utterance of his word and in the baptism of the Holy Spirit upon the Conference." [97] It was with considerable sadness that Bishop Foster took on the task of the opening sermon. It had been expected that Bishop Matthew Simpson, of the Methodist Episcopal Church, and Bishop George Foster Pierce, of the Methodist Episcopal Church, South, would both be there and open the conference. They were born in 1811, a few months apart. Converted in the same year, both had served as college presidents before election to the episcopacy.

In 1881 Bishop Simpson became Senior Bishop of his Church, and in the same year Bishop Pierce enjoyed the same rank in his Church. Bishop Pierce, at the nomination of Bishop Simpson, was appointed to preach at this hour the opening sermon of this Conference, and Bishop Simpson was designated as his alternate. Recently, and within a few days of each other, they died, in the 74th year of their age. . . . We enter the Conference through a draped portal.[98]

Bishop Foster in this lengthy and crucial address seemed to sense no need for turning the attention of the conference to its own organizational disunity. Beyond generalized sentiments of uniting passionately to fight the common foes of the church in that day, there was no reference to the unity of the church.

The Rev. J. D. Blackwell in his paper on "Methodism in 1884 and Its Outlook" in answer to the question, "What, then, is the outlook?" sets down his No. 1 answer: "We see in the near future, if it be not now at the door, a pure, vital union between all the divisions of this denomination of Christians." In the very next sentence, however, he hurries to say: "We speak not of organic union. This may co-exist with great bitterness and strife. This may be but the letter that killeth. We speak of that better, that vital, union affected by the indwelling of the eternal Spirit, that union whose bond is charity and love." [99]

[96] *Proceedings, Sermons, Essays, and Addresses of the Centennial Methodist Conference Held in Mt. Vernon Place Methodist Episcopal Church, Baltimore, Maryland, December 9-17, 1884* (New York: Phillips and Hunt, 1885), pp. 25, 29, 31.
[97] *Ibid.*, p. 38.
[98] *Ibid.*, pp. 84-85.
[99] *Ibid.*, p. 186.

The Pastoral Address of the conference was read by Bishop S. M. Merrill, for the committee appointed to draft the address. The address contained one paragraph referring to the question of reunion:

Not least among the evils we deplore as Methodists is the spirit of strife and division which, we are sorry to say, is not yet wholly eradicated from our Zion. Far be it from us to pronounce every division of the Church schismatical. There has been, doubtless, some providential ordering in the denominational organizations of Christendom, yet the multiplication of separate Churches on trivial grounds is not to be encouraged. We are happy to believe that the period of dissensions is well-nigh over. We hail the dawn of the better day, and rejoice in the rising spirit of fraternity which promises much for the future success of the cause we love. From this time onward our principal rivalries should be to excel in good works. We congratulate our Canadian brethren upon the success which has attended their movement for uniting the forces of Methodism in the Dominion. May their highest anticipations be fully realized. We of the States may not follow their example in consolidation, but we should not fall behind them in "endeavoring to keep the unity of the Spirit in the bonds of peace." [100]

The conference adopted one resolution with some bearing on the question. Dr. J. B. McFerrin, of the Methodist Episcopal Church, South, moved the suspension of the rules, in order to present a paper for the action of the conference on the seventh day in the morning session.

Dr. McFerrin's paper read as follows:

WHEREAS, we, the delegates of the Methodist Centennial Conference, held in Baltimore, December 9-17, 1884, have found the occasion one of great personal interest and spiritual profit, and, believing that it has strengthened the bond of brotherhood between the various branches of the Methodist family represented in the Conference, and with a desire to utilize and make permanent the benefit already gained, and to extend and widen its influence in the future; and,

Whereas, we desire to acknowledge, reverently, the goodness of God in thus bringing us together on the *hundredth* anniversary of our ecclesiastical family life, and especially for the peace and harmony which have pervaded all our meetings; therefore,

Resolved, 1. That we return sincere and heartfelt thanks to Almighty God, both for the occasion and for the marked prosperity he has vouchsafed to us a people for the past century.

Resolved, 2. That we part to return to our respective fields of work and life with sincere and deepened affection for each other, and with a holy purpose to consecrate ourselves anew to the great work for which our Church was, as

[100] *Ibid.,* p. 322.

we believe, raised up of God—to spread Scriptural holiness throughout the world.

Resolved, 3. That, with the spirit of true brotherhood, we will seek more than ever to co-operate together in every practical way for the accomplishment of this end.

Resolved, 4. That we respectfully commend to the bishops of the episcopal, and the chief officers of the non-episcopal, Methodist Churches represented in this Conference to consider whether informal conferences between them could not be held with profit from time to time concerning matters of common interest to their respective bodies.

Resolved, 5. That we shall be greatly pleased to see these bonds of brotherhood and fellowship increased and strengthened more and more in the future.

Resolved, 6. That any occasion that may bring our respective Churches together in convention for the promotion of these objects will always be hailed with profound satisfaction.[101]

The paper carried a variety of signatures and was responded to by several favoring speeches. Bishop A. W. Wayman, of the African Methodist Episcopal Church, moved as an amendment that while standing to approve the paper the conference join in singing:

> Together let us sweetly live;
> Together let us die;
> And each a starry crown receive,
> And reign above the sky.

This was done, but at the same time points up the obvious omission of the Methodist Protestant Church as a participating body in the Centennial Conference.

4

The Methodist Ecumenical Conferences

The factors that caused the churches to move toward reunion were intertwined. As has been seen, the impetus to the planning of the Centennial Christmas Conference came in part from a paper circulated among the delegates to the First Methodist Ecumenical Conference meeting at City Road Chapel, London, in September of 1881. The Rev.

[101] *Ibid.,* pp. 67-68.

B. F. Lee of the African Methodist Episcopal Church, speaking as a fraternal delegate to the Northern General Conference of 1880, said: "The plan for the union of the different branches of Methodism in an ecumenical council is one of great promise." [102] Quite understandably the Northern General Conference of 1884 changed the name of its Committee on the Centennial of 1884 by adding to it "and Ecumenical Conference of 1887." [103] This Second Ecumenical Conference, which met in Washington, D. C., in 1891, was the inspiration for the Southern Methodist General Conference to appoint in Memphis in 1894 a Commission on Federation.

It was again at Baltimore in 1876—a General Conference which has already engaged our attention at great length by the significant events connected with reunion which took place there—that the beginnings of the First Ecumenical Methodist Conference became evident. Report No. 1 of the Committee on the State of the Church dealt with several diverse matters, but section 3 reported on a paper presented by A. C. George and others. The committee believed that "an Ecumenical Conference of Methodism would tend in many ways to a closer alliance, a warmer fraternity, and a fuller co-operation among these various Methodist organizations for the advancement of the Redeemer's kingdom in all parts of the earth." [104] The report, therefore, called on the bishops to appoint a Committee of Correspondence to set in motion communication with all parts of world Methodism looking toward such a gathering.

The General Conference of 1880 received and approved a very full and detailed report. The Committee on Correspondence had contacted other branches of world Methodism with strongly positive results.

The Methodist Protestant Convention in 1877, also meeting in Baltimore, indorsed the proposal and appointed delegates. The bishops of the Methodist Episcopal Church, South, in their quadrennial address to the General Conference in Atlanta in 1878, said: "We have received . . . a communication which cannot fail to arrest your attention and awaken your interest." [105] The suggestion was referred to a committee which brought a recommendation to the conference which resulted in unanimous approval. The Methodist Church of Canada, the British Wesleyan Conference, the American Wesleyan Church, the Evangelical

[102] *Journal of the General Conference of the Methodist Episcopal Church*, 1880, p. 509.

[103] *Journal of the General Conference of the Methodist Episcopal Church*, 1884, p. 151.

[104] *Journal of the General Conference of the Methodist Episcopal Church*, 1876, p. 367.

[105] *Journal of the General Conference of the Methodist Episcopal Church, South*, 1878, p. 43.

Association, the Free Methodist Church, and the African Methodist Episcopal Church had all responded affirmatively and enthusiastically.

Accordingly the committee of the Northern General Conference called for a joint meeting of persons from these several branches in Cincinnati, May 6, 1880.

The report of the Joint Committee was approved by the General Conference. This report made certain things clear about the proposed Ecumenical Conference:

The Conference is not for legislative purposes, for it will have no authority to legislate. It is not for doctrinal controversies, for Methodism has no doctrinal differences. It is not for an attempt to harmonize the various polities and usages of the several branches of the one great Methodist family, for Methodism has always striven for unity, rather than uniformity. It is not, in a word, for consolidation, but for co-operation. It is to devise such means for prosecuting our home and foreign work as will result in the greatest economy and efficiency, to promote fraternity, to increase the moral and evangelical power of a common Methodism, and to secure the more speedy conversion of the world.[106]

It was determined that this conference should meet in London at City Road Chapel in August, or near that time, 1881.

Here again is evidence of the interrelated strength each of these movements drew from the other and contributed to the increased desire for reunion. It was the committee in the Southern General Conference which was raised to respond to the invitation to the Ecumenical Conference which initiated the call to the Centennial Conference of 1884.

The First Ecumenical Conference

The Rev. William Arthur of the British Wesleyan Conference, in the prefatory statement of the volume of the official proceedings, describes the joint committee meeting in Cincinnati as one the like of which had never before come together.

The representatives of the two old bodies which had been wont to assemble under the presidency of John Wesley himself (the British and Irish Conferences) met with those of bodies of very recent origin; the representatives of Episcopal Churches with those of non-Episcopal; the representatives of the African race with those of whites; the representatives of Canadian Churches with those of Churches in the United States. For the first time since 1844, when the American

[106] *Journal of the General Conference of the Methodist Episcopal Church*, 1880, pp. 419-29.

Church was divided, did Bishops of the Methodist Episcopal Church, South, meet at the same board with Bishops of the Methodist Episcopal Church.[107]

The meeting of the committee in Cincinnati was described as one "animated by a spirit of perfect harmony." [108] There was no other thought or suggestion of a meeting place other than City Road Chapel. Present-day Methodists interested in the World Methodist Council, which has grown out of these first Ecumenical Conferences, are familiar with a division of areas of work between the joint secretaries. This division originated in the first planning session. The conference was composed of four hundred delegates—half of them from churches in Europe with their missions, to be called the Eastern Section, and half from churches in America and their missions, to be called the Western Section. The president of the Wesleyan Methodist Conference was appointed chairman for the Eastern Section, and Bishop Simpson for the Western Section.

Friday, August 5, 1881, was observed as a day of special prayer on behalf of the approaching conference. On Wednesday, September 7, 1881, the delegations assembled. They represented twenty-eight different organizations of Methodists from England, Ireland, Scotland, France, Germany, Italy, Norway, Sweden, Switzerland, Africa, India, China, Japan, Australia, New Zealand, Polynesia, and from all sections of the United States, from Canada, Nova Scotia, New Brunswick, South America, and the West Indies.

The morning service was read by the president of the Wesleyan Methodist Conference, the Rev. Dr. George Osborn. The sermon was preached by the senior bishop of the Methodist Episcopal Church, Matthew Simpson. At the close of the sermon, the sacrament of the Lord's Supper was administered to the assembled delegates.

Bishop Simpson preached from the text (John 6:63): "The words that I speak unto you, they are spirit, and they are life." The phenomenal growth of Methodist bodies can only be explained, he said, because the Head of the Church had given to them "spirit and life."

What is to be said, however, to those who disparage Methodism because it has had divisions?

I am not sure that these divisions are an unmixed evil. They seem to me to have compensations also. With the different tastes and habits of men, I fancy that, through churches somewhat differently organised, and with different usages, more minds may be won for Christ. . . . Organisation has its value, and

[107] *Proceedings of the Oecumenical Methodist Conference, 1881* (London: Wesleyan Conference Office, 1881) , p. vii,
[108] *Ibid.,* p. viii,

every member of each church should be true to his association; yet the organisation is only the temple in which the life dwells. The organisation is of man.
The life is of Christ. Were there but one organisation with certain usages that
prospered, we should think its forms and usages were in themselves sacred, we
should grow narrow and bigoted. Our Church would be *the* Church, and all
others would be schismatics.[109]

Admitting the divisions, the bishop moves on to declare that they do
not mar the family likeness. There is no division of doctrine. Mr.
Wesley's sermons and the doctrinal character of the Wesley hymns have
aided in keeping a oneness. Nor is there any radical difference in usages.
The class meeting, the prayer meeting, the love feast, the watch-night
services, are known and observed everywhere.

Differ as we may, there is something in all of us which the world recognises.
Does a minister preach with unusual fervour, does he in all his duties exhibit
unusual zeal? Does not the world say, He preaches like a Methodist? Does a
congregation meet, and sing, and pray, and rejoice? Does not the world say,
They are like Methodists? This Conference evinces a yearning for closer union:
for more fraternal feeling.[110]

Wesley's expressions of a yearning for closer union with all Christians
were quoted. In this, said Bishop Simpson, "his great heart was a hundred
years in advance of the Christian world." Recently a Pan-Anglican Congress had met, as had a Pan-Presbyterian Council, and now a Methodist
Ecumenical Conference. "Do not these foreshadow an Ecumenical Protestant Conference, when Mr. Wesley's hope shall be realized, and the world
shall see that evangelical Christians are one in heart and one in effort?" [111] At any rate, the bishop declared, there will be an Ecumenical
Conference, if not on earth, at least in heaven.

Dr. Osborn in a welcoming address asked the question: "Is it a do-
nothing Conference?" Dr. Osborn emphatically denied the accusation in
the question: " 'What are you going to do?' I have been asked again and
again. 'What are you going to do?' I have said; 'What do they do in
heaven? Sing and converse, and learn to love one another.' . . . Jonathan
went to David in the wood, and strengthened his hands in God. Was that
to do nothing?" [112]

The program was skillfully designed so that by the time the four
hundred delegates from diverse places had gone through it together,

[109] *Ibid.*, p. 16.
[110] *Ibid.*, p. 17.
[111] *Ibid.*, pp. 17-18.
[112] *Ibid.*, p. 22.

adding the beneficial value of the social occasions outside the program, there would undoubtedly have resulted a closer fellowship and a stronger tie binding world Methodism.

The program and its divisions should be carefully studied in its various parts and in its total sweep. It is impressive as a unifying agent:

I. Methodism: Its History and Results
    The Grateful Recognition of the Hand of God in the Origin and Progress of Methodism
    Statistical Results
    Methodism, a Power Purifying and Elevating Society
    The Influence That Methodism Has Exerted on Other Religious Bodies, and the Extent to Which They Have Modified Methodism

II. Evangelical Agencies of Methodism
    The Itinerant Ministry
    Lay Preachers
    Women, and Their Work in Methodism
    Scriptural Holiness, and the Special Fitness of Methodist Means of Grace to Promote It

III. Methodism and the Young
    The Training of Children in Christian Homes; So as to Bring Them to Christ, and Attach Them to Methodism
    The Training of Children in the Sunday-School and Church; So as to Secure the Largest Evangelical Denominational Results

IV. The Lord's Day and Temperance
    Methodism and the Lord's Day
    Relation of Methodism to the Temperance Movement
    Juvenile Temperance Organisations and Their Promotion Through the Sunday-School and Church
    Civil Measures to Suppress Intemperance, and the Relation of the Church to Such Movements

V. Possible Perils of Methodism
    From the Papacy; from Sacerdotalism, and Its Connected Errors
    From Modern Scepticism in Its Different Forms and Manifestations
    From Formality, Worldliness, and Improper Amusements Among Our Own Members
    From Innovations Upon Established Methodist Usages and Institutions

VI. Education
    The Higher Education Demanded by the Necessities of the Church in Our Time
    The Duty of the Church to Maintain Schools Which Are Christian in Their Influence and Character
    The Education and Special Training of Ministers in Theological Schools

The Education and Special Training of Ministers While Engaged in
Ministerial and Pastoral Work

VII. The Use of the Press for the Advancement of Christianity
Denominational Literature and Its Publication
The Newspaper, and the Use to Be Made of It by the Church
Methodist Hymnology

VIII. Home Missions
The Maintenance of Home Missions Among the Most Degraded
Populations
The Important Work Which the Methodist Laity Have Performed in
This Direction, and the Great Opportunities Which They Have in
the Future
The Best Methods of Reaching the Unconverted Sections of the Richer
Classes
Methodism and Its Work for Orphans, for the Aged, and Generally for
the Dependent Classes

IX. Foreign Missions
The Results of Methodist Missions in Heathen Lands
How to Avoid Waste, Rivalries, and Confusion, Arising from Different
Methodist Bodies Occupying the Same or Contiguous Fields
The Establishment and Support of Training-Schools for Native Converts
and Native Ministers in the Foreign Field
The Use of the Press in Non-Christian Countries for the Promotion of
the Gospel
The Missionary Work Required in Papal and Semi-Infidel Nations
The Resources of Methodism for the Work of the World's Conversion,
and the Duty of Developing and Employing Those Resources

X. Christian Unity
How Christian Unity May Be Maintained and Increased Among Our-
selves, and Made Manifest in the World
The Catholicity of Methodism
Methodism as a Bond of Brotherhood Among the Nations [113]

One does not need to turn to the section on "Christian unity" to see
the cementing effect such a program would have on its participants. It
is striking that the concerns dealt with in these papers are to this day the
central characteristics of Methodism wherever found in the world. It is
not disappointing that such a conference failed to result in the immediate reunion of the many branches of the Wesleyan family. To have
joined in this study of the essentials of Methodism at this juncture in the
church's history undoubtedly secured a climate in Methodism which has
kept it a denomination with a spirit of close co-operation to this day.

In his address on "How Christian Unity May Be Maintained and

[113] *Ibid.*, pp. xxxi-xxxvi.

Increased Among Ourselves, and Made Manifest to the World," Augustus C. George (Methodist Episcopal Church) listed several specific suggestions: (a) "We ought to keep out of each other's way, and to remember that we are in no case rival bodies." (b) "We ought to help each other to do the Lord's work." (c) "We ought to have, as soon and as far as practicable, one hymn-book and one order of worship in all our congregations; and one ritual service for baptism, the Lord's Supper, consecration, and ordinations." (d) "We ought to be so thoroughly co-operative in our missionary work as to furnish to a pagan and infidel world a demonstration of our Christian love and denominational unity." (e) "We must secure a confederation of Methodist Churches in all lands." (f) "For the crowning consummation of manifest Methodist unity we must have, at least once in a decade, and twice would be better, an Ecumenical Conference, assembled in some one of the great capitals of the world." [114]

The Address of the Conference, however, moved more and more cautiously on the subject:

We are happy to observe decided tendencies to a closer, if not organic, union with each other. The example of three of the Methodist Churches in Canada, and two in Ireland, indicates that when Providence points the way, our different bodies in the same countries may be brought into one, with promise of largely increased usefulness. Such unions, we believe, should be prudently managed, and when they occur under favourable auspices, should be hailed with great joy.

But while many are praying and waiting for them, let us respect each other, especially in all matters of church discipline, and maintain just and truly fraternal relations; and being one in doctrines, aims, and essential methods, and really one spiritual organism, let us bring together annually in one year-book the results of our labours under God, and be known everywhere as one Methodist Church. To promote these most desirable results we advise that our ecclesiastical bodies frequently exchange fraternal greetings, either by letter or by deputations.[115]

The Second Ecumenical Conference

The First Ecumenical Conference planned that there should be a second one in the United States in 1887. The date was later shifted, and the ten-year cycle of the meeting of these conferences was begun.

There was less union talk in the Second Ecumenical Conference, in Washington, but there was reference to the progress made in understand-

[114] *Ibid.,* pp. 556-60.
[115] *Ibid.,* p. 583.

ing as a result of the first. The Rev. T. B. Stephenson, responding on
behalf of the Wesleyan Methodist Church to the speeches of welcome,
referred to the concrete results seen in the union of Methodist branches
in Canada in the decade between the two conferences. He goes on:

> But it has altogether altered the relation of the various bodies which constitute
> our Eastern Methodism to each other. I do not hesitate to say that there is a
> warmth of kindly feeling and a readiness and heartiness of co-operation, a frank
> and hearty recognition of each other's rights and privileges in the heritage of
> Methodism, such as did not exist before. . . . We are thankful that the change has
> come, and whatever it may lead to in the future, of this I am sure, that this
> second Ecumenical Conference will tend to promote a better mutual feeling. At
> our last meeting we buried a good many misunderstandings, and, please God,
> we shall have some more funerals this time.[116]

It is instructive that the delegate from the Northern branch of American
Methodism (Bishop C. H. Fowler) and the delegate from the Southern
branch (Bishop C. B. Galloway) could both address the conference on
the subject "The Present Status of Methodism in the Western Section"
and make no reference to the separateness of these two churches nor
express any hope for a furtherance of efforts at fraternity and union
between them. Bishop B. W. Arnett of the African Methodist Episcopal
Church, giving an address on the same subject, made no mention of
agitation for union of the three Negro branches in the United States.

In an address on "Christian Unity" T. G. Selby of Great Britain did
issue a clear call:

> Let us promote this spirit *by healing, at the earliest possible opportunity, our
> own separations and estrangements as Methodists.* We can never become a
> providential force in the reunion of evangelical Christendom unless we first
> close up our own ranks and stand shoulder to shoulder. Let us go from this
> gathering with the steadfast faith in our hearts that we shall see a united
> Methodism. Do not let us hurry on unreal amalgamations. Let the history of
> centuries teach us to keep all direct and indirect pressure out of the field. Never
> re-discuss the past or try to judge the men who led on either side. The ghoulish
> resurrectionist who digs up what is best forgotten will never hasten the coming
> of the millennium. Be patient. Keep this goal in view and ever be working for
> and stretching toward it.[117]

Similar sentiments were expressed in the discussion of this subject and
one akin to it, "Christian Co-operation." At the close of these discussions

---

[116] *Proceedings of the Second Ecumenical Methodist Conference, 1891* (New York:
Hunt and Eaton, 1892) , p. 43.
[117] *Ibid.,* pp. 114-15.

the Rev. J. C. Embry, of the African Methodist Episcopal Church, stated that a circular already had been issued by members representing the various denominations of colored people inviting them to stay for a conference immediately on the adjournment of this Ecumenical Conference, with a view to considering means of co-operation and possibly organic union.[118]

A lengthy debate, extending over several days, did result from the presentation by the Business Committee of a resolution on Methodist federation. It was finally adopted, as follows:

1. That the Conference recognizes, with gratitude to God, the growing desire for closer union among the evangelical Churches of Christendom, and especially hails with devout thankfulness the extension of that desire among the various Methodist Churches.

2. The Conference cannot doubt that concerted action among the different Methodist bodies upon many questions would be greatly to the advantage of the kingdom of God. The Conference would suggest that such concerted action might be possible and useful in the following great provinces of the Methodist world, namely: (a) Great Britain and Ireland, including affiliated Conferences and missions; (b) the United States, including its missions and Mission Conferences; (c) Australasia, with Polynesia and its other missions; (d) Canada, with its missions.

3. This Conference, therefore, respectfully requests the Churches represented in this Conference to consider whether such concerted action be possible, and if so, by what means and in what way; and directs the Secretaries to forward a copy of this resolution to the senior bishop or president of every Conference represented here.[119]

All through these conferences the question of Methodist federation became especially vital in the discussions of missionary strategy. An example of this strong sentiment is found in an address by the Rev. A. B. Leonard of the Methodist Episcopal Church: "Since organic union cannot for the present occur, is not Methodist federation possible?" [120] This was followed by the Rev. William Gibson of the Wesleyan Methodist Church, who said:

On that remarkable and never-to-be forgotten day during this Ecumenical Conference when our subject was Christian Unity and Co-operation, I ventured to say that all Methodist Churches ought to be as one on the subject of missions, whether to the heathen or in Christian lands. We ought to have a concert of

[118] *Ibid.,* p. 164.
[119] *Ibid.,* p. 434.
[120] *Ibid.,* p. 503.

Methodist organizations—a Pan-Methodistic council—as to fields of work, and not go as sections of the Methodist Church to the same spheres.[121]

In the morning session of October 17, 1891, Bishop A. W. Wayman of the A.M.E. Church made the following privileged statement to the conference:

> Mr. Chairman and Brethren: I rise to a question of high privilege. The brother in black—as we have been called by the venerable Bishop Haygood, and also by Bishop Warren, to which we have no objection—the bishops and delegates of the African Methodist Episcopal Church and the Colored Methodist Episcopal Church, have held a meeting and decided unanimously in favor of organic union; and now we say to all of our brethren in black, Come, go with us, and we will do you good; for the Lord hath spoken good concerning the brother in black.[122]

The Third Ecumenical Conference

In 1901 the Third Ecumenical Conference went back to the site of the first, City Road Chapel, London. On the subject of Methodist union T. Bowman Stephenson in the Introduction, written in retrospect, said:

> The needless existence of separate Churches is to be regretted, and separation is needless, except when sufficiently grave variations of creed, method, or polity compel it. It can scarcely be denied that in some of the now divided Churches of Methodism there are no sufficient causes for their separation. In such cases economy of men and means might well be promoted, and a larger result of the highest kind expected from labours which would be no longer in any degree expended upon rivalry or self-protection. True everywhere, this is especially true in new and sparsely-populated countries. Hence it was a cause of deep thankfulness that, whilst the second Ecumenical Conference was heralded by Methodist Union in Canada, the third could rejoice over a like Union in Australasia, all but completed.
>
> It would have added to the joy of the Conference if any decisive step could have been reported towards Union between some at least of the several Methodist Churches in Great Britain and in the United States. But it was tacitly recognised that in the countries where Methodism has been longest planted, is most widely and strongly entrenched, and has the memory of past struggles still surviving, the difficulties in the way of Union are the greatest. The Conference, however, greatly rejoiced in the fact that controversy between Methodist Churches is a thing of the past, and the relations between those churches are cordially harmonious, and

[121] *Ibid.*, p. 509.
[122] *Ibid.*, p. 521.

show promise of an increasing intimacy of relation and feeling as the years pass on.[123]

The 1901 "Address to the Churches" contained a paragraph in the same vein as Stephenson's Introduction:

It was, of course, to be expected that in our Conference the sentiment of Methodist Union should receive an impetus. All the choice spirits of Methodism are praying for it, even though for the present they may deem it to be impracticable. . . . Dreamers are already dreaming of a United, or, at least, Federated Methodism on each side of the Atlantic. Dreamers are often the truest prophets.[124]

The Fourth Ecumenical Conference

The Fourth Ecumenical Conference, in Toronto in 1911, recognized that again a union of Methodist branches had taken place in the decade since the previous conference. This had been true following each Ecumenical Conference. "It was a definite resolution then passed [London, 1901] which provided the way for the opening of the negotiations which resulted in the union of three Methodist bodies in England in 1907, the amalgamated body bearing the prophetic name of the United Methodist Church. So, then, these decennial Conferences and Methodist Union are inseparably associated." [125]

As for American Methodism, the Rev. Homer C. Stuntz spoke: "It is heartbreaking. Twelve branches of Methodists are at work in North America! That is three times the number demanded by national, racial, or strategic reasons. Many of these Churches occupy the same areas." [126] Bishop C. H. Phillips of the C. M. E. Church declared regarding the three branches of Negro Methodism: "We are not ready yet for organic union; for organic union at this time might mean more absorption [than] it would mean union. . . . Without looking forward to organic union, we have taken the preliminary steps. The bishops at the head of these Churches do enjoy, I am pleased to say, federation and co-operation." [127]

---

[123] *Proceedings of the Third Ecumenical Methodist Conference, 1901* (New York: Eaton and Mains, 1901), pp. xi-xii.

[124] *Ibid.,* p. 508.

[125] *Proceedings of the Fourth Ecumenical Methodist Conference, 1911* (New York: Eaton and Mains, 1911), pp. 724-25.

[126] *Ibid.,* p. 731.

[127] *Ibid.,* p. 738.

The Fifth Ecumenical Conference

As strong as the influence of the decennial Ecumenical Conferences were on the expression of hope for union, it still is a solemn fact that in the 1921 conference in London, forty years and five conferences from the first one, Bishop Frederick D. Leete was to report on behalf of American Methodism: "In Methodism we continue to distinguish between unity and union. Proceedings in Methodist unification—a technical term in the United States—have not reached an impasse, surely, but after five years of negotiation by commissions it will probably be generally agreed that the present step is that of hesitation." [128]

[128] *Proceedings of the Fifth Ecumenical Methodist Conference, 1921* (New York: Methodist Book Concern, 1921), p. 40.

Bibliography, Volume II

1. General Bibliography
2. Biography and Autobiography
3. Slavery and Division
4. The Methodist Protestants
5. Western Expansion
6. Language Conferences
7. Other Branches of Methodism
8. Theology and the Holiness Movement
9. Official Publications
10. Periodicals

1. General Bibliography

Abell, Aaron Ignatius. *The Urban Impact on American Protestantism, 1865-1900.* Cambridge: Harvard University Press, 1943.

Albright, Raymond W. *A History of the Evangelical Church.* Harrisburg, Pa.: The Evangelical Press, 1942.

Alexander, Gross. *A History of the Methodist Church, South, in the United States.* New York: Christian Literature Company, 1894.

Anderson, William K., ed. *Methodism.* Nashville: The Methodist Publishing House, 1947.

Archibald, F. A., ed. *Methodism and Literature.* New York: Phillips and Hunt, 1883.

Bancroft, Hubert Howe. *Works of Hubert Howe Bancroft.* 39 vols. San Francisco: A. L. Bancroft and Company, 1882-90.

Barclay, Wade Crawford. *The History of Methodist Missions.* New York: Board of Missions of The Methodist Church, Vol. I, 1949; Vol. II, 1950; Vol. III, 1957.

Bennett, William W. *A Narrative of the Great Revival Which Prevailed in the Southern Armies.* Philadelphia: Claxton, Remsen & Haffelfinger, 1877.

Bentley, George R. *A History of the Freedmen's Bureau.* Philadelphia: University of Pennsylvania Press, 1955.

Bragg, George F. *History of the Afro-American Group of the Episcopal Church.* Baltimore: Church Advocate Press, 1922.

Brown, Arlo Ayres. *A History of Religious Education in Recent Times.* New York: The Abingdon Press, 1923.

Brown, Francis J., and Roucek, Joseph S. *One America.* New York: Prentice-Hall, Inc., 1952.

Brown, S. A.; Davis, A. P.; and Lee, U. G. *The Negro Caravan.* New York: The Dryden Press, 1941.

Brunson, Alfred. *The Gospel Ministry: Its Characteristics and Qualifications.* New York, 1856.

Buckley, James M. *A History of Methodism in the United States.* 2 vols. New York: Christian Literature Company, 1897.

Bullock, Henry M. *A History of Emory University.* Nashville: Parthenon Press, 1936.

Cameron, Richard M. *Methodism and Society in Historical Perspective.* Nashville: Abingdon Press, 1961.

Cannon, James. *History of Southern Methodist Missions.* Nashville: Cokesbury Press, 1926.

Clark, Elmer T. *Healing Ourselves.* Nashville: Cokesbury Press, 1924.

Conable, F. W. *History of the Genesee Annual Conference.* 2nd ed. New York: Phillips and Hunt, 1885.

Conn, Charles W. *Like a Mighty Army Moves the Church of God.* Cleveland, Tenn.: The Church of God Publishing House, 1955.

Coulter, E. Merton. *The South During Reconstruction, 1865-1877.* Baton Rouge: Louisiana State University Press, 1947.

Curts, Lewis. *The General Conferences of the Methodist Episcopal Church from 1792 to 1896.* Cincinnati: Curts and Jennings, 1900.

Daniel, W. A. *The Education of Negro Ministers.* New York: Doran, 1925.

Daniel, W. Harrison. "The Protestant Church in the Confederate States." Unpublished dissertation, Duke University, 1957.

Daniels, Morris S. *The Story of Ocean Grove.* New York: The Methodist Book Concern, 1919.

Dannelly, Clarence Moore. "The Development of Collegiate Education in the Methodist Episcopal Church, South, 1846-1902." Unpublished dissertation, Yale University, 1933.

Deems, Charles F., ed. *Annals of Southern Methodism, 1856.* Nashville: Stevenson and Owen, 1857.

Detweiler, F. G. *The Negro Press in the United States.* Chicago: University of Chicago Press, 1922.

Du Bois, W. E. Burghardt. *Black Reconstruction.* New York: Harcourt, Brace and Company, 1935.

————. *The Negro Church.* Atlanta: Atlanta University Press, 1903.

————. *The Philadelphia Negro.* Philadelphia: University of Pennsylvania Press, 1899.

Du Bose, Horace M. *A History of Methodism* [Vol. II. of McTyeire's *History of Methodism*]. Nashville: Lamar and Smith, 1916.

Duren, William Larkin. *The Trail of the Circuit Rider.* New Orleans: Privately Printed, 1936.

Farish, Hunter Dickinson. *The Circuit Rider Dismounts: A Social History of Southern Methodism, 1865-1900.* Richmond: The Dietz Press, 1938.

Fleming, Walter Lynwood. *Civil War and Reconstruction in Alabama.* New York: Columbia University Press, 1905.

————. *The Sequel of Appomattox.* New Haven: Yale University Press, 1919.

Foster, Randolph S. *A Treatise on the Need of the M. E. Church with Respect to Her Ministry.* New York: Carlton and Phillips, 1855.

Franklin, John H. *From Slavery to Freedom: A History of American Negroes.* New York: Alfred A. Knopf, 1947.

Garber, Paul N. "The Struggle for a Trained Ministry in The Methodist Church," in *The Methodist Ministry, 1959.* Pamphlet. Nashville: Department of Ministerial Education, Board of Education of The Methodist Church, 1959.

Goldman, Eric F. *Rendezvous with Destiny.* New York: Alfred A. Knopf, 1952.

Guzman, Jessie, ed. *The Negro Year Book, 1952.* New York: William H. Wise and Company, 1952.

Hafen, LeRoy R., and Rister, Carl C. *Western America: The Exploration, Settlement, and Development of the Region Beyond the Mississippi.* New York: Prentice-Hall, Inc., 1941.

Handlin, Oscar. *The Uprooted: The Epic Story of the Great Migrations That Made the American People.* Boston: Little, Brown, 1951.

Harmon, Nolan B. *The Organization of The Methodist Church.* 2nd rev. ed. Nashville: The Methodist Publishing House, 1962.

Harrison, W. P., ed. *The Gospel Among the Slaves.* Nashville: Publishing House of the M. E. Church, South, 1893.

Hastings, Comer. "The Methodist Episcopal Church, South, During the Reconstruction Period." Unpublished dissertation, Duke University, 1932.

Haygood, Atticus G. *Our Brother in Black.* Nashville: Southern Methodist Publishing House, 1881.

Haynes, Leonard L., Jr. *The Negro Community Within American Protestantism, 1619-1844.* Boston: The Christopher Publishing House, 1953.

Hedding, Elijah. *A Discourse on the Administration of Discipline.* New York: Lane and Sanford, 1842.

Herrick, H. N., and Sweet, William Warren. *A History of the North Indiana Conference of the Methodist Episcopal Church.* Indianapolis: W. K. Stewart Company, 1917.

Holmes, Dwight O. *The Evolution of the Negro College.* New York: Bureau of Publications, Teachers College, Columbia University, 1934.

Hopkins, C. Howard. *History of the Y.M.C.A. in North America.* New York: Association Press, 1951.

Hurst, John F. *History of Methodism.* 6 vols. New York: Eaton and Mains, 1902.

Hyde, A. B. *The Story of Methodism.* Greenfield, Mass.: Willey Publishing Company, 1887.

Irby, Richard. *History of Randolph-Macon College, Virginia.* Richmond: Whittet and Shepperson, [1899].

Jones, Ilion T. *A Historical Approach to Evangelical Worship.* Nashville: Abingdon Press, 1954.

Jones, J. William. *Christ in the Camp.* Atlanta: The Martin & Hoyt Company, 1904.

Jones, John G. *A Complete History of Methodism as Connected with the Mississippi Conference of the Methodist Episcopal Church, South.* Nashville: Printed for the Author by the Publishing House of the M. E. Church, South, 1908.

Lewis, W. H. *The History of Methodism in Missouri for a Decade of Years, from 1860 to 1870.* Nashville: Privately Printed, 1890.

Luccock, Halford E.; Hutchinson, Paul; and Goodloe, Robert W. *The Story of Methodism.* Nashville: Abingdon Press, 1949.

McNeil, George E. *The Labor Movement.* New York, 1887.

McPherson, Edward. *The Political History of the United States of America During the Great Rebellion.* 2nd ed. Washington: Philp and Solomons, 1865.

McTyeire, Holland N. *History of Methodism.* Nashville: Southern Methodist Publishing House, 1884.

Mathis, William Thomas. *The Organization of the Illinois Conference of the Methodist Episcopal Church, South.* Murphysboro, Ill.: Privately Printed, 1927.

Mattingly, Lewis Edward. "A History of the Board of Missions of the Methodist Episcopal Church, South." Unpublished dissertation, Emory University, 1939.

May, Henry F. *Protestant Churches and Industrial America.* New York: Harper & Brothers, 1949.

Mode, Peter G. *The Frontier Spirit in American Christianity*. New York: The Macmillan Company, 1923.

Morrow, Ralph E. *Northern Methodism and Reconstruction*. East Lansing: Michigan State University Press, 1956.

Moss, Lemuel. *Annals of the United States Christian Commission*. Philadelphia: J. B. Lippincott and Company, 1868.

Neely, Thomas B. *American Methodism: Its Divisions and Unification*. New York: Fleming H. Revell Company, 1915.

Niebuhr, H. Richard. *The Social Sources of Denominationalism*. New York: Meridian Books, 1957.

Parrington, Vernon L. *Main Currents in American Thought*. 3 vols. New York: Harcourt, Brace and Company, 1927-30.

Penn, J. Garland. *The Afro-American Press and Its Editors*. Springfield, Mass.: Willey and Company, 1891.

Perry, J. H. *Defense of the Present Mode of Training Candidates for the Ministry in the Methodist Episcopal Church*. New York: Carlton and Phillips, 1855.

Peterson, P. A. *Hand-Book of Southern Methodism*. Richmond: J. W. Fergusson & Son, 1883.

Piette, Maximin. *John Wesley in the Evolution of Protestantism*, tr. J. B. Howard. New York: Sheed and Ward, 1937.

Potter, David M., and Manning, Thomas G. *Nationalism and Sectionalism in America, 1775-1877*. New York: Henry Holt and Company, 1949.

Redford, A. H. *History of the Organization of the Methodist Episcopal Church, South*. Nashville: A. H. Redford, 1871.

Reid, J. M., and Gracey, J. T. *Missions and Missionary Society of the Methodist Episcopal Church, Vol. I*. New York: Eaton and Mains, 1895.

Rogers, E. H. *Like unto Me*. Boston, 1876.

————. *The Relations of Christianity to Labor and Capital*. Boston, 1870.

Simkins, Francis Butler. *A History of the South*. New York: Alfred A. Knopf, 1959.

Simkins, Francis Butler, and Woody, Robert Hilliard. *South Carolina During Reconstruction*. Chapel Hill: University of North Carolina Press, 1932.

Simpson, Matthew, ed. *Cyclopaedia of Methodism*. Rev. ed. Philadelphia: Louis H. Everts, 1880.

Stephenson, George M. *The Puritan Heritage*. New York: The Macmillan Company, 1952.

Sweet, William Warren. *Methodism in American History*. Rev. ed. Nashville: Abingdon Press, 1953.

————. *The Methodist Episcopal Church and the Civil War*. Cincinnati: The Methodist Book Concern, 1912.

————. *Religion in the Development of American Culture*. New York: Charles Scribner's Sons, 1952.

————. *The Story of Religion in America*. New York: Harper & Brothers, 1930.

————. *Virginia Methodism*. Richmond: Whittet and Shepperson, 1955.

Sydnor, Charles S. *The Development of Southern Sectionalism: 1819-1848*. Baton Rouge: Louisiana State University Press, 1948.

Taylor, William. *Christian Adventures in South Africa*. New York: Hunt and Eaton, [1867].

————. *The Flaming Torch in Darkest Africa*. New York: Eaton and Mains, 1898.

Thrift, Charles T., Jr. "The History of Theological Education in the Methodist Episcopal Church, South, 1845-1915." Unpublished dissertation, Duke University, 1932.

Tigert, John J. *A Constitutional History of American Episcopal Methodism*. 6th ed. Nashville: Publishing House of the Methodist Episcopal Church, South, 1916.

Townsend, W. J.; Workman, H. B.; and Eayrs, George. *A New History of Methodism*. London: Hodder and Stoughton, 1909.

Walton, Aubrey G. "Attempts Toward Unification of the Methodist Episcopal Church and the Methodist Episcopal Church, South, 1865-1926." Unpublished dissertation, Duke University, 1931.

Warner, Wellman J. *The Wesleyan Movement in the Industrial Revolution*. London: Longmans, Green, and Company, 1930.

Warren, William F. *The True Theory of Missionary Work*. Pamphlet, 1869.

Warriner, Edwin. *Old Sands Street Methodist Episcopal Church of Brooklyn, New York*. New York: Published for the Author by Phillips and Hunt, 1885.

Wesley, John. *The Letters of the Rev. John Wesley, A.M.*, ed. John Telford. Standard Edition. 8 vols. London: Epworth Press, 1931.

————. *The Journal of the Rev. John Wesley, A.M.*, ed. Nehemiah Curnock. Standard Edition. 8 vols. New York: Eaton and Mains [1909].

Wiley, Bell Irvin. *The Life of Billy Yank, the Common Soldier of the Union*. New York: The Bobbs-Merrill Company, 1952.

————. *The Life of Johnny Reb*. Indianapolis: The Bobbs-Merrill Company, 1943.

Wilson, A. W. *Missions of the Methodist Episcopal Church, South*. Nashville: Southern Methodist Publishing House, 1882.

2. Biography and Autobiography

Allen, Richard. *The Life Experience and Gospel Labors of the Rt. Rev. Richard Allen. Written by Himself*. 200th anniversary edition; introduction by George A. Singleton. Nashville: Abingdon Press, 1960.

Asbury, Francis. *The Journal and Letters of Francis Asbury*, ed. Elmer T. Clark, J. Manning Potts, and Jacob S. Payton. 3 vols. Nashville: Abingdon Press, 1958.

Baxter, D. M. *Bishop Richard Allen and His Spirit*. Philadelphia: A. M. E. Book Concern, 1923.

Brickley, Donald P. *Man of the Morning: The Life and Work of Phineas F. Bresee*. Kansas City, Mo.: Nazarene Publishing House, 1960.

Bristol, Frank Milton. *The Life of Chaplain McCabe*. New York: Fleming H. Revell Company, 1908.

Brosnan, Cornelius. *Jason Lee: Prophet of the New Oregon*. New York: The Macmillan Company, 1932.

Cartwright, Peter. *Autobiography of Peter Cartwright*. Centennial edition; introduction by Charles A. Wallis. Nashville: Abingdon Press, 1956.

Clark, Davis W. *Life and Times of Rev. Elijah Hedding*. New York: Carlton and Phillips, 1856.

Clark, Dougan, and Smith, Joseph H. *David B. Updegraff and His Work*. Cincinnati: The Methodist Book Concern, 1895.

Clark, Robert D. *The Life of Matthew Simpson*. New York: The Macmillan Company, 1956.

Coan, J. R. *Daniel Alexander Payne, Christian Educator*. Philadelphia: A. M. E. Book Concern, 1935.

Crooks, George R. *Life and Letters of the Rev. John M'Clintock*. New York: Nelson and Phillips, 1876.

———. *The Life of Bishop Matthew Simpson*. New York: Harper & Brothers, 1890.

Du Bose, Horace M. *The Life of Joshua Soule*. Nashville: Smith and Lamar, 1911.

Dyer, John L. *The Snow-Shoe Itinerant* [autobiography]. Cincinnati: Cranston and Stowe, 1890.

Earle, A. B. *Bringing in the Sheaves* [autobiography]. Boston: J. H. Earle, 1869.

Early, Sarah J. W. *Life and Labors of Rev. Jordan W. Early*. Nashville: A. M. E. Sunday School Union, 1894.

Finney, Thomas M. *Life and Labors of Enoch Mather Marvin*. St. Louis: James H. Chambers, 1880.

Fitzgerald, O. P. *John B. McFerrin*. Nashville: Publishing House of the M. E. Church, South, 1889.

Flood, Theodore L., and Hamilton, John W., eds. *Lives of Methodist Bishops*. New York: Phillips and Hunt, 1882.

Goode, William H. *Outposts of Zion, with Limnings of Mission Life* [autobiography]. Cincinnati: Poe and Hitchcock, 1864.

Hughes, Edwin Holt. *I Was Made a Minister*. New York and Nashville: Abingdon-Cokesbury Press, 1943.

Hughes, George. *The Beloved Physician: Walter C. Palmer*. New York, 1884.

Jones, T. L. *From the Gold Mine to the Pulpit: The Story of the Rev. T. L. Jones, backwoods Methodist preacher in the Pacific Northwest, during the closing years of the nineteenth century*. Cincinnati: The Methodist Book Concern, 1904.

Kellogg, Harriet S. *Life of Mrs. Emily J. Harwood*. Albuquerque, N. M.: El Abogado Press, 1908.

McConnell, Francis J. *Borden Parker Bowne*. Cincinnati: The Abingdon Press, 1929.

McDonald, William, and Searles, John E. *The Life of Rev. John S. Inskip*. Boston: McDonald and Gill, 1887.

Marlay, John F. *The Life of Rev. Thomas A. Morris*. Cincinnati: Hitchcock and Walden, 1875.

Matlack, Lucius C. *The Life of Rev. Orange Scott: Compiled from his personal narrative, correspondence, and other authentic sources of information, in two parts*. New York: Published by C. Prindle and L. C. Matlack at the Wesleyan Methodist Book Room, 1847-48.

Moody, Granville. *A Life's Retrospect: Autobiography of Rev. Granville Moody*, ed. Sylvester Weeks. Cincinnati: Cranston and Stowe, 1890.

Paine, Robert. *Life and Times of William M'Kendree*. 2 vols. Nashville: Southern Methodist Publishing House, 1869.

Payne, Daniel. *Recollections of Seventy Years*, compiled by Sarah C. B. Scar borough, ed. C. S. Smith. Nashville: Publishing House of the A. M. E. Sunday School Union, 1888.

Pearne, Thomas Hall. *Sixty-one Years of Itinerant Christian Life in Church and State.* Cincinnati: Curts and Jennings, 1898.

Peck, George. *The Life and Times of Rev. George Peck.* New York: Nelson and Phillips, 1874.

Prentice, George. *The Life of Gilbert Haven.* New York: Phillips and Hunt, 1883.

Redford, A. H. *Life and Times of H. H. Kavanaugh.* Nashville, 1884.

Ridgaway, Henry B. *The Life of the Rev. Alfred Cookman.* New York: Harper & Brothers, 1873.

Rivers, R. H. *The Life of Robert Paine.* Nashville: Southern Methodist Publishing House, 1884.

Roberts, Benson Howard. *Benjamin Titus Roberts.* North Chili, N. Y.: The Earnest Christian Office, 1900.

Scott, John. *Recollections of Fifty Years in the Ministry.* Pittsburgh and Baltimore: Methodist Protestant Board of Publication, 1898.

Smith, David. *The Biography of Rev. David Smith of the A. M. E. Church.* Xenia, Ohio: Xenia Gazette Office, 1881.

Smith, George G. *The Life and Letters of James Osgood Andrew.* Nashville: Southern Methodist Publishing House, 1883.

———. *The Life and Times of George Foster Pierce.* Nashville: Hunter & Welburn; Sparta, Ga.: Hancock Publishing Company, 1888.

Sprague, William B., ed. *Annals of the American Pulpit: Commemorative Notices of Distinguished Clergymen. Vol. VII: Methodists.* New York: Robert Carter and Brothers, 1861.

Stanley, Edwin J. *Life of Rev. L. B. Stateler.* Nashville: Publishing House of the Methodist Episcopal Church, South, 1907.

Thoburn, James. *My Missionary Apprenticeship.* New York: Phillips and Hunt, 1886.

Tigert, John J., IV. *Bishop Holland Nimmon McTyeire, Ecclesiastical and Educational Architect.* Nashville: Vanderbilt University Press, 1955.

Wesley, Charles H. *Richard Allen, Apostle of Freedom.* Washington: Associated Publishers, 1935.

Wightman, William M. *Life of William Capers, D.D.* Nashville: Southern Methodist Publishing House, 1858.

3. Slavery Controversy and Methodist Division

Bascom, Henry B. *A Brief Appeal to Public Opinion, in a Series of Exceptions to the Course and Action of the Methodist Episcopal Church, from 1844 to 1848, Affecting the Rights and Interests of the Methodist Episcopal Church, South.* Louisville: Morton and Griswold, 1848.

———. *Methodism and Slavery: A Review of the Manifesto of the Majority in Reply to the Protest of the Minority of the Late General Conference.* Frankfort, Ky.: Hodges, Todd and Pruett, printers, 1845.

Bowen, William A. *Why Two Episcopal Methodist Churches in the United States?* Nashville: Publishing House of the Methodist Episcopal Church, South, 1901.

[Brookes, Iveson L.]. *A Defense of Southern Slavery Against the Attacks of*

Henry Clay and Alexander Campbell. Hamburg, S. C.: Robinson and Carlisle, 1851.

Elliott, Charles. *History of the Great Secession.* Cincinnati: Swormstedt and Poe, 1855.

————. *South-Western Methodism. A History of the M. E. Church in the South-West from 1844 to 1864.* Cincinnati: Poe and Hitchcock, 1868.

Harris, William L. *The Constitutional Powers of the General Conference, with a Special Application to the Subject of Slaveholding.* Cincinnati: The Methodist Book Concern, 1860.

Leftwich, W. M. *Martyrdom in Missouri, a History of Religious Proscription, the Seizure of Churches, and the Persecution of Ministers of the Gospel . . . During the Late Civil War.* St. Louis: Southwestern Book and Publishing Company, 1870.

McCarter, J. Mayland. *Border Methodism and Border Slavery, Being a Statement and Review of the Action of the Philadelphia Annual Conference Concerning Slavery, at Its Late Sessions at Easton, Pennsylvania.* Philadelphia: Collins, 1858.

Matlack, Lucius C. *The Antislavery Struggle and Triumph in the Methodist Episcopal Church.* New York: Phillips and Hunt, 1881.

————. *History of American Slavery and Methodism from 1780 to 1849; and History of the Wesleyan Methodist Connection of America.* New York, 1849.

Mattison, Hiram. *The Impending Crisis of 1860.* New York: Mason Brothers, 1859.

————. *What of the Night?* New York: Anti-Slavery Union of the Black River Conference, 1860.

Myers, Edward H. *The Disruption of the Methodist Episcopal Church, 1844-1846.* Nashville: A. H. Redford, 1875.

Norwood, John N. *The Schism in the Methodist Episcopal Church, 1844: A Study of Slavery and Ecclesiastical Politics.* Alfred, N. Y.: Alfred University Press, 1923.

Peck, George. *Slavery and the Episcopacy: Being an Examination of Dr. Bascom's Review.* New York: Lane and Tippett, 1845.

Peck, J. K. *Stevens Answered in His Appeal to the Methodist Episcopal Church.* Montrose, Pa.: "Republican" Steam Power Press, 1859.

Proceedings and Debates of the M. E. General Conference, 1856. Syracuse, N. Y.: Matlack, 1856.

Report of Debates in the General Conference of the Methodist Episcopal Church, Held in the City of New-York, 1844. New York: Lane and Tippett, 1844.

Scott, Orange. *Address to the General Conference of the Methodist Episcopal Church, by the Rev. O. Scott, a member of that body; presented during its session in . . . 1836. To which is added The Speech of the Rev. Mr. Scott, delivered on the floor of the General Conference.* New York: H. R. Piercy, printer, 1836.

Stevens, Abel. *An Appeal to the Methodist Episcopal Church Concerning What Its Next General Conference Should Do on the Question of Slavery.* New York: Trow, 1859.

Sutton, R. *The Methodist Church Property Case.* New York: Lane and Scott, 1851.

Whedon, Daniel. *Letter to Rev. Dr. Stevens on the Subject of His Late Appeal to the Methodist Episcopal Church.* New York: Alvord, 1859.

4. The Methodist Protestant Church

Bassett, Ancel H. *A Concise History of the Methodist Protestant Church.* Pittsburgh: Press of Charles A. Scott, 1877.

Carroll, J. Elwood. *History of the North Carolina Conference of the Methodist Protestant Church.* Greensboro, N. C.: McCulloh and Swain, 1939.

Constitution and Discipline of the Methodist Protestant Church. 1st ed., 1830; 2nd ed., 1831; usually revised after the General Conference.

Drinkhouse, Edward J. *History of Methodist Reform . . . with Special and Comprehensive Reference to . . . the History of the Methodist Protestant Church.* 2 vols. Baltimore and Pittsburgh: Board of Publication of the Methodist Protestant Church, 1899.

Hay, Fannie; Cargo, Ruth; and Feeman, Harlan. *The Story of a Noble Devotion: A Short History of Adrian College.* Adrian, Mich.: Adrian College Press, 1945.

Journal of the General Conference of the Methodist Protestant Church, 1834-1854, 1880-1920.

Journal of the General Conference of the Methodist Protestant Church held in Georgetown, D. C., May, 1862.

Journal of the Ninth General Conference of the Methodist Protestant Church, held in Georgetown, D. C., May, 1866. Baltimore: Printed by Sherwood & Co., 1866.

Journal of the Tenth General Conference of the Methodist Protestant Church, held in Baltimore . . . 1870. Baltimore: Printed by Sherwood & Co., 1870.

Journal of the Eleventh General Conference of the Methodist Protestant Church, held in Lynchburg, Va., May, 1874. Baltimore: Wm. J. C. Dulany & Co.

Journal of the Twelfth General Conference of the Methodist (Protestant) Church, held at Princeton, May 19-31, 1875. Pittsburgh: Methodist Board of Publication, 1875.

Journal of Proceedings of the Convention of the Methodist Protestant Church, held in Montgomery, Alabama, May, 1867. Lynchburg: Virginia Book and Job Office, Print., 1867.

Journal of Proceedings of General Conventions of the Methodist and Methodist Protestant Churches, and of the Joint Convention, held in Baltimore City, May, 1877, Resulting in the Union of the Two Churches. Baltimore: W. J. C. Dulany & Co., 1877.

Makosky, John D. *Western Maryland College in the Nineteenth Century.* Westminster, Md., 1940.

Michael, Olin Bain. *Yadkin College, a Historic Sketch.* Salisbury, N. C.: Rowan Printing Company, 1939.

Minutes of the Maryland Annual Conference, 1866, 1930.

Minutes of the Non-Episcopal Methodist Convention held in Cincinnati, Ohio, May 9-16, 1866. Springfield: Western Methodist Protestant Office, 1866.

Minutes of the First General Conference of the Methodist Church, held at Cleveland, O., May 15-22, 1867. Springfield: A. H. Bassett, Publishing Agent, 1867.

Minutes of the Second General Conference of the Methodist Church . . . 1871.
Springfield: Methodist Book Concern, 1871.

Murray, J. T., and Lewis, T. H. *History of the Maryland Annual Conference
of the Methodist Protestant Church.* Baltimore, 1882.

Proceedings of the Annual Council, 1880.

*Proceedings of the General Conference of the Methodist Protestant Church,
held at Lynchburg, Virginia, May 4, 1858.* Baltimore: Printed by Sherwood
& Co., 1858.

*Proceedings of the General Convention of Delegates from the Northern and
Western Conferences of the Methodist Protestant Church, Held at Springfield,
Ohio, Nov. 10-16, 1858.* Springfield: Office of the "Western Methodist Prot-
estant," 1859.

*Proceedings of the General Convention of Delegates from the Northern and
Western Conferences of the Methodist Protestant Church, Held at Pittsburgh,
Pa., Nov. 14-19, 1860.* Springfield: Printed at the Methodist Protestant Book
Concern, 1862.

*Proceedings of the General Convention of the Methodist Protestant Church,
held at Cincinnati, O., Nov. 5-12, 1862.* Springfield: Methodist Protestant
Book Concern, 1863.

*Proceedings of the Ninth General Conference of the Methodist Protestant
Church, held in Allegheny City, Penn., November 14-22, 1866.* Springfield:
Office of the Methodist Recorder, 1866.

5. Western Expansion

Angel, Myron, ed. *History of Nevada.* Oakland, Calif.: Thompson and West,
1881.

Anthony, C. V. *Fifty Years of Methodism. A History of the Methodist Episcopal
Church within the Bounds of the California Annual Conference from 1847
to 1897.* San Francisco: The Methodist Book Concern, 1901.

Armstrong, C. A., ed. *History of the Methodist Church in North Dakota and
Dakota Territory.* Nashville: Parthenon Press, 1960.

Babcock, S. H., and Bryce, J. Y. *History of Methodism in Oklahoma: The Story
of the Indian Mission Annual Conference of the Methodist Episcopal Church,
South, Vol. I.* 1935.

Bashford, James W. *The Oregon Missions.* New York: The Abingdon Press,
[1918].

Beardsley, Isaac. *Echoes from Peak and Plain, or Tales of Life, War, Travels,
and Colorado Methodism.* Cincinnati: Curts and Jennings, 1898.

Brill, H. E. *Story of the Methodist Episcopal Church in Oklahoma.* Oklahoma
City: Oklahoma City University Press, 1939.

Cook, Malcolm L. "The Methodist Episcopal Church in Wyoming, 1867-88."
Unpublished thesis, University of Denver, 1955.

Curl, R. F. *Southwest Texas Methodism.* Dallas: Wilkinson Printing Company.
Interboard Council, Southwest Texas Conference of The Methodist Church,
1951.

Davis, Henry T. *Solitary Places Made Glad, Being Observations and Experiences
for Thirty-two Years in Nebraska.* Cincinnati: Cranston and Stowe, 1890.

Fisher, H. D. *The Gun and the Gospel: Early Kansas and Chaplain Fisher.*
Chicago: Kenwood Press, 1896.

Harwood, Thomas. *History of New Mexico Spanish and English Missions of the Methodist Episcopal Church from 1850-1910.* 2 vols. Albuquerque: El Abogado Press, 1908, 1910.

Hines, H. K. *Missionary History of the Pacific Northwest.* Portland: H. K. Hines; San Francisco: J. D. Hammond, 1899.

Hogue, Harlan E. "A History of Religion in Southern California, 1846-80." Unpublished dissertation, Columbia University, 1958.

Jackman, Everett. *The Nebraska Methodist Story.* Nebraska Conference Methodist Historical Society, 1954.

Jervey, Edward D. *History of Methodism in Southern California and Arizona.* Nashville: Parthenon Press, 1960.

Loofbourow, Leon L. *In Search of God's Gold.* San Francisco: Historical Society of the California-Nevada Annual Conference of The Methodist Church in Co-operation with the College of the Pacific, 1950.

Marquette, David. *A History of Nebraska Methodism, 1854-1904.* Cincinnati: The Western Methodist Book Concern, 1904.

Merkel, Henry M. *History of Methodism in Utah.* Colorado Springs: The Dentan Printing Company, 1938.

Metcalf, Kenneth. "The Beginnings of Methodism in Colorado." Unpublished dissertation, Iliff School of Theology, 1948.

Mills, Edward L. *Plains, Peaks, and Pioneers: Eighty Years of Methodism in Montana.* Portland, Ore.: Binfords and Mort, 1947.

Minutes of the Twenty-fifth Anniversary of the Utah Mission. J. D. Gillilan and E. C. Hunt, 1895.

Nail, Olin W. *The First Hundred Years of the Southwest Texas Conference of the Methodist Church, 1858-1958.* San Antonio: Southwest Texas Conference of The Methodist Church, 1958.

Phelan, Macum. *A History of Early Methodism in Texas, 1817-1866.* Nashville: Cokesbury Press, 1924.

—————. *A History of the Expansion of Methodism in Texas, 1867-1902.* Dallas: Mathis, Van Nort and Company, 1937.

Simmons, J. C. *The History of Southern Methodism on the Pacific Coast.* Nashville: Southern Methodist Publishing House, 1886.

Swan, Lowell B. "A History of Methodism in Colorado, 1863-1876." Unpublished dissertation, Iliff School of Theology, 1951.

Taylor, William. *California Life Illustrated.* New York: Carlton and Porter, 1859.

—————. *Seven Years' Street Preaching in San Francisco, California, embracing Incidents, Triumphant Death Scenes, etc.,* ed. W. P. Strickland. New York: Published for the Author by Carlton and Porter, 1856.

Yarnes, Thomas D. *A History of Oregon Methodism.* Nashville: Parthenon Press, 1957.

6. Language Conferences

Andersen, Arlow W. *The Salt of the Earth: The History of Norwegian Danish Methodism in America.* Nashville: Parthenon Press, 1962.

Douglass, Paul F. *The Story of German Methodism.* New York: The Methodist Book Concern, 1939.

Fisk, Wilbur. MS letter to William Nast, March 12, 1833. Archives of the

Museum of German Methodism, Nippert Memorial Library, Bethesda Hospital, Cincinnati.

Haagensen, Andrew. *Den Norsk-Dansk Methodismes Historie paa Begge Sider Havet* [*The History of Norwegian-Danish Methodism on Both Sides of the Ocean*]. Chicago: Den Norsk-Danske Boghandels Officin [Norwegian-Danish Bookstore], 1894.

Liljegren, Nils M.; Westergreen, N. O.; and Wallenius, C. G. *Svenske Metodismen i Amerika*. Chicago: Svenska M.E. Bokhandes-Föreningens Förlag, 1895.

Mann, Henrich. *Ludwig S. Jacoby: Sein Leben und Werken*. Bremen: Verlag des Traktathauses, 1892.

Miller, Adam. *Experiences of German Methodist Preachers*. Cincinnati: The Methodist Book Concern, 1859.

Nuelsen, John L. *Der Methodismus in Deutschland nach dem Krieg*. Bremen: Buchhandlung und Verlag des Traktathauses.

————. *John Wesley und das deutsche Kirchenlied*. Bremen: Anker-Verlag, 1938.

Peter, L. *Geschichte der bischöflichen Methodistenkirchen in der Schweiz*. Zurich: Christliche Verlagsbuchhandlung, 1893.

Williams, Daniel J. *One Hundred Years of Welsh Calvinistic Methodism in America*. Philadelphia: Westminster Press, 1937.

7. Other Branches of Methodism

Alleyne, Cameron C. *Gold Coast at a Glance*. Pelham, N. Y.: Published for the Author, 1931.

The A.M.E. Hymnal. Nashville: The A.M.E. Sunday School Union, 1954.

The A.M.E. Zion Hymnal. Charlotte, N. C.: A.M.E. Zion Publishing House, 1957.

Arnett, Benjamin W. *The Budget*, 1884, 1887. [The "Budgets" were annual publications by Arnett during his term of office as financial secretary of the A.M.E. Church—1881-94, except 1889-90, 1892-93.]

————. *Colored Sunday Schools*. Nashville: A.M.E. Sunday School Union, 1896.

Berry, L. L. *A Century of Missions of the A.M.E. Church, 1840-1940*. New York: Gutenberg Printing Company, 1942.

Blews, Richard R. *Master Workmen* [Free Methodist Church]. Winona Lake, Ind.: Light and Life Press, 1939.

Bradley, David Henry, Sr. *A History of the A.M.E. Zion Church, 1796-1872*. Nashville: Parthenon Press, 1956.

Clement, Rufus E. "The Educational Work of the African Methodist Episcopal Zion Church, 1820-1920." Unpublished thesis, Northwestern University, 1922.

Discipline, A.M.E. Church.

Discipline, A.M.E. Zion Church.

Eichelberger, James W. *Manual for Directors of Christian Education in the A.M.E. Zion Church*. Nashville: Parthenon Press, n.d.

————. "A Survey of the Overhead Sunday School Organizations of the A.M.E. Zion, A.M.E., and C.M.E. Churches." Unpublished thesis, Northwestern University, 1923.

Gaines, Wesley J. *African Methodism in the South*. Atlanta: Franklin Publishing House, 1890.

Handy, James A. *Scraps of African Methodist Episcopal History*. Philadelphia: A.M.E. Book Concern, n.d.

Harris, C. R. *Zion's Historical Catechism*. Charlotte, N. C.: A.M.E. Zion Publishing House, 1916.

Hogue, Wilson T. *History of the Free Methodist Church*. Chicago: Free Methodist Publishing House, 1915.

Hood, James Walker. *One Hundred Years of the African Methodist Episcopal Zion Church*. New York: A.M.E. Zion Book Concern, 1895.

The Hymn Book of the African Methodist Episcopal Church; being a Collection of Hymns, Sacred Songs and Chants, designed to supercede all others hitherto made use of in that Church. Selected from Various Authors. Compiled by H. M. Turner, 1873.

Hymnal Adapted to the Doctrines and Usages of the African Methodist Episcopal Church. Philadelphia, 1893.

Jenifer, John T. *Centennial Retrospect History of the African Methodist Episcopal Church*. Nashville: A.M.E. Sunday School Union, 1916.

Jones, E. D. W. *Comprehensive Catechism of the A.M.E. Zion Church and Other Things You Should Know*. 1934.

Journal of the General Conference of the African Methodist Episcopal Church.

McLeister, Ira Ford. *History of the Wesleyan Methodist Church of America*, rev. by Roy Stephen Nicholson. Marion, Ind.: Wesleyan Methodist Publishing Association, 1959.

Marston, Leslie R. *A Living Witness* [Free Methodist Church]. Winona Lake, Ind.: Light and Life Press, 1960.

Moore, John Jamieson. *History of the A.M.E. Zion Church in America*. York, Pa.: Teachers Journal Office, 1884.

New Hymn and Tune Book: An Offering of Praise for the use of the African M.E. Zion Church of America. 1888.

Payne, Daniel A. *A History of the African Methodist Episcopal Church*, ed. C. S. Smith. Nashville: Publishing House of the A.M.E. Sunday School Union, 1891.

Phillips, C. H. *A History of the Colored Methodist Episcopal Church in America*. Jackson, Tenn.: Publishing House of the Colored Methodist Episcopal Church, 1900.

Ransom, Reverdy C. *Preface to the History of the A.M.E. Church*. Nashville: A.M.E. Sunday School Union, 1950.

Ridgel, Alfred. *Africa and African Methodism*. Atlanta: Franklin Publishing Company, 1896.

Roberts, Benjamin Titus. *Why Another Sect?* [Free Methodist Church]. Rochester: The Earnest Christian Publishing House, 1879.

Rush, Christopher. *A Short Account of the Rise and Progress of the African M.E. Church in America*. New York: Published by the Author, 1843.

Shaw, Beverly F. *The Negro in the History of Methodism*. Nashville: Parthenon Press, 1954.

Singleton, George A. *The Romance of African Methodism*. New York: Exposition Press, 1952.

Smith, Charles Spencer. *A History of the African Methodist Episcopal Church*. Philadelphia: Book Concern of the A.M.E. Church, 1922.

Spurgeon, F. Claude, ed. *A.M.E. Zion Handbook*. Washington, 1952-56.

Talbert, Horace. *The Sons of Allen*. Xenia, Ohio: The Aldine Press, 1906.

Tanner, Benjamin T. *An Apology for African Methodism*. Baltimore, 1867.

———. *An Outline of Our History and Government for African Methodist Churchmen*. Philadelphia: Grant, Faires & Rodgers, 1884.

Turner, H. M. *The Genius and Theory of Methodist Polity*. Philadelphia: Publications Department, A.M.E. Church, 1885.

Wright, Richard R., ed. *The Encyclopaedia of the A.M.E. Church*. 2nd ed. Philadelphia: The A.M.E. Book Concern, 1947.

8. Nineteenth Century Theology and the Holiness Movement

Bangs, Nathan. *The Present State, Prospects, and Responsibilities of the Methodist Episcopal Church*. New York: Lane and Scott, 1850.

Boland, J. M. *The Problem of Methodism: Being a Review of the Residue Theory of Regeneration and the Second Change Theory of Sanctification and the Philosophy of Christian Perfection*. Nashville: Printed for the Author by the Publishing House of the Methodist Episcopal Church, South, 1889.

Bowne, Borden Parker. *The Philosophy of Herbert Spencer,* New York: Nelson and Phillips, 1874.

Clark, Dougan. *The Offices of the Holy Spirit*. Philadelphia: The Christian Standard, 1879.

Comfort, Silas. *An Exposition of the Articles of Religion of the Methodist Episcopal Church*. New York: Published for the Author at the Conference Office, 1847.

Coward, S. L. C., ed. *Entire Sanctification from 1739 to 1901*. Louisville: Pentecostal Herald, 1901.

Crawford, Benjamin Franklin. *Theological Trends in Methodist Hymnody*. Carnegie, Pa.: Carnegie Church Press, 1939.

Danford, S. A. *Spreading Scriptural Holiness, or the North Dakota Movement*. Chicago: The Christian Witness Company, 1913.

Davies, Edward. *Illustrated History of Douglas Campmeeting*. Boston: McDonald and Gill, 1890.

The Double Cure, or Echoes from the National Campmeetings. Boston: The Christian Witness Company, 1894.

Dunn, Lewis R. *A Manual of Holiness and Review of Dr. James B. Mudge*. Cincinnati: Cranston and Curts, 1895.

———. *The Mission of the Spirit, or the Office and Work of the Comforter in Human Redemption*. New York: Carlton and Lanahan, 1871.

Flew, R. Newton. *The Idea of Perfection in Christian Theology*. London: Oxford University Press, 1934.

———. *The Nature of the Church*. New York: Harper & Brothers, 1952.

Foster, Randolph S. *Christian Purity, or the Heritage of Faith*. New York: Carlton and Lanahan, 1869.

———. *Philosophy of Christian Experience*. New York: Hunt and Eaton, 1891.

Garrison, S. Olin. *Forty Witnesses, Covering the Whole Range of Christian Experience*. New York: Phillips and Hunt, 1888.

Haynes, B. F. *Tempest-Tossed on Methodist Seas*. Kansas City, Mo.: Nazarene Publishing House, 1914.

Henkle, Moses M. *Primary Platform of Methodism; or, Exposition of the General Rules*. Louisville: Published by the Author and Company, 1851.

History of the Revival of Holiness in St. Paul's M.E. Church, Providence, R. I. Pamphlet. Providence: Privately Printed, 1887.

The Holiness Year Book. New York: W. C. Palmer, Jr., 1888.

Hughes, George. *Days of Power in the Forest Temple. A Review of the Wonderful Work of God at Fourteen National Campmeetings from 1867 to 1872.* Boston: John Bent and Company, 1874.

————. *Fragrant Memories of the Tuesday Meeting and Guide to Holiness.* New York, 1886.

Humphrey, E. P. *Our Theology and Its Development.* Philadelphia: Presbyterian Board, 1857.

Huntington, D. W. C. *Sin and Holiness.* Cincinnati: Curts and Jennings, 1898.

Jernigan, C. B. *Pioneer Days of the Holiness Movement in the Southwest.* Kansas City, Mo.: Nazarene Publishing House, 1919.

Jimeson, A. A. *Notes on the Twenty-five Articles.* Cincinnati: Applegate and Company, 1853.

Kean, Samuel Ashton. *Pentecostal Papers.* Cincinnati: The Methodist Book Concern, 1897.

Lee, Luther. *Elements of Theology; or, an Exposition of the Divine Origin, Doctrines, Morals and Institutions of Christianity.* 2nd ed. Syracuse, N. Y.: S. Lee, 1859.

Lindström, Harald. *Wesley and Sanctification,* tr. H. S. Harvey. London: Epworth Press, 1946.

Lowrey, Asbury. *Positive Theology.* Cincinnati, 1853.

————. *Possibilities of Grace.* New York: Phillips and Hunt, 1884.

McConnell, Francis J. *The Essentials of Methodism.* New York: The Methodist Book Concern, 1916.

McLean, A., and Eaton, Joel W. *Penuel; or, Face to Face with God.* New York: W. C. Palmer, Jr., 1869.

Mahan, Asa T. *Out of Darkness into Light.* Boston: Willard Tract Repository, 1876.

Mallalieu, Willard F. *The Fullness of the Blessing of the Gospel of Christ.* Cincinnati: Jennings and Pye, 1903.

Merrill, Stephen M. *Aspects of Christian Experience.* Cincinnati: Cranston and Stowe, 1882.

Miley, John. *Systematic Theology.* 2 vols. New York: Hunt and Eaton, 1892-94.

Mudge, James. *Growth in Holiness Toward Perfection.* New York: Hunt and Eaton, 1895.

Palmer, Phoebe, ed. *Pioneer Experiences, or the Gift of Power Received by Faith.* New York: W. C. Palmer, Jr., 1867.

Peck, Jesse T. *The Central Idea of Christianity.* Boston: H. V. Degen, 1856.

Peters, John L. *Christian Perfection and American Methodism.* Nashville: Abingdon Press, 1956.

Porter, John A.; Goodbey, W. B.; et. al. *Christian Perfection, an Address by the Southern Holiness Associations.* Nashville, [1890].

Proceedings of Holiness Conferences Held at Cincinnati, November 26th, 1877, and at New York, December 17, 1877. Philadelphia: National Publishing Association for the Promotion of Holiness, [1878].

Rall, Harris Franklin. *Modern Premillennialism and the Christian Hope.* New York: The Abingdon Press, 1920.

Ralston, Thomas N. *Elements of Divinity*. Louisville: Morton and Griswold, 1847.

Raymond, Miner. *A Sermon . . . before . . . the Legislature of Massachusetts at the Annual Election*. Boston: White, 1854.

——. *Systematic Theology*. 3 vols. Cincinnati: Hitchcock and Walden, 1877-79.

Roberts, Benjamin T. *Holiness Teachings Compiled from the Editorial Writings of the Late Rev. Benjamin T. Roberts*. North Chili, N. Y.: The Earnest Christian Publishing House, 1893.

Sangster, W. E. *The Path to Perfection*. New York and Nashville: Abingdon-Cokesbury Press, 1943.

Searles, J. E. *History of the Present Holiness Revival*. Boston: McDonald and Gill, 1887.

Smith, Timothy L. *Called unto Holiness: The Story of the Nazarenes, the Formative Years*. Kansas City, Mo.: Nazarene Publishing House, 1962.

——. *Revivalism and Social Reform in Mid-Nineteenth-Century America*. Nashville: Abingdon Press, 1957.

Steele, Daniel. *A Defense of Christian Perfection*. New York: Hunt and Eaton, 1896.

Summers, Thomas O. *Systematic Theology*. 2 vols. Nashville: Publishing House of the Methodist Episcopal Church, South, 1888.

Tefft, B. F. *Methodism Successful*. New York: Derby and Jackson, 1860.

Thompson, Claude H. "The Witness of American Methodism to the Historical Doctrine of Christian Perfection." Unpublished dissertation, Drew University, 1949.

Townsend, L. T. *Elements of General Christian Theology*. New York: Nelson and Phillips, 1879.

——. *Outline of Christian Theology*. New York: Nelson and Phillips, 1877.

Turner, George Allen. *The More Excellent Way: The Scriptural Basis of the Wesleyan Message*. Winona Lake, Ind.: Light and Life Press, 1951.

Wakefield, Samuel. *A Complete System of Christian Theology*. New York: Carlton and Porter, 1862.

Warren, William F. *Systematische Theologie einheitlich behandelt: Einleitung*. Bremen: Verlag des Traktathauses; Cincinnati: Poe and Hitchcock, 1865. [Not published in English.]

Watson, Richard. *Theological Institutes*. New York: Emory and Waugh, 1831.

Whedon, Daniel. *Freedom of the Will as a Basis of Human Responsibility*. New York: Carlton and Porter, 1864.

——. *Statements: Theological and Critical*. New York: Phillips and Hunt, 1887.

Wilson, George W. *Methodist Theology vs. Methodist Theologians*. Cincinnati: Jennings and Pye, 1904.

9. Conference Journals, Minutes, Other Official Publications

Annual Reports of the Freedmen's Aid Society, 1866-85.

Annual Reports of the Missionary Society of the Methodist Episcopal Church, 1820-95.

The Centenary Survey of the Board of Home Missions and Church Extension of the Methodist Episcopal Church. New York: Joint Centenary Committee, 1918.

Doctrines and Discipline of the Methodist Episcopal Church.

Doctrines and Discipline of the Methodist Episcopal Church, South. [First ed. following the 1846 General Conference.]

The Epworth Hymnal. Cincinnati: Cranston and Stowe, 1885.

Formal Fraternity, Proceedings of the General Conferences of the Methodist Episcopal Church and of the Methodist Episcopal Church, South, in 1872, 1874, and 1876, and of the Joint Commission of the Two Churches on Fraternal Relations, at Cape May, New Jersey, August 16-23, 1876. New York: Nelson and Phillips, 1876.

History of the Organization of the Methodist Episcopal Church, South: Comprehending all the Official Proceedings of the General Conference; the Southern Annual Conferences, and the General Convention; with such other matters as are necessary to a right understanding of the case. Nashville: Compiled and Published by the Editors and Publishers of the South-Western Christian Advocate, for the M. E. Church, South, by order of the Louisville Convention. William Cameron, Printer, 1845. [Reprinted by the Publishing House of the Methodist Episcopal Church, South, 1925, together with the *Journal of the General Conference,* 1846.]

Hymnal of the Methodist Episcopal Church, 1878, 1905. [The 1905 edition was published jointly with the Methodist Episcopal Church, South.]

Journal of the Baltimore Conference, 1843.

Journal of the Cincinnati Conference, 1863.

Journal of the General Conference of the Methodist Episcopal Church. [Published following each General Conference; as separate volumes after 1836.]

Journal of the General Conference of the Methodist Episcopal Church, South. [Published following each General Conference, beginning in 1846. The MS General Conference Journals of the Southern Church, including the Journal of the Louisville Convention and the 1846 Conference, are in the Library of the Methodist Publishing House, Nashville.]

Journals of the General Conference, 1796-1836. New York: Carlton and Phillips, 1855.

Journal of the Proceedings of the Board of Commissioners of the Methodist Episcopal Church, South, 1876.

Minutes of the Annual Conferences of the Methodist Episcopal Church. [Published annually; from 1878 to 1940 the Minutes were published in two sections—Spring Conferences and Fall Conferences. There have been several collected editions, published by the book agents, including *Minutes of the Methodist Conferences Annually Held in America, from 1773 to 1794, inclusive.* Philadelphia: Printed by Henry Tuckniss, sold by John Dickins, 1795. This early collection varies somewhat from later editions.]

Minutes of the Annual Conferences of the Methodist Episcopal Church, South. Published annually, beginning in 1845.

Minutes of the Cape May Convention, MS at Emory University.

Minutes of the Georgia Annual Conference of the Methodist Episcopal Church, South, 1862.

Minutes of the Mississippi Annual Conference of the Methodist Episcopal Church, South, 1865.

Minutes of the New Jersey Conference, 1845.

Minutes of the Seventy-sixth Session of the South Carolina Conference of the Methodist Episcopal Church, South, 1863.

Proceedings of the Oecumenical Methodist Conference . . . 1881. London: Wesleyan Conference Office, 1881.

Proceedings of the Second Ecumenical Methodist Conference . . . 1891. New York: Hunt and Eaton, 1892.

Proceedings of the Third Ecumenical Methodist Conference. New York: Eaton and Mains, 1901.

Proceedings of the Fourth Ecumenical Methodist Conference. New York: Eaton and Mains, 1911.

Proceedings of the Fifth Ecumenical Methodist Conference. New York: The Methodist Book Concern, 1921.

Proceedings, Sermons, Essays, and Addresses of the Centennial Methodist Conference Held in Mt. Vernon Place Methodist Episcopal Church, Baltimore, Maryland, December 9-17, 1884. New York: Phillips and Hunt, 1885.

The Sunday Service of the Methodists in North America. With Other Occasional Services. London, 1784.

The Young People's Hymnal No. 2. Nashville: Publishing House of the M. E. Church, South, 1903. [No. 1 was published in 1897.]

10. Periodicals

The A.M.E. Church Review. Authorized 1884; still published 1963, at Philadelphia.

Buffalo Christian Advocate (Buffalo, New York, Methodist Episcopal Church). Began 1850; after several title changes merged into *Northern Christian Advocate* in 1904.

Christian Advocate and Journal (New York, Methodist Episcopal Church). Began 1826; from 1828-33 published as *Christian Advocate and Journal and Zion's Herald;* became simply the *Christian Advocate* in 1866. Here referred to as the New York *Christian Advocate.*

Central Christian Advocate (St. Louis, Methodist Episcopal Church). Published under this title 1852-1929; became the Central Edition of the *Christian Advocate* in 1929. Published in Kansas City, Kansas, after 1900.

Daily Christian Advocate, Methodist Episcopal Church. Published daily during the sessions of the General Conference, beginning in 1848.

Der Christliche Apologete (Cincinnati, Methodist Episcopal Church for the German Language Conferences). Published 1839-1941.

The Guide to Holiness. Published at Boston, 1845 to 1901. Began 1839 as *Guide to Christian Perfection.*

The Journal of Negro History. Published by the Association for the Study of Negro Life and History, Washington. Began 1916; still published 1963.

The Methodist Protestant (Baltimore, Methodist Protestant Church). Published under this title 1834-1929; the *Methodist Protestant-Recorder* 1929-40; absorbed into the *Christian Advocate* at unification.

The Methodist Quarterly Review (New York, Methodist Episcopal Church). Published as *The Methodist Magazine* (1818-28); *Methodist Magazine and Quarterly Review* (1830-41); and later as *The Methodist Review* (1885-1932).

The Methodist Recorder (Springfield, Ohio, Methodist Protestant Church). Moved to Pittsburgh 1871; became *Methodist Protestant-Recorder* in 1929;

absorbed into the *Christian Advocate* at unification. Published earlier as the *Western Recorder* (1839-54) and the *Western Methodist Protestant* (1855-66).

Nashville *Christian Advocate* (Nashville, Methodist Episcopal Church, South). Began publication 1832 as *South-Western Christian Advocate;* became property of the Southern Church in 1845; absorbed into the *Christian Advocate* at unification.

New Orleans Christian Advocate (New Orleans, Methodist Episcopal Church, South). Published 1850-1946.

New York *Christian Advocate*. See *Christian Advocate and Journal*.

The Northern Independent. Published by the Free Methodist movement, beginning January, 1857, at Auburn, New York. Ended around 1863.

Phylon. The Atlanta University Review of Race and Culture; published since 1940.

Quarterly Review of the Methodist Episcopal Church, South. Published under this title 1847-61, 1879-86; 1889-94; discontinued in 1930. Also published as *Southern Methodist Review* (1887-88); *The Methodist Review* (1895-1903; 1906-8); *The Methodist Quarterly Review* (1903-6, 1908-30).

Repository of Religion and Literature. Published 1858-64 by the A.M.E. Church.

Richmond Christian Advocate (Richmond, Methodist Episcopal Church, South). Published under this title 1839-1901; became property of the Southern Church 1845; merged with the *Baltimore Christian Advocate* in 1901 to become the *Baltimore and Richmond Christian Advocate*.

St. Louis Christian Advocate (St. Louis, Methodist Episcopal Church, South). Published 1850-1931; not published in 1861-62.

Southern Christian Advocate (Charleston, Methodist Episcopal Church, South). Began publication 1837; became property of the Southern Church in 1845; continued after unification as the *South Carolina Methodist Advocate,* official organ of the South Carolina Conference.

South-Western Christian Advocate. See Nashville *Christian Advocate*.

Virginia Conference Sentinel. Published by the Virginia Conference at Richmond, March, 1836–April, 1837. Resumed publication in 1839 as the *Richmond Christian Advocate*.

Western Christian Advocate (Cincinnati, Methodist Episcopal Church). Published under this title 1834-1929; became the Western Edition of the *Christian Advocate* in 1929.

Zion's Herald (Boston, Methodist Episcopal Church). Official paper of the New England Conference; began publication 1823; still published 1963.

Index, Volume II

Abbeville School, S.C., 552
"ABC" books, 490
abolition movement, 16, 19, 20, 21, 22-39, 40, 197, 363
Adams, Charles, 186
Adams, G. H., 463
Adams, Henry, 585
"Address to Christians Throughout the World," 231-32
Adrian College, 397, 398, 401, 405, 410, 411-12, 413, 414, 418
Adriance, Jacob, 434
Advocate of Holiness, 615
Africa, 139, 158, 199, 291, 553-54
African American Methodist Episcopal Church, 579
African Methodist Episcopal Church, 526-55, 565, 566, 696, 704: doctrine and polity of, 538-42; and education, 542-47; missions of, 551-55; publishing program of, 547-50; questions of union in, 671-89; relations of, with other groups, 576-82; in the South, 255, 280, 284, 285; spread of, 527-38
African Methodist Episcopal Zion Church, 301, 531, 540, 541, 542, 555-76, 662: doctrine and polity of, 562-68; education program of, 568-72; missions of, 575-76; publications of, 573-75; questions of union in, 671-89; relations with other groups, 576-82; in South, 255, 280, 285; spread of, 555-62
African Methodist Society, Albany, 530
African Union Church, 577-78
agriculture: education in, for Negroes, 367, 368; organizations of workers in, 588
Akers, Peter, 60

Alabama, 33, 312, 362, 515, 533, 537, 578: Birmingham, 119, 684; Dadeville, Huntsville, 366; Greenville, Tuskegee, 572; Mobile, 536, 537, 571, 687; Mt. Union, 377; Russell County, 146, 282; Selma, 537, 547, 552; Tuscaloosa, 571
Alabama Colored Conference, 284
Alabama Conference: A.M.E., 537; A.M.E. Zion, 561; M.E., 45, 46; M.E.S., 107-8, 204-5, 246, 306; M.P., 395
Alaska, 535, 590
Albany Circuit, Ore., 437
Albemarle Conference A.M.E. Zion, 560
Alderson, W. W., 436
Alexander, Robert, 424
Alford, John W., 365
Allegheny College, 167
Allegheny Conference, A.M.E. Zion, 557, 571
Allen, Henry, 554
Allen, Richard, 526, 528, 530, 531, 536, 538, 542, 549, 551
Allen, Sarah, 551
Allen, Young J., 244, 245, 288
Allen C. E. League Star, 550
Allen Christian Endeavor League, 544-45, 550
Allen Christian Endeavorer, 545, 550
Allen Temple, Cincinnati, 532
Allen University, 546
Allyn, Robert, 363
A. M. E. Church Magazine, 548
A. M. E. Church Review, 548
A. M. E. Zion Quarterly Review, 573
American Antislavery Society, 25, 26, 32, 40

American Bible Society, 224, 349, 440, 441, 460, 482
American Colonization Society, 20, 21, 30, 34, 553
American Federation of Labor, 588
American Legion, 510
American Methodism . . . (Neely), 670
American Presbyterian Review, 617
American Sunday School Union, 643
Americanization of immigrants, 518
Ames, Edward R., 187, 215, 229, 249, 250, 262, 299, 365, 423, 427, 429, 435, 449, 483, 614, plate 7
amusements, attitude toward, 312, 326, 328-29, 600, 638-42
Analogy of Religion (Butler), 654, 655
Anderson, Charles, 557
Anderson, J. Harvey, 685
Anderson, James, 556
Anderson, William, 528
Andover Circuit, Ill., 496
Andover Review, 597
Andover Seminary, 618
Andrew, James O., 46, 48-49, 52, 54-59, 61-62, 64, 65, 68, 69, 75-76, 78-79, 80, 81, 82, 84, 90-96, 102-8, 110, 111, 113, 114, 116, 117, 118, 122, 123, 124, 129, 130, 132, 134, 137, 138, 144-49, 152, 154, 155, 163, 164, 177, 181, 189, 231, 237, 244, 246, 260, 272, 279, 282, plate 3
Andrew Chapel, New Bern, N.C., 691
Andrews, E. G., 691
Andrews Collegiate Institute, 377
Anglo-African, 573
Annual Conferences, A.M.E.: in Africa, 553, 554; Alabama, 537; Arkansas, 537, 552; Baltimore, 530-31,

Ann'l Conferences, A.M.E.
—cont'd
539, 543, 546; California, 534; Chicago, 535; Colorado, 535; Florida, 537; Georgia, 537; Illinois, 534-35; Indian Mission, 552; Indiana, 533, 534; Iowa, 535; Kansas, 534; Kentucky, 537, 547; Louisiana, 536-37; Michigan, 535; Mississippi, 537; Missouri, 533; New England, 531; New York, 530, 531, 539, 543; North Carolina, 537; Northwestern, 535; Ohio, 530, 532, 533, 543, 545, 546, 551; Oklahoma, 535; Philadelphia 529, 530, 534, 539, 543, 549, 552; Pittsburgh, 534; Puget Sound, 535; South Carolina, 255, 536; Tennessee, 537; Texas, 537; Upper Canada, 533, 577; Virginia, 537, 538; West Virginia, 534

Annual Conferences, A.M.E. Zion: Alabama, 561; Albemarle, 560; Allegheny, 557, 571; Arkansas, 561; Baltimore, 557; Blue Ridge, 560; California, 559; Canada-Michigan, 559; Cape Fear, 560; Florida, 561, 562; Genesee or Western New York, 558, 566; Georgia, 561-62; Indiana, 559; Kentucky, 561; Louisiana, 255, 560, 561, 566; Missouri, 559, 561; New England, 558, 560, 569, 570; New Jersey, 559; New York, 556, 573; North Carolina, 560, 566, 570, 571; Nova Scotia, 576; Ohio, 558-59; Old North Carolina, 255; Oregon, 559; Palmetto, 561; Philadelphia-Baltimore, 557, 560, 566; South Carolina, 561; South Mississippi, 561; Southern, 560; Tennessee, 560; Texas, 561; Virginia, 561; West Tennessee-Mississippi, 562

Annual Conferences, C.M.E.: Alabama, Georgia, Mississippi, Tennessee, and Texas, 284; Missouri and Kansas, 286

Annual Conferences, M.E., 12, 13, 129: reaction of, to Plan of Separation, 108-11, 156, 168, 174; Alabama, 45; Arizona Mission, 463; Arkansas, 425, 427; Baltimore, 16, 34, 35, 45, 52, 56, 84, 158, 175, 178, 207, 209, 210, 211, 298, 505, 517; Black River, 178, 474, 505; California, 441, 454, 457, 459, 460, 506, 507, 508, 511, 512; Cincinnati, 345, 484, 488, 505, 546; Colorado, 435, 436, 439, 440, 444, 445; Columbia River, 452; Delaware, 528; Des Moines, 464; Erie, 35; Florida, 64; Genesee, 45, 218, 339, 342, 343-51, 352, 354, 357, 358; Georgia, 18, 27; German, 487, 489, 492, 519; Gulf Mission, 622; Holston, 251; Idaho, 452; Illinois, 168, 175, 475, 481, 496; Indian Mission, 427; Indiana, 64, 322, 480, 484; Iowa, 64, 430, 464, 465-66; Italy, 514; Kansas, 430, 431, 434, 614; Kentucky, 186, 188, 209, 211, 261, 480; Louisiana, 514; Minnesota, 464, 465, 489, 496; Mississippi, 424, 427; Missouri, 209, 211, 213, 427, 430, 614; Montana, 452; Nebraska, 430, 431, 434, 614; Nevada, 441, 461; New England, 18, 19, 29, 34, 35, 36, 156, 178, 495, 514; New Hampshire, 32, 33; New Jersey, 52, 151, 524; New York, 34, 35, 36, 45, 151, 202, 300, 473, 480, 493, 505, 514, 517, 597; Newark, 223; North Dakota, 465; Norwegian-Danish, 501, 503, 519; Ohio, 33-34, 35, 126, 153, 164, 165, 166, 168, 477, 478, 480, 481, 488, 505; Oneida 52, 359, 505; Oregon, 448-49, 451; Oregon and California Mission, 173, 448, 454; Pacific German, 519; Peoria, 495; Philadelphia, 34, 151, 178, 209, 210, 514; Pittsburgh, 178, 480, 505, 517; Providence, 52, 151, 178; Puget Sound, 450; Rio Grande Mission,

Ann'l Conferences, M.E.—
—cont'd
425; Rock River, 218, 352-53, 494, 514; Rocky Mountain, 435, 438, 442, 452; St. Louis, 614; South Carolina, 28; Southern California, 457, 458; Swedish, 496, 498, 503, 519; Texas, 64, 425, 426, 495; Troy, 178, 475, 524; Utah, 442, 452; Vermont, 64; Virginia, 146, 209, 211; West Virginia, 182, 183; Wisconsin, 218, 500, 505; Wyoming Mission, 439, 440

Annual Conferences, M.E.S., 111, 112, 158, 244, 275: Alabama, 107-8, 114, 204-5, 246, 306; Arkansas, 102-3, 106, 113, 306; Columbia, 449, 450; Florida, 106, 114, 516; Georgia, 105-6, 114, 128, 233; Holston, 100-101, 113, 306; Illinois, 276; Indian Mission, 104-5, 114, 288, 427, 428; Kansas Mission, 191, 431-32; Kentucky, 99-100, 113, 148, 156, 158, 166, 212, 247, 260, 622; Los Angeles, 458, 463; Louisiana, 306, 475; Louisville, 212, 247; Memphis, 102, 113, 306; Mexican Border, 445; Mississippi, 102, 113, 306; Missouri, 100, 113, 267, 432, 435, 438; Montgomery, 282; New Mexico, 445; North Carolina, 103-4, 113; Pacific, 247, 449, 455, 459; St. Louis, 428, 431, 432; South Carolina, 104, 114, 254; Tennessee, 101-2, 113, 291, 306; Texas, 106-7, 114, 445, 622; Virginia, 103, 113, 158, 183; Western, 432, 435, 438; White River, 306; Wilmington, 653

Annual Conferences, M.P., 393, 394, 402-3: Alabama, 395; Colorado, 400; Indiana, 402; Iowa, 402, 413; Japan, 408; Maryland, 398, 399, 402, 407, 416, 418, 419; Michigan, 396; Minnesota, 402-3; Mississippi, 395, 400; Missouri, 403, 413; Muskingum, 402, 414; Nebraska, 403; New York, 405-6;

Ann'l Conferences, M.P.—cont'd
  North Carolina, 400, 402, 414, 416; North Illinois, 402, 413; Ohio, 402, 411, 413; Oregon, 403; Pittsburgh, 402; Tennessee, 403; Virginia, 395, 402; West Virginia, 402
Annual Conferences, Wesleyan Methodist Connection, 44
Annual Council, M.P., 405
Anthony, C. V., 460
Anthony, Elihu, 453
anti-Catholicism, 332-34
anti-Oriental feeling, 506-10
anti-Masonry, 343
Anti-Monopoly party, 588
"anti-organites," 322
antislavery movement, 8, 12, 13, 14, 15, 18, 21, 144, 167, 197, 200, 209, 214, 540. (See also abolition movement)
antislavery conventions, 38
antislavery societies, 25, 26, 32, 38, 39, 40, 44-45, 202
Antigua, 555
Apology for African Methodism (Tanner), 526-27
Appeal to the Methodist Episcopal Church . . . on the Question of Slavery (Stevens), 202
Appeals, Committee on, 354
Appleget, T. B., 406
appointive power, controversy over, 35, 41, 61, 66
Arizona, 461-63, 517, 535: Florence, Globe City, Pinal, Salt River, Tombstone, Tucson, Verde River, 463; Fort Defiance, Tubac, 462; Phoenix, 463, 535; Prescott, 462, 463
Arizona Mission Conference, M.E., 463
Arkansas, 243, 420, 426, 537: Little Rock, 242, 250, 377, 537, 547, 625; Magnolia, 404; Pine Bluff, 250; Redemption, 579; Warren, 572; Washington, 165
Arkansas Conference: A.M.E., 536, 552; A.M.E. Zion, 561; M.E., 425, 427; M.E.S., 102-3, 106, 306
Arminian Magazine, 593
Arminianism, 467, 593, 594, 602
Armstrong, John, 165, 166

Army Church, 242-43
Army Mission, 236-37
Army and Navy Herald, 237-38
Arnett, B. W., 541, 544, 582, 702
Arthur, William, 696
Articles of Religion, 43, 356, 381, 396, 629
Asbury, Francis, 13, 48, 74, 77, 296, 400, 542, 632, 650, 659
Asbury Chapel, Sacramento, 455
Asbury Church, New York City, 493, 576
Asbury Church, Wilmington, 528
Asbury College, 623, 624
Asiatic Exclusion League, 510
assistant superintendents, 564, 565
Atkinson Literary and Industrial College, 572
atonement, 601, 609
Atonement in Christ (Miley), 383
Atwood, Anthony, 612
Augusta Circuit, Ky., 166
Augustine, 389
Austria, 484, 486
authoritarianism, 19, 21, 35, 41
authority, co-ordinate understanding of, 77-82, 83, 84, 85, 100; issue of in general superintendency, 66-82, 83; unilateral understanding of, 69, 70-76, 83

Bachman, John, 24
Badger, George, 180
Bahamas, 555
Baird, I. N., 199
Baker, A., 415
Baker, Gardner, 186
Baker, James C., 193, 218, 647
Baker, Osmon C., 187
Baker Institute, 366
Baldwin, W. W., 440
Baldwin Institute, 185
Baldwin Seminary, 377
Baldwin University, Baldwin-Wallace College, 488
Baltimore African Church, 527
Baltimore Conference: A.M.E., 530-31, 539, 543, 546; A.M.E. Zion, 557; M.E., 16, 34, 35, 45, 52,

Baltimore Conf.—cont'd
  56, 84, 158, 175, 178, 207, 209, 210, 211, 298, 505, 517
"Bands," Nazarite, 345, 352, 355
Bangs, Nathan, 15, 16, 60, 63, 72, 76, 108, 127, 151, 152, 156, 169, 180, 186, 188, 202, 206, 340, 387, 593, 610, 611
Banner of Holiness, 619
baptism, 239, 600-601, 629, 636
Baptists, 264, 329, 330, 363, 617
Barbados, 555
Barris, J. S., 15
Bascom, Henry B., 90, 118, 132, 133, 136, 141, 142, 154-56, 158, 176, 177, 183, 185
Bassett, Ancel, 397, 400, 401
Bateman, A. L. S., 460
Bates, Lawrence W., 392, 401, 402
Bauer, Bruno, 384
Baxter, B. R., 438
Beanes, Scipio, 554
Bebelforscher, 490
Beecher, Henry Ward, 317, 341
Bellevue Indian mission, 429
Bennett, Jesse L., 460
Bennett, William W., 237, 238, 239
Bennett Seminary, 366, 376
Benson, Benjamin Franklin, 419
Benson, F. T., 404
Bergner, Peter, 493
Bermuda, 555, 578
Bermuda Conference, B.M.E., 578
Berrien, James C., 418
Berry, George M., 450
Berryman, Jerome, 427
Bethany Deaconess Home and Hospital, 492
Bethany Old People's Home, Stockton, Cal., 503
Bethany Society, 491, 492
Bethel Church: Baltimore, 531, 543; Columbia, Ohio, 546; Michigan, 535; Philadelphia, 526, 554; Vicksburg, 547; Wilmington, 528
Bethel Institute: Cape Town, South Africa, 554; Little Rock, Ark., 547
Bethel Literary society, 545

Bethel Ship, 493-94, 500, 501, plate 12
Bethesda Institutions, 491-92
Bewley, Anthony, 425, 426
Bible, 23-24, 593, 623, 644, 645
Bible School, 404
Bible School Quarterly, 404
biblical criticism, 595
biblical departments or schools, 193, 278, 305, 306, 309, 366, 625, 651
bilingual missions, 486-87, 504-17, 522, 523
Binder, Martha, 492
Binghamton Circuit, N.Y., 531
Birmingham Plan, 689
Birney, James G., 26
Bishop, Horace S., 462
Bishop, John M., 579
Bishop, William H., 564, 565, 575
bishops: A.M.E. Zion, 567; C.M.E., 285; defined, 72-73, 77, 78, 79, 131; M.E., 37, 48; M.E.S., 137-38, 246-47, 260, 313; office of, 55, 187; "political," 228-29; power of, 66-82, 83, 100, 103, 278, 313, 656; reaction of, to Louisville Convention, 124-26; as slaveholders, 52, 54-59. (*See also* episcopacy *and* Episcopal Addresses)
Bishops' Council (Council of Bishops), 540, 542, 686
Black, William H., 408, 409
Black Code, 530
Black Hills Mission, 439, 465, 466
Black River Conference, M.E., 178, 474, 505
Blackwell, J. D., 692
Blaine, David E. and Catherine, 450
Bland, Adam, 457
Blinn, Christian; Blinn Memorial College, 489
Bloomington College, 377
Blue Ridge Conference, A.M.E. Zion, 560
Blythe, J. F., 458
Boardman, William E., 610, 617
Boggs, John, 553
Bohemians, 517
Boland, J. M., 623
Bond, Thomas E., 45-46, 97, 108, 109, 126, 149, 151-

Bond, Thomas E.—*cont'd* 53, 156, 157, 163, 168, 179, 185, 189, 194, 199
Bonham Circuit, Tex., 425
Book Concern: A.M.E., 540; A.M.E. Zion, 574, 575; dispute over property of, 130, 134-36, 150, 156, 173, 175, 177-81, 199, 292; M.E., 128, 615; M.E.S., 118, 121-22, 128, 140-41, 190, 191; M.P. (Directory), 403, 404
Book of Common Prayer, 628
Booth, William and Catherine, 618
Bordentown Training and Industrial Institute, 547
border conferences, 150, 209-14, 253, 353
Border Methodism and Border Slavery (McCarter), 201
Borein, P. M., 195
Boring, Isaac, 157, 181
Boring, Jesse, 455, 458, 467
Boston Theological Seminary, Boston University, 193, 323, 382, 383, 648, 651, 656
boundaries, M.E.-M.E.S., 124, 127-28, 134, 142, 158, 159-67, 197, 298-99
bourgeois orientation of churches, 336-37, 339
Bowler, George, 532
Bowman, Elisha, 473
Bowman, John, 349
Bowne, Borden Parker, 385, 595, 597-98, 624
Boyer, Jean, 554
Boyle, Joseph, 183
Bradford, William, 431, 435
"brakemen," 197
Brazil, 290, 291
Breckinridge, John C., 9
Bremen Mission Conference, M.E., 483
Bremer, Karl, 480
Bresee, Phineas, 625-26
Brewster, W. H., 397
Bridges, B. T., 572
Brief Appeal to Public Opinion . . . (Bascom), 176, 177
Brier, James W., 456
British Guiana, 575, 576, 578
British Methodist Episcopal Church, 541, 577-78, 695
Brittain, Harriett, 407, 408
Brooklyn Circuit, Ill., 534
Brooks, John D., 565

Brooks, John P., 619
Brooks, Joseph, 199
Broomfield, John Calvin, 419
Brown, Arza, 164
Brown, E. D., 579
Brown, Ebenezer, 473
Brown, George, 396
Brown, George R., 418
Brown, John M., 535, 541, 548, 553
Brown, Morris, 529, 532, 536, 539, 577
Brown, O. E., 623
Brown, Paul R., 35
Brown, Samuel H., 577
Brown University (Theological Institute), Jacksonville, Fla., 546
Browning, W. H., 241
Brownlow, William G., 250, 251
Brunson, Alfred, 195
Brush, George W., 118
Bryan, William Jennings, 589
Buchanan, James, 9, 246
Bucher, August J., 490
Buckley, James M., 189, 321, 334, 616, 639
Buddhists, 511
Buell, Fayette R., 416
Buffalo Christian Advocate, 346, 351
Burke's Chapel, Cincinnati, 478
Burlingame Treaty, 507
Burlingham, Charles D., 343, 351
Bushnell, Horace, 384, 385, 387, 388
Butler, Charles, 553
Butler, W. F., 569
Button, Charles W., 406

Cahaba Conference, A.M.E. Zion, 561
Cain, R. H., 541
Calabrese, Vito L., 514
Calapooia Circuit, Ore., 448
Calhoun, John C., 3, 156
California, 4, 182, 203, 420, 421, 423, 452-59, 505, 506, 507, 509, 510, 511, 513, 517, 619: Alameda, 507, 512, 513; Berkeley, 512; Benicia, 455; Carpinteria, 458; Coloma, Marysville, Petaluma, 534; Dinuba, Manteca, Maxwell, Reedley, Walnut Grove, Willows, 513; Lexington, Sonoma, 457; Los Angeles,

California—cont'd
456, 457, 458, 492, 503,
506, 507, 512, 625, 657;
Los Nietos, 458, 463;
Monterey, Pasadena, 507;
Napa, 455, 507; north-
ern, 453-56, 467; Oakland,
511, 513, 534; Pajara,
Santa Cruz, 453; Sacra-
mento, 192, 453, 454, 455,
456, 513, 534, 613; San
Bernardino, 457, 458; San
Diego, 457, 458, 507; San
Francisco, 192, 453, 454,
455, 473, 506, 508-9, 511,
513, 534, 613; San Jose,
453, 455, 456, 506, 507,
534; San Luis Obispo,
Tulare, 457; Santa Bar-
bara, 457, 458; Santa
Clara, 613, 614; Sonora,
455; southern, 456-59;
Stockton, 453, 454, 503,
507, 513, 534
California Christian Advocate, 186, 199, 454, 458
California Conference:
A.M.E., 534; A.M.E. Zion,
559; M.E., 441, 454, 457,
459, 460, 506, 507, 508,
511, 512
California German Confer-
ence, M.E., 519
California Mission Conference, M.E., 173
California Wesleyan Col-
lege, 185, 454
Calvinism, 24, 317, 382,
593, 594, 601, 623
camp meetings, 324-26, 348,
356, 446, 487, 612-15, 621
Campbell, J. P., 534, 540
Campbell College, 547
Canada: African Methodist
societies in, 540, 544, 576,
577-78; Brandford, Hamil-
ton, St. Catherine's, 577;
British Columbia, 512,
535; Erie, 530, 577; Gam-
bia, Malden, 530; Green-
bush, 612; immigrants
from, 472, 475; Methodist
Church of, 695; Niagara,
530, 531; St. David, 531,
577; Toronto, 577, 687,
705
Canada-Michigan Confer-
ence, A.M.E. Zion, 559,
576
Candler, Asa, 656
Candler School of Theology,
656-57

Cape Fear Conference,
A.M.E. Zion, 560
Cape May Commission and
Conference, 303, 664-71
Capers, William, 27, 28,
53, 59, 66, 90, 113, 114,
122, 125, 137, 138, 162,
177, 181, 189, 203, plate 4
capitalism, Methodist sup-
port of, 316, 335-36
Cardenas, Benigno, 443, 444
Carlsson, Carl P., 498
Carman, William, 556, 557
Carnegie, Andrew, 316
Carr, A. T., 553
Carradine, Beverly, 624
Carroll, Henry K., 617
Carter, Thomas, 474
Carter, Walter S., 363
Cartersville (Ga.) Normal
and Preparatory School,
552
Cartwright, Andrew, 576
Cartwright, Peter, 14, 29,
37, 54, 67, 149, 156, 188,
340
Cass, William, 65
catechism, 139, 237
Catechism (Turner), 550
Cather, Andrew W., 440
Caughey, James, 610
Caulkins, Wilford, 378
Centenary Biblical Institute,
366
Centenary Church, St. Louis,
242
Centenary Survey, 518
Centennial of Methodism
(1884), 582, 616, 689-94
Central Christian Advocate,
199, 209, 213, 363
Central Alabama Conference,
A.M.E. Zion, 561
Central Conference of Ger-
many, M.E., 486, 491
Central Holiness University,
625
Central Idea of Christianity
(Peck), 611
Central Illinois Conference,
M.E., 475, 496
Central New York Confer-
ence: A.M.E. Zion, 560;
M.E., 597
Central Oklahoma Confer-
ence, A.M.E., 535
Central Protestant, 404
Central Swedish Conference,
M.E., 496, 519
Central Tennessee College,
365, 366, 367, 368, 370,
375, 376

Central University, 286, 306-
9, 652
Central Wesleyan College
and Orphan Asylum, 488-
89
Central Wesleyan Theologi-
cal Seminary, 657
Chamberlayne, Israel, 198
Changes of Economy, Com-
mittee on, 273, 277
Channing, William Ellery,
384
chaplains, army, in Civil
War, 220-22, 223, 236,
239, 240, 241, 242, 250,
251
Chaplains' Association, 236
Charles City (Iowa) College,
489
Charleston, John, 542
Chattanooga University, 377,
378
Chautauqua movement, 545,
647
Cherokee Mission, 427
Cherry, S. M., 238, 239
Chesbrough, Isaac M., 348,
350
Chesbrough, S. K. J., 355
Chesterfield Circuit, Va.,
146
Chicago Conference, A.M.E.,
535
Chicago Deaconess Train-
ing School, 491
Chicago Evangelistic Insti-
tute, 625
Chicago German Confer-
ence, M.E., 519
Chicago Training School,
WFMS, 652
Child's Recorder, 404, 550
China, 140, 158, 182, 244-
45, 278, 288, 290, 291
489; Shanghai, 182, 288;
Soochow, 288
Chinese in America, 506-9
Chinese Exclusion Act, 506
Chinese Mission Institute,
San Francisco, 506, 511
Chivington, John M., 434
Choate, Rufus, 178
Choctaw District, 427
choirs, 341-42
"Christ against culture," 359
Christ Hospital, Cincinnati,
491
Christian Advocate and
Journal, 38, 45, 97, 126,
129, 134, 150, 151, 152,
163-64, 176, 179, 180, 185,
189, 193, 194, 199, 209,

Christian Advocate & Journal—cont'd
248, 324, 329, 336, 593, 615
Christian Alliance Bible School, 625
Christian Associations, Southern troops, 241
Christian Commission, 221-26
Christian Endeavor Societies, 544, 569, 646
Christian Endeavor World, 404
Christian Herald (Recorder), 548
Christian Index, 285
Christian Labor Union of Boston, 337
Christian Observer, 455
Christian Perfection (Wesley), 645, 654
Christian Purity . . . (Foster), 614
Christian Standard and Home Journal, 615
Christliche Apologete, 336, 478, 490
Christmas Conference, 271, 628: of 1884, 689-94
Church of All Nations, 517
church construction, 64, 318, 321, 330-31, 437, 440, 460, 464
Church Extension Societies, 248, 330-31, 376, 442, 522, 524, 541, 553, 568
Church of God, 619
Church Lyceum, 645
"church meetings," 276
Church of the Nazarene, 622, 623, 625, 626
church property, question of ownership of, 124, 127-28. (See also Book Concern)
Cincinnati Conference, M.E., 345, 484, 488, 505, 546
Cincinnati Convention, M.P. and Wesleyans, 396, 398
Cincinnati Plan for teacher training, 544
Cincinnati Rule on slavery, 201
Cincinnati Training School, 492
circuit riders, 4, 13, 473, 628, 650
City Work, Department of, M.E., 525
Civil War, 3, 85, 208, 257, 299, 360, 420, 582, 585: and aid to freed Negroes,

Civil War—cont'd
251-55; border states in, 209-14; expansion of Northern Church into South during, 247-51; new problems brought by, 257-58; patriotism and religion in the North, 214-29; Southern Church and the Confederacy, 230-47. (See also Reconstruction)
Claflin, Lee, 336
Claflin University, 365, 367
Clark, Alexander, 403-4
Clark, Davis W., 199, 248, 251, 363
Clark, Dougan, 617
Clark, John, 195
Clark University, 365, 366, 368-70
Clarke, Homer J., 186, 189
Clarke, John, 107
class meetings and leaders, 637, 642, plate 9
class stratification, 315-16, 321, 335-39, 342, 587
Clay, Henry, 3, 97, 156
Clear Fork Circuit, Tex., 425
Clement, Rufus E., 570, 571
Clinton, Horace, 561
Clinton, J. J., 559, 560, 561, 562, 565, 566, 573
Clinton Normal and Industrial College, 572
Clopton, David, 665
Close, Benjamin, 449-50
Cocagne, John B., 474
Cocker, B. F., 385
coeducation, 412
Coke, Thomas, 74
Coke Memorial Church, Utica, 505
Coker, Daniel, 527, 539, 553
Cokesbury College, 195
Coleman, W. H., 544
Coleridge, 384, 387, 388, 389
Colhouer, T. H., 408
Collins, John A., 52, 54, 56, 58, 59, 187, 188, 197
Colorado, 228, 421, 431, 433-36, 505, 510, 535, 619, 648, 649: Central City, 434, 468; Canon City, Colorado Springs, 434; Conejos, 433; Denver, 422, 432, 434, 435, 535, 657; Golden City, 434; Loveland, 422; Pueblo, 433; San Luis Valley, 444; Sand Creek, 435; Sterling, 436

Colorado Conference: A.M.E., 535; M.E., 435, 436, 439, 440, 444, 445
Colorado Seminary, 435
Colored Congregational Methodist Church, 578
Colored Methodist Church, Sacramento, 534
Colored Methodist Episcopal Church, 281, 283-87, 314, 541, 542, 575, 681, 683, 684, 704
Colored Methodist Protestant Church, 578
Colored Methodist Society of Michigan, 535
Colored People's Church, Trenton, N.J., 530
Columbia Circuit, Pa., 543
Columbia Conference: M.E., 437, 452; M.E.S., 449, 450
"come-outers," 41, 360, 619, 622
Comfort, George, 437-38
Comfort, Silas, 18
Commission of Seven on Foreign Language Work, 518-22
Committee of Nine, 1844, 60, 62, 147, 174
Committee of Six on Foreign Language Publications, 518, 519, 521
Compendium of Christian Theology (Pope), 593
complacency, Protestant, 316-41
Complete System of Christian Theology (Wakefield), 382
Compromise of 1850, 3, 5, 8, 22
Comstock Lode, 459
Comte, Auguste, 384, 386
Confederate States of America, 156, 229, 230-47
Confederate States Bible Society, 237
"Conference" party, 69, 70-76
Congregational Church, 221, 329, 363, 617
Congregational Methodists, 410, 578
congregational participation, 341, 630-31, 632
Connecticut: Bridgeport, Hartford, Middletown, New Haven, Norwalk, Stonington, 558
Connectional Council, A.M.E. Zion, 567
conscience money, 335

constitution, Methodist: the "Constitution party," 77-82; reform of, 294-97; ultimate authority in, 76, 80
constitution, U.S., 156
Constitutional Powers of the General Conference (Harris), 200
"contrabands," 251
conversion, 238, 311, 609
Cooke, Charles P., 462
Cookman, Alfred, 240, 612, 615
Cookman Institute, 366
Cooley, William, 351
Coolidge, Calvin, 510
co-operation, Christian, 702-3, 705. (See also interdenominational endeavors)
co-operative movement, (agriculture), 588
"copperheads," 218, 262
Coppin, Levi J., 554
Corbin, John F., 517
Cornelius T. Shaffer High School, Sierra Leone, 554
Corr, Joseph M., 549
corruption in the Gilded Age, 316, 329
Corvallis Circuit, Ore., 449
Council of the Christian Union Church in Southern Illinois, 276
Council of Protestant Missionary Societies, 517
Courses of Study for ministerial candidates, 64, 546, 570, 593-94, 596, 598, 602, 650-55, 657, 658
Cousin, Victor, 384, 385, 387
Covel, James, 563
Cowan, John F., 404
Cox, J. T., 458
Cralle, A. T., 418
Cramer, Michael J., 250
Crary, B. F., 363
Craven, Braxton, 262-63
Crawford, Morris DeCamp, 664, 665
Creek Mission, 427
Crooks, George R., 198
Crowder, Thomas, 60, 119
Cuba, 290, 555, 591
Cubans in Florida, 516
Cuff, Reuben, 527-28
Cumberland Presbyterian Church, 408, 409
Cummings, Joseph, 215
Curry, Daniel, 174, 202, 316, 323, 336, 388, 621, 652

Curtis, Olin A., 594, 595, 616, 624

Dadeville (Ala.) Seminary, 366
Daily Christian Advocate, 170
Dakota Conference, M.E., 465
Dakota (Dacotah) Mission, 464, 465
Dakota Territory, 464-66
Danes, Methodism among, 499-503
Darwin, 385, 386
Daughters of the Conference, 551
Davis, Jefferson, 233
Davis, John, 55, 56
Davis, Lyman E., 404
Deaconess and Women's Home, Chicago, 503
deaconess work, 491-92
Deal, William Grove, 192
Deane, William A., 576
Deer Creek Church, Cincinnati, 532
Defence of Our Fathers (Emory), 74
Defense of the Present Mode of Training Candidates . . . (Perry), 195
Degen, Henry, 35
DeJernett, E. C., 622
Delaware, 510, 529, 530, 579: Wilmington, 528
Delaware Conference, M.E., 528
Delaware Mission, 427, 430
Demerara Mission, 575-76
Democratic Party, 9
Dempster, John, 195, 198, 383, 610
Denmark, 497, 500, 502
Dennis, L. B., 430
denominational co-operation, 222-25, 241, 259, 310, 362, 363, 407, 511, 524, 643, 646, 648
denominational rivalry, 329-31, 365, 582
Denton Circuit, Tex., 425
Denver University, 435
DePauw, Washington C., 616
Descent of Man (Darwin), 385
Des Moines Conference, M.E., 464
Devore, J. F., 450
DeWette, Wilhelm, 385
Dickerson, William F., 541, 546, 579

Dickinson College, 167
Diekmann, John A., 490
Dillon, John, 164
Dinwiddie Normal and Industrial School, 572
discipline: administration of, 636-42; decline in, 320, 326, 328-29, 340
Discipline: A.M.E., 538, 539, 540, 548, 577; A.M.E. Zion, 562-63, 565, 570, 573; M.E., 13, 14, 18, 21, 61, 73, 74, 150, 188, 329, 341, 524, 629, 650-51, 655; M.E.S., 141-42, 155, 184, 190, 191, 205, 278, 285, 295, 630, 638, 654; M.P., 392, 393
Discourse on the Administration of Discipline (Hedding), 637
discrimination: against Chinese and Japanese, 506-10; against Negroes, 526, 527
District of Columbia, 204, 406, 530, 531, 543, 557, 560, 568, 573, 579, 596, 614, 662, 682, 683, 695, 701: Georgetown, 392, 398, 531
District Conferences, 273, 276-77, 295-97
Divine Church (Brooks), 619
divorce and remarriage, 641
Dixon, James, 169, 176, 184
"Doctrines of Methodism" (Whedon), 382
Doering, Charles H., 481, 482
Doggett, David S., 276, 279, 313, 386
Dollinger, J. J. I., 333
Dominica, 555
Dominican Republic, 554
Dorcas Institute, 492
Dorcas Society, 551
Dorchester, Daniel, 19
Douglas, Stephen A., 9
Douglas Hospital, Kansas City, 552
Douglass, Frederick, 558
Dow, Lorenzo, 473
Drake, Benjamin M., 132, 137
Dred Scott decision, 9
Drew, Daniel, 316, 336, 338 n.
Drew Theological Seminary, 195-96, 323, 594, 596, 611, 648, 651, 656
Drinkhouse, E. J., 403, 404
drunkenness, 64, 297, 640

Du Bois, W. E. B., 532, 553
Duncan, Hugh, 436
Duncan, James A., 314, 661
Dunn, Lewis R., 624
Dunwoody, Samuel, 65
Durbin, John P., 61, 64, 72, 74, 75, 193, 363
Durham, Clayton, 528
Dwane, James M., 554
Dyer, John L., 435, 444, 462

Earle, A. B., 610, 617
Early, John, 90, 114, 117, 118, 122, 124, 132, 138, 141, 163, 173, 177, 191, 204, 231, 244, 246, 260, 279
Early, Jordan Winston, 533, 534, 536, 537, 543
Earnest Christian, 352
Earnest Christianity Illustrated, 610
East Baltimore Conference, M.E., 207, 209, 210-11, 517
East Florida Conference, A.M.E., 537
East Genesee Conference, M.E., 359
East German Conference, M.E., 487, 492, 519
Eastern North Carolina Industrial Academy, 572
Eastern Swedish Conference, M.E., 503, 519
Eastern Texas Conference, M.E., 425
Eatto, Timothy, 557, 575
Ebenezer Church: Georgetown, 530, 531; St. Louis, 353
economic injustice, 335, 337
ecumenical enterprises: see interdenominational endeavors
Ecumenical Methodist Conferences, 406, 582, 595, 639, 641, 683, 687, 694-706
Eddy, Thomas M., 199
Edmundson, Joseph, 427
education: A.M.E., 542-47; A.M.E. Zion, 568-72; adult, 545, 569-70; and the Freedmen's Aid Society, 364-80, 582; frontier, 450, 457, 467-68; and German Methodism, 487-90; higher, 7-8, 136-37, 185, 303-9, 323, 364-80, 545-47, 570-72; for Indians, 427, 445, 447; industrial and agricultural, 367-68; M.E.S., 123-24,

education—cont'd
136-37, 270, 278, 303-9; M.P., 410-19; ministerial, opposition to, 305, 306, 359, 650, 652; parochial school, 333, 571-72; for Negroes, 282-83, 362, 364-80, 570, 582; for poor whites in South, 378-80; theological, 193-96, 305-9, 322-24, 366, 374-75, 417-19, 488, 498, 546, 570, 571, 616, 650-58
Edward Waters College, 546
Eichelberger, James W., 568
Elderdice, Hugh Latimer, 419
Elements of General and Christian Theology (Townsend), 383
Elim Old People's Home, Minneapolis, 503
Eliza Turner School, Liberia, 553
Elizabeth Gamble Deaconess Home, 491
Ellijay (Ga.) Seminary, 377
Elliott, Charles, 60, 108, 126, 151, 152, 154-55, 156, 168, 176, 188, 189, 197, 209, 213, 215, 217, 244
Emancipation Proclamation, 231, 232, 252
Embry, J. C., 547, 549, 550, 703
Emerson, Ralph Waldo, 610
Emmanuel Institute, 489
Emmanuel Methodist Chapel, Sweden, 497
Emory, John, 74
Emory, Robert, 147, 150
Emory College, 304, 305
emotionalism, 311: decline of, 322-23. (See also revivals)
empiricism, 387: religious, 388
England: emancipation movement in, 15; London, 639, 696, 704, 706
English New Connexion Methodists, 406
Enterprise (Kan.) Normal Academy and Commercial School, 489
episcopacy: Committees on, 133-34, 137, 186-87, 279; conception of, 187; controversy over authority of, 66-82, 83, 100, 103; fear of, 405; limited, 563. (See also bishops)

Episcopal Addresses: 1844, 50-51; 1850, 181-83; 1852, 186; 1856, 196, 197; 1858, 203; 1860, 354-55; 1864, 248, 361; 1866, 272, 305; 1870, 294, 311; 1872, 333, 678; 1874, 311; 1882, 690; 1884, 689; 1888, 338, 595; 1892, 334, 646; 1894, 311, 622; 1900, 639-40; 1904, 684-85; 1908, 686; 1912, 687; 1924, 519-20
Episcopal Methodist Church, 276
Episcopalians: see Protestant Episcopal Church
Epworth Herald, 645
Epworth Hymnal, 631, 633
Epworth League, 639, 645-46
Erie Conference, M.E., 35
Erie Rule on slavery, 201
Essentials of Methodism (McConnell), 598
Estes, George W., 348-49
Ethiopia, 515
"Ethiopian" Church, South Africa, 554
Eugene Circuit, Ore., 449
Europe: contacts with intellectual developments in, 384-85; missions in, 291, 481-83, 484, 485-92, 496-98, 501-2, 514-15. (See also various countries)
Evangelical Association, 613, 695-96
Evangelical Lutheran Church, 501
evangelism, 26, 240, 319, 532, 614, 622
Evangelista Mexicana, 517
Evans, J. E., 394
Evans, John, 228
Evanston Collegiate Institute, 503
evolution, 595
Ewing, T., 180
experience: Methodism's stress on, 388; and theology, 387, 390

Faith and Its Effects (Palmer), 611, 615
Fancher, Enoch L., 178, 664, 667
fasting, 641
Federal Council of Methodism, 686
Federated Methodist Bishops, 687
Federation, Commission on, 683-84, 686, 695

Ferguson, T. P., 626
Ferguson, Vincent, 414
Few, I. A., 18
finances: Freedmen's Aid Society, 375-76, 378; language work, 522-23
Finland, 498
Finley, James B., 57, 59, 63, 69, 70, 71, 75, 76, 78, 81, 82, 91, 153, 156, 173
Finney, Charles G., 26, 610
Finney, Thomas M., 665
First Colored Wesleyan Methodist Independent Society, Baltimore, 531, 557
First Congregational Church, Schenectady, N.Y., 531
First Methodist Protestant Church, Pittsburgh, 397
First Norwegian Methodist Church, Salt Lake City, 502
Fisher, A. N., 441, 512
Fisher, George P., 385
Fisher, George W., 433, 434
Fisher, Orceneth, 449
Fisk, Clinton B., 226, 362, 363, 406, 663, 664, 668
Fisk, Wilbur, 37, 40, 477
Fitzgerald, J. N., 626
Fitzgerald, O. P., 138
Five Points Mission, 514
Flegler, S. F., 553
Flegler High School, S.C., 552
Fletcher, John W., 389
Flipper-Key-Paris College, 547
Florida, 255, 362, 515, 537: Gainesville, 372; Jacksonville, 366, 546, 580; Live Oak, 546; Key West, Palmetto Beach, Roberts City, 516; Pensacola, 562; Tallahassee, 537; Tampa, Ybor City, 515, 516
Florida Conference: A.M.E., 537; A.M.E. Zion, 561, 562; M.E., 64; M.E.S., 106, 516
Florida Latin District, 516
Florkey, William, 436
Floy, James, 35, 199
Foke Yam Tong Chapel, San Francisco, 506
Foote, Julia A., 566
Foreign Language Commission, M.E., 472, 498
foreign language work: see language ministry

foreign missions, 139, 140, 158, 182, 199, 203, 244-45, 278, 288, 289, 290, 291, 407, 408, 486, 489, 553-55, 568
Forlines, Charles E., 416, 419
Fortie, John, 543
Foss, C. D., 639
Foster, Randolph S., 195, 196, 594, 612, 614, 692
Fowler, Charles H., 498, 663, 702
Fowler, Littleton, 424, 425
Fox, George, 617
France, 420
Franco, Francisco, 515
fraternal relations between branches of Methodism, 170-73, 261-62, 299-303, 314, 396-97, 398, 399, 408-10, 456, 580-82, 660-89
Frederick, J. R., 554
Free African Society, 526, 527
Free Christian Zion Church of Christ, 579
Free Methodist Church, 339-60, 398, 611, 619, 696
freedmen: aid to, 251-55; problems of, 257, 259
Freedmen's Aid Society, 252, 362-80, 582
Freedmen's Bureau, 252, 264, 362
Freedmen's Union Commission, 362, 363
Freedom of the Will . . . (Whedon), 382
Freemen, Moses, 532
Freeman, Thomas B., 576
Freemasonry: see Masonry
Frémont, John C., 9, 252, 453
French groups, Methodist work with, 471, 472-76
Friends, Society of, 363, 617
Froebel, 644
Frothingham, O. B., 362
fugitive slaves, 251, 577
Fugitive Slave Law, 181
Fuller, Erasmus Q., 664
Fuller, James M., 353
Fulwood, C. A., 516
fundamentalism, 592, 598

Gage, W. D., 428
Gaines, W. J., 541, 686
Galbreath, George, 564
Galloway, C. B., 605, 702
Gamble, James, 478, 491
gambling, 312
Gammon Theological Seminary, 366, 657

Garibaldi, 333
Garland, Landon C., 314, 661
Garrett, Eliza, 195
Garrett Biblical Institute, 195, 196, 323, 383, 499, 648, 651, 657
Garrison William Lloyd, 8, 15, 20, 25-26
Gary, George, 447, 448
Gassaway, B. F., 619
General Conferences, A.M.E.: *1820*, 539; *1824*, 539; *1828*, 539; *1836*, 539; *1840*, 533; *1844*, 539, 546, 581; *1848*, 540, 543, 551; *1852*, 533; *1856*, 540, 549, 577; *1860*, 534; *1864*, 536, 540, 549, 552, 671-74; *1868*, 540, 676; *1872*, 541, 681-82; *1876*, 541, 544, 547, 578, 682; *1880*, 541, 546, 548, 555, 682; *1884*, 541, 545, 548; *1888*, 541, 549; *1892*, 541; *1896*, 541-42, 544, 552; *1900*, 542, 552, 553; *1904*, 542, 684-85; *1908*, 542, 553, 685-86; *1912*, 542; *1916*, 542
General Conferences, A.M.E. Zion: *1844*, 575; *1848*, 565; *1856*, 564, 575, 576; *1860*, 565, 569, 570, 574; *1864*, 560, 565, 569, 671-74; *1868*, 566, 571, 573, 675, 677-78; *1872*, 566, 574, 678; *1880*, 567, 573; *1888*, 569; *1892*, 569; *1900*, 567; *1904*, 567-68; *1908*, 568, 572; *1912*, 568; *1916*, 568, 569
General Conferences, C.M.E.: *1873*, 286; *1874*, 286
General Conferences, Free Methodist Church: *1907*, 357
General Conferences, the Methodist Church: *1871*, 399; *1875*, 399-400, 405
General Conferences, M.E.: delegated, 74, 75; question of authority of, 68-82, 83, 84, 85; *1796*, 12; *1800*, 12-13; *1804*, 13; *1808*, 13, 74, 632; *1812*, 14; *1816*, 13, 14; *1820*, 14, 83, 92, 273, 276, 632; *1824*, 14, 92, 643; *1828*, 14, 138, 273, 274, 643; *1832*, 14, 15, 274; *1836*, 15-17, 30, 36, 37, 40, 276; *1840*, 17-20, 37, 41, 274; *1844*, 15, 46, 47-82, 90, 129, 144, 145-

Gen'l Conf. M.E.—cont'd
55, 168, 169, 173-75, 179,
481, 663; *1848,* 167, 168-
76, 182, 192, 505, 661;
1852, 185-89, 193, **274,**
342-44, 428; *1856,* 196-99,
201, 346, 483, 546; *1860,*
205, 214, 274, 353; *1864,*
214, 219, 223, 224, 248, 252,
253, 266, 274, 299, 320,
324, 361, 362, 444, 462,
484, 645; *1868,* 300, 327,
496, 662, 663, 675; *1872,*
301, 329, 614, 638, 639,
645, 663, 679; *1876,* 365,
465, 498, 502, 645, 660,
695; *1880,* 376, 377, 501,
514, 695; *1884,* 377-78,
621, 689, 695; *1888,* 324,
503, 595, 616, 621, 647;
1892, 327, 496, 645, 646;
1896, 683; *1900,* 639-40;
1904, 683; *1908,* 410, 596,
597, 656, 683, 684, 686;
1912, 686-87; *1916,* 688;
1920, 498, 518, 688; *1924,*
519-20, 522, 640; *1932,*
519
General Conferences, M.E.S.,
86, 274-75; check on legislative powers of, 294-95;
post-Civil War, 265-66;
1846, 130-43, 157-59, 166;
1850, 181-85; *1854,* 189-91,
278, 292, 294, 313; *1858,*
202-5, 292, 306; *1866,* 243,
254, 266, 270-79, 283, 288-
89, 300, 305, 310, 313,
314, 681, 689; *1870,* 275,
278, 284, 290, 293, 294-97,
300, 305, 310, 311, 652,
663, 681; *1874,* 290, 292,
297-98, 309, 310, 314;
1878, 276, 291, 292, 311,
682, 690, 695; *1882,* 690-
91; *1886,* 691; *1894,* 622,
683, 695; *1898,* 622; *1902,*
653; *1906,* 684; *1910,* 686;
1914, 656, 687-88; *1938,*
119
General Conferences, M.P.:
1862, 392; *1866,* 392, 398;
1870, 399; *1874,* 399, 400;
1880, 408, 413; *1884,* 404,
408-9; *1888,* 407, 409, 413;
1892, 406, 410; *1896,* 413;
1900, 414; *1904,* 414;
Northern and Western
branch, 395-96, 407, 411,
417, 652
General Conferences, Wes-
leyan Methodist Church:
1844, 43, 44; *1864,* 397

General Holiness Assembly,
619
General Rules, 17, 18, 43,
191, 200, 201, 204-5, 252,
638, 639
general superintendency:
see episcopacy and bishops
Genesee Conference, M.E.,
45, 218, 339, 342, 343-51,
352, 354, 357, 358
Genesee conflict, 343-51
Genesee Seminary, 167
Genesee or Western New
York Conference, A.M.E.
Zion, 558, 566
George, Augustus C., 701
George, Enoch, 49
Georgia, 33, 54, 304, 373,
552, 580: Atlanta, 235, 244,
365, 366, 547, 656, 657,
690, 695; Augusta, 245,
561; Columbus, 189-91,
268; Dalton, 238, 239;
Ellijay, Mt. Zion, 377;
La Grange, 366, 370;
Macon, 237, 245, 537, 572;
Milledgeville, 147, 233;
Pierce's address to General
Assembly of, 233-35;
Rome, Waynesboro, 366;
Sparta, 45; Thomasville,
286; Wesley in, 471
Georgia Colored Conference,
284
Georgia Conference: A.M.E.,
537; A.M.E. Zion, 561;
M.E., 27; M.E.S., 105-6,
128, 233
German-English College of
Galena, 489
German Wallace College,
488
Germans in America, 288,
293, 328, 425, 431, 435,
471, 477-81, 483-85, 486-
92
Germany, 476: Bremen, 481,
482, 483, 488; Frankfurt
am Main, 486, 488, 491;
Nuremberg, 491; Winnen-
den, 484: deaconess move-
ment in, 491; Methodism
in, 199, 481-83, 484, 486;
National Socialism in,
485; Weimar Republic in,
485
Gettysburg campaign, 226,
235
Ghana, 576
Gibbon, Cardinal, 336
Gibson, Otis, 506-8, 511
Gibson, William, 703

Gilded Age, 316-39, 587
Gillespie, J. J., 406
Gilmore, Alexander, 462
Gilmore, Glezen, 60
Gilmore, J. H., 635
Gittings Seminary, 413
Gladden, Washington, 635
God's Bible School, 624
gold, discovery of, 192, 420,
433, 439, 448, 451, 456,
459, 465
Gold Coast, 576
Golder, Louise and Chris-
tian, 491
Gonzales, Ambrosio, 445
Good Way, 619
Goode, William H., 428-30,
434, 466
Goodrich, Grant, 195, 363
Gordon, George A., 604
"Gospel Society," San Fran-
cisco, 511
Gould, Jay, 316
grace, 358, 593, 601, 608,
618
Graded Lessons Conference,
644
Granberry, J. C., 241
Granger party, 588
Grant, A., 541
Grant, Ulysses S., 10, 250
Grant Memorial University,
377
Gray, S. T., 564
Gray, Valentine, 162-63
Grayson Circuit, Tex., 425
Great American Desert, 421
Greeks, 517
Green, A. L. P., 77, 131,
142, 169, 173, 180, 191
Green, A. M., 578
Green, Augustus R., 548, 578
Greenback party, 588
Greenville College, 572
Griffith, Alfred, 55, 56, 68,
69, 72, 82
Griswold E. E., 194
*Grounds for Secession from
the . . . Church* (Scott),
40
Groves, Alexander, 458, 463
Growth in Holiness . . .
(Mudge), 623
*Guide to Holiness (Chris-
tian Perfection),* 609, 615,
619
Gulf Mission Conference,
M.E., 622
Gunn, William, 119
Gurley, James, 464
Guthrie, Elizabeth, 407
Guyandotte area, W. Va.,
165

Haagensen, Andrew, 502
Hagenbach, 384, 385
Haiti, 554
Haitian Union Methodist
  Society, 555
Hale, Eli N., 531
Hale, Ira P., 460
Hall, Don Carlos, 539
Hall, James D. S., 536
Hamer, J. P., 573, 674
Hamil, Patrick, 408
Hamline, Leonidas L., 50,
  60, 61, 64, 71, 73, 75, 109,
  111, 125, 126, 154, 166,
  186, 478, 610, plate 1
Handlin, Oscar, 469
Hanner, John W., 131
Hansen, Walter, 443, 444
Hanson, A. J., 507-8
Harbor Mission Society, 492
Harding, Francis, 52, 56, 65,
  107, 122, 144, 146, 148,
  163
Hargis, James, 163
Hargrove, R. K., 665
Harlan, James, 229
Harriman, Edward H., 316
Harrington, Karl P., 635
Harris, C. R., 572, 663
Harris, Swannanoa, 415
Harris, William L., 151, 200
Harrison, John C., 119
Harrison, W. P., 408
Harper's Weekly, 229
Hartsough, Lewis, 440, 441-
  42
Harvard University, 7
Harwood, Thomas and
  Emily, 444-45
Haus und Herd, 490
Haven, E. O., 200
Haven, Gilbert,' 252, 327,
  330, 369, 370, 372, 373,
  614
Haven Normal School, 366,
  370
Hawaii, 454, 512, 591
Hayes, George H., 623
Hayes, Juliana, 291
Hayes, Rutherford B., 402
Haygood, Atticus G., 241,
  283, 310, 313, 314, 690
Haynes, B. F., 622, 623
"heart religion," 305, 311
Hebert, Martin, 475
Hedding, Elijah, 28, 35,
  45, 48, 57, 58, 60, 72,
  74, 76, 79, 109-11, 125,
  148, 149, 153, 154, 169,
  185, 186, 193, 637, plate 1
Hedge, Frederic H., 388
Hedgepeth, Lewis J., 463
Hedström, Jonas, 494-95

Hedström, Olof Gustav,
  493-97, 500
Henderson, R. C., 575
Henkle, Moses M., 141
Herald of Holiness, 623
Herbart, 644
heresy accusations, 597-98
Hibbard, F. G., 199, 200,
  346
Hickok, Laurens P., 385
High Point College, 416
Higher Christian Life
  (Boardman), 610, 617
Hill, James J., 316
Hill, Moses, 46
Hilton, G. F., 440
Hines, Gustavus, 193
History of the Organization
  of the Methodist Episcopal
  Church, South, 115-17,
  122, 141
Hitchcock, Luke, 363
Hitler, Adolf, 485, 515
Hoch, Edward and Edward
  W., 477
Hodge, Charles, 385
Hogans, Titus, 561
Hogarth, George, 539, 548
holiness movement, 311, 339,
  340, 343, 345-47, 349, 350,
  352, 356, 358, 592, 606,
  608-27: controversy and
  disruption in, 618-27
Holman, Calvin, 250
Holsey, L. H., 286
Holston Conference: M.E.,
  251; M.E.S., 100-101, 306
Home for Aged and Infirm
  Colored People, Philadel-
  phia, 551
home missions, 278, 289, 291,
  441, 522, 523, 524, 551-53,
  568
Homestead Act, 420, 500
Hood, J. W., 556, 558, 560,
  562, 570, 581, 674
Hood Theological Seminary,
  572
Hopkins, Joseph P., 557
Horton, Jotham, 41, 42, 43
Hosmer, William, 176, 189,
  200, 346, 350, 351
hospitals, 491-92, 552
Hough, A. M., 437
Hough, Alfred J., 331
Howard, Oliver Otis, 264,
  364, 365
Howell, James R., 579
Hudson's Bay Company, 445
Hughes, Edwin Holt, 656
Hughes, George, 194, 617,
  619

Hunt, A. S., 663
Hunter, William, 170
Huntington, D. W. C., 624
Hurlbut, Jesse L., 645, 647
Hurst, John F., 385
Hutchinson, Silvester, 563
hymnals, 141, 549-50, 574-
  75, 631, 632-36

Idaho, 438, 451-52, 510,
  512, 535: Boonville, Centerville, Fort Hall, Franklin, Owyhee, Placerville,
  451; Boise, Payette, Rocky
  Bar, Salmon River, 452;
  Idaho City, Pioneer City,
  Silver City, 451, 452;
  Washington, 446
Idaho Conference, M.E., 452
Iliff, T. C., 438
Iliff School of Theology, 657
Illinois, 195, 218, 413, 496,
  501, 505, 513, 533, 535,
  561, 579: Andover, Knoxville, LaFayette, Moline,
  Rock Island, 495; Batavia,
  649; Bloomington, 619;
  Chicago, 186, 473, 491,
  492, 495, 500, 503, 505-
  7, 514, 517, 535, 552, 589,
  619, 625, 652, 662, 675;
  Des Plaines, 612, 645;
  Elgin, Marengo, Wood-
  stock, 352; Evanston, 499,
  503, 611, 651, 652, 657;
  Galena, 489, 534; Galesburg, 495, 496, 499; Henry
  City, La Harpe, 413;
  Quincy, 488; St. Charles,
  352, 355; University of,
  647; Urbana, 647; Vic-
  toria, 494
Illinois Conference: A.M.E.,
  534-35; M.E., 168, 175,
  475, 481, 496; M.E.S., 276
illiteracy, 305, 444, 570
immigration, 3, 315, 326,
  328, 332-34, 379, 421, 429,
  469, 470, 492-93, 499-500,
  504, 506, 509, 513, 516,
  590; declining, 486; restricted, 506, 507, 510, 518,
  519
Immigration Act of 1924,
  510
Impending Crisis of 1860
  (Mattison), 201
imperialism, American, 591;
  cultural, 220; Japanese,
  510
Independence Circuit, Ore.,
  449

Independent A. M. E. Church, 580
Independent Methodist Episcopal Church, 541, 577, 578
Indian Manual Labor Training School, Salem, Ore., 447, 448
Indian Mission Conference: A.M.E., 552; M.E., 427; M.E.S., 104-5, 114, 288, 427, 428
Indian Removal Act (1830), 426
Indian Territory, 420, 421, 426, 428, 535
Indiana, 218, 495, 496, 561, 579, 627, 648, 649: Anderson, 619; Blue River, 533; Gary, 535, 649; Indianapolis, 196-99, 404, 548; Kokomo, 322; Lima, 612; Terre Haute, 492; Upland, 625
Indiana Conference: A.M.E., 533, 534; A.M.E. Zion, 559; M.E., 64, 322, 480, 484
Indians, 314, 426, 427, 439, 446, 462, 464; missions to, 182, 245, 278, 288, 420, 421, 423, 426-28, 448, 552
individualism, 316, 319, 335, 592, 595
industrialization, 315, 587
"Infant Manual," 237
Ingersoll, Robert G., 331
Ingham, S. W., Jr., 464
Inskip, John S., 186, 612, 614, 615
intellectual developments, 383-86, 595
Inter-Board Conference on language ministry, 518
interdenominational endeavors, 222-25, 241, 259, 310, 362, 363, 407, 511, 524, 643, 646, 648
inter-Methodist relations: see fraternal relations
Internal Revenue Act (1862), 326
International Friends Assembly, 617
International Lesson Committee, 643, 644
International Sunday School Convention (Association), 643, 644
Iowa, 42, 229, 420, 496, 500, 501, 505, 535, 614, 627: Charles City, Sioux City, 489; Mount Pleasant, 185,

Iowa—cont'd
488; New Sweden, 495; Oskaloosa, 625
"Iowa Band," 332
Iowa Conference: A.M.E., 535; M.E., 64, 430, 464-66; M.P., 402, 413
Iowa Holiness Association, 624
Iowa and Sac Mission, 427
Irish immigrants, 328
Ironsides Normal Institute, 547
Ironton Welsh Mission Circuit, Ohio, 505
Israel Bethel A. M. E. Church, Washington, 545
Israel Bethel Colored Methodist Church, Washington, 530
Israel Lyceum, 545
Isseis, 511
Italians in America, 471, 513-15, 522
Italy, 515
Italy Conference, M.E., 514
itinerancy, 18, 19, 136, 277, 319, 323, 324, 352, 473, 628

Jackson, Edward, 529
Jackson, Thomas J., 236, 241
Jacobi, J. L., 384
Jacobs, B. F., 643
Jacoby, Ludwig S., 479-83
Jakobsmüllen, Herman zur, 482
Jamaica, 555
James, William, 605
Jamison, J. M., 452
Janes, Edmund S., 50, 64, 125, 186, 193, 224, 249, 349, 425, 437, 500, 610, 614, 661, 662, 663-64, plate 1
Japan, 290, 407, 408, 510
Japan Conference, M.P., 408
Japanese, 509-13
Japanese-American Citizens League, 511
Japanese Mission House, San Francisco, 511
Japanese Mutual Aid Society, Hawaii, 512
Jenifer, J. T., 553
Jenkins, Benjamin, 182
Jennings, Martin Luther, 404
Jews, 140, 471
John of Damascus, 635
"John Wesley" (ship), 493-94

Johnson, Andrew, 269, 374, 392
Johnson, Edward, 557
Johnson, George W., 534
Johnson, Henry J., 531
Johnson, Reverdy, 178
Johnson, Thomas and William, 427
Johnson, William E., 580
Johnston, A. S., 439
Joint Commission on Fraternal Relations, 664-71
Joint Conventions: A.M.E.-A.M.E. Zion, 674-77; Methodist Protestant and Methodist Churches, 400-402, 410
Jones, Absalom, 526
Jones, John G., 97, 127
Jones, Singleton T., 566, 662, 673, 677-79, 682
Jones University, 571
Jubilee Gem, 550
Judicial Council, M.E.S., 295
justification, 346, 358. (See also sanctification)

Kanawha Valley region, 158, 164
Kansas, 9, 420, 421, 422, 428-33, 466: Atchison, Lawrence, Lecompton, 429; Fort Scott, 534; Kansas City, 534, 552; Leavenworth, 429, 430, 431, 432, 534; Manhattan, 430; Quindaro, 547; Topeka, 429, 431
Kansas City University, 413-14
Kansas Colored Conference, 286
Kansas Conference: A.M.E., 534; M.E., 430, 431, 439, 614
Kansas (Kanzas) Mission, 427
Kansas Mission Conference, M.E.S., 191, 431-32
Kansas-Nebraska Act, 4, 8, 428
Kansas-Nebraska Conference, M.E., 430-31, 434
Kant, Immanuel, 384, 386
Kant and Spencer (Bowne), 595
Kavanaugh, Hubbard H., 90, 136, 191, 246, 247, 260, 261, 265, 267, 313, 423, 456
Kean, Samuel Ashton, 626-27

Keener, John C., 301, 313
Kelley, Margaret Lavinia, 291
Kendall, William C., 347, 349
Kendall College, 503
Kentucky, 298, 353, 362, 533, 560: Covington, 165; Harrodsburg, 547; Lexington, 124, 136; Louisville, 99, 111-30, 140, 249, 286, 492, 537, 561, 661, 688; Madisonville, 572; Maysville, 127, 158, 165-67
Kentucky Conference: A.M.E., 537, 547; A.M.E. Zion, 561; M.E., 186, 188, 209, 211, 261, 480; M.E.S., 99-100, 113, 148, 156, 158, 166, 212, 247, 260, 622
Kenyon College, 477
Kickapoo Mission, 427
Kidder, Daniel P., 648
Kimball School of Theology, 657
King, B. F., 450
King, James, 437
Kingsley, C. S., 451
Kingsley, Calvin, 199, 248, 441, 442, 451
Kingsley, I. C., 345
Kingsley Seminary, 377
Kinzer, J. D., 418
Kittrell College, 547
Klein, Fred C., 408
Knights of Labor, 336, 337
Kohlstedt, E. D., 520
Korea, 290, 510
Korean Annual Conference, South, 513
Koreans, 513
Kost, John, 413
Kristelig Talsmand, 503

labor: church's responsibility to, 337-38; organization of, 5, 283, 336-337, 588; regarded as a commodity, 337
Ladies' Companion, 190
Ladies' Repository, 199, 248
laissez-faire philosophy, 317-18, 335, 338
Lambert, William, 531
Lambuth, J. W., 244, 288
Lampton College, 547
Lanahan, John, 229
Lancaster Circuit, Va., 16
Lancaster (S.C.) Normal and Industrial Institute, 572

Lane, George, 134, 157, 178
language ministry, 469-525, 654, 655: bilingual, 504-17; Chinese, 506-9; Cubans, 516; French, 471, 472-76; Germans, 471, 476-92; Italians, 471, 513-15; Japanese, 509-13; liquidation and assimilation of, 517-25; Mexicans, 516-17; Scandinavians, 492-503; Spanish-speaking, 471, 516-17; Welsh, 504-6
Larimer, William, 433, 434
Larkin, J. F., 363
Larson, John P., 496-97
Lathbury, Mary A., 507
Latta, S. A., 142
Lawlis, James Lisbon, 414
lay participation: in church, 341, 630-32; in revivals, 240
lay representation movement, 44, 185, 187, 202, 271-72, 273-75, 294, 295, 357, 393, 540, 542, 565, 567
Laymen's Conventions, 350, 351-52, 355
leadership: M.E.S., after Civil War, 313-14; A.M.E., training of, 544
Lebanon Circuit, Tenn., 291
Lee, Alfred, 224
Lee, B. F., 695
Lee, Daniel, 446
Lee, Jason, 192, 446, 447, 451
Lee, Leroy M., 115, 141, 161, 184, 394
Lee, Luther, 39, 42, 43
Lee, Robert E., 231, 235
Leech, D. D. T., 194
Leete, Frederick D., 706
Leonard, A. B., 703
Leslie, David, 446
Letter to Rev. Dr. Stevens . . . (Whedon), 202
Lewis, Thomas Hamilton, 410, 412, 416-19, 435
Libby Prison, Richmond, 221
liberalism, 598, 605
Liberator, 25
Liberia, 20, 139, 553, 576
Liberian Conference: A.M.E., 553; M.E., 199
"Library A for Small Children," 490
Liebardt, Henry, 490
Life Compass for Old and Young (Simons), 491

Lincoln, Abraham, 9, 10, 205, 214, 215-16, 220, 229, 232, 243, 249, 252, 257, 329, 459
Literary, Historical and Educational Association, A.M.E., 545
Literary Society, A.M.E. Zion, 569-70
literature: of German Methodists, 490-91; Sunday school, 404, 483, 490, 544, 550, 573-74, 582, 643
"little Benjamin" address, 410
Little Rock University, 377
Livingstone College, 572
local preachers, 246, 323-24, 422, 479, 651, 658, 659
Lockley, E. B., 458
Log Meeting House, Baltimore, 527
Loguen, Jeremiah W., 565
Lomax-Hannon High and Industrial School, Greenville, Ala., 572
Longstreet, Augustus B., 59, 114, 137, 158
Lord, Daniel, 178
Lord's Supper, 43, 629, 636
Lore, Dallas D., 444
Los Angeles Conference, M.E.S., 458, 463
Louisiana, 288, 293, 312, 420, 472-73, 513, 515, 533, 537, 543: Alexandria, Delphi, 547; Baldwin, 377; Baton Rouge, 250; Greenwood, Homer, 243; Haynesville, 404; Houma, 475; La Teche, 366; New Orleans, 244, 250, 251, 266, 270-79, 365, 366, 375, 473, 475, 480, 514, 515, 533, 536, 547, 560
Louisiana Conference: A.M.E., 536-37; A.M.E. Zion, 255, 560, 562, 566; M.E., 514; M.E.S., 306, 475
Louisville Conference, M.E.S., 212, 247
Louisville Convention, M.E.S., 111-24, 153: effects of, 155-56; reactions to, 124-30
Lovejoy, C. H., 430
Lowrey, Asbury, 613, 620
Lucas, John H., 414
Lutherans, 501
Lutkin, Peter C., 635
Lynch, James, 536

Lyng Home for Girls, Seattle, 503

McCabe, Charles C., 221-22, 240, 331, 442
McCarter, J. Mayland, 201
McClintock, John, 147-49, 167, 168, 176, 188, 198, 200, 383, 384, 387, 388, 611
McClurkan, J. O., 623
McConnell, Francis J., 597, 598, 607
McCormick, Thomas, 400
McCreery, Joseph, 342, 345, 349, 355, 359
McDonald, Frank M., 548
McDonald, William, 615, 624
Macedonian, 330
McElroy, G. B., 402, 406, 409, 412, 413
McFerrin, John B., 115, 122, 124, 128, 131, 141, 184, 201, 204, 238-40, 244, 289-93, 313, 693
McInturff, D. N., 625
McKean, Franklin, 463
McKendree, William, 48, 83, 143, 473
McKendree College, 611
McLaughlin, E. T., 437
Maclay College of Theology, 657
McLoughlin, John, 445, 446
Macon (Ga.) High and Industrial School, 572
McTyeire, Holland N., 129, 177, 244, 268, 271, 272, 279, 285, 296, 306-9, 313, 393, 394, 655, 683, plate 6
Magruder, J. W., 337
Mahan, Asa, 412, 610, 617
Maine, 33: Hallowell, 39; Old Orchard, 614; Portland, 531, 646
Maley, G. W., 164
Mallalieu, Willard F., 624
Manchuria, 290, 510
Mann, Ernest, 482
Mann, Horace, 7
Manning, Thomas G., 84
Mansel, Henry L., 385, 386
Markham, Thomas B., 429
Marley, Michael, 164, 166
Marsh, Jacob, 528
Marshall, James, 192
Martha and Mary Society, 491
Martyrdom in Missouri . . . (Leftwich), 213
Marvin, Enoch M., 242-44, 279, 290, 313, 423

Maryland, 46, 298, 353, 501, 529, 530, 560, 579: Annapolis, Kent County, 531; Baltimore, 289, 291, 366, 399, 400-404, 407, 408, 527, 531, 557, 579, 614, 660-61, 683-84, 686, 695; Elkton, 578; Westminster, 416, 418, 652, 657
Maryland Conference, M.P., 398, 399, 402, 407, 416, 418, 419
Masonry, 43, 343
Massachusetts, 32, 33, 495, 501, 513, 517, 579: Andover, 42; Boston, 42, 45, 148, 185-89, 193, 335, 337, 514, 531, 645, 651, 656; Lowell, 33, 38, 39, 40, 42; Lynn, 32, 531, 625; Nantucket, New Bedford, 558; Springfield, 33, 519, 558; Worcester, 33, 558
Masters, F. J., 508
Mather, S. F., 413
Matlack, Lucius C., 28, 35, 36, 38, 42, 43, 44, 46, 198, 397
Matthews, Jacob, 581
Mattison, Hiram, 144, 197, 198, 201
Meharry Medical College, 366
Melle, F. H. Otto, 486
membership, various branches of Methodism, 47, 211, 212, 226, 245, 246, 253, 254, 270, 276, 279-80, 284, 287, 314, 318, 401, 402-3, 425
Memphis Conference, M.E.S., 102, 113, 306
Mendenhall, J. W., 336
Meridian (Miss.) College, 624
Merrill, A. M., 418
Merrill, Stephen M., 614, 616, 693
Merritt, Timothy, 609
message of Methodism, 599-608
Methodism and Slavery (Bascom), 154-55, 156
Methodist Antislavery Society, 32
Methodist Church, The, 397-402, 419
Methodist Church of Canada, 695
Methodist Church Property Case (Sutton), 178

Methodist Episcopal Church: in Civil War, 255-56; conditions for readmitting Southern Church to, 263; division of, 3, 11, 59-64, 83, 84; expansion of, into South, 220, 247-51, 262, 265, 269, 281, 282-83, 285, 299, 301, 360-61, 668; relations with Methodist Episcopal Church, South, 145-57, 159-67, 177-81, 185-89, 207-9, 266-68; organization of, 79; proposals of reunion with Negro churches, 677-80
Methodist Episcopal Church, South, 27: in Civil War and after, 230-47, 255, 260-61, 264-70, 312-13; disorganization in, 244-47; growth of, 298-312; Louisville Convention; 111-30; organization of, 86-143; proposals to change name of, 275-76; proposals of reunion with Negro churches, 680-81; recognized by British Wesleyans, 303; work of, in territory of Northern Church, 276
Methodist Federation for Social Service, 596
Methodist General Biblical Institute, 193, 651
Methodist Hymnal, 631, 633, 635
Methodist Protestant, 391, 403, 404, 405
Methodist Protestant Church, 12, 41, 83, 92, 231, 273, 274, 681, 694, 695; activities of, after reunion 402-6; in Civil War, 391-93; Eastern and Southern Conferences of, 391-93, 394-95, 398; in Ecumenical Conferences, 406; education sponsored by, 410-19, 652; missions of, 407-8; Northern and Western Conferences of, 395-99; polity of, 404-6; publishing program of, 403-4; proposed reunion of, with other branches of Methodism, 394-95, 396-97, 408-10; reunion of Northern and Southern branches of, 263, 390, 391, 399-402; youth work of, 646

Methodist Protestant Missionary, 407

Methodist Quarterly Review, 167, 176, 188, 190, 199, 382, 384-85, 593

Methodist Recorder, 395, 398, 403, 404, 411

Methodist Review, 336, 597, 634, 642, 653

Methodist Theology vs Methodist Theologians (Wilson), 624

Metropolitan A.M.E. Church, Washington, 568

Metropolitan Church Association, Chicago, 619

Metropolitan Methodist Episcopal Church, Washington, 406

Mexican Border Conference, M.E.S., 445

Mexican Community Center, 517

Mexicans, 516-17

Mexico, 4, 290, 291, 420, 421, 517

Michigan, 410, 501, 533, 535, 559 576: Adrian, 407, 411, 412, 535; Albion, Ann Arbor, Palmyra, 612; Battle Creek, Calvin Center, Ypsilanti, 535; Detroit, 473, 474, 492, 645; Leoni, 411, 412; Wayne County, 42

Michigan Conference: A.M.E., 535; M.P., 396

Michigan Union College, 412

Middleton, E. Russell, 580

Mieyama, Kanichi, 511

Miles, William H., 285, 286

Miley, John S., 383, 594, 616, 620

Miller, Adam, 477

Miller, Jeremiah, 531, 577

Miller, William, 576

Millwood Circuit, Tex., 425

Ministerial Education Loan Fund, 653

ministers: better training for, 305-9; Negro, 253, 366-67, 374-75, 567; and preachers, distinction between, 659; preparation of, 193-96, 278, 322-24, 366, 374-75, 417-19, 488, 498, 546, 570, 571, 649-59 (*see also* Courses of Study *and* theological education); professionalism of, 322; rising demand for, 331-32. (*See also* preachers)

Ministers' and Laymen's Union, M.E., 202

Minnesota, 420, 500, 501, 505, 535: Minneapolis, 503, 686; St. Paul, 533; Winnebago, 489

Minnesota Conference, M.E., 464, 465, 489, 496

Missionaren, 503

Missionary Ridge, Battle of, 238

Missionary Seer, 573

Missionary Societies, 120, 237, 244-45, 248, 249, 251-52, 278, 288, 289, 291, 363, 376, 427, 446, 462, 470, 473, 476, 480, 481, 482, 493, 496-97, 505, 514, 515, 539, 551

missions, missionaries, 51, 64, 120-21, 134, 138-40, 158, 181-82, 203, 244, 278, 288-92, 407-8, 455, 517, 551-55, 575-76; domestic, 278, 289, 291, 441, 522, 523, 524, 551-53, 568; in far West, 192-93, 420-68; foreign, 140, 158, 182, 199, 203, 244-45, 278, 288-90, 407, 408, 486, 489, 553-55, 568; to foreign language groups, 471-517; to Indians, 182, 245, 278, 288, 420, 421, 423, 426-28, 448, 552; to soldiers, 236, 238, 239; in the South, 254, 264, 281, 220, 247-51, 299, 301

Mississippi, 373, 517, 533, 537: Coldwater, 580; Hernando, 547; Holly Springs, 365; Jackson, 250, 373; Meridian, 366, 624; Natchez, 250; Vicksburg, 235, 250, 537, 547

Mississippi Colored Conference, 284

Mississippi Conference: A.M.E., 537; M.E., 424, 427; M.E.S., 102, 113, 306; M.P., 395

Missouri, 212-13, 252, 298-99, 352, 353, 420, 515, 533: Carondelet, 533; Hannibal, 165; Kansas City, 413, 414, 492; Palmyra, 267-68, 299; St. Louis, 143, 165, 181-85, 199, 209, 242, 350, 353, 480, 481, 541, 625; Sante Fe, 286; Warrenton, 488, 657

Missouri Colored Conference, 286

Missouri Compromise, 4, 8, 22, 181

Missouri Conference: A.M.E., 533; A.M.E. Zion, 559, 561, 562; M.E., 209, 211, 213, 427, 430, 614; M.E.S., 100, 113, 267, 432, 435, 438; M.P., 403, 413

Mitchell, Hinckley G., 597, 656

Mitchell, J. T., 61, 75

mixed seating, 188

Modern Premillennialism and the Christian Hope (Rall), 598

modernism, 358, 592, 598

Mokone, M. M., 554

Monroe, Andrew, 267, 431

Monroe, Samuel Y., 198

Monrovia (Liberia) College and Industrial Institute, 553

Montana, 422, 428, 432, 436-38, 446, 500, 509, 535: Bozeman, 437, 438; Grasshopper Creek (Bannack), Virginia City (Alder Gulch), 436, 437; Helena (Last Chance), 243, 436, 437, 438; Junction, 436; Missoula, 438; Norwegian Gulch, 436-37; Willow Creek, 437

Montana Conference, M.E., 452

Montgomery Conference, M.E.S., 282

Montgomery Convention, M.P., 394

Moody, Granville, 215, 226-28

Moore, John J., 559, 566, 574, 575, 676

Moore's Academy, Lincolnton, N.C., 571

Moran, R. S., 194

Moravians, 340, 471

Morgan, Henry, 316, 337

Morgan, J. R. V., 553

Morgan, William, 343 n.

Mormons, 329, 420, 421, 433, 439-41, 451, 452, 459, 502-3

Morningside College, 489

Morell, Thomas, 384

Morrell, F. A., 194

Morris, Thomas A., 37, 48, 49, 109, 110, 111, 117, 124-26, 154, 186, 216, 220, 480, 482, 501, 661, plate 1

Morris Brown Church, Charleston, 553

Morris Brown College, 547
Morrison, A. A., 435
Morrison, Henry Clay, 622
Morrow, Ralph E., 670
Mount Pisgah Church, Salem, N.J., 527-28
Mount Pleasant College, 185, 488
Mount Union Seminary, 185, 377
Mt. Zion Seminary, 377
Mouzon, E. D., 605
Mudge, James, 623
Mueller, Christopher, 484
Murray, J. T., 406
Murray, John J., 392, 393
music, 341-42, 631, 632-36
Muskingum Conference, M.P., 402, 414
Mussolini, Benito, 515
Myers, E. H., 235, 273, 665-68
Myers, Edward, 169, 180

Nagoya College, Japan, 408
Nashville Christian Advocate, 141, 244, 270, 293, 314, 622
Nast, Albert, 490
Nast, William, 336, 476-80, 482, 483, 488, 490, plate 13
Nast Theological Seminary, 657
Natal Conference, A.M.E., 554
National Antislavery Society, 25
National Camp Meeting, 325
National Campmeeting Association for the Promotion of Holiness, 612-13, 615, 620, 624
National Council of Churches, 582
National Freedmen's Relief Association, 252
National Magazine, 189, 199
National Methodist, 404
National Primary Union, 644
National Prohibition Party, 326, 327
National Publishing Association for the Promotion of Holiness, 616
National Socialism, 485, 510
nationalism, 332, 485, 504
Native Sons of the Golden West, 510
naturalism, 317
Nazarites, 339-53, 355, 358-59

Nazrey, Willis H., 540, 577
Nebraska, 420-22, 428-33, 466, 500, 501, 505, 510, 614, 627: Nebraska City (Fort Kearney), 331, 429, 430; Omaha, 429, 430
Nebraska Conference, M.E., 430, 431, 434, 614
Neely, Thomas B., 127, 171, 670
Negroes: churches of, 255, 280, 283-87 (*see also* African Methodist Episcopal Church, African Methodist Episcopal Zion Church, *etc.*); controversy over accepting testimony of, 18-19, 33, 38; discrimination against and segregation of, 377-78, 526, 527; education of, 282-83, 362, 364-80, 570, 582; and Freedmen's Aid Society, 362-80; in Liberia, 20; missions to, 51, 138, 158, 182, 278, 281, 288; M.E. ideology and practice concerning, 361-63; Northern aid to, in Civil War, 251-55; place of in church life, 252-54; questions of union of churches of, 671-89, 704, 705; rights of, 234; work of M.E.S. with, 279-87. (*See also* freedmen *and* slavery)
Nelson, Martinus, 502
Nevada, 459-61, 509: Carson City, 459, 460, 534; Eagle Branch, Genoa, Walker River, 460; Gold Hill, Silver City, 461; Reno, 459, 461; Virginia City, 459, 460, 461, 534
Nevada Conference, M.E., 441, 461
"New Chapter," 209-14
New Connexion Methodists, England, 406
New England, 149, 473, 475, 531
New England Christian Advocate, 39
New England Conference: A.M.E., 531; A.M.E. Zion, 558, 560, 569, 570; M.E., 18, 19, 29, 34, 35, 36, 156, 178, 495, 514
New Hampshire, 501: Concord, 193, 651; New Market, 45

New Hampshire Conference, M.E., 32, 33
New Jersey, 513, 529, 557, 579: Bordentown, 547; Cape May, 303, 664-71; Gouldtown, New Brunswick, Princeton, Woodbury, 530; Madison, 651, 656; Ocean Grove, 614; Perth Amboy, 500; Salem, 527, 528; Trenton, 505, 530; Vineland, 612
New Jersey Conference: A.M.E. Zion, 559; M.E., 52, 151, 524
New Mexico, 4, 443-45, 510, 517, 535: Cherry Valley, 445; Elizabethtown, Socorro, 444; Glorieta Pass, 434; La Junta (Tiptonville), Peralta, 444, 445; Santa Fe, 431, 443, 444, 445
New Mexico Conference, M.E.S., 445
New Orleans, Society of Methodists in, 533
New Orleans University, 365
"New School Methodism," 346-49
New School Presbyterians, 26
New York, 33, 495, 501, 505, 513, 553, 579: Albany, 530, 531; Albion, 344, 350, 351, 352; Brockport, 344, 350; Brooklyn, 492, 495, 530, 531, 625, 679; Buffalo, 344, 350, 352, 530, 531, 557; Caryville, Pike, Rushford, 344; Cazenovia, 38; Lake Chautauqua, 647; Long Island, 531, 556; New York City, 32, 38, 39, 47-82, 209, 335, 473, 474, 500, 505-7, 531, 556, 564-66, 568, 573, 589, 648; Newburgh, 564; Olean, Syracuse, 352; Pekin, 347, 348, 350, 355; Rochester, 352, 530; Round Lake, 613; Schenectady, 531; Utica, 38, 42, 505, 530; Watertown, 612; West Falls, 347
New York Conference: A.M.E., 530, 531, 539, 543; A.M.E. Zion, 556, 573; M.E., 34, 35, 36, 45, 151, 202, 300, 473, 480, 493, 505, 514, 517, 597; M.P., 405-6
New York suit on property claim, 178-79, 185

Newark Conference, M.E., 223
Newburgh Reunion Platform, 564, 565
Newbury (Vt.) Biblical Institute, 651
Newman, John Henry, 346
Newman, John P., 250, 361 616, 664
Newman, Sven B., 495
Nicholson, Enoch G., 443, 444
Nippert, Louis, 482
Niseis, 511
Normal School of Galena, 489
Normal School Training Course, A.M.E., 545
North, Frank Mason, 602, 635
North Alabama Conference: A.M.E. Zion, 561; M.E.S., 306
North Carolina, 33, 268, 392, 401, 410, 414, 547, 560: Asheville, 686; Beaufort, Roanoke Island, Washington, 560; Charlotte, 566, 575; Concord, Lincolnton, 571; Edenton, 572; Greensboro, 366, 376; New Bern, 255, 560, 561, 572, 573, 582; Oxford, 374; Salisbury, 572, 575; Wilmington, 146, 537
North Carolina Conference: A.M.E., 537; A.M.E. Zion, 560, 566, 570, 571; M.E.S., 103-4, 113; M.P., 400, 402, 414, 416
North Dakota, 464-66, 500, 501, 535, 627, 648, 649: Bismarck, Goose River, Jamestown, Pembino, 465; Fargo, Grand Forks, 464, 465
North Dakota Conference, M.E., 465
North Dakota Mission, 465
North Georgia Conference, A.M.E. Zion, 561-62
North German Conference, M.E., 487, 489, 519
North Illinois Conference, M.P., 413
North Illinois Institute 413
North Indiana Conference, M.E., 64, 322
North Korea, 513
North Mississippi Conference, M.E.S., 306
North Missouri Conference, A.M.E., 533

North Ohio Conference: A.M.E., 533; M.E., 168, 488
North Ohio Conference Methodist Episcopal Alliance, 645
North Pacific Railroad Mission, 464, 465
North River Mission, 493-94
Northeast Oklahoma Conference, A.M.E., 535
Northern Christian Advocate, 176, 189, 199, 200, 346, 615
Northern Independent, 200, 346, 351, 354
Northern Louisiana Conference, A.M.E. Zion, 561
Northern Swedish Conference, M.E., 519
Northwest German Conference, M.E., 519
Northwest Iowa Conference, M.E., 464, 465-66
Northwest Mission, M.E., 496
Northwest Norwegian (and Danish) Conference (Mission), M.E., 501
Northwest Swedish Conference, M.E., 496
Northwest Texas Conference, M.E.S., 622
Northwest Texas Holiness Association, 619
Northwestern Christian Advocate, 186, 189, 199
Northwestern Conference, A.M.E., 535
Northwestern Freedmen's Aid Commission, 252
Northwestern University, 185, 499, 611, 648
Norway, 497, 500-502
Norway Conference, M.E., 502
Norwegian (and Danish) Conference, M.E., 501, 503, 519
Norwegian-Danish Girl's Home, Los Angeles, 503
Norwegian-Danish Methodism, 499-503
Norwegian-Danish Theological Seminary, 657
Norwood, John N., 57, 59, 147 165, 174
Nova Scotia, 577-78
Nova Scotia Conference; A.M.E. Zion, 576; B.M.E., 577-78
Nuelsen, Amelia and Francis, 479

Nuelsen, Henry, 480, 482
Nuelsen, John L., 471, 480, 484-86, 525

oath of allegiance, 218
Oberlin College, 412
Ogden, T. J., 406
Ohio, 33, 218, 505, 579, 627: Akron, 492, 644; Berea, 185, 488, 657; Chillicothe, 217, 532, 543; Cincinnati, 16, 126, 158, 160, 164, 226, 362, 395, 397, 481, 491, 532, 624, 643, 696-97; Cleveland, 42, 397, 517, 532, 645, 683; Columbus, 546; Danville, Gambier, 477; Hillsborough, 532; Mill Creek Valley, 487; Mount Union, 185; Munroe, Williamsfield, 42; Oberlin, 610; Springfield, 228, 395, 417; Urbana, 613; Van Wert, 649
Ohio African University, 546
Ohio Conference: A.M.E., 530, 532, 533, 543, 545, 546, 551; A.M.E. Zion, 558-59; M.E., 33-35, 126, 153, 164, 165, 166, 168, 477-78, 480, 481, 488, 505; M.P., 402, 411, 413
Ohio suit on property claim, 179, 180, 190
O'Kelly, James, 12
Oklahoma, 420, 428, 535: Oklahoma City, 687; Talihina, 547
Oklahoma Conference, A.M.E., 535
"Old School Methodists," 346
Old Union Church, Philadelphia, 214
Olin, Stephen, 53, 61, 72, 127, 151, 185, 344, 380, 387, 388, 610
Oneida Conference, M.E., 52, 359, 505
Orange River Colony Conference, A.M.E., 554
order of service, 629-31
ordination, 72, 138, 563, 566, 567, 581, 629, 658
Oregon, 4, 192, 420-22, 437, 445-49, 500, 507, 509, 510, 512, 535: Calapooia, Yamhill, 448; Chemeketa (Salem), 447, 448, 449; Clatsop, Nisqually, Umpqua (Tacoma), 447; Corvallis, Eugene Independence, 449; The Dalles,

Oregon—cont'd
Willamette Valley, 446, 448, Fort Vancouver, 446; Portland, 199, 499, 506, 512; Salem, 185, 447, 448, 449, 657; Willamette Falls (Oregon City), 447, 448
Oregon and California Mission Conference, M.E., 448, 454
Oregon City Circuit, 448
Oregon Conference: A.M.E. Zion, 559; M.E., 448, 451
Oregon Institute, 447, 448
Oregon Mission Conference, M.E., 173
Oregon Mission to the Indians, 448
Oregon Trail, 439, 446
"organ war," 322
Organic Union; Commissions on, 682; Plan for, 688
Osam-Pinanko, 576
Osbon, Abiathar, 188
Osborn, George, 697, 698
Osborn, William B., 612, 614
other-worldliness, 241, 311
Our Brother in Black (Haygood), 283
Our Morning Guide, 404
Our Sunday School Review, 550
Our Young People, 404, 646
Outline of Theology (Townsend), 383
Owen, F. A., 190
Owen, Isaac, 192, 448, 454
Oxford League, 645

Pacific, University of the, 185, 454
Pacific Christian Advocate, 199
Pacific Conference, M.E.S., 247, 449, 455, 459
Pacific German Conference, M.E., 519
Pacific Methodist, 455
Paine, Robert, 60, 90, 131, 137, 138, 177, 181, 189, 242, 246, 260, 275, 285, 306, 313, 455, 655, plate 5
Paley, William, 388
Palmer, Phoebe, 610, 611, 614, 615, 621
Palmer, Walter, 611, 614, 615
Palmetto Conference, A.M.E. Zion, 561
Palmyra Manifesto, 267-68, 299
Pan-Anglican Congress, Pan-Presbyterian Council, 698

"paper war," 97-98, 126-27, 145, 149, 180-81, 185, 200
Parent Home and Foreign Missionary Society, 539, 551
Paris, John, 399
Park, Edwards A., 385
Parker, A. P., 290
Parker, Theodore, 346, 385
Parker College, 489
parochial schools, 333, 571-72
Parrington, Vernon L., 316
Pastoral Addresses, 142, 143, 219, 268-69, 693. (See also Episcopal Addresses)
pastoral term, extension of, 271, 277, 324
Paul Quinn College, 546
Payne, Daniel A., 255, 536, 539, 540, 542, 545, 546, 549, 580, 581
Payne High School, 552
Payne Institute, 546
Payne Theological Seminary, 546
Payne University, 547
Pearne, Thomas H., 199
Peck, George, 63, 151, 154, 156, 157, 168, 169, 171, 176, 179, 180, 181, 185, 188, 197, 198, 215, 610
Peck, J. K., 202
Peck, Jesse T., 611, 614
Peck, N. R., 460
Pemberton, John C., 235
Peniel Mission (Hall), 626
Pennsylvania, 501, 505, 513, 529, 540, 579: Allegheny City, 407; Attleborough, 528-29; Bangor, Wilkes-Barre, 505; Bellefonte, Johnstown, Shippensburg, Williamsport, York, 557; Bridgeport, 530; Browns-ville, Geneva, Monmouth, Uniontown, Washington, 534; Carlisle, 167, 543, 557; Clearfield County, 223; Easton, 556; Erie, 662; Frankford, New Hope, Plemeth (Plymouth), Westchester, Whitemarsh, 530; Gettysburg, 226, 235, 543; Harrisburg, 530, 557; Kingston, 344; Lancaster, 530, 543; Lewistown, 543, 557; McKeesport, 409; Manheim, 325, 613, 614; Meadville, 661; Philadelphia, 214, 217, 226, 484, 514, 526, 527, 530, 542,

Pennsylvania—cont'd
546, 551, 554, 556, 557, 572, 645, 671-76; Pittsburgh, 42, 168-76, 395, 397, 399, 400, 403, 404, 407, 408, 481, 534, 557, 581, 661; Stroudsburg, 552
Pennsylvania Methodist Protestant, 404
Pentecostal Mission, 623
"pentecostal" sects, 619
People's United Church, Spokane, 625
Peoria Conference, M.E., 495
Peoria Mission, 427
perfectionism, 311, 340, 345, 593, 606-7, 609-27
Perry, J. H., 195
persecution: of Chinese and Japanese, 508-10; of C.M.E. Church, 286; of Freedmen's Aid Society teachers, 371-74; of Methodists, 162-64, 212-13, 299, 497
personalism, 595
Pestalozzi, 644
Petersen, Ole Peter, 500-502
Pettigrew, H. B., 572
Petty, C. C., 561, 571, 572
Petty High School, Lancaster, S.C., 571
"pewed" churches, 342
Philadelphia-Baltimore Conference, A.M.E. Zion, 560, 566
Philadelphia Conference: A.M.E., 529, 530, 534, 539, 543, 549, 552; A.M.E. Zion, 557; M.E., 34, 151, 178, 209, 210, 514
Philadelphia suit on property claim, 178
philanthropy, age of, 26
Philippines, 591
Phillips, C. H., 688, 705
Phillips, Richard, 557
Phillips, Wendell, 8
philosophical romanticism, 387, 595
Philosophy of Herbert Spencer (Bowne), 595
Phoebus, William, 556, 563
Pickens, R. T., 415
Pierce, Franklin, 5, 8, 482
Pierce, George F., 90, 132, 143, 148, 183, 191, 205, 231, 233-35, 244, 246, 260, 271, 275, 296, 306, 307, 313, 394, 692
Pierce, Gustavus M., 440, 442

Pierce, Lovick, 59, 113, 117, 122, 125, 132, 137, 138, 143, 159, 170-73, 183-84, 298, 302, 314, 660-62, 665, 666
Piette, Maximin, 605
Pike's Peak Mission, 431, 435
Pillar of Fire Church, 619
Pima Reservation, 462
Pipher, John, 430
Pitts, Fountain, 131, 158
Pittsburgh Christian Advocate, 37, 189, 199, 478
Pittsburgh Conference: A.M.E., 534; M.E., 178, 480, 505, 517
Pittsburgh Mystery, 548
Placerville Circuit, Cal., 534
Plan for Organic Union, 688
Plan of Separation, 59-64, 86, 88, 108, 116-19, 123, 125-28, 135, 149, 150-51, 158, 179: and border conferences, 159-67; fundamental principles of, 159-60; and property distribution, 292; question of constitutionality of, 156; reactions to, 96-111, 145-51, 168; repudiation of, 173-75, 182; and Southern bishops, 152-54
Plymouth Congregational Church, Adrian, Mich., 412
Pocket Hymn Book, 549
Poe, Adam, 363
Poles, 517
politics, Methodists in, 228-29, 262, 320
Pollock, D. W., 455
Pope, W. B., 593
population trends, 589
Populism, 589
Porter, David M., 84
Porter, James, 56-58, 60, 69
Portland Circuit, Ore., 449
Portuguese, 517
Potomac, Army of the, 240
Powell Valley Seminary, 377
pragmatism, 319
"prayer-meeting revivals," 240
preachers: local, 246, 323-24, 422, 479, 651, 658, 659; Negro, 253, 366-67, 374-75, 567; "refugee," 237, 242; revival, 311; traveling, 4, 13, 77, 246, 473, 628, 650, 651. (*See also* ministers)
Preachers' Aid and Mutual Relief Association, 552

Preacher's Institute, 571
preaching, 593, 628: inspirational, 193; of Northern and Southern army chaplains, 240, 241
Premillennialism, 598
Presbyterians, 24, 26, 264, 280, 330, 331, 363, 462, 464, 504, 524, 617: Cumberland, 408, 409
presiding elders, 66-82, 423, 466-67, 651
Preston, Benjamin, 35
Price, J. E., 573
Price, Sterling, 242, 243
Primitive Holiness Mission, 619
Primitive Methodists, 340, 359, 398, 410
Princeton University, 7
Principles of Psychology (James), 605
Prindle, Cyrus C., 396, 397
Problem of Methodism (Boland), 623
Problem Solved (Hayes), 623
professionalism: of ministry, 322; in sports, 328
"progressive orthodoxy," 617
prohibition movement, Prohibition Party, 312, 326, 327
property, dispute over division of, 156, 166, 174-75, 177-81, 183, 185, 190, 292, 298
"Protest of the Minority . . . ," 60-61, 77-82
Protestant Advocate, 404
Protestant Episcopal Church, 263, 363, 379, 435, 437
Protestant ethic, 317
Protestant Evangelical Theological Seminary, Blaubeuren, Germany, 476
Protestant Recorder, 404
Protestantism: and the American image, 333; and Catholicism, 333-34; complacency of, 317-39
Providence Conference, M.E., 52, 151, 178
Providence Rule on slavery, 201
Provident Hospital and Training School for Nurses, Chicago, 552
psychology, 592
publishing: A.M.E., 547-50; A.M.E. Zion, 573-75; foreign language, 518, 519,

publishing—*cont'd*
521; of German Methodists, 490-91; M.E., 127-28, 188-89, 199; M.E.S., 118, 122, 132, 140-41, 184, 190, 191, 204, 269-70, 278, 292-93; M.P., 403-4
Publishing House: A.M.E. Zion, 575; M.E.S., 245, 269, 289, 292-93
Puerto Rico, 591
Puget Sound Conference: A.M.E., 535; M.E., 450
Purdy, Fay, 350, 351
Puritanism, 316, 328, 329, 335

Quakers, 363, 617
Quarterly Review, M.E.S., 230, 314, 385-86, 623
Quinn, William Paul, 529, 532, 534, 535, 537, 539, 543, 551
Quinn Chapel: Chicago, 535; Louisville, 533
Quota Law (1921), 470

Rader, D. L., 439
Raikes, Robert, 642
Rall, Harris Franklin, 598, 599, 607
Ralston, Thomas N., 113, 114, 124, 132
Randolph-Macon College, 237
Ransom, J. J., 290
rationalism, 318, 474, 594, 595
Raymond, Miner, 197, 383, 387, 594, 616
Reconstruction, 215, 257, 259, 264, 282, 287, 293, 304, 313, 360-80, 559, 570
recruitment: of preachers, 193, 479; of soldiers, Civil War, 225-26
Redfield, John Wesley, 343, 350, 352, 353, 355
Redford, A. H., 292
Reeder, G. A., 462
Reese, Daniel E., 392
Reese, Eli Y., 391
Reese, James William, 419
reform movements, 312, 326-27, 337-38
Reformed Episcopal Church, 410
Reformed Methodist Union Episcopal Church, 579-80
Reformed Zion Union Apostolic Church, 578-79

"refugee preachers," 237, 242

Regency party, in Genesee conflict, 343-48, 350, 351, 353, 359

regeneration, personal, 605, 608

Reid, C. F., 513

Reid, Isaiah, 624

Reid, J. M., 363

Reid, John, 361

"released-time" program, 649

relief organizations, 222, 252

religion: defense of slavery based on, 23-25; "heart," 305, 311; of Indians, 443; and patriotism, 214-29; philosophies of, 386-90; religious reading, 238, 239; sociology of, 596

Religious education: see Sunday schools

Religious Education Association, 644

Religious Interests of the Colored People, Committee on, 284, 680-81

"Reply to the Protest," 64, 72-75

Repository of Religion and Literature, 548

Republican party, 9

responsive readings, 636

Rest of Faith (Earle), 610, 617

Restrictive Rules, 74, 92, 128-30, 150, 173, 174, 175, 178, 188

Reubelt, J. A., 389

reunion of churches, efforts toward, 261-62, 269, 299-301, 660-89

Review of the Manifesto . . . (Bascom), 154-55, 156

Revisals, Committee on, 187, 188

revivals, 26, 217, 296, 319, 346, 348, 350, 352, 444, 477, 495, 592, 600, 602, 604, 607, 610; in Civil War armies, 238-41; decline of, 324-26; in South, 310-11

Rhode Island, 501: Newport, 531; Providence, 42, 531, 558, 625

Rice, W. A., 547

Rich, Isaac, 336

Richardson, A. S., 573

Richardson, E. G., 522

Richardson, H., 460

Richardson, Jacob D., 557, 575

Richmond Christian Advocate, 141, 147, 161, 245

Richmond Circuit, Ohio, 533

Riemenschneider, Englehardt, 482

Rightmyer, Valentine, 461

Rinkart, Martin, 635

Rio Grande Mission Conference, M.E., 425

Roanoke Seminary, 377

"robber barons," 315-16, 335-36

Roberts, Benjamin T., 342-48, 350, 352-55, 357, 358

Roberts, Benson H., 358

Roberts, Robert R., 49, 427

Roberts, William, 192, 448, 451-54, 458

Robie, John, 344, 351

Robinson, "Bud," 622

Robinson, J. H., 406

Robinson, Richard, 554

Rochester Convention on slavery, 200

Rock River Conference, M.E., 218, 352-53, 494, 514

Rockefeller, John D., 316

Rocky Mountain Conference, M.E., 435, 438, 442, 452

Rocky Mountain Sunday School Casket, 435

Rogers, E. H., 337

Roman Catholicism, 433, 443, 451, 452, 456, 462, 475, 479; Methodism and, 332-34

romanticism, 387, 610

Roosevelt, Franklin D., 510

Roosevelt, Theodore, 509

Ross, Peter, 565

Rosser, Leonidas, 622

Roszel, S. G., 14

Rothweiler, Jacob, 488, 492

Rules for the Adjustment of Adverse Claims to Church Property, 668-69

Rumanians, 517

Rush, Christopher, 557, 558, 560, 563, 564, 570, 581

Rush Academy, 570, 571

"Rush University Fund," 571

Russell Circuit, Ala., 45

Russell Mission, Tampa, Fla., 515

Russia, 420, 498

Rust, Richard S., 363, 364, 375-76, 377

Rust University, 365

Ruter, Martin, 424, 643

Rutersville College, 424

Ryang, T. S., 513

St. George's Church, Philadelphia, 526, 527

St. James Academy and Industrial Institute, 547

St. James Methodist Church, Central City, Colo., 468

St. John, Eugenia F., 406

St. John's Church, Cleveland, 532-33

St. John's in the Wilderness, Denver, 422

St. Joseph German mission, 431, 432

St. Louis Conference: M.E., 614; M.E.S., 428, 431, 432

St. Louis German Conference, M.E., 519

St. Paul's Church: Lowell, Mass., 33; Washington, 531

St. Paul's College, 489

St. Paul's Methodist Church, Copenhagen, 502

St. Thomas, Virgin Islands, 555

St. Thomas' Protestant Episcopal Church, Philadelphia, 526

Salem Circuit, Ore., 448, 449

salvation: social, 602; universal, 593, 594, 601-3

Salvation Army, 618

"Salvation Bands," 352

Samoa, 591

San Paulo Church, Tampa, Fla., 515

sanctification, entire, 311, 339, 340, 346, 356, 358, 593, 606, 608-27. (See also holiness movement)

Sändebudet, 499, 503

Sanford, Peter, 188

Sanitary Commission, 223

Sanitary Fair, 217

Sargent, Thomas B., 60, 76

Scandinavian Methodism, 492-503

Scarborough, George P., 163

Scarritt, Nathan, 431

Schaff, Philip, 616

Schleiermacher, 385, 387-89, 605

Schmitz, Eugene, 509

Schmucker, Peter, 479, 480, 481

Schrader, Alexander von, 227

Schulyville Indian Territory Mission Circuit, 552

scientific materialism, 595

Scott, D. W., 440

Scott, Elihu, 186

Scott, John, 404

Scott, June, 576

Scott, Levi, 187, 210, 434, 456
Scott, Orange, 16, 28-31, 33, 35, 37, 38, 39-47
Scurlock, L. J., 286
Searles, J. E., 620-21
second blessing, 359, 612, 614, 616, 623, 626
Second Norwegian Methodist Church, Chicago, 502
sectionalism, 3, 25, 70, 76, 83, 262
segregation, 377-78
Sehon, Edmund W., 131, 139, 237, 289
Selby, T. G., 702
self-made man, cult of the, 317-18
Selma Institute, 552
"seminary rule," 656
Sewall, James, 193, 194
Shattuck, W. I., 523, 524
Shaw, Anna M., 405
Shaw, S. B., 619
Shawnee Mission, 427, 428
Sheldon, Henry C., 594
Shepard, Cyrus, 446
Sherman, William, 258
Shorter, J. A., 541
Shorter Chapel, Denver, 535
Shorter College, 547
Shurtleff, E. W., 635
Siberia, 290, 510
Siberian Korean Mission, 513
Sierra Leone, 553-54
Sierra Leone Conference, A.M.E., 554
Simons, George H., 491
Simonsen, Nels E., 503
Simpson, A. B., 625
Simpson, Matthew, 61, 112, 169, 174, 176, 179, 187, 207, 217-20, 224, 225, 228, 229, 249, 250, 253, 255, 319, 340, 362, 441, 442, 462, 502, 612, 613, 614, 661, 662, 692, 697-98
Simpson, Mrs. Matthew, 340-41
Simpson, Shadrach, 415
sin, universal, 593, 600-601, 608
Sin and Holiness (Huntington), 624
singing, congregational, 341-42, 631, 632-36
Sipkins, Thomas, 576
skepticism, 594-95
slavery, 3, 4, 6, 8-9, 11, 12-39, 65-66, 83, 144-47, 157, 159, 167, 184, 188, 189, 191, 196-202, 204-6, 209-

slavery—cont'd
11, 259, 429, 540: abuses of, 234; and case of Bishop Andrew, 54-59; Committee on, 52, 188; defense of, 8, 15, 22, 23-25, 27; and Emancipation Proclamation, 231, 232, 252; fugitive slaves, 251, 577; held by Methodist ministers or bishops, 28, 52-59, 68, 85; missions to slaves, 203, 254; as a moral question, 30; slave insurrections, 22; toleration of, in M.E. Church, 342, 352; and Wesleyan Methodist Church, 44-46
Sleeper, Jacob, 336
Slicer, Henry, 76, 79
Small, John B., 576
Small, Mary J., 566
Smith, A. D., 427
Smith, Charles S., 544
Smith, David, 530, 557
Smith, Henry B., 385
Smith, Henry Weston, 465
Smith, J. H., 674
Smith, J. J., 401, 409
Smith, Leven J., 556, 557
Smith, Stephen, 551
Smith, Timothy L., 207
Smith, William A., 52, 78, 116, 122, 180
Smithdeal, G. M., 415
Snow Hill Society, 529
Snow-Shoe Itinerant (Dyer), 435
social complacency, Methodist, 317-39
Social Creed of Methodism, 596
Social Darwinism, 317
social disorganization, alcohol and, 326-27
social gospel, 338, 607
social problems, 312, 588, 590, 595-96; disregard for, 335-39; legislation on, 283
social reform, 602. (See also reform movements)
social status, Methodist, 228-29, 320-21
social stratification, 315-16
Soldier's Paper, 237
Soliders' Tract Association, 237, 238
Someillan, H. B., 516
Sonntagschule Glocke, 483, 490
Soule, Joshua, 19, 36, 48, 50-51, 61, 77, 78-81, 90-96, 106, 108-11, 113-17, 122-

Soule, Joshua—cont'd
26, 130-34, 137, 138, 143, 147, 152-55, 162, 164, 165, 170, 173-74, 177, 181, 183, 189, 203, 246, 260, 279, 477, 563, plate 2
Soule Chapel, Cincinnati, 158, 160, 164-65
South: A.M.E. Church in, 535-38; A.M.E. Zion Church in, 559-62; in Civil War and after, 10, 84-85, 230-74, 308; cotton in, 5-6, 22; defense of slavery in, 8, 15, 22-25, 27; opinion of, on 1844 General Conference, 148-49
South Africa, 554
South African or Cape Colony Conference, A.M.E., 554
South and Southeast Alabama Conferences, A.M.E. Zion, 561
South Carolina, 5, 6, 9, 13, 33, 230, 255, 268, 282, 304-5, 367, 552, 578, 580: Beaufort, Edisto, 255; Charleston, 141, 245, 255, 529, 536, 553, 642; Columbia, 6, 546; Lancaster, 571; Orangeburg, 365, 366; Port Royal, 252, 255; Rock Hill, 572; Walhalla, 373
South Carolina Conference: A.M.E., 255, 536; A.M.E. Zion, 561; M.E., 28; M.E.S., 104, 114, 254
South Dakota, 464-66, 500, 501, 535, 627: Canton, Fort Randall, Richland, Sioux Falls, Vermillion, Yankton, 464; Central City, Lead City, Rapid City, 466; Crook City, Custer, 465, 466; Deadwood, 465
South Florida Conference, A.M.E. Zion, 562
South Georgia Conference, A.M.E. Zion, 561-62
South German Conference, M.E., 489, 519
South India Conference, M.E., 621
South Kansas Conference, A.M.E., 534
South Mississippi Conference, A.M.E. Zion, 562
South Ohio Conference, A.M.E., 533

Southeast Indiana Conference, M.E., 484
Southerland, S.B., 394, 406
Southern California Conference, M.E., 457, 458
Southern Conference, A.M.E. Zion, 560
Southern Christian Advance, 404
Southern Christian Advocate, 141, 153, 161, 230, 244, 245
"Southern Methodist Primer," 237
Southern Methodist University, 656, 657
Southern Pacific Railroad, 463
Southern Recorder (Christian), 548
Southern University, 305
Southwest Missouri Conference, A.M.E., 533
Southwestern Homeopathic College, 492
South-Western Methodism (Elliott), 213
Spain, 420, 421: Civil War in, 515
Spalding, H. H., 446
Spanish-American War, 591
Spanish language groups, 471, 516-17
Spencer, Herbert, 317, 337, 385, 595
Spencer, Peter, 528
Spirit, witness of, 604-5
Springer, Cornelius, 411-12
Spurlock, W. A., 458
Spywood, George A., 564
Stanberry, Henry, 180
Stanford, Leland, 316
Stanton, Edwin M., 224, 229, 249, 299, 391
Star of Zion, 573
Starr Methodist Protestant Church, Baltimore, 401
State of the Church, Committee on, 169-71, 173, 174, 301
Stateler, Learner B., 428, 432, 435, 436, 438
states' rights, 8, 9, 25
status, rising, of Methodism, 228-29, 320-21
Steele, Daniel, 616, 620, 624
Stephens, David S., 404, 414
Stephenson, Henry, 424
Stephenson, T. B., 702, 704
Stevens, Abel, 39, 40, 156, 176, 186, 189, 198-200, 202, 387

Stevens, David, 675
Stevens, Peter F., 580
Stevens, Thaddeus, 264
Stevenson, Edward, 139, 190
Stevenson, William, 424
stewards, 567
Stewart, Charles, 534
Stiles, Loren, Jr., 345, 351, 352, 356, 359
Still, Abraham, 429, 430
Stillman, J. R., 316, 363
Stillwell, William, 563
Storrs, George, 35
Stout, Benjamin, 407
Stowe, Harriet Beecher, 26
Straughn, James H., 419
Strauss, David, 384
Strawberry Alley Society, 527
strikes, 337, 588
Stringfield, Thomas, 68
Strong, James, 193-95
Stroudsburg Mission, Pa., 552
Stuart, Benjamin, 577
Stubbs, Charles O., 414
Student Volunteer Movement, 646
Stuntz, Homer C., 705
suffrage, universal, 326, 327
Summers, Thomas O., 108, 114, 132, 141, 293, 307-8, 313-14, 383, 386, 594, 616, 623, 690
Sumner, William Graham, 317
Sumter District School, S.C., 552
Sundance Circuit, Wyo., 439
Sunday observance, 312, 320, 328, 638
Sunday-School Advocate, 199
Sunday School Association, 310
Sunday School Union, 376, 481, 568, 569, 643
Sunday School Union Press, 550
Sunday schools, 310, 327, 440, 494, 542-44, 569, 581-82, 642-44, plates 10, 11. (See also literature, Sunday school)
Sunday School Visitor, 190
Sunday Service . . . (Wesley), 627, 628, 631
Sunderland, La Roy, 32, 34, 36, 39, 41-43
Supreme Court decision on Book Concern, 130
Sutter, J. A., 192
Sutton, William, 178, 572
Sweden, 496-98, 500, 501

Sweden Conference, M.E., 498, 519
Swedish Immanuel Church, Brooklyn, 495
Swedish Methodism, 492-500
Swedish Theological Seminary, 499, 651, 657
Sweet, William Warren, 65, 210, 218, 226, 236, 250, 271
Switzerland, 482
Switzerland Conference, M.E., 519
Swormstedt, Leroy, 127
Sydnor, Charles S., 84
Syrians, 517
Systematic Theology (Miley), 383
Systematic Theology (Raymond), 383
Systematic Theology (Summers), 594

Tagg, F. T., 404, 407
Talbot, Sampson, 561, 565
Talley, Alexander, 427
Taney, Roger B., 180
Tanner, Benjamin T., 526, 541, 548
Tapsico, Jacob, 549
Taylor, Charles, 181
Taylor, Georgia W., 119
Taylor, William, 192, 448, 454, 602-3, 621
Taylor University, 624-25
teachers: Negro, 364, 366-67; religious training for, 647-48
Tefft, B. F., 380
temperance, 297-98, 312, 326-27, 512
Ten Years' War, 516
Tennessee, 251, 298, 362, 533, 560, 622: Army of, 238, 240; Athen, Bloomingday, Bloomington, Fullen's Tullahoma, Well Spring, 377; Chattanooga, 235, 250, 377; Greeneville, 572; Jackson, 284; Knoxville, 560, 614; Mason, Morristown, 366; Memphis, 250, 306, 663, 683, 695; Nashville, 190, 191, 202-5, 244, 250, 269, 289, 290-92, 310, 365, 366, 370, 409, 537, 582, 622, 624, 625, 652, 681, 690; Pulaski, 623
Tennessee Colored Conference, 284

Tennessee Conference: A.M.E., 537; M.E.S., 101-2, 113, 291, 306
Tennessee Methodist, 622
Terry, Milton S., 594, 616, 620
testimony, 603, 605
Texas, 4, 288, 293, 372, 420, 421, 423-26, 510, 515, 517, 537, 578: Austin, 366, 495, 499; Brazora, Timber Creek, 425; Brenham, 489; Carthage, 284; Dallas, 404, 495, 656, 657; El Paso, 517; Fort Worth, 377, 495; Galveston, 537; Jasper, Montgomery, Nacogdoches, Pecan Point, San Augustine, Washington, 424; Marshall, 243, 366; Red River district, 423; Round Rock, 495; Rutersville, 424, 489; Tehuacana, Westminster, 414; Terry, 513; Waco, 546
Texas Colored Conference, 284
Texas Conference: A.M.E., 537; A.M.E. Zion, 561; M.E., 64, 425, 426, 495; M.E.S., 106-7, 114, 445, 622
Texas Holiness Asssociation, 619
Texas Holiness University, 623, 624
Texas Mexican Mission, 517
Texas Wesleyan College, 377
theism, 595
theological education, 193-96, 305-9, 322-24, 366, 374-75, 417-19, 488, 498, 546, 570, 571, 616, 650-58
Theological Institutes (Watson), 381, 382, 389, 593, 594, 602, 654, 655
theology, 318-19, 593-99: and advanced intellectual development, 383-86; correspondence schools of, 546; and ethics, 596; natural, 389; and religious philosophies, 386-90; systematic, 380-83
third blessing, 619
Thoburn, Isabella, 491
Thoburn, James M., 320
Tholuck, A., 384, 385
Thomas, D. C., 412
Thomas, Eleazar, 199, 343
Thompson, Abraham, 556, 576

Thompson, J. P., 575
Thompson, Mary Ann, 635
Thomson, Edward, 46, 198, 209, 248, 614
Thomson Biblical Institute, 366, 375
Thoreau, Henry David, 610
"Thousand-Dollar Proposition," 455, 458, 467
Tigert, John J., 70, 125, 594, 623
Tillett, Wilbur Fisk, 594, 624
Tippett, C. B., 134, 157
Tobago, 555
Toland, J. F. W., 182
Totten, W. T., 416
Townsend, L. T., 383
Tract House, Bremen, 483
tract societies, 224, 237, 376
transcendentalism, 346, 384, 387, 388, 610
Transvaal Conference, A.M.E., 554
Transylvania University, 124, 136, 143
traveling preachers, 4, 13, 77, 246, 473, 628, 650, 651
Treatise on the Need of the M. E. Church . . . (Foster), 195
Tredwell, George, 557
Trefren, J. L., 441
Trevecca College, 624
Tri-Council of Colored Methodist Bishops, 542, 568, 687, 688
Trimble, Joseph M., 57, 69, 169
Trinidad, 555
Trinity College, 305
Trinity Methodist Church: Cincinnati, 362; Denver, 434
Troy Conference, M.E., 178, 475, 524
True, Charles K., 35
True Wesleyan, 39, 41
Tübingen, University of, 476
Tufts College Theological School, 597
Tullahoma College, 377
Turner, Asa, 332
Turner, Henry M., 541, 548, 549, 550, 554, 671
Turner, John, 671
Turner, Nat, 22
Turner College: Miss., 547; Tenn., 547
Tuskegee Institute, 572
Tuthill, David, 462
Tuttle, Daniel, 437, 442

Twain, Mark, 587
Umatilla District, Wash., 450
Uncle Tom's Cabin (Stowe), 26
Uniform Lesson system, 544, 644
Union Church of Africans, 528-29
Union Methodist Theological Seminary, Korea, 513
Union Pacific Railroad, 439
Union Society, 576
Unitarians, 318, 329, 362, 388
United African Methodist Episcopal Church in America, 675
United Brethren, 363, 410
United States Commission for the Relief of the National Freedmen, 252
Universalism, 318-19, 597
University of the Pacific, 185, 454
Updegraff, David B., 617
Upper Canada Conference, A.M.E., 533, 577
Upper Iowa Conference, M.E., 464
urbanization, 315, 316, 318, 323, 324, 329, 589-90, 596
Utah, 420, 421, 438, 459, 502, 535: Corinne, Ogden, Tooele, 442; Salt Lake City, 441, 442, 535, 613
Utah Conference, M.E., 442, 452
Utah Mission, M.E., 439, 440, 442

Vacation Bible school, 648
Valdez, Rosa, 516
Valley Institute, 517
Van Anda, J. A., 438
Vance, Robert B., 665
Vanderbilt, Cornelius, 308-9, 316
Vanderbilt University, 279, 309, 383, 652, 656
Vanderhorst, Richard H., 285
Vanduser, Joseph E., 516
Vanhas, Peter, 557
Van Orsdel, William W. (Brother Van), 438
Varick, James, 556, 563
Varick Christian Endeavor Societies, 568, 569
Varieties of Religious Experience (James), 605
Vermont, 45, 505: Newbury, 651

Vermont Conference, M.E., 64
Vesey insurrection, 536
Vicksburg, battle of, 235
Victor Emmanuel II, 333
View of the Evidences of Christianity (Paley), 388
Vincent, B. T., 435
Vincent, John H., 633, 643, 645, 647
Virgin Islands, 555
Virginia, 6, 32, 212, 268, 298, 362, 560, 572, 578, 579: Accomac County, Guilford, 163; Alexandria, Warrenton, Westmoreland, 165; Boydton, 579; Chancellorsville, 231; Lynchburg, 399, 400; Norfolk, 537; Parkersburg, 164; Petersburg, 130-43, 157-59, 575; Portsmouth, 537, 582; Richmond, 140, 221, 231, 237, 537, 560, 691; Roanoke, 377; Salem, 162
Virginia Conference: A.M.E., 537, 538; A.M.E. Zion, 561; M.E., 146, 209, 211; M.E.S., 103, 113, 158, 183; M.P., 395, 402
Virginia Conference Sentinel, 34, 37
Voice of Missions, 548
Voltaire, 346

Wakarusa Mission, 429, 430
Wakefield, Samuel A., 382
Walden, J. M., 363
Waldensians, 514
Walker, James B., 418
Wallace, Hardin, 619
Walser, Henry, 414
Walter's Institute, Ark., 572
"War Address" of Bishop Simpson, 218
Ward, Albert Norman, 414
Ward, James T., 406, 416, 418, 419
Ward, T. M. D., 533-34, 541
Warner, Daniel S., 619
Warren, William F., 368, 377, 381-5, 483, 594
Warren College, 377
Washington, 449-51, 500, 507, 510, 512, 535, 559, 627: Olympia, 449; Seattle, 450, 503, 506, 512; Spokane, 625; Steilacoom, Walla Walla, 450
Washington, Booker T., 367, 572
Waters, Edward, 539

Waters, Francis, 392, 398
Watson, J. V., 189, 199
Watson, Richard, 18, 381, 382, 389, 593, 594, 602, 654, 655
Watson, Samuel, 285
Watts, J. C., 406
Waugh, Beverly, 19, 35, 37, 48, 49, 58, 109, 110, 111, 125, 154, 186, 192, 342, 501, plate 1
Way of Holiness, 615
Wayman, A. W., 534, 540, 694, 704
Wayman Institute, 547
wealth: and cotton, 6; danger of, 335; distribution of, 587; national, 5, 7
Webb, John, 464
Webster, Daniel, 3
weekday religious instruction, 648-49
Welch, Herbert, 602
Weld, Theodore, 26-27
Wells, John A., 351
Welsh, 504-6
Welsh Calvinistic Methodists, 504
Wesley, Charles, 632
Wesley, John, 312, 327, 328, 335, 339, 356, 389, 471-72, 504, 593, 601, 603, 606, 608, 627, 628, 632, 636, 642, 650, 654, 655, 698
Wesley Chapel (Old Stone Church), Cincinnati, 532
Wesley Church, Philadelphia, 556
Wesley Foundation, 646-47
Wesleyan Antislavery Society, 32, 38, 39
Wesleyan Antislavery Review, 40
Wesleyan Companion, 41
Wesleyan Journal, 39
Wesleyan Methodist Church, 39-47, 83, 84, 145, 169, 396-98, 554, 564-65, 695, 697, 702
Wesleyan Methodist Missionary Society, 493, 515
Wesleyan Mexican Institute, 517
Wesleyan University, 167
West Alabama Conference, A.M.E. Zion, 561
West Florida Conference, A.M.E. Zion, 562
West German Conference, M.E., 519
West Indies, 544, 555
West Kentucky Conference, A.M.E. Zion, 561

West Lafayette College, 414
West Tennessee-Mississippi Conference, A.M.E. Zion, 562
West Virginia, 212, 353: Guyandotte area, 165; Parkersburg, 164
West Virginia Conference: A.M.E., 534; M.E., 182, 183
Western Book Concern, 199, 481
Western Christian Advocate, 37, 126, 134, 150, 151, 165, 176, 189, 199, 248, 324, 477, 478
Western Christian Recorder, 548
Western Conference, M.E.S., 432, 435, 438
Western Freedmen's Aid Commission, 252
Western Laymen's Convention, 355
Western Maryland College, 401, 406, 410, 412, 416-18
Western Methodist Protestant, 398
Western Mexican Mission, 517
Western North Carolina Conference, A.M.E. Zion, 560
Western Norwegian-Danish Conference, M.E., 501, 503, 519
Western Orphan Asylum and Educational Institute, 488
Western Protestant, 404
Western Record, 404
Western Swedish Conference, M.E., 496, 519
Western Texas Conference: M.E., 64, 425, 495; M.E.S., 445
Western University, 547
Western Virginia Conference: M.E., 209, 211; M.E.S., 183
Westminster College, 414
Westminster Theological Seminary, 416, 418-19, 652, 657
Westmoreland Circuit, Va., 16, 158
Westmoreland Petition, 20-21
westward movement, 4-6, 420-68, 586-87
Whedon, Daniel D., 199, 200, 202, 261, 382, 385,

Whedon, Daniel—*cont'd*
387, 388
Whig and Rebel Ventilator,
250
White, Asa, 453-54
White River Conference,
M.E.S., 306
Whitefield, George, 504, 601
Whitman, Marcus, 192, 446
Whittier, John Greenleaf, 8
Widney, Joseph P., 626
Wightman, William M., 90,
115, 141, 149, 154, 161,
162, 184, 185, 230-31,
235, 279, 313
Wilberforce, William, 31
Wilberforce University, 546,
581
Wilbraham Academy, 652
Wilbur, James H., 448, 453
Wiley, I. W., 239, 363
Wiley University, 365-66
Wilkerson, John, 534
Willamette University, 185,
447
Willard, Frances E., 326, 337,
611
Willard, Oliver A., 435
Willerup, Christian, 501-2
William Nast College, 489,
490
Williams, James, 466
Williams, John, 560
Williamson, Charles H., 474
Wills, George S., 416
Wills, William H., 393
Wilmington   Conference,
M.E.S., 653
Wilson, C. H., 407
Wilson, George W., 624
Winans, William, 19, 28,
60, 67, 122, 130, 132, 133,
137, 140, 157
Winchell, Alexander, 385
Winchester, C. T., 635
Winnega, J. M., 463
Winner, Isaac, 67, 71, 194
Wisconsin, 496, 500, 501,
505, 535: Fond du Lac,
505; Kenosha, Madison,
Racine, 533; Milwaukee,
492, 533; Muskego, 500;
Traux Prairie, 648
Wisconsin Conference, M.E.,
218, 500, 505

Wise, Daniel, 189, 199, 200
Witting, Victor, 497
Wofford College, 230, 305
Woman's Christian Tem-
perance Union, 326
Woman's Foreign Missionary
Societies, 407, 408
Woman's Home and For-
eign Missionary Society,
A.M.E. Zion, 575
Woman's Missionary Coun-
cil, 475, 516
*Woman's Missionary Re-
corder,* 549
Woman's Missionary Society,
M.E., 292
Woman's Parent Mite Mis-
sionary Society, A.M.E.,
552, 553
Woman's Union Missionary
Society, 407
Woman's Temperance Cru-
sade, 326
women: deaconess work for,
491-92; missionary work
by, 291-92, 407, 408, 475,
516, 552, 553, 575; or-
dination of, 405, 406, 566;
suffrage for, 327; work of,
in Civil War, 225, 226
Wood, George, 178
Woodlyn, Joshua, 676
Woodson, Lewis, 543
*Worker and His Work Se-
ries,* 647
working classes, Methodism
and, 335-39
World Council of Churches,
582
World Methodist Council,
697
World War I, 484-86, 517-18
World War II, 510, 515
worship, changing patterns
of, 627-36
Wright, D. B., 463
Wright, Richard, 528, 533
Wyandott Mission, 428, 430
Wynn, A. M., 455
Wyoming, 422, 438-40, 446,
512, 535: Atlantic,
Rawlins, Rock Springs,
South Pass, 440; Cheyenne,
439-40, 535; Evanston,
440, 442; Laramie, 439,
440

Wyoming Conference, M.E.,
439, 440, 505
Wyoming Seminary, 344

Yadkin College, 392, 401,
414-16
Yale University, 7
Yamhill Circuit, Ore., 448
Young, Augustus, 550
Young, Brigham, 441, 459,
614
Young (Jung), Henry P.,
425
Young, Jacob, 153, 188
Young Allenite, 550
Young Men's (and Young
Women's) Christian As-
sociations, 222, 646
Young People's Christian
League, Boston, 645
Young People's Hymnal,
634
Young People's Methodist
Alliance, 645
Young People's Quarterly,
550
Young People's Society, De-
troit, 645
"Youth Library," 490, 491
youth work, 544-45, 550,
569, 645-47

Zambesi Conference, A.M.E.,
554
Zanjón, Treaty of, 516
Zion Church Advocate, 573
Zion Hill Collegiate Insti-
tute, 571
Zion Institute, Mobile, Ala.,
571
*Zion Standard and Weekly
Review,* 573
Zion Union Apostolic
Church, 579
Zion Wesley Institute, 571,
572
Zion's Herald, 33, 39-41,
150, 176, 200, 323, 329,
330, 369, 593, 615
Zion's Watchman, 34, 36, 39,
41
Zoar Church, Philadelphia,
527
Zwahlen, John, 477-78

DATE DUE